D0025884

AESTHETICS
IN PERSPECTIVE

AESTHETICS
IN PERSPECTIVE

Kathleen M. Higgins
University of Texas at Austin

Under the general editorship of
Robert C. Solomon
University of Texas at Austin

THOMSON

WADSWORTH

Australia • Canada • Mexico • Singapore • Spain • United Kingdom • United States

Publisher *Ted Buchholz*
Editor in Chief *Christopher P. Klein*
Senior Acquisitions Editor *David Tatom*
Developmental Editor *J. Claire Brantley*
Project Editor *Christopher Nelson*
Production Manager *Cynthia Young*
Senior Art Director *David A. Day*
Text Designer *Priscilla Mingus*

Cover Illustration "Afternoon Sunlight on Water"
Oil on Panel 32" × 44"
(1990) by Susan Hall

ISBN: 0-534-64210-1
Library of Congress Catalog Card Number: 94-79691

COPYRIGHT © 1996 Wadsworth, a division of Thomson Learning, Inc.
Thomson Learning ™ is a trademark used herein under license.

ALL RIGHTS RESERVED. No part of this work covered by the
copyright hereon may be reproduced or used in any form or by any
means — graphic, electronic, or mechanical, including photocopying,
recording, taping, Web distribution, or information storage or retrieval
systems — without the written permission of the publisher.

Wadsworth/Thomson Learning
10 Davis Drive
Belmont CA 94002-3098
USA

For information about our products, contact us:
Thomson Learning Academic Resource Center
1-800-423-0563
http://www.wadsworth.com

For permission to use material from this text, contact us by
Web: http://www.thomsonrights.com
Fax: 1-800-730-2215
Phone: 1-800-730-2214

Copyrights and acknowledgments appear on page 800, which constitutes
a continuation of this copyright page.

Printed in the United States of America
10 9 8 7 6 5 4

For Paula Fulks and Douglas Buhrer

◆◆◆

PREFACE

— ◆◆◆ —

Aesthetics in Perspective is a reader designed to accommodate the various needs of instructors in aesthetics courses. One of my reasons for undertaking the production of this anthology is that I believe aesthetics courses are greatly enhanced by the inclusion of contemporary materials in addition to classic readings. I have observed my students' enthusiasm when I have brought popular and journalistic writings to bear on aesthetic issues. Typically, they become more engrossed not only in discussion of those materials, but also in aesthetic issues more generally. I have assembled, along with some of the classics of the fields, other readings that deal with aesthetics, often outside the format of academic writing.

A second concern that motivated my interest in this project was my own growing interest in aesthetics outside the high art tradition of the West. I suspect that many instructors, myself included, will devote more time to other traditions as we come to know more about them. *Aesthetics in Perspective* includes accessible basic accounts of aesthetic values outside the West. Comparative aesthetics is a relatively new but burgeoning field, and I hope that these readings will offer a starting point for instructors who wish to introduce comparative concerns in their courses.

Instructors will find *Aesthetics in Perspective* flexible in its organization. Chapters are arranged around questions and topics that interest students as they approach aesthetics. The sequence of chapters as presented is only one reasonable ordering of the topics; other instructors may order their assignments differently. Within each chapter, readings are arranged in sequences that I think seem reasonable from a student's point of view. At the same time, I envision many instructors choosing some but not all of the readings in any given chapter and choosing some chapters but not others in constructing their courses. *Aesthetics in Perspective* offers instructors the flexibility to vary course content from term to term, always covering essential topics.

Chapters 1 and 2 provide two different entrées into aesthetics; some instructors may concentrate on one or the other, while some will use both chapters. Chapter 1 presents some historically significant background particularly, although not exclusively, as it pertains to the topic of beauty. Chapter 2 presents readings that raise questions about the nature of art, particularly in light of some of the more nontraditional art of the twentieth century. Either of these chapters form a natural beginning for an aesthetics course. Chapter 2 includes several discussions of the startling cases of twentieth-century art, while the standard theories of art are considered in subsequent chapters. My rationale for formulating this chapter is this: Beginning with recent borderline cases of art will help students see the motivation behind philosophical interest in the definition of art. The various standard approaches to the nature of art are covered in Chapters 3 through 11.

The mimesis theory of art is considered in Chapter 3; aesthetic experience as art's reason for being is presented in Chapter 4; instrumentalist views that art's purpose is moral improvement or a better society are included in Chapters 5 and 6; the view that art is optimally a manifestation of creativity or inspiration is treated in Chapter 7; readings on the formalist theory of art are in Chapter 8; the expressionist theory of art and the theory that art aims to arouse emotion are considered in Chapter 9 with related issues regarding the relevance of intention to interpretation in Chapter 10; and historicist theories of art are presented in Chapter 11.

One possible syllabus involving *Aesthetics in Perspective* might begin with Chapter 2 to consider the problematic character of art in the twentieth century and then proceed to introduce various theories by sequentially using the readings in the subsequent nine chapters. Of course, instructors should use the flexibility of the book as an advantage and construct a syllabus that most appropriately addresses their students.

Besides chapters covering familiar aesthetic territory, sometimes by way of new readings, *Aesthetics in Perspective* includes chapters on some of the challenges to traditional aesthetics that are emerging within the field. Chapter 12 looks at some of the recent theoretical challenges to traditional aesthetics (including deconstruction and postmodernism). Chapter 13 considers the allegations that the arts are sometimes sexist and racist. Chapter 14 presents popular culture in relation to fine arts, raising questions about whether the high art/low art distinction is important, and also whether some of the popular art forms deserve aesthetic accolades according to traditional standards of evaluation. Other readings examine the aesthetic character of everyday experience.

Chapter 15 includes material that contrasts with much of traditional theory—theory, that is, that has focused on Western high art. The readings are largely introductory expositions, but they are suggestive as bases for philosophical comparisons between traditions and as sources of challenges to the aesthetic standards that have prevailed in the West.

Although the majority of readings on non-Western aesthetics are located in Chapter 15, certain others appear throughout the book in chapters to which they are especially relevant. These include articles by Yuriko Saito (Chapter 3), Eugen Herrigel (Chapter 7), Mara Miller (Chapter 13), and Sei Shōnagon, Garret Sokoloff, and Barbara Sandrisser (Chapter 14).

Because some instructors prefer to place emphasis on specific artistic media, Appendix I includes a list that organizes the book's contents by medium. In order to assist instructors who wish to focus on specific artworks or to introduce reproductions or recordings of artworks in class, Appendix II lists the cases that are discussed to any significant degree. These are also listed by medium.

Aesthetics in Perspective also includes a general glossary, with important terms both in English and in foreign languages, and a general bibliography. Readings that deal with the topic of a specific chapter are listed at the end of that chapter.

ACKNOWLEDGMENTS

Many people have assisted me in the process of compiling this book. Jenene Allison, Felicia Bond, Sarah Canright, Arthur C. Danto, Matthew Daude, Stephen Davies, Marcia Muelder Eaton, Shelly Errington, Steven Feld, Henry Frankel, Douglas Kellner, Sanford Levinson, Louis Mackey, Bernd Magnus, Janet McCracken, Barbara Mundy, Martha Nussbaum, Joel Rudinow, Barbara Sandrisser, Richard Shusterman, Stephen Slawek, Garret Sokoloff, Elke Solomon, Jorge Valadez, Mary Bodine, and Leslie Kronz are among those whom I wish to thank for directing me to relevant readings and authors. I am also grateful to the Latin American Bureau of London for their assistance in my attempt to locate authors.

Thanks are also due to the following reviewers who read over portions of this manuscript in early drafts: Sherrill Begres (Indiana University of Pennsylvania), Timothy Owen Davis (Essex Community College), William J. Edgar (State University of New York—Geneseo), Karen Hanson (Indiana University), Nelson Potter (University of Nebraska at Lincoln), Anita Silvers (San Francisco State University), Robert Stecker (Central Michigan University), Julie Van Camp (California State University—Long Beach), Frans van der Bogert (Appalachian State University), and Joanne Waugh (University of South Florida). Their comments helped me to improve the structure and balance of readings, and I am appreciative for their thoughtful suggestions. I also wish to thank David Tatom, Claire Brantley, and Christopher Nelson, my editors at Harcourt Brace College Publishers, for their confidence and assistance throughout the project. I am grateful, too, to Karen Mottola, who helped me with the indexing and proofing of the final manuscript.

I would like to mention my gratitude toward my parents, Kathryn and Eugene Higgins, and my siblings, Timothy Higgins, Colleen Cook, Jeanine Felten, Maureen Daily, and James Higgins, for their continued and thoughtful encouragement. I also wish to thank Paula Fulks and Douglas Buhrer, my longtime compatriots in aesthetic experience and occasional disputes about taste. Finally, I want to thank Robert C. Solomon for inciting and (sometimes literally) supporting this project and, even more importantly, for his affection and enthusiasm.

CONTENTS

◆◆◆

◆◆◆

PART II

INTERPRETING AND
EVALUATING ART   273

————◆◆◆———

PART III

CHALLENGES TO
THE TRADITION   477

———◆◆◆———

———◆◆◆———

PART IV

BEYOND THE WEST   647

———◆◆◆———

INTRODUCTION

Aesthetic concerns are all around us, whether or not we attend to them. When we ask how to keep (or make) our environment beautiful, how to arrange our lives to reflect our personal tastes, how to assess the many appeals that our mass media send us daily—all of these are questions of aesthetics. These are also ubiquitous concerns of our everyday lives. Making aesthetic judgments and choices is unavoidable, perhaps especially in our era.

Aesthetics was a term coined by the German philosopher Alexander Gottlieb Baumgarten in the eighteenth century to refer to the philosophical investigation of perception by means of the senses. Of course, all of our interactions with our world involve sensory experience. The emphasis of the field of aesthetics as it developed, however, was primarily on sensory perceptions that seem to be particularly valuable. Thus, aesthetics is particularly concerned with our experiences of art and natural beauty, in which our perception seems to be especially worthwhile and satisfying in itself.

Because Baumgarten had his own eighteenth-century agenda in mind when he coined the term, some contemporary philosophers restrict the term *aesthetics* to the philosophical debates that were current in the eighteenth century (especially those concerning taste and its judgments). These philosophers often prefer "philosophy of art" to "aesthetics" when they refer to contemporary philosophical investigations of art. I see no reason to restrict "aesthetics" to eighteenth-century problems, however. Like many terms, its connotations have evolved over time. Philosophers were also interested in the nature of beauty and art long before the time of Baumgarten.

Moreover, the scope of aesthetics extends far beyond the realm of art. The term *art* has such detailed cultural connotations that it may not strictly apply to aesthetic productions throughout the world. (Robert Plant Armstrong argues in Chapter 2, for example, that "affecting presence" would be a more inclusive expression.) Popular media, which are often excluded from the traditional category of art, address us aesthetically. Whenever we contemplate an object with wonder, we experience aesthetically, whether or not the object is an artwork. Accordingly, the readings in this book will present aesthetic issues in connection with a broad terrain of valued and noteworthy sensory experiences, although art and experience of art will be particularly prominent.

One of the central questions aesthetics asks and seeks to answer is the question of why art itself is valuable; many of the readings in this book deal with this question, either directly or indirectly. Activities that resemble what we in the West consider "art" are prevalent worldwide (although often the results are not intended for detached contemplation or presentation in museums), which suggests that art—or something like it—is an important and basic part of human life. But we might ask why. Over the course of

Western history, philosophers have sought to explain the value of art through various lines of reasoning, all of which still figure in our expectations of art to some extent.

One possible answer is that art is beautiful. This line of reasoning immediately raises another question: Why is beauty valuable? (This question is considered in some of the readings in Chapter 1). Beauty is not a sufficient explanation of why we value art, however, for art and beauty are separable concerns of aesthetics. Natural beauty is a matter of aesthetic consideration in its own right. Art, on the other hand, *may* be intended as beautiful; but artists might alternatively aim to make stirring, disturbing, interesting, or outright ugly art. These alternative goals are themselves aesthetic values, and among the concerns of aesthetics are questions about why these aims are (or might be seen as) worthwhile.

One enduring school of thought in Western philosophical history has held that the purpose of art is to offer insight into the fundamental truths of our world, which consequently is the basis of art's importance. Although Plato himself feared that art might provide distractions from reality instead of insight into it, he suggested that art should be judged on the basis of how accurately it reflects reality. Plato's student and later philosophical antagonist, Aristotle, defended this standard in more positive terms, contending that dramatic poetry aims to reveal general truths about human beings, especially about particular types of people. For example, even in our casual judgments that a movie is or is not realistic, we implicitly refer to this standard of assessing art according to whether it reveals the truth about our world. (Chapter 3 deals with the relationships of art, truth, and reality.)

Another longstanding position is the view that art's purpose (on which it should be judged) is to facilitate certain societal goals, such as morality or social harmony. These goals, in fact, were often Plato's primary interest when he discussed art. (Chapter 3 includes one such reading from Plato.) Art can stimulate either good or bad behavior, according to Plato, who further suggests that government censorship of art is appropriate. Contemporary advocates of censorship or of warning labels on recordings are implicitly supporting the same perspective on how art should be assessed. Art, on this view, should be judged according to whether it promotes good or bad behavior and develops good or bad citizens. (Chapter 5 deals especially with art in relation to morality.)

Ancient philosophers tended to value art for its objective contributions to societal life, whether it educated its audience in truth or in moral behavior. More modern thinkers (since the seventeenth century) have tended, by contrast, to place more emphasis on psychology and the inner life of the human being. With this emphasis came a growing tendency to value the subjective impact of art. By the eighteenth century, when the term *aesthetics* was coined, philosophical debate about art focused largely on taste, the individual's subjective ability to make good judgments about what is beautiful and about the value of specific artworks. Art, accordingly, came to be understood primarily in terms of how conducive it was to producing a particularly valuable type of inner experience—aesthetic experience—in its observer. On this view, aesthetic experience is the basis of art's importance.

The assessment of art on the basis of its inward effects complicated speculation about the purpose and value of art. After all, observers might have different inner experiences. The adage that "beauty is in the eye of the beholder" reflects the conclusion drawn by some thinkers that the subjectivity of aesthetic experience renders objective judgments about art impossible. Scottish philosopher David Hume believed that taste is radically subjective (although he did not think that everyone's taste is equally good). Other philosophers, however, held that rational grounds could be given for judgments of taste, even if art is valuable primarily because of its ability to produce particular subjective experiences in the observer. Immanuel Kant, in particular, was a proponent of this latter view. (Chapter 1 includes readings from Hume and Kant that deal with these issues.)

Unprecedented artistic developments in the twentieth century have led philosophers to ponder a new set of questions about the objective nature of art. Many ask how we know something is an artwork. In much of the West's traditional art, representation of reality has been a primary objective. In the twentieth century, however, an artwork might not represent anything. We cannot even be sure that an artwork is made by an artist, or that it will appear to be anything other than an everyday object somewhat oddly presented in a museum. (Chapter 2 considers some of these unusual artworks and the philosophical efforts, in response, to determine what art is. Chapters 3–11 present some of the answers that have been proposed.)

Twentieth-century art has been denounced by many who have more traditional expectations. Some are disappointed, for example, by art that is not straightforwardly representational. Others, however, contend that even abstract art can reveal something about reality. It might show us, for instance, something about our own sense of movement or grace, or the fragmented structure of our experience. Some of the public is disappointed when art seems to have little to say about how we should live our lives. Yet others point out that some contemporary art does make statements about political matters, and that other art urges us to reflect on our social problems, even if it does not promote particular views. Contemporary art is also defended by those who think that challenges to our expectations are themselves helpful to developing the skills to live well in a world so filled with changes and surprises.

In surveying contemporary artistic developments, we may discover that certain traditional standards continue to inform this art, despite its nontraditional appearance. Contemporary art may still represent features of our experience, encourage moral and political responsibility, or stimulate inner experiences that are intrinsically valuable. On the other hand, some contemporary art is designed in explicit rejection of traditional ideals. Some of the reasons that have motivated this development include the belief that the presuppositions of previous art are no longer convincing in our fragmented and unsettling era; the conviction that much traditional art reflects and reinforces racist, sexist, and other undesirable biases; and the conviction that high art is not intrinsically superior to popular culture, which itself should become a more prominent concern of art and aesthetics. (Chapters 12, 13, and 14 deal with these challenges to tradition.)

Growing awareness of the importance of our natural environment has contributed to another recent development, the tendency within the field of aesthetics to reflect upon the value of nature and other non-art. Our efforts to adorn ourselves and to decorate our homes, to develop personal styles of living, to punctuate the passage of time with holidays and celebrations, to individualize the way we communicate, to be sensitive in our responses to other people, animals, and plants—these everyday concerns, too, are increasingly matters of aesthetic concern. (Chapter 14, in particular, considers the aesthetics of our everyday lives.)

Aesthetics is also touched by the increasing public awareness of intercultural interactions and conflicts. The aesthetic dimension is one of the first areas in which the foreignness of another culture makes itself felt. Tastes that seem unfamiliar occasion discomfort, but also, in most of us, interest. Aethetics is the arena in which unfamiliar styles and tastes can be analyzed and, one hopes, somewhat understood. Aesthetics is also a relatively unthreatening vantage for becoming acquainted with other societies, for it is possible to appreciate something of other cultures' stylistic values without abandoning one's own or being faced with the need to compete or to defend one's interests. (Chapter 15 considers some of the aesthetic values of other societies.)

I embarked on the project of editing this book because I am convinced that aesthetics is fun. I hope that the array of readings that follow will make the delightfulness of aesthetics obvious.

PART I

ART AND
THE NATURE
OF BEAUTY

WHAT IS BEAUTY AND WHERE HAS IT GONE?

If you go to a museum and see Renaissance art, you are likely to be reminded that beauty was once a major artistic aspiration in the West. Renaissance art portrays beautiful, well-proportioned human beings in contexts that are balanced and orderly. If you visit a contemporary arts museum, by contrast, you will probably not be overwhelmed by beauty. Beauty has not been the predominant aim of most twentieth-century art. Many recent artists have deliberately sought to present what is ugly, and most have viewed beauty as irrelevant to their goals.

Historically, Western philosophy has been more concerned with beauty than with art, taking beauty to be evident in people and natural phenomena, not only in human artifacts. The selected dialogues from Plato (427–347 B.C.E.), some of the most influential discussions of beauty in our tradition, take the beauty of a human being as the paradigm case. In the excerpt from Plato's *Symposium*, Plato's character Socrates recounts the instruction about beauty that he received from a wise woman named Diotima. Diotima's teaching was that the beauty we see in human beings and material things is a reflection of a more perfect and absolute Beauty. Absolute Beauty, on this account, is a spiritual reality, a **Form,** the perfect prototype for whatever is beautiful in our world. Our minds can recognize the Form of Beauty through the imperfect beauties we see around us. Insight comes when we recognize that true Beauty exists on a higher, immaterial plane of existence. The more our minds attend to this higher plane, the more we know truth, and the wiser we become.

The selection from Plato's *Phaedrus* also stars Socrates, who tells a story of human souls falling from a more perfect state of being, in which they gazed directly upon Beauty and other Forms (such as Truth and Goodness), to a less perfect state. Despite this fall, they dimly remember the Forms, including Beauty. As a consequence, they naturally respond to beauty, which they grasp even through its imperfect manifestations on the material plane. Socrates describes falling in love as a case of responding to beauty. The wisest will nurture the spiritual side of love, gaining insight and wisdom in the process. But those who do not allow themselves to be guided by reason and spiritual insight will instead respond more physically, with sexual lust and wanton behavior. The higher course results in inner peace and a blissful afterlife; but even the less noble course of physical love is not to be disdained, for the recognition of beauty involved is still a first step toward spiritual insight.

Plato's student Aristotle (384–322 B.C.E.) did not believe that Beauty was a transcendent Form. He considered the real world to be that of mundane life, and he studied this world with an eye to scientific detail. Beauty, according to Aristotle, is a property of everyday objects, characterized by order and symmetry. Aristotle's influential *Poetics* does not explicitly discuss beauty. Nevertheless, it considers the kind of ordering that is essential to beauty by discussing the way a playwright goes about structuring an ideally ordered play.

Aristotle describes the elements necessary for a tragedy, how a playwright should employ them, which plays have succeeded and why, and the relative priorities that the playwright should bear in mind. Aristotle encourages the playwright to aim at a concentrated effect, the better to elicit the emotions appropriate to tragedy—pity and fear—that the play is designed to arouse and release. The play should be modeled on the biological organism, with multiple parts all serving some function that is vital to the work as a whole. It should also exhibit **closure,** having a definite beginning and an end that resolves the threads involved in the plot. Although the *Poetics* focuses mainly on tragedy, the tradition that followed Aristotle took many of his recommendations—especially those demanding unity, closure, and organic wholeness—to apply to other art forms as well.

For all their differences, Plato and Aristotle both considered beauty to be an objective property of artworks and other things. More recent thinkers, beginning around the seventeenth century, have stressed the subjective character of all our experiences, including the experience of beauty. This emphasis led thinkers in the eighteenth century to dispute about the nature of "taste," which they took to be the faculty involved in aesthetic appreciation. Debate raged over whether one could justify one's judgments of taste, or whether these judgments were radically subjective, a purely individual matter.

Scottish philosopher David Hume's "Of the Standard of Taste" addresses this controversy. Hume (1711–1776) contends that aesthetic value is a matter of one's emotional response, which can be determined only subjectively. Every individual, accordingly, must judge for him- or herself. Nevertheless, Hume grants that some judges are especially likely to recognize artworks that will be valued by others besides themselves. These aesthetic experts are those individuals who are unusually free of bias and eccentricity in their judgment, and we do well to heed their advice if we want some idea of where to go to find artworks that we are likely to find valuable. If we want to know which works are the genuine masterpieces, however, the ultimate test is the test of time. Those works that have succeeded in inspiring durable admiration are likely to inspire our admiration as well.

Immanuel Kant (1724–1804), a German philosopher, objected to Hume's empirical account of taste as a matter of possibly eccentric individual sentiment. Kant contends that the basic structure of the human mind equips everyone to take satisfaction in beauty, and that this satisfaction stems from intellectual contemplation, not from emotional response (which he took to be relatively more variable). In "The Four Moments," the opening sections of his *Critique of Judgment,* he describes four features of the experience of beauty that are required in a purely aesthetic experience, or "judgment," of the beautiful.

First, one must enjoy the object of the experience "disinterestedly," without attending to personal interests or desires. Second, one must engage two mental faculties in what Kant describes as "free play." These faculties are imagination (the operation by which the mind converts sense impressions into "pictures" in the mind) and understanding (the operation by which we assign categories to the images formed by the imagination). In free play, our minds apprehend and attend to the object without being concerned to classify it. In free play, one enjoys the activity of contemplating the object without any particular goal in mind. Third, one must be able to consider the aesthetic object as having elements that work together to form a whole, although without being able to articulate precisely the nature of this "whole." Fourth, one must consider the beautiful object as the type of thing that others could also consider beautiful (assuming that they, too, fulfill these four requirements).

Kant concludes that judging something to be beautiful is more than an expression of personal inclinations. According to Kant, what we enjoy in aesthetic experience is the play of our mental faculties, the very faculties that are basic to our minds' operations. Since we assume that all human beings have essentially the same kind of minds, we are right to assume that they can all enjoy aesthetic experiences. When we point to something and say "That's beautiful!" we expect other people to see what we mean and be able to enjoy the beautiful object themselves, because they have the same kind of minds that we do.

Friedrich Nietzsche (1844–1900) objects to Kant's intellectualized understanding of beauty and the similar view held by Kant's nineteenth-century admirer, Arthur Schopenhauer. (Chapter 7 includes a selection from one of Schopenhauer's statements of his aesthetic theory.) Schopenhauer considered the contemplation of beauty to be an antidote to all desires, especially erotic ones. Nietzsche rejects this view, along with Kant's requirement that appreciation of beauty be disinterested. Siding with Plato on this matter, Nietzsche insists that beauty is an essentially erotic stimulus. Like beauty, art should be seen, according to Nietzsche, as stimulating a sense of life. Even tragedy functions in this way, for tragedy involves a celebration of human life in its entirety, the painful as well as the soothing.

Nietzsche's first book, *The Birth of Tragedy*, explicitly analyzed tragedy as a celebration of human existence. Reproduced here is the opening section of that book, in which Nietzsche describes the two somewhat contrary artistic principles that operate in Athenian tragedy. The principle associated with Apollo, the sun god, is the principle of order, serenity, and beautiful appearance. That associated with Dionysus, the god of wine, sexuality, and revelry, is the principle of wild dynamism, in which the participant feels a part of a throng (the phenomenon that psychologists associate with crowd behavior).

Nietzsche argues that both of these principles were celebrated by the ancient Greeks, who used them religiously as ways to understand the meaning of life in the face of the suffering that every human life involves. By drawing attention to the Dionysian principle as an alternative value to beauty, Nietzsche suggests that beauty has never been the sole aim of art and urges his own era to attend more to the Dionysian mode in its art-making. By means of Apollonian images, the Greeks transfigured the sometimes disturbing world by presenting it to themselves as beautiful. Yet the Dionysian principle reminded them that participating in the powerful flux of life was intrinsically satisfying, even if the outcome was the individual's eventual death.

By claiming that dual aesthetic principles were at work in art from the beginning of the Western tradition, Nietzsche furthered a tendency that was already evident in the eighteenth century: to see other values besides beauty as aesthetically important. The eighteenth century had been captivated by the **sublime,** the awe-inspiring, formless cases of natural grandeur (like the starry heavens or Niagara Falls) that were either too vast or too forceful for human beings to see as beautifully proportioned. Nietzsche reinforced the West's recognition that other categories besides the beautiful deserve aesthetic attention. Twentieth-century artists have taken this recognition as a starting point, often defying traditional canons of beauty with these very different objectives in mind.

Plato

THE
FORM
OF
BEAUTY

Plato (427–347 B.C.E.), an Athenian from an influential family, was accomplished as a playwright before becoming a student of Socrates. He is said to have burned his plays under the influence of Socrates, who taught reliance on reason and skepticism toward irrational appeals. Plato became one of the most influential philosophers in the Western tradition. He is the author of dialogues, philosophical conversations that usually feature Socrates as their most important figure. The following selection is taken from the Symposium, *a dialogue set at the end of a dinner party, when each of the participants takes a turn giving a speech about love. Socrates' speech, which follows, describes beauty as an absolute reality, transcending the particular beautiful things and people that we see in everyday life.*

. . . There are many spirits, and many kinds of spirits, too, and Love is one of them.

Then who were his parents? I asked.

I'll tell you, she said, though it's rather a long story. On the day of Aphrodite's birth the gods were making merry, and among them was Resource, the son of Craft. And when they had supped, Need came begging at the door because there was good cheer inside. Now, it happened that Resource, having drunk deeply of the heavenly nectar—for this was before the days of wine— wandered out into the garden of Zeus and sank into a heavy sleep, and Need, thinking that to get a child by Resource

Plato, *Symposium*, trans. Michael Joyce, *The Collected Dialogues of Plato, Including the Letters*, ed. Edith Hamilton and Huntington Cairns, Bollingen LXXI (Princeton: Princeton UP, 1961) 555–63.

would mitigate her penury, lay down beside him and in time was brought to bed of Love. So Love became the follower and servant of Aphrodite because he was begotten on the same day that she was born, and further, he was born to love the beautiful since Aphrodite is beautiful herself.

Then again, as the son of Resource and Need, it has been his fate to be always needy; nor is he delicate and lovely as most of us believe, but harsh and arid, barefoot and homeless, sleeping on the naked earth, in doorways, or in the very streets beneath the stars of heaven, and always partaking of his mother's poverty. But, secondly, he brings his father's resourcefulness to his designs upon the beautiful and the good, for he is gallant, impetuous, and energetic, a mighty hunter, and a master of device and artifice—at once desirous and full of wisdom, a lifelong seeker after truth, an adept in sorcery, enchantment, and seduction.

He is neither mortal nor immortal, for in the space of a day he will be now, when all goes well with him, alive and blooming, and now dying, to be born again by virtue of his father's nature, while what he gains will always ebb away as fast. So Love is never altogether in or out of need, and stands, moreover, midway between ignorance and wisdom. You must understand that none of the gods are seekers after truth. They do not long for wisdom, because they are wise—and why should the wise be seeking the wisdom that is already theirs? Nor, for that matter, do the ignorant seek the truth or crave to be made wise. And indeed, what makes their case so hopeless is that, having neither beauty, nor goodness, nor intelligence, they are satisfied with what they are, and do not long for the virtues they have never missed.

. . . So much, then, for the nature and the origin of Love. You were right in thinking that he was the love of what is beautiful. But suppose someone were to say, Yes, my

dear Socrates. Quite so, my dear Diotima. But what do you mean by the love of what is beautiful? Or, to put the question more precisely, what is it that the lover of the beautiful is longing for?

He is longing to make the beautiful his own, I said.

Very well, she replied, but your answer leads to another question. What will he gain by making the beautiful his own?

This, as I had to admit, was more than I could answer on the spur of the moment.

Well then, she went on, suppose that, instead of the beautiful, you were being asked about the good. I put it to you, Socrates. What is it that the lover of the good is longing for?

To make the good his own.

Then what will he gain by making it his own?

I can make a better shot at answering that, I said. He'll gain happiness.

Right, said she, for the happy are happy inasmuch as they possess the good, and since there's no need for us to ask why men should want to be happy, I think your answer is conclusive.

Absolutely, I agreed.

This longing, then, she went on, this love—is it common to all mankind? What do you think, do we all long to make the good our own?

Yes, I said, as far as that goes we're all alike.

Well then, Socrates, if we say that everybody always loves the same thing, does that mean that everybody is in love? Or do we mean that some of us are in love, while some of us are not?

I was a little worried about that myself, I confessed.

Oh, it's nothing to worry about, she assured me. You see, what we've been doing is to give the name of Love to what is only one single aspect of it; we make just the same mistake, you know, with a lot of other names.

For instance . . . ?

For instance, poetry. You'll agree that there is more than one kind of poetry in the true sense of the word—that is to say, calling something into existence that was not there before, so that every kind of artistic creation is poetry, and every artist is a poet.

True.

But all the same, she said, we don't call them all poets, do we? We give various names to the various arts, and only call the one particular art that deals with music and meter by the name that should be given to them all. And that's the only art that we call poetry, while those who practice it are known as poets.

Quite.

And that's how it is with Love. For "Love, that renowned and all-beguiling power," includes every kind of longing for happiness and for the good. Yet those of us who are subject to this longing in the various fields of business, athletics, philosophy, and so on, are never said to be in love, and are never known as lovers, while the man who devotes himself to what is only one of Love's many activities is given the name that should apply to all the rest as well.

Yes, I said, I suppose you might be right.

I know it has been suggested, she continued, that lovers are people who are looking for their other halves, but as I see it, Socrates, Love never longs for either the half or the whole of anything except the good. For men will even have their hands and feet cut off if they are once convinced that those members are bad for them. Indeed I think we only prize our own belongings in so far as we say that the good belongs to us, and the bad to someone else, for what we love is the good and nothing but the good. . . .

. . . And that being so, what course will Love's followers pursue, and in what particular field will eagerness and exertion be known as Love? In fact, what *is* this activity? Can you tell me that, Socrates?

If I could, my dear Diotima, I retorted, I shouldn't be so much amazed at *your* grasp of the subject, and I shouldn't be coming to you to learn the answer to that very question.

Well, I'll tell you, then, she said. To love is to bring forth upon the beautiful, both in body and in soul.

I'm afraid that's too deep, I said, for my poor wits to fathom.

I'll try to speak more plainly, then. We are all of us prolific, Socrates, in body and in soul, and when we reach a certain age our nature urges us to procreation. Nor can we be quickened by ugliness, but only by the beautiful. Conception, we know, takes place when man and woman come together, but there's a divinity in human propagation, an immortal something in the midst of man's mortality which is incompatible with any kind of discord. And ugliness is at odds with the divine, while beauty is in perfect harmony. In propagation, then, Beauty is the goddess of both fate and travail, and so when procreancy draws near the beautiful it grows genial and blithe, and birth follows swiftly on conception. But when it meets with ugliness it is overcome with heaviness and gloom, and turning away it shrinks into itself and is not brought to bed, but still labors under its painful burden. And so, when the procreant is big with child, he is strangely stirred by the beautiful, because he knows that beauty's tenant will bring his travail to an end. So you see, Socrates, that Love is not exactly a longing for the beautiful, as you suggested.

Well, what is it, then?

A longing not for the beautiful itself, but for the conception and generation that the beautiful effects.

Yes. No doubt you're right.

Of course I'm right, she said. And why all this longing for propagation? Because this is the one deathless and eternal element in our mortality. And since we have agreed that the lover longs for the good to be his own forever, it follows that we are bound to long for immortality as well as for the good—which is to say that Love is a longing for immortality.

So much I gathered, gentlemen, at one time and another from Diotima's dissertations upon Love.

And then one day she asked me, Well, Socrates, and what do you suppose is the cause of all this longing and all this love? Haven't you noticed what an extraordinary effect the breeding instinct has upon both animals and birds, and how obsessed they are with the desire, first to mate, and then to rear their litters and their broods, and how the weakest of them are ready to stand up to the strongest in defense of their young, and even die for them, and how they are content to bear the pinch of hunger and every kind of hardship, so long as they can rear their offspring?

With men, she went on, you might put it down to the power of reason, but how can you account for Love's having such remarkable effects upon the brutes? What do you say to that, Socrates?

Again I had to confess my ignorance.

Well, she said, I don't know how you can hope to master the philosophy of Love, if *that's* too much for you to understand.

But, my dear Diotima, I protested, as I said before, that's just why I'm asking you to teach me—because I realize how ignorant I am. And I'd be more than grateful if you'd enlighten me as to the cause not only of this, but of all the various effects of Love.

Well, she said, it's simple enough, so long as you bear in mind what we agreed was the object of Love. For here, too, the principle holds good that the mortal does all it can to put on immortality. And how can it do that except by breeding, and thus ensuring that there will always be a younger generation to take the place of the old?

Now, although we speak of an individual as being the same so long as he continues to exist in the same form, and therefore assume that a man is the same person in his dotage as in his infancy, yet, for all we call him the same, every bit of him is different, and every day he is becoming a new man, while the old man is ceasing to exist, as you can see from his hair, his flesh, his bones, his blood, and all the rest of his body. And not only his body, for the same thing happens to his soul. And neither his manners, nor his disposition, nor his thoughts, nor his desires, nor his pleasures, nor his sufferings, nor his fears are the same throughout his life, for some of them grow, while others disappear.

And the application of this principle to human knowledge is even more remarkable, for not only do some of the things we know increase, while some of them are lost, so that even in our knowledge we are not always the same, but the principle applies as well to every single branch of knowledge. When we say we are studying, we really mean that our knowledge is ebbing away. We forget, because our knowledge disappears, and we have to study so as to replace what we are losing, so that the state of our knowledge may seem, at any rate, to be the same as it was before.

This is how every mortal creature perpetuates itself. It cannot, like the divine, be still the same throughout eternity; it can only leave behind new life to fill the vacancy that is left in its species by obsolescence. This, my dear Socrates, is how the body and all else that is temporal partakes of the eternal; there is no other way. And so it is no wonder that every creature prizes its own issue, since the whole creation is inspired by this love, this passion for immortality.

Well, Diotima, I said, when she had done, that's a most impressive argument. I wonder if you're right.

Of course I am, she said with an air of authority that was almost professorial. Think of the ambitions of your fellow men, and though at first they may strike you as upsetting my argument, you'll see how right I am if you only bear in mind that men's great incentive is the love of glory, and that their one idea is "To win eternal mention in the deathless roll of fame."

For the sake of fame they will dare greater dangers, even, than for their children; they are ready to spend their money like water and to wear their fingers to the bone, and, if it comes to that, to die.

Do you think, she went on, that Alcestis would have laid down her life to save Admetus, or that Achilles would have died for the love he bore Patroclus, or that Codrus, the Athenian king, would have sacrificed himself for the seed of his royal consort, if they had not hoped to win "the deathless name for valor," which, in fact, posterity has granted them? No, Socrates, no. Every one of us, no matter what he does, is longing for the endless fame, the incomparable glory that is theirs, and the nobler he is, the greater his ambition, because he is in love with the eternal.

Well then, she went on, those whose procreancy is of the body turn to woman as the object of their love, and raise a family, in the blessed hope that by doing so they will keep their memory green, "through time and through eternity." But those whose procreancy is of the spirit rather than of the flesh—and they are not unknown, Socrates—conceive and bear the things of the spirit. And what are they? you ask. Wisdom and all her sister virtues; it is the office of every poet to beget them, and of every artist whom we may call creative.

Now, by far the most important kind of wisdom, she went on, is that which governs the ordering of society, and which goes by the names of justice and moderation. And if any man is so closely allied to the divine as to be teeming with these virtues even in his youth, and if, when he comes to manhood, his first ambition is to be begetting, he too, you may be sure, will go about in search of the loveliness—and never of the ugliness—on which he may beget. And hence his procreant nature is attracted by a comely

body rather than an ill-favored one, and if, besides, he happens on a soul which is at once beautiful, distinguished, and agreeable, he is charmed to find so welcome an alliance. It will be easy for him to talk of virtue to such a listener, and to discuss what human goodness is and how the virtuous should live—in short, to undertake the other's education.

And, as I believe, by constant association with so much beauty, and by thinking of his friend when he is present and when he is away, he will be delivered of the burden he has labored under all these years. And what is more, he and his friend will help each other rear the issue of their friendship—and so the bond between them will be more binding, and their communion even more complete, than that which comes of bringing children up, because they have created something lovelier and less mortal than human seed.

And I ask you, who would not prefer such fatherhood to merely human propagation, if he stopped to think of Homer, and Hesiod, and all the greatest of our poets? Who would not envy them their immortal progeny, their claim upon the admiration of posterity? . . .

Well now, my dear Socrates, I have no doubt that even you might be initiated into these, the more elementary mysteries of Love. But I don't know whether you could apprehend the final revelation, for so far, you know, we are only at the bottom of the true scale of perfection.

Never mind, she went on, I will do all I can to help you understand, and you must strain every nerve to follow what I'm saying.

Well then, she began, the candidate for this initiation cannot, if his efforts are to be rewarded, begin too early to devote himself to the beauties of the body. First of all, if his preceptor instructs him as he should, he will fall in love with the beauty of one individual body, so that his passion may give life to noble discourse. Next he must consider how nearly related the beauty of any one body is to the beauty of any other, when he will see that if he is to devote himself to loveliness of form it will be absurd to deny that the beauty of each and every body is the same. Having reached this point, he must set himself to be the lover of every lovely body, and bring his passion for the one into due proportion by deeming it of little or of no importance.

Next he must grasp that the beauties of the body are as nothing to the beauties of the soul, so that wherever he meets with spiritual loveliness, even in the husk of an unlovely body, he will find it beautiful enough to fall in love with and to cherish— and beautiful enough to quicken in his heart a longing for such discourse as tends toward the building of a noble nature. And from this he will be led to contemplate the beauty of laws and institutions. And when he discovers how nearly every kind of beauty is akin to every other he will conclude that the beauty of the body is not, after all, of so great moment.

And next, his attention should be diverted from institutions to the sciences, so that he may know the beauty of every kind of knowledge. And thus, by scanning beauty's wide horizon, he will be saved from a slavish and illiberal devotion to the individual loveliness of a single boy, a single man, or a single institution. And, turning his eyes toward the open sea of beauty, he will find in such contemplation the seed of the most fruitful discourse and the loftiest thought, and reap a golden harvest of philosophy, until, confirmed and strengthened, he will come upon one single form of knowledge, the knowledge of the beauty I am about to speak of.

And here, she said, you must follow me as closely as you can.

Whoever has been initiated so far in the mysteries of Love and has viewed all these aspects of the beautiful in due succession, is at last drawing near the final revelation. And

now, Socrates, there bursts upon him that wondrous vision which is the very soul of the beauty he has toiled so long for. It is an everlasting loveliness which neither comes nor goes, which neither flowers nor fades, for such beauty is the same on every hand, the same then as now, here as there, this way as that way, the same to every worshiper as it is to every other. Nor will his vision of the beautiful take the form of a face, or of hands, or of anything that is of the flesh. It will be neither words, nor knowledge, nor a something that exists in something else, such as a living creature, or the earth, or the heavens, or anything that is—but subsisting of itself and by itself in an eternal oneness, while every lovely thing partakes of it in such sort that, however much the parts may wax and wane, it will be neither more nor less, but still the same inviolable whole.

And so, when his prescribed devotion to boyish beauties has carried our candidate so far that the universal beauty dawns upon his inward sight, he is almost within reach of the final revelation. And this is the way, the only way, he must approach, or be led toward, the sanctuary of Love. Starting from individual beauties, the quest for the universal beauty must find him ever mounting the heavenly ladder, stepping from rung to rung—that is, from one to two, and from two to *every* lovely body, from bodily beauty to the beauty of institutions, from institutions to learning, and from learning in general to the special lore that pertains to nothing but the beautiful itself—until at last he comes to know what beauty is.

And if, my dear Socrates, Diotima went on, man's life is ever worth the living, it is when he has attained this vision of the very soul of beauty. And once you have seen it, you will never be seduced again by the charm of gold, of dress, of comely boys, or lads just ripening to manhood; you will care nothing for the beauties that used to take your breath away and kindle such a longing in you, and many others like you, Socrates, to be always at the side of the beloved and feasting your eyes upon him, so that you would be content, if it were possible, to deny yourself the grosser necessities of meat and drink, so long as you were with him.

But if it were given to man to gaze on beauty's very self—unsullied, unalloyed, and freed from the mortal taint that haunts the frailer loveliness of flesh and blood—if, I say, it were given to man to see the heavenly beauty face to face, would you call *his*, she asked me, an unenviable life, whose eyes had been opened to the vision, and who had gazed upon it in true contemplation until it had become his own forever?

And remember, she said, that it is only when he discerns beauty itself through what makes it visible that a man will be quickened with the true, and not the seeming, virtue—for it is virtue's self that quickens him, not virtue's semblance. And when he has brought forth and reared this perfect virtue, he shall be called the friend of god, and if ever it is given to man to put on immortality, it shall be given to him.

Plato

BEAUTY'S INFLUENCE

One of Plato's (427–347 B.C.E.) most famous dialogues is the Phaedrus, *from which the following selection is taken. Socrates describes the impact of beauty on the soul of one who beholds it. The soul itself is divided into three parts, which Socrates compares to a charioteer (representing reason) and two horses. One of the horses (who represents the appetites) is unruly, wanting to possess the beautiful human being physically. The other horse (representing spirit) is more cooperative, but it too requires guidance. Ideally, the charioteer will maintain control and direct the soul toward a more philosophical life of reverence toward the person one loves. Either way, Plato's Socrates emphasizes that beauty inspires love.*

All soul is immortal, for that which is ever in motion is immortal. . . .

. . . As to its nature there is this that must be said. . . . Let it be likened to the union of powers in a team of winged steeds and their winged charioteer. Now all the gods' steeds and all their charioteers are good, and of good stock, but with other beings it is not wholly so. With us men, in the first place, it is a pair of steeds that the charioteer controls; moreover one of them is noble and good, and of good stock, while the other has the opposite character, and his stock is opposite. Hence the task of our charioteer is difficult and troublesome.

And now we must essay to tell how it is that living beings are called mortal and immortal. All soul has the care of all that is inanimate, and traverses the whole universe, though in ever-changing forms. Thus when it is perfect and winged it journeys on high and controls the whole world, but one that has shed its wings sinks down until it can fasten on something solid, and settling there it takes to itself an earthy body which seems by reason of the soul's power to move itself. This composite structure of soul and body is called a living being, and is further termed "mortal"; "immortal" is a term applied on no basis of reasoned argument at all, but our

Plato, *Phaedrus*, trans. R. Hackforth, *The Collected Dialogues of Plato, Including the Letters*, ed. Edith Hamilton and Huntington Cairns, Bollingen LXXI (Princeton: Princeton UP, 1961) 492–502.

fancy pictures the god whom we have never seen, nor fully conceived, as an immortal living being, possessed of a soul and a body united for all time. Howbeit, let these matters, and our account thereof, be as God pleases; what we must understand is the reason why the soul's wings fall from it, and are lost. It is on this wise.

The natural property of a wing is to raise that which is heavy and carry it aloft to the region where the gods dwell, and more than any other bodily part it shares in the divine nature, which is fair, wise, and good, and possessed of all other such excellences. Now by these excellences especially is the soul's plumage nourished and fostered, while by their opposites, even by ugliness and evil, it is wasted and destroyed. And behold, there in the heaven Zeus, mighty leader, drives his winged team. First of the host of gods and daemons he proceeds, ordering all things and caring therefor, and the host follows after him, marshaled in eleven companies. For Hestia abides alone in the gods' dwelling place, but for the rest, all such as are ranked in the number of the twelve as ruler gods lead their several companies, each according to his rank. . . .

Of that place beyond the heavens none of our earthly poets has yet sung, and none shall sing worthily. But this is the manner of it, for assuredly we must be bold to speak what is true, above all when our discourse is upon truth. It is there that true being dwells, without color or shape, that cannot be touched; reason alone, the soul's pilot, can behold it, and all true knowledge is knowledge thereof. Now even as the mind of a god is nourished by reason and knowledge, so also is it with every soul that has a care to receive her proper food; wherefore when at last she has beheld being she is well content, and contemplating truth she is nourished and prospers, until the heaven's revolution brings her back full circle. And while she is borne round she discerns justice, its very self, and likewise temperance,

and knowledge, not the knowledge that is neighbor to becoming and varies with the various objects to which we commonly ascribe being, but the veritable knowledge of being that veritably is. And when she has contemplated likewise and feasted upon all else that has true being, she descends again within the heavens and comes back home. And having so come, her charioteer sets his steeds at their manger, and puts ambrosia before them and draught of nectar to drink withal.

Such is the life of gods. Of the other souls that which best follows a god and becomes most like thereunto raises her charioteer's head into the outer region, and is carried round with the gods in the revolution, but being confounded by her steeds she has much ado to discern the things that are; another now rises, and now sinks, and by reason of her unruly steeds sees in part, but in part sees not. As for the rest, though all are eager to reach the heights and seek to follow, they are not able; sucked down as they travel they trample and tread upon one another, this one striving to outstrip that. Thus confusion ensues, and conflict and grievous sweat. Whereupon, with their charioteers powerless, many are lamed, and many have their wings all broken, and for all their toiling they are balked, every one, of the full vision of being, and departing therefrom, they feed upon the food of semblance.

Now the reason wherefore the souls are fain and eager to behold the plain of Truth, and discover it, lies herein—to wit, that the pasturage that is proper to their noblest part comes from that meadow, and the plumage by which they are borne aloft is nourished thereby.

Hear now the ordinance of Necessity. Whatsoever soul has followed in the train of a god, and discerned something of truth, shall be kept from sorrow until a new revolution shall begin, and if she can do this always, she shall remain always free from hurt. But when she is not able so to follow, and sees none of it, but meeting with some mischance comes to be burdened with a load of forgetfulness and wrongdoing, and because of that burden sheds her wings and falls to the earth, then thus runs the law. In her first birth she shall not be planted in any brute beast, but the soul that hath seen the most of being shall enter into the human babe that shall grow into a seeker after wisdom or beauty, a follower of the Muses and a lover; the next, having seen less, shall dwell in a king that abides by law, or a warrior and ruler; the third in a statesman, a man of business, or a trader; the fourth in an athlete, or physical trainer, or physician; the fifth shall have the life of a prophet or a Mystery priest; to the sixth that of a poet or other imitative artist shall be fittingly given; the seventh shall live in an artisan or farmer; the eighth in a Sophist or demagogue; the ninth in a tyrant.

Now in all these incarnations he who lives righteously has a better lot for his portion, and he who lives unrighteously a worse. For a soul does not return to the place whence she came for ten thousand years, since in no lesser time can she regain her wings, save only his soul who has sought after wisdom unfeignedly, or has conjoined his passion for a loved one with that seeking. Such a soul, if with three revolutions of a thousand years she has thrice chosen this philosophical life, regains thereby her wings, and speeds away after three thousand years; but the rest, when they have accomplished their first life, are brought to judgment, and after the judgment some are taken to be punished in places of chastisement beneath the earth, while others are borne aloft by Justice to a certain region of the heavens, there to live in such manner as is merited by their past life in the flesh. And after a thousand years these and those alike come to the allotment and choice of their second life, each choosing according to her will; then does the soul of a man enter into the life of a beast, and the beast's soul that was aforetime in a man goes back to a man again. For only the soul that has beheld truth may enter into this our human form—seeing that man must needs understand the language of forms, passing from a plurality of perceptions to a unity gathered together by reasoning—and such understanding is a recollection of those things which our souls beheld aforetime as they journeyed with their god, looking down upon the things which now we suppose to be, and gazing up to that which truly is.

Therefore is it meet and right that the soul of the philosopher alone should recover her wings, for she, so far as may be, is ever near in memory to those things a god's nearness whereunto makes him truly god. Wherefore if a man makes right use of such means of remembrance, and ever approaches to the full vision of the perfect mysteries, he and he alone becomes truly perfect. . . .

. . . Such a one, as soon as he beholds the beauty of this world, is reminded of true beauty, and his wings begin to grow; then is he fain to lift his wings and fly upward; yet he has not the power, but inasmuch as he gazes upward like a bird, and cares nothing for the world beneath, men charge it upon him that he is demented.

Now, as we have said, every human soul has, by reason of her nature, had contemplation of true being; else would she never have entered into this human creature; but to be put in mind thereof by things here is not easy for every soul. Some, when they had the vision, had it but for a moment; some when they had fallen to earth consorted unhappily with such as led them to deeds of unrighteousness, wherefore they forgot the holy objects of their vision. Few indeed are left that can still remember much, but when these discern some likeness of the things yonder, they are amazed, and no longer masters of themselves, and know not what is come upon them by reason of their perception being dim.

Now in the earthly likenesses of justice and temperance and all other prized possessions of the soul there dwells no luster; nay, so dull are the organs wherewith men approach their images that hardly can a few behold that which is imaged, but with beauty it is otherwise. Beauty it was ours to see in all its brightness in those days when, amidst that happy company, we beheld with our eyes that blessed vision, ourselves in the train of Zeus, others following some other god; then were we all initiated into that mystery which is rightly accounted blessed beyond all others; whole and unblemished were we that did celebrate it, untouched by the evils that awaited us in days to come; whole and unblemished likewise, free from all alloy, steadfast and blissful were the spectacles on which we gazed in the moment of final revelation; pure was the light that shone around us, and pure were we, without taint of that prison house which now we are encompassed withal, and call a body, fast bound therein as an oyster in its shell.

There let it rest then, our tribute to a memory that has stirred us to linger awhile on those former joys for which we yearn. Now beauty, as we said, shone bright amidst these visions, and in this world below we apprehend it through the clearest of our senses, clear and resplendent. For sight is the keenest mode of perception vouchsafed us through the body; wisdom, indeed, we cannot see thereby—how passionate had been our desire for her, if she had granted us so clear an image of herself to gaze upon—nor yet any other of those beloved objects, save only beauty; for beauty alone this has been ordained, to be most manifest to sense and most lovely of them all.

Now he whose vision of the mystery is long past, or whose purity has been sullied, cannot pass swiftly hence to see beauty's self yonder, when he beholds that which is called beautiful here; wherefore he looks upon it with no reverence, and surrendering to pleasure he essays to go after the fashion of a four-footed beast, and to beget offspring of the flesh, or consorting with wantonness he has no fear nor shame in running after unnatural pleasure. But when one who is fresh from the mystery, and saw much of the vision, beholds a godlike face or bodily form that truly expresses beauty, first there come upon him a shuddering and a measure of that awe which the vision inspired, and then reverence as at the sight of a god, and but for fear of being deemed a very madman he would offer sacrifice to his beloved, as to a holy image of deity. Next, with the passing of the shudder, a strange sweating and fever seizes him. For by reason of the stream of beauty entering in through his eyes there comes a warmth, whereby his soul's plumage is fostered, and with that warmth the roots of the wings are melted, which for long had been so hardened and closed up that nothing could grow; then as the nourishment is poured in, the stump of the wing swells and hastens to grow from the root over the whole substance of the soul, for aforetime the whole soul was furnished with wings. Meanwhile she throbs with ferment in every part, and even as a teething child feels an aching and pain in its gums when a tooth has just come through, so does the soul of him who is beginning to grow his wings feel a ferment and painful irritation. Wherefore as she gazes upon the boy's beauty, she admits a flood of particles streaming therefrom—that is why we speak of a "flood of passion"—whereby she is warmed and fostered; then has she respite from her anguish, and is filled with joy. But when she has been parted from him and become parched, the openings of those outlets at which the wings are sprouting dry up likewise and are closed, so that the wing's germ is barred off. And behind its bars, together with the flood aforesaid, it throbs like a fevered pulse, and pricks at its proper outlet, and thereat the whole soul round about is stung and goaded into anguish;

howbeit she remembers the beauty of her beloved, and rejoices again. So between joy and anguish she is distraught at being in such strange case, perplexed and frenzied; with madness upon her she can neither sleep by night nor keep still by day, but runs hither and thither, yearning for him in whom beauty dwells, if haply she may behold him. At last she does behold him, and lets the flood pour in upon her, releasing the imprisoned waters; then has she refreshment and respite from her stings and sufferings, and at that moment tastes a pleasure that is sweet beyond compare. Nor will she willingly give it up. Above all others does she esteem her beloved in his beauty; mother, brother, friends, she forgets them all. Nought does she reck of losing worldly possessions through neglect. All the rules of conduct, all the graces of life, of which aforetime she was proud, she now disdains, welcoming a slave's estate and any couch where she may be suffered to lie down close beside her darling, for besides her reverence for the possessor of beauty she has found in him the only physician for her grievous suffering. . . .

Now if he whom Love has caught be among the followers of Zeus, he is able to bear the burden of the winged one with some constancy, but they that attend upon Ares, and did range the heavens in his train, when they are caught by Love and fancy that their beloved is doing them some injury, will shed blood and not scruple to offer both themselves and their loved ones in sacrifice. And so does each lover live, after the manner of the god in whose company he once was, honoring him and copying him so far as may be, so long as he remains uncorrupt and is still living in his first earthly period, and in like manner does he comport himself toward his beloved and all his other associates. And so each selects a fair one for his love after his disposition, and even as if the beloved himself were a god he fashions for himself as it were an image, and

adorns it to be the object of his veneration and worship. . . .

In the beginning of our story we divided each soul into three parts, two being like steeds and the third like a charioteer. Well and good. Now of the steeds, so we declare, one is good and the other is not, but we have not described the excellence of the one nor the badness of the other, and that is what must now be done. He that is on the more honorable side is upright and clean-limbed, carrying his neck high, with something of a hooked nose; in color he is white, with black eyes; a lover of glory, but with temperance and modesty; one that consorts with genuine renown, and needs no whip, being driven by the word of command alone. The other is crooked of frame, a massive jumble of a creature, with thick short neck, snub nose, black skin, and gray eyes; hot-blooded, consorting with wantonness and vainglory; shaggy of ear, deaf, and hard to control with whip and goad.

Now when the driver beholds the person of the beloved, and causes a sensation of warmth to suffuse the whole soul, he begins to experience a tickling or pricking of desire, and the obedient steed, constrained now as always by modesty, refrains from leaping upon the beloved. But his fellow, heeding no more the driver's goad or whip, leaps and dashes on, sorely troubling his companion and his driver, and forcing them to approach the loved one and remind him of the delights of love's commerce. For a while they struggle, indignant that he should force them to a monstrous and forbidden act, but at last, finding no end to their evil plight, they yield and agree to do his bidding. And so he draws them on, and now they are quite close and behold the spectacle of the beloved flashing upon them. At that sight the driver's memory goes back to that form of beauty, and he sees her once again enthroned by the side of temperance upon her holy seat; then in awe and reverence he falls upon his back, and therewith is compelled to pull the reins so violently that he brings both steeds down on their haunches, the good one willing and unresistant, but the wanton sore against his will. Now that they are a little way off, the good horse in shame and horror drenches the whole soul with sweat, while the other, contriving to recover his wind after the pain of the bit and his fall, bursts into angry abuse, railing at the charioteer and his yoke-fellow as cowardly treacherous deserters. Once again he tries to force them to advance, and when they beg him to delay awhile he grudgingly consents. But when the time appointed is come, and they feign to have forgotten, he reminds them of it—struggling and neighing and pulling until he compels them a second time to approach the beloved and renew their offer—and when they have come close, with head down and tail stretched out he takes the bit between his teeth and shamelessly plunges on. But the driver, with resentment even stronger than before, like a racer recoiling from the starting rope, jerks back the bit in the mouth of the wanton horse with an even stronger pull, bespatters his railing tongue and his jaws with blood, and forcing him down on legs and haunches delivers him over to anguish.

And so it happens time and again, until the evil steed casts off his wantonness; humbled in the end, he obeys the counsel of his driver, and when he sees the fair beloved is like to die of fear. Wherefore at long last the soul of the lover follows after the beloved with reverence and awe.

. . . When they lie side by side, the wanton horse of the lover's soul would have a word with the charioteer, claiming a little guerdon for all his trouble. The like steed in the soul of the beloved has no word to say, but, swelling with desire for he knows not what, embraces and kisses the lover, in grateful acknowledgment of all his kindness.

And when they lie by one another, he is minded not to refuse to do his part in gratifying his lover's entreaties; yet his yoke-fellow in turn, being moved by reverence and heedfulness, joins with the driver in resisting. And so, if the victory be won by the higher elements of mind guiding them into the ordered rule of the philosophical life, their days on earth will be blessed with happiness and concord, for the power of evil in the soul has been subjected, and the power of goodness liberated; they have won self-mastery and inward peace. And when life is over, with burden shed and wings recovered they stand victorious in the first of the three rounds in that truly Olympic struggle; nor can any nobler prize be secured whether by the wisdom that is of man or by the madness that is of god.

But if they turn to a way of life more ignoble and unphilosophical, yet covetous of honor, then mayhap in a careless hour, or when the wine is flowing, the wanton horses in their two souls will catch them off their guard, bring the pair together, and choosing that part which the multitude account blissful achieve their full desire. And this once done, they continue therein, albeit but rarely, seeing that their minds are not wholly set thereupon. Such a pair as this also are dear friends, but not so dear as that other pair, one to another, both in the time of their love and when love is past, for they feel that they have exchanged the most binding pledges, which it were a sin to break by becoming enemies. When death comes they quit the body wingless indeed, yet eager to be winged, and therefore they carry off no mean reward for their lovers' madness, for it is ordained that all such as have taken the first steps on the celestial highway shall no more return to the dark pathways beneath the earth, but shall walk together in a life of shining bliss, and be furnished in due time with like plumage the one to the other, because of their love.

Aristotle

THE FORM
OF A
TRAGEDY

Aristotle (384–322 B.C.E.) was a renowned philosopher in ancient Greece. He was a student of Plato, the tutor of Alexander the Great, a biologist, and a writer on topics in virtually all areas of human knowledge. His interest in how things work is evident in the following excerpt from Poetics, *his treatise on Greek tragedy.*

A tragedy, then, is the imitation of an action that is serious and also, as having magnitude, complete in itself; in language with pleasurable accessories, each kind brought in separately in the parts of the work; in a dramatic, not in a narrative form; with incidents arousing pity and fear, wherewith to accomplish its catharsis of such emotions. Here by "language with pleasurable accessories" I mean that with rhythm and harmony or song superadded; and by "the kinds separately" I mean that some portions are worked out with verse only, and others in turn with song.

I. As they act the stories, it follows that in the first place the Spectacle (or stage-appearance of the actors) must be some part of the whole; and in the second Melody and Diction, these two being the means of their imitation. Here by "Diction" I mean merely this, the composition of the verses; and by "Melody," what is too completely understood to require explanation. But further: the subject represented also is an action; and the action involves agents, who must necessarily have their distinctive qualities both of character and thought, since it is from these that we ascribe certain qualities to their actions. There are in the natural order of things, therefore, two causes, Thought and Character, of their actions, and consequently of their success or failure in their lives. Now the action (that which was done) is represented in the play by the Fable or Plot. The Fable, in our present sense of the term, is simply this, the combination of the incidents, or things done in the story; whereas Character is what makes us ascribe certain moral qualities to the agents; and Thought is shown in all they say when proving a particular point or, it may be, enunciating a general truth. There are six parts consequently of every tragedy, as a whole (that is) of such or such quality, viz. a Fable

Aristotle, *Poetics*, trans. Ingram Bywater, *The Basic Works of Aristotle*, ed. Richard McKeon (New York: Random House, 1941) 1460–70.

or Plot, Characters, Diction, Thought, Spectacle, and Melody; two of them arising from the means, one from the manner, and three from the objects of the dramatic imitation; and there is nothing else besides these six. Of these, its formative elements, then, not a few of the dramatists have made due use, as every play, one many say, admits of Spectacle, Character, Fable, Diction, Melody, and Thought.

The most important of the six is the combination of the incidents of the story. Tragedy is essentially an imitation not of persons but of action and life, of happiness and misery. All human happiness or misery takes the form of action; the end for which we live is a certain kind of activity, not a quality. Character gives us qualities, but it is in our actions—what we do—that we are happy or the reverse. In a play accordingly they do not act in order to portray the Characters; they include the Characters for the sake of the action. So that it is the action in it, i.e., its Fable or Plot, that is the end and purpose of the tragedy; and the end is everywhere the chief thing. Besides this, a tragedy is impossible without action, but there may be one without Character. . . . We maintain, therefore, that the first essential, the life and soul, so to speak, of Tragedy is the Plot; and that the Characters come second—compare the parallel in painting, where the most beautiful colours laid on without order will not give one the same pleasure as a simple black-and-white sketch of a portrait. We maintain that Tragedy is primarily an imitation of action, and that it is mainly for the sake of the action that it imitates the personal agents. Third comes the element of Thought, i.e., the power of saying whatever can be said, or what is appropriate to the occasion. That is what, in the speeches in Tragedy, falls under the arts of Politics and Rhetoric; for the older poets make their personages discourse like statesmen, and the modern like rhetoricians. One must not confuse it with Character. Character in a play is that which reveals the moral purpose of the agents, i.e., the sort of thing they seek or avoid, where that is not obvious—hence there is no room for Character in a speech on a purely indifferent subject. Thought, on the other hand, is shown in all they say when proving or disproving some particular point, or enunciating some universal proposition. Fourth among the literary elements is the Diction of the personages, i.e., as before explained, the expression of their thoughts in words, which is practically the same thing with verse as with prose. As for the two remaining parts, the Melody is the greatest of the pleasurable accessories of Tragedy. The Spectacle, though an attraction, is the least artistic of all the parts, and has least to do with the art of poetry. The tragic effect is quite possible without a public performance and actors; and besides, the getting-up of the Spectacle is more a matter for the costumier than the poet.

Having thus distinguished the parts, let us now consider the proper construction of the Fable or Plot, as that is at once the first and the most important thing in Tragedy. We have laid it down that a tragedy is an imitation of an action that is complete in itself, as a whole of some magnitude; for a whole may be of no magnitude to speak of. Now a whole is that which has beginning, middle, and end. A beginning is that which is not itself necessarily after anything else, and which has naturally something else after it; an end is that which is naturally after something itself, either as its necessary or usual consequent, and with nothing else after it; and a middle, that which is by nature after one thing and has also another after it. A well-constructed Plot, therefore, cannot either begin or end at any point one likes; beginning and end in it must be of the forms just described. Again: to be beautiful, a living creature, and every whole made up of parts, must not only present a certain order in its arrangement of parts, but also be a certain definite magnitude. Beauty is a matter of size and order, and therefore impossible either (1) in a very minute creature, since our perception becomes indistinct as it approaches instantaneity; or (2) in a creature of vast size—one, say, 1,000 miles long—as in that case, instead of the object being seen all at once, the unity and wholeness of it is lost to the beholder. Just in the same way, then, as a beautiful whole made up of parts, or a beautiful living creature, must be of some size, but a size to be taken in by the eye, so a story or Plot must be of some length, but of a length to be taken in by the memory. As for the limit of its length, so far as that is relative to public performances and spectators, it does not fall within the theory of poetry. If they had to perform a hundred tragedies, they would be timed by water-clocks, as they are said to have been at one period. The limit, however, set by the actual nature of the thing is this: the longer the story, consistently with its being comprehensible as a whole, the finer it is by reason of its magnitude. As a rough general formula, "a length which allows of the hero passing by a series of probable or necessary stages from misfortune to happiness, or from happiness to misfortune," may suffice as a limit for the magnitude of the story.

The Unity of a Plot does not consist, as some suppose, in its having one man as its subject. An infinity of things befall that one man, some of which it is impossible to reduce to unity; and in like manner there are many actions of one man which cannot be made to form one action. One sees, therefore, the mistake of all the poets who have written a *Heracleid*, a *Theseid*, or similar poems; they suppose that, because Heracles

was one man, the story also of Heracles must be one story. Homer, however, evidently understood this point quite well, whether by are or instinct, just in the same way as he excels the rest in every other respect. In writing an *Odyssey*, he did not make the poem cover all that ever befell his hero—it befell him, for instance, to get wounded on Parnassus and also to feign madness at the time of the call to arms, but the two incidents had no necessary or probable connexion with one another—instead of doing that, he took as the subject of the *Odyssey*, as also of the *Iliad*, an action with a Unity of the kind we are describing. The truth is that, just as in the other imitative arts one imitation is always of one thing, so in poetry the story, as an imitation of action, must represent one action, a complete whole, with its several incidents so closely connected that the transposal or withdrawal of any one of them will disjoin and dislocate the whole. For that which makes no perceptible difference by its presence or absence is no real part of the whole.

From what we have said it will be seen that the poet's function is to describe, not the thing that has happened, but a kind of thing that might happen, i.e., what is possible as being probable or necessary. The distinction between historian and poet is not in the one writing prose and the other verse—you might put the work of Herodotus into verse, and it would still be a species of history; it consists really in this, that the one describes the thing that has been, and the other a kind of thing that might be. Hence poetry is something more philosophic and of graver import than history, since its statements are of the nature rather of universals, whereas those of history are singulars. By a universal statement I mean one as to what such or such a kind of man will probably or necessarily say or do—which is the aim of poetry, though it affixes proper names to the characters; by a singular statement, one as to what, say, Alcibiades did or had done to him. In Comedy this has become clear by this time; it is only when their plot is already made up of probable incidents that they give it a basis of proper names, choosing for the purpose any names that may occur to them, instead of writing like the old iambic poets about particular persons. In Tragedy, however, they still adhere to the historic names; and for this reason: what convinces is the possible; now whereas we are not yet sure as to the possibility of that which has not happened, that which has happened is manifestly possible, else it would not have come to pass. Nevertheless even in Tragedy there are some plays with but one or two known names in them, the rest being inventions; and there are some without a single known name, e.g., Agathon's *Antheus*, in which both incidents and names are of the poet's invention; and it is no less delightful on that account. So that one must not aim at a rigid adherence to the traditional stories on which tragedies are based. It would be absurd, in fact, to do so, as even the known stories are only known to a few, though they are a delight nonetheless to all.

It is evident from the above that the poet must be more the poet of his stories or Plots than of his verses, inasmuch as he is a poet by virtue of the imitative element in his work, and it is actions that he imitates. And if he should come to take a subject from actual history, he is nonetheless a poet for that; since some historic occurrences may very well be in the probable and possible order of things; and it is in that aspect of them that he is their poet.

Of simple Plots and actions the episodic are the worst. I call a Plot episodic when there is neither probability nor necessity in the sequence of its episodes. Actions of this sort bad poets construct through their own fault, and good ones on account of the players. His work being for public performance, a good poet often stretches out a Plot

beyond its capabilities, and is thus obliged to twist the sequence of incident.

Tragedy, however, is an imitation not only of a complete action, but also of incidents arousing pity and fear. Such incidents have the very greatest effect on the mind when they occur unexpectedly and at the same time in consequence of one another; there is more of the marvellous in them then than if they happened of themselves or by mere chance. Even matters of chance seem most marvellous if there is an appearance of design as it were in them; as for instance the statue of Mitys at Argos killed the author of Mitys' death by falling down on him when a looker-on at a public spectacle; for incidents like that we think to be not without a meaning. A Plot, therefore, of this sort is necessarily finer than others.

Plots are either simple or complex, since the actions they represent are naturally of this twofold description. The action, proceeding in the way defined, as one continuous whole, I call simple, when the change in the hero's fortunes takes place without Peripety or Discovery; and complex, when it involves one or the other, or both. These should each of them arise out of the structure of the Plot itself, so as to be the consequence, necessary or probable, of the antecedents. There is a great difference between a thing happening *propter hoc* and *post hoc*.

A Peripety is the change of the kind described from one state of things within the play to its opposite, and that too in the way we are saying, in the probable or necessary sequence of events; as it is for instance in *Oedipus:* here the opposite state of things is produced by the Messenger, who, coming to gladden Oedipus and to remove his fears as to his mother, reveals the secret of his birth. And in *Lynceus:* just as he is being led off for execution, with Danaus at his side to put him to death, the incidents preceding this bring it about that he is saved and Danaus put to death. A Discovery is, as the very word implies, a change from ignorance to knowledge, and thus to either love or hate, in the personages marked for good or evil fortune. The finest form of Discovery is one attended by Peripeties, like that which goes with the Discovery in *Oedipus*. There are no doubt other forms of it; what we have said may happen in a way in reference to inanimate things, even things of a very casual kind; and it is also possible to discover whether some one has done or not done something. But the form most directly connected with the Plot and the action of the piece is the first-mentioned. This, with a Peripety, will arouse either pity or fear—actions of that nature being what Tragedy is assumed to represent; and it will also serve to bring about the happy or unhappy ending. The Discovery, then, being of persons, it may be that of one party only to the other, the latter being already known; or both the parties may have to discover themselves. Iphigenia, for instance, was discovered to Orestes by sending the letter; and another Discovery was required to reveal him to Iphigenia.

Two parts of the Plot, then, Peripety and Discovery, are on matters of this sort. A third part is Suffering; which we may define as an action of a destructive or painful nature, such as murders on the stage, tortures, woundings, and the like. The other two have been already explained.

——◆◆◆——

We assume that, for the finest form of Tragedy, the Plot must be not simple but complex; and further, that it must imitate actions arousing fear and pity, since that is the distinctive function of this kind of imitation. It follows, therefore, that there are three forms of Plot to be avoided. (1) A good man must not be seen passing from happiness to misery, or (2) a bad man from misery to happiness. The first situation is not fear-inspiring or piteous, but simply odious to us. The second is the most untragic that can be; it has no one of the requisites of Tragedy; it does not appeal either to the human feeling in us, or to our pity, or to our fears. Nor, on the other hand, should (3) an extremely bad man be seen falling from happiness into misery. Such a story may arouse the human feeling in us, but it will not move us to either pity or fear; pity is occasioned by undeserved misfortune, and fear by that of one like ourselves; so that there will be nothing either piteous or fear-inspiring in the situation. There remains, then, the intermediate kind of personage, a man not pre-eminently virtuous and just, whose misfortune, however, is brought upon him not by vice and depravity but by some error of judgement, of the number of those in the enjoyment of great reputation and prosperity; e.g., Oedipus, Thyestes, and the men of note of similar families. The perfect Plot, accordingly, must have a single, and not (as some tell us) a double issue; the change in the hero's fortunes must be not from misery to happiness, but on the contrary from happiness to misery; and the cause of it must lie not in any depravity, but in some great error on his part; the man himself being either such as we have described, or better, not worse, than that. Fact also confirms our theory. Though the poets began by accepting any tragic story that came to hand, in these days the finest tragedies are always on the story of some few houses, on that of Alcmeon, Oedipus, Orestes, Meleager, Thyestes, Telephus, or any others that may have been involved, as either agents or sufferers, in some deed of horror. The theoretically best tragedy, then, has a Plot of this description. The critics, therefore, are wrong who blame Euripides for taking this line in his tragedies, and giving many of them an unhappy ending. It is, as we have said, the right line to take. The best proof is this: on the stage, and in the public performances, such plays, properly worked out, are seen to be the most truly tragic; and Euripides, even if his execution be faulty in every other point, is seen to be nevertheless the most tragic certainly of the dramatists. After this comes the construction of Plot which some rank first, one with a double story (like the *Odyssey*) and an opposite issue for the good and the bad personages. It is ranked as first only through the weakness of the audiences; the poets merely follow their public, writing as its wishes dictate. But the pleasure here is not that of Tragedy. It belongs rather to Comedy, where the bitterest enemies in the piece (e.g., Orestes and Aegisthus) walk off good friends at the end, with no slaying of any one by any one.

The tragic fear and pity may be aroused by the Spectacle: but they may also be aroused by the very structure and incidents of the play—which is the better way and shows the better poet. The Plot in fact should be so framed that, even without seeing the things take place, he who simply hears the account of them shall be filled with horror and pity at the incidents; which is just the effect that the mere recital of the story in *Oedipus* would have on one. To produce this same effect by means of the Spectacle is less artistic, and requires extraneous aid. Those, however, who make use of the Spectacle to put before us that which is merely monstrous and not productive of fear, are wholly out of touch with Tragedy; not every kind of pleasure should be required of a tragedy, but only its own proper pleasure.

The tragic pleasure is that of pity and fear, and the poet has to produce it by a work of imitation; it is clear, therefore, that the causes should be included in the incidents of his story. Let us see, then, what kinds of incident strike one as horrible, or rather as piteous. In a deed of this description the parties must necessarily be either friends, or enemies, or indifferent to one another. Now when enemy does it on enemy, there is nothing to move us to pity either in his doing or in his meditating the deed, except so far as the actual pain of the sufferer is concerned; and the same is true when the parties are indifferent to one another. Whenever the tragic deed, however, is done within the family—when murder or the like is done or meditated by brother on brother, by son on father, by mother on son, or son on mother—these are the situations the poet should seek after.

In the Characters there are four points to aim at. First and foremost, that they shall be good. There will be an element of character in the play, if (as has been observed) what a personage says or does reveals a certain moral purpose; and a good element of character, if the purpose so revealed is good. Such goodness is possible in every type of personage, even in a woman or a slave, though the one is perhaps an inferior, and the other a wholly worthless being. The second point is to make them appropriate. The Character before us may be, say, manly; but it is not appropriate in a female Character to be manly, or clever. The third is to make them like the reality, which is not the same as their being good and appropriate, in our sense of the term. The fourth is to make them consistent and the same throughout; even if inconsistency be part of the man before one for imitation as presenting that form of character, he should still be consistently inconsistent. . . . The right thing, however, is in the Characters just as in the incidents of the play to endeavour always after the necessary or the probable; so that whenever such-and-such a personage says or does such-and-such a thing, it shall be the necessary or probable outcome of his character; and whenever this incident follows on that, it shall be either the necessary or the probable consequence of it. From this one sees (to digress for a moment) that the Denouement also should arise out of the plot itself, and not depend on a stage-artifice, as in *Medea*, or in the story of the (arrested) departure of the Greeks in the *Iliad*. The artifice must be reserved for matters outside the play—for past events beyond human knowledge, or events yet to come, which require to be foretold or announced; since it is the privilege of the Gods to know everything. There should be nothing improbable among the actual incidents. If it be unavoidable, however, it should be outside the tragedy, like the improbability in the *Oedipus* of Sophocles. But to return to the Characters. As Tragedy is an imitation of personages better than the ordinary man, we in our way should follow the example of good portrait-painters, who reproduce the distinctive features of a man, and at the same time, without losing the likeness, make him handsomer than he is. The poet in like manner, in portraying men quick or slow to anger, or with similar infirmities of character, must know how to represent them as such, and at the same time as good men, as Agathon and Homer have represented Achilles.

David Hume

OF THE
STANDARD
OF TASTE

David Hume (1711–1776) was a Scottish philosopher committed to empiricism, the view that all knowledge is ultimately grounded in sense experience. He wrote on history, art, and manners as well as on philosophy. His essay "Of the Standard of Taste" (1757) confronts the question of whether taste can be legitimated through rational argument. He argues that judgments of taste are emotional in nature and necessarily subjective, but that some judges are better than others.

The great variety of Taste, as well as of opinion, which prevails in the world, is too obvious not to have fallen under every one's observation. Men of the most confined knowledge are able to remark a difference of taste in the narrow circle of their acquaintance, even where the persons have been educated under the same government, and have early imbibed the same prejudices. But those, who can enlarge their view to contemplate distant nations and remote ages, are still more surprized at the great inconsistence and contrariety. We are apt to call *barbarous* whatever departs widely from our own taste and apprehension: But soon find the epithet of reproach retorted on us. And the highest arrogance and self-conceit is at last startled, on observing an equal assurance on all sides, and scruples, amidst such a contest of sentiment, to pronounce positively in its own favour.

As this variety of taste is obvious to the most careless enquirer; so will it be found, on examination, to be still greater in reality than in appearance. The sentiments of men often differ with regard to beauty and deformity of all kinds, even while their general discourse is the same. There are certain terms in every language, which import blame, and others praise; and all men, who use the same tongue, must agree in their application of them. Every voice is united in applauding elegance, propriety, simplicity, spirit in writing; and in blaming fustian, affectation, coldness, and a false brilliancy: But when critics come to particulars, this seeming unanimity vanishes; and it is found, that they had affixed a very different

David Hume, "Of the Standard of Taste," *Essays, Literary, Moral, and Political* (London: Ward, Lock, 1898) 134–49.

meaning to their expressions. In all matters of opinion and science, the case is opposite: The difference among men is there oftener found to lie in generals than in particulars; and to be less in reality than in appearance. An explanation of the terms commonly ends the controversy; and the disputants are surprized to find, that they had been quarrelling, while at bottom they agreed in their judgment.

Those who found morality on sentiment, more than on reason, are inclined to comprehend ethics under the former observation, and to maintain, that, in all questions, which regard conduct and manners, the difference among men is really greater than at first sight it appears. It is indeed obvious, that writers of all nations and all ages concur in applauding justice, humanity, magnanimity, prudence, veracity; and in blaming the opposite qualities. Even poets and other authors, whose compositions are chiefly calculated to please the imagination, are yet found, from HOMER down to FENELON, to inculcate the same moral precepts, and to bestow their applause and blame on the same virtues and vices. This great unanimity is usually ascribed to the influence of plain reason; which, in all these cases, maintains similar sentiments in all men, and prevents those controversies, to which the abstract sciences are so much exposed. So far as the unanimity is real, this account may be admitted as satisfactory: But we must also allow that some part of the seeming harmony in morals may be accounted for from the very nature of language. The word *virtue*, with its equivalent in every tongue, implies praise; as that of *vice* does blame: And no one, without the most obvious and grossest impropriety, could affix reproach to a term, which in general acceptation is understood in a good sense; or bestow applause, where the idiom requires disapprobation. HOMER's general precepts, where he delivers any such, will never be controverted; but it is obvious, that, when he

draws particular pictures of manners, and represents heroism in ACHILLES and prudence in ULYSSES, he intermixes a much greater degree of ferocity in the former, and of cunning and fraud in the latter, than FENELON would admit of. The sage ULYSSES in the GREEK poet seems to delight in lies and fictions; and often employs them without any necessity or even advantage: But his more scrupulous son, in the FRENCH epic writer, exposes himself to the most imminent perils, rather than depart from the most exact line of truth and veracity.

The admirers and followers of the ALCORAN insist on the excellent moral precepts interspersed throughout that wild and absurd performance. But it is to be supposed, that the ARABIC words, which correspond to the ENGLISH, equity, justice, temperance, meekness, charity, were such as, from the constant use of that tongue, must always be taken in a good sense; and it would have argued the greatest ignorance, not of morals, but of language, to have mentioned them with any epithets, besides those of applause and approbation. But would we know, whether the pretended prophet had really attained a just sentiment of morals? Let us attend to his narration; and we shall soon find, that he bestows praise on such instances of treachery, inhumanity, cruelty, revenge, bigotry, as are utterly incompatible with civilized society. No steady rule of right seems there to be attended to; and every action is blamed or praised, so far only as it is beneficial or hurtful to the true believers.

The merit of delivering true general precepts in ethics is indeed very small. Whoever recommends any moral virtues, really does no more than is implied in the terms themselves. That people, who invented the word *charity*, and used it in a good sense, inculcated more clearly and much more efficaciously, the precept, *be charitable*, than any pretended legislator or prophet, who should insert such a *maxim* in his writings. Of all expressions, those, which, together with their other meaning, imply a degree either of blame or approbation, are the least liable to be perverted or mistaken.

It is natural for us to seek a *Standard of Taste;* a rule, by which the various sentiments of men may be reconciled; at least, a decision, afforded, confirming one sentiment, and condemning another.

There is a species of philosophy, which cuts off all hopes of success in such an attempt, and represents the impossibility of ever attaining any standard of taste. The difference, it is said, is very wide between judgment and sentiment. All sentiment is right; because sentiment has a reference to nothing beyond itself, and is always real, wherever a man is conscious of it. But all determinations of the understanding are not right; because they have a reference to something beyond themselves, to wit, real matter of fact; and are not always conformable to that standard. Among a thousand different opinions which different men may entertain of the same subject, there is one, and but one, that is just and true; and the only difficulty is to fix and ascertain it. On the contrary, a thousand different sentiments, excited by the same object, are all right: Because no sentiment represents what is really in the object. It only marks a certain conformity or relation between the object and the organs or faculties of the mind; and if that conformity did not really exist, the sentiment could never possibly have being. Beauty is no quality in things themselves: It exists merely in the mind which contemplates them; and each mind perceives a different beauty. One person may even perceive deformity, where another is sensible of beauty; and every individual ought to acquiesce in his own sentiment, without pretending to regulate those of others. To seek the real beauty, or real deformity, is as fruitless an enquiry, as to pretend to ascertain the real sweet or real bitter. According to the disposition of the organs, the same object may be both sweet and bitter; and the

proverb has justly determined it to be fruitless to dispute concerning tastes. It is very natural, and even quite necessary, to extend this axiom to mental, as well as bodily taste; and thus common sense, which is so often at variance with philosophy, especially with the sceptical kind, is found, in one instance at least, to agree in pronouncing the same decision.

But though this axiom, by passing into a proverb, seems to have attained the sanction of common sense; there is certainly a species of common sense which opposes it, at least serves to modify and restrain it. Whoever would assert an equality of genius and elegance between OGILBY and MILTON, or BUNYAN and ADDISON, would be thought to defend no less an extravagance, than if he had maintained a mole-hill to be as high as TENERIFFE, or a pond as extensive as the ocean. Though there may be found persons, who give the preference to the former authors; no one pays attention to such a taste; and we pronounce without scruple the sentiment of these pretended critics to be absurd and ridiculous. The principle of the natural equality of tastes is then totally forgot, and while we admit it on some occasions, where the objects seem near an equality, it appears an extravagant paradox, or rather a palpable absurdity, where objects so disproportioned are compared together.

It is evident that none of the rules of composition are fixed by reasonings *a priori*, or can be esteemed abstract conclusions of the understanding, from comparing those habitudes and relations of ideas, which are eternal and immutable. Their foundation is the same with that of all the practical sciences, experience; nor are they any thing but general observations, concerning what has been universally found to please in all countries and in all ages. Many of the beauties of poetry and even of eloquence are founded on falsehood and fiction, on hyperboles, metaphors, and an abuse or perversion of terms from their natural meaning. To check the sallies of the imagination, and to reduce every expression to geometrical truth and exactness, would be the most contrary to the laws of criticism; because it would produce a work, which, by universal experience, has been found the most insipid and disagreeable. But though poetry can never submit to exact truth, it must be confined by rules of art, discovered to the author either by genius or observation. If some negligent or irregular writers have pleased, they have not pleased by their transgressions of rule or order, but in spite of these transgressions: They have possessed other beauties, which were conformable to just criticism; and the force of these beauties has been able to overpower censure, and give the mind a satisfaction superior to the disgust arising from the blemishes. ARIOSTO pleases; but not by his monstrous and improbable fictions, by his bizarre mixture of the serious and comic styles, by the want of coherence in his stories, or by the continual interruptions of his narration. He charms by the force and clearness of his expression, by the readiness and variety of his inventions, and by his natural pictures of the passions, especially those of the gay and amorous kind: And however his faults may diminish our satisfaction, they are not able entirely to destroy it. Did our pleasure really arise from those parts of his poem, which we denominate faults, this would be no objection to criticism in general: It would only be an objection to those particular rules of criticism, which would establish such circumstances to be faults, and would represent them as universally blameable. If they are found to please, they cannot be faults; let the pleasure, which they produce, be ever so unexpected and unaccountable.

But though all the general rules of art are founded only on experience and on the observation of the common sentiments of human nature, we must not imagine, that, on every occasion, the feelings of men will be conformable to these rules. Those finer emotions of the mind are of a very tender and delicate nature, and require the concurrence of many favourable circumstances to make them play with facility and exactness, according to their general and established principles. The least exterior hindrance to such small springs, or the least internal disorder, disturbs their motion, and confounds the operation of the whole machine. When we would make an experiment of this nature, and would try the force of any beauty or deformity, we must choose with care a proper time and place, and bring the fancy to a suitable situation and disposition. A perfect serenity of mind, a recollection of thought, a due attention to the object; if any of these circumstances be wanting, our experiment will be fallacious, and we shall be unable to judge of the catholic and universal beauty. The relation, which nature has placed between the form and the sentiment, will at least be more obscure; and it will require greater accuracy to trace and discern it. We shall be able to ascertain its influence not so much from the operation of each particular beauty, as from the durable admiration, which attends those works, that have survived all the caprices of mode and fashion, all the mistakes of ignorance and envy.

The same HOMER, who pleased at ATHENS and ROME two thousand years ago, is still admired at PARIS and at LONDON. All the changes of climate, government, religion, and language, have not been able to obscure his glory. Authority or prejudice may give a temporary vogue to a bad poet or orator; but his reputation will never be durable or general. When his compositions are examined by posterity or by foreigners, the enchantment is dissipated, and his faults appear in their true colours. On the contrary, a real genius, the longer his works endure, and the more wide they are spread, the more sincere is the admiration which he meets with. Envy and jealousy have too much place in a narrow circle; and even familiar acquaintance with his person may diminish the applause due to his performances: But when these obstructions are removed, the beauties, which are naturally fitted to excite agreeable sentiments, immediately display their energy; and while the world endures, they maintain their authority over the minds of men.

It appears then, that, amidst all the variety and caprice of taste, there are certain general principles of approbation or blame, whose influence a careful eye may trace in all operations of the mind. Some particular forms or qualities, from the original structure of the internal fabric, are calculated to please, and others to displease; and if they fail of their effect in any particular instance, it is from some apparent defect or imperfection in the organ. A man in a fever would not insist on his palate as able to decide concerning flavours; nor would one, affected with the jaundice, pretend to give a verdict with regard to colours. In each creature, there is a sound and a defective state; and the former alone can be supposed to afford us a true standard of taste and sentiment. If, in the sound state of the organ, there be an entire or a considerable uniformity of sentiment among men, we may thence derive an idea of the perfect beauty; in like manner as the appearance of objects in day-light, to the eye of a man in health, is denominated their true and real colour, even while colour is allowed to be merely a phantasm of the senses.

Many and frequent are the defects in the internal organs, which prevent or weaken the influence of those general principles, on which depends our sentiment of beauty or deformity. Though some objects, by the structure of the mind, be naturally calculated to give pleasure, it is not to be expected, that in every individual the pleasure will be equally felt. Particular incidents and situations occur, which either throw a false light on the objects, or hinder the true from conveying to the imagination the proper sentiment and perception.

One obvious cause, why many feel not the proper sentiment of beauty, is the want of that *delicacy* of imagination, which is requisite to convey a sensibility of those finer emotions. This delicacy every one pretends to: Every one talks of it; and would reduce every kind of taste or sentiment to its standard. But as our intention in this essay is to mingle some light of the understanding with the feelings of sentiment, it will be proper to give a more accurate definition of delicacy, than has hitherto been attempted. And not to draw our philosophy from too profound a source, we shall have recourse to a noted story in DON QUIXOTE.

It is with good reason, says SANCHO to the squire with the great nose, that I pretend to have a judgment in wine: This is a quality hereditary in our family. Two of my kinsmen were once called to give their opinion of a hogshead, which was supposed to be excellent, being old and of a good vintage. One of them tastes it; considers it; and after mature reflection pronounces the wine to be good, were it not for a small taste of leather, which he perceived in it. The other, after using the same precautions, gives also his verdict in flavour of the wine; but with the reserve of a taste of iron, which he could easily distinguish. You cannot imagine how much they were both ridiculed for their judgment. But who laughed in the end? On emptying the hogshead, there was found at the bottom, an old key with a leathern thong tied to it.

The great resemblance between mental and bodily taste will easily teach us to apply this story. Though it be certain, that beauty and deformity, more than sweet and bitter, are not qualities in objects, but belong entirely to the sentiment, internal or external; it must be allowed, that there are certain qualities in objects, which are fitted by nature to produce those particular feelings. Now as these qualities may be found in a small degree, or may be mixed and confounded with each other, it often happens, that the taste is not affected with such minute qualities, or is not able to distinguish all the particular flavours, amidst the disorder, in which they are presented. Where the organs are so fine, as to allow nothing to escape them; and at the same time so exact as to perceive every ingredient in the composition: This we call delicacy of taste, whether we employ these terms in the literal or metaphorical sense. Here then the general rules of beauty are of use; being drawn from established models, and from the observation of what pleases or displeases, when presented singly and in a high degree: And if the same qualities, in a continued composition and in a smaller degree, affect not the organs with a sensible delight or uneasiness, we exclude the person from all pretensions to this delicacy. To produce these general rules or avowed patterns of composition is like finding the key with the leathern thong; which justified the verdict of SANCHO'S kinsmen, and confounded those pretended judges who had condemned them. Though the hogshead had never been emptied, the taste of the one was still equally delicate, and that of the other equally dull and languid: But it would have been more difficult to have proved the superiority of the former, to the conviction of every by-stander. In like manner, though the beauties of writing had never been methodized, or reduced to general principles; though no excellent models had ever been acknowledged; the different degrees of taste would still have subsisted, and the judgment of one man been preferable to that of another; but it would not have been so easy to silence the bad critic, who might always insist upon his particular sentiment, and refuse to submit to his antagonist. But when we show him an avowed principle of art; when we illustrate this principle by examples, whose operation, from his own particular taste, he acknowledges to be conformable to the principle; when we prove, that the same principle may be applied to the present case, where he did not perceive

or feel its influence: He must conclude, upon the whole, that the fault lies in himself, and that he wants the delicacy, which is requisite to make him sensible of every beauty and every blemish, in any composition or discourse.

It is acknowledged to be the perfection of every sense or faculty, to perceive with exactness its most minute objects, and allow nothing to escape its notice and observation. The smaller the objects are, which become sensible to the eye, the finer is that organ, and the more elaborate its make and composition. A good palate is not tried by strong flavours; but by a mixture of small ingredients, where we are still sensible of each part, notwithstanding its minuteness and its confusion with the rest. In like manner, a quick and acute perception of beauty and deformity must be the perfection of our mental taste; nor can a man be satisfied with himself while he suspects, that any excellence or blemish in a discourse has passed him unobserved. In this case, the perfection of the man, and the perfection of the sense or feeling, are found to be united. A very delicate palate, on many occasions, may be a great inconvenience both to a man himself and to his friends: But a delicate taste of wit or beauty must always be a desirable quality; because it is the source of all the finest and most innocent enjoyments, of which human nature is susceptible. In this decision the sentiments of all mankind are agreed. Wherever you can ascertain a delicacy of taste, it is sure to meet with approbation; and the best way of ascertaining it is to appeal to those models and principles, which have been established by the uniform consent and experience of nations and ages.

But though there be naturally a wide difference in point of delicacy between one person and another, nothing tends further to encrease and improve this talent, than *practice* in a particular art, and the frequent survey or contemplation of a particular species of beauty. When objects of any kind are first presented to the eye or imagination, the sentiment, which attends them, is obscure and confused; and the mind is, in a great measure, incapable of pronouncing concerning their merits or defects. The taste cannot perceive the several excellences of the performance; much less distinguish the particular character of each excellency, and ascertain its quality and degree. If it pronounce the whole in general to be beautiful or deformed, it is the utmost that can be expected; and even this judgment, a person, so unpractised, will be apt to deliver with great hesitation and reserve. But allow him to acquire experience in those objects, his feeling becomes more exact and nice: He not only perceives the beauties and defects of each part, but marks the distinguishing species of each quality, and assigns it suitable praise or blame. A clear and distinct sentiment attends him through the whole survey of the objects; and he discerns that very degree and kind of approbation or displeasure, which each part is naturally fitted to produce. The mist dissipates, which seemed formerly to hang over the object: The organ acquires greater perfection in its operations; and can pronounce, without danger of mistake, concerning the merits of every performance. In a word, the same address and dexterity, which practice gives to the execution of any work, is also acquired by the same means, in the judging of it.

So advantageous is practice to the discernment of beauty, that, before we can give judgment on any work of importance, it will even be requisite, that that very individual performance be more than once perused by us, and be surveyed in different lights with attention and deliberation. There is a flutter or hurry of thought which attends the first perusal of any piece, and which confounds the genuine sentiment of beauty. The relation of the parts is not discerned: The true characters of style are little distinguished: The several perfections and defects seem wrapped up in a species of confusion, and present themselves indistinctly to the imagination. Not to mention, that there is a species of beauty, which, as it is florid and superficial, pleases at first; but being found incompatible with a just expression either of reason or passion, soon palls upon the taste, and is then rejected with disdain, at least rated at a much lower value.

It is impossible to continue in the practice of contemplating any order of beauty, without being frequently obliged to form *comparisons* between the several species and degrees of excellence, and estimating their proportion to each other. A man, who has had no opportunity of comparing the different kinds of beauty, is indeed totally unqualified to pronounce an opinion with regard to any object presented to him. By comparison alone we fix the epithets of praise or blame, and learn how to assign the due degree of each. The coarsest daubing contains a certain lustre of colours and exactness of imitation, which are so far beauties, and would affect the mind of a peasant or Indian with the highest admiration. The most vulgar ballads are not entirely destitute of harmony or nature; and none but a person, familiarized to superior beauties, would pronounce their numbers harsh, or narration uninteresting. A great inferiority of beauty gives pain to a person conversant in the highest excellence of the kind, and is for that reason pronounced a deformity: As the most finished object, with which we are acquainted, is naturally supposed to have reached the pinnacle of perfection, and to be entitled to the highest applause. One accustomed to see, and examine, and weigh the several performances, admired in different ages and nations, can only rate the merits of a work exhibited to his view, and assign its proper rank among the productions of genius.

But to enable a critic the more fully to execute this undertaking, he must preserve his mind free from all *prejudice*, and allow nothing to enter into his consideration, but the very object which is submitted to his examination. We may observe, that every work of art, in order to produce its due effect on the mind, must be surveyed in a certain point of view, and cannot be fully relished by persons, whose situation, real or imaginary, is not conformable tc that which is required by the performance. An orator addresses himself to a particular audience, and must have a regard to their particular genius, interests, opinions, passions, and prejudices; otherwise he hopes in vain to govern their resolutions, and inflame their affections. Should they even have entertained some prepossessions against him, however unreasonable, he must not overlook this disadvantage; but, before he enters upon the subject, must endeavour to conciliate their affection, and acquire their good graces. A critic of a different age or nation, who should peruse this discourse, must have all these circumstances in his eye, and must place himself in the same situation as the audience, in order to form a true judgment of the oration. In like manner, when any work is addressed to the public, though I should have a friendship or enmity with the author, I must depart from this situation; and considering myself as a man in general, forget, if possible, my individual being and my peculiar circumstances. A person influenced by prejudice, complies not with this condition; but obstinately maintains his natural position, without placing himself in that point of view, which the performance supposes. If the work be addressed to persons of a different age or nation, he makes no allowance for their peculiar views and prejudices; but, full of the manners of his own age and country, rashly condemns what seemed admirable in the eyes of those for whom alone the discourse was calculated. If the work be executed for the public, he never sufficiently enlarges his comprehension, or forgets his interest as a friend or enemy, as a rival or commentator. By this

means, his sentiments are perverted; nor have the same beauties and blemishes the same influence upon him, as if he had imposed a proper violence on his imagination, and had forgotten himself for a moment. So far his taste evidently departs from the true standard; and of consequence loses all credit and authority.

It is well known, that in all questions, submitted to the understanding, prejudice is destructive of sound judgment, and perverts all operations of the intellectual faculties: It is no less contrary to good taste; nor has it less influence to corrupt our sentiment of beauty. It belongs to *good sense* to check its influence in both cases; and in this respect, as well as in many others, reason, if not an essential part of taste, is at least requisite to the operations of this latter faculty. In all the nobler productions of genius, there is a mutual relation and correspondence of parts; nor can either the beauties or blemishes be perceived by him, whose thought is not capacious enough to comprehend all those parts, and compare them with each other, in order to perceive the consistence and uniformity of the whole. Every work of art has also a certain end or purpose, for which it is calculated; and is to be deemed more or less perfect, as it is more or less fitted to attain this end. The object of eloquence is to persuade, of history to instruct, of poetry to please by means of the passions and the imagination. These ends we must carry constantly in our view, when we peruse any performance; and we must be able to judge how far the means employed are adapted to their respective purposes. Besides, every kind of composition, even the most poetical, is nothing but a chain of propositions and reasonings; not always, indeed, the justest and most exact, but still plausible and specious, however disguised by the colouring of the imagination. The persons introduced in tragedy and epic poetry, must be represented as reasoning, and thinking, and concluding, and acting, suitably to their character and circumstances; and without judgment, as well as taste and invention, a poet can never hope to succeed in so delicate an undertaking. Not to mention, that the same excellence of faculties which contributes to the improvement of reason, the same clearness of conception, the same exactness of distinction, the same vivacity of apprehension, are essential to the operations of true taste, and are its infallible concomitants. It seldom, or never happens, that a man of sense, who has experience in any art, cannot judge of its beauty; and it is no less rare to meet with a man who has a just taste without a sound understanding.

Thus, though the principles of taste be universal, and, nearly, if not entirely the same in all men; yet few are qualified to give judgment on any work of art, or establish their own sentiment as the standard of beauty. The organs of internal sensation are seldom so perfect as to allow the general principles their full play, and produce a feeling correspondent to those principles. They either labour under some defect, or are vitiated by some disorder; and by that means, excite a sentiment, which may be pronounced erroneous. When the critic has no delicacy, he judges without any distinction, and is only affected by the grosser and more palpable qualities of the object: The finer touches pass unnoticed and disregarded. Where he is not aided by practice, his verdict is attended with confusion and hesitation. Where no comparison has been employed, the most frivolous beauties, such as rather merit the name of defects, are the object of his admiration. Where he lies under the influence of prejudice, all his natural sentiments are perverted. Where good sense is wanting, he is not qualified to discern the beauties of design and reasoning, which are the highest and most excellent. Under some or other of these imperfections, the generality of men labour; and hence a true judge in the finer arts is observed, even

during the most polished ages, to be so rare a character: Strong sense, united to delicate sentiment, improved by practice, perfected by comparison, and cleared of all prejudice, can alone entitle critics to this valuable character; and the joint verdict of such, wherever they are to be found, is the true standard of taste and beauty.

But where are such critics to be found? By what marks are they to be known? How distinguish them from pretenders? These questions are embarrassing; and seem to throw us back into the same uncertainty, from which, during the course of this essay, we have endeavoured to extricate ourselves.

But if we consider the matter aright, these are questions of fact, not of sentiment. Whether any particular person be endowed with good sense and a delicate imagination, free from prejudice, may often be the subject of dispute, and be liable to great discussion and enquiry: But that such a character is valuable and estimable will be agreed in by all mankind. Where these doubts occur, men can do no more than in other disputable questions, which are submitted to the understanding: They must produce the best arguments, that their invention suggests to them; they must acknowledge a true and decisive standard to exist somewhere, to wit, real existence and matter of fact; and they must have indulgence to such as differ from them in their appeals to this standard. It is sufficient for our present purpose, if we have proved, that the taste of all individuals is not upon an equal footing, and that some men in general, however difficult to be particularly pitched upon, will be acknowledged by universal sentiment to have a preference above others.

But in reality the difficulty of finding, even in particulars, the standard of taste, is not so great as it is represented. Though in speculation, you may readily avow a certain criterion in science and deny it in sentiment the matter is found in practice to be much more hard to ascertain in the former case than in the latter.

Theories of abstract philosophy, systems of profound theology, have prevailed during one age: In a successive period these have been universally exploded: Their absurdity has been detected. Other theories and systems have supplied their place, which again gave place to their successors: And nothing has been experienced more liable to the revolutions of chance and fashion than these pretended decisions of science. The case is not the same with the beauties of eloquence and poetry. Just expressions of passion and nature are sure, after a little time, to gain public applause, which they maintain for ever. ARISTOTLE, and PLATO, and EPICURUS, and DESCARTES, may successively yield to each other: But TERENCE and VIRGIL maintain an universal, undisputed empire over the minds of men. The abstract philosophy of CICERO has lost its credit: The vehemence of his oratory is still the object of our admiration.

Though men of delicate taste be rare, they are easily to be distinguished in society, by the soundness of their understanding and the superiority of their faculties above the rest of mankind. The ascendant, which they acquire, gives a prevalence to that lively approbation, with which they receive any productions of genius, and renders it generally predominant. Many men, when left to themselves, have but a faint and dubious perception of beauty, who yet are capable of relishing any fine stroke, which is pointed out to them. Every convert to the admiration of the real poet or orator is the cause of some new conversion. And though prejudices may prevail for a time, they never unite in celebrating any rival to the true genius, but yield at last to the force of nature and just sentiment. Thus, though a civilized nation may easily be mistaken in the choice of their admired philosopher, they never have been found long to err, in their affection for a favorite epic or tragic author.

But notwithstanding all our endeavours to fix a standard of taste, and reconcile the discordant apprehensions of men, there still remain two sources of variation, which are not sufficient indeed to confound all the boundaries of beauty and deformity, but will often serve to produce a difference in the degrees of our approbation or blame. The one is the different humours of particular men; the other, the particular manners and opinions of our age and country. The general principles of taste are uniform in human nature: Where men vary in their judgments, some defect or perversion in the faculties may commonly be remarked; proceeding either from prejudice, from want of practice, or want of delicacy; and there is just reason for approving one taste, and condemning another. But where there is such a diversity in the internal frame or external situation as is entirely blameless on both sides, and leaves no room to give one the preference above the other; in that case a certain degree of diversity in judgment is unavoidable, and we seek in vain for a standard, by which we can reconcile the contrary sentiments.

A young man, whose passions are warm, will be more sensibly touched with amorous and tender images, than a man more advanced in years, who takes pleasure in wise, philosophical reflections concerning the conduct of life and moderation of the passions. At twenty, OVID may be the favourite author; HORACE at forty; and perhaps TACITUS at fifty. Vainly would we, in such cases, endeavour to enter into the sentiments of others, and divest ourselves of those propensities, which are natural to us. We choose our favourite author as we do our friend, from a conformity of humour and disposition. Mirth or passion, sentiment or reflection; whichever of these most predominates in our temper, it gives us a peculiar sympathy with the writer who resembles us.

One person is more pleased with the sublime; another with the tender; a third with raillery. One has a strong sensibility to blemishes, and is extremely studious of correctness: Another has a more lively feeling of beauties, and pardons twenty absurdities and defects for one elevated or pathetic stroke. The ear of this man is entirely turned towards conciseness and energy; that man is delighted with a copious, rich, and harmonious expression. Simplicity is affected by one; ornament by another. Comedy, tragedy, satire, odes, have each its partizans, who prefer that particular species of writing to all others. It is plainly an error in a critic, to confine his approbation to one species or style of writing, and condemn all the rest. But it is almost impossible not to feel a predilection for that which suits our particular turn and disposition. Such preferences are innocent and unavoidable, and can never reasonably be the object of dispute, because there is no standard, by which they can be decided.

For a like reason, we are more pleased, in the course of our reading, with pictures and characters, that resemble objects which are found in our own age or country, than with those which describe a different set of customs. It is not without some effort, that we reconcile ourselves to the simplicity of ancient manners, and behold princesses carrying water from the spring, and kings and heroes dressing their own victuals. We may allow in general, that the representation of such manners is no fault in the author, nor deformity in the piece; but we are not so sensibly touched with them. For this reason, comedy is not easily transferred from one age or nation to another. A FRENCHMAN or ENGLISHMAN is not pleased with the ANDRIA of TERENCE, or CLITIA of MACHIAVEL; where the fine lady, upon whom all the play turns, never once appears to the spectators, but is always kept behind the scenes, suitably to the reserved humour of the ancient GREEKS and modern ITALIANS. A man of learning and reflection can make allowance for these peculiarities of manners; but a common audience can never divest themselves so far of their usual ideas and sentiments, as to relish pictures which in no wise resemble them.

But here there occurs a reflection, which may, perhaps, be useful in examining the celebrated controversy concerning ancient and modern learning; where we often find the one side excusing any seeming absurdity in the ancients from the manners of the age, and the other refusing to admit this excuse, or at least, admitting it only as an apology for the author, not for the performance. In my opinion, the proper boundaries in this subject have seldom been fixed between the contending parties. Where any innocent peculiarities of manners are represented, such as those above mentioned, they ought certainly to be admitted; and a man, who is shocked with them, gives an evident proof of false delicacy and refinement. The poet's *monument more durable than brass*, must fall to the ground like common brick or clay, were men to make no allowance for the continual revolutions of manners and customs, and would admit of nothing but what was suitable to the prevailing fashion. Must we throw aside the pictures of our ancestors, because of their ruffs and fardingales? But where the ideas of morality and decency alter from one age to another, and where vicious manners are described, without being marked with the proper characters of blame and disapprobation; this must be allowed to disfigure the poem, and to be a real deformity. I cannot, nor is it proper I should, enter into such sentiments; and however I may excuse the poet, on account of the manners of his age, I never can relish the composition. The want of humanity and of decency, so conspicuous in the characters drawn by several of the ancient poets, even sometimes by HOMER and the GREEK tragedians, diminishes considerably the merit of their noble performances, and gives modern authors an advantage over them. We are not interested in the fortunes and sentiments of such rough heroes: We are displeased to find the limits of vice and virtue so much confounded: And whatever indulgence we may give to the writer on account of his prejudices, we cannot prevail on our-selves to enter into his sentiments, or bear an affection to characters, which we plainly discover to be blameable.

The case is not the same with moral prin-ciples, as with speculative opinions of any kind. These are in continual flux and revolu-tion. The son embraces a different system from the father. Nay, there scarcely is any man, who can boast of great constancy and uniformity in this particular. Whatever spec-ulative errors may be found in the polite writings of any age or country, they detract but little from the value of those composi-tions. There needs but a certain turn of thought or imagination to make us enter into all the opinions, which then prevailed, and relish the sentiments or conclusions derived from them. But a very violent effort is requisite to change our judgment of man-ners, and excite sentiments of approbation or blame, love or hatred, different from those to which the mind from long custom has been familiarized. And where a man is confident of the rectitude of that moral stan-dard, by which he judges, he is justly jealous of it, and will not pervert the sentiments of his heart for a moment, in complaisance to any writer whatsoever.

Of all speculative errors, those, which regard religion, are the most excusable in compositions of genius; nor is it ever permit-ted to judge of the civility or wisdom of any people, or even of single persons, by the grossness or refinement of their theological principles. The same good sense, that directs men in the ordinary occurrences of life, is not hearkened to in religious matters, which are supposed to be placed altogether above the cognizance of human reason. On this account, all the absurdities of the pagan system of theology must be overlooked by every critic, who would pretend to form a just notion of ancient poetry; and our pos-terity, in their turn, must have the same indulgence to their forefathers. No religious principles can ever be imputed as a fault

to any poet, while they remain merely principles, and take not such strong posses-sion of his heart, as to lay him under the imputation of *bigotry* or *superstition*. Where that happens, they confound the sen-timents of morality, and alter the natural boundaries of vice and virtue. They are therefore eternal blemishes, according to the principle above mentioned; nor are the prejudices and false opinions of the age suf-ficient to justify them.

It is essential to the ROMAN catholic reli-gion to inspire a violent hatred of every other worship, and to represent all pagans, mahometans, and heretics as the objects of divine wrath and vengeance. Such senti-ments, though they are in reality very blame-able, are considered as virtues by the zealots of that communion, and are represented in their tragedies and epic poems as a kind of divine heroism. This bigotry has disfigured two very fine tragedies of the FRENCH the-atre, POLIEUCTE and ATHALIA; where an intem-perate zeal for particular modes of worship is set off with all the pomp imaginable, and forms the predominant character of the heroes. "What is this," says the sublime JOAD to JOSABET, finding her in discourse with MATHAN, the priest of BAAL, "Does the daugh-ter of DAVID speak to this traitor? Are you not afraid, lest the earth should open and pour forth flames to devour you both? Or lest these holy walls should fall and crush you together? What is his purpose? Why comes that enemy of God hither to poison the air, which we breathe, with his horrid presence?" Such sentiments are received with great applause on the theatre of PARIS; but at LONDON the spectators would be full as much pleased to hear ACHILLES tell AGAMEMNON, that he was a dog in his fore-head, and a deer in his heart, or JUPITER threaten JUNO with a sound drubbing, if she will not be quiet.

RELIGIOUS principles are also a blemish in any polite composition, when they rise up to superstition, and intrude themselves into every sentiment, however remote from any connection with religion. It is no excuse for the poet, that the customs of his country had burthened life with so many religious ceremonies and observances, that no part of it was exempt from that yoke. It must for ever be ridiculous in PETRARCH to compare his mistress LAURA, to JESUS CHRIST. Nor is it less ridiculous in that agreeable libertine, BOCCACE, very seriously to give thanks to GOD ALMIGHTY and the ladies, for their assistance in defending him against his enemies.

Immanuel Kant

THE
FOUR
MOMENTS

Immanuel Kant (1724–1804), who lived in Prussia, is probably the most influential modern philosopher in the Western world. He developed a systematic philosophy that emphasized the extent to which our minds structure the reality that we experience. His most notable works are the Critique of Pure Reason, *the* Critique of Practical Reason, *and the* Critique of Judgment *(1790), the work from which the following selection is taken. In "The Four Moments," Kant describes four characteristics necessarily involved in a pure aesthetic judgment (a judgment that an object is beautiful).*

§2
THE LIKING THAT DETERMINES A JUDGMENT OF TASTE IS DEVOID OF ALL INTEREST

Interest is what we call the liking we connect with the presentation of an object's existence. Hence such a liking always refers at once to our power of desire, either as the basis that determines it, or at any rate as necessarily connected with that determining basis. But if the question is whether something is beautiful, what we want to know is not whether we or anyone cares, or so much as might care, in any way, about the thing's existence, but rather how we judge it in our mere contemplation of it (intuition or reflection). Suppose someone asks me whether I consider the palace I see before me beautiful. I might reply that I am not fond of things of that sort, made merely to be gaped at. Or I might reply like that Iroquois *sachem* who said that he liked nothing better in Paris than the eating-houses. I might even go on, as *Rousseau* would, to rebuke the vanity of the great who spend the people's sweat on such superfluous things. I might, finally, quite easily convince myself that, if I were on some uninhabited island with no hope of ever again coming among people, and could conjure up such a splendid edifice by a mere

Immanuel Kant, *Critique of Judgment*, trans. Werner S. Pluhar (Indianapolis: Hackett, 1987) 45–90.

wish, I would not even take that much trouble for it if I already had a sufficiently comfortable hut. The questioner may grant all this and approve of it; but it is not to the point. All he wants to know is whether my mere presentation of the object is accompanied by a liking, no matter how indifferent I may be about the existence of the object of this presentation. We can easily see that, in order for me to say that an object is *beautiful*, and to prove that I have taste, what matters is what I do with this presentation within myself, and not the [respect] in which I depend on the object's existence. Everyone has to admit that if a judgment about beauty is mingled with the least interest then it is very partial and not a pure judgment of taste. In order to play the judge in matters of taste, we must not be in the least biased in favor of the thing's existence but must be wholly indifferent about it.

There is no better way to elucidate this proposition, which is of prime importance, than by contrasting the pure disinterested liking that occurs in a judgment of taste with a liking connected with interest, especially if we can also be certain that the kinds of interest I am about to mention are the only ones there are. . . .

§5
COMPARISON OF THE THREE SORTS OF LIKING, WHICH DIFFER IN KIND

Both the agreeable and the good refer to our power of desire and hence carry a liking with them, the agreeable a liking that is conditioned pathologically by stimuli (*stimuli*), the good a pure practical liking that is determined not just by the presentation of the object but also by the presentation of the subject's connection with the existence of the object; i.e., what we like is not just the object but its existence as well. A judgment

of taste, on the other hand, is merely *contemplative*, i.e., it is a judgment that is indifferent to the existence of the object: it [considers] the character of the object only by holding it up to our feeling of pleasure and displeasure. Nor is this contemplation, as such, directed to concepts, for a judgment of taste is not a cognitive judgment (whether theoretical or practical) and hence is neither *based* on concepts, nor directed to them as *purposes*.

EXPLICATION OF THE BEAUTIFUL INFERRED FROM THE FIRST MOMENT

Taste is the ability to judge an object, or a way of presenting it, by means of a liking or disliking *devoid of all interest*. The object is called *beautiful.*

SECOND MOMENT OF A JUDGMENT OF TASTE, AS TO ITS QUANTITY

§7
COMPARISON OF THE BEAUTIFUL WITH THE AGREEABLE AND THE GOOD IN TERMS OF THE ABOVE CHARACTERISTIC

As regards the *agreeable* everyone acknowledges that his judgment, which he bases on a private feeling and by which he says that he likes some object, is by the same token confined to his own person. Hence, if he says that canary wine is agreeable he is quite content if someone else corrects his terms and reminds him to say instead: It is agreeable to *me*. This holds moreover not only for the taste of the tongue, palate, and throat, but also for what may be agreeable to any one's eyes and ears. To one person the color violet is gentle and lovely, to another lifeless and faded. One person loves the sound of wind instruments, another that of string instruments. It would be foolish if we disputed about such differences with the intention of censuring another's judgment as incorrect if it differs from ours, as if the two were opposed logically. Hence about the agreeable the following principle holds: *Everyone has his own taste* (of sense).

It is quite different (exactly the other way round) with the beautiful. It would be ridiculous if someone who prided himself on his taste tried to justify [it] by saying: This object (the building we are looking at, the garment that man is wearing, the concert we are listening to, the poem put up to be judged) is beautiful *for me*. For he must not call it *beautiful* if [he means] only [that] *he* likes it. Many things may be charming and agreeable to him; no one cares about that. But if he proclaims something to be beautiful, then he requires the same liking from others; he then judges not just for himself but for everyone, and speaks of beauty as if it were a property of things. That is why he says: The *thing* is beautiful, and does not count on other people to agree with his judgment of liking on the ground that he has repeatedly found them agreeing with him; rather, he *demands* that they agree. He reproaches them if they judge differently, and denies that they have taste, which he nevertheless demands of them, as something they ought to have. In view of this . . . , we cannot say that everyone has his own particular taste. That would amount to saying that there is no such thing as taste at all, no aesthetic judgment that could rightfully lay claim to everyone's assent.

And yet, even about the agreeable we can find people standing in agreement, and because of this we do, after all, deny that some people have taste while granting it to others; in speaking of taste here we do not

mean the sense of taste, which involves an organ, but an ability to judge the agreeable in general. Thus we will say that someone has taste if he knows how to entertain his guests [at a party] with agreeable things (that they can enjoy by all the senses) in such a way that everyone likes [the party]. But here it is understood that the universality is only comparative, so that the rules are only *general* (as all empirical rules are), not *universal*, as are the rules that a judgment about the beautiful presupposes . . . or lays claim to. Such a judgment of taste about the agreeable refers to sociability as far as that rests on empirical rules. It is true that judgments about the good also rightfully claim to be valid for everyone, but in presenting the good as the object of a universal liking we do so *by means of a concept*, whereas this is the case neither with the beautiful nor with the agreeable.

§8
IN A JUDGMENT OF TASTE THE UNIVERSALITY OF THE LIKING IS PRESENTED ONLY AS SUBJECTIVE

. . . As to the agreeable we allow everyone to be of a mind of his own, no one requiring others to agree with his judgment of taste. But in a judgment of taste about beauty we always require others to agree. Insofar as judgments about the agreeable are merely private, whereas judgments about the beautiful are put forward as having general validity (as being public), taste regarding the agreeable can be called taste of sense, and taste regarding the beautiful can be called taste of reflection, though the judgments of both are aesthetic (rather than practical) judgments about an object, [i.e.,] judgments merely about the relation that the presentation of the object has to the feeling of pleasure and displeasure. But surely there is something strange here. In the case of the taste of sense, not only does experience show that its judgment (of a pleasure or displeasure we take in something or other) does not hold universally, but people, of their own accord, are modest enough not even to require others to agree (even though there actually is, at times, very widespread agreement in these judgments too). Now, experience teaches us that the taste of reflection, with its claim that its judgment (about the beautiful) is universally valid for everyone, is also rejected often enough. What is strange is that the taste of reflection should nonetheless find itself able (as it actually does) to conceive of judgments that can demand such agreement, and that it does in fact require this agreement from everyone for each of its judgments. What the people who make these judgments dispute about is not whether such a claim is possible; they are merely unable to agree, in particular cases, on the correct way to apply this ability.

Here we must note, first of all, that a universality that does not rest on concepts of the object (not even on empirical ones) is not a logical universality at all, but an aesthetic one; i.e., the [universal] quantity of the judgment is not objective but only subjective. . . .

§9

INVESTIGATION OF THE
QUESTION WHETHER
IN A JUDGMENT OF TASTE
THE FEELING OF PLEASURE
PRECEDES THE JUDGING OF
THE OBJECT OR THE JUDGING
PRECEDES THE PLEASURE

The solution of this problem is the key to the critique of taste and hence deserves full attention.

If the pleasure in the given object came first, and our judgment of taste were to attribute only the pleasure's universal communicability to the presentation of the object, then this procedure would be self-contradictory. For that kind of pleasure would be none other than mere agreeableness in the sensation, so that by its very nature it could have only private validity, because it would depend directly on the presentation by which the object *is given*.

Hence it must be the universal communicability of the mental state, in the given presentation, which underlies the judgment of taste as its subjective condition, and the pleasure in the object must be its consequence. Nothing, however, can be communicated universally except cognition, as well as presentation insofar as it pertains to cognition; for presentation is objective only insofar as it pertains to cognition, and only through this does it have a universal reference point with which everyone's presentational power is compelled to harmonize. If, then, we are to think that the judgment about this universal communicability of the presentation has a merely subjective determining basis, i.e., one that does not involve a concept of the object, then this basis can be nothing other than the mental state that we find in the relation between the presentational powers [imagination and understanding] insofar as they refer a given presentation to *cognition in general*.

When this happens, the cognitive powers brought into play by this presentation are in free play, because no determinate concept restricts them to a particular rule of cognition. Hence the mental state in this presentation must be a feeling, accompanying the given presentation, of a free play of the presentational powers directed to cognition in general. Now if a presentation by which an object is given is, in general, to become cognition, we need *imagination* to combine the manifold of intuition, and *understanding* to provide the unity of the concept uniting the [component] presentations. This state of *free play* of the cognitive powers, accompanying a presentation by which an object is given, must be universally communicable; for cognition, the determination of the object with which given presentations are to harmonize (in any subject whatever) is the only way of presenting that holds for everyone.

But the way of presenting [which occurs] in a judgment of taste is to have subjective universal communicability without presupposing a determinate concept; hence this subjective universal communicability can be nothing but [that of] the mental state in which we are when imagination and understanding are in free play (insofar as they harmonize with each other as required for *cognition in general*). For we are conscious that this subjective relation suitable for cognition in general must hold just as much for everyone, and hence be just as universally communicable, as any determinate cognition, since cognition always rests on that relation as its subjective condition.

Now this merely subjective (aesthetic) judging of the object, or of the presentation by which it is given, precedes the pleasure in the object and is the basis of this pleasure, [a pleasure] in the harmony of the cognitive powers. But the universal subjective validity of this liking, the liking we connect with the presentation of the object we call beautiful, is based solely on the mentioned universality of the subjective conditions for judging objects.

. . . This sensation, whose universal communicability a judgment of taste postulates, is the quickening of the two powers (imagination and understanding) to an activity that is indeterminate but, as a result of the prompting of the given presentation, nonetheless accordant: the activity required for cognition in general. An objective relation can only be thought. Still, insofar as it has subjective conditions, it can nevertheless be sensed in the effect it has on the mind; and if the relation is not based on a concept (e.g., the relation that the presentational powers must have in order to give rise to a power of cognition in general), then the only way we can become conscious of it is through a sensation of this relation's effect: the facilitated play of the two mental powers (imagination and understanding) quickened by their reciprocal harmony. A presentation that, though singular and not compared with others, yet harmonizes with the conditions of the universality that is the business of the understanding in general, brings the cognitive powers into that proportioned attunement which we require for all cognition and which, therefore, we also consider valid for everyone who is so constituted as to judge by means of understanding and the senses in combination (in other words, for all human beings).

EXPLICATION OF THE BEAUTIFUL INFERRED FROM THE SECOND MOMENT

Beautiful is what, without a concept, is liked universally.

THIRD MOMENT OF JUDGMENTS OF TASTE, AS TO THE *RELATION* OF PURPOSES THAT IS TAKEN INTO CONSIDERATION IN THEM

§10 ON PURPOSIVENESS IN GENERAL

What is purpose? If we try to explicate it in terms of its transcendental attributes (without presupposing anything empirical, such as the feeling of pleasure), then a purpose is the object of a concept insofar as we regard this concept as the object's cause (the real basis of its possibility); and the causality that a *concept* has with regard to its *object* is purposiveness. . . . Hence we think of a purpose if we think not merely, say, of our cognition of the object, but instead of the object itself (its form, or its existence), as an effect that is possible only through a concept of that effect. . . .

The power of desire, insofar as it can be determined to act only by concepts, i.e., in conformity with the presentation of a purpose, would be the will. On the other hand, we do call objects, states of mind, or acts purposive even if their possibility does not necessarily presuppose the presentation of a purpose; we do this merely because we can explain and grasp them only if we assume that they are based on a causality [that operates] according to purposes, i.e., on a will that would have so arranged them in accordance with the presentation of a certain rule. Hence there can be purposiveness without a purpose, insofar as we do not posit the causes of this form in a will, and yet can grasp the explanation of its possibility only by deriving it from a will. Now what we observe we do not always need to have insight into by reason (as to how it is possible). Hence we can at least observe a purposiveness as to form and take note of it in objects—even if only by reflection—without basing it on a purpose. . . .

§11
A JUDGMENT OF TASTE IS BASED ON NOTHING BUT THE *FORM OF PURPOSIVENESS* OF AN OBJECT (OR OF THE WAY OF PRESENTING IT)

Whenever a purpose is regarded as the basis of a liking it always carries with it an interest, as the basis that determines the judgment about the object of the pleasure. Hence a judgment of taste cannot be based on a subjective purpose. But a judgment of taste also cannot be determined by a presentation of an objective purpose, i.e., a presentation of the object itself as possible according to principles of connection in terms of purposes, and hence it cannot be determined by a concept of the good. For it is an aesthetic and not a cognitive judgment, and hence does not involve a *concept* of the character and internal or external possibility of the object through this or that cause; rather, it involves merely the relation of the presentational powers to each other, so far as they are determined by a presentation.

Now this relation, [present] when [judgment] determines an object as beautiful, is connected with the feeling of a pleasure, a pleasure that the judgment of taste at the same time declares to be valid for everyone. Hence neither an agreeableness accompanying the presentation, nor a presentation of the object's perfection and the concept of the good, can contain the basis that determines [such a judgment]. Therefore the liking that, without a concept, we judge to be universally communicable and hence to be the basis that determines a judgment of taste, can be nothing but the subjective purposiveness in the presentation of an object, without any purpose (whether objective or subjective), and hence the mere form of purposiveness, insofar as we are conscious of it, in the presentation by which an object is *given* us.

. . . The very consciousness of a merely formal purposiveness in the play of the subject's cognitive powers, accompanying a presentation by which an object is given, is that pleasure. For this consciousness in an aesthetic judgment contains a basis for determining the subject's activity regarding the quickening of his cognitive powers and hence an inner causality (which is purposive) concerning cognition in general, which however is not restricted to a determinate cognition. Hence it contains a mere form of the subjective purposiveness of a presentation. This pleasure is also not practical in any way, neither like the one arising from the pathological basis, agreeableness, nor like the one arising from the intellectual basis, the conceived good. Yet it does have a causality in it, namely, to *keep* [us in] the state of [having] the presentation itself, and [to keep] the cognitive powers engaged [in their occupation] without any further aim. We *linger* in our contemplation of the beautiful, because this contemplation reinforces and reproduces itself. This is analogous to (though not the sane as) the way in which we linger over something charming that, as we present an object, repeatedly arouses our attention, [though here] the mind is passive.

§13
A PURE JUDGMENT OF TASTE IS INDEPENDENT OF CHARM AND EMOTION

All interest ruins a judgment of taste and deprives it of its impartiality, especially if, instead of making the purposiveness precede the feeling of pleasure as the interest of reason does, that interest bases the purposiveness on the feeling of pleasure; but this is what always happens in an aesthetic judgment that we make about something insofar as it gratifies or pains us. Hence judgments affected in this way can make either no claim at all to a universally valid liking, or a claim that is diminished to the extent that sensations of that kind are included among the bases determining the taste. Any taste remains barbaric if its liking requires that *charms* and *emotions* be mingled in, let alone if it makes these the standard of its approval.

And yet, (though beauty should actually concern only form), charms are frequently not only included with beauty, as a contribution toward a universal aesthetic liking, but are even themselves passed off as beauties, so that the matter of the liking is passed off

as the form. This is a misunderstanding that, like many others having yet some basis in truth, can be eliminated by carefully defining these concepts.

A *pure judgment of taste* is one that is not influenced by charm or emotion (though these may be connected with a liking for the beautiful), and whose determining basis is therefore merely the purposiveness of the form.

§14
ELUCIDATION BY EXAMPLES

. . . The view that the beauty we attribute to an object on account of its form is actually capable of being heightened by charm is a vulgar error that is very prejudicial to genuine, uncorrupted, solid . . . taste. It is true that charms may be added to beauty as a supplement: they may offer the mind more than that dry liking, by also making the presentation of the object interesting to it, and hence they may commend to us taste and its cultivation, above all if our taste is still crude and unpracticed. But charms do actually impair the judgment of taste if they draw attention to themselves as [if they were] bases for judging beauty. For the view that they contribute to beauty is so far off the mark that it is in fact only as aliens that they must, indulgently, be granted admittance when taste is still weak and unpracticed, and only insofar as they do not interfere with the beautiful form.

In painting, in sculpture, indeed in all the visual arts, including architecture and horticulture insofar as they are fine arts, *design* is what is essential; in design the basis for any involvement of taste is not what gratifies us in sensation, but merely what we like because of its form. The colors that illuminate the outline belong to charm. Though they can indeed make the object itself vivid to sense, they cannot make it beautiful and worthy of being beheld. Rather, usually the requirement of beautiful form severely restricts [what] colors [may be used], and even where the charm [of colors] is admitted it is still only the form that refines the colors.

All form of objects of the senses (the outer senses or, indirectly, the inner sense as well) is either *shape* or *play;* if the latter, it is either play of shapes (in space, namely, mimetic art and dance), or mere play of sensations (in time). The *charm* of colors or of the agreeable tone of an instrument may be added, but it is the *design* in the first case and the *composition* in the second that constitute the proper object of a pure judgment of taste; that the purity of the colors and of the tones, or for that matter their variety and contrast, seem to contribute to the beauty, does not mean that, because they themselves are agreeable, they furnish us, as it were, with a supplement to, and one of the same kind as, our liking for the form. For all they do is to make the form intuitable more precisely, determinately, and completely, while they also enliven the presentation by means of their charm, by arousing and sustaining the attention we direct toward the object itself.

Even what we call *ornaments* . . . , i.e., what does not belong to the whole presentation of the object as an intrinsic constituent, but [is] only an extrinsic addition, does indeed increase our taste's liking, and yet it too does so only by its form, as in the case of picture frames, or drapery on statues, or colonnades around magnificent buildings. On the other hand, if the ornament itself does not consist in beautiful form but is merely attached, as a gold frame is to a painting so that its charm may commend the painting for our approval, then it impairs genuine beauty and is called *finery.*

———◆◆◆———

§16
A JUDGMENT OF TASTE BY WHICH WE DECLARE AN OBJECT BEAUTIFUL UNDER THE CONDITION OF A DETERMINATE CONCEPT IS NOT PURE

There are two kinds of beauty, free beauty (*pulchritudo vaga*) and merely accessory beauty (*pulchritudo adhaerens*). Free beauty does not presuppose a concept of what the object is [meant] to be. Accessory beauty does presuppose such a concept, as well as the object's perfection in terms of that concept. The free kinds of beauty are called (self-subsistent) beauties of this or that thing. The other kind of beauty is accessory to a concept (i.e., it is conditioned beauty) and as such is attributed to objects that fall under the concept of a particular purpose.

Flowers are free natural beauties. Hardly anyone apart from the botanist knows what sort of thing a flower is [meant] to be; and even he, while recognizing it as the reproductive organ of a plant, pays no attention to this natural purpose when he judges the flower by taste. Hence the judgment is based on no perfection of any kind, no intrinsic purposiveness to which the combination of the manifold might refer. Many birds (the parrot, the humming-bird, the bird of paradise) and a lot of crustaceans in the sea are [free] beauties themselves [and] belong to no object determined by concepts as to its purpose, but we like them freely and on their own account. Thus designs *à la grecque*, the foliage on borders or on wallpaper, etc., mean nothing on their own; they represent . . . nothing, no object under a determinate concept, and are free beauties. What we call fantasias in music (namely, music without a topic [*Thema*]), indeed all music not set to words, may also be included in the same class.

When we judge free beauty (according to mere form) then our judgment of taste is pure. Here we presuppose no concept of any purpose for which the manifold is to serve the given object, and hence no concept [as to] what the object is [meant] to represent; our imagination is playing, as it were, while it contemplates the shape, and such a concept would only restrict its freedom.

But the beauty of a human being (and, as kinds subordinate to a human being, the beauty of a man or woman or child), or the beauty of a horse or of a building (such as a church, palace, armory, or summer-house) does presuppose the concept of the purpose that determines what the thing is [meant] to be, and hence a concept of its perfection, and so it is merely adherent beauty. Now just as a connection of beauty, which properly concerns only form, with the agreeable (the sensation) prevented the judgment of taste from being pure, so does a connection of beauty with the good (i.e., as to how, in terms of the thing's purpose, the manifold is good for the thing itself) impair the purity of a judgment of taste.

Much that would be liked directly in intuition could be added to a building, if only the building were not [meant] to be a church. A figure could be embellished with all sorts of curlicues and light but regular lines, as the New Zealanders do with their tattoos, if only it were not the figure of a human being. And this human being might have had much more delicate features and a facial structure with a softer and more likable outline, if only he were not [meant] to represent a man, let alone a warlike one.

Now if a liking for the manifold in a thing refers to the intrinsic purpose that determines [how] the thing is possible, then it is a liking based on a concept, whereas a liking for beauty is one that presupposes no concept but is directly connected with the presentation by which the object is given (not by which it is thought). Now if a judgment of taste regarding the second liking is made to depend on, and hence is restricted by, the purpose involved in the first liking, it is a rational judgment, and so it is no longer a free and pure judgment of taste.

It is true that taste gains by such a connection of aesthetic with intellectual liking, for it becomes fixed and, though it is not universal, rules can be prescribed for it with regard to certain objects that are purposively determined. By the same token, however, these rules will not be rules of taste but will merely be rules for uniting taste with reason, i.e., the beautiful with the good, a union that enables us to use the beautiful as an instrument for our aim regarding the good, so that the mental attunement that sustains itself and has subjective universal validity may serve as a basis for that other way of thinking that can be sustained only by laborious resolve but that is universally valid objectively. Actually, however, neither does perfection gain by beauty, nor beauty by perfection. Rather, because in using a concept in order to compare the presentation by which an object is given us with that object itself (with regard to what it is [meant] to be), we inevitably hold the presentation up to the sensation in the subject, it is the *complete power* of presentation that gains when the two states of mind harmonize. . . .

— ◆◆◆ —

EXPLICATION OF THE BEAUTIFUL INFERRED FROM THE THIRD MOMENT

Beauty is an object's form of *purposiveness* insofar as it is perceived in the object *without the presentation of a purpose*.

FOURTH MOMENT OF A JUDGMENT OF TASTE, AS TO THE MODALITY OF THE LIKING FOR THE OBJECT

§19
THE SUBJECTIVE NECESSITY THAT WE ATTRIBUTE TO A JUDGMENT OF TASTE IS CONDITIONED

A judgment of taste requires everyone to assent; and whoever declares something to be beautiful holds that everyone *ought* to give his approval to the object at hand and that he too should declare it beautiful. Hence the *ought* in an aesthetic judgment, even once we have . . . all the data needed for judging, is still uttered only conditionally. We solicit everyone else's assent because we have a basis for it that is common to all. Indeed, we could count on that assent, if only we could always be sure that the instance had been subsumed correctly under that basis, which is the rule for the approval.

§22
THE NECESSITY OF THE UNIVERSAL ASSENT THAT WE THINK IN A JUDGMENT OF TASTE IS A SUBJECTIVE NECESSITY THAT WE PRESENT AS OBJECTIVE BY PRESUPPOSING A COMMON SENSE

Whenever we make a judgment declaring something to be beautiful, we permit no one to hold a different opinion, even though we base our judgment only on our feeling rather than on concepts; hence we regard this underlying feeling as a common rather than as a private feeling. But if we are to use this common sense in such a way, we cannot base it on experience; for it seeks to justify us in making judgments that contain an ought: it does not say that everyone *will* agree with my judgment, but that he *ought* to. Hence the common sense, of whose judgment I am at that point offering my judgment of taste as an example, attributing to it *exemplary* validity on that account, is a mere ideal standard. With this standard presupposed, we could rightly turn a judgment that agreed with it, as well as the liking that is expressed in it for some object, into a rule for everyone. For although the principle is only subjective, it would still be assumed as subjectively universal (an idea necessary for everyone); and so it could, like an objective principal, demand universal assent insofar as agreement among different judging persons is concerned, provided only we were certain that we had subsumed under it correctly.

That we do actually presuppose this indeterminate standard of a common sense is proved by the fact that we presume to make judgments of taste. . . .

EXPLICATION OF THE BEAUTIFUL INFERRED FROM THE FOURTH MOMENT

Beautiful is what without a concept is cognized as the object of a *necessary* liking.

Friedrich Nietzsche

ON
BEAUTY
AND
UGLINESS

Friedrich Nietzsche (1844–1900), a German philosopher, devoted many of his writings to debunking philosophical tendencies in the Western tradition that he believed were harmful or outmoded. In this selection, from his Twilight of the Idols *(1889), he takes issue with the notion that proper appreciation of beauty is disinterested, as Kant and Schopenhauer had argued. Nietzsche gives a thoroughly naturalized interpretation of beauty in this selection. The concept of beauty, he argues, derives from notions of health and vitality in human, physiological terms.*

19

Beautiful and ugly. Nothing is more conditional—or, let us say, narrower—than our feeling for beauty. Whoever would think of it apart from man's joy in man would immediately lose any foothold. "Beautiful in itself" is a mere phrase, not even a concept. In the beautiful, man posits himself as the measure of perfection; in special cases he worships himself in it. A species cannot do otherwise but thus affirm itself alone. Its *lowest* instinct, that of self-preservation and self-expansion, still radiates in such sublimities. Man believes the world itself to be overloaded with beauty—and he forgets himself as the cause of this. He alone has presented the world with beauty—alas! only with a very human, all-too-human beauty. At bottom, man mirrors himself in things; he considers everything beautiful that reflects his own image: the judgment "beautiful" is the *vanity of his species.* For a little suspicion may whisper this question into the skeptic's ear: Is the world really beautified by the fact that man thinks it beautiful? He

Friedrich Nietzsche, *Twilight of the Idols, The Portable Nietzsche,* trans. and ed. Walter Kaufmann (New York: Viking, 1968) 524–30.

has *humanized* it, that is all. But nothing, absolutely nothing, guarantees that man should be the model of beauty. Who knows what he looks like in the eyes of a higher judge of beauty? Daring perhaps? Perhaps even amusing? Perhaps a little arbitrary?

"O Dionysus, divine one, why do you pull me by my ears?" Ariadne once asked her philosophic lover during one of those famous dialogues on Naxos. "I find a kind of humor in your ears, Ariadne: why are they not even longer?"

Nothing is beautiful, except man alone: all aesthetics rests upon this naïveté, which is its *first* truth. Let us immediately add the second: nothing is ugly except the degenerating man—and with this the realm of aesthetic judgment is circumscribed. Physiologically, everything ugly weakens and saddens man. It reminds him of decay, danger, impotence; it actually deprives him of strength. One can measure the effect of the ugly with a dynamometer. Wherever man is depressed at all, he senses the proximity of something "ugly." His feeling of power, his will to power, his courage, his pride—all fall with the ugly and rise with the beautiful. In both cases we draw an inference: the premises for it are piled up in the greatest abundance in instinct. The ugly is understood as a sign and symptom of degeneration: whatever reminds us in the least of degeneration causes in us the judgment of "ugly." Every suggestion of exhaustion, of heaviness, of age, of weariness; every kind of lack of freedom, such as cramps, such as paralysis; and above all, the smell, the color, the form of dissolution, of decomposition—even in the ultimate attenuation into a symbol—all evoke the same reaction, the value judgment, "ugly." A *hatred* is aroused—but whom does man hate then? There is no doubt: the *decline of his type.* Here he hates out of the deepest instinct of the species; in this hatred there is a shudder, caution, depth, farsightedness—it is the deepest hatred there is. It is because of this that art is deep.

21

Schopenhauer. Schopenhauer, the last German worthy of consideration (who represents a *European* event like Goethe, like Hegel, like Heinrich Heine, and not merely a local event, a "national" one), is for a psychologist a first-rate case: namely, as a maliciously ingenious attempt to adduce in favor of a nihilistic total depreciation of life precisely the counter-instances, the great self-affirmations of the "will to life," life's forms of exuberance. He has interpreted *art*, heroism, genius, beauty, great sympathy, knowledge, the will to truth, and tragedy, in turn, as consequences of "negation" or of the "will's" need to negate—the greatest psychological counterfeit in all history, not counting Christianity. On closer inspection, he is at this point merely the heir of the Christian interpretation: only he knew how to approve that which Christianity had repudiated, the great cultural facts of humanity—albeit in a Christian, that is, nihilistic, manner (namely, as ways of "redemption," as anticipations of "redemption," as stimuli of the need for "redemption").

22

I take a single case. Schopenhauer speaks of *beauty* with a melancholy fervor. Why? Because he sees in it a bridge on which one will go farther, or develop a thirst to go farther. Beauty is for him a momentary redemption from the "will"—a lure to eternal redemption. Particularly, he praises beauty as the redeemer from "the focal point of the will," from sexuality—in beauty he sees the negation of the drive toward procreation. Queer saint! Somebody seems to be contradicting you; I fear it is nature. To what end is there any such thing as beauty in tone, color, fragrance, or rhythmic movement in nature? What is it that beauty evokes? Fortunately, a philosopher contradicts him too. No lesser authority than that of the divine Plato (so Schopenhauer himself calls him) maintains a different proposition: that all beauty incites procreation, that just this is the *proprium* of its effect, from the most sensual up to the most spiritual.

23

Plato goes further. He says with an innocence possible only for a Greek, not a "Christian," that there would be no Platonic philosophy at all if there were not such beautiful youths in Athens: it is only their sight that transposes the philosopher's soul into an erotic trance, leaving it no peace until it lowers the seed of all exalted things into such beautiful soil. Another queer saint! One does not trust one's ears, even if one should trust Plato. At least one guesses that they philosophized differently in Athens, especially in public. Nothing is less Greek than the conceptual web-spinning of a hermit—*amor intellectualis dei** after the fashion of Spinoza. Philosophy after the fashion of Plato might rather be defined as an erotic contest, as a further development and turning inward of the ancient agonistic gymnastics and of its *presuppositions*. What ultimately grew out of this philosophic eroticism of Plato? A new art form of the Greek agon: dialectics. Finally, I recall—against Schopenhauer and in honor of Plato—that the whole higher culture and literature of *classical* France too grew on the soil of sexual interest. Everywhere in it one may look for the amatory, the senses, the sexual contest, "the woman"—one will never look in vain.

24

L'art pour l'art. The fight against purpose in art is always a fight against the moralizing

tendency in art, against its subordination to morality. *L'art pour l'art* means, "The devil take morality!" But even this hostility still betrays the overpowering force of the prejudice. When the purpose of moral preaching and of improving man has been excluded from art, it still does not follow by any means that art is altogether purposeless, aimless, senseless—in short, *l'art pour l'art*, a worm chewing its own tail. "Rather no purpose at all than a moral purpose!"—that is the talk of mere passion. A psychologist, on the other hand, asks: what does all art do? does it not praise? glorify? choose? prefer? With all this it strengthens or weakens certain valuations. Is this merely a "moreover"? an accident? something in which the artist's instinct had no share? Or is it not the very presupposition of the artist's ability? Does his basic instinct aim at art, or rather at the sense of art, at life? at a desirability of life? Art is the great stimulus to life: how could one understand it as purposeless, as aimless, as *l'art pour l'art*?

One question remains: art also makes apparent much that is ugly, hard, and questionable in life; does it not thereby spoil life for us? And indeed there have been philosophers who attributed this sense to it: "liberation from the will" was what Schopenhauer taught as the over-all end of art; and with admiration he found the great utility of tragedy in its "evoking resignation." But this, as I have already suggested, is the pessimist's perspective and "evil eye." We must appeal to the artists themselves. What does the tragic artist communicate of himself? Is it not precisely the state *without* fear in the face of the fearful and questionable that he is showing? This state itself is a great desideratum; whoever knows it, honors it with the greatest honors, He communicates it—*must* communicate it, provided he is an artist, a genius of communication. Courage and freedom of feeling before a powerful enemy, before a sublime calamity, before a problem that arouses dread—this

*"Intellectual love of God."

triumphant state is what the tragic artist chooses, what he glorifies. Before tragedy, what is warlike in our soul celebrates its Saturnalia; whoever is used to suffering, whoever seeks out suffering, the heroic man praises his own being through tragedy—to him alone the tragedian presents this drink of sweetest cruelty.

Friedrich Nietzsche

APOLLO AND DIONYSUS

Friedrich Nietzsche (1844–1900) was a German philosopher with a background in classical philology. He was teaching classics at the University of Basel when he wrote his first book, The Birth of Tragedy *(1872). In this selection, the first section of the book, Nietzsche describes the Apollinian and Dionysian principles, which he analyzes as the fundamental impulses at work in ancient Athenian tragedy.*

1

We shall have gained much for the science of aesthetics, once we perceive not merely by logical inference, but with the immediate certainty of vision, that the continuous development of art is bound up with the *Apollinian* and *Dionysian* duality—just as procreation depends on the duality of the sexes, involving perpetual strife with only periodically intervening reconciliations, The terms Dionysian and Apollinian we borrow from the Greeks, who disclose to the discerning mind the profound mysteries of their view of art, not, to be sure, in concepts, but in the intensely clear figures of their gods. Through Apollo and Dionysus, the two art deities of the Greeks, we come to recognize that in the Greek world there existed a tremendous opposition, in origin and aims, between the Apollinian art of sculpture, and the nonimagistic, Dionysian art of music. These two different tendencies run parallel to each other, for the most part openly at variance; and they continually incite each other to new and more powerful births, which perpetuate an antagonism, only superficially reconciled by the common term "art"; till eventually, by a metaphysical miracle of the Hellenic "will" they appear coupled with each other, and through this coupling ultimately generate an equally Dionysian and Apollinian form of art—Attic tragedy.

In order to grasp these two tendencies, let us first conceive of them as the separate art worlds of *dreams* and *intoxication*. These physiological phenomena present a contrast analogous to that existing between the Apollinian and the Dionysian. It was in dreams, says Lucretius, that the glorious diving figures first appeared to the souls of men; in dreams the great shaper beheld the splendid bodies of superhuman beings; and the Hellenic poet, if questioned about the mysteries of poetic inspiration, would

Friedrich Nietzsche, *The Birth of Tragedy*, trans. Walter Kaufmann (New York: Random House, 1967) 33–38.

likewise have suggested dreams and he might have given an explanation like that of Hans Sachs in the *Meistersinger:*

> The poet's task is this, my friend,
> to read his dreams and comprehend.
> The truest human fancy seems
> to be revealed to us in dreams:
> all poems and versification
> are but true dreams' interpretation.

The beautiful illusion of the dream worlds, in the creation of which every man is truly an artist, is the prerequisite of all plastic art, and, as we shall see, of an important part of poetry also. In our dreams we delight in the immediate understanding of figures; all forms speak to us; there is nothing unimportant or superfluous. But even when this dream reality is most intense, we still have, glimmering through it, the sensation that it is *mere appearance:* at least this is my experience, and for its frequency—indeed, normality—I could adduce many proofs, including the sayings of the poets.

Philosophical men even have a presentiment that the reality in which we live and have our being is also mere appearance, and that another, quite different reality lies beneath it. Schopenhauer actually indicates as the criterion of philosophical ability the occasional ability to view men and things as mere phantoms or dream images. Thus the aesthetically sensitive man stands in the same relation to the reality of dreams as the philosopher does to the reality of existence; he is a close and willing observer, for these images afford him an interpretation of life, and by reflecting on these processes he trains himself for life.

It is not only the agreeable and friendly images that he experiences as something universally intelligible: the serious, the troubled, the sad, the gloomy, the sudden restraints, the tricks of accident, anxious expectations, in short, the whole divine comedy of life, including the inferno, also pass before him, not like mere shadows on a wall—for he lives and suffers with these

scenes—and yet not without that fleeting sensation of illusion. And perhaps many will, like myself, recall how amid the dangers and terrors of dreams they have occasionally said to themselves in self-encouragement, and not without success: "It is a dream!" I have likewise heard of people who were able to continue one and the same dream for three and even more successive nights—facts which indicate clearly how our innermost being, our common ground, experiences dreams with profound delight and a joyous necessity.

This joyous necessity of the dream experience has been embodied by the Greeks in their Apollo: Apollo, the god of all plastic energies, is at the same time the soothsaying god. He, who (as the etymology of the name indicates) is the "shining one," the deity of light, is also ruler over the beautiful illusion of the inner world of fantasy The higher truth, the perfection of these states in contrast to the incompletely intelligible everyday world, this deep consciousness of nature, healing and helping in sleep and dreams, is at the same time the symbolical analogue of the soothsaying faculty and of the arts generally, which make life possible and worth living. But we must also include in our image of Apollo that delicate boundary which the dream image must not overstep lest it have a pathological effect (in which case mere appearance would deceive us as if it were crude reality). We must keep in mind that measured restraint, that freedom from the wilder emotions, that calm of the sculptor god. His eye must be "sunlike," as befits his origin; even when it is angry and distempered it is still hallowed by beautiful illusion. And so, in one sense, we might apply to Apollo the words of Schopenhauer when he speaks of the man wrapped in the veil of *māyā* (*Welt als Wille und Vorstellung*, I, p. 416): "Just as in a stormy sea that, unbounded in all direction, raises and drops mountainous waves howling, a sailor sits in a boat and trusts in his frail bark: so in the midst of a world of torments the individual human being sits quietly, supported by and trusting in the *principium individuationis.*" In fact, we might say of Apollo that in him the unshaken faith in this *principium* and the calm repose of the man wrapped up in it receive their most sublime expression; and we might call Apollo himself the glorious divine image of the *principium individuationis*, through whose gestures and eyes all the joy and wisdom of "illusion," together with its beauty, speak to us.

In the same work Schopenhauer has depicted for us the tremendous *terror* which seizes man when he is suddenly dumfounded by the cognitive form of phenomena because the principle of sufficient reason, in some one of its manifestations, seems to suffer an exception. If we add to this terror the blissful ecstasy that wells from the innermost depths of man, indeed of nature, at this collapse of the *principium individuationis*, we steal a glimpse into the nature of the *Dionysian*, which is brought home to us most intimately by the analogy of intoxication.

Either under the influence of the narcotic draught, of which the songs of all primitive men and peoples speak; or with the potent coming if spring that penetrates all nature with joy, these Dionysian emotions awake, and as they grow in intensity everything subjective vanishes into complete self-forgetfulness. In the German Middle Ages, too, singing and dancing crowds, ever increasing in number, whirled themselves from place to place under this same Dionysian impulse. In these dancers of St. John and St. Vitus, we rediscover the Bacchic choruses of the Greeks, with their prehistory in Asia Minor, as far back as Babylon and the orgiastic Sacaea. There are some who, from obtuseness or lack of experience, turn away from such phenomena as from "folk-diseases," with contempt or pity born of the consciousness of their own "healthy-mindedness." But of course such poor wretches have no idea how corpselike and ghostly their so-called "healthy-mindedness" looks when

the glowing life of the Dionysian revelers roars past them.

Under the charm of the Dionysian not only is the union between man and man reaffirmed, but nature which has become alienated, hostile, or subjugated, celebrates once more her reconciliation with her lost son, man. Freely, earth proffers her gifts, and peacefully the beasts of prey of the rocks and desert approach. The chariot of Dionysus is covered with flowers and garlands; panthers and tigers walk under its yoke. Transform Beethoven's "Hymn to Joy" into a painting; let your imagination conceive the multitudes bowing to the dust, awestruck—then you will approach the Dionysian. Now the slave is a free man; now all the rigid, hostile barriers that necessity, caprice, or "impudent convention" have fixed between man and man are broken. Now, with the gospel of universal harmony, each one feels himself not only united, reconciled, and fused with his neighbor, but as one with him, as if the veil of *māyā* had been torn aside and were now merely fluttering in tatters before the mysterious primordial unity.

In song and in dance man expresses himself as a member of a higher community; he has forgotten how to walk and speak and is on the way toward flying into the air, dancing. His very gestures express enchantment. Just as the animals now talk, and the earth yields milk and honey, supernatural sounds emanate from him, too: he feels himself a god, he himself now walks about enchanted, in ecstasy, like the gods he saw walking in his dreams. He is no longer an artist, he has become a work of art: in these paroxysms of intoxication the artistic power of all nature reveals itself to the highest gratification of the primordial unity. The noblest clay, the most costly marble, man, is here kneaded and cut, and to the sound of the chisel strokes of the Dionysian world-artist rings out the cry of the Eleusinian mysteries: "Do you prostate yourselves, millions? Do you sense your Maker, world?"

DISCUSSION QUESTIONS

1. Do you agree with Plato that we have an innate notion of beauty that we refer to when we judge someone or something beautiful? How much do you think our cultural background and experiences influence our notion of beauty?
2. How do Aristotle's criteria for a successful tragedy apply to contemporary tragic films and plays? Consider specific cases.
3. Do you think that judgments of taste can be justified by means of reasons? Do some people have better taste than others? If so, what are the grounds for this assessment?
4. Do you think that beauty should be contemplated from a disinterested point of view? Why or why not?
5. What is the role of beauty in our lives? How important do you think it is in the lives of individuals and societies?
6. What other aims besides beauty are important in twentieth-century art?

FURTHER READING

Historical Works—Primary Sources

Aristotle. *Basic Works of Aristotle.* Ed. Richard McKeon. New York: Random House, 1941.

Burke, Edmund. *A Philosophical Enquiry into the Origin of Our Ideas of the Sublime and Beautiful.* 2nd ed. London: Routledge, 1958.

Hume, David. *"Of the Standard of Taste" and Other Essays.* Ed. J. W. Linz. New York: Bobbs-Merrill, 1965.

Hutcheson, Francis. *An Inquiry into the Origins of Our Idea of Beauty and Virtue.* London: J. Dabny, 1725.

Kant, Immanuel. *Critique of Judgment.* Trans. Werner S. Pluhar. Indianapolis: Hackett, 1987.

Nietzsche, Friedrich. *The Birth of Tragedy* [together with *The Case of Wagner*]. Trans. Walter Kaufmann. New York: Random House, 1967.

————— *Twilight of the Idols. The Portable Nietzsche.* Trans. and ed. Walter Kaufmann. New York: Viking, 1968.

Plato. *The Collected Dialogues of Plato, Including the Letters.* Ed. Edith Hamilton and Huntington Cairns. Princeton: Princeton UP, 1961.

Historical Works—Secondary Sources

Bowie, Andrew. *Aesthetics and Subjectivity: From Kant to Nietzsche.* Manchester: Manchester UP, 1990.

Guyer, Paul. *Kant and the Claims of Taste.* Cambridge: Harvard UP, 1979.

Halliwell, Stephen. *Aristotle's Poetics.* London: Duckworth, 1986.

Krukowski, Lucian. *Aesthetic Legacies.* Philadelphia: Temple UP, 1992.

Moravcsik, Julius, and Philip Temko, eds. *Plato on Beauty, Wisdom, and the Arts.* Totowa: Rowman and Littlefield, 1982.

Beauty

Danto, Arthur C. "What Happened to Beauty?" *The Nation* 254.12 (1992): 418–21.

Gadamer, Hans-Georg. *The Relevance of the Beautiful and Other Essays.* Trans. Nicholas Walker. Cambridge: Cambridge UP, 1986.

Mothersill, Mary. *Beauty Restored.* Oxford: Oxford UP, 1984.

Osborne, Harold. *Theory of Beauty.* London: Routledge, 1952.

Santayana, George. *The Sense of Beauty.* New York: Dover, 1896.

WHAT
IS
ART?

Although Western philosophy focused more on beauty than art throughout most of its history, the nature of art is nevertheless an issue of longstanding philosophical speculation. Plato held that art is essentially **mimetic,** or imitative. According to this view, art mimics the behavior or appearance of certain things in the real world, and its audience recognizes and enjoys these imitations. A recent related view, the **representationalist** position, contends that art represents reality by employing a representational vocabulary that is conventionally understood by its audience. (Plato, by contrast, did not see imitation as a matter of convention. He believed that art's imitations could be identified by anyone, without any necessary background in a representational vocabulary.)

Aristotle's interest in tragedy's arousal and catharsis of pity and fear (see Chapter 1) inspired some thinkers to focus on art's potential to arouse emotion.[1] The **arousal** theory (termed **emotionalism** in the reading by Morris Weitz in this chapter) is another consistent approach in the debate over the defining purpose of art. Still others contend that while art is fundamentally concerned with emotion, it aims to express emotions rather than to arouse them. This view is often termed the **expressionist** view of art.

Eighteenth-century theorists like Immanuel Kant, along with many of their intellectual descendents, offer another account of art's nature. This

---

[1]In fact, Plato's and Aristotle's theories of art were not so different on this point, although they had different opinions of art's influence on society. Plato, like Aristotle, assumed that emotions are aroused by art, in accordance with what it imitates. Aristotle also believed, like Plato, that art was inherently imitative.

formalist account contends that art's main purpose is to present formal elements in significant relationship.[2] The proponent of formalism often contrasts artistic form with **content,** the subject matter presented in representational art.

Yet another view of art is proposed by the **instrumentalists,** who insist that art's primary purpose is to serve as a means toward some other goal, such as the moral improvement or education of its audience. In practice, many philosophers who believed that art sought to imitate reality or to arouse emotion also believed that it had valuable instrumental effects. The instrumentalist position, however, is the view that such effects are the basic purpose of art.

In the early nineteenth century, G. W. F. Hegel advanced a particular instrumentalist view that can be called the **dialectical** theory of art. "Dialectic," according to Hegel, is the ongoing process by which we enhance our self-knowledge; it occurs when partial understandings of the self confront one another and are ultimately integrated into a more complete picture. Art's fundamental purpose is to make our self-understandings clear to us, as these alter and improve over the course of human history. By facilitating self-knowledge, art serves an important role in humanity's basic enterprise of striving for a complete understanding of self and reality (at least as long as art is still adequate to this task, a matter further considered in Chapter 11).

Still other theories of art have been proposed. Several are mentioned in the reading from Weitz. These include the **intuitionist** theory, the view that art incites our spiritual awareness on a level that is not conceptual or verbally specifiable; the **organicist** view, an Aristotelian variant of the formalist position, which holds that art aims to integrate its elements into a unity that is modeled on the organic body; and the **voluntarist** view, which holds that art's basic purpose is to provide imaginary fulfillments to our desires.

Twentieth-century art has challenged many of the traditional theories about the purpose of art. In particular, the mimesis and representation theories have become questionable in the twentieth century, for much recent art does not seem to aim at representing reality. In fact, much twentieth-century art defies traditional conventions for keeping the domains of art and reality separate. The casts of certain avant-garde theater productions step offstage and interact with the audience, for example; and many contemporary paintings are unframed or portray partial figures, suggesting that the world of the painting extends beyond the borders of the canvas.

One individual who did much to undercut the dominance of traditional ideas in the Western visual arts was French artist Marcel Duchamp (1887–1968). Many of his artworks resemble jokes, for they make witty commentaries on the artistic tradition. Among the most famous of these are his "readymades," ordinary objects uprooted from their pedestrian vocations

---

[2]Significant form," in fact, is twentieth-century formalist Clive Bell's technical term for what art achieves. An excerpt from Bell is included in Chapter 9. Although Bell considers form to be fundamental to the nature of art, he insists that significant form inspires an emotional response.

and exhibited as art by Duchamp. These readymades include a snow shovel, a bottle dryer, and, most notoriously, several urinals. Duchamp's readymades, not surprisingly, inspired controversy. Many saw and still see them as offensive, an insult to the public, and an arrogant appropriation of objects that were not even made by the artist. "Anyone could do that" is a common reaction. Some feel that they would be as edified by the contents of their own basements as they would by Duchamp's displays.

Arthur C. Danto's article "The Artworld" considers what "art" means in a context in which real things can become art. He contends that at every point in history, art has been seen as art because of theory. The artworld—all the producers, institutions, and appreciators who form the context of art at any given time—has some notion of what art is, and this notion determines what sorts of things are seen as art. Theories change from time to time, Danto argues. In the twentieth century, the traditional theory that art imitates reality has been abandoned in favor of a view that emphasizes the "real," material character of the artwork. In this theoretical atmosphere of our time, even ordinary objects can be "transfigured" into art, according to Danto. And only by means of a theory of this sort could anyone come to see Duchamp's "Fountain" (the name he gave to one of the urinals) as art.

Danto sees no reason to assume that our culture's current conception of art will remain static. Other features of objects besides their imitative character or their materiality might serve as future bases for seeing a thing as an artwork. In the meantime, however, our current definition of art gives us a basis for seeing certain real objects as art. Perhaps, Danto suggests, our theory gives a new sense to the ancient claim that art "mirrors" reality. Our art may serve the purpose of a mirror, namely, to reveal us to ourselves.[3]

Morris Weitz is less confident than Danto that theory can establish why a thing is an artwork. After reviewing some of the rival theories about what makes art art, Weitz concludes that none of them can fully account for art. The reason, according to Weitz, is that "art" is an open concept. In other words, the meaning of the term continues to change as new works extend the range to which it applies. In the expression of Ludwig Wittgenstein, artworks are included in the category because they have a general "family resemblance" to other works, not because all artworks share certain specific properties. Philosophers should not look for a set of necessary and sufficient criteria for calling something an artwork,[4] for the nature of art is evolving. The theories can be of use to aesthetics, not because any one of them gives us the "correct" account of what art is, but because each helps us to attend to features of art that might otherwise be neglected.

George Dickie rejects Weitz's conclusion. Artworks can be defined in terms of necessary conditions, according to Dickie. The most important of

---

[3]This suggestion resembles Hegel's theory of art. For more insight into Danto's Hegelianism, see the Hegel and Danto readings of Chapter 11.

[4]Necessary criteria are those that must be fulfilled for the term to apply. Sufficient criteria are those whose presence is all that is necessary to establish that the term applies to the case at hand.

these is that the status of art be conferred on an object by the informal network of institutions called the artworld.[5] This **institutional** definition of art is a **procedural** definition, in the terminology of Stephen Davies. In other words, it designates the standard procedures that render a thing an artwork. A procedural definition contrasts with a **functional** definition, a definition that stipulates the function that an object must perform in order to be an artwork.

In Dickie's view, a thing is an artwork because of the procedure that makes it so, the institutional conferral of the status of artwork on it. Dickie also contends that an artwork is necessarily an **artifact,** a product or by-product of human construction. Even a natural object such as a piece of driftwood can be given "artifactuality," however, by being picked up and exhibited. Dickie's institutional theory of art defines art in terms of human practices. An artwork is an artwork precisely because of how it relates to us and our institutions. (More recently, Dickie has deemphasized institutions as such, focusing instead on the "art circle," the practices and relationships that connect artists, artworks, and the appreciative public.)

Timothy Binkley agrees with Dickie that art should be procedurally defined, but disagrees about the relevant procedure. He even denies that an artwork must be an object, at least in the sense of being material. In "Piece: Contra Aesthetics," Binkley argues that art need not be "aesthetic"; in other words, it need not involve beautiful, sensuous objects presented for contemplation. Duchamp shows us that the sensuous object is not crucial to art at all. One gets the point of some of Duchamp's works simply by hearing about them; sensuous experience of the work is unnecessary. Duchamp has also demonstrated that an artist need not construct certain objects called artworks, according to Binkley. All that "making art" involves is "indexing," pronouncing that something is art. Anyone can do this, although not everyone can make a living at it. "Art" is no longer the set of artworks; instead it is the set of all "pieces" indexed by anyone as art.

Like Danto and Binkley, Walter Benjamin considers the impact that twentieth-century developments have had on our understanding of art. Benjamin is concerned with technology's negative effect on our ability to appreciate art in his 1939 essay, "The Work of Art in the Age of Mechanical Reproduction." The mechanical reproduction of artistic images, Benjamin argues, has robbed artworks of their aura, the unique presence that surrounds an original work of art. In the past, the aura of each artwork linked it to the ritual role that art had originally served. Now, by contrast, artworks have become objects of exhibition instead of objects of ritual. Technology has made the appearance of artworks available to those who cannot travel to the sites of originals; but this advance in accessibility has meant a concomitant reduction in the value and impact of the artwork.

---

[5]Although Dickie takes the term *artworld* from Danto, Dickie considers the artworld to be more determinately structured than Danto does. Certain institutions, such as museums, are included in Danto's artworld, but so is the audience, hardly a formal institution.

Robert Plant Armstrong reminds us that our ideas about art are not shared by the entire world. The Western concepts of aesthetic experience, art, and beauty are local cultural phenomena. In approaching the aesthetics of the rest of the world, Armstrong urges us to adopt the more inclusive concept of "affecting presence" instead of relying on "art," which has ethnocentric associations. Affecting presences are humanly made things and events that are principally concerned with emotion, values, and potency. These presences are presented to convey affect, or feeling, to those who come into contact with it. Armstrong sees these presences as the tutors of a culture's feelings and the prototypes for its ways of organizing daily life. Far from offering an escape from everyday life, on Armstrong's account, affecting presences are central to a culture's experiences as a whole and so vital that one can experience a kind of starvation without them.

Arthur C. Danto

THE ARTWORLD

Arthur C. Danto is professor emeritus of philosophy at Columbia University and art critic for The Nation. *His books on art include* The Transfiguration of the Commonplace, The Philosophical Disenfranchisement of Art, The State of Art, *and* Encounters and Reflections. *In his essay "The Artworld," Danto explores the boundary that divides art from non-art, concluding that art is art because prevailing theory makes it so.*

Hamlet:
  Do you see nothing there?
The Queen:
  Nothing at all; yet all that is I see.

       Shakespeare: Hamlet, Act III, Scene IV

Hamlet and Socrates, though in praise and deprecation respectively, spoke of art as a mirror held up to nature. As with many disagreements in attitude, this one has a factual basis. Socrates saw mirrors as but reflecting what we can already see; so art, insofar as mirrorlike, yields idle accurate duplication of the appearances of things, and is of no cognitive benefit whatsoever. Hamlet, more acutely, recognized a remarkable feature of reflecting surfaces, namely that they show us what we could not otherwise perceive— our own face and form—and so art, insofar as it is mirrorlike, reveals us to ourselves, and is, even by socratic criteria, of some cognitive utility after all. As a philosopher, however, I find Socrates' discussion defective on other, perhaps less profound grounds than these. If a mirror-image of *o* is indeed an imitation of *o*, then, if art is imitation, mirror-images are art. But in fact mirroring objects no more is art than returning weapons to a madman is justice; and reference to mirrorings would be just the sly sort of counterinstance we would expect Socrates to bring forward in rebuttal of the theory he instead uses them to illustrate. If that theory requires us to class *these* as art, it thereby shows its inadequacy: "is an imitation" will not do as a sufficient condition for "is art" Yet, perhaps because artists *were* engaged in imitation, in Socrates' time and after, the insufficiency of the theory was not noticed until the invention of photography. Once rejected as a sufficient condition, mimesis was quickly discarded as even a necessary one; and since the achievement of Kandinsky, mimetic features have been relegated to the periphery of critical concern, so much so that some works survive in spite of possessing those virtues, excellence in which was once celebrated as the essence of art, narrowly escaping demotion to mere illustrations.

It is, of course, indispensable in socratic discussion that all participants be masters of the concept up for analysis, since the aim is to match a real defining expression to a term in active use, and the test for adequacy presumably consists in showing that the former analyzes and applies to all and only those things of which the latter is true. The popular disclaimer notwithstanding, then, Socrates' auditors purportedly knew what art was as well as what they liked; and a theory of art, regarded here as a real definition of "Art," is accordingly not to be of great use in helping men to recognize instances of its application. Their antecedent ability to do this is precisely what the adequacy of the theory is to be tested against, the problem being only to make explicit what they already know. It is our use of the term that the theory allegedly means to capture, but we are supposedly able, in the words of a recent writer, "to separate those objects which are works of art from those which are not, because . . . we know how correctly to use the word 'art' and to apply the phrase 'work of art.'" Theories, on this account, are somewhat like mirror-images on Socrates' account, showing forth what we already know, wordy reflections of the actual linguistic practice we are masters in.

But telling artworks from other things is not so simple a matter, even for native speakers, and these days one might not be aware he was on artistic terrain without an artistic theory to tell him so. And part of the reason for this lies in the fact that terrain is constituted artistic in virtue of artistic theories, so that one use of theories, in addition to helping us discriminate art from the rest, consists in making art possible. Glaucon and the others could hardly have known what was art and what not: Otherwise they would never have been taken in by mirror-images.

. . . Two of our pioneers—Robert Rauschenberg and Claes Oldenburg—have made genuine beds.

Rauschenberg's bed hangs on a wall, and is streaked with some desultory housepaint. Oldenburg's bed is a rhomboid, narrower at one end than the other, with what one might speak of as a built-in perspective: ideal for small bedrooms. As beds, these sell at singularly inflated prices, but one *could sleep* in either of them: Rauschenberg has expressed the fear that someone might just climb into his bed and fall asleep. Imagine, now, a certain Testadura—a plain speaker and noted philistine—who is not aware that these are art, and who takes them to be reality simple and pure. He attributes the paintstreaks on Rauschenberg's bed to the slovenliness of the owner, and the bias in the Oldenburg bed to the ineptitude of the builder or the whimsy, perhaps, of whoever had it "custom-made." These would be mistakes, but mistakes of rather an odd kind, and not terribly different from that made by the stunned birds who pecked the sham grapes of Zeuxis. They mistook art for reality, and so has Testadura. . . .

How shall we describe Testadura's error! What, after all, prevents Oldenburg's creation from being a misshapen bed? This is equivalent to asking what makes it art, and with this query we enter a domain of conceptual inquiry where native speakers are poor guides: *they* are lost themselves.

To mistake an artwork for a real object is no great feat when an artwork is the real object one mistakes it for. The problem is how to avoid such errors, or to remove them once they are made. The artwork is a bed, and not a bed-illusion; so there is nothing like the traumatic encounter against a flat surface that brought it home to the birds of Zeuxis that they had been duped. Except for the guard cautioning Testadura not to sleep on the artworks, he might never have discovered that this was an artwork and not a bed; and since, after all, one cannot discover that a bed is not a bed, how is Testadura to realize that he has made an error? A certain sort of explanation is required, for the error here is a curiously philosophical one, rather like, if we may assume as correct some well-known view of P. F. Strawson, mistaking a person for a material body when the truth is that a person *is* a material body in the sense that a whole class of predicates, sensibly applicable to material bodies, are sensibly, and by appeal to no different criteria, applicable to persons. So you cannot *discover* that a person is not a material body.

We begin by explaining, perhaps, that the paintstreaks are not to be explained away, that they are *part* of the object, so the object is not a mere bed with—as it happens— streaks of paint spilled over it, but a complex object fabricated out of a bed and some paintstreaks: a paint-bed. Similarly, a person is not a material body with—as it happens— some thoughts superadded, but is a complex entity made up of a body and some conscious states: a conscious-body. Persons, like artworks, must then be taken as irreducible to *parts* of themselves, and are in that sense primitive. Or, more accurately, the paintstreaks are not part of the real object—the bed—which happens to be part of the artwork, but are, *like* the bed, part of the artwork as such. And this might be generalized into a rough characterization of artworks that happen to contain real objects as parts of themselves: not every part of an artwork *A* is part of a real object *R* when *R* is part of *A* and can, moreover, be detached from *A* and seen merely as *R*. The mistake thus far will have been to mistake *A* for *part* of itself, namely *R*, even though it would not be incorrect to say that *A* is *R*, that the artwork is a bed. It is the "is" which requires clarification here.

There is an *is* that figures prominently in statements concerning artworks which is not the *is* of either identity or predication; nor is it the *is* of existence, of identification, or some special *is* made up to serve a philosophic end. Nevertheless, it is in common usage, and is readily mastered by children. It is the sense of *is* in accordance with which a child, shown a circle and a triangle and asked which is him and which his sister, will point to the triangle saying "That is me"; or, in response to my question, the person next to me points to the man in purple and says "That one is Lear"; or in the gallery I point, for my companion's benefit, to a spot in the painting before us and say "That white dab is Icarus." We do not mean, in these instances, that whatever is pointed to stands for, or represents, what is said to be, for the *word* "Icarus" stands for or represents Icarus: yet I would not in the same sense of *is* point to the word and say "That is Icarus." The sentence "That *a* is *b*" is perfectly compatible with "That *a* is not *b*" when the first employs this sense of *is* and the second employs some other, though *a* and *b* are used nonambiguously throughout. Often, indeed, the truth of the first *requires* the truth of the second. The first, in fact, is incompatible with "That *a* is not *b*" only when the *is* is used nonambiguously throughout. For want of a word I shall designate this the *is of artistic identification;* in each case in which it is used, the *a* stands for some specific physical property of, or physical part of, an object; and, finally, it is a necessary condition for something to be an artwork that some part or property of it be designable by the subject of a sentence that employs this special *is*. It is an *is*, incidentally, which has near-relatives in marginal and mythical pronouncements. (Thus, one *is* Quetzalcoatl; those *are* the Pillars of Hercules.)

Let me illustrate. Two painters are asked to decorate the east and west walls of a science library with frescoes to be respectively called *Newton's First Law* and *Newton's Third Law*. These paintings, when finally unveiled, look, scale apart, as follows:

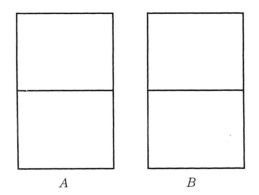

A   B

As objects I shall suppose the works to be indiscernible: a black, horizontal line on a white ground, equally large in each dimension and element. *B* explains his work as follows: a mass, pressing downward, is met by a mass pressing upward: the lower mass reacts equally and oppositely to the upper one. *A* explains his work as follows: the line through the space is the path of an isolated particle. The path goes from edge to edge, to give the sense of its *going beyond*. If it ended or began within the space, the line would be curved: and it is parallel to the top and bottom edges, for if it were closer to one than to another, there would have to be a force accounting for it, and this is inconsistent with its being the path of an *isolated* particle.

Much follows from these artistic identifications. To regard the middle line as an edge (mass meeting mass) imposes the need to identify the top and bottom half of the picture as rectangles, and as two distinct parts (not necessarily as two masses, for the line could be the edge of *one* mass jutting up—or down—into empty space). If it is an edge, we cannot thus take the entire area of the painting as a single space: it is rather composed of two forms, or one form and a non-form. We could take the entire area as a single space only by taking the middle horizontal as a *line* which is not an edge. But this almost requires a three-dimensional identification of the whole picture: the area

can be a flat surface which the line is *above* (*Jet-flight*), or *below* (*Submarine-path*), or *on* (*Line*), or *in* (*Fissure*), or *through* (*Newton's First Law*)—though in this last case the area is not a flat surface but a transparent cross section of absolute space. We could make all these prepositional qualifications clear by imagining perpendicular cross sections to the picture plane. Then, depending upon the applicable prepositional clause, the area is (artistically) interrupted or not by the horizontal element. If we take the line as *through* space, the edges of the picture are not really the edges of the space: the space goes beyond the picture if the line itself does; and we are in the same space as the line is. As *B*, the edges of the picture can be *part* of the picture in case the masses go right to the edges, so that the edges of the picture are *their* edges. In that case, the vertices of the picture would be the vertices of the masses, except that the masses have four vertices more than the picture itself does: here four vertices would be part of the art work which were not part of the real object. Again, the faces of the masses could be the face of the picture, and in looking at the picture, we are looking at these faces: but *space* has no face, and on the reading of *A* the work has to be read as faceless, and the face of the physical object would not be part of the artwork. Notice here how one artistic identification engenders another artistic identification, and how, consistently with a given identification, we are *required* to give others and *precluded* from still others: indeed, a given identification determines how many elements the work is to contain. These different identifications are incompatible with one another, or generally so, and each might be said to make a different artwork, even though each artwork contains the identical real object as part of itself—or at least parts of the identical real object as parts of itself. There are, of course, senseless identifications: no one could, I think, sensibly read the middle horizontal as

Love's Labour's Lost or *The Ascendency of St. Erasmus.* Finally, notice how acceptance of one identification rather than another is in effect to exchange one *world* for another. We could, indeed, enter a quiet poetic world by identifying the upper area with a clear and cloudless sky, reflected in the still surface of the water below, whiteness kept from whiteness only by the unreal boundary of the horizon.

And now Testadura, having hovered in the wings throughout this discussion, protests that *all he sees is paint:* a white painted oblong with a black line painted across it And how right he really is: that is all he sees or that anybody can, we aesthetes included. So, if he asks us to show him what there is further to see, to demonstrate through pointing that this is an artwork (*Sea and Sky*), we cannot comply, for he has overlooked nothing (and it would be absurd to suppose he had, that there was something tiny we could point to and he, peering closely, say "So it is! A work of art after all!"). We cannot help him until he has mastered the *is of artistic identification* and so *constitutes* it a work of art. If he cannot achieve this, he will never look upon artworks: he will be like a child who sees sticks as sticks.

But what about pure abstractions, say something that looks just like *A* but is entitled No. 7? The 10th Street abstractionist blankly insists that there is nothing here but white paint and black, and none of our literary identifications need apply. What then distinguishes him from Testadura, whose philistine utterances are indiscernible from his? And how can it be an artwork for him and not for Testadura, when they agree that there is nothing that does not meet the eye? The answer, unpopular as it is likely to be to purists of every variety, lies in the fact that this artist has returned to the physicality of paint through an atmosphere compounded of artistic theories and the history of recent and remote painting, elements of which he is trying to refine out of his own work; and

as a consequence of this his work belongs in this atmosphere and is part of this history. He has achieved abstraction through rejection of artistic identifications, returning to the real world from which such identifications remove us (he thinks), somewhat in the mode of Ch'ing Yuan, who wrote:

> Before I had studied Zen for thirty years, I saw mountains as mountains and waters as waters. When I arrived at a more intimate knowledge, I came to the point where I saw that mountains are not mountains, and waters are not waters. But now that I have got the very substance I am at rest. For it is just that I see mountains once again as mountains, and waters once again as waters.

His identification of what he has made is logically dependent upon the theories and history he rejects. The difference between his utterance and Testadura's "This is black paint and white paint and nothing more" lies in the fact that he is still using the *is* of artistic identification, so that his use of "That black paint is black paint" is not a tautology. Testadura is not at that stage. To see something as art requires something the eye cannot decry—an atmosphere of artistic theory, a knowledge of the history of art: an artworld.

◆◆◆

Mr. Andy Warhol, the Pop artist, displays facsimiles of Brillo cartons, piled high, in neat stacks, as in the stockroom of the supermarket. They happen to be of wood, painted to look like cardboard, and why not? To paraphrase the critic of the *Times*, if one may make the facsimile of a human being out of bronze, why not the facsimile of a Brillo carton out of plywood? The cost of these boxes happens to be 2×10^3 that of their homely counterparts in real life—a differential hardly ascribable to their advantage in durability. In fact the Brillo people might, at some slight increase in cost, make their boxes out of plywood without these becoming artworks, and Warhol might make *his* out of cardboard without their ceasing to be art. So we may forget questions of intrinsic value, and ask why the Brillo people cannot manufacture art and why Warhol cannot *but* make artworks. Well, his are made by hand, to be sure. Which is like an insane reversal of Picasso's strategy in pasting the label from a bottle of Suze onto a drawing, saying as it were that the academic artist, concerned with exact imitation, must always fall short of the real thing: so why not just *use* the real thing? The Pop artist laboriously reproduces machine-made objects by hand, e.g., painting the labels on coffee cans (one can hear the familiar commendation "Entirely made by hand" falling painfully out of the guide's vocabulary when confronted by these objects). But the difference cannot consist in craft: a man who carved pebbles out of stones and carefully constructed a work called *Gravel Pile* might invoke the labor theory of value to account for the price he demands; but the question is, What makes it art? And why need Warhol *make* these things anyway? Why not just scrawl his signature across one? Or crush one up and display it as *Crushed Brillo Box* ("A protest against mechanization . . .") or simply display a Brillo carton as *Uncrushed Brillo Box* ("A bold affirmation of the plastic authenticity of industrial . . .")? Is this man a kind of Midas, turning whatever he touches into the gold of pure art? And the whole world consisting of latent artworks waiting, like the bread and wine of reality, to be transfigured, through some dark mystery, into the indiscernible flesh and blood of the sacrament? Never mind that the Brillo box may not be good, much less great art. The impressive thing is that it is art at all. But if it is why are not the indiscernible Brillo boxes that are in the stockroom? Or *has* the whole distinction between art and reality broken down?

Suppose a man collects objects (readymades), including a Brillo carton; we praise the exhibit for variety, ingenuity, what you will. Next he exhibits nothing but Brillo cartons, and we criticize it as dull, repetitive, self-plagiarizing—or (more profoundly) claim that he is obsessed by regularity and repetition, as in *Marienbad*. Or he piles them high, leaving a narrow path; we tread our way through the smooth opaque stacks and find it an unsettling experience, and write it up as the closing in of consumer products, confining us as prisoners: or we say he is a modern pyramid builder. True, we don't say these things about the stockboy. But then a stockroom is not an art gallery, and we cannot readily separate the Brillo cartons from the gallery they are in, any more than we can separate the Rauschenberg bed from the paint upon it. Outside the gallery, they are pasteboard cartons. But then, scoured clean of paint, Rauschenberg's bed is a bed, just what it was before it was transformed into art. But then if we think this matter through, we discover that the artist has failed, really and of necessity, to produce a mere real object. He has produced an artwork, his use of real Brillo cartons being but an expansion of the resources available to artists, a contribution to *artists' materials*, as oil paint was, or *tuche*.

What in the end makes the difference between a Brillo box and a work of art consisting of a Brillo box is a certain theory of art. It is the theory that takes it up into the world of art, and keeps it from collapsing into the real object which it is (in a sense of *is* other than that of artistic identification). Of course, without the theory, one is unlikely to see it as art, and in order to see it as part of the artworld, one must have mastered a good deal of artistic theory as well as a considerable amount of the history of recent New York painting. It could not have been art fifty years ago. But then there could not have been, everything being equal, flight insurance in the Middle Ages, or Etruscan typewriter erasers. The world has to be ready for certain things, the artworld no less than the real one. It is the role of artistic

Morris Weitz

THE ROLE
OF THEORY
IN AESTHETICS

Morris Weitz (1916–1981) was a professor of philosophy at Ohio State University. He is author of Philosophy of the Arts, Hamlet and the Philosophy of Literary Criticism, *and* Philosophy in Literature: Shakespeare, Voltaire, Tolstoy and Proust. *In the classic essay "The Role of Theory in Aesthetics," Weitz considers a variety of theories about the nature of art and concludes that we should abandon efforts to give a comprehensive definition of art.*

Is aesthetic theory, in the sense of a true definition or set of necessary and sufficient properties of art, possible? If nothing else does, the history of aesthetics itself should give one enormous pause here. For, in spite of the many theories, we seem no nearer our goal today than we were in Plato's time. Each age, each art-movement, each philosophy of art, tries over and over again to establish the stated ideal only to be succeeded by a new or revised theory, rooted, at least in part, in the repudiation of preceding ones. Even today, almost everyone interested in aesthetic matters is still deeply wedded to the hope that the correct theory of art is forthcoming. We need only examine the numerous new books on art in which new definitions are proffered; or, in our own country especially, the basic textbooks and anthologies to recognize how strong the priority of a theory of art is.

In this essay I want to plead for the rejection of this problem. I want to show that theory—in the requisite classical sense—is *never* forthcoming in aesthetics, and that we would do much better as philosophers to supplant the question, "What is the nature of art?," by other questions, the answers to which will provide us with all the understanding of the arts there can be. I want to show that the inadequacies of the theories are not primarily occasioned by any legitimate difficulty such, e.g., as the vast complexity of art, which might be corrected by further probing and research. Their basic inadequacies reside instead in a fundamental misconception of art. Aesthetic theory—all of it—is wrong in principle in thinking

Morris Weitz, "The Role of Theory in Aesthetics," *Journal of Aesthetics and Art Criticism* 15.1 (1956): 27–35.

that a correct theory is possible because it radically misconstrues the logic of the concept of art. Its main contention that "art" is amenable to real or any kind of true definition is false. Its attempt to discover the necessary and sufficient properties of art is logically misbegotten for the very simple reason that such a set and, consequently, such a formula about it, is never forthcoming. Art, as the logic of the concept shows, has no set of necessary and sufficient properties, hence a theory of it is logically impossible and not merely factually difficult. Aesthetic theory tries to define what cannot be defined in its requisite sense. But in recommending the repudiation of aesthetic theory I shall not argue from this, as too many others have done, that its logical confusions render it meaningless or worthless. On the contrary, I wish to reassess its role and its contribution primarily in order to show that it is of the greatest importance to our understanding of the arts.

Let us now survey briefly some of the more famous extant aesthetic theories in order to see if they do incorporate correct and adequate statements about the nature of art. In each of these there is the assumption that it is the true enumeration of the defining properties of art, with the implication that previous theories have stressed wrong definitions. Thus, to begin with, consider a famous version of Formalist theory, that propounded by Bell and Fry. It is true that they speak mostly of painting in their writings but both assert that what they find in that art can be generalized for what is "art" in the others as well. The essence of painting, they maintain, are the plastic elements in relation. Its defining property is significant form, i.e., certain combinations of lines, colors, shapes, volumes—everything on the canvas except the representational elements—which evoke a unique response to such combinations. Painting is definable as plastic organization. The nature of art,

what it *really* is, so their theory goes, is a unique combination of certain elements (the specifiable plastic ones) in their relations. Anything which is art is an instance of significant form; and anything which is not art has no such form.

To this the Emotionalist replies that the truly essential property of art has been left out. Tolstoy, Ducasse, or any of the advocates of this theory, find that the requisite defining property is not significant form but rather the expression of emotion in some sensuous public medium. Without projection of emotion into some piece of stone or words or sounds, etc., there can be no art. Art is really such embodiment. It is this that uniquely characterizes art, and any true, real definition of it, contained in some adequate theory of art, must so state it.

The Intuitionist disclaims both emotion and form as defining properties. In Croce's version, for example, art is identified not with some physical, public object but with a specific creative, cognitive and spiritual act. Art is really a first stage of knowledge in which certain human beings (artists) bring their images and intuitions into lyrical clarification or expression. As such, it is an awareness, non-conceptual in character, of the unique individuality of things; and since it exists below the level of conceptualization or action, it is without scientific or moral content. Croce singles out as the defining essence of art this first stage of spiritual life and advances its identification with art as a philosophically true theory or definition.

The Organicist says to all of this that art is really a class of organic wholes consisting of distinguishable, albeit inseparable, elements in their causally efficacious relations which are presented in some sensuous medium. In A. C. Bradley, in piece-meal versions of it in literary criticism, or in my own generalized adaptation of it in my *Philosophy of the Arts*, what is claimed is that anything which is a work of art is in its nature a unique complex of interrelated parts—in painting, for example, lines, colors volumes, subjects, etc., all interacting upon one another on a paint surface of some sort. Certainly, at one time at least it seemed to me that this organic theory constituted the one true and real definition of art.

My final example is the most interesting of all, logically speaking. This is the Voluntarist theory of Parker. In his writings on art, Parker persistently calls into question the traditional simple-minded definitions of aesthetics. "The assumption underlying every philosophy of art is the existence of some common nature present in all the arts." "All the so popular brief definitions of art—'significant form,' 'expression,' 'intuition,' 'objectified pleasure'—are fallacious, either because, while true of art, they are also true of much that is not art, and hence fail to differentiate art from other things; or else because they neglect some essential aspect of art." But instead of inveighing against the attempt at definition of art itself, Parker insists that what is needed is a complex definition rather than a simple one. "The definition of art must therefore be in terms of a complex of characteristics. Failure to recognize this has been the fault of all the well-known definitions." His own version of Voluntarism is the theory that art is essentially three things: embodiment of wishes and desires imaginatively satisfied, language, which characterizes the public medium of art, and harmony, which unifies the language with the layers of imaginative projections. Thus, for Parker, it is a true definition to say of art that it is ". . . the provision of satisfaction through the imagination, social significance, and harmony. I am claiming that nothing except works of art possess all three of these marks."

Now, all of these sample theories are inadequate in many different ways. Each purports to be a complete statement about the defining features of all works of art and yet each of them leaves out something which the others take to be central. Some

are circular, e.g., the Bell-Fry theory of art as significant form which is defined in part in terms of our response to significant form. Some of them, in their search for necessary and sufficient properties, emphasize too few properties, like (again) the Bell-Fry definition which leaves out subject-representation in painting, or the Croce theory which omits inclusion of the very important feature of the public, physical character, say, of architecture. Others are too general and cover objects that are not art as well as works of art. Organicism is surely such a view since it can be applied to *any* causal unity in the natural world as well as to art. Still others rest on dubious principles, e.g., Parker's claim that art embodies imaginative satisfactions, rather than real ones; or Croce's assertion that there is nonconceptual knowledge. Consequently, even if art has one set of necessary and sufficient properties, none of the theories we have noted or, for that matter, no aesthetic theory yet proposed, has enumerated that set to the satisfaction of all concerned.

Then there is a different sort of difficulty. As real definitions, these theories are supposed to be factual reports on art. If they are, may we not ask, Are they empirical and open to verification or falsification? For example, what would confirm or disconfirm the theory that art is significant form or embodiment of emotion or creative synthesis of images? There does not even seem to be a hint of the kind of evidence which might be forthcoming to test these theories; and indeed one wonders if they are perhaps honorific definitions of "art," that is, proposed redefinitions in terms of some *chosen* conditions for applying the concept of art, and not true or false reports on the essential properties of art at all.

But all these criticisms of traditional aesthetic theories—that they are circular, incomplete, untestable, pseudo-factual, disguised proposals to change the meaning of concepts—have been made before. My intention is to go beyond these to make a much more fundamental criticism, namely, that aesthetic theory is a logically vain attempt to define what cannot be defined, to state the necessary and sufficient properties of that which has no necessary and sufficient properties, to conceive the concept of art as closed when its very use reveals and demands its openness.

The problem with which we must begin is not "What is art?," but "What sort of concept is 'art'?" Indeed, the root problem of philosophy itself is to explain the relation between the employment of certain kinds of concepts and the conditions under which they can be correctly applied. If I may paraphrase Wittgenstein, we must not ask, What is the nature of any philosophical x?, or even, according to the semanticist, What does "x" mean?, a transformation that leads to the disastrous interpretation of "art" as a name for some specifiable class of objects; but rather, What is the use or employment of "x"? What does "x" do in the language? This, I take it, is the initial question, the begin-all if not the end-all of any philosophical problem and solution. Thus, in aesthetics, our first problem is the elucidation of the actual employment of the concept of art, to give a logical description of the actual functioning of the concept, including a description of the conditions under which we correctly use it or its correlates.

My model in this type of logical description or philosophy derives from Wittgenstein. It is also he who, in his refutation of philosophical theorizing in the sense of constructing definitions of philosophical entities, has furnished contemporary aesthetics with a starting point for any future progress. In his . . . work, *Philosophical Investigations*, Wittgenstein raises as an illustrative question, What is a game? The traditional philosophical, theoretical answer would be in terms of some exhaustive set of properties common to all games. To this Wittgen-

stein says, let us consider what we call "games": "I mean board-games, card-games, ball-games, Olympic games, and so on. What is common to them all?—Don't say: 'there *must* be something common, or they would not be called "games"' but *look and see* whether there is anything common to all.— For if you look at them you will not see something that is common to *all*, but similarities, relationships, and a whole series of them at that . . ."

Card games are like board games in some respects but not in others. Not all games are amusing, nor is there always winning or losing or competition. Some games resemble others in some respects—that is all. What we find are no necessary and sufficient properties, only "a complicated network of similarities overlapping and crisscrossing," such that we can say of games that they form a family with family resemblances and no common trait. If one asks what a game is, we pick out sample games, describe these, and add, "This and *similar things* are called 'games.'" This is all we need to say and indeed all any of us knows about games. Knowing what a game is is not knowing some real definition or theory but being able to recognize and explain games and to decide which among imaginary and new examples would or would not be called "games."

The problem of the nature of art is like that of the nature of games, at least in these respects: If we actually look and see what it is that we call "art," we will also find no common properties—only strands of similarities. Knowing what art is is not apprehending some manifest or latent essence but being able to recognize, describe, and explain those things we call "art" in virtue of these similarities.

But the basic resemblance between these concepts is their open texture. In elucidating them, certain (paradigm) cases can be given, about which there can be no question as to their being correctly described as "art" or "game," but no exhaustive set of cases can be given. I can list some cases and some conditions under which I can apply correctly the concept of art but I cannot list all of them, for the all-important reason that unforeseeable or novel conditions are always forthcoming or envisageable.

A concept is open if its conditions of application are emendable and corrigible; i.e., if a situation or case can be imagined or secured which would call for some sort of *decision* on our part to extend the use of the concept to cover this, or to close the concept and invent a new one to deal with the new case and its new property. If necessary and sufficient conditions for the application of a concept can be stated, the concept is a closed one. But this can happen only in logic or mathematics where concepts are constructed and completely defined. It cannot occur with empirically-descriptive and normative concepts unless we arbitrarily close them by stipulating the ranges of their uses.

I can illustrate this open character of "art" best by examples drawn from its subconcepts. Consider questions like "Is Dos Passos' *U. S. A.* a novel?," "Is V. Woolf's *To the Lighthouse* a novel?," "Is Joyce's *Finnegan's Wake* a novel?" On the traditional view, these are construed as factual problems to be answered yes or no in accordance with the presence or absence of defining properties. But certainly this is not how any of these questions is answered. Once it arises, as it has many times in the development of the novel from Richardson to Joyce (e.g., "Is Gide's *The School for Wives* a novel or a diary?"), what is at stake is no factual analysis concerning necessary and sufficient properties but a decision as to whether the work under examination is similar in certain respects to other works, already called "novels," and consequently warrants the extension of the concept to cover the new case. . . .

What is true of the novel is, I think, true of every sub-concept of art: "tragedy," "comedy," "painting," "opera," etc., of "art" itself.

No "Is X a novel, painting, opera, work of art, etc.?" question allows of a definitive answer in the sense of a factual yes or no report. "Is this *collage* a painting or not?" does not rest on any set of necessary and sufficient properties of painting but on whether we decide—as we did—to extend "painting" to cover this case.

"Art," itself, is an open concept. New conditions (cases) have constantly arisen and will undoubtedly constantly arise; new art forms, new movements will emerge, which will demand decisions on the part of those interested, usually professional critics, as to whether the concept should be extended or not. Aestheticians may lay down similarity conditions but never necessary and sufficient ones for the correct application of the concept. With "art" its conditions of application can never be exhaustively enumerated since new cases can always be envisaged or created by artists, or even nature, which would call for a decision on someone's part to extend or to close the old or to invent a new concept. (E.g., "It's not a sculpture, it's a mobile.")

What I am arguing, then, is that the very expansive, adventurous character of art, its ever-present changes and novel creations, makes it logically impossible to ensure any set of defining properties. We can, of course, choose to close the concept. But to do this with "art" or "tragedy" or "portraiture," etc., is ludicrous since it forecloses on the very conditions of creativity in the arts.

Of course there are legitimate and serviceable closed concepts in art. But these are always those whose boundaries of conditions have been drawn for a *special* purpose. Consider the difference, for example, between "tragedy" and "(extant) Greek tragedy." The first is open and must remain so to allow for the possibility of new conditions, e.g., a play in which the hero is not noble or fallen or in which there is no hero but other elements that are like those of plays we already call "tragedy." The second is closed. The plays it can be applied to, the conditions under which it can be correctly used are all in, once the boundary, "Greek," is drawn. Here the critic can work out a theory or real definition in which he lists the common properties at least of the extant Greek tragedies. Aristotle's definition, false as it is as a theory of all the plays of Aeschylus, Sophocles, and Euripides, since it does not cover some of them, properly called "tragedies," can be interpreted as a real (albeit incorrect) definition of this closed concept; although it can also be, as it unfortunately has been, conceived as a purported real definition of "tragedy," in which case it suffers from the logical mistake of trying to define what cannot be defined—of trying to squeeze what is an open concept into an honorific formula for a closed concept.

What is supremely important, if the critic is not to become muddled, is to get absolutely clear about the way in which he conceives his concepts; otherwise he goes from the problem of trying to define "tragedy," etc., to an arbitrary closing of the concept in terms of certain preferred conditions or characteristics which he sums up in some linguistic recommendation that he mistakenly thinks is a real definition of the open concept. Thus, many critics and aestheticians ask, "What is tragedy?," choose a class of samples for which they may give a true account of its common properties, and then go on to construe this account of the chosen closed class as a true definition or theory of the whole open class of tragedy. This, I think, is the logical mechanism of most of the so-called theories of the sub-concepts of art: "tragedy," "comedy," "novel," etc. In effect, this whole procedure, subtly deceptive as it is, amounts to a transformation of correct criteria for *recognizing* members of certain legitimately closed classes of works of art into recommended criteria for *evaluating* any putative member of the class.

◆◆◆

The elucidation of the descriptive use of "Art" creates little difficulty. But the elucidation of the evaluative use does. For many, especially theorists, "This is a work of art" does more than describe; it also praises. Its conditions of utterance, therefore, include certain preferred properties or characteristics of art. I shall call these "criteria of evaluation." . . .

There is nothing wrong with the evaluative use; in fact, there is good reason for using "Art" to praise. But what cannot be maintained is that theories of the evaluative use of "Art" are true and real definitions of the necessary and sufficient properties of art. Instead they are honorific definitions, pure and simple, in which "Art" has been redefined in terms of chosen criteria.

But what makes them—these honorific definitions—so supremely valuable is not their disguised linguistic recommendations; rather it is the *debates* over the reasons for changing the criteria of the concept of art which are built into the definitions. In each of the great theories of art, whether correctly understood as honorific definitions or incorrectly accepted as real definitions, what is of the utmost importance are the reasons proffered in the argument for the respective theory, that is, the reasons given for the chosen or preferred criterion of excellence and evaluation. It is this perennial debate over these criteria of evaluation which makes the history of aesthetic theory the important study it is. The value of each of the theories resides in its attempt to state and to justify certain criteria which are either neglected or distorted by previous theories. Look at the Bell-Fry theory again. Of course, "Art is significant form" cannot be accepted as a true, real definition of art; and most certainly it actually functions in their aesthetics as a redefinition of art in terms of the chosen condition of significant form. But what gives it its aesthetic importance is what lies behind the formula: In an age in which literary and representational elements have become paramount in painting, *return* to the plastic ones since these are indigenous to painting. Thus, the role of the theory is not to define anything but to use the definitional form, almost epigrammatically, to pin-point a crucial recommendation to turn our attention once again to the plastic elements in painting.

Once we, as philosophers, understand this distinction between the formula and what lies behind it, it behooves us to deal generously with the traditional theories of art; because incorporated in every one of them is a debate over and argument for emphasizing or centering upon some particular feature of art which has been neglected or perverted. If we take the aesthetic theories literally, as we have seen, they all fail; but if we reconstrue them, in terms of their function and point, as serious and argued-for recommendations to concentrate on certain criteria of excellence in art, we shall see that aesthetic theory is far from worthless. Indeed, it becomes as central as anything in aesthetics, in our understanding of art, for it teaches us what to look for and how to look at it in art. What is central and must be articulated in all the theories are their debates over the reasons for excellence in art—debates over emotional depth, profound truths, natural beauty, exactitude, freshness of treatment, and so on, as criteria of evaluation—the whole of which converges on the perennial problem of what makes a work of art good. To understand the role of aesthetic theory is not to conceive it as definition, logically doomed to failure, but to read it as summaries of seriously made recommendations to attend in certain ways to certain features of art.

George Dickie

ART
AS A
SOCIAL
INSTITUTION

George Dickie, professor of philosophy at the University of Illinois at Chicago, describes and defends the institutional theory of art in the following excerpt, which is taken from his Aesthetics: An Introduction. *Dickie contends here that artworks are artifacts that are taken to be suitable candidates for appreciation because this status has been conferred upon them by a social institution on behalf of the artworld.*

In what follows it is maintained that Weitz is wrong and that the generic sense of "art" can be defined, although it is admitted that he may be right to the extent that all or some of the subconcepts of art such as novel, tragedy, ceramics, sculpture, painting, etc., may lack necessary conditions *for their application as subconcepts*. For example, there may not be any characteristics common to all tragedies which would distinguish them from comedies, satyr plays, happenings, and the like *within the domain of art*, but it may be that there are characteristics which works of art have which would distinguish them from nonart.

The first obstacle to defining art is Weitz's contention that artifactuality is not a necessary condition for art. Most people assume that there is a sharp distinction between works of art and natural objects, but Weitz has argued that the fact that we sometimes say of natural objects such as driftwood that they are works of art breaks down the distinction. In short, there appear to be works of art which are not artifacts. However, Weitz's argument is inconclusive because he fails to take account of the two senses of "work of art"—the evaluative and classificatory. . . .

There is a certain irony here because Weitz makes the distinction in his article, but he does not see that it undercuts his own argument. The evaluative sense of "work of art" is used to praise an object—for example, "That driftwood is a work of art" or "That painting is a work of art." In

George Dickie, *Aesthetics: An Introduction* (Indianapolis: Pegasus, 1971) 98–108.

these examples we are saying that the drift-wood and the painting have qualities worthy of notice and praise. In neither case do we mean that the object referred to by the subject of the sentence is a work of art in the classificatory sense: we are speaking evaluatively about the driftwood and the painting. It would be silly to take "That painting is a work of art" as a classificatory statement; ordinarily to utter the expression "That painting" is to commit oneself to meaning that the referent of the expression is a work of art. The classificatory sense is used simply to indicate that a thing belongs to a certain category of artifacts. We rarely utter sentences in which we use the classificatory sense because it is such a basic notion. We are rarely in situations in which it is necessary to raise the question of whether or not an object is a work of art in the classificatory sense. We generally know straight away whether or not an object is a work of art. Generally, no one needs to say, by way of classification, "That is a work of art." However, recent developments in art such as junk sculpture and found art may occasionally force such remarks. For example, I was recently in a room at the Museum of Modern Art in which a work of art consisting of 144 one-foot-square metal plates was spread out on the floor. A man walked through the room and right across the work of art, apparently without seeing it. I did not, but I could have said, "Do you know that you are walking across a work of art?" The point is that the classificatory sense of "work of art" is a basic concept which structures and guides our thinking about our world. The whole point can perhaps be made clear by considering what would happen if one tried to understand the sentence "That painting is a work of art" in the classificatory sense. As indicated above, the expression "That painting" already contains the information that the object referred to is a work of art. Consequently, if the expression "That painting" is replaced in the sentence with its approximate equivalent, "That work of art

which was created by putting paint on a surface such as canvas," the resulting sentence would be "That work of art which was created by putting paint on a surface such as canvas is a work of art." Thus, if one tries to understand this sentence by taking the last occurrence of "work of art" in the classificatory sense, the whole sentence turns into a tautology; that is, it is redundant. However, one would scarcely utter "That painting is a work of art" meaning to utter a tautology, that is, simply to say that a work of art in the classificatory sense is a work of art in the classificatory sense. It is clear that what would generally be meant by such a sentence about a painting is that a work of art in the classificatory sense is a work of art in the evaluative sense. A parallel analysis could be given for the sentence about the driftwood, except that if one tried to understand "That piece of driftwood is a work of art" by construing "work of art" in the classificatory sense, a contradiction would result rather than a redundancy. It is, however, easy to understand this sentence construing "work of art" in the evaluative sense.

Weitz's conclusion that *being an artifact* is not a necessary condition for being a work of art rests upon a confusion. What his argument proves is that it is not necessary for an object to be an artifact in order to be called (quite correctly) a work of art, when this expression is understood in the evaluative sense. It is, by the way, not at all surprising that the members of the class of objects which we find worthy of notice and praise do not all have a characteristic in common. Such a class would naturally be large and varied. Once we grasp the significance of the *two* senses of "work of art" and see that Weitz's argument is misleading, we are free to reflect clearly on our understanding of the classificatory sense. And surely when we do so reflect, we realize that *part* of what is meant when we think of or assert of something (not in praise) that it is a work of art is that it is an artifact. . . . The point is that artifactuality, unlike such properties as color, shape, and size, is not exhibited when the artifact is observed, except in those infrequent cases in which the act of creation of the artifact is observed. Artifactuality is a relational, nonexhibited property, and perhaps this is also true of the other property or properties which distinguish art from nonart and which are involved in the definition of art.

Although he does not try to formulate a definition of art, Arthur Danto in his provocative article, "The Artworld," draws conclusions which suggest the direction such attempts at definition must take. In reflecting upon art and its history in general and such present-day developments as Warhol's "Brillo Carton" and Rauschenberg's "Bed" in particular, Danto writes, "To see something as art requires something the eye cannot descry—an atmosphere of artistic theory, a knowledge of history of art: an artworld." Danto seems to agree with Mandelbaum about the importance of nonexhibited properties (what the eye cannot descry), but he perhaps goes further than Mandelbaum by speaking provocatively, if vaguely, of atmosphere and history—of an artworld. Perhaps the substance of Danto's remark can be captured in a formal definition. The definition will first be formulated and then its implications and adequacy will be examined.

> A work of art in the classificatory sense is 1) an artifact 2) upon which some person or persons acting on behalf of a certain social institution (the artworld) has conferred the status of candidate for appreciation.

The definition speaks of conferring status and what is involved in this must be made clear. The most obvious and clear-cut examples of the conferring of status are certain actions of the state in which legal status is involved. A king's conferring of knighthood, a grand jury's indicting someone, the chairman of the election board certifying that someone is a candidate for office, or a minister pronouncing a couple man and wife are examples in which a person acting on behalf of a social institution (the state) confers *legal* status. These examples suggest that pomp and ceremony are required to establish a legal status; but this is not so. For example, in some jurisdictions common-law marriage is possible—a legal status acquired without ceremony.

The conferring of a Ph.D. degree on someone by a university, the election of someone as president of the Rotary, and the declaring of an object as a relic of the church are examples in which a person or persons confer nonlegal status. As before, ceremony is not required to establish this kind of status; for example, a person can acquire without ceremony the status of wise man within a community. What the offered definition of a work of art suggests is that just as a person can be certified as a candidate for office or two persons can acquire the status of common-law marriage within a legal system and as a person can be elected president of the Rotary or a person can acquire the status of wise man within a community, an artifact can acquire the status of candidate for appreciation within the social system which Danto has called "the artworld."

Two questions arise about the *conferring* of the status of candidate for appreciation: how does one know when the status has been conferred, and how is it conferred? An artifact's hanging in an art museum as part of a show or a performance at a theater are sure signs that the status has been conferred; these are paradigm cases of knowing that the status has been conferred. There is, of course, no guarantee that one can always know whether something is a candidate for appreciation, just as one cannot always tell that a given person is a knight or is married. The second question of how the status is conferred is the more important of the two questions, however. The examples mentioned—hanging in a museum and a performance in a theater—seems to suggest that a number of persons is required for the actual conferring of the status in question. In one sense, a number of persons is required, and in another sense, only one person is required. A number of persons are required to make up the social institution of the artworld, but only one person is required to act on behalf of or as an agent of the artworld and to confer the status of candidate for appreciation. Many works of art are never seen by anyone but the persons who create them, but they are still works of art. The status in question may be acquired by *a single person's treating an artifact as a candidate for appreciation.* Of course nothing prevents a group of persons conferring the status, but it is usually conferred by a single person, the artist who creates the artifact.

In may be helpful to compare and contrast the notion of conferring the status of candidate for appreciation with a case in which something is simply presented for appreciation; this device may throw light on the notion of conferring the status of candidate. Consider the case of a salesman of plumbing supplies who spreads his wares before us. There is an important difference between "placing before" and "conferring the status of candidate," and this difference can be brought out by comparing the salesman's action with the superficially similar act of Duchamp in entering a urinal which he christened "Fountain" in that now famous art show. The difference is that Duchamp's action took place within the institutional setting of the artworld, and the plumbing salesman's action took place outside of it. The salesman could do what Duchamp did, that is, convert a urinal into a work of art, but such a thing probably would not occur to him. Please remember that calling "Fountain" a work of art does not mean that it is a good one, nor does this qualification insinuate that it is a bad one either.

It may be felt that the notion of conferring status within the artworld is excessively vague. Certainly this notion is not as clear-cut as is the conferring of status within the legal system, where procedures and lines of authority are explicitly defined and incorporated into law. The counterparts in the artworld to specified procedures and lines of authority are nowhere codified, and the artworld carries on its business at the level of customary practice. Still there *is* a practice and this defines a social institution. A social institution need not have a formally established constitution, officers, and bylaws in order to exist and have the capacity to confer status. Some social institutions are formal and some are informal. The artworld could become formalized, but most people who are interested in art would probably consider this a bad thing: Such formality would threaten the freshness and exuberance of art. Every person who sees himself as a member of the artworld is an "officer" of it and is thereby capable of conferring status in its name. One present-day artist has in the case of one of his works even gone through the motions—no doubt as a burlesque—of using a formal procedure characteristic of many legal and some nonlegal institutions. Walter de Maria's "High Energy Bar," which is a stainless-steel bar, is accompanied by a certificate which bears the name of the work and states that the bar is a work of art only when the certificate is present. This amusing example serves to suggest the significance of the act of naming works of art. An object may acquire the status of art without ever being named, but giving it a title makes clear to whomever is interested that an object is a work of art. Specific titles function in a variety of ways—for example, as aids in understanding a work or as a convenient way of identifying a work—but any title at all (even the name "Untitled") is a badge of status.

Let us now pass on to a discussion of the notion of appreciation. Notice that the definition speaks of the conferring of the status of *candidate* for appreciation. Nothing is said about actual appreciation, and this leaves open the possibility for works of art which, for whatever reason, are not appreciated. It is important not to build into the definition of the classificatory sense of "work of art" value properties such as actual appreciation: to do so would make it impossible to speak of unappreciated works of art and of bad works of art, and this is clearly undesirable. Any theory of art must preserve certain central features of the way in which we talk about art, and we do find it necessary sometimes to speak of bad art. It should also be noted that not every aspect of a work of art is included in the candidacy for appreciation. For example, the color of the back of a painting is not ordinarily an object of appreciation. . . .

The definition of art given above ought for the sake of completeness to include a qualification about the various aspects of works of art, but such a qualification would make the definition unduly complicated and the reader should understand the definition with the qualification in mind.

There is a second consideration about appreciation which must be brought out in order to counter the suspicion which may arise in the minds of some that the definition depends on there being a special kind of aesthetic appreciation. . . . All that is meant by "appreciation" in the definition is something like "in experiencing the qualities of a thing one finds them worthy or valuable," and this meaning applies quite generally both inside and outside the domain of art.

The institutional theory of art which is set forth here has quite consciously been worked out with the practices of the art-world in mind—especially developments of the last seventy-five years, such as dadaism, pop art, found art, and happenings. The institutional theory and these developments raise a number of questions, and a few of these will be dealt with here.

First, if Duchamp can convert a urinal, a snowshovel, and a hatrack into works of art, can't natural objects such as driftwood also become works of art? Such natural objects can become works of art if any one of a number of things is done to them. One thing which would do the trick would be to pick a natural object up, take it home, and hang it on the wall. Another thing would be to pick it up and enter it in an exhibition. It was being assumed earlier that Weitz's sentence about the driftwood referred to a piece of driftwood in its ordinary situation on a beach and untouched by human hand. Please keep in mind that for something to be a work of art in the classificatory sense does not mean that it has any actual value. Natural objects which become works of art in the way being discussed are artifactualized without the use of tools—the artifactuality is conferred on the object rather than worked on it.

Second, a question which frequently arises in connection with discussions of the concept of art and which seems especially relevant in the context of institutional theory is, "How are we to conceive of paintings done by individuals such as Betsy the chimpanzee from the Baltimore Zoo?" Calling Betsy's products "paintings" here is not meant to prejudge that they are works of art; it is just that some word is needed to refer to them. The question of whether or not Betsy's paintings are art depends on what is done with them. For example, a year or two ago The Field Museum of Natural History in Chicago exhibited some chimpanzee and gorilla paintings. In the case of these paintings we must say that they are not works of art. However, if they had been exhibited a few miles away at the Chicago Art Institute they would have been works of art—the paintings would have been art if the director of the Art Institute had, so to speak, gone out on a limb. It all depends on the institutional setting—the one setting is congenial to conferring the status of art and the other is not. What would make Betsy's paintings works of art would be some agent's conferring the status on behalf of the artworld. Despite the fact that Betsy did the painting, the resulting works of art would not be Betsy's but the work of the person who does the conferring. Betsy cannot do the conferring because she cannot see herself as an agent of the artworld—she is unable to participate (fully) in our culture.

Weitz's charge that the defining of art or its subconcepts forecloses creativity requires discussion. Some of the traditional definitions of art may have and some of the traditional definitions of its subconcepts probably did foreclose creativity, but the institutional definition of art certainly will not. The requirement of artifactuality can scarcely prevent creativity, since artifactuality is a necessary condition of creativity. How could there be an instance of creativity without an artifact of some kind being produced? The other requirement involving the conferring of status could not inhibit creativity; in fact, it encourages it. Since it is possible that anything whatever may become art, the definition imposes no restraints on creativity. Weitz is probably right that the definition of some of the subconcepts of art have foreclosed creativity, but this danger is now a thing of the past. In the past, it may very well have happened that, for example, a playwright conceived of and wished to write a play with tragic features but which lacked a defining characteristic of, say, Aristotle's definition of tragedy. Faced with this dilemma, the playwright might have been intimidated and put his project aside. However, with the present-day disregard for established genres and the clamor for novelty in art, this obstacle to creativity probably no longer exists. Today, if a new and unusual work is created and it is fairly similar to some members of an established type, then it will usually be accommodated within that type, or if the new work is very unlike any existing works, then a new subconcept will probably be

created. Artists today are not easily intimidated, and they regard art genres as loose guidelines rather than as rigid specification.

The institutional theory of art may sound like saying, "A work of art is an object of which someone has said, 'I christen this object a work of art.'" And it is rather like that; although this does not mean that the conferring of the status of art is a simple matter. Just as christening a child has as its background the history and structure of the church, conferring the status of art has as its background the Byzantine complexity of the artworld. Some persons may find it strange that in the nonart cases discussed it appears that there are ways in which the conferring can go wrong, while there does not appear to be a way in which conferring the status of art can be invalid. For example, a king might say the wrong words or use the wrong instrument and the person who was to be knighted would not be a knight; or an indictment might have been improperly drawn up, and the person charged would not actually be indicted. But nothing parallel seems possible in the case of art. This fact reflects the differences between the artworld and legal institutions. The legal system deals with matters of grave personal consequences and its procedures must reflect this; the artworld deals with important matters also, but they are of a different sort entirely. The artworld does not require rigid procedures; it admits and even encourages frivolity and caprice without losing its serious purpose. However, if it is not possible to make a mistake *in* conferring the status of art, it is possible to make a mistake *by* conferring it. In conferring the status of art on an object one assumes a certain kind of responsibility for the object in its new status; presenting a candidate for appreciation always faces the possibility that no one will appreciate it and that the person who did the conferring will thereby lose face. One *can* make a work of art out of a sow's ear, but that does not necessarily make it a silk purse.

Timothy Binkley

PIECE:
CONTRA
AESTHETICS

*Timothy Binkley is professor of humanities at the
School of Visual Arts in New York City. He is author of*
Wittgenstein's Language *and is particularly interested
in the uses of computers in art. In this selection
Binkley argues that the only requirement for
something to be a work of art is that it be "indexed"
as such.*

I. WHAT IS THIS PIECE?

1. The term "aesthetics" has a general
meaning in which it refers to the philosophy
of art. In this sense, any theoretical writing
about art falls within the realm of aesthetics.
There is also a more specific and more
important sense of the term in which it
refers to a particular type of theoretical
inquiry which emerged in the eighteenth
century when the "Faculty of Taste" was
invented. In this latter sense, "aesthetics" is
the study of a specific human activity involving the perception of aesthetic qualities such
as beauty, repose, expressiveness, unity,
liveliness. Although frequently purporting to
be a (or even *the*) philosophy of art, aesthetics so understood is not exclusively about
art; it investigates a type of human experience (aesthetic experience) which is elicited
by artworks, but also by nature and by

nonartistic artifacts. The discrepancy is generally thought to be unimportant and is
brushed aside with the assumption that if
aesthetics is not exclusively about art, at
least art is primarily about the aesthetic.
This assumption, however, also proves to be
false, and it is the purpose of this piece to
show why. Falling within the subject matter
of aesthetics (in the second sense) is neither
a necessary nor a sufficient condition for
being art.

2. Robert Rauschenberg erases a
DeKooning drawing and exhibits it as his
own work, "Erased DeKooning Drawing."
The aesthetic properties of the original work
are wiped away, and the result is not a non-
work, but another work. No important information about Rauschenberg's piece is
presented in the way it *looks*, except perhaps *this* fact, that looking at it is artistically
inconsequential. It would be a mistake to

Timothy Binkley, "Piece: Contra Aesthetics," *Journal of Aesthetics and Art Criticism* 35.3 (1977):
265–77.

search for aesthetically interesting smudges on the paper. The object may be bought and sold like an aesthetically lush Rubens, but unlike the Rubens it is only a souvenir or relic of its artistic meaning. The owner of the Rauschenberg has no privileged access to its artistic content in the way the owner of the Rubens does who hides the painting away in a private study. Yet the Rauschenberg piece is a work of art. Art in the twentieth century has emerged as a strongly self-critical discipline. It has freed itself of aesthetic parameters and sometimes creates directly with ideas unmediated by aesthetic qualities. An artwork is a piece; and a piece need not be an aesthetic object, or even an object at all.

3. This piece is occasioned by two works of art by Marcel Duchamp, *L.H.O.O.Q.* and *L.H.O.O.Q. Shaved.* How do I know they are works of art? For one thing, they are listed in catalogues. So I assume they are works of art. If you deny that they are, it is up to you to explain why the listings in a Renoir catalogue are artworks, but the listings in a Duchamp catalogue are not. And why the Renoir show is an exhibition of artworks, while the Duchamp show is not, and so forth. Anyway, whether the Duchamp pieces are works of art is ultimately inconsequential, as we shall see.

This piece is also, shall we say, about the philosophical significance of Duchamp's art. This piece is primarily about the concept "piece" in art; and its purpose is to reformulate our understanding of what a "work of art" is.

II. WHAT IS *L.H.O.O.Q.*?

These are Duchamp's words:

This Mona Lisa with a moustache and a goatee is a combination readymade and iconoclastic Dadaism. The original, I mean the original readymade is a cheap chromo 8×5 on which I inscribed at the bottom

four letters which pronounced like initials in French, made a very risque joke on the Gioconda.

Imagine a similar description of the *Mona Lisa* itself. Leonardo took a canvas and some paint and put the paint on the canvas in such-and-such a way so that—presto—we have the renowned face and its environs. There is a big difference between this description and Duchamp's description. The difference is marked by the unspecified "such-and-such" left hanging in the description of Leonardo's painting. I could, of course, go on indefinitely describing the look of the *Mona Lisa*, and the fidelity with which your imagination reproduced this look would depend upon such things as how good my description is, how good your imagination is, and chance. Yet regardless of how precise and vivid my description is, one thing it will never do is acquaint you with the painting. You cannot claim to know that work of art on the basis of reading the most exquisite description of it, even though you may learn many interesting things *about* it. The way you come to know the *Mona Lisa* is by looking at it or by looking at a decent reproduction of it. The reason reproductions count is not that they faithfully reproduce the work of art, but rather because what the work of art is depends fundamentally upon how it looks. And reproductions can do a more or less acceptable job of duplicating (or replicating) the salient features of the appearance of a painting. This does not mean that a person is entitled to limit his or her aesthetic judgments to reproductions. What it means is that you can't say much about a painting until you know how it looks.

Now reconsider the description of Duchamp's piece: *L.H.O.O.Q.* is a reproduction of the Mona Lisa with a moustache, goatee, and letters added. There is no amorphous "such-and-such" standing for the most important thing. The description tells you what the work of art is; you now know the piece without actually having seen it (or a reproduction of it). When you do see the artwork there are no surprises: Yes, there is the reproduction of the *Mona Lisa;* there is the moustache, the goatee; there are the five letters. When you look at the artwork you learn nothing of artistic consequence which you don't already know from the description Duchamp gives, and for this reason it would be pointless to spend time attending to the piece as a connoisseur would savor a Rembrandt. Just the opposite is true of the *Mona Lisa.* If I tell you it is a painting of a woman with an enigmatic smile, I have told you little about the work of art since the important thing is how it *looks;* and that I can only *show* you, I cannot tell you.

This difference can be elucidated by contrasting ideas and appearances. Some art (a great deal of what is considered traditional art) creates primarily with appearances. To know the art is to know the look of it; and to know that is to *experience* the look, to perceive the appearance. On the other hand, some art creates primarily with ideas. To know the art is to know the idea; and to know an idea is not necessarily to experience a particular sensation, or even to have some particular experience. This is why you can know *L.H.O.O.Q.* either by looking at it or by having it described to you. (In fact, the piece might be better or more easily known by description than by perception.) The critical analysis of appearance, which is so useful in helping you come to know the *Mona Lisa,* bears little value in explaining *L.H.O.O.Q.* Excursions into the beauty with which the moustache was drawn or the delicacy with which the goatee was made to fit the contours of the face are fatuous attempts to say something meaningful about the work of art. If we do look at the piece, what is important to notice is that there is a reproduction of the *Mona Lisa,* that a moustache has been added, etc. It hardly matters exactly *how* this was done, how it looks. One views the *Mona Lisa* to see what it

looks like, but one approaches Duchamp's piece to obtain information, to gain access to the thought being expressed.

III. WHAT IS *L.H.O.O.Q. SHAVED?*

Duchamp sent out invitations to preview the show called "Not Seen and/or Less Seen of/by Marcel Duchamp/Rrose Selavy 1904–64: Mary Sisler Collection." On the front of the invitation he pasted a playing card which bears a reproduction of the *Mona Lisa.* Below the card is inscribed, in French, "L.H.O.O.Q. Shaved." This piece looks like the *Mona Lisa* and the *Mona Lisa* looks like it: since one is a reproduction of the other, their aesthetic qualities are basically identical. Differences in how they look have little, if any, artistic relevance. We do not establish the identity of one by pointing out where it looks different from the other. This is due to the fact that Duchamp's piece does not articulate its artistic statement in the language of aesthetic qualities. Hence, its aesthetic properties are as much a part of *L.H.O.O.Q. Shaved* as a picture of a mathematician in an algebra book is part of the mathematics.

Appearances are insufficient for establishing the identity of a work of art if the point is not in the appearance. And if the point is in the appearance, how do we establish that? What is to keep a Duchamp from stealing the look for ulterior purposes? Here occurs the limit of the ability of aesthetics to cope with art, since aesthetics seeks out appearances. To see why and how, we need to examine the nature of aesthetics.

IV. WHAT IS AESTHETICS?

1. *The Word.* The term "aesthetics" has come to denote that branch of philosophy which deals with art. The word originated in the eighteenth century when Alexander Gottlieb Baumgarten adopted a Greek word for perception to name what he defined to

be "the science of perception." Relying upon a distinction familiar to "the Greek philosophers and the Church fathers," he contrasted things perceived (aesthetic entities) with things known (noetic entities), delegating to "aesthetics" the investigation of the former. Baumgarten then gathered the study of the arts under the aegis of aesthetics. The two were quickly identified and "aesthetics" became "the philosophy of art" in much the way "ethics" is the philosophy of morality.

2. *Aesthetics and Perception.* From the outset aesthetics has been devoted to the study of "things perceived," whether reasoning from the "aesthetic attitude" which defines a unique way of perceiving, or from the "aesthetic object" of perception. The commitment to perceptual experience was deepened with the invention of the Faculty of Taste by eighteenth-century philosophers anxious to account for the human response to Beauty and to other aesthetic qualities. The Faculty of Taste exercises powers of discrimination in aesthetic experiences. A refined person with highly developed taste is enabled to perceive and recognize sophisticated and subtle artistic expressions which are closed to the uncultured person with poorly developed taste. This new faculty was characterized by its operation in the context of a special "disinterested" perception, a perception severed from self-interest and dissociated from so-called "practical concerns." The development of the concept of disinterestedness reinforced the perceptual focus of aesthetics, since removing "interest" from experience divests it of utility and invests its value in immediate awareness. An aesthetic experience is something pursued "for its own sake." Eventually aesthetics came to treat the object of aesthetic perception as a kind of illusion since its "reality"—i.e., the reality of disinterested perception—stands disconnected from the reality of practical interest. The two realities are incommensurable: The cows in Turner's paintings can be seen, but not milked or heard.

It is important to note that aesthetics is an outgrowth of the ancient tradition of the philosophy of the Beautiful. Beauty is a property found in both art and nature. A man is beautiful; so is his house and the tapestries hung inside. Aesthetics has continued the tradition of investigating a type of experience which can be had in the presence of both natural and created objects. As a result, aesthetics has never been strictly a study of artistic phenomena. The scope of its inquiry is broader than art since aesthetic experience is not an experience unique to art. This fact has not always been sufficiently emphasized, and as a result aesthetics frequently appears in the guise of philosophy-of-art-in-general.

As aesthetics and the philosophy of art have become more closely identified, a much more serious confusion has arisen. The work of art has come to be construed as an aesthetic object, an object of perception. Hence the meaning and essence of all art is thought to inhere in appearances, in the looks and sounds of direct (though not necessarily unreflective) awareness. The first principle of philosophy of art has become: all art possesses aesthetic qualities, and the core of a work is its nest of aesthetic qualities. This is why "aesthetics" has become just another name for the philosophy of art. Although it is sometimes recognized that aesthetics is not identical to the philosophy of art, but rather a complementary study, it is still commonly assumed that all art is aesthetic in the sense that falling within the subject matter of aesthetics is at least a necessary (if not a sufficient) condition for being art. Yet as we shall see, being aesthetic is neither a necessary nor a sufficient condition for being art. . . .

3. *The Theory of Media.* What does it mean to have the requisite "direct experience" of an aesthetic object? How do you specify *what* it is that one must experience in order to know a particular artwork? Here we encounter a problem. Aesthetic qualities cannot be communicated except through

direct experience of them. So there is no way of saying just what the aesthetic qualities of a work are independently of experiencing them. As Isabel Hungerland puts it, there are no intersubjective criteria for testing the presence of aesthetic qualities. This is why one cannot communicate the *Mona Lisa* by describing it. It is impossible to establish criteria for identifying artworks which are based on their aesthetic qualities. And this is the point where aesthetics needs the concept of a medium. Media are the basic categories of art for aesthetics, and each work is identified through its medium. Let's see how this is done.

In recent aesthetics, the problem of the relationship between the aesthetic and the non-aesthetic properties of an object has been much discussed. Whatever the particular analysis given, it is generally conceded that aesthetic qualities *depend* in some way upon non-aesthetic qualities. There is no guarantee that a slight change in color or shape will leave the aesthetic qualities of a painting unaffected, and this is why reproductions often have aesthetic qualities different from those of the original. Changing what Beardsley calls the "physical" properties, however slightly, can alter those features of a work of art which are experienced in the "aesthetic experience" of the object. Aesthetic objects are vulnerable and fragile, and this is another reason why it is important to have identity criteria for them.

Since aesthetic qualities depend on non-aesthetic qualities, the identity of an aesthetic artwork can be located through conventions governing its non-aesthetic qualities. These conventions determine the non-aesthetic parameters which must remain invariant in identifying particular works. A medium is not simply a physical material, but rather a network of such conventions which delimits a realm over which physical materials and aesthetic qualities are mediated. For example, in the medium of painting there is a convention which says

that the paint, but not the canvas, stretcher, or frame, must remain invariant in order to preserve the identity of the artwork. On the other hand, paint is not a conventional invariant in the art of architecture but is applied to buildings (at least on the inside) according to another art, interior decorating. The same architectural work could have white walls or pink walls, but a painting could not have its white clouds changed to pink and still remain the same painting. Similarly, the medium of painting is invariant through modifications of the frame holding a painting, while a building is not invariant through modifications in, say, the woodwork. Moving a Rubens from an elaborate Baroque frame into a modern Bauhaus frame will not change the work of art, but making a similar change in the woodwork of a building will change, however slightly, the architectural work.

In its network of conventions, each artistic medium establishes non-aesthetic criteria for identifying works of art. By being told which medium a work is in, we are given the parameters within which to search for and experience its aesthetic qualities. As we watch a dance, we heed how the dancers move their bodies. As we watch a play on the same stage, we concentrate instead on what is being acted out. Treating a piece of writing as a poem will make us focus on different non-aesthetic features than if we approach it as a short story: when the type is set for a poem the individual lines are preserved, as they are not in a short story. . . .

In the twentieth century we have witnessed a proliferation of new media. A medium seems to emerge when new conventions are instituted for isolating aesthetic qualities differently on the basis of new materials or machines. Film became an artistic medium when its unique physical structure was utilized to identify aesthetic qualities in a new way. The filmmaker became an artist when he or she stopped recording the creation of the playwright and discovered that film has resources for creation which theater lacks. The aesthetic qualities that can be presented by a film photographed from the orchestra and obedient to the temporal structure of the play are, basically, the aesthetic properties of the play itself. But when the camera photographs two different actions in two different places at two different times, and the images end up being seen at the same time and place, aesthetic properties can be realized which are inaccessible to theater. A new convention for specifying aesthetic properties had emerged. We say "See this film" instead of "See this play." In each case, what you look for is determined by the conventions of the medium.

The aesthetic theory of media has given rise to an analogy which seems to be gaining acceptance: a work of art is like a person. The dependence of aesthetic qualities on non-aesthetic ones is similar to the dependence of character traits on the bodily dispositions of persons. . . .

Although not universally accepted, this person analogy appears frequently in aesthetic theory because it provides a suitable model for understanding the artwork as a single entity appealing to two markedly different types of interest. It explains, for example, the basis of the connection between Beauty and Money.

The analogy has recently been carried to the extent of claiming that works of art, like persons, have rights. To deface a canvas by Picasso or a sculpture by Michelangelo is not only to violate the rights of its owner, but also to violate certain rights of the work itself. The work is a person; to mar the canvas or marble is to harm this person. So we see that aesthetic works of art are also mortal. Like people, they age and are vulnerable to physical deterioration.

4. *Art and Works.* Aesthetics has used the conventions of media to classify and identify artworks, but its vision of the nature of art does not adequately recognize the thoroughly conventional structure within which artworks appear. This is because aesthetics tends to view a medium as a kind of substance (paint, wood, stone, sound, etc.) instead of as a network of conventions.

Its preoccupation with perceptual entities leads aesthetics to extol and examine the "work of art," while averting its attention almost entirely from the myriad other aspects of that complex cultural activity we call "art." In other words, art for aesthetics is fundamentally a class of things called works of art which are the sources of aesthetic experience. To talk about art is to talk about a set of objects. To define art is to explain membership in this class. Thus we frequently find aesthetic discussions of the question "What is art?" immediately turning to the question "What is a work of art?" as though the two questions are unquestionably identical. Yet they are not the same.

What counts as a work of art must be discovered by examining the practice of art. Art, like philosophy, is a cultural phenomenon, and any particular work of art must rely heavily upon its artistic and cultural context in communicating its meaning. *L.H.O.O.Q. Shaved* looks as much like the *Mona Lisa* as any reproduction of it does, but their artistic meanings could hardly be more different. Just as I cannot tell you what the word "rot" means unless you say whether it is English or German, I cannot explain the meaning of a painting without viewing it immersed in an artistic milieu. The shock value of Manet's *Olympia*, for example, is largely lost on modern audiences, although it can be recovered by studying the society in which the painting emerged. Even so simple a question as what a painting represents cannot be answered without some reference to the conventions of depiction which have been adopted. Whether a smaller patch of paint on the canvas is a smaller person or a person farther away—or something else—is determined by conventions of representation. The moribund prejudice against much of the "unrealistic" art of the past comes from misjudging it according to standards which are part of the alien culture of the present.

Thus trying to define "art" by defining "work of art" is a bit like trying to define philosophy by saying what constitutes a philosophy book. A work of art cannot stand alone as a member of a set. Set membership is not the structure of that human activity called art. To suppose we can examine the problem of defining art by trying to explain membership in a class of entities is simply a prejudice of aesthetics, which underplays the cultural structure of art for the sake of pursuing perceptual objects. yet even as paradigmatic an aesthetic work as the *Mona Lisa* is a thoroughly cultural entity whose artistic and aesthetic meanings adhere to the painting by cultural forces, not by the chemical forces which keep the paint intact for a period of time.

As media proliferated, the aesthetic imperatives implied in their conventions weakened. Art has become increasingly nonaesthetic in the twentieth century, straining the conventions of media to the point where lines between them blur. Some works of art are presented in "multi-media," others (such as Duchamp's) cannot be placed within a medium at all. The concept of a medium was invented by aesthetics in order to explain the identity of artworks which articulate with aesthetic qualities. As art questions the dictates of aesthetics, it abandons the conventions of media. Let us see why.

V. ART OUTSIDE AESTHETICS

Art need not be aesthetic. *L.H.O.O.Q. Shaved* makes the point graphic by duplicating the appearance of the *Mona Lisa* while depriving it of its aesthetic import. The two works look exactly the same but are completely different. As the risque joke is compounded by *L.H.O.O.Q. Shaved*, the *Mona Lisa* is humiliated. Though restored to its original appearance, it is not restored to its original state. Duchamp added only the moustache and goatee, but when he removed them the sacred aura of aesthetic qualities vanished as well—it had been a conventional artistic covering which adhered to the moustache and goatee when they were removed, like paint stuck to tape. The original image is intact but literalized; its function in Duchamp's piece is just to denote the *Mona Lisa*. *L.H.O.O.Q.* looked naughty, graffiti on a masterpiece. It relies upon our seeing both the aesthetic aura and its impudent violation. But as its successor reinstates the appearance, the masterpiece is ironically ridiculed a second time with the disappearance of the dignity which made *L.H.O.O.Q.* a transgression. The first piece makes fun of the Gioconda, the second piece destroys it in the process of "restoring" it. *L.H.O.O.Q. Shaved* reindexes Leonardo's artwork as a derivative of *L.H.O.O.Q.*, reversing the temporal sequence while literalizing the image, i.e., discharging its aesthetic delights. Seen as "*L.H.O.O.Q.* shaved," the image is sapped of its artistic/aesthetic strength—it seems almost vulgar as it tours the world defiled. This is because it is placed in a context where its aesthetic properties have no meaning and its artistic "person" is reduced to just another piece of painted canvas.

It has already been pointed out that one can know the work *L.H.O.O.Q.* without having any direct experience of it, and instead by having it described. This it shares with a great deal of recent art which eschews media. When Mel Bochner puts lines on a gallery wall to measure off the degrees of an arc, their purpose is to convey information, not to proffer aesthetic delights. The same is true of On Kawara's "I GOT UP" postcards, which simply note his time of rising each day. What you need to see, to experience, in order to know this art is subject to intersubjective tests—unlike aesthetic art— and this is why description will sometimes be adequate in communicating the artwork.

When Duchamp wrote "*L.H.O.O.Q.*" beneath the image of the *Mona Lisa*, he was not demonstrating his penmanship. The beauty of a script depends upon aesthetic properties of its line. The meaning of a sentence written in the script, however, is a function of how the lines fit into the structure of an alphabet. Aesthetics assumes that artistic meaning must be construed according to the first type of relation between meaning and line, but not the second. It mistakes the experience of aesthetic qualities for the substance of art. Yet the remarkable thing about even aesthetic art is not its beauty (or any other of its aesthetic qualities), but the fact that it is human-created beauty *articulated* in a medium.

The flaw in aesthetics is this: how something looks is partly a function of what we bring to it, and art is too culturally dependent to survive in the mere look of things. The importance of Duchamp's titles is that they call attention to the cultural environment which can either sustain or suffocate the aesthetic demeanor of an object. Duchamp's titles do not name objects; they put handles on things. They call attention to the artistic framework within which works of art are indexed by their titles and by other means. The culture infects the work.

A great deal of art has chosen to articulate in the medium of an aesthetic space, but there is not *a priori* reason why art must confine itself to the creation of aesthetic objects. It might opt for articulation in a semantic space instead of an aesthetic one so that artistic meaning is not embodied in a physical object or event according to the conventions of a medium. Duchamp has proven this by creating non-aesthetic art, i.e., art whose meaning is not borne by the appearance of an object. In particular, the role of line in *L.H.O.O.Q.* is more like its role in a sentence than in a drawing or painting. This is why the appearance of the moustache and goatee are insignificant to the art. The first version of *L.H.O.O.Q.* was executed not by Duchamp, but by Picabia on Duchamp's instructions, and the goatee was left off. It would be an idle curiosity to speculate about whose version is better or more interesting on the basis of how each looks. The point of the artwork cannot be ascertained by scrutinizing its appearance. It is not a person-like union of physical and perceptual qualities. Its salient artistic features do not *depend* upon non-aesthetic qualities in the sense of being embodied in them. The aesthetic qualities of *L.H.O.O.Q.*, like the aesthetic qualities of Rauschenberg's erased DeKooning, are not offered up by the artist for aesthetic delectation, but rather are incidental features of the work like its weight or its age. Line is perceived in Duchamp's piece just as it is in a sentence in a book, and in both cases we can descry the presence of aesthetic qualities. But the point of neither can be read off its physiognomy. The lines are used to convey information, not to conjure up appearances; consequently the relationship of meaning to material is similar to what it is in a drawing of a triangle in a geometry book.

If an artwork is a person, Duchamp has stripped her bare of aesthetic aura. *L.H.O.O.Q.* treats a person as an object by means of the joke produced by reading the letters in French. It also treats an artwork as a "mere thing." The presence of the moustache violates the *Mona Lisa's* aesthetic rights and hence violates the artwork "person." In making fun of these persons, Duchamp's piece denies its own personhood.

Aesthetics is limited by reading the artwork on the model of a person. Some person-like entities are works of art, but not all artworks are persons. If not a person, what is an artwork?

VI. WHAT IS AN ARTWORK?

An artwork is a piece. The concept "work of art" does not isolate a class of peculiar aesthetic personages. The concept marks an indexical function in the artworld. To be a piece of art, an item need only be indexed as an artwork by an artist. Simply recategorizing an unsuspecting entity will suffice. Thus "Is it art?" is a question of little interest. The question is "So what if it is?" Art is an epiphenomenon over the class of its works. . . .

. . . Anyone can be an artist. To be an artist is to utilize (or perhaps invent) artistic conventions to index a piece. These might be the conventions of a medium which provide for the indexing of an aesthetic piece by means of non-aesthetic materials. But even the aesthetic artist has to stand back from the painting or play at a certain point and say *"That's* it. It's done." This is the point where the artist relies upon the basic indexing conventions of art. The fundamental art-making (piece-making) act is the specification of a piece: "The piece is ——." Putting paint on canvas—or making any kind of product—is just one way of specifying what the work of art is. When Duchamp wrote *"L.H.O.O.Q."* below the reproduction, or when Rauschenberg erased the DeKooning, it was not the work (the labor) they did which made the art. A work of art is not necessarily something worked on; it is basically something conceived. To be an artist is not always to make something, but rather to engage in a cultural enterprise in which artistic pieces are proffered for consideration. . . .

. . . *L.H.O.O.Q. Shaved* could, for the sake of argument, be construed as residing in the same physical object as the *Mona Lisa* itself. Then there is one extensionally specified object, but two intensionally specified artworks. Rauschenberg has suggested this possibility since the only things of substance he changed by erasing the DeKooning drawing were aesthetic qualities. To complete the cycle in the way Duchamp did, Rauschenberg should buy a DeKooning painting and exhibit it in his next show: "Unerased DeKooning." The point is that artworks are identified intensionally, not extensionally. The reason *L.H.O.O.Q. Shaved* and the *Mona Lisa* are different artworks is not that they are different objects, but rather that they are different ideas. They are specified as different pieces in the art practice.

That an artwork is a piece and not a person was established by the Readymade. Duchamp selected several common objects and converted them into art simply by indexing them as artworks. Sometimes this was accomplished in conjunction with explicit indexing ceremonies, such as signing and dating a work, giving it a title, entering it in a show. But always what separates the readymade artwork from the "readymade" object it was ready-made from is a simple act of indexing. Duchamp says, "A point I want very much to establish is that the choice of these Readymades was never dictated by aesthetic delectation. The choice was based on a reaction of *visual indifference* with a total absence of good or bad taste." The Readymade demonstrates the indexical nature of the concept "work of art" by showing that whether something is an artwork is not determined by its appearance but by how it is regarded in the artworld. The same shovel can be a mere hardware item at one time and an artwork at another depending upon how the artworld stands in relation to it. Even an old work of art can be converted into a new one without changing the appearance of the old work, but only "creating a new idea for it," as Duchamp has said of the urinal readymade called *Fountain.* The significance of the title of this piece has not been fully appreciated. A urinal is a fountain; that is, it is an object designed for discharging a stream of water. The reason most urinals are *not* fountains, despite their designs, is that their locations and use differ from similar devices we do consider fountains. The objects are structurally similar, but their cultural roles are very different. Putting a urinal in a gallery makes it visible as a "fountain" and as a work of art because the context has been changed. Cultural contexts endow objects with special meanings; and they determine arthood.

It has been pointed out that *Fountain* was accepted as a work of art only because Duchamp had already established his status as an artist by producing works in traditional forms. This is probably true: not just anyone could have carried it off. You cannot revolutionize the accepted conventions for indexing unless you have some recognition in the artworld already. However, this does not mean that Duchamp's piece is only marginal art and that anyone desiring to follow his act of indexing has to become a painter first. When Duchamp made his first non-aesthetic work, the conventions for indexing artworks were more or less the media of aesthetics: to make an artwork was to articulate in a medium. Duchamp did not simply make an exception to these conventions, he instituted a new convention, the indexing convention which countenances non-aesthetic art, though perhaps it should be said rather that Duchamp *uncovered* the convention, since it lies behind even the use of media, which are specialized ways of indexing aesthetic qualities. In any event, once the new convention is instituted anyone can follow it as easily as he or she can follow the indexing conventions of aesthetics. The Sunday Indexer can have just as good a time as the Sunday Painter.

Walter Benjamin

THE WORK OF ART IN THE AGE OF MECHANICAL REPRODUCTION

Walter Benjamin (1892–1940) was a philosopher, art critic, and literary theorist. He considered art to be essentially bound up with politics, and he emphasized both the material character of the artwork and its social and historical context. In the following selection from one of his most influential essays, he ponders the impact that reproductions of artwork have on our experience of art.

. . . In principle a work of art has always been reproducible. Man-made artifacts could always be imitated by men. Replicas were made by pupils in practice of their craft, by masters for diffusing their works, and, finally, by third parties in the pursuit of gain. Mechanical reproduction of a work of art, however, represents something new. Historically, it advanced intermittently and in leaps at long intervals, but with accelerated intensity. The Greeks knew only two procedures of technically reproducing works of art: founding and stamping. Bronzes, terra cottas, and coins were the only art works which they could produce in quantity. All others were unique and could not be mechanically reproduced. With the woodcut graphic art became mechanically reproducible for the first time, long before script became reproducible by print. The enormous changes which printing, the mechanical reproduction of writing, has brought about in literature are a familiar story. However, within the phenomenon which we are here examining from the perspective of world history, print is merely a special, though particularly important, case. During the Middle Ages engraving and etching were added to the woodcut; at the beginning of the nineteenth century lithography made its appearance.

With lithography the technique of reproduction reached an essentially new stage. This much more direct process was distinguished by the tracing of the design on a stone rather than its incision on a block of

Walter Benjamin, *Illuminations: Essays and Reflections*, trans. Harry Zohn (New York: Shocken, 1968) 217–215.

wood or its etching on a copperplate and permitted graphic art for the first time to put its products on the market, not only in large numbers as hitherto, but also in daily changing forms. Lithography enabled graphic art to illustrate everyday life, and it began to keep pace with printing. But only a few decades after its invention, lithography was surpassed by photography. For the first time in the process of pictorial reproduction, photography freed the hand of the most important artistic functions which henceforth devolved only upon the eye looking into a lens. Since the eye perceives more swiftly than the hand can draw, the process of pictorial reproduction was accelerated so enormously that it could keep pace with speech. A film operator shooting a scene in the studio captures the images at the speed of an actor's speech. Just as lithography virtually implied the illustrated newspaper, so did photography foreshadow the sound film. The technical reproduction of sound was tackled at the end of the last century. These convergent endeavors made predictable a situation which Paul Valéry pointed up in this sentence: "Just as water, gas, and electricity are brought into our houses from far off to satisfy our needs in response to a minimal effort, so we shall be supplied with visual or auditory images, which will appear and disappear at a simple movement of the hand, hardly more than a sign." . . . Around 1900 technical reproduction had reached a standard that not only permitted it to reproduce all transmitted works of art and thus to cause the most profound change in their impact upon the public; it also had captured a place of its own among the artistic processes. For the study of this standard nothing is more revealing than the nature of the repercussions that these two different manifestations—the reproduction of works of art and the art of the film—have had on art in its traditional form.

Even the most perfect reproduction of a work of art is lacking in one element: its presence in time and space, its unique existence at the place where it happens to be. This unique existence of the work of art determined the history to which it was subject throughout the time of its existence. This includes the changes which it may have suffered in physical condition over the years as well as the various changes in its ownership. The traces of the first can be revealed only by chemical or physical analyses which it is impossible to perform on a reproduction; changes of ownership are subject to a tradition which must be traced from the situation of the original.

The presence of the original is the prerequisite to the concept of authenticity. Chemical analyses of the patina of a bronze can help to establish this, as does the proof that a given manuscript of the Middle Ages stems from an archive of the fifteenth century. The whole sphere of authenticity is outside technical—and, of course, not only technical—reproducibility. Confronted with its manual reproduction, which was usually branded as a forgery, the original preserved all its authority; not so *vis à vis* technical reproduction. The reason is twofold. First, process reproduction is more independent of the original than manual reproduction. For example, in photography, process reproduction can bring out those aspects of the original that are unattainable to the naked eye yet accessible to the lens, which is adjustable and chooses its angle at will. And photographic reproduction, with the aid of certain processes, such as enlargement or slow motion, can capture images which escape natural vision. Secondly, technical reproduction can put the copy of the original into situations which would be out of reach for the original itself. Above all, it enables the original to meet the beholder halfway, be it in the form of a photograph or a phonograph record. The cathedral leaves its locale to be received in the studio of a lover of art; the choral production, performed in an auditorium or in the open air, resounds in the drawing room.

The situations into which the product of mechanical reproduction can be brought may not touch the actual work of art, yet the quality of its presence is always depreciated. This holds not only for the art work but also, for instance, for a landscape which passes in review before the spectator in a movie. In the case of the art object, a most sensitive nucleus—namely, its authenticity—is interfered with whereas no natural object is vulnerable on that score. The authenticity of a thing is the essence of all that is transmissible from its beginning, ranging from its substantive duration to its testimony to the history which it has experienced. Since the historical testimony rests on the authenticity, the former, too, is jeopardized by reproduction when substantive duration ceases to matter. And what is really jeopardized when the historical testimony is affected is the authority of the object.

One might subsume the eliminated element in the term "aura" and go on to say: that which withers in the age of mechanical reproduction is the aura of the work of art. This is a symptomatic process whose significance points beyond the realm of art. One might generalize by saying: the technique of reproduction detaches the reproduced object from the domain of tradition. By making many reproductions it substitutes a plurality of copies for a unique existence. And in permitting the reproduction to meet the beholder or listener in his own particular situation, it reactivates the object reproduced. These two processes lead to a tremendous shattering of tradition which is the obverse of the contemporary crisis and renewal of mankind. Both processes are intimately connected with the contemporary mass movements. Their most powerful agent is the film. Its social significance, particularly in its most positive form, is inconceivable without its destructive, cathartic aspect,

that is, the liquidation of the traditional value of the cultural heritage. This phenomenon is most palpable in the great historical films. It extends to ever new positions. In 1927 Abel Gance exclaimed enthusiastically: "Shakespeare, Rembrandt, Beethoven will make films . . . all legends, all mythologies and all myths, all founders of religion, and the very religions . . . await their exposed resurrection, and the heroes crowd each other at the gate." Presumably without intending it, he issued an invitation to a far-reaching liquidation.

. . . The concept of aura which was proposed above with reference to historical objects may usefully be illustrated with reference to the aura of natural ones. We define the aura of the latter as the unique phenomenon of a distance, however close it may be. If, while resting on a summer afternoon, you follow with your eyes a mountain range on the horizon or a branch which casts its shadow over you, you experience the aura of those mountains, of that branch. This image makes it easy to comprehend the social bases of the contemporary decay of the aura. It rests on two circumstances, both of which are related to the increasing significance of the masses in contemporary life. Namely, the desire of contemporary masses to bring things "closer" spatially and humanly, which is just as ardent as their bent toward overcoming the uniqueness of every reality by accepting its reproduction. Every day the urge grows stronger to get hold of an object at very close range by way of its likeness, its reproduction. Unmistakably, reproduction as offered by picture magazines and newsreels differs from the image seen by the unarmed eye. Uniqueness and permanence are as closely linked in the latter as are transitoriness and reproducibility in the former. To pry an object from its shell, to destroy its aura, is the mark of a perception whose "sense of the universal equality of things" has increased to such a degree that it extracts it even from a unique object by means of reproduction. Thus is manifested in the field of perception what in the theoretical sphere is noticeable in the increasing importance of statistics. The adjustment of reality to the masses and of the masses to reality is a process of unlimited scope, as much for thinking as for perception.

◆◆◆

The uniqueness of a work of art is inseparable from its being imbedded in the fabric of tradition. This tradition itself is thoroughly alive and extremely changeable. An ancient statue of Venus, for example, stood in a different traditional context with the Greeks, who made it an object of veneration, than with the clerics of the Middle Ages, who viewed it as an ominous idol. Both of them, however, were equally confronted with its uniqueness, that is, its aura. Originally the contextual integration of art in tradition found its expression in the cult. We know that the earliest art works originated in the service of a ritual—first the magical, then the religious kind. It is significant that the existence of the work of art with reference to its aura is never entirely separated from its ritual function. In other words, the unique value of the "authentic" work of art has its basis in ritual, the location of its original use value. This ritualistic basis, however remote, is still recognizable as secularized ritual even in the most profane forms of the cult of beauty. The secular cult of beauty, developed during the Renaissance and prevailing for three centuries, clearly showed that ritualistic basis in its decline and the first deep crisis which befell it. With the advent of the first truly revolutionary means of reproduction, photography, simultaneously with the rise of socialism, art sensed the approaching crisis which has become evident a century later. At the time, art reacted with the doctrine of *l'art pour l'art*, that is, with a theology of art. This gave rise to what might be called a negative theology in the form of the idea of "pure" art, which not only denied any social function of art but also any categorizing by subject matter. (In poetry, Mallarmé was the first to take this position.)

An analysis of art in the age of mechanical reproduction must do justice to these relationships, for they lead us to an all-important insight: for the first time in world history, mechanical reproduction emancipates the work of art from its parasitical dependence on ritual. To an ever greater degree the work of art reproduced becomes the work of art designed for reproducibility. From a photographic negative, for example, one can make any number of prints; to ask for the "authentic" print makes no sense. But the instant the criterion of authenticity ceases to be applicable to artistic production, the total function of art is reversed. Instead of being based on ritual, it begins to be based on another practice—politics.

◆◆◆

Works of art are received and valued on different planes. Two polar types stand out: with one, the accent is on the cult value; with the other, on the exhibition value of the work. Artistic production begins with ceremonial objects destined to serve in a cult. One may assume that what mattered was their existence, not their being on view. The elk portrayed by the man of the Stone Age on the walls of his cave was an instrument of magic. He did expose it to his fellow men, but in the main it was meant for the spirits. Today the cult value would seem to demand that the work of art remain hidden. Certain statues of gods are accessible only to the priest in the cella; certain Madonnas remain covered nearly all year round; certain sculptures on medieval cathedrals are invisible to the spectator on ground level. With the emancipation of the various art practices from ritual go increasing opportunities for the exhibition of their products. It is easier to exhibit a portrait bust that can be sent here and there than to exhibit the statue of a divinity that has its fixed place in the interior of a temple. The same holds for the painting as against the mosaic or fresco that preceded it. And even though the public presentability of a mass originally may have been just as great as that of a symphony, the latter originated at the moment when its public presentability promised to surpass that of the mass.

With the different methods of technical reproduction of a work of art, its fitness for exhibition increased to such an extent that the quantitative shift between its two poles turned into a qualitative transformation of its nature. This is comparable to the situation of the work of art in prehistoric times when, by the absolute emphasis on its cult value, it was, first and foremost, an instrument of magic. Only later did it come to be recognized as a work of art. In the same way today, by the absolute emphasis on its exhibition value the work of art becomes a creation with entirely new functions, among which the one we are conscious of, the artistic function, later may be recognized as incidental.

Robert Plant Armstrong

THE AFFECTING PRESENCE

Robert Plant Armstrong (1919–1984) had a multifaceted career. He was a prize-winning creative writer, an editor at Alfred A. Knopf and director of Northwestern University Press, and professor of anthropology at Northwestern University and at the University of Texas at Dallas. In his anthropological writings, which focused primarily on African art, Armstrong contended that standards of beauty are not universal. His writings include Forms and Processes of African Sculpture, The Powers of Presence: Myth, Consciousness, and the Affecting Presence, *and* The Affecting Presence: An Essay in Humanistic Anthropology, *the source of the following excerpt.*

I shall speak of *affecting things and events*, which are those cultural objects and happenings resulting from human actions directed toward producing *them* rather than anything else, which is to say that they are not accidental. These objects and happenings in any given culture are accepted by those native to that culture as being purposefully concerned with potency, emotions, values, and states of being or experience—all, in a clear sense, *powers*. Further, irrespective of such considerations, under certain circumstances and in some cultures such things and events may be admired for the excellence of their own properties; thus, this admiration is in itself of an affecting nature. In other words, such things and events are characterized by some people in some cultures as having "beauty." These affecting things and events may be *depictions* of subjects, objects, and states of affairs, or they may be *abstractions* from or *variations* upon such subjects, objects, or conditions. In any case, they are regarded by those co-cultural with them, thus *appropriately* regarded, as being in and of the real world, however constituted, including the mythical.

Robert Plant Armstrong, *The Affecting Presence: An Essay in Humanistic Anthropology* (Urbana: U of Illinois P, 1971) 3–12, 25–29.

The "powers" with which these affecting things and events are concerned tend not to be clearly separable one from the other in any specific thing or event. Indeed, these categories may, and often do, simultaneously characterize an affecting thing or event. A sculpture, for example, may be asserted to have potency and thus to accomplish good, yet at the same time forcefully constitute the abstraction derived from the contemplation of the form or significance of a hero. The concepts of potency, bravery, force, and hero clearly produce affect, and it is to this affect that the thing or event is dedicated, and thereafter is the work, affecting us when we enter into transaction with it. By *work*, which is the body through which the act of presentation occurs, I mean the thing or event as a depiction of, an abstraction from, or a variation upon an object, an event, or a theme in the internal or external world achieved by means of the affecting media, those components of volume, movement and experience which eventuate in the affecting work. . . .

Each such work, which is in enduring media, is a perpetual act because it is self-contained and wholly committed. Those which are in evanescent media become perpetual when recorded. The totality of such acts constitutes a separate universe—not of discourse, but of feeling. This is the domain of *presentation* and the ultimate objective of the creation of things and events in the affecting universe. Presentation, not representation, is the goal of the artist; even though representation is sometimes achieved, this is another and quite different function of the work—not necessarily an *affecting* function, irrespective of the fact that emotional attachment may exist between the model for and the perceptor of the work.

Because such works are perpetual and perpetuating acts—the act ever in the process of being enacted—I find it accurate to speak of the *affecting* things and events. By the use of this participial form, I intend to convey the idea that the perpetual and perpetuating act is also perpetually and perpetuatingly in affect. It is thus to be seen as a very special kind of action that is of concern here; and as action, it is particularly recommended to the serious attention of all students of human action and behavior. Affecting things and events are not negligible doodads in culture but constitute a distinct and significant category of human existence. If understanding of this category is not achieved, it follows that there is no full understanding of human behavior, and the social sciences are solely of society—not of man—and thus incomplete.

Inherent to this approach is the creator's intention to produce a work conveying affect. . . .

———◆◆◆———

. . . There are many kinds of affecting works, but only some of these are intentionally created to be such. It is in these latter ones alone that we are interested. In the first place, there are some affecting things and events that are not created at all, but these are obviously outside the area of our interest if we are to isolate a class somewhat like but yet differently constituted from "art." A tree in Java or in Nigeria may be thought to house spirits and thus to be affecting; or a rock in Samoa may be said to contain power. Animals may be considered as being sacred, as may certain fruits and vegetables. A storm may fill one with terror if it is regarded as an expression of the wrath of a god. The criterion of intention thus helps us eliminate from our consideration natural things and events which have come to be affecting.

———◆◆◆———

It is not too difficult to determine the presence of the intention to be affecting.

Interrogation, of course, is one way. Perhaps it is even the best way. But there is another method as well. Frequently such objects and events as are intended to be invested with feelings are accorded special treatment—they are placed in galleries or in shrines; they surround important persons; they are used in rituals; or they are hidden away from public gaze and ordinary use. . . .

In contrast to this inductive approach, it would prove unrewarding to proceed in an investigation based upon the notion of art, and the beauty which presumably is its foremost characteristic, for "art" is difficult to communicate as a concept, to say nothing of "beauty," and would not make a useful basis from which to organize one's inquiry. To attempt to study the affecting things and events of another people by using the concepts of "art" and "the beautiful" would constitute a surpassing example of ethnocentrism, the exportation to an alien context of our own values, our own structures, our own grid. And yet there are numerous instances in which anthropologists, those professionally most sensitive to the subtle insistencies of ethnocentrism, have themselves ethnocentrically used "art" to categorize certain phenomena. Whether as a result of their lack of clarity about what "art" is in their own culture, or out of some residual determination to be sensitive to the variability of data, they have sometimes tended to emerge with a congeries rather than a class of things and events—when they have included events at all. Their congeries have included non-affecting items from the material culture as readily as intentionally affecting ones, axes as readily as works of sculpture. As for "beauty," I have heard more than one anthropologist assert something to the effect that one could not convince him that the Yoruba, for example, have no notion of beauty; they must have—how else could they create objects as "beautiful" as certain figure carvings he has seen.

The terms provided here must take the place of "art" and "beauty" in the analytical vocabulary of the individual who would identify and study a class of phenomena of which all the components, in any given culture, would share common, critical, definitive characteristics; and of the student who would define, in any given culture, a class of like-featured things and events which would bear the mark of the individuality of that culture and embody many of its powers.

We have established a category, or a class of things and events, based upon affect—feeling—and have maintained that these are works and that such works are intentionally affecting and are amenable to identification. It is also maintained here that the intentional creation of affecting things and events is a cultural universal. Even in those parts of the world where materials for such works are most rare, the creation of affecting things occurs. The Eskimos engrave ivory, and the pygmies of the Kalahari Desert decorate ostrich eggs—the vessels in which life-sustaining water is carried and which must therefore be greatly accompanied by feeling—and they also sing and dance.

But although the realm of affect is universal, there is great diversity among its works. Affecting things and events range from depiction to abstraction, from the passionate to the removed, from the extravagant to the austere, from the complex to the simple—not only from culture, but also even within one culture.

The affecting presence acts as subject, asserting its own being, inviting the perceptor's recognition and, in culturally permitted ways, structuring that subsequent relationship which someone has called "transaction" in recognition of the fact that while the presence informs the man, the man, in his unique way, to some extent and in some fashion informs the presence. But although the presence is subject, it is a limited subject. Its limitations are described by its restrictedness, by the extent, indeed, to which it is at the same time an object. It obviously cannot perceive the perceptor; it can only be perceived, owned, created, and disposed of. It is not uncommon, however, to find that its sense of being is so acknowledged that the affecting presence is accorded special treatment—sometimes it receives the attentions and services accorded a person: it may, as is true of some of the sculptured figures and masks of West Africa, be bathed, clothed, fed, and, when its usefulness has ended, buried. Indeed, in certain kinds of magical situations, it can be "sickened," "deprived," "wounded," or "killed."

In the recognition of this quality of personality which characterizes the affecting presence lies the refutation of those who would deny, the work's selfhood and maintain that it is not a presence as herein described but a symbol, carrying some meaning or feeling from the mind of the artist to the mind of the perceptor, with offhand rejection accorded the view that the work does not symbolize but *is* its own affecting.

The symbolistic fallacy is especially beguiling in those cases in which the affecting presence is a representation of some model external to itself. But representation, lying within the genius of all the media, is in this sole respect a burden that must be borne—or rather that representation may give rise to confusions is a situation to be abided. The affecting presence is perpetrated by an artist after an affecting "idea"; it is the artist who brings about the work, but it is the work that presents. Once created, the work embodies the idea and, insofar as it is representation, its model is irrelevant to its existence—the work has also embodied the model. The artist is no longer important. Thus, the work stands in the relationship of

immediacy, not of mediation, and does not fulfill the role of the symbol. Indeed, in the long run its frame of reference, as described by the affecting media, is—as affecting presence—solely itself. That there was a model in a different universe is irrelevant to the affecting presence in that special and self-contained world of affect. . . .

The affecting work, then, is an affecting presence, a self-contained, perpetuating actor on the one hand and a human-perceptor related affectant on the other. But there are other complexities characteristic of the affecting presence which must also be noted. In terms of its recognition by a perceptor, any affecting presence is universal, cultural, and particular. Inasmuch as the affective realm is universal, affecting presences may be expected to be recognized outside their producing cultures—not in terms of the specific nature of their affecting existence, perhaps, but identified as an affecting presence. To a certain extent, the attempt to perceive such works from an exotic culture *in their own terms* is probably of doubtful merit, problematic to accomplish, and perhaps characteristic chiefly of a highly educated and sophisticated culture characterized by intensive and frequent international, inter-cultural contacts. Nonetheless, at the very least, there might be identification of the forms of one culture among the peoples of a great many more cultures, irrespective of such "sophistication."

It is this aspect of universality which has led to many foolish statements by those who, knowledgeable of the arts but not of the important cultural and individual variables of man, have been beguiled into judgments and interpretations based upon the universal aspect. Such judgments have understandably alienated many anthropologists from much of the writing in the field of "primitive art" and have driven them to their own cautious statements, based upon close observation and abhorring the imaginative, as both an area of study and a technique involving the leap into pertinence and revelation. . . .

The recognition of the affecting presence, I have mentioned, is universal. This is true in two respects—formal and emotional. In the first instance, recognition occurs because all peoples who create affecting works do so by virtue of either depiction of, variation upon, or abstraction from the perceivable world and its experiences, and therefore they recognize such depictions, variations, or abstractions as indicating the likely existence of a work characterized by a present affecting purpose. Similarly, one can often know when affect is present in a work by observing whether it is greeted by its perceptors with feeling, even though the exact content or the precise boundaries of the feeling may not be obvious.

Each affecting presence is inescapably individual; equally, by definition, all such presences are cultural, since together, in respect of their own kind, they constitute a cultural order of phenomena. In the instance of a given culture, however, *individualism* may be a cultural value, in which event both intra-form diversity and the radical differentiation of pieces are more highly prized than is the assertion of familial characteristics. Late twentieth-century England, for example, asserts the desirability of the radical differentiation of pieces and of intra-form diversity more markedly than did Renaissance Italy, which, despite the marked differentiation of pieces by virtue of a style demanding individuation of subjects, nonetheless did not exhibit as wide a range of intra-form experimentation. In other words, the Italian Renaissance did not produce a situation in which there were simultaneously practiced styles as far apart as are primitivism, realism, surrealism, and abstract expressionism.

Although culture is a collectivity, it is also much more. It is not passive as a statistic is passive but viable as a master system from which one cannot escape and within which

one finds his meaning, deriving his conscious knowledge as well as his unconscious attitudes and perceiving the world through its grids. The affecting presence is the tutor of our feelings, and that part of existence it teaches is capable of infinite instruction. Further, feeling is with us early—and it is articulate earlier than the intellect. It is, in fact, a primitive level of existence; and what relationship it has to thought, to the structure and content of behavior that is not affective, one cannot easily say. One can with safety assert that it is not irrelevant. I would be tempted to suspect that the way in which one organizes his feelings and the motifs he stresses are not at all unrelated to the rest of his life. This holds true for culture as well, for culture is man writ large, simultaneously both superman and supraman.

The feelings crave extension and definition of being as ardently as the mind, and thus one learns new affecting idioms—through experimentation, acculturation, and the rise of new philosophical attitudes, such as that of individualism in the Western world. In West Africa, prior to the last decade or so, the affecting works of any given type were characterized by little differentiation in any given tribal group. Representations appear to have been generalized and were, by and large, myth-related. Perhaps because myth is itself general, the sculptures had to be general also. In any case, the two generalizations of myth and affecting work were functionally related, and their reciprocity doubtless magnified the content and the force of the work. But today shows us that the more experimentation, individualism, and acculturation intervene, the more the individual is alienated from this coherent, affecting dialectic—from myth to form—and under certain circumstances a radical starvation of affect can occur and disorganization and affecting anemia can result. Of course, there can even be a free-floating surge of affect which, only vaguely known, seeks to create new and socialized works in order that it might, defined, emerge into being. Such, for example, were the works of the cargo cults which occurred notably at various places in the Pacific after World War II.

Affecting presences are culturized, by which I mean that necessary to the relationship between presence and person is the guided production within the person in culturally approved ways of affective responses, which are similar from one person to the next irrespective of happenings in one's own history that might, and indeed do, give added affective resonance to the experience. Since this is the case, works clearly do not lose their presentation, when they are deprived of their native audience, but do lose something of their originally intended presentation, and thus their native import. In such a case, an alien perceptor perceives with referred affect, accepting the affecting presence in those terms he reserves for what he presumes to be like works in his own culture. In such an instance, there might be something of that affecting which was originally intended, which is yet inherent in the transaction; but if this is so, it is the result of purely fortuitous convergences. Under such circumstances of being erroneously perceived, or reinterpreted, the affecting presence does not cease to be what it was created; it is simply confined to the slavery of misapprehension, of inapposite interchange.

DISCUSSION QUESTIONS

1. Do any of the theories of art advocated in this chapter strike you as compelling? If so, why?
2. Do you think that Duchamp's readymades are appropriately called "art"? Why or why not?
3. Do the nonrepresentational artworks of the twentieth century establish that the mimetic theory or representationalist theory of art should be rejected? Why or why not?
4. Is there any specific function that an artwork must fulfill in order to be art, in your view? How would you defend your answer?
5. Do you think more is required for a thing to be art than its being indexed by someone as art (or its being designated art by the artworld)?
6. Do you agree with Benjamin that the prevalence of artistic reproduction undercuts the impact of artworks? Does an original artwork have a distinctive "aura," as he claims?
7. Do you think we typically consider artworks to have a dignity (akin to the dignity of a human being)? If so, what do you think is the basis for this impression?
8. Does Armstrong's notion of "affecting presence" accommodate the kinds of things we call art in the West? Do you agree with him that our notion of "art" has associations that are ill-suited to certain aesthetic objects and events in non-Western cultures?

FURTHER READING

Beardsley, Monroe C. "The Definitions of the Arts." *Journal of Aesthetics and Art Criticism* 20 (1960): 175–87.

Danto, Arthur C. *The Transfiguration of the Commonplace.* Cambridge: Harvard UP, 1981.

———*The Philosophical Disenfranchisement of Art.* New York: Columbia UP, 1986.

Davies, Stephen. *Definitions of Art.* Ithaca: Cornell UP, 1991.

Dickie, George. *Art and the Aesthetic: An Institutional Analysis*. Ithaca: Cornell UP, 1974.

Eaton, Marcia Muelder. "Art, Artifacts, and Intentions." *American Philosophical Quarterly* 6 (1969): 165–69.

Levinson, Jerrold. "Defining Art Historically." *British Journal of Aesthetics* 19 (1979): 232–50.

Mandelbaum, Maurice. "Family Resemblances and Generalizations Concerning the Art." *American Philosophical Quarterly* 2 (1965): 219–28.

Sclafani, Richard J. "'Art,' Wittgenstein, and Open-textured Concepts." *Journal of Aesthetics and Art Criticism* 29 (1971): 333–41.

Sparshott, Francis. *The Theory of the Arts*. Princeton: Princeton UP, 1982.

Tolstoy, Leo. *What Is Art?* Trans. Aylmer Maude. Indianapolis: Bobbs-Merrill, 1980.

Walton, Kendall. "Categories of Art." *Journal of Aesthetics and Art Criticism* 79 (1970): 334–67.

Ziff, Paul. "The Task of Defining a Work of Art." *The Philosophical Review* 62 (1953): 58–78.

ART, TRUTH,
AND REALITY

When we confront a glossy advertisement, we are encouraged to imagine ourselves transformed. The merchandise displayed is insinuated to be the key to a better lifestyle. A fashionable purse or a new pair of jeans are not only presented as desirable objects in such advertising; they are usually depicted as a part of a more perfect world, a world that would include us, if only we made such purchases. Of course, we need only buy the purse or the jeans to realize that they cannot change our lives very much. Yet strangely, despite the disappointment we experience after succumbing to the propaganda of one ad, we usually find ourselves still susceptible to others, dimly convinced that we are offered glamour if we make the right purchase.

Although the high gloss of contemporary advertising is relatively new, the kinds of appeals that it makes are not. Nor are critics of these appeals. In Plato's *Republic*, Socrates, the central character, expresses grave reservations about the wholesomeness of the fantasies that are induced and celebrated by art. The excerpt in this chapter reveals an ambivalent perspective on art. On the one hand, art's power to imitate the human world is wondrous. (Plato, like Aristotle, took this imitation, or **mimesis,** to be the primary aim of art.) On the other hand, art can have a bad influence on its audience, making inappropriate behavior look glamorous and distorting reality.

Plato complains that even the poetic works of Homer, the basic texts for ancient Athenian education, give young people bad role models through their depictions of crafty and lust-driven deities. Worst of all, the representations of art distract people from real knowledge. By imitating the way things appear in the material world (and then only from a single point of view), art can distract attention from the higher realm of true reality (the abode of absolute Beauty, discussed in the excerpts from Plato in Chapter 1).

Plato is worried about the obstacles that stand between us and genuine insight, and he is convinced that art is often such an obstacle. Yet not everyone would agree that fantasy and appearance are so harmful. Oscar Wilde, in his essay "The Decay of Lying," emphasizes the charming nature of aesthetic dissembling. Through art and fantasy, we improve our world by protesting the flaws in nature and beautifying our conceptions of things. Wilde's character Vivian insists that there are not enough "lies" of this sort. Wilde agrees with Plato that art is an important influence on our understanding of reality. But he disagrees with Plato about the significance of this fact. Vivian theorizes that "Life imitates art far more than Art imitates life." In other words, art gives us the prototypes for making sense of our experience. The products of our imaginations, the "lies" that Plato denounces, are our means of focusing on our world and enhancing our ordinary lives.

Joseph Lyons suggests another basis for disagreeing with Plato. He contends that prehistoric cave paintings, usually found in particularly inaccessible places within the caves, are located in deliberately chosen sites. Lyons speculates that these sites were chosen to separate the unreal world of representation from the real world of everyday life. Far from being distractions from higher reality, as Plato contends, such art served to stimulate ideas of a different reality, according to Lyons. Such proto-religious notions as magic and ritual developed, he suggests, from our ancestors' early artistic practices. Art was the key, not the obstruction, to a sense of a world beyond this one.

The authenticity of an artwork itself is sometimes called into question, and this is another sense in which art's relation to reality can be problematic. Is the artwork what it seems to be? Does its audience know its real story? Denis Dutton considers why artistic forgeries distress us. When an artwork's alleged authorship is shown to be false, it is usually considered less valuable than before. But this is perplexing. If the work looks just the same, we might wonder, why should it matter who made it?

Dutton suggests an explanation for the impression that a work is less valuable if it is a forgery than it would be if it were not. Besides placing value on aesthetic appearance, Dutton argues, we also value the achievement that we take a particular work to display. An artwork is more than its surface appearance; and our aesthetic experience of an artwork depends on our understanding of its context and origin. If we learn that a work is a forgery, we discover that we had faulty information for judging the nature of the achievement. We cannot really understand a work of art when its origin is misrepresented. So we discount our earlier evaluation when we discover that a work is a forgery, for we conclude that our assessment was unreliable.

Although art has been contrasted with reality in the Western tradition, nature, an aspect of reality, is seen as having aesthetic value. The beauty of nature is legendary, and the sublimity (the awesome power and expanse) of nature has been aesthetically valued in our tradition since the eighteenth century. Yuriko Saito contrasts Western attitudes toward nature with those of the Japanese, who do not tend to see nature as sublime. The Western notion of sublimity depends on our seeing nature as a force in opposition to human beings, even as a potential threat. By contrast, the Japanese emphasize human beings' connection with nature, construing emotional identification with nature as aesthetically valuable. The Japanese also find the transience of nature to be extremely moving, while Westerners tend toward John Keats's perspective that "A thing of beauty is a joy forever." The Western approach regards beauty as a means of escaping the ravages of time, while the Japanese see the temporal vulnerability of an aesthetic object as an enhancement of its beauty and value.

John Cage believes twentieth-century technology gives us new opportunities to use art as a means of restoring our intimacy with nature. Cage considers music to be the play of sounds, both intentional and environmental. He describes some of his experimental music, which explores the range of "sonic space," the entirety of sound in our world. Cage hopes that these experiments will help us to hear our environment as resounding, with nature itself making music.

Plato

ART
AND
APPEARANCE

Plato (427–347 B.C.E.) believed that art had tremendous power to influence its audience, and sometimes not for the better. In this excerpt from The Republic, *Socrates proposes that censorship must be part of the ideal state, so that young people are not presented with bad role models, and so that citizens are not inspired to behave in ways that are not consistent with reason.*

. . . And truly, I said, many other considerations assure me that we were entirely right in our organization of the state, and especially, I think, in the matter of poetry.

What about it? he said.

In refusing to admit at all so much of it as is imitative, for that it is certainly not to be received is, I think, still more plainly apparent now that we have distinguished the several parts of the soul.

What do you mean?

Why, between ourselves—for you will not betray me to the tragic poets and all other imitators—that kind of art seems to be a corruption of the mind of all listeners who do not possess as an antidote a knowledge of its real nature.

What is your idea in saying this? he said.

I must speak out, I said, though a certain love and reverence for Homer that has possessed me from a boy would stay me from speaking. For he appears to have been the first teacher and beginner of all these beauties of tragedy. Yet all the same we must not honor a man above truth, but, as I say, speak our minds. . . .

Could you tell me in general what imitation is? For neither do I myself quite apprehend what it would be at. . . .

In the present case, then, let us take any multiplicity you please; for example, there are many couches and tables.

Of course.

But these utensils imply, I suppose, only two ideas or forms, one of a couch and one of a table.

Yes.

And are we not also in the habit of saying that the craftsman who produces either of them fixes his eyes on the idea or form,

Plato, *The Republic*, trans. Paul Shorey, *The Collected Dialogues of Plato, Including the Letters*, ed. Edith Hamilton and Huntington Cairns, Bollingen LXXI, Book X (Princeton: Princeton UP, 1961) 819–33.

and so makes in the one case the couches and in the other the tables that we use, and similarly of other things? For surely no craftsman makes the idea itself. How could he?

By no means.

But now consider what name you would give to this craftsman.

What one?

Him who makes all the things that all handicraftsmen severally produce.

A truly clever and wondrous man you tell of.

Ah, but wait, and you will say so indeed, for this same handicraftsman is not only able to make all implements, but he produces all plants and animals, including himself, and thereto earth and heaven and the gods and all things in heaven and in Hades under the earth.

A most marvelous Sophist, he said.

Are you incredulous? said I. Tell me, do you deny altogether the possibility of such a craftsman, or do you admit that in a sense there could be such a creator of all these things, and in another sense not? Or do you not perceive that you yourself would be able to make all these things in a way?

And in what way, I ask you, he said.

There is no difficulty, said I, but it is something that the craftsman can make everywhere and quickly. You could do it most quickly if you should choose to take a mirror and carry it about everywhere. You will speedily produce the sun and all the things in the sky, and speedily the earth and yourself and the other animals and implements and plants and all the objects of which we just now spoke.

Yes, he said, the appearance of them, but not the reality and the truth.

Excellent, said I, and you come to the aid of the argument opportunely. For I take it that the painter too belongs to this class of producers, does he not?

Of course.

But you will say, I suppose, that his creations are not real and true. And yet, after a

fashion, the painter too makes a couch, does he not?

Yes, he said, the appearance of one, he too.

What of the cabinetmaker? Were you not just now saying that he does not make the idea or form which we say is the real couch, the couch in itself, but only some particular couch?

Yes, I was.

Then if he does not make that which really is, he could not be said to make real being but something that resembles real being but is not that. But if anyone should say that being in the complete sense belongs to the work of the cabinetmaker or to that of any other handicraftsman, it seems that he would say what is not true.

That would be the view, he said, of those who are versed in this kind of reasoning.

We must not be surprised, then, if this too is only a dim adumbration in comparison with reality.

No, we must not.

Shall we, then, use these very examples in our quest for the true nature of this imitator?

If you please, he said.

We get, then, these three couches, one, that in nature, which, I take it, we would say that God produces, or who else?

No one, I think.

And then there was one which the carpenter made.

Yes, he said.

And one which the painter. Is not that so?

So be it.

The painter, then, the cabinetmaker, and God, there are these three presiding over three kinds of couches.

Yes, three.

Now God, whether because he so willed or because some compulsion was laid upon him not to make more than one couch in nature, so wrought and created one only, the couch which really and in itself is. But two or more such were never created by God and never will come into being.

How so? he said.

Because, said I, if he should make only two, there would again appear one of which they both would possess the form or idea, and that would be the couch that really is in and of itself, and not the other two.

Right, he said.

God, then, I take it, knowing this and wishing to be the real author of the couch that has real being and not of some particular couch, nor yet a particular cabinetmaker, produced it in nature unique.

So it seems.

Shall we, then, call him its true and natural begetter, or something of the kind?

That would certainly be right, he said, since it is by and in nature that he has made this and all other things.

And what of the carpenter? Shall we not call him the creator of a couch?

Yes.

Shall we also say that the painter is the creator and maker of that sort of thing?

By no means.

What will you say he is in relation to the couch.

This, said he, seems to me the most reasonable designation for him, that he is the imitator of the thing which those others produce.

Very good, said I. The producer of the product three removes from nature you call the imitator?

By all means, he said.

This, then, will apply to the maker of tragedies also, if he is an imitator and is in his nature three removes from the king and the truth, as are all other imitators.

It would seem so.

We are in agreement, then, about the imitator. But tell me now this about the painter. Do you think that what he tries to imitate is in each case that thing itself in nature or the works of the craftsmen?

The works of the craftsmen, he said.

Is it the reality of them or the appearance? Define that further point.

What do you mean? he said.

This. Does a couch differ from itself according as you view it from the side or the front or in any other way? Or does it differ not at all in fact though it appears different, and so of other things?

That is the way of it, he said. It appears other but differs not at all.

Consider, then, this very point. To which is painting directed in every case, to the imitation of reality as it is or of appearance as it appears? Is it an imitation of a phantasm or of the truth?

Of a phantasm, he said.

Then the mimetic art is far removed from truth, and this, it seems, is the reason why it can produce everything, because it touches or lays hold of only a small part of the object and that a phantom, as, for example, a painter, we say, will paint us a cobbler, a carpenter, and other craftsmen, though he himself has no expertness in any of these arts, but nevertheless if he were a good painter, by exhibiting at a distance his picture of a carpenter he would deceive children and foolish men, and make them believe it to be a real carpenter.

Why not?

But for all that, my friend, this, I take it, is what we ought to bear in mind in all such cases. When anyone reports to us of someone, that he has met a man who knows all the crafts and everything else that men severally know, and that there is nothing that he does not know more exactly than anybody else, our tacit rejoinder must be that he is a simple fellow, who apparently has met some magician or sleight-of-hand man and imitator and has been deceived by him into the belief that he is all-wise, because of his own inability to put to the proof and distinguish knowledge, ignorance, and imitation.

Most true, he said.

Then, said I, have we not next to scrutinize tragedy and its leader Homer, since some people tell us that these poets know all the arts and all things human pertaining to virtue and vice, and all things divine? For the good poet, if he is to poetize things rightly, must, they argue, create with knowledge or else be unable to create. So we must consider whether these critics have not fallen in with such imitators and been deceived by them, so that looking upon their works they cannot perceive that these are three removes from reality, and easy to produce without knowledge of the truth. For it is phantoms, not realities, that they produce. Or is there something in their claim, and do good poets really know the things about which the multitude fancy they speak well?

We certainly must examine the matter, he said.

Do you suppose, then, that if a man were able to produce both the exemplar and the semblance, he would be eager to abandon himself to the fashioning of phantoms and set this in the forefront of his life as the best thing he had?

I do not.

But, I take it, if he had genuine knowledge of the things he imitates he would far rather devote himself to real things than to the imitation of them, and would endeavor to leave after him many noble deeds and works as memorials of himself, and would be more eager to be the theme of praise than the praiser.

I think so, he said, for there is no parity in the honor and the gain.

Let us not, then, demand a reckoning from Homer or any other of the poets on other matters by asking them, if any one of them was a physician and not merely an imitator of a physician's talk, what men any poet, old or new, is reported to have restored to health as Asclepius did, or what disciples of the medical art he left after him as Asclepius did his descendants, and let us dismiss the other arts and not question them about them. But concerning the greatest and finest things of which Homer undertakes to speak, wars and generalship and the administration of cities and the education of men, it surely is fair to question him and ask, "Friend Homer, if you are not at the third remove from truth and reality in human

excellence, being merely that creator of phantoms whom we defined as the imitator, but if you are even in the second place and were capable of knowing what pursuits make men better or worse in private or public life, tell us what city was better governed owing to you, even as Lacedaemon was because of Lycurgus, and many other cities great and small because of other legislators. But what city credits you with having been a good legislator and having benefited them? Italy and Sicily say this of Charondas and we of Solon. But who says it of you?" Will he be able to name any?

I think not, said Glaucon. . . .

Shall we, then, lay it down that all the poetic tribe, beginning with Homer, are imitators of images of excellence and of the other things that they "create," and do not lay hold on truth, but, as we were just now saying, the painter will fashion, himself knowing nothing of the cobbler's art, what appears to be a cobbler to him and likewise to those who know nothing but judge only by forms and colors?

Certainly.

And similarly, I suppose, we shall say that the poet himself, knowing nothing but how to imitate, lays on with words and phrases the colors of the several arts in such fashion that others equally ignorant, who see things only through words, will deem his words most excellent, whether he speak in rhythm, meter, and harmony about cobbling or generalship or anything whatever. So mighty is the spell that these adornments naturally exercise, though when they are stripped bare of their musical coloring and taken by themselves, I think you know what sort of a showing these sayings of the poets make. For you, I believe, have observed them.

I have, he said.

Do they not, said I, resemble the faces of adolescents, young but not really beautiful, when the bloom of youth abandons them?

By all means, he said.

Come, then, said I, consider this point. The creator of the phantom, the imitator, we say, knows nothing of the reality but only the appearance. Is not that so?

Yes.

Let us not, then, leave it half said but consider it fully.

Speak on, he said.

The painter, we say, will paint both reins and a bit.

Yes.

But the maker will be the cobbler and the smith.

Certainly.

Does the painter, then, know the proper quality of reins and bit? Or does not even the maker, the cobbler, and the smith know that, but only the man who understands the use of these things, the horseman?

Most true.

And shall we not say that the same holds true of everything?

What do you mean?

That there are some three arts concerned with everything, the user's art, the maker's, and the imitator's.

Yes.

Now do not the excellence, the beauty, the rightness of every implement, living thing, and action refer solely to the use for which each is made or by nature adapted?

That is so.

It quite necessarily follows, then, that the user of anything is the one who knows most of it by experience, and that he reports to the maker the good or bad effects in use of the thing he uses. As, for example, the flute player reports to the flute maker which flutes respond and serve rightly in flute playing, and will order the kind that must be made, and the other will obey and serve him.

Of course.

The one, then, possessing knowledge, reports about the goodness or the badness of the flutes, and the other, believing, will make them.

Yes.

Then in respect of the same implement the maker will have right belief about its excellence and defects from association with the man who knows and being compelled to listen to him, but the user will have true knowledge.

Certainly.

And will the imitator from experience or use have knowledge whether the things he portrays are or are not beautiful and right, or will he, from compulsory association with the man who knows and taking orders from him for the right making of them, have right opinion?

Neither. . . .

On this, then, as it seems, we are fairly agreed, that the imitator knows nothing worth mentioning of the things he imitates, but that imitation is a form of play, not to be taken seriously, and that those who attempt tragic poetry, whether in iambics or heroic verse, are all altogether imitators.

By all means. . . .

And the same things appear bent and straight to those who view them in water and out, or concave and convex, owing to similar errors of vision about colors, and there is obviously every confusion of this sort in our souls. And so scene painting in its exploitation of this weakness of our nature falls nothing short of witchcraft, and so do jugglery and many other such contrivances.

True.

And have not measuring and numbering and weighing proved to be most gracious aids to prevent the domination in our soul of the apparently greater or less or more or heavier, and to give the control to that which has reckoned and numbered or even weighed?

Certainly.

But this surely would be the function of the part of the soul that reasons and calculates.

Why, yes, of that.

And often when this has measured and declares that certain things are larger or that some are smaller than the others or equal, there is at the same time an appearance of the contrary.

Yes. . . .

This, then, was what I wished to have agreed upon when I said that poetry, and in general the mimetic art, produces a product that is far removed from truth in the accomplishment of its task, and associates with the part in us that is remote from intelligence, and is its companion and friend for no sound and true purpose.

By all means, said he.

Mimetic art, then, is an inferior thing cohabiting with an inferior and engendering inferior offspring.

It seems so.

Does that, said I, hold only for vision or does it apply also to hearing and to what we call poetry?

Presumably, he said, to that also.

Let us not, then, trust solely to the plausible analogy from painting, but let us approach in turn that part of the mind to which mimetic poetry appeals and see whether it is the inferior or the nobly serious part.

So we must.

Let us, then, put the question thus. Mimetic poetry, we say, imitates human beings acting under compulsion or voluntarily, and as a result of their actions supposing themselves to have fared well or ill and in all this feeling either grief or joy. Did we find anything else but this?

Nothing.

Is a man, then, in all this of one mind with himself, or just as in the domain of sight there was faction and strife and he held within himself contrary opinions at the same time about the same things, so also in our actions there is division and strife of the man with himself? But I recall that there is no need now of our seeking agreement on this point, for in our former discussion we were sufficiently agreed that our soul at any one moment teems with countless such self-contradictions.

Rightly, he said. . . .

When a good and reasonable man, said I, experiences such a stroke of fortune as the loss of a son or anything else that he holds most dear, we said, I believe, then too, that he will bear it more easily than the other sort.

Assuredly.

But now let us consider this. Will he feel no pain, or, since that is impossible, shall we say that he will in some sort be moderate in his grief?

That, he said, is rather the truth.

Tell me now this about him. Do you think he will be more likely to resist and fight against his grief when he is observed by his equals or when he is in solitude alone by himself?

He will be much more restrained, he said, when he is on view.

But when left alone, I fancy, he will permit himself many utterances which, if heard by another, would put him to shame, and will do many things which he would not consent to have another see him doing.

So it is, he said.

Now is it not reason and law that exhorts him to resist, while that which urges him to give way to his grief is the bare feeling itself?

True. . . .

And is it not obvious that the nature of the mimetic poet is not related to this better part of the soul and his cunning is not framed to please it, if he is to win favor with the multitude, but is devoted to the fretful and complicated type of character because it is easy to imitate?

It is obvious.

This consideration, then, makes it right for us to proceed to lay hold of him and set him down as the counterpart of the painter, for he resembles him in that his creations are inferior in respect of reality, and the fact that his appeal is to the inferior part of the soul and not to the best part is another point of resemblance. And so we may at last say that we should be justified in not admitting him into a well-ordered state, because he stimulates and fosters this element in the soul, and by strengthening it tends to destroy the rational part, just as when in a state one puts bad men in power and turns the city over to them and ruins the better sort. Precisely in the same manner we shall say that the mimetic poet sets up in each individual soul a vicious constitution by fashioning phantoms far removed from reality, and by currying favor with the senseless element that cannot distinguish the greater from the less, but calls the same thing now one, now the other.

By all means.

But we have not yet brought our chief accusation against it. Its power to corrupt, with rare exceptions, even the better sort is surely the chief cause for alarm.

How could it be otherwise, if it really does that?

Listen and reflect. I think you know that the very best of us, when we hear Homer or some other of the makers of tragedy imitating one of the heroes who is in grief, and is delivering a long tirade in his lamentations or chanting and beating his breast, feel pleasure, and abandon ourselves and accompany the representation with sympathy and eagerness, and we praise as an excellent poet the one who most strongly affects us in this way.

I do know it, of course.

But when in our own lives some affliction comes to us, you are also aware that we plume ourselves upon the opposite, on our ability to remain calm and endure, in the belief that this is the conduct of a man, and what we were praising in the theater that of a woman.

I do note that.

Do you think, then, said I, that this praise is rightfully bestowed when, contemplating a character that we would not accept but would be ashamed of in ourselves, we do not abominate it but take pleasure and approve?

No, by Zeus, he said, it does not seem reasonable.

Oh yes, said I, if you would consider it in this way.

In what way?

If you would reflect that the part of the soul that in the former case, in our own misfortunes, was forcibly restrained, and that has hungered for tears and a good cry and satisfaction, because it is its nature to desire these things, is the element in us that the poets satisfy and delight, and that the best element in our nature, since it has never been properly educated by reason or even by habit, then relaxes its guard over the plaintive part, inasmuch as this is contemplating the woes of others and it is no shame to it to praise and pity another who, claiming to be a good man, abandons himself to excess in his grief, but it thinks this vicarious pleasure is so much clear gain, and would not consent to forfeit it by disdaining the poem altogether. That is, I think, because few are capable of reflecting that what we enjoy in others will inevitably react upon ourselves. For after feeding fat the emotion of pity there, it is not easy to restrain it in our own sufferings.

Most true, he said.

Does not the same principle apply to the laughable, namely, that if in comic representations, or for that matter in private talk, you take intense pleasure in buffooneries that you would blush to practice yourself, and do not detest them as base, you are doing the same thing as in the case of the pathetic? For here again what your reason, for fear of the reputation of buffoonery, restrained in yourself when it fain would play the clown, you release in turn, and so, fostering its youthful impudence, let yourself go so far that often ere you are aware you become yourself a comedian in private.

Yes, indeed, he said.

And so in regard to the emotions of sex and anger, and all the appetites and pains and pleasures of the soul which we say accompany all our actions, the effect of poetic imitation is the same. For it waters and fosters these feelings when what we ought to do is to dry them up, and it establishes them as our rulers when they ought to be ruled, to the end that we may be better and happier men instead of worse and more miserable.

I cannot deny it, said he.

Then, Glaucon, said I, when you meet encomiasts of Homer who tell us that this poet has been the educator of Hellas, and that for the conduct and refinement of human life he is worthy of our study and devotion, and that we should order our entire lives by the guidance of this poet, we must love and salute them as doing the best they can, and concede to them that Homer is the most poetic of poets and the first of tragedians, but we must know the truth, that we can admit no poetry into our city save only hymns to the gods and the praises of good men. For if you grant admission to the honeyed Muse in lyric or epic, pleasure and pain will be lords of your city instead of law and that which shall from time to time have approved itself to the general reason as the best.

Most true, he said.

Let us, then, conclude our return to the topic of poetry and our apology, and affirm that we really had good grounds then for dismissing her from our city, since such was her character. For reason constrained us. And let us further say to her, lest she condemn us for harshness and rusticity, that there is from of old a quarrel between philosophy and poetry. For such expressions as "the yelping hound barking at her master and mighty in the idle babble of fools," and "the mob that masters those who are too wise for their own good," and the subtle thinkers who reason that after all they are poor, and countless others are tokens of this ancient enmity. But nevertheless let it be declared that, if the mimetic and dulcet

poetry can show any reason for her existence in a well-governed state, we would gladly admit her, since we ourselves are very conscious of her spell. But all the same it would be impious to betray what we believe to be the truth. Is not that so, friend? Do not you yourself feel her magic and especially when Homer is her interpreter?

Greatly.

Then may she not justly return from this exile after she has pleaded her defense, whether in lyric or other measure?

By all means.

And we would allow her advocates who are not poets but lovers of poetry to plead her cause in prose without meter, and show that she is not only delightful but beneficial to orderly government and all the life of man. And we shall listen benevolently, for it will be clear gain for us if it can be shown that she bestows not only pleasure but benefit.

How could we help being the gainers? said he.

But if not, my friend, even as men who have fallen in love, if they think that the love is not good for them, hard though it be, nevertheless refrain, so we, owing to the love of this kind of poetry inbred in us by our education in these fine polities of ours, will gladly have the best possible case made out for her goodness and truth, but so long as she is unable to make good her defense we shall chant over to ourselves as we listen the reasons that we have given as a countercharm to her spell, to preserve us from slipping back into the childish loves of the multitude, for we have come to see that we must not take such poetry seriously as a serious thing that lays hold on truth, but that he who lends an ear to it must be on his guard fearing for the polity in his soul and must believe what we have said about poetry.

By all means, he said, I concur.

Oscar Wilde

THE
DECAY
OF
LYING

Oscar Wilde (1854–1900) was an Irish poet and playwright, known especially for his devastating wit. He was an advocate of the "art for art's sake movement" (also called "aestheticism"). Among his most famous works are his plays Lady Windermere's Fan *and* The Importance of Being Earnest, *and his novel,* The Picture of Dorian Gray. *In "The Decay of Lying" (1889), which is presented as a dialogue, one of Wilde's characters defends lying as an important display of imagination.*

CYRIL: . . . I should like to ask you a question. What do you mean by saying that life, "poor, probable, uninteresting human life," will try to reproduce the marvels of art? I can quite understand your objection to art being treated as a mirror. You think it would reduce genius to the position of a cracked looking-glass. But you don't mean to say that you seriously believe that Life imitates Art, that Life in fact is the mirror, and Art the reality?

VIVIAN: Certainly I do. Paradox though it may seem—and paradoxes are always dangerous things—it is none the less true that Life imitates art far more than Art imitates life. We have all seen in our own day in England how a certain curious and fascinating type of beauty, invented and emphasised by two imaginative painters, has so influenced Life that whenever one goes to a private view or to an artistic salon one sees, here the mystic eyes of Rossetti's dream, the long ivory throat, the strange square-cut jaw, the loosened shadowy hair that he so ardently loved, there the sweet maidenhood of *The Golden Stair,* the blossom-like mouth and weary loveliness of the *Laus Amoris,* the passion-pale face of

Oscar Wilde, "The Decay of Lying," *Intentions* (New York: Brentano's, 1905) 31–43.

Andromeda, the thin hands and lithe beauty of the Vivien in *Merlin's Dream*. And it has always been so. A great artist invents a type, and Life tries to copy it, to reproduce it in a popular form, like an enterprising publisher. Neither Holbein nor Vandyck found in England what they have given us. They brought their types with them, and Life, with her keen imitative faculty, set herself to supply the master with models. The Greeks, with their quick artistic instinct, understood this, and set in the bride's chamber the statue of Hermes or of Apollo, that she might bear children as lovely as the works of art that she looked at in her rapture or her pain. They knew that Life gains from Art not merely spirituality, depth of thought and feeling, soul-turmoil or soul-peace, but that she can form herself on the very lines and colours of art and can reproduce the dignity of Pheidias as well as the grace of Praxiteles. Hence came their objection to realism. They disliked it on purely social grounds. They felt that it inevitably makes people ugly, and they were perfectly right. We try to improve the conditions of the race by means of good air, free sunlight, wholesome water, and hideous bare buildings for the better housing of the lower orders. But these things merely produce health; they do not produce beauty. For this, Art is required, and the true disciples of the great artist are not his studio-imitators, but those who become like his works of art, be they plastic as in Greek days, or pictorial as in modern times; in a word, Life is Art's best, Art's only pupil. . . .

. . . All that I desire to point out is the general principle that Life imitates Art far more than Art imitates Life, and I feel sure that if you think seriously about it you will find that it is true.

Life holds the mirror up to Art, and either reproduces some strange type imagined by painter or sculptor, or realizes in fact what has been dreamed in fiction. Scientifically speaking, the basis of life—the energy of life, as Aristotle would call it—is simply the desire for expression, and Art is always presenting various forms through which this expression can be attained. Life seizes on them and uses them, even if they be to her own hurt. Young men have committed suicide because Rolla did so, have died by their own hand because by his own hand Werther died. Think of what we owe to the imitation of Christ, of what we owe to the imitation of Cæsar.

CYRIL: The theory is certainly a very curious one, but to make it complete you must show that Nature, no less than Life, is an imitation of Art. Are you prepared to prove that?

VIVIAN: My dear fellow, I am prepared to prove anything.

CYRIL: Nature follows the landscape painter then, and takes her effects from him?

VIVIAN: Certainly. Where, if not from the Impressionists, do we get those wonderful brown fogs that come creeping down our streets, blurring the gas-lamps and changing the houses into monstrous shadows? To whom, if not to them and their master, do we owe the lovely silver mists that brood over our river, and turn to faint forms of fading grace curved bridge and swaying barge? The extraordinary change that has taken place in the climate of London during the last ten years is entirely due to this particular school of Art. You smile. Consider the matter from a scientific or a metaphysical point of view, and you will find that I am right. For what is Nature?

Nature is no great mother who has borne us. She is our creation. It is in our brain that she quickens to life. Things are because we see them, and what we see, and how we see it, depends on the Arts that have influenced us. To look at a thing is very different from seeing a thing. One does not see anything until one sees its beauty. Then, and then only, does it come into existence. At present, people see fogs, not because there are fogs, but because poets and painters have taught them the mysterious loveliness of such effects. There may have been fogs for centuries in London. I dare say there were. But no one saw them, and so we do not know anything about them. They did not exist till Art had invented them. Now, it must be admitted, fogs are carried to excess. They have become the mere mannerism of a clique, and the exaggerated realism of their method gives dull people bronchitis. Where the cultured catch an effect, the uncultured catch cold. And so, let us be humane, and invite Art to turn her wonderful eyes elsewhere. She has done so already, indeed. That white quivering sunlight that one sees now in France, with its strange blotches of mauve, and its restless violet shadows, is her latest fancy, and, on the whole, Nature reproduces it quite admirably. Where she used to give us Corots and Daubignys, she gives us now exquisite Monets and entrancing Pisaros. Indeed there are moments, rare, it is true, but still to be observed from time to time, when Nature becomes absolutely modern. Of course she is not always to be relied upon. The fact is that she is in this unfortunate position. Art creates an incomparable and unique effect, and, having done so, passes on to other things. Nature, upon the other hand, forgetting that imitation can be made the sincerest form of insult, keeps on repeating this effect until we all become absolutely wearied of it. Nobody of any real culture, for instance, ever talks now-a-days about the beauty of a sunset. Sunsets are quite old-fashioned. They belong to the time when Turner was the last note in art. To admire them is a distinct sign of provincialism of temperament. Upon the other hand they go on. Yesterday evening Mrs. Arundel insisted on my coming to the window, and looking at the glorious sky, as she called it. Of course I had to look at it. She is one of those absurdly pretty Philistines, to whom one can deny nothing. And what was it? It was simply a very second-rate Turner, a Turner of a bad period, with all the painter's worst faults exaggerated and over-emphasized. Of course, I am quite ready to admit that Life very often commits the same error. She produces her false Renés and her sham Vautrins, just as Nature gives us, on one day a doubtful Cuyp, and on another a more than questionable Rousseau. Still, Nature irritates one more when she does things of that kind. It seems so stupid, so obvious, so unnecessary. A false Vautrin might be delightful. A doubtful Cuyp is unbearable. However, I don't want to be too hard on Nature. I wish the Channel, especially at Hastings, did not look quite so often like a Henry Moore, grey pearl with yellow lights, but then, when Art is more varied, Nature will, no doubt, be more varied also. That she imitates Art, I don't think even her worst enemy would deny now. It is the one thing that keeps her in touch with civilized man.

Joseph Lyons

PALEOLITHIC AESTHETICS: THE PSYCHOLOGY OF CAVE ART

◆◆◆

Joseph Lyons is professor of psychology at the University of California at Davis. His books include Psychology and the Measure of Man, Experience: An Introduction to a Personal Psychology, *and* Ecology of the Body: Styles of Behavior in Human Life. *Lyons suggests that the placement of cave paintings reveals that primitive humanity had a sense of framing, of separating one order of reality from another.*

DISCOVERIES AND THEORIES

The story of the modern discovery of paleolithic cave art is now widely known. Once the notion had been accepted, in the face of curious personal and scholarly resistance, that artistic achievement of a very high order had existed at least as far back as 20,000 B.C., a mounting tempo of exploration led in a very short time to most of the major discoveries of cave painting and shelter sculpture. Sufficient material is now available for answering the major questions of dating—when and in what sequence the works were produced.

A "schedule" presented by Movius, based on data from radiocarbon tests, gives the following as the time spans of the major paleolithic cultures. The Mousterian culture appeared about 46,000 B.C. and lasted until about 27,000 B.C.; overlapping with it was the culture known as Perigordian I (43,000 B.C.–30,000 B.C.), of which a later version, the Gravettian, lasted from 25,000 B.C. to 20,000 B.C. Aurignacian culture, in five phases, extended from 35,000 B.C. to 17,000 B.C.; the Magdalenian from 18,000 B.C. to 11,000 B.C.; and the Solutrean from 20,000 B.C. to 15,000 B.C.

In all these phases, remarkably high levels of technical skill and artistic achievement are apparent, beginning with the earliest known artistic works which were produced for their own sake rather than as more or less useful decorative additions to other objects. These were the engraved, and probably painted, blocks or slabs of stone produced by Aurignacian hunters about 30,000 B.C., and followed very soon by engravings on pieces of bone and antler.

Joseph Lyons, "Paleolithic Aesthetics: The Psychology of Cave Art," *Journal of Aesthetics and Art Criticism* 26.1 (1967): 107–14.

Beginning about 25,000 B.C., these people were replaced over large areas of Europe by a vigorous and far-ranging group of hunters, the Gravettian, who produced mainly small, and therefore portable, sculptured objects, or *art mobilier*, many of them in the form of figurines of the female figure. One of the most striking of these Venuses, as they have been collectively named, suggests the technical level that had already been attained. Discovered at a campsite at Dolńi Věstonice, in Czechoslovakia, this is a wonderfully stylized female figure about 11.5 cm. in height, in which the lines emphasizing the sexual characteristics have been organized into a continuous flow of curves. Even in technique it is outstanding: it was modelled in a yellow clay that had been mixed with ash from burnt mammoth bones and then baked. Similarly, a skilled engraver has described the Aurignacian artifact known as the "La Colombière pebble" as the work of "a highly experienced artisan who had developed complete control of his technique and the medium in which he was working. He was an exceedingly skillful engraver, and not a beginner in any sense of the word." On this pebble, clearly and strikingly delineated, appear, on the one side, a horse, a reindeer, an ibex, an incomplete bear, a lion, and a bison, and on the other side, one complete and two incomplete rhinoceroses, a horse, a reindeer, a lion's head, and parts of three other horses—all in correct proportion, all lively and detailed, with some use of shading to represent mane or fur, and with attempts at depicting perspective. The size of this stone is 11.5 cm. by 8.3 cm.

The very high level of skill, the wide range of techniques, and the great artistic merit of the major part of these productions, all suggest that we have here not simply a historical problem concerning the emergence of novel cultural patterns—although there is this element—but more significantly, a socio-psychological problem of fundamental importance. That is, what is to be explained here is not the fact that art of a certain type emerged, but more important, the appearance of an endeavor that must have enlisted the total vital energy of a culture, resulting in an artistic explosion not to be equalled for another ten thousand years.

The significance of this phenomenon has hardly escaped the attention of historians of art, and as a consequence a number of theories have been proposed in answer to what may be termed the *historical* question: what were the causative factors which led to the emergence of art? That is to say, *how* did art first appear? For purposes of summary, theories in this regard may be reduced to two, paralleling two major trends in the history of aesthetics: a theory of "play," and a theory of "utility." The first of these, which in its modern form perhaps goes back to the influence of Johann Herder, postulates a natural and non-practical impulse, an art for art's sake; and so it stresses Croce's "divine joy of the creator" as well as the idea of art serving no end other than itself. An original version has recently been offered by Bataille, who argued that art is that form of play in which primitive man, in toying with the transgression of limits imposed by death and sexuality, expressed his deepest relation to the taboos that defined his very humanness. In the utility theory of art, it is suggested that all activity, including the artistic, subserves practical and ultimately social ends. Such primitive customs as smearing corpses or skeletons with red paint, presumably to indicate life, have been proposed as origins of the practice of adorning the body, which in turn is thought to have led to development of the graphic arts. . . . In its most extreme form, the utility theory is maintained by anthropologists who stress social and economic influences on the forms of human activity. Weltfish, for example, considers the "close relationship between art and industrial production" and concludes that "art emerges not as an abstract vision but as a celebration of the skill of work well done and enjoyed." . . .

REQUIREMENTS FOR A THEORY

Although the theory of sympathetic magic appears to explain a great deal and to bring together a large number of facts, it shares the difficulty common to all such explanations of *how* art came about; it attempts to elucidate the very behaviors and psychological processes that it assumes in order to make the theory hang together. Because explanations of the origin of art are also attempts at understanding the genesis of certain modes of behavior, they are at bottom essays in psychological theory. Thus, the view that cave paintings were produced as central items in an elaborate group ritual assumes the prior existence of rather complex societal and religious patterns, with all the symbolic and imaginative developments presupposed by this view. If, as Giedion remarks, "art came in being as a direct response to his inner sight," a theory concerning art must become a theory concerning the genesis of the psychological phenomenon of "inner sight." If "inner sight" developed, or if, as Luquet argued, the resemblance of "accidental appearances" to common animals was so striking as to lead to deliberate imitation, an acceptable theory can hardly avoid, first of all, an explanation of the perceptual processes involved. Animals do not seem to notice such striking resemblances, nor do children before the age of two years; and the 50,000 or more years of humanoid development, including the discovery of fire and the use of tools, before this discovery occurred suggests that it was not a simple but a radical step to take. It should therefore provide us with a starting point, in the form of a general question: what is the nature of the psychological and behavioral innovation that was necessary in order to make art possible?

An equally important question, concerning *locus*, must also fit into a viable theory. By *locus* I mean, not simply the facts of the location of art works—although this too provides a major, and significant, puzzle in regard to cave paintings—but broadly speaking, the question of the kind and style of art that was produced in each time and place and by each culture. It has long been recognized that the major cultures each produced a style and kind of art work that was unique to it, and further that this resulted in a clear-cut sequence over the span of some 25,000 years. The earliest productions, in the form of engravings on movable rock slabs, gave way to engravings on pieces of bone, and then to portable figurines; subsequent groups specialized in life-size rock friezes at the entrances to their open-air shelters; and Paleolithic art culminated in wall paintings placed deep within caves. The locations of the latter are, additionally, invariably striking in terms of their accessibility—that is, they are always either extremely inaccessible, located in places that can be reached only with great difficulty, or else they are found in spots so chosen as to be difficult to reach but strikingly obvious once they are found. The painting of a woolly rhinoceros in the cave of Font-de-Gaume is a not atypical example of the former: it is in a "cleft so narrow that it had to be drawn reflected in a mirror for there was no possibility of getting a straight view of it." [Brown] The famous "Black Hall" of Niaux exemplifies the latter phenomenon, for it is located some 800 yards into the cave, at the end of twisting, narrow, pitch-dark corridors—but the paintings themselves, like the remarkable figure known as the "Sorcerer" in the cave of Les Trois Frères, are set off in unmistakable fashion on a sharply delimited panel. Even more decisive evidence concerning the importance of a precise location for cave painting is the fact that the same spot may have been used over and over, almost without regard for clarity of presentation. In one shelter in Spain, Kühn found persistent overpainting on some areas which had unpainted spots immediately on either side. The use of a favored spot sometimes persisted over a period of a thousand years, as is evidenced in the changing fauna depicted at Niaux.

FIELD AND FRAME IN PERCEPTION

When a particular spot which stands out from its background is selected for painting a picture, it suggests a kind of natural *frame*. This device, in constant use since perhaps the second century B.C., has now become so familiar to us, either in the form of a structural line around a picture or in the form of a location or a base for sculpture, that we are prone to overlook its perceptual import. From *Gestalttheorie* we learn that the contour is perceived as part of what it outlines; and so it is perceptually feasible that a frame will be fitted around the picture so as to bind and contain it. But to what purpose? Why do we invariably thus mark off the area of the picture or the space occupied by the statue? It can only be because we mean to indicate in this way the simultaneous presence of two *kinds* of space—and if one of these spaces is the familiar real one in which we move and act, the other can be none other than a less familiar, an *un*real space. We all know this, of course, perhaps without even thinking about the matter. Adults who see a painting on a wall are not likely to perceive its scene as part of the visual field to which the wall itself belongs. Yet, they accomplish this trick of separating the larger from the smaller space without giving thought to the process as it occurs nor to the long development necessarily involved. Animals below the level of the higher apes apparently never learn to make the separation, as witness the inability of even intelligent dogs to respond appropriately to a two-dimensional representation such as a drawing or a TV picture. Within the human culture, the trick is learned by every growing child: finally, he comes to recognize each unreal representation of a known object, even if it is a never-seen view of horse, colored green, and one-twenty-fifth the size of the real thing. In this way he grows into the typically human world, a

world of symbols; and in the end, though he shares emotion with animals, he is alone in his possession of a "symbolic imagination."

At this point some speculation is in order so as to re-create a supposed beginning toward this perceptual achievement. If an animal comes across a rock which happens to bear an accidental resemblance to some other object, such as an animal, he will pass it by. But consider what ensues when once this kind of resemblance is grasped by a Cro-Magnon hunter. He finds a rock which, when held in his hand, seems to him to "look like" a mammoth standing off in the distance. He looks down at the rock, then up at the real animal—and in that instant, we may suppose, there is created for him the first small bit of imagined and unreal space. This "accident" which he holds is unique in all his experience; it is both real and not real. Now whenever he determines to look at this rock in a certain special way, he has at his command a new and different, above all an infinitely unlimited, world which can exist together with the real and accustomed world of action.

We should note this, that the distinction the hunter makes is not a perceptual one, for by perception alone—as infrahuman animals clearly show us—the distinction might never be made. But once it has occurred—in whatever manner and by whatever miracle of change—then two classes of perceptual object become available, one to be gained through the world of real action, the other reserved for occasions which deserve the effort of creation. In a strictly utilitarian sense, nothing has been gained; and we can imagine one sage Perigordian hunter saying sternly to another, "Resemblance carves no flints." It is at first merely perceptual play; for this is what play is, the manipulation of one's sensory experience in new dimensions that eventuate in no change in the world's significance. One learns to find stones that "look like," one treasures them and carries them around;

they become talismans, worn smooth by lifetimes and perhaps even centuries of such use. Indeed, such stones have been dug out of Neanderthal debris, and so the apperceptive trick which first gave rise to the life of the imagination may be even older than we had thought.

Now, we may suppose, these Mousterian nomads were ready for the next step. They were already familiar with the *representing* object, which existed in its own ideal space and had already become the first token to be venerated, even if only in terms of fiercely insistent possession. Their toolmaking skills had been developed to a high degree. Surely it must have happened, as they tried to express the full meaning of their attachment to the huge wandering herds on which their own lives depended, that some toolmakers more or less accidentally formed, or shaped, or improved, stone figures that resembled the animals of their dreams. The accident of fortuitous realism became the deliberate act of intentional realism: here imagination was tied to action, and so all the vitality of these people might now be directed, in one great surge of creative expression, toward fashioning replicas. But a problem, almost technical in nature, presented itself very soon. How was the representing object known? In what way did it identify itself? It had no frame, so to speak. It was distinguished from the perceived real object primarily by the fact that it could be hefted and turned, caressed or crushed at will. If it were placed at a distance, to be viewed like any other percept, would it now differ from the real thing? In short, how could its magical quality be guaranteed?

The problem must have become especially acute when engraving—a skill already highly developed in the crafts of decorative carving on bone and antler—began to be utilized to represent the *outline* of the representing object. We know that this occurred during the Perigordian era. What had next to be mastered was the idea of the encompassing frame, a limit that would mark off the unreal from the real space and thus would enclose the unreal object in its own space. Whereas the initial step had been one in which imagination was born, in the realization that one object resembled another, the new step of creating a frame was largely a conceptual achievement. It meant, essentially, that not merely the unreal object as such, but the unreal space in which this object resided, had come to be grasped. The frame was the device for isolating and setting off this space. And with this achievement, the way was opened for the graphic arts of wall sculpture and painting. Paleolithic man was no longer tied to representing the world of his imagination in objects that were small enough to be carried from one real place to another. He could apply hi enormous technical skills to the creation of art forms that were limited only by one demand: that they repeat, over and over, the miraculous evocation of the space of the imagined within a stated frame.

The next great artistic explosion occurred among the Solutrean peoples, dwellers in open-air shelters along the sides of great valleys in southern France; and quite naturally, it consisted of life-size, monumental friezes of animals which they carved into the rock walls of their living places. Freed to express their imaginative efforts, they found just the kind of location that would serve as frame for the space they meant to fill. This was the protected overhang with a smooth back wall, forming almost a natural chapel in which the sculptured frieze could dominate the real space around it. A quite different culture, whose people lived along the Mediterranean coast of Spain some few thousand years later—the dates are not known with any certainty at all—also discovered this location as frame in their own open-air shelter. Their distinctive form of Levantine art was a lively kind of small drawing of persons in frantic action, charming, detailed, and wonderfully skilled and sophisticated. And a group of hunters who occupied the Lascaux cave at about the time of the Solutreans made still another discovery, that an area within can also serve as chapel. The Great Hall of Lascaux, where the majority of their paintings are on permanent exhibit, formed in effect a natural art gallery—a sheet of gleaming white calcite, marked off by a ledge about waist high, which covered the walls of that mysterious, cavernous room.

The sequence in which the forms of paleolithic art developed now falls into a logical order. It began with portable pieces of sculpture, the result of the discovery of the representing object. The second major form, the life-size, deep bas relief, helped to make a bridge between sculpture and painting following the discovery of the frame. Finally, at the high point of prehistoric art, painting became possible—at first in the form of outlines and silhouettes, then gradually with the elaborate use of colors and shading—when the concept of the frame was adapted to the conditions of locations within caves. The painters of the Magdalenian era had to find a location for each work which was startling, set off from the real world; and this they achieved by seeking out the innermost recess, or by discovering a panel or alcove that formed figure against a ground, or on rare occasions by the fortunate circumstance of a naturally occurring gallery, as at Lascaux, or a natural set of sculptured forms in the rock, as at Altamira. In each case the goal and purpose were the same: first, to find a canvas for their talents, which meant to find a naturally occurring frame, and then to use and re-use this selected space. Without exception, the location of the great works of prehistoric cave art can be understood in these terms.

ART AND MAGIC

Now, we may suppose, still another momentous development occurred. The places self-selected for these enduring works, into which the greatest energy of these people was poured, invariably possessed characteristics that made them special. They were deep within the caves, in darkness that required flickering and smoky lights to be seen, in locations that demanded almost the effort one would need to enter another world. Even after the viewer had come to this strange place, the works could be fully seen only if he placed himself in the proper stance, participating, as it were, in the full effect of a shadowed, flickering, shimmering, and unreal world. In particular, the primitive hunter whose life pattern was one of direct action, when brought to this place and required to let himself be caught up in the mystery of viewing these vibrant totems, must have been particularly overcome. To him this must have seemed like the very entrance to a different world. And so, we suppose, this is how magic was born—as the child of man's new found imagination and of the circumstances in which he had to display his imagination's works. In place of the claim that art arose in the service of magic, we have now proposed a reversed sequence, to make the argument psychologically sound: that art arose first, in an apperceptive and perceptual leap forward, and that magic developed as a set of practices taking full advantage of the viewer's participation in the unreal world of represented objects. Ritual practices, and perhaps even forms of sympathetic magic to insure success in the hunt, would then have emerged within a short time—and may have been developed by later generations of viewers who had already lost track of their ancestors who had produced the first paintings. But even the painters who succeeded the earliest artists and utilized the same magical locations over and over never deviated from their primary aim—to make, and remake, a single overwhelming discovery, thereby creating for themselves the realm of the represented, the symbolized, the imagined. Only in these terms can we make sense out of the curious fact that, though they were quite capable of doing so, they never attempted to organize the area *within* a frame so as to depict a real setting. "Although there may sometimes have been an attempt to make use of natural surfaces, no deliberate effort to indicative vegetation, a horizon, or any kind of landscape was ever made."* The artists of the Stone Age were occupied only with separating out a represented object from the real object of Nature which appeared in the visual field. Indeed, the solution to the major problems posed by the geometry of represented space was not fully achieved until the fifteenth century, when methods for representing pictorial perspective were finally understood.

Only recently have we ourselves taken to displaying paintings that are not marked off by the ubiquitous frame—thereby recognizing at long last that viewers may be capable, without assistance, of keeping apart the two spaces, the real and the represented. This change may have one other significance as well. When the frame is removed, and the boundary between real and unreal eliminated, then the viewer is invited to join the artist in his own magical space. Recent trends in the visual arts, whether of painting or sculpture or theater, seem to be pointing in just this direction: the artist invites the viewer to join him, and they become collaborative partners in a living experience, not simply two role-bound persons whose places are fixed by a frame or a proscenium. The circle may have now come full swing, after more than 30,000 years. If art, beginning in imagination, led to magic, it may be that now, in the rediscovery of the magical experience, we will be led back into the pristine experience of art.

*A. Laming, *Lascaux* (London, 1959) 26.

Denis Dutton

ARTISTIC CRIMES: THE PROBLEM OF FORGERY IN THE ARTS

Denis Dutton is senior lecturer in philosophy at the University of Canterbury in Christchurch, New Zealand, and the editor of Philosophy and Literature. *He has also done fieldwork in New Guinea. His books include* The Concept of Creativity in Science and Art *and* The Forger's Art: Forgery and the Philosophy of Art. *Dutton believes that we are justified in our disappointment when we discover that an artwork is a foregery. When we judge an artwork, we rely on what we know about the kind of achievement it represents, precisely the knowledge that forgery undercuts.*

The concept of forgery is a touchstone of criticism. If the existence of forgeries—and their occasional acceptance as authentic works of art—has been too often dismissed or ignored in the theory of criticism, it may be because of the forger's special power to make the critic look ridiculous. Awkward as it is, critics have heaped the most lavish praise on art objects which have turned out to be forged. The suspicion this arouses is, of course, that the critics were led to praise the forgery for the wrong reasons in the first place. Since the aesthetic object as perceived is no different after the revelation that it is forged, the inference to be drawn is that it had previously been critically valued not for its intrinsic aesthetic properties, but because it was believed to be the work of an esteemed artist.

Natural as this suspicion is, it represents a point of view I shall seek to discredit in the following discussion. Everyone recognizes that the proper identification of an art object as genuine or forged is crucial as regards monetary value, that forgery has moral implications, that there are important historical reasons for wanting to distinguish the genuine from the faked art object. But there are many who also believe that when we come down to assessing the *aesthetic*

Denis Dutton, "Artistic Crimes: The Problem of Forgery in the Arts," *British Journal of Aesthetics* 19:4 (1979): 302–14.

merits of an art object the question of authenticity is irrelevant. Take, for example, the celebrated case of Han van Meegeren. The facts are familiar enough: van Meegeren tried to make for himself a career as a painter in Holland in the years after the First World War. Critics refused to recognize what he took to be his genius, and he decided to get even. His plan was to forge a Vermeer, and after the painting had been discovered and lauded by critics, he would reveal to the world that Han van Meegeren had painted it. The critics would have either to admit that they were fallible (and perhaps fallible in their previous estimate of his talents) or, if they were to uphold their claims to authority, they would have to allow that he stood with Vermeer among the supreme masters of art. Van Meegeren went about his business with the greatest care, using only badger hair brushes lest a modern bristle imbedded in the paint should give him away, crushing his own lapis lazuli for pigment, studying seventeenth-century formulae for varnishes, collecting old canvases, and perfecting a method for producing a very convincing *craquelure* in the painted surface.

He might have started out with the notion of humiliating the critics, but, as it turned out, his first forgery was too profitable for that. He decided to make another, and then another. Before the end of his career as a forger, he had painted over a dozen Vermeers, Terborchs, and de Hoochs. How was he found out? Interestingly, not on account of suspicions about the authenticity of his paintings, some of which might even have been accepted to this day were it not for the fact that one had found its way into the collection of Hermann Göring. Since van Meegeren was known to have dealt with these paintings, he was arrested soon after the end of the war and tried for having sold a Dutch national treasure to the enemy. It was only at his trial that he confessed to having created this famous "masterpiece" and others himself. Some critics refused to believe it then and even continued to disbelieve it in later years (though new dating techniques dealing with the relative quantities of lead and certain radium isotopes in the pigment have now confirmed that van Meegeren was telling the truth).

But, of course, why should anybody have believed him then? Here was an accused criminal claiming that he had painted acknowledged masterpieces by Vermeer, including *Christ and the Disciples at Emmaus.* . . .

The van Meegeren story is just one good example of the general problem of forgery in the arts. I say "arts" in the plural because I believe that in one form or another the problem can arise in all of them. The problem may be stated quite simply thus: if an aesthetic object has been widely admired and is discovered to be a forgery, a copy, or a misattribution, why reject it? A painting has hung for years on a museum wall, giving delight to generations of art lovers. One day it is revealed to be a forgery, and is immediately removed from view. But why? The discovery that a work of art is forged, as say, a van Meegeren Vermeer, does not alter the perceived qualities of the work. Hence it can make no *aesthetic* difference whether a work is forged or not. At least this is how one approach to this question goes, an approach which has had the support of such able defenders as Alfred Lessing and Arthur Koestler. Koestler, for instance, insists that an object's status as original or forged is extraneous information, incidental to its intrinsic aesthetic properties. Thus the person who pays an enormous sum for an original but who would have no interest in a reproduction which he could not tell from the original (perhaps a Picasso pen and ink drawing), or worse, who chooses an aesthetically inferior original in preference to an excellent and superior forgery (or reproduction), is said to be at best confused and at worst a snob.

In a discussion which is largely in agreement with this, Lessing mentions that the possibility of forgery exists only in the "creative" but not in the "performing" arts. While I will argue that in certain respects this distinction itself is dubious, regarding the possibility of forgery it is surely misleading. Consider for a moment Smith and Jones, who have just finished listening to a new recording of Liszt's Transcendental Études. Smith is transfixed. He says, "What beautiful artistry! The pianist's tone is superb, his control absolute, his speed and accuracy dazzling. Truly an electric performance!" Jones responds with a sigh. "Yeah, it was electric all right. Or to be more precise, it was electronic. He recorded the music at practice tempo and the engineers speeded it up on a rotating head recorder." Poor Smith—his enthusiasm evaporates.

But, really, ought it to? If Smith cannot with his ears discriminate between the pianist's technical accomplishments and an engineer's turning a knob, why should it make any difference to him? In fact, looking at the situation from Koestler's perspective, we will have to consider that Smith is a snob, or at least somehow confused. But surely there is something legitimate in Smith's response; surely there is more to this than can be accounted for by saying that Smith is simply letting extra-aesthetic considerations influence his aesthetic response to the piano performance.

I raise this example in connection with Lessing's claim that "the concept of forgery applies only to the creative and not the performing arts." The distinction between so-called creative and performing arts has certain obvious uses: we would not wish to confuse the actor and the playwright, the conductor and the composer, the dancer and the choreographer. And yet this distinction (often employed invidiously against the performer) can cause us to lose sight of the fact that in certain respects all arts are creative, and correlatively, all arts are performing. It is this latter fact which is of particular relevance in understanding what is wrong with forgeries. For it can be argued that every work of art—every painting, statue, novel, symphony, ballet, as well as every interpretation or rendition of a piece of music, every reading of a poem or production of a play—involves the element of performance.

When we speak of a performance we usually have in mind a human activity which stands in some sense complete in itself: we talk of the President's performance at a press conference, or a student's performance in an examination, with the intention of marking off these particular activities from the whole of a presidential administration or the quality of the student's work done throughout a course. Moreover, as these examples also indicate, performances are said to involve some sense of accomplishment, of achievement. As objects of contemplation, art works stand in differing relations to the performances of artists, depending on the art form in question. On the one hand, we have such arts as the dance, where the human activity involved in creating the object of contemplation and the object itself are one and the same thing. In such a case it would be odd to say that the object somehow represents the performance of the artist, because to perceive the object is to perceive the performance. On the other hand, we have painting, where we normally perceive the work of art without perceiving those actions which have brought it into being. Nevertheless, in cases such as the latter what we see is the end-product of human activity; the object of our perception can be understood as representative of a human performance. That arts differ with respect to how or whether we actually perceive at the moment of creation the artist's performance makes no difference to the relevance of the concept to understanding all of the arts. In fact, the concept of performance is internal to our whole notion of art.

Every work of art is an artifact, the product of human skills and techniques. If we see an actor or a dancer or a violinist at work, we are constantly conscious of human agency. Less immediately apparent is the element of performance in a painting which has hung perhaps for generations in a museum, or a long-familiar musical composition. Yet we are in such cases no less confronted with the results of human agency. As performances, works of art represent the ways in which artists solve problems, overcome obstacles, make do with available materials. The ultimate product is designed for our contemplation, as an object of particular interest in its own right, perhaps in isolation from other art objects or from the activity of the artist. But this isolation which frequently characterizes our mode of attention to aesthetic objects ought not to blind us to a fact that we may take for granted: that the work of art has a human origin, and must be understood as such.

We begin to see this more clearly when we consider our aesthetic response to natural beauty. In a passage in *Art as Experience*, John Dewey asks us to imagine that some object we had come to enjoy, believing it to be a primitive artifact, is revealed to us to be an "accidental natural product." In Dewey's view, this revelation changes our "appreciative perception" of the object. His point is that aesthetic appreciation is "inherently connected with the experience of making." This is well taken; imagine, for instance, the sorts of things we might say of the object before and after its natural origin is revealed. We could continue to appreciate those features from among the object's purely physical qualities which please us, such as shape and texture. But aspects of the object which we had previously assumed to be expressive will no longer be understood as such: it could still be called "angular" or "jagged," but not "energetic" or "restless"; it could still be "fragile," perhaps even "graceful," but no longer "economical" or "witty." It could in general still be described in terms of predicates which

indicate that it is agreeably shaped, but not in terms of predicates implying that it is well wrought. We could continue to enjoy the object, but we would no longer find ourselves admiring it in the same way: "to admire" usually means in part "to enjoy," but it also carries with it implications of *esteem* (one can even admire a work of art without particularly enjoying it). . . .

And so it is whenever we observe the work of an artist, be that artist a composer developing a theme, or inventing one (compare the usual performances of Beethoven with Tchaikovsky in these regards); be that artist a poet writing an elegy for his deceased parrot; be that artist a painter trying to figure out how to give some unity to the family portrait now that the duke insists on having his favorite hunting dogs included too; be that artist a playwright who must resolve a complex and tangled plot—in all of these cases it is appropriate to speak of the performance of a task, and of the success or failure of the task at hand.

Again, in order to grasp what it is that is before us, we must have some notion of what the maker of the object in question has done, including some idea of the limitations, technical and conventional, within which he has worked. It may be perfectly true (and not necessarily obviously so) to remark that in a painting of the Madonna the pale pink of the Virgin's robe contrasts pleasantly with the light blue-grey of her cloak. But it is far from irrelevant to know that the artist may be working within a canon (as, for example, fifteenth-century Italian artists did) according to which the robe must be some shade of red, and the cloak must be blue. The demand (to juxtapose fundamentally warm and cool colours) poses difficulties for creating harmony between robe and cloak, in the face of which Ghirlandajo may reduce the size of the cloak and tone it down with grey, Perugino may depict the cloak thrown over the Virgin's knees and allow a green shawl with red and yellow stripes to dominate the composition, while Filippino Lippi may simply cover the robe completely with the cloak. To say that the resulting assemblage of colours is pleasant may, again, be true enough; a fuller appreciation and understanding, however, would involve recognizing how that pleasing harmony is a response to a problematic demand put upon the artist.

Artistic performances in general, like musical or dramatic performances in particular, are assessed according to how they succeed or fail—the notions of success or failure are as much internal to our idea of performance as the idea of performance is to our concept of art. In this respect, there is an important truth in a view such as Goethe's which insists that criticism must begin by finding out what the artist intended to do and then ask whether he succeeded in doing it. Before we can determine whether or not a particular artistic performance can be said to succeed or fail, we must have some notion of *what counts as success or failure in connection with the kind of artistic performance in question.* . . .

The fundamental question then is, what has the artist done, what has he achieved? The question is fundamental, moreover, not because of any contingent facts about the psychology of aesthetic perception, but because of the nature of the concept of art itself. As I have noted, Smith's initial disappointment in the piano recording may later be replaced by admiration for the skill and sensitivity with which the engineer has varied the tempi of the recording. This does not indicate that Smith's response can be understood as merely conditioned by his beliefs about what he perceives. On the contrary, Smith's beliefs are about what he takes to be a work of art, and hence are centered on what he understands to be the achievement implicit in what he perceives. Technological advances in the arts in general, the inventions of airbrushes, electric stage lighting, sound synthesizers, and so forth, have

tended progressively to alter what counts as achievement in the arts; these advances have in no way altered the relevance of the concept of achievement in art or criticism and hence have not changed to that extent the concept of art *überhaupt*. Smith's mistake about the nature of the achievement before him, or the experts' mistakes about the van Meegeren Vermeers, simply requires that the question of what the achievement is should be recast: indeed, the achievement of the engineer may be worthy of admiration, just as the achievement of van Meegeren was far from negligible. Under its (corrected) description, van Meegeren's performance was one of producing in the twentieth century paintings in effective imitations of the seventeenth-century Dutch style. Some of his canvases, *e.g. Emmaus* and at least one of the Terborch forgeries, had they their origins in the seventeenth century, might well have been worth placing in museums, at least as examples of an antique genre. Still, just as the achievement of an engineer, however notable, is different in kind from (though not necessarily inferior to) the achievement of a pianist, so the achievement of van Meegeren could never be of the same sort of that of Vermeer.

I can believe that the painting before me is a Vermeer instead of a van Meegeren, and adjust my perception accordingly. But I cannot similarly believe that it makes *no difference* whether it is a Vermeer or a van Meegeren, not at any rate if I am to continue to employ the concept of art in terms of which we think about Vermeers, van Meegerens, piano virtuosi, and the rest. This is not a contingent matter of belief or taste; reference to origins is a necessary constituent of the concept of a work of art. Nor is it merely a cultural question. Cultural considerations can influence how we talk about art, can alter in various ways our attitude towards it. It is frequently pointed out, for instance, that criticism as customarily practised in the European tradition places great emphasis on the individual artist in a way that art and criticism in the Orient traditionally do not. Modern critics in the Occident tend to care deeply, perhaps sometimes excessively, about who created a work of art. But this does not mean that, say, Chinese critics have been unconcerned with the origins of art works: it does not entail that they would be uninterested in ever distinguishing a copy from a newly invented composition, or a marvelously carved stone from one smoothed by the waters of a brook. To be sure, culture shapes and changes what various peoples believe about art, their attitudes towards it. This may be strikingly different from ours, as in the case of the elaborately carved *Malagan* of New Ireland which is unceremoniously discarded after its one-time use. Anyone who concluded from this that the people of New Ireland had no concept of art would be open to ridicule; they may have different views about how art is to be treated—to that extent we could even say loosely that theirs is a "different conception of art from ours." But, limiting ourselves only to that consideration germane to the present discussion, *it is a conception of art* so long as according to it art is treated among other things as human performance, the work of art having implicit in it the possibility of achievement of some kind. Thus the concept of art is constituted *a priori* of certain essential properties. I do not propose to enumerate those features (the question of the contents of any such list lies at the heart of the philosophy of art); but I do insist that reference to origins and achievement must be included among these properties. This whole issue is what gives the problem of forgery such central philosophical importance: theorists who claim that it ought to make no difference to appreciation whether a work is forged or not do not merely challenge a few dearly held cultural beliefs about what is important in art. They attack rather the very idea of art itself. . . .

In developing a view which finds the aesthetic significance of forgery in the extent to which it misrepresents artistic achievement, I have hitherto avoided discussion of a concept often contrasted with forgery: originality. It is of course easy to say that originality is a legitimate source of value in art, that forgeries lack it, and that therefore they are to be discredited on that account. This seems true enough so far as it goes, but the difficulty is that it does not go far enough. One problem centers on deciding what "original" means, or ought to mean, in contrast to "forged." Originality is often associated with novelty in art, but this sense alone will not do, since there are many fine works of art whose outstanding features have little to do with novelty. Stravinsky's musical ideas, or Wagner's, were more novel in their respective epochs than Mozart's or Bach's; yet it would be odd on that account to call the latter composers relatively unoriginal in their contribution to music. Furthermore, even forgeries—those putative paradigm cases of unoriginal effort—can have strikingly original aspects. Not, perhaps, with those forgeries which are mere copies; but indeed, the most interesting cases of forgery involve works which are precisely not slavish copies, but pastiches, or works in the style of another artist. Here there is room for originality. Consider the heavy-lidded, sunken eyes of van Meegeren's faces: they may be insipid, but they are certainly original, and not to be found in Vermeer. In fact, we must remind ourselves that stripped of its pretensions, each of the van Meegeren Vermeers *is an original van Meegeren.* For what it is worth, each of these canvases is in that sense an original work of art: my point is precisely that it may not be worth much.

A crux here is that an artistic performance can be quite perfectly original and yet at the same time share with forgery the essential element of being misrepresented in terms of its actual achievement. The concept of originality is important in this context: part of what disturbs us about such cases as the van Meegeren episode is that aesthetically significant aspects of the paintings at issue did not have their origins with Vermeer but with an artist who lived several hundred years later. In that sense, we can call the van Meegeren fakes "unoriginal"; though they are original van Meegerens, elements which we especially value in them did not originate with Vermeer—and part of what would make those elements valuable is that they should be the product of seventeenth-century Vermeer performances rather than twentiety-century van Meegeren performances. But even where all aspects of the performance in question did in fact originate with the single individual who is credited with it, even where the performance is in that sense pluperfectly original, it is possible for it to share with forgery the essential feature of misrepresentation of achievement. Consider an instrumental performer who announces he will play an improvisation and then proceeds to play a carefully premeditated composition of his own creation. What is performed originates entirely with the performer; it is in no sense a copy of the work of another, and one would not want to call it "unoriginal." But it is surely a performance which shares with forgery the fact that its true nature is misrepresented. (Still, even though its status as composition or improvisation is indifferent to the fact that the same person is performing, origins remain important: an improvisation is distinguished from a composition in that it is originated spontaneously, on the spur of the moment—it is heard as it is created.)

And just as there can be cases of misrepresentation of achievement which do not, strictly speaking, involve any misunderstanding of the identity of the individual with whom the art object originates, so there can be misattributions of origin which do not entail significant misrepresentation of achievement. There are stanzas counting as decent Keats which would not have to be radically reappraised in terms of the artistic achievement they represent if they were discovered to have actually been written by Shelley. The same might be said of certain canvases by Derain and Cézanne, or sonatas by Kuhlau and Telemann. (This is not to deny that there are crucial differences between these artists and many of their works: but to mistake Mozart for Haydn is not *always* a foolish or naïve blunder.) In other cases, subtle and interesting shifts in our understanding of particular works might result: a piece of music perceived as run-of-the-mill Beethoven might be seen as outstanding Spohr. In such a case, however, our reassessment of the achievement involved is relative only to the career of the individual artist, and not to the historical achievement the work represents.

The significant opposition I find then is not between "forged" and "original," but between correctly represented artistic performance and misrepresented artistic performance. Originality remains a highly relevant concept here, however, insofar as it shows us that some notion of the origins of a work is always germane to appreciation. Without such concern, we cannot understand the full nature of the achievement a work represents, and such understanding is intrinsic to a proper grasp of the work of art. The predictable challenge to this involves the insistence that while I have been directing attention to human performances, what is really in question in appreciating works of art is *aesthetic experience*. On this account, aesthetic experience is said to refer to the visual or auditory experience of the sensuous surface of the work of art. Yet who is it who ever has these curious "aesthetic experiences"? In fact, I would suppose they are never had, except by infants perhaps—surely never by informed lovers of painting, music, or literature (the latter always a difficult case for aestheticians who like talking about "sensuous surface"). The encounter with a work of art does not consist in merely hearing a succession of pretty sounds or seeing an assemblage of pleasing shapes and colours. It is as much a matter of hearing a virtuoso perform a dazzling and original interpretation of a difficult piece of music or of experiencing a new vision of a familiar subject provided by a painter. Admittedly, there is an attraction in wanting to look past these thorny complexities to concentrate on the sensuous surface, and it is the same attraction that formalism in all its various guises has always had. It is a marvelously simple view, but (alas!) art itself is even more marvelously complex. Against those who insist that an object's status as forged is irrelevant to its artistic merit, I would hold that when we learn that the kind of achievement an art object involves has been radically misrepresented to us, it is not as though we have learned a new fact about some familiar object of aesthetic attention. On the contrary, insofar as its position as a work of art is concerned, it is no longer the same object.

Yuriko Saito

THE JAPANESE APPRECIATION OF NATURE

Yuriko Saito teaches philosophy in the Division of Liberal Arts of the Rhode Island School of Design. She specializes in aesthetics, Buddhism, and environmental philosophy. In the reading that follows, she contrasts Japanese and Western ideas about the aesthetic appreciation of nature.

1. THE LACK OF SUBLIME OBJECTS IN JAPANESE APPRECIATION OF NATURE

Many commentators have noted that the Japanese appreciation of nature is directed exclusively towards those objects and phenomena which are small, charming and tame. This characteristic becomes conspicuous especially when we compare it with the Western and other Oriental (such as Chinese and Korean) traditions which appreciate not only those small, tame objects of nature but also gigantic or frightful aspects of nature.

Citing various short ancient poems which are perhaps the best record of the traditional Japanese appreciation of nature, Hajime Nakamura points out that "the love of nature, in the case of the Japanese, is tied up with their tendencies to cherish minute things and treasure delicate things." Even when a grand landscape is appreciated, it is not the grandeur or awesome scale of the scene but rather its composition compressed into a compact design that is praised. . . .

A graphic illustration of the Japanese appreciation of mountains as friendly and warm rather than hostile and formidable can be found in some of the wood block prints of the Edo period. Consider, for example, Andō Hiroshige's depiction of Mount Hakone from the *Fifty-Three Sceneries of Tōkaidō*. While successfully conveying the difficulty of passing this steep mountain by fantastically exaggerating its profile, this print does not give the viewer an impression that the mountain is hostile, or that it challenges us to conquer it. Moreover, despite its steep shape, the size of the mountain relative to the size of men in procession is rather reduced, avoiding the impression that the mountain is overbearing. In addition, the colour used for the men in procession and

Yuriko Saito, "The Japanese Appreciation of Nature," *British Journal of Aesthetics* 25.3 (1985): 239–51.

the mountain are almost indistinguishable, again avoiding a stark contrast between the two.

The same observation can be made of the Japanese depiction of the sea. . . .

Even when a rough sea is depicted in visual art (which is not frequent), it never gives the impression of ferociousness. Take, for example, the famous wood block print by Katsushika Hokusai of a gigantic wave almost swallowing boats, with Mount Fuji seen at a distance. While the represented state of affairs might be horrifying, the work does not convey such a feeling at all. Although highly evocative of dynamic movement, because of a fairly contrived and calculated composition with a distant Mount Fuji as a static focal point, this print gives us a feeling which is neither insecure nor dreadful.

Likewise, creatures depicted by the Japanese are often small, harmless ones such as butterflies, warblers, copper pheasants, cuckoos. On the other hand, ferocious, life-endangering animals such as tigers are frequently objects of appreciation in other traditions. Indeed, in the Japanese tradition we do not find a praise for "forests filled with wild beasts"; instead there is a constant appreciation of things which are "small, gentle and intimate."

Some thinkers ascribe this conspicuous absence of the sublime in the Japanese appreciation of nature wholly to Japan's relatively tame landscape and mild climate. Tall cliffs, unbounded landscapes and soaring mountains may indeed be lacking in Japanese topography. However, the lack of appreciation of the sublime in the Japanese tradition cannot be wholly accounted for by reference to this factor. The fierce and awful aspects of nature such as annual autumn typhoons, earthquakes and rough seas are fully experienced by the Japanese, perhaps most eloquently documented by a mediaeval Buddhist recluse, Kamo no Chōmei, in his *An Account of My Hut* (1212).

In spite of the frequent occurrences of devastating typhoons, however, it is noteworthy that the morning *after* a typhoon, not the typhoon itself, is praised for its aesthetic appeal in three major classics in the Japanese tradition. *The Pillow Book* (c. 1002), *The Tale of Genji* (c. 1004) and *Essays in Idleness* (c. 1340). For example, in *The Pillow Book*, a series of anecdotes and essays concerning the Heian period court life, Sei Shōnagon praises the beauty of the morning after the storm without describing her experience of the storm itself during the previous night. The only reference made to the storm is her amazement at recognizing the arrangement of leaves "one by one through the chinks of the lattice-window" is the work of "the same wind which yesterday raged so violently."

How do we then account for the fact that the grand and fearful aspects of nature, while experienced by the Japanese, are not acknowledged as objects of aesthetic appreciation in their tradition? It may be helpful here first to examine, as a point of comparison, the Western notion regarding the appreciation of the sublime. Perhaps the most theoretical discussion of man's appreciation of the sublime in the West can be found in Kant's aesthetic theory. In his theory of the sublime, Kant proposes that man's appreciation of the sublime in nature (either vast or powerful parts of nature) is based upon the fundamental contrast between nature and man. The contrast is twofold. First, man is contrasted with nature because of his apparent inadequacy to grasp the magnitude of a vast part of nature or to have dominion over its powerful part. However, second, man is also contrasted with nature because of his ultimate dominion and superiority over nature. That is, in experiencing the vast parts of nature, the feeling of pleasure is generated because we recognize that our rational faculty is capable of *thinking of* infinity in spite of the inability of our sensible faculty to grasp it. Our appreciation of the powerful aspects of nature is brought about by a similar recognition. While the power of nature may have dominion over our physical being we have ultimate dominion over nature due to our super-sensible faculty of reason which is free from those causal laws governing the phenomenal world. Indeed, Kant describes the play of mental faculties (imagination and reason) involved in our experience of the sublime to be "harmonious *through their very contrast.*"

The lack of appreciation of the sublime in the Japanese appreciation of nature, then, is explained by the Japanese view of nature in its relation to man. Rather than conceiving the relationship between man and nature as contrasting, I shall argue that the Japanese appreciate nature primarily for its identity with man. As Masaharu Anesaki observes:

> Both Buddhism and Shintoism teach that the things of nature are not essentially unlike mankind, and that they are endowed with spirits similar to those of men. Accordingly awe and sublimity are almost unknown in Japanese painting and poetry, but beauty and grace and gentleness are visible in every work of art.

In what way then is nature considered to be essentially the same as man in the Japanese tradition? There are two ways in which the Japanese have traditionally identified with nature. One may be called emotional identification and the other is identification based upon the transience of both man and nature.

2. EMOTIVE IDENTIFICATION WITH NATURE

There is a long tradition in Japanese literature of emotional expression in terms of natural objects or phenomena. Lament and love, two strong emotions which constitute the major subject-matters of Japanese literature, are often expressed not directly but in terms of or by reference to nature. This tradition goes as far back as the oldest anthology of Japanese poems, *Manyōshū*, compiled in the eighth century. Shūichi Katō explains that this anthology indicates "the court poets of the *Manyōshū* expressed their profound feelings in terms of their daily natural surroundings."

Perhaps the most explicit expression of this tradition in Japanese literature is found in Ki no Tsurayuki's preface to *Kokinshū, another* anthology of poetry, compiled in 1905. In this preface Tsurayuki explicitly defines the nature of poetry as expression of emotion *in terms of* nature. Its opening paragraph states:

> Japanese poetry has the hearts of men for its seeds, which grow into numerous leaves of words. People, as they experience various events in life, speak out their hearts *in terms of* what they see and hear. On hearing a warbler chirp in plum blossoms or a kajika frog sing on the water, what living thing is not moved to sing out a poem?

This identification of man and nature through emotive affinity is developed into an important aesthetic concept by an Edo-period philologist and literary critic, Motoori Norinaga (1730–1801) in his theory of *mono no aware*. Variously translated as "pathos of things" or "sensitivity of things," and sometimes compared to the Latin notion of "*lacrimae rerum*" ("tears of things"), *mono no aware* refers to the essential experience of sympathetic identification with natural objects or situations.

The experience and appreciation of the identification with natural objects or situations occur in two ways. Sometimes we intuit the *kokoro* (essence, spirit) of the object or situation and sympathize with it: this results in an aesthetic experience of the object based upon *mono no aware*. Hence, with respect to situations (*koto*), Norinaga claims,

> What does it mean for one to be moved by knowing *mono no aware?* It is, for example, when one is confronted by some

situation which is supposed to be happy, one feels happy. One feels happy because one apprehends the *koto no kokoro* which is happiness in this case. By the same token, one feels sad when confronted with what is supposed to be sad; because one apprehends its *koto no kokoro*. Therefore, to know *mono no aware* is to apprehend the *koto no kokoro*, which is sometimes happy and sometimes sad, depending upon the situation in question.

Regarding natural objects (*mono*), he makes a similar point:

> To see cherry blossoms in full bloom and to see them as beautiful flowers is to know *mono no kokoro*. To recognize their beauty and to be moved by feeling that they are deeply beautiful is to know *mono no aware*.

Some other times, when we are possessed with a strong emotion, we experience an identification with natural objects and events by colouring these objects with our emotion. Norinaga claims that the aesthetic appeal of many classical Japanese literary works is derived from descriptions of this kind of emotional identification with nature. He agrees with Ki no Tsurayuki that "*mono no aware*, which is so intense that any verbal expression seems inadequate, can be expressed in a profound manner if one expresses it by what one sees or hears" such as "the sound of wind or crickets, . . . the colour of flowers or snow." Indeed, according to Norinaga, the most important aesthetic appeal of *The Tale of Genji*, the work he praises for its expression of *mono no aware*, is its description of nature which has affinity with the characters' emotive states.

Some natural objects and phenomena are associated with certain emotive content in Japanese literature so frequently that they have been established as symbols for expressing particular emotions. For example, cherry blossoms (especially when they are falling) are often associated with

sorrow in classical Japanese literature because they epitomize the transience of beauty. The autumn evening is a favourite symbol among mediaeval poets for expressing desolation and loneliness.

Whether the emotive identification between man and nature is rendered primarily as a result of man's intuitive grasp of the essence of a natural object or as a result of the imposition of feeling onto the outward reality, this appreciation of nature for being emotionally charged constitutes an important aspect of the Japanese aesthetic appreciation of nature: the appreciation of nature for its expressive quality. . . .

Emotion is also often associated with a natural object or phenomenon. Emotion can be said to be aesthetically expressed by a natural object when we can *see* the landscape as emotionally charged. If the emotive content remains distinct from the object and the viewer's experience is dominated by the emotion he experiences, then the aesthetic component in the appreciation diminishes. In other words, if the appreciation is directed merely towards the feeling of loneliness, the appreciation does not seem to be aesthetic; but if it is directed towards the way in which the feeling of loneliness is embodied by the actual landscape, then the appreciation is aesthetic. While this mode of appreciating nature as a mirror of one's emotion is not limited to the Japanese tradition, it constitutes an important aspect of the Japanese aesthetic appreciation of nature.

3. THE JAPANESE APPRECIATION OF THE TRANSIENCE OF NATURE

The Japanese appreciation of nature for its affinity rather than contrast with man has another basis. In addition to appreciating the relatively small and gentle objects and phenomena of nature, the Japanese are also known for their appreciation of the transitory aspects of nature. This fact is most significantly reflected in the traditional phrase by which the Japanese refer to nature as an object of appreciation—*kachōfūgetsu*, flower, bird, wind and moon. Flowers (most notably cherry blossoms) do not stay in bloom forever; the bird song is always changing and passing; wind is literally passing and transitory by definition; and the moon is constantly changing its appearance and location. Indeed these natural objects and phenomena form the favourite subjects for Japanese art. Other natural objects and phenomena frequently referred to in Japanese art are also short-lived: rain, dew, fog, insects, and various seasonal flowers.

The Japanese preoccupation with the change of seasons should be understood in this regard. In many instances of appreciation of nature from the earliest record, the Japanese have been most sensitive to the characteristics of each season and the transition from one to the other. Consider the following examples. *The Pillow Book* begins with the famous description of the best of each season; the first six volumes of *Kokin-shū* is organized according to the four seasons; a famous passage in *Essays in Idleness* (a well-known series of essays by a fourteenth-century retired Buddhist monk, Yoshida Kenkō) also is directed towards appreciating the transition of seasons.

The Japanese sensitivity towards seasonal change is even today manifested in the following aesthetic phenomena. Some natural objects or phenomena are celebrated for their symbolic presentation of their respective seasons. This symbolic import has been established throughout the long tradition of the required use of the season word, *kigo*, in haiku poetry and the celebration of the seasonal festivals. . . .

The importance of seasons in the Japanese appreciation of nature is not limited to the symbolic import vested in various individual objects and phenomena. Just as emotion often organizes various components of nature into a unified expressive whole, seasons are also used as an aesthetic organizing principle. In other words, sometimes a composition made up of various natural objects and phenomena is praised for the "fittingness" of the objects which creates a unified whole suggestive of a particular season. For example, one of the norms of flower arrangement is to suggest the mood of a season. Master Sennō advises: "when there comes the season for autumn flowers like chrysanthemums and gentians, your work must suggest the desolation of a withered winter moor." Japanese cooking also reflects the Japanese appreciation of seasonal changes by its emphasis on seasonable dishes and the incorporation of appropriate materials for garnish and decoration. Accordingly, many contemporary Japanese cookbooks are arranged by season.

What is the basis for this Japanese appreciation of the transitory nature of natural objects and phenomena? There is an immediate aesthetic appeal of something which does not last for long. Psychologically we tend to cherish and appreciate objects or events more if we know that they will never be the same. Hence, commentators discussing the notion of Japanese wisdom point out that the Japanese appreciation of the flower, moon and snow is based upon "regret for the transience of phenomena" which compels them to cherish "those rare occurrences fitting to each season and time."

A contemporary Japanese painter, Higashiyama Kaii, indicates that his experience of viewing the full moon in the spring against the foreground of drooping cherry blossoms in full bloom in the Maruyama district of Kyoto is intensified by the recognition of the transitory and non-recurring nature of the phenomenon.

Flowers look up at the moon. The moon looks at the flowers. . . . This must be what is called an encounter. Flowers stay in their fullest bloom only for a short period of time and it is very difficult for them to encounter the moon. Moreover, the full moon is only for this one night. If cloudy or rainy, this view cannot be seen. Furthermore, I must be there to watch it. . . .

If flowers are in full bloom all the time and if we exist forever, we won't be moved by this encounter. Flowers exhibit their glow of life by falling to the ground.

Higashiyama, therefore, recommends that we "think of the encounter with a particular landscape occurring only once." Such advice would have us avoid the fatigue factor which is detrimental to the aesthetic experience of any object. It is not yet clear whether transitoriness itself directly contributes to the aesthetic quality of the object, but it is aesthetically relevant in the sense that it predisposes the viewer to attend very carefully to the object and fully savour whatever the object has to offer at the moment.

Another appeal of the transitoriness of natural objects and phenomena is also aesthetic. It is based upon the pleasure we derive from imagining the condition of the object before or after the present stage and comparing them. This aspect of the appeal of the transitory and changeable nature of natural objects and phenomena is discussed by Yoshida Kenkō. In a well-known passage in *Essays in Idleness* he claims that natural objects such as flowers or the moon are best appreciated before or after their full stage. "Branches about to blossom or gardens strewn with faded flowers are worthier of our admiration" than blossoms in full bloom. As in a love affair between a man and a woman, "in all things, it is the beginnings and ends that are interesting" because such stages of the phenomena are more stimulating to one's imagination. In particular, we appreciate the exquisite contrast between the present condition and the imagined condition of the previous or following stage. Even when an object or phenomenon is at the peak of its beauty, the appreciation is deepened by pathos based upon the apparent contrast between its present appearance and what will become of it later on.

The Japanese taste for such natural objects as cherry blossoms and moon, therefore, can be explained from the aesthetic point of view: these objects most eloquently exhibit to one's senses the transience of nature in general. Cherry blossoms are more effective than other flowers for symbolizing transience because they look most fragile and delicate, they stay in full bloom for only a short period of time, and they drift down slowly petal by petal, giving an impression that they regret falling. But why is such sensuous manifestation of transience so cherished and appreciated? Why not appreciate the (apparent) permanence and stability of a rock, for example? After all, isn't transience of everything, including ourselves, considered a primary source of man's suffering?

The Japanese traditional appreciation of the transient aspect of nature stems from a further metaphysical consideration. One of the most important ideas spread by the introduction of Buddhism in the sixth century was the impermanence of everything. Everything, both nature and man, will sooner or later change through modification, destruction or death. Transience of human life was often considered a source of people's suffering and an object of lament. Youth and beauty pass. Wealth and power do not last. And, of course, no one avoids death.

Lament over these facts is the subject-matter of major literary pieces in Japan. *An Account of My Hut*, for example, presents in the first chapter the following observation on the human condition.

> It might be imagined that the houses, great and small, which vie roof against proud roof in the capital remain unchanged from one generation to the next, but when we examine whether this is true, how few are the houses that were there of old. Some were burnt last year and only since rebuilt;

great houses have crumbled into hovels and those who dwell in them have fallen no less. The city is the same, the people are as numerous as ever, but of those I used to know, a bare one or two in twenty remain. They die in the morning, they are born in the evening, like foam on the water. (197)

The same theme is expressed in the beginning paragraph of perhaps the most famous tale from the Japanese mediaeval period, *The Tale of the Heike:*

Yes, pride must have its fall, for it is as unsubstantial as a dream on a spring night. The brave and violent man—he too must die away in the end, like a whirl of dust in the wind . . .

What interests us here in these two passages is not merely their rather pessimistic outlook on man's life. What is noteworthy is that the description of the transience of human life is compared to the transience of natural phenomena. Kamo no Chōmei's passage is preceded by: "The flow of the river is ceaseless and its water is never the same. The bubbles that float in the pools, now vanishing, now forming, are not of long duration: so in the world are man and his dwellings" (197). The passage from *The Tale of Heike* is also preceded by the famous beginning: "The bell of the Gion Temple tolls into every man's heart to warn him that all is vanity and evanescence. The faded flowers of the sala trees by the Buddha's deathbed bear witness to the truth that all who flourish are destined to decay." . . .

This frequent association between transience of nature and transience of human life stems from the conviction that nature and man are essentially the same, rooted in the same principle of existence. As Higashiyama remarks, referring to his discussion of viewing the full moon against the cherry blossoms at Maruyama,

Nature is alive and always changing. At the same time, we ourselves, watching nature

change, are also changing day by day. Both nature and ourselves are rooted in the same fated, ever-changing cycle of birth, growth, decline and death.

This belief concerning the co-identity of man and nature is the ground of the Japanese appreciation of the evanescent aspects of nature. Grief experienced at the transience of human life is transformed to aesthetic pathos when it is compared to the transience of nature. By identifying human life with nature, the Japanese find a way to justify the transience of life. That is, since *everything* is in constant flux there is no escaping change and this recognition leads to resignation and finally to an acceptance of the sorrow of human existence.

As a psychologist, Hiroshi Minami, commenting on Japanese psychological characteristics, suggests, this preoccupation with the co-identity of man and nature and the appreciation of the transient are based upon "the perception of nature and life as one and the same, and the ascription of unhappiness and misfortune to the transiency and evanescence of nature and things impermanent." This identity between man and nature leads to resignation before the facts of life and then to acceptance of life, with all its sorrow and suffering. "Unhappiness in life is expressed through the guise of nature; because of the evanescence of nature, man realizes that it is senseless to grieve and should become reconciled to fate."

Many contemporary thinkers, in particular those concerned with ecological matters, often praise the Japanese attitude of "man in harmony with nature" for being ethically more desirable than the Western tradition of "man over nature" or "man against nature." I believe that a further critical study is needed to determine whether their praise of the Japanese attitude towards nature for its ecological implication is justified. However, the preceding discussion does suggest that the Japanese regard man and nature as fundamentally identical and appreciate nature for its unity with man. The content of this unity and co-identity between man and nature should be understood in the sense that both man and nature share the most important principle of existence in common: transience. The Japanese appreciation of the evanescent aspects of nature is rooted in the psychological benefit the Japanese derive from them: justification of the impermanence of human existence.

John Cage

EXPERIMENTAL MUSIC

John Cage (1912–1992) was an avant-garde composer, famous for his employment of randomness in composition and his conviction that all sounds are potentially music. His notorious work 4'33" consisted of a performer or performers sitting on a stage for precisely four minutes and thirty-three seconds. The following selection describes some of Cage's experiments with multitrack taping, experiments which he sees as explorations of the environment's sonic possibilities.

Formerly, whenever anyone said the music I presented was experimental, I objected. It seemed to me that composers knew what they were doing, and that the experiments that had been made had taken place prior to the finished works, just as sketches are made before paintings and rehearsals precede performances. But, giving the matter further thought, I realized that there is ordinarily an essential difference between making a piece of music and hearing one. A composer knows his work as a woodsman knows a path he has traced and retraced, while a listener is confronted by the same work as one is in the woods by a plant he has never seen before.

Now, on the other hand, times have changed; music has changed; and I no longer object to the word "experimental." I use it in fact to describe all the music that especially interests me and to which I am devoted, whether someone else wrote it or I myself did. What has happened is that I have become a listener and the music has become something to hear. Many people, of course, have given up saying "experimental" about this new music. Instead, they either move to a halfway point and say "controversial" or depart to a greater distance and question whether this "music" is music at all.

For in this new music nothing takes place but sounds: those that are notated and those that are not. Those that are not notated appear in the written music as silences, opening the doors of the music to the sounds that happen to be in the environment. This openness exists in the fields of modern sculpture and architecture. The glass houses of Mies van der Rohe reflect their environment, presenting to the eye

John Cage, *Silence* (Middletown: Wesleyan UP, 1961) 7–12.

images of clouds, trees, or grass, according to the situation. And while looking at the constructions in wire of the sculptor Richard Lippold, it is inevitable that one will see other things, and people too, if they happen to be there at the same time, through the network of wires. There is no such thing as an empty space or an empty time. There is always something to see, something to hear. In fact, try as we may to make a silence, we cannot. For certain engineering purposes, it is desirable to have as silent a situation as possible. Such a room is called an anechoic chamber, its six walls made of special material, a room without echoes. I entered one at Harvard University several years ago and heard two sounds, one high and one low. When I described them to the engineer in charge, he informed me that the high one was my nervous system in operation, the low one my blood in circulation. Until I die there will be sounds. And they will continue following my death. One need not fear about the future of music.

But this fearlessness only follows if, at the parting of the ways, where it is realized that sounds occur whether intended or not, one turns in the direction of those he does not intend. This turning is psychological and seems at first to be a giving up of everything that belongs to humanity—for a musician, the giving up of music. This psychological turning leads to the world of nature, where, gradually or suddenly, one sees that humanity and nature, not separate, are in this world together; that nothing was lost when everything was given away. In fact, everything is gained. In musical terms, any sounds may occur in any combination and in any continuity.

And it is a striking coincidence that just now the technical means to produce such a free-ranging music are available. When the Allies entered Germany towards the end of World War II, it was discovered that improvements had been made in recording sounds magnetically such that tape had become suitable for the high-fidelity recording of music. First in France with the work of Pierre Schaeffer, later here, in Germany, in Italy, in Japan, and perhaps, without my knowing it, in other places, magnetic tape was used not simply to record performances of music but to make a new music that was possible only because of it. Given a minimum of two tape recorders and a disk recorder, the following processes are possible: 1) a single recording of any sound may be made; 2) a rerecording may be made, in the course of which, by means of filters and circuits, any or all of the physical characteristics of a given recorded sound may be altered; 3) electronic mixing (combining on a third machine sounds issuing from two others) permits the presentation of any number of sounds in combination; 4) ordinary splicing permits the juxtaposition of any sounds, and when it includes unconventional cuts, it, like rerecording, brings about alterations of any or all of the original physical characteristics. The situation made available by these means is essentially a total sound-space, the limits of which are ear-determined only, the position of a particular sound in this space being the result of five determinants: frequency or pitch, amplitude or loudness, overtone structure or timbre, duration, and morphology (how the sound begins, goes on, and dies away). By the alteration of any one of these determinants, the position of the sound in sound-space changes. Any sound at any point in this total sound-space can move to become a sound at any other point. But advantage can be taken of these possibilities only if one is willing to change one's musical habits radically. That is, one may take advantage of the appearance of images without visible transition in distant places, which is a way of saying "television," if one is willing to stay at home instead of going to a theatre. Or one may fly if one is willing to give up walking.

Musical habits include scales, modes, theories of counterpoint and harmony, and the study of the timbres, singly and in combination of a limited number of sound-producing mechanisms. In mathematical terms these all concern discrete steps. They resemble walking—in the case of pitches, on steppingstones twelve in number. This cautious stepping is not characteristic of the possibilities of magnetic tape, which is revealing to us that musical action or existence can occur at any point or along any line or curve or what have you in total sound-space; that we are, in fact, technically equipped to transform our contemporary awareness of nature's manner of operation into art.

Again there is a parting of the ways. One has a choice. If he does not wish to give up his attempts to control sound, he may complicate his musical technique towards an approximation of the new possibilities and awareness. (I use the word "approximation" because a measuring mind can never finally measure nature.) Or, as before, one may give up the desire to control sound, clear his mind of music, and set about discovering means to let sounds be themselves rather than vehicles for man-made theories or expressions of human sentiments.

This project will seem fearsome to many, but on examination it gives no cause for alarm. Hearing sounds which are just sounds immediately sets the theorizing mind to theorizing, and the emotions of human beings are continually aroused by encounters with nature. Does not a mountain unintentionally evoke in us a sense of wonder? otters along a stream a sense of mirth? night in the woods a sense of fear? Do not rain falling and mists rising up suggest the love binding heaven and earth? Is not decaying flesh loathsome? Does not the death of someone we love bring sorrow? And is there a greater hero than the least plant that grows? What is more angry than the flash of lightning and the sound of thunder? These responses to nature are mine and will not necessarily correspond with another's. Emotion takes place in the person who has it.

And sounds, when allowed to be themselves, do not require that those who hear them do so unfeelingly. The opposite is what is meant by response ability.

New music: new listening. Not an attempt to understand something that is being said, for, if something were being said, the sounds would be given the shapes of words. Just an attention to the activity of sounds.

Those involved with the composition of experimental music find ways and means to remove themselves from the activities of the sounds they make. Some employ chance operations, derived from sources as ancient as the Chinese *Book of Changes*, or as modern as the tables of random numbers used also by physicists in research. Or, analogous to the Rorschach tests of psychology, the interpretation of imperfections in the paper upon which one is writing may provide a music free from one's memory and imagination. Geometrical means employing spatial superimpositions at variance with the ultimate performance in time may be used. The total field of possibilities may be roughly divided and the actual sounds within these divisions may be indicated as to number but left to the performer or to the splicer to choose. In this latter case, the composer resembles the maker of a camera who allows someone else to take the picture.

Whether one uses tape or writes for conventional instruments, the present musical situation has changed from what it was before tape came into being. This also need not arouse alarm, for the coming into being of something new does not by that fact deprive what was of its proper place. Each thing has its own place, never takes the place of something else; and the more things there are, as is said, the merrier.

But several effects of tape on experimental music may be mentioned. Since so many inches of tape equal so many seconds of time, it has become more and more usual that notation is in space rather than in symbols of quarter, half, and sixteenth notes and so on. Thus where on a page a note appears will correspond to when in a time it is to occur. A stop watch is used to facilitate a performance; and a rhythm results which is a far cry from horse's hoofs and other regular beats.

Also it has been impossible with the playing of several separate tapes at once to achieve perfect synchronization. This fact has led some towards the manufacture of multiple-tracked tapes and machines with a corresponding number of heads; while others—those who have accepted the sounds they do not intend—now realize that the score, the requiring that many parts be played in a particular togetherness, is not an accurate representation of how things are. These now compose parts but not scores, and the parts may be combined in any unthought ways. This means that each performance of such a piece of music is unique, as interesting to its composer as to others

listening. It is easy to see again the parallel with nature, for even with leaves of the same tree, no two are exactly alike. The parallel in art is the sculpture with moving parts, the mobile. . . .

Where do we go from here? Towards theatre. That art more than music resembles nature. We have eyes as well as ears, and it is our business while we are alive to use them.

And what is the purpose of writing music? One is, of course, not dealing with purposes but dealing with sounds. Or the answer must take the form of paradox: a purposeful purposelessness or a purposeless play. This play, however, is an affirmation of life—not an attempt to bring order out of chaos nor to suggest improvements in creation, but simply a way of waking up to the very life we're living, which is so excellent once one gets one's mind and one's desires out of its way and lets it act of its own accord.

DISCUSSION QUESTIONS

1. Do you think that Plato is right to worry that art can give us danger-ously false ideas about reality? Can you think of any contemporary cases in which his concerns seem warranted?
2. Do you agree with Wilde that life imitates art? Can you think of any instances of this phenomenon in your experience?
3. How do the imaginary worlds that we sometimes enter through art relate to our everyday lives? Do you think that art aims to inspire us to change our lives or our world? If so, do you think that it ever succeeds?
4. Why do you think we are so annoyed when we discover that an art-work is a forgery? Do you think there are other reasons for this reac-tion besides the one that Dutton offers?
5. Does the transience or vulnerability of an artwork or a craftwork ever seem to add to the work's aesthetic value, in your opinion?
6. Do you agree with Cage that artworks can help us to become more aware of nature? Do you think that contemporary sound technology serves this function? If not, could it?

FURTHER READING

Art

Coomaraswamy, Ananda K. *The Transformation of Nature in Art*. Cam-bridge: Harvard UP, 1934.

Dutton, Denis, ed. *The Forger's Art: Forgery and the Philosophy of Art*. Berkeley: U of California P, 1983.

Gombrich, Ernst, and Richard Langton Gregory. *Illusion in Nature and Art*. London: Duckworth, 1973.

Haywood, Ian. *Art and the Politics of Forgery*. Brighton: Harvester, 1983.

Heidegger, Martin. "The Origin of the Work of Art." *Poetry, Language, and Thought*. Trans. Albert Hofstadter. New York: Harper & Row, 1971. 17–75.

Kivy, Peter. *Sound and Semblance: Reflections on Musical Representation.* Princeton: Princeton UP, 1984.

Sagoff, Mark. "The Aesthetic Status of Forgeries." *The Journal of Aesthetics and Art Criticism* 35 (1976): 169–80.

Sartwell, Crispin. "The Aesthetics of the Spurious." *The British Journal of Aesthetics* 28 (1988): 360–67.

Ucko, Peter J., and Andree Rosenfeld. *Paleolithic Cave Art.* London: Wendenfeld and Nicolson, 1967.

Nature

Crawford, Donald. "Nature and Art: Some Dialectical Relationships." *Journal of Aesthetics and Art Criticism* 42 (1983): 49–58.

Hepburn, Ronald W. "Aesthetic Appreciation of Nature." *Aesthetics in the Modern World.* Ed. Harold Osborne. London: Thames and Hudson, 1968. 49–66.

Kemal, Salim, and Ivan Gaskell, eds. *Landscape, Natural Beauty, and the Arts.* Cambridge: Cambridge UP, 1993.

Turner, Frederick. "Cultivating the American Garden: Toward a Secular View of Nature." *Harper's*, August 1985: 45–52.

ART AS A VEHICLE FOR AESTHETIC EXPERIENCE

What would human beings be like if they did not make art and did not attempt to decorate their tools and environments? Arguably, they would be radically different kinds of creatures. Human beings in societies throughout the world construct artifacts and arrange their homes and communities, not solely with attention to practical function, but also to reflect their tastes. Art and decoration are fundamental activities of our species. But why are they such important activities for human beings? Why does this dimension of our lives matter so much?

One possible explanation—common in the West at least since Plato—has been that aesthetic experience makes a powerful impression that reinforces whatever it accompanies. By presenting art that provokes aesthetic experience in connection with important societal events, a culture educates its citizens in its values and history. On this instrumentalist view, aesthetic experience is important because it functions to promote other ends that are valuable, such as the development of social cohesiveness or moral education.

Certainly, aesthetic experience seems to incite enthusiasm. Rika Burnham's "It's Amazing and It's Profound" indicates the excitement art provokes in her high school students. When not discouraged from believing themselves capable of understanding and appreciating art, Burnham insists, students in their early teen years are capable of experiencing art in ways that are both amazing and profound. Burnham lets her students speak for themselves as they describe why they find their aesthetic experiences so meaningful.

But is the importance of aesthetic experience to be found in its ability to further nonaesthetic goals, as the instrumentalist argues? Walter Pater would say no. Pater describes the value of art in terms of the type of experience it produces, which he takes to be valuable for its own sake. He urges both critics and audiences of art to pay less attention to abstract theories about art and more direct attention to things of beauty. Too often, we pay little attention to the things around us, proceeding mostly on "automatic pilot" and going through our habitual motions. The real joy of living, however, stems from genuinely experiencing and passionately responding to objects we encounter, both in art and in everyday experience. Art's value is to offer us occasions for such experiences and responses. Art gives our moments "the highest quality" that they can have, and it gives us a quickened sense of life.

What is the nature of aesthetic experience? Many thinkers have argued that it involves taking a particular attitude toward what one observes. Usually this attitude has been described as contrasting with our usual practical attitude, in which we consider things with an eye to how they might be useful for our various projects. Edward Bullough defends the view that aesthetic experience requires a particular attitude, which he characterizes in terms of psychological "distance" from what one observes. In the appropriate state of distance, one does not consider one's personal motivations or projects, but instead contemplates the object. Bullough insists, however, that the attitude of aesthetic distance should not be understood merely negatively, as the suppression of our practical motivations. Instead, by inhibiting these concerns, we make room for a positive engagement in contemplating the object. (Bullough's account of aesthetic distance is similar to Kant's account of "disinterestedness," included in Chapter 1.)

José Ortega y Gasset suggests that disinterested contemplation is also characteristic of the artist's attitude. Ortega was interested in explaining the art of the early twentieth century to a largely uncomprehending public. He analyzes what he calls the recent "dehumanization of art," the abandonment of the goal of representing everyday human reality. While most people's attitudes toward their experience is that of participants, the artist assumes the stance of observer toward life, according to Ortega. Recent art emphasizes the artist's detachment from the human world to an exaggerated degree. Vastly more interested in style than in representation, many of Ortega's artistic contemporaries considered their lack of concern with reality and sentiment as evidence of liberation. Their art may strike some as "inhuman," but Ortega applauds what he sees as their achievement, that of constructing something that does not copy "nature" and "yet possesses substance of its own."

George Dickie, by contrast, questions the theory that aesthetic experience involves a distanced "aesthetic" attitude. Although he, too, takes aesthetic experience to involve contemplation, he finds most theoretical accounts of aesthetic experience to be short on information about what details of an object are aesthetically relevant. Moreover, aesthetic attitude theories make too sharp a distinction between the art critic's role and that of the ordinary observer. Perhaps most problematically, according to Dickie, this theory divorces aesthetic appreciation from moral concerns. Dickie objects that one's moral judgment of an artwork is not irrelevant to one's aesthetic appreciation, but rather is importantly involved in aesthetic experience.

Rika Burnham

IT'S AMAZING
AND
IT'S PROFOUND

Rika Burnham is museum educator in the education department of the Metropolitan Museum of Art in New York City. In the following essay, her students describe their experiences of art in their own words. Burnham cautions that theory can be damaging if it mediates the relationship between the artwork and its beholder. She reminds us that spending time actually looking and listening to artworks is more important to aesthetics than learning technical vocabularies.

I have been teaching high school students at the Metropolitan Museum of Art for the past 15 years, primarily in an after-school program that students come to out of their own interest and choosing. It is my intent . . . to represent the voices of the high school students I teach: to report their thoughts and chronicle an aesthetic experience in the museum. . . .

In most museums, high school students are generally a feared group of visitors. People who teach them worry they will be recalcitrant at best, openly and verbally hostile at worst. The image is of the sullen high school student, barely civil enough to remove a headset, wearing hats or too many beads, wandering off or whispering among themselves. Museum instructors feel they have to dazzle the students in exchange for their attention, showing them works of art that deal with subjects thought to be appealing to the adolescent, such as sex, scenes of violence, or the surreal.

It is my experience that this is an approach that underrates, belittles, and in fact chokes off, the very significant capacity high school students have for aesthetic experience. On the threshold of an adult world, they have not yet learned to fear being labeled "corny" in our language, "nerdy" in theirs, for expressing thoughts about the nature of the human condition: life, death, fear, loneliness, love, despair, exclusion, inclusion, the meaning of existence and the acceptance of ambiguity. Nor have they learned the convention of an art

Rika Burnham, "If You Don't Stop, You Don't See Anything," *Teachers College Record* 95:4 (Summer 1994): 1–5.

history–loaded language that can preempt experience and teach art appreciation through the narrow lens of historical and formal analysis. The high school students instead bring honesty and visual acuity to looking at works of art, a courage to see and think, an extraordinary ability to consider art on their own terms. They can appreciate with aplomb great masterpieces, and in fact, almost relish them, seeming to prefer works of art with "big ideas" instead of "little" ones. As John Melendez, a senior at Seward Park High School in New York said, a masterpiece "makes your heart pound, your mind think, it fills you up with emotions you never knew you had. It's not like every day life, it's amazing, and it's profound."

Recently, I was with some students in front of one of Ad Reinhardt's black paintings. One of the students who had been coming to the museum for several years said suddenly, "I get it, I finally get it. . . . if you don't stop, you don't see anything." And we admired in silence how out of the blackness comes the slow risings of dark reds and brooding greens and impossible yellows. And then we laughed, because in that moment we realized it was always true. Of course you have to stop to see a work of art, but you have to *really* stop. You have to stop in the deepest sense: out of your life, out of your own time and space, out of conventions and even out of your expectations. Otherwise you don't see anything. The high school students, much more than we, understand that only then will the work of art begin to interface with your life and thoughts, only then will experience begin and meaning unfold. Everything else, all other information, becomes irrelevant. In the words of Amy Chen, a junior at Stuyvesant High School:

> I sit there and try not to think of anything around me. I just sit there and forget about everything else around it and then I look at it and look at it. Soon it will come to you. Whatever you see first will lead you

through the rest of it. Somehow, the painting flows and eventually comes together inside your mind.

This may sound like a relatively simple proposition, but in fact most museums are constructed so this sustained encounter with a work of art does not happen. My high school students tell me their confidence to look at art sometimes fails as they approach the museum. There it is, they say, in all its architectural splendor, an imposing presence easily confused with libraries and courts of law. Big banners wave with names they don't recognize ("Annenberg," "Majolica," "Verrocchio" to name a few from recent times). Up the steps, they meet armed guards who tell them to check their belongings. Information desks suggest visitors need information; acoustiguide desks suggest they need acoustiguides; bookstores, books; lecture kiosks, lectures. If they are brave enough to continue, they may encounter lecturers in the galleries who, astonishingly, stand there and describe in detail what they already see, or worse, refer to concepts like "Siennese school" or "caravaggiste" that sound like a foreign language. Labels may offer up information about patrons and provenance, but none about mysterious iconography or unusual visual phenomena. In fact, what one sees may be obfuscated by the discussion of information so tangential as to seem opposed.

The parenthetical message is stifling. Students quickly become aware that other people not only know names and dates, but that they have "answers." It has already been decided what is significant, what one is supposed to see first, what is a correct response, and that there *is* right and wrong. Their participation seems irrelevant, and they do not respond. No wonder we fear recalcitrance and hostility.

My students have taught me that given the chance, they can and do find the museum a place that is neither forbidding nor exclusive, but a place where significant and extraordinary understandings of works of art can occur—for all of us. Not just for the art historians, or the critics, or the artists, but for all of us. It is a profoundly democratic notion that aesthetic experience is available to all of us if we can only come to believe in our own ability to see and feel and think. Given the time and space to do so, we find that the experience comes from within. It does not get told or given or memorized. There is absolute meaning, but only if its one's own. A student, Siddarth Shah, was discussing a painting in the Metropolitan's collection by the Italian Renaissance painter Vittore Carpaccio. He said:

> This painting proves that everyone has a different perception of art. You'll never find a true answer. Everyone has their own feeling, their own meaning, and that's good because it stays in your mind. You keep asking, "Where am I? Where am I in this situation?" Everything is surrounding you and you have to pick the right path, but any path you pick will be right.

The distinction between teacher and student breaks down; for both the experience is about mutual discovery and experience. It is about the ultimate acceptance of the mysterious interfacing between art and the self. The possibilities for significant aesthetic experience, for what Dr. Judith Burton of Columbia Teachers College calls "meaning-making," are endless.

The objective of the aesthetic experience is no longer the transfer of information, but the realignment of values whereby visual experience and individual response count. It becomes necessary to put the viewers' experience first, before one's own, before the museums', before art history. To encourage free and interactive response means that teachers need to create a domain in which the student can question, search, challenge, be moved by, and ultimately bring the work into the context of his or her own life

without being intimidated or made to feel inadequate. This freedom is the confidence to make a substantial judgment about a work of art in front of you, and to take possession of the work of art for yourself. It demands your concentration and your participation at the very center.

I ask students to sit in front of works of art for long periods of time. I invite them to respond and to listen to each other. Ideas will start to come slowly forward, to fill the perceptual space. They may be generated by any aspect of the work of art—the narrative, the colors, the way the paint is applied, the atmosphere. All points of entry are good, all visual thinking valuable. The collective experience builds its own truth, it places enormous value on the here and now, what we see and what the significance of that seeing is. The instructor is a collector of thoughts, thoughts that can be moved along and prodded into an evolving experience, one of increasing revelation and awareness. Everyone contributes to the flow of ideas, to the exploration of the imagery. As Karen Zaidberg, a junior in high school, said:

> It doesn't really work to try to look at paintings by yourself. I've come to the museum and stood there and asked myself the how-do-you-feel thing and I look at it and I come up with a thought or two. But when I'm by myself it doesn't seem as great as it does when there are people around you raising their hands and having thoughts. By yourself, once you have exhausted those two thoughts, you're standing there looking at this painting and the painting is standing there looking at you, and there's nothing interactive about it. You're not with other people who can bring out things you didn't see, or explain things you couldn't figure out, or describe feelings you couldn't put into words.

To sit with a work of art for an hour or more is not our usual experience. Living in a time when things move quickly, we easily spend an hour or more watching television, two hours with a movie, ten hours with a novel. Only rarely do we construct an encounter with a visual work of art that lasts more than a few minutes. To do so requires slowing down, stopping in order to see, and then actively engaging our perceptions in a dialogue with the work of art and with our co-observers. But the rewards are great, as we begin to see ourselves in relation to a larger, more comprehensive, complex, and moving experience of art. We can examine the art in the context of our lives, and extend our appreciation in all directions.

Walter Pater

A
QUICKENED
SENSE OF LIFE

Walter Pater (1839–1894) was an English critic, essayist, and humanist. He was a major proponent of aestheticism, or the position that art should be appreciated for its own sake, not as a tool of moral instruction. His books include Marius the Epicurean, Appreciations, Essays on Literature and Art, *and* The Function of Criticism at the Present Time. *In the following excerpts from* The Renaissance *(1873), Pater argues that art criticism should not aim at abstract theorizing but instead should facilitate our heightened experience of art.*

PREFACE

Many attempts have been made by writers on art and poetry to define beauty in the abstract, to express it in the most general terms, to find some universal formula for it. The value of these attempts has most often been in the suggestive and penetrating things said by the way. Such discussions help us very little to enjoy what has been well done in art or poetry, to discriminate between what is more and what is less excellent in them, or to use words like beauty, excellence, art, poetry, with a more precise meaning than they would otherwise have. Beauty, like all other qualities presented to human experience, is relative; and

the definition of it becomes unmeaning and useless in proportion to its abstractness. To define beauty, not in the most abstract but in the most concrete terms possible, to find not its universal formula, but the formula which expresses most adequately this or that special manifestation of it, is the aim of the true student of aesthetics.

"To see the object as in itself it really is," has been justly said to be the aim of all true criticism whatever; and in aesthetic criticism the first step towards seeing one's object as it really is, is to know one's own impression as it really is, to discriminate it, to realise it distinctly. The objects with which aesthetic criticism deals—music, poetry, artistic and accomplished forms of

Walter Pater, *The Renaissance* (New York: Boni and Liveright, 1919) xxv–xxvii, 194–99.

human life—are indeed receptacles of so many powers or forces: they possess, like the products of nature, so many virtues or qualities. What is this song or picture, this engaging personality presented in life or in a book, to *me?* What effect does it really produce on me? Does it give me pleasure? and if so, what sort or degree of pleasure? How is my nature modified by its presence, and under its influence? The answers to these questions are the original facts with which the aesthetic critic has to do; and, as in the study of light, of morals, of number, one must realise such primary data for one's self, or not at all. And he who experiences these impressions strongly, and drives directly at the discrimination and analysis of them, has no need to trouble himself with the abstract question what beauty is in itself, or what its exact relation to truth or experience—metaphysical questions, as unprofitable as metaphysical questions elsewhere. He may pass them all by as being, answerable or not, of no interest to him.

The aesthetic critic, then, regards all the objects with which he has to do, all works of art, and the fairer forms of nature and human life, as powers or forces producing pleasurable sensations, each of a more or less peculiar or unique kind. This influence he feels, and wishes to explain, by analysing and reducing it to its elements. To him, the picture, the landscape, the engaging personality in life or in a book, *La Gioconda,* the hills of Carrara, Pico of Mirandola, are valuable for their virtues, as we say, in speaking of a herb, a wine, a gem; for the property each has of affecting one with a special, a unique, impression of pleasure. Our education becomes complete in proportion as our susceptibility to these impressions increases in depth and variety. And the function of the aesthetic critic is to distinguish, to analyse, and separate from its adjuncts, the virtue by which a picture, a landscape, a fair personality in life or in a book, produces this special impression of beauty or pleasure, to indicate

what the source of that impression is, and under what conditions it is experienced. His end is reached when he has disengaged that virtue, and noted it, as a chemist notes some natural element, for himself and others. . . .

What is important, then, is not that the critic should possess a correct abstract definition of beauty for the intellect, but a certain kind of temperament, the power of being deeply moved by the presence of beautiful objects. He will remember always that beauty exists in many forms. To him all periods, types, schools of taste, are in themselves equal. In all ages there have been some excellent workmen, and some excellent work done. The question he asks is always:—In whom did the stir, the genius, the sentiment of the period find itself? where was the receptacle of its refinement, its elevation, its taste? "The ages are all equal," says William Blake, "but genius is always above its age.". . .

1873.

CONCLUSION

. . . To regard all things and principles of things as inconstant modes or fashions has more and more become the tendency of modern thought. Let us begin with that which is without—our physical life. Fix upon it in one of its more exquisite intervals, the moment, for instance, of delicious recoil from the flood of water in summer heat. What is the whole physical life in that moment but a combination of natural elements to which science gives their names? But those elements, phosphorus and lime and delicate fibres, are present not in the human body alone: we detect them in places most remote from it. Our physical life is a perpetual motion of them—the passage of the blood, the waste and repairing of the lenses of the eye, the modification of the tissues of the brain under every ray of light and sound—processes which science reduces to simpler and more elementary forces. Like the elements of which we are composed, the action of these forces extends beyond us: it rusts iron and ripens corn. Far out on every side of us those elements are broadcast, driven in many currents; and birth and gesture and death and the springing of violets from the grave are but a few out of ten thousand resultant combinations. That clear, perpetual outline of face and limb is but an image of ours, under which we group them—a design in a web, the actual threads of which pass out beyond it. This at least of flame-like our life has, that it is but the concurrence, renewed from moment to moment, of forces parting sooner or later on their ways.

Or, if we begin with the inward world of thought and feeling, the whirlpool is still more rapid, the flame more eager and devouring. There it is no longer the gradual darkening of the eye, the gradual fading of colour from the wall—movements of the shore-side, where the water flows down indeed, though in apparent rest—but the race of the mid-stream, a drift of momentary acts of sight and passion and thought. At first sight experience seems to bury us under a flood of external objects, pressing upon us with a sharp and importunate reality, calling us out of ourselves in a thousand forms of action. But when reflexion begins to play upon those objects they are dissipated under its influence; the cohesive force seems suspended like some trick of magic; each object is loosed into a group of impressions—colour, odour, texture—in the mind of the observer. And if we continue to dwell in thought on this world, not of objects in the solidity with which language invests them, but of impressions, unstable, flickering, inconsistent, which burn and are extinguished with our consciousness of them, it contracts still further: the whole scope of observation is dwarfed into the narrow chamber of the individual mind. Experience,

already reduced to a group of impressions, is ringed round for each one of us by that thick wall of personality through which no real voice has ever pierced on its way to us, or from us to that which we can only conjecture to be without. Every one of those impressions is the impression of the individual in his isolation, each mind keeping as a solitary prisoner its own dream of a world. Analysis goes a step farther still, and assures us that those impressions of the individual mind to which, for each one of us, experience dwindles down, are in perpetual flight; that each of them is limited by time, and that as time is infinitely divisible, each of them is infinitely divisible also; all that is actual in it being a single moment, gone while we try to apprehend it, of which it may ever be more truly said that it has ceased to be than that it is. To such a tremulous wisp constantly reforming itself on the stream, to a single sharp impression, with a sense in it, a relic more or less fleeting, of such moments gone by, what is real in our life fines itself down. It is with this movement, with the passage and dissolution of impressions, images, sensations, that analysis leaves off—that continual vanishing away, that strange, perpetual weaving and unweaving of ourselves.

Philosophiren, says Novalis, *ist dephlegmatisiren, vivificiren.** The service of philosophy, of speculative culture, towards the human spirit, is to rouse, to startle it to a life of constant and eager observation. Every moment some form grows perfect in hand or face; some tone on the hills or the sea is choicer than the rest; some mood of passion or insight or intellectual excitement is irresistibly real and attractive to us,—for that moment only. Not the fruit of experience, but experience itself, is the end. A counted number of pulses only is given to us of a variegated, dramatic life. How may we see in

---

*"To philosophize is to become less phlegmatic, to become enlivened."

them all that is to be seen in them by the finest senses? How shall we pass most swiftly from point to point, and be present always at the focus where the greatest number of vital forces unite in their purest energy?

To burn always with this hard, gemlike flame, to maintain this ecstasy, is success in life. In a sense it might even be said that our failure is to form habits: for, after all, habit is relative to a stereotyped world, and meantime it is only the roughness of the eye that makes any two persons, things, situations, seem alike. While all melts under our feet, we may well grasp at any exquisite passion, or any contribution to knowledge that seems by a lifted horizon to set the spirit free for a moment, or any stirring of the senses, strange dyes, strange colours, and curious odours, or work of the artist's hands, or the face of one's friend. Not to discriminate every moment some passionate attitude in those about us, and in the very brilliancy of their gifts some tragic dividing of forces on their ways, is, on this short day of frost and sun, to sleep before evening. With this sense of the splendour of our experience and of its awful brevity, gathering all we are into one desperate effort to see and touch, we shall hardly have time to make theories about the things we see and touch. What we have to do is to be for ever curiously testing new opinions and courting new impressions, never acquiescing in a facile orthodoxy of Comte, or of Hegel, or of our own. Philosophical theories or ideas, as points of view, instruments of criticism, may help us to gather up what might otherwise pass unregarded by us. "Philosophy is the microscope of thought." The theory or idea or system which requires of us the sacrifice of any part of this experience, in consideration of some interest into which we cannot enter, or some abstract theory we have not identified with ourselves, or of what is only conventional, has no real claim upon us.

One of the most beautiful passages of Rousseau is that in the sixth book of the *Confessions*, where he describes the awakening in him of the literary sense. An undefinable taint of death had clung always about him, and now in early manhood he believed himself smitten by mortal disease. He asked himself how he might make as much as possible of the interval that remained; and he was not biassed by anything in his previous life when he decided that it must be by intellectual excitement, which he found just then in the clear, fresh writings of Voltaire. Well! we are all *condamnés* as Victor Hugo says: we are all under sentence of death but with a sort of indefinite reprieve—*les hommes sont tous condamnés à mort avec des sursis indéfinis*:* we have an interval, and then our place knows us no more. Some spend this interval in listlessness, some in high passions, the wisest, at least among "the children of this world," in art and song. For our one chance lies in expanding that interval, in getting as many pulsations as possible into the given time. Great passions may give us this quickened sense of life, ecstasy and sorrow of love, the various forms of enthusiastic activity, disinterested or otherwise, which come naturally to many of us. Only be sure it is passion—that it does yield you this fruit of a quickened, multiplied consciousness. Of such wisdom, the poetic passion, the desire of beauty, the love of art for its own sake, has most. For art comes to you proposing frankly to give nothing but the highest quality to your moments as they pass, and simply for those moments' sake.

1868.

*"Human beings are all condemned to death with indefinite delays."

Edward Bullough

PSYCHICAL DISTANCE

Edward Bullough (1880–1934) was the author of
Aesthetics, Cambridge Readings in Italian Literature,
and The Philosophy of St. Thomas Aquinas. *In this
excerpt from his classic article "'Psychical Distance'
as a Factor in Art and an Aesthetic Principle,"
Bullough contends that aesthetic experience of art
depends on adopting the proper amount of distance
from the artwork.*

"PSYCHICAL DISTANCE" AS A FACTOR IN ART AND AN AESTHETIC PRINCIPLE.

I.

1. The conception of "Distance" suggests, in connexion with Art, certain trains of thought by no means devoid of interest or of speculative importance. Perhaps the most obvious suggestion is that of *actual spatial* distance, i.e., the distance of a work of Art from the spectator, or that of *represented spatial* distance, i.e., the distance represented within the work. Less obvious, more metaphorical, is the meaning of *temporal* distance. The first was noticed already by Aristotle in his *Poetics;* the second has played a great part in the history of painting in the form of perspective; the distinction between these two kinds of distance assumes special importance theoretically in the differentiation between sculpture in the round, and relief-sculpture. Temporal distance, remoteness from us in point of time, though often a cause of misconceptions, has been declared to be a factor of considerable weight in our appreciation.

It is not, however, in any of these meanings that "Distance" is put forward here, though it will be clear in the course of this essay that the above mentioned kinds of distance are rather special forms of the conception of Distance as advocated here, and derive whatever *aesthetic* qualities they may possess from Distance in its *general* connotation. This general connotation is "Psychical Distance."

A short illustration will explain what is meant by "Psychical Distance." Imagine a fog at sea: for most people it is an experience of acute unpleasantness. Apart from the physical annoyance and remoter forms of discomfort such as delays, it is apt to produce feelings of peculiar anxiety, fears of invisible dangers, strains of watching and listening for distant and unlocalised signals. The listless movements of the ship and her warning calls soon tell upon the nerves of the passengers; and that special, expectant, tacit anxiety and nervousness, always associated with this experience, make a fog the dreaded terror of the sea (all the more terrifying because of its very silence and gentleness) for the expert seafarer no less than for the ignorant landsman.

Nevertheless, a fog at sea can be a source of intense relish and enjoyment. Abstract from the experience of the sea fog, for the moment, its danger and practical unpleasantness, just as every one in the enjoyment of a mountain-climb disregards its physical labour and its danger (though, it is not denied, that these may incidentally enter into the enjoyment and enhance it); direct the attention to the features "objectively" constituting the phenomenon—the veil surrounding you with an opaqueness as of transparent milk, blurring the outline of things and distorting their shapes into weird grotesqueness; observe the carrying-power of the air, producing the impression as if you could touch some far-off siren by merely putting out your hand and letting it lose itself behind that white wall; note the curious creamy smoothness of the water, hypocritically denying as it were any suggestion of danger; and, above all, the strange solitude and remoteness from the world, as it can be found only on the highest mountain tops: and the experience may acquire, in its uncanny mingling of repose and terror, a flavour of such concentrated poignancy and delight as to contrast sharply with the blind and distempered anxiety of its other aspects. This contrast, often emerging with startling suddenness, is like a momentary switching on of some new current, or the passing ray of a brighter light, illuminating

the outlook upon perhaps the most ordinary and familiar objects—an impression which we experience sometimes in instants of direst extremity, when our practical interest snaps like a wire from sheer over-tension, and we watch the consummation of some impending catastrophe with the marvelling unconcern of a mere spectator.

It is a difference of outlook, due—if such a metaphor is permissible—to the insertion of Distance. This Distance appears to lie between our own self and its affections, using the latter term in its broadest sense as anything which affects our being, bodily or spiritually, e.g., as sensation, perception, emotional state or idea. Usually, though not always, it amounts to the same thing to say that the Distance lies between our own self and such objects as are the sources or vehicles of such affections.

Thus, in the fog, the transformation by Distance is produced in the first instance by putting the phenomenon, so to speak, out of gear with our practical, actual self; by allowing it to stand outside the context of our personal needs and ends—in short, by looking at it "objectively," as it has often been called, by permitting only such reactions on our part as emphasise the "objective" features of the experience, and by interpreting even our "subjective" affections not as modes of *our* being but rather as characteristics of the phenomenon.

The working of Distance is, accordingly, not simple, but highly complex. It has a *negative*, inhibitory aspect—the cutting-out of the practical sides of things and of our practical attitude to them—and a *positive* side— the elaboration of the experience on the new basis created by the inhibitory action of Distance.

2. Consequently, this distanced view of things is not, and cannot be, our normal outlook. As a rule, experiences constantly turn the same side towards us, namely, that which has the strongest practical force of appeal. We are not ordinarily aware of those

aspects of things which do not touch us immediately and practically, nor are we generally conscious of impressions apart from our own self which is impressed. The sudden view of things from their reverse, usually unnoticed, side, comes upon us as a revelation, and such revelations are precisely those of Art. In this most general sense, Distance is a factor in all Art.

3. It is, for this very reason, also an aesthetic principle. The aesthetic contemplation and the aesthetic outlook have often been described as "objective." We speak of "objective" artists as Shakespeare or Velasquez, of "objective" works or art forms as Homer's *Iliad* or the drama. It is a term constantly occurring in discussions and criticisms, though its sense, if pressed at all, becomes very questionable. For certain forms of Art, such as lyrical poetry, are said to be "subjective"; Shelley, for example, would usually be considered a "subjective" writer. On the other hand, no work of Art can be genuinely "objective" in the sense in which this term might be applied to a work on history or to a scientific treatise; nor can it be "subjective" in the ordinary acceptance of that term, as a personal feeling, a direct statement of a wish or belief, or a cry of passion is subjective. "Objectivity" and "subjectivity" are a pair of opposites which in their mutual exclusiveness when applied to Art soon lead to confusion.

Nor are they the only pair of opposites. Art has with equal vigour been declared alternately "idealistic" and "realistic," "sensual" and "spiritual," "individualistic" and "typical." Between the defence of either terms of such antitheses most aesthetic theories have vacillated. It is one of the contentions of this essay that such opposites find their synthesis in the more fundamental conception of Distance.

Distance further provides the much needed criterion of the beautiful as distinct from the merely agreeable.

Again, it marks one of the most important steps in the process of artistic creation and serves as a distinguishing feature of what is commonly so loosely described as the "artistic temperament."

Finally, it may claim to be considered as one of the essential characteristics of the "aesthetic consciousness,"—if I may describe by this term that special mental attitude towards, and outlook upon, experience, which finds its most pregnant expression in the various forms of Art.

II.

. . . 1. Distance does not imply an impersonal, purely intellectually interested relation of such a kind. On the contrary, it describes a *personal* relation, often highly emotionally coloured, but *of a peculiar character.* Its peculiarity lies in that the personal character of the relation has been, so to speak, filtered. It has been cleared of the practical, concrete nature of its appeal, without, however, thereby losing its original constitution. One of the best-known examples is to be found in our attitude towards the events and characters of the drama: they appeal to us like persons and incidents of normal experience, except that side of their appeal, which would usually affect us in a directly personal manner, is held in abeyance. . . .

2. This personal, but "distanced" relation (as I will venture to call this nameless character of our view) directs attention to a strange fact which appears to be one of the fundamental paradoxes of Art: it is what I propose to call "the antinomy of Distance."

It will be readily admitted that a work of Art has the more chance of appealing to us the better it finds us prepared for its particular kind of appeal. Indeed, without some degree of predisposition on our part, it must necessarily remain incomprehensible, and to that extent unappreciated. The success and intensity of its appeal would seem, therefore, to stand in direct proportion to the completeness with which it corresponds with our intellectual and emotional peculiarities and the idiosyncracies of our experience. The absence of such a concordance between the characters of a work and of the spectator is, of course, the most general explanation for differences of "tastes."

At the same time, such a principle of concordance requires a qualification, which leads at once to the antinomy of Distance.

Suppose a man, who believes that he has cause to be jealous about his wife, witnesses a performance of "Othello." He will the more perfectly appreciate the situation, conduct and character of Othello, the more exactly the feelings and experiences of Othello coincide with his own—at least he *ought* to on the above principle of concordance. In point of fact, he will probably do anything but appreciate the play. In reality, the concordance will merely render him acutely conscious of his own jealousy; by a sudden reversal of perspective he will no longer see Othello apparently betrayed by Desdemona, but himself in an analogous situation with his own wife. This reversal of perspective is the consequence of the loss of Distance.

If this be taken as a typical case, it follows that the qualification required is that the coincidence should be as complete as is compatible with maintaining Distance. The jealous spectator of "Othello" will indeed appreciate and enter into the play the more keenly, the greater the resemblance with his own experience—*provided* that he succeeds in keeping the Distance between the action of the play and his personal feelings: a very difficult performance in the circumstances. It is on account of the same difficulty that the expert and the professional critic make a bad audience, since their expertness and critical professionalism are *practical* activities, involving their concrete personality and constantly endangering their Distance. [It is, by the way, one of the reasons why Criticism is an art, for it requires the constant interchange from the practical to the distanced attitude and *vice versâ*, which is characteristic of artists.]

The same qualification applies to the artist. He will prove artistically most effective in the formulation of an intensely *personal* experience, but he can formulate it artistically only on condition of a detachment from the experience *quâ personal*. Hence the statement of so many artists that artistic formulation was to them a kind of catharsis, a means of ridding themselves of feelings and ideas the acuteness of which they felt almost as a kind of obsession. Hence, on the other hand, the failure of the average man to convey to others at all adequately the impression of an overwhelming joy or sorrow. His personal implication in the event renders it impossible for him to formulate and present it in such a way as to make others, like himself, feel all the meaning and fulness which it possesses for him.

José Ortega y Gasset

THE
DEHUMANIZATION
OF ART

José Ortega y Gasset (1883–1955) was a Spanish philosopher and humanist who defended the importance of the individual in a world that he saw as increasingly controlled by mass culture. His aesthetic works include The Dehumanization of Art and Other Essays on Art, Culture, and Literature, Meditations on Quixote, *and* The Idea of the Theatre. *In "The Dehumanization of Art" (1925), he offers a defense of those artists of his time who had abandoned the representation of human life in their work.*

A FEW DROPS OF PHENOMENOLOGY

A great man is dying. His wife is by his bedside. A doctor takes the dying man's pulse. In the background two more persons are discovered: a reporter who is present for professional reasons, and a painter whom mere chance has brought here. Wife, doctor, reporter, and painter witness one and the same event. Nonetheless, this identical event—a man's death—impresses each of them in a different way. So different indeed that the several aspects have hardly anything in common. What this scene means to the wife who is all grief has so little to do with what it means to the painter who looks on impassively that it seems doubtful whether the two can be said to be present at the same event.

It thus becomes clear that one and the same reality may split up into many diverse realities when it is beheld from different points of view. And we cannot help asking ourselves: Which of all these realities must then be regarded as the real and authentic one? The answer, no matter how we decide, cannot but be arbitrary. Any preference can be founded on caprice only. All these realities are equivalent, each being authentic for its corresponding point of view. All we can do is to classify the points of view and to determine which among them seems, in a practical way, most normal or most

José Ortega y Gasset, "The Dehumanization of Art," *The Dehumanization of Art and Other Essays on Art, Culture, and Literature* (Princeton: Princeton UP, 1968) 14–23.

spontaneous. Thus we arrive at a conception of reality that is by no means absolute, but at least practical and normative.

As for the points of view of the four persons present at the deathbed, the clearest means of distinguishing them is by measuring one of their dimensions, namely the emotional distance between each person and the event they all witness. For the wife of the dying man the distance shrinks to almost nothing. What is happening so tortures her soul and absorbs her mind that it becomes one with her person. Or to put it inversely, the wife is drawn into the scene, she is part of it. A thing can be seen, an event can be observed, only when we have separated it from ourselves and it has ceased to form a living part of our being. Thus the wife is not present at the scene, she is in it. She does not behold it, she "lives" it.

The doctor is several degrees removed. To him this is a professional case. He is not drawn into the event with the frantic and blinding anxiety of the poor woman. However it is his bounden duty as a doctor to take a serious interest, he carries responsibility, perhaps his professional honor is at stake. Hence he too, albeit in a less integral and less intimate way, takes part in the event. He is involved in it not with his heart but with the professional portion of his self. He too "lives" the scene although with an agitation originating not in the emotional center, but in the professional surface, of his existence.

When we now put ourselves in the place of the reporter we realize that we have traveled a long distance away from the tragic event. So far indeed that we have lost all emotional contact with it. The reporter, like the doctor, has been brought here for professional reasons and not out of a spontaneous human interest. But while the doctor's profession requires him to interfere, the reporter's requires him precisely to stay aloof; he has to confine himself to observing. To him the event is a mere scene, a pure spectacle on which he is expected to report in his newspaper column. He takes no feeling part in what is happening here, he is emotionally free, an outsider. He does not "live" the scene, he observes it. Yet he observes it with a view to telling his readers about it. He wants to interest them, to move them, and if possible to make them weep as though they each had been the dying man's best friend. From his schooldays he remembers Horace's recipe: *"Si vis me flere dolendum est primum ipsi tibi"*—if you want me to weep you must first grieve yourself.

Obedient to Horace the reporter is anxious to pretend emotion, hoping that it will benefit his literary performance. If he does not "live" the scene he at least pretends to "live" it.

The painter, in fine, completely unconcerned, does nothing but keep his eyes open. What is happening here is none of his business; he is, as it were, a hundred miles removed from it. His is a purely perceptive attitude; indeed, he fails to perceive the event in its entirety. The tragic inner meaning escapes his attention which is directed exclusively toward the visual part—color values, lights, and shadows. In the painter we find a maximum of distance and a minimum of feeling intervention.

The inevitable dullness of this analysis will, I hope, be excused if it now enables us to speak in a clear and precise way of a scale of emotional distances between ourselves and reality. In this scale, the degree of closeness is equivalent to the degree of feeling participation; the degree of remoteness, on the other hand, marks the degree to which we have freed ourselves from the real event, thus objectifying it and turning it into a theme of pure observation. At one end of the scale the world—persons, things, situations—is given to us in the aspect of "lived" reality; at the other end we see everything in the aspect of "observed" reality.

At this point we must make a remark that is essential in aesthetics and without which neither old art nor new art can be satisfactorily analyzed. Among the diverse aspects of reality we find one from which all the others derive and which they all presuppose: "lived" reality. If nobody had ever "lived" in pure and frantic abandonment a man's death, the doctor would not bother, the readers would not understand the reporter's pathos, and the canvas on which the painter limned a person on a bed surrounded by mourning figures would be meaningless. The same holds for any object, be it a person, a thing, or a situation. The primal aspect of an apple is that in which I see it when I am about to eat it. All its other possible forms—when it appears, for instance, in a Baroque ornament, or on a still life of Cézanne's, or in the eternal metaphor of a girl's apple cheeks—preserve more or less that original aspect. A painting or a poem without any vestiges of "lived" forms would be unintelligible, i.e., nothing—as a discourse is nothing whose every word is emptied of its customary meaning.

That is to say, in the scale of realities "lived" reality holds a peculiar primacy which compels us to regard it as "the" reality. Instead of "lived" reality we may say "human" reality. The painter who impassively witnesses the death scene appears "inhuman." In other words, the human point of view is that in which we "live" situations, persons, things. And, vice versa, realities—a woman, a countryside, an event—are human when they present the aspect in which they are usually "lived."

As an example, . . . let us mention that among the realities which constitute the world are our ideas. We use our ideas in a "human" way when we employ them for thinking things. Thinking of Napoleon, for example, we are normally concerned with the great man of that name. A psychologist, on the other hand, adopts an unusual, "inhuman" attitude when he forgets about Napoleon and, prying into his own mind,

tries to analyze his idea of Napoleon as such idea. His perspective is the opposite of that prevailing in spontaneous life. The idea, instead of functioning as the means to think an object with, is itself made the object and the aim of thinking. We shall soon see the unexpected use which the new art has made of this "inhuman" inversion. . . .

Far from going more or less clumsily toward reality, the artist is seen going against it. He is brazenly set on deforming reality, shattering its human aspect, dehumanizing it. With the things represented on traditional paintings we could have imaginary intercourse. Many a young Englishman has fallen in love with Gioconda. With the objects of modern pictures no intercourse is possible. By divesting them of their aspect of "lived" reality the artist has blown up the bridges and burned the ships that could have taken us back to our daily world. He leaves us locked up in an abstruse universe, surrounded by object with which human dealings are inconceivable, and thus compels us to improvise other forms of intercourse completely distinct from our ordinary ways with things. We must invent unheard-of gestures to fit those singular figures. This new way of life which presupposes the annulment of spontaneous life is precisely what we call understanding and enjoyment of art. Not that this life lacks sentiments and passions, but those sentiments and passions evidently belong to a flora other than that which covers the hills and dales of primary and human life. What those ultra-objects* evoke in our inner artist are secondary passions, specifically aesthetic sentiments.

It may be said that, to achieve this result, it would be simpler to dismiss human forms—man, house, mountain—altogether

---

*"Ultraism" is one of the most appropriate names that have been coined to denote the new sensibility.

and to construct entirely original figures. But, in the first place, this is not feasible.* Even in the most abstract ornamental line a stubborn reminiscence lurks of certain "natural" forms. Secondly—and this is the crucial point—the art of which we speak is inhuman not only because it contains no things human, but also because it is an explicit act of dehumanization. In his escape from the human world the young artist cares less for the *"terminus ad quem,"* the startling fauna at which he arrives, than for the *"terminus a quo,"* the human aspect which he destroys. The question is not to paint something altogether different from a man, a house, a mountain, but to paint a man who resembles a man as little as possible; a house that preserves of a house exactly what is needed to reveal the metamorphosis; a cone miraculously emerging—as the snake from his slough—from what used to be a mountain. For the modern artist, aesthetic pleasure derives from such a triumph over human matter. That is why he has to drive home the victory by presenting in each case the strangled victim.

It may be thought a simple affair to fight shy of reality, but it is by no means easy. There is no difficulty in painting or saying things which make no sense whatever, which are unintelligible and therefore nothing. One only needs to assemble unconnected words or to draw random lines. But to construct something that is not a copy of "nature" and yet possesses substance of its own is a feat which presupposes nothing less than genius.

---

*An attempt has been made in this extreme sense—in certain works by Picasso—but it has failed signally.

George Dickie

THE MYTH
OF THE
AESTHETIC
ATTITUDE

George Dickie is professor of philosophy at the University of Illinois at Chicago. He is a major proponent of the institutional theory of art, the view that something is an artwork because it is deemed so by the institutions (such as galleries, museums, and institutions of higher education) that comprise the artworld. Dickie's works include Aesthetics: An Introduction, Art and the Aesthetic: An Institutional Analysis, The Art Circle: A Theory of Art, *and* Evaluating Art. *In the following excerpt, Dickie argues against the view that aesthetic experience depends on a particular attitude on the part of the audience member.*

I

Psychical distance, according to Bullough, is a psychological process by virtue of which a person *puts* some object (be it a painting, a play, or a dangerous fog at sea) "out of gear" with the practical interests of the self. Miss [Sheila] Dawson maintains that it is "the beauty of the phenomenon, which captures our attention, puts us out of gear with practical life, and forces us, if we are receptive, to view it on the level of aesthetic consciousness."

Later she maintains that some persons (critics, actors, members of an orchestra, and the like) "distance deliberately." Miss Dawson, following Bullough, discusses cases in which people are unable to bring off an act of distancing or are incapable of being induced into a state of being distanced. She uses Bullough's example of the jealous ("under-distanced") husband at a

George Dickie, "The Myth of the Aesthetic Attitude," *American Philosophical Quarterly* 1.1 (1964): 56–65.

performance of *Othello* who is unable to keep his attention on the play because he keeps thinking of his own wife's suspicious behavior. On the other hand, if "we are mainly concerned with the technical details of its [the play's] presentation, then we are said to be over-distanced." There is, then, a species of action—distancing—which may be deliberately done and which initiates a state of consciousness—being distanced.

The question is: Are there actions denoted by "to distance" or states of consciousness denoted by "being distanced"? When the curtain goes up, when we walk up to a painting, or when we look at a sunset are we ever induced into a state of being distanced either by being struck by the beauty of the object or by pulling off an act of distancing? I do not recall committing any such special actions or of being induced into any special state, and I have no reason to suspect that I am atypical in this respect. The distance-theorist may perhaps ask, "But are you not usually oblivious to noises and sights other than those of the play or to the marks on the wall around the painting?" The answer is of course—"Yes." But if "to distance" and "being distanced" simply mean that one's attention is focused, what is the point of introducing new technical terms and speaking as if these terms refer to special kinds of acts and states of consciousness? The distance-theorist might argue further, "But surely you put the play (painting, sunset) 'out of gear' with your practical interests?" This question seems to me to be a very odd way of asking (by employing the technical metaphor "out of gear") if I attended to the play rather than thought about my wife or wondered how they managed to move the scenery about. Why not ask me straight out if I paid attention? Thus, when Miss Dawson says that the jealous husband under-distanced *Othello* and that the person with a consuming interest in techniques of stagecraft over-distanced the play, these are just technical and misleading ways of describing two different cases of inattention. In both cases something is being attended to, but in neither case is it the action of the play. To introduce the technical terms "distance," "under-distance," and "over-distance" does nothing but send us chasing after phantom acts and states of consciousness.

Miss Dawson's commitment to the theory of distance (as a kind of mental insulation material necessary for a work of art if it is to be enjoyed aesthetically) leads her to draw a conclusion so curious as to throw suspicion on the theory.

> One remembers the horrible loss of distance in *Peter Pan*—the moment when Peter says "Do you believe in fairies? . . . If you believe, clap your hands!" the moment when most children would like to slink out of the theatre and not a few cry—not because Tinkerbell may die, but because the magic is gone. What, after all, should we feel like if Lear were to leave Cordelia, come to the front of the stage and say, "All the grown-ups who think that she loves me, shout 'Yes.'"

It is hard to believe that the responses of any children could be as theory-bound as those Miss Dawson describes. In fact, Peter Pan's request for applause is a dramatic high point to which children respond enthusiastically. The playwright gives the children a momentary chance to become actors in the play. The children do not at that moment lose or snap out of a state of being distanced because they never had or were in any such thing to begin with. The comparison of Peter Pan's appeal to the hypothetical one by Lear is pointless. *Peter Pan* is a magical play in which almost anything can happen, but *King Lear* is a play of a different kind. There are, by the way, many plays in which an actor directly addresses the audience (*Our Town, The Marriage Broker, A Taste of Honey*, for example) without causing the play to be less valuable. Such plays are unusual, but what is unusual is not necessarily bad; there is no point in trying to lay down rules to which every play must conform independently of the kind of play it is.

It is perhaps worth noting that Susanne Langer reports the reaction she had as a child to this scene in *Peter Pan*. As she remembers it, Peter Pan's appeal shattered the illusion and caused her acute misery. However, she reports that all the other children clapped and laughed and enjoyed themselves.

II.

The second way of conceiving of the aesthetic attitude—as the ordinary action of attending done in a certain way (disinterestedly)—is illustrated by the work of Jerome Stolnitz and Eliseo Vivas. Stolnitz defines "aesthetic attitude" as "disinterested and sympathetic attention to and contemplation of any object of awareness whatever, for its own sake alone." Stolnitz defines the main terms of his definition: "disinterested" means "no concern for any ulterior purpose"; "sympathetic" means "accept the object on its own terms to appreciate it"; and "contemplation" means "perception directed toward the object in its own right and the spectator is not concerned to analyze it or ask questions about it."

The notion of disinterestedness, which Stolnitz has elsewhere shown to be seminal for modern aesthetic theory, is the key term here. Thus, it is necessary to be clear about the nature of disinterested attention to the various arts. It can make sense to speak, for example, of listening disinterestedly to music only if it makes sense to speak of listening interestedly to music. It would make no sense to speak of walking *fast* unless walking could be done *slowly*. Using Stolnitz' definition of "disinterestedness," the two situations would have to be described as "listening with no ulterior purpose" (disinterestedly) and "listening with an ulterior purpose" (interestedly). Note that what

initially appears to be a perceptual distinction—listening in a certain way (interestedly or disinterestedly)—turns out to be a motivational or an intentional distinction—listening for or with a certain purpose. Suppose Jones listens to a piece of music for the purpose of being able to analyze and describe it on an examination the next day and Smith listens to the same music with no such ulterior purpose. There is certainly a difference between the motives and intentions of the two men: Jones has an ulterior purpose and Smith does not, but this does not mean Jones's *listening* differs from Smith's. It is possible that both men enjoy the music or that both be bored. The attention of either or both may flag and so on. It is important to note that a person's motive or intention is different from his action (Jones's listening to the music, for example). There is only one way to *listen* to (to attend to) music, although the listening may be more or less attentive and there may be a variety of motives, intentions, and reasons for doing so and a variety of ways of being distracted from the music.

In order to avoid a common mistake of aestheticians—drawing a conclusion about one kind of art and assuming it holds for all the arts—the question of disinterested attention must be considered for arts other than music. How would one look at a painting disinterestedly or interestedly? An example of alleged interested viewing might be the case in which a painting reminds Jones of his grandfather and Jones proceeds to muse about or to regale a companion with tales of his grandfather's pioneer exploits. Such incidents would be characterized by attitude-theorists as examples of using a work of art as a vehicle for associations and so on, i.e., cases of interested attention. But Jones is not looking at (attending to) the painting at all, although he may be facing it with his eyes open. Jones is now musing or attending to the story he is telling, although he had to look at the painting at first to notice that it resembled his grandfather. Jones is not now looking at the painting interestedly, since he is not now looking at (attending to) the painting. Jones's thinking or telling a story about his grandfather is no more a part of the painting than his speculating about the artist's intentions is and, hence, his musing, telling, speculating, and so on cannot properly be described as attending to the painting interestedly. What attitude-aestheticians are calling attention to is the occurrence of irrelevant associations which distract the viewer from the painting or whatever. But distraction is not a special kind of attention, it is a kind of inattention.

Consider now disinterestedness and plays. I shall make use of some interesting examples offered by J. O. Urmson, but I am not claiming that Urmson is an attitude-theorist. Urmson never speaks in his article of aesthetic attitude but rather of aesthetic satisfaction. In addition to aesthetic satisfaction, Urmson mentions economic, moral, personal, and intellectual satisfactions. I think the attitude-theorist would consider these last four kinds of satisfaction as "ulterior purposes" and, hence, cases of interested attention. Urmson considers the case of a man in the audience of a play who is delighted. It is discovered that his delight is *solely* the result of the fact that there is a full house—the man is the impresario of the production. Urmson is right in calling *this* impresario's satisfaction economic rather than aesthetic, although there is a certain oddness about the example as it finds the impresario sitting *in the audience*. However, my concern is not with Urmson's examples as such but with the attitude theory. This impresario is certainly an interested party in the fullest sense of the word, but is his behavior an instance of interested attention as distinct from the supposed disinterested attention of the average citizen who sits beside him? In the situation as described by Urmson it would not make any sense to say that the impresario is attending to the play at all, since his *sole* concern at the moment is the till. If he can be said to be attending to anything (rather than just thinking about it) it is the size of the house. I do not mean to suggest that an impresario could not attend to his play if he found himself taking up a seat in a full house; I am challenging the sense of disinterested attention. As an example of personal satisfaction Urmson mentions the spectator whose daughter is in the play. Intellectual satisfaction involves the solution of technical problems of plays and moral satisfaction the consideration of the effects of the play on the viewer's conduct. All three of these candidates which the attitude-theorist would propose as cases of interested attention turn out to be just different ways of being distracted from the play and, hence, not cases of interested attention to the play. Of course, there is no reason to think that in any of these cases the distraction or inattention must be total, although it could be. In fact, such inattentions often occur but are so fleeting that nothing of the play, music, or whatever is missed or lost.

The example of a playwright watching a rehearsal or an out-of-town performance with a view to rewriting the script has been suggested to me as a case in which a spectator is certainly attending to the play (unlike our impresario) and attending in an interested manner. This case is unlike those just discussed but is similar to the earlier case of Jones (not Smith) listening to a particular piece of music. Our playwright—like Jones, who was to be examined on the music—has ulterior motives. Furthermore, the playwright, unlike an ordinary spectator, can change the script after the performance or during a rehearsal. But how is our playwright's *attention* (as distinguished from his motives and intentions) different from that of an ordinary viewer? The playwright might enjoy or be bored by the performance as any spectator might be. The playwright's attention might even flag. In short, the kinds of things which may happen to the playwright's attention are no different from those that may happen to an ordinary spectator, although the two may have quite different motives and intentions.

The above cases of alleged interested attending can be sorted out in the following way. Jones listening to the music and our playwright watching the rehearsal are both attending with ulterior motives to a work of art, but there is no reason to suppose that the attention of either is different in kind from that of an ordinary spectator. The reader who reads a poem as history is simply attending to an aspect of a poem. On the other hand, the remaining cases—Jones beside the painting telling of his grandfather, the gloating impresario, daydreaming while "reading" a poem, and so on—are simply cases of not attending to the work of art.

In general, I conclude that "disinterestedness" or "intransitiveness" cannot properly be used to refer to a special kind of attention. "Disinterestedness" is a term which is used to make clear that an action has certain kinds of motives. Hence, we speak of disinterested findings (of boards of inquiry), disinterested verdicts (of judges and juries), and so on. Attending to an object, of course, has its motives but the attending itself is not interested or disinterested according to whether its motives are of the kind which motivate interested or disinterested action (as findings and verdicts might), although the attending may be more or less close.

I have argued that the second way of conceiving the aesthetic attitude is also a myth, or at least that its main content—disinterested attention—is; but I must now try to establish that the view misleads aesthetic theory. I shall argue that the attitude-theorist is incorrect about (1) the way in which he wishes to set the limits of aesthetic relevance; (2) the relation of the critic to a work

of art; and (3) the relation of morality to aesthetic value.

First, what is meant by "aesthetic relevance"? Stolnitz defines the problem by asking the question: "Is it ever 'relevant' to the aesthetic experience to have thoughts or images or bits of knowledge which are not present within the object itself?" Stolnitz begins by summarizing Bullough's experiment and discussion of single colors and associations. Some associations absorb the spectator's attention and distract him from the color and some associations "fuse" with the color. Associations of the latter kind are aesthetic and the former are not. Stolnitz draws the following conclusion about associations:

> If the aesthetic experience is as we have described it, then whether an association is aesthetic depends on whether it is compatible with the attitude of "disinterested attention." If the association re-enforces the focusing of attention upon the object, by "fusing" with the object and thereby giving it added "life and significance," it is genuinely aesthetic. If, however, it arrogates attention to itself and away from the object, it undermines the aesthetic attitude.

It is not clear how something could *fuse* with a single color, but "fusion" is one of those words in aesthetics which is rarely defined. . . .

It is a confusion to take compatibility with disinterested attention as a criterion of relevance. If, as I have tried to show, *disinterested attention* is a confused notion, then it will not do as a satisfactory criterion. . . .

A second way in which the attitude theory misleads aesthetics is its contention that a critic's relationship to a work of art is different in kind from the relationship of other persons to the work. H. S. Langfeld in an early statement of this view wrote that we may "slip from the attitude of aesthetic enjoyment to the attitude of the critic." He characterizes the critical attitude as "intellectually occupied in coldly estimating . . . merits" and the aesthetic attitude as responding "emotionally to" a work of art. At the beginning of his book in the discussion of the aesthetic attitude, Stolnitz declares that if a percipient of a work of art "has the purpose of passing judgment upon it, his attitude is not aesthetic." He develops this line at a later stage of his book, arguing that appreciation (perceiving with the aesthetic attitude) and criticism (seeking for reasons to support an evaluation of a work) are (1) distinct and (2) "psychologically opposed to each other." The critical attitude is questioning, analytical, probing for strengths and weakness, and so on. The aesthetic attitude is just the opposite: "It commits our allegiance to the object freely and unquestioningly"; "the spectator 'surrenders' himself to the work of art." "Just because the two attitudes are inimical, whenever criticism obtrudes, it reduces aesthetic interest." Stolnitz does not, of course, argue that criticism is unimportant for appreciation. He maintains criticism plays an important and necessary role in preparing a person to appreciate the nuances, detail, form, and so on of works of art. We are quite right, he says, thus to read and listen perceptively and acutely, but he questions, "Does this mean that we must analyze, measure in terms of value-criteria, etc., *during* the supposedly aesthetic experience?" His answer is "No" and he maintains that criticism must occur "*prior* to the aesthetic encounter," or it will interfere with appreciation.

How does Stolnitz know that criticism will always interfere with appreciation? His conclusion sounds like one based upon the observations of actual cases, but I do not think it is. I believe it is a logical consequence of his definition of aesthetic attitude in terms of disinterested attention (no

ulterior purpose). According to his view, to appreciate an object aesthetically one has to perceive it with no ulterior purpose. But the critic has an ulterior purpose—to analyze and evaluate the object he perceives—hence, in so far as a person functions as a critic he cannot function as an appreciator. But here, as previously, Stolnitz confuses a perceptual distinction with a motivational one. If it were possible to *attend* disinterestedly or interestedly, then perhaps the critic (as percipient) would differ from other percipients. But if my earlier argument about attending is correct, the critic differs from other percipients only in his motives and intentions and not in the way in which he attends to a work of art.

. . . Stolnitz' remarks suggest that one reason he thinks criticism and appreciation incompatible is that they compete with one another for time (this would be especially bad in the cases of performed works). But seeking and finding reasons (criticism) does not compete for time with appreciation. First, to seek for a reason means to be ready and able to notice something and to be thus ready and able as one attends does not compete for time with the attending. In fact, I should suppose that seeking for reasons would tend to focus attention more securely on the work of art. Second, finding a reason is an achievement, like winning a race. (It takes time to run a race but not to win it.) Consider the finding of the following reasons. How much time does it take to "see" that a note is off key (or on key)? How long does it take to notice that an actor mispronounces a word (or does it right)? How much time does it take to realize that a character's action does not fit his already established personality? (One is struck by it.) How long does it take to apprehend that a happy ending is out of place? It does not take time to find any of these reasons or reasons in general. Finding a reason is like coming to understand—it is done in a flash. I do not mean to suggest that one cannot be mistaken in finding a reason. What may appear to be a fault or a merit (a found reason) in the middle of a performance (or during one look at a painting and so forth) may turn out to be just the opposite when seen from the perspective of the whole performance (or other looks at the painting).

A third way in which the attitude theory misleads aesthetic theory is its contention that aesthetic value is always independent of morality. This view is perhaps not peculiar to the attitude theory, but it is a logical consequence of the attitude approach. . . .

This conception of the aesthetic attitude functions to hold the moral aspects and the *aesthetic* aspects of the work of art firmly apart. Presumably, although it is difficult to see one's way clearly here, the moral aspects of a work of art cannot be an object of aesthetic attention because aesthetic attention is by definition disinterested and the moral aspects are somehow practical (interested). I suspect that there are a number of confusions involved in the assumption of the incompatibility of aesthetic attention and the moral aspects of art, but I shall not attempt to make these clear, since the root of the assumption—disinterested attention—is a confused notion. Some way other than in terms of the aesthetic attitude, then, is needed to discuss the relation of morality and aesthetic value.

David Pole in a recent article has argued that the moral vision which a work of art may embody is *aesthetically* significant. It should perhaps be remarked at this point that not all works of art embody a moral vision and perhaps some kinds of art (music, for example) cannot embody a moral vision, but certainly some novels, some poems, and some films and plays do. I assume it is unnecessary to show how novels and so on have this moral aspect. Pole notes the curious fact that while so many

critics approach works of art in "overtly moralistic terms," it is a "philosophical commonplace . . . that the ethical and the aesthetic modes . . . form different categories." I suspect that many philosophers would simply say that these critics are confused about their roles. But Pole assumes that philosophical theory "should take notice of practice" and surely he is right. In agreeing with Pole's assumption I should like to reserve the right to argue in specific cases that a critic may be misguided. This right is especially necessary in a field such as aesthetics because the language and practice of critics is so often burdened with ancient theory. Perhaps *all* moralistic criticism is wrong but philosophers should not rule it out of order at the very beginning by use of a definition.

Pole thinks that the moral vision presented by a particular work of art will be either true or false (perhaps a mixture of true and false might occur). If a work has a false moral vision, then something "is lacking within the work itself. But to say that is to say that the [work] is internally incoherent; some particular aspect must jar with what—on the strength of the rest—we claim a right to demand. And here the moral fault that we have found will count as an aesthetic fault too." Pole is trying to show that the assessment of the moral vision of a work of art is just a special case of coherence or incoherence, and since everyone would agree that coherence is an aesthetic category, the assessment of the moral vision is an aesthetic assessment.

I think Pole's conclusion is correct but take exception to some of his arguments. First, I am uncertain whether it is proper to speak of a moral vision being true or false, and would want to make a more modest claim—that a moral vision can be judged to be acceptable or unacceptable. (I am not claiming Pole is wrong and my claim is not inconsistent with his.) Second, I do not see that a false (or unacceptable) moral vision makes a work incoherent. I should suppose that to say a work is coherent or incoherent is to speak about how its parts fit together and this involves no reference to something outside the work as the work's truth or falsity does.

In any event, it seems to me that a faulty moral vision can be shown to be an aesthetic fault independently of Pole's consideration of truth and coherence. As Pole's argument implies, a work's moral vision is a *part* of the work. Thus, any statement—descriptive or evaluative—about the work's moral vision is a statement about the *work;* and any statement about a *work* is a critical statement and, hence, falls within the aesthetic domain. To judge a moral vision to be morally unacceptable is to judge it defective and this amounts to saying that the work of art has a defective part. (Of course, a judgment of the acceptability of a moral vision may be wrong, as a judgment of an action sometimes is, but this fallibility does not make any difference.) Thus, a work's moral vision may be an aesthetic merit or defect just as a work's degree of unity is a merit or defect. But what justifies saying that a moral vision is a part of a work of art? Perhaps "part" is not quite the right word but it serves to make the point clear enough. A novel's moral vision is an essential part of the novel and if it were removed (I am not sure how such surgery could be carried out) the novel would be greatly changed. Anyway, a novel's moral vision is not like its covers or binding. However, someone might still argue that even though a work's moral vision is defective and the moral vision is part of the work, that this defect is not an *aesthetic* defect. How is "aesthetic" being used here? It is being used to segregate certain aspects or parts of works of art such as formal and stylistic aspects from such aspects as a work's moral vision. But it seems to me that the separation is only nominal. "Aesthetic" has been selected as a name for a certain sub-set of characteristics of works of art. I certainly cannot object to such a stipulation, since an underlying aim of this essay is to suggest the vacuousness of the term "aesthetic." My concern at this point is simply to insist that a work's moral vision is a part of the work and that, therefore, a critic can legitimately describe and evaluate it. I would *call* any defect or merit which a critic can legitimately point out an aesthetic defect or merit, but what we call it does not matter.

It would, of course, be a mistake to judge a work solely on the basis of its moral vision (it is only one part). The fact that some critics have judged works of art in this way is perhaps as much responsible as the theory of aesthetic attitude for the attempts to separate morality from the aesthetic. In fact, such criticism is no doubt at least partly responsible for the rise of the notion of the aesthetic attitude.

DISCUSSION QUESTIONS

1. How would you describe aesthetic experience? Can you control when you have an aesthetic experience, in your opinion?
2. Is the production of aesthetic experience the primary function of art? What are the pros and cons of defining art in terms of aesthetic experience?
3. Is aesthetic distance necessary for aesthetic experience, in your opinion? Why or why not? Can you be too close or too far from the subject matter of an artwork to have an aesthetic experience in connection with it?
4. Do you think that an artistic performer must be having an aesthetic experience in order for the audience to have one?
5. Does the perspective of the artist in Ortega y Gasset's account strike you as strange or inhuman? Why or why not?
6. Does aesthetic experience have any lingering effects or influence? Is aesthetic experience inherently valuable? Why or why not?

FURTHER READING

Dickie, George. *Art and the Aesthetic: An Institutional Analysis*. Ithaca: Cornell UP, 1974.

——— *The Art Circle: A Theory of Art*. New York: Haven, 1984.

Dufrenne, Mikel. *Phenomenology of Aesthetic Experience*. Trans. Edward Casey. Evanston: Northwestern UP, 1973.

Korsmeyer, Carolyn. "On Distinguishing 'Aesthetic' from 'Artistic,'" *The Journal of Aesthetic Education* 22 (1977): 45–57.

Saxena, Sushil Kumar. "The Aesthetic Attitude." *Philosophy East and West* 28 (1978): 81–90.

Stolnitz, Jerome. *Aesthetics*. New York: Macmillan, 1965.

Chapter

⑤

ART AND
ETHICS

In one of Monty Python's sketches, John Cleese plays a pope who insists on having an artist, "Michelangelo," brought to see him. The "pope" reprimands the artist for painting a "Last Supper" with too many characters (not only too many disciples, but three Christs, and even a kangaroo). "Michelangelo" claims that he has merely taken some artistic license, since everyone knows that the real Last Supper had twelve disciples and one Christ. He suggests changing the title, a solution that the pope in the sketch rejects, but precisely the solution employed by Paolo Veronese when he was brought before the Tribunal of the Inquisition for painting irrelevant characters in his "Last Supper." (Paolo Veronese's painting did not include a kangaroo, but the presence of Germans, buffoons, and a disciple using a toothpick struck the Inquisitors as blasphemous.)

The demand that art portray religiously and ethically suitable content has been voiced since Plato, if not before. (See the selection from Plato's *Republic* in Chapter 3 for some of his arguments.) One longstanding position on the purpose of art is the instrumentalist view that art's purpose is to reflect sound values and to provide moral education for its audience. Although the instrumentalist view is not the presumption of the twentieth century, the view that art should at least *not* reflect or promote bad moral values is implicit in the demands that morally offensive art not be exhibited, that music with the wrong moral message be banned from the airwaves, and that sex and violence in Hollywood movies be restricted.

The selections from Alexander Nehamas and Allan Bloom each relate these current demands to Plato's arguments. Nehamas compares Plato's complaint that his contemporaries will likely imitate the behavior portrayed in plays to contemporary denunciations of television. Nehamas argues that we often fail to notice the similarity because television seems mere entertainment, while we consider the works of Homer and the tragedians to be fine art. But these classics were themselves popular entertainment for the ancient Athenians. While agreeing with the critics who claim that much television is vapid, Nehamas nevertheless observes that it is the use of the medium, not the medium itself, that causes television programs to be of low caliber. In principle, he concludes, nothing inherent in the medium precludes television from being employed as a fine art that is neither aesthetically insipid nor morally harmful.

Allan Bloom endorses Plato's lines of attack on the art of his era and updates Plato's arguments to criticize rock music. Bloom accepts Plato's analysis of beauty as a stimulus to reflection on spiritual matters. Rock, according to Bloom, makes a travesty of this aim. Geared to immediate gratification, rock does not instill spiritual ardor. Instead, it promotes an ideology of cheap thrills and gluttonous appetites. Bloom compares the influence of rock to the influence of drugs, both of which, he claims, kill sensitivity and the potential to appreciate anything finer.

Opponents of rock music often insist that the message of the music is morally pernicious. But should art function as a kind of propaganda for the right things, as Plato suggests, encouraging or manipulating us to behave in certain desirable ways? Karsten Harries considers the question of whether art ought to promote a positive moral agenda. His answer is "no," but not because he denies that art has a role to play in our ethical lives. Art's ethical role is not to induce moral conformity, argues Harries, but to disrupt our habits and to raise important questions. Art that states a message too directly cannot achieve this moral vocation. Art conveys ethical import most effectively when it upsets our moral complacency and stimulates us to do the hard work of moral thinking in a world where simple answers will not do.

Far from urging that art challenge accepted values, Iran's Ayatollah Khomeini pronounced a death sentence on Salman Rushdie in 1989 for allegedly committing blasphemy in his novel *The Satanic Verses*. This pronouncement resulted in furor among defenders of artistic freedom around the world. It also raised questions about the extent to which it is appropriate for an artwork to challenge a society's moral or religious values. Are there limits to an artist's right to criticize or offend those who are more conventional?

Carlos Fuentes defends Salman Rushdie, claiming that Rushdie has accomplished an important religious and ethical service by artistically reflecting the challenges of our world, in which different cultures encounter one another. Rushdie's novel reveals tensions in our world, and it aims to disturb us. Fuentes' description is reminiscent of Harries' analysis of the ethical significance of art. Ironically, although Khomeini and those who support him dismiss the rights of the artist, Fuentes argues, they have enhanced the potency of literature, taking it so seriously that they view a death sentence as an appropriate response.

William H. Gass denies that we should judge art in terms of morality. He grants that an artwork can reflect moral values, but he insists that an artwork's aesthetic value is independent of moral values. Artists, in his view, should aspire to achieve beauty, balance, pleasing structure, and whatever perfection they can in their works. Gass defends the thesis that art is **autonomous,** that its function is not to serve some other purpose (such as morality), but that it has intrinsic value of a particularly artistic sort.

The theory of art's autonomy is emphatically not accepted by many contemporary college students. Liza Mundy describes cases on various campuses across the United States in which students have protested and even vandalized artworks on the grounds that they are morally offensive or insulting to particular groups. One interesting aspect of such protests is that they often pit seeming allies against one another. Feminists are divided, for instance, on whether pornography is harmful to women. Mundy's article focuses attention on the discrepancy that sometimes emerges between the artist's intended message and that interpreted by a work's audience. (Jerrold Levinson's "Messages in Art," in Chapter 10, offers a related analysis of meaning and interpretation.)

Donald Kuspit is less sympathetic to the idea that art ought to facilitate better political attitudes. In "Art and the Moral Imperative," he criticizes recent activist art that straightforwardly aims to convey a particular political message. Such art tends to be blatant and aesthetically shallow, according to Kuspit. Art with aesthetic impact does not proceed from moralistic motivations; instead it proceeds from the more Dionysian soil of eroticism and desire. Activist art is bent on imposing restrictions, but aesthetically rich art revitalizes its observer.

Museums are more often thought to contain art than to be art, but Philip Gourevitch analyzes Washington, D.C.'s Holocaust Museum as one might an artwork. He considers its appeals, its intentions, and what it actually achieves. Despite its effort to respond in a morally sensitive way to the atrocities committed in Nazi Germany, the Holocaust Museum fails to achieve what it attempts, according to Gourevitch. It is too much like mass entertainment, promoting complacency by encouraging a false sense that the Holocaust and its motivations are safely in the past. Gourevitch asks again one of Plato's central questions: Does our art yield, or prevent, real insight as to where we stand?

Alexander Nehamas

PLATO
AND THE
MASS MEDIA

Alexander Nehamas is professor of philosophy and humanities at Princeton University, and he works primarily in ancient philosophy, Nietzsche scholarship, and literary theory. He is author of Nietzsche: Life as Literature *and translator (with Paul Woodruff) of Plato's* Symposium. *Nehamas argues that recent complaints about the influence of television resemble Plato's complaints against the drama of his own time. This is appropriate, Nehamas contends, for Plato's allegations about poetry are attacks on the popular entertainment of the day, not on art in general.*

The metaphysics of Pygmalion is still in the center of our thinking about the arts. To see that this is so, and why, we must change subjects abruptly and recall Newton Minnow's famous address to the National Association of Broadcasters in 1961. Though Minnow admitted that some television was of high quality, he insisted that if his audience were to watch, from beginning to end, a full day's programming,

I can assure you that you will observe a vast wasteland. You will see a procession of game shows, violence, audience participation shows, formula comedies about totally unbelievable families, blood and thunder, mayhem, violence sadism, murder, western badmen, western goodmen, private eyes, gangsters, more violence, and cartoons.

This general view of the vulgarity of television has been given a less extreme expression, and a rationale, by George Gerbner and Larry Gross:

Unlike the real world, where personalities are complex, motives unclear, and outcomes ambiguous, television presents a world of clarity and simplicity. . . . In order to complete a story entertainingly in only an hour or even half an hour conflicts on TV are usually personal and solved by action. Since violence is dramatic and relatively simple to produce, much of the action tends to be violent.

Alexander Nehamas, "Plato and the Mass Media," *The Monist* 71.2 (1988): 214–34.

An extraordinary, almost hysterical version of such a view, but nevertheless a version that is uncannily close to Plato's attitude that the lowest part of the soul is the subject-matter of poetry, is given by Jerry Mander. Television, he writes, is inherently suited for

> expressing hate, fear, jealousy, winning, wanting, and violence . . . hysteria or ebullience of the kind of one-dimensional joyfulness usually associated with some objective victory—the facial expressions and bodily movements of antisocial behavior.

Mander also duplicates, in connection with television, Plato's view that poetry directly influences our life for the worse: "We slowly evolve into the images we carry, we become what we see." This, of course, is the guiding premise of the almost universal debate concerning the portrayal of sex, violence, and other disapproved or antisocial behavior on television on the grounds that it tends to encourage television's audience to engage in such behavior in life. And a very sophisticated version of this Platonic point, making use of the distinction between form and content, has been accepted by Wayne Booth:

> The effects of the medium in shaping the primary experience of the viewer, and thus the quality of the self during the viewing, are radically resistant to any elevation of quality in the program content: as viewer, I become *how* I view, more than *what* I view. . . . Unless we change their characteristic forms, the new media will surely corrupt whatever global village they create; you cannot build a world community out of misshapen souls.

. . . Plato's reason for thinking that our reactions to life duplicate our reactions to poetry is that imitations are superficially identical with the objects of which they are imitations. Exactly this explanation is also given by Rudolph Arnheim, who wrote that television "is a mere instrument of transmission, which does not offer any new means for the artistic interpretation of reality." Television, that is, presents us the world just as it is or, rather, it simply duplicates its appearance. Imitations are substitutes for reality. In Mander's words,

> people were believing that an *image* of nature was equal . . . to the experience of nature . . . that images of historical events or news events were equal to the events . . . the confusion of . . . information with a wider, direct mode of experience was advancing rapidly.

Plato's argument against poetry is repeated in summary form, and without an awareness of its provenance, in connection with television by Neil Postman: "Television," he writes, "offers viewers a variety of subject-matter, requires minimal skills to comprehend it, and is largely aimed at emotional gratification." The inevitable result, strictly parallel to "the bad government in the soul" which Plato would go to all lengths to avert, is, according to Postman, an equally dangerous "spiritual devastation."

Parallels between Plato's view and contemporary attitudes such as that expressed in the statement that "daily consumption of 'Three's Company' is not likely to produce a citizenry concerned about, much less committed to, Madisonian self-government," are to be found wherever you look. Simply put, the greatest part of contemporary criticisms of television depends on a moral disapproval which is identical to Plato's attack on epic and tragic poetry in the fourth century B.C. In this respect, at least, we are most of us Platonists. We must therefore reexamine both our grounds for disapproving of Plato's attack on poetry and our reasons for disapproving of television. . . .

◆◆◆

My effort to establish a parallel between Plato's deep, complex, and suspicious hostility toward Homer and Aeschylus on the one hand and the obviously well-deserved contempt with which many today regard *Dynasty* or *Dallas* may well appear simply ridiculous. Though classical Greek poetry still determines many of the criteria that underlie the literary canon of our culture, most of television hardly qualifies as entertainment. Yet my position does not amount to a trivialization of Plato's views. On the contrary, I believe, we are bound to miss (and have already missed) the real urgency of Plato's approach if we persist in taking it as an attack against art as such. Plato was neither insensitive to art nor inconsistent in his desire to produce, as he did, artworks of his own in his dialogues; he neither discerned a deep characteristic of art that pits it essentially against philosophy nor did he envisage a higher form of art which he would have allowed in his city. Plato's argument with poetry concerns a practice which is today paradigmatically a fine art, but it is not an argument directed at it as such a fine art. At this point, the history of art becomes essential for an understanding of its philosophy. Though Plato's attack against poetry in the *Republic* may be the originating text of the philosophy of art, his argument, without being any less profound or disturbing, dismisses poetry as what it was in his time: and poetry then was popular entertainment.

The audience of Attic drama, as far as we now know, was "a 'popular' audience in the sense that it was a body fully representative of the great mass of the Athenian people" and included a great number of foreign visitors as well. During the Greater Dionysia in classical times no fewer than 17,000 people, perhaps more, were packed into the god's theater. Pericles, according to Plutarch, established the *theōrikon*, a subsidy to cover the price of admission and something more, which ended up being distributed to rich and poor alike, and made of the theater a free entertainment.

The plays were not produced in front of a well-behaved audience. The dense crowd was given to whistling . . . and the theater resounded with its "uneducated noise." . . . Plato expresses profound distaste for the tumult with which audiences, in the theater and elsewhere, voiced their approval or dissatisfaction (*Rep.* 492c). Their preferences were definitely pronounced if not often sophisticated. Since four plays were produced within a single day, the audience arrived at the theater with large quantities of food. Some of it they consumed themselves—hardly a silent activity in its own right, unlikely to produce the quasi-religious attention required of a fine-art audience today and more reminiscent of other sorts of mass entertainments. Some of their food was used to pelt those actors whom they did not like, and whom they often literally shouted off the stage. In particular, and though this may be difficult to imagine today, the drama was considered a realistic representation of the world: we are told, for example, that a number of women were frightened into having miscarriages or into giving premature birth by the entrance of the Furies in Aeschylus' *Eumenides*.

The realistic interpretation of Attic drama is crucial for our purposes. Simon Goldhill, expressing the recent suspiciousness toward certain native understandings of realism, has written that Electra's entrance as a peasant in the play Euripides named after her "is upsetting not because it represents reality but because it represents reality in a way which transgresses the conventions of dramatic representations, indeed the representations of reality constructed elsewhere in the play," In fact, he continues, "Euripides constantly forces awareness of theatre as theatre." This, along with the general contemporary claim that all art necessarily contains hints pointing toward its artificial nature and undermining whatever naturalistic pretensions it makes, may well be true. But it doesn't alter the fact that it is of the essence of popular entertainment that these hints are not, while the entertainment still remains popular, consciously perceived. Popular entertainment, in theory and practice, is generally taken to be inherently realistic.

To be inherently realistic is to seem to represent reality without artifice, without mediation and convention. Realistic art is, just in the sense in which Plato thought of imitation, transparent. This transparency, I believe, is not real. It is only the result of our often not being aware of the mediated and conventional nature of the representations to which we are most commonly exposed. As Barish writes in regard to the theater, "it has an unsettling way of being received by its audiences, at least for the moment and with whatever necessary mental reserves, as reality pure and simple." Whether or not we are aware of it, however, mediation and convention are absolutely essential to all representation. But since, in such cases, they cannot be attributed to the representation itself, which, transparent as it is, cannot be seen as an object with its own status and in its own right, they are instead attributed to the represented subject-matter: the slow-moving speech and action patterns of soap operas, for example, are considered (and criticized) as representations of a slow-moving world.

Attributed to subject-matter, mediation and convention appear, almost by necessity, as distortions. And accordingly . . . the reality the popular media [is] supposed to represent has always been considered, while the media in question are still popular, as a distorted, perverted, and dismal reality. And it has regularly involved campaigns to abolish or reform the popular arts or efforts on the part of the few to distance themselves from the arts as far as possible. And insofar as the audience of these media has been supposed, and has often supposed itself, to react directly to that reality, the audience's undisputed enjoyment of the popular arts has been interpreted as the enjoyment of this distorted, perverted, and dismal reality. It has therefore also been believed that this enjoyment both reflects and contributes to a distorted, perverted, and dismal life—a vast wasteland accurately reflected in the medium which mirrors it.

This is the essence of Plato's attack against poetry and, I believe, the essential idea behind a number of attacks against television today. Nothing in Plato's time answered to our concept of the fine arts, especially to the idea that the arts are a province of a small and enlightened part of the population (which may or may be not be interested in attracting the rest of the people to them), and Plato holds no views about them. His quarrel with poetry is not disturbing because anyone seriously believes that Plato could have been right about Homer's pernicious influence. Plato's view is disturbing because we are still agreed with him that representation is transparent—at least in the case of those media which, like television, have not yet acquired the status of art and whose own nature, as opposed to what they depict, has not yet become in serious terms a subject in its own right. And because of this view, we may indeed react to life, or think that we do, as we react to its representations: what is often necessary for a similarity between our reactions to life and our reactions to art is not so much the fact that the two are actually similar but only the view that they are. Many do in fact enjoy things on television which, as Plato wrote in regard to poetry, some at least would be ashamed, even horrified, to enjoy in life.

The problem here is with the single word "things," which applies both to the contents of television shows and to the situations those represent. What this suggests is that what is presented on television is a duplicate of what occurs in the world. No interpretation seems to be needed in order to reveal and to understand the complex relations that actually obtain between them.

By contrast, no one believes that the fine arts produce such duplications. Though we are perfectly willing to learn about life from literature and painting (a willingness which, in my opinion, requires close scrutiny in its own right), no one would ever project directly the content of a work of fine art onto the world. The fine arts, we believe, bear an indirect, interpretative relationship to the world, and further interpretation on the part of audience and critics is necessary in order to understand it. It is precisely for this sort of interpretation that the popular arts do not seem to call.

———◆◆◆———

Yet the case of the *Republic* suggests that the line between the popular and the fine arts is much less settled than is often supposed. If my approach has been right so far, Plato's quarrel with poetry is to a great extent, as much of the disdain against television today is, a quarrel with a popular form of entertainment. Greek drama, indeed, apart from the fact that it was addressed to a very broad audience, exhibits a number of features commonly associated with popular literature. One among them is the sheer volume of output required from any popular genre. "Throughout the fifth century B.C. and probably, apart from a few exceptional years, through the earlier part of the fourth century also," Pickard-Cambridge writes, "three tragic poets entered the contest for the prize in tragedy, and each presented four plays." If we add to these the plays produced by the comic poets, the plays produced at all the festivals other than the City Dionysia (with which Pickard-Cambridge is exclusively concerned), and the plays of the poets who were not chosen for the contest, we can see that the actual number of dramas must have been immense. The three great tragedians alone account for roughly three hundred works. And this is at least a partial explanation of the fact that so many plays were different treatments of the same stories. This practice is imposed on popular authors by the demands of their craft and is in itself a serious source of satisfaction for their audience.

The most important feature of popular art, however, is the transparency to which we have already referred. The idea is complex, and it is very difficult to say in general terms which of a popular work's features are projected directly onto reality since, obviously, not all are. A television audience knows very well that actors shot during a show are not really dead, but other aspects of the behavior of such fictional characters are actually considered as immediate transcriptions of reality. On a very simple level, for example, it is difficult to explain otherwise the fact that the heroines of *Cagney and Lacey* invariably buckle their seat belts when they enter their car, whether to chase a murderer or to go to lunch. And many aspects of their relationship are considered as perfectly accurate transcriptions of reality. Popular art is commonly perceived as literally incorporating parts of reality within it; hence the generally accepted, and mistaken, view that it requires little or no interpretation.

Arthur Danto has recently drawn attention to art which aims to incorporate reality directly within it, and has named it the "art of disturbation." This is not art which represents, as art has always represented, disturbing reality. It is art which aims to disturb precisely by eradicating the distance between it and reality, by placing reality squarely within it. Disturbational art aims to frustrate and unsettle its audience's aesthetic, distanced, and contemplative expectations: "Reality," Danto writes, "must in some way . . . be an actual component of disturbatory art and usually reality of a kind itself disturbing. . . . And these as components in the art, not simply collateral with its production and appreciation." "Happenings" or Chris Burden's viciously self-endangering projects fall within this category. And so did, until relatively recently, obscenity in the cinema and the theatre.

The purpose of disturbational art, according to Danto, is atavistic. It aims to reintroduce reality back into art, as was once supposedly the norm: "Once we perceive statues as merely designating what they resemble . . . rather than containing the reality through containing the form, a certain power is lost to art." But contemporary disturbational art, which Danto considers "pathetic and futile," utterly fails to recapture this lost "magic."

This failure is not an accident. The disturbational art with which Danto is concerned consists mainly of paintings, sculptures, and "happenings" that are essentially addressed to a sophisticated audience through the conventions of the fine arts: you dress to go see it. But part of what makes the fine arts fine is precisely the distance they have managed, over time, to insert between representation and reality; this distance can no longer be eliminated. Danto finds that disturbational art still poses some sort of vague threat: "Perhaps it is for this reason that the spontaneous response to disturbational art is to disarm it by cooptation, incorporating it instantaneously into the cool institutions of the artworld where it will be rendered harmless and distant from forms of life it meant to explode." My own explanation is that the cool institutions of the artworld are just where the art of disturbation, which is necessarily a fine art, has always belonged.

Disturbational art aims to restore "to art some of the magic purified out when art became *art*." This, I believe, is not a reasonable goal: once a genre has become fine, it seldom if ever loses its status; too much is invested in it. And yet, I want to suggest, "the magic purified out when art became *art*" is all around us, and just for that reason almost totally invisible. The distinction between representation and reality is constantly and interestingly blurred by television—literally an art which has not yet become *art*—and which truly disturbs its audience: consider, as one instance among innumerably many, the intense debate over the influence on Soviet-American relations

of the absurd mini-series *Amerika* in the spring of 1987.

As a medium, television is still highly transparent. Though, as I have admitted, I don't yet have a general account of which of its features are projected directly onto the world, television clearly convinces us on many occasions that what we see *in* it is precisely what we see *through* it. This is precisely why it presents such a challenge to our moral sensibility. The "magic" of television may be neither admirable nor even respectable. But it is, I am arguing, structurally identical to the magic Plato saw and denounced in Greek poetry, which also, of course, was not *art*.

Plato's attack on poetry is duplicated today even by those who think of him as their great enemy and the greatest opponent of art ever to have written. It is to be found not only in the various denunciations of television, many of which are reasonable and well-supported, but even more importantly in the total neglect of television on the part of our philosophy of art. Aesthetics defends the arts which can no longer do harm and against which Plato's strictures hardly make sense. His views are thus made incomprehensible and are not allowed to address their real target. Danto writes that every acknowledged literary work is "about the 'I' that reads the text . . . in such a way that each work becomes a metaphor for each reader." The key word here is "metaphor": we do not literally emulate our literary heroes, in the unfortunate manner of Don Quixote; we understand them through interpretation and transformation, finding their relevance to life, if anywhere, on a more abstract level. But such literal emulation was just what Plato was afraid of in the case of tragic poetry, and what so many today are afraid of in regard to television: "we become what we see." Plato's attack on "art" is still very much alive.

Allan Bloom

MUSIC

Allan Bloom (1930–1992) was professor in the Committee on Social Thought and co-director of the John M. Olin Center for Inquiry into the Theory and Practice of Democracy at the University of Chicago. His books include his translation and interpretation of The Republic of Plato, Love and Friendship, *and* The Closing of the American Mind. *The selection below discusses rock music, which Bloom considers a pernicious influence on the education and spiritual development of young people.*

. . . Plato's teaching about music is, put simply, that rhythm and melody, accompanied by dance, are the barbarous expression of the soul. Barbarous, not animal. Music is the medium of the *human* soul in its most ecstatic condition of wonder and terror. Nietzsche, who in large measure agrees with Plato's analysis, says in *The Birth of Tragedy* (not to be forgotten is the rest of the title, *Out of the Spirit of Music*) that a mixture of cruelty and coarse sensuality characterized this state, which of course was religious, in the service of gods. Music is the soul's primitive and primary speech and it is *alogon*, without articulate speech or reason. It is not only not reasonable, it is hostile to reason. Even when articulate speech is added, it is utterly subordinate to and determined by the music and the passions it expresses.

Civilization or, to say the same thing, education is the taming or domestication of the soul's raw passions—not suppressing or excising them, which would deprive the soul of its energy—but forming and informing them as art. The goal of harmonizing the enthusiastic part of the soul with what develops later, the rational part, is perhaps impossible to attain. But without it, man can never be whole. Music, or poetry, which is what music becomes as reason emerges, always involves a delicate balance between passion and reason, and, even in its highest and most developed forms—religious, warlike and erotic—that balance is always tipped, if ever so slightly, toward the passionate. Music, as everyone experiences, provides an unquestionable justification and a fulfilling pleasure for the activities it accompanies: the soldier who hears the

Allan Bloom, *The Closing of the American Mind* (New York: Simon and Schuster, 1987) 68–81.

marching band is enthralled and reassured; the religious man is exalted in his prayer by the sound of the organ in the church; and the lover is carried away and his conscience stilled by the romantic guitar. Armed with music, man can damn rational doubt. Out of the music emerge the gods that suit it, and they educate men by their example and their commandments. . . .

This is the significance of rock music. I do not suggest that it has any high intellectual sources. But it has risen to its current heights in the education of the young on the ashes of classical music, and in an atmosphere in which there is no intellectual resistance to attempts to tap the rawest passions. Modern-day rationalists, such as economists, are indifferent to it and what it represents. The irrationalists are all for it. There is no need to fear that "the blond beasts" are going to come forth from the bland souls of our adolescents. But rock music has one appeal only, a barbaric appeal, to sexual desire—not love, not *eros*, but sexual desire undeveloped and untutored. It acknowledges the first emanations of children's emerging sensuality and addresses them seriously, eliciting them and legitimating them, not as little sprouts that must be carefully tended in order to grow into gorgeous flowers, but as the real thing. Rock gives children, on a silver platter, with all the public authority of the entertainment industry, everything their parents always used to tell them they had to wait for until they grew up and would understand later.

Young people know that rock has the beat of sexual intercourse. That is why Ravel's *Bolero* is the one piece of classical music that is commonly known and liked by them. In alliance with some real art and a lot of pseudo-art, an enormous industry cultivates the taste for the orgiastic state of feeling connected with sex, providing a constant flood of fresh material for voracious appetites. Never was there an art form directed so exclusively to children.

Ministering to and according with the arousing and cathartic music, the lyrics celebrate puppy love as well as polymorphous attractions, and fortify them against traditional ridicule and shame. The words implicitly and explicitly describe bodily acts that satisfy sexual desire and treat them as its only natural and routine culmination for children who do not yet have the slightest imagination of love, marriage or family. This has a much more powerful effect than does pornography on youngsters, who have no need to watch others do grossly what they can so easily do themselves. Voyeurism is for old perverts; active sexual relations are for the young. All they need is encouragement.

The inevitable corollary of such sexual interest is rebellion against the parental authority that represses it. Selfishness thus becomes indignation and then transforms itself into morality. The sexual revolution must overthrow all the forces of domination, the enemies of nature and happiness. From love comes hate, masquerading as social reform. A worldview is balanced on the sexual fulcrum. What were once unconscious or half-conscious childish resentments become the new Scripture. And then comes the longing for the classless, prejudice-free, conflictless, universal society that necessarily results from liberated consciousness—"We Are the World," a pubescent version of *Alle Menschen werden Brüder*, the fulfillment of which has been inhibited by the political equivalents of Mom and Dad. These are the three great lyrical themes: sex, hate and a smarmy, hypocritical version of brotherly love. Such polluted sources issue in a muddy stream where only monsters can swim. A glance at the videos that project images on the wall of Plato's cave since MTV took it over suffices to prove this. Hitler's image recurs frequently enough in exciting contexts to give one pause. Nothing noble, sublime, profound, delicate, tasteful or even decent can find a place in such tableaux. There is room only for the intense, changing, crude and immediate, which Tocqueville warned us would be the character of democratic art, combined with a pervasiveness, importance and content beyond Tocqueville's wildest imagination.

Picture a thirteen-year-old boy sitting in the living room of his family home doing his math assignment while wearing his Walkman headphones or watching MTV. He enjoys the liberties hard won over centuries by the alliance of philosophic genius and political heroism, consecrated by the blood of martyrs; he is provided with comfort and leisure by the most productive economy ever known to mankind; science has penetrated the secrets of nature in order to provide him with the marvelous, lifelike electronic sound and image reproduction he is enjoying. And in what does progress culminate? A pubescent child whose body throbs with orgasmic rhythms; whose feelings are made articulate in hymns to the joys of onanism or the killing of parents; whose ambition is to win fame and wealth in imitating the drag-queen who makes the music. In short, life is made into a nonstop, commercially prepackaged masturbational fantasy.

This description may seem exaggerated, but only because some would prefer to regard it as such. The continuing exposure to rock music is a reality, not one confined to a particular class or type of child. One need only ask first-year university students what music they listen to, how much of it and what it means to them, in order to discover that the phenomenon is universal in America, that it begins in adolescence or a bit before and continues through the college years. It is *the* youth culture and, as I have so often insisted, there is now no other countervailing nourishment for the spirit. Some of this culture's power comes from the fact that it is so loud. It makes conversation impossible, so that much of friendship must be without the shared speech that Aristotle asserts is the essence of friendship

and the only true common ground. With rock, illusions of shared feelings, bodily contact and grunted formulas, which are supposed to contain so much meaning beyond speech, are the basis of association. None of this contradicts going about the business of life, attending classes and doing the assignments for them. But the meaningful inner life is with the music.

This phenomenon is both astounding and indigestible, and is hardly noticed, routine and habitual. But it is of historic proportions that a society's best young and their best energies should be so occupied. People of future civilizations will wonder at this and find it as incomprehensible as we do the caste system, witch-burning, harems, cannibalism and gladiatorial combats. It may well be that a society's greatest madness seems normal to itself. The child I described has parents who have sacrificed to provide him with a good life and who have a great stake in his future happiness. They cannot believe that the musical vocation will contribute very much to that happiness. But there is nothing they can do about it. The family spiritual void has left the field open to rock music, and they cannot possibly forbid their children to listen to it. It is everywhere; all children listen to it; forbidding it would simply cause them to lose their children's affection and obedience. When they turn on the television, they will see President Reagan warmly grasping the daintily proffered gloved hand of Michael Jackson and praising him enthusiastically. Better to set the faculty of denial in motion—avoid noticing what the words say, assume the kid will get over it. If he has early sex, that won't get in the way of his having stable relationships later. His drug use will certainly stop at pot. School is providing real values. And popular historicism provides the final salvation: there are new life-styles for new situations, and the older generation is there not to impose its values but to help the younger one to find its own. TV, which compared to music plays a comparatively small role in the formation of young people's character and taste, is a consensus monster—the Right monitors its content for sex, the Left for violence, and many other interested sects for many other things. But the music has hardly been touched, and what efforts have been made are both ineffectual and misguided about the nature and extent of the problem.

The result is nothing less than parents' loss of control over their children's moral education at a time when no one is seriously concerned with it. . . .

This strong stimulant . . . was for a very long time, almost fifteen years, epitomized in a single figure, Mick Jagger. A shrewd, middle-class boy, he played the possessed lower-class demon and teen-aged satyr up until he was forty, with one eye on the mobs of children of both sexes whom he stimulated to a sensual frenzy and the other eye winking at the unerotic, commercially motivated adults who handled the money. In his act he was male and female, heterosexual and homosexual; unencumbered by modesty, he could enter everyone's dreams, promising to do everything with everyone; and, above all, he legitimated drugs, which were the real thrill that parents and policemen conspired to deny his youthful audience. He was beyond the law, moral and political, and thumbed his nose at it. Along with all this, there were nasty little appeals to the suppressed inclinations toward sexism, racism and violence, indulgence in which is not now publicly respectable. Nevertheless, he managed not to appear to contradict the rock ideal of a universal classless society founded on love, with the distinction between brotherly and bodily blurred. He was the hero and the model for countless young persons in universities, as well as elsewhere. I discovered that students who boasted of having no heroes secretly had a passion to be like Mick Jagger, to live his life, have his fame. They were ashamed to admit this in a university, although I am not certain that the reason has anything to do with a higher standard of taste. It is probably that they are not supposed to have heroes. Rock music itself and talking about it with infinite seriousness are perfectly respectable. It has proved to be the ultimate leveler of intellectual snobbism. . . .

My concern here is not with the moral effects of this music—whether it leads to sex, violence or drugs. The issue here is its effect on education, and I believe it ruins the imagination of young people and makes it very difficult for them to have a passionate relationship to the art and thought that are the substance of liberal education. The first sensuous experiences are decisive in determining the taste for the whole of life, and they are the link between the animal and spiritual in us. The period of nascent sensuality has always been used for sublimation, in the sense of making sublime, for attaching youthful inclinations and longings to music, pictures and stories that provide the transition to the fulfillment of the human duties and the enjoyment of the human pleasures. Lessing, speaking of Greek sculpture, said "beautiful men made beautiful statues, and the city had beautiful statues in part to thank for beautiful citizens." This formula encapsulates the fundamental principle of the esthetic education of man. Young men and women were attracted by the beauty of heroes whose very bodies expressed their nobility. The deeper understanding of the meaning of nobility comes later, but is prepared for by the sensuous experience and is actually contained in it. What the senses long for as well as what reason later sees as good are thereby not at tension with one another. Education is not sermonizing to children against their instincts and pleasures, but providing a natural continuity between what they feel and what they can and should be. But this is a lost art. Now we have come to exactly the opposite point. Rock music encourages passions and provides models that have no relation to any life the young people who go to universities can possibly lead, or to the kinds of admiration encouraged by liberal studies. Without the cooperation of the sentiments, anything other than technical education is a dead letter.

Rock music provides premature ecstasy and, in this respect, is like the drugs with which it is allied. It artificially induces the exaltation naturally attached to the completion of the greatest endeavors—victory in a just war, consummated love, artistic creation, religious devotion and discovery of the truth. Without effort, without talent, without virtue, without exercise of the faculties, anyone and everyone is accorded the equal right to the enjoyment of their fruits. In my experience, students who have had a serious fling with drugs—and gotten over it—find it difficult to have enthusiasms or great expectations. It is as though the color has been drained out of their lives and they see everything in black and white. The pleasure they experienced in the beginning was so intense that they no longer look for it at the end, or as the end. They may function perfectly well, but dryly, routinely. Their

energy has been sapped, and they do not expect their life's activity to produce anything but a living, whereas liberal education is supposed to encourage the belief that the good life is the pleasant life and that the best life is the most pleasant life. I suspect that the rock addiction, particularly in the absence of strong counterattractions, has an effect similar to that of drugs. The students will get over this music, or at least the exclusive passion for it. But they will do so in the same way Freud says that men accept the reality principle—as something harsh, grim and essentially unattractive, a mere necessity. These students will assiduously study economics or the professions and the Michael Jackson costume will slip off to reveal a Brooks Brothers suit beneath. They will want to get ahead and live comfortably. But this life is as empty and false as the one they left behind. The choice is not between quick fixes and dull calculation. This is what liberal education is meant to show them. But as long as they have the Walkman on, they cannot hear what the great tradition has to say. And, after its prolonged use, when they take it off, they find they are deaf.

Karsten Harries

THE ETHICAL
SIGNIFICANCE
OF MODERN ART

Karsten Harries is Mellon Professor of Philosophy at Yale University. His books include The Meaning of Modern Art *and* The Bavarian Rococo Church: Between Faith and Aestheticism. *In the selection that follows, Harries argues that contemporary art serves an ethical function, not in the traditional sense of promoting specific moral values, but in the currently more important sense of disrupting our complacency about ethical matters.*

In a televised debate that was part of the discussion that preceded the establishment of the National Endowment for the Arts in 1965, John Kenneth Galbraith declared arts legislation to be the "final step now that recognizes that the artist is a first-class citizen, that he is worthy of being taken as seriously as the scientist, the businessman, or even the economist." Like many such declarations, this one asserted what is readily granted: do we really need the artist as much as we do the scientist, the businessman, and perhaps even, although here there is more reason for doubt, the economist? While I should like to agree with Galbraith, I do not find his claim easy to defend.

In *The Painted Word* Tom Wolfe claimed that art and the public today are linked mostly by mutual indifference: while the art world is self-contained and unconcerned about the public, the public in turn is not paying much attention to modern art and cares little whether it thrives or not. To be sure, Tom Wolfe's sketch of the art world, including the artists and a small well-to-do aesthetic elite, restricted to eight cities in five countries, offered only a caricature. But that caricature still has its point: an enormous gap separates modern art from the general public and its concerns. Only the most serious art seems to have a little public significance, less certainly than professional sports, soap operas, or popular music. Because so many value the latter and are willing to pay for what they enjoy, here there is neither need nor demand for federal

Karsten Harries, "The Ethical Significance of Modern Art," *Design for Arts in Education* 89.6 (1988): 2–12.

funding. Why not entrust the future of art, too, to the forces of a free market? If there is an aesthetic elite that values and is willing to support modern art, fine—why not leave it at that? But does a democratic government have any more business supporting the arts than it does supporting baseball or gourmet cooking? And if widespread indifference should threaten the survival of modern art, who is to say that something essential would be lost? What today is the social significance of art?

We are given a hint by a response that goes beyond indifference: by the widespread hostility to modern art. Usually such hostility expresses itself in nothing more damaging than a cutting comment, directed perhaps at a curator unfortunate enough to have hung some work of abstract art upside down, or in the delight that tends to greet reports that yet another art expert has been taken in by the forger's skill or that a janitor inadvertently used a Duchamp ready-made as the simple snow shovel it once was. Tom Wolfe's clever barbs directed at what he calls Cultureburg betray more than a trace of such hostility.

Hostile reactions are not always as harmless. As a recent article in *Art News* pointed out, vandalism directed against works of modern art has become a serious problem. I will give just two examples.

What caused a 29-year-old student of veterinary medicine to punch holes into Barnett Newman's *Who's Afraid of Red, Yellow, and Blue?*, which Berlin's New National Gallery had just acquired for one million dollars? The vandal, one Josef Klein, claimed that the painting had made him afraid; also that the sum paid for it had scandalized him. Both claims must be taken seriously. How can such an expenditure be justified? Should money and time be spent on art as long as there are persons who go homeless, hungry, and lack adequate medical care? Such questions become more difficult to answer when the money is the taxpayer's.

Given the painting's title, Klein's assertion that it made him afraid is of special interest. I well understand reacting to a Barnett Newman with some nameless fear: given this modern version of the sublime, Klein's reaction can hardly be called altogether inappropriate, although Klein could be accused of a failure to preserve aesthetic distance. That Klein's attack on the Newman possessed a social significance is shown by the way the Berliners elevated him into a minor hero—if not quite into an Oliver North, at least into a Bernard Goetz. By punching holes into the canvas, Klein seemed to strike blows against forces threatening to unravel the social fabric. Reader's responses to Newman's painting were predictable: any house painter's apprentice could have created that sort of object at a fraction of the cost; visit any first- or second-grade classroom and you will find works of comparable quality; not the vandal is crazy, but those willing to pay one million dollars for the Newman.

Equally revealing is the decision of some local politicians in the Rhineland to use an enamel bathtub, which Josef Beuys, emulating Duchamp, had transformed into a readymade-aided, as a wine cooler. What provoked these representatives of the people to scrub and clean the tub, in which the artist as baby had been bathed and which was now awaiting exhibition in some German castle? What prompted them to thus "destroy and desecrate," as the art work's owner put it, a work of art? Once again public opinion tended to side with the vandals. Outrage was directed not so much against the deed, as against the court's subsequent award of DM 80,000 in damages, plus interest, to the owner.

It would be easy to go on. All I want to suggest here is that such acts of vandalism have an ethical significance. The perpetrators understand themselves as defenders of good sense that they see being mocked and threatened by art works that defy expectations of what art should be. That this threat is taken seriously suggests that the works, too, are perceived to possess ethical and political significance, albeit of a negative, subversive sort. Does that perception presuppose a more positive significance? What is the ethical significance of art? The following remarks attempt an answer.

I will begin with three statements, three voices from the not-too-distant past. Although they come from very different quarters, they yet agree in their condemnation of modern art. Each assumes the ethical significance of art; each accuses modern art of subversion.

The first belongs to Congressman George A. Dondero, who in 1949, when many feared Moscow's diabolically clever scheming, thought it his duty to awaken his presumably nodding colleagues in Congress to the dangers of modern art. Art, he proclaimed,

> is considered a weapon of communism, and the Communist doctrinaire names the artist as a soldier in the revolution against our form of government, and against any government or system other than communism.

Had the Russian revolution not used this weapon successfully against the Czarist government? And did the fact that this revolution, once it had become the new establishment, was quick to divorce itself from modern art not testify to this art's corrosive power? The Soviet leadership knew very well what it was doing when at home it enforced an edifying realism "extolling the imaginary wonders, benefits, and happiness of existence under the socialized state" while abroad it continued to use modern art against its adversaries, especially against the United States, resorting to a more subtle form of germ warfare. The congressman was particularly disturbed by the fact that this foreign pest had not only invaded but actually taken over this country's art education.

> We are now face to face with the intolerable situation, where public schools, colleges, and universities, art and technical schools, invaded by a horde of foreign art manglers, are selling to our young men and women a subversive doctrine of "isms," Communist-inspired and Communist-connected, which have one common goal— the destruction that awaits if this Marxist trail is not abandoned.

I do not know how many of those who heard the congressman were able to take his remarks seriously—were able to take art that seriously, for what power must art possess to be capable of seducing our young men and women, threatening our free society with destruction. Today Dondero's speech would seem to provide little more than an unpleasant footnote to the triumphant progress of modern art in this country. Have we not learned to take pride in the fact that New York has replaced Paris as the world's artistic capital? Who today would blame this country's ills on modern art? The very suggestion seems preposterous. Is not art by its very nature innocent, harmless, wonderfully irrelevant?

Given the congressman's assertion of a deep link between modern art and communism, it is interesting to note that at just about the same time communists saw in modern art the tool of decadent capitalism. The second voice belongs to Vladimir Kemenov, the former director of Moscow's Tretjakow Gallery. The passage is taken from an article published in 1947.

According to Kemenov, those who plead for the political innocence of modern art are mistaken. By assuming the mask of such innocence, by insisting that art be for art's sake and as such free of all ideological content, modern artists only hide the true political function of their work.

> As a matter of fact, this "pure" art actually disseminated reactionary ideas, ideas that were advantageous or useful to the capitalists. Formalistic artists ceased to be rebels and became the abject slaves of capital, even though from time to time they did assail capitalism, sometimes even sincerely.

But such professions of solidarity with the suffering masses are belied by an art that, born of narcissistic self-preoccupation, idealizes the individual. Instead of giving voice to the proletariat, art for art's sake cannot but subvert revolutionary fervor. To such decadent art, Kemenov opposed what he called "a vital Soviet art, ideologically forward-looking and artistically wholesome: socialist in content and national form; an art worthy of the great Stalin epoch."

The third voice is national and socialist with a vengeance. It belongs to Adolf Hitler, who, unable to forgive those who had twice denied the would-be artist a place in the Vienna Academy, vowed to make vandalism public policy, promising to unleash a tornado that would destroy modern art and to put its practitioners into asylums or prisons. The occasion for the following remarks was the inauguration of the Great Exhibition of German Art in 1937 in Munich's newly built House of German Art.

> I do not want anybody to have false illusions: National-Socialism has made it its primary task to rid the German Reich, and thus, the German people and its life of all those influences which are fatal and ruinous to its existence. And although this purge cannot be accomplished in one day, I do not want to leave the shadow of doubt as to the fact that sooner or later the hour of liquidation will strike for those phenomena which have participated in this corruption.

Different as they are, all three statements agree in attributing to art the power to subvert the health of the community. Modern art is judged by political criteria and found wanting. All three statements presuppose that art has an ethical function, even, and indeed especially, when it disavows this function and claims to exist only for art's sake; they presuppose that art helps to mold the ethos of those who come under its spell, the way individuals understand themselves and their place in society; and they presuppose that modern art does so irresponsibly. And regardless of our distaste for these particular advocates of political control of the arts, can the presupposition that art possesses an ethical function really be dismissed? If not, must we not insist that the guardians of the state make sure that art exercise this function responsibly?

Insistence that art be subject to political control is, of course, not at all a new phenomenon. The statements above are but three of countless variations on a theme first stated in Plato's *Republic*. Socrates there challenges poetry and her sister arts of imitation to prove their right to exist in a well-ordered state. Such a proof, he insists, would have to show, not only that art is pleasant, but that it is "useful to States and to human life." The primacy of the political is taken for granted. The rulers of the state would be negligent, did they not recognize and control the ethical function of art. To assume that responsibility is to assume also the responsibility of censorship.

Plato's critique of the arts would hardly have been so vigorous had it been directed only against the uselessness of art. Such uselessness is easily defended. As Aristotle knew, life would be hollow were it not for activities that we engage in for their own sake, for experiences that are their own justification. We would not delight in such experiences as we do, were it not for their uselessness.

But when Plato's Socrates questions the right of the poets to a place in his *Republic*, and we can extend his questioning to all the arts, he does so not because they give pleasure, but because, while giving pleasure, they also usurp, perhaps unwittingly, the role of the educator. That ancient quarrel between poetry and philosophy of which Socrates speaks is a quarrel about who should be entrusted with moral education. Is it not obvious that it should be entrusted to those who know best, because they have thought most responsibly about such matters? If Socrates considers expelling the poets from his Republic, this is first of all because although perhaps disguised as entertainers, they do shape, or rather mis-shape, the self-understanding of the citizens. Their work is measured by the philosophers' understanding of truth and found wanting. The poets lie too much, and they especially lie too much about the gods. Such tales of idealized human beings should guide and illuminate human existence; they should communicate edifying truths and thus rein-force what is good in us and make it more difficult for us to give in to selfish impulses. But what do poets like Homer tell us of the gods? That they fight, whine, despair, lie, commit adultery. The poets' gods are all too human, entertaining perhaps, but hardly edi-fying. Nor should this surprise us: Vice is more interesting and thus more entertaining than virtue. Consider the heroes of our own popular art, our movies, our soap operas.

Plato is convinced of the ethical power of poetry and, more generally, of art. He knows that even if philosophers may possess a bet-ter grasp of moral truths than poets or artists do, we do not change human behav-ior with clear reasons as much as with affecting images and words. Just because of this he insists that the philosopher's reason controls art, just as the doctor's reason should control the use of drugs.

In spite of familiar arguments for the autonomy of the aesthetic realm, it is not easy to dismiss claims that poetry, and more generally art, can have an ethical function. Think of Plato's own poetic portrayal of Socrates as a new kind of hero, whose calm reason, selfless love, and fearless courage are to replace the virtues of Homer's Achilles. Or think of the Gospels, which tell stories of a very different courage and love.

We do not have to limit ourselves to such extraordinary examples. Most art of the past has served a particular way of life, has called human beings to a particular ethos. It would be easy to be specific. I could discuss, for example, the educational func-tion the Jesuits assigned to art; or the way art helped shape the ethos of Victorian gen-tlemen. Or the function of social realism.

But what of modern art? What is the ethi-cal function of Frank Stella's protractor paintings or of Roy Lichtenstein's pop fan-tasies? Has modern art not lost or, if you prefer, shed its ethical function and become art for art's sake? I shall return to these questions. But regardless of how they are answered, can we deny an ethical function to today's popular art and entertainment? To give just the most obvious examples, must the endless hours so many spend before their television sets not shape their ethos, and not only because of what appears on the screen, but because of the nature of the medium? Can the casual way in which these screen heroes love and kill be a matter of indifference to society? And if such images and stories do indeed help shape the ethos of those exposed to them, would it not be irresponsible to entrust that power to artists and entertainers who may care little whether what is offered is a destructive lie, as long only as this lie finds its public and becomes a commercial success? In the *Republic* Plato reserves thus the privilege of lying for the rulers. They alone "may be allowed to lie for the public good. But nobody else should meddle with anything of the kind."

The rulers' monopoly on lying assumes that they know what is in the public's best interest. Do we have such confidence in our statesmen? Plato solves this problem by making the philosopher king. In him reason and political power are joined. Today we are likely to insist that there be no such state monopoly on lying; that free discussion and democratic practices, while no doubt imper-fect, are yet better suited to bring about the desired union of reason and political power. But can we disagree with Plato when he insists that art be ruled by a thoughtful determination of what is in the public's best interest? This raised a more basic question: is unprejudiced reason capable of determining the public good? An affirmative answer is presupposed by all attempts to subject the arts to its control.

Like so many philosophers, Plato calls for the subjection of passion and emotion to reason, for a domestication of eros by the power of logos. Just because, as Plato reminds us, the point of art is not "to please or to affect the rational principle in the soul," but rather man's "passionate and fitful temper," we have to guard against its seductions.

Can we divorce reason and passion in this manner? I have suggested that Plato's own discourse owes its effectiveness to eros as much as to logos, to the siren charms of poetry as much as to the cooler voice of reason. The hold that Plato's Socrates still has on us today is due not only, perhaps not even primarily, to the arguments Plato presents in support of this way of life, but also to the story that he tells. That story communicates something of Socrates' quite distinctive eros, which continues to affect us and invites us to follow Plato's example and to choose Socrates as our hero.

Could Plato the philosopher have dispensed with Plato the poet? One might answer that the telling of the story was not necessary to establish the truth that mattered to Plato, although it may well have been necessary to let that truth become effective in the world. But is Plato's poetry no more than a concession to those who will not heed the truth unless it appears dressed up in poetic garments? At issue is the more fundamental question: does reason have the power to determine the true ends of human existence, objectively and dispassionately, free from all personal or cultural prejudice? If that is granted, if we can indeed determine the truth and falsity of moral discourse just as we can determine the truth and falsity of the discourse of science, if there are such things as moral facts,

then there is no need to quarrel with Plato's claim that the philosopher must be declared the winner in his contest with the poet. We should then call on philosophers as on society's experts in all moral matters. They would draw boundaries that human beings should not violate. The highest vocation of art would then be to become the handmaid of moral philosophy.

Philosophers, increasingly on the fringes of the academic establishment, may find it tempting to thus see themselves as the guardians of the spiritual health of the nation, at, or at least close to, the centers of power: the highly paid advisers of doctors, lawyers, and artists. It is a dream philosophers and society should resist.

Can reason be practical? Of course, if by practical reasoning we mean reasoning about means or reasoning that seeks to articulate and systematize individual or social preferences. But can unprejudiced reason discover the true ends of human action? From Plato to Kant and indeed right down to the present, philosophers have certainly tried to show that it can. That such attempts continue is itself a comment on what is being attempted. I cannot make sense of objective values or of categorical imperatives. Both seem to me contradictions in terms.

For what would be meant by objective values? Presumably that values are very much like facts. To be sure, these would not be ordinary facts; values do not exist as the things of this world do. But these ideal facts, too, would be what they are, regardless of what anyone would take them to be. Correspondence with these facts would make moral judgments true or false. Just as the pursuit of truth in science demands unprejudiced inquiry, so to gain proper access to values, one would first have to free oneself from all personal or cultural prejudice, rise beyond one's all too subjective interests and desires, transcend oneself as an engaged, embodied self.

But values must engage and claim us. To recognize an asserted value as a value, an individual must recognize it as an articulation of what more immediately affects him. To communicate values, discourse must touch this affective base, which cannot be divorced from our concrete biological and historical being in the world. A disinterested and, in this sense, truly objective knowing could never discover values.

Just as it makes no sense to speak of objective values, so it makes no sense to speak of a categorical imperative, an unconditional ought, with no regard to reward or punishment, to happiness or unhappiness. We may indeed feel that to be true to our own self we must respect the dignity of every human being or be convinced that we truly gain ourselves only when ready to sacrifice ourselves for a larger whole, a whole that may include only one other loved person or embrace all humanity. But such self-understanding rests on passion or faith rather than on the voice of pure reason.

Like the poets' tales of gods or heroes, the philosopher's moral speculations are born of his necessarily precarious attempt to articulate what he feels to matter. The philosopher may cast these feelings into a form that claims the agreement of all unprejudiced inquirers, but this is first of all a rhetorical appearance. Values are human creations. They have their ground in the affective life of individuals, who, while concerned with their own survival and welfare, also experience themselves as parts of larger social wholes, and are caught in the tensions this amphibian state brings with it. If we are to acknowledge the validity of such creations, we must recognize them as articulating what more immediately claims us. We must, as Plato would say, recollect their truth, but that truth should be sought, not above, in a timeless Platonic heaven, but below, in what Plato calls our "passionate and fitful temper." That is to say, to be effective, the communication of values must be sufficiently rhetorical, or poetic, or artistic to touch the hearts of those to whom it is addressed. Without this, asserted values will seem but arbitrary constructions. Similarly arbitrary will seem laws enacted to enforce obedience to values that have died, that is, lost their affective base. And as particular laws lose their authority, the authority of all law is threatened, as it comes to be understood as first of all a matter of mere power.

But must this suggestion that moral discourse inevitably objectifies subjective interests and desires not threaten that shared sense of values on which society depends? How can there be a responsible exercise of political power, if there is no practical reason to guide it?

Confident in the power of reason to determine what ought to be, Plato offers us his vision of a state where reason rules. Reasonable challenge to such rule would appear to be impossible. In such an ideal state individuals would have learned to understand themselves as parts of the political whole and to keep the place they have been assigned. Plato knew of course about the dangers of basing public policy on utopian thinking. The confusion of human beings with angels or gods has often proved disastrous and those in power have rarely been blessed with a particularly developed moral sense. All too often private passion has masked itself by claiming the authority of reason.

The problem is, however, not just a problem of the inevitable distance that separates every ideal from reality. The very assumption of a pure practical reason, capable of offering the one true determination of what ought to be, must be challenged. What fashions a multiplicity of persons into a community is not so much reason as common sense. This common sense is itself a historical product, precariously established out of countless individual feelings and desires, some selfish, some selfless. Attempts to ground this common sense in reason put the cart before the horse.

There will always be tension between private desires and common sense. Nor are desires and common sense constant. They can be expected to change as conditions change. Such change calls for an ongoing interpretation, reappropriation, and recasting of values that have come to be articulated, established, and accepted. Attempts to shore up and secure inherited values by appealing to supposedly timeless dictates of reason are likely to have the opposite effect. By freezing common sense, by covering up the affective base of values, such appeals prepare for the erosion of common sense and for the devaluation of old values.

To be sure, society needs stability. But we need not fear that by grounding values in necessarily subjective affects we surrender morality "to our random and changing appetite." The very existence of societies argues that human beings are sufficiently alike to share enough desires to allow for the emergence of a common sense. Even Hobbes takes for granted that, atomized as they are, human beings have certain interests in common: if human beings did not fear death, seek power, and love liberty, they could not arrive at a covenant that allows them to escape from the state of war. All effective government is supported by an already established common sense. Not that such a common sense is fixed once and for all. To live, common sense, too, must grow and change. Current discussions centering on equal rights or on the abortion issue are part of the ongoing evolution of this society's common sense. It would be a mistake to cut such discussions short by invoking the authority of some supposedly timeless truth.

But how does common sense get established? How do private feelings gain a public voice? Plato already points in this connection to art. Art awakens, communicates, reinforces, and shapes affective states. Thus it can help to establish and maintain, but also to subvert, a common ethos. It is precisely this power that gives art its ethical significance.

If this is right, no state can afford to neglect the aesthetic education of its future citizens, for at stake is the establishment and continuing support of that common sense without which the social order threatens to unravel. This, however, is not to say that government should prescribe to art what it is to say. For where would such prescription find its norms? In moral reasoning? But such reasoning must ground itself in common sense. In common sense then? But common sense does not furnish anything like a secure and stable ground. It is itself the changing product of changing personal convictions. Art is one instrument serving the evolution of common sense. The artist has his necessarily precarious place between the already established and what still struggles to gain voice. Art must dare venture beyond the boundaries of what has come to be judged acceptable; it must be a place of experimentation; it therefore cannot be justified by appeals to accepted criteria. Creative achievement and nonsense are uncomfortably close neighbors.

I have challenged the assumption that practical reason can ground political practice. Such reason must rather ground itself in and serve evolving common sense, recognizing the need for stability as well as the need for change, the right of the past as well as the right of the future. Nor can censorship invoke the authority of pure reason. Reason, too, is only an instrument of evolving common sense. That evolution cannot be determined in advance. The precariousness of censorship is thus the inverse of the precariousness of artistic creation. If one is conservative, the other counsels change. What has come to be established does not as such have authority, and what presents itself as new liberating insight may only be a willful and self-indulgent fancy. In their different ways censors and artists both make a significant contribution. The struggle between them is part of a healthy society. . . .

Often the mask of the fool has proved insufficient to protect the artist. The hostility that a good part of the public has so often felt when confronted with modern art is not altogether unlike the hostility that led the Athenians to condemn Socrates to death. Socrates was accused of being "a doer of evil, who corrupts the youth; and who does not believe in the gods of the state, but has other divinities of his own." Both charges had their point. By calling on the individual to think of himself, Socrates did shake further an already shaken confidence in the established and usually taken for granted. Thus Socrates made people uncomfortable. His questioning touched something that threatened the self-understanding that they had come to acquire as good Athenians. The deity that presided over Socrates' life and called him to his subversive life of questioning did not belong with the public deities, which always appear to give supernatural blessing to what is being done. This deity demanded of the individual that, instead of simply living as one lived, he step back from and examine inherited and taken-for-granted conventions.

Like Socrates, the modern artist dislocates and thereby liberates. If Socrates wanted to lead others to think for themselves, the artist lets us see, feel, and also think for ourselves. Kandinsky claimed that the task of art is to make things visible. That this should be a task presupposes that because we usually do not see or only half see the things that are closest to us, the clothes we wear, the room we live in, the street we cross every day, we take them for granted. We are too busy in the world, too accustomed to it, to open ourselves to its reality. That goes also for our own reality. Just as the mysterious presence of things is veiled by the established and the accepted, so are our own needs and desires. To open ourselves to our own selves and to the world around us, we must first free ourselves from the everyday, from its talk, from its cares and concerns; take leave from the familiar but only to return to it, now with clearer and more questioning eyes. In this sense art may be said to help us recover the affective base without which all talk of values rings hollow or false.

Earlier I suggested that one task of art is to make public affective states. Art furnishes shared metaphors of what is essentially private; thus it helps bridge the gap that separates individuals and society and contributes to the establishment of a genuinely common sense. But common sense loses its roots in the affective states of individuals, when shared commitments give way to the rule of what one says and does. When this happens art gains another function: its second task is to plough the crust of convention, to call individuals in danger of losing themselves to what has come to be taken for granted back to the affective ground in which all effective common sense must finally be rooted. There appears to be tension between these two tasks: while the first seems edifying and constructive, the second seems subversive and destructive. And yet such subversion is itself an essential part of the life of common sense. To be sure, the guardians of the established would rather see the artist serve the existing order, express what has already been approved. But a healthy society must allow for places where its presuppositions and commitments, its established ways of thinking and seeing, are challenged and new alternatives are hinted at, presented, and explored. Without such challenge, what has come to be taken for granted tends to be mistaken for what has to be. The achievements of the past threaten to become obstacles to new creation; the future is sacrificed to the past. Common sense offers no final security. It must be tested by a constant pushing toward its boundaries. Without such testing it becomes rigid and dies.

Especially today, in this rapidly changing world, art should be a place of challenge and experimentation. Its primary point should be not to amuse or titillate, nor to comfort. Art should both excite us and make us uneasy, even afraid. If it is to do so, if it is to lead us to and beyond the boundaries of established common sense, we must make sure that the distance that separates the fool and the king, art and politics, is preserved; we must recognize that there is a sense in which the artist must be left alone, just as the artist must preserve his distance from the community and protect the apolitical character of his art and his fool's freedom. But paradoxically, just this apolitical character gives genuine art its profoundly political and ethical significance. A society that possesses the courage to face an unknown future will support a free art, knowing full well that often the return for such support will be questions and provocations, or even nonsense.

Carlos Fuentes

WORDS
APART

Carlos Fuentes is a Mexican novelist, critic, short story writer, playwright, and diplomat, who has served as ambassador to France. He has written many books, both fiction and nonfiction, including Don Quixote: or the Critique of Reading, The Buried Mirror: Reflections on Spain and the New World, Cristopher Unborn, The Old Gringo, Whither Latin America?, *and* The New Hispano-American Novel. *He lives in Mexico City. In the following article, he defends the moral significance of Salman Rushdie's novel* The Satanic Verses. *According to Fuentes, the novel can help us to become more sensitive to the current complexity of our world, in which cultural confrontation and collision are rampant.*

Mikhail Bakhtin was probably the greatest theorist of the novel in our century. His life, in a way, is as exemplary as his books. Shunted off to remote areas of the Soviet Union by the minions of Stalinism for his unorthodox ideas, Bakhtin could not profit from rehabilitation when it came under Brezhnev, simply because he had never been accused of anything. A victim of faceless intolerance, his political nemesis was Stalin, but his literary symbol was Kafka.

His case was and is not unique. I have thought a lot about Bakhtin while thinking about Salman Rushdie during these past few weeks. Rushdie's work perfectly fits the Bakhtinian contention that ours is an age of competitive language. The novel is the privileged arena where languages in conflict can meet, bringing together in tension and dialogue not only opposing characters but also different historical ages, social levels, civilization, and other . . . realities of human life. In the novel, realities that are normally separated can meet, establishing a dialogic encounter, a meeting with the other.

This is no gratuitous exercise. It reveals a number of things. The first is that in dialogue no one is absolutely right; neither speaker holds an absolute truth or, indeed, has an absolute hold over history. Myself and the other, as well as the history that both of us are making . . . are unfinished.

Carlos Fuentes, "Words Apart," *The Guardian*, 24 Feb. 1989: 24–30.

The novel, by its very nature, indicates that we are becoming. There is no final solution. There is no last word.

This is what Milan Kundera means when he proposes that the novel is a constant redefinition of men and women as problems, never as sealed, concluded truths. But this is precisely what the ayatollahs of this world cannot suffer. For the ayatollahs, reality is dogmatically defined once and for all in a sacred text. But a sacred text is, by definition, a completed and exclusive text. You can add nothing to it. It does not converse with anyone. It is its own loudspeaker. It offers perfect refuge for the insecure who then, having the protection of a dogmatic text over their heads, proceed to excommunicate those whose security lies in their search for the truth. I remember Luis Buñuel saying: "I would give my life for a man who is looking for the truth. But I would gladly kill a man who thinks that he has found the truth."

This . . . surrealist sally is now being dramatically acted out in reversal. An author who is looking for the truth has been condemned to death by a priestly hierarchy whose deep insecurity is disguised by its pretension to holding the truth.

The ayatollahs, nevertheless, have done a great service to literature, if not to Islam. They have debased and caricatured their own faith. But they have shifted the wandering attention of the world to the power of words, literature, and the imagination, in ways totally unforeseen by their philosophy. . . . The intolerance of the ayatollahs not only sheds light on Salman Rushdie and his uses of the literary imagination. By making this imagination so dangerous that it deserves capital punishment, the sectarians have made people everywhere wonder what it is that literature can say that can be so powerful and, indeed, so dangerous. . . .

I have always conceived of the novel (at least those I try to write) as a crossroads between the individual and the collective destinies of men and women. Both tentative, both unfinished, but both only sayable and minimally understandable if it is previously understood that in fiction truth is the search for truth, nothing is pre-established, and knowledge is only what both of us—reader and writer—can imagine. There is no other way to freely and fruitfully explore the possibilities of our unfinished humanity. No other way to refuse the death of the past, making it present through memory. No other way of effectively giving life to the future, through the manifestation of our desire.

That these essential activities of the human spirit should be denied in the name of a blind yet omniscient, paralytical yet actively homicidal dogmatism is both a farce and a crime in itself. Salman Rushdie has done the true religious spirit a service by brilliantly imagining the tensions and complements that it establishes with the secular spirit. Humor, certainly, cannot be absent, since there is no contemporary language that can utter itself without a sense of the diversification of that same language. When we all understood everything, the epic was possible. But not fiction. The novel is born from the very fact that we do not understand one another any longer, because unitary, orthodox language has broken down. Quixote and Sancho, the Shandy brothers, Mr. and Mrs. Karenin: their novels are the comedy (or the drama) of their misunderstandings. Impose a unitary language: you kill the novel, but you also kill the society.

. . . After what has happened to Salman Rushdie and *The Satanic Verses*, I hope that everyone now understands this. Fiction is not a joke. It is but an expression of the cultural, personal, and spiritual diversity of mankind. Fiction is a harbinger of a multipolar and multicultural world, where no single philosophy, no single belief, no single solution, can shunt aside the extreme wealth of mankind's cultural heritage. Our future depends on expanding the freedom for the multiracial and the polycultural to express themselves in a world of shifting, decaying, and emerging power centers. . . .

The defense of Salman Rushdie is a defense of ourselves. It is a matter of pride to say that Rushdie has given us all a better reason to understand and protect the profession of letters at the highest level of creativity, imagination, intelligence, and social responsibility.

William H. Gass

GOODNESS KNOWS NOTHING OF BEAUTY

William H. Gass is David May Distinguished University Professor in the Humanities at Washington University. He is also an award-winning novelist. Many of his nonfiction works are concerned with art, especially literature. Among these are Fiction and the Figures of Life, The World within the Word, On Being Blue, *and* Habitations of the Word, *which won a National Book Critics Circle Award. Gass defends the distinction between aesthetic and moral values in the essay that follows. Certainly, ethical values are evident in artworks, Gass argues; but they are not the basis of aesthetic value.*

In life, values do not sit in separate tents like harem wives; they mix and mingle rather like sunlight in a room, or pollution in the air. A dinner party, for example, will affect the diners' waists, delight or dismay their palates, put a piece of change in the grocer's pocket, bring a gleam to the vintner's eye. The guests may be entertained or stupefied by gossip, chat, debate, wit. I may lose a chance to make out, or happily see my seduction advance past hunt and peck. The host may get a leg up in the firm whose boss he's entertaining, serious arguments may break out, new acquaintances may be warmly made. And if I, Rabbi Ben Ezra, find myself seated next to Hermann Goering, it may put me quite off the quail—quail which the *Reichsminister* shot by machine gun from a plane. We should all be able to understand that. It would be a serious misjudgment, however, if I imagined that the quail was badly cooked on account of who shot it, or to believe that the field marshal's presence had soured the wine, although it may have ruined the taste in my mouth. It might be appropriate to complain of one who enjoyed the meal and laughed at the fat boy's jokes. Nevertheless, the meal will be well prepared or not quite independently of the guests' delightful or obnoxious presence, and it would be simple-minded to imagine that because these values were

William H. Gass, "Goodness Knows Nothing of Beauty," *Harper's Magazine* 274.643 (1987): 37–44.

realized in such close proximity they therefore should be judged on other than their own terms—the terms, perhaps, of their pushier neighbors.

The detachment it is sometimes necessary to exercise in order to disentangle aesthetic qualities from others is often resented. It is frequently considered a good thing if moral outrage makes imbeciles of us. The aesthete who sees only the poppies blowing in Flanders fields is a sad joke, to be sure, but the politicized mind is too dense and too dangerous to be funny.

I have been mentioning some differences between moral acts as they are normally understood (keeping promises, saving the baby) and what might be called artistic ones (dancing the fandango, painting the Botticelli), and I have been drawing our attention to the public and private qualities of the several arts lest they be treated en bloc. Finally, I have suggested that values have to be judged by sharply different standards sometimes, though they come to the same table. However, my dinner party differs from Petronius' banquet in another essential: it is "thrown" only once. Even if the evening is repeated down to the last guest's happy gurgle, the initial party can be only vaguely imitated, since you can't swallow the same soup twice (as a famous philosopher is supposed to have said). The events of my party were like pebbles tossed into a pond. The stones appear to shower the surface of the water with rings, which then augment or interfere with one another as they widen, although eventually they will enlarge into thin air, the pond will become calm, and the stones' effects negligible.

Art operates at another level altogether. Petronius' story does not fling itself like a handful of stones at the public and then retire to contemplate the recession of its consequences, but occurs continually as readers reenact it. Of course these readings will not be identical (because no reading is written or a part of the text), but the text,

unless it has been mutilated or reedited, will remain the same. I shall recognize each line as the line I knew, and each word as the word that was. The letter abides and is literal, though the spirit moves and strays. In short, the mouth may have an altered taste, but not the soup.

For this reason the powers of events are known to be brief, even when loud and unsettling, and unless they can reach the higher levels of historical accounts—unless they can reach language—the events will be forgotten and their effects erased. Accounts, too, can be lost or neglected, so those texts which are truly strong are those whose qualities earn the love and loyalty of their readers, and enlist the support and stewardship of the organizations those readers are concerned with and control (schools, societies, academies, museums, archives), because the institutions encourage us to turn to these now canonical texts again and again, where their words will burn in each fresh consciousness as if they had just been lit.

Moralists are right to worry about works of art, then, because they belong to a higher level of reality than most things. Texts can be repeated; texts can be multiplied; texts can be preserved; texts beget commentaries, and their authors energize biographers; texts get quoted, praised, reviled, memorized; texts become sacred.

The effect of a text (as every failed commission on pornography has demonstrated) cannot be measured as you measure blows; the spread of a text cannot be followed like the course of an epidemic; there is no dye which can be spilled upon the ground to track the subtle seepages of its contamination. Texts are not acts of bodies but acts of minds; for the most part, then, they do not act on bodies as bodies act, but on minds as minds do.

So my position is not that literature has no relation to morality, or that reading and writing, or composing, or painting, aren't also moral, or possibly immoral, acts. Of course they can be. But they are economic acts as well. (They contribute to their author's health or illness, happiness or melancholy.) My position, however, is that the artistic value of a book is different from its economic value, and is differently determined, as is its weight in pounds, its utility as a doorstop, its elevating or edifying or life-enhancing properties, its gallery of truths: new truths, known truths, believed truths, important truths, alleged truths, trivial truths, absolute truths, coming truths, plain unvarnished truths. Artistic quality depends upon a work's internal, formal, organic character, upon its inner system of relations, upon its structure and its style, and not upon the morality it is presumed to recommend, or upon the benevolence of its author, or its emblematic character, when it is seen as especially representative of some situation or society.

. . . Values may reinforce one another, or interfere with their realization in some thing or person. The proximity of Herr Goering may put me off my feed. Perhaps I ought to be put off. Perhaps the chef should have poisoned the quail. Perhaps all of the guests should have left in a huff. And the housemaid and the butler grin as they quaff champagne in the kitchen, grin so little bones appear between their open teeth. How's the pâté no one would eat? Deelish.

Wagner's works are not wicked simply because he was; nor does even the inherent vulgarity deep within the music quite destroy it. Frost's poetry seems written by a better man than we've been told he was. In fact, we are frequently surprised when an author of genius (like Chekhov) appears to be a person of some decency of spirit. The moral points of view in works of art differ as enormously as Dante's do from Sophocles', or Shakespeare's from Milton's. Simply consider what we should have to say if the merit of these writers depended at all upon their being correct, even about anything. In any case, Balzac sees the world quite differently than Butor does; Goethe and Milton cannot both be right; so if being right mattered, we should be in a mess indeed, and most of our classics headed for the midden.

If author and art ought not to be confused, neither should art and audience. If we were to say, as I should prefer, that it is the moral world of the work which ought to matter to the moralist, not the genes of the author's grandfather, or the Jean who was a longtime lover, or a lean of the pen-holder toward the political right or left, we ought also to insist that the reactions of readers aren't adequate evidence either. If Wagner's anti-Semitism doesn't fatally bleed into his operas, and, like a bruise, discolor them, and if Balzac's insufferable bourgeois dreams don't irreparably damage his fictions, then why should we suppose the work itself, in so much less command of its readers than its author is of it, will communicate its immoral implications like a virus to the innocents who open its covers?

To be sure, authors often like to think of their works as explosive, as corrupting, as evil. It is such fun to play the small boy. Lautréamont asks Heaven to "grant the reader the boldness to become ferocious, momentarily, like what he is reading, to find, without being disoriented, his abrupt and savage path through the desolate swamps of these somber and poison-filled pages." Yet this is an operatic attitude; reading is never more than reading, and requires a wakeful understanding—that is all. Certainly we should like to think that we had written some "poison-filled" pages, but no luck. Even chewing them won't make you sick, not even queasy.

If the relation of morality to art were based simply on the demand that art be concerned with values, then almost every author should satisfy it even if they wrote with their pricks in their sleep. (Puritans will object to the language in that sentence, and feminists to the organ, and neither will admire or even notice how it was phrased.) Henry Miller's work has been condemned, but Henry Miller is obsessed with ethical issues, and his work has a very pronounced moral point of view. *Madame Bovary* was attacked; *Ulysses* was forbidden entry into the United States; *Lady Chatterley's Lover* was brought to court, where they worried about signs of sodomy in it; *Lolita*, of course, was condemned; and, as someone has said, who also has suffered such censorship, so it goes. How long the list would be, how tiresome and dismaying and absurd its recital, if we were to cite every work that has been banned, burned, or brought into the dock.

It is simply not possible to avoid ethical concerns; they are everywhere; one is scarcely able to move without violating someone's moral law. Nor are artists free of the desire to improve and instruct and chastise and bemoan their fellow creatures, whether they call themselves Dickens, D. H. Lawrence, or Hector Berlioz. Céline is so intensely a moral writer that it warps his work. That is the worry. "There are still a few hatreds I'm missing," he wrote. "I am sure they exist." Hate, we mustn't forget, is a thoroughly moralized feeling.

It is the management of all these impulses, attitudes, ideas, and emotions (which the artist has as much as anyone) that is the real problem, for each of us is asked by our aims, as well as by our opportunities, to overcome our past, our personal aches and pains, our beloved prejudices, and to enlist them in the service of our skills, the art we say we're loyal to and live for. If a writer is in a rage, the rage must be made to energize the form, and if the writer is extended on the rack of love, let pain give the work purpose and disappointment its burnished point. So the artistic temperament is called cold because its grief becomes song instead of wailing. To be a preacher is to bring your sense of sin to the front of the church, but to be an artist is to give to every mean and ardent, petty and profound, feature of the soul a glorious godlike shape.

It is actually not the absence of the ethical that is complained of, when complaints are made, for the ethical is never absent. It is the absence of the *right* belief, the *right* act, which riles. Our pets have not been fed; repulsive enthusiasms have been encouraged; false gods pursued; obnoxious notion noised about; so damn these blank and wavy paintings and these hostile drums, these sentences which sound like one long scratch of chalk. Goodness knows nothing of Beauty. They are quite disconnected. If I say *shit* in a sentence, it is irrelevant what else I say, whether it helps my sentence sing or not. What is relevant is the power of certain principles of decorum, how free to be offensive we are going to be allowed to be. When the Empress Dowager of China, Ci Xi, diverted funds intended for the navy to construct a large and beautiful marble boat, which thousands now visit at the Summer Palace in Beijing, she was guilty of expropriation. If her choice had been a free one, she would seem to have chosen to spend her money on a thing of peace rather than on things of war (a choice we might applaud); in fact, we know she simply spent the money on herself. She cannot have chosen the beauty she received because beauty is beyond choice. The elegant workmanship which went into the boat, the pleasure it has given to many, its rich and marvelous material, are serendipitous, and do not affect the morality of the case.

When a government bans nonobjective art, it is the threat of the very look it has, its veer from the upright, its deviationism, that is feared—a daub is just as dangerous. Finally, when the Soviet authorities decide to loosen their restrictions on the publication of books and the holding of performances, this is not suddenly a choice of art over politics on their parts; it *is* politics, and has to do with issues such as the freedom of information, the quashing of the Stalin cults, not with art. They know what the novels in the drawers are about.

I do happen to feel, with Theodor Adorno, that writing a book is a very important moral act indeed, consuming so much of one's life, and that, in these disgusting times, a writer who does not pursue an alienating formalism, but rather tries to buck us up and tell us not to spit in the face of the present, this to serve a corrupt and debauched society in any way, is, if not a pawn of the system (a lackey, we used to say), then probably a liar and a hypocrite. It is a moral obligation to live in one's time, and to have a just and appropriate attitude toward it, not to live in the nineteenth century or to be heartless toward the less fortunate or to deny liberty and opportunity to others or to fall victim to nostalgia.

But good books have been written by bad people, by people who served immoral systems, who went to bed with snakes, by people who were frauds in various ways, by schemers and panderers. And beautiful books have been written by the fat and old and ugly, the lonely, the misbegotten (it is the same in all the arts), and some of these beautiful books are like Juan Goytisolo's, ferociously angry, and some of them are even somewhat sinister like Baudelaire's, and some are shakingly sensuous like those of Colette, and still others are dismayingly wise, or deal with terror tenderly, or are full of lamentable poppycock. (I am thinking most immediately of Pope's *Essay on Man.*)

I think it is one of the artist's obligations to create as perfectly as he or she can, not regardless of all other consequences, but in full awareness, nevertheless, that in pursuing other values—in championing Israel or fighting for women or defending the faith or exposing capitalism or speaking for your race—you may simply be putting a saving scientific, religious, political false face on your failure as an artist. Neither the world's truth nor a god's goodness will win you that race.

Finally, in a world which does not provide beauty for its own sake, but where the loveliness of flowers, landscapes, faces, trees, and sky are adventitious and accidental, it is the artist's task to add to the world objects and ideas—delineations, symphonies—which ought to be there, and whose end is contemplation and appreciation; things which deserve to become the focus of a truly disinterested affection.

There is perhaps a moral in that.

Liza Mundy

THE NEW CRITICS

Liza Mundy is an editor at Washington, D.C.'s The City Paper *and an occasional contributor to* Lingua Franca. *In the reading that follows she describes some recent on-campus debates about morally offensive art.*

The things were balls—that much was clear. More specifically, they were truck-tire inner tubes that had been inflated and coated with fiberglass to produce a clump of large bulbous shapes. So it's not entirely surprising that last fall, when students at St. Mary's College awoke to find Marcia Kaplan's abstract sculpture installed on campus near the dining hall, many of them believed they were beholding a gigantic set of male genitalia.

Others believed they were seeing a gigantic set of female genitalia.

Still others wondered why, in order to get their breakfast, they had to hike past a gigantic pair of female breasts.

A few felt Kaplan's sculpture resembled oversize hot dogs.

"There was an incredible range of descriptions of what people saw in them," says Douglas Tyler, chair of the art department at St. Mary's, a small Catholic women's school near South Bend, Indiana. "It was kind of hilarious."

St. Mary's students were not amused. And if they couldn't agree on what the balls were, exactly, the young women were united in thinking them lewd and hence intolerable.

"I can't remember anything else on this campus that people got so upset about," recalls then senior Karen Fordham, who promptly drew up a petition demanding that the offending artwork be removed. While she was canvasing dorms and collecting some 300 signatures, a few classmates expressed their displeasure more directly: They rolled around on the sculpture until one of the balls was, ahem, busted.

Flustered St. Mary's officials swiftly stored Kaplan's damaged sculpture for safekeeping.

Kaplan may not have known it, but she had just joined a growing company of artists whose work has fallen afoul of censorious students. Around the same time that St. Mary's students were fulminating against obscenity on campus, students at Colgate University joined with faculty to challenge the school's decision to exhibit groundbreaking new works by noted American photographer Lee Friedlander. The protesters claimed that Friedlander's black-and-white, painstakingly unglamorous pictures of women's naked bodies—hailed by *The New York Times* as "masterly images by one of the most important photographers of our

Liza Mundy, "The *New* Critics," *Lingua Franca* 3.6 (1993): 26–33.

time"—created an atmosphere hostile to women. At the University of Alabama at Birmingham, the student government last year voted to condemn the purchase of an Andres Serrano photograph, calling it a "hate crime" against religious students. At the University of Ohio at Lancaster, students were revolted by—and revolted against—an exhibit that included photos of men kissing. At the University of Arizona in Tucson, students railed against a group of self-portraits showing the artist, a graduate student named Laurie Blakeslee, posing in her skivvies. When words failed, the Arizona students resorted to spitting on the photos, tearing at them, and, finally, flinging food at them, until the manager of the student union removed Blakeslee's photos to prevent them from being destroyed. Students at the University of Pittsburgh banned an "obscene" painting from last year's open exhibit of student art. The painting showed a naked woman drowning in a pool of semen; according to the male artist who created it, this surreal vision was meant to depict women victimized by masculine desire. To the all-female student panel, it constituted sexual harassment.

Holy water buffalo! In these days of cultural sensitivity and interpretative chaos, even artists can't know their own true motives. "In this culture, there isn't uniformity of opinion," notes Columbia University anthropologist Carole Vance, who has written about the Meese Commission's report on pornography. "What may strike me as sexist might not strike you as sexist."

The ambiguity poses a real problem for artists—who trade, after all, in ambiguity. Indeed, it may be campus art—not campus conversation—that becomes the lasting casualty of speech codes and the atmosphere they create: Faced with images that are troubling or ugly or carnal or merely unclear, a vocal minority among today's undergrads simply concludes that what it is really witnessing is the visual equivalent of hate speech.

"Students are increasingly seduced by these code-word excuses," notes Marjorie Heins, director of the Arts Censorship Project of the American Civil Liberties Union and author of *Sex, Sin and Blasphemy: A Guide to America's Censorship Wars*. "There's a tendency to describe anything you don't like in a work of art as sexual harassment, so that it becomes a civil rights violation."

The most irritating part is that even now, in the post–Robert Mapplethorpe era—when thinking people are supposed to know better—more and more administrators are letting themselves be bullied into a kind of moral paralysis. Muttering noncommittal bromides about "a conflict of liberal principles," secretly quaking at the prospect of an unseemly lawsuit and the bad press it would bring, bent on mollifying the most fractious voices on campus, and silently (sometimes vocally) endorsed by a comatose and complicit faculty, these university leaders are ceding their mission to educate—and to lead—and allowing overwrought twenty-year-olds to determine what can and cannot be displayed on a college campus. "Administrations that really show inertia when it comes to addressing problems of sexism and so on will snap to when someone says that a film or work of art is offensive," says Vance. "It's a relatively inexpensive way for an administration to show its concern."

Or as one frustrated artist put it, "There's no way to win doing sculpture for a campus."

Nowhere have the battles over campus art been more passionate than in those cases where clashing visions of feminism are at stake. Young women and men influenced by crusading law professor Catharine MacKinnon—and these are in the ascendance on many campuses—believe that pornography and other sexually explicit imagery create an atmosphere in which rape is tolerated and even encouraged. MacKinnonite ideas underlie many of the student-led attacks on campus art; ironically, they often pit feminist students against feminist artists. And nowhere has this clash been more evident than at the University of Michigan Law School, where MacKinnon herself teaches, and where, last fall, a group of students were inspired by her theories and, possibly, by her, to pull a "pornographic" videotape from an art exhibit they themselves had commissioned.

"Have you seen the tape?" MacKinnon asks me on the phone. Surprisingly (her secretary had said she would be unavailable for comment), the renowned feminist has returned my call requesting her views on the Michigan flap. For some reason, MacKinnon refuses to say where she's calling from. That in itself is unnerving; even more unnerving is MacKinnon's response when I admit I have not seen the videotape in question.

"Depending on your own history of sexual abuse," she comments offhandedly, "you might want to be prepared for what it might do to you."

With that introduction, the tape arrives in my mailbox, dispatched from the office of Detroit artist Carol Jacobsen. A two-hour work, more documentary than art, really, assembled by Jacobsen and featuring segments by five video artists, it explores the lives and livelihoods of street walkers and call girls. In the opening segment, former hooker Carol Leigh interviews prostitutes from various countries. Another, "The Salt Mines," tells the stories of homeless male prostitutes living in a road-salt repository outside of New York City.

Sandwiched between these two sobering presentations is an autobiographical segment produced by porn-star-and-proud-of-it Veronica Vera. In her "Portrait of a Sexual Evolutionary," Vera sets out to prove just how gratifying pornography can be for the women who make it. "Portrait," MacKinnon argues, is little more than "a puff piece for [Vera] as a pornographic model," and it's easy to see what MacKinnon means: It opens with a heavily made-up Vera, wearing a gauzy gold blouse and sitting before a

translucent scrim, discussing certain, um, seminal moments in her life in such breathy, bad-actressy tones that it's hard to believe she's serious.

The film is cheesy, amateurish, fascinating. To show how pornography satisfied her early erotic yearnings, Vera shifts between childhood experiences—usually involving her Catholic upbringing—and adult ones. . . .

. . . Vera moved to New York City, became a secretary, began performing oral sex on men in her office, began publishing erotica, began performing in porn movies. She portrays this subterranean universe as populated by strong women who instructed her about sexual independence. Her guru is Annie Sprinkle, formerly an actress in X-rated films who has gained a certain cachet as a downtown performance artist—Sprinkle calls herself a "post-porn modernist" and is often mentioned in the same breath as National Endowment for the Arts outlaws Karen Finley and Holly Hughes. Sprinkle appears several times in Vera's feature. In one of the video's scenes Vera is supposed to be behind the camera, helping produce a Sprinkle video. Before long, however, the action on stage gets so hot that Vera is moved to join it. . . .

Jacobsen assembled the video for a show titled "Porn'imag'ry: Picturing Prostitutes." The exhibit, which also includes a Jacobsen documentary about Detroit prostitutes, "Street Sex," was commissioned last fall by the Michigan law students to accompany a conference on prostitution. The conference, in turn, was convened to launch the flagship issue of the students' new feminist legal journal, *The Michigan Journal of Gender and Law*.

Jacobsen says she had her doubts when the students approached her about the project, suspecting that some (if not all) were MacKinnon acolytes. As do many feminists, Jacobsen strongly disagrees with MacKinnon about the ideological significance of sex workers. Where MacKinnon sees women who are cruelly exploited by diabolic male pornographers and pimps, Jacobsen sees potential feminists trying to make a buck. But the students assured her that speakers who favored the legalization of prostitution would be invited to balance those who opposed it, and that the point of view of so-called pro-sex feminists would be represented. Jacobsen's misgivings returned, however, when she learned that the students had changed their minds and invited only MacKinnonite speakers—including MacKinnon herself and her longtime ally Andrea Dworkin. According to student organizer Ann Kraemer, the group decided that the MacKinnon camp represented the "newer" and more interesting feminist take on the world's oldest profession. However, another student, Lisa Lodin, told *The New York Times* that some of the antiprostitution speakers refused to appear if the "other side" was invited. Lodin said the students felt "manipulated," but agreed to their demands.

At this point, Jacobsen says, the students told her that her exhibit was more important than ever; it would provide the sole alternative viewpoint in an increasingly one-sided discourse. So she went ahead, assembling and installing it in the student union, a block from where the three-day conference would be held. She missed the first day of the conference but on the second day stopped by the exhibit and noticed that the five-part tape was missing. Assuming it had been stolen, she installed a backup. On her way to the conference, she ran into a law student who told her that another student had removed the tape after some of the speakers objected to it. The student acknowledged that neither of them had watched the tape, nor could they tell her which part was deemed offensive. She assumes it was Vera's segment.

Outraged, Jacobsen retorted that she had replaced the tape. In response, she says, the students announced to the conference audience that the tape must go. Jacobsen protested, arguing that female artists deserved better treatment from a feminist conference and saying that "if the conference organizers want to censor any part of the exhibit they'll have to censor the entire thing." Whereupon the students held a hasty meeting with MacKinnon, Dworkin, and other speakers, according to Kraemer; the students then went into a separate room and independently decided to ask Jacobsen to take down the entire exhibit. Jacobsen did so. She immediately called the local papers and, a few days later, contacted the ACLU. It threatened to sue the University of Michigan for depriving Jacobsen of her right to free speech.

In doing so, however, the ACLU had to confront a difficult question: Can students censor? Strictly speaking, censorship is an act in which the state suppresses speech. Do students who have received money from a state institution represent the state itself? Kraemer maintains that they did not; the ACLU's Marjorie Heins concedes the point, but argues that the students clearly censored the artists in the broadest sense of the word. As Heins defines it in her book, "Censorship happens whenever some people succeed in imposing their political or moral values on others by suppressing words, images, or ideas they find offensive." Of Vera's video segment, she writes, "The work is by a woman, speaks to issues of women's liberation and sexuality, presents a libertarian political viewpoint—and was censored by people claiming to be feminists."

The ACLU sought to strengthen its case by arguing that the students acted at MacKinnon's behest—something which, if true, might lend credence to the notion that the university, and by extension the state, quashed the tape. MacKinnon denies the charge. . . . She says she spoke with the students only twice, and never told them to remove the tape. When a speaker at the conference called her to complain about the video, she says, she phoned the students and advised them to take a look at it. Later, she spoke with them again and warned them of the dangers of showing pornography, even in an academic context: She had felt compelled to stop teaching a class she and Dworkin gave on the subject, she told them, after "several students had mental breakdowns as a result of remembering things that happened to them as children." Then she urged the students again to look at the tape: "I said, 'I haven't seen this stuff, I don't know if it is pornography, but, if it is, people need to think about its impact in an academic setting—and not assume that an academic setting is stronger than the pornography.'"

MacKinnon adds, "The one thing I asked them to do, they didn't do, did they?"

The students agree that MacKinnon played no part in their decision. Beyond that, their defense is confused: Several students told reporters they pulled the tape because some of the speakers at the conference felt physically endangered by it. An angry Michigan undergrad who spoke out at a recent conference on censorship and the arts said she and other students felt the tape could incite men to rape. Kraemer, however, says only that the students did not wish to have "commercial pornography" shown in any context and that, in fact, Jacobsen interfered with *their* freedom of expression.

To MacKinnon's feminist critics, however, the dustup over Vera's video segment is yet another reminder of the naïveté with which the other camp reads images and theorizes what their effect is on us. "I think the idea that an image per se is harassing is actually quite mistaken and is totally incompatible with how we normally think about images," says Columbia's Carole Vance. "Context matters, so does interpretive frame, and viewers differ in how they interpret an image. If the question is posed as, Which images are sexually harassing? half of an important question has already been ceded to those who have a reductionist, simplified view of art and culture."

Vance and others fear that those most harmed by the MacKinnonite approach to art will be female artists—and with them, students who are deprived of the opportunity to see and study what one critic has described as the "most interesting" development in contemporary art: sexual art by women. "We're beginning to open up areas of women's lives that have not been visualized: They're unfamiliar, unladylike, disturbing, difficult images," notes Jacobsen. "and they can so easily be labeled pornographic and then suppressed."

MacKinnon, of course, disagrees. Female artists, she says, haven't begun to escape the miserable self-image foisted upon them by dastardly pornographers. Luckily, though, she has: "What you need is people who see through literature like Andrea Dworkin, who see through law like me, to see through art and create the uncompromised women's visual vocabulary."

In any case, after protracted negotiations between the ACLU and Michigan Law School dean Lee Bollinger, a settlement was eventually reached. It was decided that Jacobsen will reinstall her exhibit this fall, when the law school (not the students) will present a conference on sexual art and censorship. Bollinger, a First Amendment scholar, says the students "made a mistake," but otherwise seems to sympathize with their desire to orchestrate their own conference.

But what about Bollinger's colleagues on the Michigan faculty? Did this top ten law school cough up any homegrown Alan Dershowitzes, First Amendment zealots bellowing about the marketplace of ideas? Well, no. Jacobsen says she received not so much as a Hallmark sympathy card, much less an amicus brief, from Michigan faculty, though one art professor did help her take her exhibit down. Noting the "deafening silence" of the people who are paid by the state to educate the taxpaying citizens of tomorrow, Carole Vance ventures that "no one wanted to cross Catharine MacKinnon."

But come now. We can't blame MacKinnon for everything. Nor should we assume that sex is the only thing provoking frenzies of outrage in today's ban-happy undergrads. An equally bitter—if less publicized—dispute broke out in May 1992 at Colby College in Waterville, Maine, where a poster advertising the senior art exhibit was removed by a black student. At Colby, as at Michigan, the artist took an incendiary image and placed it in an artistic context; however, many students felt the image retained its original shock value. In this case, the image consisted of a still from the videotape of the Rodney King beating. Hoping to galvanize Colby's apathetic white population, Greg Long, a white student, took that image and superimposed slogans intended to demonstrate the superficiality of modern culture upon it. AS EXCITING AS POLICE BRUTALITY, said one; another read, IT'LL HIT YOU LIKE A BLOW TO THE HEAD. The morning the posters appeared, Long says, a dean asked him to take them down. He refused, but no matter: within hours, all fifty had vanished. The Colby administration quickly issued a memo deploring Long's "insensitivity" and "poor judgment" and stating that other student artists were taking down the posters.

Actually, that's not quite what happened. "I went around and took them all down," says biology major Leonard Baker. To Long, the poster was an ironic commentary on an uncaring culture. To Baker, it was an affront to himself as a black student in a white-dominated school—a school he had paid good money to attend. "The fact that I pay tuition to this school means that I shouldn't have to walk around seeing pictures of a black man being beaten," Baker says. "I didn't want to have to go to classes and look at that."

The tumult dominated the remaining days of the term at the liberal arts college. "It was the only thing that people talked about," says a still-shaken Long. "It completely swept the school. There was a meeting in the chapel, with some 200 students, and I had to get up and defend what I did. Some people called me a racist; others defended me. People were weeping and breaking down. It was nuts."

Long was hard-pressed to find advocates among Colby's administration—or its faculty, aside from some tepid support from the art department. One government professor was quoted in the student newspaper saying that Long had "screwed up big time"; a dean suggested that Long should seek a refund from Colby, since he had obviously learned nothing there. Even Baker was shocked by the swiftness with which President William R. Cotter capitulated: When Baker visited the president's office to complain, he says, Cotter "had the apology all typed out before he even heard what I had to say." Baker feels Colby's administration—terrified of alienating black students—wanted to pacify him as quickly as it could.

Long's ordeal is a textbook example of thwarted good intentions—a case of an artist who thought he was the good guy finding, to his surprise, that his audience felt otherwise. "I never intended to hurt anybody with the piece," says Long. "It was very painful to me to see that I had done that."

If Long thought his intentions were misread, he might take comfort in the case of Connecticut artist Julia Balk, who in 1990 was commissioned by the University of North Carolina at Chapel Hill's class of '85 to create a sculpture called *The Student Body*. In an effort to reflect the diversity of UNC's 23,000 students, Balk came up with a group of attenuated bronze figures in poses designed to blend with pedestrian traffic at the main entrance to UNC's Davis Library. Seeking a central figure, Balk sculpted a tall man twirling a basketball, and—in tribute to UNC grad Michael Jordan—made the basketball player black; similarly, she gave an African-American appearance to a female student shown balancing a book on her head. Another female student was depicted walking with a male, his arm around her shoulder and hers around his waist; he was reading a book and she was eating an apple—showing, in a subtle biblical allusion, who had the real knowledge.

For all her multiculti carefulness, Balk caught it from all sides. Campus feminists wanted to know why the man got the book, and why the women appeared subservient. Black students wanted to know why the athlete was black—did UNC see black men only as jocks?—and whether the woman was modeled after an African basket-carrier. Not to be left out, Asian students wanted to know why a figure with a vaguely Asian face was shown carrying a violin case.

Students formed a Committee Against Offensive Statues. Somebody vandalized Balk's work one night, toppling one of the figures and making off with the basketball. In the face of the uproar, UNC chancellor Paul Hardin agreed to have the $65,000 sculpture moved to a nearby garden, where students would not be obliged to confront it. Hardin describes himself as "almost a First Amendment absolutist" but justifies his concession with what he describes as the "captive audience" exception—the theory that the First Amendment doesn't apply when people cannot avoid the speech being directed at them.

When it's pointed out to him that undergrads are by nature captive audiences, Hardin chuckles. "I had the advantage that I was legally trained and they weren't," he says. "And I felt I had a good feeling for where the balance might be."

Whether or not Hardin made the right choice, decisions like his will surely encourage campus art committees to stick with the abstract stuff. "The further you get from realism, the less likely a piece of work is to be vandalized," says William Massey, a UNC grad who ran interference between Balk and the administration. "People will be looking at the texture of the hair, or the size of the nose, or the bone structure—the more identifiable they are, the more likely the work is to be criticized."

Once upon a time—that is to say, in the 1960s and 1970s—students would have been overjoyed to see some outrageous, preferably sexual, piece of art installed in the campus quad or gallery. Anything would be better than those dreary statues of the university's first trustees donated by the class of '26 or the Wedgwood snuffboxes collected by the president's wife. But once upon a time students also agitated for free speech on campus and took libertarian foulmouths like Lenny Bruce and Germaine Greer as their heroes. A lot has happened since then: MacKinnon; speech codes that encourage students to seek and destroy any expression—verbal or visual—that offends them; the religious right's attacks on "blasphemous" and "obscene" art funded by the NEA; an economic downturn. St. Mary's art prof Douglas Tyler speculates that students of the 1990s, obsessed with careers and tuition and shrinking opportunities, have undergone a withering of the imagination.

Students are also influenced by a powerful consumer mentality—a conviction that the art they've "paid for" must be art they like. Witness a long-standing series of protests at the University of Arizona in Tucson, which for more than a decade has administered an ambitious public art program. To augment its purchases of art by professionals, the school launched a program in 1985 in which an art student would be selected each year to display a piece of sculpture in front of the administration building. The art students reacted with gratification and pride. Their classmates reacted with mockery and vandalism. A student sculptor named John Davis designed the first work of art, a large wooden structure supporting a group of fiberglass trout swimming upstream toward a net. The message was that, like AU undergrads, some of the trout would make it out, while others would be netted.

"It was a whimsical piece, quite innocuous really," recalls Robert Cauthorn, art critic for the *Arizona Daily Star*. Therein lay the problem. Arizona students didn't want whimsy. They wanted ART. So they denounced the sculpture and sawed off the trout. Every time Davis replaced a trout, somebody sawed it off.

"Students thought that it was a waste of money, that it was stupid, that there was no reason our tuition money should go for a sculpture that didn't represent them," recalls AU student Bridget David.

"They want an equestrian sculpture," snorts Cauthorn. "They want art that conforms to some failed notion of dignity that they have. They believe in having dignified expressions, so that when people come to campus they won't think it's a silly campus. That matters to them."

Art committees take note: Whimsy is out. But so is provocative art. Recently, Arizona students objected to another student piece, an old travel trailer that had been transformed into a rather realistic depiction of a shelter for the homeless. They protested a sculpture by a professional artist that was to be displayed in a grassy area where people sunbathed. ("I found myself defending art against freedom of lounging!" marvels Peter Bermingham, who chairs the campus art committee.) And, of course, they protested the seminude photographs of Laurie Blakeslee, in which she made a statement about the female condition by donning underwear and, among other things, sticking her head in an oven.

Faced with such an unpleasant commotion, what's a university helmsman to do? Apparently the answer depends on where the commotion is coming from—that is to say, who's doing the yelling. Last year, the art department of the University of Alabama at Birmingham raised private funds to purchase a work by Andres Serrano, creator of the "Piss Christ" photograph so reviled by Senator Jesse Helms. In the University of Alabama's Serrano, a small replica of Michelangelo's Pieta sculpture is submerged in a tank of cow's blood and urine. The body fluids, notes art department chair Sonja Rieger, gave the statue a wondrous glow; nonetheless, when the student government realized where the glow came from, it passed a resolution demanding that the work, called "Pieta II," be returned—prompting the Alabama faculty, in a remarkable act of courage, to pass a resolution condemning the students. "It was almost a reverse 1960s situation, where the faculty was pushing the radical side, and the students were saying no," gleefully notes Jon Griswold, the libertarian/Native American/ Christian/older student who led the undergraduate protest.

UAB president Charles MacCallum also sided against the students—sort of—and, in the face of conservative criticism from around the state, issued a memorandum stating, "While many people in the community, including myself, find the work offensive, the Department of Art feels that the work has significant artistic and educational merit."

Similarly, when a group of students protested an exhibit of homoerotic art at the University of Ohio at Lancaster last year, the administration was prepared, and the exhibit stayed put.

Such staunchness is admirable. But it makes you wonder whether in the arts—as in questions of offensive speech—campus administrators are on the verge of developing a bad case of the double standards. Whenever the intent or effect of an artwork is unclear, some university presidents seem all too ready to cave in to the superior wisdom (or media visibility) of lefty student activists—while at other schools, the arguments of fundamentalist students are made in vain. In any case, many administrators have been going through a marvelous series of contortions: At Michigan, Lee Bollinger trod a careful line between feminist camps, pleasing neither side. But at least Bollinger did something: At Colby, Greg Long was left to twist slowly in the wind. At UNC, the administration relocated Julia Balk's vision of a student body. At St. Mary's, Marcia Kaplan's sculpture was exhibited for only a few days before it was shipped back to her. At Pitt, the administration sided with the female students and reinstated the "obscene" painting only after the artist, represented by the ACLU, filed suit.

By far the most singular compromise was struck at Colgate. There, students and faculty objected to the Lee Friedlander photographs of nudes being shown on the top floor of the Picker Art Gallery, which serves as a corridor to several offices. Rather than move the works to a self-contained lower-floor gallery, Bruce Selleck, provost and dean of faculty, opted to remove them during the week, when the gallery served as a "workplace," and reinstall them on weekends, when the Picker was merely a "gallery." In a memo, Selleck acknowledged that the arrangement was "awkward," but said that "it will permit interested members of the community to view the photographs."

In the Colgate students' defense, it should be noted that Selleck seems to have been reacting primarily to angry faculty members and only secondarily to nonplussed students whose responses were cited by faculty in a number of tart memos. ("They comment that they feel embarrassed and uncomfortable when they walk down the hallway on their way to a class," writes Lynn Schwartzer, a professor in the Art and Art History Department who proposed that the exhibit be relocated.) It should also be noted that some Colgate students were moved to defend the Friedlander exhibit, and that one English professor had the temerity to circulate a petition urging that the question of censorship at least be discussed, if only in conjunction with harassment. But in the end, of course, awkward compromise carried the day.

The compromise that will allow Carol Jacobsen's work to be shown has also failed to reconcile the pro- and anti-porn feminists on the University of Michigan campus. Indeed, Catharine MacKinnon and her supporters are sure Jacobsen's video will only strengthen their claim that porn cannot be transformed by context. Asked whether the video, as porn that at least aspires to be art, is still porn, MacKinnon replies, "It's not even a close call. This is sexually explicit material; women are being hurt, used, violated, stripped."

But perhaps the most telling outcome of all the art wars on campus occurred at the University of Arizona. There, an administration worn down by repeated anti-art stampedes eventually opted to suspend the student sculpture program, replacing the works with a bed of red flowers in the shape of an A. Not every student is happy with this solution. Remembering the infamous trout sculpture, Bridget David recalls fondly: "It was funny, though the students didn't think so. The piece—it wasn't, like, the greatest piece I've ever seen, but it was a fine piece, and it was a good idea, and now we don't have art there anymore."

Donald Kuspit

ART AND THE MORAL IMPERATIVE: ANALYZING ACTIVIST ART

Donald Kuspit is professor of art history and philosophy at the State University of New York at Stony Brook and Andrew Dixon White Professor at Large at Cornell University. In 1983 he received the Frank Jewett Mather Award for Distinction in Art Criticism, awarded by the College Art Association. His books include Louise Bourgeois *and* The New Subjectivism: Art of the 1980s. *The following reading is an abbreviated version of the original article of the same title. Kuspit argues that the political art of our era is an aesthetic failure.*

What is of interest to me is the cast of mind that leads the artist to attribute unique moral grandeur to himself. He is of course hardly the only member of society who does so. And, in his case, as in those of the others, moral pretentiousness serves an indispensable psychic function. But his case is different, for his emphasis on the moral purpose of art is at odds with the assumption that its essential purpose is aesthetic. Whatever else it might articulate, and as important as that may be, is secondary to its goal of achieving aesthetic importance. In other words, the moralizing artist uses art in a fundamentally inappropriate way. He misapplies it, as it were. No doubt art can and does have moral implications, but these are beside the point of its aesthetic intention. However, the moralizing artist thinks righteousness is more important than aesthetics. The latter, he believes, must serve the former, not vice versa. How does he come to believe this? Why does he perversely justify art in moral rather than aesthetic terms? Why, psychologically speaking, does he stand the meaning of art on its head, making a secondary meaning it might have primary and its primary meaning secondary? . . .

The social protest of the moralizing artist, and his general conception of art as inherently moral—which he thinks makes him a more authentic, authoritative artist than the

Donald Kuspit, "Art and the Moral Imperative: Analyzing Activist Art," *New Art Examiner* 18.5 (1991): 18–25.

aesthetically oriented artist—is necessary to his self-regard. This is especially so in the Modern situation of artistic decadence, so-called pluralism, indicative of stylistic insecurity and, even more fundamentally, basic uncertainty about the character and necessity of art. Nothing any longer seems innately artistic—perhaps the basic meaning of artistic decadence. Decadence is an ambiguous concept, traditionally having to do with the dialectic of decay and rejuvenation. But it can also be regarded positively: the splitting of art into a variety of conflicting factions, seemingly weakening it as a whole, in fact signals its healthy differentiation, that is, the discovery of new artistic possibilities. But the fragmentation of art is no doubt also an enfeeblement of it, and suggests general uncertainty about its effect on the individual and society—its impact. It is as though art must try out a variety of stylistic and conceptual strategies in the hopes that one will hit the psychosocial mark—take hold in human as well as art history.

The activist artist's moral intention is not simply the latest instance of the old belief, traceable to antiquity, that art must have a moral purpose to be socially credible, but the facile answer to a complex epistemological and narcissistic crisis—to art's seemingly unresolvable self-conflict and undefinability, inherent uncertainty and lack of self-identity, leading to its ambiguous fragmentation. Activist art is one subliminally anxious response to the modern inability to achieve a totally cohesive, seemingly self-adequate work of art, whose parts are decisively equilibrated—an art emblematic of ego strength and self-integration. In lieu of what increasingly looks like a modern incapacity to achieve a work of art that seems integral in itself—a seamlessly whole yet subtly differentiated work, ripe despite the incommensurateness of its parts—activist art offers a totalitarian conception of art as moralistic. That is, it totalizes art as morally responsible or dispenses with it as

next to nothing at all. Activist art believes in effect that the only hope of putting the pieces of the Humpty Dumpty of art together again is by giving it an exclusively moral determination.

The artist's claim to moral authority has escalated in the last decade. He presents himself as though he alone was sufficiently fit to wear the mantle of moral authority. He in effect exhibits himself as society's super-ego—its most authentic moral force. Indeed, in the last decade we have seen the virtual institutionalization of moralizing activist art. In certain quarters it is assumed that an art without an overt moral mission is necessarily immoral. This is the current version of the artist-moralist's case against doggedly aesthetic art. So influential is this view, that art without an overt moral point feels compelled to insist that it has a covert one, as in the case of Richard Serra's steel plate sculpture. Supposedly a moral protest against capitalistic society, especially in the way the sculpture presumably "defeats" the capitalistic skyscraper, if Serra's work must have sociomoral meaning, it can in fact be said to epitomize rather than resist the social order. For its crudity and delusional grandiosity, and especially the contradiction between its heroic look and inner shakiness—bold, self-confident appearance and structural unsoundness, giving one the sense of its inner insecurity—are exactly the traits of capitalistic society.

Similarly, Ross Bleckner declares his black paintings memorials to people with AIDS, as though their aesthetic elegance was insufficient to give them artistic credibility. The need Bleckner feels to wrap his refined pictures in the cloak of moral concern suggests the defensive posture aesthetic artists must take to survive in today's self-righteous art world. Support for the victims of AIDS is without doubt an important moral, sociopolitical cause, and one is grateful for an artist's sensitivity to it. But to use it to justify an art that needs no justification is another matter. Bleckner feels compelled to apologize for producing an essentially aesthetic art, as though that is not good enough. In fact, he admits that the idea of associating his melancholy images with people who have died from AIDS occurred to him after he painted them. It was presumably a way of adding to their inherent gravity, and above all giving them a social weight and moral credential they did not originally have or need. No doubt if an artist says so his work can spontaneously acquire an overlay of moral meaning—a specious moral depth—at will. Such determination to give art moral meaning seems to allow for spurious superegoism, that is, conscience as an adaptational, art-politically judicious afterthought.

Moreover, it should be noted that in finding social targets the artist often avoids the most psychosocially consequent ones, e.g., the entertainment industry, with its mass production of false subjectivity. Perhaps this is because the contemporary artist unconsciously regards himself as an entertainer manque—the persona of Warhol seems to imply as much, seems to generalize itself over the scene like a blight. Is he envious of entertainment's mass appeal and enormous social effect? I suggest the art of Barbara Kruger and Jenny Holzer, among others, is the confused result of such emulative, even identificative envy, as well as the wish to make an explicitly public, socially influential, and communicative art. Similarly, ecologically concerned art, while intending to be socially catalytic, deals with an issue that has become not just an urgent matter of survival but entertaining, "popular." It seems that part of the motivation of moralizing activist art is its wish to be socially accepted—to belong—as though that, perhaps in and of itself, will make it credible.

The activist argument is that if art is not explicitly in the moral opposition, it finds itself naively in the service of the immoral status quo. Activist art has not only become a standard part of the art scene—

mainstream rather than marginal—but ruthlessly passes judgment on it. . . .

In fact, contemporary activist art is a caricature of avant-garde art. For, while avant-garde art originates in antagonism to existing society and art, as Renato Poggioli remarks, its value ultimately resides in the stylistic innovation which is the aesthetic result of its antagonism—its answer to some sense of the questionableness of existing society and art. In contrast, contemporary activist art, however antagonistic, is more avant-gardistic than avant-garde, for it eschews aesthetic innovation—it is not stylistically challenging. Indeed, the activist artist cannot truly call his style his own. He uses conventionalized avant-garde styles, so simplified and stereotyped that they are no longer either a social threat or intellectual challenge—no longer provocative. He modifies them—with a shrewd sense of art world Realpolitik, so that his work will seem art historically credible—to his facile communicative purpose. He offers nothing artistically new, and indeed avoids stylistic experimentation as a threat to communication. This suggests that oppositionality and subversiveness—part of the standard expectation (catechism?) of avant-garde art, automatic guarantees of avant-gardeness—have become trendy cliches, very much in need of a critique. Activist art of course offers none, for it depends on the cliche of oppositionality and subversiveness. . . . The question is whether that is enough. . . .

The artist-moralist attempts to impose a moral limit or construction on art, as its most serious, ultimate meaning, in order to repress, even deny, its fundamental aestheticity, because that aestheticity is the emblem of desire. Aestheticity affords the illusion that desire can exist in a free, pure state—that there can be free passage of pure desire. It assumes that desire can be precipitated out of history by art, even as desire makes history happen, flow. This is an illusion, for desire always exists both constructively and subversively within the semiotics of events. But it is a necessary illusion, luring life on—indeed, justifying it to itself—with the belief that it can know its own depths, renew contact with what is most basic in itself, and as such revitalize itself.

The idea that one must perpetually renew desire to exist in the fullness of one's being—work with fresh desire, desire that has been liberated from its sedimentation in semiosis, and that can be a source of new semioticization of existence—is the motivation for art, or rather aestheticity, which at its best is experienced as desire rejuvenated and re-energizing life. Every aesthetic innovation is an attempt at the restoration of desire. The artist-moralist attempts to immobilize covert aesthetic desire—arrest its vital and vitalizing passage—by making stridently super-egotistic art. In doing so, he reveals the conflict of his own mental life—the conflict, already described, implicit in his experience of bad beautifulness of the lifeworld. . . .

Activist art, the latest version of moralistic art, is at bottom opposed to the free display and play of desire. Indeed, that is what oppositionality in general and opposition to the aesthetic in particular is fundamentally about. As such, activist art is inherently anti-art, for the task of art is to find new ways of articulating desire, freeing it all of all ideological—that is, didactic—predetermination. Desire has neither social, moral, nor generally ideological meaning, however much it may fuel such meanings—which it will revolt against when they become reified, as they invariably do, when there is an attempt to indoctrinate people with them.

Philip Gourevitch

BEHOLD
NOW
BEHEMOTH

Philip Gourevitch is cultural editor of The Forward, *a weekly Jewish newspaper with national circulation in the United States. In the essay that follows, Gourevitch criticizes the Holocaust Memorial in Washington, D.C. This memorial is too much like other public attractions, in Gourevitch's view. Even worse, it insinuates that the evil that is memorialized is a unique occurrence in the past, instead of the ever-present danger it is.*

I am a first-generation American, born, like the nation, in Philadelphia, the child of refugees from European barbarism. Both my parents, in their separate youths, escaped the Nazi effort to murder all Jews; many in my family were not so lucky. I knew this fact, in some form, from as early in my life as I remember knowing anything significant. To a degree, I derived pride and a sense of romance from the distinctiveness of this awful yet dramatic heritage: I was glad to have a story that gave shape and meaning to my origins, and thereby provided me with a consciousness of destiny. I understood that my life belonged not only to me but to the course of history.

Yet the story, the details of which I knew only sketchily until I was nearly twenty, worried me too. I had a dream around the age of seven or eight, a dream I may have dreamed more than once, of a vast, darkened plain across which masses of people fled in chaotic haste, pursued and at times surrounded by other equally chaotic masses. Fire at the margins of the scene illuminated the action, the only possible outcome of which seemed to be isolation and annihilation. I survived, of course, because I woke up; the slaughter ended before I did.

The phrase that became attached to this hateful vision was, "The Nazis are coming." I don't know if I thought the words in my sleep, or if I added them afterward. The experience seemed at once absolutely true and absolutely useless. Nothing could be learned from it, nothing taken away; there was nothing in it for life.

I was reminded of this dream of terror last April, when I visited the newly opened United States Holocaust Memorial Museum, the latest addition to the federal museum system—a $168 million facility built by

Philip Gourevitch, "Behold Now Behemoth," *Harper's Magazine* 287.1718 (1993): 55–62.

federal decree on a plot of priceless federal land just off the National Mall in Washington, D.C. There I spoke with Michael Berenbaum, who was the museum's project director throughout its planning and construction. A rabbi and professor of theology at Georgetown University, he explained to me that the museum's mission is twofold: to memorialize the victims of Nazism by providing an exhaustive historical narrative of the Holocaust; and, at the same time, to present visitors with an object lesson in the ethical ideals of American political culture by presenting the negation of those ideals. Berenbaum has coined a phrase to describe the latter part of this mission. He calls it "The Americanization of the Holocaust."

"In America," he said, "we recast the story of the Holocaust to teach fundamental American values. What are the fundamental values? For example—when America is at its best—pluralism, democracy, restraint on government, the inalienable rights of individuals, the inability of government to enter into freedom of the press, freedom of assembly, freedom of religion, and so forth."

The museum, then, is meant to serve as an ideological vaccine for the American body politic. A proper dose of Holocaust, the thinking goes, will build up the needed antibodies against totalitarianism, racism, and state-sponsored mass murder. "The Holocaust," Berenbaum has written, "can become a symbolic orienting event in human history that can prevent recurrence." He and his colleagues have designed the national Holocaust museum so that as much of the American public as possible—particularly the school groups that are expected to make up a large percentage of visitors—will, in a sense, walk through my childhood nightmare. This experience, they believe, will teach Americans both to celebrate and to think critically about their political culture.

"When America is at its best," Berenbaum told me, "the Holocaust is impossible in the United States."

The fact remains, however, that the Holocaust was a European event, and that even at its utter worst, America has been a place where the Holocaust—a program of genocidal extermination mandated and implemented by every organ of a nation-state—has never entered the realm of possibility. America's problems and America's faults, however extreme, have been and remain different from those of fascist Germany. To suggest that there are meaningful comparisons can only distort our already feeble understanding of European history and—worse—obscure our perception of current American reality.

The museum's dedication ceremony on April 22 was an exercise in official pageantry and speechifying, attended by virtually unanimous celebration in the nation's press. President Clinton addressed the gathered thousands—survivors, foreign heads of state, American dignitaries, and assorted citizens—describing the museum as "an investment in a secure future against whatever insanity lurks ahead." He went on to say that "if this museum can mobilize morality, then those who have perished will thereby gain a measure of immortality."

The President's "if" had a particularly sinister resonance on that day; as he spoke, Serbian forces in the former Yugoslavia were pressing forward with the slaughter of their Bosnian Muslim neighbors. There, in the heart of Europe, the Serbian program of murdering innocents, and the sickening euphemism "ethnic cleansing" (with which even the American press masked the bloodiness), was glaringly reminiscent of—though not equivalent to—the Holocaust. As of that moment, the international response to this atrocity had amounted to expressions of outrage and the decision to stand by. Indeed, many of the world's leaders stood in Washington with the National Mall as their backdrop, the Washington Monument and the Jefferson Memorial looming in the near distance, and applauded President Clinton's suggestion that the Holocaust museum could redeem the deaths of Nazism's victims by serving as "a constant reminder of our duty to build and nurture the institutions of public tranquility and humanity."

In Yiddish, the language Hitler sought to eliminate along with the Jews of Europe, such talk is called *chutzpah*. There is something dangerously facile about opposing evil fifty years after the fact. Yet that is the price one pays for Americanizing the Holocaust; as soon as the Holocaust is set up as a metaphor for national ideology, it comes back to haunt us, making its utterance a constant potential embarrassment and tainting the otherwise irreproachable impulse to commemorate the dead. As an American, and as a Jew, I am deeply discomforted to have to point out these things. I do not, for a moment, want to suggest that the Holocaust should be forgotten, remembered in silence, or ignored. I want only to serve a reminder, as this museum becomes a major new touchstone in America's narrative of national identity, that denouncing evil is a far cry from doing good. . . .

To draw people into this strange new American civics lesson, exhibition designers have devised a gimmick for audience participation in the Holocaust narrative. Upon admission, visitors are issued an identity card—matched to their age and gender—imprinted with the name and vital statistics of an actual Holocaust victim or survivor. As they pass through the three floors of the museum's permanent exhibition, museum-goers will be periodically able to plug these bar-coded cards into computerized stations and measure their progress against the fate of their phantom surrogates, most of whom were murdered.

The sample I.D. card included in the promotional materials that the museum sent me is stamped with the name and photograph of Haskel Kernweis, who was born in 1920 and lived in the rural village of Kolbushova, Poland. "His family is very religious," the card explains, although it does not name their religion. For the years 1933–1939, we read that "Haskel now calls himself 'Charley,' for his passion is no longer religion but English. . . . He writes to Eleanor Roosevelt telling her that he loves English and wants to speak it in America one day. She responds enthusiastically. The German police order Charley to work for them." Between 1940 and 1944, Charley fled to the woods with a group of Jews after learning that the Germans meant to kill him. Returning to town one day to buy bread, he was caught by Polish peasants and, the card announces, "his friends found him—dead, a pitchfork stuck into his chest." The card's final entry is: "1945– . Charley's entire family was gassed at Belzec. Only one of the Jewish fighters who went to the woods with him survived the war."

There are some five hundred visitor I.D. cards, but it is no accident that the one selected for publicity purposes should tell the story of a man who is described as having converted from Judaism to Americanism before his death at the hands of Nazi collaborators. The card's narrative even implies that the animosity of the Nazis was a consequence of Haskel/Charley's Americanism. When I asked Berenbaum about this, he said, "Clearly, when they're sending out fund-raising things they want to attract American people—to attract and interest the Americans without falsifying events."

Entering the Holocaust museum from southwest Fifteenth Street (now renamed Raoul Wallenberg Place, after the Swedish diplomat who saved thousands of Hungarian Jews from Nazi extermination), one is confronted by a black marble wall engraved with the passage from the Declaration of Independence celebrating "life, liberty, and the pursuit of happiness." Opposite this, chiseled in gray limestone, are words from

George Washington: "The government of the United States . . . gives to bigotry no sanction, to persecution no assistance."

From the I.D.-card dispensary one is ushered directly into an elevator, where a video monitor plays footage of an armored vehicle rumbling over bleak European terrain while the voice of an American soldier describes coming upon a Nazi death camp without knowing what it was. After less than a minute, the elevator doors open on the fourth floor and the permanent exhibition begins with a wall-sized photograph of some twenty American G.I.'s looking down on a massive heap of charred logs and charred corpses. These are the calcined remains of concentration camp inmates at Ohrdruf, Germany, in April 1945—twisted limbs, broken torsos, blackened skin crumbling from skull bones. Along the same wall, video monitors play ghastly color footage of the liberation of Dachau, and a giant color photo presents a starved Buchenwald inmate sipping a post-liberation meal from a tin bowl. This man is the picture of cosmic woe; cadaverous in his short-panted, striped pajamas, he sits in dazzling sunshine, squinting up at his photographer with a face so harrowed by unhappiness that it calls into permanent question just what it means to say that he has survived.

Before visitors even reach the first exhibit on the rise of Nazism, they have been dealt a visceral, emotional wallop with the graphic evidence of the end result: Jewish corpses. The effect is, at the least, shocking. A wincing, uncomfortable silence hangs over the crowded gallery, punctuated only by clucked tongues and staccato gasps of outrage—sounds that become less frequent as the museum tour continues and visitors recoup their defenses or become accustomed to images of horror.

The museum's designers explain the decision to begin the exhibition with the American liberation of the camps as a means of orienting visitors who may have no knowledge whatever of history. The idea is to ease the passage from the festive present of a visit to the Mall to the alien hell of Nazi Europe by discovering that hell through American eyes. Of course, opening the show from this vantage point will also comfort Americans by identifying them immediately as heroes. An odd spin, this: clutching their I.D. cards, museumgoers are asked to identify simultaneously with the victims and their saviors. Placing the American liberation of the camps in the foreground of the exhibition also nudges to the background the third role visitors are being asked to consider: that of the bystanders who participate in history by an acquiescent failure to act. The decision further blurs the understanding of the role of bystanders by creating the impression that Americans knew nothing of Hitler's "Final Solution of the Jewish Problem" until the end of the war. That was true of many American G.I.'s, but the American government, some members of the press, and some of the public, especially the American Jewish community, had known of the death camps for years. This is matter examined at several points later in the exhibition. By then, however, the issue is likely to be confused for anyone who does not already have a firm grasp of the events under examination.

Shortly before he committed suicide, Primo Levi, the most lucid and probing of survivor-authors, wrote about receiving a lecture from a fifth-grader on how he should and could have escaped Auschwitz, a detailed plan of action that the child concluded with the words "If it should happen to you again, do as I told you. You'll see that you'll be able to do it." To Levi, the boy's remarks illustrated "the gap that exists and grows wider every year between things as they were 'down there' and things as they are represented by the current imagination fed by approximative books, films, and myths." Every aspect of the Holocaust museum's exhibition that promotes

Americanization drives the museum deeper into that gap.

On either side of a darkened hallway, the history of Germany from 1933 to 1939 looms behind glass—a montage of photographs, artifacts, text and video displays. The section headings tell the story: "Nazi Takeover of Power," "The Terror Begins," "The Boycott," "The Burning of Books," "Nazi Propaganda," "The Nuremberg Laws." Here is an exhibit devoted to Nazi race science: photo charts of human heads describing various "racial types," images of scientists taking cranial measurements from human specimens, a pair of metal calipers, a sampler of different types and colors of human hair hanging from the wall. Here is a giant color photograph of a Nazi rally, radiant blond children frozen as they give the stiff-armed "Heil Hitler" salute. Here is a school desk from the period, and over it a photograph of a little German girl cheerfully reading *The Poisoned Mushroom*, a popular anti-Semitic children's book that took its title from Hitler's description of Jews in *Mein Kampf*. Here is a section on laws against interracial relations, with images of Jewish-Aryan couples forced to wear signs confessing their crimes before mocking crowds in the public streets.

In the section titled "Expansion Without War," the Anschluss is seen on video: the Nazis' triumphal arrival in Vienna, the joyous Austrians swarming to welcome them. Next to the monitor hang the famous images of Vienna's Jews, forced on all fours to scrub the city's streets with hand-held brushes while passersby stop to enjoy the show. Europe's indifference to such goings-on is conveyed by a large color photograph of Neville Chamberlain, beaming and doffing his bowler hat in an open car beneath snapping swastika banners in Munich, 1938.

In an alcove dedicated to the "Mosaic of Victims," an authentic Gypsy caravan stands beneath images of Gypsies and Jehovah's Witnesses and mug shots of German men arrested on charges of homosexuality.

Desecrated Torah scrolls spill over the floor beneath a defaced ark from a German synagogue in the exhibition's treatment of *Kristallnacht*. Four video monitors play footage from that night showing stores being smashed, synagogues burning. Festive martial tunes drift across the gallery from a nearby display on Nazi high society. Further along, a wall of photographs tells of the torture and murder of the Polish intelligentsia in the winter of 1939: mass executions, mass graves, blindfolded people stumbling through the woods to their deaths. Around the corner is a display on the murder of the handicapped: a metal hospital cot with restraint bands stands before a 1941 photo of the Hadamar Euthanasia center in Hadamar, Germany—a large, factory-like building at the edge of a quiet-looking town. Smoke jetting from its chimney comes from a crematorium. Another photo shows a naked girl held upright on a bed by a strong-armed attendant. The caption informs that she is mentally disabled and about to be murdered.

After this, there is a long gallery on American reactions to the events in Europe, a chronicle of journalistic alarm and official isolationism that provides a short breather before one descends to the third floor and the story of the Final Solution. Here, the exhibition halls narrow and lift onto a bridge over a pavement of cobblestones imported from the Warsaw Ghetto. The process of herding Jews into ghettos, moving them about in railroad transports, and finally deporting them to death camps is carefully chronicled. Ghetto life is evoked in all its grim and hopeless detail.

By the time I reached the exhibit on the *Einsatzgruppen*, or mobile killing squads, I felt I'd had enough. In just a few hours I had already seen images of hundreds of dead bodies, many of them naked, and hundreds more people starving, beaten, and otherwise brutalized. Now a photograph hung before me of a man squatting at the edge of a mass grave, corpses beneath him, Nazis behind him, a pistol at his head about to be fired.

Below this picture, the crowd—which was impossibly dense throughout the gallery—was even thicker than usual. I waited to draw closer and found, behind a low "privacy wall" designed to keep young children from particularly graphic material, two video monitors playing footage of the killing squads at work.

This is what I wrote in my notebook: "Peep-show format. Snuff films. Naked women led to execution. People are being shot. Into the ditch, shot, spasms, collapse, dirt thrown in over. Crowds of naked people. Naked people standing about to be killed, naked people lying down dead. Close-up of a woman's face and throat as a knife is plunged into her breast—blood all over. Someone holds a severed head in his hand. Mass graves of thousands. Naked. Naked corpses. Naked corpses. Street beatings. The gun, the smoke, a figure crumbles. Naked corpses. Naked women dragged to death. Shooting. Screaming. Blackout. The film begins again." . . .

I hurried on, up a platform, past images of deportation, and into a railroad freight car, an actual railroad car on actual iron railroad tracks—one of the gifts to the museum from the Polish government. During the war, cars just like this one hauled Jews to Treblinka to be murdered. It was small and dark inside. I felt like a trespasser, someone engaged in an unwholesome experience, the way I might feel if I were asked to lie in someone else's coffin.

On the exit ramp, I stood behind another family group, a stout older man with his wife and two daughters. They were examining a wall of mug shots of Auschwitz inductees, and after a minute the man said, "Nope, these are all 1942."

"You were there the next year?" his wife said.

"Yup." He turned to his kids. "Let's move it, eh?" He glanced ahead to see where he was going and found that he was about to pass under a cast of the metal gate that hangs over the entry to Auschwitz with the message ARBEIT MACHT FREI ("Work makes one free"). For a moment the man appeared to hesitate. Then he grinned and said, "Oh, yeah, I want to be free." . . .

Violence and the grotesque are central to the American aesthetic, and the Holocaust museum provides both amply. It is impossible to take in the exhibition without becoming somewhat inured to the sheer graphic horror on display; indeed, it would be unbearable to be defenseless in such a place. A flat response, however, is less unsettling than is the potential for *excitement*, for titillation, and even for seduction by the overwhelmingly powerful imagery. The museum courts the viewer's fascination, encouraging familiarity with the incomprehensible and the unacceptable; one is repeatedly forced into the role of a voyeur of the prurient. (By contrast, Claude Lanzman's wrenching film *Shoah* holds one mesmerized for nine hours without a single violent image.)

During the American Civil War, people used to go out to the battlefield to watch the fighting, an activity that was known as "going to see the elephant." They were out for the show, something enormous and exotic and terrifying. The spectacle was its own reward. There is already an elephant on the National Mall, a trumpeting bull elephant stuffed in the lobby of the National Museum of Natural History; there are already train cars in the National Museum of American History; there are even airplanes, rocket ships, blimps, and fabulous films that make you feel that you are flying in the National Air and Space Museum. But the new show in town is more wondrous strange yet. Never mind the elephant; as the Lord said to Job: "Behold now behemoth."

When General Dwight Eisenhower toured the mass graves at the Ohrdruf concentration camp, he said, "We are told that the American soldier does not know what he was fighting for. Now at least he will know what he is fighting against." Ike's remark could serve as the Holocaust museum's motto. Americans, it seems, are no longer confident asserting their principles and ideals affirmatively. The new museum has been compared with Maya Lin's Vietnam Veterans Memorial as providing a critique of the iconography of progress and state power that abounds on the Mall. But the Holocaust museum seems less to repudiate traditional American boosterism than to invert the rhetoric in which its claims are made. Here we are told not what we stand for but what we stand against.

When I asked various museum officials why America should set aside one of the last remaining plots of land on the Mall to commemorate the Holocaust, they responded by pointing out that national museums of Native-American and African-American history are also planned. The comparison explains nothing. Those museums will present American history, not European history, and they will cover hundreds of years of each people's history, their accomplishments as well as their tragedies. Nobody talks about a Trail of Tears museum or a museum of slavery.

The Holocaust museum, on the other hand, installs Jews on the Mall as a people identified by their experience of mass murder. If Jews had not had that experience, Jews would not have this museum. This fact points to the centrality of victimology in contemporary American identity politics. At a time when Americans seem to lack the confidence to build national monuments to their ideas of good, the Holocaust has been seized as an opportunity to build instead a monument against absolute evil. The absolute, however, is a treacherous place to seek lessons. By definition, it does not yield. Like the God of Exodus, it is what it is and it shall be what it shall be. For that reason, the absolute is useless as metaphor. It is incomparable. While it is common to hear something referred to as "like the Holocaust," references to the Holocaust as like something else—except, of course, that other absolute, hell—are unheard.

Among the forces that the Holocaust museum is explicitly designed to combat are the "historical revisionists," those crank historians who deny that there ever was a Holocaust. This objective is in keeping with the one certain lesson I am willing to draw from the Holocaust—that it happened. That is reason enough to study it, to remember it. Beyond the fact that it happened, however, all claims made in the name of the Holocaust are suspect.

When I say that there is nothing in my childhood dream of Nazism for life, I mean that political and ethical madness, however methodical, teaches nothing about political and ethical sanity. Sanity cannot be asserted by its negative. Racism, hatred, the dehumanization of one's fellow human beings are bad not because they can lead to Auschwitz, not even because they can lead to murder. These things are bad because they are not good. They are unethical and unjust. Justice requires that all be treated with equal humanity. If there is a lesson that needs to be taught in the world today, it is this difficult affirmative lesson in the most fundamental of American values—what true justice is and why it is good. . . .

One way history *is* doomed to repetition at the Holocaust museum is that day in and day out, year after year, the videos of the *Einsatzgruppen* murders will play over and over. There, just off the National Mall in Washington, the victims of Nazism will be on view for the American public, stripped, herded into ditches, shot, buried, and then the tape will repeat and they will be herded into the ditches again, shot again, buried again. I cannot comprehend how anyone can enthusiastically present this constant recycling of slaughter, either as a memorial to those whose deaths are exposed or as an edifying spectacle for the millions of visitors a year who will be exposed to them. Didn't these people suffer enough the first time their lives were taken from them?

DISCUSSION QUESTIONS

1. Do Plato's moral criticisms of art apply to contemporary television, in your opinion?
2. Do you agree with Bloom's depiction of rock music? Do you think his criticisms apply to the category of rock music as a whole? Do you think they apply to any instances of rock music? If you disagree with Bloom's critique, how would you construct a defense of rock music?
3. Do you think that art can be a bad moral influence? If so, under what circumstances? Do you think that art can be a good moral influence? If so, under what circumstances? Can an artwork have a moral impact in itself, or does its influence depend on how it is used?
4. Do you think the morality of an artwork's apparent message should be considered in your aesthetic evaluation of it? Why or why not?
5. Do you think that various critics of the artworks that Mundy describes are right in their opinions? Do you agree with their tactics?
6. Can a memorial be morally misguided or offensive? How?

FURTHER READING

Beardsmore, R. W. *Art and Morality.* London: Macmillan, 1971.

Cavell, Marcia. "Taste and Moral Sense." *Journal of Aesthetics and Art Criticism* 34.1 (1975): 29–33.

Eaton, Marcia Muelder. *Aesthetics and the Good Life.* Madison: F. Dickinson UP, 1989.

Eldridge, Richard. *On Moral Personhood: Philosophy, Literature, Criticism, and Self-Understanding.* Chicago: U of Chicago P, 1989.

Higgins, Kathleen Marie. *The Music of Our Lives.* Philadelphia: Temple UP, 1991.

Korthals, Michiel. "Art and Morality: Critical Theory about the Conflict and Harmony between Art and Morality." *Philosophy and Social Criticism* 15.3 (1989): 241–51.

Nussbaum, Martha C. *Love's Knowledge: Essays on Philosophy and Literature.* New York: Oxford UP, 1991.

Radford, Colin. "How Can Music Be Moral?" *Midwest Studies in Philosophy* 16 (1991): 421–38.

Read, Alan. *Theatre and Everyday Life: An Ethics of Performance.* New York: Routledge, 1993.

Robinson, Jenefer, and Stephanie Ross. "Women, Morality, and Fiction." *Aesthetics in Feminist Perspective.* Ed. Hilde Hein and Carolyn Korsmeyer. Bloomington: Indiana UP, 1993. 105–18.

Schiller, Friedrich. *Letters on the Aesthetic Education of Man.* 1794. Trans. E. M. Wilkinson and L. A. Willoughby. Oxford: Clarendon, 1967.

Tirell, M. Lynne. "Storytelling and Moral Agency." *Journal of Aesthetics and Art Criticism* 48.2 (1990): 115–26.

Chapter
⟨6⟩

ART AND
OUR INSTITUTIONS

The government's appropriate relationship to art, if any, has become a topic of hot debate in the United States in recent years. The National Endowment for the Arts has been criticized for providing funding to assist artists who made "obscene" and "immoral" works and to support museums that sometimes exhibited them. Particularly vilified have been the homoerotic and sadistic photographs by the late Robert Mapplethorpe and a sacrilegious artwork entitled *Piss Christ* by Andres Serrano, which features a plastic crucifix immersed in the artist's urine. Many have asked why government funding should support such artists and exhibitions, or why the government should be in the business of supporting art at all.

Paul Mattick, Jr., makes the case for government support of artistic enterprises. Government funding is the way we, as a society, encourage cultural activities in general, according to Mattick. The National Endowment for the Arts has not primarily been in the business of supporting obscenity and blasphemy; instead, it has made art-making possible for artists of modest means and given the public access to art that would not otherwise have been available to it. Mattick takes issue with proposals by Senator Jesse Helms and others that would withhold government funding from artists and exhibitions presenting art that is repugnant to community standards. Art often expresses criticisms of the status quo and draws attention to tensions within community standards. Mattick sees these to be important services that art provides. This whistle-blowing aspect of art is indeed among the reasons for considering art a valuable enterprise that the community should support.

As Carole S. Vance reports, the U.S. Congress did pass legislation to prohibit the use of government funding for obscene art. But she suggests that the high-tempered debate over the issue has obscured the public's understanding of the legal definition of obscenity. Several criteria need to be met before the legal standards apply. (In fact, in cases where exhibits of Mapplethorpe's photographs were alleged to include obscene content, juries decided that these exhibitions did not meet the legal criteria.) The mere presence of erotic content does not make an artwork legally obscene. But Vance fears that the move to withhold funding from "obscene" art may lead NEA administrators and judges to deny support in some cases merely because art makes reference to sexuality.

Tom Wolfe reflects on a nongovernmental institution that influences the art that is available to us, the museum. He criticizes the museum's presentation of "serious art," which most of the public has difficulty comprehending. Wolfe believes, however, that this art does serve a real purpose in our society—to function as a religion in a secular world. Religions in the past have typically been used to distance their followers from the world and to legitimate wealth, Wolfe argues. Contemporary art now serves both of these functions. If contemporary art is incomprehensible to many who see it, Wolfe concludes, this only reinforces the new "religious" status of art.

Americans often are proud of their freedom to express themselves. The body of law protecting the freedom of artists is also growing in the United States. One impact of recent legislation is that artworks no longer have the status of other private property; instead, buyers of artworks are no longer legally entitled to change or destroy artworks as casually as in the past.

Such laws are clearly designed to protect the rights of artists—but do artworks themselves have rights? Artworks have sometimes been compared to human beings on the ground that they have individualities. If this comparison makes sense, does it follow that artworks have a *right* to exist? James O. Young considers the arguments against destroying works of art. While he thinks that destroying good art is usually wrong, even for the artist, there are exceptions to this general rule. Nevertheless, Young is convinced that the destruction of an artwork should never be taken lightly.

Douglas Stalker and Clark Glymour approach the issue of destroying or dismantling art from a different point of view. Focusing on public sculpture, they contend that the burden of proof should be placed on those who claim that public sculpture benefits the public. In fact, much evidence suggests that public art can actually harm the public. At the very least, they argue, there is no good reason to keep harmful public sculpture in the public's view. Moreover, without evidence demonstrating that the public genuinely benefits from public sculpture, the government has no interest in promoting it.

Arthur C. Danto's discussion of the Vietnam Veterans Memorial suggests that at least some public art does importantly benefit the public, even when some of the public does not like it. The Vietnam Veterans Memorial, denounced by some because it is not representational, is profoundly moving to most of the public who come to see it. Danto suggests that the nearby statue of veterans, eventually installed to placate those who wanted a "real" memorial, derives any artistic power it has only by its placement. Besides urging us to reconsider our expectations of monuments, Danto also reminds us of the importance of an artwork's context, which may enhance or diminish its impact.

Paul Mattick, Jr.

ARTS
AND
THE
STATE

Paul Mattick, Jr., is professor of philosophy at Adelphi University. He is also author of Social Knowledge: An Essay on the Nature and Limits of Social Science. *Mattick defends government funding of the arts as a way of culturally encouraging an activity that we, as a society, believe to be valuable.*

Visiting the exhibition of Robert Mapplethorpe's photographs at the Institute of Contemporary Art in Boston a month ago, it was hard at first to see what all the fuss was about. The controversy that has dogged the show since its organization by the Institute of Contemporary Art in Philadelphia certainly made itself felt in the huge numbers of visitors (tickets sold out well in advance) and in the aura of decorous excitement that enveloped those who managed to get in. Most of the pictures, however, were unexciting. With the exception of a handful of striking images from the artist's last years, we saw celebrity portraits shot in 1940s fashion style, arty flowers, naked black men in a venerable art-nude tradition. In a distinct area, however, reached only by waiting in a patient line of cultured scopophiles, were the pictures which more than the others had called down upon the National Endowment

for the Arts, partial funder of the Philadelphia I.C.A., the wrath of America's self-appointed guardians of morality.

There were more flowers, more naked black men and a set of s&m photos that was undeniably gripping. Here the subject matter overcame Mapplethorpe's tendency to artiness and commercial finish in a set of documents with the power of the once dark and hidden brought to light. Here are some things some people like to do, they say; this is part of our world; you can look or not, but now you know they exist, whatever you think of them. In an age saturated with sexual imagery of all kinds, these pictures were perhaps not as disturbing as they might have been to more innocent eyes. At any rate, the visiting public was not so horrified as to fail to crowd the museum store to purchase bookfuls of Mapplethorpe's pictures (along with black nude–emblazoned T-shirts, floral

Paul Mattick, Jr., "Arts and the State," *The Nation* 251.10 (1990): 348–58.

porcelain plates and bumper stickers proclaiming support for freedom of the arts). Nonetheless, these photographs, in the company of a few other pictures and performances, have evoked a storm of Congressional and popular indignation that now threatens to sweep away the N.E.A. itself. This, in turn, has given rise to attempts to defend the current mode of state patronage of the arts.

It is difficult to speak of real controversy in this area, as the two discourses at work are to a great degree at cross-purposes. That of the naysaying politicians tends toward expressions of traditional American anti-intellectualism, portraying state arts funding as the use, basically for the gratification of a degenerate Eastern elite, of money better spent on local pork barrels and military projects. Art, in this view, has a natural affinity with sex, subversion and fraudulence. On the other hand, the statements of opposition to censorship and calls for arts funding by artists, dealers, other art professionals and liberal politicians take as given the social value of the arts, their consequent claim on the public purse and (with some disagreement) the current mode of distribution of the goodies. Without being in favor of either censorship or the diversion of yet more money to produce new bombers and missiles, one may step back and attempt to rethink the question.

Lacking a feudal heritage, a tradition of princely magnificence such as that which stands behind state cultural policy in European countries, the United States has no long history of governmental patronage of the arts. Under American law, corporations themselves were forbidden to engage in philanthropy, including support of the arts, until 1935. Washington was supposed, in this most purely capitalist of all nations, to spend only the minimum needed to control labor and defend business's national interests. Theater, including opera, functioned in

the nineteenth century as a commercial enterprise across the country, and the visual arts were for the most part produced for private purchase. When growing economic power stimulated the mercantile and industrial upper classes of the later nineteenth century to call for the establishment of museums, symphony orchestras and other cultural institutions, they had to put up the money themselves. Thus, while the revolutionary regime in France, for example, took over the King's palace and its contents to create the Musée du Louvre for the nation, the United States did not have a National Gallery in Washington until Andrew Mellon gave his personal collection to the country and started building a structure to house it in 1938.

The arts began to attract more public attention with the start of the twentieth century, as can be seen in the national publicity gained by the Armory Show, which introduced European modernism to the United States in 1913. Whereas art and all those things called "culture" in general had earlier been largely identified with the European upper class, Regionalism, given national exposure by a *Time* cover story in 1934, claimed to be a uniquely American style. At the time of the New Deal, a few farsighted individuals conceived the idea of government aid to the arts as part of the general federal effort to combat the Depression. Two programs for the employment of artists, one run out of the Treasury Department and a much larger one as part of the Works Progress Administration, represented the national government's first entry into patronage (aside from the commissioning of official buildings, statuary and paintings). In the view of the organizers of these projects, their long-term rationale was support for the arts as a fundamental part of American life; but they could be realized, in the face of much opposition from Congress (and professional artists' associations, true to the principles of free enterprise), only as relief programs, employing otherwise starving (and potentially subversive) artists and preserving their productive skills during the emergency. Both programs died, after a period of reduction, with America's entry into the war.

Institutional concern with the arts developed markedly with the U.S. rise to world supremacy after the war. The war reversed the normal flow of American artists to Europe, bringing refugee artists to New York and California and thus stimulating artistic life, at least on the edges of North America. More important, its segue into the cold war joined to the growing desire of the American upper class to play social roles equal to its expanded global importance a new use for American modern art as a symbol of the advantages of a free society. New York abstraction, still unappreciated by any sizable public, was not only promoted by the mass media that had once publicized Regionalism but was shipped around the world along with jazz music and industrial design, by government bodies like the United States Information Agency and by the Rockefeller-dominated Museum of Modern Art. In modern art, it seemed, America was now number one; while still incomprehensible (as critic Max Kozloff once observed), art that celebrated the autonomy of the creative individual no longer seemed so subversive. In the realm of classical music, Van Cliburn's victory in a piano competition in Moscow in 1958 was an event of political as well as cultural importance.

More fundamentally, beyond issues of international political prestige and the aristocratic pretensions of the very rich, the idea was gaining ground among America's elite— particularly in the Northeast but in a city like Chicago as well—that art is a Good Thing, a glamorous thing, even (more recently) a fun thing. This attitude rapidly trickled down to the middle class, whose self-assertion as leading citizens of an affluent and powerful nation was expressed in a new attachment to culture. As interest in art spread throughout the country, the 1950s saw galleries in department stores, rising museum and concert attendance and the commercial distribution of classical LPs and inexpensive reproductions of famous paintings. Studio training and art history departments proliferated in the universities. A handful of corporate executives, in alliance with cultural entrepreneurs like Mortimer Adler and R. M. Hutchins, discovered that culture, whether classic or modern, could be both marketed and used as a marketing medium.

In part this reflected the changing nature of the business class; while fewer than 50 percent of top executives had some college education in 1900, 76 percent did by 1950. The postwar rise of the professional manager helped break down the traditional barrier between the worlds of business and culture, affecting the self-image of American society as a whole. To this was joined— with the growth of academia, research institutions and all levels of government— the emergence of the new professional-intellectual stratum, connected in spirit to the power elite in a way unknown to the alienated intelligentsia of yesteryear. In 1952 the editors of *Partisan Review* introduced a symposium on "Our Country and Our Culture" with the observation that just a decade earlier, "America was commonly thought to be hostile to art and culture. Since then, however, the tide has begun to turn. . . . Europe . . . no longer assures that rich experience of culture which inspired and justified a criticism of American life. . . . [N]ow America has become the protector of Western civilization."

Thus politics, business and culture joined hands. Art's growing value as an area of investment and domestic public relations could only be reinforced by its emergence as a marker of international prestige. The Kennedys' Camelot was a watershed, with its transformation of the Europhilia typical of the American elite into the representation of the White House as a world cultural center. Kennedy counselor Arthur Schlesinger Jr. put it this way, in arguing for a government arts policy: "We will win world understanding of our policy and purposes not through the force of our arms or the array of our wealth but through the splendor of our ideals."

Such efforts both led to and were enormously enhanced by the founding of the National Endowment for the Arts in 1965 and its rapid development thereafter. While it represented the fulfillment of ideas bruited about various levels of government since the Eisenhower days, the N.E.A. was realized as an accompaniment to Lyndon Johnson's Great Society; like that program as a whole (and like the W.P.A.), it reflected the principle of the state's responsibility for those aspects of the good life not automatically taken care of by market forces. It should not be thought that it was established without opposition (as of course no Great Society program was); in fact, the N.E.A. achieved legislative reality only as a unit of a National Foundation for the Arts and Humanities, of which the National Endowment for the Humanities was the more respectable half. In addition, the arts were carefully defined to include the productions of the culture industry—movies, radio, fashion and industrial design—along with the traditional "high" arts. The Endowment not only survived numerous challenges to legitimacy but saw its budget rise between 1969 and 1977 from $8 million to more than $82 million, and by 1990 to $171 million. This, moreover, is only a portion of total arts spending, which includes sums directed, for some examples, to museum development, to the Smithsonian Institution and to projects under the aegis of the National Park System. In addition, the big push to culture given by Congress since the mid-1960s included changes in tax laws—in

recent years to a certain extent undone—encouraging donations of art and money to museums and other institutions.

One must not exaggerate: The sums spent on its arts agency by the American government have always been derisorily small, both relative to other government programs and in comparison with the spending of other industrialized capitalist nations. West Germany, the world leader, spent about $73 per inhabitant on the arts last year; the Netherlands spent $33, and even Margaret Thatcher's Britain laid out $12; the United States indulged its culture-mongers with a measly 71 cents per capita. This amounted to less than 0.1 percent of the federal budget (the Smithsonian alone receives a larger appropriation than the N.E.A., as does the Pentagon's military band program, budgeted in 1989 at $193 million). Even this, however, has seemed too much to many conservative politicians, and the current effort to eliminate or restrict the N.E.A. must be seen as one more protest by conservative forces against a relatively novel effort with which they have never been happy. . . .

The N.E.A. has indeed provided space at the margins which made life easier for many artists and provided an expansion of cultural production beyond that which would have been fostered by the market or private philanthropy alone. To take the case of theater, for example, while there were just fifty-six nonprofit theaters in the United States in 1965, there are more than 400 at present—and every Pulitzer Prize–winning play since 1976 has had its initial production at a nonprofit. Given the endowment's important role in direct arts financing and in stimulating private patronage (on average, N.E.A. funding brings with it three times as much in private and state moneys) in the mainstream as well as at the margins, the Helms amendment and its ilk have a chilling effect on artists and institutions. I am not qualified to judge whether restrictions such as those proposed by Helms are, as some lawyers claim, unconstitutional. But that is certainly political—it is the use of the state to foster some tastes at the expense of others—and it is certainly censorship. Lipman makes the issue clear: "In a free society, it is neither possible nor desirable to go very far [!] in prohibiting the private activities that inspire this outré art," he wrote apropos of Mapplethorpe. But, he continues, to believe that "because we are not compelled to witness what we as individuals find morally unacceptable, we cannot refuse to make it available for others" ignores the dreadful effects of "this decadence" on us and our children and "our responsibility for others." The president of the Massachusetts branch of Morality in Media put it more pithily: "People looking at these kind of pictures become addicts and spread AIDS."

This faith in the power of images for good or evil appears to involve a deep suspicion that seemingly decent Americans will be overwhelmed by dark forces within them that such images might unleash. It is no accident that the assault on the N.E.A. gathered steam during the regime that produced the Meese Report on obscenity. The current denunciations of "filth" continue key aspects of the traditional discourse on pornography: When Helms displayed the offending Mapplethorpes to his colleagues in the Senate, he first asked that the room be cleared of women and children. Sexual imagery, however distasteful, is permissible as the private possession of (exclusive groups of) males. What has made pictures like Mapplethorpe's an issue is, in Kramer's words, "the demand that is now being made to accord these hitherto forbidden images the status of perfectly respectable works of art," thus eligible for exhibition in public institutions. Kramer, like other antipornographers, is no doubt fighting a losing battle; the principle of the free-enterprise system so loved by all the advocates of decency—we may note here the double celebrity of Charles Keating, once chief enemy of sin in Cincinnati and now defending his haul from the Lincoln savings and loan—that the customer is always right, leads ineluctably to the free flow of all categories of images throughout society. And art, having for centuries been a home of the erotic and (especially since the invention of photography) the documentary, is hardly likely to cease supplying images of powerful and fascinating sorts to publics seeking titillation, exaltation or even the shock of the horrific.

The argument that the state ought not to fund work repugnant to "community standards" is not a good one, since it rests on the idea of a homogeneous community, with clearly demarcated standards, which does not in fact exist. (This is of course a basic problem with the going legal definition of obscenity, even apart from that definition's dependence on such undefined concepts as an appeal to "prurient interest" and lack of serious "artistic value.") On the other hand, the argument that art should be allowed to develop freely typically rests (as in Oldenburg's formulation quoted above) on the assumption that the development of the arts represents an interest of "society"—a unified interest that also does not exist. Present-day society is made up not only of classes with antagonistic interests but of a multitude of groups whose differences are expressed in aesthetic as well as other terms. For this reason, the idea that there exists an aesthetic sphere untouched by social and political meaning is an ideological fiction, one recognized even in the muddled thinking of a would-be censor like Kramer. The problem is not that art has been politicized; the existence of state funding shows that the generally hidden political side of the arts has existed all along. The struggle over the N.E.A. is a struggle for control of this political side.

Carole S. Vance

MISUNDERSTANDING OBSCENITY

Carole S. Vance is an anthropologist who teaches at Columbia University School of Public Health. She is editor of Pleasure and Danger: Exploring Female Sexuality. *In this reading Vance argues that the popular conception of obscenity is not the same as the legal definition, but that the popular conception is nonetheless harmful to art.*

When the House and the Senate voted to prohibit the use of NEA and NEH money to fund "obscene" art, the intent of Congress was to apply the current legal definition of obscenity, spelled out in Miller v. California, a 1973 Supreme Court case. The Miller ruling provided a narrow definition of obscenity and made clear that only a small portion of sexually explicit material would fall within its boundary. According to what has come to be known as the "three prongs" of the Miller standard, work can be found obscene only when it meets *all three* of the following criteria stated in the ruling:

1) the average person, applying contemporary community standards, would find that the work, taken as a whole, appeals to prurient interest [translation: "prurient interest" here means that the work leads to sexual arousal], and
2) the work depicts or describes, in a patently offensive way, sexual conduct specified by the statute, and

3) the work, taken as a whole, lacks serious literary, artistic, political, or scientific value.

The Miller ruling does not prohibit specific sexual subjects or depictions and takes into account intent and context. And although parts of the definition are problematic and far from crystal clear (what are "contemporary community standards," for example, and how do you assess them?), winning an obscenity conviction under Miller is difficult. The most explicit, prurient and offensive image, for example, cannot be found obscene if it can be shown to have serious value. As a result, obscenity prosecutions directed at literature and art have virtually disappeared. Even prosecutions against X-rated material found in adult sex shops have dwindled, conservatives and fundamentalists lament, because convictions are so expensive, time-consuming and difficult to obtain.

Carole S. Vance, "Misunderstanding Obscenity," *Art in America* 78.5 (1990): 49–55.

For all these reasons, the crafters of the compromise legislation believed that the obscenity regulation would have no impact on the NEA and NEH. In practice, nothing that either agency has ever funded, including the photographs of Robert Mapplethorpe, could ultimately be upheld as obscene by a higher court. Indeed, it can be argued that the very choice of an endowment panel to award funds in a competition based on artistic excellence or the decision of an arts institution to show a particular work indicates a priori that the work in question has serious artistic value and thus could not be found obscene.

Despite the protective stringency of the Miller definition, the actual effect of this new regulation has been alarming, chilling and far from meaningless, even in these few months since its passage. The regulation has lifted the discussion of obscenity out of the public scrutiny of the courts and landed it in private rooms, where anxious arts administrators, untrained in law, worry about what obscenity *might* mean and perhaps decide to play it safe and fund landscapes this year.

One evident problem with the new regulation is that the procedures used to implement it operate entirely outside the structure of the court system. The determination of obscenity is made by NEA panelists and administrators—not by judges or juries—in private, following procedures that are totally unspecified. Since few arts administrators are attorneys, the "three prongs" of the Miller standard are replaced by gut feelings and vague intuitions. The injunction to avoid funding art that "*may* be considered" obscene, for instance, can suggest that panelists should reject any work that *might* offend any group, no matter how small. The phrase "may be considered" also creates a linguistic elasticity that conservatives exploit, since they already call any act or image that exceeds their notions of propriety "obscene." Moreover, the "may be considered obscene" phrase implicitly acknowledges that definitions of obscenity

will not be legally tested. Ultimately, applicants whose work is deemed obscene have no right to defend their work before the persons judging them and no right of appeal. By contrast, in a legal obscenity trial, the prosecutor would have to prove beyond a reasonable doubt that a work or image was obscene; the defendant would be informed of all charges and be able to answer them in open court; expert witnesses could be called if necessary to challenge prosecutorial assertions that a specific work was obscene; and, even if convicted, producers of obscenity have full rights of appeal.

A second problem with the new regulation is the confusion that its language has sowed, even among those most friendly to the NEA. Serious misunderstandings exist about the precise legal definition of obscenity. Despite the rarity and difficulty of Miller-defined convictions, many well-meaning people now seem to believe that obscenity lurks everywhere. Consider two examples. An artist I know, who has already served on NEA panels, recently articulated to me her concern about whether or not she will be able to tell what is obscene when she serves on an upcoming panel, apparently anticipating difficult and wrenching deliberations over what is in fact a null set. (Question: Is there any reason for those who serve on an NEA panel to act any differently given the new obscenity regulation? Answer: A resounding "no," because serious art by definition cannot be obscene.) In another case, a sympathetic article in the liberal *Village Voice* nevertheless expresses some doubt about the legality of recently attacked art works, saying that "Robert Mapplethorpe's homoerotic photographs, and even Andres Serrano's *Piss Christ*, might well pass" the Supreme Court's Miller test. Of course they would pass. Both have serious artistic value, and *Piss Christ* is not even sexually explicit.

The various misreadings of "obscenity" can be traced to the peculiar wording of the compromise regulation, patched together in conference committee. The compromise bill states: the NEA is prohibited from funding "obscene materials *including but not limited to* depictions of sadomasochism, homoeroticism, the sexual exploitation of children, or individuals engaged in sex acts" (my emphasis). This phrasing derives almost word for word from the Helms amendment introduced by the senator at the height of the furor over the Mapplethorpe show. (Helms originally proposed to prohibit, among other things, the funding of "obscene or indecent material, including but not limited to depictions of sadomasochism, homoeroticism, the exploitation of children, or individuals engaged in sex acts.") The purpose of this sexual laundry list was to provide specific examples of what Sen. Helms and, more generally, conservatives and fundamentalists find indecent. Although in the course of negotiations arts advocates succeeded in removing the term "indecent," the laundry list remained. And many now take this list as an explanation of what obscenity means.

What does the wording of the current compromise legislation really mean? The trick here is to understand that the list of sexual acts simply gives examples of depictions that *might* fall under the legal definition of obscenity, *after* the three prongs of the Miller test are met. But these sexual depictions or acts are not by themselves obscene. (Or, to take another example, more easily understood because it is not about sex, consider the phrase "obscene material including but not limited to black-and-white photographs, color slides and Cibachromes." We grasp immediately that the terms here are not interchangeable: obscenity may include black-and-white photographs, but not all black-and-white photographs are obscene.) Yet when the sexual laundry list is attached to the word "obscenity," many carelessly read the phrase to mean that any depiction of sadomasochism or homoeroticism is in itself obscene. This is no accident, since the original Helms list

contains typical right-wing linguistic ploys that play on the readers' own sexual prejudices. It is a list that mixes up acts that are stigmatized (homoeroticism and sadomasochism), illegal (child pornography) and conventional (any individuals engaged in sex acts, the unspecified form of sex here being heterosexuality). Typically the stigmatized acts appear first and are intended to set off the readers' anxiety, their negativity about sex and homophobia. Critical thinking stops, and the sexual red alert flashes. Although many readers would realize that the mere depiction of (hetero)sexual acts is not necessarily obscene, the placement of the topic so late in the list makes this realization less likely.

The NEA regulation, then, contains a prejudicial sleight of hand, and it comes as no surprise that this language promotes conservative goals. The wide-ranging use of the term obscene has been an important and consistent ploy of conservative and fundamentalist sexual politics, familiar from recent debates over pornography and abortion. Frustrated by their limited ability to attack sexually explicit material through existing obscenity law, conservatives have pioneered new ways of expanding the rhetorical meaning of obscenity. In their own rhetoric, conservatives now routinely equate premarital sex and homosexuality with obscenity. Indeed, the list targets not just homosexual sex but the even broader category of homoeroticism, thus constituting an attack on all gay and lesbian images. If it were stated explicitly, this viewpoint would not be very convincing to the mainstream public. It is not difficult to imagine the fate of conservative legislation which attempted to define representations of premarital relations or homosexuality as obscene. Yet the almost unnoticed migration of conservative language into the widely circulated compromise legislation plays havoc with people's ability to think critically about obscenity.

How else do we understand the actions of *both* John Frohnmayer, head of the NEA, and Susan Wyatt, executive director of Artists Space, who each believed that the ban on funding obscene art somehow applied to "Against Our Vanishing," a 23-artist exhibition about AIDS that contained images of homosexuality? Or, how do we explain a recent feature in *Art News*, "What is Pornography?" which responded to the NEA crisis by providing ample evidence of widely differing subjective definitions of pornography, art and obscenity without ever informing readers that obscenity has a specific legal meaning? Or a recent *New York Times* article about the "loyalty oaths" that NEH grantees are now required to sign? Writers must swear that they will not produce obscene works with endowment funds, but many erroneously believe that the oath prohibits them from *writing* on specific sexual or erotic topics. The *Times* never corrects the error, but compounds it by stating: "grant recipients are now being asked to refrain from producing artworks that include, but are not limited to, 'depictions of sadomasochism, homoeroticism, the sexual exploitation of children, or individuals engaged in sex acts. . . .'" In this morass of confusion, the folk definitions of obscenity—though legally mistaken—are dismayingly compatible with the views and political goals of the right wing, though the vehicle which now endlessly circulates them—the NEA regulation—is no longer identifiably right wing.

The equation between obscenity and sexuality has already achieved wide currency. Consider the distribution of the NEA regulation with no effort to provide guidance about the legal meaning of obscenity or to clarify the relationship between the sex laundry list and that legal definition of obscenity. The unvarnished regulation is now routinely included in all NEA and NEH application packets. Each grant recipient must sign a form agreeing to the terms of the new law, under the threat of not receiving funds. Members of peer-review panels are also instructed to consider in the course of their evaluations whether the art works are obscene. For all concerned, the terms of this regulation are sobering, freighted with a foreboding sense of responsibility and imagined legal penalties for mistaken judgment. What is most fantastic about this regulation, however, is that it covertly circulates and legitimizes conservative definitions of obscenity among liberal, educated people who would, in other circumstances, indignantly reject them.

Tom Wolfe

THE WORSHIP
OF ART:
NOTES ON
THE NEW GOD

Tom Wolfe helped to found the "new journalism" with such works as The Electric Kool-Aid Acid Test *and* The Right Stuff. *He has more recently written the best-selling novel* Bonfire of the Vanities. *As an art critic, Wolfe is given to debunking, as he demonstrates in his books* The Painted Word *and* From Bauhaus to Our House. *In the reading below, Wolfe suggests that contemporary art is designed to confuse most of the public, since this aim is consistent with its real functions in our society.*

Let me tell you about the night the Vatican art show opened at the Metropolitan Museum of Art in New York. The scene was the Temple of Dendur, an enormous architectural mummy, complete with a Lake of the Dead, underneath a glass bell at the rear of the museum. On the stone apron in front of the temple, by the lake, the museum put on a formal dinner for 360 souls, including the wife of the President of the United States, the usual philanthropic dowagers and corporate art patrons, a few catered names, such as Prince Albert of Monaco and Henry Kissinger, and many well-known members of the New York art world. But since this was, after all, an exhibition of the Vatican art collection, it was necessary to include some Roman Catholics. Cardinal Cooke, Vatican emissaries, prominent New York Catholic laymen, Knights of Malta—there they were, devout Christians at a New York art world event. The culturati and the Christians were arranged at the tables like Arapaho beads: one culturatus, one Christian, one culturatus, one Christian, one culturatus, one Christian, one culturatus, one Christian.

Gamely, the guests tried all the conventional New York conversation openers—real estate prices, friends who have been mugged recently, well-known people whose children have been arrested on drug charges, Brits, live-in help, the dishonesty of helipad contractors, everything short of the desperately trite subjects used in the rest of the country, namely the weather and

Tom Wolfe, "The Worship of Art," *Harper's Magazine* 269.1613 (1984): 61–68.

front-wheel drive. Nothing worked. There were dreadful lulls during which there was no sound at all in that antique churchyard except for the pings of hotel silver on earthenware plates echoing off the tombstone facade of the temple.

Shortly before dessert, I happened to be out in the museum's main lobby when two Manhattan art dealers appeared in their tuxedos, shaking their heads.

One said to the other: "Who *are* these *unbelievable people?*"

But of course! It seemed not only *outré* to have these . . . these . . . these . . . these *religious types* at an art event, it seemed sacrilegious. The culturati were being forced to rub shoulders with heathens. That was the way it hit them. For today art—not religion—is the religion of the educated classes. Today educated people look upon traditional religious ties—Catholic, Episcopal, Presbyterian, Methodist, Baptist, Jewish—as matters of social pedigree. It is only art that they look upon religiously.

When I say that art is the religion of the educated classes, I am careful not to use the word in the merely metaphorical way people do when they say someone is religious about sticking to a diet or training for a sport. I am not using "religion" as a synonym for "enthusiasm." I am referring specifically to what Max Weber identified as the objective functions of a religion: the abnegation or rejection of the world and the legitimation of wealth. . . .

Today there are a few new religions that appeal to educated people—Scientology, Arica, Synanon, and some neo-Hindu, neo-Buddhist, and neo-Christian groups—but their success has been limited. The far more common way to reject the world, in our time, is through art. I'm sure you're familiar with it. You're on the subway during the morning rush hour, in one of those cars that is nothing but a can of meat on wheels, jammed in shank to flank and haunch to paunch and elbow to rib with people who talk to themselves and shout obscenities into the void and click their teeth and roll back their upper lips to reveal their purple gums, and there is nothing you can do about it. You can't budge. Coffee, adrenaline, and rogue hate are squirting through every duct and every vein, and just when you're beginning to wonder how any mortal can possibly stand it, you look around and you see a young woman seated serenely in what seems to be a perfect pink cocoon of peace, untouched, unthreatened, by the growling mob around her. Her eyes are lowered. In her lap, invariably, is a book. If you look closely, you will see that this book is by Rimbaud, or Rilke, or Baudelaire, or Kafka, or Gabriel García Márquez, author of *One Hundred Years of Solitude.* And as soon as you see this vision, you understand the conviction that creates the inviolable aura around her: "I may be forced into this rat race, this squalid human stew, but I do not have to be *of* it. I inhabit a universe that is finer. I can reject all this." You can envision her apartment immediately. There is a mattress on top of a flush door supported by bricks. There's a window curtained in monk's cloth. There's a hand-thrown pot with a few blue cornflowers in it. There are some Paul Klee and Modigliani prints on the wall and a poster from the Acquavella Galleries' Matisse show. "I don't need your Louis Bourbon bergères and your fabric-covered walls. I reject your whole Parish-Hadley world—through art."

And what about the legitimation of wealth? It wasn't so long ago that Americans of great wealth routinely gave 10 percent of their income to the church. The practice of tithing was a certification of worthiness on earth and an option on heaven. Today the custom is to give the money to the arts. When Mrs. E. Parmalee Prentice, daughter of John D. Rockefeller Sr. and owner of two adjoining mansions on East Fifty-third Street, just off Fifth Avenue, died in 1962, she did not leave these holdings, worth about $5 million, to her church. She left them to the Museum of Modern Art for the building of a new wing. Nobody's eyebrows arched. By 1962, it would have been more remarkable if a bequest of that size had gone to a religion of the old-fashioned sort. . . .

Today, what American corporation would support a religion? Most would look upon any such thing as sheer madness. So what does a corporation do when the time comes to pray in public? It supports the arts. I don't need to recite figures. Just think of the money raised since the 1950s for the gigantic cultural complexes—Lincoln Center, Kennedy Center, the Chandler Pavillion, the Woodruff Arts Center—that have become *de rigueur* for the modern American metropolis. What are they? Why, they are St. Patrick's, St. Mary's, Washington National, Holy Cross: the American cathedrals of the late twentieth century.

We are talking here about the legitimation of wealth. The worse odor a corporation is in, the more likely it is to support the arts, and the more likely it is to make sure everybody knows it. The energy crisis, to use an antique term from the 1970s, was the greatest bonanza in the Public Broadcasting Service's history. The more loudly they were assailed as exploiters and profiteers, the more earnestly the oil companies poured money into PBS's cultural programming. Every broadcast seemed to end with a discreet notice on the screen saying: "This program was made possible by a grant from Exxon," or perhaps Mobil, or ARCO. . . .

In this age of the art clerisy, the client is in no position to say what will save him. He is in no position to do anything at all except come forward with the money if he wants salvation and legitimation.

Today large corporations routinely hire curators from the art village to buy art in their behalf. It is not a mere play on words to call these people curates, comparable to the Catholic priests who at one time were attached to wealthy European families to conduct daily masses on their estates. The corporations set limits on the curators' budgets and reserve the right to veto their choices. But they seldom do, since the entire purpose of a corporate art program is legitimation of wealth through a spiritually correct investment in art. The personal tastes of the executives, employees, clients, or customers could scarcely matter less. The corporate curators are chiefly museum functionaries, professors of art, art critics, and dealers, people who have devoted themselves not so much to the history of art as to the theories and fashions that determine prestige within the art world—that village of 3,000 souls—today, in the here and now.

Thus Chase Manhattan Bank hired a curator who was a founding trustee of the scrupulously devout and correct New Museum in New York. IBM hired a curator from the Whitney Museum to direct the art program at its new headquarters in New York. Philip Morris, perhaps the nation's leading corporate patron of the arts, did IBM one better. In its new headquarters in New York, Philip Morris has built a four-story art gallery and turned it over directly to the Whitney. Whatever the Whitney says goes.

For a company to buy works of art simply because they appeal to its executives and its employees is an absolute waste of money, so far as legitimation is concerned. The Ciba-Geigy agricultural chemical company started out collecting works of many styles and artists, then apparently realized the firm was getting no benefit from the collection whatsoever, other than aesthetic pleasure. At this point Ciba-Geigy hired an artist and a Swiss art historian, who began buying only Abstract Expressionist works by artists such as Philip Guston and Adolph Gottlieb. These works were no doubt totally meaningless to the executives, the employees, and the farmers of the world who use agricultural chemicals, and were, therefore, a striking improvement.

If employees go so far as to protest a particular fashionable style, a corporation will usually switch to another one. Corporations are not eager to annoy their workers. But at the same time, to spend money on the sort of realistic or symbolic work employees might actually enjoy would be pointless. The point is to be acclaimed for "support of the arts," a phrase which applies only to the purchase of works certified by the curates of the art village. This was quite openly the aim of the Bank of America when it hired a curator in 1979 and began buying works of art at the rate of 1,000 a year. The bank felt that its corporate image was suffering because it was not among those firms receiving "credit for art support."

The credit must come from the art clerisy. It is for this reason that IBM, for example, has displayed Michael Heizer's *Levitated Mass* at its outdoor plaza at Madison Avenue and Fifty-sixth Street. The piece is a 25-foot-by-16-foot metal tank containing water and a slab of granite. It is meaningless in terms of IBM, its executives, its employees, its customers, and the thousands of people who walk past the plaza every day. Far from being a shortcoming, that is part of *Levitated Mass*'s exemplary success as a spiritual object.

It is precisely in this area—public sculpture—that the religion of art currently makes its richest contribution to the human comedy. . . .

. . . The Rockefellers' Number One Chase Manhattan Plaza was the first glass skyscraper on Wall Street. Out front, on a bare Bauhaus-style apron, the so-called plaza, was installed a sculpture by Jean Dubuffet. It is made of concrete and appears to be four toadstools fused into a gelatinous mass with black lines running up the sides. The title is *Group of Four Trees*. Not even *Group of Four Rockefellers*. After all, there *were* four at the time: David, John D. III, Nelson, and Laurance. But the piece has absolutely nothing to say about the glory or even the existence of the Rockefellers, Wall Street, Chase Manhattan Bank, American business, or the building it stands in front of. Instead, it proclaims the glory of contemporary art. It fulfills the new purpose of public sculpture, which is the legitimation of wealth through the new religion of the educated classes.

Six years after Number One Chase Manhattan Plaza was built, the Marine Midland Bank building went up a block away. It is another glass skyscraper with a mean little Bauhaus-style apron out front, and on this apron was placed a red cube resting on one point by Isamu Noguchi. Through the cube (a rhombohedron, strictly speaking) runs a cylindrical hole. One day I looked through that hole, expecting at the very least that my vision would be led toward the board room, where a man wearing a hard-worsted suit, and with thinning, combed-back hair, would be standing, his forefinger raised, thundering about broker loan rates. Instead what I saw was a woman who appeared to be part of the stenographic pool probing the auditory meatus of her left ear with a Q-Tip. So what is it, this red cube by Noguchi? Why, nothing more than homage to contemporary art, the new form of praying in public. . . .

If people want to place Turds in the Plazas as a form of religious offer or prayer, and they own the plazas, there isn't much anybody else can do about it. But what happens when they use public money, tax money, to do the same thing on plazas owned by the public? At that point you're in for a glorious farce. . . .

In 1976, the city of Hartford decided to reinforce its reputation as the Athens of lower central midwestern New England by having an important piece of sculpture installed downtown. It followed what is by now the usual procedure, which is to turn the choice over to a panel of "experts" in the field—i.e., the clerisy, in this case, six curators, critics, and academicians, three of them chosen by the National Endowment for the Arts, which put up half the money. So one day in 1978 a man named Carl Andre arrived in Hartford with thirty-six rocks. Not carved stones, not even polished boluses of the Henry Moore sort—rocks. He put them on the ground in a triangle, like bowling pins. Then he presented the city council with a bill for $87,000. Nonplussed and, soon enough, furious, the citizenry hooted and jeered and called the city council members imbeciles while the council members alternately hit the sides of their heads with their hands and made imaginary snowballs. Nevertheless, they approved payment, and the rocks—entitled *Stone Field*—are still there.

One day in 1981, the Civil Service workers in the new Javits Federal Building in Manhattan went outside to the little plaza in front of the building at lunchtime to do the usual, which was to have their tuna puffs and diet Shastas, and there, running through the middle of it, was a wall of black steel twelve feet high and half a city block long. Nonplussed and, soon enough, furious, 1,300 of them drew up a petition asking the GSA to remove it, only to be informed that this was, in fact, a major work of art, entitled *Tilted Arc*, by a famous American sculptor named Richard Serra. Serra did not help things measurably by explaining that he was "redefining the space" for the poor Civil Service lifers and helping to wean them away from the false values "created by advertising and corporations." Was it his fault if "it offends people to have their preconceptions of reality changed"? This seventy-three-ton gesture of homage to contemporary art remains in place.

The public sees nothing, absolutely nothing, in these stone fields, tilted arcs, and Instant Stonehenges, because it was never meant to. The public is looking at the arcana of the new religion of the educated classes. At this point one might well ask what the clerisy itself see in them, a question that would plunge us into doctrines as abstruse as any that engaged the medieval Scholastics. Andre's *Stone Field*, for example, was

created to illustrate three devout theories concerning the nature of sculpture. One, a sculpture should not be placed upon that bourgeois device, the pedestal, which seeks to elevate it above the people. (Therefore, the rocks are on the ground.) Two, a sculpture should "express its gravity." (And what expresses gravity better than rocks lying on the ground?) Three, a sculpture should not be that piece of bourgeois pretentiousness, the "picture in the air" (such as the statues of Lee and Duke); it should force the viewer to confront its "object-ness." (You want object-ness? Take a look at a plain rock! Take a look at thirty-six rocks!) . . .

The public is nonplussed and, soon enough, becomes furious—and also uneasy. After all, if understanding such arcana is the hallmark of the educated classes today, and you find yourself absolutely baffled, what does that say about your level of cultivation? Since 1975, attendance at museums of art in the United States has risen from 42 million to 60 million people per year. Why? In 1980 the Hirshhorn Museum did a survey of people who came to the museum over a seven-month period. I find the results fascinating. Thirty-six percent said they had come to the museum to learn about contemporary art. Thirty-two percent said they had come to learn about a particular contemporary artist. Thirteen percent came on tours. Only 15 percent said they were there for what was once the conventional goal of museumgoers: to enjoy the pictures and sculptures. The conventional goal of museumgoers today is something quite different. Today they are there to learn—and to see the light. At the Hirshhorn, the people who were interviewed in the survey said such things as: "I know this is great art, and now I feel so unintelligent." And: "After coming to this museum, I now feel so much better about art and so much worse about me."

In other words: "I believe, O Lord, but I am unworthy! Reveal to me Thy mysteries!"

James O. Young

DESTROYING
WORKS
OF ART

James O. Young teaches philosophy at the University of Victoria in Victoria, British Columbia. He is author of articles on metaphysics and philosophy of language. In this reading Young argues that one should never take the destruction of artworks lightly, even though it may sometimes be warranted.

A visit to any collection of modern art prompts questions about whether the destruction of artworks is ever permissible. Museums are increasingly saddled with very bad art: bedabbled canvasses, scraps of twisted and rusted metal and plastic bottles hanging on fluorescent tubes. The acquisition of almost worthless art is not new; the cellars of many institutions are crammed with poor nineteenth century paintings. However, with the proliferation of bad art, questions about whether art may be destroyed have become more pressing. Many examples of public art have also brought these questions to the fore. Since 1977, when Carl Andre's *Stone Field* (a collection of thirty-six glacial boulders arranged in a triangle) appeared in a Hartford, Connecticut, churchyard, there have been calls for its removal. A thirty-five meter long sheet of metal, Richard Serra's *Tilted Arc*, located in Manhattan's Federal Plaza,

has proved even more controversial. Any suggestion that artworks may be destroyed is usually condemned and dismissed as philistinism or vandalism or both. Any destruction of works of art is often regarded as unjustifiable interference with artists' rights. There are, however, conditions under which the intentional destruction of some artworks is unobjectionable.

A couple of methodological points are necessary before the argument begins. The first point is that works whose destruction is mooted are works of art. This is important because there is room to doubt whether some putative artworks are art. Someone may intend to engage in scientific inquiry but only succeed in producing pseudo-science. The scientific failure and others may, mistakenly, believe that he has produced a scientific theory. Similarly, a failed artist may create, not bad art but, rather, something not art at all. If some work were not art, the present philosophical problem would not arise. If there were no suspicion that some pile of scrap metal is art, no one would cavil at putting it out with the rubbish. It is important to allow that the works in question are still art.

A second methodological point concerns the sorts of artworks at issue. This essay will focus on the destruction of works, such as paintings and sculptures, which depend for their continued existence on the integrity of some particular object or objects. There is, of course, nothing objectionable about the destruction of old musical scores or tattered novels so long as other copies survive. If there is only one copy of a score, the same considerations will apply as in the cases of painting and sculpture. Works such as engravings and statues cast from a single mould form a problematic class of works. The destruction of one engraving leaves others in existence. Moreover, if the plate remains intact, more can be printed. However, plates and moulds wear out with time and use. Unlike, say, novels they cannot be reproduced at will forever. So engravings and the like should probably be regarded as items whose destruction is potentially objectionable.

Questions about whether artworks may be destroyed cannot be answered simply by reflection on matters of ownership and property. While it may be wrong to destroy a work that belongs to someone else, the ownership of a work of art plainly does not convey what might be called the aesthetic prerogative to dispose of the work. Suppose that the privatization of public resources continues and I am able to purchase da Vinci's *Portrait of Genevra de' Benci*. Suppose, moreover, that according to the laws of the land there is no doubt that I possess legal title to the portrait. I would still act wrongly if, for whatever reason, I decided to destroy the painting. The law in many jurisdictions recognizes that the destruction of artworks, at least architectural works, in private hands is wrong. Underlying these laws and the wrongness of destroying the da Vinci is a loosely consequentialist principle: some works are of such great aesthetic value that there must be restrictions on what anyone may do to them. Restrictions on what individuals may do with artworks they possess are similar to restrictions on other sorts of property. Real estate is, for example, subject to laws governing eminent domain, zoning, mineral rights and the like. This point raises, of course, the deeper question of whether anyone can ever be said to own a work of art. If ownership is the right to freely dispose of property, there is reason to doubt that anyone ever owns art except in a purely legalistic sense of "own." This question need not be decided here. Suffice it to say that legal title to some artwork does not, by itself, convey the right to destroy that work.

The destruction of many artworks is certainly wrong under most circumstances. Artworks are things of value. Regardless of whether works of art exist to make aesthetic experiences possible, to display emotion or to convey truth and meaning, they contribute to human well-being and, therefore, have value. The imperative not to destroy artworks is simply a special case of more general imperative not . . . to destroy things of value. When it is wrong to destroy some artwork, it is wrong for the same sort of reason it is wrong to vandalize public buildings, kill whales or deface scenes of natural beauty: all of these things are valuable. When something is valuable there is always a prima facie case against destroying it. But sometimes this case can be overcome. Sometimes preserving something of value requires that something else of value be sacrificed. In cases of such conflict, difficult calculations of value must be made. Such calculations are difficult because things are valuable for different reasons and in varying degrees. There are some calculations of value which justify the destruction of artworks.

A few examples will illustrate the general point that the destruction of valuable things is sometimes unobjectionable. Freedom of expression is certainly valuable but there are conditions when it may be limited or even temporarily abolished. Freedom of expression is limited by laws against slander and (in Canada, for example) incitement to hatred. In times of war or other national emergencies civil liberties may be suspended altogether. In both cases, freedom of expression is sacrificed to some other public good. Consider another example. A forest may have great scenic value. There are, however, some circumstances where the logging of the forest could be justified by an appeal to considerations of economic value. In general, things of value may sometimes be destroyed.

Consider now the question of whether works of art may be destroyed. It is not difficult to imagine uncontroversial circumstances under which even good artworks could unobjectionably be destroyed. Consider the following variation on the classic lifeboat problem. Someone might be adrift in a lifeboat full of Rembrandts. The only way to prevent the lifeboat from sinking and ruining all of the paintings is to throw some of the pictures overboard. The occupant of the boat, an authority on seventeenth century Dutch painting, makes a quick calculation of the relative aesthetic values of the paintings. The best available evidence suggests that a couple of portraits, fortunately rather heavy, are relatively mediocre. The art historian tosses them over the gunwale. Plainly, anyone who consigned paintings to the deep under such circumstances would not act wrongly. Or suppose that a group of terrorists is barricaded in a lovely Norman church and that only by destroying the church can the terrorists be prevented from killing thirty children. Surely, one would not act wrongly in destroying the church— indeed, one would act wrongly in not destroying it. (If thirty children seems like too small a number, choose whatever number seems sufficient.)

Two conclusions can be drawn from these examples. In both of these examples, artworks may be destroyed because, although works of value are lost, more is to be gained by destroying them. Secondly, the second example illustrates that non-aesthetic considerations can be brought to bear on the question of whether or not some artwork may be destroyed. In neither of these cases, however, are artworks being destroyed qua artworks. In the first case paintings are being destroyed qua ballast and in the second case the church is being destroyed qua redoubt. The interesting question is whether a work of art may be destroyed just qua work of low aesthetic value.

This question should be answered in the affirmative. Suppose that every year for a century the curators of a gallery have brought some painting up from the vaults and displayed it for a panel of artists, critics and philosophers. Suppose, moreover, that every year for centuries the panelists have decided that the work has a vanishingly small amount of aesthetic value. Finally, after hundreds of years, a curator tries to sell the despised painting but finds no bidders. (This recently happened at the Art Gallery of New South Wales.) The curator then hangs the offending painting in the cafeteria but diners complain that they are being put off their food. (This happened at the Sydney museum.) Finally, in despair, the museum attempts to give away the painting but no one is willing to take it away. If the painting is returned to the vault, it will occupy much-needed storage space. (The museum has made other unwise investments.) Effort must be expended to keep the painting warm and dry. The curator decides that, on balance, the painting is of such little value that it is not worth preserving. He leaves it in the dumpster in the lane behind the gallery. In doing so, I submit, he does not act wrongly. Nor does anyone act wrongly who destroys bad art under similar circumstances: when the aesthetic value of a work of art is so small that it cannot outweigh the disadvantages of preserving it.

The conclusion that it is not wrong to destroy bad artworks faces a number of possible objections. Someone might object that no matter how bad some work is, it possesses historical interest. No one will ever confuse rudely-decorated pre-Columbian peasant pottery with good art, someone might reason, but it would be wrong to destroy such works. It is interesting to know how past cultures lived and, in particular, how they adorned various items. Similarly, it might be argued, no matter how bad some contemporary artwork might be, future generations may be curious about what has passed for art in this century. Perhaps, the worse the art the better: some future generation might be fascinated by the odd things we generate. So, it might be concluded, considerations of aesthetic quality can never, by themselves, justify the destruction of an artwork.

There is a good deal to be said for the argument from historical interest. Questions about whether or not to destroy a work of art are questions about the value—and not just the aesthetic value—of the work. While something may possess little value qua artwork it may be valuable for some other reason, perhaps for its historical interest. Other works may possess value as, say, a windbreak. These other reasons should be taken into account when contemplating the destruction of an artwork. Even if this is true, however, it does not follow that works of art ought never to be destroyed. A community may have reason to believe that the mild curiosity some future generation may feel does not outweigh the ennui they daily suffer because of some banal piece of public sculpture. Moreover, the argument from historical interest shows, at most, that it is wrong to destroy all of some sort of bad artwork. So long as a representative sample of some sort of artwork is preserved together, perhaps, with photographs of others, there would be no objection to disposing of some. In any case, it is plain that we should not take the argument from historical interest too seriously, for if we did, we could throw nothing away. Ten thousand years from now, a glass that is given away (with a minimum purchase) at a service station may be of enormous historical interest. Surely, however, we are under no obligation to preserve all such glasses.

Another objection may be called the argument from contrast. According to this argument, we are only able to apprehend the virtues of the best art because we can contrast it with poor art. Perhaps if the only artworks were great masterpieces, we would grow insensitive to the greatness of these works. Since it is obviously undesirable that we lose the capacity to appreciate great art, the argument concludes, it is wrong to destroy bad art.

There is some reason to doubt that we can apprehend the virtues of good art only if we are familiar with the vices of bad art. In general, it is not obvious that the apprehension of one property depends on the prior experience of an opposite property. The awareness of pleasure arguably does not require an earlier experience of pain. An experience of some neutral state would suffice. Similarly, experience of the worst art may not be necessary if the best is to be appreciated. Experience of mediocre art may suffice. But even if we grant the initial premise of the argument from contrast, its conclusion still does not follow. A weaker conclusion may follow: that it would be wrong to destroy *all* bad art. But since there is little doubt that new bad art will always be created, perhaps not even this weaker conclusion follows. In any case, the argument from contrast does not establish that bad art may never be destroyed.

A further objection starts from the premise that any destruction violates the rights of artists. Serra has claimed that those who would dismantle *Tilted Arc* would violate his rights. It is unclear precisely which rights are violated by the destruction of artworks when the artist has no legal title to a work. It is rather ad hoc to posit the right of artists not to have their work destroyed. It is much more likely that there is some general right which is violated by the act of destroying an artwork, such as the right to freedom of expression. Someone might argue that destroying an artwork is tantamount to interfering with freedom of the press or like stopping someone from speaking in public. Perhaps there are conditions which must be met before freedom of expression is permitted: permission to hold a rally or erect a sculpture in a public place may be required. But, someone might argue, once these conditions are met, a rally cannot be stopped or an artwork destroyed simply because we do not approve of what is being expressed. Since it is wrong to limit freedom of expression, someone might conclude, it is wrong to destroy works of art.

The argument from artists' right is not without force. There can be no doubt that everyone ought to be allowed to create art, even free to create bad art. However, it does not follow from this that artists have the right to have their art preserved for them. No one should deny that any political party has the right to print its views. But, equally, if a pamphlet is placed in my mailbox, I am under no obligation to preserve it. Even if all copies of a pamphlet are thrown away, no wrong has been done. This example illustrates that it is acts of expression which are protected by freedom of expression, not the results of the acts. So while artists may freely express themselves in their art, no one is under an obligation to preserve the results of their artistic activity. There may be other reasons why the results of artistic activity are protected. For example, someone has legal title to it and does not want it destroyed. But the mere fact that the expression of artists should be unconstrained is not sufficient reason to preserve art.

There is, moreover, another reason why freedom of expression does not protect all artworks from destruction. In many cases poor artworks fail to express anything. Artworks can be used by artists to make a statement about how things are, seem or ought to be. Alternatively, a work can be indirectly expressive. It may, for example, be intended to shock its audience so that they see other things differently. When presented to an audience a work of art may fail to convey anything. If it conveys nothing to anyone, it expresses nothing. If it expresses nothing, no freedom of expression is violated if it is destroyed.

Even if works of art are not protected from destruction by the rights of artists, perhaps they are protected by their own rights. In recent years a number of writers have proposed that many things besides persons are bearers of rights. Even the enfranchisement of artworks has been proposed. Alan Tormey has argued that artworks have rights. He argues that anything that imposes obligations has rights. Now, the abuse, including destruction, of works of art pains those who value the abused works. (Call this pain "aesthetic pain.") Since one ought to avoid causing pain, artworks impose (on all rational creatures) the obligation not to abuse them. Tormey concludes that artworks have rights. Just as the right to life is the most basic right a person may have, the right on which all others depend, presumably the most basic right of artworks is the right not to be destroyed. Since works of art possess such a right, it might be argued, it is wrong to destroy them.

The claim that artworks have rights has been subjected to telling criticisms. The most serious problem is that, even if the abuse of artworks involves the violation of rights, the rights do not seem to belong to the artworks in question. It seems more likely that rational persons have an obligation not to cause aesthetic pain to those who value the arts. Only because people can be pained by the abuse of art (the artworks themselves do not suffer) is there reason to protect works of art. (If there were no appreciators of art, it is hard to see what would make the destruction of art objectionable.) If there is an obligation to appreciators of the arts, then it is they, not artworks who have rights. We often do speak of abusing works of art. But this does not entail that artworks have rights any more than talk of the sun rising entails that it moves. If works of art have no rights, destroying them is not a violation of their rights.

Suppose, however, that artworks can have rights. The destruction of some bad works would still be unobjectionable. At most the argument shows that valued works, works whose abuse causes aesthetic pain, have rights. Suppose that there are works so bad that no one values them. The abuse of such works pains no one and, hence, these works have no rights to violate. So unvalued works may be destroyed without violating any rights.

Even works of art with rights could be destroyed under some conditions. Any right can be overridden in some circumstances. The just war theorist says that even the right to life may be overridden. It would not take a great deal to override the rights of works of art valued less than the time and effort required to maintain them. The consequentialist will have no difficulty demonstrating that the rights of artworks would be forfeit under such circumstances. Even those who think that only another right can override a right would not object to the destruction of bad art. Surely the rights of curators and the viewing public could, in some cases, override the rights of bad artworks. Such individuals plausibly have the right to be free of the aesthetic pain caused by bad art. And it seems a violation of rights to require individuals to preserve what no one values.

A fifth argument against destroying artworks may be called the slippery slope argument. Someone might argue that it is always wrong to destroy works of art because it may lead to the destruction of other artworks. Perhaps if museum curators were to get into the habit of destroying bad art, they might find the habit difficult to break. The result of such destruction may be the devaluing, at a social level, of art in general, which may lead to the destruction of more artworks. The advocates of such a line of reasoning may admit that it is not certain that destroying some artworks will have this result. They will still maintain, however, that it is not unreasonable to suppose that it might and that the risk, even if small, is not worth running.

It is difficult to assess the slippery slope argument without a better idea about the probability that the destruction of some artworks will lead to the devaluation of art and so, perhaps, to the destruction of valuable items. On the face of the matter, however, it is much more likely that the preservation of bad artworks leads to the devaluation of art. There is little doubt that the proliferation of bad art in this century has led to a fall in public esteem for the arts. If the low standing of the arts has not led to increased vandalism and other instances of art being destroyed, this has only been good fortune. The proposed destruction of Serra's *Twain* by the St. Louis City Council can probably be attributed to the low standing of the arts. Few of the objections to *Tilted Arc* apply to *Twain*: it does not, for example, render a large public space unusable. It seems likely that its destruction is proposed because there is a public backlash against what the public and its elected representatives perceive as charlatanism on the part of artists. (There remarks are not intended as a comment on the quality of *Twain*. It may be an innocent victim of this backlash.) If poor art contributes to a low public opinion of the arts, there is all the more reason to destroy at least some of it.

Perhaps the most trenchant argument against the destruction of bad artworks is an epistemological argument. The view that bad works of art may be destroyed implicitly presupposes that bad works are distinguishable from good ones. Now, someone might argue, there is no completely reliable way to decide which works of art are good and which are bad. Since there is no reliable test of the quality of an artwork, the argument might continue, we ought not to destroy any works lest we destroy good ones by mistake. This argument becomes even more worrisome when we consider that, in some cases, estimates of the aesthetic merit of works have changed. In some cases the value of a work is not recognized for some time. There is a danger that such works will be destroyed before their aesthetic worth is realized.

This epistemological argument is worrisome. Certainly the possibility of error is, at very least, reason to employ utmost caution. I do not, however, take the epistemological argument to provide decisive grounds for not destroying bad art. I believe that there is a distinction between good art and bad and that we can reliably tell the difference. In the context of this essay I cannot argue for this view. I can, however, show that even if this view is mistaken, the epistemological argument does not succeed. There are two grounds on which to object to the claim that there is good and bad art and a way to tell the difference between them. One could object that there is no difference. Or one could object that there is a difference but no reliable way to discern it. On either ground, the epistemological argument cannot give us reason to refrain from destroying artworks.

Consider the first objection. The view that the destruction of some art is unobjectionable is controversial, according to the epistemological argument, because there is a fear that good art will be lost. But if there is no distinction between good and bad art, this cannot be a worry. Moreover, if the categories of bad and good do not apply to art, concerns about the destruction of art become much less pressing. If there are no qualitative distinctions among works of art, it does not matter so much what we keep

and what we destroy. Quantitative considerations are all that remain and there will always be plenty of art. The second objection collapses into the first. Suppose that there is no reliable way to tell the difference between good and bad art. A verificationist argument, unobjectionable in this context, can then be made: if we cannot tell the difference, there is no distinction. And, again, if there is no distinction between good and bad art, the epistemological objection fails.

The destruction of art by the artists who created them raises some important issues. In November, 1948, Georges Rouault burned 315 of his own paintings. The paintings were not, perhaps, among his very best and they were not completely finished. Nevertheless, there is good reason to suppose that the works were of considerable aesthetic value. According to the view adopted in this essay artworks may be destroyed if and only if their aesthetic (and other) value is insufficient to outweigh the disadvantages of preserving the work. On the present view, therefore, Rouault acted wrongly in burning his paintings. Someone might claim, however, that artists may unobjectionably destroy their own works without reference to the aesthetic value of the works. Someone might argue for this claim by holding that, unless artists sell or otherwise grant their works to others, the works belong to them. Since people may do what they like with what belongs to them, the argument might run, artists may do what they like with their works. Certainly, it would have been a great tragedy if Jane Austen had decided to burn the manuscript of *Persuasion* or if da Vinci had decided to destroy the *Portrait of Genevra de' Benci*. But they would, on this view, not have acted wrongly.

The question of whether artists may destroy their own works raises again the thorny issue of the ownership of artworks. It does not seem unreasonable, on the surface, to suppose that if anyone can own some artwork, it is the artist who creates it. If an artist owns an artwork, he may dispose of it as he pleases, even destroy it. While this may seem a plausible line of argument it is, in fact, seriously misguided. The cause of some artwork is that without which the work would not have existed. This being the case, it is plain that a single individual is never the sole cause, or creator, of an artwork. It is much more accurate to say that artworks, especially the best artworks, are the product of an artistic tradition. The individual artist is simply the last stage in a causal chain which has included many other artists. To suggest otherwise is to adopt an implausible Romantic conception of the artist as lonely hero.

The classic illustration of this point is the music of Johann Sebastian Bach. No doubt, much of the magnificence of Bach's work is due to his own genius. But, equally, the works are the culmination of a tradition of North German music and much is due, as well, to the contribution of an Italian musical tradition. More, of course, is owed to a Bach family tradition which ran from Johann Bach (?–1626) through to Johann Michael Bach and Johann Ambrosius Bach, Johann Sebastian's father. These traditions did not end with J. S. Bach. They stretch through other musicians and, in particular, through his sons, into the future.

Since works of art are the product of traditions, if artworks are owned, they are owned by traditions, by communities of artists. This being the case, it is absurd to suppose that individual members of traditions are free to dispose, as they see fit, of the products of the tradition. J. S. Bach would have acted wrongly had he destroyed the manuscript of the *St. Matthew Passion*, and not merely because he would have destroyed something of great value. He would have destroyed something that was not his to destroy. If something is owned by a group of people, it cannot be destroyed without permission of all members of the group.

There is one exception to the rule that not even artists are free to destroy good artworks. This exception applies in the case of works intended by their creators to be temporary. The works by artists such as Cristo would fall into this class. There are works which can only express what their artists intend if they are dismantled after a period of time. Such works are complete only when they are destroyed. There can be no objection to the destruction of these artworks for to interfere with their destruction would be to interfere with artists' freedom of expression. In general artists should be the judge of when their temporary works are to be dismantled. There may, however, be exceptions to this rule. If a work remains intact for a sufficient period, a community may obtain a degree of control over it. If the designer of the Eiffel Tower had somehow survived to the present day, he would not be free to dismantle it, even though it was designed to be a temporary structure.

Any decision to destroy a work of art should not be taken lightly. The act of destroying an artwork, even a bad artwork, is not to be compared, say, with throwing away an unuseful kitchen appliance—an electric wok, say, or an inefficient fish-slice. The arts are central to a culture in a way that appliances are not: domestic utensils make life easier but the arts make it worthwhile. The importance of the arts requires that they be accorded a measure of respect and protection not accorded to the kitchen appliances. So any proposal that some artwork be destroyed should be the occasion of very careful consideration. It does not follow, however, that artworks are never to be destroyed. Some works of art are simply not worth preserving.

Douglas Stalker and Clark Glymour

THE MALIGNANT OBJECT: THOUGHTS ON PUBLIC SCULPTURE

Douglas Stalker is professor of philosophy at the University of Delaware. Clark Glymour is professor of history and philosophy of science at the University of Pittsburgh. They have collaborated on the book Examining Holistic Medicine. *They have also jointly produced the essay from which the following reading is excerpted. The burden of proof, they argue, should be on those who claim that public sculpture benefits the public, not on those who would prefer to remove certain public sculptures.*

Millions of dollars are spent in this country on public sculpture—on sculpture that is created for the explicit purpose of public viewing, placed in public settings, and constructed generally by contemporary artists without any intention of commemorating or representing people or events associated with the site. The objects in question may be clothespins, boulders, or tortuous steel shapes. The money may sometimes come from private sources, but much of it comes from public treasuries.

One of the clearest and most general attempts to provide a justification for financing and placing these objects in public spaces is given by Janet Kardon, who is the Director of Philadelphia's Institute of Contemporary Art. "Public art," Ms. Kardon writes, "is not a style or a movement, but a compound social service based on the premise that public well-being is enhanced by the presence of large scale art works in public spaces." Large scale art works executed, to be sure, not to public taste but to the taste of the avant-garde art community. Elsewhere, she writes: "Public art is not a style, art movement or public service, but a compound event, based on the premise that our lives are enhanced by good art and that good art means work by advanced artists thrust into the public domain." The justification here is moral rather than aesthetic, phrased in terms of well-being rather than those of beauty. Public art is good for us.

Douglas Stalker and Clark Glymour, "The Malignant Object: Thoughts on Public Sculpture," *The Public Interest* 66 (1982): 3–21.

Her thesis is put simply and with clarity; it is perhaps the same thesis as that put forward by many writers who claim that public art "enhances the quality of life" or "humanizes the urban environment," even "speaks to the spirit."

Our view is that much pubic sculpture, and public art generally as it is created nowadays in the United States, provides at best trivial benefits to the public, but does provide substantial and identifiable harm. This is so for a variety of reasons having to do with the character of contemporary artistic enterprises and with prevalent features of our society as well. We will discuss these issues in due course, but for now we want to make our view as clear as we can.

There is abundant evidence, albeit circumstantial, pointing directly to the conclusion that many pieces of contemporary public sculpture, perhaps the majority, are not much enjoyed by the public at large— even though the public firmly believes in a general way that art is a very good thing. In short, the outright aesthetic benefits are few and thin. Perhaps the public is wrong in its distaste or indifference, perhaps members of the public *ought* to take (in some moral sense, if you like) more pleasure in these objects thrust upon them, but these questions are wholly beside the point. Government, at whatever level, only has a legitimate interest in publicly displaying contemporary art in so far as that display provides *aesthetic* benefits to the citizenry. Many artists, critics and art administrators think otherwise, and claim for contemporary public sculpture, and for contemporary art more generally, various intellectual, pedagogical, or economic virtues which are appropriate for the state to foster. By and large the objects in question have no such virtues, so even if governments did wish to foster them, they could not properly or efficiently do so by placing contemporary sculpture in public environs. Further, there are identifiable harms caused by public contemporary art.

These harms are akin in structure, though perhaps not in degree, to the harms often said to be caused by the public display of pornography. After considering the arguments developed subsequently, we hope the reader will conclude that this last contention is not so outrageous as it may seem to be at the outset. Thus, our argument runs, public contemporary sculpture does little or nothing to enhance the quality of life generally, and governments have no intrinsic interest in promoting it. Whatever legitimacy there is to government support of such displays derives from the tradition of serving the special interests of a very limited group of citizens—those served, for example, by museums of contemporary art. But this justification is overwhelmed by the fact that publicly displayed contemporary sculpture causes significant offense and harm, and does so in a way that intrudes repeatedly into people's normal living routines. . . .

The public distaste for today's public sculpture often goes well beyond mere words. The common responses include petitions, assemblies, litigation, and, occasionally, direct action. Enraged by what is thrust at them, the public often takes up a kind of vigilantism against contemporary public sculpture, and in community after community spontaneous bands of Aesthetic Avengers form, armed with hammers, chisels, and spray-paint cans. Jody Pinto's "Heart Chambers for Gertrude and Angelo," erected on the University of Pennsylvania campus for Ms. Kardon's own Institute of Contemporary Art, was turned into rubble overnight. Barnett Newman's "Broken Obelish" was rapidly defaced when it was put on display in 1967. Removed to Houston, Texas, it is now placed in a pool away from errant paint. Claes Oldenburg's "Lipstick" was so thoroughly defaced at Yale that the sculptor retrieved it. Of course, for any object there is some thug or madman willing or eager to destroy what he can of it, but the defacement of some pieces of public sculpture seems to enjoy a measure of community support or at least tolerance.

The examples could be continued into tedium. On the whole, the public does not like today's public art. . . .

MONUMENTS TO THE MUNDANE

What basis can there be, then, for the claim that contemporary public sculpture enhances public well-being? The most obvious value of an aesthetic object—the aesthetic pleasure in seeing it and touching it and living with it—is apparently not present in today's public sculpture. By and large, the members of the public feel no pleasure, or very little, in seeing and touching and having such things. What else can be said in Ms. Kardon's defense? Perhaps that people become accustomed to public sculpture. After a piece has been in place for a while, the outrage, the shouts, the complaints cease. Children play on the thing if it can be played on. Old people may sit by it. This is a sorry defense, in which people's adaptability, and their impotence to control their environs, is used against them. People will, in fact, make what they can of *almost anything*, no matter how atrocious or harmful, if they have no choice. They will adapt to burned out tenements, to garbage in the streets, to death on the sidewalks. However horrible, tasteless, pointless, or insipid an object may be, if children can make a plaything of it they will. Bless them, not the artists.

Today's public sculpture, like the rest of contemporary art, is often defended for its intellectual value, for what the piece says or expresses, rather than for what it looks like. If this is to be any serious defense at all, it must be shown that typical pieces—or at least *some* pieces—of contemporary public sculpture are saying something serious and interesting, and doing so in a way that makes what is being expressed especially

accessible to the public. None of these requirements is met—and moreover these requirements are *obviously* not met—by today's public sculpture.

Attempts to articulate the thought expressed by various pieces are, virtually without exception, trivial or fatuous or circular. Consider some remarks in *Newsweek* in defense and interpretation of a notable piece of public art: "Claes Oldenburg's work—his 'Batcolumn' in Chicago, for example—is formally strong as well as ironic. Oldenburg's silly subjects state a truth often overlooked: inside those self-important glass boxes, people are really thinking hard about such things as baseball bats or clothes-pins." We have no evidence that this is not the very thought that occurs to people when they see Oldenburg's column—but we doubt it. But even if it were, it is a patently trivial thought, and if the object is justified by the expression rather than the sensation, would not a small sign have been in better taste? . . .

. . . What is undeniable about nearly every critical account of the message of one or another school of contemporary art is that the message—whether it is about physics or philosophy—is *esoteric*, and cannot be garnered from any amount of gazing at, climbing on, or even vandalizing of the object.

MORE FAILED JUSTIFICATIONS

Inevitably, today's public sculpture is justified in a kind of circular way: The very fact that the public dislikes it, or even violently abhors it, is taken to warrant its presentation. Thus Jody Pinto, rather typically, remarked after her sculpture at the University of Pennsylvania was destroyed that "Tons of letters were written to the *Daily Pennsylvanian*, both pro and con, which is wonderful. If art can stimulate that kind of discussion and really make people think, then it's accomplished probably more than most artists could even hope for." Thus the justification for public art is that it causes people to think about why they do not like it, or about the propriety of having destroyed it. That is indeed a virtue, one supposes, but a virtue shared quite as much by every calamity.

There is also the common suggestion that, like travel, contemporary art in public places is broadening. It introduces the public to the fact that there are other and different tastes and sensitivities, alternative and unconventional standards of beauty. It makes people *tolerant.* In fact, there is no case at all that public sculpture makes people tolerant of anything that matters. Today's public sculpture may well make people tolerant of public sculpture, for the simple reason that if the object is too large, too strong, or too well fortified, they have no choice. Does it make people tolerant of, or sensitive to, the aesthetic expectations of other cultures or times? One doubts that it does, and surely not as well as an exhibition of Chinese calligraphy, or American ghetto art, or Tibetan dance, or the treasures of King Tut.

It is sometimes urged, rather opaquely, that there are significant economic benefits to be derived from public art. The case is seldom developed in any detailed fashion, and there is good reason to doubt that public support of permanent or quasi-permanent public art structures can lean very much on such considerations. . . .

THE PROPRIETY OF GOVERNMENT SUPPORT

Government at various levels may be legitimately concerned to promote the public welfare, but it cannot be legitimately concerned to promote activities with no demonstrable or even very plausible connection with the well-being of the citizenry. The argument for public art fails entirely if it is based on considerations of direct general welfare. What remains to be said in defense of public sculpture is only a kind of analogy. Governments at various levels support museums, even museums wholly or partly given over to contemporary art, and such support is ordinarily thought to be entirely proper. The public at large is thought to benefit by having art collections available, and a small segment of the public does benefit from active and repeated use of such collections. Why, it might reasonably be asked, is public sculpture any different? Granted that only a small segment of the population actively enjoys the things, why should not the government support that interest while providing to others the benefits of availability in case they change their minds or their tastes? The answer brings us to another conclusion: The objects of contemporary public sculpture are not benign or indifferent.

. . . The moral questions associated with the public display of large pieces of contemporary art are rather like the moral issues surrounding the public display of pornography. The analogy between public contemporary art and public pornography is revealing, and we will pursue it, not because we believe that the harms caused by public contemporary art are the same harms as those caused by public pornography, but because the different harms in the two cases arise in similar ways, and belong to similar categories.

PUBLIC SCULPTURE, PUBLIC PORNOGRAPHY

The public display of pornography is widely claimed to cause several kinds of harm in several ways. In the first place, merely seeing pornographic depictions of events offends many people who do the seeing. The offensiveness of these displays to such people is at least partly aesthetic— it involves their immediate repugnance at what they perceive. (It is in that way different from the repugnance which is expressed by evangelical prudes at anyone, anywhere, gazing upon pornographic displays, no matter how much pleasure the gazer may find.) . . .

Second, the public display of pornography is claimed to have a kind of reflective effect on some people. On reflection, if one is a woman, one is *humiliated* by the depiction of women as simply and rightfully objects of lust who are nothing more than sexual slaves. Third, the public display of pornography is claimed to have indirect effects which do substantial harm: It is alleged to promote sex crimes, for example, and to cause or to sustain the repression of women and discrimination against them. More clearly, the public display of pornography violates the interests of those who value modesty, who are offended by pornographic displays, and who wish society not to develop in such a way that immodesty and pornography are ubiquitous. The public display of pornography can be reasonably expected to contribute to the further erosion of taboos against immodesty and public sexuality in various forms, and thus to cause the evolution of society in such a way that is inimical to the interests of those who prefer a society whose members confine their eroticism to private circumstances. These are rather familiar objections to public pornography, and anyone who has thought or talked much of the subject has met versions of them. Most have a valid analogue in public art.

A good deal of today's public sculpture offends the public eye. It offends twice: once because it is simply unsightly, as with garbage, auto salvage yards, and scrap heaps; and again because it is unsightly *art*. It is offensive to be presented with rags and scrap metal, but perhaps equally offensive to be told that an unsightly mess must be respected as art. . . .

There is a related harm of the second kind, a reflective harm which is a kind of insult or humiliation. Viewing public sculpture and finding it ugly or silly or simply commonplace, the common person brings his own eye and mind into direct conflict with the judgment of the aesthetic and political authorities. He can only draw one of three conclusions. Either his own judgment is hopelessly flawed, so that he is a complete aesthetic incompetent; or else that of the authorities is flawed in like fashion; or, finally, he and his fellow citizens have been made the butt of a joke by the artist, his associates, and his admirers. The second conclusion is not widely held, though it is a logical possibility, and is doubtless sometimes true. In the first case, the citizen can only be humiliated by an object which, try as he will, he cannot find the beauty of; in the third case, he can only be insulted and righteously indignant at those who have erected an object which is an expression of contempt for the public. Both to the timid and to the self-confident, the object acts with malice. We are not sure that the harm associated with the humiliation and insult given by public sculpture is altogether less intense than the humiliation some people feel at public pornography. And the harm is repeated and repeated and repeated. The citizen can only escape by moving his domicile or work or normal activities, or by cultivating indifference.

In a third way, as well, the erection of public sculpture of the contemporary kind harms the interests of citizens who find it offensive: It begets more of the same. It does so directly by means of artistic influence, through mechanisms familiar to everyone. It does so indirectly by influencing the sense of beauty in the youthful, and thus causing them to welcome more of the same. Everyone has an interest in society developing in such a way that his own aesthetic sensibilities are not everywhere outraged; for much of the citizenry, most works of today's public sculpture act against that interest. . . .

Artists, critics, and art administrators may find this argument to be simply an endorsement of philistinism, but that is a grievous confusion. Philistines are people too, and, whether or not one shares their tastes, the moral point of view requires that their interests be considered. If art is serious then aesthetic values must interact with moral values and aesthetic reactions must also help determine moral obligations. The artistic community generally is constitutionally allergic to close argument and clear statement, preferring allusion and non-sequitur. But any serious discussion about art and social obligation cannot be so self-indulgent, and that is why we have found Ms. Kardon's statements so welcome. If there is a serious defense of the view that today's public art enhances public well-being, it is not enough to presuppose it, allude to it, imply it, or suggest it. Give it.

Arthur C. Danto

THE
VIETNAM
VETERANS
MEMORIAL

Arthur C. Danto is art critic for The Nation *as well as professor emeritus of philosophy at Columbia University. The following is one of his articles from* The Nation. *Danto describes the controversy that surrounded the Vietnam Veterans Memorial in Washington, D.C., both during and after its construction. Danto considers the memorial, with its walls and roster of names, to be vastly more powerful from an aesthetic point of view than the figurative sculpture that was erected nearby to placate the memorial's critics. Nevertheless, Danto contends, the sculpture gains power by virtue of its proximity to the memorial.*

We erect monuments so that we shall always remember, and build memorials so that we shall never forget. Thus we have the Washington Monument but the Lincoln Memorial. Monuments commemorate the memorable and embody the myths of beginnings. Memorials ritualize remembrance and mark the reality of ends. The Washington Monument, vertical, is a celebration, like fireworks. The Lincoln Memorial, even if on a rise, presses down and is a meditation in stone. Very few nations erect monuments to their defeats, but many set up memorials to the defeated dead. Monuments make heroes and triumphs, victories and conquests, perpetually present and part of life. The memorial is a special precinct, extruded from life, a segregated enclave where we honor the dead. With monuments we honor ourselves.

Memorials are often just lists of those killed. Herodotus describes a megalith that carried the names of all 300 Spartans slain at Thermopylae in a defeat so stunning as to elevate their leader, Leonidas, to what Ivan

Arthur C. Danto, "The Vietnam Veterans Memorial," *The Nation* 241.5 (1985): 152–55.

Morris once called the nobility of failure. Lists figure prominently in the hundreds of Civil War memorials, where the names of fallen townsmen bear the iconographic significance that those who were lost meant more than what had been won. The paradox of the Vietnam Veterans Memorial in Washington is that the men and women killed and missing would not have been memorialized had we won the war and erected a monument instead. Among the specifications for the memorial's commission was the stipulation that it show the names of all the U.S. dead and missing (the battlestone of Thermopylae only memorialized the Spartans, not their Theoan or Thespian allies) and that it make no political statement about the war. But just being called a memorial is as eloquent as not being called a monument: not being forgotten is the thin compensation for not having participated in an event everyone wants to remember. The list of names, as a collective cenotaph, situates the memorialized war in the consciousness of the nation.

The Washington Monument is an obelisk, a monumental form with connotations of the trophy in Western art. Augustus carried obelisks to Alexandria, whence they were in time borne off to London and New York; Constantine brought one to Rome, where it was appropriated by Pope Sixtus V for San Giovanni in Laterano; Napoleon was obliged to cart an obelisk to Paris. The Lincoln Memorial is in the form of a classical temple, in which Lincoln is enthroned like a brooding god. It is a metaphor for sacrifice and a confession of the limits of human power. The Veterans Memorial carries no explicit art-historical references, though it consists of two symmetrical walls, mirror images of one another, right triangles sharing a common vertical base, which point, like a pair of long wings, east, to the obelisk of triumph, and west, to the temple of submission. Everything about it is part of a text. Even the determination to say nothing political is inscribed by the absence of a political statement.

A third stipulation for the memorial was that it harmonize with its surroundings. It does more: it integrates the two structures it points to into a moral landscape. Because the two wings form an angle, the Veterans Memorial together with the Washington Monument and the Lincoln Memorial compose a large triangle, with the long reflecting pool as a segment of the base.

The memorial was dedicated on November 13, 1982—Veterans Day—when there were only the walls and the names, each wall composed of seventy granite panels, with about 58,000 names and room for several hundred more. Two years later a bronze statue of three servicemen, done in an exacting realism, was added to the site. Their backs are to the axis that connects the Monument and the Memorial, as though they are oblivious to the historical meanings to which the walls return us by pointing. Like innocents who look at the pointer rather than that to which it points, they see only rows and columns of names. They are dazed and stunned. The walls reflect their obsessed gaze, as they reflect the flag to which the servicemen's back is also turned, as they reflect the Monument and the Memorial. The gently flexed pair of walls, polished black, is like the back of Plato's cave, a reflecting surface, a dark mirror. The reflections in it of the servicemen, the flag, the Monument and the Memorial are appearances of appearances. It also reflects us, the visitors, as it does the trees. Still, the living are in it only as appearances. Only the names of the dead, on the surface, are real.

The reflecting walls constituted the Veterans Memorial at the time of its dedication, but before they were in place a concession was made to a faction that demanded figurative realism instead of what it perceived as an abstract monument to the liberal establishment. Thus the bronze servicemen. Those walls could have stood on their own, artistically, but the bronze group could not have. As a piece of free-standing sculpture it is intrinsically banal. Its three figures belong to obligatorily distinct racial types: a black and someone vaguely ethnic—a Jew, perhaps, or some Mediterranean type—stand on either side of a Nordic figure. The central figure has a holstered pistol, but the end figures carry more powerful weapons—though not held in a position for use—and there are no empty spaces in the cartridge belts: fighting is suspended. The garb and gear of this war are precisely documented: visitors will learn how many eyelets were in G.I. boots and that soldiers carried two canteens. More realistic than the military figures that guard the honor rolls in Civil War memorials, they look too much like specimens for a military museum, at least when considered alone. But they are greatly enhanced by their relationship to the great walls. In a way, the harmonization of their presence in the triangle generated by the walls is a monument to the triumph of political compromise rather than a memorial to artistic strife. The dead are remembered in their gaze, even when there are no living to look.

The walls are the design of Maya Ying Lin, who won a competition against 1,421 contestants when she was 21 and a student at Yale University. An Asian-American from Athens, Ohio, she was a child at the time of the memorialized conflict, too young to remember the tumult and the protest, which for her are simply history, like the War of Independence or the Civil War. The bronze group was done by Frederick Hart, a Washington sculptor, who was, ironically, a demonstrator against the Vietnam War. The irony is that artistic realism was associated with patriotism and endorsement of the war in the minds of those who insisted on figuration. They regarded the walls as a symbol for peaceniks. "A wailing wall for liberals"; "a tribute to Jane Fonda"; "a degrading ditch"; "the most insulting and demeaning memorial to our experience that was possible": these were among the nasty things said. The walls are nonfigurative, of course,

but they are deeply representational, given the textual nature of memorial art (of all art, when it comes to that), and the question of the meaning of Lin's text was acknowledged by those who rejected what they took to be its supposed representation of reality. Its being black, for example, was loudly read as a sign of shame until a black general brought an abrupt end to that effort to preempt the language of color.

The winning design was the unanimous choice of a panel of eight experts, and it was accepted by the group that pushed the idea of a memorial as an expression of the feelings they wanted to have objectified. It gave a form to those feelings, as public art is supposed to do: the issues are never solely esthetic. It was accepted by 150,000 participants at the dedication. No one has defaced it, no one has tried to blow it up, though there was a threat of this once. It has been accepted by the nation at large, which did not even know it wanted such a memorial. It is now one of the sites most visited in the capital. Still, it was wholly appropriate that the design should have been put in question when a schism opened up, that intense emotion and antagonism should have raged, that terrible and foolish things should have been said by everyone. Lin mounted the same high horse favored by artists whose work is publicly criticized and accused the critics of sexism. Even so, her design held. It was not replaced by a monument, as though the tacit rules that govern the distinction between monuments and memorials finally prevailed. Those who wanted realism finally got their mannequins, not exactly where they wanted them, with the walls to their back and a proud flag flying at the vee, but off to one side, up a gentle slope, and at a certain distance, with the flag still farther away. By a miracle of placement, Hart's shallow work has acquired a dignity and even a certain power. The complex of walls and figures reminded me of a memorial sculpture of Canova, in which a single figure sits in white silence outside a pyramidal sepulcher. A dimension is even added to the triangular walls, wonderful as they are. The entire complex is an emblem of the participation of the public in the framing of public art. It did not, to paraphrase Richard Serra, cost the government a dime. More than 275,000 Americans responded to the call for funds with contributions in small denominations—those bearing the faces of Washington and Lincoln.

Lin's instructor told her that the angle where the walls meet had to mean something, and I asked myself, when I pilgrimed down one hot Tuesday in July, what its meaning was. A writer in the "Talk of the Town" section of *The New Yorker* described it as "a long open hinge, its leaves cut vertically into the ground, which descends very gradually toward the vertex." The hinge is a powerful symbol—we speak of "the hinge of fate"—and it has the mysterious property of opening and closing at once. Still, that is something of a misdescription. A hinge 140 feet long sounds too much like Claes Oldenburg, who might, consistent with his *oeuvre*, have submitted the Vietnam Veterans Memorial Hinge had he entered the competition. The *New Yorker* writer does better on a nearer approach: "a little like facing a huge open book with black pages." The book lies open now that the episode is closed and all or nearly all the dead are known. A book of the dead. And that would fit with their being listed in chronological order, from the first one killed in 1959 to the last one killed in 1975, when the remaining Americans were evacuated from Saigon as the Republic of Vietnam surrendered, on April 30.

This brings me to my chief criticism of Lin's work, which concerns an incongruity between narrative and form. An effort has been made to make the slight angle meaningful by having the narrative begin and end there: RICHARD VANDE GEER is at the bottom right of the west panel and DALE R. BUIS is at the top left of the east panel on either side of the joint. As though a circle were closed, and after the end is the beginning. But a circle has the wrong moral geometry for a linear conflict: the end of a war does not mean, one hopes, the beginning of a war. As it stands now, we read from the middle to the end, then return to the other end and read again our way to the middle. This means that the terminal panels, architecturally the most important, carry one name each, but the end points of the walls are not the end points of the list. If the first were first, we would read through to the last, from left to right. The panels grow larger, which is to say the space in which the walls are set grows deeper, as we approach the center. So there are more names on the central panels than on the rest. But that exactly reflects the shape of the war itself, our involvement being greatest in the late 1960s. So the angle could represent a high point and a turning point. And you would leave with the Monument before you, as you entered with the Memorial behind you, and the whole complex would acquire the direction of time and, perhaps, hope. . . .

. . . There is really no way to imagine the memorial from . . . any pictures I have seen. For that you must make a visit. If you know someone who was killed, an attendant from the National Parks Service will help you locate his or her name. They are all listed alphabetically in directories near the site.

Be prepared to weep. Tears are the universal experience even if you don't know any of the dead. I watched reverent little groups count down the rows of a panel and then across to the name they sought. Some place a poignant, hopeless offering underneath: a birthday card, a flag, a ribbon, a flower. Some leave little notes. Most photograph the name, but many take rubbings of it on pamphlets handed out by the Parks Service. You can borrow a ladder to reach the top names. The highest panels are about ten feet high—or, more accurately, their bottom edges are about ten feet below ground level. Someday, I suppose, visiting it will be like standing before a memorial from the Civil War, where the bearers of the names really have been forgotten ánd, since the theory is that the meaning of a name is its denotation, the names themselves will have lost their meaning. They will merely remain powerful as names, and there will only be the idea of death to be moved by. Now, however, we are all moved by the reality of death, or moved by the fact that many who stand beside us are moved by its reality. I copied down two of the names of which rubbings were made:

EDWARD H. FOX
WILBUR J. MILLER

DISCUSSION QUESTIONS

1. Is government funding of the arts ever warranted? If funding should be available, should it be limited to works that conform to community standards? Justify your position.
2. Is sexual content compatible with artistic merit? Can it ever enhance the artistic merit of an artwork?
3. Do you think that it is ever legitimate for a government to restrict or censor art?
4. Do you agree with Wolfe that the "serious art" typically presented in contemporary art museums is deliberately intended to be difficult for the public to understand? Does the museum have any responsibility to alleviate public misunderstanding of contemporary art?
5. Would you compare art to religion in any respect? Do you think Wolfe's comparison is appropriate?
6. Should the legal burden of proof be on those who want to erect public sculptures or on those who want to remove them?

FURTHER READING

Art, Law, and Censorship

Dubin, Steven C. *Arresting Images: Impolitic Art and Uncivil Actions.* New York: Routledge, 1992.

Duboff, Leonard D. *Art Law: In a Nutshell.* St. Paul: West, 1984.

Feldman, Franklin, and Stephen E. Weil. *Art Law: Rights and Liabilities of Creators and Collectors.* Boston: Little, Brown, 1986.

Heins, Marjorie. *Sex, Sin and Blasphemy: A Guide to America's Censorship Wars.* New York: New Press, 1993.

Hoffman, Barbara. "Law for Art's Sake in the Public Realm." *Critical Inquiry* 17.3 (1991): 540–73.

Hughes, Robert. *Culture of Complaint: The Fraying of America.* New York: Oxford UP, 1993.

Merryman, John Henry, and Albert E. Elsen. *Law Ethics, and the Visual Arts.* Philadelphia: U of Pennsylvania P, 1987.

Senie, Harriet F., and Sally Webster. *Critical Issues in Public Art: Content, Context, and Controversy.* New York: HarperCollins, 1992.

Serra, Richard. "Art and Censorship." *Critical Inquiry* 17.3 (1991): 574–81.

Smith, Ralph A. and Ronald Berman, eds. *Public Policy and the Aesthetic Interest: Critical Essays on Defining Cultural and Educational Relations.* Urbana: U of Illinois P, 1992.

Museums

Bazin, Germain. *The Museum Age.* New York: Universe, 1967.

Crimp, Douglas. *On the Museum's Ruins.* Cambridge: M.I.T. P, 1993.

Fisher, Philip. *Making and Effacing Art: Modern American Art in a Culture of Museums.* New York: Oxford UP, 1991.

Karp, Ivan, and Steven D. Lavine, eds. *Exhibiting Cultures: The Poetics and Politics of Museum Display.* Washington, D.C.: Smithsonian Institution, 1991.

Malraux, André. *Museum without Walls.* Trans. Stuart Gilbert and Francis Price. London: Secker and Warburg, 1967.

PART II

INTERPRETING
AND
EVALUATING
ART

CREATION AND INSPIRATION

Human creativity has a mythical dimension. Most of us have heard the story that Mozart wrote whole symphonies in his head and once requested that stories be read to him while he copied parts directly from his mind. Chemist Friedrich August Kekulé allegedly made his discovery of benzene's "ring" structure by dreaming of a snake biting its own tail, an image that suggested the solution to the structural problem. Creativity seems miraculous and impervious to conscious control.

Plato's *Ion* promotes the view that artistic creation is mysterious. The dialogue portrays a conversation between Socrates and a performer named Ion. Technically a rhapsode, who performed poetry for the public in Athenian society, Ion asks why he can move his audiences when he presents Homer, but not when he presents any other poetry. Socrates explains that Ion is divinely inspired when he performs Homer. Socrates compares inspiration to magnetism. A god inspired Homer, who transmits this inspiration to Ion; Ion, in turn, transmits it to his audience. While inspired, an artist is not his ordinary self; the artist is borrowing power from the inspiring god. The claim that the artist is moved by divine powers sounds like a compliment, but Socrates is actually insulting Ion. By saying that Ion works through inspiration, Socrates is saying that he lacks real knowledge of his art; for if Ion knew the art of performing, he could utilize it in all his performances without depending on inspiration.

Aristotle had differences with Plato on virtually every topic, and the topic of artistic creation is no exception. In the selection from his *Poetics*, Aristotle offers sound practical advice for those who want to write tragedies. Plato's account of inspiration depicts the artist as a passive recipient of irrational forces. Aristotle's account, by contrast, suggests that there are reliable methods for writing a good play.

Since the eighteenth century, inspiration has more often been thought to stem from the artist's own mind than from an external power. According to Immanuel Kant, for example, great art is inspired by genius. Although genius resides in the artist, it is like a force of nature. In fact, Kant claims that genius is the means by which nature "gives the rule" to art. Genius, in other words, gives art its shape, and it is not subject to human control. One genius might inspire another, but no formula or recipe can explain or ensure artistic greatness.

Arthur Schopenhauer, too, believes that great art arises from genius. The selection below, from his major work *The World as Will and Representation* (1819), describes genius as the ability to take a serene, dispassionate stance toward the world around one. Schopenhauer believes that everyone is occasionally able to contemplate without ulterior motives, but he thinks that most people do so very seldomly. The genius, by contrast, is able to contemplate in a will-less fashion much more often than most, and is also able to communicate this state to other individuals through art. From Schopenhauer's thoroughly pessimistic point of view, a person can attain real salvation only through living an ascetic life and by relinquishing all desire. Recognizing that few people (including himself) will pursue that route, he considers artistic works of genius to be havens of liberation in an otherwise miserable existence.

Rainer Maria Rilke, Anne Truitt, and Christopher Middleton each describe the activity of art-making from a practitioner's point of view. Rilke's letters to a young poet recommend solitude and self-reliance. He also urges his correspondent to respect the creative process within himself and to avoid analyzing it too closely. Like Kant, Rilke is convinced that genius follows its own laws, and that it cannot be subjected to conscious control.

Anne Truitt's journal reflects her deliberate attempt to chronicle the dynamics of the creative process. She suggests that the process of art-making is more complex than traditional inspiration accounts suggest. An exhilarating experience of art-making does not necessarily yield art of high quality. Yet the activities of the mind bear an intimate relationship to the shape and the value of what is ultimately produced.

Poet Christopher Middleton is convinced that mental images play a basic role in shaping an artwork. The appearance of a fertile mental image is involuntary, Middleton contends, agreeing this far with Plato. Nevertheless, the image is usually a mere fragment. It must be nurtured if it is to develop into a full-blown artwork, and Middleton believes that an artist can assist the nurturing process by taking a somewhat ironic attitude. Such an attitude helps to prevent a type of artistic failure that is particularly common in our time, the deterioration of an image from the germ of art to kitsch. (The phenomenon of kitsch is considered in Chapter 9 in the selections by Kundera and Calinescu.)

The final reading in this chapter considers the creative process involved in artistic performance. Taken from Eugen Herrigel's *Zen in the Art of Archery* (1953), the passage describes discoveries Herrigel made while studying with an archery master. The selection offers an interesting glimpse at a successful case of communication between teacher and art student. Inspiration theories have sometimes been thought to imply that the important aspects of art cannot be taught. Herrigel focuses on the way the teacher elicits artistic discoveries from the student. His picture of the student–teacher relationship is subtle, and it hints that we should reconsider what both teaching and learning involve.

Plato

INSPIRATION AS MAGNETISM

*Plato (427–347 B.C.E.) had an ambivalent view of art.
He admired its power but opposed art that did not
subordinate this power to the aims of reason. Plato's
ambivalence is evident in his depiction of Ion, a
rhapsode (a performer of poetry) who performs
Homer—but only Homer—brilliantly. Plato's character
Socrates concludes that Ion is divinely inspired but
ignorant of his art. Although a vehicle for a force that
is greater than himself, Ion lacks what every one of us
should seek—genuine knowledge.*

SOCRATES: We may therefore generalize, and say: When several persons are discussing a given subject, the man who can distinguish the one who is talking well on it, and the one who is talking badly, will always be the same. Or, if he does not recognize the one who is talking badly, then, clearly, neither will he recognize the one who is talking well, granted that the subject is the same.

ION: That is so.

SOCRATES: Then the same man will be skilled with respect to both?

ION: Yes.

SOCRATES: Now you assert that Homer and the other poets, among

them Hesiod and Archilochus, all treat of the same subjects, yet not all in the same fashion, but the one speaks well, and the rest of them speak worse.

ION: And what I say is true. . . .

SOCRATES: Well then, my best of friends, when we say that Ion has equal skill in Homer and all other poets, we shall not be mistaken. It must be so, since you yourself admit that the same man will be competent to judge of all who speak of the same matters, and that the poets virtually all deal with the same subjects.

ION: Then what can be the reason, Socrates, for my behavior? When anyone discusses any other poet, I pay no

Plato, *The Ion*, trans. Lane Cooper, *The Collected Dialogues of Plato, Including the Letters*, ed. Edith Hamilton and Huntington Cairns, Bollingen LXXI (Princeton: Princeton UP, 1961) 218–22.

attention, and can offer no remark of any value. I frankly doze. But whenever anyone mentions Homer, immediately I am awake, attentive, and full of things to say.

SOCRATES: The riddle is not hard to solve, my friend. No, it is plain to everyone that not from art and knowledge comes your power to speak concerning Homer. If it were art that gave you power, then you could speak about all the other poets as well. There is an art of poetry as a whole? Am I not right?

ION: Yes.

SOCRATES: And is not the case the same with any other art you please, when you take it as a whole? The same method of inquiry holds for all the arts? . . . Let us reason the matter out. There is an art of painting taken as a whole?

ION: Yes.

SOCRATES: And there are and have been many painters, good and bad?

ION: Yes indeed.

SOCRATES: Now, take Polygnotus, son of Aglaophon. Have you ever seen a man with the skill to point out what is good and what is not in the works of Polygnotus, but without the power to do so in the works of other painters? A man who, when anybody shows the works of other painters, dozes off, is at a loss, has nothing to suggest, but when he has to express a judgment on one particular painter, say Polygnotus or anyone else you choose, wakes up, and is attentive, and is full of things to say?

ION: No, on my oath, I never saw the like. . . . But of this thing I am conscious, that I excel all men in speaking about Homer, and on him have much

to say, and that everybody else avers I do it well, but on the other poets I do not. Well then, see what that means.

SOCRATES: I do see, Ion, and in fact will proceed to show you what to my mind it betokens. As I just now said, this gift you have of speaking well on Homer is not an art; it is a power divine, impelling you like the power in the stone Euripides called the magnet, which most call "stone of Heraclea." This stone does not simply attract the iron rings, just by themselves; it also imparts to the rings a force enabling them to do the same thing as the stone itself, that is, to attract another ring, so that sometimes a chain is formed, quite a long one, of iron rings, suspended from one another. For all of them, however, their power depends upon that loadstone. Just so the Muse. She first makes men inspired, and then through these inspired ones others share in the enthusiasm, and a chain is formed, for the epic poets, all the good ones, have their excellence, not from art, but are inspired, possessed, and thus they utter all these admirable poems. So is it also with the good lyric poets; as the worshiping Corybantes are not in their senses when they dance, so the lyric poets are not in their senses when they make these lovely lyric poems. No, when once they launch into harmony and rhythm, they are seized with the Bacchic transport, and are possessed—as the bacchants, when possessed, draw milk and honey from the rivers, but not when in their senses. So the spirit of the lyric poet works, according to their own report. For the poets tell us, don't they, that the melodies they bring us are gathered from rills that run with honey, out of glens and gardens of the Muses, and they bring them as the bees do honey, flying like the bees?

And what they say is true, for a poet is a light and winged thing, and holy, and never able to compose until he has become inspired, and is beside himself, and reason is no longer in him. So long as he has this in his possession, no man is able to make poetry or to chant in prophecy. Therefore, since their making is not by art, when they utter many things and fine about the deeds of men, just as you do about Homer, but is by lot divine—therefore each is able to do well only that to which the Muse has impelled him— one to make dithyrambs, another panegyric odes, another choral songs, another epic poems, another iambs. In all the rest, each one of them is poor, for not by art do they utter these, but by power divine, since if it were by art that they knew how to treat one subject finely, they would know how to deal with all the others too. Herein lies the reason why the deity has bereft them of their senses, and uses them as ministers, along with soothsayers and godly seers; it is in order that we listeners may know that it is not they who utter these precious revelations while their mind is not within them, but that it is the god himself who speaks, and through them becomes articulate to us. The most convincing evidence of this statement is offered by Tynnichus of Chalcis. He never composed a single poem worth recalling, save the song of praise which everyone repeats, well-nigh the finest of all lyrical poems, and absolutely what he called it, an "Invention of the Muses." By this example above all, it seems to me, the god would show us, lest we doubt, that these lovely poems are not of man or human workmanship, but are divine and from the gods, and that the poets are nothing but interpreters of the gods, each one possessed by the divinity to whom he is in bondage. And to prove this, the deity on purpose sang the loveliest of all lyrics through the most miserable poet. Isn't it so, Ion? Don't you think that I am right?

ION: You are indeed, I vow! Socrates, your words in some way touch my very soul, and it does seem to me that by dispensation from above good poets convey to us these utterances of the gods.

———◆◆◆———

SOCRATES: Well, do you see that the spectator is the last of the rings I spoke of, which receive their force from one another by virtue of the loadstone? You, the rhapsodist and actor, are the middle ring, and the first one is the poet himself. But it is the deity who, through all the series, draws the spirit of men wherever he desires, transmitting the attractive force from one into another. And so, as from the loadstone, a mighty chain hangs down, of choric dancers, masters of the chorus, undermasters, obliquely fastened to the rings which are suspended from the Muse. One poet is suspended from one Muse, another from another; we call it being "possessed," but the fact is much the same, since he is *held*. And from these primary rings, the poets, others are in turn suspended, some attached to this one, some to that, and are filled with inspiration, some by Orpheus, others by Musaeus. But the majority are possessed and held by Homer, and, Ion, you are one of these, and are possessed by Homer. And whenever anyone chants the work of any other poet, you fall asleep, and haven't a thing to say, but when anybody gives tongue to a strain of this one, you are awake at once, your spirit dances, and you have much to say, for not by art or science do you say of Homer what you say, but by dispensation from above and by divine possession. So the worshiping Corybantes have a lively feeling for that strain alone which is of the deity by whom they are possessed, and for that melody are well supplied with attitudes and utterances, and heed no others. And so it is with you, Ion. When anyone mentions Homer, you are ready, but about the other poets you are at a loss. You ask me why you are ready about Homer and not about the rest. Because it is not by art but by lot divine that you are eloquent in praise of Homer.

Aristotle

CONSTRUCTING A TRAGEDY

Aristotle (384–322 B.C.E.) was especially interested in how things of all sorts come into being. In this excerpt from his Poetics, *he describes the process by which the playwright successfully writes a tragedy, implicitly offering recommendations to would-be dramatists.*

At the time when he is constructing his Plots, and engaged on the Diction in which they are worked out, the poet should remember (1) to put the actual scenes as far as possible before his eyes. In this way, seeing everything with the vividness of an eyewitness as it were, he will devise what is appropriate, and be least likely to overlook incongruities. This is shown by what was censured in Carcinus, the return of Amphiaraus from the sanctuary; it would have passed unnoticed, if it had not been actually seen by the audience; but on the stage his play failed, the incongruity of the incident offending the spectators. (2) As far as may be, too, the poet should even act his story with the very gestures of his personages. Given the same natural qualifications, he who feels the emotions to be described will be the most convincing; distress and anger, for instance, are portrayed most truthfully by one who is feeling them at the moment. Hence it is that poetry demands a man with a special gift for it, or else one with a touch of madness in him; the former can easily assume the required mood, and the latter may be actually beside himself with emotion. (3) His story, again, whether already made or of his own making, he should first simplify and reduce to a universal form, before proceeding to lengthen it out by the insertion of episodes. The following will show how the universal element in *Iphigenia*, for instance, may be viewed: A certain maiden having been offered in sacrifice, and spirited away from her sacrificers into another land, where the custom was to sacrifice all strangers to the Goddess, she was made there the priestess of this rite. Long after that the brother of the priestess happened to come; the fact, however, of the oracle having for a certain reason bidden him go thither, and his object in going, are outside the Plot of the play. On his coming he was arrested, and about to be sacrificed, when he revealed who he was—either as

Aristotle, *The Poetics*, trans. Ingram Bywater, *The Basic Works of Aristotle*, ed. Richard McKeon (New York: Random House, 1941) 1471–73.

Euripides puts it, or (as suggested by Polyidus) by the not improbable exclamation, "So I too am doomed to be sacrificed, as my sister was"; and the disclosure led to his salvation. This done, the next thing, after the proper names have been fixed as a basis for the story, is to work in episodes or accessory incidents. One must mind, however, that the episodes are appropriate, like the fit of madness in Orestes, which led to his arrest, and the purifying, which brought about his salvation. In plays, then, the episodes are short; in epic poetry they serve to lengthen out the poem. The argument of the *Odyssey* is not a long one. A certain man has been abroad many years; Poseidon is ever on the watch for him, and he is all alone. Matters at home too have come to this, that his substance is being wasted and his son's death plotted by suitors to his wife. Then he arrives there himself after his grievous sufferings; reveals himself, and falls on his enemies; and the end is his salvation and their death. This being all that is proper to the *Odyssey*, everything else in it is episode.

Immanuel Kant

THE
NATURE
OF
GENIUS

German philosopher Immanuel Kant (1724–1804)
described genius as nature's means of shaping art.
Genius is original; therefore we cannot give formulas
to explain how a genius went about creating an
artwork. The mind of the genius, according to Kant,
produces aesthetic ideas, which inform the work.
Aesthetic ideas occasion much thought, but they are
not reducible to any particular thought.

§ 46
FINE ART IS THE ART OF GENIUS

Genius is the talent (natural endowment) that gives the rule to art. Since talent is an innate productive ability of the artist and as such belongs itself to nature, we could also put it this way: *Genius* is the innate mental predisposition . . . *through which* nature gives the rule to art. . . .

For every art presupposes rules, which serve as the foundation on which a product, if it is to be called artistic, is thought of as possible in the first place. On the other hand, the concept of fine art does not permit a judgment about the beauty of its product to be derived from any rule whatsoever that has a *concept* as its determining basis,

i.e., the judgment must not be based on a concept of the way in which the product is possible. Hence fine art cannot itself devise the rule by which it is to bring about its product. Since, however, a product can never be called art unless it is preceded by a rule, it must be nature in the subject (and through the attunement of his powers) that gives the rule to art; in other words, fine art is possible only as the product of genius.

What this shows is the following: (1) Genius is a *talent* for producing something for which no determinate rule can be given, not a predisposition consisting of a skill for something that can be learned by following some rule or other; hence the foremost property of genius must be *originality*. (2) Since nonsense too can be original, the

Immanuel Kant, *Critique of Judgment*, trans. Werner S. Pluhar (Indianapolis: Hackett, 1987) 174–89.

products of genius must also be models, i.e., they must be *exemplary;* hence, though they do not themselves arise through imitation, still they must serve others for this, i.e., as a standard or rule by which to judge. (3) Genius itself cannot describe or indicate scientifically how it brings about its products, and it is rather as *nature* that it gives the rule. That is why, if an author owes a product to his genius, he himself does not know how he came by the ideas for it; nor is it in his power . . . to devise such products at his pleasure, or by following a plan, and to communicate [his procedure] to others in precepts that would enable them to bring about like products. (Indeed, that is presumably why the word genius is derived from [Latin] *genius,* [which means] the guardian and guiding spirit that each person is given as his own at birth, and to whose inspiration . . . those original ideas are due.) (4) Nature, through genius, prescribes the rule not to science but to art, and this also only insofar as the art is to be fine art.

§ 49
ON THE POWERS OF THE MIND WHICH CONSTITUTE GENIUS

Of certain products that are expected to reveal themselves at least in part to be fine art, we say that they have no *spirit,* even though we find nothing to censure in them as far as taste is concerned. A poem may be quite nice and elegant and yet have no spirit. A story may be precise and orderly and yet have no spirit. An oration may be both thorough and graceful and yet have no spirit. Many conversations are entertaining, but they have no spirit. Even about some woman we will say that she is pretty, communicative, and polite, but that she has no spirit. Well, what do we mean here by spirit?

Spirit [Geist] in an aesthetic sense is the animating principle in the mind. But what

this principle uses to animate [or quicken] the soul, the material it employs for this, is what imparts to the mental powers a purposive momentum, i.e., imparts to them a play which is such that it sustains itself on its own and even strengthens the powers for such play.

Now I maintain that this principle is nothing but the ability to exhibit *aesthetic ideas;* and by an aesthetic idea I mean a presentation of the imagination which prompts much thought, but to which no determinate thought whatsoever, i.e., no [determinate] *concept,* can be adequate, so that no language can express it completely and allow us to grasp it. It is easy to see that an aesthetic idea is the counterpart (pendant) of a *rational idea,* which is, conversely, a concept to which no *intuition* (presentation of the imagination) can be adequate.

For the imagination ([in its role] as a productive cognitive power) is very mighty when it creates, as it were, another nature out of the material that actual nature gives it. We use it to entertain ourselves when experience strikes us as overly routine. We may even restructure experience; and though in doing so we continue to follow analogical laws, yet we also follow principles which reside higher up, namely, in reason (and which are just as natural to us as those which the understanding follows in apprehending empirical nature). In this process we feel our freedom from the law of association (which attaches to the empirical use of the imagination); for although it is under that law that nature lends us material, yet we can process that material into something quite different, namely, into something that surpasses nature.

If, after this analysis, we look back to the above explication of what we call *genius,* we find: *First,* genius is a talent for art, not for science, where we must start from distinctly known rules that determine the procedure we must use in it. *Second,* since it is an artistic talent, it presupposes a determinate concept of the product, namely, its purpose; hence genius presupposes understanding, but also a presentation (though an indeterminate one) of the material, i.e., of the intuition, needed to exhibit this concept, and hence presupposes a relation of imagination to understanding. *Third,* it manifests itself not so much in the fact that the proposed purpose is achieved in exhibiting a determinate concept, as, rather, in the way *aesthetic ideas,* which contain a wealth of material [suitable] for that intention, are offered or expressed; and hence it presents the imagination in its freedom from any instruction by rules, but still as purposive for exhibiting the given concept. Finally, *fourth,* the unstudied, unintentional subjective purposiveness in the imagination's free harmony with the understanding's lawfulness presupposes such a proportion and attunement of these powers as cannot be brought about by any compliance with rules, whether of science or of mechanical imitation, but can be brought about only by the subject's nature.

———◆◆◆———

§ 50
ON THE COMBINATION OF TASTE WITH GENIUS IN PRODUCTS OF FINE ART

. . . Taste, like the power of judgment in general, consists in disciplining (or training) genius. It severely clips its wings, and makes it civilized, or polished; but at the same time it gives it guidance as to how far and over what it may spread while still remaining purposive. It introduces clarity and order into a wealth of thought, and hence makes the ideas durable, fit for approval that is both lasting and universal, and [hence] fit for being followed by others and fit for an ever advancing culture. Therefore, if there is a conflict between these two properties in a product, and something has to be sacrificed, then it should rather be on the side of genius; and judgment, which in matters . . . of fine art bases its pronouncements on principles of its own, will sooner permit the imagination's freedom and wealth to be impaired than that the understanding be impaired.

Hence fine art would seem to require *imagination, understanding, spirit,* and *taste.*

Arthur Schopenhauer

ON
GENIUS

Arthur Schopenhauer (1788–1860) was a German philosopher most noted for his extreme pessimism about the human condition. Although he did not think that art could be our ultimate salvation, he did think that aesthetic experience was about the closest most people ever got to liberation from their desires, the source of all our problems in Schopenhauer's view. He defines genius in terms of the ability to see things from a disinterested aesthetic point of view and to communicate this condition to others.

. . . Originally and by its nature, knowledge is completely the servant of the will, and, like the immediate object which, by the application of the law of causality, becomes the starting-point of knowledge, is only objectified will. And so all knowledge which follows the principle of sufficient reason remains in a nearer or remoter relation to the will. For the individual finds his body as an object among objects, to all of which it has many different relations and connections according to the principle of sufficient reason. Hence a consideration of these always leads back, by a shorter or longer path, to his body, and thus to his will. As it is the principle of sufficient reason that places the objects in this relation to the body and so to the will, the sole endeavor of knowledge, serving this will, will be to get to know concerning objects just those relations that are laid down by the principle of sufficient reason, and thus to follow their many different connections in space, time, and causality. For only through these is the object *interesting* to the individual, in other words, has it a relation to the will. Therefore, knowledge that serves the will really knows nothing more about objects than their relations, knows the objects only in so far as they exist at such a time, in such a place, in such and such circumstances, from such and such causes, and in such and such effects—in a word, as particular things. If all these relations were eliminated, the objects also would have disappeared for knowledge, just because it did not recognize in them anything else. . . .

Now as a rule, knowledge remains subordinate to the service of the will, as indeed it came into being for this service; in fact, it

Arthur Schopenhauer, *The World as Will and Representation*, 2 vols., trans. E. F. J. Payne, vol. 1 (New York: Dover, 1969) 176–95.

sprang from the will, so to speak, as the head from the trunk. With the animals, this subjection of knowledge to the will can never be eliminated. With human beings, such elimination appears only as an exception, as will shortly be considered in more detail. . . .

As we have said, the transition that is possible, but to be regarded only as an exception, from the common knowledge of particular things to knowledge of the Idea takes place suddenly, since knowledge tears itself free from the service of the will precisely by the subject's ceasing to be merely individual, and being now a pure will-less subject of knowledge. Such a subject of knowledge no longer follows relations in accordance with the principle of sufficient reason; on the contrary, it rests in fixed contemplation of the object presented to it out of its connection with any other, and rises into this. . . .

Raised up by the power of the mind, we relinquish the ordinary way of considering things, and cease to follow under the guidance of the forms of the principle of sufficient reason merely their relations to one another, whose final goal is always the relation to our own will. Thus we no longer consider the where, the when, the why, and the whither in things, but simply and solely the *what*. Further, we do not let abstract thought, the concepts of reason, take possession of our consciousness, but, instead of all this, devote the whole power of our mind to perception, sink ourselves completely therein, and let our whole consciousness be filled by the calm contemplation of the natural object actually present, whether it be a landscape, a tree, a rock, a crag, a building, or anything else. We *lose* ourselves entirely in this object, to use a pregnant expression; in other words, we forget our individuality, our will, and continue to exist only as pure subject, as clear mirror of the object, so that it is as though the object alone existed without anyone to perceive it, and thus we

are no longer able to separate the perceiver from the perception, but the two have become one, since the entire consciousness is filled and occupied by a single image of perception. If, therefore, the object has to such an extent passed out of all relation to something outside it, and the subject has passed out of all relation to the will, what is thus known is no longer the individual thing as such, but the *Idea*, the eternal form, the immediate objectivity of the will at this grade. Thus at the same time, the person who is involved in this perception is no longer an individual, for in such perception the individual has lost himself; he is *pure will-less, painless, timeless subject of knowledge.* . . . Now in such contemplation, the particular thing at one stroke becomes the *idea* of its species, and the perceiving individual becomes the *pure subject of knowing.* The individual, as such, knows only particular things; the pure subject of knowledge knows only Ideas. For the individual is the subject of knowledge in its relation to a definite particular phenomenon of will and in subjection thereto. This particular phenomenon of will is, as such, subordinate to the principle of sufficient reason in all its forms; therefore all knowledge which relates itself to this, also follows the principle of sufficient reason, and no other knowledge than this is fit to be of any use to the will; it always has only relations to the object. The knowing individual as such and the particular thing known by him are always in a particular place, at a particular time, and are links in the chain of causes and effects. The pure subject of knowledge and its correlative, the Idea, have passed out of all these forms of the principle of sufficient reason. Time, place, the individual that knows, and the individual that is known, have no meaning for them. . . .

. . . But now, what kind of knowledge is it that considers what continues to exist outside and independently of all relations, but which alone is really essential to the world, the true content of its phenomena, that which is subject to no change, and is therefore known with equal truth for all time, in a word, the *Ideas* that are the immediate and adequate objectivity of the thing-in-itself, of the will? It is *art*, the work of genius. It repeats the eternal Ideas apprehended through pure contemplation, the essential and abiding element in all the phenomena of the world. According to the material in which it repeats, it is sculpture, painting, poetry, or music. Its only source is knowledge of the Ideas; its sole aim is communication of this knowledge. Whilst science, following the restless and unstable stream of the fourfold forms of reasons or grounds and consequents, is with every end it attains again and again directed farther, and can never find an ultimate goal or complete satisfaction, any more than by running we can reach the point where the clouds touch the horizon; art, on the contrary, is everywhere at its goal. For it plucks the object of its contemplation from the stream of the world's course, and holds it isolated before it. This particular thing, which in that stream was an infinitesimal part, becomes for art a representative of the whole, an equivalent of the infinitely many in space and time. It therefore pauses at this particular thing; it stops the wheel of time; for it the relations vanish; its object is only the essential, the Idea. . . . Only through the pure contemplation described above, which becomes absorbed entirely in the object, are the Ideas comprehended; and the nature of *genius* consists precisely in the preeminent ability for such contemplation. Now as this demands a complete forgetting of our own person and of its relations and connections, the *gift of genius* is nothing but the most complete *objectivity*, i.e., the objective tendency of the mind, as opposed to the subjective directed to our own person, i.e., to the will. Accordingly, genius is the capacity to remain in a state of pure perception, to lose oneself in perception, to remove from the service of the will

the knowledge which originally existed only for this service. In other words, genius is the ability to leave entirely out of sight our own interest, our willing, and our aims, and consequently to discard entirely our own personality for a time, in order to remain *pure knowing subject*, the clear eye of the world; and this not merely for moments, but with the necessary continuity and conscious thought to enable us to repeat by deliberate art what has been apprehended, and "what in wavering apparition gleams fix in its place with thoughts that stand for ever!" For genius to appear in an individual, it is as if a measure of the power of knowledge must have fallen to his lot far exceeding that required for the service of an individual will; and this superfluity of knowledge having become free, now becomes the subject purified of will, the clear mirror of the inner nature of the world. This explains the animation, amounting to disquietude, in men of genius, since the present can seldom satisfy them, because it does not fill their consciousness. This gives them that restless zealous nature, that constant search for new objects worthy of contemplation, and also that longing, hardly ever satisfied, for men of like nature and stature to whom they may open their hearts. The common mortal, on the other hand, entirely filled and satisfied by the common present, is absorbed in it, and, finding everywhere his like, has that special ease and comfort in daily life which are denied to the man of genius. Imagination has been rightly recognized as an essential element of genius; indeed, it has sometimes been regarded as identical with genius, but this is not correct. The objects of genius as such are the eternal Ideas, the persistent, essential forms of the world and of all its phenomena; but knowledge of the Idea is necessarily knowledge through perception, and is not abstract. Thus the knowledge of the genius would be restricted to the Ideas of objects actually present to his own person, and would be dependent on the concatenation of circumstances that brought them to him, did not imagination extend his horizon far beyond the reality of his personal experience, and enable him to construct all the rest out of the little that has come into his own actual apperception, and thus to let almost all the possible scenes of life pass by within himself. Moreover, the actual objects are almost always only very imperfect copies of the Idea that manifests itself in them. Therefore the man of genius requires imagination, in order to see in things not what nature has actually formed, but what she endeavored to form, yet did not bring about, because of the conflict of her forms with one another. . . . We shall return to this later, when considering sculpture. Thus imagination extends the mental horizon of the genius beyond the objects that actually present themselves to his person, as regards both quality and quantity. For this reason, unusual strength of imagination is a companion, indeed a condition, of genius. But the converse is not the case, for strength of imagination is not evidence of genius; on the contrary, even men with little or no touch of genius may have much imagination. . . .

As we have said, the common, ordinary man, that manufactured article of nature which she daily produces in thousands, is not capable, at any rate continuously, of a consideration of things wholly disinterested in every sense, such as is contemplation proper. He can direct his attention to things only in so far as they have some relation to his will, although that relation may be only very indirect. . . .

. . . On the other hand, the man of genius, whose power of knowledge is, through its excess, withdrawn for a part of his time from the service of his will, dwells on the consideration of life itself, strives to grasp the Idea of each thing, not its relations to other things. In doing this, he frequently neglects a consideration of his won path in life, and therefore often pursues this with insufficient skill. Whereas to the ordinary man his faculty of knowledge is a lamp that lights his path, to the man of genius it is the sun that reveals the world. This great difference in their way of looking at life soon becomes visible even in the outward appearance of them both. The glance of the man in whom genius lives and works readily distinguishes him; it is both vivid and firm and bears the character of thoughtfulness, of contemplation. We can see this in the portraits of the few men of genius which nature has produced here and there among countless millions. On the other hand, the real opposite of contemplation, namely spying or prying, can be readily seen in the glance of others, if indeed it is not dull and vacant, as is often the case. Consequently a face's "expression of genius" consists in the fact that a decided predominance of knowing over willing is visible in it, and hence that there is manifested in it a knowledge without any relation to a will, in other words, a *pure knowing*. On the other hand, in the case of faces that follow the rule, the expression of the will predominates, and we see that knowledge comes into activity only on the impulse of the will, and so is directed only to motives.

As the knowledge of the genius, or knowledge of the Idea, is that which does not follow the principle of sufficient reason, so, on the other hand, the knowledge that does follow this principle gives us prudence and rationality in life, and brings about the sciences. Thus individuals of genius will be affected with the defects entailed in the neglect of the latter kind of knowledge. Here, however, a limitation must be observed, that what I shall state in this regard concerns them only in so far as, and while, they are actually engaged with the kind of knowledge peculiar to the genius. Now this is by no means the case at every moment of their lives, for the great though spontaneous exertion required for the will-free comprehension of the Ideas necessarily relaxes again, and there are long intervals during which men of genius stand in very much the same position as ordinary persons, both as regards merits and defects. On this account, the action of genius has always been regarded as an inspiration, as indeed the name itself indicates, as the action of a superhuman being different from the individual himself, which takes possession of him only periodically. . . . A prudent man will not be a genius insofar as and while he is prudent, and a genius will not be prudent insofar as and while he is a genius. Finally, knowledge of perception generally, in the province of which the Idea entirely lies, is directly opposed to rational or abstract knowledge which is guided by the principle of the ground of knowing. It is also well known that we seldom find great genius united with preeminent reasonableness; on the contrary, men of genius are often subject to violent emotions and irrational passions. But the cause of this is not weakness of the faculty of reason, but partly unusual energy of that whole phenomenon of will, the individual genius. This phenomenon manifests itself through vehemence of all his acts of will. The cause is also partly a preponderance of knowledge from perception through the sense and the understanding over abstract knowledge, in other words, a decided tendency to the perceptive. In such men the extremely energetic impression of the perceptive outshines the colorless concepts so much that conduct is no longer guided by the latter, but by the former, and on this very account becomes irrational. Accordingly, the impression of the present moment on them is very strong, and carries them away into thoughtless actions, into emotion and passion. Moreover, since their knowledge has generally been withdrawn in part from the service of the will, they will not in conversation think so much of the person with whom they are speaking as of the thing they are speaking about, which is vividly present in their

minds. Therefore they will judge or narrate too objectively for their own interests; they will not conceal what it would be more prudent to keep concealed, and so on. Finally, they are inclined to soliloquize, and in general may exhibit several weaknesses that actually are closely akin to madness. . . .

. . . That which exists in the actual individual thing, only imperfectly and weakened by modifications, is enhanced to perfection, to the Idea of it, by the method of contemplation used by the genius. Therefore he everywhere sees extremes, and on this account his own actions tend to extremes. He does not know how to strike the mean; he lacks cool-headedness, and the result is as we have said. He knows the Ideas perfectly, but not the individuals. Therefore it has been observed that a poet may know *man* profoundly and thoroughly, but *men* very badly; he is easily duped, and is a plaything in the hands of the cunning and crafty.

Now according to our explanation, genius consists in the ability to know, independently of the principle of sufficient reason, not individual things which have their existence only in the relation, but the Ideas of such things, and in the ability to be, in face of these, the correlative of the Idea, and hence no longer individual, but pure subject of knowing. Yet this ability must be inherent in all men in a lesser and different degree, as otherwise they would be just as incapable of enjoying works of art as of producing them. Generally they would have no susceptibility at all to the beautiful and to the sublime; indeed, these words could have no meaning for them. We must therefore assume as existing in all men that power of recognizing in things their Ideas, of divesting themselves for a moment of their personality, unless indeed there are some who are not capable of any aesthetic pleasure at all. The man of genius excels them only in the far higher degree and more continuous duration of this kind of knowledge. These enable him to retain that thoughtful contemplation necessary for him to repeat what is thus known in a voluntary and intentional work, such repetition being the work of art. Through this he communicates to others the Idea he has grasped. Therefore this Idea remains unchanged and the same, and hence aesthetic pleasure is essentially one and the same, whether it be called forth by a work of art, or directly by the contemplation of nature and of life. The work of art is merely a means of facilitating that knowledge in which this pleasure consists. That the Idea comes to us more easily from the work of art than directly from nature and from reality, arises solely from the fact that the artist, who knew only the Idea and not reality, clearly repeated in his work only the Idea, separated it out from reality, and omitted all disturbing contingencies.

Rainer Maria Rilke

LETTERS TO A YOUNG POET

Rainer Maria Rilke (1875–1926) was a Czech-born Austrian poet. His most famous works are the "Duino Elegies" and "The Sonnets to Orpheus." The Letters to a Young Poet *(1929) stem from Rilke's correspondence with a nineteen-year-old military student. The latter discovered that Rilke had spent a year at the same military school and wrote to Rilke asking for advice about his writing.*

You ask whether your verses are any good. You ask me. You have asked others before this. You send them to magazines. You compare them with other poems, and you are upset when certain editors reject your work. Now (since you have said you want my advice) I beg you to stop doing that sort of thing. You are looking outside, and that is what you should most avoid right now.

No one can advise or help you—no one. There is only one thing you should do. Go into yourself. Find out the reason that commands you to write; see whether it has spread its roots into the very depths of your heart; confess to yourself whether you would have to die if you were forbidden to write. This most of all: ask yourself in the most silent hour of your night: *must* I write? Dig into yourself for a deep answer. And if this answer rings out in assent, if you meet this solemn question with a strong, simple "*I must*," then build your life in accordance with this necessity; your whole life, even into its humblest and most indifferent hour, must become a sign and witness to this impulse. Then come close to Nature. Then, as if no one had ever tried before, try to say what you see and feel and love and lose. Don't write love poems; avoid those forms that are too facile and ordinary: they are the hardest to work with, and it takes a great, fully ripened power to create something individual where good, even glorious, traditions exist in abundance. So rescue yourself from these general themes and write about

Rainer Maria Rilke, *Letters to a Young Poet*, trans. Stephen Mitchell (New York: Random House, 1984) 5–8, 54–56.

what your everyday life offers you; describe your sorrows and desires, the thoughts that pass through your mind and your belief in some kind of beauty—describe all these with heartfelt, silent, humble sincerity and, when you express yourself, use the Things around you, the images from your dreams, and the objects that you remember. If your everyday life seems poor, don't blame *it*; blame yourself; admit to yourself that you are not enough of a poet to call forth its riches . . .

What is necessary, after all, is only this: solitude, vast inner solitude. To walk inside yourself and meet no one for hours—that is what you must be able to attain. To be solitary as you were when you were a child, when the grownups walked around involved with matters that seemed large and important because *they* looked so busy and because you didn't understand a thing about what they were doing.

And when you realize that their activities are shabby, that their vocations are petrified and no longer connected with life, why not then continue to look upon it all as a child would, as if you were looking at something unfamiliar, out of the depths of your own world, from the vastness of your own solitude, which is itself work and status and vocation? Why should you want to give up a child's wise not-understanding in exchange for defensiveness and scorn, since not-understanding is, after all, a way of being alone, whereas defensiveness and scorn are a participation in precisely what, by these means, you want to separate yourself from. . . .

Anne Truitt

DAYBOOK:
THE JOURNAL
OF AN ARTIST

Anne Truitt is a sculptor with works in the collections of the Museum of Modern Art, the National Gallery of Art, and the Metropolitan Museum of Art. Truitt kept a journal about her activity as an artist over a seven-year period. The selection consists of excerpts from this journal, published as Daybook: The Journal of an Artist. *Truitt is also author of* Turn.

Flying over the desert yesterday, I found myself lifted out of my preoccupations by noticing suddenly that everything was curved. Seen whole from the air, circumscribed by its global horizon, the earth confronted me bluntly as a context all its own, echoing that grand sweep. I had the startling impression that I was looking at something intelligent. Every delicate pulsation of color was met, matched, challenged, repulsed, embraced by another, none out of proportion, each at once unique and a proper part of the whole. The straight lines with which human beings have marked the land are impositions of a different intelligence, abstract in this arena of the natural. Looking down at these facts, I began to see my life as somewhere between these two orders of the natural and the abstract, belonging entirely neither to the one nor to the other.

In my work as an artist I am accustomed to sustaining such tensions: A familiar position between my senses, which are natural, and my intuition of an order they both mask and illuminate. When I draw a straight line or conceive of an arrangement of tangible elements all my own, I inevitably impose my own order on matter. I actualize this order, rendering it accessible to my senses. It is not so accessible until actualized.

An eye for this order is crucial for an artist. I notice that as I live from day to day, observing and feeling what goes on both inside and outside myself, certain aspects of what is happening adhere to me, as if magnetized by a center of psychic gravity. I have learned to trust this center, to rely on its acuity and to go along with its choices although the center itself remains mysterious to me. I sometimes feel as if I *recognize*

Anne Truitt, *Daybook: The Journal of an Artist* (New York: Penguin, 1982) 10–13, 41, 63–64, 66–68, 93–94, 117–19, 142–43.

my own experience. It is a feeling akin to that of unexpectedly meeting a friend in a strange place, of being at once startled and satisfied—startled to find outside myself what feels native to me, satisfied to be so met. It is exhilarating.

I have found that this process of selection, over which I have virtually no control, isolates those aspects of my experience that are most essential to me in my work because they echo my own attunement to what life presents me. It is as if there are external equivalents for truths which I already in some mysterious way know. In order to catch these equivalents, I have to stay "turned on" all the time, to keep my receptivity to what is around me totally open. Preconception is fatal to this process. Vulnerability is implicit in it; pain, inevitable.

———◆◆◆———

8 JUNE

My hand is out. I feel it a numb weight hanging off my right arm as if no longer quick with life. The marks on my fine-grained drawing paper are simply marks, physical traces as meaningless as chicken tracks in the dirt. This is not a new thing to me and is, I suppose, the analogue of writer's block. Some vital connection in my spirit has gone flaccid. I have learned over the years (there is always the frightening shadow—is it forever?) how to behave. Rest is a concept that seems easy to understand, but I do not find it so, for it is precisely those overstrained parts of myself that persist most obstinately to jangle. . . .

9 JUNE

Consciousness seems to me increasingly inconceivable. I know more and more that I know nothing of its nature, range, and force except what I experience through the slot of this physical body. The tie to my body may *feel* stronger than it *is*. So it seems anyway when I remember how I occasionally hold myself separate from it. Yet I baulk. When

we love one another the most delicate truth of that love is held in the spirit, but my body is the record of those I have loved. I feel their bones as my bones, almost literally. This record is autonomous. It continues, dumbly, to persist. Its power is independent of time. The love is fixed, instantly accessible to memory, somehow stained into my body as color into cloth.

All bodies have this record. It is the magic of drawing them. Here, where my pencil touches the paper, is the place at which a body holds itself intact. The line marks, with infinite tenderness, the experience of a body—a separate unknowable experience inside the line, space outside it. . . .

25 JULY

The terms of the experience and the terms of the work itself are totally different. But if the work is successful—I cannot ever know whether it is or not—the experience becomes the work and, through the work, is accessible to others with its original force.

For me, this process is mysterious. It's like not knowing where you're going but knowing how to get there. The fifteen years that David Smith thought it took to become an artist are spent partly in learning how to move ahead sure-footedly as if you did actually know where you are going.

——————

10 SEPTEMBER

The familiar strain of sustaining the various demands of daily life is once again a whine in the back of my mind. As I move from cleaning the house to washing and ironing to cooking to work in the studio to helping the children with their homework, even in the atmosphere of satisfaction these activities evoke, their inexorable sequence jerks my body into a faster pattern of response than is natural to it.

I could lower my standards but in so doing would sink with them, taking my children with me. It is not necessary for us to have candlelit dinners every night. But the ceremony of meals has always been important to regard. Where else can children learn so easily and pleasantly, and at such range when guests are included, what it is to be grown-up? The world of children is fascinating but very personal. The presence of adults in the full cry of conversation, with opinions, interests, engagements, and responsibilities discussed, crisscrossed by agreements and disagreements, laced with rhetoric, is so pungent with variety that children can learn without harm to their self-respect that they are, for all their interest to themselves, on their way to larger definitions.

Doing my duty as well as I can is essentially self-serving. It is only by attending to tasks and responsibilities as they arise that I can prevent myself from feeling angry that I cannot work in the studio as much as I want to. This is particularly true now, fresh as I am from the time at Yaddo when I was free from all demands other than those I made of myself. Anger at once excites and deadens my mind. The only answer to it I have found is efficiency. So I have tried to train myself always to keep abreast of the household routine in order to set myself free for clear concentration in the studio.

18 SEPTEMBER

I did not see a painting of high quality until I was thirteen. One hot afternoon, my father took my sisters and me to a friend's house to swim. We were led through a wide central hall at the end of which a screen door opened out onto a sunny lawn bordering a broad river. On the left of this door hung a small painting, the head of a girl in brilliant, clear colors. I gazed, transfixed. I remember swiftly calculating whether it would be rude to ask about it. I felt shy to thrust my curiosity forward, but I was

blocking the way as I stood in front of it and I finally found it less awkward to ask who had made it. "Reno," was the answer, "a French painter." Pressed by our small group, I moved on, but I have remembered the radiance of that little painting ever since, along with the dazzling insight that such beauty could be *made*.

Now, when I am called upon to look critically at the work of another artist, I watch for this response—the spontaneous rise of my whole being.

This instantaneous recognition of quality has been very, very rare in my experience with artists I am called upon to gauge, and in these modest circumstances I make it a habit to start by coming to respectful attention. It is such an act of courage to put pencil to paper that I begin by honoring the artist's intention.

Usually the work falls into a range I have to examine with my mind, in the light of what I know about the history of art and about its techniques. If the work is the result of honest effort, I acknowledge its validity but I look for the skill and talent that set apart potentially significant art. I try to discern the range of the artist's gift. When this range coincides with contemporary artistic concerns, the work has cogency in an historical context. This seems to me to be a matter of luck. A perfectly articulated range of sensibility may be just plain irrelevant to the problems confronting artists ambitious to make work of the highest quality in this historical sense. The degree to which an artist addresses these problems usually indicates the degree of his or her ambition. There is a sort of "feel" that marks relevant art. To some extent it can be learned, and here I find that young artists can badly deceive themselves: They can fall into using intelligence the wrong way; they can fail to realize that the purpose of scanning contemporary art is to use its articulations for the purer realization of their own work. As a carpenter might reach out for a newly invented saw, the work of other artists may suggest techniques or even solutions. But the essential struggle is private and bears no relation to anyone else's. It is of necessity a solitary and lonely endeavor to explore one's own sensibility, to discover how it works and to implement honestly its manifestations.

It is ultimately character that underwrites art. The quality of art can only reflect the quality and range of a person's sensitivity, intellect, perception, and experience. If I find an artist homing in on himself or herself, I bring maximum warmth to bear, knowing full well that the process is painful and, lonely as it is, susceptible to encouragement. Companionship helps. And the pleasure of being with younger or less experienced artists can be intense—the delight of watching people grow into themselves, becoming more than they have known that they are.

Sometimes artists use their work for ends that have nothing to do with art, placing it rather in the service of their ambitions for themselves in the world. This forces their higher parts to serve their lower parts in a sad inversion of values. And is, in art perhaps more than in any other profession, self-defeating. Purity of aspiration seems virtually prerequisite to genuine inspiration.

—◆◆◆—

2 NOVEMBER

In the last few months, I have become more conscious of how my work takes form. It sometimes happens unexpectedly. Just as I wake up, a series of three sculptures may present themselves somewhere that seems high over my head in my consciousness. They simply materialize, whole and themselves, in a rather stately way, and stand there, categorical in their simplicity. This can happen anywhere, not necessarily just after waking, but, characteristically, without any preparation on my part. Sometimes a single piece will appear; never more than three at once. I cannot make them all. Less than a quarter of them ever reach actuality.

Other pieces result from a more or less conscious concentration on a particular area of emotionally charged personal experience—a person, say, or a series of events, or a period in my life. I have some small degree of control over this kind of formation in that I decide whether or not to accept it. I can postpone crystallization until I have finished a previous piece that is already begun and for which I have a structure fabricated, undercoated, and ready to accept its being into itself. I try to hold the process of conception to a reasonable pace. There seems no end to this kind of formulation. These concepts hover, already complete, it would seem, on the edge of my consciousness. In the early sixties, when all this was new to me, I used to be overwhelmed and would wake up in the middle of the night flooded, inundated by peremptory demands for making these sculptures. We, they and I, have by now worked out a *modus vivendi*.

The force of my concentration can also be directed toward single visual events: a glimpse of radiant space, a plant in a lake, a juxtaposition of weights and shapes that matches, touches off, some powerful resonance in me. Certain sensory experiences elicit, draw forth into clarity, what visually they only infer. The laws they exemplify seem to spring from behind them, organizing a whole of form and color that lies just beyond what my senses apprehend.

Landfall, for example, came to me by itself, unexpectedly. I was driving to the studio at 1928 Calvert Street about 10:00 A.M. on a cool, rainy, windy day. I had opened the window beside me to feel the air, and rain hit my face in gusts. I put my head out into it and on the inside, behind my eyes, I was in a long, shallow, open wooden boat, multi-oared and with belling, rectangular, maroon sails, in wind-roughened waves. It was just after dawn; the sun, still tender, was behind me. Ahead, low on the western horizon, lay a coast just discernible as beach: landfall.

——◆◆◆——

10 JANUARY

There is an appalling amount of mechanical work in the artist's life: lists of works with dimensions, prices, owners, provenances; lists of exhibitions with dates and places; bibliographical material; lists of supplies bought, storage facilities used. Records pile on records. This tedious, detailed work, which steadily increases if the artist exhibits to any extent, had been something of a surprise to me. It is all very well to be entranced by working in the studio, but that has to be backed up by the common sense and industry required to run a small business. In trying to gauge the capacity of young artists to achieve their ambition, I always look to see whether they seem to have this ability to organize their lives into an order that will not only set their hands free in the studio but also meet the demands their work will make upon them when it leaves the studio. The "enemies of promise," in Kyrie Connolly's phrase, are subtle, guileful, and resourceful. Talent is mysterious, but the qualities that guard, foster, and direct it are not unlike those of a good quartermaster.

11 JANUARY

. . . The point at which decision is brought to bear on process is that at which two opposing forces meet and rebound, leaving an interval in which a third force can act. The trick of acting is to catch this moment. When it all happens well, a happy feeling of swinging from event to event results, a sort of gymnastic pleasure. Yesterday Renato thought an exhibition room should be unified by pigeon gray; John thought the photographs would line up into nonentity in such a flat environment. They turned to me. I suggested a third solution incorporating both insights; we all rose to it and took the wave of decision as one.

It was Gurdjieff who dissected this process for me to examine, and I like to watch it happening. His analysis of process into octaves is also fascinating to me, and very helpful. An undertaking, he says, begins with a surge of energy that carries it a certain distance toward completion. There then occurs a drop in energy, which must be lifted back to an effective level by conscious effort, in my experience by bringing to bear hard purpose. It is here that years of steady application to a specific process can come into play. It is, however, in the final stage, just before completion, that Gurdjieff says pressure mounts almost unendurably to a point at which it is necessary to bring to bear an even more special kind of effort. It is at this point, when idea is on the verge of bursting into physicality, that I find myself meeting maximum difficulty. I sometimes have the curious impression that the physical system seems in its very nature to *resist* its invasion by idea. The desert wishes to lie in the curves of its own being: It resists the imposition of the straight line across its natural pattern. Matter itself seems to have some mysterious intransigency.

It is at this critical point that most failures seem to me to occur. The energy required to push the original concept into actualization, to finish it, has quite a different qualitative feel from the effort needed to bring it to this point. It is this strange, higher-keyed energy to which I find I have to pay attention—to court, so to speak, by living in a particular way. Years of training build experience capable of holding a process through the second stage. The opposition of purpose to natural indolence, the friction of this opposition, maintained year after year, seems to create a situation that attracts this mysterious third force, the curious fiery energy required to raise an idea into realization. Whether or not it does so attract remains a mystery.

——◆◆◆——

6 MARCH

The tendency to complete a *Gestalt* is so strong that it is surprising so many people have trouble finishing tasks. It just shows the inherent difficulty of getting anything physical accomplished. Matter is stubborn. Only dogged effort brings a concept into an arena in which it can demand the serious attention we give a challenge to our own physical selves. It is here that "conceptual art" tends to be, using Alexandra's adjective, "lame." The concept, remaining merely conceptual, falls short of the bite of physical presence. Just one step away is the debilitating idea that a concept is as forceful in its conception as in its realization.

I see that this might be considered an intelligent move. The world is cluttered with objects anyway. The ideas in my head are invariably more radiant than what is under my hand. But something puritanical and tough in me won't take that fence. The poem has to be written, the painting painted, the sculpture wrought. The beds have to be made, the food cooked, the dishes done, the clothes washed and ironed. Life just seems to me irremediably about coping with the physical.

—◆◆◆—

27 MARCH

The change itself was set off by a weekend trip to New York with my friend, Mary Pinchot Meyer, in November 1961, almost one year to the day after Sam's birth. We went up on Saturday and spent the afternoon looking at art. This was my first concentrated exposure since 1957, when I had moved to San Francisco, and I was astonished to note the freedom with which materials of various sorts were being used. More specifically, how they were being *put to use*. That is, I noticed that the materials were used without particular attention to their intrinsic bent, as if what I had always thought of as their natural characteristics was being disregarded. For the first time, I grasped the fact that art could spring from concept, and medium could be in its service.

I had always rooted myself in process, the thrust of my endeavor being to seek patiently and unremittingly how an idea would *emerge* from a material. My insight into the art I saw that afternoon reversed this emphasis, throwing the balance of meaning from material to idea. And this reversal released me from the limitations of material into the exhilarating arena of my own spirit.

At the Guggenheim Museum, I saw my first Ad Reinhardt. I was baffled by what looked to be an all black painting and enchanted when Mary pointed out the delicate changes in hue. I remember feeling a wave of gratitude—to her for showing me such an incredibly beautiful fact and to the painter for having made it to be seen. Farther along the museum's ramp, a painting constructed with wooden sticks and planes also caught my attention, setting off a kind of home feeling; I do not remember the artist's name but I liked his using plain old wood such as I had seen all my life in carpentry. And when we rounded into the lowest semi-circular gallery, I saw my first Barnett Newman, a universe of blue paint by which I was immediately ravished. My whole self lifted into it. "Enough" was my radiant feeling—for once in my life enough space, enough color. It seemed to me that I had never before been free. Even running in a field had not given me the same airy beautitude. I would not have believed it possible had I not seen it with my own eyes. Such openness wiped out with one swoop all my puny ideas. I staggered out into the street, intoxicated with freedom, lifted into a realm I had not dreamed could be caught into existence. I was completely taken by surprise, the more so as I had only earlier that day been thinking how I felt like a plowed field, my children all born, my life laid out; I saw myself stretched like brown earth in furrows, open to the sky, well planted, my life as a human being complete. My yearning for a family, my husband and my children, had been satisfied. I had looked for no more in the human sense and had felt content.

I went home early to Mary's mother's apartment, where we were staying, thinking I would sleep and absorb in self-forgetfulness the fullness of the day. Instead, I stayed up almost the whole night, sitting wakeful in the middle of my bed like a frog on a lily pad. Even three baths spaced through the night failed to still my mind, and at some time during these long hours I decided, hugging myself with determined delight, to make exactly what *I* wanted to make. The tip of balance from the physical to the conceptual in art had set me to thinking about my life in a whole new way. What did I *know*, I asked myself. What did I *love?* What was it that meant the very most to me inside my very own self? The fields and trees and fences and boards and lattices of my childhood rushed across my inner eye as if borne by a great, strong wind. I saw them all, detail and panorama, and my feeling for them welled up to sweep me into the knowledge that I could make them. I knew that that was exactly what I was going to do and how I was going to do it.

Christopher Middleton

ON THE
MENTAL
IMAGE

Christopher Middleton is a poet, essayist, translator, maker of collages, and professor emeritus of German languages and literature at the University of Texas at Austin. He has written many books of poetry, including The Pursuit of the Kingfisher, Pataxanadu, Two Horse Wagon Going By, *and* The Balcony Tree. *In the following excerpt from his essay "On the Mental Image," Middleton describes the capricious and volatile way that mental images operate in the creation of art on the basis of his experience as a poet.*

Le temps vu à travers l'image est un temps perdu de vue. L'être et le temps sont bien différents. L'image scintille éternelle, quand elle a dépassé l'être et le temps.

[The time that is seen through an image is a time that is lost from view. Being and time are very different. The image scintillates eternally, having transcended being and time.]

—René Char

I should begin by saying that the term *mental image* which shifts through several contexts here has no connection with recently popular ideas about "visualization." Those ideas seem to have been marketed with a view to reminding people that imagination is by no means the privilege of a few. Yet world peace, or whatever else besides, is not likely to be achieved just because some people are busy visualizing it. My concern is really the disruptive and eruptive character of a certain kind of mental image. It is a kind that cannot be willed across the gaps that yawn, or through the shadow that falls, between possibilities of being which are mystically imagined, and the way this world historically unfolds.

Certainly a large mental image can sweep through a whole nation and achieve consensual or hegemonic status. Hence in ancient Israel and Byzantium the sustained and ruthless politicking against idolatry, as if excessive reification of mental image could unbridle demons, threaten the numinous itself with lifeterm imprisonment, and promote (among illiterates) an urge to pester

Another version of this essay appeared in *P. N. Review* 102 (1995).

with primitive desires the subtlest presences. Social benefits of widespread floating visualization, as well as blockage of life by idolatries, are unquantifiable matters, to say the least. Moreover, as E. P. Thompson has remarked, "It is quite possible for statistical averages and human experience to run in opposite directions."[1] Positive thinking can certainly help people who are otherwise not inclined to think at all; but who is to measure what total outcome a massive act of imagination might have? True, the simplistic visualization idea opposes mass-media hypnotism. It may even intend to mitigate or reverse such hypnotism. But taking the economic status quo for granted it overlooks the labyrinthine obstacles which beset the best of wills in any modern community. Such ideas betray, too, their wide-eyed utopian character: often the marketers of wishful thinking (visualized or not) are instruments of evil, evil as a real though mysterious obstructive power in the mass urban-technological frameworks into which most people are locked.

The conception of a mental image that I will be outlining does arise from questions that occur to most of us. How do mental images occur in the first place, presenting themselves unbidden? How do they imbed ideas, how do ideas come to be mounted on them? Is any kind of mental activity accompanied by involuntarily produced mental images, whether sharp or vague? How do mental images regulate perspectives in which, individually or collectively, we come to view and interpret experience? What is the role of language in shaping mental images, those we entertain in dreams and those we navigate by when awake?

Questions like these have often been asked. The answers have been many and not always conflicting. For the patriarchs of modern philosophy, Kant and Hegel, the mental image is something of a nuisance: at worst an obstacle in the path of intellect toward a "pure" concept, at best a forceps

for delivering the concept. For psychoanalysts a mental image is a deep, commanding, and flexible apparatus, but one that can come unstuck. The unstuck apparatus may be a source of suffering; it may also be a breach through which identifiable and pacifiable subconscious structures are assaulting the sufferer's ego. My argument is that anyone's fugitive images fuel their dominant mental images; the dominant ones, however, may derive from a ferment which occurs spontaneously in the nervous system after certain key experiences have been repeatedly channelled into the system. Dominant mental images take on emotional qualities so impressive that their carrier, the person, dances to their tune. Further, a mental image will have a core and rind; its repetitious intrinsic features as well as fugitive extrinsic features may sometimes be barely distinguishable.

Next, a strong mental image is resistant and positive: it shapes the stuff of experience and posits your tacit perspective on experience. With no mental image to navigate with, experience might crush you. Thanks to it, experience can enliven and enlighten you—it can be distanced and made significant. Blent as it is from sensory experience that you assimilate, blent into intrinsic patterns dictated (or at least sketched) by your nervous system, any strong (but not necessarily dominant) mental image that you project upon experience serves you as a kind of compass. The compass may not be altogether reliable. An image in which a dominant idea is secretly imbedded, an idea mounted upon an unacknowledged or quaking image, can together dilate monstrous delusions. Yet an uncertainty proper to the image or to the relation between image and idea does open up the realms of choice and combination. You can choose what to think and do (either this or that), but you can also combine options (both this and that) without confusing them. Hence the usefulness of the uncertain or unacknowledged image; its power is propulsive as long as it does not warp or inhibit intelligence.

The behaviour of a mental image, unpredictable as it may be, is one means by which you experience discrepancy, difference, variance, conflict, tension. A mental image, let's say, works as a compass equipped with a shock-absorber. It absorbs and distills pleasurable and painful experiences and combines them—the extrinsic aspect; yet that blended distillation is already patterned by intrinsic impulses from "deep down" inside the secret, or culturally imprinted, recesses of the nervous system. Its deeper patterning sets a dominant mental image off against the spaces and times which we vaguely differentiate into foreground, middle ground, and background (to each his own chronotope). Here I might brashly rephrase Kafka: The Messenger has memorized the message confided to him by the dying Emperor and through impenetrable interiors of time and space he is carrying it to you. Instead of dreaming that this is so, you can get up and go seek the Messenger. An imagineer needs to withdraw from ego-addiction and advance individuality by working with the psyche.

Observations as general as these suggest that a distinction now needs to be made between two orders of mental imagery. Each of these orders is a labyrinth of variables. Whether or not the labyrinths touch or embrace each other along a sliding axis, who knows. Closer to the forefront of a brain's operations, first, there will be the play of images around a thought. An image will shadow thought, before, around, or behind. Nouns we utter—ice cream, highrise, music, liberty—whether the referents are concrete or abstract, each of us "pictures" the referents in an individual way. During reflection also the retina is not inactive. A picture on it may be vestigial and fugitive, but it can become sharp, it can take on a fuller shape, when what we name is not there for the asking or for the beholding. With picturing fictions we people the unseen. Even when thought has been rigorously exercised to arrive at a "hard concept," thus even in abstraction, some concrete residue is apt to cling to discourse, weakly or marginally visualized (proleptically or analeptically) as an image of this forefrontal order, which may harden into a world view.

Then there is another order of imagery. This does not merely shadow but can possibly engender the concept; it is an imagery, too, which may recoil from contact with discourse. This other imagery, no less volatile than the shadowing kind, is psychologically potent. What is more, this other imagery cannot be willed or bidden into discourse. It cannot be bidden, somewhat as a breathtaking metaphor cannot be forced and cannot be transcoded. The oft mistaken foreign language of the unconscious makes cryptic even the voices of the dead. The arousal of this other imagery is involuntary, I suggest, and its forms are wild and complex. Emphatically it is other than things and other than representations. If it is ever akin to the image such as Bergson conceived of it, then it might intervene between things and representations. A person who has experienced the way this other imagery erupts spontaneously into thought and disaggregates ordinary language, or I might say disconcerts the hierarchy of language duties that we call decorum, is likely to suspect that a projective mode of imagining such as this might be a womb for thought, generally antecedent even to the keenest philosophical modes of conceiving and thinking—antecedent to any containing dialectic.

But is it a picture at all that this other imagery designs as it flies across a field of consciousness? What it designs may certainly possess some pictorial features. The fact often overlooked is that the pictorial rind adhering to images of this order is often rather makeshift, often a sensory consortium. The flesh itself—to pursue the analogy—is vivid with aural, tactile, and olfactory tones, which, even without displacing the visual rind, are singularly patterned as drama or narrative. The singular patterning includes intervals also, silences that can be divined as having volume. Volatile as the patterning may be, it surrounds a core that is we know not what: perhaps a furnace in which neural energy is refined, desire condensed and directed, the craving for life prepared. Some kind of nemesis follows abuse of this other imagery—a burning out or shutting down of the furnace in madness or in melancholy. History tells how such consequences may be inflicted catastrophically on whole societies.

Here I should bring, sketchily enough, art into the outline. The profound antagonism between truth and words, or else their tacit contract of mutual evasion, procures a freedom of play, active somehow in the genesis of mental images. Perhaps in a general way they are safeguards against a complete and suffocating enclosure of the psyche in the prison of language. The freedom to play, the ludic factor in imagination, also sets certain kinds of aesthetically actualized images apart from ordinary nominal ones. The counterordinary, sometimes countersensically mental images are the ones we value in works of art, pictures or poems. We may call such ludic images "representations of reality," but that is only a fraction of a larger story in which non-mimetic events may be paramount. What is represented is what is different, discrepant, and conflictual for and in the imagination which has shaped into the actuality of writing or painting an image of its own desperate and delighted making. The oddity of the image communicated in a work of art may consist in its being altogether independent of reference to any acknowledged phenomenon. So the image in art points through the known to the unknown. The "unknown" can also be

the way in which this or that object of imagination is perceived and so presented: not a fancy mystery at all, nothing absolutely other, but a technical mode of beholding and articulating the altogether ordinary. The medium with a strange moulding (*pétrissage* is what Francis Ponge calls it) rescues the object, pronounces it afresh, as a field of events. For that is how an iconic organization works. "Experience," Oliver Sacks tells us, "is not *possible* unless it is organized iconically . . . 'The brain's record' of everything—everything alive—must be iconic. This is the final form of the brain's record, even though the preliminary form may be computational or programmatic. . . ."[2] The neurological data should warn (but have not, apparently) levellers, whatever their socio-philosophical persuasion, that language is misconstrued if its heterogeneous functions, vistas, and horizons, are reduced to any one allegedly inclusive "discourse." Poetic structures properly fired, small or large, arise more directly and more resistantly from the iconogonic (image-creating, imaginative) sources of conceptualization than such texts as do lend themselves to levelling paraphrase. Networks of concepts have, too, their "dark sides"—their iconic organization.

◆◆◆

Anticipatory or not, a mental image can seldom be seized on as a complete picture. It tends to be fragmentary, until a great artist comes along and creates a synthesis which tells people what they didn't know they were thinking. A mental image also tends to compose itself in leaps, rather than continuously, as new elements flow into it, fresh contradictions oppose it. It is capricious, whether vague or sharp. It blends into thinking, but it is not thought. It is volatile, but into feeling it presses graphic shapes, designs that glow, independently of appetition. Perhaps there is a relatively constant dynamic in its emergence, marked by observable stages. The initial ferment impinges, unbidden, on the outer "skin" of consciousness. Then gradually it engages with experience, including language, and the image ascends, irresistible, freed from the ferment, living a many-layered life of its own, but soon to be modified by further experience, modified and possibly distorted. Then it comes to persist, in your knowledge that distortion, though anomalous, is essential to its force. Later the image may subside, you view it in the round, and are not at all attached to it. Or it will go back into the ferment, until, revived, there it is again, actively otherwise.

I'd like next to illustrate in concrete terms the outline so far suggested.

After the five-hour bus ride from Antalya to Anamur, on the Turkish Mediterranean coast, I am ready to find the little hotel described in my French guidebook: rose-colored rooms upstairs, overlooking a charmed garden. A taxi takes me at top speed up the usual battered and dusty streets, between the usual dusty and battered buildings, and I arrive: upstairs I step out on to the little balcony and see the peaks of mountains inland.

Below me there is a walled garden with a willow tree in it, poplars I notice next, then palm trees and pines. A vine spreads its web across the wooden supports of a trellis. Unidentifiable edible plants grow in a dozen rows, dusty green. Some chickens, some goats are rambling around, engrossed in their search for food. I'd thought I might hear the sea but discover that it is two miles away.

A description like this—nominal language again—relays no sense of the excitement with which I was perceiving what I saw and heard from the balcony. Setting the words down in their order I drain the substance off my images. What about the smells, for instance? Woodsmoke, diesel fumes, goat,

the hot and thickish smell of Turkish dust. And sounds: relayed by loudspeaker the taped chant of the muezzin calling now from his minaret, a forlorn trumpeting, criss-crossed with another taped chant from another minaret. And chickens clucking. Also the color of the walls: with dismay I see they aren't really rose, but a dull peach, cheery enough but reminiscent of an asylum. Rose, in my imagination it had evoked a velvet feeling. I had anticipated nightfall, a kiosk, Turkish music, a vine-embroidered emerald kiosk with silken girls bringing sherbet. Those features of the image in my mind outran all the nominal words and all the real objects I saw and smelled and heard. No doubt a false transcendence. Mental images can easily bind together the fibers of false consciousness. But at least I was now a step beyond the facile language of the guidebook.

So out I soon went to search for my velvet and emerald kiosk. Where is the lute being softly plucked? Where is the imaginary Orient? Then quelling these chimeras of mine, quelling all images that delight or delude, those hybrid images, half woman, half bird, hybrids that ancient people knew the tricks of, I soldiered on till I found a stark sort of popular eating place on the highway. Timber trucks were thundering past, there were flies on the plates, flies in the air. At the counter I asked for chicken, peppers, and rice. At the white plastic table I waited among the flies. Eventually, in each morsel of chicken, skewered and grilled, I find either a piece of bone or a sinew, or both. I put the chicken pieces into the round flat bread, rolled the bread, and took a bite. The next moments were spent extracting bones and sinews, but the bread was good, and while negotiating the hideous chicken I saw a fine young cat. This leopard of a cat had black ears for a crown, black spots of its white sides, black hind legs and white forelegs. It was catching moths, skipping from empty table to empty table, but to my occupied table it would not come. Mine were the only feet under a table, the cat knew this, knew that feet, even beneath a table loaded with expendable chicken, are dangerous. It went on chasing its moths, doing its ballet, rolling and play-acting, all around the empty tables, but it would not come to my feet.

Instead, an experience now began to come to me. It was a kind of reflexive duplication of the actual goings-on, but it was not supported by anticipatory images or vexed by chimeras. By transference of thought through the cat, I saw into the workings of my own imagination. I had my fictions—the rose-coloured room, the Oriental kiosk, the music, the velvet feeling—and a hideous chicken had dispelled them. The cat, too, had its fictions. The cat was living its fictions, as a ballet with moths, and fiercely it clung to those fictions, shielding them from my feet. Here I was now, in the actual Anamur, still picturing another Anamur; and that other Anamur of mine was as far from me as I was far from the cat in its empire of moths.

Even then, I reflected, setting the chicken now aside, you do need the fictions and you can't help it, they erupt and they disrupt. The fiction draws out the imagination it springs from, it makes for hope. Like revolution or materialism, fictions may devour their children, us; we are made stupid, vulnerable, manipulable, by the dreams that we initiate but which end up dreaming us, turning us into their toys. Become inflexible, or exclusive, become idols and totalitarian, dreams and fictions actualized on a large historical scale can unleash terrible powers of destruction. Yet an individual's aptitude for making fictions, fictions which mediate worlds known or unknown, need never lapse toward destructiveness at all. Like Shiva, I was thinking, perhaps the aptitude performs a ring dance: a dance by turns destructive and creative. Like the cat, the dance is more intelligible once you notice that it shuns human feet.

These reflections were the fabric now weaving itself as I left the restaurant, a fabric that would reveal its design only later, in the depths of sleep, only after I had set aside the notion of the dance of Shiva being performed, up and down the centuries, across the ravaged features of Turkish Western Asia. Upstairs in the room again I left the glass balcony doors open and went to sleep.

What happened next can neither be exactly described nor rigorously accounted for, because I slept for about four hours and can have no idea what sensory experiences, if any, were congregating in my body. In sleep a body is not actually unconscious (except in a manner of speaking), rather it is suspended between its ever-watchful animal awareness of outside stimuli and the unbidden workings of its secret (or culturally imprinted) desires. I woke up to hear a loud octet of voices in the half moonlit dark. Frogs were croaking fortissimo. A donkey was braying. A rooster crowed. Goats were bleating. Nocturnal insects were beating rhythmically their tambourines. Chickens, too, were clucking for all they were worth. A great throb of mixed animal sounds beat through the darkness, the hot darkness in which I lay sweating. Then the muezzin joined in. The muezzin began his forlorn trumpeting chant, and another muezzin from another minaret answered with a different text. When the muezzins stopped, the donkey brayed again, the frogs had never lost a beat, nor had the insects, now throwing their tambourines away and scratching the hot night's heart with fingernails, a different music.

Again I slept. And in my sleep an image came to me. I saw, bathed in a dark gold light, an enormous carousel. It was turning round and round, and its vehicles were going up and down, undulating as they turned. It was also as if I had eyes not only to look ahead but eyes that saw sideways; as if I had taken a step back, or else had no body and was not there at all, because all the space of vision was occupied by this gyrating and undulating caroussel—nothing behind it, nothing to the sides of it or in front of it where I might have been but was not. It was impossible to tell if the vehicles were animal or mechanical, in fact I did not even need to take a closer look. But they went round and round like the vehicles on an ordinary fairground roundabout. Inside it was dark too. Yet it was bathed in this golden light, or a light the colour of a blond patina on bronze. Because the caroussel turned anti-clockwise, the image must have had some duration. Certainly, though, it had condensed millennia into an instant, or so I was thinking as the image faded and left me. But at what precise moment did I assign to the caroussel a semantic value and recall it as a figure belonging in time? While waking up, and just as it left me, I told myself (before being fully awake) that it represented "the cultures" (without troubling myself to specify which cultures). The words "it's the cultures" that came to me as the image faded were to that extent *continuous* with the image, not an afterthought. The vehicles were the cultures of earth, and they went round and round, up and down in their gyrating undulation, suspended from their rods, thus fixed to a turning roof as the stars were once supposed to be (but had my caroussel had a roof at all?). Once awake, I sensed that I had seen something that had no counterpart in space and time as we think we know them. The image was a distillation, with no ordinary single time or single space identifiable as its source or as a source of verifiable co-ordinates.

Later I was able to identify some possible sources, even then. Three weeks before, I had seen my grandsons riding the little old carousel in the Luxembourg Gardens, the one that Rilke had written a poem about in 1906. Only a few days before, I had stood in the immense Greco-Roman amphitheatre at Aspendos, near Antalya, thinking of Osip

Mandelstam's conception of the cultures of earth as an immense dynamic theater of styles, circling, changing styles, rising and falling. Yet the visual mass and the all-inclusive field occupied by my Anamur caroussel removed it really from the scope of my private cultural references and gave it a luminous character of its own. It was only an image, only a figure. My verbal interpretation was part of it; although the figure floated free from bondage to words, still it could be verbally designated as "representing" the complicated, gyrating, immediate contemporaneity of all cultures earth had ever known.

Yet it is no detraction from the power of that image to suggest that it was insinuated into my sleeping consciousness by the swirl of natural sounds all around me, by the aforesaid octet, only minus the muezzins. A body in sleep does tend to centre itself and range its perceptions around it in a ring. The great orbiting of individual cultures through their times and spaces, the turning of the luminous vehicles around the dark core, might well have been acoustically activated, by frogs, goats, and a donkey. My sense of the myriad ethnic and historical flux from earliest times to the present across the length and breadth of Turkey, as well as my interpretation of the little cat's cautious view of my feet in the midst of its whirling moth ballet, these too might have curiously crystallized into the image.

A mental image, even when fraught with language, even as it arises in sleep out of image-débris imbedded in language, may seem to bring an insight. Linear thinking might negotiate some such insight, but it could never deliver it so vividly that it seizes the beholder with rapture or pain. At the same time, a critique of the caroussel suggests itself. While deploying whole consistent image-configurations themselves, most religions that are mounted on a body of myth (communal stories memorializing origins and sacred centres), even more so those that are accounted historical (counter-worldly and individualistic religions) have cautioned devotees against mental images as deceptive signals of any "spirit."[3] What is now called anthropism—respectfully in the new physics—has had its dangerously trite, capriciously hubristic adventures in the past. There are sound psychological reasons for these old cautions. Only after lengthy testing do images obtain consensual value. Centuries may pass before they are encoded as appropriate symbols—like Solomon's nut-palace (*klifah/hekal*) in the Zohar.[4]

By way of conclusion, let me develop somewhat a critique of image-making. In doing so I am wary of the possibility that nature is about to jettison it, so that the species may brace itself more vigorously for its next convulsion in the cosmic sack. The image occurs through a spatializing that the *cogito* imposes on iconogonic drives. Such spatializing is usually "dyadic": polarized schemata arise, such as homology, analogy, complementarity, or opposition.[5] All kinds of irregular nuances, countless sliding axes of complex reference are submerged by rhetorics mounted and mapped upon or metaphorically spatial prejudice. My caroussel was "visible" to me—did no part of it squeak, was there no calliope? I heard nothing, and there I failed. The emergent image ought to articulate the entire sensorium as it burgeons in time, to the music of time; but it seems that the sensorium is all too inclined (by a cultural program) to prod reality with its ocular forefinger, and refrain from spreading, generously, all five fingers of its hand (as Rilke phrased it in his *"Urgeräusch"* essay).

The spreading of those five fingers in the act of imagining might check the spatializing drive, integrate it with other and perhaps less falsifiable ones: the devalorizing futility of Kitsch might then lose at last its deadly grip on average imaginations. The spatial models which active imagination seems to invoke for its humblest articulation, are they not saturated, in any case, with time, time which is a solvent to rigid oppositional, dyadic systems? Doesn't the cosmic harp of the sensorium resonate in the winds of time? There must be ways—and aesthetic experience is one of them—to dismantle such figments of spatializing as deaden human behavior in the universal relationship. For sure, ultimate images, images of first and last things, do turn out often enough to have been "fictions"; they only become figments when Kitsch fabricates them, or as long as puppeteer evangelists are giving tongue. There are supreme fictions to be cultivated. They choose us, not we them. Those are the fictions which channel imagination, renew its life at times of drooping, and sometimes send it whirling away into the unknown, or into a time no thought can touch. *"La musique savante manque à notre désir,"* wrote Rimbaud. It is conceivable that certain varieties of aesthetic experience clarified, mercurial as ever, transforming by its images space into time, might catch up with a "wise music" ordinarily absent from its designs.

[1]E. P. Thompson, *The Making of the English Working Class.* New York: Penguin Books, 1968, p. 231.

[2]Oliver Sacks, *The Man Who Mistook his Wife for a Hat.* New York: Harper & Row, 1987, p.148. Sacks refers to the researches of D. Marr: *Vision: A Computational Investigation of Visual Representation in Man.* San Francisco: W. H. Freeman, 1982.

[3]Homer's image of the twin gates (*geminae portae* in Vergil) of horn and ivory surely came from older Mediterranean folklore. It is the gate of

Eugen Herrigel

ZEN IN THE ART OF ARCHERY

Eugen Herrigel (1884–1955) was a professor of philosophy at the University of Tokyo between the two world wars. He is also author of The Method of Zen. *In this reading, Herrigel describes some of his interactions with a master of archery. The master's suggestions that help Herrigel perfect his performance refer to archery, but they are suggestive for the practice of other arts as well.*

Perhaps it was chance, perhaps it was deliberately arranged by the Master, that we one day found ourselves together over a cup of tea. I seized on this opportunity for a discussion and poured my heart out.

"I understand well enough," I said, "that the hand mustn't be opened with a jerk if the shot is not to be spoiled. But however I set about it, it always goes wrong. If I clench my hand as tightly as possible, I can't stop it shaking when I open my fingers. If, on the other hand, I try to keep it relaxed, the bowstring is torn from my grasp before the full stretch is reached—unexpectedly, it is true, but still too early. I am caught between these two kinds of failure and see no way of escape." "You must hold the drawn bowstring," answered the Master, "like a little child holding the proffered finger. It grips it so firmly that one marvels at the strength of the tiny fist. And when it lets the finger go, there is not the slightest jerk. Do you know why? Because a child doesn't think: I will now let go of the finger in order to grasp this other thing. Completely unself-consciously, without purpose, it turns from one to the other, and we would say that it was playing with the things, were it not equally true that the things are playing with the child."

"Maybe I understand what you are hinting at with this comparison," I remarked. "But am I not in an entirely different situation? When I have drawn the bow, the moment comes when I feel: unless the shot comes at once I shan't be able to endure the tension. And what happens then? Merely that I

Eugen Herrigel, *Zen in the Art of Archery*, trans. R. F. C. Hull (New York: Random House, 1981) 29–39.

get out of breath. So I must loose the shot whether I want to or not, because I can't wait for it any longer."

"You have described only too well," replied the Master, "where the difficulty lies. Do you know why you cannot wait for the shot and why you get out of breath before it has come? The right shot at the right moment does not come because you do not let go of yourself. You do not wait for fulfillment, but brace yourself for failure. So long as that is so, you have no choice but to call forth something yourself that ought to happen independently of you, and so long as you call it forth your hand will not open in the right way—like the hand of a child. Your hand does not burst open like the skin of a ripe fruit."

I had to admit to the Master that this interpretation made me more confused than ever. "For ultimately," I said, "I draw the bow and loose the shot in order to hit the target. The drawing is thus a means to an end, and I cannot lose sight of this connection. The child knows nothing of this, but for me the two things cannot be disconnected."

"The right art," cried the Master, "is purposeless, aimless! The more obstinately you try to learn how to shoot the arrow for the sake of hitting the goal, the less you will succeed in the one and the further the other will recede. What stands in your way is that you have a much too willful will. You think that what you do not do yourself does not happen."

"But you yourself have told me often enough that archery is not a pastime, not a purposeless game, but a matter of life and death!"

"I stand by that. We master archers say: one shot—one life! What this means, you cannot yet understand. But perhaps another image will help you, which expresses the same experience. We master archers say: with the upper end of the bow the archer pierces the sky; on the lower end, as though attached by a thread, hangs the earth. If the

shot is loosed with a jerk there is a danger of the thread snapping. For purposeful and violent people the rift becomes final, and they are left in the awful center between heaven and earth."

"What must I do, then?" I asked thoughtfully.

"You must learn to wait properly."

"And how does one learn that?"

"By letting go of yourself, leaving yourself and everything yours behind you so decisively that nothing more is left of you but a purposeless tension."

"So I must become purposeless—on purpose?" I heard myself say.

"No pupil has ever asked me that, so I don't know the right answer."

"And when do we begin these new exercises?"

"Wait until it is time."

This conversation—the first intimate talk I had had since the beginning of my instruction—puzzled me exceedingly. Now at last we had touched on the theme for whose sake I had undertaken to learn archery. Was not this letting go of oneself, of which the Master had spoken, a stage on the way to emptiness and detachment? Had I not reached the point where the influence of Zen on the art of archery began to make itself felt? What the relation might be between the purposeless waiting-capacity and the loosing of the shot at the right moment, when the tension spontaneously fulfilled itself, I could not at present fathom. But why try to anticipate in thought what only experience can teach? Was it not high time to drop this unfruitful habit? How often I had silently envied all those pupils of the Master who, like children, let him take them by the hand and lead them. How delightful it must be to be able to do this without reserve. Such an attitude need not necessarily lead to indifference and spiritual stagnation. Might not children at least ask questions?

During the next lesson the Master—to my disappointment—went on with the previous exercises: drawing, holding, and loosing. But all his encouragement availed nothing. Although I tried, in accordance with his instructions, not to give way to the tension, but to struggle beyond it as though no limits were set by the nature of the bow; although I strove to wait until the tension simultaneously fulfilled and loosed itself in the shot—despite all my efforts every shot miscarried; bewitched, botched, wobbling. Only when it became clear that it was not only pointless to continue these exercises but positively dangerous, since I was oppressed more and more by a premonition of failure, did the Master break off and begin on a completely new tack.

"When you come to the lessons in the future," he warned us, "you must collect yourselves on your way here. Focus your minds on what happens in the practice-hall. Walk past everything without noticing it, as if there were only one thing in the world that is important and real, and that is archery!"

The process of letting go of oneself was likewise divided into separate sections which had to be worked through carefully. And here too the Master contented himself with brief hints. For the performance of these exercises it is sufficient that the pupil should understand, or in some cases merely guess, what is demanded of him. Hence there is no need to conceptualize the distinctions which are traditionally expressed in images. And who knows whether these images, born of centuries of practice, may not go deeper than all our carefully calculated knowledge?

The first step along this road had already been taken. It had led to a loosening of the body, without which the bow cannot be properly drawn. If the shot is to be loosed right, the physical loosening must now be continued in a mental and spiritual loosening, so as to make the mind not only agile, but free; agile because of its freedom, and free because of its original agility; and this original agility is essentially different from everything that is usually understood by mental agility. Thus, between these two states of bodily relaxedness on the one hand and spiritual freedom on the other there is a difference of level which cannot be overcome by breath-control alone, but only by withdrawing from all attachments whatsoever, by becoming utterly egoless: so that the soul, sunk within itself, stands in the plenitude of its nameless origin.

The demand that the door of the senses be closed is not met by turning energetically away from the sensible world, but rather by a readiness to yield without resistance. In order that this actionless activity may be accomplished instinctively, the soul needs an inner hold, and it wins it by concentrating on breathing. This is performed consciously and with a conscientiousness that borders on the pedantic. The breathing in, like the breathing out, is practiced again and again by itself with the utmost care. One does not have to wait long for results. The more one concentrates on breathing, the more the external stimuli fade into the background. They sink away in a kind of muffled roar which one hears with only half an ear at first, and in the end one finds it no more disturbing than the distant roar of the sea, which, once one has grown accustomed to it, is no longer perceived. In due course one even grows immune to large stimuli, and at the same time detachment from them becomes easier and quicker. Care has only to be taken that the body is relaxed whether standing, sitting, or lying, and if one then concentrates on breathing one soon feels oneself shut in by impermeable layers of silence. One only knows and feels that one breathes. And, to detach oneself from this feeling and knowing, no fresh decision is required, for the breathing slows down of its own accord, becomes more and more economical in the use of breath, and finally, slipping by degrees into a blurred monotone, escapes one's attention altogether.

This exquisite state of unconcerned immersion in oneself is not, unfortunately, of long duration. It is liable to be disturbed from inside. As though sprung from nowhere, moods, feelings, desires, worries and even thoughts incontinently rise up, in a meaningless jumble, and the more far-fetched and preposterous they are, and the less they have to do with that on which one has fixed one's consciousness, the more tenaciously they hang on. It is as though they wanted to avenge themselves on consciousness for having, through concentration, touched upon realms it would otherwise never reach. The only successful way of rendering this disturbance inoperative is to keep on breathing, quietly and unconcernedly, to enter into friendly relations with whatever appears on the scene, to accustom oneself to it, to look at it equably and at last grow weary of looking. In this way one gradually gets into a state which resembles the melting drowsiness on the verge of sleep.

To slip into it finally is the danger that has to be avoided. It is met by a peculiar leap of concentration, comparable perhaps to the jolt which a man who has stayed up all night gives himself when he knows that his life depends on all his senses being alert; and if this leap has been successful but a single time it can be repeated with certainty. With its help the soul is brought to the point where it vibrates of itself in itself—a serene pulsation which can be heightened into the feeling, otherwise experienced only in rare dreams, of extraordinary lightness, and the rapturous certainty of being able to summon up energies in any direction, to intensify or to release tensions graded to a nicety.

This state, in which nothing definite is thought, planned, striven for, desired or expected, which aims in no particular direction and yet knows itself capable alike of the possible and the impossible, so unswerving is its power—this state, which is at bottom purposeless and egoless, was called by the Master truly "spiritual." It is in fact charged with spiritual awareness and is therefore also called "right presence of mind." This means that the mind or spirit is present everywhere, because it is nowhere attached to any particular place. And it can remain present because, even when related to this or that object, it does not cling to it by reflection and thus lose its original mobility. Like water filling a pond, which is always ready to flow off again, it can work its inexhaustible power because it is free, and be open to everything because it is empty. This state is essentially a primordial state, and its symbol, the empty circle, is not empty of meaning for him who stands within it.

Out of the fullness of this presence of mind, disturbed by no ulterior motive, the artist who is released from all attachment must practice his art. But if he is to fit himself self-effacingly into the creative process, the practice of the art must have the way smoothed for it. For if, in his self-immersion, he saw himself faced with a situation into which he could not leap instinctively, he would first have to bring it to consciousness. He would then enter again into all the relationships from which he had detached himself; he would be like one wakened, who considers his program for the day, but not like an Awakened One who lives and works in the primordial state. It would never appear to him as if the individual parts of the creative process were being played into his hands by a higher power; he would never experience how intoxicatingly the vibrancy of an event is communicated to him who is himself only a vibration, and how everything that he does is done before he knows it.

The necessary detachment and self-liberation, the inward-turning and intensification of life until full presence of mind is reached, are therefore not left to chance or to favorable conditions, the less so as the more depends on them, and least of all are they abandoned to the process of creation itself—which already demands all the artist's powers—in the hope that the desired concentration will appear of its own accord. Before all doing and creating, before ever he begins to devote and adjust himself to his task, the artist summons forth this presence of mind and makes sure of it through practice. But, from the time he succeeds in capturing it not merely at rare intervals but in having it at his fingertips in a few moments, the concentration, like the breathing, is brought into connection with archery. In order to slip the more easily into the process of drawing the bow and loosing the shot, the archer, kneeling to one side and beginning to concentrate, rises to his feet, ceremoniously steps up to the target and, with a deep obeisance, offers the bow and arrow like consecrated gifts, then nocks the arrow, raises the bow, draws it and waits in an attitude of supreme spiritual alertness. After the lightning release of the arrow and the tension, the archer remains in the posture adopted immediately following the shot until, after slowly expelling his breath, he is forced to draw air again. Then only does he let his arms sink, bows to the target and, if he has no more shots to discharge, steps quietly into the background.

DISCUSSION QUESTIONS

1. Do you think that an artwork is more likely to be good if the artist making it feels inspired than if the artist does not?
2. Can an artist do anything to make creativity or inspiration more likely to happen? To what extent is creativity subject to the artist's control?
3. Can all aspects of art-making be taught? Can any?
4. Do you think that genius is an original gift, unique to an individual? Do you think that the societies that cultivated artists who we now consider geniuses were responsible in any respect for their achievements?
5. Do you think that genius (if you believe that it exists) is evenly distributed among groups within society? For example, are women as likely to be geniuses as men?
6. Do any of the realizations that Herrigel makes about archery strike you as relevant to other creative processes? Explain.
7. Is scientific discovery creative in the same way that art can be creative? Explain.

FURTHER READING

Beardsley, Monroe. "On the Creation of Art." *Journal of Aesthetics and Art Criticism* 23.3 (1965): 291–304.

Boden, Margaret A. *The Creative Mind: Myth and Mechanisms*. London: Weidenfeld and Nicolson, 1990.

Casey, Edward S. *Imagining: A Phenomenological Study*. Bloomington: U of Indiana P, 1976.

Dutton, Denis, and Michael Krausz, eds. *The Concept of Creativity in Science and Art*. The Hague: Martinus Nijhoff, 1981.

Freud, Sigmund. *The Standard Edition of the Complete Psychological Works of Sigmund Freud*. Trans. and ed. James Strachey. London: Hogarth Press, 1966–1974. Vol. 7: *A Case of Hysteria, Three Essays on Sexuality, and Other Works*. Vol. 9: *Jensen's "Gradiva" and Other Works*. Vol. 13: *Totem and Taboo and Other Works*. 24 vols.

Hindemith, Paul. *A Composer's World*. Cambridge: Harvard UP, 1952.

Jung, C. G. *The Collected Works of C. G. Jung*. Trans. R. F. C. Hull. Bollingen
    Series. Vol. 15: *The Spirit in Man, Art and Literature*. Princeton:
    Princeton UP, 1966. 24 vols.

Koestler, Arthur. *The Act of Creation*. New York: Macmillan, 1964.

Scruton, Roger. *Art and Imagination*. London: Methuen, 1979.

Tomas, V., ed. *Creativity in the Arts*. Englewood Cliffs: Prentice-Hall, 1964.

Warnock, Mary. *Imagination*. Berkeley: U of California P, 1976.

Chapter 8

SHOULD WE FOCUS ON FORM?

Anton Chekhov famously remarked that if a playwright brought a gun into the first act of the play, it should be fired before the play was finished. This principle follows a basic aspiration for an artwork that has been revered in the West since Aristotle: an artwork, according to this ideal, should integrate every element into an overall effect. Ideally, the work's structure should be so perfectly unified that changing a single part would result in an inferior work.

Aristotle certainly emphasized structural ideals in his account of tragedy; but Kant, in the eighteenth century, took the demand for formal integrity to a new plane. Kant considered form (or, strictly speaking, the form of our mental image of an object) to be the basis for aesthetic contemplation. Emotion, charm, and even color are relatively unimportant, according to Kant, and potentially distractions from genuine aesthetic experience.

In order to make sense of formalistic theories like Kant's, we need to understand what artistic "form" is. DeWitt H. Parker itemizes several aspects of an artwork's form. He includes organic unity, principle or theme, thematic variation, balance, hierarchy, and evolution. Parker takes these to be general principles of form in any medium, although he focuses primarily on painting.

Roger Fry also emphasizes an example from painting in his consideration of form and content. Fry takes issue with formalist Clive Bell (who is included in the following chapter because of his emphasis on emotional response to form). Bell contends that one properly reponds to the "significant form" of an artwork, and that the subject matter of representational art is aesthetically irrelevant. Fry takes issue with this final claim. The content depicted often affects our response to art, Fry argues, and appropriately so. To ignore the subject matter of certain works of art, such as religious paintings, is to miss something important.

The visual arts may provide the most frequent examples considered in general discussions of formalism, but formalism has been applied to other media as well. Eduard Hanslick, a nineteenth-century music critic, applied Kantian formalism to music. In the excerpt from his "On the Musically Beautiful," Hanslick contends that musical beauty depends solely on "tonally moving forms." Hanslick objects to the popular view that musical beauty is primarily emotional. While not denying that music arouses emotion, he considers intellectual appreciation of musical form to be the basis of aesthetic experience. He also defends the autonomy of music, insisting on its intrinsic value and attacking those who look to music for moral edification. Such listeners, according to Hanslick, see music as a mere neural stimulus and do not respect music's status as art.

David Michael Levin indicates how formalism can be understood in the dance. Levin contends that formalism in dance pertains to the sensuousness and grace of the dancer's body, aside from any considerations of theatrical representation. Levin applauds both the formalism and the **modernism** of choreographer George Balanchine. Modernism in the visual arts was described by its proponents, and critic Clement Greenberg in particular, as aiming to reveal the essence of the artistic medium itself. Greenberg applauded abstraction in art. Art should be about art itself, in his view, and not aim to represent reality. Greenberg called for art whose content was the formal nature of its own medium. Painting, for example, should emphasize the flatness of the canvas, for flatness is the fundamental formal characteristic of that art. Levin applies modernist premises to Balanchine's choreography, which was austerely abstract. Balanchine's emphasis on abstract form, as opposed to anything representational, revealed the essence of dance—the human body gracefully controlling the dynamic tension between weight and weightlessness.

Art historian Leo Steinberg takes a less sanguine view of the rejection of representation by many contemporary artists, particularly that attempted in the name of modernism. Steinberg presents the case against formalism in his attack on the "high modernist" theory of art criticism enunciated by Greenberg. Steinberg defends the importance of artistic content that is narrative and representational. He insists that Greenberg is making a false dichotomy between painting that creates pictorial illusion and painting that emphasizes its flatness. Human interest is relevant in the criticism of any art, modernist or not, according to Steinberg. To say that a painting emphasizes "flatness" is not to say much, in Steinberg's view. Imagistic paintings as well as abstract paintings can flaunt their flat character; and the most interesting things to say about paintings refer to other considerations, including the way the art represents and symbolizes the living concerns of human beings.

Umberto Eco and Mark Crispin Miller both consider the applicability of traditional emphasis on artistic form to the aesthetics of our popular entertainment. Eco asks whether the typical television program seeks to be "a complete whole" or "an organic unity." He concludes that television shows do reflect traditional ideals, but that these are evident in the series as a whole, not in the individual episode. While this might appear to be a recent development, at odds with the entire previous aesthetic tradition, Eco suggests that the series has roots as old as Aristotle's precepts. Greek tragedies themselves, he contends, were in effect "serial" productions, with each new play a repeat of a story that its audience had seen many times before.

Mark Crispin Miller takes a more skeptical look at one of our popular forms, that of the Hollywood movie. Hollywood movies have lost whatever claim they once had to good artistic form, Miller contends, for their structure is now determined largely by the interests of advertising. Miller analyzes the many ways in which advertising has undercut aesthetic considerations in movies. The outlook for aesthetics in movies is dismal, he thinks, but occasionally a film still rises above all the pressures to advertise and achieves the status of art.

DeWitt H. Parker

AESTHETIC FORM

DeWitt H. Parker (1885–1949) was professor of philosophy at the University of Michigan. He was author of The Principles of Aesthetics, The Analysis of Art, *and* Human Values. *In this selection Parker specifies several basic features that are included in the notion of artistic form.*

. . . We must first consider the general characteristics of aesthetic form. These I shall try to reduce to their simplest principles, hoping to provide the elements of what might be called a logic of aesthetic form. These principles are, I think, very few; as few, indeed, as six: the principle of organic unity, or unity in variety, as it has been called; the principle of the theme; the principle of thematic variation; balance; the principle of hierarchy; and evolution. I do not assert that there are no more principles, but I at least have been unable to find any of equal generality. Others that have been suggested can be shown either to be identical with the six mentioned or to be special cases of them. I shall consider each at some length.

First, the long-established principle of organic unity. By this is meant the fact that each element in a work of art is necessary to its value, that it contains no elements that are not thus necessary, and that all that are needful are there. The beautiful object is organized all through, "baked all through like a cake." Since everything that is necessary is there, we are not led to go beyond it to seek something to complete it; and since there are no unnecessary elements, there is nothing present to disturb its value. Moreover, the value of the work as a whole depends upon the reciprocal relations of its elements: each needs, responds to, demands, every other element. . . .

In a melody, each tone requires its successor to continue the trend that is being established. In short, the meaning of the whole is not something additional to the elements of the work of art, but their cooperative deed.

This principle cannot, however, be described in so external a fashion. For the unity of a work of art is the counterpart of a unity within the experience of the beholder. Since the work of art becomes an embodiment not only of the imagination of the artist, but of the imagination of the spectator as well, his own experience is, for the

DeWitt H. Parker, *The Analysis of Art* (New Haven: Yale UP, 1926) 34–43.

moment, concentrated there. He is potentially as completely absorbed in it as he is in a dream; it is for the moment, in fact, his dream. And he can and does remain in the dream because the artist has so fashioned his work that everything there tends to continue and deepen it, and nothing to disturb and interrupt it. Art is the expression of the whole man, because it momentarily makes of man a whole. . . . This does not mean, of course, that the work of art is not related to other things or that it is actually isolated; but only that its relations are irrelevant to its value, and that it cuts itself off from the rest of the world during appreciation; and this it does, first, because it embodies my dream and, second, because it is so constructed as to make me dream on. The marble of which the statue is made comes from a certain quarry and has an interesting geological history there; it stands in a certain part of space, and hence is related to other parts of space; but all such facts are of no account to its beauty. By placing the statue on a pedestal, we indicate its isolation from the space of the room, as by putting a frame around a picture we isolate it, too, from everything else in the world. It is true that, in order to understand a work of art in its historical relations, I must connect it with the artist's personality, with other works of his, with the "moral temperature" of the age, with the development of artistic styles, and the full appreciation of its beauty depends upon acquaintance with its spiritual background. Who, for example, can appreciate the whole meaning of Signorelli's Pan . . . without some knowledge of classical antiquity and the Italian Renaissance? Yet at the moment of appreciation, all such knowledge becomes focused in the work of art, gathered and contained there like rays in a prism, and does not divert us from it.

The ancient law of organic unity is the master principle of aesthetic form; all the other principles serve it. First among them is what I would call the principle of the theme. . . . In every complex work of art there is some one (or there may be several) pre-eminent shape, color, line, melodic pattern or meaning, in which is concentrated the characteristic value of the whole. It contains the work of art in little; represents it; provides the key to our appreciation and understanding of it. Thus every good pattern is built up of one or more shapes, the disposition of which constitutes the design. When there is color as well as shape, there is some dominant color that appears again and again or in related degrees of saturation, or else there is a color chord that is similarly repeated or is analyzed. In architecture, each style has its characteristic shape, line, or volume, as the pointed arch of the Gothic, the round arch of the Roman, the ellipse of the baroque. In music, there are the one or more themes that express the essential significance of each composition. Likewise, every sculptor, every draughtsman, has his unique and inimitable line. In every poem, there is a peculiar inflection and a regnant idea which constitute the basis of the design. In the drama or the novel, there is some one, or there may be several persons, whose character and fate create the plot.

The third principle is thematic variation. It is not sufficient to state the theme of a work of art; it must be elaborated and embroidered. One of the prominent ways of doing this is to make it echo and re-echo in our minds. Usually, if the theme can be repeated once only we are better pleased than with a single appearance. Yet to find the same thing barely repeated is monotonous; hence what we want is the same, to be sure, but the same with a difference: thematic variation. The simplest type of thematic variation is recurrence of the theme, as in any pattern built upon a repeat. Here is the maximum of sameness with the minimum of difference: mere difference of spatial or temporal position. A slight acquaintance with primitive art is sufficient to convince one of the overwhelming importance of recurrence there. Yet it is needless to say that recurrence is not confined to primitive art. We find it in all civilized art: the recurrence of the same shape and proportions in architecture and sculpture; the recurrence of the theme in music; the recurrence of the same type of foot in meter; repetition of the same color in painting; recurrence of lines and directions of lines (parallelism) in painting and sculpture and architecture; the refrain in poetry; the reappearance of the hero in different scenes in the drama and novel. However, because of the monotony of mere repetition, recurrence gives place to what may be called, in a generalized sense, transposition of theme, as when a melody is transposed to another key or tempo; or when in a design the same shape appears in a different color, or a color appears in different degrees of saturation or brightness; or in architecture, where a shape occurs in different sizes or members—in doors, windows, gables, choir-stalls, and the like. Still another kind of thematic variation is alternation, which requires, of course, more than one theme, or at least two different transpositions of the same theme. Of this, again, the illustrations are legion. Finally, there is inversion of theme, as when a melody is inverted or, in painting or sculpture, a curve is reversed. These are not all the possible types of thematic variation, but they are, I think, the most important and usual.

Another principle of aesthetic form is balance. Balance is equality of opposing or contrasting elements. Balance is one kind of aesthetic unity, for despite the opposition of the elements in balance, each needs the other and together they create a whole. Thus the blue demands the gold and the gold the blue, and together they make a new whole, gold-and-blue. Opposition or contrast is never absent from balance, for even in symmetry, where the balancing elements are alike, the directions of these elements are opposed, right and left. But contrast is never by itself aesthetically satisfactory, for the contrasting elements must offset each other, they must balance. In color, the warm offsets the cold; in a picture, the small object, properly placed, offsets the large one. Hence, just as only equal weights will balance in a scale pan, so only elements that are somehow equal in value, despite their opposition, will balance aesthetically. Not every tint of blue will balance every shade of yellow; that depth of blue must reappear in a corresponding depth of yellow; a light, superficial blue would never balance a deep yellow. But the identity of the opposites is even greater than this. For, as has been remarked, the elements of a balanced unity demand each other; the blue demands the yellow; the line which falls in one direction demands the line that falls in the opposite direction. Now the demand which the color or line makes for its opposite is itself a foreshadowing of the latter; in its demand it already contains the prophecy of its opposite. And even when, as may occur in painting, there is balance between elements of unlike quality—balance, say, of brightness of color against distance or size—the attention value of each must be the same, though opposed in direction. The essential thing about balance is equality of opposed values, however unlike be the things that embody or carry the values.

The pervasiveness of the principle of balance is too generally recognized to need much illustration or argument. In painting we expect, with a reservation that I shall consider in a moment, a threefold balance: horizontal, perpendicular, and radial or diagonal—between the right and left sides, the upper and lower portions, and between what may roughly be called the corners. This last has not received the attention which it deserves; but in many pictures, as for example, Tintoretto's Mercury and the Three Graces, the diagonal axis is the main axis; and in all cases of circular composition, radial balance is fundamental. In architecture, we find balance between right and left, and often between upper and lower parts. In music, there is not seldom a balance between earlier and later parts of a composition, or between opposing themes. In sculpture, there is the balance characteristic of the human body made more perfect by the artist.

Pervasive as balance is, its universality has not stood unquestioned. Nevertheless, many apparent exceptions can be explained away, as is well known, as cases of disguised or subtle balance. The older interpretation of balance after the analogy of symmetry—the balance of like parts—is only a special kind of balance, and has to be supplemented by the wider conception of balance of unlike parts. With this richer conception in mind, we can understand the balance—as in Bruegel's Harvesters . . . —between prominent objects in the right-hand part and little except a vista on the left. Similarly, there is a balance—as in the same picture—between the upper and lower halves of a painting, even when the horizon line is high, and the upper part seems therefore to be relatively empty of masses; for the distance values in the sky balance the heavier lower part. No more difficult of explanation are some cases where asymmetry appears to be definitely sought, as when a girl will put a patch on one cheek but not on another, or will tie the lock of hair on the right with a ribbon, but not the lock on the left. For the piquancy of this procedure comes from the fact that there is a background of decisive symmetry, against which the asymmetrical element stands out. This is quite different from absolute lack of balance. One finds similar eccentric elements in all complex patterns; but always with a background of emphatic balance. And if it is true that such elements disturb symmetry, it is equally true that they serve to emphasize it. The triangle of passion is another illustration; for there also a balanced relationship is the background against which the unbalanced derives its interest.

There are, however, more difficult cases to consider. Many works of art, of the temporal arts in particular, are superficially considered rhythmical rather than balanced, and rhythm may seem to be opposed to balance. Yet an analysis of rhythm shows it to be built upon the two fundamental aesthetic forms, thematic repetition and balance. For what are the typical characteristics of rhythm? Every rhythm is a motion of waves, all of a relatively constant or lawfully varying shape and temporal and spatial span, with balancing crests and troughs. The crest may be an accent or the swing up of a line; the trough may be one or more unaccented syllables, a pause, or the swing back of a line in the opposite direction. The rhythm may begin with the trough, as in iambic meter. The swing up and the swing back may both be very complex, as in free verse, yet the fundamental pattern, as it has just been described, is maintained: in every case there is the recurrence of a certain type of wave form, and the opposition—and balance—between the rising and falling swings. The simplest repeat, if you take its elements in succession, is a rhythm. In the diaper pattern, for example, there is the recurrence of the rising and falling lines, and their opposition and balance, two by two. Or a colonnade, as you apprehend the columns in succession, is a rhythm of identical and balancing filled and empty spaces, the columns corresponding to the arsis, and the spatial interval to the thesis.

Hence when balance seems to be replaced by rhythm, balance is still present, only it is not the simple type of balance so easily recognized, but balance as an element in the complex structure we call rhythm. This more subtle type of balance exists oftentimes in pictorial composition—in "open" as opposed to "closed" forms—where the ordinary mode of balance is rejected. I remember one of Monet's Lily Ponds, in which I searched vainly for the usual type of balance with reference to some axis, only to find that the elements of the picture were arranged in a clear-cut rhythm. Rhythm often replaces right-and-left balance in wall paintings, as in those of Puvis de Chavannes. . . .

Another and last type of unity I call evolution. By this I mean the unity of a process when the earlier parts determine the later, and all together create a total meaning. For illustrations, one naturally turns first to the temporal arts. The course of a well-fashioned story is a good example, for each incident determines its follower and all the incidents determine the destiny of the characters involved. The drama offers similar illustrations: the form is the same, only transposed to theatrical presentation. In the older, orthodox story or play there were three stages in the development, an initial one of introduction of characters, a second stage of complication, ending in the climax, and then the unraveling. But these stages may be compressed. The story may begin with the complication already there; the play may begin with the climax and proceed to the unraveling, and go back, as in Ibsen, to the preparation. But in every case, there is a necessary relation between means and consequences, causes and effects, and a total resulting meaning. Illustrations of this type of unity abound also in the static arts. Any line which we appreciate as having a beginning, middle, and end, and any composition of figures where we are led on from one figure or group of figures to another, is an illustration; for there, too, although the figures be physically static, our appreciation of them is a process in time, and through the process the meaning of the whole is evolved. Of all painters, I think El Greco offers the best illustrations of evolution, as in the Crucifixion . . . where we follow an intensely dramatic movement from the lower to the upper part of the picture.

Roger Fry

THE LIMITS
OF FORMAL
ANALYSIS

Roger Fry (1866–1934) was a British art critic and historian, as well as a painter. His works include Art History as an Academic Study, Reflections on British Painting, Transformations: Critical and Speculative Essays on Art, *and* Vision and Design.

Clearly the expression in art has some similarity to the expression of these emotions in actual life, but it is never identical. It is evident that the artist feels these emotions in a special manner, that he is not entirely under their influence, but sufficiently withdrawn to contemplate and comprehend them. My "Essay in Aesthetic" . . . elaborates this point of view. . . .

I conceived the form of the work of art to be its most essential quality, but I believed this form to be the direct outcome of an apprehension of some emotion of actual life by the artist, although, no doubt, that apprehension was of a special and peculiar kind and implied a certain detachment. I also conceived that the spectator in contemplating the form must inevitably travel in an opposite direction along the same road which the artist had taken, and himself feel the original emotion. I conceived the form and the emotion which it conveyed as being inextricably bound together in the aesthetic whole.

About the time I had arrived at these conclusions the discussion of aesthetic stimulated by the appearance of Post-Impressionism began. It became evident through these discussions that some artists who were peculiarly sensitive to the formal relations of works of art, and who were deeply moved by them, had almost no sense of the emotions which I had supposed them to convey. Since it was impossible in these cases to doubt the genuineness of the aesthetic reaction it became evident that I had not pushed the analysis of works of art far enough, had not disentangled the purely aesthetic elements from certain accompanying accessories.

It was, I think, the observation of these cases of reaction to pure form that led Mr. Clive Bell in his book, "Art," to put forward the hypothesis that however much the emotions of life might appear to play a part in the work of art, the artist was really not concerned with them, but only with the expression of a special and unique kind of

Roger Fry, *Vision and Design* (New York: Brentano, 1920) 193–97.

emotion, the aesthetic emotion. A work of art had the peculiar property of conveying the aesthetic emotion, and it did this in virtue of having "significant form." He also declared that representation of nature was entirely irrelevant to this and that a picture might be completely non-representative.

This last view seemed to me always go too far since any, even the slightest, suggestion of the third dimension in a picture must be due to some element of representation. . . .

Let us take as an example of what I mean Raphael's "Transfiguration," which a hundred years ago was perhaps the most admired picture in the world, and twenty years ago was one of the most neglected. It is at once apparent that this picture makes a very complex appeal to the mind and feelings. To those who are familiar with the Gospel story of Christ it brings together in a single composition two different events which occurred simultaneously at different places, the Transfiguration of Christ and the unsuccessful attempt of the Disciples during His absence to heal the lunatic boy. This at once arouses a number of complex ideas about which the intellect and feelings may occupy themselves. Goethe's remark on the picture is instructive from this point of view. "It is remarkable," he says, "that anyone has ever ventured to query the essential unity of such a composition. How can the upper part be separated from the lower? The two form one whole. Below the suffering and the needy, above the powerful and helpful— mutually dependent, mutually illustrative."

It will be seen at once what an immense complex of feelings interpenetrating and mutually affecting one another such a work sets up in the mind of a Christian spectator, and all this merely by the content of the picture, its subject, the dramatic story it tells.

Now if our Christian spectator has also a knowledge of human nature he will be struck by the fact that these figures, especially in the lower group, are all extremely incongruous with any idea he is likely to have formed of the people who surrounded Christ in the Gospel narrative. And according to his prepossessions he is likely to be shocked or pleased to find instead of the poor and unsophisticated peasants and fisherfolk who followed Christ, a number of noble, dignified, and academic gentlemen in impossible garments and purely theatrical poses. Again the representation merely as representation, will set up a number of feelings and perhaps of critical thoughts dependent upon innumerable associated ideas in the spectator's mind.

Now all these reactions to the picture are open to anyone who has enough understanding of natural form to recognise it when represented adequately. There is no need for him to have any particular sensibility to form as such.

Let us now take for our spectator a person highly endowed with the special sensibility to form, who feels the intervals and relations of forms as a musical person feels the intervals and relations of tones, and let us suppose him either completely ignorant of, or indifferent to, the Gospel story. Such a spectator will be likely to be immensely excited by the extraordinary power of co-ordination of many complex masses in a single inevitable whole, by the delicate equilibrium of many directions of line. He will at once feel that the apparent division into two parts is only apparent, that they are co-ordinated by a quite peculiar power of grasping the possible correlations. He will almost certainly be immensely excited and moved, but his emotion will have nothing to do with the emotions which we have discussed since in the former case, ex-hypothesi, our spectator has no clue to them.

It is evident then that we have the possibility of infinitely diverse reactions to a work of art. We may imagine, for instance, that our pagan spectator, though entirely unaffected by the story, is yet conscious that the figures represent men, and that their gestures are indicative of certain states of mind and, in consequence, we may suppose that according to an internal bias his emotion is either heightened or hindered by the recognition of their rhetorical insincerity. Or we may suppose him to be so absorbed in purely formal relations as to be indifferent even to this aspect of the design as representation. We may suppose him to be moved by the pure contemplation of the spatial relations of plastic volumes. It is when we have got to this point that we seem to have isolated this extremely elusive aesthetic quality which is the one constant quality of all works of art, and which seems to be independent of all the prepossessions and associations which the spectator brings with him from his past life.

A person so entirely pre-occupied with the purely formal meaning of a work of art, so entirely blind to all the overtones and associations of a picture like the "Transfiguration" is extremely rare. Nearly every one, even if highly sensitive to purely plastic and spatial appearances, will inevitably entertain some of those thoughts and feelings which are conveyed by implication and by reference back to life. The difficulty is that we frequently give wrong explanations of our feelings. I suspect, for instance, that Goethe was deeply moved by the marvellous discovery of design, whereby the upper and lower parts cohere in a single whole, but the explanation he gave of this feeling took the form of a moral and philosophical reflection.

Eduard Hanslick

ON THE MUSICALLY BEAUTIFUL

Eduard Hanslick (1825–1904) was a renowned music critic and theorist of the aesthetics of music in the nineteenth century. The following selection is taken from his influential treatise On the Musically Beautiful *(1854). Hanslick takes issue with the popular view that musical beauty is primarily a matter of emotion. He concludes that the beauty of music is a matter of intellectual appreciation of musical structure.*

. . . What kind of beauty is the beauty of a musical composition?

It is a specifically musical kind of beauty. By this we understand a beauty that is self-contained and in no need of content from outside itself, that consists simply and solely of tones and their artistic combination. Relationships, fraught with significance, of sounds which are in themselves charming—their congruity and opposition, their separating and combining, their soaring and subsiding—this is what comes in spontaneous forms before our inner contemplation and pleases us as beautiful.

The primordial stuff of music is regular and pleasing sound. Its animating principle is rhythm: rhythm in the larger scale as the co-proportionality of a symmetrical structure; rhythm in the smaller scale as regular alternating motion of individual units within the metric period. The material out of which the composer creates, of which the abundance can never be exaggerated, is the entire system of tones, with their latent possibilities for melodic, harmonic, and rhythmic variety. Unconsumed and inexhaustible, melody holds sway over all, as the basic form of musical beauty. Harmony, with its thousandfold transformations, inversions, and augmentations, provides always new foundations. The two combined are animated by rhythm, the artery which carries life to music, and they are enhanced by the charm of a diversity of timbres.

If now we ask what it is that should be expressed by means of this tone-material, the answer is musical ideas. But a musical idea brought into complete manifestation in

Eduard Hanslick, *On the Musically Beautiful*, trans. Geoffrey Payzant (Indianapolis: Hackett, 1986) 28–32.

appearance is already self-subsistent beauty; it is an end in itself, and it is in no way primarily a medium or material for the representation of feelings or conceptions.

The content of music is tonally moving forms.

How music is able to produce beautiful forms without a specific feeling as its content is already to some extent illustrated for us by a branch of ornamentation in the visual arts, namely arabesque. We follow sweeping lines, here dipping gently, there boldly soaring, approaching and separating, corresponding curves large and small, seemingly incommensurable yet always well connected together, to every part a counterpart, a collection of small details but yet a whole. Now let us think of an arabesque not dead and static, but coming into being in continuous self-formation before our eyes. How the lines, some robust and some delicate, pursue one another! How they ascend from a small curve to great heights and then sink back again, how they expand and contract and forever astonish the eye with their ingenious alternation of tension and repose! There before our eyes the image becomes ever grander and more sublime. Finally, let us think of this lively arabesque as the dynamic emanation of an artistic spirit who unceasingly pours the whole abundance of his inventiveness into the arteries of this dynamism. Does this mental impression not come close to that of music?

As children, all of us have much enjoyed the play of colour and shape in a kaleidoscope. Music is a kind of kaleidoscope, although it manifests itself on an incomparably higher level of ideality. Music produces beautiful forms and colours in ever more elaborate diversity, gently overflowing, sharply contrasted, always coherent and yet always new, self-contained and self-fulfilled. The main difference between such a musical, audible kaleidoscope and the familiar visible one is that the former presents itself as the direct emanation of an artistically creative spirit, while the latter is no more than a mechanically ingenious plaything. If, not merely in thought but in actuality, we want to raise colour to the level of music, we get involved in the tasteless frivolity of colour organs and the like. The invention of these devices, for all that, does at least show how the formal aspects of both music and colour rest on the same basis. . . .

All musical elements have mysterious bonds and affinities among themselves, determined by natural laws. These, imperceptibly regulating rhythm, melody, and harmony, require obedience from human music, and they stamp as caprice and ugliness every noncompliant relationship. They reside, though not in a manner open to scientific investigation, instinctively in every cultivated ear, which accordingly perceives the organic, rational coherence of a group of tones, or its absurdity and unnaturalness, by mere contemplation, with no concept as its criterion. . . .

One particular musical conception is, taken by itself, witty; another is banal. A particular final cadence is impressive; change two notes, and it becomes insipid. Quite rightly we describe a musical theme as majestic, graceful, tender, dull, hackneyed, but all these expressions describe the musical character of the passage. To characterize this musical expressiveness of a motive, we often choose terms from the vocabulary of our emotional life: arrogant, peevish, tender, spirited, yearning. We can also take our descriptions from other realms of appearance, however, and speak of fragrant, vernal, hazy, chilly music. Feelings are thus, for the description of musical characteristics, only one source among others which offer similarities. We may use such epithets to describe music (indeed we cannot do without them), provided we never lose sight of the fact that we are using them only figuratively and take care not to say such things as "This music portrays arrogance," etc.

David Michael Levin

BALANCHINE'S FORMALISM

David Michael Levin is professor of philosophy at Northwestern University. He is author of Three Essays in Dance, The Body's Recollection of Being, Modernity and the Hegemony of Vision, *and* The Listening Self: Personal Growth, Social Change and the Closure of Metaphysics. *In the following selection, Levin argues that the choreography of George Balanchine achieves a formalism of abstract bodily movement.*

What are the elements that constitute the singular beauty of classical ballet? One might say: Among other things, certainly, a tension between weight and weightlessness. But George Balanchine was one of the first to regard this tension as the concealed essence of the ballet art, and especially as the essence of the phenomenon of grace. Discriminating this essence as the telos of a new ballet aesthetic, Balanchine was also one of the first to demonstrate how it so informs the classical idiom that, when it is properly isolated, exhibited and—in a word—released, it can be exquisitely expressive entirely on its own. The expressivity of classical dance is indeed possible without the various resources of mimetic and symbolic convention. Or, in other words, classical ballet is not essentially mimetic, not essentially representational; rather, these functions merely enclose what *is* of the essence: the immanent sensuous

beauty and grace of the dancing body. Balanchine has mastered the deepest logic of this intrinsic, expressive power of the human body; has followed, in particular, its surprising constraints on costume and stage décor. To release such an essence requires a very delicate touch. For it is most easily presented in concealment. As we shall see, costuming and staging can make all the difference.

Modernism, in this context, is the aesthetic principle that accounts for the privilege being given to the revelation of this essence, this sort of essence. And modernism demands the exclusion of every element that might veil, or mute, or distract from the conditions of the revelation. Formalism is a direct consequence of this chosen aesthetic. It is not, and never has been, for Balanchine, an end in itself. The cherished essence of classical ballet—its syntactical treasures—will remain deeply sublimated, to the extent that there are any semantic elements in the presentation of the dance that must be taken as mimetic or in some other way representational.

The timelessness of Balanchine's miraculous art amounts to this: that he found the possibility of drama in a ballet form, which lets the semantical transparencies of modernism articulate, or heighten, the innermost syntactical treasures of classicism. Or, considering this timelessness in a different focus, it amounts to the tense simultaneity of the body's weight and weightlessness. And in this supernatural instant, a sublime essence is brought to presence: the dancer's capacity to suspend the natural condition of his body in the very act of acknowledging it. . . .

My principal contention is that this master choreographer came to understand, more profoundly perhaps than anyone before him, the possibility of abstracting the pure classical syntax of the mobile human body as the defining condition, or essence, of the ballet art (the essence toward which, he thought, his favorite precursors were variously striving?); and that, consenting to this possibility, he boldly completed the development of a modernist formalism, which would be phenomenologically adequate—as no other possible aesthetic could be—to the consummate release and expression of this sublime, or implicit, essence. (I do not mean to suggest that Balanchine never has chosen to set aside this formalism. He has, indeed, many times preferred to produce ballets in the older, more "theatrical" style. His traditional ballets—such as the narrative *La Valse*—will also be admired and remembered; but simply because they are exquisite inventions, and not because they introduce another possible aesthetic.) More particularly, I would like to concentrate on the striking affinities I am wont to discern between Balanchine's altogether original interpretation of the ballet art and the no less original aesthetic that defines the paint-

ings and sculptures we shall call, after Clement Greenberg, "modernist art."

According to Greenberg, modernist painting and sculpture consummate an intrinsically logical progression of these traditional arts, which have passed through four stages: first, a painterly aesthetic (the theory of Alberti's treatise *On Painting* of 1435), committed to the simplicity of actual *mimesis*, the faithful representation of the human reality; second, an aesthetic which subordinated the demand for exact representation to the demand for a sensuous yet still lucid figuration (as in Matisse's 1916 *The Piano Lesson* and Klee's 1912 *Actor's Mask*); third, an aesthetic which kept figuration, but distorted and perplexed it and rendered it entirely abstract, so that the expressiveness of the art—powerfully heightened—became a function, not of some discriminable symbol or subject-matter faithfully transcribed, but rather of the sensuous properties of the abstractly presented structure (as in Picasso's 1912 *Torero* and de Kooning's 1957 *Parc Rosenberg*); finally, an aesthetic which demanded the total annihilation—or anyway, the precarious suppression—of all figurative tendencies. We might summarize this progression by saying that an aesthetic of immanence (an aesthetic of self-revealing presence) has come to replace the earlier aesthetic of mimetic connotation and transcendent symbolism. For the modernist aesthetic (exhibited to various degrees, for example, in the paintings of Jackson Pollack, Morris Louis, Barnett Newman, Kenneth Noland, and Frank Stella; the sculptures of Anthony Caro and David Smith) challenges the work of art to reveal, to make present (I do not say: to represent) its defining condition as art. It requires moreover that the work accomplish this in a self-referential, or reflexive, manner—solely in terms of the abstract, sensuous properties residing in, and constitutive of, the structure itself. Thus, for the modernist aesthetic, the "form" of the work and its "content" (prepared for its formal role because of its pure abstractness) are one and the same—identical in the strictest sense of this word. If the modernist painting or sculpture represents nothing, refers to nothing outside itself (refers to nothing transcendent), then the sense that it nonetheless expresses and makes totally present may be fittingly described as a revelation. Modernist art, to speak paradoxically, reveals . . . itself! Less paradoxically, it exists solely for the revelation of its ownmost (and latent, or immanent) defining conditions. (Needless to say, I am bent on purging the term "revelation" of every metaphysical association—using it, indeed, in a specifically Kantian, antimetaphysical sense. Thus employed, the term implies a repudiation of all symbolism and intellectual interpretation and invokes, rather, the significant qualities that are immanent in the purely sensuous structures of perceptual experience.)

But what are the conditions that define its being and its unique mode of phenomenological givenness (or presence)? Greenberg and Michael Fried have suggested the answer. So too has Martin Heidegger, in his *Holzwege* essay entitled "Der Ursprung des Kunstwerkes." And it may be significant that here their lines of thought coincide. A work of art is of course a material object; yet, at the same time, it also is the negation of this objecthood. So what the modernist work of art is meant to reveal, what it must reveal, is precisely this contradiction. And if it suppresses one or the other of these two modalities of its being, it has simply failed to articulate the truth about art which seems logically imperative at this given point in its history.

On Fried's view, the two ineluctable defining conditions of painting are its flatness and its shape. No painting can conceivably exist unless it is reduced to flatness and has assumed a certain shape. But, since material objects are also shaped and may also be flat, painting can defeat, or suspend, its own objecthood if—and only if—it accomplishes what no mere object can possibly do: it must somehow materially acknowledge these conditions, rendering them totally present. Discussing modernist sculpture, Greenberg writes: "To render substance entirely optical, and form, whether pictorial, sculptural, or architectural, as an integral part of ambient space—this brings anti-illusionism full circle. Instead of the illusion of things, we are now offered the illusion of modalities: namely, that matter is incorporeal, weightless, and exists only optically, like a mirage."

Not surprisingly, the role of color has posed a serious problem for the modernist aesthetic. Painters must take care lest their colors create an illusion that would prevent the wholly optical acknowledgment of the painting's flatness. Sculptors risk the danger that their coloring may create a surface bespeaking the objecthood of a sculptural mass whose interior it simply conceals: a surface unable to present itself as a merely optical extension. Robert Morris, we know, simply relinquished the use of color, while those sculptors who have dared to use color (David Smith and Calder) somehow succeeded in negating the very (material) surface, which color must logically also affirm. If the structure itself cannot jeopardize this implicit mass behind the color surface, the work will fail to halt its reduction to mere objecthood. Color similarly imperils modernist painting. The work must simultaneously acknowledge, or make present, the flatness and shape which root it in the earth, and yet somehow employ its color in a purely optical way, so that the space of the painting—the "world" created through the act of painting—will be truly accessible (aesthetically intelligible) only to a disembodied eye. (Unlike the visual illusion that emerges in the painting of a representation on a flat canvas, offering the illusion of a tactile accessibility, the modernist illusion offers itself as an illusion accessible only to the eye, hence only to an eye that does not have a tactile and mobile support.)

Fried asseverates, moreover, that the imperative defeat or suspension of object-hood entails that modernist art defeat or suspend its possible "theatricality." Unfortu-nately, he does not establish the terms of this entailment with compelling clarity. The connection, however, can be made. The pos-sibility of "theatre" requires the situatedness of a spectator with regard to the theatrical object. Thus, the theatricality of the object is possible only insofar as the spectator can be oriented towards it in a temporal and spatial perspective. This means that the spectator/object relationship is to be defined (in part) through a heightened con-sciousness of the limiting co-ordinates of the spectator's corporeality and the object's objecthood. Now, it is precisely this sort of relationship that the opticality of modernist art is meant to defeat. So Fried is right, after all, in claiming that theatricality and mod-ernist formalism contradict one another.

We may note a parallel progression toward modernism in the history of the bal-let. In Europe, ballet originated as a species of court entertainment. Long after it entered the public domain, however, it continued to be, in essence, a divertissement, a merely theatrical event. The early ballet consisted of artificial and rigidly determined dance move-ments. Gradually, though, it submitted to the desire for a more stylized, but also more "natural," expressiveness. Beyond this stage, the ballet has mainly developed along four distinct routes. Two of these are rather akin to Abstract Expressionism. The one is cer-tainly theatrical and, even in its incipient for-mal abstractness, it sustains the confident expressiveness of intelligible gestural sym-bols. (I am thinking, for example, of the works of Antony Tudor, and of the sort of productions we associate with Martha Gra-ham.) The other belongs to those ballets that have tried to mix a formal abstractness of movement with a theatricality which often substitutes the expressiveness of stage décor, lighting, and costumes for the expres-siveness of symbols intrinsic to the move-ments of the dancers. (Here I am thinking of the Joffrey Ballet's *Clowns* and *Astarte*.) A third, and very different sort of route is rep-resented by the dance of Merce Cunningham, Yvonne Rainer, and perhaps Twyla Tharp. This form is entirely abstract; the movement is very expressive, although it rigorously excludes every quality of expression not wholly immanent in the dancers' abstract movements. At the same time, however, the production as a whole does not exclude the-atricality, which is latent in the various items (including costumes) that may be employed as props. In addition, the acceptable dance syntax, here, is unlike the classical syntax (however abstract), not only in regard to some of its formal properties, but also in regard to the extent of its vocabulary. (So the inventions of Cunningham, Tharp, and Rainer differ from those of Balanchine, even when they are scarcely more abstract.) The fourth route, of course, is the one paved and traveled by George Balanchine. . . .

Viewed against the classical tradition, Bal-anchine's unique aesthetic can seem exceed-ingly austere. It calls for a "bare-bones" reduction of the ballet essence. Yes—but only because this asceticism is designed to release a beauty and a grace which the older, seemingly richer essence had in principle to suppress. Whereas the older art sought expressiveness, both in the decorations of stage and costume and in the familiar sym-bolism of immediately intelligible gestures and postures (a symbolism certainly meant to evoke "transcendent longings"), the new Balanchine art refuses the expressiveness of stage costumes and excludes, too, all these resources of corporeal syntax that cannot achieve their expressiveness without the encumbrance of some mimetic or transcen-dent symbolism.

The abstractness of dance formalism does not exclude the sensuous expressiveness of the body. Indeed, this is the only truly intrinsic expressiveness that is possible in the formal syntax; what formalism excludes, rather, are such modes of expressiveness and meaning as do not directly reveal their presence through a wholly abstract, a purely syntactic medium. A form, as such, may be either representational or abstract, and if abstract, either abstracted from the semantic materials of a prior representation or else originally abstract. A form may be abstract, and none the less sensuous, insofar as the perception of the form is capable of inducing modes of kinetic and kinaesthetic pleasure. So, odd though it may seem, the Balanchine aesthetic has adopted a profoundly anti-theatrical approach to ballet, amply demonstrating that the theatricality of stage and costume, as well as the theatricality of distinctly allusive movement, are not, in fact, the necessary conditions of drama in a performing art. (I have described the tendency of Balanchine's works as "anti-theatrical." But I am most definitely not suggesting that his ballets mute, or are meant to defeat, the tensions and resolutions of drama.) . . .

To achieve a modernist drama, the syntax of dance must be so presented that it is aesthetically accessible neither as purely literal movement (an objective modification, in Euclidian space, of the dancer's "real" body) nor as wholly figurative movement (a subjective qualification of the dancer's formally expressive "phenomenal" body), but rather as both simultaneously. This possibility derives from the fact that the human body spans a dynamic tension between the objectively actual and the inwardly virtual. Formalism can heighten this tension to the degree that it achieves a disclosure of the body that demonstrates the dancer's objective spatialization, at the same time that it suspends, or annihilates, this condition through the peculiar, deep expressivity of a syntax reduced to pure self-reference. The syntax must utilize and acknowledge the tangible weight, the massive balances of the body, but only in order to defeat or suspend them, and to render the objective body as a magically weightless, optically intangible presence. (Actually, as we shall see, this *presence* of the dancing body is also a sort of *absence*, since the sublimity of grace, unlike the beauty of poise, is up-lifting, and releases the body from the horizontal space-field of the stage.)

The reader of Nabokov's *Ada* will find, near the beginning of the novel, the following curious passage: "Presently the vegetation assumed a more southern aspect as the lane skirted Ardis Park. At the next turning, the romantic mansion appeared on the gentle eminence of old novels. It was a splendid countryhouse, three stories high, built of pale brick and purplish stone." Nabokov, of course, has used language, here, so that it accuses itself. The words create, or posit, a world of representational validity; at the same time, they nullify this world by an acknowledgment of their act of creation. Similarly, George Balanchine sometimes deploys the dancer's weight in a way that especially fits the human body to betray this declaration of objecthood, and indeed to betray this in the very act of declaring it. The drama in the metamorphosis of corporeality (objecthood)—the drama we behold in the sublime immanence of grace—thus replaces the older ballet intention, transcendence through the grace of "longing." . . .

The Persian dervish poet Rumi tells us that, "Whosoever knoweth the power of the dance, dwelleth in God." In the myths of cosmology, Grace is a gift from the Sky of God. Grace acknowledges the supernatural destination of the soul, everlastingly released from the circumstantial field of Earth. Through Grace, the soul casts off its autochthonous embodiment (and consequently its objecthood) and returns to the Sky of God. Thus, in beholding the spectacle of Grace, our productive imagination surpasses its sensible ground, and we witness the joining of Earth and Sky.

We have seen that the graceful dancer appears to be weightless. But now we can also see that Grace is the necessary condition for this weightlessness, this unearthly suspension of objecthood. For it is precisely from the Sky of God that the supervenient order of Grace, up-lifting, descends. But why is the gift of Grace thus bestowed upon the dancer? Is it not—paradoxically—because, through the skillful body, the dancer is so eloquently praising the gravity of the body, acknowledging in gratitude the Earth of the body? And is it not because, in order fully to acknowledge this, the dancer has skillfully perfected the releasing possibilities of the body? The dancer's gracefulness is a sublime presence (or, more accurately, a presence/absence), which belongs to the horizontal field of gratitude, of spatialized skill, but—at the same time—belongs totally and immortally to the vertical time-field of Grace, the Sky of God. And finally, we are in a position to understand the costuming and stage requirements for the modernist presentation of grace. For costuming and staging are elements that constitute the horizontal field of space within which the dancer must move. But, if modernism is to reveal the sublime essence of grace, and not just show the beauty of poise, the stage-space must be cleared of everything that would locate the dancer within the binding coordinates of the horizontal field, thus defeating the possibility of a vertical release into the Time of Grace.

Leo Steinberg

OTHER
CRITERIA

Leo Steinberg is a prominent art historian and professor of art history at the University of Pennsylvania. He is well known for his critique of Clement Greenberg's brand of formalism in art criticism and for his interpretation of Renaissance depictions of Christ (for example, in Michelangelo's "Pietà") as erotic in character. His books include Jasper Johns, Michelangelo's Last Paintings, The Sexuality of Christ in Renaissance Art and Modern Oblivion *(winner of a 1984 National Book Critics Circle Award), and* Other Criteria, *from which the following selection is taken.*

THE STRAIGHT AND NARROW MAINSTREAM

Contemporary American formalism owes its strength and enormous influence to the professionalism of its approach. It analyzes specific stylistic changes within a linear conception of historic development. Its theoretical justification was furnished by Clement Greenberg, whose essay "Modernist Painting" (1965) reduces the art of a hundred years to an elegant one-dimensional sweep. Following is a brief summary, given as far as possible in the author's own words.[1]

"The essence of Modernism lies . . . in the use of the . . . methods of a discipline to criticize the discipline itself—not in order to

subvert it, but to entrench it more firmly in its area of competence." As Kant used logic to establish the limits of logic, so, argues Greenberg, "Modernism criticizes from the inside, through the procedures themselves of that which is being criticized." How then does this self-criticism proceed? "The task of self-criticism became to eliminate from the effects of each art any . . . effect that might conceivably be borrowed from . . . any other art. Thereby each art would be rendered 'pure.' . . . "This purity, Greenberg continues, "meant self-definition, and the enterprise of self-criticism in the arts became one of self-definition with a vengeance." How did this process of self-definition find expression in painting? Pictorial art, Greenberg

Leo Steinberg, "Other Criteria," *Other Criteria: Confrontations with Twentieth-Century Art* (New York: Oxford UP, 1972) 66–82.

explains, "criticized and defined itself under Modernism" by "stressing the ineluctable flatness of the support (i.e., the stretched canvas or panel). . . . Flatness alone was unique and exclusive to that art. . . . and so, Modernist painting oriented itself to flatness as it did to nothing else."

We may take it for granted that in this system all narrative and symbolic content had to drain out of painting because that kind of content was held in common with literature. The depiction of solid forms was abandoned because "three-dimensionality is the province of sculpture, and for the sake of its own autonomy painting has had above all to divest itself of everything it might share with sculpture." Recognizable entities had to go because they "exist in three-dimensional space and the barest suggestion of a recognizable entity suffices to call up associations of that kind of space . . . and by doing so, alienates pictorial space from the two-dimensionality which is the guarantee of painting's independence as an art."

Whatever else one may think of Greenberg's construction, its overwhelming effect is to put all painting in series. The progressive flattening of the pictorial stage since Manet "until its backdrop has become the same as its curtain"[2]—the approximation of the depicted field to the plane of its material support—this was the great Kantian process of self-definition in which all serious Modernist painting was willy-nilly engaged. The one thing which painting can call its own is color coincident with the flat ground, and its drive towards independence demands withdrawal from anything outside itself and single-minded insistence on its unique property. Even now, two hundred years after Kant, any striving for other goals becomes deviationist. Despite the continual emergence in our culture of cross-border disciplines (ecology, cybernetics, psycholinguistics, biochemical engineering, etc.), the self-definition of advanced painting is still said to require retreat. It is surely cause

for suspicion when the drift of third-quarter twentieth-century American painting is made to depend on eighteenth-century German epistemology. Are there no contractionist impulses nearer at hand? Was it Kantian self-definition which led the American woman into what Betty Friedan calls the "Feminine Mystique," wherein "the only commitment for women is the fulfilment of their own femininity"?[3]

ILLUSIONISM NEW AND OLD

A graver objection concerns Greenberg's management of pre-modern art, and this needs discussion because Greenberg's Modernism defines itself in opposition to the Old Masters. If that opposition becomes unstable, Modernism may have to be redefined—by other criteria.

The problem, it seems, hinges on the illusionism of Old Master paintings—the supposed intent of their art to deceive and dissemble. Now, there can be no doubt that there are, and that there have always been, people who look at realistic images as though they were real—but what kind of people? On August 13, 1971, the cover of *Life* magazine featured a nude *Eve* by Albrecht Dürer side by side with the photograph of a modern young woman in dungarees. In the weeks following, close to 3000 Middle American readers cancelled their subscriptions to *Life*, protesting the shamelessness of the nude. Many took her for real and thought she had stripped for the photographer. But these people, whatever their moral standards, are not the definers of art.

Yet Greenberg's contrasting definition of Old Master art relies on just this sort of reading. "Realistic, illusionist art had dissembled the medium, using art to conceal art"; whereas "Modernism used art to call attention to art."[4] It is as though we were told that modern poetry for the first time draws attention to its own process, whereas

Dante, Shakespeare, and Keats had merely used meter and rhyme to tell stories. Has Greenberg been taken in by the illusionism of the Old Masters? Obviously not, for he has a good eye for painting. And in fact his actual observations continually overturn the polarity he seeks to establish. Thus: "The Old Masters always took into account the tension between surface and illusion, between the physical facts of the medium and its figurative content—but in their need to conceal art with art, the last thing they had wanted was to make an explicit point of this tension."[5] The defining contrast then is not a matter of essence, but only of emphasis; the Old Masters do acknowledge the physical facts of the medium—but not "explicitly." On closer inspection the difference between their goals and those of Modernist painting becomes even more elusive:

> The Old Masters had sensed that it was necessary to preserve what is called the integrity of the picture plane: that is, to signify the enduring presence of flatness under the most vivid illusion of three-dimensional space. The apparent contradiction involved—the dialectical tension, to use a fashionable but apt phrase—was essential to the success of their art, as it is indeed to the success of all pictorial art. The Modernists have neither avoided nor resolved this contradiction; rather, they have reversed its terms. One is made aware of the flatness of their pictures before, instead of after, being made aware of what the flatness contains. Whereas one tends to see what is *in* an Old Master before seeing it as a picture, one sees a Modernist painting as a picture first. This is, of course, the best way of seeing any kind of picture, Old Master or Modernist, but Modernism imposes it as the only and necessary way, and Modernism's success in doing so is a success of self-criticism.[6]

Are we still on firm factual ground? The "objective" difference between Old Master and Modernist reduces itself to subjective tendencies in the viewer. It is he who in looking at an Old Master painting *tends* to see the illusion "before seeing it as a picture." But what if he doesn't? What if he sees a Giotto, a Poussin, or a Fragonard as a picture first, habitually screening out the deep space indications until he has seen the surface disposition of its formal elements? Does an Old Master painting forego its Old Master status if it is seen in primary flatness and only secondly as a vivid illusion? Consider that typical Old Master expression, the rapid sketch. Does Rembrandt's drawing become Modernist if its pen strokes and bister washes emerge for us before, or along with, the old lady's image? It seems to me that the last thing this draughtsman wants is to dissemble his medium, or conceal his art; what he wants, and gets, is precisely a tension, made fully explicit, between the figure evoked and the physicality of paper, pen stroke, and ink. And yet, in terms of style, such a sketch as this is integral to Old Master art. It merely dramatizes the quality that enables Baudelaire to see a Delacroix as nothing but arabesques.

And, contrariwise, what if the viewer tends to see Modernist paintings as spatial abstractions of landscape? The sculptor Don Judd complains that New York School paintings of the 1950's keep him intensely aware of what their flatness contains—"airiness" and "illusionistic space." He said recently: "Rothko's whole way of working depended on a good deal of illusionism. It's very aerial. The whole thing is about areas floating in space. Compared to Newman there is distinctly a certain depth. But I finally thought that all painting was spatially illusionistic."[7]

Where does this leave us? The difference between Old Master and Modernist is not, after all, between illusion and flatness; it turns out that both are present in each. But if the difference is in the *order* in which these two presences are perceived, then do the subjective approaches of Baudelaire and Judd reverse the distinction between historic and modern art?

Greenberg is fully conscious of the airy illusionism observed by Judd in Modernist painting. But though open atmospheric effects, such as are found in Rothko or Jules Olitski, clearly deny and dissemble the picture's material surface, he nevertheless finds them congruent with Painting's self-definition because the illusion conveyed is visual, rather than tactile or kinesthetic. And visual art should, to conform with Kantian self-criticism and scientific consistency, "confine itself exclusively to what is given in visual experience." "Where the Old Masters created an illusion of space into which one could imagine oneself walking, the illusion created by a Modernist is one into which one can look, can travel through, only with the eye."[8]

The difference, then, reduces itself to distinct *kinds* of spatial illusion, but this last saving distinction is one which defines "Modernism" by pre-industrial standards of locomotion. How, in what kind of painted space, do you let yourself roam? Greenberg apparently can imagine himself trudging through a Rembrandtesque gloom, but he cannot conceive journeying through an Olitski. Do we need to be reminded that in an age of space travel a pictorial semblance of open void is just as inviting to imaginary penetration as the pictorial semblance of a receding landscape was formerly to a man on foot? Are we now to define Modernist painting against a Kantian concept of transportation? Greenberg's theoretical schema keeps breaking down because it insists on defining modern art without acknowledgment of its content, and historical art without recognizing its formal self-consciousness.

All major painting, at least of the last six hundred years, has assiduously "called attention to art." Except for *tour de force* demonstrations and special effects, and before their tradition collapsed in nineteenth-century academicism, the Old Masters always took pains to neutralize the effect of reality, presenting their make-believe worlds, as it were, between quotation marks. The means they chose were, of course, those of their day, not of ours; and often their careful controls are annulled by our habit of lifting a partial work from its setting—transposing a detached fresco or predella panel into the category of easel painting. But a dramatic narrative painted by Giotto resembles neither nineteenth-century easel painting nor a movie screen. When it is not wrenched from its context (as in most art history books), it works within a wall system, each wall supporting multiple scenes set between elaborate framing bands, within which, in turn, other scenes on different scales are described. You are shown simultaneous and incompatible systems whose juxtaposition cancels or checks the illusion. Similarly, the Sistine Ceiling when seen in its entirety: the work is a battleground for local illusion, counter-illusion, and emphasized architectural surface—art turning constantly back on itself. . . .

Where the Old Masters do seem to dissolve the picture plane to gain an unambiguous illusion of depth, they usually have a special objective in mind, an objective understood and shared by the viewer. Michelangelo's *Last Judgment*, unlike the Ceiling, obliterates the supporting wall plane so that the vision of a Christ "come to judge the quick and the dead" gives immediate urgency to the words of the Creed. Caravaggio's pictures, whether erotic or religious in their address, were similarly intended to induce a penetrating experience. But their relentless, surface-dissolving illusionism was largely repudiated by the Old Masters. Until the nineteenth century, the kind of painting which utterly broke the consistency of the surface remained a special, even exceptional resource of Old Master art.

The more realistic the art of the Old Masters became, the more they raised internal safeguards against illusion, ensuring at every point that attention would remain focused upon the art.

Again and again, in so-called illusionist art, it is illusionism that is under discussion, the art "calling attention to art" in perfect self-critical consciousness. And this is why the Old Masters are forever inventing interferences with spatial recession. They do not merely "take account" of the tension between surface and depth, as if for the sake of decorative coherence, while reserving their thrust for the depiction of depth. Rather, they maintain an explicit, controlled, ever-visible dualism. Fifteenth-century perspective was not a surface-denying illusion of space, but the symbolic form of space as an intelligible coordinate surface pattern. Good illusionist painting not only anchors depth to the plane; it is almost never without built-in devices designed to suspend the illusion, and the potency of these devices depends—like the appreciation of counterpoint or of puns—on the spectator's ability to register two things in concert, to receive both the illusion and the means of illusion at once.

Some of the Old Masters overruled the apparent perspective by dispersing identical color patches as an allover carpet spread (Pieter Bruegel, for instance). Some worked with chromatic dissonances to weave a continuous surface shimmer like mother-of-pearl. Many—from Titian onward—insured their art against realism by the obtrusive calligraphy of the brush—laying a welter of brush-strokes upon the surface to call attention to process. Some contrived implausible contradictions within the field, as when the swelling bulk of a foreshortened form is collapsed and denied the spatial ambience to house it. All of them counted on elaborate framing as an integral part of the work ("advertising the literal nature of the support," as Greenberg says of Collage)—so that the picture, no matter how deep its illusionism, turned back into a thing mounted there like a gem. It was Michelangelo himself who designed the frame of the

Doni Madonna, an element essential to the precious-mirror effect of its surface.

Greenberg wants all Old Master and Modernist painters to reduce their differences to a single criterion, and that criterion as mechanistic as possible—either illusionistic or flat. But what significant art is that simple? Have you ever asked how deep the thrones of the Sistine Prophets and Sibyls are? Perfectly shallow if you glance across the whole sequence; but they run ten to twenty feet deep as soon as you focus on one alone. Perspective illusionism and anatomic foreshortening sustain a ceaseless optical oscillation.

"The abiding effect is a constant shuttling between surface and depth, in which the depicted flatness is "infected" by the undepicted. Rather than being deceived, the eye is puzzled; instead of seeing objects in space, it sees nothing more than—a picture."[9] These words, in which Greenberg describes Cubist collage, apply as well to Michelangelo's Ceiling, and to thousands of Old Master works. They describe the effect of a not untypical early-fifteenth-century manuscript page . . . : *Missus est Gabriel angelus*. Three reality levels oscillate in and compete for that capital *M*: an arcade opening on a bedchamber; a trellis for ivy ornament; and a letter at the head of a word. All three at once. The eye is puzzled; instead of seeing objects in space it sees a picture.[10]

The notion that Old Master paintings in contrast to modern dissemble the medium, conceal the art, deny the surface, deceive the eye, etc., is only true for a viewer who looks at the art like those ex-subscribers to *Life* magazine. The distinction a critic makes between Modern–self-analytical and Old Master–representational refers less to the works compared than to his own chosen stance—to be analytic about the one and polemically naive about the other.

It is poor practice, when modern art is under discussion, to present the Old Masters as naively concerned with eye-fooling trickery, while reserving for modern art both the superior honesty of dealing with the flat plane of painting and the maturer intellectual discipline of self-analysis. All important art, at least since the Trecento, is preoccupied with self-criticism. Whatever else it may be about, all art is about art. All original art searches its limits, and the difference between the old and the modernist is not in the fact of self-definition but in the direction which this self-definition takes. This direction being part of the content.

At this point Greenberg might answer that self-definition does not deserve its name unless it aims at purity, and that this in turn requires stripping painting down to its irreducible essence, i.e., the coincidence of flattened color with its material support. I reply that this mistakes a special case for a necessity. The process of Painting's self-realization can go either way. For Jan van Eyck, for example, the self-realization of painting is not reductive but expansive. He turns to the sculptor and says, "Anything you can do I can do better"; then to the goldsmith—"Anything *you* can do I can do better"; and so to the architect. He redesigns everything in the flat and even banishes metallic gold to create the effect of it—like Manet—in pure color and light. Anything anybody can do, painting does better—and that's where, for van Eyck, painting realizes itself—discovering its autonomy literally in its ability to do without external aid.

Art's perpetual need to redefine the area of its competence by testing its limits takes many forms. Not always does it probe in the same direction. Jacques Louis David's ambition to make art a force of national moral leadership is as surely a challenge to the limits of art as is Matisse's elimination of tonal values. At one historical moment painters get interested in finding out just how much their art can annex, into how much non-art it can venture and still remain art. At other times they explore the opposite end to discover how much they can renounce and still stay in business. What is constant is art's concern with itself, the interest painters have in questioning their operation. It is a provincialism to make the self-critical turn of mind the sufficient distinction of Modernism; and once it is understood as not its peculiar distinction, then the specific look of contemporary abstract art—its object quality, its blankness and secrecy, its impersonal or industrial look, its simplicity and tendency to project a stark minimum of decisions, its radiance and power and scale—these become recognizable as a kind of content—expressive, communicative, eloquent in their own way.[11]

THE CORPORATE MODEL OF DEVELOPING ART

It is astonishing how often recent Abstract American painting is defined and described almost exclusively in terms of internal problem-solving. As though the strength of a particular artist expressed itself only in his choice to conform with a set of existent professional needs and his inventiveness in producing the answers. The dominant formalist critics today tend to treat modern painting as an evolving technology wherein at any one moment specific tasks require solution—tasks set for the artist as problems are set for researchers in the big corporations. The artist as engineer and research technician becomes important insofar as he comes up with solutions to the right problem. How the choice of that problem coincides with any personal impulse, psychological predisposition, or social ideal is immaterial; the solution matters because it answers a problem set forth by a governing technocracy.

In America this corporate model of artistic evolution appears full-blown by the mid-1920's. It inhabits the formalist doctrine that Painting aspires towards an ever-tightening synthesis of its design elements. The theory in its beginnings was fairly simple. Suppose a given painting represents a reclining nude; and suppose the figure outlined with a perceptible contour. Within that contour lies a distinct shape. That shape is of a certain color, and the color—modulated from light to dark or from warm to cool—reflects a specific quantity or kind of light. We have then four formal elements—line, shape, color, and light—which can be experienced and thought of as separate and distinct. Now, it is argued, the test of significantly advanced painting will be the progressive obliteration of these distinctions. The most successful picture will so synthesize the means of design that line will be no longer separable from shape, nor shape from color, nor color from light. A working criterion, easily memorized and applied. It tells you not necessarily which picture is best, but which is in line to promote the overall aspiration of Painting—this alignment being a *sine qua non* of historic importance. By this criterion, the painter of the Sistine Ceiling is, with due respect, relegated to one of the byways of Painting since his inventions, for all their immediate interest, do not ultimately promote the direction in which Painting must go; Michelangelo's forms are "realized in a sculptural rather than a pictorial manner" (Albert C. Barnes).[12] Indeed, the elements of Michelangelo's depictions are remarkable for separability—specific shapes sharply delineated by bounding lines, tinted by local color, modulated by chiaroscuro. Though Michelangelo will (I am convinced) be emerging within the next several years as one of the most original colorists of all time, by the criteria enunciated above he fails to contribute—as did Titian's coloristic diffusion—to the synthesis of the means of design. For the critic-collector Albert C. Barnes he remains a dead end, whereas the course initiated by

Titian leads irresistibly to its culmination in Renoir and William Glackens.

This single criterion for important progressive art, moving as by predestination towards utter homogeneity of the elements of design, is still with us, now considerably more analytical, more prestigious than ever, and celebrating its latest historical denouement in the triumph of color field painting.

In formalist criticism, the criterion for significant progress remains a kind of design technology subject to one compulsive direction: the treatment of "the whole surface as a single undifferentiated field of interest." The goal is to merge figure with ground, integrate shape and field, eliminate foregound-background discontinuities; to restrict pattern to those elements (horizontals or verticals) that suggest a symbiotic relationship of image and frame; to collapse painting and drawing in a single gesture, and equate design and process (as Pollock's drip-paintings do, or Morris Louis's *Veils*); in short, to achieve the synthesis of all separable elements of painting, preferably—but this is a secondary consideration—without that loss of incident or detail which diminishes visual interest.

There is, it seems to me, a more thoroughgoing kind of synthesis involved in this set of descriptions—the leveling of end and means. In the criticism of the relevant paintings there is rarely a hint of expressive purpose, or recognition that pictures function in human experience. The painter's industry is a closed loop. The search for the holistic design is simply self-justified and self-perpetuating. Whether this search is still the exalted Kantian process of self-criticism seems questionable; the claim strikes me rather as a remote intellectual analogy. And other analogies suggest themselves, less intellectual, but closer to home. It is probably no chance coincidence that the descriptive terms which have dominated American formalist criticism these past fifty years run parallel to the contemporaneous evolution of the Detroit automobile. Its ever-increasing symbiosis of parts—the ingestion of doors, running boards, wheels, fenders, spare tires, signals, etc., in a one-piece fuse-lage—suggests, with no need for Kant, a similar drift towards synthesizing its design elements. It is not that the cars look like the paintings. What I am saying here relates less to the pictures themselves than to the critical apparatus that deals with them. Pollock, Louis, and Noland are vastly different from each other; but the reductive terms of discussion that continually run them in series are remarkably close to the ideals that govern the packaging of the all-American engine. It is the critics' criterion far more than the painters' works which is ruled by a streamlined efficiency image.

But the reference to industrial ideals can serve to focus on certain distinctions within art itself. If, for instance, we question the work of the three painters just mentioned from the viewpoint of expressive content, they immediately separate out. There is obviously no affinity for industrialism in Pollock or Louis, but it does characterize an important aspect of the younger man's work. His thirty-foot-long stripe paintings, consisting of parallel color bands, embody, beyond the subtlety of their color, principles of efficiency, speed, and machine-tooled precision which, in the imagination to which they appeal, tend to associate themselves with the output of industry more than of art. Noland's pictures of the late sixties are the fastest I know.

The painter Vlaminck used to say that he wished to make pictures which would be readable to a motorist speeding by in an automobile. But Vlaminck's belated expressionism could no more incorporate such an ideal than Robert Henri's impressionist portraits incorporated his admiration for mechanical tools. Vlaminck's palette-knifed snowscapes lacked every access to his ostensible goal. They possessed neither the scale,

the format, the color radiance, nor even the appropriate subject matter: good motorists look for signals and signs, not at messages from a painter's easel. Vlaminck's statement remains naive because it is essentially idle. But there is nothing naive in Noland's determination to produce, as he put it, "'one-shot' paintings perceptible at a single glance." I quote from a recent article by Barbara Rose, who continues: "To achieve maximum immediacy, Noland was ready to jettison anything interfering with the most instantaneous communication of the image."[13]

Noland's stated objective during the 1960's confirms what his pictures reveal—an idealization of efficient speed and, implicitly, a conception of the humanity at whom his "one-shots" are aimed. The instantaneity which his pictures convey implies a different psychic orientation, a revised relationship with the spectator. Like all art that ostensibly thinks only about itself, they create their own viewer, project their peculiar conception of who, what, and where he is.

Is he a man in a hurry? Is he at rest or in motion? Is he one who construes or one who reacts? Is he a man alone—or a crowd? Is he a human being at all—or a function, a specialized function or instrumentality, such as the one to which Rauschenberg's *Chairs* (1968) reduced the human agent. (A room-size transparent screen whose illumination was electronically activated by sound; the visibility of the chairs which constituted the image depending on the noises made by the spectator—his footsteps when entering, his coughing or speaking voice. One felt reduced to the commodity of a switch.) I suspect that all works of art or stylistic cycles are definable by their built-in idea of the spectator. Thus, returning once more to the Pollock-Louis-Noland procession, the younger man, who separates himself from his elders by the criterion of industrial affinity, parts from them again by his distinct view of the viewer.

Considerations of "human interest" belong in the criticism of modernist art not because we are incurably sentimental about humanity, but because it is art we are talking about. And it appears to me that even such professional technicalities as "orientation to flatness" yield to other criteria as soon as the picture is questioned not for its internal coherence, but for its orientation to human posture.

What is "pictorial flatness" about? Obviously it does not refer to the zero curvature of the physical plane—a cat walking over pictures by Tiepolo and Barnett Newman gets the same support from each one. What is meant of course is an ideated flatness, the sensation of flatness experienced in imagination. But if that's what is meant, is there anything flatter than the *Olympia* (1950) of Dubuffet? If flatness in painting indicates an imaginative experience, then the pressed-leaf effect, the graffito effect, the scratched-gravel or fossil-impression effect of Dubuffet's image dramatizes the sensation of flatness far beyond the capacity, or the inten-

tion, of most color field painting. But in fact, these different "flatnesses" are not even comparable. And the word "flat" is too stale and remote for the respective sensations touched off by the visionary color *Veils* of Morris Louis . . . and the bedrock pictographs of Dubuffet. Nor need flatness be an end product at all—as Jasper Johns demonstrated in the mid-1950's, when his first *Flags* and *Targets* relegated the whole maintenance problem of flatness to "subject matter." However atmospheric his brushwork or play to tonalities, the depicted subject ensured that the image stayed flat. So then one discovers that there are recognizable entities, from flags even to female nudes, which can actually promote the sensation of flatness.

This discovery is still fairly recent, and it is not intelligible in terms of design technology. It demands consideration of subject and content, and, above all, of how the artist's pictorial surface tilts into the space of the viewer's imagination.

---

[1] See Clement Greenberg, "Modernist Painting," in *The New Art*, ed. Gregory Battcock, New York, 1966, pp. 101 ff. The essay first appeared in *Art and Literature*, Spring 1965.

[2] Greenberg, "Abstract, Representational, and so forth," in *Art and Culture*, Boston: Beacon, 1961, p. 136.

[3] Betty Friedan, *The Feminine Mystique*, New York, 1963. p. 37. Cf. her analysis (pp. 29–30) of the ideal American woman as presented in an issue of *McCalls* (July 1960)—"pared down to pure femininity, unadulterated."

[4] "Modernist Painting," p. 102.

[5] "Cézanne," *Art and Culture*, p. 53.

[6] "Modernist Painting," pp. 103–4.

[7] *Art News*, October 1971, p. 60.

[8] "Modernist Painting," p. 107.

[9] Greenberg, "Collage," in *Art and Culture*, pp. 73–74.

[10] The deliberate exploitation of surface-to-depth oscillation characterizes all major painting. It is the inexhaustible resource of the art. But the degree to which the resultant duality registers on

the viewer's attention depends on the culture and the set of expectancies he brings to his appreciation. He mistakes the goal of the Old Masters if he imagines them aiming for that near-absolute dissolution of the picture plane which distinguishes late nineteenth-century academic painting.

To take an outstanding example of illusionist Old Master art—Velázquez' *Menippus*: the heavy impasto that molds the scrolls and books in the foreground tells you explicitly where the paint is. But the jug and bench in the "background," where the raw canvas appears barely stained by a thin wash of pigment, says—"this is where the canvas is." And the palpable mystery of the painting is the old Cynic's material presence inserted in the non-dimensional film between canvas and paint. No painting was ever more self-defining than this.

[11] On this question of content: during the 1960's many American sculptors made boxes, some of them highly impressive. By some marvelous coincidence, the moment when this plain box, cube, or die first emerged as a sufficient sculptural

statement was also the moment when the Black Box of the computer entered the general consciousness, sometimes with fateful meaning. Remember Senator Morse of the Senate Foreign Relations Committee interrogating Secretary of State Rusk in March 1968 (*New York Times*, March 12, 1968, p. 16). The Senator was referring to the Tonkin Gulf incident, when the North Vietnamese attacked the American destroyer *Maddox*. The vessel was claimed to be on a routine patrol in international waters, but, according to Morse, was engaged in an act of deliberate provocation. "Why didn't the Administration tell this committee on August 6, 1964," he asked, "that the Maddox . . . was completely equipped with spy equipment, including the big black box . . . that that big black box on the Maddox had made possible to stimulate the electronic instruments of North Vietnam? . . ."

It may well be that the electronic black box, the faceless housing of invisible functions, is to the modern imagination what muscular strength was to Cellini and mechanical energy to the generation of the Futurists. As the aged Thomas Hart Benton said in a recent interview (*New York Times*, June 5, 1968, p. 38): "Look at that train! The machines of that day really had something for an artist. They weren't afraid to exhibit their

power. Today's machines enclose it, cover it up." Cf. Derek J. de Solla Price, "Gods in Black Boxes," in *Computers in Humanistic Research*, ed. E. Bowles, Englewood Cliffs, 1967, p. 6: "Although the concept of a 'black box' has now become commonplace in such diverse fields as computers, cybernetics, and psychology, the historical origin of the phrase is not . . . clear. . . . So far as I know, the black box was first used as a pedagogic device in the 1880's when it entered teaching laboratories of physics, particularly the Cavendish Laboratory in Cambridge, as a box containing a network of resistances, inductances and capacitances which were led out to a set of terminals mounted on the box. . . . Such boxes were actually used, and in the late 1930's some of them had been painted black, presumably to go along with the symbolism of the dark nature of their interior. . . . I do not know who publicized the term, . . . I understand the term to mean a piece of apparatus with known input and output properties but unknown interior mechanism."

[12]Albert C. Barnes, *The Art of Painting*, New York, 1925, p. 408. For the author's insistence on synthesizing the elements of design, see pp. 55, 61, 67 f.

[13]"Quality in Louis," *Art News*, October 1971, p. 65.

Umberto Eco

REPETITION
AND
THE SERIES

Umberto Eco, an Italian philosopher, has written on medieval and contemporary aesthetics, semiotics (the study of signs), and mass communication and culture. He has also written two novels, The Name of the Rose *and* Foucault's Pendulum. *In the following selection, he considers the way in which our mass media format of the series has its own aesthetic character, which should not be dismissed as a "merely" popular form.*

THE SERIES

The *series* works upon a fixed situation and a restricted number of fixed pivotal characters, around whom the secondary and changing ones turn. The secondary characters must give the impression that the new story is different from the preceding ones, while in fact the narrative scheme does not change. . . .

With a series one believes one is enjoying the novelty of the story (which is always the same) while in fact one is enjoying it because of the recurrence of a narrative scheme that remains constant. The series in this sense responds to the infantile need of hearing again always the same story, of being consoled by the "return of the Identical," superficially disguised.

The series consoles us (the consumers) because it rewards our ability to foresee: we are happy because we discover our own ability to guess what will happen. We are satisfied because we find again what we had expected, but we do not attribute this happy result to the obviousness of the narrative structure, but to our own presumed capacities to make forecasts. We do not think, "The author has constructed the story in a way that I could guess the end," but rather, "I was so smart to guess the end in spite of the efforts the author made to deceive me." . . .

Umberto Eco, "Innovation and Repetition: Between Modern and Post-Modern Aesthetics," *Daedalus* 114.4 (1985): 161–84.

Every text presupposes and constructs always a double Model Reader (let us say, a naive and a "smart" one). The former uses the work as semantic machinery and is the victim of the strategies of the author who will lead him little by little along a series of previsions and expectations; the latter evaluates the work as an aesthetic product and enjoys the strategies implemented in order to produce a model reader of the first level. This second-level reader is the one who enjoys the seriality of the series, not so much for the return of the same thing (that the ingenuous reader believed was different) but for the strategy of the variations; in other words, he enjoys the way in which the same story is worked over to appear to be different.

This enjoyment of variations is obviously encouraged by the more sophisticated series. Indeed, we can classify the products of serial narratives along a continuum that takes into account the different gradations of the reading agreement between the text and the "smart" reader (as opposed to the naive one). It is evident that even the most banal narrative product allows the reader to become, by an autonomous decision, a critical reader, able to recognize the innovative strategies (if any). But there are serial works that establish an explicit agreement with the critical reader and thus, so to speak, challenge him to acknowledge the innovative aspects of the text.

Belonging to this category are the television films of Lieutenant Columbo. It is worth noticing that in this series the authors spell out from the beginning who the murderer is. The spectator is not so much invited to play the naive game of guessing (whodunit?) as (1) to enjoy Columbo's detection technique, appreciated as an encore to a well-known piece of bravura (and in this sense the pleasure provided by Columbo is not so different from the one provided by Nero Wolfe); and (2) to discover in what way the author will succeed in winning his bet, which consists in having

Columbo do what he always does, but nevertheless in a way that is not banally repetitive. . . . Every episode of Columbo is directed by a different person. The critical addressee is invited to pronounce a judgment on the best variation.

I use the term "variation" thinking of the classical musical variations. They, too, were "serial products" that aimed very little at the naive addressee and that bet everything on an agreement with the critical one. The composer was fundamentally interested only in the applause of the critical listener, who was supposed to appreciate the fantasy displayed in his innovations on an old theme.

In this sense, seriality and repetition are not opposed to innovation. Nothing is more "serial" than a tie pattern, and yet nothing can be so personalized as a tie. The example may be elementary, but that does not make it banal. Between the elementary aesthetics of the tie and the recognized "high" artistic value of the Goldberg Variations, there is a gradated continuum of repetitious strategies, aimed at the response of the "smart" addressee.

The problem is that there is not, on the one hand, an aesthetics of "high" art (original and not serial), and on the other a pure sociology of the serial. Rather, there is an aesthetics of serial forms that requires an historical and anthropological study of the ways in which, at different times and in different places, the dialectic between repetition and innovation has been instantiated. When we fail to find innovation in the serial, this is perhaps less a result of the structures of the text, than of our "horizon of expectations" and our cultural habits. We know very well that in certain examples of non-Western art, where we always see the same thing, the natives recognize infinitesimal variations and feel the shiver of innovation. Where we see innovation, at least in the serial forms of the Western past, the original addressees were not at all interested in that aspect and conversely enjoyed the recurrences of the scheme.

◆◆◆

If we re-read Aristotle's *Poetics* we see that it was possible to describe the model of a Greek tragedy as a *serial* one. From the quotations of the Stagirite we realize that the tragedies of which he had knowledge were many more than have come down to us, and they all followed (by varying it) one fixed scheme. We can suppose that those that have been saved were those that corresponded better to the canons of the ancient aesthetic sensibility. But we could also suppose that the decimation came about on the basis of political-cultural criteria, and no one can forbid us from imagining that Sophocles may have survived by virtue of a political maneuver, by sacrificing better authors (but "better" according to what criteria?).

If there were many more tragedies than those we know, and if they all followed (with variations) a fixed scheme, what would happen if today we were able to see them and read them all together? Would our evaluations of the originality of Sophocles or Aeschylus be different from what they are currently? Would we find in these authors variations on topical themes where today we see indistinctly a unique (and sublime) way of confronting the problems of the human condition? Perhaps where we see absolute invention, the Greeks would have seen only the "correct" variation on a single scheme, and sublime appeared to them, not the single work, but precisely the scheme. It is not by chance that, when speaking of the art of poetry, Aristotle dealt mainly with schemes before all else, and

mentioned single works only for the sake of an example.

Since at this point I am playing what Peirce called "the play of musement" and I am multiplying the hypotheses—in order to find out, maybe later, a single fruitful idea—let us now reverse our experiment and look at a contemporary TV serial from the point of view of a future neo-romantic aesthetics which, supposedly, has assumed again that "originality is beautiful." Let us imagine a society in the year 3000 A.D., in which 90 percent of all our present cultural production had been destroyed and of all our television serials only *one* show of lieutenant Columbo had survived.

How would we "read" this work? Would we be moved by such an original picture of a little man in the struggle with the powers of evil, with the forces of capital, with an opulent and racist society dominated by WASPs? Would we appreciate this efficient, concise, and intense representation of the urban landscape of an industrial America?

When—in a single piece of a series—something is simply *presupposed* by the audience, which knows the whole series, would we speak perhaps of an art of synthesis of a sublime capacity of telling through essential allusions?

In other words, how would we read a "piece" of a series, if the whole of the series remained unknown to us?

Such a series of questions could continue indefinitely. I started to put them forth because I think that we still know very little about the role of repetition in the universe of art and in the universe of mass media.

Mark Crispin Miller

ADVERTISING— END OF STORY

Mark Crispin Miller is professor of media studies at Johns Hopkins University. He is author of Boxed In: The Culture of Television *and editor of* Seeing through Movies. *The following reading is excerpted from a longer essay that appears in the latter volume. Here Miller argues that the advertising industry has intervened in filmmaking to such an extent that a well-constructed story is virtually a thing of the past.*

"This approach to human beings strikes me as utterly cynical, and directly contrary to the democratic ideal." Such was the sharp response of Dr. Lewis Webster Jones, head of the National Conference of Christians and Jews. Other clergymen agreed: this new technique could mean the twilight of democracy. "Such a weapon," wrote one rabbi, "could result in the molding of our population's social and political attitudes and beliefs to the point where democracy would be a mockery and freedom meaningless." Nor was it only God's ministers who sensed a terminal threat: "Put to political propaganda purposes," warned Republican congressman William A. Dawson of Utah, this infamous device "would be made to order for the establishment and maintenance of a totalitarian government." Many intellectuals were equally perturbed by this new

instrument, which could, suggested Aldous Huxley, make "nonsense of the whole democratic procedure, which is based on conscious choice on rational ground." Huxley had not, he said, foreseen this invention when writing *Brave New World*—which, he feared, might now come true.

Such were the apprehensions not only of a few edgy pundits but of the nation generally. The public protest was immense. The National Association of Radio and Television Broadcasters felt obliged to ban the use of the technique by any of its members, and the three major television networks also publicly rejected it. The New York State Senate unanimously passed a bill outlawing the technique. When KTLA, an independent TV station in Los Angeles, announced that it would soon start using the invention to discourage littering and unsafe driving, the

Mark Crispin Miller, "Advertising—End of Story," *Seeing through Movies*, ed. Mark Crispin Miller (New York: Pantheon, 1990) 186–246.

station "received such a torrent of adverse mail," *Life* magazine reported, "that it cancelled the campaign."

Meanwhile, there were some who were not emitting "yelps of alarm," according to the *Wall Street Journal*. Indeed, certain forward-looking managers were rather taken with the idea, despite its dangers, or perhaps because of them. These men regarded the new instrument not with foreboding but with a wry and jovial fascination. "Chuckles one TV executive with a conscious eye on the future," reported *Time* magazine in its coverage of the controversy, "'It smacks of brain washing, but of course it would be tempting.'"

The invention that had sparked the national panic, and that was also quietly thrilling certain corporate salesmen, was "subliminal advertising"—a phrase coined by the first of its practitioners, James M. Vicary, "a young motivational researcher and amateur psychologist," as the *Journal* dubbed him. On September 12, 1957, Vicary, vice-president of Subliminal Projection Company, held a press conference to tout the results of an experiment he had just concluded at a movie theater in Fort Lee, New Jersey. For six weeks, using special equipment, he had flashed imperceptible allurements onto the screen during the theater's showing of *Picnic*, a Columbia release. Projected every five seconds for one three-thousandth of a second, those unnoticed coaxings, Vicary said, had dramatically boosted sales out at the concession stand of the items subliminally hyped. Vicary had projected two terse bits of copy: "Hungry? Eat popcorn" and "Drink Coca-Cola."

Today what matters most about Vicary's experiment is not its "findings"—which Vicary fabricated. His device turned out to have had no effect at all on how much Coke or popcorn people swallowed but was a mere sales gimmick used to promote the Subliminal Projection Company itself. However,

while Vicary's "results" were valueless, the outrage stirred by his announcement was important. Back in 1957 the rumor that one movie had been temporarily polluted with an advertising pitch—"Drink Coca-Cola"— was enough to elicit a great wave of angry protest from the American public.

What is the difference between James Vicary's ploy and . . . later cinematic tricks to make an audience "Drink Coca-Cola"? In 1957, Vicary tried to boost his business by implanting a commercial message in a Columbia release (and then by making false claims for the failed experiment). In 1982, Coca-Cola purchased 49 percent of Columbia Pictures and began at once to plug (its own) products in (its own) movies—trying, just like Vicary, to profit by turning movies into advertising. (The company kept it up until it sold Columbia Pictures to Sony in 1989.) Certainly, there is a difference in degree. Whereas Vicary's method was a furtive imposition on the movie, used only in one theater, and only temporarily, the come-ons embedded in Coke's movies are there forever, in whatever prints or tapes you choose to see, because they are worked—overtly—right into the movies' scripts and *mise-en-scène*.

These later exhortations to "Drink Coca-Cola," one might argue, differ crucially from Vicary's gimmick, since his appeal was "subliminal," whereas the later cans and signs beckon us openly, like illuminated billboards. Such a distinction, however, rests on too crude an understanding of "subliminal" effects—which result not from invisible "implants" but from words and/or images that are explicitly presented yet only, at best, half-perceived. These latter-day plugs for Coca-Cola work as "subliminal" inducements because their context is— ostensibly—the movie, not the ad, so that each of them comes sidling toward us dressed as something not an ad and therefore welcome, just as other kinds of ads nowadays routinely come at us disguised as "magalogues" and "advertorials," rock videos, "educational" broadcasts and newsletters, filmstrips and posters, as well as many concerts, art exhibits, sports events, magazines, newspapers, books, TV shows, and a good deal of your daily mail—in short, as anything and everything but advertising.

The "subliminal" impact of the Coke plugs arises not only from their cinematic camouflage but from the rich and pleasant welter of associations that, within each movie, efficiently glamorizes every Coca-Cola can or logo: James Garner's personal warmth and fine old car, and John Candy's would-be riotous antics (as well as each man's patent stardom) are attractions serving as oblique—that is, "subliminal"—enhancements to the all-important product. Precisely because of this benefit, Coca-Cola has been very careful in its choice of cinematic vehicles. And for the same reason, Coca-Cola also used the movies to stigmatize the competition.

This practice represented a sly refinement on official company policy. Shortly after buying into Columbia in 1982, the managers of Coca-Cola sent the studio executives a memo forbidding the use, at company events as well as (by implication) in Columbia productions, of any goods produced by PepsiCo or Philip Morris: Pepsi, Miller, Löwenbräu, 7-Up, Stolichnaya vodka, and Frito-Lay potato chips. Columbia, however, sometimes went beyond mere omission to the deliberate sabotage of rival images. In *Murphy's Romance*, for instance, Field's nice son goes looking for a job; and while "Coca-Cola" sheds its deep-red warmth throughout Murphy's homey general store, in a big supermarket where the kid is told abruptly that he isn't needed, two (blue) Pepsi signs loom coldly on the wall like a couple of swastikas. In fact, the company

used such tactics before its purchase of Columbia. In Costa-Gavras's *Missing* (1982), made just before the acquisition, Jack Lemmon plays a very decent father searching in Chile for his son, who has been kidnapped by Pinochet's soldiers. In one scene this haggard, loyal dad, while talking things out, takes rare (and noticeable) solace in a bottle of Coke—whereas inside the nightmare stadium where the army does its torturing and murdering, there stands a mammoth Pepsi machine, towering within this underworld like a dark idol.

Although PepsiCo owns no movie studio (yet), its officers began fighting back at once. A special manager tackled the job of keeping Pepsi on the silver screen, and from that moment the circular Pepsi logo (white/blue/red) became a film presence almost as ubiquitous as big handguns. In the movies Pepsi is the choice of a new generation—that is, of every generation. The suburban kids are drinking Pepsi in *Ferris Bueller's Day Off*, the poor kids are drinking Pepsi in *Stand and Deliver* and in *Lean on Me*, the old folks are drinking Pepsi in *Cocoon: The Return*. Jennifer Beals is drinking Diet Pepsi in *Flashdance*, Kathy Baker is buying Pepsi in *Clean and Sober*, and in *Legal Eagles* Debra Winger keeps her Pepsi cold and blatant in a refrigerator otherwise full of blank containers. Pepsi glides through the Texas of the fifties in *Everybody's All-American*, Pepsi glows among the Texans of today in *True Stories*, Pepsi pops into the cute Manhattan of *Crossing Delancey*, Pepsi drops in on Norman Bates's milieu in *Psycho II* and *Psycho III*. In *Cobra* a huge neon Pepsi logo shines right outside Sylvester Stallone's apartment (he kicks some ass, fatally, in its cool light), and in **batteries not included* a huge neon Pepsi logo high above Times Square forms the immediate backdrop to a pivotal scene (in which cuddly metal critters zoom back down to save the day, and frolic in the Pepsi sign's warm light). And PepsiCo, too, has tried to move against its major rival, refusing to place a Pepsi ad on the cassette of *Dirty Dancing* unless Vestron, the video company, would cut every scene that showed a Coca-Cola sign. Vestron passed. (All these movies have happy endings.)

Such "subliminal" tactics are certainly not peculiar to the mighty cola rivals, for they are also used today—aggressively—by every other major advertiser. Indeed, cinematic "product placement" has become so common in the eighties that it now sustains a veritable industry. Formerly, plugging was a marginal (if common) practice in the movie industry, the result of direct battering between studio and advertiser: MGM (say) would use a box of (say) Rice Krispies in a movie, and for such exposure Kellogg's would keep the studio commissary stocked with cold cereals for a year. Although a serviceable system, it was not wholly pleasing to the advertiser, who had no guarantee that the all-important footage would not be cut before the film's release, or that the product would be set off vividly enough.

In the eighties the plugging process became "rationalized" as dozens of companies formed to broker deals between advertisers and film producers. Such companies, said one "product placement" manager in 1984, "are getting specific guarantees of exposure now. It's no longer a hit-or-miss situation with the producers or prop masters." Usually the advertisers keep the brokers on retainer with an annual fee and are then charged extra for specific "placements." In return for the plug the manufacturer will help defray the ever-rising costs of filmmaking, not only by providing props or costumes but—more important—by mounting a tie-in promotional campaign that will sell the movie in many ads, in thousands of bright aisles, on millions of clean boxes. . . .

The arrangement seems to work wonders for the budgets of all concerned.

—◆◆◆—

In a few recent films, the subtle use of products does make the fictive milieu more believable than generic items would. Usually, however, "product placement" does not seem "natural" at all but is, in fact, deliberately *anti*-realistic: its sole purpose is to enhance the product by meticulously placing it within the sort of idealized display that occurs nowhere in real life but everywhere in advertising—which is itself just such display. In the world as advertised, the label or logo always shines forth like the full moon, whereas in our world, where "people go shopping and drive cars and drink beer," the crucial symbols reach us (if at all) with none of that sudden, startling clarity: for the very ubiquitousness of advertising has also, paradoxically, worked to hide it from us. To live the "daily life in which people go shopping" is to be bombarded into numbness; and it is this stupefaction that movie plugs (like advertising proper) have been devised to penetrate.

Sailing through the movies, the multitudinous labels and logos of our daily lives appear (or so the advertisers hope) renewed, their stale solicitations freshened up by the movie's magical, revivifying light—and by the careful steps taken to glamorize them. As such plugs are anti-realistic, so are they also anti-narrative, for the same movie-glow that exalts each product high above the "clutter" of the everyday also lifts it out of, and thereby makes it work against, the movie's story (if any). Even when half-turned toward us, coquettishly, and/or placed in some marginal position, the crucial can or box or bottle tends (as it were) to make a scene. An expert rhetorical missile in the first place, and with its force enhanced a thousandfold by advertising, the product cannot even sneak by without distracting us at least a little, its vivid, pleasant features calling, *Hey! It's me!*". . . .

The rise of "product placement" has, however, damaged movie narrative not only through the shattering effect of individual plugs but, more profoundly, through the fundamental shift of power that the practice has wrought within the movie industry: the transfer of creative authority out of the hands of filmmaking professionals and into the purely quantitative universe of the CEOs. All the scenes, shots, and lines mentioned above overemphasizing Coca-Cola, Pepsi, *Fortune*, Pampers, Tylenol, Grey Poupon, Nike, Molson Light, etc., represent the usurpation, by advertising, of those authorial prerogatives once held by directors and screen writers, art directors and set designers—and by studio heads, who at least cared (with widely varying results) about how their films were put together, whereas the managers now in charge are thinking only of their annual reports. "Hollywood has changed," says Edward Meyer of ad agency Saatchi & Saatchi DFS Compton. "Unlike the old days, the bankers and MBAs are calling the shots, and producers have discovered that product placements and tie-in promotions can help cut the movies' production and advertising costs."

Thus the basic decisions of filmmaking are now often made, indirectly, by the advertisers, who are focused not on a movie's narrative integrity but *only* on its viability as a means of pushing products.

END OF STORY: THE MOVIE

. . . Of course, the movies have always used gratuitous tricks to keep viewers riveted: pointless close-ups of a baby's smile to get the women cooing, martial music to tense up the men, sad violins to get the whole house sniffling. Indeed, some of cinema's basic rhetorical devices, it could be argued, are inherently non-narrative, subvisual: cross-cutting for suspense, say, or the weepy reaction shot (which moves the viewers to weep). The point, however, is not that such tricks are new but that they now

are all-important—for their power has been fantastically augumented by computer science, Dolby sound, great strides forward in the art of mock mayhem, and other technological advances.

As the special effects have, since *Star Wars*, become more mind-blowing and yet more believable, they have also advanced in their importance to the spectacle, and have changed in tone. First of all, the effects, in many instances, now *are* the movie, whether it's *Indiana Jones and the Last Crusade* or *Nightmare on Elm Street 3*, films you can sleep through for twenty minutes without then having to ask, "What did I miss?" And as the effects have become the whole show, they have ceased to represent some ambiguous looming force, uncanny or apocalyptic—as in the first *King Kong, The Day the Earth Stood Still*, or *2001: A Space Odyssey*—and have instead become the tools for a light-show that both stimulates and reassures, like fireworks on the Fourth.

Whereas the effects, in other words, were once used, by and large, to fake some scary Threat to All Humanity, they now routinely fake, in one way or another, someone's annihilation—and it is *good*. The wipeout might be violent, as at the end of *Raiders of the Lost Ark* (1981), the Nazis melted down or shriveled up by the wrathful ark light, or as in the horror movies where (say) Jason burns, zaps, and mangles several teens, until some teen then zaps or burns or mangles Jason. Whether the killing force is righteous or demonic, the spectacle of its/his/her destructiveness/destruction invites your rapt gaze of wondering assent—just like those movies that present the wipeout as a sweet translation into outer space (i.e., Heaven): *E.T., Close Encounters of the Third Kind, Cocoon, Cocoon: The Return*—films whose (grateful) characters finally disappear into the all-important light show, just like the films themselves.

WHEN YOU WISH UPON A STAR

Over and over, conventional narrative requirements are broken down by the imperative of violence—which need not only be inflicted by "us," through the movie's hero, but which is just as often used against us, by the movie's anti-hero: for what matters above all, it seems, is that we feel the stimulus. Thus we are victimized by the "sight" of the vampires in *The Lost Boys* (1987) biting off bright-red gobbets of their victims' heads ("Ow!"), or by the sound of Freddy Krueger's razor-nails scraping metal just like fingernails raked across a blackboard, or by the sight/sound of the good guy having his fingers broken *(Blade Runner, Blue Thunder)* or receiving a ballistic kick between the legs *(Shoot the Moon, Black Moon Rising)*. Likewise, the movies now, more than ever, shock us with the old (nonvisual) trick of going "Boo!", a crude startler once used mainly in horror films (and sparingly at that) but now recurring in thriller after thriller (often heightened by the deep "*lub*-dub-*lub*-dub" that simulates your fearful heart-beat.)

The primacy of stimulation has, in short, made the movies more and more cartoonlike. In the cartoon world, nothing stands between the wish to see/feel violence and the enactment of that violence: no demands of plot or character, no physical limitations (space, gravity), no mortality. Ingeniously, and with cruel wit, the cartoon presents a universe wherein the predatory are, over and over, punished for their appetite by the very trees and doors and crockery. Full of rage and purpose, those victim/predators get nowhere and yet never die, pushing on forever, despite the anvils landing on their heads, the steamrollers flattening their bodies out like massive pancakes, the cannonballs zooming down their throats—torments at once severe and harmless, and that occur exclusively because we want to see them happen. . . .

The convergence of the movies with both cartoons and ads makes sense, because the ad and the cartoon each present a fantasy of perfect wish fulfillment: that is, a wish fulfillment that seems both immediate and absolute, arising, on the one hand, from a purchase (which will make life perfect *now*) or, on the other hand, from the animated spectacle itself (in which the universe appears responsive to your wishes). This has been compounded in the movies, which now purvey a wish fulfillment fantasy as extreme as, and far more compelling than, any Coke spot or Tom and Jerry free-for-all.

Although as old as Hollywood itself, the fantasy has, since the late seventies, changed in several crucial ways. First of all, the element of wish fulfillment no longer recurs primarily in a last-minute payoff, obviously tacked on, as it did in so many movies of the past—most notably Hitchcock's *Suspicion* and Frank Capra's *Meet John Doe* (both 1941)—where troubling implications would then have to be negated through some sudden, terminal change of heart or unexpected gift of money. This kind of hasty ending is still used today, although the "problems" dramatized, and then dismissed, are generally much slighter than they used to be, and the "solutions" are even more perfunctory. . . .

Often, however, today's cinematic wish fulfillment comes not in an abrupt and gratuitous final moment, as if the writer(s) didn't know what else to do, but as an obviously calculated piling up of surplus triumphs—triumph upon triumph upon triumph—not as a quick way to end the film, in other words, but as its very purpose. Many movies now purvey such surplus wish fulfillment, film after film repeatedly screaming: "You *can* have it all!"

. . . Formerly the movie was (like many ads before the seventies) a sort of exit visa from the working world, proffering an "escape" through empathy with some intrepid hero/heroine, who has a lofty job to do in some exotic or aristocratic setting. By contrast, today's movies tend to extol not the lucky, plucky character who marries up or wins a war but the star who plays that character—and who shines as the true object of your empathy, sheerly because s/he is the center of attention. The change is evident in all those closing-credit sequences that feature outtakes of the stars euphorically kidding on the set, and in those numerous sequences of teen heroes lip-synching famous hits and posturing like rock stars before imaginary crowds of loving fans, and in the frequent "comic" bit that has a character do the rapturous sportscast commentary on his own athletic horseplay, also performed before imaginary cheering crowds. In short, *feeling warmly watched by everyone* now seems a sweeter fantasy than the fictitious heroisms of past cinema, in which the star's fame helped to glamorize the story—whereas celebrity now is the story, just as in the ads.

Abrupt, illogical, unmotivated, the new happy ending is, as narrative, a total washout. And that is precisely what it's meant to be: each cheery climax functions not to end the story but to liquefy it. As everybody seems to melt into the spectacle, the "problems" that had kept the story going, however minimally, need no longer be resolved, because this sweetest of all pleasures has *dissolved* them: the bliss of being in the spectacle, of being (like the stars) lovingly looked up to and (also like the stars) watched over. . . .

Thus the movies promise us no distance, no difference—and *no ending*. Made for, and helping to create, an audience terrified of time itself, an audience eager to "forget tomorrow and forget yesterday," the movies now conclude their "narratives" without seeming to terminate them, as if to assure us

that the spectacle will never end at all. Such is the implicit promise of the gimmick that now ends, or rather stops, most movies, a gimmick that, in film after film, follows even the new happy ending, as a bit of (as it were) surplus reassurance: the freeze-frame, whereby the movie actually negates the crucial power of its own cameras to make a keen, enduring record of the passage of time.

"IF HISTORY HAS TAUGHT US ANYTHING . . ."

Formerly the movies sold a vision of utopia, allowing—indeed, exploiting—the impulse to escape into another place: a balmy land of plenty, where the people would be kind (and, in most movies, all the same). This vision often made the movies memorable. In 1939, for instance, the best big productions ended—albeit naïvely, or dishonestly—with their gazes outward, looking past the whole dispiriting mechanism of production: toward that place "across the border" where Dallas and the Ringo Kid are headed, or toward that Paradise beyond the snows where Heathcliff will love Cathy for all time, or toward Jefferson Smith's rejuvenated nation, or toward that new Union wherein Rhett and Scarlett now will go their separate ways, or toward that homey farm where Dorothy *will* now find her "heart's desire."

Today's movies offer no utopia, since everything you'd ever want, they say, is here on sale. They make this pitch first of all by concentrating on, and glamorizing, the closed sites of shopping and consumption: nice restaurants and luminous department stores, and the clean and roomy cell wherein the star keeps his/her posters, sweaters, jackets, copper pots, appliances. And the movie makes the pitch by packaging *itself* as a commodity—as an item, like any smoke or Coke or burger, whose appeal does not outlast the moment that it takes to suck it in.

And so going to the movies now is about as memorable as going to the airport. Conceived and sold as "product," just like the many products that it sells, so does the movie pass right through you, leaving nothing in you but the vague, angry craving for another one. Today, that craving is what keeps the movies going—and so the movies sell that kind of appetite, that infantile ravenousness, even as they offer you a daydream of your own tremendous strength. Reconsider the famous bat sign that, in 1989, sold *Batman* on several million bits of merchandise. Seen the obvious way, that logo is a stylized emblem of the bat in flight, a sign inviting you to think of Batman and to feel yourself as zooming likewise high above the lethal city. Seen another way, it shows the open mouth of an insatiable half-wit: Pac-Man seen from the front, about to take another bite.

But this is much too grim an ending; because the movies, at their best, have reminded us, forcefully, that things should be otherwise—which is why advertising urges us to laugh them off, to "see right through them." Those movies have to be suppressed, revised, their power forgotten, because they don't just bedazzle us with a blurred promissory vision of utopia but actually enable us to *see*, through them, the real workings of the very system that produced them, and that is now degrading them and us.

"The cinema is a more or less modern thing, and it ought to be used, now and again, as a means of getting something clear about the life that takes hold of us, and our attempts to pretend that the hold is a handshake." Thus, in 1936, one critic expressed the promise of the movies, which have, at times, made good: by treating us not as wired "consumers" but respectfully, as persons (somehow) still outside that system, and so still able to be moved and challenged by its devastations. . . .

DISCUSSION QUESTIONS

1. Do you think that Parker's list of general aspects of form applies to artworks in every medium? Can you think of any counterexamples (artworks in which one or more of these elements do not apply)?
2. Hanslick is so convinced that form is the basis of aesthetic appreciation of music that he considers the written score, performed or not, to be a complete work of music. Do you agree with him on this point?
3. How might a formalist respond to the criticism that content is also an important feature of our experience of representational art?
4. Do you agree with the modernists that artworks should reveal the essence of their media? Do you think that Hanslick concurred, in effect, with the more recent modernist doctrine?
5. Could a formalist agree with Steinberg that art refers to the living concerns of human beings? If so, on what basis?
6. Do you think that Miller is implicitly defending an Aristotelian ideal of organic unity when he complains about what advertising has done to the movies? Why or why not?

FURTHER READING

Babbitt, Milton. "Who Cares If You Listen?" *High Fidelity* (1958). Rpt. as "The Composer as Specialist," *Esthetics Contemporary*. Ed. Richard Kostelanetz. Buffalo: Prometheus, 1978. 280–287.

Bell, Clive. *Art.* Ed. J.B. Bullen. New York: Oxford UP, 1987.

———. *Enjoying Pictures.* London: Chatto and Windus, 1934.

———. *Since Cézanne.* London: Chatto and Windus, 1922.

Burke, Kenneth. "On Form." *Esthetics Contemporary*. Ed. Richard Kostelanetz. Buffalo: Prometheus, 1978. 132–138.

Greenberg, Clement. *Art and Culture: Critical Essays.* Boston: Beacon, 1961.

Hanslick, Eduard. *On the Musically Beautiful.* Trans. Geoffrey Payzant. Indianapolis: Hackett, 1986.

Rosenblum, Robert. *Modern Art and the Northern Romantic Tradition.* London: Thames and Hudson, 1975.

ART AS EXPRESSING
OR AROUSING EMOTION

For several decades during the twentieth century, the government of the now defunct Soviet Union waged campaigns against artists accused of "formalism." By formalism, the Soviets meant art that was pursued for its own sake, not in an effort to promote moral or social ideals. Even composers such as Prokofiev and Shostakovich were required to recant their "formalism" and were instructed instead to compose music that would speak to the workers, employing melodies from the "folk" tradition, structured in ways that would be clearly intelligible to them.

Some of the artistic consequences of the Soviet admonition to avoid formalism seem, at least from a distance, rather dubious achievements. The "socialist realist" art that sought to depict workers as they joined the march of socialism through human society was often plodding and exaggeratedly obvious in its efforts to ensure intelligibility, even to those with little exposure to art. Nevertheless, the Soviet position is not unique in Western history. The view that art should speak to the community as a whole, and not just to a narrow elite, has been and remains the assumption of many of the more democratically minded analysts of art, and also of those who see art as a vehicle for moral education of the masses.

Russian novelist Leo Tolstoy, for example, contends that responses to art should be communal experiences. He fears, however, that too many have lost sight of art's real purpose. The purpose of art is to unite a community in sympathetic emotion, which the artwork transmits to its audience. Art is fundamentally a form of communication, and the bonds it forms among members of its audience are vital to the health of a society. When art becomes merely decorative, as Tolstoy believes that it has for many of the well-to-do, it has become decadent and is no longer socially justifiable.

Clive Bell, a twentieth-century British art critic, also believes that art aims to arouse emotion. Bell insists, however, emotions aroused by art are features of *aesthetic* experience only when they respond to formal elements. Concerned with explaining French Postimpressionist painting to a British audience, Bell defends the new style with formalist arguments. Our primary focus in genuinely aesthetic experience of art, he contends, is "significant form," the fundamental relations among lines and colors. Significant form is as important in traditional painting as in the less representational works coming from France; but the latter more directly invite contemplation of form from their audiences. Bell resembles Kant in insisting that form is the primary object of aesthetic contemplation. But more like Kant's nemesis, David Hume, Bell claims that the appropriate response to significant form is emotional.

Susanne K. Langer, an American philosopher of the twentieth century, also conjoins formalism with a theory that art is concerned with emotion. She agrees with Bell that art of aesthetic value arouses aesthetic emotion, but she insists that the pleasure involved in aesthetic experience is more importantly an intellectual than an emotional satisfaction. Aesthetic experience is akin to the experience of discovering truth; and indeed, art does help us to discover certain truths about ourselves. Art bears an isomorphism, or a similarity of shape, with our mental and emotional lives. It presents these shapes for our reflection. The thrill we experience in connection with art arises because it offers intellectual insight into our own nature.

According to Robin G. Collingwood, art's defining purpose is not to arouse emotion. Instead, he contends that art *expresses* emotion. A person can arouse emotions in others without personally experiencing those emotions. Artists, however, are not involved in such manipulative endeavors. Instead, the process of making art is an exploration of the artist's own emotions. Like Langer, Collingwood sees art as a means by which we make our emotional lives clear to ourselves.

The concept of expression, however, is not straightforwardly obvious. John Hospers's essay "The Concept of Artistic Expression" does not develop a positive theory of expression; instead, it presents objections to the casual equation that many of us make between emotions we take art to express and those experienced by the artist or the audience. Hospers analyzes some of the problems posed by assertions, like Collingwood's, that the artist is exploring his or her own emotions when making art. Hospers questions whether we are justified in attributing particular emotional experiences (or any other subjective states) to artists on the basis of their works. He also raises objections to views, such as Tolstoy's, that associate artistic expression of emotion with the communication of emotion from artist to audience.

Whether or not an artwork can be said to *communicate* the artist's emotion, David Novitz believes that the emotional response of the reader can be crucial to understanding fiction fully. Emotional engagement results when we imaginatively "make believe" that the fictional account is actual, according to Novitz. Like Langer, Novitz emphasizes both our intellectual and our emotional engagement in art. Our ability to respond emotionally depends on the thinking process involved in "making believe." At the same time, our understanding of a work depends on our emoting in response to the story.

Those who take emotion to be fundamental to aesthetic experience usually think that these emotions figure in our enjoyment of art. But certain emotions allegedly provoked by art do not seem obviously enjoyable. Stephen Davies considers the "sad" feelings inspired by certain music. Our enjoyment of such music is puzzling, he observes, for we deliberately listen to such music but try to avoid sadness in real life. The explanation becomes evident when we consider why we are interested in music in general, Davies contends. What we enjoy about art is the process of coming to understand it, even if this process sometimes occasions unpleasant emotions. While this predilection for a sometimes unpleasant process might seem perplexing, Davies contends that this is simply a human tendency that is evident in other human activities as well as art.

Opponents of theories that emphasize the arousal of emotion have sometimes complained about the quality of emotions aroused. Milan Kundera describes the emotional reactions induced by kitsch, art of low aesthetic merit whose appeal is mainly the emotions it elicits. Taking the example of a Czechoslovakian May Day parade, Kundera suggests that kitsch plays with stock images that allow the audience the wallow in "feel-good" emotions. Kitsch makes no effort to represent reality as it is, Kundera maintains. Instead it presents deceptive images of absolute good and absolute evil that hinder our understanding of reality, which is far more complicated.

Matei Calinescu is also interested in kitsch and the historical context from which it emerged. Kitsch, he points out, is a recent phenomenon, dependent on specific technological and social developments. Calinescu analyzes kitsch as a manifestation of middle-class sensibilities. Kitsch does not aspire to artistic entertainment. Kitsch, according to Calinescu, is a product of contemporary consumer society, with its particular conceptions of relaxation and fun.

Leo Tolstoy

WHAT IS ART?

Leo Tolstoy (1828–1910) was a Russian writer and one of the world's great novelists. His novels War and Peace *and* Anna Karenina *are considered classics. He also wrote nonfictional works on art and religion, defending the view that art has a primarily moral function. In the excerpts that follow, he contends that art serves its true purpose only when it communicates emotion, and that the upper classes, with their preference for mere decoration, have lost sight of this purpose.*

Every work of art causes the receiver to enter into a certain kind of relationship both with him who produced, or is producing, the art, and with all those who, simultaneously, previously, or subsequently, receive the same artistic impression.

Speech, transmitting the thoughts and experiences of men, serves as a means of union among them, and art acts in a similar manner. The peculiarity of this latter means of intercourse, distinguishing it from intercourse by means of words, consists in this, that whereas by words a man transmits his thoughts to another, by means of art he transmits his feelings.

The activity of art is based on the fact that a man, receiving through his sense of hearing or sight another man's expression of feeling, is capable of experiencing the emotion which moved the man who expressed it. To take the simplest example: one man laughs, and another who hears becomes merry; or a man weeps, and another who hears feels sorrow. A man is excited or irritated, and another man seeing him comes to a similar state of mind. By his movements or by the sounds of his voice, a man expresses courage and determination or sadness and calmness, and this state of mind passes on to others. A man suffers, expressing his sufferings by groans and spasms, and this suffering transmits itself to other people; a man expresses his feeling of admiration, devotion, fear, respect, or love to certain objects, persons, or phenomena, and others are infected by the same feelings of admiration,

Leo Tolstoy, *What Is Art?*, trans. Almyer Maude (Indianapolis: Bobbs-Merrill, 1960) 49–51, 71–73.

devotion, fear, respect, or love to the same objects, persons, and phenomena.

And it is upon this capacity of man to receive another man's expression of feeling and experience those feelings himself, that the activity of art is based.

If a man infects another or others directly, immediately, by his appearance or by the sounds he gives vent to at the very time he experiences the feeling; if he causes another man to yawn when he himself cannot help yawning, or to laugh or cry when he himself is obliged to laugh or cry, or to suffer when he himself is suffering—that does not amount to art.

Art begins when one person, with the object of joining another or others to himself in one and the same feeling, expresses that feeling by certain external indications. To take the simplest example: a boy, having experienced, let us say, fear on encountering a wolf, relates that encounter; and, in order to evoke in others the feeling he has experienced, describes himself, his condition before the encounter, the surroundings, the wood, his own lightheartedness, and then the wolf's appearance, its movements, the distance between himself and the wolf, etc. All this, if only the boy, when telling the story, again experiences the feelings he had lived through and infects the hearers and compels them to feel what the narrator had experienced, is art. If even the boy had not seen a wolf but had frequently been afraid of one, and if, wishing to evoke in others the fear he had felt, he invented an encounter with a wolf and recounted it so as to make his hearers share the feelings he experienced when he feared the wolf, that also would be art. And just in the same way it is art if a man, having experienced either the fear of suffering or the attraction of enjoyment (whether in reality or in imagination), expresses these feelings on canvas or in marble so that others are infected by them. And it is also art if a man feels or imagines to himself feelings of delight, gladness,

sorrow, despair, courage, or despondency and the transition from one to another of these feelings, and expresses these feelings by sounds so that the hearers are infected by them and experience them as they were experienced by the composer.

The feelings with which the artist infects others may be most various—very strong or very weak, very important or very insignificant, very bad or very good: feelings of love for one's own country, self-devotion and submission to fate or to God expressed in a drama, raptures of lovers described in a novel, feelings of voluptuousness expressed in a picture, courage expressed in a triumphal march, merriment evoked by a dance, humor evoked by a funny story, the feeling of quietness transmitted by an evening landscape or a lullaby, or the feeling of admiration evoked by a beautiful arabesque—it is all art.

If only the spectators or auditors are infected by the feelings which the author has felt, it is art.

To evoke in oneself a feeling one has experienced, and having evoked it in oneself, then, by means of movements, lines, colors, sounds, or forms expressed in words, so to transmit that feeling that others may experience the same feeling—that is the activity of art.

Art is a human activity consisting in this, that one man consciously, by means of certain external signs, hands on to others the feelings he has lived through, and that other people are infected by these feelings and also experience them.

For the great majority of working-people, our art, besides being inaccessible on account of its costliness, is strange in its very nature, transmitting as it does the feelings of people far removed from those conditions of laborious life which are natural to the great body of humanity. That which is enjoyment to a man of the rich classes is incomprehensible as a pleasure to a work-ingman, and evokes in him either no feeling at all or only a feeling quite contrary to that which it evokes in an idle and satiated man. Such feelings as form the chief subjects of present-day art—say, for instance, honor, patriotism, and amorousness—evoke in a workingman only bewilderment and con-tempt, or indignation. So that even if a possi-bility were given to the laboring classes in their free time to see, to read, and to hear all that forms the flower of contemporary art (as is done to some extent in towns by means of picture galleries, popular concerts, and libraries), the workingman (to the extent to which he is a laborer and has not begun to pass into the ranks of those per-verted by idleness) would be able to make nothing of our fine art, and if he did under-stand it, that which he understood would not elevate his soul but would certainly, in most cases, pervert it. To thoughtful and sin-cere people there can, therefore, be no doubt that the art of our upper classes never can be the art of the whole people. But if art is an important matter, a spiritual blessing, essential for all men ("like religion," as the devotees of art are fond of saying), then it should be accessible to everyone. And if, as in our day, it is not accessible to all men, then one of two things: either art is not the vital matter it is represented to be or that art which we call art is not the real thing.

The unbelief of the upper classes of the European world had this effect—that instead of an artistic activity aiming at trans-mitting the highest feelings to which human-ity has attained, those flowing from religious perception, we have an activity which aims at affording the greatest enjoyment to a cer-tain class of society. And all of the immense domain of art, that part has been fenced off and is alone called art which affords enjoy-ment to the people of this particular circle.

Apart from the moral effects on Euro-pean society of such a selection from the whole sphere of art of what did not deserve such a valuation, and the acknowledgement of it as important art, this perversion of art has weakened art itself and well-nigh destroyed it. The first great result was that art was deprived of the infinite, varied, and profound religious subject matter proper to it. The second result was that having only a small circle of people in view, it lost its beauty of form and became affected and obscure; and the third and chief result was that it ceased to be either natural or even sincere and became thoroughly artificial and brain-spun.

Clive Bell

EMOTION IN RESPONSE TO SIGNIFICANT FORM

Clive Bell (1881–1964) was an English art critic whose works, such as Art *and* Since Cézanne, *were instrumental in achieving the acceptance of Postimpressionist art in Britain. The following selection includes a statement of his theory of significant form. Bell contends that the aesthetic merits of an artwork depend on its formal relations and that aesthetic emotion responds to these relations.*

The starting-point for all systems of aesthetics must be the personal experience of a peculiar emotion. The objects that provoke this emotion we call works of art. All sensitive people agree that there is a peculiar emotion provoked by works of art. I do not mean, of course, that all works provoke the same emotion. On the contrary, every work produces a different emotion. But all these emotions are recognisably the same in kind; so far, at any rate, the best opinion is on my side. That there is a particular kind of emotion provoked by works of visual art, and that this emotion is provoked by every kind of visual art, by pictures, sculptures, buildings, pots, carvings, textiles, &c., &c., is not disputed, I think, by anyone capable of feeling it. This notion is called the aesthetic emotion; and if we can discover some quality common and peculiar to all the objects that provoke it, we shall have solved what I take to be the central problem of aesthetics. We shall have discovered the essential quality in a work of art, the quality that distinguishes works of art from all other classes of objects.

For either all works of visual art have some quality, or when we speak of "works of art" we gibber. Everyone speaks of "art," making a mental classification by which he distinguishes the class "works of art" from all other classes. What is the justification of this classification? What is the quality common and peculiar to all members of this class? Whatever it be, no doubt it is often found in company with other qualities; but

Clive Bell, *Art* (London: Chatto and Windus, 1914) 6–10, 27–30.

they are adventitious—it is essential. There must be some one quality without which a work of art cannot exist; possessing which, in the least degree, no work is altogether worthless. What is this quality? What quality is shared by all objects that provoke our aesthetic emotions? What quality is common to Sta. Sophia and the windows at Chartres, Mexican sculpture, a Persian bowl, Chinese carpets, Giotto's frescoes at Padua, and the masterpieces of Poussin, Piero della Francesca, and Cézanne? Only one answer seems possible—significant form. In each, lines and colours combined in a particular way, certain forms and relations of forms, stir our aesthetic emotions. These relations in combinations of lines and colours, these aesthetically moving forms, I call "Significant Form"; and "Significant Form" is the one quality common to all works of visual art.

At this point it may be objected that I am making aesthetics a purely subjective business, since my only data are personal experiences of a particular emotion. It will be said that objects that provoke this emotion vary with each individual, and that therefore a system of aesthetics can have no objective validity. It must be replied that any system of aesthetics which pretends to be based on some objective truth is so palpably ridiculous as not to be worth discussing. We have no other means of recognizing a work of art than our feeling for it. The objects that provoke aesthetic emotion vary with each individual. Aesthetic judgments are, as the saying goes, matters of taste; and about taste, as everyone is proud to admit, there is no disputing. A good critic may be able to make me see, in a picture that had left me cold, things that I had overlooked, till at last, receiving the aesthetic emotion, I recognise it as a work of art. To be continually pointing out those parts, the sum, or rather the combination, of which unite to produce significant form, is the function of criticism. But it is useless for a critic to tell me that something is a work of art; he must make me feel it for myself. This he can do only by making me see; he must get at my emotions through my eyes. Unless he can make me see something that moves me, he cannot force my emotions. I have no right to consider anything a work of art to which I cannot react emotionally; and I have no right to look for the essential quality in anything that I have not *felt* to be a work of art. The critic can affect my aesthetic theories only by affecting my aesthetic experience. All systems of aesthetics must be based on personal experience—that is to say, they must be subjective.

To appreciate a work of art we need bring with us nothing but a sense of form and colour and a knowledge of three-dimensional space. That bit of knowledge, I admit, is essential to the appreciation of many great works, since many of the most moving forms ever created are in three dimensions. To see a cube or a rhomboid as a flat pattern is to lower its significance, and a sense of three-dimensional space is essential to the full appreciation of most architectural forms. Pictures which would be insignificant if we saw them as flat patterns are profoundly moving because, in fact, we see them as related planes. If the representation of three-dimensional space is to be called "representation," then I agree that there is one kind of representation which is not irrelevant. Also, I agree that along with our feeling for line and colour we must bring with us our knowledge of space if we are to make the most of every kind of form. Nevertheless, there are magnificent designs to an appreciation of which this knowledge is not necessary: so, though it is not irrelevant to the appreciation of some works of art it is not essential to the appreciation of all. What we must say is that the representation of three-dimensional space is neither irrelevant nor essential to all art, and that every other sort of representation is irrelevant.

That there is an irrelevant representative or descriptive element in many great works of art is not in the least surprising. Why it is not surprising I shall try to show elsewhere. Representation is not of necessity baneful, and highly realistic forms may be extremely significant. Very often, however, representation is a sign of weakness in an artist. A painter too feeble to create forms that provoke more than a little aesthetic emotion will try to eke that little out by suggesting the emotions of life. To evoke the emotions of life we must use representation. Thus a man will paint an execution, and, fearing to miss with his first barrel of significant form, will try to hit with his second by raising an emotion of fear or pity. But if in the artist an inclination to play upon the emotions of life is often the sign of a flickering inspiration, in the spectator a tendency to seek, behind form, the emotions of life is a sign of defective sensibility always. It means that his aesthetic emotions are weak or, at any rate, imperfect. Before a work of art people who feel little or no emotion for pure form find themselves at a loss. They are deaf men at a concert. They know that they are in the presence of something great, but they lack the power of apprehending it. They know that they ought to feel for it a tremendous emotion, but it happens that the particular kind of emotion it can raise is one that they can feel hardly or not at all. And so they read into the forms of the work those facts and ideas for which they are capable of feeling emotion, and feel for them the emotions that they can feel—the ordinary emotions of life. When confronted by a picture, instinctively they refer back its forms to the world from which they came. They treat created form as though it were imitated form, a picture as though it were a photograph. Instead of going out on the stream of art into a new world of aesthetic experience, they turn a sharp corner and come straight home to the world of human interest. For them the significance of a work of art depends on what they bring to it; no new thing is added to their lives, only the old material is stirred. A good work of visual art carries a person who is capable of appreciating it out of life into ecstasy: to use art as a means to the emotions of life is to use a telescope for reading the news. You will notice that people who cannot feel pure aesthetic emotions remember pictures by their subjects; whereas people who can, as often as not, have no idea what the subject of a picture is. They have never noticed the representative element, and so when they discuss pictures they talk about the shapes of forms and the relations and quantities of colours. Often they can tell by the quality of a single line whether or no a man is a good artist. They are concerned only with lines and colours, their relations and quantities and qualities; but from these they win an emotion more profound and far more sublime than any that can be given by the description of facts and ideas.

Susanne K. Langer

THE
SYMBOL
OF FEELING

Susanne K. Langer (1865–1985) was an American philosopher whose works focused on linguistic analysis and aesthetics. A student of Alfred North Whitehead, Langer developed a theory of artistic meaning in terms of Whitehead's theory of symbolic modes. Her books on aesthetics include Philosophy in a New Key, Mind: An Essay on Human Feeling, Problems of Art, *and* Feeling and Form: A Theory of Art. *Langer defines art as the creation of symbolic forms for human feeling. In the reading that follows, she clarifies what she means by such symbolic forms by taking music as her primary example.*

In language, which is the most amazing symbolic system humanity has invented, separate words are assigned to separately conceived items in experience on a basis of simple, one-to-one correlation. A word that is not composite (made of two or more independently meaningful vocables, such as "omni-potent," "com-posite") may be assigned to mean any object *taken as one.* We may even, by fiat, take a word like "omnipotent," and regarding it as one, assign it a connotation that is not composite, for instance by naming a race horse "Omnipotent." Thus Praisegod Barbon ("Barebones") was an indivisible being although his name is a composite word. He had a brother called "If-Christ-had-not-come-into-the-world-thou-wouldst-have-been-damned." The simple correlation between a name and its bearer held here between a whole sentence taken as one word and an object to which it was arbitrarily assigned. Any symbol that names something is "taken as one"; so is the object. A "crowd" is a lot of people, but *taken as a lot,* i.e., as one crowd.

So long as we correlate symbols and concepts in this simple fashion we are free to pair them as we like. A word or mark used arbitrarily to denote or connote something may be called an associative symbol, for its meaning depends entirely on association. As soon, however, as words taken to denote

Susanne K. Langer, *Feeling and Form* (London: Routledge, 1953) 30–32.

different things are used in combination, something is expressed by the way they are combined. The whole complex is a symbol, because the combination of words brings their connotations irresistibly together in a complex, too, and this complex of ideas is analogous to the word-complex. To anyone who knows the meanings of all the constituent words in the name of Praisegod's brother, the name is likely to sound absurd, because it is a sentence. The concepts associated with the words form a complex concept, the parts of which are related in a pattern analogous to the word-pattern. Word-meanings and grammatical forms, or rules for word-using, may be freely assigned; but once they are accepted, propositions emerge automatically as the meanings of sentences. One may say that the elements of propositions are *named* by words, but propositions themselves are *articulated* by sentences.

A complex symbol such as a sentence, or a map (whose outlines correspond formally to the vastly greater outlines of a country), or a graph (analogous, perhaps, to invisible conditions, the rise and fall of prices, the progress of an epidemic) is an *articulate form*. Its characteristic symbolic function is what I call *logical expression*. It expresses relations; and it may "mean"—connote or denote—any complex of elements that is of the same articulate form as the symbol, the form which the symbol "expresses."

Music, like language, is an articulate form. Its parts not only fuse together to yield a greater entity, but in so doing they maintain some degree of separate existence, and the sensuous character of each element is affected by its function in the complex whole. This means that the greater entity we call a composition is not merely produced by mixture, like a new color made by mixing paints, but is *articulated*, i.e., its internal structure is given to our perception.

Why, then, is it not a *language* of feeling, as it has often been called? Because its

elements are not words—independent associative symbols with a reference fixed by convention. Only as an articulate form is it found to fit anything; and since there is no meaning assigned to any of its parts, it lacks one of the basic characteristics of language—fixed association, and therewith a single, unequivocal reference. We are always free to fill its subtle articulate forms with any meaning that fits them; that is, it may convey an idea of anything conceivable in its logical image. So, although we do receive it as a significant form, and comprehend the processes of life and sentience through its audible, dynamic pattern, it is not a language, because it has no vocabulary.

Perhaps, in the same spirit of strict nomenclature, one really should not refer to its content as "meaning," either. Just as music is only loosely and inexactly called a language, so its symbolic function is only loosely called meaning, because the factor of conventional reference is missing from it. . . . But meaning, in the usual sense recognized in semantics, includes the condition of conventional reference, or the consummation of the symbolic relationship. Music has *import*, and this import is the pattern of sentience—the pattern of life itself, as it is felt and directly known. Let us therefore call the significance of music its "vital import" instead of "meaning," using "vital" not as a vague laudatory term, but as a qualifying adjective restricting the relevance of "import" to the dynamism of subjective experience.

So much, then, for the theory of music; music is "significant form," and its significance is that of a symbol, a highly articulated sensuous object, which by virtue of its dynamic structure can express the forms of vital experience which language is peculiarly unfit to convey. Feeling, life, motion and emotion constitute its import.

Here, in rough outline, is the special theory of music which may, I believe, be generalized to yield a theory of art as such. The basic concept is the articulate but non-discursive form having import without conventional reference, and therefore presenting itself not as a symbol in the ordinary sense, but as a "significant form," in which the factor of significance is not logically discriminated, but is felt as a quality rather than recognized as a function. If this basic concept be applicable to all products of what we call "the arts," i.e., if all works of art may be regarded as significant forms in exactly the same sense as musical works, then all the essential propositions in the theory of music may by extended to the other arts, for they all define or elucidate the nature of the symbol and its import.

At this point I will make bold to offer a definition of art, which serves to distinguish a "work of art" from anything else in the world, and at the same time to show why, and how, a utilitarian object may be *also* a work of art; and how a work of so-called "pure" art may fail of its purpose and be simply bad, just as a shoe that cannot be worn is simply bad by failing its purpose. It serves, moreover, to establish the relation of art to physical skill, or making, on the one hand, and to feeling and expression on the other. Here is the tentative definition, on which the following chapters are built: Art is the creation of forms symbolic of human feeling.

The word "creation" is introduced here with full awareness of its problematical character. There is a definite reason to say a craftsman *produces* goods, but *creates* a thing of beauty; a builder *erects* a house, but *creates* an edifice if the house is a real work of architecture, however modest. An artifact as such is merely a combination of material parts, or a modification of a natural object to suit human purposes. It is not a creation, but an arrangement of given factors. A work of art, on the other hand, is more than an "arrangement" of given things—even qualitative things. Something emerges from the arrangement of tones or colors, which was not there before, and this, rather than the arranged material, is the symbol of sentience.

The making of this expressive form is the creative process that enlists a man's utmost technical skill in the service of his utmost conceptual power, imagination. Not the invention of new original turns, nor the adoption of novel themes, merits the word "creative," but the making of any work symbolic of feeling, even in the most canonical context and manner. A thousand people may have used every device and convention of it before. A Greek vase was almost always a creation, although its form was traditional and its decoration deviated but little from that of its numberless forerunners. The creative principle, nonetheless, was probably active in it from the first throw of the clay.

To expound that principle, and develop it in each autonomous realm of art, is the only way to justify the definition, which really is a philosophical theory of art in miniature.

Robin G. Collingwood

EXPRESSING
EMOTION

Robin G. Collingwood (1889–1943) was a British historian and philosopher. He was the author of books in a variety of areas of philosophy, including Outlines of a Philosophy of Art *and* Principles of Art. *In this excerpt from the latter, Collingwood differentiates between arousing, describing, betraying, and expressing emotion. Only the last of these is the province of art, according to Collingwood.*

EXPRESSING EMOTION AND AROUSING EMOTION

Our first question is this. Since the artist proper has something to do with emotion, and what he does with it is not to arouse it, what is it that he does? It will be remembered that the kind of answer we expect to this question is an answer derived from what we all know and all habitually say; nothing original or recondite, but something entirely commonplace.

Nothing could be more entirely commonplace than to say he expresses them. The idea is familiar to every artist, and to every one else who has any acquaintance with the arts. To state it is not to state a philosophical theory or definition of art; it is to state a fact or supposed fact about which, when we have sufficiently identified it, we shall have later to theorize philosophically. For the present it does not matter whether the fact that is alleged, when it is said that the artist expresses emotion, is really a fact or only supposed to be one. Whichever it is, we have to identify it, that is, to decide what it is that people are saying when they use the phrase. Later on, we shall have to see whether it will fit into a coherent theory.

They are referring to a situation, real or supposed, of a definite kind. When a man is said to express emotion, what is being said about him comes to this. At first, he is conscious of having an emotion, but not conscious of what this emotion is. All he is conscious of is a perturbation or excitement, which he feels going on within him, but of whose nature he is ignorant. While in this state, all he can say about his emotion is: "I feel . . . I don't know what I feel." From this helpless and oppressed condition he extricates himself by doing something which we call expressing himself. This is an activity which has something to do with the thing we call language: he expresses himself

Robin G. Collingwood, *The Principles of Art* (Oxford: Clarendon, 1938) 109–124.

by speaking. It has also something to do with consciousness: the emotion expressed is an emotion of whose nature the person who feels it is no longer unconscious. It has also something to do with the way in which he feels the emotion. As unexpressed, he feels it in what we have called a helpless and oppressed way; as expressed, he feels it in a way from which this sense of oppression has vanished. His mind is somehow lightened and eased.

This lightening of emotions which is somehow connected with the expression of them has a certain resemblance to the "catharsis" by which emotions are earthed through being discharged into a make-believe situation; but the two things are not the same. Suppose the emotion is one of anger. If it is effectively earthed, for example by fancying oneself kicking some one down stairs, it is thereafter no longer present in the mind as anger at all: we have worked it off and are rid of it. If it is expressed, for example by putting it into hot and bitter words, it does not disappear from the mind; we remain angry; but instead of the sense of oppression which accompanies an emotion of anger not yet recognized as such, we have that sense of alleviation which comes when we are conscious of our own emotion as anger, instead of being conscious of it only as unidentified perturbation. This is what we refer to when we say that it "does us good" to express our emotions.

The expression of an emotion by speech may be addressed to someone; but if so it is not done with the intention of arousing a like emotion in him. If there is any effect which we wish to produce in the hearer, it is only the effect which we call making him understand how we feel. But, as we have already seen, this is just the effect which expressing our emotions has on ourselves. It makes us, as well as the people to whom we talk, understand how we feel. A person arousing emotion sets out to affect his audience in a way in which he himself is not necessarily affected. He and his audience stand in quite different relations to the act, very much as physician and patient stand in quite different relations towards a drug administered by the one and taken by the other. A person expressing emotion, on the contrary, is treating himself and his audience in the same kind of way; he is making his emotions clear to his audience, and that is what he is doing to himself.

It follows from this that the expression of emotion, simply as expression, is not addressed to any particular audience. It is addressed primarily to the speaker himself, and secondarily to any one who can understand. Here again, the speaker's attitude towards his audience is quite unlike that of a person desiring to arouse in his audience a certain emotion. If that is what he wishes to do, he must know the audience he is addressing. He must know what type of stimulus will produce the desired kind of reaction in people of that particular sort; and he must adapt his language to his audience in the sense of making sure that it contains stimuli appropriate to their peculiarities. If what he wishes to do is express his emotions intelligibly, he has to express them in such a way as to be intelligible to himself; his audience is then in the position of persons who overhear him doing this. Thus the stimulus-and-reaction terminology has no applicability to the situation.

The means-and-end, or technique, terminology too is inapplicable. Until a man has expressed his emotion, he does not yet know what emotion it is. The act of expressing it is therefore an exploration of his own emotions. He is trying to find out what these emotions are. There is certainly here a directed process: an effort, that is, directed upon a certain end; but the end is not something foreseen and preconceived, to which appropriate means can be thought out in the light of our knowledge of its special character. Expression is an activity of which there can be no technique.

EXPRESSION AND INDIVIDUALIZATION

Expressing an emotion is not the same thing as describing it. To say "I am angry" is to describe one's emotion, not to express it. The words in which it is expressed need not contain any reference to anger as such at all. Indeed, so far as they simply and solely express it, they cannot contain any such reference. The curse of Ernulphus, as invoked by Dr. Slop on the unknown person who tied certain knots, is a classical and supreme expression of anger; but it does not contain a single word descriptive of the emotion it expresses.

This is why, as literary critics well know, the use of epithets in poetry, or even in prose where expressiveness is aimed at, is a danger. If you want to express the terror which something causes, you must not give it an epithet like "dreadful." For that describes the emotion instead of expressing it, and your language becomes frigid, that is inexpressive, at once. A genuine poet, in his moments of genuine poetry, never mentions by name the emotions he is expressing.

Some people have thought that a poet who wishes to express a great variety of subtly differentiated emotions might be hampered by the lack of a vocabulary rich in words referring to the distinctions between them; and that psychology, by working out such a vocabulary, might render a valuable service to poetry. This is the opposite of the truth. The poet needs no such words at all; the existence or nonexistence of a scientific terminology describing the emotions he wishes to express is to him a matter of perfect indifference. If such a terminology, where it exists, is allowed to affect his own use of language, it affects it for the worse.

The reason why description, so far from helping expression, actually damages it, is that description generalizes. To describe a thing is to call it a thing of such and such a kind: to bring it under a conception, to classify it. Expression, on the contrary, individualizes. The anger which I feel here and now, with a certain person, for a certain cause, is no doubt an instance of anger, and in describing it as anger one is telling truth about it; but it is much more than mere anger: it is a peculiar anger, not quite like any anger that I ever felt before, and probably not quite like any anger I shall ever feel again. To become fully conscious of it means becoming conscious of it not merely as an instance of anger, but as this quite peculiar anger. Expressing it, we saw, has something to do with becoming conscious of it; therefore, if being fully conscious of it means being conscious of all its peculiarities, fully expressing it means expressing all its peculiarities. The poet, therefore, in proportion as he understands his business, gets as far away as possible from merely labelling his emotions as instances of this or that general kind, and takes enormous pains to individualize them by expressing them in terms which reveal their difference from any other emotion of the same sort.

This is a point in which art proper, as the expression of emotion, differs sharply and obviously from any craft whose aim it is to arouse emotion. The end which a craft sets out to realize is always conceived in general terms, never individualized. However accurately defined it may be, it is always defined as the production of a thing having characteristics that could be shared by other things. A joiner, making a table out of these pieces of wood and no others, makes it to measurements and specifications which, even if actually shared by no other table, might in principle be shared by other tables. A physician treating a patient for a certain complaint is trying to produce in him a condition which might be, and probably has been, often produced in others, namely, the condition of recovering from that complaint. So an "artist" setting out to produce a certain emotion in his audience is setting out to produce not an individual emotion, but an emotion of a certain kind. It follows that the means appropriate to its production will be not individual means but means of a certain kind: that is to say, means which are always in principle replaceable by other similar means. As every good craftsman insists, there is always a "right way" of performing any operation. A "way" of acting is a general pattern to which various individual actions may conform. In order that the "work of art" should produce its intended psychological effect, therefore, whether this effect be magical or merely amusing, what is necessary is that it should satisfy certain conditions, possess certain characteristics: in other words be, not this work and no other, but a work of this kind and of no other.

This explains the meaning of the generalization which Aristotle and others have ascribed to art. We have already seen that Aristotle's *Poetics* is concerned not with art proper but with representative art, and representative art of one definite kind. He is not analysing the religious drama of a hundred years before, he is analysing the amusement literature of the fourth century, and giving rules for its composition. The end being not individual but general (the production of an emotion of a certain kind) the means too are general (the portrayal, not of this individual act, but of an act of this sort; not, as he himself puts it, what Alcibiades did, but what anybody of a certain kind would do). Sir Joshua Reynolds's idea of generalization is in principle the same; he expounds it in connexion with what he calls "the grand style," which means a style intended to produce emotions of a certain type. He is quite right; if you want to produce a typical case of a certain emotion, the way to do it is to put before your audience a representation of the typical features belonging to the kind of thing that produces it: make your kings very royal, your soldiers very soldierly, your women very feminine, your cottages very cottagesque, your oak-trees very oakish, and so on.

Art proper, as expression of emotion, has nothing to do with all this. The artist proper is a person who, grappling with the problem of expressing a certain emotion, says, "I want to get this clear." It is no use to him to get something else clear, however like it this other thing may be. Nothing will serve as a substitute. He does not want a thing of a certain kind, he wants a certain thing. This is why the kind of person who takes his literature as psychology, saying "How admirably this writer depicts the feelings of women, or bus-drivers, or homosexuals . . . ," necessarily misunderstands every real work of art with which he comes into contact, and takes for good art, with infallible precision, what is not art at all.

EXPRESSING EMOTION AND BETRAYING EMOTION

Finally, the expressing of emotion must not be confused with what may be called the betraying of it, that is, exhibiting symptoms of it. When it is said that the artist in the proper sense of that word is a person who expresses his emotions, this does not mean that if he is afraid he turns pale and stammers; if he is angry he turns red and bellows; and so forth. These things are no doubt called expressions; but just as we distinguish proper and improper senses of the word "art," so we must distinguish proper and improper senses of the word "expression," and in the context of a discussion about art this sense of expression is an improper sense. The characteristic mark of expression proper is lucidity of intelligibility; a person who expresses something thereby becomes conscious of what it is that he is expressing, and enables others to become conscious of it in himself and in them. Turning pale and stammering is a natural accompaniment of fear, but a person who in addition to being afraid also turns pale and stammers does not thereby become conscious of the precise quality of his emotion. About that he is as much in the dark as he would be if (were that possible) he could feel fear without also exhibiting these symptoms of it.

Confusion between these two senses of the word "expression" may easily lead to false critical estimates, and so to false aesthetic theory. It is sometimes thought a merit in an actress that when she is acting a pathetic scene she can work herself up to such an extent as to weep real tears. There may be some ground for that opinion if acting is not an art but a craft, and if the actress's object in that scene is to produce grief in her audience; and even then the conclusion would follow only if it were true that grief cannot be produced in the audience unless symptoms of grief are exhibited by the performer. And no doubt this is how most people think of the actor's work. But if his business is not amusement but art, the object at which he is aiming is not to produce a preconceived emotional effect on his audience but by means of a system of expressions, or language, composed partly of speech and partly of gesture, to explore his own emotions: to discover emotions in himself of which he was unaware, and, by permitting the audience to witness the discovery, enable them to make a similar discovery about themselves. In that case it is not her ability to weep real tears that would mark out a good actress; it is her ability to make it clear to herself and her audience what the tears are about.

This applies to every kind of art. The artist never rants. A person who writes or paints or the like in order to blow off steam, using the traditional materials of art as means for exhibiting the symptoms of emotion, may deserve praise as an exhibitionist, but loses for the moment all claim to the title of artist. Exhibitionists have their uses; they may serve as an amusement, or they may be doing magic. The second category will contain, for example, those young men who, learning in the torment of their own bodies and minds what war is like, have stammered their indignation in verses, and published them in the hope of infecting others and causing them to abolish it. But these verses have nothing to do with poetry.

Thomas Hardy, at the end of a fine and tragic novel in which he has magnificently expressed his sorrow and indignation for the suffering inflicted by callous sentimentalism on trusting innocence, spoils everything by the last paragraph fastening his accusation upon "The president of the immortals." The note rings false, not because it is blasphemous (it offends no piety worthy of the name), but because it is rant. The case against God, so far as it exists, is complete already. The concluding paragraph adds nothing to it. All it does is to spoil the effect of the indictment by betraying a symptom of the emotion which the whole book has already expressed; as if a prosecuting counsel, at the end of his speech, spat in the prisoner's face.

The same fault is especially common in Beethoven. He was confirmed in it, no doubt, by his deafness; but the cause of it was not his deafness but a temperamental inclination to rant. It shows itself in the way his music screams and mutters instead of speaking, as in the soprano part of the Mass in D, or the layout of the opening page in the *Hammerklavier* Sonata. He must have known his failing and tried to overcome it, or he would never have spent so many of his ripest years among string quartets, where screaming and muttering are almost, one might say, physically impossible. Yet even there, the old Adam struts out in certain passages of the *Grosse Fuge*.

It does not, of course, follow that a dramatic writer may not rant in character. The tremendous rant at the end of *The Ascent of F6*, like the Shakespearian[*] ranting on which it is modelled, is done with tongue in cheek. It is not the author who is ranting, but the unbalanced character he depicts; the emotion the author is expressing is the emotion with which he contemplates that character; or rather, the emotion he has towards that secret and disowned part of himself for which the character stands.

[*]Shakespeare's characters rant (1) when they are characters in which he takes no interest at all, but which he uses simply as pegs on which to hang what the public wants, like Henry V; (2) when they are meant to be despicable, like Pistol; or (3) when they have lost their heads, like Hamlet in the graveyard.

John Hospers

THE CONCEPT
OF ARTISTIC
EXPRESSION

John Hospers is professor emeritus of philosophy at the University of Southern California. He specializes in philosophy of mind as well as aesthetics. He is author of Introductory Readings in Aesthetics, Meaning and Truth in the Arts, *and* Artistic Expression.

What, then, is expression? One answer seems obvious, though we shall see that it is not the only one: expression is an activity of the artist in the process of creation; expressing is something that the artist *does*. What precisely is it that the artist does when he expresses? On this point accounts differ from each other considerably, and I can do no more than mention a few main points to indicate briefly the area in which aesthetic philosophers are working when they discuss expression.

. . . It becomes of interest for the philosopher when it is presented, as it often is, as a theory of art. And as such there are a few questions which should be put to it:

1. Expression theories usually speaking of *emotions* as what is being expressed, although sometimes the phrase "expression of *feelings*" is employed; but the meaning of these two terms, and their relation to each other, is not usually made clear. But let that pass: why, one wonders, cannot other things be expressed as well, such as ideas? One wants to know more about *what* it is that the artist *qua* artist is expressing, and, if some things can be expressed and not others, why the limitation.

2. But no matter what the artist is said to be expressing, why should one assume that the artist in his distinctively artistic activity is always expressing? Why not say that he is sometimes representing, for example, or just playing around with tones and colours? And would it really be true to say that doing these things is only a means of expressing? Artists have been creating great works for many centuries, yet only in the last two centuries would it have been customary, or even seemed natural, to say that the distinctive activity of the artist was that of expression. . . .

John Hospers, "The Concept of Artistic Expression," *Proceedings of the Aristotelian Society* 55 (1954–55): 313–44.

Indeed, the written records left by artists, when we have them, sometimes flatly contradict the expression theory—even though artists as a whole probably tend to glamourise themselves and like to leave the impression that they are solitary geniuses engaged in mysterious acts of self-expression. Thus, Poe gives us an account of cold-blooded calculation in the composition of his poem "The Raven," which is such a far cry from the description of the artistic process given us by the expression theory that it would be difficult to make it fit in at any point. And T. S. Eliot said in *The Sacred Wood* that "poetry is not a turning loose of emotion but an escape from emotion." One may, of course, say that if these men did not go through the process described by the theory, they were therefore not artists; but this is surely to allow an *a priori* dogma to take precedence over cold facts. It is, I think, more certain that these men were artists than that any single theory of art, such as the expression theory, is true. And if the theory is presented, not as an *a priori* pronouncement but as an actual account of the creative process in artists, it will have to stand the empirical test, namely: in all cases of admitted works of art, was the process of its creation such as the expression theory describes? And I do not see any evidence that it holds true in all cases.

3. If it is true that not all great art was created in the way the theory describes, it is, I think, even more plainly true that not everything created in the way the theory describes is great art. Let us assume that Shakespeare, Virgil, Mozart, Rembrandt and Hokusai all went through the throes of creation described by the expression theory; the same can be said of any number of would-be poets, painters, and composers whom one has never heard of for the very good reason that they have never produced anything worth looking at twice. I do not mean, now, the deliberate hacks and quacks, the detective-story writers who spin out half a dozen books a year with an eye on next season's market—these could be accused of trying to arouse emotions in others instead of expressing emotions of their own; I mean that host of deeply earnest would-be artists with delusions of grandeur, so dedicated to Art that they would starve if need be to give proper expression to their genius—but who have neither genius nor, sometimes, even talent. The same turmoil and excitement, the same unpredictability of outcome, the feelings of compulsion and dedication, the surcease from emotion from working in a medium, are experienced not alone by the great creators of art but by their hosts of adoring imitators and camp-followers as well as the supreme individualists who sigh and die alone, ignored and unrecognised but devoted still. . . .

4. In any case, can anything at all relating to the artistic process be validly used as a criterion for evaluating an artistic product? Even if all artists did in fact go through the process described by the expression theory, and even if nobody but artists did this, would it be true to say that the work of art was a good one *because* the artist, in creating it, went through this or that series of experiences in plying his medium? Once the issue is put thus baldly, I cannot believe that anyone could easily reply in the affirmative; it seems too plain that the merits of a work of art must be judged by what we can observe in the work of art, quite regardless of the conditions under

which the work of art came into being. Its genesis is strictly irrelevant; what we must judge is the work of art before us, not the artist who created the work. . . .

Our conclusion is, then, that when we make a judgment of aesthetic value upon a work of art, we are in no way judging the process, including any expressive process, which led to its completion, and therefore the act of expression does not enter into a critical judgment. If we do not know what the process was like, we need not on that account hold our judgment of the work in abeyance; and if we do happen to know what it was like, we should not let it sway our judgment of the work. But there *are* times when we *seem* to invoke the process as a criterion of judgment, and these we should now briefly examine. Here is an example from Dewey:

> If one examines into the reason why certain works of art offend us, one is likely to find that the cause is that there is no personally felt emotion guiding the selecting and assembling of the materials presented. We derive the impression that the artist . . . is trying to regulate by conscious intent the nature of the emotion aroused.

One example of this occurs, I suppose, when we feel that a novel is "plot-ridden"—for example, that the novelist has forced his characters into conformity with the demands of a plot which he had outlined in full before giving much thought to his characters. This feeling, I take it, is familiar enough. But is our criticism here really of the author's creative processes? Are we blaming the novel because he outlined the plot first and then manufactured the characters to fit the plot? I do not think so: we criticise the work because the actions that these characters are made to perform are not such as characters of this kind would do; in other words, they oversimplify and

falsify human nature, and it is because of this that we are offended. If the characters strike us as real human beings, we do not care what process the artist went through in creating them: whether he thought of the plot first and the characters afterward, or whatever it may have been. . . .

Thus far we have been discussing the sense of "express" in which expressing is something that the artist does. Let us now turn to another sense, that in which we say that a work of art expresses something, or is expressive. Here we need not bring in the artist's creative process, which we found to be so damaging to the expression theory. . . .

1. There is, I think, a sense in which we can bring in the artist even here. We may say, "The music expresses sadness," meaning thereby the sadness which the artist felt; this sense means approximately the same as "reveal." In this sense there *is* a biographical commitment, for if it should turn out that the artist did not feel any sadness, then this would falsify our statement that the music expressed his sadness: X cannot reveal Y if there is no Y. Just as Jones' face does not express Jones' grief if Jones is not feeling grief, so Jones' music cannot reveal his grief if he feels none. . . .

   Whether the "reveal" sense of "express" is much used of art is doubtful. At any rate, it is primarily used in speaking of a person's state-of-mind as being expressed (revealed) by his facial expression or gestures. If Jones was not feeling joyful, we would retract our statement that his face expressed his joy; but if Mozart was not feeling joy, we would probably not retract our statement that Mozart's rondo expresses joy. This shows that when we make the expression-claim of music we are not involving ourselves in any biographical commitment, anything that could be falsified by knowing more about the composer's biography. We would insist that the music was expressive of joy even if we learned that Mozart hadn't had a joyful moment in his life. Since in this case we do not test our statement by facts about Mozart's life, what *do* we mean when we say that the music expresses, or is expressive of, the emotion?

2. One obvious answer is that to say that the music expresses joy is to say that it *evokes* joy in the listener. (Expression in the rest of the sense in this section is a "to me" characteristic: it may express *X* to you and not to me because it evokes *X* in you but not in me.)

   But this analysis is, I think, at once seen to be too crude to do the job. Music which I say expresses joy may not make me joyful at all, especially if I am in a sour mood today or have just been jilted in love or have already heard the same composition twenty times this week.

3. Perhaps, then, we should say, not that it actually *does* make me feel so-and-so, but that when I hear it I have a *disposition* to feel so-and-so, the fulfilment of this disposition depending on the non-occurrence of certain inhibiting factors such as fatigue, boredom, worry, and sleep. In short, in normal circumstances (and we can specify what these are) the music will make me feel so-and-so, but it will not always do so, just as normally light-waves of a certain character impinging on my retina will make me see red but will not do so if I am drugged or colour-blind.

4. But this, though an improvement, will not do either. Does "The music expresses sadness" ever mean "I am disposed to feel sad when I hear the music"? If it did, why should I ever wish to hear it? Sad experiences, such as suffering personal bereavement or keen disappointment, are not the kind of things we wish to repeat or prolong. Yet sad music does not affect us in this way: it may bring relief, pleasure, even happiness. Strange kind of sadness that causes pleasure!

One may, of course, reply to this as follows: Sadness expressed in music is a very different thing from sadness in life; it is only by a kind of analogy that we use the same word for both. Sadness in music is depersonalised; it is taken out of, or abstracted from, the particular personal situation in which we ordinarily feel it, such as the death of a loved one or the shattering of one's hopes. In music we get what is sometimes called the "essence" of sadness without all the accompanying accidents, or causal conditions which usually bring it into being. In view of this, it is said, we can continue to say music expresses sadness, but we should distinguish the music-sadness, which is a happy experience, from life-sadness, which is not.

Now, this view is not beyond criticism. Why, one might ask, should the experience of sadness come into being when it is cut off from its usual causal conditions? And if it is replied that the experience is, after all, very different, why call it sadness? Is not sadness the kind of experience that accompanies events like bereavement and disappointment, and would it be sadness without these things? . . .

Here, then, is a possible meaning for "The music expresses sadness": "I am disposed, in response to hearing the music, to feel music-sadness." But there are other possible meanings as well.

5. A person may intellectually *recognise* music as expressive of sadness without being disposed to feel it or to have any effective response at all: that is, I may recognise this music as the kind of music which, under other conditions, made me feel music-sadness, and therefore I call this music sad. But this is surely a derivative sense; unless I had at least once actually *had* the feeling, I would be unable to recognise it.

6. I may even say that the music expresses sadness without having ever felt anything in response at all; perhaps I am tone-deaf. But I have heard others say that it expressed sadness and I may recognise this composition as similar to other compositions of which I have heard people say this, and therefore say that this one, too, expresses sadness. Again this is clearly derivative: if I have not experienced the music-sadness, someone else must have. This is strictly a trying-to-keep-up-with-the-Joneses sense: not having a musical sense myself, I disguise this fact by aping the locutions of others.

7. All these are rough characterisations of states of mind evoked in us by the music which may be the criterion for our calling them expressive. But there are other, more demanding and complicated, criteria, which there is not time to discuss in detail. I shall select only one, perhaps the best known, that of Santayana, who says in *The Sense of Beauty* that A (an element in a work of art) does not express B (an emotion) to me unless A and B are confounded with one another in my mind; or, as he says in another passage, A and B are so indissolubly fused together in my mind that I do not think of them as separate entities. The music does not express joy to me unless the joy is felt as being "in the very notes I hear"; if I merely associated joy with the notes, then the

one would merely remind me of the other and the two would not have fused in my mind, and without this fusion there is no expression. . . .

Personally, I am not inclined to say either that a work is better art, or that it is more beautiful, when I say that it is expressive of something. (1) When I hear several compositions and say what they express to me, and then hear some entirely non-descriptive compositions (a Mozart quintet, a Bach fugue) and cannot say what they seem to me expressive of, in fact I cannot honestly say I find them expressive of anything at all, I do not value them any less as music on this account. My judgment of their merit as music remains unchanged by whether I do or do not attribute to them any expressive character. I can say that some passages of *Tristan und Isolde* express longing but I cannot say that the *Prelude and Fugue in G Minor* is expressive of anything, but I still prefer the *Prelude and Fugue* for all that. (2) When I say that a composition expresses this or that, I do not think that its beauty or its merit as music depends on this: I may find many mediocre compositions also expressive of the same emotion. Expressiveness is one thing, then, and beauty is another; why should expressiveness be any more an indicator of beauty in a tune than in a face? Just as there may be faces which are expressive but not beautiful, so also with works of art. (3) On those occasions when I hold the same composition to be both beautiful and expressive, I do not mean to imply that it is beautiful *because* it is expressive. Its beauty seems to depend on an extremely complex, subtle, and delicate combination of tones; and while I cannot say why I find this melody beautiful and another one, almost exactly like it, repulsive, I find the recourse to expressiveness quite unhelpful in explaining the difference. Indeed, when I say that it expresses so-and-so, the expressiveness seems to be as far from constituting its beauty, or even being an explanation of its beauty, as a heap of scattered clothes on the floor constitutes or explains the living beauty of face and form. (4) The expressive quality attributed to a composition by a person or a generation of people may alter, while leaving the attribution of beauty and musical merit unchanged. When Mozart's compositions first appeared, they struck the public as being full of storm and stress as opposed to the serenity and peace characterising the works of Haydn. When Beethoven appeared on the scene, the compositions of Mozart joined those of Haydn in the Olympian realm of calm. And when Beethoven was followed by Brahms, Wagner and Mahler, the expressive qualities attributed to the works of music again shifted. In all this the attribution of musical merit remained fairly stable; the beauty of Mozart's compositions, for example, was nowhere questioned. Again: Hanslick reports that he found the opening passage of the great E flat trio by Schubert "the *ne plus ultra* of energy and passion," while Schumann called that same passage "tender, girlish, and confiding." Yet these two sensitive listeners did not disagree in their judgments about its beauty; if they had been called upon to make a list of all Schubert's works in order of merit, they might well have constructed identical lists. I am not trying to show here that our verdict of expressiveness has nothing to do with our verdict of beauty, but only that it is far from being the only thing, and, in fact, far from being the most important thing. At the very least it should dispose of the notion that beauty *is* expressiveness. Even if we held that all beautiful works were *also* expressive, and *vice versa*, the material equivalence would not constitute an identity.

Expressiveness, then, as constituting, or even being an indicator of, beauty in a work of art is a view I believe we must reject. If one simply stipulates the alleged identity in a definition, "beauty = expression," then I can only say I see no reason to adopt such a

use of terms, and would no more equate them than I would be inclined to say "Blue = solid." If, on the other hand, we tone down the assertion to read, "Whenever you say that something is beautiful, then you will also find that you will want to call that object expressive," then I think we shall find that in many cases this correlation does not hold. In this area, of course, each person can only state how he feels about the matter; if anyone honestly says that all those things he finds beautiful he also finds expressive, and *vice versa*, then I cannot deny what he says, but would still remind him that what he is stating, at most, is a correlation which he has found to hold thus far in his experience between two different things—a correlation which could conceivably be upset by the next instance that appeared. This, indeed, is the possible fate of any contingent connexion.

But we may long since have become impatient with the line of reasoning pursued. . . . What we have been talking about all through it (it will be said) is *evocation*—trying to analyse expression in terms of certain effects, of whatever kind, evoked in the listener or reader or observer. And whatever expression is, it is not evocation; no theory of expression is merely a theory about evocation. So we shall have to look elsewhere if we want a sensible meaning for the term "expression," when used to characterise not artistic processes but works of art.

Why is the evocation-talk inadequate, one might ask, to deal with expression? One could imagine the following reply: To say that a work of art expresses something is not to say that the artist underwent certain creative processes . . . , nor to say that the listener had certain experiences. . . . Rather, it is to say that the artist has communicated something *to* the listener by means of his work. Expression is not just something evoked in us, it is something which the artist *did* which he then *communicated to* us. Thus far we have dealt with the two aspects—artist and audience—in isolation from each other; but we should have considered them both together; this has been our error. . . .

. . . Let me state some objections. . . .

1. There are many experiences which the artist undergoes in the process of creation—the divine agonies of inception, the slow working through of ideas to fruition, and the technical details of execution—which the audience need not and probably should not share. This part of the artist's creative activity need in no sense be communicated. For example, much of the creative process may be agonising or even boring, but the audience on viewing or hearing the work of art should not feel either agonised or bored. At most, then, it is only a selection of the artist's experiences in creation that should be communicated. One should not speak as if somehow the artist's whole experience (including emotion) in creation were somehow transferred bodily to the observer or listener.

2. Even for the part that the artist wants to communicate to his audience, it is not necessary that he be feeling this at the time of creation, as the theory so often seems to imply. When the artist is under the sway or spell of an emotion, he is all too inclined to be victim and not master of it, and therefore not to be in a good position to create a work of art, which demands a certain detachment and distance as well as considerable lucidity and studied self-discipline. Wordsworth himself said that the emotion should be recollected in tranquility; and others, such as Eliot, have gone further and expunged emotion from the

account altogether. Perhaps, then, it might be held essential only that the artist *have had* the emotion at some time or other. But if all that is required is that the artist have had some emotion or other of type X, then, since most people of any sensitivity have experienced a considerable part of the gamut of human emotions, including some from type X or any other one chooses to mention, this feature in no way distinguishes the artist, and the theory loses all its punch: it becomes innocuous and, like all highly diluted solutions, uninteresting and undistinctive.

3. To say that the audience should feel the same kind of emotion as the artist seems often to be simply not true. Perhaps, in lyric poems and some works of music, the listener may feel an emotion of the same kind as the artist once felt; but in many cases this is not so at all. Even when we do feel emotions in response to works of art (and most of the time what we experience should probably not be called "emotions" at all), they are often of a quite different sort: if the author has expressed anger, we feel not anger but (perhaps) horror or repulsion; if he has expressed anguish, we may feel not anguish but pity. . . .

4. Epistemologically the most ticklish point for the expression theory is simply this: how can we ever know for sure that the feeling in the mind of the artist was anything like the feeling aroused in a listener or observer? Our judgments on this point, in cases where we do have some evidence, have notoriously often been mistaken. We might feel absolutely certain that Mozart felt joy when he composed the Haffner Symphony, and be amazed to discover that during this whole period of his life he was quite miserable, full of domestic dissension, poverty, and

disease. A happy composition does not imply a happy composer. . . .

This consequence is fatal if the expression theory is made a criterion of good art. For it would follow that, if we cannot know whether the emotion felt by a listener is of the same kind as that felt by the artist, we cannot know whether or not his is a good work of art. Therefore, in those cases where we have no records or they are of dubious value, we must hold our judgment of the work of art in abeyance. And such a consequence, it would seem, makes the theory in this form pass the bounds of the ridiculous.

"But," it may be said, "we don't have to find out from the artist himself or from written records what emotion the artist felt—we can tell this from seeing or hearing the work of art!" But this is precisely what we cannot do. Though in this area conviction is strong and subjective feelings of certainty run high, our inferences from work of art to artist are as likely as not to be mistaken. . . .

We might, in the light of these objections, wish to revise the theory so as not to require that the audience should feel what the artist felt, but only what the artist *intended* the audience feel. But when this is done, difficulties again confront us: (1) The same difficulties that attend our knowing how the artist felt are also present, though sometimes in lesser degree, in our knowing what he intended. (2) The artist's whole intention may have misfired; he may have intended us to feel one thing, but if even the most careful and sensitive listeners for generations fail to feel anything like this when they hear his composition, shall we still say that we should feel what the artist intended us to feel? (3) The moment we abandon the stipulation that the audience should feel, not as the artist felt but as the artist intended the

audience to feel, we seem to abandon anything that could be called the expression theory. For it is characteristic of the expression theory that the artist must have felt something which he wants us also to feel; if he did not feel it, but only tried to make us feel it or intended us to feel it, this is no longer an expression of feeling on his part but a deliberate attempt to evoke it in others—in other words, not expression but arousal. . . .

"To say," we might object, "that the artist went through a certain series of experiences, or (if you prefer) interactions with his artistic medium, is indeed to talk about expression, in the sense of the expressive *process;* this is chiefly of importance if we are interested in the psychology of artistic creation; it says nothing about the expressive *product.* The attempt to talk about the expressive product in terms of what feelings it evokes in an audience is, I think, a mistake; and so is the attempt to talk about it as a transaction between the artist and the audience. It is neither the artist nor the audience that matters here; it is the work of art itself. It is *the music* which is expressive; and the music may be expressive even if the artist had no emotions when he wrote it, and even if the audience is composed of such insensitive clods that they feel nothing when they hear it. The expressiveness of the music is dependent on neither of these things." . . .

Yet how are we in the final analysis to defend such a claim? If our opponent in the controversy has just as long an experience of music as we have, and is just as learned, sincere and intelligent, and after repeated hearings he retains his conviction, what now can we do? Shall we simply say, "Now ends the argument and begins the fight"? Or is there some way in which we can defend the view that the music *really does* express what we say it does? I shall conclude this paper by offering two possible suggestions or lines of approach, though I am dubious about the helpfulness of either of them.

1. We may take pains to define the music's expressive character in terms of certain configurations of tones or rhythmic patterns in the music. We may say, for example, that music is expressive of sadness if it falls within a certain range or (rather slow) tempo, is in the minor key, has more than a certain proportion of sixths or diminished thirds among its harmonic intervals, etc. The formula will have to be extremely complex, for the characteristics of music which make us say that a composition expresses sadness are extremely numerous. Moreover, it may be that no single one of them is necessary; for example, sad music does not *have* to be in the minor key; it is only necessary that some of them be present. . . .

   The reason why this suggestion may not be helpful is, of course, that our opponent may reject these patterns of notes as expressive of sadness. He will, perhaps, present a counter-list of sad-making features. The difficulty is that which features of the music we are willing to include on our list of sad-making features is dependent on which features of the music make us feel the music-sadness, or, at any rate, make us inclined to say that the music is sad. And those features in virtue of which you call the music sad *may* be quite different from those in virtue of which I call it sad. And when this happens, what are we to do?

2. We might seek a basis for our claim in the expressiveness of human gestures and facial expressions. Certain configurations of facial expression and gestures *are* expressive of sadness; these features are hard to describe but are easily recognisable, even by children and dogs. Anybody who said that these features did not express sadness would be wrong. Why should he be wrong? Because people when they are sad *do* exhibit these features and not other ones. Or, if we prefer: these features are part of the total complex of features which together constitute sadness; and we say we know this because these are features which do, as a matter of empirical fact, go together—this kind of feeling goes with tears and not with smiles and exuberance, and so on. Now similarly, we might hold, certain features of the music go with the sadness we feel.

Will this approach be successful? (1) Certain facial configurations do express sadness, quite objectively, that is, they *reveal* them; and what they reveal to us is that the person is sad. But what do musical configurations reveal? Surely not that the composer is sad—we have already tried to refute this contention. . . .

(2) How in practice is one to defend his judgment of expressiveness against others? About what features make music-sadness we would probably agree pretty well. It may well be, as Professor Bouwsma says, that "sad music has some of the characteristics of people who are sad. It will be slow, not tripping; it will be low, not tinkling. People who are sad move more slowly, and when they speak, they speak softly and low." But what about more complex claims, especially when disagreement continues? How would we defend against attack our judgment that this movement is, after all, not joyful, as we had always thought, but a bit frenzied, and that its rapidity is that of tension rather than of exuberance? Or that a composition which we had always thought to be highly dramatic in character is not really so but pompous, ostentatious, and posed?

David Novitz

FICTION,
IMAGINATION
AND EMOTION

David Novitz (1945–2001) was reader in philosophy at the University of Canterbury in New Zealand. His books include Knowledge, Fiction and Imagination *and* The Boundaries of Art. *In the following selection, Novitz argues that experiencing appropriate emotion is essential to understanding fiction. In order to do this, one must "make-believe," imagining the fictional account as real without believing it to be literally true.*

It is a commonplace of literary theory that anyone who mistakes a fictional work for a factual report or a history has not properly understood it. A person who responds to *Hamlet* by rushing to Elsinore in search of Yorick's skull, or to *Anna Karenina* by attempting to locate the fateful locomotive, has only partially, and at best improperly, understood these works.

Equally commonplace is the view that an appropriate emotional response to a fictional work is often integral to a proper understanding of it. But this is puzzling, for such a response seems to involve treating fiction as fact. We all tend to believe that we can only rationally be moved or upset by what we take to be actual calamities or real quandaries. It is silly, we think, to mourn fictional deaths or celebrate imagi-

nary victories. Hence it would seem that in order to be rationally moved by the fate of Othello one must believe that Othello is a real person. Put differently, one must believe that Shakespeare's play is a history or a factual report—and, as we have just seen, anyone who believes this has not properly understood the play. Consequently it appears that any reader who is rationally moved by a fictional work does not properly understand it. Conversely, if the reader does adequately understand the fiction, an emotional response to it must be irrational.

This conclusion, however, is as muddled as it is unwarranted. In what follows I shall argue that far from an emotional response to fiction precluding a proper understanding of it, one can *only* properly understand fiction if one is in a position to be appropriately

David Novitz, "Fiction, Imagination and Emotion," *Journal of Aesthetics and Art Criticism* 38.3 (1980): 279–88.

moved by the fortunes or misfortunes of its characters. A condition of being appropriately moved by, and so understanding, fiction is that one should respond imaginatively to it. Rather than treat *Anna Karenina* and *Hamlet* as histories, the reader must take it as if there are certain people who occupy imaginary worlds: he must make-believe, fantasize, or imagine that they live in certain places or do certain things.

What precisely this amounts to is by no means clear. Nor is there much clarity about what is to count as *properly* understanding fiction. Both questions can only be adequately answered as the paper progresses. Despite this, though, it is obvious, even at this early stage, that talk about properly understanding a literary work is by no means incomprehensible. We know that it is possible to grasp the meaning of an utterance without realizing, for example, that it was intended as a joke. We might mistakenly think it a warning or a threat, and in such a case we fail, in a perfectly ordinary sense, to understand it properly. In a similar way, one may grasp the meaning of most, even all, the sentences in a fictional work, and still not understand the work properly—perhaps because one has not recognized it as fiction or because one is unable to grasp its theme. Obviously there is much that remains to be said about this, and it is a point to which I shall return presently.

For the time being let us consider a likely objection to the claim that we need to become imaginatively involved in fiction if we are to understand it properly. In this way we shall be able both to explain the claim and, hopefully, initiate a defense of it, eventually resulting in the provision of an adequate epistemological framework in terms of which we shall be able to explain the interpretation of fiction, and to furnish a viable account of how we can rationally be moved by the fortunes or misfortunes of fictional characters.

IMAGINATION AND UNDERSTANDING

While it is true that one will not properly understand a novel like *The Pickwick Papers* unless one treats Pickwick as a fictional person, it is nonetheless arguable that this does not require that a reader should imagine Pickwick. The author, it may be said, has already imagined this. All that the reader has to do in order to understand the work is to understand these imaginings—where this involves recognizing them as imaginings of a certain sort. And (the argument continues) just as one does not have to imagine that there is a wolf present in order to recognize or understand that a child imagines this, so one does not have to fantasize in order to understand the imaginings of an author.

The advocates of this view need not deny that readers may, and often do, respond imaginatively to novels and plays. The claim, though, is that even if this does occur, such responses are not necessary for a thoroughgoing comprehension of fictional literature. Rather it is maintained that one responds appropriately to, and begins to understand, *The Pickwick Papers* by noting in the first instance that the statements which it contains are not true of our world. The comprehending reader may be said to preface the novel with the words "It is imagined that . . ." where the sentences which follow tell us what has been imagined. All of this is understood first, by *knowing* what to expect of fictional literature; and second, by *knowing* the meanings of its constitutive sentences. Hence it is concluded that understanding *The Pickwick Papers* requires knowledge of a certain sort, but does not require the reader's imaginative participation in the life of the novel.

But this leaves something important out of account. Consider the case of a child playing wolves. The view, as we have seen, is that one understands not merely *that* a game is in progress, but the game itself, by entertaining statements like: "The child imagines that the shadow is a wolf." "She imagines that it is eating the boy." "She imagines that it is smacking its lips." Here, it is maintained, one understands the game by understanding what is imagined, and one understands this without imagining it himself.

Certainly one will be able to understand aspects of the game in this way, but it soon becomes apparent that one will not be able to grasp it fully. The trouble is that by responding in the suggested way one prevents himself from entering into the spirit of the game. By prefacing my descriptions of the child's cries of alarm, her ravings, raptures, and distress with the words "She imagines that . . ." one effectively denies that these events are real, that her reports apply to the actual world, and so by discounting her utterances and refusing to take them seriously, one "distances" himself from the game and becomes unable to experience its nuances of feeling and heights or depths of passion. One becomes a mere bystander who is prevented from feeling the fears, excitement, and tensions which the game generates. As a result one is increasingly unlikely to know what to look for in the game: one will not have the appropriate expectations and beliefs, and after a while one will, in all probability, be bored by the increasingly meaningless gestures, grimaces, and growls, and will consider the whole unworthy of attention.

It would seem, then, that one is unable to grasp the full impact of the game, and so properly understand it, by responding in this way. Of course, the use of the words "full impact" to explain the notion of properly understanding a game is not intended to suggest that a "complete" grasp of all aspects of the make-believe (whatever that could amount to!) is required in order to ensure that one has properly understood it. "Properly" in this context must be understood adverbially, not adjectivally. Conse-

quently, whether or not one understands the game properly depends on whether or not one has adopted an adequate *way* of understanding it—where the latter is to be explained as a mode of understanding which permits or enables one to grasp (but which can never ensure that one will grasp) all of what are normally regarded as the salient or important features of the game. Hence, one can be said to understand a game properly without grasping all of its salient features and so without having a proper or full understanding of it.

It is in this sense that one cannot properly understand a child's game of wolves by prefacing one's descriptions of it with the words "She imagines that. . . ." For to do so is to adopt a skeptical attitude towards it: an attitude which prevents one form becoming involved in the game, and so from experiencing the emotional tensions which are part and parcel of it. And, as I have said, emotional involvement of this sort creates certain expectations and so directs the player's attention to some of the game's more important features. The curl of a lip or the shape of a hand may be vital to the game, but are only noticed, and only achieve significance, because of our expectations which are bred of emotional involvement. Not to be able to notice these features is to fail to understand the make-believe properly.

These considerations apply equally to the problem of understanding fiction. Understanding a novel like *The Pickwick Papers* is not merely a matter of understanding that Dickens has imagined certain things. Of course, if one is to understand the novel at all one has to understand that Dickens imagined that there was a man called Pickwick, that he was fat and jovial, and so on. But this, although in some sense necessary for properly understanding the novel, is by no means sufficient. The trouble is that in this context the phrase "It is imagined that . . ." is used to assert that the propositions which follow it are not true of the actual world:

that they describe events and states of affairs which do not actually obtain. By attending to this fact, one effectively discounts the narrative by regarding it as inapplicable to one's actual situation: one refuses either to believe or to disbelieve it since it does not purport to describe the actual world.

It is a fact of our experience, and a commonplace of psychology, that we cannot become emotionally involved in the plight of characters in a narrative if we actively discount the narrative in this way. It goes without saying that by constantly reminding oneself that the narrative is neither true nor false of the actual world, that it is a mere product of fancy or a total fabrication, one effectively "distances" oneself from the action of the novel. One does not allow oneself to be "drawn into" its imaginary world or to be "caught up in" its various intrigues and romances. As a result one cannot share the emotional turmoil of its fictional characters, nor can one experience the tensions generated by its plot. To respond to fiction in a way which does not permit such involvement is to respond to it in a way which cannot promote a full understanding of the work. For, as we have seen, it will deprive the reader of emotional experiences integral to understanding fiction: emotional experiences which would otherwise furnish whole sets of expectations in terms of which it is possible to notice other, sometimes vital, aspects of the work.

The same, I think, would be true of anyone who responds to *The Pickwick Papers* by actively disbelieving it. Incredulity is an obvious psychological barrier to emotional involvement. It prevents a reader from being emotionally "caught up in" the fiction and so from properly understanding it. This, however, is not to say that one has to believe the novel in order to understand it. Statements of fiction, I have stressed, are not intended as assertions about the actual world, but are assertions about an imaginary world. For this reason they are neither false nor true of our world, and it is as misguided to believe them as it is to disbelieve them. The person who refuses to leave the room with J. Alfred Prufrock or who journeys to Elsinore in search of Yorick's skull, is as silly as the person who doubts whether Anna Karenina really came to grief under the wheels of a locomotive. If one is to understand fiction properly, one has to do so not by believing or disbelieving it, nor, indeed, by discounting it. One has to entertain its statements in a different and rather special way by making-believe—that is, by imagining or taking it as if there is a man called Pickwick who does certain things and visits certain places. Such make-believe, far from involving belief or disbelief, involves responding to Dickens's descriptions of Pickwick not, as we shall see, by considering what Pickwick would be like if he actually existed, but by considering what Pickwick is like in a possible, but nonactual—that is, in an imaginary—world. This alone enables the reader to know what Pickwick is actually like in the imaginary world delineated by Dickens. And such knowledge, we shall find, is often the occasion of our emotional responses to fiction.

To respond to *The Pickwick Papers*, or, indeed, to any work of fiction, by considering what the hero would be like if he existed in our world, is not to respond appropriately to the novel. Such a response fails to take account of the fact that the imaginary or possible world of the hero is delineated by a set of statements, not all of which will (in all likelihood) be compatible with statements about the actual world. Hence to consider what Pickwick would be like if he existed in our world is not strictly relevant to one's comprehension of *The Pickwick Papers*. To understand this novel we have to know what Pickwick *is* like in *his own* world, not what he would be like in ours. In other words, to treat the statements of fiction as counterfactual conditionals is not to treat the fiction as an imaginative construction at all. It is to suppose that the statements of fiction, although hypothetical, are nonetheless assertions about the actual world. And this is not the case. What is more, to treat such statements as counterfactuals in anticipation of coming to understand the work is to assume that the world of the novel is in all respects the same as the actual world. And this, of course, is hardly likely.

It seems, then, that in order to understand fiction a reader must neither believe nor disbelieve the statements of a work, but, by making-believe, must regard them as true or false of an imaginary world. A reader does this in much the way that a geometrician does when he supposes that the short line sketched on his blotter is four meters long. He knows that the line is not really this length, but like the reader who knows that Pickwick is not really a person, he disregards (certain of) the facts of his immediate situation. His is an imaginative act: an act of fancy, if you like.

Such imaginative acts, however, are by no means free to take whatever form we wish. They are importantly constrained—either, as it were, by authorial decree, or by pencil marks on our geometrician's blotter. One is not at liberty when reading *The Pickwick Papers* to respond to it by creating one's own imaginary world. Anyone who does so will not have understood the novel. . . .

They are directed and constrained by Dickens's descriptions. Consequently, we may say that in order to understand a fictional work (rather than understand *that* it is fiction) the reader has, as it were, to imagine along with the author: he has to make-believe by thinking his way into the author's imaginary world. And once immersed in this world the reader treats fictional characters as persons, allowing them their rights, fearing for them, laughing at them, pitying them.

To believe fiction, we have seen, is to be deceived by it, and while deception may promote an appropriate emotional response, it can never promote a proper understanding of the work. To disbelieve or to discount the work, on the other hand, prevents us from acquiring those beliefs necessary for an appropriate emotional response to it. Rather than respond to fiction by believing, disbelieving, or discounting it, one must respond imaginatively by making-believe. Such imagining, we have seen, is for the most part derivative, and involves thinking of or considering the fictional world described by the author without a mind to the factual vacuity of his descriptions. It is this which allows us to acquire beliefs about creatures of fiction which are capable of moving us.

Stephen Davies

WHY LISTEN TO SAD MUSIC IF IT MAKES ONE FEEL SAD?

Stephen Davies is associate professor of philosophy at the University of Auckland. He has written extensively on aesthetics, often on musical aesthetics. His books include Definitions of Art *and* Musical Meaning and Expression. *Davies analyzes the anomaly that even though sad music makes us feel sad, we enjoy listening to it. Davies argues that negative emotion is experienced in many of our activities, including those we value most highly. The pleasure we take in sad music is akin to that which we experience in many of our other activities. Grappling with difficulty and pain are not just evils to be borne, but are part of what gives these activities their significance.*

Let me begin with some assumptions for which I will not argue, though some of them might be regarded as controversial. (a) Some purely instrumental music expresses emotions. (b) These usually are of a rather general character. (c) Music's expressiveness does not consist in its power to move the listener; that is, the expressive qualities of music are distinct from its effect on the listener. (d) Some listeners sometimes are moved, nevertheless, to feel emotions that mirror the expressive character of the music; that is, happy music sometimes induces happiness in the listener and music expressive of sadness sometimes leads the listener to feel sad.

Now the problem to be discussed can be stated: if it is sadness that sad music makes people feel, why would they bother to listen to sad music? To put what I take to be a related point: why would one value being made to feel sad?

Stephen Davies, *Musical Meaning and Expression* (Ithaca: Cornell UP, 1994) 307–319.

THE DILEMMA POSED BY THE SAD RESPONSE

It seems that one is trapped on the horns of a dilemma. If we enjoy the sadness that we claim to feel, then it is not plainly sadness that we are talking of, because sadness is not an enjoyable experience. On the other hand, if the sadness is unpleasant, we would not seek out, as we do, artworks leading us to feel sad. . . .

. . . At this stage I recommend a new approach, one that calls into question the formulation of the problem. I suggest in this section that one should ask not "Why do people concern themselves with music that makes them feel sad?" but instead "Why do people concern themselves with music?" Part of the puzzle, I suggest, arises from too narrow a focus.

The problem posed by negative responses to artworks frequently seems to be presented as one concerning our interest in a subset of artworks. [Colin] Radford says, "If there is a problem about sad music making people sad, because why then should they want to listen to it, there is no corresponding problem about why people would and would want to listen to happy music." But there is a problem, as I see it, concerning happy music, though I admit the difficulty is less obvious. Much happy music is trite and boring. That a musical work expresses happiness is not, just like that, a good reason for wanting to listen to it, and if a person is addicted to such music their commitment might be no less puzzling than is that of the person who willingly listens to sad music. To see the puzzle as arising only in connection with a subset of artworks is to misconceive the problem and to do so in a way making it difficult to answer.

Whereas there are many motivations for an interest in music, to be interested in music "aesthetically," "for its own sake," is to aim at understanding a work, such as Beethoven's Symphony No. 5, for the piece it is. Those of us who have this concern have it because we derive pleasure from music in understanding it. Not every work affords pleasure when it is understood, though. To the contrary, it is just because some works are appreciated that they are avoided, for they are revealed to be overblown, lifeless and mechanical in their predictability, or whatever. My point is a general one: much music presents a content such that the deeper one's understanding, the more enjoyable is the experience, and we value as great those works providing such enjoyment.

Now, if it is true that (many) people concern themselves with music for the sake of the enjoyment that comes with understanding it, and if it also is true that works dealing with "negative" emotions are no less worth understanding than those dealing with "positive" feelings, the listener should be as interested in the one kind of work as the other. And in either case, if the listener aims at understanding and appreciating the music, and if the emotional response is an aspect of the understanding she gains, then it is to be welcomed. If one desires comprehension, and if a response of sadness can indicate an appreciation of the nature of the given situation, just because it is appropriate to that situation, then the response, despite being negative, allows the satisfaction that goes with understanding. The response is not merely a by-product of the process of understanding; it is not merely a pleasant bonus or an irritant to be accepted with resignation. The response is not an incidental accompaniment but rather something integral to the understanding achieved. It is not something with which one puts up for the sake of understanding; it is an element in that understanding. If negative responses are no less an aspect of artistic appreciation than are positive responses, and if the concern lies with artistic understanding rather than, say, emotional titillation, and if understanding requires effort and commitment whatever emotions might arise in connection with it, then the question to be asked cannot narrow the focus to the negative emotions without losing touch with the wider context in which the explanation should be sought. Many people engage with music for the enjoyment of understanding and appreciating it, or at least in anticipation of its meriting these in an enjoyable way. Understanding sometimes leads to responses, some of which are pleasant and some of which are unpleasant. The enjoyment of appreciating art is not reducible to the enjoyment of responding to it with pleasant emotions, no more than it is inhibited by a negative emotional response; the enjoyment of understanding is no less consistent with the one response than the other.

We pursue artworks that are liable to give rise to negative emotional responses no less avidly than those likely to produce positive emotional responses because what motivates our interest is a concern with locating those artworks that merit understanding and these are as likely to be works causing negative as causing positive responses. The works to avoid are those that are unlikely to repay the effort of appreciation—works that are clichéd, banal, boring. Some works might generate pleasant reactions to their expressive character, others unpleasant ones, but the latter works are neither more nor less to be avoided than the former if one is motivated to seek the pleasure that goes with understanding rather than with mere titillation.

Personally, I avoid many films and books depicting gore and violence. Equally, though, there are books and films I avoid no less assiduously because I believe them to be happy in a trite, overly sentimental fashion. Also, there are books and films I seek out though I know in advance that they are gory or violent. The issue for me in these cases is neither that of whether "negative" emotions are dealt with nor that of whether the work might make me feel sad or depressed; it is,

instead, whether I predict that the work presents a content worth appreciating and understanding. The distinction rests on my anticipated judgment of the work's artistic merits. If it strikes me as worth the effort, I accept that what I understand, through its very comprehension, might generate experiences that are not in themselves enjoyable. My attitude is not one of resignation, because I do want to understand works that richly reward the effort involved.

I am not always so high-minded; sometimes I choose mindless entertainment over the artistically demanding (I have nothing against the pursuit of titillation as such). When I do, I prefer those entertainments that I expect to amuse me or make me feel happy over those I expect to make me sad. In the case of art, I doubt that its powerful attraction can be explained merely as a mindless pursuit of emotional frissons.

Some individuals are not much interested in any art, and many of those who are interested in some kind of art are not much interested in all forms of art. But to love music from the late eighteenth-century, say, is to be interested in understanding all such music if it rewards the effort required. For some (good) artworks, negative emotions come with the understanding we seek. These are not enjoyable emotions, but they are, for some people at least, an inevitable aspect of the understanding and appreciation they seek from art. The response would not be better for lacking this aspect because the response would, for the works and people concerned, not then be an understanding, appreciative one. . . .

LIFE AND SUFFERING

I have argued that the issue is not so much why we concern ourselves with a subset of artworks that lead us to feel sad as why we take pleasure in understanding art that might involve a negative response to some of the properties of the given work. Someone might take the point but claim that it shifts, rather than answers, the problem with which we began. My earlier answer to the problem was that art is enjoyable through the understanding of it. Now, though, the problem is revived in this form: why should we find *that* enjoyable? Why do we enjoy understanding art, given that an aspect of that understanding sometimes can be unpleasant; and, more generally, given that an appreciation of art can require hard work and practice; and, finally, given that the understanding often does not serve obvious, practical goals? The answer to such a grand question lies beyond the scope both of my subject and my powers, but I cannot resist pursuing it a short distance.

Many people watch or listen to the daily news broadcasts (and do so knowing that much of the news will be depressing). Why? Presumably because they would rather know what is happening than not; they would rather know the worst than live in blissful ignorance. Much of what is reported in the news deals with events that do not touch one directly—accidents on freeways in foreign countries and the like—but one attends to the news despite this obvious fact. We are interested in understanding the actions of people and the complex products of human society not always for the sake of the benefits flowing to us from doing so, though there may be many such, but because such things have an abiding interest. Given the importance of information, it is not surprising that curiosity has considerable motivating power. Curiosity motivates us, I believe, even when it is not regarded as a means to some particular end. We are curious on occasions when no obvious, immediate, practical value derives from the trait.

Our interest in art, I have suggested elsewhere . . . , is a spin-off, activated by curiosity. We are a creature concerned (up to a point) with understanding and appreciation for their own sakes, in the sense that not all

the things that concern us are tied directly to specifiable, practical goals. An interest in art in general may have many practical consequences of value (as a source of knowledge, heightened moral sensibility, character development, and so on), and perhaps the arts would not be regarded as a good thing were this not so, but to be interested in art usually is to be interested in works approached not for the sake of their typicality but of their individuality. We are capable of finding enjoyment in attempting to comprehend such works in their particularity; to the extent that the identity of works is relative to context, an interest in their individuality involves a concern with the piece as of a genre, of an oeuvre, of a style, of a school, of an artistic period.

In reply to the question "Why do we enjoy art (and the news for that matter) if the experience sometimes is constituted in part by features leading, through our grasp of their character, to negative responses?" I have said, "We are just like that." One way of elaborating that answer would be explaining why we find interest in human action and the complex products of human agency. In turn, this would involve an account of human nature and psychology in terms of evolutionary theory, the demands of social life, and whatever else might be relevant. Rather than taking that course, I settle for emphasizing how much and how often we are "just like that." If the puzzle is one about the meaning of life (not just about the importance of both art and the broadcast news), I might hope to be excused from answering it.

Loss, deprivation, pain, struggle and discomfort—all are part of life. Sometimes these things are avoidable; sensible navigators on the ocean of existence give rocky outcrops a wide berth. But also, such things are, as it were, inherent to the medium of life rather than merely a part of its content that one might try to skirt. They come unavoidably with life itself, so the living of a life includes one's dealing with such things as an inescapable part of existence. (So it is that prudence, courage, fortitude, stalwartness, endurance, and commitment are numbered among the moral virtues, or are the stuff from which virtuous actions might be forged, and their opposites are counted as vices. If the world yielded without resistance to our every whim and desire, the virtues as we understand them could have no social significance, for there would be no occasion for the exhibition of the qualities of character they involve.) In this world, to choose life also is to choose loss, pain, and the like. And we do choose life, even at an age when we know what that choice includes. The evidence of attempted suicides suggests that pain, loneliness, grief, humiliation, and the like can be so acute that death is to be preferred to life. But suicide is far from the most common form of death overall. Suffering and discomfort are by no means always worse than death or unconsciousness. Sometimes they are preferable to sensory deprivation, or to being ignored, as is apparent from the behavior of children who, if they cannot attract attention to themselves in any other way, do so by being naughty, even knowing that their actions will lead to penalties.

Negative emotions and feelings are not unavoidably a part of life merely as the price of admission, as an unpleasant extra tolerated so long as it does not prevent our participation in the games that give us pleasure. They are more intimately elements in the activities giving our lives meaning and importance than this view suggests. Some of the projects providing the greatest fulfilment demand fearful risks and known costs. Yet people commit themselves cheerfully to intellectually and physically demanding professions, to intense personal relationships, to birthing and raising children, and so on—and they do so not entirely in ignorance of what the future holds in store. Often the hard work, pain, anxiety, and stress are so

much a part of the project that it would no longer be the same project were their possibility removed. One expects to bring up children, not angels, so one expects all the difficulties and disappointments, as well as all the rewards, that go with trying to teach slowly maturing human beings how to become adults who might respect themselves and deserve the respect and affection of others. There is no gain without pain, as they say. The deepest satisfactions depend sometimes not just on what was gained but on how hard it was to attain.

These observations cannot be dismissed as covering merely the serious side of life. People race in cars at speed, crawl through mud and water in narrow tunnels in the bowels of the earth, wrestle with the intellectual problems posed by chess, crosswords, and the like, throw themselves off bridges with bits of elastic tied to their ankles, attempt time and again to improve their ability to hit a small ball into a slightly larger hole a quarter of a mile away, and so on, and so forth. They do such things not always for money, or esteem, or fame, or glory, or because they have a duty to engage in such activities, or for the sake of their health and character-development (though they may be mindful of such matters sometimes) but also, and mainly, out of love of the activity. These activities are engaged in for fun! Many involve unpleasantness in one way or another, if only as hard work directed to no obvious payout beyond what is found in the activity itself.

In some cases the unpleasant aspects might be regarded merely as inconveniences that must be tolerated, but in others the unpleasant side of the activity is integral to it—integral not in the sense that, masochistically, the unpleasantness is to be enjoyed for its own sake but, rather, in the sense that the activity found enjoyable would no longer be what it is if that unpleasantness (or the risk of it) were absent. For example, the danger faced by the mountaineer is not tolerated merely for the sake of the view from the top; if it were, the person would opt for a safe helicopter ride if she had the choice. The dedicated mountaineer's enjoyment is taken in the activity of climbing mountains. Now, to ask if climbing would be the more enjoyable if the climb were always without danger is to ask a strange question. Climbing on mountains is inherently dangerous, so it is not clear how to make sense of the question. And to ask if climbing would be more enjoyable for the person if she were always without fear also is to ask a far from straightforward question. If the enjoyment derived from climbing comes from meeting the demands of the activity, then the climber must display the requisite skills, and these include a proper assessment of the dangers posed by the mountain and, in view of this, the adoption of methods making the climb as safe as it can be, given the route, and so on. It is far from clear how someone could recognize the danger for what it is while never feeling fear, though the person might display the courage or nerve required to overcome that fear calmly. The fear comes from understanding the conditions of climbing, and it is that very same understanding that provides point to enjoying the exercise of the skills required in climbing (one among many of which is that of controlling one's own anxieties). The climber takes pleasure in mountaineering—in its challenge and so forth—and, if the activity were to be such that it might be climbing-in-a-context-in-which-fear-could-not-naturally-arise, then it would no longer be the climbing she enjoys; climbing of that kind just is not mountaineering, it might be said. To understand why the mountaineer takes on a scary sport is to understand how she can find enjoyment in a complex activity including among its elements the possibility of ever-present fear.

Why do people climb mountains for fun? For the same sort of reason they take an interest in the appreciation of music, or marry, or work at carpentry as a hobby. Because they choose the enjoyment that comes with taking charge of their own lives, even if that means taking on the negative as well as the positive constituents making life what it is. One's own life is what one does, and what happens to one, and what one makes of what happens to one, in the time between one's birth and death. A person who rehearsed too hard or waited too long for the right moment would find, not that he was prepared for life, but that the life he had lived was the life that consisted in preparing for something else, not the life he took himself to be preparing for. And a person who tried always to shun confrontation with pain and suffering would miss out on everything normally judged to make life worth living, while condemning himself to the sadness of realizing that the wait was in vain. At least some of the pleasure life can give comes from one's attempting with a degree of success to deal with one's situation and circumstanes—controlling what can be controlled, accepting with grace and equanimity the unavoidable. If the appreciation of art is specially important in this process, it is so not because it is a training or a substitute for life (as sometimes is held) but because it is a celebration of the ways people engage with each other and the world in giving significance to their existence.

Milan Kundera

THE
NATURE
OF
KITSCH

Milan Kundera is a Czech writer of novels, short stories, plays, and poetry. His works tend to take an ironic look at politics and sexuality. Among his novels are The Book of Laughter and Forgetting, The Joke, Immortality, *and* The Unbearable Lightness of Being. *He has also written a literary critical study called* The Art of the Novel. *In the following passage from* The Unbearable Lightness of Being, *Kundera's character Sabina witnesses a parade for the Communist holiday May Day and reflects on its character as kitsch.*

Sabina's initial inner revolt against Communism was aesthetic rather than ethical in character. What repelled her was not nearly so much the ugliness of the Communist world (ruined castles transformed into cow sheds) as the mask of beauty it tried to wear—in other words, Communist kitsch. The model of Communist kitsch is the ceremony called May Day.

She had seen May Day parades during the time when people were still enthusiastic or still did their best to feign enthusiasm. The women all wore red, white, and blue blouses, and the public, looking on from balconies and windows, could make out vari-ous five-pointed stars, hearts, and letters when the marchers went into formation. Small brass bands accompanied the individ-ual groups, keeping everyone in step. As a group approached the reviewing stand, even the most blasé faces would beam with daz-zling smiles, as if trying to prove they were properly joyful or, to be more precise, in proper *agreement*. Nor were they merely expressing political agreement with Com-munism; no, theirs was an agreement with being as such. The May Day ceremony drew its inspiration from the deep well of the cat-egorical agreement with being. The unwrit-ten, unsung motto of the parade was not

Milan Kundera, *The Unbearable Lightness of Being*, trans. Michael Henry Heim (New York: Harper & Row, 1984) 248–51.

"Long live Communism!" but "Long live life!" The power and cunning of Communist politics lay in the fact that it appropriated this slogan. For it was this idiotic tautology ("Long live life!") which attracted people indifferent to the theses of Communism to the Communist parade.

Ten years later (by which time she was living in America), a friend of some friends, an American senator, took Sabina for a drive in his gigantic car, his four children bouncing up and down in the back. The senator stopped the car in front of a stadium with an artificial skating rink, and the children jumped out and started running along the large expanse of grass surrounding it. Sitting behind the wheel and gazing dreamily after the four little bounding figures, he said to Sabina, "Just look at them." And describing a circle with his arm, a circle that was meant to take in stadium, grass, and children, he added, "Now, that's what I call happiness."

Behind his words there was more than joy at seeing children run and grass grow; there was a deep understanding of the plight of a refugee from a Communist country where, the senator was convinced, no grass grew or children ran.

At that moment an image of the senator standing on a reviewing stand in a Prague square flashed through Sabina's mind. The smile on his face was the smile Communist statesmen beamed from the height of their reviewing stand to the identically smiling citizens in the parade below.

How did the senator know that children meant happiness? Could he see into their souls? What if, the moment they were out of sight, three of them jumped the fourth and began beating him up?

The senator had only one argument in his favor: his feeling. When the heart speaks, the mind finds it indecent to object. In the realm of kitsch, the dictatorship of the heart reigns supreme.

The feeling induced by kitsch must be a kind the multitudes can share. Kitsch may not, therefore, depend on an unusual situation; it must derive from the basic images people have engraved in their memories: the ungrateful daughter, the neglected father, children running on the grass, the motherland betrayed, first love.

Kitsch causes two tears to flow in quick succession. The first tear says: How nice to see children running on the grass!

The second tear says: How nice to be moved, together with all mankind, by children running on the grass!

It is the second tear that makes kitsch kitsch.

The brotherhood of man on earth will be possible only on a base of kitsch.

And no one knows this better than politicians. Whenever a camera is in the offing, they immediately run to the nearest child, lift it in the air, kiss it on the cheek. Kitsch is the aesthetic ideal of all politicians and all political parties and movements.

Matei Calinescu

KITSCH
AND
HEDONISM

*Matei Calinescu is professor of comparative literature
at Indiana University. He is particularly interested
in the phenomena of postmodernism. His books
include* Exploring Postmodernism, The Faces of
Modernity: Modernism, Avant-Garde, Decadence, Kitsch,
Postmodernism, *and* Rereading. *Calinescu argues
that kitsch appeals to the sensibilities and tastes of
the middle class, particularly its conceptions of
leisure and fun.*

The term kitsch is, like the concept it designates, quite recent. It came into use in the 1860s and 1870s in the jargon of painters and art dealers in Munich, and was employed to designate cheap artistic stuff. It was not before the first decades of the twentieth century that kitsch became an international term. As frequently happens with such rather loose and widely circulating labels, its etymology is uncertain. Some authors believe that the German word derives from the English "sketch," mispronounced by artists in Munich and applied derogatorily to those cheap images bought as souvenirs by tourists, especially the Anglo-Americans. . . . According to others its possible origin should be looked for in the German verb *verkitschen,* meaning in the Mecklenburg dialect "to make cheap." . . . Ludwig Giesz in his *Phänomenologie des Kitsches* also mentions the hypothesis that links kitsch to the German verb *kitschen,* in the sense of "collecting rubbish from the street" (*den Strassenschlamm zusammenscharren*); *kitschen* has indeed this specific meaning in the southwestern part of Germany; it can also mean "to make new furniture from old" (*neue Möbel auf alt zurichten*).

These three main etymological hypotheses, even if erroneous, seem to me equally suggestive of certain basic characteristics of kitsch. First, there is often something sketchy about kitsch. Second, in order to be affordable, kitsch must be relatively cheap. Last, aesthetically speaking, kitsch may be considered rubbish or junk. . . .

Matei Calinescu, *The Faces of Modernity: Avant-Garde, Decadence, Kitsch* (Bloomington: Indiana UP, 1977) 234–48.

Whatever its origin, kitsch was and still is a strongly derogatory word, and as such lends itself to the widest range of subjective uses. To call something kitsch is in most cases a way of rejecting it outright as distasteful, repugnant, or even disgusting. Kitsch cannot be applied, however, to objects or situations that are completely unrelated to the broad domain of aesthetic production or aesthetic reception. Generically, kitsch dismisses the claims or pretensions of quality of anything that tries to be "artistic" without genuinely being so. It may, then, apply derogatorily to architecture, landscaping, interior decoration and furnishing, painting and sculpture, music, cinema and TV programs, literature, and virtually anything subject to judgments of taste. If we think of kitsch in terms of aesthetic deception and self-deception, there are obviously as many types of kitsch as there are possibilities of misusing or counterfeiting the signs of art. Limiting ourselves, for the moment, to literature, we can distinguish two very comprehensive categories, each one comprising an indefinite number of species and subspecies: (1) Kitsch produced for *propaganda* (including political kitsch, religious kitsch, etc.) and (2) kitsch produced mainly for *entertainment* (love stories, Rod McKuen-type giftshop poetry, potboilers, slicks, etc.). We should recognize, however, that the division between the two categories can become extremely vague: propaganda can masquerade as "cultural" entertainment and, conversely, entertainment can be directed toward subtle manipulative goals. From the psychological point of view we can use the distinction proposed by Hans Egon Holthusen between "sweet kitsch"— the sentimental "saccharine type"—and the sour variety, with innumerable nuances in between.

No matter how we classify its contexts of usage, kitsch always implies the notion of *aesthetic inadequacy.* Such inadequacy is often found in single objects whose formal qualities (material, shape, size, etc.) are inappropriate in relation to their cultural content or intention. A Greek statue reduced to the dimensions of a *bibelot* can serve as illustration. But the "law of aesthetic inadequacy" has a much wider scope, and we may well speak of kitsch effects in connection with combinations or arrangements of objects that, taken individually, have absolutely nothing kitschy about them. Thus, a real Rembrandt hung in a millionaire's home elevator would undoubtedly make for kitsch. Obviously, this is a hypothetical example and a caricature but it has the merit of suggesting the *use* of genuine great art as mere ostentatious decoration. An aesthetic object displayed as a symbol of affluence does not become kitsch itself, but the role it plays is typical of the world of kitsch. Certainly, the opposite happens more frequently, that is, a variety of easily affordable things, which have little if anything to do with art, may be given aesthetic significance and treated with the respect due to true art objects. We have only to think of the horrendous old "curiosities" that are on sale in the increasingly numerous nostalgia shops—rotten boots, broken cart wheels, porcelain night-pots, unwieldy rusty bathtubs of two or three generations ago, and innumerable other shabby junky "antiques," which many people enjoy as poetic relics from the better world of our grandfathers. Between the two extremes of authentic art reduced to signifying mere wealth and patent nonart vested with aesthetic prestige, there are countless instances to which the concept of aesthetic inadequacy applies. . . .

Certainly, one of the main reasons for the growth of kitsch since the beginning of the nineteenth century, to quote another sociologist of modern culture, Dwight Macdonald, is the fact that "business enterprise found a profitable market in the cultural demands of the newly awakened masses, and the advance technology made possible the cheap production of books, pictures, music, and furniture in sufficient quantities to satisfy the market." But even if the association between kitsch and low cost is often inescapable, we should not overlook the fact that the latter notion is very relative and can therefore become, when used as a unique criterion, dangerously misleading. What is regarded as cheap by a member of the upper-middle class can be prohibitively expensive for somebody less well off. Let us also repeat that sometimes bad taste can enjoy the possession of important financial means for the satisfaction of its ostentatious whims and fancies.

We have, then, to recognize the existence, along with the humbler varieties of kitsch, of a gorgeous kitsch that is the privilege of the rich. Moreover, even when it is inexpensive, kitsch is often supposed to suggest richness and superfluity: imitation gold or silver objects and colored-glass jewelry sold in drugstores undoubtedly have something to do with kitsch. As for actual rich, upper-class kitsch, the second half of the nineteenth century and then the time span that has been called *la belle époque* can furnish a great number of examples. Even the kings who happened to reign in that blessed period were sometimes converts to kitsch, like Ludwig II of Bavaria, who indulged frenetically in the most luxurious kind of bad taste. For some writers (for instance, Abraham A. Moles), the real kitsch has to be looked for precisely in that epoch, our own time being characterized by the formation of a "neo-kitsch" style, in keeping with the demands of an affluent consumer society. Even if we accept such a periodization of kitsch—and I do not see why we should not—the cheaper contemporary variety has, so to speak, its traditional roots in the pseudo-aristocratic aesthetic notions of the rich nineteenth-century bourgeoisie. . . .

Cheap or expensive, kitsch is sociologically and psychologically the expression of a life style, namely, the life style of the bourgeoisie or the middle class. This style can appeal to members of both the upper and lower classes and, in fact, become the *ideal life style* of the whole society—all the more so when the society grows affluent and more people have more spare time. Insofar as man chooses the ambience that suits his tastes, he can have several distinct types of relations with the objects that make up the decor or his home life. Abraham Moles distinguishes no less than seven modes of behavior in this respect: ascetic, hedonist, aggressive, acquisitive, surrealist, functionalist or cybernetic, and kitsch. And the kitsch mode is absolutely opposed to the ascetic one, combining all others in various proportions. The number of these modes can easily be increased or reduced. But the basic conflict between asceticism and hedonism remains in any ordering of these attitudes. Thus, keeping Moles's classification in mind, it is not difficult to show that, asceticism excepted, all the other categories can be subsumed under hedonism. Aggressiveness, like possessiveness, cannot be dissociated from the pleasure principle. Surrealism is nothing else than an extreme case of enjoyment of quaint, unpredictable combinations, and functionalism (in this context) is just another word for the "comforts of civilization."

To understand the nature of kitsch we should, then, analyze the particular hedonism characteristic of the middle-class mentality. Its primary feature is perhaps that it is a middle-of-the-road hedonism, perfectly illustrated by the "principle of mediocrity" that always obtains in kitsch (this all-pervading mediocrity is easier to notice in the more elaborate and exaggeratedly complicated forms of kitsch). The middle class being an active class, its hedonism is confined to the use of spare time. It is a hedonism of relaxation and, therefore, compensatory in nature. That is why kitsch lends itself to a definition in terms of a systematic attempt to fly from daily reality: in *time* (to a personal past, as indicated by the kitsch cult of the souvenir; to the "idyll of history"; to an adventurous future by means of the clichés of science fiction, etc.); and in *space* (to the most diverse imaginary and exotic lands). At a practical level, the pursuit of relaxation requires that household activities be performed with as little effort and as much fun as possible: this is how the gadget appears (gadgets being produced by a specialized sector of the industry of kitsch objects). Middle-class hedonism is in principle open, unprejudiced, eager for new experience; this openness, unhampered by any critical sense, accounts for the tolerant and sometimes heteroclite character of the world of kitsch. The superficiality of this hedonism can be matched only by its desire for universality and totality, and by its infinite capacity for acquiring beautiful junk.

The fundamental trait of modern middle-class hedonism is perhaps that it stimulates the *desire to consume* to the point that consumption becomes a sort of regulating social ideal. Obviously, consumption and production have always implied each other, but the ethical significance attached to these correlative concepts and activities has varied widely. Traditional civilizations—even those that do not hold labor as such in particularly high esteem—are for diverse reasons inclined to praise the virtues of *saving*, frugality, thrift, etc. (which are nothing but forms of postponing consumption), and will consequently guard against the dangers involved in immoderate consumption (a word that in common language still means primarily "destruction," "waste," "squandering," and that is naturally associated with notions of "luxury," "affluence," and even "decadence"). Although modernity is largely a product of the famous Protestant work ethic (in which Max Weber saw the main cause of capitalism), the dynamics of present-day economics and the whole temporal framework in which social activities are performed encourage a drastic revision, indeed a reversal, of the traditional outlook: consumption is totally vindicated,

whereas old temperance, restraint, and saving habits tend to appear as outmoded and touchingly ridiculous relics of the past. More than a mere fulfillment of certain basic needs, consumption has somehow become almost a duty—a way of helping the economic health of the nation—and, beyond mere economics, a way of apprehending and understanding the world.

To better comprehend what underlies today's frenzy of consumption (the "have it now" urge of both cultural and countercultural hedonism) we also have to consider another major characteristic of modernity, namely, its all-pervasive sense of change. The psychological consequences of modernity's increasing pace of change—and in the first place the ensuing axiological relativism—account for a decreasing trust in stability or continuity, without which no ethos of postponement or restraint is possible. In traditional societies, a homogeneous time that perpetually renews itself in a circular movement offers the guarantee that tomorrow will not be substantially different from yesterday or today. Individual anxieties and tragedies are of course possible, and within the framework of an essentially harmonious universe (the Greek Cosmos, for instance, as opposed to Chaos) the accidents and irregularities of chance may provoke untold personal and collective disasters. However, such mishaps do not contradict the belief in the basic unity of existence or the deep sense of continuity derived from respect for tradition. . . .

. . . In our age the myth of progress appears to have been largely exhausted. It has been replaced by the myth of modernity itself. The future has become almost as unreal and empty as the past. The widespread sense of instability and discontinuity makes instant enjoyment about the only "reasonable" thing to strive for. Hence, the drive toward consumption and the whole paradoxical concept of a "throw-away economy" and, more generally, civilization. . . .

Kitsch, therefore, is "efficient" art, the expendable cultural aspect of today's society, and one of the most direct manifestations of the triumphant aesthetics and ethics of consumerism. Originally, as pointed out before, kitsch emerged as an expression of the taste of the middle class and of its peculiar spare-time hedonism. . . .

. . . Kitsch is the direct artistic result of an important ethical mutation for which the peculiar time awareness of the middle classes has been responsible. By and large, kitsch may be viewed as a reaction against the "terror" of change and the meaninglessness of chronological time flowing from an unreal past into an equally unreal future. Under such conditions, spare time—whose quantity is socially increasing—is felt as a strange burden, the burden of emptiness. Kitsch appears as an easy way of "killing time," as a pleasurable escape from the banality of both work and leisure. The fun of kitsch is just the other side of terrible and incomprehensible boredom.

DISCUSSION QUESTIONS

1. Must an artist experience a particular emotion in order to arouse it in the audience? Must an artist experience a particular emotion in order to express it? Does expression depend on anyone's having a particular emotional experience?
2. Do you think that emotion experienced in connection with art produces feelings of social solidarity, as Tolstoy argues? Are such feelings a sign that the art involved is kitsch, as Kundera suggests?
3. Tolstoy argues that art that is primarily decorative has lost touch with the real purpose or art. Do you agree? Why or why not?
4. How important is empathy to understanding art fully? Can you have a full understanding of an artwork without being emotionally engaged?
5. What does the audience gain from expressive art? An experience of the emotion being expressed? Insight into their own emotional nature? Insight into the artist's emotional nature?
6. What, in your view, makes kitsch kitsch? Can you think of counterexamples to Kundera's characterization of kitsch?
7. Is kitsch morally or intellectually harmful, in your opinion? Explain.

FURTHER READING

Emotion

Carroll, Noël. *The Philosophy of Horror, or Paradoxes of the Heart.* New York: Routledge, 1990.

Davies, Stephen. *Musical Meaning and Expression.* Ithaca: Cornell UP, 1994.

Kivy, Peter. *Sound Sentiment: An Essay on the Musical Emotions.* Philadelphia: Temple UP, 1989.

Langer, Susanne K. *Feeling and Form.* New York: Routledge, 1953.

———. *Philosophy in a New Key.* 3rd ed. Cambridge: Harvard UP, 1953.

———. *Problems of Art.* New York: Scribner's, 1957.

Meyer, Leonard B. *Emotion and Meaning in Music*. Chicago: U of Chicago P, 1956.

Tolstoy, Leo. *What Is Art?* Trans. A. Maude. Indianapolis: Bobbs-Merrill, 1960.

Tormey, Alan. *The Concept of Expression*. Princeton: Princeton UP, 1971.

Bad Taste and Kitsch

Calinescu, Matei. *Five Faces of Modernity: Modernism, Avant-Garde, Decadence, Kitsch, Postmodernism*. Durham: Duke UP, 1987.

Crick, Philip. "Kitsch." *British Journal of Aesthetics* 23.1 (1983): 48–52.

Dorfles, Gillo. *Kitsch: An Anthology of Bad Taste*. London: Studio Vista, 1969.

Graycyk, Theodor A. "Having Bad Taste." *British Journal of Aesthetics* 30.2 (1990): 117–31.

Greenberg, Clement. "Avant-Garde and Kitsch." *Art and Culture*. Boston: Beacon, 1961.

Higgins, Kathleen. "Sweet Kitsch." *Philosophy of the Visual Arts*. Ed. Philip Alperson. New York: Oxford UP, 1992. 568–81.

Morreall, John, and Jessica Loy. "Kitsch and Aesthetic Education." *Journal of Aesthetic Education* 23.4 (1989): 63–73.

Solomon, Robert C. "On Kitsch and Sentimentality." *Journal of Aesthetics and Art Criticism* 49.1 (1990): 1–14.

INTENTION AND
INTERPRETATION

When Charles Manson blamed the Beatles' song "Helter Skelter" for the mass murder he instigated, few were impressed. Whatever the Beatles may have intended to convey through the song, most found the suggestion that they were advocating murder implausible. Manson's beliefs about "Helter Skelter" seemed to stem from his own psychological disturbance. Balanced people simply did not hear what he claimed to hear in the song.

A number of recent rap musicians, however, have been criticized for promoting cop killing and rape with their lyrics. Their lyrics clearly touch on these matters. Rappers often claim that their songs describe rather than advocate. Their critics, however, do not see much difference when the descriptions make criminal behavior appear glamorous. (No comparable furor among the American public was instigated by Eric Clapton's rendition of Bob Marley's "I Shot the Sheriff" a couple of decades ago, even though the lyrics referred unmistakably to the shooting of law enforcement officials.)

When, if ever, should artists be blamed if violent or immoral behavior is inspired by their work? Cases such as Manson's lead some to think that artists should be blamed only if they intend to incite such activities. But how can we ascertain an artist's intentions? Certain recent schools of thought, such as the "New Criticism" movement in literary criticism, contend that speculation about artists' intentions is idle and irrelevant. The "meaning" of a work should be found in its immediately evident features, not in largely fabricated accounts of what the artist "intended" to say through it.

William K. Wimsatt, Jr., and Monroe C. Beardsley argue the New Critics' position in "The Intentional Fallacy": We have no real access to the intentions that motivated artists in the production of their works. To take such intentions as a standard for judging a work is to abandon any ground for judgment at all and to reduce criticism to mere speculation. Wimsatt and

Beardsley do not entirely reject historical and contextual evidence; these can be relevant to determining how a writer was using a given word or the genre in which a work is written. But the fundamental basis for an assessment of the work should be the intrinsic features of the work itself.

Opponents of this approach counter that the intrinsic features of an artwork are often evident only with reference to artists' intentions. P. D. Juhl takes this position in his consideration of poetry produced by a computer. Computer-generated poetry has sometimes been considered a demonstration that authors' intentions are irrelevant to meaning in literature. Juhl denies this, arguing that any interpretation depends on construing the arrangement of lines as something other than random. But to do this amounts to interpreting it as a product of intentions. We may know that a computer produced the poem, and we may not believe that computers have intentions of the sort that human beings have. Nevertheless, Juhl argues, we can interpret a computer poem as meaningful only if we read it as "intentional."

Juhl's discussion underscores the fact that multiple interpretations are often attributed to the same work of literature. The same seems to be true of other kinds of artworks. Controversial artworks are often problematic precisely because audience members differ in their interpretations. In "Messages in Art," Jerrold Levinson considers such a case and concludes that an artist's message is not straightforward. Nevertheless, some possible interpretations can be ruled out. Significantly, the constraints on interpretation that Levinson indicates are supplied by features of the work itself (the genre chosen, for example), not by speculation about the artist's psychology. Although some interpretations of art may be unjustified, Levinson concludes that artists may bear some responsibility for meanings that others find in their works, even if these meanings do not reflect the artists' own views.

The "historical performance" movement has occasioned similar debates about composer's intentions. This movement urges that a classical work is best performed when it accords with the performance practices of its time and whatever we can ascertain of the composer's intentions. Should we seek to replicate the contingencies of the first performance of a work, or should we try to reproduce what the composer would have wanted?

Peter Kivy is supportive of the ideal of the historically authentic performance. Many of the complaints raised against the authenticity movement, he argues, stem from misinterpretations of its goal. For example, some have complained that authenticity would require an "average" performance, which would likely include performers of mediocre ability and a sprinkling of outright mistakes. Kivy counters that this is a silly construal of the aims of the authentic performance movement, which actually urges the recreation of the sound of an *optimal* performance in the manner of the period that produced a work. Despite his sympathy for the movement, Kivy cautions against literalism. If we could travel through time to Bach's era, Kivy argues, we would hear his works as alive and spontaneous, not as meticulous products of scholarship. Kivy urges those involved in the debate to recognize that performances can be authentic in some respects but not in others, and also that a performance that is "authentic" in some respects is not necessarily good.

Perhaps the audience, as well as the performer, has an obligation to respect the artist's intentions. This, at least, is an argument often made with regard to the colorization of black-and-white movies, as Yuriko Saito's article indicates. Interestingly, both defenders and detractors of colorization often appeal to artists' intentions. Opponents contend that to colorize is to ignore the director's intentions. But colorization enthusiasts argue that, since most filmmakers have chosen to film in color once high-quality color film has become available, colorization respects what might well have been earlier filmmakers' intentions had color technology been available sooner. Besides, colorization defenders argue, it is safe to assume that filmmakers want a large audience for their work. Since color films are shown much more often than their black-and-white counterparts, colorization facilitates the most basic artistic intention of filmmakers: to have their films seen and enjoyed by the widest possible audience.

William K. Wimsatt, Jr., and Monroe C. Beardsley

THE
INTENTIONAL
FALLACY

Monroe C. Beardsley (1915–1985) was a professor of philosophy at Swarthmore College and Temple University. His works on aesthetics include Aesthetic Inquiry: Essays on Art Criticism and the Philosophy of Art, The Aesthetic Point of View: Selected Essays, Aesthetics from Classical Greece to the Present: A Short History, *and* Aesthetics: Problems in the Philosophy of Criticism. *William K. Wimsatt (1907–1975) was a literary critic and professor of English at Yale University. His writings include* Literary Criticism, Idea and Act: The English Institute *and* Day of the Leopards: Essays in Defense of Poems. *The following is an abridged version of one of the seminal declarations of the New Criticism movement, which insisted that literary criticism should focus on formal features of the text itself, not on the background of its author or on its alleged moral effect. In this essay they claim that authors' intentions are private mental conditions to which the reader has no access.*

The claim of the author's "intention" upon the critic's judgment has been challenged in a number of recent discussions, notably in the debate entitled *The Personal Heresy*, between Professors Lewis and Tillyard. But it seems doubtful if this claim and most of its romantic corollaries are as yet subject to any widespread questioning. The present writers, in a short article entitled "Intention" for a *Dictionary* of literary criticism, raised the issue but were unable to pursue its implications at any length. We argued that the design or intention of the author is neither available nor desirable as a standard for

William K. Wimsatt, Jr., and Monroe C. Beardsley, *The Verbal Icon: Studies in the Meaning of Poetry* (Lexington: UP of Kentucky, 1954) 3–18.

judging the success of a work of literary art, and it seems to us that this is a principle which goes deep into some differences in the history of critical attitudes. It is a principle which accepted or rejected points to the polar opposites of classical "imitation" and romantic expression. It entails many specific truths about inspiration, authenticity, biography, literary history and scholarship, and about some trends of contemporary poetry, especially its allusiveness. There is hardly a problem of literary criticism in which the critic's approach will not be qualified by his view of "intention."

"Intention," as we shall use the term, corresponds to *what he intended* in a formula which more or less explicitly has had wide acceptance. "In order to judge the poet's performance, we must know *what he intended*." Intention is design or plan in the author's mind. Intention has obvious affinities for the author's attitude toward his work, the way he felt, what made him write.

We begin our discussion with a series of propositions summarized and abstracted to a degree where they seem to us axiomatic.

1. A poem does not come into existence by accident. The words of a poem, as Professor Stoll has remarked, come out of a head, not out of a hat. Yet to insist on the designing intellect as a *cause* of a poem is not to grant the design or intention as a *standard* by which the critic is to judge the worth of the poet's performance.

2. One must ask how a critic expects to get an answer to the question about intention. How is he to find out what the poet tried to do? If the poet succeeded in doing it, then the poem itself shows what he was trying to do. And if the poet did not succeed, then the poem is not adequate evidence, and the critic must go outside the poem— for evidence of an intention that did not become effective in the poem.

"Only one *caveat* must be borne in mind," says an eminent intentionalist in a moment when his theory repudiates itself; "the poet's aim must be judged at the moment of the creative act, that is to say, by the art of the poem itself."

3. Judging a poem is like judging a pudding or a machine. One demands that it work. It is only because an artifact works that we infer the intention of an artificer. "A poem should not mean but be." A poem can *be* only through its *meaning*—since its medium is words— yet it *is*, simply *is*, in the sense that we have no excuse for inquiring what part is intended or meant. Poetry is a feat of style by which a complex of meaning is handled all at once. Poetry succeeds because all or most of what is said or implied is relevant; what is irrelevant has been excluded, like lumps from pudding and "bugs" from machinery. In this respect poetry differs from practical messages, which are successful if and only if we correctly infer the intention. They are more abstract than poetry.

4. The meaning of a poem may certainly be a personal one, in the sense that a poem expresses a personality or state of soul rather than a physical object like an apple. But even a short lyric poem is dramatic, the response of a speaker (no matter how abstractly conceived) to a situation (no matter how universalized). We ought to impute the thoughts and attitudes of the poem immediately to the dramatic *speaker*, and if to the author at all, only by an act of biographical inference.

5. There is a sense in which an author, by revision, may better achieve his original intention. But it is a very abstract sense. He intended to write a better work, or a better work of a certain kind, and now has done it. But it

follows that his former concrete intention was not his intention. "He's the man we were in search of, that's true," says Hardy's rustic constable, "and yet he's not the man we were in search of. For the man we were in search of was not the man we wanted."

"Is not a critic," asks Professor Stoll, "a judge, who does not explore his own consciousness, but determines the author's meaning or intention, as if the poem were a will, a contract, or the constitution? The poem is not the critic's own." He has accurately diagnosed two forms of irresponsibility, one of which he prefers. Our view is yet different. The poem is not the critic's own and not the author's (it is detached from the author at birth and goes about the world beyond his power to intend about it or control it). The poem belongs to the public. It is embodied in language, the peculiar possession of the public, and it is about the human being, an object of public knowledge. What is said about the poem is subject to the same scrutiny as any statement in linguistics or in the general science of psychology.

A critic of our *Dictionary* article, Ananda K. Coomaraswamy, has argued that there are two kinds of inquiry about a work of art: (1) whether the artist achieved his intentions; (2) whether the work of art "ought ever to have been undertaken at all" and so "whether it is worth preserving." Number (2), Coomaraswamy maintains, is not "criticism of any work of art *qua* work of art," but is rather moral criticism; number (1) is artistic criticism. But we maintain that (2) need not be moral criticism: that there is another way of deciding whether works of art are worth preserving and whether, in a sense, they "ought" to have been undertaken, and this is the way of objective criticism of works of art as such, the way which enables us to distinguish between a skillful murder and a skillful poem. A skillful murder is an example which Coomaraswamy

uses, and in his system the difference between the murder and the poem is simply a "moral" one, not an "artistic" one, since each if carried out according to plan is "artistically" successful. We maintain that (2) is an inquiry of more worth than (1), and since (2) and not (1) is capable of distinguishing poetry from murder, the name "artistic criticism" is properly given to (2).

It is not so much a historical statement as a definition to say that the intentional fallacy is a romantic one. When a rhetorician of the first century A.D. writes: "Sublimity is the echo of a great soul," or when he tells us that "Homer enters into the sublime actions of his heroes" and "shares the full inspiration of the combat," we shall not be surprised to find this rhetorician considered as a distant harbinger of romanticism and greeted in the warmest terms by Saintsbury. One may wish to argue whether Longinus should be called romantic, but there can hardly be a doubt that in one important way he is.

Goethe's three questions for "constructive criticism" are "What did the author set out to do? Was his plan reasonable and sensible, and how far did he succeed in carrying it out?" If one leaves out the middle question, one has in effect the system of Croce— the culmination and crowning philosophic expression of romanticism. The beautiful is the successful intuition-expression, and the ugly is the unsuccessful; the intuition or private part of art is *the* aesthetic fact, and the medium or public part is not the subject of aesthetic at all.

> The Madonna of Cimabue is still in the Church of Santa Maria Novella; but does she speak to the visitor of to-day as to the Florentines of the thirteenth century?

> *Historical interpretation* labours . . . to reintegrate in us the psychological conditions which have changed in the course of

history. It . . . enables us to see a work of art (a physical object) as its *author saw it* in the moment of production.

The first italics are Croce's, the second ours. The upshot of Croce's system is an ambiguous emphasis on history. With such passages as a point of departure a critic may write a nice analysis of the meaning or "spirit" of a play by Shakespeare or Corneille—a process that involves close historical study but remains aesthetic criticism—or he may, with equal plausibility, produce an essay in sociology, biography, or other kinds of nonaesthetic history.

—◆◆◆—

There is criticism of poetry and there is author psychology, which when applied to the present or future takes the form of inspirational promotion; but author psychology can be historical too, and then we have literary biography, a legitimate and attractive study in itself, one approach, as Professor Tillyard would argue, to personality, the poem being only a parallel approach. Certainly it need not be with a derogatory purpose that one points out personal studies, as distinct from poetic studies, in the realm of literary scholarship. Yet there is danger of confusing personal and poetic studies; and there is the fault of writing the personal as if it were poetic.

There is a difference between internal and external evidence for the meaning of a poem. And the paradox is only verbal and superficial that what is (1) internal is also public: it is discovered through the semantics and syntax of a poem, through our habitual knowledge of the language, through grammars, dictionaries, and all the literature which is the source of dictionaries, in general through all that makes a language and culture; while what is (2) external is private or idiosyncratic; not a part of the work as a linguistic fact: it consists of revelations (in journals, for example, or letters or reported conversations) about how or why the poet

wrote the poem—to what lady, while sitting on what lawn, or at the death of what friend or brother. There is (3) an intermediate kind of evidence about the character of the author or about private or semiprivate meanings attached to words or topics by an author or by a coterie of which he is a member. The meaning of words is the history of words, and the biography of an author, his use of a word, and the associations which the word had for *him*, are part of the word's history and meaning. But the three types of evidence, especially (2) and (3), shade into one another so subtly that it is not always easy to draw a line between examples, and hence arises the difficulty for criticism. The use of biographical evidence need not involve intentionalism, because while it may be evidence of what the author intended, it may also be evidence of the meaning of his words and the dramatic character of his utterance. On the other hand, it may not be all this. And a critic who is concerned with evidence of type (1) and moderately with that of type (3) will in the long run produce a different sort of comment from that of the critic who is concerned with (2) and with (3) where it shades into (2).

The whole glittering parade of Professor Lowes' *Road to Xanadu*, for instance, runs along the border between types (2) and (3) or boldly traverses the romantic region of (2). "'Kubla Khan,'" says Professor Lowes, "is the fabric of a vision, but every image that rose up in its weaving had passed that way before. And it would seem that there is nothing haphazard or fortuitous in their return." This is not quite clear—not even when Professor Lowes explains that there were clusters of associations, like hooked atoms, which were drawn into complex relation with other clusters in the deep well of Coleridge's memory, and which then coalesced and issued forth as poems. If there was nothing "haphazard or fortuitous" in the way the images returned to the surface, that may mean (1) that Coleridge could not produce what he did not have, that he was limited in his creation by what he had read or otherwise experienced, or (2) that having received certain clusters of associations, he was bound to return them in just the way he did, and that the value of the poem may be described in terms of the experiences on which he had to draw. The latter pair of propositions (a sort of Hartleyan associationism which Coleridge himself repudiated in *Biographia*) may not be assented to. There were certainly other combinations, other poems, worse or better, that might have been written by men who had read Bartram and Purchas and Bruce and Milton. And this will be true no matter how many times we are able to add to the brilliant complex of Coleridge's reading. In certain flourishes (such as the sentence we have quoted) and in chapter headings like "The Shaping Spirit," "The Magical Synthe-

sis," "Imagination Creatrix," it may be that Professor Lowes pretends to say more about the actual poems than he does. There is a certain deceptive variation in these fancy chapter titles; one expects to pass on to a new stage in the argument, and one finds— more and more sources, more and more about "the streamy nature of association."

We mean to suggest by the above analysis that whereas notes tend to seem to justify themselves as external indexes to the author's *intention*, yet they ought to be judged like any other parts of a composition (verbal arrangement special to a particular context), and when so judged their reality as parts of the poem, or their imaginative integration with the rest of the poem, may come into question.

P. D. Juhl

COMPUTER POEMS

P. D. Juhl is a professor of German, who has taught at Princeton University. He is author of Interpretation: An Essay in the Philosophy of Literary Criticism. *Juhl responds to those who deny the relevance of intention to interpretation on the basis of computer-generated poetry. One cannot interpret even this poetry, he contends, without some reference to intention.*

1

It is often claimed that poems produced by a computer show that there is no logical connection between the meaning of a literary work and its author's intention. I shall argue in the following that this is not the case; and in particular, that to "interpret" a computer "poem" is not to interpret a poem.

It is certainly true that a syntactically and semantically well-formed sentence has meaning quite independently of what a particular person who utters the sentence on some occasion might mean by his utterance. Thus what the example of computer "poetry" is thought to show is that the interpretation of literary works (or of utterances in ordinary discourse) does not, as a matter of logic, involve any appeal to the author's intention. In other words, the claim is that to interpret a literary work written by a person *is* (as a matter of logic) to interpret the word sequence of which it consists in abstraction from anyone's (in particular, the author's) use of that word sequence. That this should be so is not obvious. For the literary works commonly read and interpreted do have authors (although some of them may be anonymous), and in writing a work, they are using words and sentences in a particular way to convey something. But in interpreting a poem produced by a computer, that is, by a random combination of a certain set of words, punctuation marks, spaces, etc., we are not dealing with anyone's use of the words or sentences which constitute the text (except possibly the programmer's; thus a better case for the anti-intentionalist argument would be, e.g., a text produced by a monkey randomly depressing keys on a typewriter or marks produced on a rock by water erosion).

The question then is this: Would we necessarily interpret a poem which has been

P. D. Juhl, "Do Computer Poems Show That an Author's Intention Is Irrelevant to the Meaning of a Literary Work?" *Critical Inquiry* 5.3 (1979): 481–88.

written by a person in the same way if it had been produced by a computer (i.e., if we considered the word sequence of which it consists in abstraction from its use by anyone)? To put it differently: Is the meaning of a poem necessarily the same whether it has been written by a person or produced by chance?

2

Suppose a computer prints out the following little "poem":

The shooting of the hunters she heard;
But to pity it moved her not.

What can we say about the meaning of this "poem"? We can say that it is ambiguous. It could mean:

(1)   She heard the hunters shooting at animals, people, etc., but she had no pity for the victims.

Let us assume that on this interpretation the first line does not mean "She heard the hunters being shot." Or it could mean:

(2)   She heard the hunters being shot but did not pity them.

Let us assume that on this interpretation the first line does not mean "She heard the hunters shooting at someone or something." Or it might conceivably mean:

(3)   She heard the hunters shooting at someone or something and she heard the hunters being shot (at) but did not pity either.

An author could use the above word sequence (the text of the "poem") to convey either (1), (2), or (3). But since (by hypothesis) we cannot treat the text produced by the computer as anyone's use of the words in question, it would not make sense *to decide* among its linguistically possible readings, just as it would not make sense to choose among the linguistically possible readings of

an ambiguous sentence if it is considered in abstraction from its use by a speaker on a particular occasion. For example, it would not make sense to say of the sentence "He saw the man who is carrying the suitcase" that it just means "He saw the man who is carrying the suitcase" if we know that and in what ways the sentence is ambiguous. If someone did say this, we would be inclined to think either that he does not know that the sentence is ambiguous or that he is talking not about the sentence but about an utterance (i.e., a use) of that sentence by a speaker on some occasion.

Hence all we can do in interpreting the computer "poem" is to specify the set of its (linguistically) possible readings, namely, {(1), (2), (3)}. But it would not make sense to select (1), for example, and say "That is what the computer poem means, not (2), nor (3)."

3

Now suppose that the above lines were not produced by a computer but were written by a contemporary poet. One difference is obvious at once: Would it not now *make sense* to choose between the possible readings of the text and to say, for example, that it means (1), not (2), nor (3)? . . .

. . . Under the present assumption (that the text has been produced by a person), it would not only make sense to choose one of its linguistically possible readings, and to say "This interpretation is correct but not that," it would be necessary to choose between them since the three possible readings are incompatible. But even if this were not necessary, it is certainly possible—if the text was written by a person—that only one of its linguistically admissible readings is correct. It follows that in interpreting a literary text produced by a person (i.e., not by chance), we cannot be *just* interpreting the word sequence of which the text consists as though it had been produced by, say, a computer. Consequently, if it turns out that the text of what was hitherto regarded as a poem by a certain author was in fact produced by a computer, then at least in certain cases it might not be correct to interpret the "poem" in the same way as before (i.e., under the assumption that it has been written by a person).

4

Furthermore, there is at least one important difference between the way we would go about interpreting a computer "poem" and the way we would attempt to determine the meaning of a text written by a person. This difference brings out perhaps more clearly that in interpreting a poem written by a person, we are construing an utterance, that is, the *use* of certain words, not a word sequence taken *in abstracto*.

In the case of poems which have authors, we frequently look at so-called parallel passages (by the same author) in order to determine the connotations of a word, the significance of a certain image, etc. Although an appeal to parallel passages may be frequently inconclusive, it would be difficult to deny that parallel passages are relevant to determining what a particular line or the whole text of a poem means. Let us suppose that our poem was written by an author among whose works are a number of poems in which hunters and shooting figure prominently. These would certainly be relevant to determining the significance of the words "hunters" and "shooting" in this poem; they would be relevant, for example, to determining whether these words occur here in their literal or in some figurative sense. But would the parallel passages still be relevant if it turned out that the poem had not been written by anyone but produced by a computer or by a monkey randomly depressing keys on a typewriter? Suppose the computer had produced a

number of "poems" about hunters and shooting. Would these be relevant to determining the connotations and figurative meaning (if any) of the "hunters" in this poem? Clearly something essential is missing: a connection between the "poems."

5

In my interpretation of the computer "poem," I have tacitly assumed that the two lines of the "poem" belong together, are parts of a whole. Suppose someone challenged my interpretation of the "poem"—and indeed any interpretation of the "poem" as a whole—on the grounds that the two lines do not, in the relevant sense, *belong together?* How could we answer this objection?

To say that the two sentences make sense together clearly will not do. . . . We could obviously pair a large number of sentences from different authors. . . .

Can we then dispose of the objection on typographical grounds, that is, on the grounds that the computer printed them out together? Is this sufficient to warrant the claim that the lines in fact belong together? Suppose that an inch below the second line of our "poem," there are two further lines which the computer typed out. Is that the second "stanza" or is it a separate "poem"?

Clearly, the idea that certain words, lines, or sentences produced by chance belong together or constitute a whole is unintelligible. In order for us to take certain words, lines, or sentences as belonging together or constituting a whole, we must assume that they have been produced by a person and with certain intentions.

6

It follows from this that a computer "poem" is not a poem. Hence the fact that some computer "poems" have meaning or can, in some sense, be interpreted does not show that a statement about the meaning of a poem is not a statement about the author's intention. . . .

There is clearly something very odd about *interpreting* a computer "poem" or any "text" produced by chance. Would it be possible to interpret a series of marks on a rock which closely resemble words of an English sentence if we knew that they had been produced by water erosion? Could one even call them "words"? Could one say of an appropriate "word" or "words" that they *refer* to so-and-so? That they are an *allusion* to such-and-such? That they are ironic? What could it mean to say of such marks that they mean so-and-so? It might be possible to construe this in terms of Grice's natural sense or senses of "mean," for example, the sense in which we say of certain spots that they mean measles. But that is obviously not the sense in which we say of a literary work or of an utterance in ordinary discourse that it means so-and-so.

The only other possibility (and this is what I have assumed above) is that the sense of "mean" here is that in which we speak of the meaning of a word in a language, that is, the sense of "mean" in which we say, for example, "The word 'man' in English means. . . ." It should be noted that a statement about the meaning of the marks on the rock cannot be a statement about the meaning of a particular utterance of the corresponding words, or about their meaning on a particular occasion of utterance, since of course there is no such utterance. It can only be a statement about what Grice has called the "timeless meaning(s)" of the words in question; for example, a statement about the meaning of the word "man" in English, as opposed to a statement about the meaning of a particular *utterance* of the word, or about the meaning of the word on a particular occasion on which it is used. Thus what we are interpreting is quite independent of the existence of the marks on the rock or the production of the "poem" by the computer; that is, the computer "poem" exists even before the computer produces it or even if it never does. Something one would surely not want to say of a poem.

In other words, it would be possible to "interpret" a "text" produced by chance in the sense in which we might be said to "interpret" a sentence when we explain its meaning to a foreigner, that is, when we explain to him what the individual words mean, how they function in the sentence, and thus how the sentence *could* be used or what it *could* be used to express or convey. But while that is the only possible way to "interpret" a computer "poem," it is not, as I have tried to show, to interpret a poem.

Jerrold Levinson

MESSAGES
IN
ART

Jerrold Levinson is professor of philosophy at the University of Maryland. He has written many articles on aesthetics, especially the aesthetics of music, some of which appear in his Music, Art, and Metaphysics: Essays in Philosophical Aesthetics. *Levinson explains why the "message" involved in many artworks is not as obvious as many take it to be.*

I.

I begin with the well-known anecdote attributed to early Hollywood mogul Jack Warner.[1] When asked what the message was in one of his recent offerings, he replied that he just makes movies, and that if he had wanted to send a message, he would have used Western Union. It's worth noting that Warner was, after all, a producer, and that his directors might have had a different opinion, but certainly such an attitude is widespread in the arts, and has been given respectability by formalists and art-for-art's-sakers, as well as those who are happy to see art of any sort as only entertainment or diversion. A more high-minded expression of the attitude is Archibald MacLeish's "a poem should not mean, but be." However, despite such disclaimers by artists or their representatives, it seems hard to deny that artworks—and by that I mean poems and films, as well as paintings and sculptures—very often do have messages, and far from inexpressible ones. In other words, many works are reasonably taken as **saying** something, in an extended sense, that is, as implicitly advancing some proposition, endorsing some perspective, or affirming some value. What's more, the imparting of such a message often appears to be a primary motivation of the artist who fashions the work as he or she does. Of course message in art is not, in the sense I have in mind, anywhere near the whole of the content of a work of art, or even the totality of what it conveys. But it is an evident and important part of such content, at least for a good many works of art.

In this paper I will touch on three questions regarding message in art. The first, which will primarily occupy me, is what we

Jerrold Levinson, "Messages in Art" *Australasian Journal of Philosophy* 73.2 (June 1995): 189–203.

might **mean** by message in art—that is, what does an artwork's saying something amount to, and how do we discern what, if anything, it says? My approach to that question will be through a number of examples, traditional and nontraditional, from which I will try to wring some illumination. The second question, which will not get its due here, is the partly ethical one of **who** is responsible for the message in an artwork, i.e., for what it broadly says, and **in what ways,** responsible? A third question, which I will supply an answer to in closing, is this: how can art remain **artistic** when in the business of conveying messages, and how can we attend to such messages and still appreciate the art **as art,** rather than as mere instrument of communication, dispensable once the message has been received?

II.

Now for my examples.

Ibsen's *An Enemy of the People* is a play set in a small coastal town in southern Norway, whose mainstay is a set of baths serving as a spa. The town doctor, Thomas Stockmann, discovers that the source of the baths is polluted, and that the waters are contaminated by microorganisms and a danger to health. Public disclosure of this would lead to substantial, if temporary, economic loss for the town, and would require a great sum of money to set right. Nevertheless, people's lives are at issue and so the doctor presses to make his discovery public, only to be opposed in sequence by all the public figures in town, including his own brother the mayor, all of whom look to their selfish interests first and bow to expediency. The doctor loses his post and is even forced out of his home. Eventually, joined by his wife and sons and an honest sea captain who offers the use of his house, he resolved to open a school for poor children which will educate them in true citizenship and independence of mind. No one can doubt,

when Ibsen has his protagonist pronounce at the end of *An Enemy of the People* that "the strongest man in the world is the one who stands most alone," that the play is affirming that as well, nor that the characterization in the play's title, which refers to Stockmann, is to be understood as a badge of honor. At least, no one familiar with the premises of realist drama, the political history of nineteenth century Europe, Ibsen's earlier plays, and Ibsen's appreciation of Kierkegaard on the importance of the individual. Ibsen would not have written the play as he did if he did not mean to advocate a certain position about the perils of majority thinking and the herd instinct.

Goya's *The Third of May, 1808*, which depicts the casual execution of a number of apparently guiltless citizens of Madrid by Napoleon's occupying troops, clearly embodies as well the painter's horror at this scene. The pitiful expression on the main figure's face, the blazing color and dramatic lighting, the faceless, impassive soldiers arrayed in a line against their victims, all contribute to making the painting a passionate protest against political tyranny; it says, implicitly, that military occupations such as this one are evil, and their victims are martyrs. No one who did not view matters in that way would have painted the picture as Goya did. And our conviction of this is underscored, one might add, by the evident sympathy with the oppressed and the distrust of power manifested in other works by Goya, even his portraits of the Spanish Royal Court.

A last example of the traditional sort, but more indirect in its address to the audience, is Browning's well-known poem, *My Last Duchess*. In this poem Browning creates a character, the Duke of Ferrara, who speaks to a silent emissary from the court of a count who has come to negotiate the marriage of the count's daughter to the Duke, who is apparently in need of another wife. The Duke discourses to his guest about his former wife in front of a striking portrait of her, to which he closely controls access. In the course of this we are made to realize the Duke's cruelty, jealousy, and arrogance, all of which have led him to have his late wife killed, but without any trace of remorse or regret in that regard. We can only hope the count's emissary will at this point turn back the Duke's overtures in regard to his patron's daughter, but we fear that, men being men, and the **realpolitik** of the Renaissance being what it was, that this will not occur. The poem's disapproval, even condemnation, of behavior and personality such as that displayed by the Duke is clear; it is saying, at the least, that such men are evil, and perhaps the more dangerous in their obliviousness to their wrongdoings.[2]

I have claimed that these works of Ibsen, Goya, and Browning say certain things. But what does this mean? Are these artists **literally** stating these things through such works? That seems rather unlikely. Such works do not consist of statements, even when, as in the case of two of them, they are composed of language. Ibsen's play and Browning's poem are no more being asserted than is Goya's painting, nor can assertions attributable **directly** to Ibsen or Browning or Goya be found within them. Dr. Stockmann says, in the play, that the majority is always wrong, Ibsen does not; the Duke says, in the poem, that his ex-wife was too free with her approval, Browning does not; and no one says anything in Goya's painting.

Yet, once again, our intuitions are that these works **are** saying certain things. It seems we must look for some more liberal construal of "saying" to account for what is going on here. Perhaps an artwork says suchandsuch if its creator believed suchandsuch when he or she made the work? One trouble with that is that we have little access to what artists believe, apart from their works, yet we often have fairly clear ideas as to what their works are saying. A second worry with the proposal is that it would

render the connection between what a work says and how it appears or strikes us completely external and adventitious. But thirdly, and conclusively, an artwork surely cannot be **saying,** even in a liberal sense, everything its creator believed while making it. For example, Ibsen believed in the emancipation of women as he penned *An Enemy of the People*, and for that matter in the existence of France, but the play says nothing on either score. Perhaps, then, an artwork says what its creators intended that those who experienced it should come to believe? No, for first, such intentions can famously misfire, which seems to amount to works saying something other than what their creators intended them to, and second, saying something about a subject should not, it seems, be tied so closely to the goal of converting belief; surely one can say something without aiming to change anyone's mind on the subject. (For example, I might declare out loud that the sun was shining, or that slavery was wrong, just for the heck of it, without caring if anyone was in hearing, or what, if they **happened** to be, were their beliefs on those subjects. Perhaps—this is now a third proposal—a work of art says suchandsuch—communicates that to us in some way—if it is inconceivable that someone could have created the work as it is **unless** he or she believed suchandsuch. Although this is getting closer to the mark, it still falls short: for it will always be possible, will it not, to come up with **other** explanations of why a work is as it is, making the inconceivability test unmeetable.

Suppose, though, that we relax this last proposal a bit. The following formula may be roughly what we are seeking: a work of art says suchandsuch if it would be **reasonable** to **hypothesize,** on the basis of the work offered, that the artist believed suchandsuch.

Now even if this is roughly right, two qualifications are rather quickly in order.[3] The first is that a work cannot be saying

everything it would be reasonable, from the work, to hypothesize that the artist believed about its subject, but only some subset thereof, which we might characterize as those beliefs to which the work appears to be drawing **attention,** or alternatively, those which it seems the artist is intending to foreground or make manifest to us. A work does not say **everything** that, when understood, it provides evidence of the artist's believing. For example, in the case of the *Third of May*, the painting gives reason to credit Goya with the belief that men have eyes and limbs, but the painting doesn't **say** this, in the sense we are after. It's not part of what the painting seems designed to get across. It's not part of the painting's message.

The second qualification of the rough formula is that such hypothesizing of the artist's mind cannot go on in a vacuum, if it is to be reasonably identified with what a work says as an artistic vehicle of a historically placed individual. Rather, any such plausible hypothesizing—any responsible "psyching out" of the attitudes or values embodied in and put forward by a work— must be informed and constrained by a work's position in a communicative matrix whose dimensions include the artist's time and place, the artist's social climate, the artist's predecessors, the artist's oeuvre as a whole, the particular artform, tradition, genre, and problematic within which the artist is working, and even the artist's public self or identity. We have similar concerns, of course, when engaged in deciding what construction to put on someone's utterance in normal conversational situations; we cannot determine with accuracy what has been said, on even the literal level, from words alone. It may very well be relevant who is speaking, what they have previously said on this or other occasions, where and when the speaking is taking place, what the speaker can be taken to be aware of and thus possibly alluding to, and so on. Now art is utterance too, I have been suggesting, but

its context is generally more complex and wide-ranging than that of speech. So there is all the greater danger of misunderstanding if that context is misgauged or even overlooked entirely.

Putting these qualifications in place, we get more or less this: A work of art says what, on the basis of the work contextually construed, it would be reasonable to impute to its artist as a view that he or she both significantly held and was concerned to say.[4] Now, by this criterion, many, if not all, works of art, and surely those discussed earlier by Ibsen, Goya, and Browning, end up saying something. Of course in many other cases this will be less clear, often because we will be unable to decide whether a view we discern in a work is indeed plausibly attributed to its maker as **held,** rather than merely considered, explored, or tried on for size.[5]

Some have thought to capture the drift of the preceding reflections in terms of the notion of an **implied artist** or **author,** that is, the agent a work seems to have been created by or to have issued from, "the creating person who is implied by the totality of a given work when it is offered to the world," in the words of Wayne Booth, the original proponent of the notion.[6] The implied author of a work may, as it turns out, coincide fairly closely with the **actual** author as regards personality and viewpoint, but often this is not the case, and in any event, there is no necessity of it. Given this notion, then instead of speaking of beliefs or attitudes that would be **reasonably attributed** to the actual author on the basis of the work, contextually grasped, we can speak of the beliefs or attitudes that **just straightforwardly belong** to the implied author—he or she being a construction tailor-made to bear them.

But here we must distinguish two ways of engaging in this construction, leading to two kinds of implied author. The first we may call the superficially (or "thinly") implied author—this is roughly the mind you would infer is behind a work on the basis of the work alone, given only general information about the period of creation, genre conventions, and prevailing language involved. The second we may call the deeply (or "thickly") implied author—this is roughly the mind you would infer is behind a work given the work and the aforementioned minimal historical context, but also the author's previous works, his public self or image, and the specifics of his situatedness in relation to his surrounding culture and society.

To see that these are not the same, consider again my Ibsen example. The mind we infer is behind *An Enemy of the People*, the beliefs we hypothesize drove its making, and thus ultimately, the message we take from it, varies according to whether we approach the text as merely a piece of nineteenth century drama of naturalistic stripe—that is to say, thinly—or as the product of Ibsen in particular, with his own concrete formative experiences, artistic track record, and public persona—that is to say, thickly. On the former approach it is open that there is an element of satire or caricature in the heroic extremity of Stockmann's stand of one against all, but not on the latter. Whereas on the latter approach, but not the former, the individualistic thrust of *Enemy* is corroborated by those of Ibsen's earlier *Wild Duck* and *Doll's House*, and its concerns naturally related to the failure of the popular revolutions of 1848—whose great effect on him Ibsen acknowledged repeatedly in his letters and journals. Lastly, we can clearly see reflected in the play an appreciation of the earthshattering importance of Pasteur's recent discoveries about microbes if we approach it thickly, but not so clearly otherwise.

So does a work say what it seems to when we project its implied author thinly or thickly? The latter, I suggest. Even though with art there is always an inclination to take works in isolation, to let them speak as they will as independent offerings, unteth-ered to their creators and unbeholden to their antecedents, the fact is, first, that they are **not** independent offerings, and second, that taken in isolation—from the artist and his or her known circumstances—works tend to have impoverished meanings and dampened resonances, as well as verging undesirably often on wholesale ambiguity or indeterminacy. Each work of art takes its place in an ongoing expressive endeavor, one in which the artist's whole self and activity are implicated. An artwork is a complex situated utterance, not a structure fallen from the sky of possibilities, nor something on the order of a found object. What it says, accordingly, can be identified most nearly with what can be ascribed to its thickly implied artist, i.e., with what it would be reasonable to infer, from the work taken in its full publicly accessible context, are views importantly held by the actual artist and that he or she wanted to transmit.

Now that—what a situated work of art says—coincides necessarily neither with what the actual artist actually believes and hopes to convey, nor with what the implied authors of other works of the artist can be said to believe. So there is still a difference between what works say and what their authors say—or would say if directly queried—and between what one work says and what another says—even if a certain amount of mutual inflection is here inescapable.

It is high time we acknowledged, though, that most works of art do not have messages as unequivocally as the three with which I began, and some have no discernible messages at all. We have only to think of any of Magritte's paintings, of Kafka's novel *The Castle*, of Wallace Stevens' poem *The Jar*, of the Beatles' songs *Blackbird* or *I Am the Walrus*, of Joyce's *Finnegan's Wake* or David Lynch's *Eraserhead*, of Chris Burden's or Vito Acconci's exercises in self-mutilation or self-fashioning,[7] in the first instance, or Kandinsky's *Improvisations*, or Beethoven's

First Symphony, or Brancusi's *Bird in Space*, or Brakhage's *Mothlight*, or Balanchine's *The Four Temperaments* in the second. In these cases we have difficulty, at the least, in arriving at reasonable inferences, based on those works taken even in thick artistic context, as to what their makers saliently believed and wished to impart. In other words, we are either not impelled univocally, or not impelled at all, toward hypotheses of views the creators of such works must have had, and had in mind to transmit, given the works put forward for our appreciation. But instead of pursuing any of those patently elusive examples, I turn rather to their opposite number, namely, works that appear all-too-plainly to have messages. The public waters have been roiled more often of late by works of this sort than ones of the preceding sort. This is perhaps not surprising: obscurity, detachment, and paradoxicality can be ignored, but blatancy, engagement, and bluntness seem to call for a response. I will consider first a manifestation that occurred not long ago at my home institution,[8] and second, a contemporary rap music offering.

III.

At the center of the furor on my campus was an art project generated by twelve students in a class on feminist art, all of whom were members of a group called Women's Coalition for Change, and which was exhibited during an annual campus event called Art Attack. It consisted of a large wall erected to display the names, in alphabetical order, of all the male students listed in the campus student directory. At the head of this wall of names, this giant poster, was the rubric "Potential Rapists." Some of the individuals named and most of the columnists in the school paper denounced this project, parents complained to the university, suits were threatened, if idly, and eventually the president of the university had to issue a public condemnation of the work and an apology to the university community.[9]

In my view, the students named on the giant poster had no cause for complaint, parents and columnists overreacted, and the president of the university acted unwisely in responding to pressure in that manner. Part of the problem, as you might imagine, was confusion about what the messages in works of art are, and how to determine them. What do artworks "say," and how does one tell what they are "saying"? The Art Attack item—which I will call *Rape Piece*—though not particularly subtle or original, clearly was such a work. Was it saying anything? If so, what?

Rape Piece appears to be—that is to say, on the surface it looks like—an item in the category of public notices or announcements. As such, it would be ranged with "Wanted" posters in the post office, with announcements of openings for engineers in the local firm, with advertisements for upcoming lectures, with political proclamations in favor of some candidate or against some municipal policy, and with Martin Luther's "Ninety-five Theses." In short, so classified, it would be taken as non-fiction declarative communication, pure and simple.

But clearly it is not. *Rape Piece* is not strictly an item of that category, it only resembles such; what it is, at base, is an artistic representation of such an item. That is to say, the creators of *Rape Piece* have borrowed the form of a public proclamation of warning and used it in an image—an image, however, which is knowingly indiscernible from the thing itself, at least if intention and framing context are ignored or left out of account.

Now *Rape Piece* **might** in fact be saying, ultimately, what the literal proclamation whose form and look it imitates or appropriates would be saying, but we are not in a position to decide that unless we recognize from the outset that *Rape Piece* is not simply such a proclamation **tout court**. To regard *Rape Piece* as a public notice is to ascribe a certain meaning to it and a certain state of mind to its author or authors; to regard *Rape Piece* as an artwork in a certain avant-garde tradition which fictively embodies a public notice might be to ascribe a meaning to it obliquely related to that of the public notice it mimics, and a state of mind to its creators equally obliquely related to that we would attribute to the author of such a notice in reality. Of course the meanings might, as it turns out, be fairly coincident, i.e., we might decide we are justified in identifying the attitude of the actual artist with that of the implied proclaimer in the work. But as a conceptual matter they are not identical, and we must at least consider the ways in which, and the reasons for which, they might diverge.

Rape Piece is an artwork: it was presented in a setting explicitly identified as artistic, it was intended to be seen as the product of artistic activity and thinking, and to be viewed in the context of earlier endeavors of that sort. But what sort is that? *Rape Piece* echoes and is informed by various modes of avant-garde artmaking in the twentieth century. Like Conceptual Art its materials seem to be ideas and conventions more than the physical stuff out of which it is composed. Like Minimal Art it simplifies its forms and eschews visual elaboration for its own sake, yet like Concrete Poetry it calls attention to the shape of words and sentences as visual facts with their own weights and resonances. Like Pop Art it borrows and adapts images from the surrounding culture and reflects them back to us. Like Dada it is purposely provocative. None of this means that it is any good as art, only that in order to decide what if anything it says and whether it was worth saying that way, it must first be perceived in an art context, with the activities of Duchamp, Warhol, Bob Dylan, Allen Ginsburg, Laurie Anderson and Conceptualists such as Joseph Kosuth or Adrian Piper as points of reference,

rather than the actions of notice-posters and thesis-tackers per se.

Just situating an utterance in its proper context is not sufficient, of course, to determine what it is saying, in the broad sense already invoked. We now have to ask, in line with the formula proposed earlier: What significant views—if any—is it reasonable to hypothesize the makers of *Rape Piece* both held and hoped to convey, **on the basis of the work taken in its full context of presentation?** The question is fairly easy to pose, but answering it is considerably more difficult.

Perhaps *Rape Piece*'s simulacrum of a proclamation does not, ultimately, make that proclamation at all, but only invites us to imagine that proclamation being made, and so indirectly, to reflect on whether it should be made. Perhaps *Rape Piece* is knowingly the image of a hyperbolic statement, recognized as hyperbolic by its mounters, and whose glaring over-the-top-ness, as well as their awareness of it, they would take to be evident to all. Perhaps *Rape Piece* simply asks us to consider whether things have come to such a pass that the sexes have no choice but to view each other with probabilistic suspicion.[10]

Now while a case could be made for such construals, I would not be overly confident of them. *Rape Piece* is not only a work of Conceptual or Documentation art, it is the product of a political action group, a radical feminist one at that, and this, I think, makes it implausible that its address to the issues is as indirect as these last hypotheses of intent make it out to be. Let us suppose then, that the piece is best seen, artistic envelope acknowledged, as actually saying what its contained proclamation says, because that is, all told, the most reasonable hypothesis of what its authors believe, and accounts in the most convincing way for their making and exhibiting such a work. How, then, should the proclamation be understood? In other words, what construction should be put on the listing of male student names under the rubric of "potential rapist"?

A point of utmost significance, which I have not heretofore underlined, is that **all** the male names in the student directory were employed in the piece, without selection or discrimination. In other words, though individuals' names were used, for reasons of immediacy and impact, it was not any individuals **in particular** who were the target of the fictive proclamation. Rather, it was clearly men in general, or else young men in college. Now why should anyone think that all college men are potential rapists—or even represent that as proclaimed in a work of Documentation Art? What does "potential" plausibly mean here?

One way to take it would be: that all college men are already disposed to rape, and that they need only the right trigger or favorable conditions to set them off. Now perhaps the makers intended that reading. If so, it is undoubtedly false, and arguably offensive to men collectively. But is that the most plausible construal? Recall that this was the work of students in a course on Feminist Art on a campus which, like many others, is subject to the problems of sexual attacks, poor lighting, acquaintance rape, and insufficient caution on the part of female students. More likely, given the political context and a principle of charity, is an epistemic reading of the word "potential," as meaning roughly, "for all I know, might turn out to be." In other words, the force of the proclamation-within-the-work is not that there's a good chance any college man will commit rape if the circumstances are right, but that there's some chance that among the college men on campus you encounter, even among those you know, there are some that will commit rape in certain, not inconceivable, circumstances, and you cannot tell with assurance who they are. And so therefore, you cannot be too careful. Perhaps this is a bit paranoid as an attitude, but it is neither offensive to individual men, nor **wholly** unreasonable.[11]

V.

. . . But acknowledging these points hardly absolves artists of responsibility for messages that are, in the last analysis, ascribable to their products nonetheless. Even though the message implicit in a work is logically distinct from the message the artist, as a private individual, might vouchsafe one on that topic, the artist **has** generated the work's message, and usually is in **as good** a position as anyone to assess what it is. Who then should be responsible for the message in a work if not the artist, and for the social repercussions, if any, of its reception? And this remains true in cases where the resulting message is not intended by the artist, or even not recognized by him, so long as it is discerned there fairly and squarely.

In addition, artists may even bear some responsibility for messages **not** rightly ascribable to their works seen in proper context, though widely **thought** to be so, where such misreading could easily have been foreseen. Artists who don't appear to reckon on likely ways of being misunderstood are, at best, being disingenuous, and indeed there are artists who want to be generally misunderstood, their messages received intact only by cognoscenti. But at worst, the artist apparently oblivious to likely misreading is just a bad, or sloppy, artist. Art is a dangerous business, for artists as well as audiences: it isn't always enough, at least in terms of the wider community of one's fellows, to be right, i.e., to make a work say what you want it to say. Concern may also have to be carried to whether the message will, to less-than-ideal audiences in imperfect conditions, have much of a chance of getting across. It's one thing to **epater la bourgeoisie** for **epater**ing's sake; it's another for a work to **epater** when it doesn't mean to, or to **epater** so crassly that whatever else it said is simply not heard at all. An artist cannot both style himself an **agent provocateur** and also claim full artistic immunity when he succeeds in provoking, arguing that his work is not being seen or taken in the right way, knowing all along that it generally would not be.

As is evident, this discussion of artistic accountability is far from complete. My observations are meant to be suggestive, and not to constitute proper defense of a full position on this subject. But one further statement of clarification is in order. In saying that an artist has some responsibility for unintended but eminently foreseeable misinterpretations of her works I don't mean to imply that an artist is therefore blameworthy for all undesirable consequences thereof. "Responsible" is a broader, more neutral ascription than either "blameworthy" or "praiseworthy," being in fact presupposed by them. What I would, though, insist on, is an irreducible kernel of responsibility in cases of the sort we have been discussing: an artist cannot simply disavow any concern for the consequences of likely misreadings of her work where such misreading might easily have been predicted, merely on the grounds that such are indeed misreadings, and thus not a reflection of or reaction to the content of that work.

I have still one promissory note to redeem. Granted there are, at least in many cases, messages in art—something the artwork, as an utterance, understood in context, is broadly saying—how is it possible to look for and attend to such messages while still treating the art as art? Doesn't this reduce art, as Warner irreverently suggested, to the status of telegraphy? The answer is that, although with telegrams, the typeface and paper color don't matter, and the telegram itself may be discarded once it is understood, with art we appreciate the **unique way in which** the artwork embodies and carries its message. We don't simply "take the message and run," to adapt a title of Woody Allen's. That is to say, we value the vehicle of the message as much as, or more than, we do the message **per se,** or better, we value precisely the message-as-conveyed-by-that-specific-vehicle. One might even argue—though I will not—that message in art regarded as art is properly **only** that vehicle qualified thing, the generically-expressible-idea-as-embodied-in-the-concrete-work; in other words, content inseparable from form. Of course there is no danger that in attending to "message" in that sense that we could ever lose sight of the art itself, for such messages do not exist apart from the very works which contain them. But without jettisoning our familiar idea of detachable messages—ones that can be formulated in words, more or less, and that might be equally well conveyed by entirely different works of art—we can still state a rule for aesthetic appreciation of them: that it always be with reference to their particular embodiment in, and way of being uttered by, the work of art at hand.

---

[1] Though it is also attributed to Darryl Zanuck.

[2] A structurally similar example from popular art is the rock ballad by Simon & Garfunkel called "I Am a Rock." In this song the lyric persona aggressively proclaims his independence from others and his imperviousness to emotional pain, but it's clear the song is not endorsing, but rather regretting and challenging, such sentiments.

[3] What follows echoes, though without paralleling entirely, the account of literary meaning as utterance meaning I have set out at length in my "Intention and Interpretation: A Last Look," in G. Iseminger (ed.), *Intention and Interpretation* (Temple UP, 1992) 221–56.

[4] A possible objection to this working formula is that it may exclude from the potentially sayable by a work anything it appears the author would likely disavow, even when strongly suggested by what is in the work. But perhaps there is little, in the way of possible content, that could actually meet that double condition.

[5] One writer who pinpoints this difficulty in interpretation well is Robert Stecker, in a discussion of perspective embodied in works of literature:

"This is not to say that perspectives are not some-times held in the strong sense of affirmed by writers or that it is never worth asking whether a perspective is affirmed or merely entertained by its writer. It may be part of understanding a work to understand this." ["Apparent, Implied, and Postulated Authors," *Philosophy and Literature*, 1987] Indeed, I have been arguing that such asking, in a hypothetical vein, is crucial to deciding what, if anything, a work **says.**

[6] From his *Critical Understanding: The Powers and Limits of Pluralism* (U Chicago P, 1979) 269. Booth's account of "implied authors" was first set out in his *The Rhetoric of Fiction* (U Chicago P, 1961).

[7] A step further, or a somewhat different direction, has been taken recently by the French performance artist Orlan. Orlan is engaged in a project-in-progress of redefining her self through surgical self-transformation. So far she has had five operations, which are themselves conducted as a sort of ritual, and appears to have enjoyed them all.

[8] The University of Maryland, College Park, April 1993.

[9] I am simplifying the event involved, for my own rhetorical purposes. The art project actually consisted of two parts, the wall of names described, but also leaflets with randomly selected male student names, posted on kiosks around campus. The second part of this project might indeed be rightly criticized on the grounds that were applied to the project as a whole, but I here leave that out of account.

[10] Foreshadowing the worst kind of scenario that might result in this new battle of the sexes, some male students wrote letters of complaint to the school newspaper about *Rape Piece* proposing that all the female names in the student directory be emblazoned on posters under the heading "Potential Prostitutes."

[11] There is a reflection of it, curiously, in these observations of the narrator of Ford Madox Ford's *The Good Soldier*: "For who in this world can give anyone a character [i.e., a character reference]? Who in this world knows anything of any other heart—or of his own? I don't mean to say that one cannot form an average estimate of the way a person will behave. But one cannot be certain of the way any man will behave in every case—and until one can do that a 'character' is of no use to anyone." [Penguin, 1915/1990, 144]. Of course Ford's sorry spokesperson in the novel has ample reason to align himself with those who regard suspicion about one's fellows in matters of sex as only sensible, having himself come multiply to grief in that arena.

Peter Kivy

THE "HISTORICALLY AUTHENTIC" PERFORMANCE

Peter Kivy is professor of philosophy at Rutgers University and author of many books on aesthetics, especially the aesthetics of music. Among these are Sound Sentiment, Music Alone, *and* The Fine Art of Repetition: Essays in the Philosophy of Music. *Kivy defends the ideal of "historically authentic" performance of music, but he suggests that authenticity can be understood in a number of ways.*

What has knowledge of the history of music to do with its performance? Not so long ago the answer would have been "Nothing." And not so very long before that the history of music was a non-subject.

Today the situation is radically altered. As Joseph Kerman writes in his recent, and refreshingly irreverent survey of the current musicological scene,

> Musicology . . . has a whole long catalogue of music to contribute to the repertory and a definite theory as to how it should be performed. The catalogue consists mostly of "early music"—early by comparison with that of the so-called standard repertory—but also includes later works . . . which never got into the repertory or else dropped out. All this music, according to musicological doctrine, should be presented—as far as this is possible—according to the reconstructed performing traditions and conditions of its own time and place.

This performance idea, nurtured by the theory and practice of modern musicology, has come to be referred to generally as the concept of "historical authenticity" in performance.

Two questions have quite naturally arisen, in the musicological and music-critical literature, with regard to the historically authentic performance. *What* is it? And, of course, *why* is it; that is to say, *why* should we want an "historically authentic" performance, whatever we may construe it to be? . . .

AUTHENTICITY AND INTENTION

It may not seem obvious why, on first reflection; but often the concept of historical authenticity in performance is identified with the realizing of the composer's intentions. Richard Taruskin quite correctly observes that "the usual answer" to the question of

Peter Kivy, "On the Concept of 'The Historically Authentic' Performance," *The Monist* 71.2 (1988): 278–90.

why we should (as Wimsatt and Beardsley put it) "consult the oracle" is that we want our performance to be authentic." . . .

It is frequently advanced, as a *reductio ad absurdum* of the "authentic performance" movement that it endorses "bad" performances by endorsing, to use Kerman's description, the reconstructed performing conditions and traditions of the music's own time and place. For, as Charles Rosen observes, in his article, "Should Music Be Played 'Wrong'?," the title of which just about sums up the argument,

> Like most things, music is generally badly played. . . . I have heard a tape of a new composition in which most of the rhythms were at least slightly wrong, the players were rarely quite together, and often they forgot to come in at all. The composer lamented that if this tape were exhumed in the twenty-second century, students would conclude that it represented the performance practice of the twentieth century. As a matter of fact, they would be quite right.

Rosen's point, of course, . . . is that if we are committed, without qualification, to the reconstruction of the performance practice of any period whatever, we are committed to the perpetuation of what is bad in that practice as well as what is good, under the quite reasonable assumption that, on *any* reasonable standard of good and bad, *any* performance practice will contain both.

What this points up is that the reconstruction of performance practice, like any purely historical reconstruction, is non-normative, value free. But the concept of compositional intention is not; and that is what allows it to circumvent Rosen's objection. For, I take it, we have a right to assume that the composer intends, among other things, the best possible performance of his or her work. Indeed, that is what, presumably, all of the specific intentions add up to. If, therefore, we construe the historically authentic performance to be identical with the performance intended by the composer

(to the extent that the composer had specific intentions in this regard), we need not include any "bad" performance practice. We need not play Berlioz' music out of tune, if that was the practice of his times; for we can reasonably assume that he did not intend it to be played that way. Nor, to take a more interesting case, need we conduct eighteenth-century music by "beating a rolled-up sheet of music paper on the desk to keep the orchestra in time . . . ," even though, as Rosen points out, "this practice was traditional and part of the immediately audible experience of eighteenth-century opera." Indeed, we may even assume that the eighteenth-century composer intended the music to be conducted this way; for, of course, this was an intermediate intention, serving the primary intention of keeping the orchestra in time, in the most effective possible way. And if we can think of a better, more effective way, we *are* realizing the composer's intention more fully, under the methodological assumption that the composer intended his or her music to be played as well as possible.

A second objection to the historically authentic performance, even more obviously avoided by identifying authenticity with intention, is that it is a mistake to assume composers acquiesce in all aspects of the performance practice of their time, even when it is not obviously bad practice, and therefore, that in being authentic, we are violating the composers' intentions and wishes as to the performance of their works. As Taruskin correctly surmises, "performance styles in the past, no less than in the present, had their proponents and their detractors . . ."; and it is surely likely that at least some composers were among the detractors. Authenticity and intention, then, may frequently be at cross purposes; and it is intention, so the argument goes, that should be honored. But, needless to say, if authenticity and intention are identified, this conflict cannot occur, and the objection to authenticity is quite blunted.

. . . The mere mention of the word "intention" in regard to any art-critical or art-theoretical question is liable to elicit, these days, the most violent reaction, as if one had just dropped a snake in a crowded room, so discredited has the concept become in some circles, where it is deemed as metaphysically suspect and closed to human scrutiny as the will of God. . . . Let me just state what seem to me to be some simple, and reassuring truths about intentions in general, composers' intentions in particular. We all have intentions; and so did our ancestors, as far back as we wish to trace the history of *homo sapiens*. Intentions are not mysterious or inaccessible, either in principle or in practice. They are inferred, or known directly, through actions, documents, circumstances, both present and past; through art-works, artifacts, fossils, and ways of living. If the intentions of dead composers cannot, at least some of them, be known, then the intentions of dead kings and ministers cannot be known, nor the intentions of dead philosophers and scientists; so a good deal of what we think of as political and intellectual history goes up the spout along with what we think of as a legitimate part of the history of music. But this is a *reductio ad absurdum*. Unless we are raising the kind of doubts about other minds that are raised in epistemology seminars, we should be no less comfortable with knowledge claims, or at least well-founded conjectures, about the intentions of Bach or Dufay than with similar claims or conjectures about the intentions of Newton or Archimedes, Henry VIII or Solon. And if we are raising such skeptical doubts, then we might just as well give up music history, or the history of anything else, across-the-board. . . .

. . . I want to make out what I think are some important points about historically authentic performance that would only be obscured by the flap over intention, and are better explicated using another concept of authenticity.

AUTHENTICITY AND RECONSTRUCTION

Let us revert, then, to Kerman's way of putting it: the reconstructed performing traditions and conditions of the music's own time and place. How can we cash that out as a description of the historically authentic performance? To begin with, we are faced immediately with the problem, avoided, as we have seen, by authenticity as intention, of playing the music "wrong." We must assume, therefore, that any attempt to reconstruct a performance tradition of the past, for the purpose of playing real music to real audiences, and not just as a scholarly exercise, will be an attempt to reconstruct only the "optimal" one. We do not want to reconstruct an incompetent performance—at least not one incompetent by the standards of *its* time as well as ours. . . .

A second consideration is this. We will have to ask, when we state our formula, about whom we are talking when we talk about a performance sounding the way it would have at some historical period: that is to say, we will have to ask, *to whom* it sounded "the" way it did. For, clearly, a performance will sound differently to different auditors: differently to an educated listener than to an uneducated one; differently to an Italian than to a German; and, most importantly, differently to *me* than to a contemporary of the music. For *I* can hear a piece of music (say) as anticipating the harmonic techniques of Brahms or Wagner; and Bach could not. No matter how hard I try to reproduce the "sound" of an eighteenth-century performance, it will, it seems, never be the "sound" of an eighteenth-century performance in a way that is so musically deep and significant that even after the last treatise is perused, the last instrument reconstructed and mastered, the last notation deciphered, we will still be light-years away from an "historically authentic performance."

Imagine the following extreme science fiction example. With the help of H. G. Wells and Stephen Spielberg, I return, via time machine, to eighteenth-century Leipzig, just in time to hear a performance of the *St. Matthew Passion* under the direction of the master himself. I think this is the kind of conceptual ideal that many perpetrators of "authentic historical performance" have. But this does not, for the reasons rehearsed above, give me the opportunity of hearing an authentic performance in the sense of one that would sound the way it sounded in Bach's time, *if* we mean by that the "sound" that was in the ears of Bach or his contemporaries. Undaunted, however, I obtain, this time through the good offices of Robert Louis Stevenson, a drug that completely obliterates my twentieth-century self and provides me with an eighteenth-century one, "memories" and all. Back again I go; now I am an "eighteenth-century" man hearing Bach performing the *St. Matthew Passion*. The trouble is, in a quite obvious sense, I am no longer myself. *I'm* not finding out how Baroque music sounded to Baroque ears because I have turned myself into someone else: into a Baroque man.

Not to worry, though; I have anticipated all of that. The drug is of a temporary kind, and wears off soon after my time machine returns me to 1986. So although I can't hear Baroque music with Baroque ears, I can *remember* what Baroque music sounds like to Baroque ears, since I was so recently a Baroque bloke. *(Recently?)*

However, it should be clear that that stratagem is not going to work. Because all I will be doing when I *remember* hearing Bach's performance is what I would be doing if I were remembering any other performance: that is to say, hearing the music running through my head, as best I can. And I will be mentally "hearing" it through twentieth-century ears of the mind. I am up against a metaphysical stone wall.

I have gone through this little exercise in musical science fiction partly for the sheer fun of it—but partly, too, to keep it very prominent before our minds that "historically authentic performances," whatever they are, are for twentieth-century audiences. . . . Be that as it may, perhaps I should conclude this train of thought with some consolation, if consolation is needed. It is *not* a misfortune not to be able to hear Bach with the ears of his time. If it is even *intelligible* to conceive of it as a goal, it is a goal that no sensible music lover should want to achieve. For what Bach or Josquin means to me, in terms of appreciation and greatness, neither could possibly have meant for their contemporaries. Were I a contemporary of Bach, chances are I wouldn't enjoy his music much at all, let alone see it as one of the deepest and most sublime experiences music has to offer; for we all know, if only from Nicholas Slonimsky's *Lexicon of Musical Invective*, that contemporary audiences, with few exceptions, have trouble appreciating the music of their times that later achieves the status of "masterpiece." This, just to remind us again that it is the performance that is supposed to be reconstructed, not us. . . .

AUTHENTICITIES

. . . I shall assume, for purposes of argument, that what we mean by an historically authentic performance of a given piece of music is one sonically like a performance we would hear if we were transported by Wells, Spielberg, et al., to the right time and place.

Again, though, we must ask who the "we" is in our formula. It is not a person of that time and that place; that we have already established. But *who?* Clearly, the sounds that Leonard Bernstein would hear if he were our time traveler, would be different from those of a completely untutored music lover would hear: that finely tuned, superbly educated ear would hear far more than the average concert-goer's. For argument's sake, I will simply stipulate the "we" as *me:* somewhat more musically perceptive and educated than the average concert-goer, some orders of magnitude less so than Leonard Bernstein. I shall mean, then, by an historically authentic performance of a musical work, a performance sonically like one I would hear if I were at the right historical time and place for performances of that particular work, and were hearing an optimal performance of it. . . .

. . . Surely, if we are to reasonably construe our phrase "sonically like," we must construe "like" as "approximately like," "something like," or something of the kind, and allow, therefore, for *degrees* of authenticity. We will want, then, to say that some performances are more authentic, historically, than others. We will want to say in what respects some performance is historically authentic and some other not. A most important implication of all of this is that we will come to see authenticity, for all practical purposes, as a trade-off: that is to say, one will have to choose in which respects one wants one's performance to be authentic, because, in practice, various authenticity-producing features are incompatible with one another. . . .

Clearly, the time travel model of historically authentic performance throws the doors wide open to every kind of historical research into the way music was performed in any given period, and the kinds of physical means at the disposal of performers. It sanctions the use of old and reconstructed instruments, the following of instructions about how to phrase, ornament, articulate, and so forth, that can be culled from treatises and documents of the period. It licenses, indeed, the whole institution that has come to be called the "early music movement," loudly trumpeted (on valveless trumpets, of course) by its supporters as the

only way to perform, just as stridently put down by the so-called musical establishment as the work of pedants and philistines (although it is beginning to be a real question these days as to which group has the right to "establishment" status: Steinway and Co. may be running scared).

But before we throw away our Steinways, and tear the keys off our clarinets and oboes, it might be well to think a little bit more carefully about just what, *exactly*, our musical time traveler will hear if he or she returns to the scene of the crime. Let's go back, then, to Leipzig, for that performance of the *St. Matthew Passion*. What will we hear? Well, certainly we will hear oboes and (wooden) flutes without keys, short-necked fiddles, and all the rest of it. We will hear the ornaments played in whatever way they really were, the phrasing and articulation likewise, and we will, or won't hear vibrato, double-dotting, *notes inégales*, little *sforzandi* at the beginning of phrases, a pause before the final chord—depending upon which, if any, of the students of these things are right. We will hear, in short, all of those things that the early music enthusiasts try to reproduce in their carefully researched, original-instrument performances. To the extent that they succeed—to the extent that their research is sound and its realization accurate—their performances will be historically authentic: more or less sonically like what I would hear if I had that musical time machine.

But what else would I hear? To introduce my answer to that question, let me call attention to two frequently voiced objections to what its critics call "authentic" performance. The first objection is that authentic performances are dull, pedantic affairs, in which the performers have substituted rule-following and calculation for aesthetic sensibility and imaginative musicality. The authentic performance movement, they charge, has tried to transform the art of performing into a science of the thing, with dire, mind-deadening results. Secondly, so the critics believe, true, live, convincing musical performance must come out of a living musical tradition, a laying on of hands; but, it is argued, authentic musical performance is the vain attempt to revive a dead tradition, on dead instruments, rather than to carry on a live one with the living tools of one's trade.

With these objections in mind, let us imagine once again what our musical time traveler will hear at Bach's performance of his *St. Matthew Passion.* Will he hear a dull, pedantic, scholarly performance where rule-following is substituted for musical imagination and artistic spontaneity gives place to "musicological" calculation? Will there be the absence of a living musical tradition that some feel at an historically authentic performance today? The answers are so obvious that the questions need hardly be put. Bach was not reproducing an eighteenth-century performance of his work, he was giving one. Bach was not reviving a tradition, he was living one. He was not "following the rules": he was in the dynamic process of making and breaking them. . . . Thus, what our time traveler would hear in Leipzig would be a performance full of the spontaneity, vigour, liveliness, musicality, aesthetic imagination that critics of the "early music" movement find lacking in its "authentic" performances.

The lesson to be learnt from this *gedankenexperiment* is that we are creating a false dichotomy in contrasting *the* historical authenticity of (say) a musicologically correct performance of a Mozart sonata on one of Mozart's fortepianos with the historically *inauthentic* performance by Rudolph Serkin on a Steinway grand. And the question, remember, is not which is better, but which is historically authentic. The answer is, *both* and *neither,* not in some metaphorical or attenuated sense of "historically authentic" but in the rich, full-blooded, and quite literal sense that the time traveler model is intended to convey. The musicologically correct performance on a period forte-

piano is indeed historically authentic in ways in which Serkin's is not. The instrumental sound of a modern concert grand would be. And, let us assume, the phrasing, articulation, dynamics, ornamentation, balance, and "expression" are more like a Mozart performance too. In all these ways, then, the performance on the fortepiano by the musicologist-performer is more historically authentic than Serkin's on the Steinway. But in (at least) two very important ways, which result in a host of sonic features, Serkin's performance, on the modern piano, is more historically authentic than the musicologist's on Mozart's fortepiano. For, like Mozart, Serkin is giving a performance based not on historical judgment but on musical imagination, and all the rest of those "good things" that the great performer brings to the art of musical interpretation, on the instrument to which he was born. And, like Mozart's performance again, and unlike the musicologist's "reconstruction," Serkin's performance comes out of a living musical tradition, a laying on of hands, that give such performances qualities of vibrancy and spontaneity that musicologically "correct" ones are felt to lack. . . .

It is in this sense that, I suggested earlier, historically authentic performance involves a trade-off. We cannot have it entirely both ways. For there are historically authentic features of the musicologist's performance that I simply cannot have if I want the "living tradition" performance; but, contrariwise, there are, in the true, literal sense, historically authentic features of the "living tradition" performance that I cannot have in the musicologist's. If I am giving myself over entirely to the "archaeological" reconstruction of Mozartian performance (and I mean no disparagement of that enterprise), then I *must* renounce the kind of musically imaginative spontaneity that the "living tradition" performance relies on and throw myself into the arms of "scientific" historical judgment; and in so doing I lose those historically authentic features that the "living tradition" performance bestows—historically authentic because the Mozartian performance that the musicologist is trying to "reconstruct" was itself a "living tradition" performance, not a "reconstruction." But if I am after the historical authenticity of the "living tradition" performance—the spontaneity of imagination, artistic judgment, laying on of hands, etc. etc.—that a Mozart performance had in Mozart's day, then I must abrogate my "scientific," historical judgment (if I have any) and throw myself into the arms of musicality, intuition, aesthetic sensibility, and all of those good things that a "living tradition" performance is supposed to have. In a word, I cannot serve two masters at the same time. I can, indeed, give a "mixed" performance (as all performances to a certain extent will always be): serving one master here, the other there. What I cannot do is have it entirely both ways, at least in practice, if not in principle as well. . . .

In sum, then, there are aspects in which the musicologically reconstructed performance is historically authentic and the performance by the "establishment" performer, on a modern instrument, is not—this needs no arguing, and provides ample justification, if it were needed, for musicological research into performance practice and the construction of "ancient" instruments. What has apparently escaped notice, and what I have argued for here, is that in a literal, full-blooded sense of "historically authentic," the "establishment" performance is historically authentic in ways that the musicological performance cannot be. What weight may be given to the various features of these performances that are seen to lend historical authenticity to them is a question of real interest and depth; but I shall not attempt an answer here. . . .

The debate between defenders and critics of historically authentic performance becomes, at its worst, largely a matter of self-congratulation and name-calling, with "authentic" and "inauthentic" as the epithets of choice, the parties to the debate doing no more than biting their thumbs. Where the debate is real and interesting, it seems to me it is either over a matter of historical fact or critical evaluation. In the former case, the issue is whether or not a performance has come close to duplicating what, given the present state of knowledge, the musicologist construes as the historically correct performance. In the latter case, the issue is whether the "authentic" performance was a good one. Where the debate collapses into rhetoric is just where "good" collapses into "authentic." It is my hope that the present paper will help to prevent that collapse, which is to say, help to keep the debate about authenticity authentic.

Yuriko Saito

THE
COLORIZATION
CONTROVERSY

Yuriko Saito, who teaches philosophy at the Rhode Island School of Design, considers in the following selection the pros and cons of colorizing black-and-white movies.

Many oppose colorization primarily because of the rather blatant financial motivation they see behind it. The sale of videotapes of old films was sagging, and market research indicated that a majority of viewers prefer seeing movies in color. Given the computer capability of colorizing old films, several studios seized classics which essentially existed in the public domain, colorized them, and acquired exclusive copyrights to these new versions in the belief that this "face-lift" would give a boost to the otherwise declining market for old movies.

Indeed, most supporters of colorization, of whom Ted Turner is representative, are those who own and reap financial benefit from colorized films, and most likely their support is primarily motivated by this economic prospect. However, this circumstance should be ignored in discussing the aesthetic dimension of the controversy to prevent the criticism of colorization from resolving itself into *ad hominem* accusations. We should separate our judgment of

Ted Turner, the capitalist, from our judgment concerning the aesthetic merit or demerit of his venture.

We should also disregard two other criticisms of colorization that are often cited. One concerns current technical problems of colorization. Because of present technological limitations, new colors must be added *over* the black-and-white images, resulting in the persistent presence of shades of gray. Many critics complain of "mostly washed-out" colors that give everything "the look of a tinted Victorian postcard." The other criticism of colorization charges that the lab technicians' incompetence results in crude or inaccurate color assignments. . . . However, both of these problems can be overcome either with more advanced and sophisticated technology or with more careful and sensitive work by technicians. We should therefore dismiss these technical problems from the aesthetic discussion on colorization, as they do not call into question the desirability of colorization itself.

Yuriko Saito, "Contemporary Aesthetic Issue: The Colorization Controversy" *Journal of Aesthetic Education* 23.2 (1989): 21–31.

I

Let us now turn to those challenges to colorization that involve deeper disagreements over aesthetic matters. One of the prevailing criticisms voiced against colorization appeals to an analogy between coloring a film and coloring a drawing or a painting. . . . The late John Huston, incensed by the colorization of his *The Maltese Falcon*, also claimed that "freedom does not entitle people to . . . hand-tint drawings by Leonardo da Vinci." If it is undesirable to add colors to da Vinci's *Virgin and Child*, then, the critics conclude, by analogy it is undesirable to add colors to monochrome films.

Does this argument from analogy support the critics' objection to colorizing monochrome films? One obvious problem with this analogy is this: while there is one and only one *Virgin and Child*, there are many copies of *It's a Wonderful Life* and *Yankee Doodle Dandy*. That is, coloring the *Virgin and Child* will result in an irreparable alteration of this work of art, while colorizing a monochrome film will not have the same consequences. Indeed, one of the companies engaging in colorization defends its practice by saying: "We're not destroying the 'Mona Lisa.' You bring us the 'Mona Lisa,' we transfer it to tape and give the original back to you." The supporters of colorization do have a point. A more exact analogy would be to color a reproduction of the *Virgin and Child* without touching the original. Is *this* as undesirable as coloring the original drawing?

Whether desirable or not, modifications of a work of art in reproduction have become prevalent, especially since the advent of mechanical reproduction. Many classical visual images have become subjected to a number of modifications and transformations. The image of *Mona Lisa* has been reproduced not only in monochrome and in various sizes but has been used for various commercial purposes, from a pattern for wrapping paper to an advertisement for

spaghetti sauce. Contemporary artists are also responsible for creating variously transformed images of *Mona Lisa*, starting with Duchamp's *I.H.O.O.Q.* Despite all these treatments of the reproduced images, the original *Mona Lisa* remains intact in the Louvre. Supporters of colorizing films can thus point out that if colorization of video copies of a film is to be condemned, then all kinds of modifications to reproduced images in other art media such as painting also ought to be criticized.

Critics of colorization, however, may note the following difference between the aforementioned two cases of modification. Although not everyone can afford to go to the Louvre to experience the original *Mona Lisa*, it is still available to the public at large. In the case of films, on the other hand, the "original" monochrome films, while still existent, are often not readily available. They may be stored, for example, in a film archive, "available for viewing by people *who make the effort to find them.*" Furthermore, at present our experience of old films is for the most part facilitated by television and video cassettes. Since these media show colorized versions, it would be much more difficult to experience an unadulterated original film than to experience an original painting. Hence, the fact that the original monochrome film still exists does not by itself indicate that we can experience the original whenever we want to.

Supporters of colorization, however, can point out that we can still easily obtain the monochrome visual image of these colorized films by turning off the color on the television set. "A quick twist of the color-tint knob on [the viewer's] set will, in an instant, wipe away the colorizer's work and return the classic to its prelapsarian glory." Colorization does not prevent us from seeing the original monochrome image.

The above reply would not satisfy the opponents, however. True, colorization may not prevent the audience from experiencing the original black-and-white version (either in an archive or on a television set with its color turned off). But once colorization takes place, our experience of the original version is significantly and inevitably altered, just as our perception of the world, especially of its colors, has not been the same since the introduction of impressionist paintings. We may enjoy the original more, for example, by appreciating the stark contrast between light and dark which often becomes muted in the colorized version. Or, after seeing a particularly good colorized version, we may develop a negative reaction toward the original because the original may strike us as dreary and boring.

The fact that our perception of the original changes after we have experienced its modifications is not, however, unique to colorized films. The image of *Mona Lisa* has never been quite the same after the satirical treatment given it by Duchamp and other artists. The difference between the colorization of films and modifications in other art media (e.g., painting) seems to be one of degree rather than kind. That is, we experience only one modified version of an original film, while we are exposed to many different modified versions of *Mona Lisa*. But in both cases our perception and subsequent interpretation and appreciation of the originals are bound to be affected by the later modifications to their images. Those who criticize colorization by the foregoing argument from analogy therefore have the burden of either condemning modifications on copies of a work of art *in general* or of showing why various changes made on the copies of the *Mona Lisa*, e.g., are acceptable while colorizing monochrome films is not.

II

Another argument against colorization often cited is this: colorizing a film is disrespectful of the artist's intention. A remarkable aspect of the colorization controversy is that those "artists" whose works have been, or are going to be, colorized are still alive, expressing their views on the fate of their creations. According to the critics, those artists' outcry indicates that colorizing monochrome films amounts to desecration.

It is reasonable to suppose that in general the artists hold a privileged position with regard to their creations and that we ought to respect their wishes concerning what happens to their works. However, it is not clear whether the artists should have the sole or the last say regarding the fate of their works. We *in fact* sometimes override the artist's intention in this respect. Consider the following examples. We feel that the publisher was justified in not destroying Tolstoy's masterpieces though instructed to do so as a result of the author's conviction about art expressed in *What Is Art?* Or take our modern institution, the art museum. We take art objects out of their original context (e.g., a cathedral), put them into a wholly foreign environment, and sometimes display them in parts, most likely against the artists' intentions. But we justify these acts by supposing that whatever problems they cause are outweighed by other considerations, such as making these objects accessible to a large number of people.

Finally, consider the following incident in the colorization controversy. Opponents of colorization who gathered at a meeting called by the American Film Institute in October 1986 were reportedly unaffected by the surprise revelation by the defense that the cinematographer for *It's a Wonderful Life* worked closely with its colorization team. Neither were they impressed by the fact that Frank Capra, the director of this film, was at first opposed to its colorization but in the end reconciled himself to the adaptation. Thus, at worst, respecting the artist's intention might result in a straightforward endorsement of colorization; at best, it will be one important consideration to be weighed against others.

There is a curious twist in the argument regarding the artist's intention in the colorization controversy. That is, not only the opponents but also the proponents of colorization refer to the artist's intention in their defense. The proponents' argument goes as follows. Many black-and-white films were made either when color film technology was not available or by those directors who could not afford to use the color technology. But if such technology had been available or affordable, they would have made their films in color. Colorizing their films, therefore, amounts to a belated fulfillment of their original intention. For example, one commentator points out that "these Laurel and Hardy shorts, as well as the much earlier Mack Sennet comedies, were shot in black-and-white because that was the only film stock available or affordable." This consideration leads a proponent of colorization to suggest that "if the original producers had had a choice *they* would have made them in color."

However, this argument invoking the artist's original plan serves the proponents of colorization no better than the argument from the artist's intention serves the opponents. That is, some directors may indeed agree that they would have chosen the color film medium had it been available or affordable. On the other hand, others may contend that even if such an option had been available to them, they still would have chosen the monochrome medium in much the same way Woody Allen (in *Manhattan*) or Martin Scorsese (in *Raging Bull*) chose it.

Whatever the original circumstances concerning the production of these films, however, the proponents of colorization must acknowledge one important factor: they were made *as* black-and-white films. That is, all the artistic decisions (concerning lighting, make-up, camera angles, etc.) involved in producing these films were made on the basis of their monochromatic effects.

Perhaps the best example of a black-and-white film that derives its expressive power from the expert manipulation of monochromatic aesthetics is *Citizen Kane*. This film is celebrated for its effective use of contrasts between dark and light to convey expressive import. To cite one instance, in one scene Kane appears completely dark, in contrast to the other reporters present, when signing his "Declaration of Principles," as if to suggest that the "I" of those principles is only a phantom. Such expressive content is possible only with monochromatic images; colorization will weaken the contrast, hence diminishing the expressive power of this scene.

Such purely cinematographic considerations constitute a powerful argument against the colorization of films such as *Citizen Kane* and *The Maltese Falcon*. But the same aesthetic considerations can be an argument *for* colorizing some films; it is possible that *some* monochrome films can be improved artistically by colorization. Indeed, one critic admits that "in color . . . *Gunga Din* is one of the great epic pictures. There's a scene where the Scotties go marching right into a trap with their colors flying and their bagpipes blaring. It brought us right off our seats." Other films that some critics claim are improved by colorization include *Mutiny on the Bounty* (for a clearer storm scene), *Yankee Doodle Dandy* (for better stage sets and waving flags), and *Way out West* (for more effective portrayal of the mock-historical period).

The above observations indicate that the cinematographic consideration, while a powerful argument against colorizing many films, cannot lead to an opposition to colorization *in general* or *in principle*. As one commentator satirically entitles his editorial, "a little color doesn't hurt sometimes." Neither proponents nor opponents of colorization can argue for their respective stance by reference to the artist's intention or to purely aesthetic considerations.

III

The above argument against colorization from the artist's intention is based on a fundamental belief that works of art belong to the artists and that artists should be given priority over others in deciding the fate of their work. Proponents of colorization, however, make the opposite assumption: that a work of art (especially a film) belongs to the public and *the public* has a right to decide what happens to the object.

Market research has indicated that the general audience finds monochrome films boring and prefers to see them in color. This is particularly true of young audiences who have grown up watching color TV. Without colorization, today's young audiences will most likely not be interested in watching classic films. Colorization, therefore, is rescuing these old films from eventual obscurity.

A number of questions can be raised regarding this support for colorization. *So what* if the public at large finds colorization desirable? Would colorization then become desirable? Should aesthetic matters be subjected to democratic determination? What if the majority of people decided that some old masterpieces in painting can be made more pleasing by various alterations? . . .

. . . Neither respect for the artist's intention nor purely aesthetic considerations would yield a general prohibition against modifying works of art. Perhaps the following line of argument is more promising in explaining why we should not subject art objects to various modifications and alterations prompted by the present audience's capacities, interests, and preferences. One might say that a work of art possesses several different values, only one of which is aesthetic. Our concern with preserving the original condition of a work of art is based upon valuing it as a historical object, an object determined by the specific cultural/historical context of its creation. . . .

Furthermore, there is a profound sense of the moral function of art which makes our experience of art so significant. In addition to providing us aesthetic pleasure, the experience of art can and should facilitate establishing the most important basis for our moral life: transcendence of our own egocentric viewpoint. Art enables us to see, interpret, and evaluate the world from somebody else's viewpoint which is often spatially or temporally removed from our own. In stressing the importance of understanding and appreciating the art of a civilization different from our own, John Dewey claims that "works of art are means by which we enter, through imagination and the emotion they evoke, into other forms of relationship and participation than our own."

Once we agree that art is not only an object of aesthetic appreciation but also a vehicle for overcoming our egocentricity, we can explain why it is objectionable (other things being equal) to modify works of art to suit our own tastes, needs, and capacities. Doing so would cater to our egocentric attitudes and viewpoints instead of helping us overcome them. Specifically, colorization would produce generations whose acquaintance with film classics is limited to the colorized versions. As a result, they will not have a chance to develop the sensitivity needed to appreciate the drama created by monochrome cinematography. . . . We can conclude from the above that, other things being equal, it is objectionable to modify a work of art so that it becomes more accessible and appealing to the current audience.

However, in this age of democratizing art, some serious questions can be raised about the extent of our commitment against making works of art accessible and appealing to us. The art museum was the first means of democratizing art—and possibly the first step toward cultural vandalism. For example, old objects that were site specific were taken out of their contexts and sometimes divided into parts so that more people could see them in museums. Modern reproduction techniques, which make museums without walls possible, also minimize our direct encounter with the original works of art. From the aesthetic point of view, therefore, democratizing art exacted a heavy price.

When we turn to film, we should recognize that we have already accepted (tacitly perhaps) a kind of cultural vandalism even before colorization took place. We rarely question this form of vandalism, probably because of its surreptitious introduction and subsequent pervasiveness. In addition to dubbing, which has Gary Cooper mosey up to a bar and say, *"Ein Bier, bitte,"* the most serious deviation from the original films tolerated by us is that of media change. Most often we experience an old film (even without colorization) in the medium of video rather than film. . . . Furthermore, if it is presented on TV by a commercial network, each film will be compressed into a two-hour slot with enough time-outs for commercials. The effects of this change are staggering. In light of this fact, the proponents of colorization are justified in challenging the inconsistency in their opponents' attitude. . . .

A commercial art medium such as film may be more susceptible to modification according to popular demand and preference. Erwin Panofsky defines "commercial art" as "all art . . . not primarily produced in order to gratify the creative urge of its maker but primarily intended to meet the requirements of a patron or a buying public," and he includes Dürer's prints and Shakespeare's plays as well as film among examples of commercial art. I believe that there is a difference between film and other fine arts even if the motivation for creation is the same. As David Blum points out, "The outrageous costs and fees connected with moviemaking have long since separated it [film] from all other art forms—to the point where directors will go out and ask the public for their advice on a picture *before* it's been released." In other words, film presupposes the necessity of satisfying the audience's taste in order to justify the prohibitive cost of production. Hence, while there are good *general* reasons against modifying works of art, with respect to film, it may be that "there is such a thing as being too pious about art. Especially art from Hollywood."

DISCUSSION QUESTIONS

1. Do you agree with the New Critics that artworks should be judged in terms of their intrinsic features, not on the basis of the artists' intentions? To what extent do you think that we can ascertain the intentions of the artists?
2. Do artists have privileged information about the meaning of their works? Justify your view.
3. What do you think computer poems show us about the nature of artistic creation, if anything?
4. Do artists have any responsibility for the meanings that their audiences find in their works when they themselves did not intend these meanings? Why or why not?
5. Do you think that historical authenticity should be a goal of all performers of music? Is historical authenticity an effective means of honoring a composer's intentions?
6. Is colorization of black-and-white movies ever appropriate? Are there any circumstances in which colorization of black-and-white movies would not be appropriate? Justify your answers.

FURTHER READING

Artists' Intentions

Beardsely, Monroe C., and William K. Wimsatt. "The Intentional Fallacy." *Sewanee Review* 54 (1946): 3–23.

Feagin, Susan L. "On Defining and Interpreting Art Intentionalistically." *The British Journal of Aesthetics* 22 (1982): 65–77.

Hirsch, E. D. *Validity in Interpretation.* New Haven: Yale UP, 1976.

Hoy, David Couzens. *The Critical Circle: Literature, History, and Philosophical Hermeneutics.* Berkeley: U of California P, 1978.

Trilling, Lionel. *Sincerity and Authenticity.* New York: Oxford UP, 1972.

Authenticity in Music

Davies, Stephen. "Authenticity in Musical Performance." *The British Journal of Aesthetics* 27 (1987): 39–50.

Dipert, Randall R. "The Composer's Intentions: An Examination of Their Relevance for Performance." *Musical Quarterly* 66 (1980): 205–18.

Edidin, Aron. "Look What They've Done to My Song: 'Historical Authenticity' and the Aesthetics of Musical Performance." *Midwest Studies in Philosophy* 16 (1991): 394–420.

Kenyon, Nicholas, ed. *Authenticity and Early Music.* New York: Oxford UP, 1988.

Colorization

Daniels, Charles E. "Notes on Colorization." *British Journal of Aesthetics* 30.1 (1990): 68–70.

Levinson, Jerrold. "Colorization Ill-Defended." *British Journal of Aesthetics* 30.1 (1990): 62–67.

Young, James. "In Defense of Colorization." *British Journal of Aesthetics* 18 (1988): 368–72.

ART AS THE SIGN OF
ITS TIME AND PLACE

Andy Warhol quipped that eventually everyone would have fifteen minutes of fame. Besides implying that his own celebrity was a mere accident, the comment reminded his contemporaries that nothing endures, that change is a condition of life. Warhol's remark is expressed in emphatic terms, but his basic point has been a staple in philosophy of art since the nineteenth century. Art itself has a history. It has undergone transformations; and in order to understand an artwork, we need to understand the period from which it came.

Among the many European philosophers of the early nineteenth century who emphasized the importance of historical change, G. W. F. Hegel is the most prominent. Hegel contends that all things that people produce—whether art, technology, cities, or legal institutions—reflect humanity's central spiritual concerns. History, as Hegel understands it, is the development of the human spirit, the unity that encompasses all individuals. An artwork is a deliberate reflection of the central spiritual insights of its era, according to Hegel, and it can be judged according to how well it embodies such spiritual ideas in physical form.

The ways in which these ideas are embodied in art, however, have changed over the course of history. Hegel divides art history into three basic phases. The first of these phases, that of **symbolic art,** is characterized by spiritual ideas that have not yet become very articulate. Because the ideas are not precisely formulated, they do not have the power to give shape to the art that expresses them. Instead, artworks represent ideas symbolically, more because they are associated with the ideas than because they display them straightforwardly. In Hegel's view, for example, the multiple limbs shown in Hindu sculptures of Shiva symbolize a divine power that exceeds that of humanity, but they do not depict this power.

The second phase of art began when ideas became sufficiently articulate to dictate the structure of art. This phase is evident in the art of the ancient Greeks, particularly in Greek sculpture. The gods and goddesses depicted in Greek sculpture embody human notions of perfection, for they appear as perfectly formed, active human beings. Hegel calls the art of this phase **classical art.**

Ultimately, however, the spiritual ideas of humanity became too refined to be captured in physical form. At this point, art began to point beyond itself, gesturing toward the inner life of humanity that is not shown but only suggested. Romantic music, which sought to convey the dynamic of our inner life, is one of Hegel's examples of this type of art, which he terms **romantic art.**

Like Hegel, artist Wassily Kandinsky sees art as a reflection of its era's spiritual life. Unlike Hegel, however, Kandinsky focuses attention on the differences between artworks within an era. Some, he contends, mirror their age more effectively than others. Artists produce relatively ineffective art, according to Kandinsky, when they mimic styles of previous eras instead of devising styles appropriate to their own times. Such artists refuse the real challenge of their vocation as artists. They also abandon the possibility of deeply moving their audience.

Arthur C. Danto agrees with Hegel that art has developed over the course of history. He also agrees with Hegel's predictions that thought would eventually outstrip art as a means of embodying spiritual insight, and that art would cease to play a central role in a society's understanding of its identity and values. In his essay "Approaching the End of Art," Danto claims that Western art has lost its once dominant objective, the goal of representing reality. More recent schools of art have proposed alternative aspirations for art; but Danto concludes that, ultimately, Hegel was right to think that the narrative of art history would reach an end. The direction of art is no longer internally motivated, but art remains to enhance our lives. This Danto considers a worthy vocation in its own right.

In many societies, music has served more as a means of transcending time than as a means of expressing a particular era. D. M. Gruver analyzes the social function of the hula dance in the tradition of the Hawaiian Islands. The relative priority of static arts over performed arts in the West, Gruver notes, is reversed in traditional Hawaii, where chant and dance were the crucial modes of artistic expression. Always conjoined, hula and chant were means of maintaining traditional accounts of the Hawaiians' genealogy and the adventures of their ancestors. At the same time, the performers introduced their own nuances into their art, interpenetrating their individuality with the historical narrative of their people. Hula, in Gruver's analysis, preserves the Hawaiians' traditional cultural ideology, which comes to life anew in each performance.

Hegel interpreted art and other human productions as reflections of spiritual ideas. His philosophical descendent Karl Marx, however, saw them as reflections of economic circumstances. Following Marx in this view, John Berger correlates the development of oil painting with the rise of the class of property owners. Oil paints, unlike earlier pigments, were particularly well suited to depict the materiality of objects, by suggesting the lushness or gleam of particular textures. Berger contends that oil paintings presented the desirability of objects as property. Not surprisingly, he claims, the very economic class that was accumulating wealth and property became the primary audience for oil paintings, which celebrated their acquisitions.

Peter Wicke offers an economically based historical account of a more recent artistic phenomenon—rock music. Wicke considers the Beatles' aesthetic, which he describes as one of sensuousness, in light of the context that produced it. The popularity of the Beatles' music and subsequent rock stemmed from the socioeconomic situation of the young British working class, which used this music as an assertion of identity. Wicke suggests that the widespread availability of rock recordings provided a new opportunity for young people to utilize the music in social situations of their own choosing. This enabled them to insert their own meanings into rock songs by adding their own layers of associations.

G. W. F. Hegel

THE
AGES
OF
ART

G. W. F. Hegel (1770–1831) was a German philosopher of the early nineteenth century and the academic superstar of his era. His philosophy emphasized the historical development of human ideas and enterprises, which he took to be the expression of human spirit, a collective dimension of our existence. In the following excerpt from his lectures on fine arts, he considers the evolution of art, which he understands as each era's attempt to embody its most important spiritual insights in material form.

. . . The content of art is the Idea, and its form lies in the plastic use of images accessible to sense. These two sides art has to reconcile into a full and united totality. The *first* attribution which this involves is the requirement that the content, which is to be offered to artistic representation, shall show itself to be in its nature worthy of such representation. Otherwise we only obtain a bad combination, whereby a content that will not submit to plasticity and to external presentation, is forced into that form, and a matter which is in its nature prosaic is expected to find an appropriate mode of manifestation in the form antagonistic to its nature.

The *second* requirement, which is derivable from this first, demands of the content of art that it should not be anything abstract in itself. . . .

Only in the highest art are the Idea and the representation genuinely adequate to one another, in the sense that the outward shape given to the Idea is in itself essentially and actually the true shape, because the content of the Idea, which that shape expresses, is itself the true and real content. It is a corollary from this, . . . that the Idea must be defined in and through itself as concrete totality, and thereby possess in itself the principle and standard of its

Georg Wilhelm Friedrich Hegel, *The Introduction to Hegel's Philosophy of Fine Art*, trans. Bernard Bosanquet (London: Kegan Paul, Trench, Trübner, 1905) 169–93.

particularization and determination in external appearance. . . .

We have here to consider *three* relations of the Idea to its outward shaping.

(a) First, the Idea gives rise to the beginning of Art when, being itself still in its indistinctness and obscurity, or in vicious untrue determinateness, it is made the import of artistic creations. As indeterminate it does not yet possess in itself that individuality which the Ideal demands; its abstractness and one-sidedness leave its shape to be outwardly bizarre and defective. The first form of art is therefore rather a mere search after plastic portrayal than a capacity of genuine representation. The Idea has not yet found the true form even within itself, and therefore continues to be merely the struggle and aspiration thereafter. In general terms we may call this form the *Symbolic* form of art. In it the abstract Idea has its outward shape external to itself in natural sensuous matter, with which the process of shaping begins, and from which, *qua* outward expression, it is inseparable.

Natural objects are thus primarily left unaltered, and yet at the same time invested with the substantial Idea as their significance, so that they receive the vocation of expressing it, and claim to be interpreted as though the Idea itself were present in them. At the root of this is the fact that natural objects have in them an aspect in which they are capable of representing a universal meaning. But as an adequate correspondence is not yet possible, this reference can only concern *an abstract attribute*, as when a lion is used to mean strength.

On the other hand, this abstractness of the relation brings to consciousness no less strongly the foreignness of the Idea to natural phenomena; and the Idea, having no other reality to express it, expatiates in all these shapes, seeks itself in them in all their unrest and disproportion, but nevertheless does not find them adequate to itself. Then it proceeds to exaggerate the natural shapes and the phenomena of reality into indefiniteness and disproportion, to intoxicate itself in them, to seethe and ferment in them, to do violence to them, to distort and explode them into unnatural shapes, and strives by the variety, hugeness, and splendor of the forms employed to exalt the phenomenon to the level of the Idea. For the Idea is here still more or less indeterminate and non-plastic, but the natural objects are in their shape thoroughly determinate.

Hence, in view of the unsuitability of the two elements to each other, the relation of the Idea to objective reality becomes a *negative* one, for the former, as in its nature inward, is unsatisfied with such an externality, and as being its inner universal substance persists in exaltation or *Sublimity* beyond and above all this inadequate abundance of shapes. In virtue of this sublimity the natural phenomena and the human shapes and incidents are accepted, and left as they were, though at the same time understood to be inadequate to their significance, which is exalted far above every earthly content.

These aspects may be pronounced in general terms to constitute the character of the primitive artistic pantheism of the East, which either charges even the meanest objects with the absolute import, or again coerces nature with violence into the expression of its view. By this means it becomes bizarre, grotesque, and tasteless, or turns the infinite but abstract freedom of the substantive Idea disdainfully against all phenomenal being as null and evanescent. By such means the import cannot be completely embodied in the expression, and in spite of all aspiration and endeavor the reciprocal inadequacy of shape and Idea remains insuperable. This may be taken as the first form of art, Symbolic art with its aspiration, its disquiet, its mystery and its sublimity.

(b) In the second form of art, which we propose to call "Classical," the double defect of symbolic art is cancelled. The plastic shape of symbolic art is imperfect, because, in the first place, the Idea in it only enters into consciousness in *abstract* determinateness or indeterminateness, and, in the second place, this must always make the conformity of shape to import defective, and in its turn merely abstract. The classical form of art is the solution of this double difficulty; it is the free and adequate embodiment of the Idea in the shape that, according to its conception, is peculiarly appropriate to the Idea itself. With it, therefore, the Idea is capable of entering into free and complete accord. Hence, the classical type of art is the first to afford the production and intuition of the completed Ideal and to establish it as a realized fact.

The conformity, however, of notion and reality in classical art must not be taken in the purely *formal* sense of the agreement of a content with the external shape given to it, any more than this could be the case with the Ideal itself. Otherwise every copy from nature, and every type of countenance, every landscape, flower, or scene, etc., which forms the purport of any representation, would be at once made classical by the agreement which it displays between form and content. On the contrary, in classical art the peculiarity of the content consists in being itself concrete idea, and, as such, the concrete spiritual; for only the spiritual is the truly inner self. To suit a content, then, we must search out that in Nature which on its own merits belongs to the essence and actuality of the mind. It must be the absolute notion that *invented* the shape appropriate to concrete mind, so that the *subjective notion*—in this case the spirit of art—has merely *found* it, and brought it, as an existence possessing natural shape, into accord with free individual spirituality. This shape, with which the Idea as spiritual—as individually determinate spirituality—invests itself when manifested as a temporal phenomenon, is *the human form*. Personification and anthropomorphism have often been decried as a degradation of the spiritual; but art, in as far as its end is to bring before perception the spiritual in sensuous form, must advance to such anthropomorphism, as it is only in its proper body that mind is adequately revealed to sense. The migration of souls is in this respect a false abstraction, and physiology ought to have made it one of its axioms that life had necessarily in its evolution to attain to the human shape, as the sole sensuous phenomenon that is appropriate to mind. The human form is employed in the classical type of art not as mere sensuous existence, but exclusively as the existence and physical form corresponding to mind, and is therefore exempt from all the deficiencies of what is merely sensuous, and from the contingent finiteness of phenomenal existence. The other shape must be thus purified in order to express in itself a content adequate to itself; and again, if the conformity of import and content is to be complete, the spiritual meaning which is the content must be of a particular kind. It must, that is to say, be qualified to express itself completely in the physical form of man, without projecting into another world beyond the scope of such an expression in sensuous and bodily terms. This condition has the effect that Mind is by it at once specified as a particular case of mind, as human mind, and not as simply absolute and eternal, inasmuch as mind in this latter sense is incapable of proclaiming and expressing itself otherwise than as intellectual being.

Out of this latter point arises, in its turn, the defect which brings about the dissolution of classical art, and demands a transition into a third and higher form, viz. into the *romantic* form of art.

(c) The romantic form of art destroys the completed union of the Idea and its reality, and recurs, though in a higher phase, to that difference and antagonism of two aspects which was left unvanquished by symbolic art. The classical type attained the highest excellence, of which the sensuous embodiment of art is capable; and if it is in any way defective, the defect is in art as a whole, i.e., in the limitation of its sphere. This limitation consists in the fact that art as such takes for its object mind—the conception of which is *infinite* concrete universality—in the shape of *sensuous* concreteness, and in the classical phase sets up the perfect amalgamation of spiritual and sensuous existence as a Conformity of the two. Now, as a matter of fact, in such an amalgamation Mind cannot be represented according to its true notion. For mind is the infinite subjectivity of the Idea, which, as absolute inwardness, is not capable of finding free expansion in its true nature on condition of remaining transposed into a bodily medium as the existence appropriate to it.

As *an escape from such a condition* the romantic form of art in its turn dissolves the inseparable unity of the classical phase, because it has won a significance which goes beyond the classical form of art and its mode of expression. This significance—if we may recall familiar ideas—coincides with what Christianity declares to be true of God as Spirit, in contradistinction to the Greek faith in gods which forms the essential and appropriate content for classical art. In Greek art the concrete import is potentially, but not explicitly, the unity of the human and divine nature; a unity which, just because it is purely *immediate* and *not explicit*, is capable of adequate manifestation in an immediate and sensuous mode. The Greek god is the object of naïve intuition and sensuous imagination. His shape is, therefore, the bodily shape of man. The circle of his power and of his being is individual and individually limited. In relation with the subject, he is, therefore, an essence and a power with which the subject's inner being is merely in latent unity, not itself possessing this unity as inward subjective knowledge. Now the higher stage is the *knowledge* of this *latent* unity, which as

latent is the import of the classical form of art, and capable of perfect representation in bodily shape. The elevation of the latent or potential into self-conscious knowledge produces an enormous difference. It is the infinite difference which, e.g., separates man as such from the animals. Man is animal, but even in his animal functions he is not confined within the latent and potential as the animal is, but becomes conscious of them, learns to know them, and raises them—as, for instance, the process of digestion—into self-conscious science. By this means Man breaks the boundary of merely potential and immediate consciousness, so that just for the reason that he knows himself to be animal, he ceases to be animal, and, as *mind*, attains to self-knowledge.

If in the above fashion the unity of the human and divine nature, which in the former phase was potential, is raised from an *immediate* to a *conscious* unity, it follows that the true medium for the reality of this content is no longer the sensuous immediate existence of the spiritual, the human bodily shape, but *self-conscious inward intelligence*. Now, Christianity brings God before our intelligence as *spirit*, or mind—not as particularized individual spirit, but as absolute, in *spirit* and in truth. And for this reason Christianity retires from the sensuousness of imagination into intellectual inwardness, and makes this, not bodily shape, the medium and actual existence of its significance. So, too, the unity of the human and divine nature is a conscious unity, only to be realized by *spiritual* knowledge and in *spirit*. Thus the new content, won by this unity, is not inseparable from sensuous representation, as if that were adequate to it, but is freed from this immediate existence, which has to be posited as negative, absorbed, and reflected into the spiritual unity. In this way, romantic art must be considered as art transcending itself, while remaining within the artistic sphere and in artistic form.

Therefore, in short, we may abide by the statement that in this third stage the object (art) is *free*, concrete intellectual being, which has the function of revealing itself as spiritual existence for the inward world of spirit. In conformity with such a subject matter, art cannot work for sensuous perception. It must address itself to the inward mind, which coalesces with its object simply and as though this were itself, to the subjective inwardness, to the heart, the feeling, which, being spiritual, aspires to freedom within itself, and seeks and finds its reconciliation only in the spirit within. It is this *inner* world that forms the content of the romantic, and must therefore find its representation as such inward feeling, and in the show or presentation of such feeling. The world of inwardness celebrates its triumph over the outer world, and actually in the sphere of the outer and in its medium manifests this its victory, owing to which the sensuous appearance sinks into worthlessness.

But, on the other hand, this type of Art, like every other, needs an external vehicle of expression. Now the spiritual has withdrawn into itself out of the external and its immediate oneness therewith. For this reason, the sensuous externality of concrete form is accepted and represented, as in Symbolic art, as something transient and fugitive. And the same measure is dealt to the subjective finite mind and will, even including the peculiarity or caprice of the individual, of character, action, etc., or of incident and plot. The aspect of external existence is committed to contingency and left at the mercy of freaks of imagination, whose caprice is no more likely to mirror what is given as it is given, than to throw the shapes of the outer world into chance medley, or distort them into grotesqueness. For this external element no longer has its notion and significance, as in classical art, in its own sphere, and in its own medium. It has come to find them in the feelings, the display of which is *in themselves* instead of being in the external and *its* form of reality, and which have the power to preserve or to regain their state of reconciliation with themselves, in every accident, in every unessential circumstance that takes independent shape, in all misfortune and grief, and even in crime.

Owing to this, the characteristics of symbolic art, in difference, discrepancy, and severance of Idea and plastic shape, are here reproduced, but with an essential difference. In the sphere of the romantic, the Idea, whose defectiveness in the case of the symbol produced the defect of external shape, has to reveal itself in the medium of spirit and feelings as perfected in itself. And it is because of this higher perfection that it withdraws itself from any adequate union with the external element, inasmuch as it can seek and achieve its true reality and revelation nowhere but in itself.

This we may take as in the abstract the character of the symbolic, classical, and romantic forms of art, which represent the three relations of the Idea to its embodiment in the sphere of art. They consist in the aspiration after, and the attainment and transcendence of, the Ideal as the true Idea of beauty.

Wassily Kandinsky

CONCERNING THE SPIRITUAL IN ART

Wassily Kandinsky (1866–1944) was a Russian abstract painter. His essay "Concerning the Spiritual in Art" (1911), from which the following selection is taken, defends the effort to liberate art from the project of depicting reality.

Every work of art is the child of its age and, in many cases, the mother of our emotions. It follows that each period of culture produces an art of its own which can never be repeated. Efforts to revive the art-principles of the past will at best produce an art that is still-born. It is impossible for us to live and feel, as did the ancient Greeks. In the same way those who strive to follow the Greek methods in sculpture achieve only a similarity of form, the work remaining soulless for all time. Such imitation is mere aping. Externally the monkey completely resembles a human being; he will sit holding a book in front of his nose, and turn over the pages with a thoughtful aspect, but his actions have for him no real meaning.

There is, however, in art another kind of external similarity which is founded on a fundamental truth. When there is a similarity of inner tendency in the whole moral and spiritual atmosphere, a similarity of ideals, at first closely pursued but later lost to sight, a similarity in the inner feeling of any one period to that of another, the logical result will be a revival of the external forms which served to express those inner feelings in an earlier age. An example of this today is our sympathy, our spiritual relationship, with the Primitives. Like ourselves, these artists sought to express in their work only internal truths, renouncing in consequence all consideration of external form.

This all-important spark of inner life today is at present only a spark. Our minds, which are even now only just awakening after years of materialism, are infected with the despair of unbelief, of lack of purpose and ideal. The nightmare of materialism, which has turned the life of the universe into an evil, useless game, is not yet past; it holds the awakening soul still in its grip. Only a feeble light glimmers like a tiny star in a vast gulf of darkness. This feeble light is but a presentiment, and the soul, when it sees it, trembles in doubt whether the light

Wassily Kandinsky, *Concerning the Spiritual in Art*, trans. M. T. H. Sadler (New York: Dover, 1977) 1–5.

is not a dream, and the gulf of darkness reality. This doubt, and the still harsh tyranny of the materialistic philosophy, divide our soul sharply from that of the Primitives. Our soul rings cracked when we seek to play upon it, as does a costly vase, long buried in the earth, which is found to have a flaw when it is dug up once more. For this reason, the Primitive phase, through which we are now passing, with its temporary similarity of form, can only be of short duration.

These two possible resemblances between the art forms of today and those of the past will be at once recognized as diametrically opposed to one another. The first, being purely external, has no future. The second, being internal, contains the seed of the future within itself. After the period of materialist effort, which held the soul in check until it was shaken off as evil, the soul is emerging, purged by trials and sufferings. Shapeless emotions such as fear, joy, grief, etc., which belonged to this time of effort, will no longer greatly attract the artist. He will endeavour to awake subtler emotions, as yet unnamed. Living himself a complicated and comparatively subtle life, his work will give to those observers capable of feeling them lofty emotions beyond the reach of words.

The observer of today, however, is seldom capable of feeling such emotions. He seeks in a work of art a mere imitation of nature which can serve some definite purpose (for example a portrait in the ordinary sense) or a presentment of nature according to a certain convention ("impressionist" painting), or some inner feeling expressed in terms of natural form. . . . All those varieties of picture, when they are really art, fulfil their purpose and feed the spirit. Though this applies to the first case, it applies more strongly to the third, where the spectator does feel a corresponding thrill in himself. Such harmony or even contrast of emotion cannot be superficial or worthless; indeed the *Stimmung* of a picture can deepen and purify that of the spectator. Such works of art at least preserve

the soul from coarseness; they "key it up," so to speak, to a certain height, as a tuning-key the strings of a musical instrument. But purification, and extension in duration and size of this sympathy of soul, remain one-sided, and the possibilities of the influence of art are not exerted to their utmost.

Imagine a building divided into many rooms. The building may be large or small. Every wall of every room is covered with pictures of various sizes; perhaps they number many thousands. They represent in colour bits of nature—animals in sunlight or shadow, drinking, standing in water, lying on the grass; near to, a Crucifixion by a painter who does not believe in Christ; flowers; human figures sitting, standing, walking; often they are naked; many naked women, seen foreshortened from behind; apples and silver dishes; portrait of Councillor So and So; sunset; lady in red; flying duck; portrait of Lady X; flying geese; lady in white; calves in shadow flecked with brilliant yellow sunlight; portrait of Prince Y; lady in green. All this is carefully printed in a book—name of artist—name of picture. People with these books in their hands go from wall to wall, turning over pages, reading the names. Then they go away, neither richer nor poorer than when they came, and are absorbed at once in their business, which has nothing to do with art. Why did they come? In each picture is a whole lifetime imprisoned, a whole lifetime of fears, doubts, hopes, and joys.

Whither is this lifetime tending? What is the message of the competent artist? "To send light into the darkness of men's hearts—such is the duty of the artist," said Schumann. "An artist is a man who can draw and paint everything," said Tolstoi.

Of these two definitions of the artist's activity we must choose the second, if we think of the exhibition just described. On one canvas is a huddle of objects painted with varying degrees of skill, virtuosity and vigour, harshly or smoothly. To harmonize the whole is the task of art. With cold eyes and indifferent mind the spectators regard the work. Connoisseurs admire the "skill" (as one admires a tightrope walker), enjoy the "quality of painting" (as one enjoys a pasty). But hungry souls go hungry away.

The vulgar herd stroll through the rooms and pronounce the pictures "nice" or "splendid." Those who could speak have said nothing, those who could hear have heard nothing. This condition of art is called "art for art's sake." This neglect of inner meanings, which is the life of colours, this vain squandering of artistic power is called "art for art's sake."

The artist seeks for material reward for his dexterity, his power of vision and experience. His purpose becomes the satisfaction of vanity and greed. In place of the steady co-operation of artists is a scramble for good things. There are complaints of excessive competition, of over-production. Hatred, partisanship, cliques, jealousy, intrigues are the natural consequences of this aimless, materialist art.

The onlooker turns away from the artist who has higher ideals and who cannot see his life purpose in an art without aims.

Sympathy is the education of the spectator from the point of view of the artist. It has been said above that art is the child of its age. Such an art can only create an artistic feeling which is already clearly felt. This art, which has no power for the future, which is only a child of the age and cannot become a mother of the future, is a barren art. She is transitory and to all intent dies the moment the atmosphere alters which nourished her.

The other art, that which is capable of educating further, springs equally from contemporary feeling, but is at the same time not only echo and mirror of it, but also has a deep and powerful prophetic strength.

The spiritual life, to which art belongs and of which she is one of the mightiest elements, is a complicated but definite and easily definable movement forwards and upwards. This movement is the movement of experience. It may take different forms, but it holds at bottom to the same inner thought and purpose.

Veiled in obscurity are the causes of this need to move ever upwards and forwards, by sweat of the brow, through sufferings and fears. When one stage has been accomplished, and many evil stones cleared from the road, some unseen and wicked hand scatters new obstacles in the way, so that the path often seems blocked and totally obliterated. But there never fails to come to the rescue some human being, like ourselves in everything except that he has in him a secret power of vision.

He sees and points the way. The power to do this he would sometimes fain lay aside, for it is a bitter cross to bear. But he cannot do so. Scorned and hated, he drags after him over the stones the heavy chariot of a divided humanity, ever forwards and upwards.

Often, many years after his body has vanished from the earth, men try by every means to recreate this body in marble, iron, bronze, or stone, on an enormous scale. As if there were any intrinsic value in the bodily existence of such divine martyrs and servants of humanity, who despised the flesh and lived only for the spirit! But at least such setting up of marble is a proof that a great number of men have reached the point where once the being they would now honour, stood alone.

Arthur C. Danto

APPROACHING
THE END
OF ART

Arthur C. Danto, professor emeritus of philosophy at Columbia University, considers the progress of art history in this selection from his essay "Approaching the End of Art." Art, he contends, has fulfilled its historical mission of increasingly accurate representation of reality. As Hegel predicted, the narrative development of art, its internally motivated progress and culmination, has reached an endpoint. Nevertheless, art-making continues to have value for us as a practice that enhances human life.

The idea that art should come to an end like this was advanced in . . . Hegel's *Vorlesungen uber die Aesthetik*, which he delivered for the last time in 1828, three years before his death—a very long time ago indeed—and a great deal of art has been made since Hegel last held forth in Berlin. So there is a natural temptation to say, Well, Hegel was just wrong, and drop the matter there. Philosophers have said some crazy things about the real world. Aristotle insisted, for reasons I can only guess at, that women have fewer teeth than men. In medieval representations of him, Aristotle is often depicted on all fours, being ridden by a woman with a whip in her hand. This was Phyllis, the mistress of Aristotle's pupil, Alexander. One might suppose, from his posture of erotic domination by a woman he was mad about, that Aristotle would have supposed she had more teeth than men, showing that even masochists can be sexist. In any case, one need only look in the nearest female mouth to refute that mighty thinker. Hegel himself had a proof that as a matter of cosmic necessity there must be exactly seven planets, but Neptune was discovered in 1846 and Pluto in 1930—and if we reckon in the minor planets, of which there are more than a thousand, an argument on rational grounds that there must be seven shatters against the universe. So the claim that art must be over by 1828 sounds like another of those unfortunate thoughts

Arthur C. Danto, "Approaching the End of Art," *The State of the Art* (New York: Prentice-Hall, 1987), 209–18.

philosophers have from time to time about the uncooperating world. Heidegger, whose essay on the *origins* of art appeared in 1950, was not much impressed by a refutation of Hegel based on the continuation of art since his death.

> The judgment that Hegel passes . . . cannot be evaded by pointing out that since Hegel's lectures were given for the last time during the winter of 1828–29, we have seen many new artworks and movements arise. Hegel did not mean to deny this possibility. The question, however, remains: is art still an essential and necessary way in which truth that is decisive for our historical existence happens, or is art no longer of this character? . . . The truth of Hegel's judgment has not yet been decided.

I suppose the simplest way to connect the possible truth of Hegel's judgment with the facts of art history since 1828 is to distinguish between something stopping, and something coming to an end. Stopping is an external matter, in that something is caused to stop when it could have continued. But coming to an end is an internal matter of pattern and consummation, when, as in a melody or a narrative, there is nothing else that can happen to cause the melody or narrative to go on. A storyteller breaks a tale off, to continue it the next night, when we learn what happens next. A novelist puts her novel aside and never takes it up again, so that though it stopped we have no way of knowing how it would have ended. Or a writer drops dead and we are asked, as with *The Mystery of Edwin Drood,* to imagine alternative endings. We all understand this difference even if we are not prepared with a good theory of narrative closure that will explain the fact that there are stories that stop *because* they have reached the end. But in such cases, though the story has ended, life goes on: A lot happens when the prince and princess live happily ever after—the king, his father, dies, so he is now ruler and

she his queen, they have their children, she conducts discreet affairs with Sir Lancelot, there are border uprisings . . . but still the story ended when the love toward which their destinies drove them came to mutual consciousness when they knew, each knowing the other knew, that they were meant for each other.

Hegel thought that art had come to an end in the *narrative* sense of ending, namely as an episode in a larger narrative in which art played a certain role. The story of art is the story of art's role in the grand history of the spirit. There was art before and there will be art after, but the highest vocation of art was to advance some grander matter. There was a moment when the energies of art coincided with the energies of history itself—and then it subsided into something else. If there could have been a change of that order, then it would have been change of a different order than the changes that preceded and succeeded it. So there is a question of whether there is a narrative structure to the history of art, in which case coming to an end would be almost a matter of logic, or whether the history of art is merely a chronicle, first this and then that, the record of which is so many columns of art criticism, one after the other, as in the present collection. The record of insistent change, which . . . is the philosophy of history of the practicing journalist, following the day-by-day events in the art world: the news, the latest, the next. So the question then is whether art has the one sort of structure or the other (which is a nonstructure); hence, whether it can come or can have come to end—or whether it can merely stop. One could imagine art stopping, as under some terrible government or during the chill darknesses of the nuclear winter when all our energy goes into keeping ourselves alive.

Now once upon a time painting was certainly thought of as narrativistic, as the progressive conquest of visual appearances.

The artists sought cumulatively to present the eye with what it would receive as a matter of course from natural appearances. . . .

This must certainly have been the aim of Greek art if the severe criticisms found in Plato have any basis in practice, though the Greek artists were severely limited in what they could do by way of constructing appearances that could not be told apart, by merely optical means, from what reality itself would present. There are famous legends that confirm this goal and even record some startling successes at fooling the birds into pecking at sham and two-dimensional grapes.

In terms of this sense of the history of art, the discovery of perspective would have marked a climax, and perhaps the discovery of aerial perspective marked another. Who, unless concerned with changes in atmosphere induced by distance, would have chosen the grayed pale hues needed to register distal objects? Who even needed to register distance, unless verisimilitude was an objective? The great dramas of medieval art take place in mystical spaces, whose geometry and optics have little to do with the body's eyes. In any case, we can readily imagine this narrative coming to an end, namely with those discoveries in which, finally, the progress is achieved. Of course painting might very well continue to be made, but its real history would be over with. It could not any longer have climaxes of the order of the work of Michelangelo, according to Vasari's stirring account:

> While the best and most industrious artists were laboring, by the light of Giotto and his followers, to give the world examples of such power as the benignity of their stars and the varied character of their fantasies enabled them to command, and while desirous of imitating the perfection of nature by the excellence of art . . . The Ruler of Heaven was pleased to turn the eye of his clemency toward earth, and perceiving the fruitlessness of so many labors,

> the ardent studies pursued without any result . . . he resolved, by way of delivering us from such great errors, to send the world a spirit endowed with universality of power in each art. . . .

This highflown and manneristic passage gives an incidental reason why imitation should have enjoyed a renaissance as a theory in the Renaissance. The artist, in imitating nature, imitates God: Artistic creativity is the emulation of divine creation. In any case, with Michelangelo, the story is over, but of course art goes on and on: halls had to be decorated, portraits executed, marriage chests embellished.

There are certain inherent limits to this progress, simply because there are certain properties of things discernible to vision that cannot be directly represented in painting. Motion is clearly one such property—an artist can represent, as it were, *the fact* that something is in motion, but he cannot imitate the motion itself. Rather, the viewer must infer that the subject shown is in movement as the best explanation of why the painting looks the way it does—the man's feet do not touch the ground, say. Here I must rather ruthlessly cut my account, but I have argued at length elsewhere that the entire concept of painting had to change when it was discovered that only through an altogether different technology could motion be directly shown, namely that of cinematography or one of its ruder predecessors.

The history of art as the discovery of perceptual equivalences did not come to an end with cinema, but the history of painting so far as it was regarded as the mimetic art par excellence came to an end. The goal of history could no longer be believed attainable by painters, and the torch had been handed on. My own sense of history suggests that the history of painting took a very different turn when this was recognized. It is striking that photography presented no such challenge—it provided, rather, an ideal. But motion picture photography showed something not in principle attainable by painting, and by 1905, when we are roughly at the period of the Fauves, all the structures for narrative cinema were in place.

The very fact of the Fauves recommends the view that at some level of consciousness, artists realized that they must rethink the meaning of painting, or accept the fact that from the defining perspective of mimetic progress, painting was finished. Painters could behave archaistically just as sword-makers carry on a ceremonial trade in the era of firearms. But instead they began to reexamine the foundation of their practice, and the decades since have been the most astonishing period in the history of art. This is mainly, I believe, because the immense problem of self-definition had been imposed on painting, which could no longer acquiesce in a characterization taken for granted through two-and-a-half millennia, with some interruptions. Cinematography was immensely liberating for art, but it also changed the direction of art. Art must now, whatever else it does, come to terms with its own nature. It must discover what that nature really is. In Hegelian terms, it had reached a kind of consciousness of itself as a problem. Up to now, art had a set of problems, but it was not a problem for itself. Perhaps it had been a problem for philosophers. But now, in becoming a problem for itself, it began to attain a certain philosophical dimension. It faced that crisis of self-identity a sensitive person may face at a certain moment of her of his life, when existence can no longer be taken as given, where one can only go ahead by discovering whom one is—and consciousness of that problem henceforward becomes *part* of what one is. Heidegger speaks of man as a being for whom the question of his being is part of his being. It is a profoundly philosophical moment when this becomes a matter of consciousness in one's life, and it is

my claim that such a consciousness began to define art after the advent of cinematography. In rethinking its identity, art had of course to rethink the meaning of its history. It could no longer assume that its history had to be the progressive endeavor it had seemed up to then to be.

There are two theoretical responses to this problem that I know of, one of which is quite familiar today. This is a theory of art history best exemplified perhaps in the great and groundbreaking thought of the art historian Erwin Panofsky. Panofsky put forward a remarkable thesis in a no-less remarkable paper of 1927 (just a century after Hegel's prediction). Called *Die Perspektive als symbolische Form—Perspective as Symbolic Form*—Panofsky's bold thesis was that, instead of marking a certain stage in the advancing conquest of visual appearances, perspective marked a certain change in historical direction: It was a form through which its civilization began to represent the world on a symbolic level, as though optics was a matter more of meaning than mimesis. Perspective, or optical exactitude, for example, would have no meaning for an artistic tradition in which even if it were known about, its practitioners were concerned with other ways of symbolizing the world. It plays no role in the mask-making artforms of the Guro people of the Ivory Coast, whose works, concerned with magic and dark powers, with a different intervention of art into life than optical similitude would allow, would have no use for the kind of knowledge perspective represents. For Panofsky, perspective then was symbolic of what one might call the "Renaissance philosophy of man and world." It is certainly true that painting in the period after 1905 abandoned perspective, not because artists had lost the technique but because it bore no relevance to what they were seeking. Indeed, if perspective was symbolic, its rejection would be symbolic as well, and part of the meaning of the new work would be carried by its palpable absence or by distortion. And with this new symbolic form, a shift analogous to what has come to be called a "paradigm shift" in science took place. So in Panofsky's view, there is no progress in the history of art, simply the working out of different symbolic forms until, in whatever way it takes place, some internal upheaval gives rise to a new culture and new sets of symbolic forms. Panofsky's own discipline, what he termed "iconology," was concerned specifically to identify those points in history at which such transformative changes took place, and to map the symbolic forms through which the new period was defined. Its art, but its art no more that anything else distinctive to it, expressed the culture as our behavior and speech express our personality.

In any case it is clear that Panofsky's view of art history is that it has no narrative structure. There is instead just the chronicle of symbolic form succeeding symbolic form. The history of art can stop, though it is not clear that there would ever be a social life without some idiom of symbolic representation, however bleak its reality. There is no story to tell. It must have been something like this that Gombrich meant when, somewhat inconsistently with his own progressive theories of history, he suggested in his textbook on art that there is no such thing as art, only the lives of the artists.

This is one way of thinking about the history of art. Hegel's is the other.

I have often said that there is no nutshell capacious enough to contain the philosophy of Hegel in the extravagance of its mad totality—but in a nutshell, his thesis about history is that it consists in the progressive coming to philosophical consciousness of its own processes, so that the philosophy of history is the end of history, and internally related to its drive. Hegel congratulated history for having achieved consciousness of itself through him, for his philosophy, he supposed, was the meaning of history. This

coming to consciousness proceeds by discontinuous stages, which is the dialectic of which certain theories of history make so much. So that in a way Hegel's model of history combined features of both the models I have discussed here: It is narrative, in that it has an end, but it is discontinuous in that there is an internal reason why there are those cataclysmic changes outwardly expressed by symbolic forms. (Panofsky's idea of symbolic forms is in fact a rephrasing of Hegel's own theory of the spirit or *Geist* of a given time.) Once more, the best example of something that exhibits this structure would be a single life, not as one event after another, say as it would be represented at a low level of biography, but as the moving from stage to stage of consciousness through growth until the person comes to understand his or her own history at some moment of maturity—after which one's life is up to oneself. Hegel, and Marx as well, supposed that once we become aware of history—or history becomes aware of itself through us—we enter the realm of freedom, no longer subject to the iron laws of development and transformation. The whole of history is the structure of a full human life writ large. It is a progress, but not a linear progress. Each stage is the revolutionization of the preceding stages, until the seeds of revolution have worked themselves out.

Now something like this structure is what I want to say is illustrated by the history of art. My sense is that with the trauma to its own theory of itself, painting had to discover, or try to discover, what its true identity was. With the trauma, it entered onto a new level of self-awareness. My view, again, is that painting had to be the avant-garde art just because no art sustained the kind of trauma it did with the advent of cinema. But its quest for self-identity was limited by the fact that it was *painting* which was the avant-garde art, for painting remains a nonverbal activity, even if more and more verbality began to be incorporated into works of art—"painted words" in Tom Wolfe's apt but shallow phrase. Without theory, who could see a blank canvas, a square lead plate, a tilted beam, some dropped rope, as works of art? Perhaps the same question was being raised all across the face of the art world but for me it became conspicuous at last in the show of Andy Warhol at the Stable Gallery in 1964, when the Brillo box asked, in effect, why it was art when something just like it was not. And with this, it seemed to me, the history of art attained that point where it had to turn into its own philosophy. It had gone, as art, as far as it could go. In turning into philosophy, art had come to an end. From now on progress could only be enacted on a level of abstract self-consciousness of the kind which philosophy alone must consist in. If artists wished to participate in this progress, they would have to undertake a study very different from what the art schools could prepare them for. They would have to become philosophers. Much as art on one model of its history turned the responsibility for progress over to cinema, it turned the responsibility for progress over to philosophy on another model of its history. Painting does not stop when it ends like this. But it enters what I like to term its post-historical period.

In its great philosophical phase, from about 1905 to about 1964, modern art undertook a massive investigation into its own nature and essence. It set out to seek a form of itself so pure as art that nothing like what caused it to undertake this investigation in the first place could ever happen to it again. It realized that it had identified its essence with something it could exist without, namely the production of optical equivalences, and it is no accident that abstraction should be among the first brilliant stages in its marvelous ascent to self-comprehension. There have been more projected definitions of art, each identified with a different movement of art, in the six or seven decades of the modern era, than in

the six or seven centuries that preceded it. Each definition was accompanied by a severe condemnation of everything else as *not* art. There was an almost religious fervor, as though historical salvation depended upon having found the truth of one's own being. It was like the strife of warring sects. That has all but vanished from the art scene today. And this returns me to the decade of the 1970s, with which I began this philosophical narrative. The 1970s were the period of relaxed toleration, a period of benign pluralism, a period of "do as you like," after the great style wars had subsided.

Those were the first years of the post-historical period, and because it was, as a period, so new, how could it not have been incoherent? On the one hand there was the sense that something had come to an end. On the other hand there was the sense that things had to go on as before, since the art world was possessed by a historical picture that called for a next thing. I am suggesting that in that sense there are to be no next things. The time for next things is past. The end of art coincides with the end of a history of art that has that kind of structure. After that there is nothing to do but live happily ever after. It was like coming to the end of the world with no more continents to discover. One must now begin to make habitable the only continents that there are. One must learn to live within the limits of the world.

As I see it, this means returning art to the serving of largely human ends. There is after all something finally satisfying in making likenesses, and it is not surprising that there should have been a great upsurge in realism. There is something finally satisfying in just moving paint around. Drawing pictures and playing with mud are very early manifestations of the impulses that become art. So it is not surprising that there should have been an upsurge in expressionism. These were next things, but not the kinds of next things that the art world with its view of history as

D. M. Gruver

HAWAIIAN
HULA

D. M. Gruver was a graduate student in philosophy at the University of Hawaii when he wrote this paper. Gruver describes Hawaiian hula as a means of expressing and preserving the cultural worldview from which it emerged.

Ke lu la i na pua lehua
Nana i kai o Hopoe,
Ka wahine 'ami i kai,
'O Nanahuki la,
Hula le'a wale,
I ke kai o Nanahuki e-e!

[Scattering the lehua blossoms,
Look towards the sea, there is Hopoe,
The woman swaying near the sea,
Of Nanahuki,
Pure delightful dancing,
Near the sea of Nanahuki!]

[This is part of the
Pele-Hi'iaka-i-ka-poli-o-peli chant saga
as recorded by Morrison and Chun.]

. . . Nietzsche offers the idea that, in the West, the turning away from the emotively expressive acts of dance and song began when the impulsive Dionysian consciousness was first compromised by the representational Apollonian notion of art. Finally, dance and song as transcendent unifying practices of expression were eventually eclipsed by the Socratic scheme of rationale and dialectic. From Socrates onward, so Nietzsche would say, the autographic per-

forming arts have suffered a generally lower aesthetic status and an accompanying lack of philosophical significance.

In Polynesia the converse of this model was true. If there ever was a tension between representational and expressive art, the materially static forms of creative activity only rarely rose beyond utility and functionality. It was in the purely nonliterate practices of *hula* and *oli* (chant) that Hawaiian culture most dynamically expressed its aesthetic sense.

In old Hawai'i, *hula* and *oli* were but two sides of the same cloak. One always appeared with the other, the resulting combination constituting a complementary relationship in which words and movement were used to express a unified concept. Within the narrative of words and motion were recorded the history and cosmology of the Hawaiian people. This contextualization comprised a unique "World Book," in which could be read, in Nathaniel Emerson's words, ". . . the great themes of life and death, of ambition and jealousy, of sexual passion, of romantic love, of conjugal love . . . attitudes toward nature and the dread forces of earthquake and storm, and the mysteries of spirit and the hereafter."

In traditional times *hula* was performed in order to preserve the ideology of the Island culture. This ideology was a religio-philosophical structure that reinforced the lines of relationship uniting the people, particularly the *ali'i* (the royal, or upper class) through a complex chain of interrelated genealogies. The genealogies were a crucial factor in justifying the transfer of political power from one generation to the next. They also expressed in symbol and metaphor the metaphysical foundations of culture. The *ali'i* were able to trace their ancestry to the primal mother–father dyad, Papa and Wakea, and, with such proof of divine ancestry, exercised their warrant to rule. At many points in these long family histories, incidents could be teased out and developed into horizontal story lines. These were then performed as dramatic poetic narratives in song and dance. The saga of the volcano goddess, Pele, and her youngest sister, Hi'i-aka-i-ka-poli-o-pele, is one such side development which was extended into a great chronicle of adventure that has strong moral overtones. A large percentage of modern *hula* has to do with the Pele–Hi'iaka cycle.

Though each oral and physical performance was in certain ways unique and unrepeatable, there was an overall structure that strictly influenced virtually every aspect of composition and presentation. *Hula* was more than just "movement" as Snoe Yen Bos indicates in his definition of dance. The movements of hands, feet, and eyes all closely followed precise formulas. The same held true for the chants: particular stories were repeated in certain patterns and rhythms. There was a structure, an architecture, that reflected the Hawaiians' view of universal order. This order was adumbrated

in a grand scheme of relationships that included all elements of the universe.

Revision and creation were watched and analyzed to make sure that continuity was maintained in each story line. *Kumu hula* (dance masters) were responsible for their groups of dancers (*halau*), a responsibility that included not only the correct performance of *hula* and *oli*, but the proper observance of religions rites and tabus as well. The dancers themselves were professionals, specially educated and trained for their central role in society. Their role was nothing less than to be living repositories and expressors of Hawaiian cosmology and tradition.

In performing *hula* and *oli*, the performers themselves became part of the narrative. The audience, through the act of empathetic observation, became part of the hermeneutic circle of understanding, bringing the full force of individual and collective historicity to bear. In situations of this nature, understanding itself proves to be an event and a vivification of tradition.

In Hawai'i the *hula* dancer would present a performance that was intentionally beautiful and pleasing according to local standards while at the same time communicating a multi-leveled symbolical narrative in synergistic complement to the accompanying *oli*. This "artist as art" amounted to what Elizabeth Bentzel Buck calls "the primary form of symbolic creation" in traditional Hawaiian society.

. . . Hawaiian *hula* was, and in some sense still is, a classic example of art as an immediate expression of being. It combined intuited expression with intended meaning in an unadulterated oral tradition. This is a state unattainable to individuals in a literate culture. Nevertheless, the artist as dancer comes close, perhaps as close as is possible in human terms, to unifying the major elements of the aesthetic experience. Dance is a dialect of the language we use as a species for the ceaseless conversation that constitutes our being.

Pa'i ana no pahu a hula le'a;
O ka'u hula no keia.

[Let the better-enjoyed hula chanters beat their own drums; this is the hula chant that I know.]*

*A retort: "Let those who claim to know a lot produce their knowledge; this is what I know" (Pukui 1983, 283).

John Berger

OIL
PAINTING

John Berger is a contemporary British art critic, as well as a novelist and screenplay writer. His books on art, such as Ways of Seeing, Art and Revolution, *and* The Success and Failure of Picasso, *emphasize the role that historical and political contexts play in the structure of artworks. Berger considers here the role that the burgeoning merchant class played in the rise of oil paint as a preferred medium for painting.*

Oil paintings often depict things. Things which in reality are buyable. To have a thing painted and put on a canvas is not unlike buying it and putting it in your house. If you buy a painting you buy also the look of the thing it represents.

This analogy between *possessing* and the way of seeing which is incorporated in oil painting, is a factor usually ignored by art experts and historians. Significantly enough it is an anthropologist who has come closest to recognizing it.

Lévi-Strauss writes:

> It is this avid and ambitious desire to take possession of the object for the benefit of the owner or even of the spectator which seems to me to constitute one of the outstandingly original features of the art of Western civilization.

If this is true—though the historical span of Lévi-Strauss's generalization may be too large—the tendency reached its peak during the period of the traditional oil painting.

The term *oil painting* refers to more than a technique. It defines an art form. The technique of mixing pigments with oil had existed since the ancient world. But the oil painting as an art form was not born until there was a need to develop and perfect this technique (which soon involved using canvas instead of wooden panels) in order to express a particular view of life for which the techniques of tempera or fresco were inadequate. When oil paint was first used— at the beginning of the fifteenth century in Northern Europe—for painting pictures of a new character, this character was somewhat inhibited by the survival of various medieval artistic conventions. The oil painting did not fully establish its own norms, its own way of seeing, until the sixteenth century.

Nor can the end of the period of the oil painting be dated exactly. Oil paintings are still being painted today. Yet the basis of its traditional way of seeing was undermined by impressionism and overthrown by Cubism. At about the same time the photograph took

John Berger, *Ways of Seeing* (New York: Penguin, 1972) 83–89.

the place of the oil painting as the principal source of visual imagery. For these reasons the period of the traditional oil painting may be roughly set as between 1500 and 1900.

The tradition, however, still forms many of our cultural assumptions. It defines what we mean by pictorial likeness. Its norms still affect the way we see such subjects as landscape, women, food, dignitaries, mythology. It supplies us with our archetypes of "artistic genius." And the history of the tradition, as it is usually taught, teaches us that art prospers if enough individuals in society have a love of art.

What is a love of art?

The art of any period tends to serve the ideological interests of the ruling class. If we were simply saying that European art between 1500 and 1900 served the interests of the successive ruling classes, all of whom depended in different ways on the new power of capital, we should not be saying anything very new. What is being proposed is a little more precise; that a way of seeing the world, which was ultimately determined by new attitudes to property and exchange, found its visual expression in the oil painting, and could not have found it in any other visual art form.

Oil painting did to appearances what capital did to social relations. It reduced everything to the equality of objects. Everything became exchangeable because everything became a commodity. All reality was mechanically measured by its materiality. The soul, thanks to the Cartesian system, was saved in a category apart. A painting could speak to the soul—by way of what it referred to, but never by the way it envisaged. Oil painting conveyed a vision of total exteriority.

Pictures immediately spring to mind to contradict this assertion. Works by Rembrandt, El Greco, Giorgione, Vermeer, Turner, etc. Yet if one studies these works in relation to the tradition as a whole, one discovers that they were exceptions of a very special kind.

The tradition consisted of many hundreds of thousands of canvases and easel pictures distributed throughout Europe. A great number have not survived. Of those which have survived only a small fraction are seriously treated today as works of fine art, and of this fraction another small fraction comprises the actual pictures repeatedly reproduced and presented as the work of "the masters."

Visitors to art museums are often overwhelmed by the number of works on display, and by what they take to be their own culpable inability to concentrate on more than a few of these works. In fact such a reaction is altogether reasonable. Art history has totally failed to come to terms with the problem of the relationship between the outstanding work and the average work of the European tradition. The notion of Genius is not in itself an adequate answer. Consequently the confusion remains on the walls of the galleries. Third-rate works surround an outstanding work without any recognition—let alone explanation—of what fundamentally differentiates them.

The art of any culture will show a wide differential of talent. But in no other culture is the difference between "masterpiece" and average work so large as in the tradition of the oil painting. In this tradition the difference is not just a question of skill or imagination, but also of morale. The average work—and increasingly after the seventeenth century—was a work produced more or less cynically: that is to say the values it was nominally expressing were less meaningful to the painter than the finishing of the commission or the selling of his product. Hack work is not the result of either clumsiness or provincialism; it is the result of the market making more insistent demands than the art. The period of the oil painting corresponds with the rise of the open art market.

And it is in this contradiction between art and market that the explanations must be sought for what amounts to the contrast, the antagonism existing between the exceptional work and the average.

Whilst acknowledging the existence of the exceptional works, to which we shall return later, let us first look broadly at the tradition.

What distinguishes oil painting from any other form of painting is its special ability to render the tangibility, the texture, the lustre, the solidity of what it depicts. It defines the real as that which you can put your hands on. Although its painted images are two-dimensional, its potential of illusionism is far greater than that of sculpture, for it can suggest objects possessing colour, texture and temperature, filling a space and, by implication, filling the entire world.

Peter Wicke

"LOVE ME DO": THE AESTHETICS OF SENSUOUSNESS

◆◆◆

Peter Wicke is professor of the theory and history of popular music and director of the Center for Popular Music Research at Humboldt University in Berlin. He has written on a number of forms of popular music; the following excerpt is taken from his book Rock Music: Culture, Aesthetics and Sociology. *Wicke contends that rock music's significance depended, originally, on the way it was appropriated by working-class young people. Its meaning, according to Wicke, cannot be fully appreciated without this social context.*

Rock'n'roll contained the seeds of a development which was to advance into new musical dimensions in the sixties. The foundations of this development were laid in British beat music.

. . . British beat music penetrated even music production itself, establishing within it an aesthetic which suited both the cultural contexts of use which had evolved as well as the technical creation of music. The first song which made this clear was the Beatles' "Love Me Do"; a song which, not least because of this, became a legend. Twenty years after its first release in October 1962 it even reappeared in the British top forty.

"Love Me Do," with "P.S. I Love You" on the flip side, was the Beatles' first official single. The song itself is not particularly exciting, nor is it difficult to identify its precursors. . . . The song itself consists of a constant repetition of its rather thin basic elements: a scant rhythm-set phrase in the backing vocals, a short melodic motif and the repeated "Love, love me do, you know I love you." The arrangement, with three guitars and drums as well as the harmonica, could hardly be any simpler. The bass guitar swings back and forth between the roots of the three chords used while the rhythm guitar adds the regularly strummed triads and

Peter Wicke, *Rock Music: Culture, Aesthetics and Sociology*, trans. Rachel Fogg (New York: Cambridge UP, 1990) 48–72.

the lead guitar simply follows the melody line. Beneath this is a stereotyped drum pattern which marks the beat. The interplay of Paul McCartney's vocals, supported by George Harrison and John Lennon, with the harmonica insertions is the only distinctive element of the song, and even that was copied.

What is it then that makes a song like this legendary? How does it mark a cultural turning point of such significance that George Melly actually considered it the starting point of a "revolution"?

. . . The remarkable thing about this recording was that it had audibly broken consistently maintained professional standards in music production. The young men who had stood in the studio were dilettantes in the eyes of the professional musicians. The material they played no longer came from the desks of the professional songwriters of London's Denmark Street—the home of the great British music publishers—but had been confirmed by their audience a long time ago in countless live appearances. It was impossible to work with studio musicians which, even in rock'n'roll, was otherwise customary with new groups, since the songs were arranged for the instruments which the group themselves played. And the way they played those instruments, with their naive lack of concern and their enthusiastic greenness, contradicted every norm.

Of course the Beatles were not by any means the only group playing this kind of music at the time. . . . But in spite of this, thanks to their clever manager Brian Epstein, the Beatles were the first band to sign a contract with one of the large market-leading record companies. At the time it was like opening a floodgate and this was what gave this song its legendary significance. "Love Me Do" was the first song coming out of the broad amateur music movement of the time which achieved unlimited media presence, which was on national radio and which was available in the large record shops. . . .

Looked at more closely, "Love Me Do" represented not only the beginning of a structural change within the music industry which resulted in pop music being taken out of the hands of a small group of professional songwriters, but also a different conception of popular music, one which showed the basic form of rock.

The first obvious break with the traditional aesthetic communication model of pop music was the fact that it was now the whole group who were the focus of identification for the audience, not an individual singer. What had been concealed in rock'n'roll—seen from outside it appeared to be the same as the conventional pop song, simply in another musical form—here became quite clear. The Beatles' "Love, love me do, you know I love you" no longer concealed the stylised role play of the languishing lover undertaken for the entertainment of the audience. Sung by more than one person this no longer made any sense. Thus, this song was spared the theatricality which the traditional pop song had acquired from its roots in the musical stage entertainment of the nineteenth century—operetta, music hall and later the talking picture. And this inevitably shifted the aesthetic coordinates of the music, which could no longer be taken as a code representing individual expression and the emotions which the singer personified. The idea that a pop song should be constructed like a conversation between singer and audience, that the singer should give a personal significance to the music, finally collapsed with this change. There was no longer a romanticised "I" behind the Beatles' songs but, visibly, a collective "we," and this lifted the music out of a communication pattern in which it was understood as the musical symbol of personal emotions. Instead of expressing emotions with great feeling, which the text of "Love Me Do" actually suggested, and for which a suitable reservoir of musical means were available in the conventional pop song, this song was, by way of complete contrast, totally unsentimental in style.

The intensity of "Love, love me do . . ." was created in a very genuine way, without following the conventions which always necessitated the musical expression of great love in "great" melodic phrases. In the construction of this song the rhythmic organisation dominated all other musical factors. Even the vocal part did not have a particularly original or concise melody, in fact had no individual melodic form, but was nothing more than one element of a rhythmically constructed whole. The act of listening to this song was coordinated with a rhythmically organised progression of movement, one which seemed full of intensity because of its almost manic uniformity instead of merely portraying this intensity according to the conventional rules. The ceaseless repetition of the basic musical elements of the song had a rather hypnotic effect. Every dancer knows what intensity of feeling can be produced by a repeated pattern of steps and it was as dance music that "Love Me Do" originated. In other words, instead of transposing emotions into musical structures according to a handed down aesthetic code, these emotions were *presented* in movement, a movement which demanded the active participation of the listener so that the emotions could be created in reality. In his research into Afro-American music, in which this form of music has its roots, Bram Dijkstra correctly established: "Such movement does not actually have to happen. Just as a dancer can dance to music in his head, the seemingly passive listener always reacts mentally to the rhythmic pattern which his senses are registering, even if he is not consciously listening." The basis of what Dijkstra is describing is the direct sensuous power of music. Here musical performance takes place according to an aesthetic of sensuousness.

The force behind this concept of music was American rock'n'roll, particularly Afro-

American forms. But since in Britain this musical import from the USA encountered completely different conditions and was removed from its original context, in Britain it evolved far beyond its inherent boundaries. The key to the conception of British beat music—and all that followed—lies in the particular way in which rock'n'roll was received. It was in this context that the aesthetic of rock was created, an aesthetic which runs through all its playing styles and stylistic forms with their continually changing emphases and their new attempts at developing its musical possibilities. The individual nature of this aesthetic resulted from the relationships which rock'n'roll entered in fifties Britain. . . .

In the fifties the BBC, in its role as the British national cultural institution, still possessed almost unlimited authority in all questions of the nation's musical entertainment. . . .

The BBC considered itself a cultural educational institution. It only granted entertainment an independent status in programming structures during the Second World War, when the radio was used to mobilise a spirit of resistance in the civilian population as well as in the armed forces. The Light Programme was introduced in 1946 to replace the Forces Programme (introduced at the beginning of the forties for troop entertainment). To a large extent it took over the Forces Programme's view of entertainment, but was still based on a concept which did not see any difference between entertainment and education. Sir William Haley, director of the BBC, described this concept in 1946 in a pamphlet on programming entitled "The Responsibilities of Broadcasting": "Each programme at any given moment must be ahead of its public, but not so much as to lose their confidence. The listener must be led from good to better by curiosity, liking and a growth of understanding." The concept of musical entertainment was thus linked to the idea that the listener would be completely uncritical and have no standards of comparison. . . .

. . . The programmes were designed for home and family and the tastes and cultural values of the lower middle classes therefore reigned unchallenged. It is not surprising that from the mid-fifties rock'n'roll imported from America became the enthusiastically accepted alternative to all this, particularly among working-class teenagers, for they were unable to recognise themselves in the BBC's model listener.

Another factor was that the BBC was not allowed to use records on its music programmes for more than twenty-two hours per week, an anachronism remaining from the early thirties. The BBC was bound by an agreement with the British Musicians' Union which limited the so-called "needle time," the broadcasting of records, in order to secure jobs for professional musicians in live studio music broadcasts. In addition only every third piece of music broadcast could be a piece of vocal music. Consequently the BBC clung unwaveringly to an aesthetic concept of pop music which was oriented towards the instrumental swing standards of the thirties. . . .

The large record companies, foremost among them EMI, naturally adjusted to the guidelines of BBC programming policy and only concentrated on those releases which, in view of the existing limitations of the needle time agreement, had any chance of being considered for the broadcasting playlist, one of the main tools of sales promotion. . . .

Bill Haley's "Rock Around the Clock," released in Britain in 1954 on the Decca Brunswick label, really exploded onto this soft British musical entertainment scene. The contrast could not have been greater. It was also the first single to sell more than a million copies in Britain. This was the signal for a radically different style of leisure behaviour, particularly among British working-class teenagers, for as the sociologists and consumer strategists quickly found out:

the teenage market is almost entirely working class. Its middle class members are either still at school and college or else just beginning on their careers: in either case they dispose of much smaller incomes than their working class contemporaries and it is highly probably, therefore, that not far short of 90 per cent of all teenage spending is conditioned by working class taste and values.

Rock'n'roll made it obvious for the first time in Britain that working-class teenagers were beginning to form cultural value patterns in their leisure which were increasingly clearly contrasted with the official cultural institutions. Just the fact that "Rock Around the Clock" was an American production shocked the officials of British culture.

The first direct contacts with highly commercialised American mass culture were via the American forces stationed in England in 1942 and their radio station, the American Forces Network (AFN), set up as part of the troop welfare operation. Since then a massive campaign had been running in British public opinion against the "American influence," fearing that it would undermine British cultural traditions. Even in 1942 the British Government limited the transmission radius of the AFN stations to 10 miles in order to protect their own population from it as far as possible. As Dick Hebdige wrote later: "By the early 50s, the very mention of the word 'America' could summon up a cluster of negative associations."

In order to "prove" the corrupting influence of American culture there was also no lack of exaggerated scandal reports in the British press about young criminal offenders and their rock'n'roll background. . . .

In fact these arguments about rock'n'roll really concealed a conflict of a quite different nature from the one which was pushed into the foreground and in which people were encouraged to believe—the danger of the "Americanisation" of British culture. Since the thirties, pop music in Britain had been nurtured by American influences and the pre-war Hollywood film successes had left deeper marks on Britain's cultural life than rock'n'roll, linked as it was mainly to working-class teenagers, could ever bring with it. Conservative Britain was far more afraid of the political consequences which might arise from an undirected commercial generalisation of the cultural needs of the masses. The real problem was a concept of mass culture which threatened to undermine the authority of the official British cultural institutions, supported by Crown and Government, a concept of mass culture which, merely because of its numerical supremacy, was bound to lead to a shift in cultural processes towards the needs and lifestyle of the working class. As Iain Chambers commented: "It was the novel and unsolicited ingression of new tastes coming from 'below,' and their evident powers to challenge and redraw some of the traditional maps of cultural habits, that generated many an acid but apprehensive rebuttal." Class divisions in Britain—reaching as they did deep into the structure of the cities, with their socially sharply distinct residential districts—were reinforced culturally. In people's minds the working-class culture and lifestyle, once given the opportunity to develop, were linked to the spectre of the decline of the nation. . . .

Fifties Britain also saw the conservative revitalisation of existing social relations. The collapse of the British Empire after the Second World War, when it had to relinquish sovereignty to its colonies, plunged British capitalism into a deep crisis. In order to solve this crisis all possible forces were mobilised. . . .

. . . While on the one hand British capital interests tried to solve the problems occasioned by the loss of markets and cheap labour in the former British colonies with a cynical contempt for the working class, on the other hand they promoted a "classless" consumer paradise, a superb screen for the genuine interests of capital. In order to give a certain reality to the promised "classlessness," without even touching real class conditions, a consumer culture was cobbled together in which social differences genuinely seemed to have disappeared. . . . Ian Birchall described the situation in the following terms:

> Britain in the late fifties and early sixties saw an unprecedented degree of political stability and general prosperity. . . . But above all society was fragmented and individualistic. Improvements in living standards in a boom situation came from local bargaining and direct action—politics or identification with a social class seemed increasingly irrelevant to the real concerns of life. More and more working-class people, especially the young, told social scientists and opinion pollsters that they were not working class. Political apathy was defined, in the phrase of the distinguished historian E. P. Thompson, as "private solutions to public problems." For youth above all frustration and satisfaction were defined, not in social terms, but in relation to personal, and particularly sexual relations. It was this pattern of life that found its cultural reflection in the rock music of the years 1963 to 1966.

At first the "pattern of life" which Birchall describes here was linked to American rock'n'roll, which gave British working-class teenagers a medium of self-portrayal. Even if they no longer considered themselves working-class, their experiences were still class-specific. Their search for cultural forms which suited them and which differed from the official consumer model, in which they could rediscover themselves and which they could relate to their everyday experiences, was nothing more than an expression of this. . . .

Rock'n'roll promoted the utopia of a distant America, an utopia which could encompass the everyday experiences of British working-class teenagers with all their longings, desires, hopes, frustrations and leisure needs. Rock'n'roll mediated a self-image to these teenagers, which—influenced by the values and leisure patterns of American high school students—was literally miles away from their actual situation, but which despite this could only find its basis in the structure of their daily lives. It took the experience of daily life in the dismal English working-class suburbs, where the cinema was the only remaining alternative to the street, to see rock'n'roll as an opportunity for cultural realisation, an opportunity which was able to break down the constricting boundaries of school, work and the family home by making them able to feel an undefined longing for something "real" which had to exist somewhere beyond the oppressive ordinariness of life. Thus, with a provocative challenge rock'n'roll bore witness to the social and cultural claims of British working-class teenagers, even though these claims were expressed via a foreign identity. . . .

Against this background, rock'n'roll achieved a significance in Britain which it had never possessed in America. In fifties Britain it became the cultural symbol of working-class teenagers. . . . When the rise of British beat music made the argument that British culture was being swamped by American music imports untenable, reactions sharpened, thereby reinforcing the link between the music and the social problems of the working-class teenager. Music became a convenient symbol in the increasingly sharp conflict. The fact that teenagers themselves took this conflict quite personally—equating it with clashes with their parents, with school, with the world around them, with the problems of getting a job, with their superiors at work—did not change the social nature of the conflict at all. This was not the private conflict of a restless youth, the so-called "generation conflict," but was rather concerned with the opportunities for developing a lifestyle

and culture suited to the class-specific experience of the changing face of British capitalism. It is not surprising that ruling conservative opinion considered this a threat. The *New Statesman*, the opinion leader of the political establishment, in 1964 described the "menace of Beatleism":

> Both T.V. channels now run weekly programmes in which popular records are played to teenagers and judged. While the music is performed, the cameras linger savagely over the faces of the audience. What a bottomless chasm of vacuity they reveal. Huge faces, bloated with cheap confectionery and smeared with chain-store make-up, the open, sagging mouths and glazed eyes, the hands mindlessly drumming in time to the music, the broken stiletto heels, the shoddy, stereotyped, "with-it" clothes: here, apparently, is a collective portrait of a generation enslaved by a commercial machine.

Such distorted images dominated public discussion about British beat music and also formed the background which gave a song like the Beatles' "Love Me Do" its explosive force. . . .

Of course, when a new market began to appear with the rock'n'roll craze among working-class teenagers the British music industry also reacted promptly, despite the public arguments. However, right from the start the music business adapted rock'n'roll to suit its concept of "excellent entertainment for the whole family," as David Jacobs, compere of the television programme "Juke Box Jury," a pop music programme for teenagers, put it at the time. Practically every month a new young star appeared on the record market, gushingly billed as "Britain's answer to Elvis Presley." Tommy Steele and Cliff Richard in particular represented the British form of soft rock'n'roll blend with their cliched "good boy" style, a style which actually robbed rock'n'roll of precisely those elements which had initially made it an alternative to the bourgeois British pop music productions of the fifties. This ultimately resulted in young people playing rock'n'roll themselves, once the skiffle craze had made playing music fashionable. . . .

. . . The most significant effect of playing rock'n'roll was that it helped to create a leisure environment which working-class teenagers could call their own. The beat clubs which sprang up in disused cellars, former jazz clubs and pubs were their world and provided a centre for their leisure needs where only the rules that *they* made counted. They were not allowed into bars, dance halls and pubs, since these sold alcohol and were therefore barred to young people under 18. The few youth clubs which existed were under educational supervision and were usually organised by church-based charitable organisations, who not only did not have rock'n'roll in mind but considered their "cultural" leisure activities—handicrafts circles, games and community singing—an alternative to it. In contrast to all this, playing music themselves created an independent leisure environment, supported by the way the music was used and developed by the teenagers themselves. Their leisure activities shifted away from the streets and into the beat clubs.

. . . Form and content now followed other rules than those which correspond to the conversion of content into the dialectic of form, into the unity of lyrics and music. The most important thing about this music is no longer the wealth of emotion, the fulfillment of the content and the diversity of associations developed in the artistic structures, but rather the ability of these elements to be open to the symbolic meanings which they receive from their listeners. . . .

What was important was rock'n'roll's dance music qualities and the songs from the Afro-American tradition were the ones which suited this best. The songs which

exercised the greatest influence on early British beat music were those with the most motoric energy, like Chuck Berry's "Roll Over Beethoven." It was not by chance that this song was in the Beatles' repertoire together with a number of other Berry songs. Dancing itself was, of course, already a central element of teenage leisure activity and, together with music, created their own leisure environment. But at the same time it was the form of the literal appropriation of the rock'n'roll songs which made them open to *their* meanings and open to being *their* medium of expression. In sensuous identification with the music through bodily movement in dance the structures of the songs were dissolved into patterns and images of movement. It was not their meaning, their content, that was "read" but their movement; they were not merely heard but rather physically deciphered. And it was exactly this which formed the basis for the construction of a second, symbolic, system of meaning over the immediate content, a system of meaning which, without being obvious in the songs and without being fixed in meaning by the lyrics and music, is nevertheless not independent of them. Teenagers stripped rock'n'roll songs of their concrete determinacy of meaning by changing them into patterns of movement while they were dancing. And as patterns of movement they could be assimilated into the structures of their lifestyle and leisure and could then themselves function as the material such as clothes, hairstyles, gestures (coolness, etc.) and styles of speech (slang) as elements in a complex cultural style of behaviour. . . .

. . . As a result a complex multi-dimensionality was established, both in performance and in involvement with the music, which became the foundation of rock music and which established an analogous multi-dimensional song concept for further development. The French semiotician, Roland Barthes, found a very accurate model for this when he was working on similar multi-level systems of meaning in images and literary texts:

> In the same way, if I am in a car and I look at the scenery through the window, I can at will focus on the scenery or on the window-pane. At one moment I grasp the presence of the glass and the distance of the landscape; at another, on the contrary, the transparence of the glass and the depth of the landscape; but the result of this alternation is constant: the glass is at once present and empty to me, and the landscape unreal and full.

Even if it may perhaps seem erroneous, rock songs can be compared to the window of the car in Barthes' model. Just as the form and composition of the window determine the segment of reality which is visible through it, yet it is not the window but the scenery beyond which attracts the eye of the onlooker, so it is with rock songs. Lyrics and music anchor them in the cultural contexts of leisure, the everyday life and lifestyle in which they function, determining in the same way a particular, social, segment of reality. But beyond these contexts more comprehensive meanings are enclosed which are as equally little formulated in lyrics and music as the scenery is displayed on the window; but just as much linked with the lyrics and music of the songs as the view of the scenery remains determined by the form and composition of the window. And just as the car moves through the scenery so that new segments of reality become visible without the form and composition of the window changing—these always limit the onlooker's field of view in the same way—so rock songs can be moved through the cultural scenery, always encompassing new meanings without the lyrics and music changing. The same songs had a quite different meaning in American high schools than they did in the leisure structures of British working-class teenagers. If we focus on the songs, we become aware of their internal composition and the content formulated with this. But just as in Roland Barthes' model the form of the window and its material composition—its streaks and air bubbles, the structure of its surface—are not at all the object of interest of the person looking at the scenery; they limit his field of view and influence the colour and perspective of the visible piece of scenery and are therefore not unimportant since the window and the scenery seem to melt into one unity, so the internal composition of the songs is not in the slightest of real importance to the listener. What is of importance is the ability they have, like the window, to be transparent to the symbolic meanings lying beyond them, meanings with which they form a single unity, as the window does with the piece of scenery. . . .

However complicated this relationship may appear, it is quite easily achieved by the musicians. They only have to succeed in providing a music with which each audience identifies. They do not have to track down the complex secondary plane of meaning which their songs receive from the audience, nor do they have to understand the open nature of their songs. Indeed, as long as they keep their relationship with their audience in mind, something which they always professed if only for commercial reasons, they may even believe that they are only expressing their own thoughts and emotions. . . .

These relationships constituted a song concept which was freed from the functional narrowness of traditional pop music, from its reduction to dancing and entertainment, but which on the other hand was able to realise very complex meanings without being overlooked in terms of content and without having to desert the functional planes of dancing and entertainment. This song concept needed no complex and differentiated "significant" musical structures in order to realise those symbolic meanings. Quite the reverse, the more open the songs remained, open to different possibilities of meaning and of use, the more flexibly they followed the meanings which had developed in the teenagers' leisure behaviour. Their concrete acquisition through translation into patterns and images of movement, the sensuous development of their content of movement, in spite of everything made possible a performance that was always different, especially since to a great extent this was developed from the musicians' consciousness of their own bodies and did not simply follow some principles of construction which would have had to have been learnt and which would have required an understanding recognition from the listener. . . .

Thus there is a sensuous truth behind rock music which is not attached to the logic of the structural detail but rather to the sound of the surface characteristics of the musical form. Put together from a style-dependent repertoire from more or less fixed "standard" playing formulas, rhythmic models and stereotyped sounds which, like the parts of a kaleidoscope, form continually changing patterns, this musical form corresponds to a mode of perception and use in which music is not taken as a form of expression similar to speech with prescribed structures of meaning but as a body-oriented sensuous experience. The Who's Keith Moon put it this way: "Of course we take our music seriously. But we don't give any messages. People can take what they want from our songs" [translated from German]. The essential nature of the rock experience does not consist of decoding the music as a structure of meaning but rather in being able to place one's own significance on the sensuous experience which it provides. Thus music is performed according to an aesthetic of sensuousness.

DISCUSSION QUESTIONS

1. Do you agree with Hegel and Danto that the era of art's most important spiritual vocation lies behind us? What evidence would you use to defend your opinion?
2. Do you think that art has evolved over time, as Hegel argues? Is contemporary art progressing, in your opinion?
3. Can you think of examples of contemporary art that express our current times, in your opinion? How do they accomplish this?
4. Is it possible to agree with Hegel that an era's artwork reflects its highest spiritual values and also agree with Hume that durable admiration is the best test of a work's aesthetic merit? Explain.
5. Do you think the meaning of a song depends on the context in which it is used? What examples would you use to defend your opinion?

FURTHER READING

Benjamin, Walter. *Aesthetics and Politics.* Ed. R. Taylor. London: New Left, 1977.

Berger, John. *About Looking.* New York: Random House, 1980.

————. *Ways of Seeing.* New York: Penguin, 1972.

Danto, Arthur C. *The Philosophical Disenfranchisement of Art.* New York: Columbia UP, 1986.

Eagleton, Terry. *The Ideology of the Aesthetic.* Oxford: Basil Blackwell, 1990.

Lang, Berel, ed. *The Death of Art.* New York: Haven, 1984.

Solomon, Maynard, ed. *Marxism and Art.* New York: Knopf, 1973.

Wolff, Janet. *The Social Production of Art.* London: Macmillan, 1975.

PART III

CHALLENGES
TO THE
TRADITION

BEYOND
TRADITIONAL MODELS

One scene in Luis Bunuel's film *The Phantom of Liberty* opens with a man sitting on a sofa and contemplating the mantel above his fireplace. On the mantel is a clock of a common sort, rounded at the top, with flared sides and a flat base. The clock, rather predictably, rests in the center of the mantelpiece. The man suddenly leaps from the couch and says, "I'm sick of symmetry." He moves to the mantle, shoves the clock to one side, and props a square "artwork" on the other side—a spider displayed under glass.

A visit to any exhibition of contemporary art will alert us to the fact that many twentieth-century artists have been fed up with symmetry—and with many other traditional values besides. If traditional models are not dead, they are at least no longer reigning. Marcel Duchamp's readymades would not traditionally have been considered candidates for the label "art." Neither would rap music, despite its popularity. The aesthetics of rap diverge from the traditional aesthetics of music (even popular music). Rap plays on unresolved tensions, generated both by the music and the lyrics; it also employs many "noise" elements and nonstandard techniques of sound production, such as sampling and the amplification of the sound caused by scratching records. Richard Shusterman confronts the tendency to dismiss such forms, arguing that rap music should be considered as a fine art. The techniques employed in rap, he claims, are as sophisticated and artful as those endemic to the traditional handful of "fine" arts.

Such arts could hardly have been included in the usual list of traditional fine arts (even if subcategories of music were listed individually), for the technology on which they depend has only recently been invented. The nontraditional "performance" pieces that are considered art in the late twentieth century also contrast with the traditional canons of art. Many involve their audiences in active participation (rather than disinterested contemplation), and the objects and props employed are often nonstandard, if not straight-forwardly bizarre. Thomas Heyd considers the charge that performance artists have contradictory goals when they want their work to be taken seriously as art but also want it to "go beyond art." Heyd defends the performance artist's position. Whether a given performance is art might be subject to debate; but confusion about the status of a performance can itself be an artistic device that engages the attention of the audience. In Heyd's view, much effective performance art has succeeded in going "beyond art" in the important—but traditional—sense of having real impact on its viewers' lives.

The changes art has undergone in the twentieth century have been attended by changes in theory about art. One approach that has had immense influence on thought about the arts, especially literature, is **structuralism**. Structuralism is a form of "deep interpretation," which looks beneath the surface presentation of a work in order to find a more fundamental structure. Often the structures that are postulated are analyzed in terms of basic oppositions (for example, "sign" and "signified"). Structuralism considers literary texts as akin to language, treating them as a system of interconnected signs that are interpreted by means of conventions. Literary critic Roland Barthes describes his understanding of structuralism in "The Structuralist Activity." As his title indicates, Barthes emphasizes that structuralism is an active way of engaging with art or other human productions. Structuralists look for patterns that might help to crack the code of a text— or, more generally, of a society's way of conveying meaning.

Jenene J. Allison describes the characteristic methodology of a movement that has challenged structuralism and has accordingly been termed "**deconstruction**." The deconstructionists question whether simple patterns and oppositions of the sorts employed by structuralists can really decode the "meaning" of any human production. Instead, they contend, meaning is a slippery and sometimes arbitrary business. Any text is also susceptible to continual reinterpretation as one rearranges what one puts in the foreground of one's attention. Structuralism, on this account, is not so much a method for unlocking the fundamental meanings of texts and artworks. Instead, it is a means of *imposing* meanings, and it obstructs our ability to see other interpretive possibilities.

Deconstruction is sometimes associated with **postmodernism**, an approach to art and society that rejects the "modernist" perspective—that dream of comprehensive progress that occasioned much enthusiasm among artists earlier in the twentieth century. Modernists emphasized utopian ideals, such as the aim of universal communication and the possibility that human efforts might be coordinated. They considered art to be an autonomous realm, separate from the rest of life, and they endorsed artistic experiments that explored the formal possibilities inherent in given media, or "art about art."

Postmodernists, by contrast, are suspicious of universalistic aspirations, which they see as evidence of authoritarian tendencies. They reject the idea that art is autonomous, insisting that art is always linked to its context and related to the world. Postmodernists also emphasize the gaps between the perspectives of different societies and social subgroups and stress the fragmentary and provisional nature of each of our efforts to know the world. Postmodernist art reflects these emphases by exploring the diversity of human perspectives and the fragmentary and eclectic character of contemporary experience. To some, such art and the postmodern orientation it reflects are desirable because they explore the gaps between various perspectives. This exploration can help us to diagnose and confront the problems involved in our contemporary social situation.

Kwame Anthony Appiah is less convinced that postmodernism is a constructive force in the contemporary social world. While the postmodernist gospel calls for a celebration of "the Other," Appiah suggests that postmodernists may be more interested in celebrating their own message than in what "the Other" actually has to say. Postmodernists speak from the standpoint of the privileged, Appiah reminds us. Their "celebration" of the Other, he fears, is all too often a reinforcement of their position of power in the world.

Tomas Ybarra-Frausto does not discuss postmodernism as such, but he is enthusiastic about the eclecticism and cultural dialogue exhibited in recent Chicano art. Chicano art employs materials drawn from everyday Chicano experience, such as theater posters, religious images, and home shrines. This art, according to Ybarra-Frausto, is engaged in a process of cultural negotiation, simultaneously challenging the mainstream power structure and initiating new conversations between ethnic groups. This art has a characteristic dynamism because it is grounded in the practical and adaptable sensibility that typifies Chicano life, a sensibility that is aptly expressed by images from popular culture.

Richard Shusterman

THE FINE ART OF RAP

Richard Shusterman is professor of philosophy at Temple University and author of a number of books on aesthetics. These include Analytic Aesthetics, The Object of Literary Criticism, *and* Pragmatist Aesthetics: Living Beauty, Rethinking Art. *This reading is based on a much longer study of rap that appears in* Pragmatist Aesthetics *and, in abbreviated form, in* New Literary History.

In the view of both the culturally elite and the so-called general public, rap music lurks in the underworld of aesthetic respectability. Though it is today's "fastest growing genre of popular music," its claim to artistic status has been drowned under a flood of abusive critique. Rap has not only suffered moral and aesthetic condemnations but also organized censorship, blacklists, arrests, and the police-enforced stopping of concerts. Moreover, on a different level of cultural combat, we find attempts to dilute and undermine rap's ethnic and political content by encouraging and exploiting its most bland, "sanitized," and commercialized forms. None of this should be surprising. For rap's cultural roots and prime following belong to the black underclass of American society; and its militant black pride and thematizing of the ghetto experience represent a threatening siren to that society's compla-

cent status quo. The threat is of course far more audible and urgent for the middle-brow public who not only interact more closely and competitively with the poor black population, but who rely on (and thus compete for) the same mass-media channels of cultural transmission, and who have a greater need to assert their sociocultural (and ultimately political) superiority over black America.

Armed with such powerful political motives for opposing rap, one can readily find aesthetic reasons which seem to discredit it as a legitimate art form. Rap songs are not even sung, only spoken or chanted. They typically employ neither live musicians nor original music; the sound track is instead composed from various cuts (or "samples") of records already made and often well known. Finally, the lyrics seem to be crude and simple-minded, the diction

Richard Shusterman, "The Fine Art of Rap," *New Literary History* 22 (1991): 613–632.

substandard, the rhymes raucous, repetitive, and frequently raunchy. Yet, as my title suggests, these same lyrics insistently claim and extol rap's status as poetry and fine art.

. . . Rap, I believe, is a postmodern popular art which challenges some of our most deeply entrenched aesthetic conventions, conventions which are common not only to modernism as an artistic style and ideology but to the philosophical doctrine of modernity and its differentiation of cultural spheres. By considering rap in the context of postmodern aesthetics, I hope not only to provide academic aestheticians with a better understanding of this much maligned but little studied genre of popular art. I also hope to enhance our understanding of postmodernism through the concrete analysis of one of its unique cultural forms.

Postmodernism is a vexingly complex and contested phenomenon, whose aesthetic consequently resists clear and unchallengeable definition. Nonetheless, certain themes and stylistic features are widely recognized as characteristically postmodern, which is not to say that they cannot also be found to varying degrees in some modernist art. These characteristics include: recycling appropriation rather than unique originative creation, the eclectic mixing of styles, the enthusiastic embracing of the new technology and mass culture, the challenging of modernist notions of aesthetic autonomy and artistic purity, and emphasis on the localized and temporal rather than the putatively universal and eternal. Whether or not we wish to call these features postmodern, rap not only saliently exemplifies them, but often consciously highlights and thematizes them. Thus, even if we reject the whole category of postmodernism, these features are essential for understanding rap.

APPROPRIATIVE SAMPLING

Artistic appropriation is the historical source of hip-hop music and still remains the core of its technique and a central feature of its aesthetic form and message. The music derives from selecting and combining parts of prerecorded songs to produce a "new" soundtrack. This soundtrack, produced by the DJ on a multiple turntable, constitutes the musical background for the rap lyrics. These in turn are frequently devoted both to praising the DJ's inimitable virtuosity in sampling and synthesizing the appropriated music, and to boasting of the lyrical and rhyming power of the rapper (called the MC). While the rapper's vaunting self-praise often highlights his sexual desirability, commercial success, and property assets, these signs of status are all presented as secondary to and derivative from his verbal power.

. . . Failure to recognize the traditional tropes, stylistic conventions, and constraint-produced complexities of Afro-American English (such as semantic inversion and indirection, feigned simplicity, and covert parody—all originally designed to conceal the real meaning from hostile white listeners) has induced the false belief that all rap lyrics are superficial and monotonous, if not altogether moronic. But informed and sympathetic close reading will reveal in many rap songs not only the cleverly potent vernacular expression of keen insights but also forms of linguistic subtlety and multiple levels of meaning whose polysemic complexity, ambiguity, and intertextuality can sometimes rival that of high art's so-called "open work."

Like its stylized aggressively boasting language, so rap's other most salient feature—its dominant funky beat—can be traced back to African roots, to jungle rhythms which were taken up by rock and disco and then reappropriated by the rap DJs. . . . But for all its African heritage, hip hop was born in the disco era of the mid-seventies in the grim ghettos of New York, first the Bronx, and then Harlem and Brooklyn. As it appropriated disco sounds and techniques, it undermined and transformed them, much as jazz (an earlier black art of appropriation) had done with the melodies of popular songs. But in contrast to jazz, hip hop did not take mere melodies or musical phrases, that is, abstract musical patterns exemplifiable in different performances. . . .

Thus, unlike jazz, its borrowing and transfiguration did not require skill in playing musical instruments but only in manipulating recording equipment. DJs in ordinary disco clubs had developed the technique of cutting and blending one record into the next, matching tempos to make a smooth transition without violently disrupting the flow of dancing. Dissatisfied with the tame sound of disco and commercial pop, self-styled DJs in the Bronx reapplied the technique of cutting to concentrate and augment those parts of the records which could provide for better dancing. . . .

In short, hip hop began explicitly as dance music to be appreciated through movement, not mere listening. It was originally designed only for live performance (at dances held in homes, schools, community centers and parks), where one could admire the dexterity of the DJ and the personality and improvisational skills of the rapper. It was not intended for a mass audience, and for several years remained confined to the New York City area and outside the mass media network. Though rap was often taped informally on cassette and then reproduced and circulated by its growing body of fans and bootleggers, it was only in 1979 that rap had its first radio broadcast and released its first records. These two singles, "Rapper's Delight" and "King Tim III (Personality Jock)," which were made by groups outside the core rap community but which had connections with the record industry, provoked competitive resentment in the rap world and the incentive and example to get out of the underground and onto disc and radio. However, even when the groups moved from the street to the studio where they could use live music, the DJ's role of appropriation was not generally abandoned and continued to be thematized in rap lyrics as central to the art.

From the basic technique of cutting between sampled records, hip hop developed three other formal devices which contribute significantly to its sound and aesthetic: "scratch mixing," "punch phrasing," and simple scratching. The first is simply overlaying or mixing certain sounds from one record to those of another already playing. Punch phrasing is a refinement of such mixing, where the DJ moves the needle back and forth over a specific phrase of chords or drum slaps of a record so as to add a powerful percussive effect to the sound of the other record playing all the while on the other turntable. The third device is a wilder and more rapid back and forth scratching of the record, too fast for the recorded music to be recognized but productive of a dramatic scratching sound which has its own intense musical quality and crazed beat.

These devices of cutting, mixing, and scratching give rap a variety of forms of appropriation, which seem as versatilely applicable and imaginative as those of high art—as those, say, exemplified by Duchamp's mustache on the Mona Lisa, Rauschenberg's erasure of a De Kooning canvas, and Andy Warhol's multiple re-representation of prepackaged commercial images. Rap also displays a variety of appropriated content. Not only does it sample from a wide range of popular songs, it feeds on classical music, TV theme songs, advertising jingles, and the electronic music of arcade games. It even appropriates nonmusical content, such as media news reports and fragments of speeches by Malcolm X and Martin Luther King.

Though some DJs took pride in appropriating from very unlikely and arcane sources and sometimes tried to conceal (for fear of competition) the exact records they were sampling, there was never any attempt to conceal the fact that they were working from prerecorded sounds rather than composing their own original music. On the contrary, they openly celebrated their method of sampling. What is the aesthetic significance of this proud art of appropriation?

First, it challenges the traditional ideal of originality and uniqueness that has long enslaved our conception of art. Romanticism and its cult of genius likened the artist to a divine creator and advocated that his works be altogether new and express his singular personality. Modernism with its commitment to artistic progress and the avant-garde reinforced the dogma that radical novelty was the essence of art. Though artists have always borrowed from each other's works, the fact was generally ignored or implicitly denied through the ideology of originality, which posed a sharp distinction between original creation and derivative borrowing. Postmodern art like rap undermines this dichotomy by creatively deploying and thematizing its appropriation to show that borrowing and creation are not at all incompatible. It further suggests that the apparently original work of art is itself always a product of unacknowledged borrowings, the unique and novel text always a tissue of echoes and fragments of earlier texts.

Originality thus loses its absolute originary status and is reconceived to include the transfiguring reappropriation and recycling of the old. In this postmodern picture there are no ultimate, untouchable originals, only appropriations of appropriations and simulacra of simulacra; so creative energy can be liberated to play with familiar creations without fear that it thereby denies itself the opportunity to be truly creative by not producing a totally original work. Rap songs simultaneously celebrate their originality and their borrowing. And as the dichotomy of creation/appropriation is challenged, so is the deep division between creative artist and appropriative audience; transfigurative appreciation can take the form of art.

CUTTING AND TEMPORALITY

Rap's sampling style also challenges the work of art's traditional ideal of unity and integrity. Since Aristotle, aestheticians have often viewed the work as an organic whole so perfectly unified that any tampering with its part would damage the whole. Moreover, the ideologies of romanticism and art for art's sake have reinforced our habit of treating artworks as transcendent and virtually sacred ends in themselves, whose integrity we should respect and never violate. In contrast to the aesthetic of organic unity, rap's cutting and sampling reflects the "schizophrenic fragmentation" and "collage effect" characteristic of the postmodern aesthetic. In contrast to an aesthetic of devotional worship of a fixed untouchable work, hip hop offers the pleasures of deconstructive art—the thrilling beauty of dismembering (and rapping over) old works to create new ones, dismantling the prepackaged and wearily familiar into something stimulatingly different.

The DJ's sampling and the MC's rap also highlight the fact that the apparent unity of the original artwork is often an artificially constructed one, at least in contemporary popular music where the production process is frequently quite fragmented: an instrumental track recorded in Memphis, combined with a back-up vocal from New York, and a lead voice from Los Angeles. Rap simply continues this process of layered artistic composition by deconstructing and differently reassembling prepackaged musical products and then superimposing the MC's added layer of lyrics so as to produce a new work. But rap does this without the pretense that its own work is inviolable, that the artistic process is ever final, that there is ever a product which should be so fetishized that it could never be submitted to appropriative transfiguration. Instead, rap's sampling implies that an artwork's integrity as object should never outweigh the possibilities for continuing creation through use of that object. Its aesthetic thus suggests the Deweyan message that art is more essentially process than finished product, a welcome message in our culture whose tendency to reify and commodify all artistic expression is so strong that rap itself is victimized by this tendency while defiantly protesting it.

In defying the fetishized integrity of artworks, rap also challenges traditional notions of their monumentality, universality, and permanence. . . . In contrast to the standard view that "a poem is forever," rap highlights the artwork's temporality and likely impermanence. . . . By rap's postmodern aesthetic, the ephemeral freshness of artistic creations does not render them aesthetically unworthy; no more than the ephemeral freshness of cream renders its sweet taste unreal. For the view that aesthetic value can only be real if it passes the test of time is simply an entrenched but unjustified presumption, ultimately deriving from the pervasive philosophical bias toward equating reality with the permanent and unchanging.

By refusing to treat art works as eternal monuments for permanent hands-off devotion, by reworking works to make them work better, rap also questions their assumed universality—the dogma that good art should be able to please all people and all ages by focusing only on universal human themes. Hip hop does treat universal themes like injustice and oppression, but it is proudly localized as "ghetto music," thematizing its commitment to the black urban ghetto and its culture. While it typically avoids excluding white society (and white artists), rap focuses on features of ghetto life that whites and middle-class blacks would rather ignore: pimping, prostitution, and drug addiction, as well as rampant venereal disease, street killings, and oppressive harassment by white policemen. Most rappers define their local allegiances in quite specific terms, often not simply by city but by neighborhood, like Compton, Harlem, Brooklyn, or the Bronx. Even when rap goes international, it remains proudly local; we find in French rap, for example, the same targeting of specific neighborhoods and concentration on local problems. . . .

TECHNOLOGY AND MASS-MEDIA CULTURE

Rap's complex attitude toward mass circulation and commercialization reflects another central feature of postmodernism: its fascinated and overwhelming absorption of contemporary technology, particularly that of the mass media. While the commercial products of this technology seem so simple and fruitful to use, both the actual complexities of technological production and its intricate relations to the sustaining socioeconomic system are, for the consumer public, frighteningly unfathomable and unmanageable. Mesmerized by the powers technology provides us, we postmoderns are also vaguely disturbed by the great power it has over us, as the all-pervasive but increasingly incomprehensible medium of our lives. But fascination with its awesome power can afford us the further (perhaps illusory) thrill that in effectively employing technology, we prove ourselves its master. . . .

Hip hop powerfully displays this syndrome, enthusiastically embracing and masterfully appropriating mass-media technology, but still remaining unhappily oppressed and appropriated by that same technological system and its sustaining society. Rap was born of commercial mass-media technology: records and turntables, amplifiers and mixers. Its technological character allowed its artists to create music they could not otherwise make, either because they could not afford the musical instruments required or because they lacked the musical training to play them. Technology constituted its DJs as artists rather than consumers or mere executant technicians. . . .

The creative virtuosity with which rap artists have appropriated new technology is indeed astounding and exhilarating, and it is often acclaimed in rap lyrics. By acrobatically juggling the cutting and changing of many records on multiple turntables, skillful DJs showed their physical as well as artistic mastery of commercial music and its technology. From the initial disco equipment, rap artists have gone on to adopt more (and more advanced) technologies: electronic drums, synthesizers, sounds from calculators and touchtone phones, and sometimes computers which scan entire ranges of possible sounds and then can replicate and synthesize the desired ones.

Mass-media technology has also been crucial to rap's impressively growing popularity. As a product of black culture, an essentially oral rather than written culture, rap needs to be heard and felt immediately, through its energetically moving sound, in order to be properly appreciated. No notational score could transmit its crazy collage of music, and even the lyrics cannot be adequately conveyed in mere written form, divorced from their expressive rhythm, intonation, and surging stress and flow. Only mass-media technology allows for the wide dissemination and preservation of such oral performance events. Both through radio and television broadcasting and through the recording media of records, tapes, and compact discs, rap has been able to reach out beyond its original ghetto audience and thus give its music and message a real hearing, even in white America and Europe. Only through the mass media could hip hop become a very audible voice in our popular culture, one which middle America would like to suppress since it often stridently expresses the frustrating oppression of ghetto life and the proud and pressing desire for social resistance and change. . . . Similarly, only through the mass media could hip hop have achieved artistic fame and fortune, its commercial success enabling renewed artistic investment and serving as a undeniable source of black cultural pride.

Rap not only relies on mass-media techniques and technologies, it derives much of its content and imagery from mass culture. Television shows, sports personalities, arcade games, and familiar name-brand commercial products (for example, Adidas sneakers) are frequently referred to in the lyrics, and their musical themes or jingles are sometimes sampled; a whole series of rap records was based on the Smurf cartoons. Such items of mass-media culture help provide the common cultural background necessary for artistic creation and communication in a society where the tradition of high culture is largely unknown or unappealing, if not also oppressively alien and exclusionary.

But for all its acknowledged gifts, the mass media is not a trusted and unambiguous ally. It is simultaneously the focus of deep suspicion and angry critique. Rappers inveigh against its false and superficial fare, its commercially standardized and sanitized but unreal and mindless content. . . .

Finally, apart form their false, superficial content and repressive censorship, the media are linked to a global commercial system and society which callously exploits and oppresses hip hop's primary audience. Recognizing that those who govern and speak for the dominating technological-commercial complex are indifferent to the enduring woes of the black underclass . . . , rappers protest how our capitalist society exploits the disenfranchised blacks both to preserve its sociopolitical stability (through their service in the military and police) and to increase its profits by increasing their demand for unnecessary consumer goods. One very prominent theme of hip hop is how the advertised ideal of conspicuous consumption—luxury cars, clothes, and high-tech appliances—lures many ghetto youth to a life of crime, a life which promises the quick attainment of such commodities but typically ends in death, jail, or destitution, thus reinforcing the ghetto cycle of poverty and despair.

It is one of the postmodern paradoxes of hip hop that rappers extol their own achievement of consumerist luxury while simultaneously condemning its uncritical idealization and quest as misguided and dangerous for their audience in the ghetto community to which they ardently avow their solidarity and allegiance. In the same way, self-declared "underground" rappers at once denigrate commercialism as an artistic and political sell-out, but nonetheless glorify their own commercial success, often even regarding it as indicative of their artistic power. Such contradictions are perhaps expressive of the postmodern fragmentation of the self into inconsistent personae, but they may be equally expressive of more fundamental contradictions in the sociocultural fields of ghetto life and so-called noncommercial art. Certainly there is a very deep connection in Afro-American culture between independent expression and economic achievement which would impel even noncommercial rappers to tout their commercial success and property. For, as Houston Baker so well demonstrates, Afro-American artists must always, consciously or unconsciously, come to terms with the history of slavery and commercial exploitation which forms the ground of black experience and expression. As slaves were converted from independent humans to property, their way to regain independence was to achieve sufficient property of their own so as to buy their manumission (as in the traditional liberation narrative of Frederick Douglass). Having long been denied a voice because they were property, Afro-Americans could reasonably conclude "that *only* property enables expression." For underground rappers, then, commercial success and its luxury trappings may function essentially as signs of an economic independence which enables free artistic and political expression and which is conversely also enabled by such expression. A major dimension of this celebrated economic independence is its independence from crime.

AUTONOMY AND DISTANCE

. . . Modernity, according to Weber and others, was bound up with the project of occidental rationalization, secularization, and differentiation which disenchanted the traditional religious worldview and carved up its organic domain into three separate and autonomous spheres of secular culture: science, art, and morality, each governed by its own inner logic of theoretical, aesthetic, or moral-practical judgment. This tripartite division was of course powerfully reflected and reinforced by Kant's critical analysis of human thinking in terms of pure reason, practical reason, and aesthetic judgment.

In this division of cultural spheres, art was distinguished from science as not being concerned with the formulation or dissemination of knowledge, since its aesthetic judgment was essentially nonconceptual and subjective. It was also sharply differentiated from the practical activity of the realm of ethics and politics, which involved real interests and appetitive will (as well as conceptual thinking). Instead, art was consigned to a disinterested, imaginative realm which Schiller later described as the realm of play and semblance. As the aesthetic was distinguished from the more rational realms of knowledge and action, it was also firmly differentiated from the more sensate and appetitive gratifications of embodied human nature—aesthetic pleasure residing, rather, in distanced, disinterested contemplation of formal properties.

Hip hop's genre of "knowledge rap" (or "message rap") is dedicated to the defiant violation of this compartmentalized, trivializing, and eviscerating view of art and the aesthetic. Such rappers repeatedly insist that their role as artists and poets is inseparable from their role as insightful inquirers into reality and teachers of truth, particularly those aspects of reality and truth which get neglected or distorted by establishment history books and contemporary media coverage. . . .

Of course, the realities and truths which hip hop reveals are not the transcendental eternal verities of traditional philosophy, but rather the mutable but coercive facts and patterns of the material sociohistorical world. Yet this emphasis on the temporally changing and malleable nature of the real (reflected in rap's frequent time tags and its popular idiom of "knowing what time it is") constitutes a respectably tenable metaphysical position associated with American pragmatism. Though few may know it, rap philosophers are really "down with" Dewey, not merely in metaphysics but in a non-compartmentalized aesthetics which highlights social function, process, and embodied experience.

For knowledge rap not only insists on uniting the aesthetic and the cognitive, but equally stresses that practical functionality can form part of artistic meaning and value. Many rap songs are explicitly devoted to raising black political consciousness, pride, and revolutionary impulses; some make the powerful point that aesthetic judgments, and particularly the question of what counts as art, involve political issues of legitimation and social struggle in which rap is engaged as progressive praxis and which it advances by its very self-assertion as art. Other raps function as street-smart moral fables, offering cautionary narratives and practical advice on problems of crime, drugs, and sexual hygiene (for example, Ice-T's "Drama" and "High Rollers," Cool Moe Dee's "Monster Crack" and "Go See the Doctor," BDP's "Stop the Violence" and "Jimmy"). Finally, we should note that rap has been used effectively to teach writing and reading skills and black history in the ghetto classroom. . . .

. . . Why does proper aesthetic response traditionally require distanced contemplation by a putatively transcendent and coolly disinterested subject? This assumption of the necessity of distance is yet another manifestation of the modernist convention of artistic purity and autonomy which hip hop repudiates. Indeed, rather than an aesthetic of distanced, disengaged, formalist judgment, rappers urge an aesthetic of deeply embodied participatory involvement, with content as well as form. They want to be appreciated primarily through energetic and impassioned dance, not through immobile contemplation and dispassionate study. . . . This aesthetic of divine yet bodily possession is strikingly similar to Plato's account of poetry and its appreciation as a chain of divine madness extending from the Muse through the artists and performers to the audience, a seizure which for all its divinity was criticized as regrettably irrational and inferior to true knowledge. More importantly, the spiritual ecstasy of divine bodily possession should remind us of Vodun and the metaphysics of African religion to which the aesthetics of Afro-American music has indeed been traced.

What could be further from modernity's project of rationalization and secularization, what more inimical to modernism's rationalized, disembodied, and formalized aesthetic? No wonder the established modernist aesthetic is so hostile to rap and to rock music in general. If there is a viable space between the modern rationalized aesthetic and an altogether irrational one whose rabid Dionysian excess must vitiate its cognitive, didactic, and political claims, this is the space for a postmodern aesthetic. I think the fine art of rap inhabits that space, and I hope it will continue to thrive there.

Thomas Heyd

UNDERSTANDING PERFORMANCE ART

Thomas Heyd teaches philosophy at the University of Victoria. Heyd argues that performance artists are not being self-contradictory when they claim that performance art "goes beyond art." Challenging the boundary that separates art from non-art is a significant artistic endeavor in its own right, and some performance artists succeed in producing work that does indeed cross this boundary.

INTRODUCTION

Rat Sniffy as prime performer of Rick Gibson's "rat piece" (*Free Art Lesson*, 1990) recently made the headlines when media and animal activists found out that the script included the annihilation, compliments of a 25 kg. concrete block, of Sniffy. Disregarding here the complex moral dimension, it is clear that many may wonder where the *art* is meant to be in this piece. Performance art pieces, probably more frequently than pieces from the other arts, have elicited from the public the puzzled question "is it art?"

Such queries are not entirely unjustified since performance artists themselves have sought to question the relation between art and the institution of art. At least for some

performance pieces it is claimed that they deliberately seek to break through the limitations imposed on the role of art by convention; such pieces are meant to go *beyond art*, while *remaining*, in some sense, *under the auspices of art*. I propose that the conception of art that lies behind these attempts at going beyond art deserves our attention and makes performance an especially interesting art form.

There are some problems that performance art has to face, though. It may be claimed that artists who attempt to go beyond art are oblivious of the past, since history has *already* shown that such attempts must end in failure. Moreover, it may be argued that the attempt to make art that *transcends* art must be doomed simply because it is *self-contradictory*.

Thomas Heyd, "Understanding Performing Art: Art Beyond Art," *British Journal of Aesthetics* 31.1 (1991): 68–73.

In reply I shall suggest, first, that history is not un-ambiguous in its verdict with regard to the success or failure of previous attempts to go beyond art; and, second, that such attempts are only *apparently* self-contradictory.

As we shall see, art which goes beyond art indeed makes some traditional art-identificatory requirements the mere result of historical accident. I will also briefly note that this alternative conception of art has received support from thinkers of both ancient and modern times. I shall close by providing some examples of performances that most obviously seem to succeed in being art beyond art.

Earlier this century the movements which have been called the historical avant-garde (by which generally is meant Dada, Futurism, Surrealism and the Russian Avant-Garde) had already sought to transcend art by seeking the integration of art and life. According to avant-garde theorist Peter Bürger, art was to be "sublated" (*aufgehoben*) in the praxis of life, which means not only that art was to be *eliminated qua* art through its integration in life, but also that it was to *survive* in some sense by the transformation which it was to effect in life. . . .

If Bürger were correct in his assessment of those expressions of contemporary art that retain the aims of the historical avant-garde, namely that such art is doomed to fail since in his view it merely imitates ploys of failed avant-garde movements, we should be able to find significant signs of failure, for example, in contemporary performance art. In fact, apparent symptoms can readily be found. Instead of inciting new life praxes, performance pieces are sometimes received as works merely carried out in a new style or fashion. Such perceptions may be strengthened by poorly thought out pieces that are unable to maintain the interest of their audience because of their simplistic minimalism.

Actually, it may be supposed that the apparent difficulties in attaining the goal of integrating art and life encountered by avant-garde and performance artists are *inevitable* since avant-gardiste art seems *self-contradictory* in intention: either the sublation of art in life is successful, in which case it stops being perceived, and becomes invisible, as art, or the sublation is not successful, in which case art remains strictly within the institution of art and may not be perceived as relevant to life concerns; in either case the avant-gardiste project apparently *fails*. Hence Bürger speaks of happenings and "the neo-avant-garde" as attempts to repeat the impossible, because contradictory, project of the avant-garde.

In the following I will suggest that it is *not* so clear that the avant-garde really *did* fail. Moreover, I will claim that the attempt to produce art that goes *beyond art* need not be self-contradictory, since the intentional ambiguity inherent in this sort of art may actually be instrumental in the *achievement* of the sought-for integration of art and life.

PERFORMANCE ART THAT GOES BEYOND ART DOES MAKE SENSE

Bürger's negative assessment of the avant-garde project seems to rely largely on the fact that he expects the avant-garde to bring about a *thoroughgoing* transformation of the relation between the institution of art and life, perhaps on the scale of a revolution. Since art still exists as a recognizable institution, and life has not become a work of art for any significant fraction of humanity, it might indeed seem that the avant-garde failed. The effect of the avant-garde, however, may be more *subtle* than that.

Some performance pieces, such as those introduced below, quite evidently do accomplish the aim of being art beyond art, despite the problems in production and reception noted above. And precisely in so far as art, which comes close to the achievement of avant-gardiste aims, *is* made today, one may suppose that the avant-garde *has* had an effect on art and life.

Moreover, art which tries to go beyond art *need not* be self-contradictory since we may conceive of pieces that show their relevance to life concerns while remaining recognizable as art. Such pieces indicate their artistic character by drawing attention to their *signal value*, while they show their relevance to life by addressing issues that are of concern *outside* the world of art. In fact, the inherent ambiguity of avant-gardiste art may play an important role in its effectiveness: as long as a piece keeps one wondering if it is art or not, attention will be focused on making sense of it. In other words, art which *is* successful in its attempts to go beyond art may achieve its effectiveness by keeping the audience unsure about the category to which a piece should be assigned.

This way of conceiving of art emphasizes the life-transformative role which a piece may play, and de-emphasizes the importance of aesthetic qualities and the role of the artist *qua* intentional creator. As a consequence, pieces of this sort may be judged by some to fall outside the parameters of art. In one sense unconcern with these particular aspects of traditional art need not be seen as a break with Western thinking about art, however, because art repeatedly has been conceived as a life-reformative force ever since Plato proposed that in the ideal state poetry should suit the educational purposes required for a just state.

One of the most interesting occasions, in our context, in which art has been called upon in this manner occurred in modern times when the term "avant-garde" was first applied to art. Its use there serves the intent of singling out the arts as the *leading force in social change*. . . .

To conclude I describe some performance art pieces to illustrate that art beyond art may be realizable, and that this art form may be particularly apt for this life-transformative purpose.

ART BEYOND ART: SOME PERFORMANCE ART PIECES

As is to be expected, the pieces that perhaps best exemplify art beyond art often may be perceived as something other than art. Among the works that achieve the goal of integrating art and life most effectively we may count Bené Fonteles's 1984, 1986 and 1987 garbage delivery performances. These performances consisted of the delivery to the main square of the city of Cuiabá, Brazil, of whole truckloads of garbage. The point of the pieces was that Fonteles wanted to "bring back to the people of Cuiabá the garbage and litter they left behind in the forest, creeks and waterfalls during weekend picnics."

Fonteles's actions would ordinarily be classed as a kind of eco-political protest. These actions, however, are also an integral part of his performance and installation work which consistently addresses itself to the natural environment and human interactions with it.

Greenpeace's dramatic actions, such as the plugging of chemical effluent pipes and the hanging of banners on tall smokestacks, on bridges, and at symbol-laden locations such as on the Statue of Liberty (1984) or on Mount Rushmore (1987), also tend to be seen as solely political. None the less, it has been argued that these types of actions should be included in "the history of protest theater" or "guerrilla theater."

These Greenpeace pieces should be considered as performances that exemplify art beyond art because, despite their rational appeal for changes in societal/corporate behavior, they achieve their political effect through the creation of potentially ambivalent imagery. Their imagery incites reflection since these actions usually are provocative and sometimes appear to bring on the defilement of quasi-sacred locations. They are, however, not merely meant as gestures of resentment but as "bearing witness" to, or taking responsibility for, injustices. These pieces are also exemplars of the integration of art and life in so far as they involve the demonstration of serious personal commitment, to the point of personal risk.

Art that effectively goes beyond art, of course, takes on many forms. Among the many other performance pieces concerning which there is no doubt that art and life have met one may count, for example, Stuart Brisley's *Artist Project Peterlee* (1976) or Joseph Beuys's *7000 Oaks* (1982–87). Brisley's piece involved a long residence in the newly created industrial town where he gathered accounts of the experiences of the original inhabitants of the area in order to help the new people settled there develop a sense of rootedness. Beuys's piece involved the gathering of support, in the face of considerable resistance, for the planting of 7000 oaks throughout Kassel, Germany. Even Gibson's "rat piece" must be considered a success *qua* art beyond art since its apparently ambivalent character forced the public to focus on a very life-related event (i.e., the killing of a rat) that, despite its frequency, ordinarily causes little interest or active concern.

In each of these cases one may only note the effect that the actions have on immediate socio-political conditions, and conclude that they merely are *local* interventions for limited practical purposes, or one may only note the place that these actions occupy in the dialectical development of art. As I have tried to suggest above, though, there is another way to frame these events; it is based on the assumption that art may be go *beyond* institutionalized art on the premiss that "the function of art [is] . . . creating images that have an impact on people's lives."

Roland Barthes

THE
STRUCTURALIST
ACTIVITY

Roland Barthes (1915–1980) was a flamboyant French literary critic who developed theories on the nature of writing, codes and systems of signs, and the mythology of everyday life. He was also a part of the "New Criticism" movement, which urged that literary criticism should focus on literary works themselves, instead of the sentiment they produce or the background of their production. Barthes utilized structuralist analyses in some of his theorizing. The following essay states his understanding of the structuralist approach and its value.

. . . The first thing to be said is that in relation to *all* its users, structuralism is essentially an *activity*, i.e., the controlled succession of a certain number of mental operations: we might speak of structuralist activity as we once spoke of surrealist activity (surrealism, moreover, may well have produced the first experience of structural literature, a possibility which must some day be explored). But before seeing what these operations are, we must say a word about their goal.

The goal of all structuralist activity, whether reflexive or poetic, is to reconstruct an "object" in such a way as to manifest thereby the rules of functioning (the "functions") of this object. Structure is therefore actually a *simulacrum* of the object, but a directed, *interested* simulacrum, since the imitated object makes something appear which remained invisible, or if one prefers, unintelligible in the natural object. Structural man takes the real, decomposes it, then recomposes it; this appears to be little enough (which makes some say that the structuralist enterprise is "meaningless," "uninteresting," "useless," etc.). Yet, from another point of view, this "little enough" is decisive: for between the two objects, or the two tenses, of structuralist activity, there occurs *something new*, and what is new is nothing less than the

Roland Barthes, *Essais Critiques*, trans. Richard Howard (Paris: Editions du Seuil, 1964); *Partisan Review* 34.1 (1967): 82–88.

generally intelligible: the simulacrum is intellect added to object, and this addition has an anthropological value, in that it is man himself, his history, his situation, his freedom and the very resistance which nature offers to his mind.

We see, then, why we must speak of a structuralist *activity*: creation or reflection are not, here, an original "impression" of the world, but a veritable fabrication of a world which resembles the first one, not in order to copy it but to render it intelligible. Hence one might say that structuralism is essentially *an activity of imitation*, which is also why there is, strictly speaking, no *technical* difference between structuralism as an intellectual activity on the one hand and literature in particular, art in general on the other: both derive from a *mimesis*, based not on the analogy of substances (as in so-called realist art), but on the analogy of functions. . . .

It is of little consequence whether the initial object liable to the simulacrum-activity is given by the world in an already assembled fashion (in the case of the structural analysis made of a constituted language or society or work) or is still scattered (in the case of the structural "composition"); whether this initial object is drawn from a social reality or an imaginary reality. It is not the nature of the copied object which defines an art (though this is a tenacious prejudice in all realism), it is the fact that man adds to it in reconstructing it: technique is the very being of all creation. It is therefore to the degree that the goals of structuralist activity are indissolubly linked to a certain technique that structuralism exists in a distinctive fashion in relation to other modes of analysis or creation: we recompose the object *in order* to make certain functions appear, and it is, so to speak, the way that makes the work; this is why we must speak of the structuralist activity rather than the structuralist work.

The structuralist activity involves two typical operations: dissection and articula-

tion. To dissect the first object, the one which is given to the simulacrum-activity, is to find in it certain mobile fragments whose differential situation engenders a certain meaning; the fragment has no meaning in itself, but it is nonetheless such that the slightest variation wrought in its configuration produces a change in the whole; a *square* by Mondrian, a *series* by Pousseur, a *versicle* of Butor's *Mobile*, the "mytheme" in Lévi-Strauss, the phoneme in the work of the phonologists, the "theme" in certain literary criticism—all these units (whatever their inner structure and their extent, quite different according to cases) have no significant existence except by their frontiers: those which separate them from other actual units of the discourse (but this is a problem of articulation) and also those which distinguish them from other virtual units, with which they form a certain class (which linguistics calls a *paradigm*); this notion of a paradigm is essential, apparently, if we are to understand the structuralist vision: the paradigm is a group, a reservoir—as limited as possible—of objects (of units) from which one summons, by an act of citation, the object or unit one wishes to endow with an actual meaning; what characterizes the paradigmatic object is that it is, vis-à-vis other objects of its class, in a certain relation of affinity and dissimilarity: two units of the same paradigm must resemble each other somewhat *in order* that the difference which separates them be indeed evident. . . .

The American automobiles (in Butor's *Mobile*) must be constantly regarded in the same way, yet they must differ each time by both their make and color; the episodes of the Oedipus myth (in Lévi-Strauss's analysis) must be both identical and varied—in order that all these languages, these works may be intelligible. . . .

Once the units are posited, structural man must discover in them or establish for them certain rules of association: this is the activity of articulation, which succeeds the summoning activity. The syntax of the arts and of discourse is, as we know, extremely varied; but what we discover in every work of structural enterprise is the submission to regular constraints whose formalism, improperly indicted, is much less important than their stability; for what is happening, at this second stage of the simulacrum-activity, is a kind of battle against chance; this is why the constraint of recurrence of the units has an almost demiurgic value: it is by the regular return of the units and of the associations of units that the work appears constructed, i.e., endowed with meaning; linguistics calls these rules of combination *forms*, and it would be advantageous to retain this rigorous sense of an overtaxed word: the work of art is what man wrests from chance. This perhaps allows us to understand on the one hand why so-called nonfigurative works are nonetheless to the highest degree works of art, human thought being established not on the analogy of copies and models but with the regularity of assemblages; and on the other hand why these same works appear, precisely, fortuitous and thereby useless to those who discern in them no *form*: in front of an abstract painting, Khrushchev was certainly wrong to see only the traces of a donkey's tail whisked across the canvas; at least he knew in his way, though, that art is a certain con-

quest of chance (he simply forgot that every rule must be learned, whether one wants to apply or interpret it).

The simulacrum, thus constructed, does not render the world as it has found it, and it is here that structuralism is important. First of all, it manifests a new category of the object, which is neither the real nor the rational, but the *functional*, thereby joining a whole scientific complex which is being developed around information theory and research. Subsequently and especially, it highlights the strictly human process by which men give meaning to things. Is this new? To a certain degree, yes; of course the world has never stopped looking for the meaning of what is given it and of what it produces; what is new is a mode of thought (or a "poetics") which seeks less to assign completed meanings to the objects it discovers than to know how meaning is possible, at what cost and by what means. Ultimately, one might say that the object of structuralism is not man endowed with meanings, but man fabricating meanings, as if it could not be the *content* of meanings which exhausted the semantic goals of humanity, but only the act by which these meanings, historical and contingent variables, are produced. *Homo significans*: such would be the new man of structural inquiry.

Jenene J. Allison

DECONSTRUCTION AND THE ENERGIZER BUNNY RABBIT

Jenene J. Allison is the director of the DuBarry Foundation, based in Boston, Massachusetts. She is a specialist in eighteenth-century French literature and author of Revealing Difference: The Fiction of Isabelle de Charrière. *In this selection (written in 1994), Allison describes the basic moves involved in deconstructive criticism, taking as her point of departure a well-known series of Energizer battery advertisements.*

Alice Jardine, a feminist theorist well versed in the complexities of deconstruction, has suggested that "entering into a text with Derrida is like getting lost in a funhouse where no One is home."[1] Such a pithy description nonetheless highlights all the salient factors. In bringing the philosophical reflections of Jacques Derrida to bear on a text, be it literary or otherwise, one (not the "One" who is seemingly absent) engages in a progression governed by parameters that contest our everyday sense of what makes sense. Derrida himself, responding to a question at a conference in 1966, said: "I am trying, precisely, to put myself at a point so that I do not know any longer where I am going."[2] Yet the way of thinking designated by the term "deconstruction," once the exclusive property of academics, has also been simplified (one might say domesticated) and appropriated by less exclusive groups. Deconstruction has been integrated into spoken English to such a degree that a recent made-for-TV movie could be entitled "Deconstructing Sara." In what follows I offer an illustration of deconstruction. This illustration, designed to be faithful to the original, philosophical sense of the word rather than to its current, colloquial meaning, is drawn from the media and is offered in the spirit of entering into a funhouse albeit with a serious objective. By way of giving a sense of deconstruction, I propose to consider the advertising campaign for Energizer batteries, specifically ads showing the Energizer bunny rabbit.

To begin with a historical note it is necessary to bear in mind that originally deconstruction was not a methodology. Thus in 1979, Geoffrey Hartman's preface to *Deconstruction and Criticism* refers to "Deconstruction, as it has come to be called. . . ."[3] At first it represented a reaction against a certain direction in philosophy, a reaction that may be understood in two different ways. In one sense, deconstruction was an effort to think outside of philosophy and in another sense it was an effort to think through the very center of philosophical inquiry.

Working along the line of reasoning that tended to situate deconstruction outside philosophy, critics drew attention to a certain area of discomfort in philosophy, namely the issue of writing. In order to do philosophy, one writes philosophical texts. At the same time, philosophers have the suspicion that in writing they may be betrayed. This discomfort is hardly new. Francis Bacon (1561–1626) complained about what happened when philosophers tried to write exceptionally well: "men began to hunt more after words than matter; and more after . . . tropes and figures, than after the weight of matter, . . . soundness of argument."[4] Philosophers are becoming more involved in how prettily or how astutely they express themselves, and this is to the detriment of the enquiry they are pursuing. Bacon's complaint sets up an opposition. He is distinguishing, on the one hand, tropes, metaphors, rhetorical expression, and, on the other hand, the meat of philosophy, the weight of the matter, the soundness of the argument. In expressing this discomfort relative to writing Bacon sets up an opposition: it is at this point that deconstruction, in the twentieth century, will be situated. In effect, the critics who elaborated deconstruction took the discomfort felt by the philosopher in the act of writing and exacerbated it.

The problem of distinguishing between the intellectual matter of a statement and the language in which it is couched is not just a problem for philosophy. In art, we make a distinction between what is extraneous to the art work and the force of the art work itself. Indeed, playing with this distinction, inverting it, subverting it, denying it, has itself become an influence on artists. The problem is perhaps most complex in literature, for example, where the language

may not be considered extrinsic. Consider the anecdote cited by Deirdre Bair in her not-unauthorized biography of Samuel Beckett.[5] James Joyce was losing his eyesight and Beckett was acting as his secretary. This meant that Joyce would speak while Beckett listened and wrote down what he heard. Joyce was dictating what would eventually be canonized as one of the masterpieces of literature and as Beckett continued to transcribe, someone knocked at the door. "Come in," said Joyce. Later, when Beckett reread to Joyce what he had transcribed, he came across this odd "Come in," and realized what had happened. Just as he was going to erase it, however, Joyce stopped him and requested that it be left in the text. How can we assess the idea that an event so trivial as someone knocking on the door should be integrated into one of our greatest works of literature?

The distinction we make, whether we respect it, deplore it, or subvert it, between language and what it conveys rests on another fundamental concept, that of presence. The role that this term plays within deconstruction represents an effort to think through the very center of philosophical inquiry. When I have a sudden, visceral reaction to what another person has said or done to me, when I think abruptly, "She's lying," for example, I have a sense that I am fully present in that statement. Those are my words, my very thought. We do not always communicate so directly, and in the context of a formal lecture delivered to a class on a specific topic, I am less fully present in the statement I make. I follow a prescribed outline, I suppress any irrelevant thoughts that pop into my mind, I choose my words carefully with the particular audience in mind. At a further remove from the statement I think in my mind would be the case of an actor reading a script. To follow the possibilities to their furthest extreme, consider the movie in which the actor Clint Eastwood said the line "Go ahead—make my day." The first time he said that, he was an actor following a script.

Then "Go ahead—make my day" became a cliché and everyone was using it to express an emotion similar to the one represented by the character Eastwood was playing in the film. In the final form or deformation of this phrase, it would be possible to parody Clint Eastwood movies and to use the machismo implied by "Go ahead—make my day" to mock the very idea of a superhero.

Somewhere within the various contexts in which a given statement may signify, we like to believe that there is a speech act grounded in reality, a speech act on the order of "I swear to tell the truth, the whole truth, and nothing but the truth" as delivered in a judicial act within a functional court of law. But it is difficult to construct an epistemological framework that could enumerate, flawlessly, the rules governing the distinction between Clint Eastwood saying "Go ahead—make my day" in an action movie and a comedian mimicking that phrase in a parody of an action movie.[6] To be able to say that one is more present, more real, more truthful than the other in an absolute and exhaustive way leads to such complications that the complications themselves become of interest. It was this line of inquiry that the critics who originally worked on deconstruction followed. In the words of Geoffrey Hartman,

> Deconstruction . . . refuses to identify the force of literature with any concept of embodied meaning and shows how deeply such logocentric or incarnationist perspectives have influenced the way we think about art. We assume that, by the miracle of art, the "presence of the word" is equivalent to the presence of meaning. But the opposite can also be urged, that the word carries with it a certain absence or indeterminacy of meaning.[7]

Of particular interest was the idea that just when one is depending on being able to distinguish between these two types of truth, one is going to be tripped up by the difficulty of so doing.

The status of writing, or language, and the meaning of presence are, then, the two focal points of the criticism leveled by deconstruction at philosophy. At this point I would like to outline deconstruction. (Here I refer to deconstruction as it has come to be practiced, as a methodology.) This outline will involve four steps. The first step is to observe an opposition. In the course of a deconstruction the critic will show that this opposition is not an opposition but a hierarchy.

In a hierarchy, one part dominates and one part is suppressed, so that the situation in a hierarchy is much less innocuous than the situation in a simple opposition. The second step in a deconstruction is to take the hierarchy and to reverse it, so that what formerly dominated is suppressed, and what was suppressed comes to dominate. As an example of this we may take Derrida's own signature, such as he appended it to one of the founding documents of deconstruction: the article entitled "Signature, Event, Context."[8] Derrida's signature appears at the conclusion of his text, and to the left of the signature, and so parallel with it, he wrote, "the—written—text of this—oral—communication was to be delivered to the Association des sociétés de philosophie de langue française before the meeting. That dispatch should thus have been signed. Which I do, and counterfeit, here. Where? There. J. D."[9] A counterfeit is the opposite of a true signature. What Derrida is doing when he signs and states that in signing he is counterfeiting, is reversing a hierarchy. In principle, between a signature and a counterfeit, one feels that the signature is truer, more valid, whereas the counterfeit is derivative, less valid, a mere copy. Here Derrida reverses that by asserting that in signing his name he is actually counterfeiting it because it can now be duplicated infinitely. His signature is no longer a one-time-only gesture, a unique item. It is an item that can be duplicated. (By pulling the rug pulled out from the authority traditionally attributed to a signature, Derrida's serious/provocative/mischievous gesture at the conclusion of "Signature, Event, Context" provides a good example of what it feels like to be in the funhouse to which Jardine refers.)

The third step of a deconstruction would be the displacement of the system within the original opposition obtained. Jonathan Culler, who has written extensively and, I believe, eloquently about deconstruction puts it in these terms: "The practitioner of deconstruction works within the terms of the system but in order to breach it."[10] That's the point at which one moves from reversing the hierarchy to displacing the system supporting it. After this third step, a deconstruction would involve having put the whole system into question. This general and perhaps vague notion may be clarified by the example which follows.

Before embarking on the example of the Energizer battery ads featuring a pink, drum-beating bunny, it is perhaps helpful to think of a different rabbit: the rabbit in the famous duck-rabbit drawing. This picture looks like a duck with a beak pointing to the left, or else like a rabbit looking to the right with his ears pointed left depending on how you focus.[11] The ability to change what is seen depending on the focus used is what counts in this instance. This is a useful warm-up exercise before thinking about deconstruction.

It is unfortunate, but significant, that the Energizer battery ads I will discuss have been superseded by more conventional ones, a matter to which I will return. The ads that pertain to deconstruction were ads that worked on two levels and they ranged from the mundane to the sublime. A good first example is the ad that began with a couple in a hot air balloon. One person says to the other person, "Boy, I'll bet you're glad you don't have to go the bathroom. You had diarrhea earlier on, and you couldn't do this if you still did." The other person answers that having taken a particular stomach remedy they feel fine. While the name given to the remedy might strike the viewer as a bit

unsophisticated, the ad, up until this point, seemed like an ad for the stomach remedy in question. Then suddenly the sound of a little electric drum being pounded is heard, and the Energizer bunny rabbit appears in the corner of the screen, powered by its Energizer battery, moving through the air toward the couple in the balloon. Only at this point did the viewer become aware that the ad was for batteries, not for medicine.

Another such ad showed a white, middle-aged man in a lab coat, standing in a computer-filled laboratory. He would say, "If you have allergies and need relief, use Nasex." While the approach to selling the product seemed, once again, unsophisticated, it was not unduly so. Then suddenly the sound of the drum being pounded is heard, and the Energizer bunny rabbit appears, waddling across the top of a table, pushing off lab equipment. The pseudo-doctor stares at the little toy and the viewer "gets it": the ad is for batteries, not for medicine.

What these ads shared in common, apart from the battery in question, was a form that mimicked ads, a form that was intended to be undermined. A more elegant example than the preceding ones will illustrate this. The ad opens with a young couple running through the fields. Soon they lie down and become amorous to the tune of genuine classical music playing in the background. The voice-over begins and announces a new film by a French director. The title appears in white on black script, and until the Energizer bunny rabbit suddenly appeared, I was wondering why I had never heard of this particular French director.

To begin illustrating deconstruction using this type of ad, we start with an opposition: in the case of a television ad the opposition is between how the message is conveyed and the message itself. The scenarios featuring characters or endorsing the product may vary, but the message remains the same: buy product X. What the Energizer battery ads did was to show the hierarchy in this opposition, a gesture equivalent to the second step in a deconstruction. The hierarchy that obtained in the hot air balloon ad or in the French film ad, and that obtains in any television advertising, sets the message itself (buy product X) above how the message is conveyed (the scenarios used). When the pink toy bunny comes booming along, this hierarchy is reversed: now what is important is how the message is conveyed (the false scenario for a stomach remedy, the false clip from a non-existent French movie) because the viewer's sense of having "been had," their startled discovery that the ad was not a real ad but a fake ad for a completely different product, is what makes the Energizer battery ad effective and gives it a particular and memorable forcefulness. Going back to what Jonathan Culler wrote about deconstruction, "The practitioner of deconstruction works within the terms of the system but in order to breach it," we might say that the Energizer bunny works within the terms of television advertising but in order to subvert it and, in so doing, sell more batteries.

After the reversal of the hierarchy, we need the displacement of the system that is characteristic of a deconstruction. After a viewer has watched one of these battery ads, maybe they will choose Energizer batteries over another brand the next time they are shopping; in addition, however, they have been confronted with the falseness of the reality depicted in television advertising. As soon as the pink toy bunny comes into the picture, the viewer is reminded that the reality in which they had been temporarily engaged, the hot air balloon trip, the medical lab, the film about an amorous couple, is pure fabrication. This continues to be true well after appeal to buy Energizer batteries has been exhausted.

If this example was not drawn from popular culture, if it was a real deconstruction, one would not stop here. One would have to deconstruct what happens when the pink toy bunny shows up the falseness of the ad apparently under way. Because the ads in question are just that, they go on further. In fact, these subversive ads have been replaced by ads that depend on other stories: *The Wizard of Oz, Dracula, King Kong.*[12] The newer ads are more conservative and less interesting, in that they draw on fictions that are not particular to the medium of television itself. On the other hand, the pink toy bunny with its penchant for showing up in unexpected places has itself become a cliché, much like Eastwood's "Go ahead—make my day." In *Hot Shots, Part Deux,* Charlie Sheen is shown in a particularly murderous moment, killing off his enemies in a continuous barrage of machine gun fire. The Energizer bunny rabbit walks determinedly into this carnage, beating its little drum. Sheen blows it to bits saying, "At last," perhaps giving voice to the force against which the original ads exercised their light-hearted contestation.

To go beyond the ads discussed here, to carry out a deconstruction in this context, would involve thinking of a way to undermine the very form of representation for which television is the vehicle. To keep the bunny going, as it were, through its own deconstruction. Yet it is crucial to bear in mind that deconstruction, as Derrida has said, "has nothing to do with destruction. That is to say, it is simply a question of (and this is a necessity of criticism in the classical sense of the word) being alert to the implications, to the historical sedimentation of the language we use—and that is not destruction."[13] To enter the funhouse and discover that "no One" is home is hardly the same as never going anywhere at all.

[1]Alice Jardine, *Gynesis: Configurations of Woman and Modernity* (Ithaca: Cornell University Press, 1985), 127.

[2]Jacques Derrida, "Structure, Sign, and Play in the Discourse of the Human Sciences" in Richard Macksey and Eugenio Donato, *The Structuralist Controversy: The Languages of Criticism and*

Kwame Anthony Appiah

IS THE POST-
IN POSTMODERNISM
THE POST-
IN POSTCOLONIAL?

*Kwame Anthony Appiah is Laurance S. Rockefeller
University Professor of Philosophy at the University
Center for Human Values at Princeton University. His
books include* For Truth in Semantics, Necessary Questions,
and In My Father's House, *which analyzes the situation of
postcolonial Africa. In this selection, Appiah considers
whether the imbalance of power involved in the
postcolonial situation is also evident in "postmodernist"
concern with African art and literature.*

In 1987, the Center for African Art in New York organized a show entitled "Perspectives: Angles on African Art." The curator, Susan Vogel, had worked with a number of "cocurators," whom I list in order of their appearance in the table of contents of the exhibition catalogue: Ekpo Eyo, quondam director of the department of antiquities of the National Museum of Nigeria; William Rubin, director of the department of painting and sculpture at the museum of Modern Art and organizer of its controversial exhibit, "Primitivism and Twentieth-Century Art"; Romare Bearden, African-American painter; Ivan Karp, curator of African ethnology at the Smithsonian; Nancy Graves, European-American painter, sculptor, and filmmaker; James Baldwin, who surely needs no qualifying glosses; David Rockefeller, art collector and friend of the mighty; Loela Kouakou, Baule artist and diviner from the Ivory Coast (this a delicious juxtaposition, richest and poorest, side by side); Iba N'Diaye, Senegalese sculptor; and Robert Farris Thompson, Yale professor and African and African-American art historian. In her introductory essay, Vogel describes the process of selection used to pick artworks for the show. The one woman and nine men were each offered a hundred-odd photographs of "African art as varied in type and origin, and as high in quality, as we could manage" and asked to select ten for the show. Or, I should say more exactly, this

Kwame Anthony Appiah, "Is the Post- in Postmodernism the Post- in Postcolonial?" *Critical Inquiry* 17 (1991): 336–57.

is what was offered to eight of the men. For Vogel adds "in the case of the Baule artist, a man familiar only with the art of his own people, only Baule objects were placed in the pool of photographs." . . . At this point we are directed to a footnote to the essay, which reads:

> Showing him the same assortment of photos the others saw would have been interesting, but confusing in terms of the reactions we sought here. Field aesthetics studies, my own and others, have shown that African informants will criticize sculptures from other ethnic groups in terms of their own traditional criteria, often assuming that such works are simply inept carvings of their own aesthetic tradition.

I shall return to this irresistible footnote in a moment. But let me pause to quote further, this time from the words of David Rockefeller, who would surely never "criticize sculptures from other ethnic groups in terms of [his] own traditional criteria," discussing what the catalogue calls a "Fanti female figure":

> I own somewhat similar things to this, and I have always liked them. This is a rather more sophisticated version than the ones that I've seen, and I thought it was quite beautiful. . . . the total composition has a very contemporary, very Western look to it. It's the kind of thing, I think, that goes very well with . . . contemporary Western things. It would look very good in a modern apartment or house.

We may suppose that Rockefeller was delighted to discover that his final judgment was consistent with the intentions of the sculpture's creators. For a footnote to the earlier checklist—the list of artworks ultimately chosen for the show—reveals that the Baltimore Museum of Art desires to "make public the fact that the authenticity of the Fante figure in its collection has been challenged." Indeed, work by Doran Ross

suggests this object is almost certainly a modern piece produced in my hometown of Kumasi by the workshop of a certain Francis Akwasi, which "specializes in carvings for the international market in the style of traditional sculpture. Many of its works are now in museums throughout the West, and were published as authentic by Cole and Ross" (yes, the same Doran Ross) in their classic catalogue, *The Arts of Ghana*.

But then it is hard to be *sure* what would please a man who gives as his reason for picking another piece, this time a Senufo helmet mask, "I have to say that I picked this because I own it. It was given to me by President Houphouet Boigny of the Ivory Coast"; or who remarks "concerning the market in African art":

> the best pieces are going for very high prices. Generally speaking, the less good pieces in terms of quality are not going up in price. And that's a fine reason for picking the good ones rather than the bad. They have a way of becoming more valuable.
>
> I look at African art as objects I find would be appealing to use in a home or an office. . . . I don't think it goes with everything, necessarily—although the very best perhaps does. But I think it goes well with contemporary architecture.

There is something breathtakingly unpretentious in Rockefeller's easy movement between considerations of finance, aesthetics, and decor. In these responses, we have surely a microcosm of the site of the African in contemporary—which is, then, surely to say, postmodern—America.

I have quoted so much from Rockefeller not to emphasize the familiar fact that questions of what we call "aesthetic" value are crucially bound up with market value, nor even to draw attention to the fact that this is known by those who play the art market. Rather I want to keep clearly before us the fact that David Rockefeller is permitted to say *anything at all* about the arts of Africa because he is a *buyer* and because he is at the *center*, while Lela Kouakou, who merely makes art and who dwells at the margins, is a poor African whose words count only as parts of the commodification—both for those of us who constitute the museum public and for collectors, like Rockefeller—of Baule art. I want to remind you, in short, of how important it is that African art is a *commodity*.

But the cocurator whose choice will set us on our way is James Baldwin, the only cocurator who picked a piece that was not in the mold of the Africa of "Primitivism." The sculpture that will be my touchstone is a Yoruba piece that carries the museum label, *Man with a Bicycle*. Here is some of what Baldwin said about it:

> This something. This has got to be contemporary. He's really going to town! It's very jaunty, very authoritative. His errand might prove to be impossible. . . . He is challenging something—or something has challenged him. He's grounded in immediate reality by the bicycle. . . . He's apparently a very proud and silent man. He's dressed sort of polyglot. Nothing looks like it fits him too well.

Baldwin's reading of this piece is, of course and inevitably, "in terms of [his] own . . . criteria," a reaction contextualized only by the knowledge that bicycles are new in Africa and that this piece, anyway, does not look anything like the works he recalls seeing from his earliest childhood at the Schomburg Museum in Harlem. His response torpedoes Vogel's argument for her notion that the only "authentically traditional" African—the only one whose responses, as she says, could have been found a century ago—must be refused a choice among Africa's art cultures because he—unlike the rest of the cocurators, who are Americans and the European-educated Africans—will use his "own . . . criteria." The message is that this Baule diviner, this authentically African villager, does not know what *we*,

authentic postmodernists, now know: that the first and last mistake is to judge the Other on one's own terms. And so, in the name of this relativist insight, we impose our judgment: that Lela Kouakou may not judge sculpture from beyond the Baule culture zone, because he, like all the other African "informants" we have met in the field, will read them as if they were meant to meet those Baule standards.

Worse than this, it is nonsense to explain Kouakou's responses as deriving from an ignorance of other traditions—if indeed he is, as he no doubt is supposed to be, like most "traditional" artists today, if he is, for example, like Francis Akwasi of Kumasi. Kouakou may judge other artists by his own standards (what on earth else could he, could anyone, do save make no judgment at all?), but to suppose that he is unaware that there are other standards within Africa (let alone without) is to ignore a piece of absolutely basic cultural knowledge, common to most precolonial as well as to most colonial and postcolonial cultures on the continent: the piece of cultural knowledge that explains why the people we now call "Baule" exist at all. To be Baule, for example, is, for a Baule, not to be a white person, not to be Senufo, not to be French.

But Baldwin's *Man with a Bicycle* does more than give the lie to a point of entry to my theme, a piece of contemporary African art that will allow us to explore the articulation of the postcolonial and the postmodern. *Man with a Bicycle* is described as follows in the exhibition catalogue:

> Man with a Bicycle
> Yoruba, Nigeria 20th century
> Wood and paint H. 35¾ in.
> The Newark Museum
>
> The influence of the Western world is revealed in the clothes and bicycle of this neo-traditional Yoruba sculpture which probably represents a merchant en route to market.

It is this word *neotraditional*—a word that is almost right—that provides, I think, the fundamental clue. . . .

. . . I do not (this will come as no surprise) have a definition of the postmodern to put in the place of Jameson's or Lyotard's, but there is now a rough consensus about the structure of the modern/postmodern dichotomy in the many domains—from architecture to poetry to philosophy to rock music to the movies—in which it has been invoked. In each of these domains there is an antecedent practice that laid claim to a certain exclusivity of insight, and in each of them "postmodernism" is a name for the rejection of that claim to exclusivity, a rejection that is almost always more playful, though not necessarily less serious, than the practice it aims to replace. That this will not do as a *definition* of postmodernism follows from the fact that in each domain this rejection of exclusivity assumes a particular shape, one that reflects the specificities of its setting. To understand the various postmodernisms this way is to leave open the question of how their theories of contemporary social, cultural, and economic life relate to the actual practices that constitute that life—to leave open, then, the relations between postmodern*ism* and postmodern*ity.*

It is an important question *why* this distancing of the ancestors should have become so central a feature of our cultural lives. The answer surely has to do with the sense in which art is increasingly commodified. To sell oneself and one's products as art in the marketplace, one must, above all, clear a space in which one is distinguished from other producers and products—and one does this by the construction and the marking of differences. To create a market for bottled waters, for example, it was necessary, first, to establish that subtle (even untestable) differences in mineral content

and source of carbonation were essential modes of distinction.

It is this need for distinctions in the market that accounts for a certain intensification of the long-standing individualism of post-Renaissance art production: in the age of mechanical reproduction, aesthetic individualism, the characterization of the artwork as belonging to the oeuvre of an individual, and the absorption of the artist's life into the conception of the work can be seen precisely as modes of identifying objects for the market. The sculptor of the man with a bicycle, by contrast, will not be known by those who buy this object; his individual life will make no difference to the future history of his sculpture. (Indeed, he surely knows this, in the sense in which one knows anything whose negation one has never even considered.) Nevertheless, there is *some*thing about the object that serves to establish it for the market: the availability of Yoruba culture and of stories about Yoruba culture to surround the object and distinguish it from "folk art" from elsewhere.

Postmodern culture is the culture in which all postmodernisms operate, sometimes in synergy, sometimes in competition; and because contemporary culture is, in a certain sense to which I shall return, transnational, postmodern culture is global—though that emphatically does not mean that it is the culture of every person in the world. . . .

I do not know when *Man with a Bicycle* was made or by whom; African art has, until recently, been collected as the property of "ethnic" groups, not of individuals and workshops, so it is not unusual that not one of the pieces in the "Perspectives" show was identified in the checklist by the name of an individual artist, even though many of them are twentieth-century works. (And no one will be surprised, by contrast, that most of them *are* kindly labeled with the names of the people who own the largely private collections where they now live.) As a result I cannot say if the piece is literally postcolonial, produced after Nigerian independence in 1960. But the piece belongs to a genre that has certainly been produced since then: the genre that is here called *neotraditional*. Simply put, what is distinctive about this genre is that it is produced for the West.

I should qualify. Of course, many of the buyers of first instance live in Africa; many of them are juridically citizens of African states. But African bourgeois consumers of neotraditional art are educated in the Western style, and, if they want African art, they would often rather have a "genuinely" traditional piece, by which I mean a piece that they believe to be made precolonially, or at least in a style and by methods that were already established precolonially. These buyers are a minority. Most of this art— *traditional* because it uses actual or supposed precolonial techniques but *neo-*(this, for what it is worth, is the explanation I promised earlier) because it has elements that are recognizably colonial or postcolonial in reference—has been made for Western tourists and other collectors.

The incorporation of these works in the West's museum culture and its art market has almost nothing, of course, to do with postmodernism. By and large, the ideology through which they are incorporated is modernist: it is the ideology that brought something called "Bali" to Antonin Artaud, something called "Africa" to Pablo Picasso, and something called "Japan" to Roland Barthes. (This incorporation as an official Other was criticized, of course, from its beginnings: hence Oscar Wilde's observation that "the whole of Japan is a pure invention. There is no such country, there are no such people.") What *is* postmodernist is Vogel's muddled conviction that African art should not be judged "in terms of [someone else's] traditional criteria." For modernism, primitive art was to be judged by putatively *uni-* *versal* aesthetic criteria, and by these standards it was finally found possible to value it. The sculptors and painters who found it possible were largely seeking an Archimedean point outside their own cultures for a critique of a Weberian modernity. For *post-* modernisms, by contrast, these works, however they are to be understood, cannot be seen as legitimated by culture- and history-transcending standards.

The *neotraditional* object is useful as a model, despite its marginality in most African lives, because its incorporation in the museum world (as opposed to the many objects made by the same hands that live peacefully in nonbourgeois homes: stools, for example) reminds one that in Africa, by contrast, the distinction between high culture and mass culture, insofar as if it makes sense at all, corresponds, by and large, to the distinction between those with and those without Western-style formal education as cultural consumers.

The fact that the distinction is to be made this way—in most of sub-Saharan Africa, excluding the Republic of South Africa— means that the opposition between high culture and mass culture is available only in domains where there is a significant body of Western formal training. This excludes (in most places) the plastic arts and music. There are distinctions of genre and audience in African music, and for various cultural purposes there is something we call "traditional" music that we still practice and value; but village and urban dwellers alike, bourgeois and nonbourgeois, listen, through discs and, more important, on the radio, to reggae, to Michael Jackson, and to King Sonny Adé.

And this means that, by and large, the domain in which such a distinction makes the most sense is the one domain where that distinction is powerful and pervasive: in African writing in Western languages. So that it is here that we find, I think, a place for consideration of the question of the *post-* coloniality of contemporary African culture.

Postcoloniality is the condition of . . . a relatively small, Western-style, Western-trained group of writers and thinkers, who mediate the trade in cultural commodities of world capitalism at the periphery. In the West they are known through the Africa they offer; their compatriots know them both through the West they present to Africa and through an Africa they have invented for the world, for each other, and for Africa.

All aspects of contemporary African cultural life—including music and some sculpture and painting, even some writings with which the West is largely not familiar—have been influenced, often powerfully, by the transition of African societies *through* colonialism, but they are not all in the relevant sense *post*colonial. For the *post-* in postcolonial, like the *post-* in postmodern, is the *post-* of the space-clearing gesture I characterized earlier, and many areas of contemporary African cultural life—what has come to be theorized as popular culture, in particular—are not in this way concerned with transcending, with going beyond, coloniality. Indeed, it might be said to be a mark of popular culture that its borrowings from international cultural forms are remarkably insensitive to, not so much dismissive of as blind to, the issue of neocolonialism or "cultural imperialism." This does not mean that theories of postmodernism are irrelevant to these forms of culture, for the internationalization of the market and the commodification of artworks are both central to them. But it *does* mean that these artworks are not understood by their producers or their consumers in terms of a postmodern*ism*: there is no antecedent practice whose claim to exclusivity of vision is rejected through these artworks. What is called "syncretism" here is a consequence of the international exchange of commodities, but not of a space-clearing gesture. . . .

If there is a lesson in the broad shape of this circulation of cultures, it is surely that we are all already contaminated by each other, that there is no longer a fully autochthonous *echt*-African culture awaiting salvage by our artists (just as there is, of course, no American culture without African roots). And there is a clear sense in some postcolonial writing that the postulation of a unitary Africa over against a monolithic West—the binarism of Self and Other—is the last of the shibboleths of the modernizers that we must learn to live without.

In *Le Devoir de violence*, in Ouologuem's withering critique of "Shrobéniusologie," there were already the beginnings of this postcolonial critique of what we might call "alteritism," the construction and celebration of oneself as Other. . . .

. . . Ouologuem articulates . . . the interconnections of Africanist mystifications with tourism and the production, packaging, and marketing of African artworks.

Already it had become more than difficult to procure old masks, for Shrobenius and the missionaries had the good fortune to snap them all up. And so Saif—and the practice is still current—had slapdash copies buried by the hundredweight, or sunk into ponds, lakes, marshes, and mud holes, to be exhumed later on and sold at exorbitant prices to unsuspecting curio hunters. These three-year-old masks were said to be *charged with the weight of four centuries of civilization*.

Ouologuem here forcefully exposes the connections we saw earlier in some of Rockefeller's insights into the international system of art exchange, the international art world: we see the way in which an ideology of disinterested aesthetic value—the "baptism" of "Negro art" as "aesthetic"—meshes with the international commodification of African expressive culture, a commodification that requires, by the logic of the space-clearing gesture, the manufacture of Otherness. . . .

Tomas Ybarra-Frausto

THE CHICANO MOVEMENT/ THE MOVEMENT OF CHICANO ART

Tomas Ybarra-Frausto is Dean of Students at Bellevue Community College in Bellevue, Washington. He is a specialist in Chicano art and literature, whose works include The Marvelous/The Real, Modern Chicano Writers, *and* Arte Chicano: A Comprehensive Annotated Bibliography of Chicano Art, 1965–1981. *In this essay Ybarra-Frausto summarizes some of the recent developments in Chicano art, emphasizing the way in which everyday objects and experiences are used as artistic material.*

Born in the tumultuous decade of the 1960s, Chicano art has been closely aligned with the political goals of Chicano struggles for self-determination. As an aesthetic credo, Chicano art seeks to link lived reality to the imagination. Going against mainstream cultural traditions of art as escape and commodity, Chicano art intends that viewers respond both to the aesthetic object and to the social reality reflected in it. A prevalent attitude toward the art object is that it should provide aesthetic pleasure while also serving to educate and edify. In its various modalities, Chicano art is envisioned as a model for freedom, a call to both conscience and consciousness.[1]

PHASE I, 1965–1975: CREATION OF THE PROJECT

Although struggles for social, political, and economic equality have been a central tenet of Chicano history since 1848, the efforts to unionize California farmworkers launched by Cesar Chavez in 1965 signaled a national mobilization, known as La Causa, among people of Mexican descent in the United States. The Chicano movement, or El Movimiento, was an ideological project closely aligned with the tactics, formulations, and beliefs of the civil-rights movement, the rise of Black Power, the political agenda of the New Left, the onset of an

Tomas Ybarra-Frausto, "The Chicano Movement/The Movement of Chicano Art, *Exhibiting Cultures: The Poetics and Politics of Museum Display,* ed. Ivan Karp and Steven P. Lavine (Washington, D.C.: Smithsonian Institution P, 1991) 128–50.

international student movement, and struggles of liberation throughout the Third World. In retrospect, the Chicano movement was extremely heterogeneous, cutting across social class and regional and generational groupings.

Impelled by this mass political movement, Chicano artists, activists, and intellectuals united to articulate the goals of a collective cultural project that would meld social practice and cultural production. A primary aim of this project was to surmount strategies of containment by struggling to achieve self-determination on both the social and aesthetic planes. It was the Chicano movement—through various political fronts such as the farmworkers' cause in California, urban civil-rights activities, the rural-land-grant uprisings in New Mexico, the student and antiwar movements on college campuses, the labor struggles of undocumented workers, and the rise of feminism—that gave cogency to the cultural project.

Artists were integrated into the various political fronts of El Movimiento in unprecedented numbers and in significant ways. They organized, wrote the poems and songs of struggle, coined and printed the slogans, created the symbols, danced the ancient rituals, and painted ardent images that fortified and deepened understanding of the social issues being debated in Chicano communities. An urgent first task was to repudiate external vision and destroy entrenched literary and visual representations that focused on Mexican Americans as receptors rather than active generators of culture. For the creative artist, whether painter, dancer, musician, or writer, this meant appropriation of his or her own self. Novelist Tomas Rivera further defines the enterprise:

The invention of ourselves by ourselves is in actuality an extension of our will. Thus, as the Chicano invents himself he is complementing his will. Another complement. This is of great importance because these lives are trying to find form. This development is becoming a unifying consciousness. The thoughts of the Chicano are beginning to constantly gyrate over his own life, over his own development, over his identity, and as such over his own conservation. . . . Chicano literature has a triple mission: to represent, and to conserve that aspect of life that the Mexican American holds as his own and at the same time destroy the invention by others of his own life. That is—conservation, struggle and invention.[2]

This triad of conservation, struggle, and invention became a theme of Chicano literature. It served also as a core assumption in the production of energetic new forms of visual culture. . . .

This *"nuevo arte del pueblo"* (a new art of the people) was to be created from shared experience and based on communal art traditions. Necessarily, a first step was to investigate, and give authority to, authentic expressive forms arising within the heterogeneous Chicano community. In opposition to the hierarchical dominant culture, which implicitly made a distinction between "fine art" and "folk art," attempts were made to eradicate boundaries and integrate categories. An initial recognition was that the practices of daily life and the lived environment were primary constituent elements of the new aesthetic.

In the everyday life of the barrio, art objects are embedded in a network of cultural sites, activities, and events. "The way folk art fits into this cultural constellation reveals time-tested aesthetic practices for accomplishing goals in social, religious and economic life. And these practices are ongoing; they point not to an absolute standard or set of truths."[3] Inside the home, in the yard, and on the street corner—throughout the barrio environment—a visual culture of accumulation and bold display is enunciated. Handcrafted and store-bought items from the popular culture of Mexico and the mass culture of the United States mix freely and exuberantly in a milieu of inventive appropriation and recontextualization. The barrio environment is shaped in ways that express the community's sense of itself, the aesthetic display projecting a sort of visual biculturalism.

As communal customs, rituals, and traditions were appropriated by Movimiento artists, they yielded boundless sources of imagery. The aim was not simply to reclaim vernacular traditions but to reinterpret them in ways useful to the social urgency of the period.

SOME VERNACULAR SOURCES OF CHICANO ART

ALMANAQUES *Almanaques* (calendars) are a common feature in Chicano households, given to favored customers each year by barrio businesses. *Almanaques* traditionally feature images from Mexican folklore. Favorite images include nostalgic rural landscapes, interpretations of indigenous myths or historical events, bullfighting and cockfighting scenes, and the full pantheon of Catholic saints. Two of the most common images from the *almanaque* tradition are the Virgin of Guadalupe and an Aztec warrior carrying a sleeping maiden, which is a representation of the ancient myth of Ixtacihuatl and Popocatepetl (two snow-covered volcanoes in the Valley of Mexico).

Almanaques are printed in the United States, but the lithographed or chromolithographed images are generally imported from Mexico because of the immense popularity of famous *almanaque* artists such as Jesus Helguera and Eduardo Catano.[4] Their pastel, romanticized versions of Mexican types and customs are saved from year to year and proudly displayed in homes.

In the *almanaque* tradition, many community centers began issuing *calendarios Chicanos* in the mid-1970s.

ESTAMPAS RELIGIOSAS In many Chicano households, images of Catholic saints, martyrs of the faith, and holy personages are mingled with family photographs and memorabilia and prominently displayed on home altars or used as wall decorations.

Dispensed at churches or purchased in religious-specialty stores, the *estampas religiosas* (religious images) vary from calling-card-size to poster-size. *Estampas* represent Catholic saints with their traditional symbols: for example, St. Peter with a set of two crossed keys, St. Clement with an anchor, or St. Catherine with a wheel. The images are folk religious narratives, depicting miracles, feats of martyrdom in defense of the faith, or significant stories from the lives of the saints. Parents refer to the *estampas* as they recount the heroic episodes depicted, both socializing their children and introducing them to the tenets of the Catholic church. The saints of the *estampas* become guides to proper behavior and are many a child's first encounter with traditional Christian symbols.

ALTARES Artists also focused on *altares* (home religious shrines) as expressive forms of cultural amalgamation. In their eclectic composition, they fuse traditional items of folk material culture with artifacts from mass culture. Typical constituents of an *altar* include crocheted doilies and embroidered cloths, *recuerdos* (such as flowers or favors saved from some dance or party), family photographs, personal mementos, *santos* (religious chromolithographs or statues) especially venerated by the family, and many other elements. The grouping of the various objects in a particular space—atop a television set, on a kitchen counter, atop a bedroom dresser, or in a specially constructed *nicho* (wall shelf)—appears to be random but usually responds to a conscious sensibility and aesthetic judgment of what things belong together and in what arrangement. *Altares* are organic and ever-changing. They are iconic representations of the power of relationships, the place of contact between the human and the divine. *Altares* are a sophisticated form of vernacular *bricolage*, and their constituent elements can be used in an infinite number of improvised combinations to generate new meanings. A number of Chicano artists, among them Amalia Mesa-Bains and Rene Yanez, became known as *altaristas* (makers of altars), experimenting with the *altar* form in innovative ways.

CARTELES   Mexican *carteles* (theatrical posters) and the ubiquitous commercially designed advertisements for barrio social events, such as dances or artistic caravans of visiting Mexican entertainers, were also significant image sources.

EXPRESSIVE FORMS FROM YOUTH CULTURES   Chicano youth cultures were acknowledged as guardians and generators of a style, stance, and visual discourse of pride and identity. Urban iconography melds customs, symbols, and forms of daily-life practices in the metropolis. *Placas* (graffiti), tattoos, customized *ranflas* (low-rider cars), gang regalia, and countless other expressive forms evoke and embody a contemporary barrio sensibility. It is a sense of being that is defiant, proud, and rooted in resistance. Gilbert Lujan, Willie Herron, John Valadez, Judith Baca, and Santos Martinez are among legions of artists who experiment with barrio symbology in their work.

RASQUACHISMO: A CHICANO SENSIBILITY

Beyond grounding themselves in vernacular art forms, Movimiento artists found strength from and recovered meaning sedimented in consistent group stances such as *rasquachismo*. *Rasquachismo*[5] is neither an idea nor a style, but more of a pervasive attitude or taste. Very generally, *rasquachismo* is an underdog perspective—a view from *los de abajo*. It is a stance rooted in resourcefulness and adaptability, yet ever mindful of aesthetics.

In an environment in which things are always on the edge of coming apart (the car, the job, the toilet), lives are held together with spit, grit, and *movidas*. *Movidas* are whatever coping strategies one uses to gain time, to make options, to retain hope. *Rasquachismo* is a compendium of all the *movidas* deployed in immediate, day-to-day living. Resilience and resourcefulness spring from making do with what is at hand (*hacer rendir las cosas*). This utilization of available resources makes for syncretism, juxtaposition, and integration. *Rasquachismo* is a sensibility attuned to mixtures and confluence. Communion is preferred over purity.

Pulling through and making do are not guarantors of security, so things that are *rasquache* possess an ephemeral quality, a sense of temporality and impermanence—here today and gone tomorrow. While things might be created using whatever is at hand, attention is always given to nuances and details. Appearance and form have precedence over function.

In the realm of taste, to be *rasquache* is to be unfettered and unrestrained, to favor the elaborate over the simple, the flamboyant over the severe. Bright colors (*chillantes*) are preferred to somber, high intensity to low, the shimmering and sparkling over the muted and subdued. The *rasquache* inclination piles pattern on pattern, filling all available space with bold display. Ornamentation and elaboration prevail and are joined with a delight in texture and sensuous surfaces. A work of art may be *rasquache* in multiple and complex ways. It can be sincere and pay homage to the sensibility by restating its premises, i.e., the underdog worldview actualized through language and behavior, as in the dramatic presentation *La Carpa de los Rasquaches*, by Luis Valdez. Another strategy is for the artwork to evoke a *rasquache* sensibility through self-conscious manipulation of materials of iconography. One thinks of the combination of found materials and the use of satiric wit in the sculptures of Ruben Trejo, or the manipulation of *ras-quache* artifacts, codes, and sensibilities from both sides of the border in the performance pieces of

Guillermo Gomez-Peña. Many Chicano artists continue to investigate and interpret facets of *rasquachismo* as a conceptual lifestyle or aesthetic strategy.

FRONTS OF STRUGGLE, FORMS OF ART

The initial phase of the Chicano cultural project (circa the mid-1960s) was seminal in validating emancipatory communal practices and codifying the symbols and images that would be forcefully deployed in adversarial counterrepresentations. By that time, visual artists had been well integrated into the various political fronts of El Movimiento, within which they were gestating a Chicano art movement that was national in scope and developed outside the dominant museum, gallery, and arts-publication circuit. Fluid and tendentious, the art produced by this movement underscored public connection instead of private cognition.

Inscribed in multiple arenas of agitation, artists continued to evolve *un arte del pueblo* that aimed to close the gap between radical politics and community-based cultural practices. The rural farmworkers' cause and the urban student movement are prime examples of this rapprochement.

La Causa, the farmworkers' struggle, was a grass-roots uprising that provided the infinitely complex human essence necessary for creating a true people's art. One of the early purveyors of *campesino* expression was the newspaper *El Malcriado* (The Ill-Bred). Established primarily as a tool for organizing, the periodical soon came to function as a vehicle that promoted unity by stressing a sense of class consciousness while building cultural and political awareness. In artistic terms, *El Malcriado* lived up to its name by focusing on art forms outside the "high-art" canon, such as caricature and cartoons. The pervasive aesthetic norm was *rasquachismo*, a bawdy, irreverent, satiric, and ironic worldview. . . .

As a primary impetus toward collaboration between workers and artists, *El Malcriado* planted the seed that would come to fruition in many other cooperative ventures between artists and workers. The creative capacities of artists were placed at the service of and welcomed by those struggling for justice and progress.

Simultaneously with the cultural expression of the farmworker's cause, a highly vocal and visible Chicano student movement emerged during the mid-1960s. Related to the worldwide radicalization of youth and inspired by international liberation movements, especially the Cuban revolution, the Black Power movement, and varied domestic struggles, the Chicano student movement developed strategies to overcome entrenched patterns of miseducation. Institutionalized racism was targeted as a key detriment, and cultural affirmation functioned as an important basis for political organization.

Chicano culture was affirmed as a creative, hybrid reality synthesizing elements from Mexican culture and the social dynamics of life experience in the United States. Scholars such as Octavio Romano published significant essays debunking orthodox views of Chicano life as monolithic and ahistorical. Contrary to these official notions, Chicano culture was affirmed as dynamic, historical, and anchored in working-class consciousness.

Within the student movement, art was assigned a key role as a maintainer of human signification and as a powerful medium that could rouse consciousness. Remaining outside the official cultural apparatus, the student groups originated alternative circuits for disseminating an outpouring of artistic production. As in the nineteenth century, when Spanish-language newspapers became major outlets for cultural expression in the Southwest, contemporary journals functioned as purveyors of cultural polemics and new representations. Although varying in emphasis and quality, most student-movement periodicals shared a conscious focus on the visual arts as essential ingredients in the formation of Chicano pride and identity. . . .

Knowledge about the Hispanic–Native American art forms of the Southwest came from neither academic nor scholarly sources, but rather from venues within the movement such as *El Grito del Norte*, a newspaper issued from Espanola, New Mexico, starting in 1968. This journal had a gross-roots orientation and placed emphasis on preserving the culture of the rural agrarian class. Often, photographic essays focusing on local artisans or documenting traditional ways of life in the isolated *pueblitos* of northern New Mexico were featured. . . .

Asserting that Chicano art had a basic aim to document, denounce, and delight, individual artists and artists' groups resisted the formulation of a restricted aesthetic program to be followed uniformly. The Chicano community was heterogeneous, and the art forms it inspired were equally varied. Although representational modes became dominant, some artists opted for abstract and more personal expression. Artists in this group felt that internal and subjective views of reality were significant, and that formal and technical methods of presentation should remain varied.

ALTERNATIVE VISIONS AND STRUCTURES

By the early 1970s, Chicano artists had banded together to create networks of information, mutual support systems, and alternative art circuits. Regional artists' groups such as the Royal Chicano Air Force (R.C.A.F.) in Sacramento, the Raza Art and Media Collective in Ann Arbor, Michigan, the Movimiento Artistico Chicano (MARCH) in Chicago, the Con Safos group in San Antonio, Texas, and many others persisted in the vital task of creating art forms that strengthened the will and fortified the cultural identity of the community.

With militant and provocative strategies, Chicano arts organizations developed and shared their art within a broad community context. They brought aesthetic pleasure to the sort of working people who walk or take the bus to work in the factories or in the service sector of the urban metropolis. In its collective character, in its sustained efforts to change the mode of participation between artists and their public, and, above all, as a vehicle for sensitizing communities to a pluralistic rather than a monolithic aesthetic, the Chicano alternative art circuit played a central and commanding role in nurturing a visual sensibility in the barrio.

POSTERS   The combative phase of El Movimiento called for a militant art useful in the mobilization of large groups for political action. Posters were seen as accessible and expedient sources of visual information and indoctrination. Because they were inexpensive to reproduce and portable, they were well suited for mass distribution. Moreover, posters had historical antecedents in the Chicano community.[6] Many of the famous *planes* or political programs of the past had been issued as broadsides or posters to be affixed on walls, informing the populace and mustering them for political action.

The initial phase of Chicano poster production was directly influenced by both the work of Jose Guadalupe Posada and images from the Agustin Casasola photographic archives, which contained photos documenting the Mexican revolution.[7] Early Chicano poster makers appropriated images from these two primary sources and merely reproduced and massively distributed Posada and Casasola images embellished with slogans such as *Viva La Causa* and *Viva La Revolución*. Francisco "Pancho" Villa and Emiliano Zapata, iconic symbols of the Mexican Revolution, were among the first images that assaulted Chicano consciousness via the poster. Poster images of Villa and Zapata were attached to crude wooden planks and carried in picket lines and countless demonstrations. Quoting from Mexican antecedents was an important initial strategy of Chicano art. Having established a cultural and visual continuum across borders, Chicano artists could then move forward to forge a visual vocabulary and expressive forms corresponding to a complex bicultural reality.

Used to announce rallies, promote cultural events, or simply as visual statements, Chicano posters evolved as forms of communication with memorable imagery and pointed messages. . . .

Formal elements such as color, composition, and lettering style echoed diverse graphic traditions: the powerful, socially conscious graphics of the Taller de Grafica Popular in Mexico, the colorful, psychedelic rock-poster art of the hippie counterculture, and the boldly assertive style of the Cuban *affiche*.

Such eclectic design sources taught graphic artists how to appeal and communicate with brevity, emphasis, and force. Chicano posters did not create a new visual vocabulary, but brilliantly united various stylistic influences into an emphatic hybrid expression. The two salient categories are political posters and event posters. The primary function of both forms was ideological mobilization through visual and verbal means.

Chicano posters generally were issued in hand-silkscreened editions of several hundred or lithographed runs of several thousand. They were posted on walls, distributed free at rallies, or sold for nominal prices. Within many sectors of the community, Chicano posters were avidly collected and displayed in personal spaces as a matter of pride and identification with their message. For a mass public unaccustomed and little inclined to visit museums and art galleries, the Chicano poster provided a direct connection to the pleasures of owning and responding to an art object. Chicano posters were valued both as records of historical events and as satisfying works of art.

MURALS   The barrio mural movement is perhaps the most powerful and enduring contribution of the Chicano art movement nationwide. Created and nurtured by the humanist ideals of Chicano struggles for self-determination, murals functioned as a pictorial reflection of the social drama.

Reaching back to the goals and dicta of the Mexican muralists, especially the pronouncements of David Alfaro Siqueiros, in the mid-1960s Chicano artists called for an art that was public, monumental, and accessible to the common people. The generative force of Chicano muralism was also a mass social movement, but the artists as a whole did not have the same kind of formal training as the Mexican muralists, and they fostered mural programs through an alternative circuit independent of official sanction and patronage.

For their visual dialogue, muralists used themes, motifs, and iconography that gave ideological direction and visual coherence to the mural programs. In the main, the artistic vocabulary centered on the indigenous heritage (especially the Aztec and Mayan past), the Mexican Revolution and its epic heroes and heroines, renderings of both historical and contemporary Chicano social activism, and depictions of everyday life in the barrio. Internationalism entered the pictorial vocabulary of Chicano murals via iconographic references to liberation struggles in Vietnam, Africa, and Latin America and motifs from cultures in those areas. The muralists' efforts were persistently directed toward documentation and denunciation.

Finding a visual language adequate to depict the epic sweep of the Chicano movement was not simple. Some murals became stymied, offering romantic, archaicizing views of indigenous culture, uncritically depicting Chicano life, and portraying cultural and historical events without a clear political analysis. Successful mural programs, however, were most significant in reclaiming history. As the community read the visual chronicles, it internalized an awareness of the past and activated strategies for the future.

Apart from the aesthetic content, muralism was significant in actualizing a communal approach to the production and dissemination of art. Brigades of artists and residents worked with a director who solicited community input during the various stages of producing the mural. Through such collaborative actions, murals became a large-scale, comprehensive public-education system in the barrio.

In retrospect, it can be affirmed that Chicano art in the 1960s and 1970s encompassed both a political and an aesthetic one. That art underscored a consciousness that helped define and shape fluid and integrative forms of visual culture. Artists functioned as visual educators, with the important task of refining and transmitting through plastic expression the ideology of a community striving for self-determination.

A Chicano national consciousness was asserted by a revival in all the arts. Aesthetic guidelines were not officially promulgated but arose within the actual arena of political practice. As opposed to mainstream art movements, where critical perspectives remain at the level of the work (art about itself and for itself), the Chicano art movement sought to extend meaning beyond the aesthetic object to include transformation of the material environment as well as of consciousness.

PHASE II, 1975–1990: NEUTRALIZATION AND RECUPERATION OF THE PROJECT

The late 1970s and the 1980s have been a dynamically complex juncture for the Chicano cultural project. Many of its postulates and aims have come to fruition during this time. Three of these aims are: (1) the creation of a core of visual signification, a bank of symbols and images that encode the deep structures of Chicano experience. Drawing from this core of commonly understood iconography, artists can create counterrepresentations that challenge the imposed "master narrative" of elite art practice; (2) the maintenance of alternative art structures, spaces, and forms. For more than two decades, Chicano arts organizations have persisted in the arduous task of creating a responsive working-class audience for art. A principal goal of these efforts has been to make art accessible, to deflect its rarefied, elitist aura, and especially to reclaim the art from its commodity status with the ideal of returning it to a critical role within the social practices of daily living; and (3) the continuation of mural programs. Although there has been a diminution in the number of public art forms such as murals and posters, what has been produced since 1975 is of deeper political complexity and superior aesthetic quality. . . .

Such accomplishments are especially praiseworthy, having transpired during a period of intense change and transformation in Chicano communities. The utopian buoyancy that sustained a national Chicano art movement has eroded. As the groundswell of collective political action has dispersed, as more Chicanos enter the professional class and are affected by its implied social mobility, and as public art forms have diminished in frequency, tracings of a new agenda of struggle have surfaced.

Given demographic data indicating that the number of people of Latin American descent in the United States is growing, and given sociological data indicating that Spanish-speaking groups remain definitely "other" for several generations, new cultural undercurrents among Chicanos call for an awareness of America as a continent and not a country. In the new typology an emergent axis of influence might lead from Los Angeles to Mexico City and from there to Bogotá, Lima, Buenos Aires, Managua,

Barcelona, and back to the barrio. For the creative artists, such new political and aesthetic filiations expand the field with hallucinatory possibilities. . . .

Contemporary revisions of identity and culture affirm that both concepts are open and offer the possibility of making and remaking oneself from within a living, changing tradition.

In contemporary Chicano art, no artistic current is dominant. Figuration and abstraction, political art and self-referential art, art of process, performance, and video all have adherents and advocates. The thread of unity is a sense of vitality and continual maturation. The mainstream art circuit continues to uphold rigid and stereotypical notions in its primitivistic and folkloristic categorizations of "ethnic art." This is an elite perspective that blithely relegates highly trained artists into a nether region in which Chicano art is inscribed in an imagined world that is a perpetual fiesta of bright colors and folk idioms—a world in which social content is interpreted as a cultural form unconnected to political and social sensibilities. . . .

In the visual arts, . . . cultural negotiation occurs in different ways. At the level of iconography and symbolism, for example, the Chicano artist often creates a personal visual vocabulary freely blending and juxtaposing symbols and images culled from African American, Native American, European, and mestizo cultural sources. Resonating with the power ascribed to the symbols within each culture, the new combination emerges dense with multifarious meaning. Beyond symbols, artistic styles and art-historical movements are continually appropriated and recombined in a constant and richly nuanced interchange. Current Chicano art can be seen as a visual narration of cultural negotiation.

Presently in the United States, entrenched systems of control and domination affirm and uphold distinctions between "us" and "them." Dichotomies such as white/non-white, English-speaking/Spanish-speaking, the haves/the have-nots, etc., persist and are based on social reality. We should not dissemble on this fact, but neither should we maintain vicious and permanent divisions or permit dogmatic closure.

My own sense of the dialectic is that in the current struggle for cultural maintenance and parity within the Chicano community, there are two dominant strategies vying for ascendancy. On the one hand, there is an attempt to fracture mainstream consensus with a defiant "otherness." Impertinent representations counter the homogenizing desires, investments, and projections of the dominant culture and express what is manifestly different. On the other hand, there is the recognition of new interconnections and filiations, especially with other Latino groups in the United States. Confronting the dominant culture leads to a recognition that Anglos' visions of Chicanos and Chicanos' visions of themselves support and to an extent reflect each other.

Rather than flowing from a monolithic aesthetic, Chicano art forms arise from tactical, strategic, and positional necessities. What Carlos Monsivais has called *la cultura de la necesidad* (the culture of necessity) leads to fluid multivocal exchanges among shifting cultural traditions. A consistent objective of Chicano art is to undermine imposed models of representation and to interrogate systems of aesthetic discourse, disclosing them as neither natural nor secure but conventional and historically determined.

Chicano art and artists are inscribed within multiple aesthetic traditions, both popular and elite. Their task is to record themselves and move beyond dichotomies in a fluid process of cultural negotiation. This negotiation usually reflects cultural change, variation by gender and region, and tensions within and among classes and groups of people, such as Mexican nationals or other ethnic minorities in the United States.

In the dynamism of such a contemporary social reality, interests are culturally medi-ated, replaced, and created through what is collectively valued and worth struggling for. The task continues, and remains open.

[1]This text is a reworking of my unpublished manuscript *Califas: California Chicano Art and Its Social Background*. Sections have been excerpted in *Chicano Expressions: A New View in American Art* (New York: INTAR Latin American Gallery, 1986) and *The Mural Primer* (Venice, Calif.: Social and Public Resource Center, 1987). My analysis parallels ideas in James Clifford, *The Predicament of Culture: Twentieth-Century Ethnography, Literature and Art* (Cambridge: Harvard University Press, 1988).

[2]Tomas Rivera, *Into the Labyrinth: The Chicano in Literature* (Edinburg, Texas: Pan American University, 1971).

[3]Kay Turner and Pat Jasper, "La Causa, La Calle y La Esquina: A Look at Art Among Us," in *Art Among Us: Mexican American Folk Art of San Antonio* (San Antonio: San Antonio Museum Association, 1986).

[4]See the catalog *Jesus Helguera: El Calendario Como Arte* (Mexico City: Subsecretaria de Cultura/Programa Cultural de Las Fronteras, 1987).

[5]Tomas Ybarra-Frausto, "Rasquachismo: A Chicano Sensibility," in *Rasquachismo: Chicano Aesthetic* (Phoenix: Movimiento Artistico Del Rio Salado, 1988).

[6]See Shifra M. Goldman, "A Public Voice: Fifteen Years of Chicano Posters," *Art Journal 44*, no. 1 (Spring, 1984).

[7]Victor Sorell, "The Photograph as a Source for Visual Artists: Images from the Archivo Casasola in the Works of Mexican and Chicano Artists," in *The World of Agustin Victor Casasola: Mexico 1900–1938* (Washington, D.C.: Fonda del Sol Visual Arts and Media Center, 1984).

DISCUSSION QUESTIONS

1. What traditional values do Duchamp's readymades defy? What alternative aims for art do they implicitly endorse?
2. Are the political aims of the performance art that Heyd describes compatible with such traditional aesthetic values as the principle of closure and organic unity? Why or why not?
3. Do you think that deconstruction is an essentially negative strategy? Can you think of any positive insights that emerge from deconstructive strategies of interpretation?
4. How would you deconstruct the Energizer Rabbit's own "deconstructive" project?
5. Do you think that postmodernist strategies in art such as eclecticism, fragmentariness, and the presentation of multiple perspectives inform us about the character of our times? Do you think these strategies have political implications? If so, what implications are there?
6. Do you agree with Appiah that postmodernism is more self-celebration than a celebration of "the Other"? Why or why not?
7. Can you think of any postmodern artworks that you think are particularly effective? If so, what do they succeed in doing?

FURTHER READING

Modern Art and the Avant-Garde

Bürger, Peter. *Theory of the Avant-Garde.* Trans. Michael Shaw. Minneapolis: U of Minnesota P, 1984.

Danto, Arthur C. *The Transfiguration of the Commonplace.* Cambridge: Harvard UP, 1981.

Eco, Umberto. *The Open Work.* Trans. Anna Cancogni. Cambridge: Harvard UP, 1989.

Gass, William H. "Vicissitudes of the Avant-Garde." *Harper's* 277.1661 (1988): 64–70.

Goldsmith, Steven. "The Readymades of Marcel Duchamp: The Ambiguities of an Aesthetic Revolution." *The Journal of Aesthetics and Art Criticism* 42 (1983): 197–308.

Harries, Karsten. *The Meaning of Modern Art: A Philosophical Interpretation*. Evanston: Northwestern UP, 1968.

Herwitz, Daniel. *Making Theory/Constructing Art: On the Authority of the Avant-Garde*. Chicago: Chicago UP, 1993.

Hughes, Robert. *The Shock of the New: Art and the Century of Change*. Rev. and enl. ed. London: Thames and Hudson, 1991.

Krauss, Rosalind E. *The Originality of the Avant-Garde and Other Modernist Myths*. Cambridge: M.I.T.P, 1987.

Wolfe, Tom. *The Painted Word*. New York: Bantam, 1976.

Deconstruction

Bloom, Harold, et. al. *Deconstruction and Criticism*. New York: Seabury, 1979.

Norris, Christopher. *The Deconstructive Turn*. New York: Methuen, 1983.

Postmodernism

Best, Steven, and Douglas Kellner. *Postmodern Theory: Critical Interrogations*. New York: Guilford, 1991.

Calinescu, Matei. *Five Faces of Modernity: Modernism, Avant-Garde, Decadence, Kitsch, Postmodernism*. Durham: Duke UP, 1987.

Foster, Hal. *The Anti-Aesthetic: Essays on Postmodern Culture*. Port Townsend: Bay, 1983.

Structuralism and Signs

Barthes, Roland. *The Elements of Semiology*. Trans. A. Lavers and C. Smith. New York: Hill and Wang, 1967.

———. *The Pleasures of the Text*. Trans. P. Miller. New York: Hill and Wang, 1975.

Culler, Jonathan. *Structuralism and Poetics*. London: Routledge, 1975.

Lévi-Strauss, Claude. *The Raw and the Cooked: Introduction to a Science of Mythology, I*. Trans. John and Doreen Weightman. London: Jonathan Cape, 1969.

———. *The Savage Mind*. London: Weidenfeld and Nicolson, 1966.

RACISM AND SEXISM
IN THE ARTS

Rock 'n' roll videos have been criticized on many grounds, but one of the most steady complaints is that they encourage a sexist view of women. Male rock stars swagger through videos wearing black leather with spikes and chains, while women in videos are often depicted as admiring audiences or passive objects for male aggression. Rock lyrics have long been criticized on similar grounds. Too many endorse the worst clichés of sexism, portraying women as "under men's thumbs" or as toys for male amusement.

Popular entertainment, however, is not the only arena in which art forms are accused of abetting sexism. The Western high art tradition, according to some critics, also treats women as property and playthings for men. Critics such as John Berger have pointed to such conventions in painting as the vulnerable female nude gazing provocatively at the (male) owner of the painting and to the frequency of women appearing in reclining positions. Berger considers high art to be just as sexist as popular art and advertising. Feminists have often charged that women have been placed on a pedestal in the past few centuries as a means of preventing them from having an impact on everyday reality. What more obvious pedestal is there, feminist art critics ask, than that of our high art tradition?

Similar complaints have been raised about the racist biases of both popular and high art. Critics attack such allegedly classic movies as D. W. Griffith's *The Birth of a Nation* (1915), which sympathetically portrays the early days of the Ku Klux Klan, and Leni Riefenstahl's *Triumph of the Will* (1935), which celebrates Hitler's 1934 Nuremberg Rally, as racist propaganda. Literary critic Edward Said has accused most of our tradition's artistic and literary depictions of the East (especially of the Middle East) of "orientalism," the ideological division of the world into "the West" and "the East," with the East portrayed as exotic, alien, and backward so as to legitimate Western imperialist attitudes. Others, too, have complained that our society's traditional notions of "classics" and "masterpieces" are ethnocentric. Such critics argue that to include ethnocentric, sexist, and racist art among "the masterpieces of our tradition" is offensive to many and discouraging to nonwhites and women.

Leo Marx takes seriously the argument that certain works within the traditional canon may offend some people, and that Mark Twain's beloved *Huckleberry Finn* may be among them. Marx concludes that the many grounds for valuing Twain's book provide arguments for continuing to think of it as a "classic." Moreover, Twain's work depicts characters with racist attitudes, but it does not endorse those attitudes. Nevertheless, he believes that the sensibilities of those who are offended by some of its language and characterizations should be treated with respect. His concrete suggestion is that educators be less rigid in their procedures and reconsider whether *Huckleberry Finn* should be required reading for every American high school student.

Marx believes that Twain depicts but does not express racist attitudes. But other artists, presumably, are less obviously ironic in their portrayals. How prevalent are works that actually *express* racist attitudes? Robert Gooding-Williams argues that racial representations, depictions that classify individuals as members of one race or another, are rampant in our society. The functions that black characters play in popular film, for example, encourage the impression that African Americans are facilitating sidekicks for whites, peripheral to the main story. This impression has an impact on how Americans, in general, think of black citizens, according to Gooding-Williams. Until such representations are demythified, Americans will continue to think of their country as a white nation with some outsiders in its midst.

How did the present condition of artistic portrayal of women and ethnic minorities originate? Some feminists argue that one reason why art has been a vehicle for expressing visions that reinforce male privilege is that the creation of art has been largely foreclosed to women.

Linda Nochlin employs this type of analysis in addressing the question "Why are there no great women artists?" The scarcity of female artists in art historical accounts has led some to conclude that women simply are not as talented as their male counterparts. Nochlin suggests, however, that in the context of Western history, *any* female achievement is remarkable. Besides being trained from their infancy for a life without room for art, women have traditionally been taught not to aspire to greatness in any pursuit. Even those rare women who sought to be artists were refused admittance to the best schools and denied access to nude models (on grounds of moral propriety). Moreover, women were, for the most part, forced to choose between life as a woman and life as an artist. It is remarkable, Nochlin observes, that we can find any historical examples of women artists at all.

Is the situation of minority group members in the arts similar to that of women? Their absence in certain artistic roles suggests some similarities. That Bill Cosby was noteworthy as an African American starring in his own television show suggests that race has sometimes impeded certain kinds of success in popular entertainment. The relegation of the Lone Ranger's Indian friend Tonto to the position of television's most famous sidekick offers further evidence of this point.

Nevertheless, in certain performing arts, African Americans have held prominent positions. Jazz and blues music and certain dance forms are cases in point. Brenda Dixon Gottschild contends, however, that even in dance, race interferes with the stature of black performers. Dance styles that are viewed as "black" (usually because they are performed by groups of black dancers) are marginalized. Black dancers who perform in otherwise all-white companies, moreover, are usually viewed as "different." Gottschild notes that black dancers were straightforwardly excluded from the popular "Rockettes."

Gottschild also argues that once a "black" style becomes sufficiently popular, it is no longer identified as black. Instead, it is appropriated by the white artistic establishment. Joel Rudinow considers the comparable case in connection with blues music. Rudinow is sympathetic to the complaint that the history of blues music shows white musicians making fortunes on music that they stole from its black originators, a saga that Amiri Baraka calls "the Great Music Robbery."

In asking whether white people can sing the blues, however, Rudinow raises a question of the ownership of the arts. Can an art form be the property of a particular ethnic group and authentic only when produced by its members? Rudinow suggests that ethnicity does not give or deprive one of a claim to having an authentic connection with an art form. Although blues music is integrally related to the experience of African Americans, it is possible for others to become initiated into the blues tradition and thus join the ranks of those who can "authentically" play the blues.

One approach to countering such phenomena as "the Great Music Robbery" and the erasure of women and nonwhites from historical accounts of artistic achievement is to rewrite the history. Some feminists have suggested, for example, that despite the various impediments that Nochlin describes, there were more women artists through history than most of us realize. Employing such theoretical models as Marxism (with its emphasis on economic conditions) and psychoanalysis (with its explanations of inner psychological constraints), feminists have sought not only to include more women in the canonical story but also to provide a new historical account in general, in which women's achievements and the pressures mounted against them are given significant weight.

The psychoanalytic model has also been employed by feminists to indicate sexism in the appeals of popular art. A common concern of many feminists writing on film, for instance, is that most movies (at least those of the Hollywood variety) presuppose "the male gaze," the orientation of the male viewer. Unlike male characters, with whom the viewer can straightforwardly identify, the female characters are typically presented in ways that incite somewhat prurient interests on the part of viewers. The viewer becomes a voyeur, privy to the female character's intimate behavior and able to take gratification in the very act of looking.

Noël Carroll agrees that is the way that women are typically represented in films. But he disagrees that psychoanalysis is the best approach to understanding them. Carroll contends that these representations of women make more sense if we take them to instantiate our paradigm notions about the way women are. As opposed to psychoanalytic efforts to expose the embarrassing gratification the viewer gets from representations of women, Carroll urges us to seek a more fundamental paradigm shift. If we as a culture change our beliefs about the way women are and should be, what we will accept and enjoy in cinematic portrayals of women will also change, hopefully for the better.

Feminist complaints about artistic representations of women might seem discouraging. If art reflects our cultural attitudes and our culture is sexist, must our art inevitably reinforce sexism? And if there are alternatives, do we need to abandon eroticism as a theme in art? In considering these questions, Mara Miller turns outside the Western tradition to the art of Japan, specifically, to the erotic paintings called ***shunga*** (literally, "spring paintings"). The depictions of women in these paintings, Miller observes, stand in striking contrast with the erotically tinged depictions of women in Western art. Women in *shunga* are shown as active sexual participants, pursuing pleasure as enthusiastically as men, and as likely to be subjects as objects of "the gaze." Miller is convinced that these Japanese depictions of women demonstrate the compatibility of the goals of feminism with erotic art.

Most critics who allege that artworks are sometimes racist or sexist are convinced, like Gooding-Williams, that representations of women and members of racial minority groups have repercussions for the way we see actual women and minority group members. María Lugónes points out that we imaginatively represent other individuals to ourselves even outside the artistic context. She contrasts "arrogant perception" with "loving perception." These different modes of perception result, respectively, in divergent aestheticized images of other people, especially those that we view as unlike ourselves. Arrogant perception is essentially self-centered and involves viewing the other person as being a different kind of being from oneself. In loving perception, by contrast, one assumes the perspective of the other person, imaginatively visiting that person's "world." Loving perception depends on adopting a playful attitude, in which one is open to surprise and vulnerability. In effect, loving perception is a mode of aesthetic receptiveness. Lugónes considers it to have ethical significance in human relationships, especially with those whose backgrounds differ from our own.

Leo Marx

HUCK
AT
100

Leo Marx is professor in the Department of Technology and Human Affairs at Massachusetts Institute of Technology and editor of the annotated edition of Huckleberry Finn. *He is also author of* The Machine in the Garden: Technology and the Pastoral Ideal in America *and* The Americanness of Walt Whitman. *Marx considers the complaint sometimes made that Mark Twain's* Huckleberry Finn *reflects racist attitudes. While he disagrees with the move to eliminate the book from the literary canon, Marx encourages sensitivity on the part of those who consider assigning the text.*

Ever since it was published, exactly one hundred years ago, Mark Twain's *Adventures of Huckleberry Finn* has been a target of moral disapproval. Many of the novel's first reviewers found it disturbing and offensive. They called it, among other things, vulgar, inelegant, ungrammatical, coarse, irreverent, semi-obscene, trashy and vicious. The library in Concord, Massachusetts, promptly banned it, but the book soon won the affection of a large audience, and during the next fifty years critics, scholars and writers succeeded in rescuing it from the mincingly refined standards of what George Santayana aptly named "the genteel tradition." In the 1930s Ernest Hemingway praised *Huckleberry Finn* as the work from which all modern American writing stems, and T. S. Eliot later described Mark Twain's vernacular style as nothing less than "a new discovery in the English language." By the 1950s the initial objections to the novel had been dispelled, and it was quietly installed, along with *The Scarlet Letter* and some other "classic" American books in the more or less standard high-school English curriculum.

But then, having survived the disdain of the genteel critics, the book became the object of another, angrier and more damaging kind of moral condemnation. In 1957 the

Leo Marx, "Huck at 100," *The Nation* 241.5 (1985): 150–52.

National Association for the Advancement of Colored People called *Huckleberry Finn* racially offensive, and since then we have seen a mounting protest against this novel whose first-person narrator, the 14-year-old son of the town drunk, routinely refers to blacks as "niggers." Huck's repeated use of that demeaning epithet is enough to convince many black Americans that schoolchildren should not be required to read the book. (Another, somewhat less obvious reason for their disquiet is a certain resemblance between the novel's leading black character, the escaped slave, Jim, and the stereotypical minstrel-show darkie.) In the last few years the protest has been gaining adherents. In a number of cities across the country, indignant parents, educators and school-board members have demanded that the book be removed from the curriculum and even, in some instances, that it be banned from school or public libraries. This past year a group of black parents succeeded in having the novel taken off the list of required reading in Waukegan, Illinois, and John H. Wallace, an educator with the school board in Chicago, is now conducting a nationwide campaign against Mark Twain's greatest work, which he calls "the most grotesque example of racist trash ever written."

One result of this protest is that the centenary of *Huckleberry Finn* has been marked by a curious conjunction of celebration and denunciation. In March, when Shelley Fisher Fishkin, a literary scholar at Yale University, came to Mark Twain's defense, she attracted national attention to the dispute about his racial views. In an announcement treated as front-page news by *The New York Times*, she reported the authentication of an 1885 letter in which Twain offered to provide financial support for a black student at Yale Law School. There he wrote that "we have ground the manhood out of . . . [black men] & the shame is ours, not theirs; and we should pay for it." (He subsequently did provide the money.) Because the letter reveals

"the personal anguish that Twain felt regarding the destructive legacy of slavery," Fishkin evidently thought that it might help to overcome the objections of black people to *Huckleberry Finn*. The implication was that a man of such enlightened views could not possibly have written a racially offensive novel and that once those views were established, the controversy would be resolved.

But as it turned out, the Yale letter merely provoked the contending parties to recast their arguments in less compromising, more strident language. Thus Sterling Stuckey, a historian at Northwestern University who is black, was moved to reaffirm the received scholarly-critical estimate of Mark Twain's masterwork. Of the letter he said that it "couldn't be a clearer, more categorical indictment of racism in American life," and he went on to praise *Huckleberry Finn* as "one of the most devastating attacks on racism ever written." But Wallace, perhaps the novel's most outspoken critic, was unmoved by Fishkin's announcement. When asked to comment on the new evidence of Mark Twain's sympathy for blacks, he said that it "still does not mitigate the problems that children have with *Huck Finn*. . . . The book teaches blatant racism. . . . We ought to get it off the school reading list."

What shall we make of this unusual controversy? Unlike most issues of public policy involving opposed literary judgments, the current argument about the place of *Huckleberry Finn* in the public school curriculum does not involve censorship or First Amendment rights. Whether or not high-school students are required to read a particular novel has nothing to do with anyone's freedom of speech. (I am putting aside the very different and, to my mind, intolerable proposal to remove the book from school or public libraries.) Another striking feature of the dispute is the extremity of the antagonists' views. Most public quarrels about the merit of literary works turn on relatively subtle questions of interpretation, but in this case an enormous gulf separates those who consider *Huckleberry Finn* to be "one of the most devastating attacks on racism ever written" from those who denounce it as "racist trash"—who claim that it actually "teaches" blatant racism. At first sight, indeed, the two parties seem to be so far apart as to make the controversy irresolvable, and perhaps it is. But it may be useful, as a step toward a resolution, to consider why this novel lends itself to such antithetical readings. How is it possible for *Huckleberry Finn* to convey such diametrically opposed attitudes toward American racism?

The explanation should begin, I think, with a decisive though perhaps insufficiently appreciated fact: the racial attitudes to which this novel lends overt expression are not Mark Twain's, they are those of an ignorant adolescent boy. This fact also explains, incidentally, why evidence from other sources about what the writer, Samuel L. Clemens, may have thought or said on the subject of race (as in the Yale letter) proves to be largely beside the point. That a considerable disparity often exists between what writers believe and what their work conveys is an axiom of modern criticism. In the case of a first-person narrative like *Huckleberry Finn*, of course, Clemens's viewpoint is manifestly disguised, and can only make itself felt obliquely, in the voice of—from behind the mask of—the boy narrator, Huck.

In accounting for the ability of readers to arrive at radically opposed conclusions about the racial attitudes embodied in this novel, the importance of the first-person narrative method cannot be exaggerated. Every word, every thought, every perception, emanates from Huck or, in passages where other characters speak, is reported by him—filtered through his mind. *Adventures of Huckleberry Finn* is a tour de force of sustained impersonation. It is a tale told by a boy who is a vagrant and a virtual outcast, who has no mother (she is never mentioned), whose father is an illiterate drunk,

bigot and bully, and who is inclined to accept society's view of people like himself as being, in his own words, irremediably "wicked and low-down and ornery."

Of course Huck calls black people "niggers"; for him to refer to them any other way would be inconceivable. But to say this can be misleading if it is taken to imply that the difficulty comes down to a mere question of usage, as if Mark Twain might have absolved his narrator (and himself) of the charge of racism merely by cleaning up Huck's vocabulary. The truth is that *Huckleberry Finn* is written from the viewpoint of a racist, or, to be more precise, a semiracist—a racist with a difference. The difference stems in part from Huck's exceptionally empathic nature (or, as Mark Twain puts it, his "sound heart") and in part from his disreputable upbringing on the fringe of antebellum Southern society. Unlike Tom Sawyer and his other friends whose parents belong to "the quality," Huck has been spared much of the formative influence of family, church and school. His racial prejudice is not supported by a sense of family or social superiority. On the contrary, he is a distinct outsider, a boy who is only half "civilized" or, in social science idiom, he has been incompletely acculturated. Although he has picked up the received version of white racism along with other bits and pieces of the dominant belief system, that viewpoint has been less deeply implanted in him than in respectable children like Tom Sawyer.

In moments of crisis, accordingly, Huck comes up against the discrepancy between the standard conception of black people as "niggers"—a conception he shares—and what he has learned as a result of his direct experience with Jim. During such crises his inner struggle characteristically begins with an unquestioning endorsement of the culture's stock prejudices, but then, when he tries to enact them, he balks and, in consequence, he inadvertently reveals their inhumanity. When, for example, it suddenly occurs to him that his journey with an escaped slave will determine what people back home think about him, his first reaction is wholly conventional: "It would get all around that Huck Finn helped a nigger to get his freedom; and if I was ever to see anybody from that town again, I'd be ready to get down and lick his boots for shame." He knows what he is supposed to do if he wants the respect of law-abiding citizens, but the thought of turning Jim in calls up vivid memories of Jim's loyalty and friendship, and he finally decides that he can't do it; he would rather go to hell. The conflict between Huck's stock racist ideas and his compassionate nature exemplifies the way the controlling irony works: when he thinks he is behaving ignobly, we are invited to recognize his innate nobility. What makes the outcome so powerful is that the novel's readers are compelled to effect the ironic reversal. That Huck can acknowledge Jim's humanity only by violating the moral code of a racist society is an implication that the boy is unable to grasp or put into words. It is a thought that Mark Twain's readers must formulate for themselves.

But of course the centrality of that irony also explains why some readers consider *Huckleberry Finn* a racist book. For whatever reason, and one can imagine several, they mistake the hero's flagrant if erratic racism for the novel's—the author's—viewpoint. It may be difficult, admittedly, for admirers of this wonderful book to believe that an average, reasonably competent reader could fail to recognize that its satirical thrust is directed against slavery and racial bigotry, but it does happen. Leaving aside the incontrovertible evidence that some adult readers do miss the point, it must be emphasized that Wallace and those who share his views are not chiefly concerned about the novel's effect on mature, competent readers. They are concerned about its effect on schoolchildren, all schoolchildren,

but especially black American children, whose special experience might very well hinder their responsiveness to the ironic treatment of racial oppression. How much do we know, actually, about the ability of teachers, or of children of various ages and social backgrounds, to make sense of ironic discourse? I have taught this book with pleasure to hundreds of college students, but I'm not at all confident about my ability to persuade a class of inner-city adolescents—or any literal-minded adolescents, for that matter—that a book can say, or seem to say, one thing and mean another; or that in this case we should not be troubled by the fact that the hero calls black people "niggers" because, after all, that's what all white Southerners called them back then, and anyway, look, in the end he is loyal to Jim.

And besides, what does one say about Jim? There can be no doubt that Mark Twain wants us to admire him; he is a sympathetic, loving, self-abnegating, even saintly, "Christ-like" man. But what does one tell black children about his extreme passivity, his childlike credulity, his cloying deference toward the white boy? Aren't these the traits of a derisory racial stereotype, the fawning black male? To overcome objections on that score, one would have to stress Jim's cunning and his occasional refusal to play the minstrel darkie, especially the great episode in which he drops his habitual pose of docility, if it is a pose, and angrily denounces Huck for making him the victim of a cruel joke. "It was fifteen minutes," Huck says about his reluctant apology, "before I could work myself up to go and humble myself to a nigger—but I done it, and I wasn't ever sorry for it afterwards, neither." It is a splendid moment, but is it splendid enough to offset the inescapable doubts of black readers about Jim's customary pliancy? Is it enough that Jim, the only black male of any significance in the novel, asserts his dignity in this one moving episode?

To raise these complex issues, it need hardly be said, is not to condone the denunciation of the novel as racist trash. But even if that opinion is as wrongheaded as I believe it to be, it does not follow that those who hold it are necessarily wrong about the inappropriateness of requiring high-school teachers to teach, and students to read, the *Adventures of Huckleberry Finn*. The point at issue, then, is the justification for that requirement. To claim that it should be required reading because it is a great American book is unconvincing: we don't require students to read most great books. Objections to the requirement become more understandable if we recognize the unique character of the niche Twain's novel tends to occupy in the high-school English course. It often is the only book that is centrally concerned with racial oppression.

All of which suggests that educators could take a large step toward resolving the current controversy simply by eliminating the requirement. This would open the way for the ideal solution: allow each teacher to decide whether his or her students should be asked to read *Huckleberry Finn*. It is the teachers, after all, who are best qualified to make a sensible and informed decision, one that would rest on their confidence in their own ability to convey, and their students' ability to grasp, the irony that informs every word of this matchless comic novel.

Robert Gooding-Williams

"LOOK, A NEGRO!"

Robert Gooding-Williams is professor of philosophy and adjunct professor of African-American studies at Northwestern University. He is author of Nietzsche's Dionysian Modernism *and editor of* Reading Rodney King/Reading Urban Uprising. *In this essay Gooding-Williams argues that the representations of blacks in Hollywood movies has a harmful influence on American attitudes toward African Americans. He urges the demythification of these racial representations.*

My body was given back to me sprawled out, distorted, recolored, clad in mourning in that white winter day. The Negro is an animal, the Negro is bad, the Negro is mean. . . .

—Frantz Fanon

Your country? How came it yours?

—W. E. B. DuBois

INTRODUCTION

In this essay, I will investigate the impact of racial ideology (by which I mean, roughly, the interpretation of racial identities in the representation of racially classified individuals or groups) on the trial of the policemen who beat Rodney King and on media coverage of the L.A. uprising. My principal aim will be to analyze critically the ways in which racial ideology, during the policemen's trial and the media's coverage of the uprising, functioned to characterize black bodies and, implicitly, to interpret the sociopolitical status of blacks in the United States.

In pursuing this aim, my critique of racial ideology will differ from a more familiar approach to ideology critique that, owing most of its influence to the writings of Marx and Freud, attempts to demystify social phenomena by identifying their social origins. Marx, for example, criticizes the fetishism of commodities by showing that exchange values are not simply properties of things, but also effects of capitalist social relations. Similarly, psychoanalysis reveals the significance of otherwise unintelligible neurotic symptoms by relating them to prior contexts

Robert Gooding-Williams, "Look, a Negro!" *Reading Rodney King/Reading Urban Uprising*, ed. Robert Gooding-Williams (New York: Routledge, 1993) 157–77.

of childhood trauma.[1] Black bodies, however, unlike Marx's exchange values and Freud's neurotic symptoms, do not ordinarily strike us as resembling mysterious fetishes or "hieroglyphics" that have been waiting to have meaning attributed to them.[2]

Black bodies, in fact, have been supersaturated with meaning, as they have been relentlessly subjected to characterization by newspapers, newscasters, popular film, television programming, public officials, policy pundits and other agents of representation. Characterizations of black bodies often represent their actions and/or attributes as consequences of discrimination, social pathology, state policy, unemployment, jungle chaos, physical prowess, genial good-heartedness, or some other cause or causes. Many of these characterizations are false, and so need to be vigorously contested. But, over and beyond contesting such false characterizations, a critique of racial ideology should also explore the ways in which explanations and other representations of black bodies function as forms of sociopolitical imagination. To be more precise, it should investigate the ways in which these representations present themselves as allegories of social organization and political community. The point of such an investigation would not be to *demystify* black bodies (that is, the point would not be to identify the social causes of their actions and attributes), but to *demythify* them, that is, to subject to critical scrutiny the allegories of American social and political life intimated in characterizing them.[3]

In what follows, I will elaborate further my concept of racial ideology, drawing on Toni Morrison's discussion of Africanism in American literature and on a recent popular film (popular film being one of the most influential sources of racial ideology in our time) for my examples. I will then use my concept of racial ideology to analyze, first, the defense lawyers' representation of Rodney King to the jurors who exonerated his assailants, and second, the media's representation of black participation in the uprising prompted by the jurors' verdicts. I present this analysis as a possible starting point for further inquiry. It is not intended to be exhaustive of the issues it addresses.

THE CONCEPT OF RACIAL IDEOLOGY

I understand the concept of racial ideology to have as its extension (i.e., the scope of its reference) all *racial representations*, that is, all representations of racially classified individuals or groups (of individuals). Thus, in contemporary American society, where all individuals and groups are subject to racial classification, the concept of racial ideology applies in fact to all representations of social activity. Though the notion of racial ideology I am proposing may seem at first glance to be *too* inclusive, since it identifies *all* representations of racially classified individuals or groups as ideological, its inclusiveness is in fact one of its strengths. By advocating a relatively broad and encompassing concept of racial ideology, I mean to resist the temptation to restrict in advance the proper domain of a critique of racial ideology.

Michael Omi and Howard Winant have argued that "In US society . . . a kind of 'racial etiquette' exists, a set of interpretive codes and racial meanings which operate in the interactions of daily life. . . . Everybody learns some combination, some version, of the rules of racial classification, and of their own racial identity, often without conscious teaching or conscious inculcation. Race becomes 'common sense'—a way of comprehending, explaining, and acting in the world."[4] Here, Omi and Winant remind us that racial classification is pervasive in American society. In the most familiar cases, e.g., the classification of individuals as "black" or "white," it proceeds on the basis of visible physical characteristics that almost everyone learns to read on sight as signifiers of racial identity.[5] Most Americans take it for granted that they are competent and even adept participants in the practice of racial classification; they tend to acknowledge explicitly their participation in this practice only when they encounter individuals whom they cannot immediately racially categorize. First of all and most of the time, racial classification operates as an unthematized but constitutive dimension of social interaction in American society.

Because racial classification is pervasive; because, in fact, there are no occasions in American society in which racial classification is not present as a dimension of social interaction, it is possible and even reasonable to read all representations of the individuals or groups present in American society—by which I mean all visual, verbal, and written depictions of these individuals or groups, fictional depictions included—as interpretations of the racial identities which all racial classifications posit.[6] In a society in which racial classification is a constitutive feature of social life, all representations of social life make implicit reference to racial identities. Thus, all representations of social life can be read as interpretations of racial identities. The critique of racial ideology, as I conceive it, proceeds from the heuristic assumption that all such representations *should be* read as interpretations of racial identities.[7]

To be sure, readings of the sort I envision are not always informative or illuminating. And readings of this sort, far from being exhaustive, constitute just *one* of many viable and politically significant perspectives on the representation of American social life.[8] Still, an essential part of a critique of racial ideology is to produce such readings, without presupposing that some racial representations should be excluded a priori from the set of potentially fruitful objects of ideology critique.

THE CONCEPT OF IDEOLOGY CRITIQUE: GENEALOGY, SOCIOPOLITICAL ALLEGORY, AND DEMYTHIFICATION

The conception of ideology critique I wish to elaborate has three components: (1) the genealogical exposure of racial representations; (2) the reading of genealogically exposed racial representations as sociopolitical allegories; and (3) the demythification of the allegorical content of genealogically exposed racial representations.

My conception of genealogical exposure draws its inspiration from Nietzsche.[9] As I conceive it, a genealogical exposure of racial representations discloses the interpretive origins of those representations. Its point, more exactly, is to identify the acts of interpretation which constitute racial representations. Following Nietzsche, I regard an act of interpretation as a characterization of a physical object, individual, practice, or other subject matter that ascribes to it some purpose(s) or function(s) or other significance (e.g., the characterization of the practice of punishment as having the purpose of preventing further harm).[10] To disclose the interpretive origin of a racial representation is, for my purposes, to show that that representation has been constituted through the ascription of some purpose(s) or function(s) or other significance to a racially classified individual or group of individuals, and to the racial identity(ies) which he, she, or it has been classified as embodying.

The best examples I know of the genealogical exposure of racial representations can be found in Toni Morrison's study of American Africanism, *Playing in the Dark: Whiteness and the Literary Imagination*. As Morrison defines it, "American Africanism" refers to "the ways in which a nonwhite, Africanlike (or Africanist) presence or persona was constructed in the United States, and the imaginative uses this fabricated presence served."[11] In her analysis of American Africanism, Morrison attempts to show that in American literature "black matters," that it makes a difference.[12] Her aim, as I read her, is to disclose and explore the many ways in which works of American literature adapt themselves to and characterize individuals who have been racially classified as black. The questions she asks—"How does literary utterance arrange itself when it tries to imagine the Africanist other? What are the signs, the codes, the literary strategies designed to accommodate this encounter? What does the inclusion of Africans or African-Americans do to and for the work?"—clearly implicate the genealogical dimensions of her project, as they pertain explicitly to the functions which literary works assign to racially classified individuals (what the inclusion of such individuals does to and for a work), and to the ways in which literary works "arrange" themselves so as to "accommodate" these functions.[13]

Morrison's genealogical exposures of Africanist racial representations in American literature show that these representations were constituted through the ascription of multiple purposes and functions to individuals racially classified as black (the black characters appearing in the fictions Morrison discusses). Some of the purposes and functions she identifies are: "surrogate and enabler of self-reflexion"; figure for what is "hip, sophisticated, (and) ultra-urbane"; means to defining the goals and enhancing the qualities of white characters; and "means of meditation—both safe and risky on one's own humanity."[14] What Morrison calls "the serviceability of the African presence" is a constitutive force in American literature, whose pervasiveness she wishes to highlight.[15] By bringing into view the many roles and purposes which American writers have ascribed to black characters and figures of blackness, she lets us see a large

part of the quite complicated network of meanings which American culture has attributed to what it construes as a black racial identity.[16]

Let me now turn to an example of American Africanism, in order to begin to explain the possibility of reading genealogically exposed racial representations as sociopolitical allegories. The example I have in mind is that of the male-nurse figures who appear in Hemingway's fiction. These male nurses, Morrison points out, are almost always black. "Cooperative or sullen," she writes, "they are Tontos all, whose role is to do everything possible to serve the Lone Ranger without disturbing his indulgent delusion that he is indeed alone."[17] Morrison goes on to discuss at length the functions of these figures, noting both their enabling and disenabling qualities vis-à-vis their white male patrons.[18] Her remarks along these lines are striking, in part because of the insight they bring to Hemingway's writings, but likewise because they remind us that fictive individuals of the sort she analyzes pervade American culture. In popular film, for example, figures of black nurses and sidekicks abound, gendered sometimes as male, sometimes as female, bound often to Lone Rangers, but sometimes to romantic lovers. A by-now classic example is the figure of Sam (Dooley Wilson), who in *Casablanca* appears as nurse, as sidekick, and as a desexualized Cupid figure whose raison d'être is to keep alive the myth of (white) heterosexual romance. A more recent example is the figure of Oda Mae Brown (Whoopi Goldberg), who in *Ghost* reprises the role of the Cupid figure by appearing literally as the medium through whom two white heterosexual lovers, estranged by death, can touch each other one last time.[19]

The nurse, sidekick, and Cupid figures appearing in *Casablanca* and *Ghost*, no less than those cropping up in Hemingway's fiction, serve various functions within the narratives in which they occur. Once the representations of these black characters have been genealogically exposed, the assignment to these characters of particular roles can be read allegorically as commenting on the social and political status of blacks in America. In the cases of *Casablanca* and *Ghost*, for example, allegorical readings let us see how the assignment of particular narrative functions to black characters can intimate the view that the African presence in American social and political life, though serviceable, is expendable. More familiar to contemporary audiences than Hemingway's fiction, and, for that matter, than classical Hollywood films like *Casablanca*, the example of *Ghost* is especially significant, because it highlights the fact that American Africanism, besides being an essential feature of an established American literary tradition, continues to be perpetuated in contemporary American culture.

Based loosely on Shakespeare's *Macbeth* (the dead protagonist's ghost is meant to recall Banquo's ghost), *Ghost* is about the effort of a dead but "legitimate" white American patriarch and capitalist to defend his realm against the designs of an "illegitimate" usurper. The film persuades its audiences to endorse this effort, by conflating it with the expression of an intensely passionate heterosexual love. Personifying a (socially posited) black racial identity, Oda Mae functions in the film to facilitate both the communication of this love and the protagonist's destruction of the "tyrant" who has displaced him. Once she fulfills her function, she is dispensable (as is Sam in *Casablanca*). Read as an allegorical commentary on contemporary American society, Oda Mae represents the claim that though the black presence in America is *not essential* to America's identity as a political community, it constitutes a useful, convenient, and sometimes welcome means for propping up and stabilizing the patriarchal and capitalist social order which is the foundation of that

community.[20] *Ghost*'s dominant fantasy, reminiscent of the "indulgent delusion" Morrison attributes to the Lone Ranger, is that America can use blacks for its purposes, and yet retain an identity to which a black presence is not essential.[21]

By discussing *Ghost*, I have hoped to show how a genealogically exposed racial representation can be read as a sociopolitical allegory.[22] I have hoped, too, to begin to explain my concept of demythification. "Demythification," as I use that term, refers to the critical use of evidence and argument to gauge the truth value of the sociopolitical allegories implicit in racial representations.[23] Demythifying *Ghost*, for example, could involve an appeal to evidence and argument contradicting the view that the black presence in America, though convenient, is not an essential part of America's identity as a nation.[24] Such evidence is readily available and has been for a long time. W. E. B. DuBois used it, when almost a century ago he attacked the myth which *Ghost* embraces.

Your country? How came it yours? Before the Pilgrims landed we were here. Here we have brought our three gifts and mingled them with yours: a gift of story and song . . . ; the gift of sweat and brawn to beat back the wilderness . . . ; the third a gift of Spirit. Around us the history of the land has centered for thrice a hundred years; out of the nation's heart we have called all that is best to throttle and subdue all that was worst, . . . Actively we have woven ourselves with the warp and woof of the nation,—we fought their battles, shared their sorrow, mingled our blood with theirs, and generation after generation have pleaded with a headstrong careless people to despise not Justice, Mercy, and Truth, lest the nation be smitten with a curse. Our song, our toil, our cheer, and warning have been given to the nation in blood-brotherhood. Are not these gifts worth the giving? Is not this work and striving? *Would America be America without her Negro people?*[25] (emphasis mine)

DuBois argues that the Negro has given America its song, built its foundations, and, weaving him/herself with the warp and woof of the nation, born the brunt of its struggle for justice, mercy, and truth. His point is that the Negro has played so important a role in creating America, and in fostering its highest aspirations, that America's identity as a distinct political community is not conceivable absent the centuries-long presence of blacks in America. DuBois demythifies the claim set forth allegorically in *Ghost*, that this presence has been a peripheral and inessential one, by insisting that America would not be America without its Negro people.[26]

DuBois's eloquence is unusually compelling. But *Ghost*, it is important to see, is just one of many film and television events that can be usefully subjected to ideological criticism. Less important, therefore, than the details of my analysis of this film is the recognition that what *Ghost* exemplifies, namely, the use of racial representations to interpret racial identities, pervades American culture. Although the interpretation of racial identities varies from one racial representation to another, and though the complexity of some racial representations far and away exceeds that of others, the fact remains that American culture lives and breathes by racial representations, using them relentlessly to make sense of American history, society, and politics.

Thus, when we consider the role of racial ideology in the trial of the policemen who beat Rodney King and in the media's depiction of the L.A. uprising, we should acknowledge from the beginning that courtroom and media representations of black bodies grow out of a long and ongoing tradition of American Africanism. The racial representations present in *Ghost*, *Casablanca*, and the works of fiction Toni Morrison discusses are but a small sample of the great storehouse of interpreted images of black people that American jurors, lawyers, and media pundits

have available to them as elements of the culture they have in common. That particular jurors, lawyers, and pundits should have made use of some of these images in the contexts of the Simi Valley trial and the television coverage of the L.A. uprising simply marks them as Americans.

Racial ideology in contemporary America works relentlessly to exclude blacks from many white Americans' conceptions of who their fellow citizens are. The antiblack sentiment reported in a recent *New York Times* article about the Greenwood section of Chicago begins to tell the story. Putting succinctly all he claims to know about black Americans, 23-year-old William Knepper says that "they came from Africa, and they can get away with a lot of stuff because they're black, they're a minority." Peggy O'Connor, a waitress and the wife of a police officer, is a bit more blunt: "I don't want to be too close to them. I think they've been whining too long, and I'm sick of it."[27] As it turns out, the image of the whining black recurs frequently among white Americans, as according to a poll CNN reported on the weekend of the L.A. uprising, 46% of the whites queried agreed that blacks "[a]re always whining about racism."[28] For many whites, then, black speech is not the speech of fellow citizens, but the always-complaining speech of spoiled children. Casting blacks in the infantilizing role of whiners from Africa, the racial ideology of these white folk works against the possibility of recognizing blacks as partners in a broadly conceived social and political enterprise.[29]

Read as sociopolitical allegory, the remarks and thoughts of Knepper, O'Connor, and many others can be said to envision America as a white nation that has got itself beset by a bunch of whimpering interlopers who get away with too much. DuBois's words . . . exemplify [a] discursive strategy for demythifying and resisting this vision.

Other discursive strategies are possible as well. Absent demythification and resistance, we should anticipate endless echoes of Fanon's leitmotif:

> Look at the nigger! . . . Mama, a Negro! . . . Hell, he's getting mad. . . . Take no notice,

sir, he does not know that you are as civilized as we. . . ."

My body was given back to me sprawled out, distorted, recolored, clad in mourning in that white winter day. The Negro is an animal, the Negro is bad, the Negro is mean, the Negro is ugly; look, a nigger. . . .[30]

[1]For a clear discussion of Marx's critique of the fetishism of commodities, see Seyla Benhabib, *Critique, Norm, and Utopia: A Study of the Foundations of Critical Theory* (New York: Columbia University Press, 1986), 114–23. For an account of Freud that points implicitly to the affinity between Freud and Marx to which I have alluded, see Jürgen Habermas, "The Hermeneutic Claim to Universality," in *Contemporary Hermeneutics*, ed. Joseph Bleicher (London: Routledge, 1980), 193–94. I should add, finally, that the conception of ideology critique as demystification depends on the assumption that a form of consciousness is ideological if, to borrow the words of Raymond Geuss, "it contains essentially an 'objectification' mistake, i.e., if it contains a false belief to the effect that some social phenomenon is a natural phenomenon, or, to put it another way, human agents or 'subjects' are suffering from ideologically false consciousness if they falsely 'objectify' their own activity, i.e., if they are deceived into taking that activity to be something 'foreign' to them, especially if they take that activity to be a natural process outside their control." See Raymond Geuss, *The Idea of a Critical Theory: Habermas and the Frankfurt School* (Cambridge: Cambridge University Press, 1981), 14.

[2]Marx himself uses the figure of the hieroglyphic in his discussion of the fetishism of commodities. See Karl Marx, *Capital: A Critique of Political Economy*, vol. 1, trans. Samuel Moore and Edward Aveling (New York: International Publishers, 1967), 74.

[3]My conception of allegory is the standard one, according to which an allegorical text narrates events that "make sense in themselves . . . but also . . . signify a second, correlated order of persons, things, concepts, or events" (see M. H. Abrams, *A Glossary of Literary Terms* (New York: Holt, Rinehart, and Winston, 1971), 4). My conceptualization of ideology as allegory and as sociopolitical imagination draws its inspiration from Frederic Jameson, *The Political Unconscious: Narrative as a Socially Symbolic Act* (Ithaca: Cornell University Press), 9–102, and Benedict Anderson, *Imagined Communities* (London: Verso, 1991), 1–7.

For the recent use of a distinction between demystification and demythologization that differs slightly from the distinction I have drawn between demystification and demythification see Cornel West, "The New Cultural Politics of Difference," in *Out There: Marginalization and Contemporary Cultures*, ed. Russel Ferguson, Martha Gever, Trinh T. Minh-ha, and Cornel West (New York: New Museum of Contemporary Art; and Cambridge: MIT Press, 1990), 29–32.

[4]Michael Omi and Howard Winant, *Racial Formation in the United States* (New York: Routledge, 1986), 62.

[5]Cf. Robert Miles, *Racism* (New York: Routledge, 1989), 69–84. Here, I also wish to emphasize that the rules of racial classification differ from place to place, and that in a single place they may change over time. For more on this, see Omi and Winant, *Racial Formation in the United States*, 60ff. I should also note here that when, in this essay, I write of "whites," "blacks," "antiblack sentiment," etc., I am myself producing racial representations and, therefore, racial ideology. Thus, my own discourse can itself be taken as an object of ideology critique as I have conceived it.

[6]Some of these interpretations will be contesting received interpretations. Sometimes the object of contestation will be racial classifications themselves. (See, for example, Michael Jackson's "Black or White" MTV video.)

[7]My conception of racial ideology, as a system of racial representations that can be read as interpreting the racial identities which racial classifications posit, seems to me to be logically compatible with Barbara Fields's conceptions of racial ideology as a "medium" that mediates the comprehension of social reality. See Barbara Fields, "Ideology and Race in American History," *in Region, Race, and Reconstruction: Essays in Honor of C. Vann Woodward*, ed. James Morgan Kousser and James M. Mcpherson (New York: Oxford University Press, 1982), 143–75.

[8]In general, a complete analysis of any given instance of racial ideology must also take into account those analytical perspectives that focus on the interpretation of class, gender, and sexual identities in the representation of American social life. Still, it seems to me that a critique of racial ideology can be usefully undertaken as a distinct endeavor. Thus, I believe that we can approach racial ideology more or less as Eve Sedgwick suggests we should approach gender and sexuality: "[I]n twentieth-century Western culture gender and sexuality represent two analytic axes that may productively be imagined as distinct from one another as, say, gender and class, or class and race. Distinct, that is to say, no more than minimally, but nonetheless usefully." See Eve Kosofsky Sedgwick, *Epistemology of the Closet* (Berkeley: University of California Press, 1990), 30.

[9]Friedrich Nietzsche, *On the Genealogy of Morals*, trans. Walter Kaufmann and R. J. Hollingdale, in *On the Genealogy of Morals and Ecce Homo* (New York: Random House, 1969), 76–9.

[10]Cf. Nietzsche, *On the Genealogy of Morals*, 79–81.

[11]Toni Morrison, *Playing in the Dark: Whiteness and the Literary Imagination* (Cambridge, MA: Harvard University Press, 1992), 6.

[12]Ibid., 1.

[13]Ibid., 16.

[14]Ibid., 51–53.

[15]Ibid., 76.

[16]Here, I want to emphasize that genealogical exposure and the critique of racial ideology need not restrict themselves, as does Morrison's discussion, to works by whites. Wilson Moses, for example, discusses the figures of the black Messiah and the Uncle Tom as they appear in literary representations of blacks produced by blacks as well as whites. See Wilson Jeremiah Moses, *Black Messiahs and Uncle Toms: Social and Literary Manipulations of a Religious Myth* (University Park: Pennsylvania State University Press, 1982). For a helpful historical perspective on some of the issues Morrison raises, see George Frederickson, *The Black Image in the White Mind* (Middletown: Wesleyan University Press, 1987). For an interesting and provocative attempt to raise similar issues as regards children's literature about black children, see Keith Millner, "By the Color of Their Skin *and* the Content of Their Character: Representing Race for Children in African-American Picture Books," Senior Thesis, Amherst College, 1992.

[17]Morrison, *Playing in the Dark*, 82.

[18]Ibid., 82ff.

[19]The reading of *Ghost* I sketch below derives from an essay in progress, entitled "Black Cupids, White Desires: A Reading of *Casablanca* and *Ghost*." For a brief but helpful discussion of *Ghost* that begins to address some of the issues I think important, see Tania Modleski, *Feminism without Women: Culture and Criticism in a "Postfeminist" Age* (New York: Routledge, 1991), 131–34. Modleski's treatment of *Ghost* comes at the end of an insightful chapter ("Cinema and the Dark Continent: Race and Gender in Popular Film") on the interplay of racial and gender ideologies in a number of well-known American films. For an older but still-useful analysis of the representation of race in American film, see James Baldwin's *The Devil Finds Work* (New York: Dell, 1976). See also Thomas Cripps, *Slow Fade to Black: The Negro in American Film, 1900–1942* (New York: Oxford University Press, 1977).

[20]A fuller reading would also take into account issues of gender and sexuality.

[21]The paradigmatic cinematic expression of this claim is the portrait of the black "good souls" in D. W. Griffith's *The Birth of a Nation*.

[22]The tendency to overlook issues of race in allegorical readings of popular film is striking. Consider, for example, Frederic Jameson's reading of *Something Wild*, which completely ignores the film's obsession with figures of racial blackness, including its deployment of black cupid figures. Jameson's discussion of *Something Wild* is contained in chapter 9 of his *Postmodernism, or, The Cultural Logic of Late Capitalism* (Durham:

Duke University Press, 1991). For a helpful corrective to his racially blind reading of the film, see Cameron Bailey, "Nigger Lover—The Thin Sheen of Race in 'Something Wild,'" *Screen 4* (Autumn 1988): 28–40.

[23]Here, I mean to leave open the possibility that not *all* allegorical commentaries or messages are false. See, for example, my discussion below of the Amherst College effigy protest.

[24]The claims set forth by a demythifying critique will vary with the allegorically expressed claims under consideration. Thus, a demythifying critique of the Cosby show would proceed along different lines than a demythifying critique of *Ghost*.

[25]W. E. B. DuBois, *The Souls of Black Folk* (New York: Bantam, 1989), 186–87.

[26]As far as I can tell, DuBois's argument does *not* entail the questionable view that the history of America can be readily comprehended by means of an organic model of historical development. For more on this issue, see Robert Gooding-Williams, "Evading Narrative Myth, Evading Prophetic Pragmatism: Cornel West's *The American Evasion of Philosophy*," *The Massachusetts Review* (Winter 1991–92): 517–42.

[27]*New York Times*, 21 June 1992.

[28]The poll was taken on 30 April 1992 by the firm of Yankelovich Clancy Shulman, located in Westport, Connecticut.

[29]Television media's tendency to use images of black bodies to represent people on welfare contributes substantially to the view that black people, *in general*, are clients but not citizens of the larger political community. Note also Gertrude Ezorsky's observation that "15 to 19 percent of whites would not vote for a qualified black candidate nominated by their own party either for governor or president. According to Linda Williams, senior research associate at the Joint Center for Policy Studies, their 1986 poll showed that 'the higher the office, the more whites there were who would admit that they would never vote for a black.'" See Gertrude Ezorsky, *Racism and Justice*, 13.

For an insightful discussion of the ways in which the failure of whites to recognize blacks as fellow citizens has (mis)shaped contemporary policy debates about race in America, see Adolph Reed and Julian Bond, "Equality: Why We Can't Wait," *The Nation* 20 (December 1991): 736. For a provocative *philosophical* discussion of the issues of recognition, membership, and citizenship which I have raised here, see Michael Walzer, *Spheres of Justice* (New York: Basic Books, 1983), 31–63.

[30]Fanon, *Black Skin, White Masks*, 113.

Linda Nochlin

WHY ARE THERE
NO GREAT
WOMEN ARTISTS?

Linda Nochlin is professor of art history at Yale University. Her work focuses particularly on the political dimensions of art. Her books include Art and Architecture in the Service of Politics, The Politics of Vision, *and* Woman as Sex Object: Studies in Erotic Art. *In the following excerpt from her classic essay "Why Are There No Great Women Artists?" Nochlin describes some of the structural barriers that have historically worked to prevent women from achieving stature in the visual arts.*

"Why are there no great women artists?" This question tolls reproachfully in the background of discussions of the so-called woman problem, causing men to shake their heads regretfully and women to grind their teeth in frustration. Like so many other questions involved in the red-hot feminist controversy, it falsifies the nature of the issue at the same time that it insidiously supplies its own answer: "There are no great women artists because women are incapable of greatness." The assumptions lying behind such a question are varied in range and sophistication, running anywhere from "scientifically" proven demonstrations of the inability of human beings with wombs rather than penises to create anything signif-

icant, to relatively open-minded wonderment that women, despite so many years of near-equality—and after all, a lot of men have had their disadvantages too—have still not achieved anything of major significance in the visual arts.

The feminist's first reaction is to swallow the bait, hook, line and sinker and to attempt to answer the question as it is put: that is, to dig up examples of worthy or insufficiently appreciated women artists throughout history; to rehabilitate rather modest, if interesting and productive careers; to rediscover forgotten flower painters or David-followers and make out a case for them; to demonstrate that Berthe Morisot was really less dependent upon

Linda Nochlin, "Why Are There No Great Women Artists?" *Women in Sexist Society*, ed. Vivian Gornick and Barbara K. Moran (New York: Basic Books, 1971) 344–66.

Manet than one had been led to think—in other words, to engage in activity not too different from that of the average scholar, man or woman, making out a case for the importance of his own neglected or minor master. Whether undertaken from a feminist point of view, such attempts, like the ambitious article on women artists which appeared in the 1858 *Westminster Review*, or more recent scholarly studies and reevaluations of individual woman artists like Angelica Kauffmann or Artemisia Gentileschi, are certainly well worth the effort, adding to our knowledge both of women's achievement and of art history generally; and a great deal still remains to be done in this area. Unfortunately, such efforts, if written from an uncritically feminist viewpoint, do nothing to question the assumptions lying behind the question "Why are there no great women artists?"; on the contrary, by attempting to answer it and by doing so inadequately, they merely reinforce its negative implications.

At the same time that champions of women's equality may feel called upon to falsify the testimony of their own judgment by scraping up neglected female artistic geniuses or puffing up the endeavors of genuinely excellent but decidedly minor women painters and sculptors into major contributions, they may resort to the easily refuted ploy of accusing the questioner of using "male" standards as the criterion of greatness or excellence. This attempt to answer the question involves shifting the ground slightly; by asserting, as many contemporary feminists do, that there is actually a different kind of greatness for women's art than for men's, one tacitly assumes the existence of a distinctive and recognizable feminine style, differing in both its formal and its expressive qualities from that of male artists and positing the unique character of women's situation and experience.

This, on the surface of it, seems reasonable enough: in general, women's experience and situation in society, and hence as artists, is different from men's; certainly, the art produced by a group of consciously united and purposefully articulate women intent on bodying forth a group consciousness of feminine experience might be stylistically identifiable as feminist, if not feminine art. Unfortunately, this remains within the realm of possibility; so far, it has not occurred. While the Danube School, Caravaggio's followers, the painters gathered around Gauguin at Pont Aven, the Blue Rider, or the Cubists may be recognized by certain clearly defined stylistic or expressive qualities, no such common qualities of femininity would seem to link the styles of women artists generally, any more than such qualities can be said to link all women writers. . . . In every instance women artists and writers would seem to be closer to other artists and writers of their own period and outlook than they are to each other.

Women artists are more inward-looking, more delicate and nuanced in their treatment of their medium, it may be asserted. But which of the women artists cited above is more inward turning than Redon, more subtle and nuanced in the handling of pigment than Corot at his best? Is Fragonard more or less feminine than Elisabeth Vigée-Lebrun? Or is it not more a question of the whole rococo style of eighteenth-century France being "feminine," if judged in terms of a two-valued scale of masculinity versus femininity? Certainly, though, if daintiness, delicacy, and preciousness are to be counted as earmarks of a feminine style, there is nothing very fragile about Rosa Bonheur's *Horse Fair*, or dainty and introverted about Helen Frankenthaler's giant canvases. If women have indeed at times turned to scenes of domestic life or of children, so did men painters like the Dutch Little Masters, Chardin, and the impressionists—Renoir and Monet as well as Berthe Morisot and Mary Cassatt. In any case, the mere choice of a certain realm of subject matter, or the restriction to certain subjects, is not to be equated with a style, much less with some sort of quintessentially feminine style.

The problem here lies not so much with the feminists' concept of what femininity is, but rather with their misconception of what art is: with the naive idea that art is the direct, personal expression of individual emotional experience, a translation of personal life into visual terms. Art is almost never that, great art certainly never. The making of art involves a self-consistent language of form, more or less dependent upon, or free from, given temporally defined conventions, schemata, or systems of notation, which have to be learned or worked out, either through teaching, apprenticeship, or a long period of individual experimentation. The language of art is, more materially, embodied in paint and line on canvas or paper, in stone or clay or plastic or metal—it is neither a sob story nor a hoarse, confidential whisper. The fact of the matter is that there have been no great women artists, as far as we know—although there have been many interesting and good ones who have not been sufficiently investigated or appreciated—or any great Lithuanian jazz pianists, or Eskimo tennis players, no matter how much we might wish there had been. That this should be the case is regrettable, but no amount of manipulating the historical or critical evidence will alter the situation; neither will accusations of male-chauvinist distortions of history and obfuscation of actual achievements of women artists (or black physicists or Lithuanian jazz musicians). The fact is that there *are* no women equivalents for Michelangelo or Rembrandt, Delacroix or Cézanne, Picasso or Matisse, or even, in very recent times, for de Kooning or Warhol, any more than there are any black American equivalents for the same. If there actually were large numbers of "hidden" great women artists, or if there really should be different standards for women's art as opposed to men's—and logically, one cannot

have it both ways, then what would feminists be fighting for? If women have in fact achieved the same status as men in the arts, then the status quo is fine as it is.

But in actuality things as they are and as they have been in the arts, as in a hundred other areas, are stultifying, oppressive, and discouraging to all who did not have the good fortune to be born white, preferably middle-class or above, males. The fault lies not in our stars, our hormones, our menstrual cycles, or our empty internal spaces, but in our institutions and our education—education understood to include everything that happens to us from the moment we enter, head first, into this world of meaningful symbols, signs, and signals. The miracle is, in fact, that given the overwhelming odds against women, so many have managed to achieve so much in bailiwicks of masculine prerogative like science, politics, or the arts. In some areas, indeed, women have achieved equality. While there may have been no great women composers, there have been great women singers; if no female Shakespeares, there have been Rachels, Bernhardts, and Duses, to name only a few great women stage performers. Where there is a need there is a way, institutionally speaking: once the public and the authors themselves demanded more realism and range than boys in drag or piping castrati could offer, a way was found to include women in the institutional structure of the performing arts, even if in some cases they might have to do a little whoring on the side to keep their careers in order. In fact, in some of the performing arts like the ballet, women have exercised a virtual monopoly on greatness, though, it is true, they generally had to serve themselves up to Grand Dukes or aspiring bankers as an added professional obligation.

Under the institution of the British monarchy, weak women like Elizabeth I and Victoria were deemed fit to control the fate of entire nations and did so with noteworthy success. During World War II, the institutional structure of factory work found a way to transform fragile little women into stalwart Rosy the Riveters; after the war, when these jobs were needed by muscular males, the same riveters were found to be too frail to do anything more strenuous than checking out groceries at supermarkets, where they could stand on their feet lifting heavy packages all day long at much lower salaries—or housework and childcare, where they could cope with three or four children on a sixteen-hour shift at no salary at all. Wondrous are the works of man and the institutions he has established, or disestablished at his will!

When one really starts thinking about the implications of "Why are there no great women artists?" one begins to realize to what extent our very consciousness of how things are in the world has been conditioned—and too often falsified—by the way the most important questions are posed. We tend to take it for granted that there really are an East Asian problem, a poverty problem, a black problem—and a woman problem. But first we must ask ourselves who is formulating these "questions," and then, what purposes such formulations may serve; we may, of course, refresh our memories with the unspeakably sinister connotations of the Nazi's "Jewish problem." Obviously, for wolves, be they in sheep's clothing or in mufti, it is always best to refer to the lamb problem in the interests of public relations, as well as for the good of the lupine conscience. Indeed, in our time of instant communication, "problems" are rapidly formulated to rationalize the bad conscience of those with power. Thus, for example, what is in actuality the problem posed by the unwanted and unjustifiable presence of Americans in Vietnam and Cambodia is referred to by these intruding and destructive Americans as the East Asian problem, whereas East Asians may view it, more realistically, as the American problem; the so-

called poverty problem might more directly and concretely be viewed as the wealth problem by the poor and hopeless denizens of urban ghettos or rural wastelands; the same not-so-foolish irony twists the white problem—what blacks are going to do to wrest their rights from a dominating, hypocritical, and often outright hostile white majority—into its opposite: a black problem; and the same inverse, but certainly not ineffective or unmotivated, logic turns up in the formulation of our own present state of affairs as the Woman Problem.

Now the women problem, like all human problems, so-called (and the very idea of calling anything to do with human beings a problem is, of course, a fairly recent one), and unlike mathematical or scientific ones, is not amenable to solution at all, since what human problems involve is an actual reinterpretation of the nature of the situation, or even a radical alteration of stance or program of action *on the part of the problems themselves*; recourses unavailable to mathematical symbols, molecules, or microbes. In other words, the "objects" involved in the solution to human problems are at the same time *subjects*, capable of turning on that other group of human beings who has decided that their fellows are problem-objects to be solved, and capable of refusing both the solution, and, at the same time, the status of being problematic at all. Thus, women and their situation in the arts, as in other realms of endeavor, are not a problem to be viewed through the eyes of the dominant male power elite, at whose will or whose whim their demands may possibly some day be answered, at masculine convenience, of course. Women must conceive of themselves as potentially—if not actually—equal subjects, willing to look the facts of their situation as an institutional and objective problem not merely as a personal and subjective one, full in the face, without self-pity or copouts. Yet at the same time, they must view their situation with that high degree of emotional and intellectual commitment necessary to create a world in which truly equal achievement will be not only made possible, but actively encouraged by social institutions.

It is certainly not realistic to hope, as some feminists optimistically do, that a majority of men in the arts or in any other field will soon see that it is actually in their own self-interest to grant complete equality to women or to maintain that men themselves will soon realize that they are diminished by denying themselves access to traditionally feminine realms and emotional reactions. After all, there are few areas that are really denied to men, if the level of operations demanded be transcendant, responsible, or rewarding enough: men who have a need for feminine involvement with babies or children can certainly fulfill their needs adequately, and gain status and a sense of achievement to boot, in the field of pediatrics or child psychology, with a female nurse to do the more routine work; those who feel the urge for creativity at the stove may gain fame as master chefs or restaurateurs; and of course, men who yearn to fulfill themselves through what are often termed feminine artistic interests can easily find themselves as painters or sculptors, rather than as volunteer museum aides or as part-time ceramicists, as their presumably more aesthetically oriented female counterparts so often end up. As far as scholarship is concerned, how many men would really be willing to exchange their roles as teachers and researchers for that of unpaid, part-time research assistants and typists as well as full-time nannies and domestic workers? . . .

Thus, the question of women's equality—in art as in any other realm—devolves not upon the relative benevolence or ill-will of individual men, or the self-confidence or abjectness of individual women, but rather on the very nature of our institutional structures themselves and the view of reality that they impose on the human beings who are part of them. As John Stuart Mill pointed out more than a century ago: "Everything which is usual appears natural. The subjection of women to men being a universal custom, any departure from it quite naturally appears unnatural." Most men, despite lip service to equality, are reluctant to give up this natural order of things in which their advantages so far outweigh their disadvantages; for women the case is further complicated by the fact that, as Mill astutely pointed out, theirs is the only oppressed group or caste whose masters demand not only submission, but unqualified affection as well; thus, women are often weakened by the internalized demands of the male-dominated society itself, as well as by a plethora of material goods and comforts: the middle-class woman has a great deal more to lose than her chains. . . .

Beneath the question lie naive, distorted, uncritical assumptions about the making of art in general, much less the making of great art. These assumptions, conscious or unconscious, link together such unlikely superstars as Michelangelo and Van Gogh, Raphael and Jackson Pollock under the rubric of Great Artist—an honorific attested to by the number of scholarly monographs devoted to the artist in question—and the Great Artist is conceived of as one who has genius; genius, in turn, is thought to be an atemporal and mysterious power somehow embedded in the person of the Great Artist. Thus, the conceptual structure underlying the question "Why are there no great women artists?" rests upon unquestioned, often unconscious, meta-historical premises that make Hippolyte Taine's race-milieu-moment formulation of the dimensions of historical thought seem like a model of sophistication. Such, unfortunately, are the assumptions lying behind a great deal of art history writing. It is no accident that the whole crucial question of the conditions *generally* productive of great art has so rarely been investigated, or that attempts to investigate such general problems have, until fairly recently, been dismissed as unscholarly, too broad, or the province of some other discipline like sociology. To encourage such a dispassionate, impersonal, sociological, and institutionally oriented approach would reveal the entire romantic, elitist, individual-glorifying, and monograph-producing substructure upon which the profession of art history is based, and which has only recently been called into question by a group of younger dissidents within the discipline.

Underlying the question about woman as artist, then, we find the whole myth of the Great Artist—unique, godlike subject of a hundred monographs—bearing within his person since birth a mysterious essence, rather like the golden nugget in Mrs. Grass's chicken soup, called genius or talent, which must always out, no matter how unlikely or unpromising the circumstances.

The magical aura surrounding the representational arts and their creators has given birth to myths since earliest times. Interestingly enough, the same magical abilities attributed by Pliny to the Greek painter Lysippos in antiquity—the mysterious inner call in early youth, the lack of any teacher but nature herself—is repeated as late as the nineteenth century by Max Buchon in his biography of the realist painter Courbet. The supernatural powers of the artist as imitator, his control of strong, possibly dangerous powers, have functioned historically to set him off from others as a godlike creator, one who creates being out of nothing like the demiurge. The fairy tale of the boy wonder, discovered by an older artist or discerning patron, usually in the guise of a lowly shepherd boy, has been a stock in trade of artistic mythology ever since Vasari immortalized the young Giotto, whom the great Cimabue discovered drawing sheep on a stone, while the lad was guarding his flocks; Cimabue, overcome with admiration for the realism of the drawing, immediately invited the humble youth to be his pupil. Through some mysterious coincidence, later artists like Beccafumi, Andrea Sansovino, Andrea del Castagno, Mantegna, Zurbaran, and Goya were all discovered in similar pastoral circumstances. Even when the Great Artist was not fortunate enough to come equipped with a flock of sheep as a lad, his talent always seems to have manifested itself very early, independent of any external encouragement: Filippo Lippi, Poussin, Courbet, and Monet are all reported to have drawn caricatures in the margins of their schoolbooks, instead of studying the required subjects—we never, of course, hear about the myriad youths who neglected their studies and scribbled in the margins of their notebooks without ever becoming anything more elevated than department store clerks or shoe salesmen—and the great Michelangelo himself, according to his biographer and pupil, Vasari, did more drawing than studying as a child. So pronounced was the young Michelangelo's talent as an art student, reports Vasari, that when his master, Ghirlandaio, absented himself momentarily from his work in Santa Maria Novella and the young Michelangelo took the opportunity to draw "the scaffolding, trestles, pots of paint, brushes, and the apprentices at their tasks," he did so so skillfully that upon his return his master exclaimed: "This boy knows more than I do."

As is so often the case, such stories, which may indeed have a grain of truth in them, tend both to reflect and to perpetuate the attitudes they subsume. Despite the actual basis in fact of these myths about the early manifestations of genius, the tenor of the tales is itself misleading. It is no doubt true, for example, that the young Picasso passed all the examinations for entrance to the Barcelona, and later to the Madrid, Academy of Art at the age of fifteen in a single day, a feat of such difficulty that most candidates required a month of preparation; however, one would like to find out more about similar precocious qualifiers for art academies, who then went on to achieve nothing but mediocrity or failure—in whom, of course, art historians are uninterested—or to study in greater detail the role played by Picasso's art professor father in the pictorial precocity of his son. What if Picasso had been born a girl? Would Señor Ruiz have paid as much attention or stimulated as much ambition for achievement in a little Pablita?

What is stressed in all these stories is the apparently miraculous, nondetermined, and asocial nature of artistic achievement. This gratuitous, semi-religious conception of the artist's role was elevated into a true hagiography in the nineteenth century, when both art historians, critics, and, not least, some of the artists themselves tended to erect the making of art into a substitute religion, the last bulwark of higher values in a materialistic world. The artist in the nineteenth-century Saints' Legend struggles onward against the most determined parental and social opposition, suffering the slings and arrows of social opprobrium like any Christian martyr, and ultimately succeeds against all odds—generally, alas, after his death—because from deep within himself radiates that mysterious, holy effulgence: genius. Here we have the mad Van Gogh, spinning out sunflowers despite epileptic seizures and near-starvation, or perhaps because of them; Cézanne, braving paternal rejection and public scorn in order to revolutionize painting; Gauguin, throwing away respectability and financial security with a single existential gesture to pursue his calling in the tropics, unrecognized by crass Philistines on the home front; or Toulouse-Lautrec, dwarfed, crippled, and alcoholic, sacrificing his aristocratic birthright in favor of the squalid surroundings that provided him with inspiration.

Of course, no serious contemporary art historian ever takes such obvious fairy tales at their face value. Yet it is all too often this sort of mythology about artistic achievement and its concomitants that forms the unconscious or unquestioned assumptions of art scholars, no matter how many crumbs are thrown to social influences, ideas of the times, economic crises, and so on. Behind the most sophisticated investigations of great artists, more specifically, the art history monograph, which accepts the notion of the Great Artist as primary, and the social and institutional structures within which he lived and worked as mere secondary "influences" or "background," lurks the golden nugget theory of genius and the free enterprise conception of individual achievement. On this basis, women's lack of major achievement in art may be formulated as a syllogism: if women had the golden nugget of artistic genius, then it would reveal itself. But it has never revealed itself. Q.E.D. Women do not have the golden nugget of artistic genius. If Giotto, the obscure shepherd boy, and Von Gogh, the epileptic, could make it, why not women?

Yet as soon as one leaves behind the world of fairy tale and self-fulfilling prophecy and instead casts a dispassionate eye on the actual situations in which important art has been produced, in the total range of its social and institutional structures throughout history, one finds that the very questions that are fruitful or relevant for the historian to ask shape up rather differently. One would like to ask, for instance, from what social classes, from what castes and subgroups, artists were most likely to come at different periods of art history? What proportion of painters and sculptors, or more specifically, of major painters and sculptors, had fathers or other close relatives engaged in painting, sculpture, or related professions? As Nikolaus Pevsner points out in his discussion of the French Academy in the seventeenth and eighteenth centuries, the transmission of the artistic profession from father to son was considered a matter of course (as in fact it was with the Coypels, the Coustous, the Van Loos, and so forth); indeed, sons of academicians were exempted from the customary fees for lessons. Despite the noteworthy and dramatically satisfying cases of the great father-rejecting révoltés of the nineteenth century, a large proportion of artists, great and not-so-great, had artist fathers. In the rank of major artists, the names of Holbein and Dürer, Raphael and Bernini immediately spring to mind; even in our more recent, rebellious times, one can cite the names of Picasso, Calder, Giacometti, and Wyeth as members of artist families.

As far as the relationship of artistic occupation and social class is concerned, an interesting parallel to "why are there no great women artists?" might well be: "why have there been no great artists from the aristocracy?" One can scarcely think, before the antitraditional nineteenth century at least, of any artist who sprang from the ranks of any more elevated class than the upper bourgeoisie; even in the nineteenth century, Degas came from the lower nobility—more like the *haute bourgeoisie*, in fact—and only Toulouse-Lautrec, metamorphosed into the ranks of the marginal by accidental deformity, could be said to have come from the loftier reaches of the upper classes. While the aristocracy has always provided the lion's share of the patronage and the audience for art—as indeed, the aristocracy of wealth does even in our more democratic days, it has rarely contributed anything but a few amateurish efforts to the actual creation of art itself, although aristocrats, like many women, have had far more than their share of educational advantage and leisure, and, indeed, like women, might often be encouraged to dabble in the arts or even develop into respectable amateurs. Napoleon III's cousin, the Princess Mathilde, exhibited at the official salons; Queen Victoria and Prince Albert studied art with no less a figure than Landseer himself. Could it be possible that the little golden nugget—genius—is as absent from the aristocratic make-up as from the feminine psyche? Or is it not rather that the demands and expectations placed on both aristocrats and women—the amount of time necessarily devoted to social functions, the very kinds of activities demanded—simply made total devotion to professional art production out of the question and unthinkable?

When the right questions are finally asked about the conditions for producing art (of which the production of great art is a subtopic), some discussion of the situational concomitants of intelligence and talent generally, not merely of artistic genius, has to be included. As Piaget and others have stressed in their studies of the development of reason and the unfolding of imagination in young children, intelligence—or, by implication, what we choose to call genius—is a dynamic activity, rather than a static essence, and an activity of a subject *in a situation*. As further investigations in the field of child development reveal, these abilities or this intelligence are built up minutely, step by step, from infancy onward, although the patterns of adaptation-accommodation may be established so early within the subject-in-an-environment that they may indeed *appear* to be innate to the unsophisticated observer. Such investigations imply that, even aside from metahistorical reasons, scholars will have to abandon the notion, consciously articulated or not, of individual genius as innate and primary to the creation of art.

The question "Why are there no great women artists?" has so far led to the conclusion that art is not a free, autonomous activity of a superendowed individual, "influenced" by previous artists, and, more vaguely and superficially, by "social forces," but rather, that art making, both in terms of the development of the art maker and the nature and quality of the work of art itself, occurs in a social situation, is an integral element of the social structure, and is mediated and determined by specific and definable social institutions, be they art academies, systems of patronage, mythologies of the divine creator and artist as he-man or social outcast.

THE QUESTION OF THE NUDE

We can now approach our question from a more reasonable standpoint, since it seems probable that the answer to why there are no great women artists, or so few women artists at all, lies not in the nature of individual genius or the lack of it, but in the nature of given social institutions and what they forbid or encourage in various classes or groups of individuals. Let us first examine such a simple, but critical issue as availability of the nude model to aspiring women artists in the period extending from the Renaissance until near the end of the nineteenth century, a period in which careful and prolonged study of the nude model was essential to the training of every young artist, to the production of any work with pretensions to grandeur, and to the very essence of history painting, generally accepted as the highest category of art. Indeed, it was argued by defenders of traditional painting in the nineteenth century that there could be no great painting *with* clothed figures, since costume inevitably destroyed both the temporal universality and the classical idealization required by great art. Needless to say, central to the training programs of art academies since their inception late in the sixteenth and early in the seventeenth centuries, was life drawing from the nude, generally from the male, model. In addition, groups of artists and their pupils often met privately for life-drawing sessions from the nude model in their studios. In general, while individual artists and private academies employed the female model extensively, the female nude was forbidden in almost all public art schools as late as 1850 and after—a state of affairs which Pevsner rightly designates as "hardly believable." Far more believable, unfortunately, was the complete unavailability to the aspiring woman artist of *any* nude models at all, be they male or female. As late as 1893

"lady" students were not admitted to life drawing at the official academy in London; even when they were admitted after that date, the model had to be "partially draped."

The very plethora of surviving "Academies"—detailed, painstaking studies from the nude studio model—in the youthful work of artists down through the time of Seurat and well into the twentieth century attests to the central importance of this branch of study in the pedagogy and development of the talented beginner. The formal academic program itself normally proceeded, as a matter of course, from copying from drawings and engravings, to drawing from casts of famous works of sculpture, to drawing from the living model. To be deprived of this ultimate stage of training meant, in effect, to be deprived of the possibility of creating major art works, unless one were a very ingenious lady indeed, or simply, as most of the few women aspiring to be painters ultimately did, restricted oneself to the "minor" and less highly regarded fields of portraiture, genre, landscape, or still life. It is rather as though a medical student were denied the opportunity to dissect or even examine the naked human body.

There exist, to my knowledge, no representations of artists drawing from the nude model that include women in any role but that of the nude model itself, an interesting commentary on rules of propriety: it is all right for a ("low," of course) woman to reveal herself naked-as-an-object for a group of men, but forbidden to a woman to participate in the active study and recording of naked-man-as-an-object, or even a fellow woman! An amusing example of this taboo on confronting a dressed lady with a naked man is embodied in Zoffany's group portrait of the members of the Royal Academy in London in 1772; all the distinguished members are gathered in the life room before two nude male models, with one noteworthy exception—the single female member, the renowned Angelica Kauffmann, who for propriety's sake, one assumes, is merely present in effigy, in the form of a portrait hanging on the wall. A slightly earlier drawing of *Ladies in the Studio* by the Polish artist Daniel Chodowiecki shows the ladies portraying a modestly dressed member of their own sex. In a lithograph dating from the relatively liberated epoch following the French Revolution, the lithographer Marlet has represented some women sketchers in a group of students working from the male model, but the model himself has been chastely provided with what appears to be a pair of bathing trunks, a garment hardly conducive to a sense of classical elevation; no doubt, such license was considered daring in its day, and the young ladies in question suspected of doubtful morals, but even this state of affairs seems to have lasted only a short while. In an English stereoscopic color view of the interior of a studio of about 1865, the standing, bearded male model is so heavily draped that not an iota of his anatomy escapes from the discreet toga, save for a single bare shoulder and arm: even so, he obviously had the grace to avert his eyes in the presence of the crinoline-clad young sketchers, who so clearly outnumber the men that one suspects this is a ladies' drawing class.

The women in the Women's Modeling Class at the Pennsylvania Academy were evidently not even allowed this modest privilege. A photograph by Thomas Eakins of about 1885 reveals these students modeling from a cow (bull? the nether regions are obscure in the photograph), a naked cow to be sure, perhaps a daring liberty when one considers that even piano legs might be concealed beneath pantalettes during this era; the idea of introducing a bovine model into the artist's studio stems directly from Courbet, who brought a living bull into his short-lived studio academy in the 1860s.

The question of the availability of the nude model is but a single aspect of the automatic, institutionally maintained discrimination against women. It reveals both the universality of the discrimination and its consequences, as well as the institutional rather than individual nature of but one facet of the necessary preparation and equipment for achieving mere proficiency, much less greatness, in the realm of art. One could equally well have examined other dimensions of the situation, such as the apprenticeship system, the academic educational pattern that, in France especially, was almost the only key to success; there was a regular progression and set competitions, crowned by the Prix de Rome, which enabled the young winner to work in the French Academy in that city; this was unthinkable for women, of course, and they were unable to compete for the prize until the end of the nineteenth century, when the whole academic system had lost its importance anyway. If one uses as an example nineteenth-century France—a country with the largest proportion of women artists—it seems clear that "women were not accepted as professional painters." In the middle of the century, there were only a third as many women as men artists, but even this mildly encouraging statistic is deceptive, when we discover that even out of this relatively meager number, *none* had attended that major stepping stone to artistic success, the Ecole des Beaux-Arts; only 7 percent had received any official commission or had held any official office—and these might include the most menial sort of work—only 7 percent had ever received any salon medal; and *none* had ever received the Legion of Honor. Deprived of encouragements, educational facilities, and rewards, it is almost incredible that a certain percentage of women, admittedly a small one, actually sought out a profession in the arts.

It also becomes apparent why women were able to compete on far more equal terms with men—and even become innovators—in the field of literature. While art making has traditionally demanded the learning of specific techniques and skills, in a certain sequence, in an institutional setting outside the home, as well as becoming familiar with a specific vocabulary of iconography and motifs; the same is by no means true for the poet or novelist. Anyone, even a woman, has to learn the language, can learn to read and write, and can commit personal experiences to paper in the privacy of the home. Naturally, this oversimplifies the very real difficulties and complexities involved in creating good or great literature, whether by man or woman, but it still gives a clue as to the possibility of the existence of an Emily Dickinson or a Virginia Woolf, and the lack of their counterparts, at least until quite recently, in the visual arts.

Then, of course, there were the "fringe" requirements for major artists, which were for the most part both psychically and socially closed to women, even if they hypothetically could have achieved the requisite grandeur in the performance of their craft. In the Renaissance and after, the great artist, aside from participating in the affairs of an academy, might well be intimate with members of humanist circles with whom he could exchange ideas, establish suitable relationships with patrons, travel widely and freely, perhaps politic and intrigue; in addition, he had to possess the sheer organizational acumen and ability required to run a major atelier-factory, like that of Rubens. An enormous amount of self-confidence and worldly knowledgeability, as well as a natural sense of well-earned dominance and power, was needed by the great *chef d'école*, both in running the production end of painting and in controlling and instructing the numerous students and assistants who might flock to his studio.

THE LADY'S ACCOMPLISHMENT

In contrast to the single-mindedness and commitment demanded of a *chef d'école*, we might set the image of the "lady painter"

established by nineteenth-century etiquette books and reinforced by the literature of the times. It is precisely the insistence upon a modest, proficient, self-demeaning level of amateurism, the looking upon art, like needlework or crocheting, as a suitable "accomplishment" for the well-brought up young woman, who naturally would want to direct her major attention toward the welfare of others—family and husband—that militated, and still militates today, against any real accomplishment on the part of women. It is this emphasis that transforms serious commitment to frivolous self-indulgence, busy work, or occupational therapy, and today, more than ever, in suburban bastions of the feminine mystique, tends to distort the whole notion of what art is and what kind of social role it plays. In Mrs. Ellis's widely read *The Family Monitor and Domestic Guide*, a book of advice popular both in the United States and in England, published before the middle of the nineteenth century, women were warned against the snare of trying too hard to excel in any one thing. Lest we are tempted to laugh, we may refresh ourselves with more recent samples of exactly the same advice cited in Betty Friedan's *Feminine Mystique* or in the pages of recent issues of popular women's magazines.

> It must not be supposed that the writer is one who would advocate, as essential to woman, any very extraordinary degree of intellectual attainment, especially if confined to one particular branch of study. "I should like to excel in something" is a frequent, and, to some extent, laudable expression; but in what does it originate, and to what does it tend? *To be able to do a great many things tolerably well, is of infinitely more value to a woman, than to be able to excel in any one. By the former, she may render herself generally useful; by the latter, she may dazzle for an hour. By being apt, and tolerably well skilled in every thing, she may fall into any situation in life with dignity and ease—by*

devoting her time to excellence in one, she may remain incapable of every other.

So far as cleverness, learning, and knowledge are conducive to woman's moral excellence, they are therefore desirable, and no further. *All that would occupy her mind to the exclusion of better things, all that would involve her in the mazes of flattery and admiration, all that would tend to draw away her thoughts from others and fix them on herself, ought to be avoided as an evil to her, however brilliant or attractive it may be in itself.*

. . . As far as painting specifically is concerned, Mrs. Ellis finds that it has one immediate advantage for the young lady over its rival branch of artistic activity, music—it is quiet and disturbs no one (this negative virtue, of course, would not be true of sculpture, but accomplishment with the hammer and chisel simply never occurs as a suitable accomplishment for the weaker sex); in addition, says Mrs. Ellis, "it [drawing] is an employment which beguiles the mind of many cares. . . . Drawing is of all other occupations, the one most calculated to keep the mind from brooding upon self, and to maintain that general cheerfulness which is a part of social and domestic duty. . . . It can also be laid down and resumed, as circumstance or inclination may direct, and that without any serious loss." Again, lest we feel that we have made a great deal of progress in this area in the past hundred years, I might bring up the remark of a bright young doctor who, when the conversation turned to his wife and her friends "dabbling" in the arts, contemptuously snorted: "Well, at least it keeps them out of trouble!" Amateurism and lack of real commitment, as well as snobbery and emphasis on chic on the part of women in their artistic "hobbies," feeds the contempt of the successful, professionally committed man who is engaged in "real" work and can, with a certain justice, point to his wife's lack of seriousness in her artistic activities. For such men, the "real" work

of women is only that which directly or indirectly serves themselves and their children: any other commitment falls under the rubric of diversion, selfishness, egomania, or, at the unspoken extreme, castration. The circle is a vicious one, in which philistinism and frivolity mutually reinforce each other, today as in the nineteenth century.

In literature, as in life, even if the woman's commitment to art was apparently a serious one, she was naturally expected to drop her career and give up this commitment at the behest of love and marriage: this lesson is still inculcated in young girls, directly or indirectly, from the moment they are born. . . . Then, as so often is the case now, despite men's greater "tolerance," the choice for women seems always to be marriage *or* a career: solitude as the price of success *or* sex and companionship at the price of professional renunciation. If such were the alternatives presented to men, one wonders how many great artists, or even mediocre ones, would have opted for commitment to their art—especially if they had been constantly reminded from their earliest moments that their only true fulfillment *as* men could come from marriage and raising a family. That achievement in the arts, as in any field of endeavor, demands struggle and sacrifice, no one would deny; that this has certainly been true after the middle of the nineteenth century, when the traditional institutions of artistic support and patronage no longer fulfilled their customary obligations, is incontrovertible. One has only to think of Delacroix, Courbet, Degas, Van Gogh, and Toulouse-Lautrec, who all gave up the distractions and obligations of family life, at least in part, so that they could pursue their artistic careers more singlemindedly; yet none of them was automatically denied the pleasures of sex or companionship on account of this choice—on the contrary! Nor did they ever feel that they had sacrificed their manhood or their sexual role in order to achieve professional fulfillment. But if the artist in question happens to be a woman, a thousand years of guilt, self-doubt, and objecthood have been added to the undeniable difficulties of being an artist in the modern world. . . .

SUCCESSES

But what of the small band of heroic women, who, throughout the ages, despite obstacles, have achieved preeminence, if not the pinnacles of grandeur of a Michelangelo, a Rembrandt, or a Picasso? Are there any qualities that may be said to have characterized them as a group and as individuals? While such an investigation in depth is beyond the scope of this essay, we can point to a few striking characteristics of women artists generally: they all, almost without exception, were either the daughters of artist fathers, or generally later, in the nineteenth and twentieth centuries, had a close personal connection with a stronger or more dominant male artistic personality. Neither of these characteristics is, of course, unusual for men artists; it is simply true almost *without exception* for their feminine counterparts, at least until quite recently. . . .

It would be interesting to investigate the role of benign, if not outright encouraging, fathers in the formation of women professionals in the field: both Käthe Kollwitz and Barbara Hepworth, for example, recall the influence of unusually sympathetic and supportive fathers on their artistic pursuits. In the absence of any thoroughgoing investigation, though, one can only gather impressionistic data about the presence or absence of rebellion against parental authority in women artists, and about whether there may be more or less rebellion on the part of women, rather than men, artists. One thing, however, is clear: for a woman to opt for a career at all, much less for a career in art, has required a certain amount of unconventionality, both in the past and at present; whether or not the woman artist rebels

against or finds strength in the attitude of her family, she must in any case have a good, strong streak of rebellion in her to make her way in the world of art at all, rather than conform to the socially approved role of wife and mother, the only role to which every social institution consigns her automatically, simply by virtue of her birth. It is only by adopting, however covertly, the "masculine" attributes of singlemindedness, concentration, tenaciousness, and absorption in ideas and craftsmanship for their own sake that women have succeeded and continue to succeed in the world of art. . . .

CONCLUSION

We have tried to deal with one of the perennial questions used to challenge women's demand for true, rather than token, equality, by examining the whole erroneous intellectual substructure upon which the question "Why are there no great women artists?" is based; by questioning the validity of the formulation of so-called problems in general and the problem of women specifically; and by probing some of the limitations of the discipline of art history itself. By stressing the *institutional*—that is, the public—rather than the *individual* or private preconditions for achievement in the arts, we have provided a model for the investigation of other areas in the field. By examining in some detail a single instance of deprivation and disadvantage—the unavailability of nude models to women art students—we have suggested that it was made *institutionally* impossible for women to achieve artistic excellence or success on the same footing as men, *no matter what* the potency of their so-called talent or genius, or their lack of this mysterious ingredient. The existence of a tiny band of successful, if not great, women artists throughout history does nothing to gainsay this fact, any more than does the existence of a few superstars or token achievers among the members of any minority group. A brief glance at the inner conflicts—and real difficulties—experienced by two highly successful women artists confirms the obvious truth that while great achievement is rare and difficult at best, it is still rarer and more difficult if you must wrestle with inner demons of self-doubt and guilt and outer monsters of ridicule or patronizing encouragement, none of which have any specific connection with the quality of the art work as such.

What is important is that women face up to the reality of their history and of their present situation, without making excuses or puffing mediocrity. Disadvantage may indeed be an excuse; it is not, however, an intellectual position. Rather, using their situation as underdogs in the realm of grandeur and outsiders in the realm of ideology as a vantage point, women can reveal institutional and intellectual weaknesses in general, and, at the same time that they destroy false consciousness, take part in the creation of institutions in which clear thought—and true greatness—are challenges open to anyone, man or woman, courageous enough to take the necessary risk, the leap into the unknown.

Brenda Dixon Gottschild

BLACK DANCE AND DANCERS AND THE WHITE PUBLIC— A PROLEGOMENON TO PROBLEMS OF DEFINITION

Brenda Dixon Gottschild teaches dance at Temple University. In the following article, she argues that black dance should not be defined in terms of the race of the performer. Instead, it should be understood as a product of a particular tradition and judged in terms that are appropriate to its cultural background.

What conflicts arise when Black dance forms become public domain? Must the Black roots of a particular dance be reaffirmed publicly, even after that dance has become popular in the White world? What is the responsibility of the White or Black researcher, critic, or educator whose subject is Black dance? Must the Black choreographer make aesthetic/artistic adjustments when choreographing works targeted for White, rather than Black, audiences?

These questions form the opening paragraph of a report I authored which appeared in the Fall, 1984 issue of the *Dance Research Journal.* Sally Banes, Julinda Lewis and I organized a one-day seminar (sponsored by the Dance Critics Association and held at the Dance Theater Workshop/Bessie Schoenberg Theater in New York on Novem-

ber 5, 1983) entitled *You've Taken My Blues and Gone; A Seminar on Black Dance in White America.* The report was a summation of that effort in establishing a forum for these issues.

Reflecting here on those issues, I want to use the example of choreographers Alvin Ailey and Arthur Mitchell to make observations on how the White public might approach the work of Black choreographers and to illustrate the difficulties inherent in defining Black dance.

It is not easy to address Black dance, because the phenomenon has not been defined. Clearly, we can address Black performance in traditional African and African-based new world forms such as the danced ceremonies in religions such as Vodun, Santeria, and Macumba. However, the situation

Brenda Dixon-Stowell, "Black Dance and Dancers and the White Public—A Prolegomenon to Problems of Definition," *The Black Tradition in American Modern Dance*, ed. Gerald E. Myers (Durham: American Dance Festival, 1988) 20–21.

in the United States in particular, and in concert dance in general, is different. In using Black forms to create concert dance, we face a multi-layered example of syncretism. In using Black dancers to perform in White concert programs, we face the American cultural reflex of seeing Blacks as outsiders in any White context. Add to this the ever-present and shifting influences of Black-on-White-on-Black in American society—a basic, although oft-unacknowledged integer—and the problem of defining Black dance becomes apparent.

I do not believe Alvin Ailey and Arthur Mitchell conceive their choreography as Black dance. Black influences are one of the many influences in their work. However, both the Dance Theater of Harlem (DTH) and the Alvin Ailey American Dance Theater(AAADT) are considered Black dance companies by the White public. This is not only because the majority of performers in both groups are Black, but also because, in general terms, the White public considers that regardless of style, *Black dance is what Black dancers do*. This point of view is one major source of friction among Black dancers/choreographers and the White public, and it is a double-edged nemesis.

First, it means that the Ailey troupe and the DTH are relegated to a separate status that classifies them as different, somehow, from the New York City Ballet (NYCB), the Paul Taylor or Twyla Tharp companies, or any other White company, regardless of dance style. Arlene Croce addressed this is a review some years ago (*The New Yorker*, January 28, 1980, p. 78). In introducing her comments on the DTH, she stated:

> Subdivision is one way of holding onto the exclusivity of an art form, but amateurish distinctions can interest no one for long.

Further on, she said:

> The Dance Theater of Harlem quite naturally occupies a category of its own: else

there would be no reason for it to exist. That black (sic) classicists are classicists with a difference is visibly evident, but because the style [ballet] both isolates and neutralizes their color it's as if they'd shuffled their cards of identity. Either they're not exotic enough for some people or they're too exotic—the difference amounts to inadmissible deviation. Well, classical norms are set by classical dancers, not their critics. The D.T.H. norm is there to be seen. The trouble is, not enough people are going to see it.

I quote her at length in order not to misrepresent her point of view. The entire article begs analysis, but what is interesting in this portion is that after ridiculing subdivisions Croce separately categorized DTH in what she perceives as a justifiable subdivision—namely, that of Black classicism. Thus, she suggests that, even in their unquestionable mastery of European-based ballet, this company performs a Black dance style. America has learned that separate is, inherently, unequal. No dancer or choreographer wants a separate category created for his or her work.

Secondly, it means that a Black dancer in an all-White company is perceived and treated as "different." (This is not always the case, with the example of Carolyn Adams' years as a Paul Taylor dancer as one of the most refreshing exceptions.) I think of the exceptionally gifted Mel Tomlinson, underused at NYCB, initially dancing the roles to which his mentor, Arthur Mitchell, had been circumscribed over two decades earlier in the same company. And I cite my experience as a young modern dancer: after auditioning for a major modern dance choreographer, I was told that I could not be used because my skin color would "destroy the unity of the corps" (which was all-White) in a dance which had no racial or social connotations. In the popular dance arena, this is why Blacks were excluded from the Rockettes, even though a range of both skin and hair colors was represented among the white "hoofers" of that group.

So, black dance remains undefined, but Black dancers are defined and delimited, so to speak, by the White consensus that Black dance and Black dancers are synonymous. Printed statements by choreographers ranging from Mitchell to Rod Rodgers indicate that these people see themselves as *artists who happen to be Black, rather than Black artists.* Printed statements by White reviewers—and not only Croce—suggest that the White viewpoint is the reverse. This seemingly subtle distinction has created unfortunate pigeonholing and stereotyping of the work of artists who happen to be Black.

In returning to the issue of defining Black dance, another point of contention arises in the area of public domain. Black dance, music, language, and lifestyles have become the general means of expression in American popular culture. American culture is syncretistic, with many cultural strains as part of this fusion but, undeniably, the two main strains are Black (rooted in West African traditions) and White (rooted in Western European traditions). Tap dance, jazz dance, and disco (or, formerly, ballroom) social dances are examples of the Black/White American fusion. All of these styles have passed, in greater or lesser degree, to the concert stage. It may be difficult to backtrack, separate, prioritize and figure out what parts of American dance are the Black-rooted parts. In a positive light, responding to the need to define an existing but unexplored quantity, Pearl Primus has made a plea, each time I have heard her speak in the past few years, that dance researchers address the definition, analysis, and documentation of Black dance. In a negative light, due to the persistence of racial oppression socially, politically, and economically in the United States, the issue of definition becomes a crucial matter of identity and legal rights. Historically, rather than reaping benefits from the public domain,

Blacks have been shortchanged financially and in the area of public recognition for their contributions to mainstream American culture.

It seems to me that one of the reasons why AAADT's contribution is belittled is, ironically, because it is so popular. A vocabulary of Ailey signature movements has, in two decades, become public domain. (This is true also of West African dance forms which, for years, have been taught in dance studios as a motley, derivative, and bastardized new form often termed "primitive" or "Afro" dance.) Often White and Black dancers alike have appropriated Black elements of Ailey's fusion style, both in patent and subliminal ways. The double irony is that Ailey's choreography is in itself a fusion of Black forms, modern dance, and ballet. (This tradition dates back to the beginnings of concert dance by Black choreographers. Katherine Dunham's pioneering fusion of Caribbean forms with concert forms was the original model.) Only certain parts of certain Ailey works can be classified as Black dance.

Any serious attempt to *study* Black dance demands a study of African and New World Black cultures. Any attempt to *evaluate* Black dance—or the Black dance elements in White forms—on the concert stage demands an emic approach, so as to understand the phenomenon also in the context of its Black origins, and not only in the context of the White, western frame of reference. There are many fine works on African and New World, African-based cultures which can give the researcher or the layperson a Black-contexted frame of reference. I recommend the work of authors such as Harold Courlander, Melville Herskovits, Joanne Kealiinohomoku, Judith Lynne Hanna, Drid Williams, Robert Farris Thompson, Veve Clark, Karen Kramer, Maya Deren, Katherine Dunham, Judith Gleason, John Szwed, Robert Abrams, Errol Hill, Marshall Stearns, Janheinz Jahn, Katrina Hazzard Gordon, Zora Neale Hurston, Gregory Tate, Imamu

Amiri Baraka. Many of the scholars on Black aesthetics are White but, to paraphrase James Hatch, it is a strength for a cultural group to have spheres of interest and power among positive forces in other cultures, and a reinforcement of its future survival and continuity.

For example, in terms of evaluating the many dances choreographed by Ailey, Rodgers, and other Black choreographers to vocalized Black ballads, it would be a contextual error to evaluate the choreography on modern dance principles of Louis Horst. Instead, the roots of this genre of Black dance, as epitomized by a work such as Ailey's solo song cycle for dancer Dudley Williams (Love Songs, 1972), lie in a Black tradition of song-as-survival, here applied to choreography.

To understand this aesthetic requires some research into Black music and culture, since little has been said about its permutations in Black-inspired dance forms. For decades, jazz musicians have used the Scottish-based ballad form as a prime vehicle for creative expression, ranging from the direct, upbeat versions by swing-era big bands, through complex inversions by the likes of Charlie Parker, to the third-stream, Miles Davis-influenced renditions of later decades, and the jazz-pop-fusion pyrotechnics of contemporary musicians such as Keith Jarrett and Al Jarreau. Contemporary music critics, including Stephen Holden and Gregory Tate, have addressed the Black ballad form. According to Holden, it ". . . equates erotic love with divine insight" (*The New York Times*, Sunday, January 30, 1983, sect. 2, p. 23, "Smokey Robinson Builds a Pop Paradise"). According to Tate, it represents ". . . the transference of religious rapture onto songs of romance, bespeaking an unshakable faith in the black [sic] pop lovesong as a form of salvation" (*Village Voice*, September 20, 1983, pp. 75, 78, "Something Real").

It behooves the White critic, educator or researcher in dance, then, to be aware of this tradition and to recognize its legacy in Black ballad dances, reflecting particular Black aesthetic/cultural principles rather than principles from another cultural context.

Another example of a possible contextual misconception is the printed opinion of some White critics that the Ailey approach to making dances is dense and overchoreographed. Here, too, I recommend a culturally appropriate or culture-specific look at the choreography in his Black-inspired works in terms of the African-based, Black aesthetic. Although Ailey's work can be considered a syncretistic fusion of Black styles, jazz dance (already a fusion), modern dance, and ballet, some of his works, such as *Phases* (1980), seem to be highly *informed* by a Black aesthetic. This dance genre is based on clusters of movement rather than linear exposition and is characterized in movement by the equivalent of polyrhythms, call-and-response, and multiple meter which are signatures of African-based music. It helps to have some knowledge of these features of Black performance, so that a Black-inspired Ailey work is not evaluated/perceived as a weak exercise in choreographic principles from another frame of reference. Perhaps it would be more appropriate to compare the density of such a dance with the density synesthetically described by Robert Farris Thompson in his comparisons of counterpoint, percussive composition of African fabric to similar structure in Black performance modes.

It would appear that, due to inaccuracies in critical frame of reference and due to the great popularity—or public domain—of his works, Ailey is one of the least appreciated yet most deserving of American choreographers. Anna Kisselgoff is one of the few White American critics who perceives his work as a contribution on a par with that of major modern dance choreographers. She has said that "in his own brand of third-stream idiom, Mr. Ailey has made a little noticed but genuine contribution toward the extension of the dance vocabulary" (*The New York Times*, Sunday, December 13, 1981, p. 18).

Again referring to the realm of music, I quote Amiri Baraka to address the problem of misinterpretation through application of aesthetically alien cultural frameworks. In an article on White critics of Black music he states: ". . . many of these white [sic] critics . . . all too often imposed a critical standard on the music that was opposed to the standard the music itself carried with it and described" (*The Village Voice*, August 16, 1983, pp. 22–23, "Other Voices" column).

That I have used musical analogues in addressing Black dance styles highlights the fact that there is no body of research addressing Black forms in concert dance. This leads back to the Peal Primus plea for serious research in this area.

To conclude, I cite some observations that were voiced at the group I led at the November 5, 1983 seminar on Black dance. They were made by two veterans of dance whose interest and enthusiasm have not waned and whose quest for understanding is evident in this comment:

> What we, as critics, are trying to do is to find a multilingual perception in looking at dance, based on the fact that dance is not one language, but many languages. As an example, I still look at African art through the eyes of Picasso, because that is the way I was brought up; it's a problem for me. It means that I am always "translating," in this regard. I'm seeing it from a distance, with a western, selected gathering of certain attitudes. —Madeleine Gutman.

> [After attending the Black Dance America Conference and Symposium at BAM and realizing that] . . . a lot of people, including myself, had not really looked at Black dance as if it were "up there" and for us to really see. I don't think people really see it the way they see other things that they're more accustomed to. And my reaction to that was after the conference I looked at things very differently, and I was seeing minimal structure in the pieces Charles Moore did outdoors there is in Brooklyn . . . I don't think people notice [things like] that [in Black dance]. —Pauline Tish.

Craig Bromberg made a valuable statement in suggesting that we ought ". . . not to think of any kind of aesthetic as an ideal that is transcendent of history."

The above statement is applicable interdisciplinarily and cross-culturally. In a shrinking, global world community we cannot afford the luxury of ethnocentrism. If need be, we must metaphorically walk across hot coals to loosen ". . . the invisible limitations placed on us by our assumptions" (Adam Smith, *Esquire*, January 1984, p. 12, "Walking on Fire").

Joel Rudinow

CAN
WHITE PEOPLE
SING
THE BLUES?

Joel Rudinow teaches philosophy at Santa Rosa Junior College. His writings on aesthetics have appeared in the Journal of Aesthetics and Art Criticism, Philosophy and Literature, Critical Inquiry, *and the* British Journal of Aesthetics. *He also plays the piano with a number of American roots music bands in the San Francisco area. The following article considers the question of whether non-African Americans can be authentic performers of the blues.*

The idea of a white blues singer seems an even more violent contradiction of terms than the idea of a middle class blues singer.

   Amiri Baraka (LeRoi Jones), *Blues People*

It is unlikely that [the blues] will survive through the imitations of the young white college copyists, the "urban blues singers," whose relation to the blues is that of the "trad" jazz band to the music of New Orleans: sterile and derivative. The bleak prospect is that the blues probably has no real future; that, folk music that it is, it served its purpose and flourished whilst it had meaning in the Negro community. At the end of the century it may well be seen as an important cultural phenomenon—and someone will commence a systematic study of it, too late.

   Paul Oliver, *Blues Off the Record*

Can white people sing the blues? Can white people play the blues? On the surface, these may seem to be silly questions. Why not? What is Mose Allison, if not a white blues singer? Surely the performances of guitarists Eric Clapton and Stevie Ray Vaughan and pianist Dr. John must count as playing the blues. But the question, "Can white people sing (or play) the blues?" is much more persistent, elusive and deep than such ready responses acknowledge. The above passage from Paul Oliver exemplifies a tradition of criticism which distinguishes between the performances of black and white blues musicians, preferring those of black musicians and refusing to recognize as genuine those of white musicians. This tradition raises

Joel Rudinow, "Race, Ethnicity, Expressive Authenticity: Can White People Sing the Blues?" *Journal of Aesthetics and Art Criticism* 52.1 (1994): 127–37.

questions of race, ethnicity and expressive authenticity which go to the heart of the contemporary debate over multi-culturalism, the canon and the curriculum. I derive my title, and take my theme, from the late jazz critic Ralph J. Gleason, who raised the issue definitively, at least for white liberals in the late 1960's, saying:

> [T]he blues is black man's music, and whites diminish it at best or steal it at worst. In any case they have no moral right to use it.

When I raise this issue in my Aesthetics classes, I find I must first get my students to appreciate it as a genuine and genuinely deep issue. They tend to dismiss it rather quickly by simple appeal to their own musical experience. They tend to think that the mere mention of the name "Stevie Ray Vaughan" settles it. It doesn't. Nevertheless, there's something in this naive response. It reflects the central dialectic of the issue— the difficulty of appreciating its depth and significance in the face of its apparent implications. In an age of renewed and heightened racial and cultural sensitivity such a critical stance seems paradoxically to be both progressive and reactionary, and to stand in need of both clarification and critique. It seems to embody, as well as any, the problematic of "political correctness." The stance taken, as in the case of Gleason and Oliver, by white critics and scholars seems progressive in that it unambiguously credits African American culture as the authoritative source of the blues as musical genre and style, something the dominant culture has by and large systematically neglected. And yet it seems reactionary—indeed, prima facie racist—to restrict access to the blues as a medium of artistic expression. . . .

A "RACIST" ARGUMENT?

Part of appreciating the issue is rescuing it from a racist reading. Let us first get clear about what would make the negative position "racist." "Racism" is widely discussed and many would say even more widely practiced, but it is rarely defined or clarified conceptually. For present purposes I will consider as racist any doctrine or set of doctrines which presupposes that there are "races" whose members share genetically transmitted traits and characteristics not shared by members of other "races" and which makes moral distinctions or other (for example aesthetic) distinctions with moral implications, on this basis alone. Essentially racism seeks to establish a scientific, in this case biological, basis for differential treatment of human beings—a basis in the nature of things for discrimination.

Thus critiques of racism have attempted to establish that there is no genetic, or biological, (i.e., scientific) basis for *morally significant* classification of human beings into races, by arguing that those genetically determined gross morphological characteristics whereby individuals are assigned to racial categories (pigmentation, bone structure, and so on) are not morally significant and that those human characteristics which *are or can be* morally significant (intelligence, linguistic capability, and so on), though genetically determined, do not vary significantly with race. A more radical critique of racism would undercut the concept of "race" itself as an artificial and harmful construct without objective foundation in science, arguing in effect that there is no foundation in biology or genetics for *any* system of classification of humans by "race." This might be based on the observation that the degree of variation, with respect even to gross morphological characteristics, within a given "racial" group exceeds that between "typical" members of different groups, and on the generally accepted finding in genetics that the probability of any particular genetic difference occurring between two members of the same "racial" group is roughly the same as for any two human beings. We might do well to wonder whether, if either of these critiques has force (and they both seem forceful to me), we can raise the issue of the authenticity of white blues musicians at all. Is there a way to enter into such a discussion without reifying "race" and investing it with moral significance? Doesn't the very question presuppose race as a morally significant human category with a verifiable basis of some sort?

Suppose we begin to answer this by distinguishing between race and ethnicity. Unlike race, let us say, which is supposed to be innate and in nature, ethnicity requires no genetic or biological foundation. Ethnicity is a matter of acknowledged common culture, based on shared items of cultural significance such as experience, language, religion, history, habitat, and the like. Ethnicity is essentially a socially conferred status—a matter of communal acceptance, recognition and respect.

Thus the negative position may *seem* racist since it may appear that nothing other than race is available as a basis for what is evidently both an aesthetic and moral distinction between black and white blues artists and performances. The negative position would *be* racist if, for example, it held that white people were genetically incapable of producing the sounds essential to the blues. Is there a difference between John Lee Hooker's blues and John Hammond's blues? Well, certainly. There are many. The diction, phrasing and intonation of each as vocalist, as well as their techniques of instrumental self-accompaniment are distinctive and immediately identifiable (which shows that whatever differences there are are relevant *aesthetically*). If someone proposed to explain these differences on the basis of the genetically inherited expressive capacities and limitations of members of different races, and then went on to argue for some form of differential assessment of performances or treatment of artists on this basis, that would qualify as a racist account.

However the question raised by the negative position is not one of genetically transmissable expressive or musical capabilities and limitations, but rather one of "authenticity." Again, the negative position would *be* racist if it held that music made by white people, however much it may resemble blues and be intended as blues, isn't authentic blues *simply because it is made by people of the wrong race.* But nobody says this. Nor does any serious adherent of the negative position hold that white people are somehow *genetically* incapable of delivering an authentic blues performance. What makes one blues performance authentic and another inauthentic? The question of authenticity is really a matter of "credentials."

THE AUTHENTICITY QUESTION

Authenticity is a value—a species of the genus credibility. It's the kind of credibility that comes from having the appropriate relationship to an original source. Thus authenticity's most precise, formal, and fully institutionalized application in the artworld is to distinguish from the forgery a work "by the author's own hand." When we authenticate a work in this sense, what we want to know is whether or not the putative author is who (s)he is represented to be. In this application the "authentic/inauthentic" distinction is dichotomous, the alternatives both mutually exclusive and exhaustive, and the appropriate relationship is one of identity.

More broadly, less precisely, but in an essentially similar way, "authenticity" is applicable to the artifacts and rituals which are a culture's "currency," conferring value on those "acceptably derived" from original sources. So, for example, an authentic restoration of a turn of the century Victorian house might be one reconstructed according to original plans and specifications and perhaps using only the tools, techniques and building materials of the period. An authentic cajun recipe might be one traceable to a source within the culture using ingredients traditionally available within the region. In such applications authenticity admits of degrees. A given piece of work may be more or less authentic than another. And the standards or criteria of authenticity admit of some flexibility of interpretation relative to purpose.

In the literature of musical aesthetics the authenticity question has been focussed largely on the relation between performances and "the work"—or, because the work is conceived of as a composition, between performances and what the composer intended—and the criteria for authenticity have been understood in terms of accuracy or conformity with performance specifications which constitute the work. As applied to blues performances the authenticity question must be focussed somewhat differently, for although we may speak of blues "compositions," what we thereby refer to consist of no more typically than a simple chord progression shared by many other such "compositions," with no definite key signature, no particular prescribed instrumentation, and a lyrical text which itself is open to *ad lib* interruption, interpretation and elaboration in performance. As a musical genre, the blues is characterized by what we might call "compositional minimalism" and a complementary emphasis on expressive elements. The question of the authenticity of a given blues performance is thus one of stylistic and expressive authenticity, and our question becomes, "Is white blues 'acceptably enough derived' from the original sources of the blues to be stylistically authentic and authentically expressive within the style?" The negative position can now be understood as: white musicians cannot play the blues in an authentic way because they do not have the requisite relation or proximity to the original sources of the blues. No one has made the case for the negative position more provocatively, eloquently, profoundly, and forcefully than

Amiri Baraka (LeRoi Jones). In what follows I will consider that case, which I believe consists of two interrelated arguments, which I will call the "Proprietary Argument" and the "Experiential Access Argument."

THE PROPRIETARY ARGUMENT

The proprietary argument addresses the question of ownership. Who "owns" the blues? Who has legitimate authority to use the blues as an idiom, as a performance style, to interpret it, to draw from it and to contribute to it as a fund of artistic and cultural wealth, to profit from it? The originators and the major innovative elaborators of the blues were in fact members of the African American community. Women and men like Ma Rainey, Bessie Smith, Charlie Patton, Robert Johnson, Muddy Waters, Howlin' Wolf, John Lee Hooker, T-Bone Walker, Professor Longhair, and so on. The question arises, to whom does this cultural and artistic heritage belong? Who are Robert Johnson's legitimate cultural and artistic heirs and conservators?

The proprietary argument says in effect that the blues as genre and style belongs to the African American community and that when white people undertake to perform the blues they misappropriate the cultural heritage and intellectual property of African Americans and of the African American community—what Baraka refers to as "the Great Music Robbery." Baraka describes a systematic and pervasive pattern throughout the history of black people in America—a pattern of cultural and artistic cooptation and misappropriation in which, not just the blues, but every major black artistic innovation, after an initial period of condemnation and rejection as culturally inferior, eventually wins recognition for superior artistic significance and merit, only to be immediately appropriated by white imitators whose imitations are very profitably mass produced and distributed, and accepted in the cultural mainstream as definitive, generally without due credit to their sources. Calling the blues "the basic national voice of the African-American people," he writes:

> . . . after each new wave of black innovation, i.e., New Orleans, big band, bebop, rhythm and blues, hard bop, new music, there was a commercial cooptation of the original music and an attempt to replace it with corporate dilution which mainly featured white players and was mainly intended for a white middle-class audience.

. . . Let's consider a possible objection, or set of objections, to this argument: The crucial claim is the ownership claim: that the blues as genre and style belongs to the African American community. How is this claim warranted? Part of the warrant is the factual claim that the originators and major innovative elaborators of the blues were members of the African American community like Ma Rainey, Bessie Smith, Charlie Patton, Robert Johnson, Muddy Waters, Howlin' Wolf, John Lee Hooker, T-Bone Walker, Professor Longhair, and so on. There is an interpretive tradition which holds, contrary to this, that the blues is an oral folk form with an ancient and untraceable pre-history, but in spite of this let us take the factual claim as true. But what is the principle or set of principles which connects this factual claim with the ownership claim that the blues belongs to the African American *community?*

The crucial assumption underlying this as a *critical* question—as the basis for a series of objections—is the modern notion of intellectual property as applied to the blues. On this assumption, an *individual* is understood to have certain rights regarding the products of his or her original creative work, including the right to control access to the work for the purposes of commercial exploitation, etc. So one could say that the musical literature of the blues rightly belongs to *certain members* of the African

American community like Ma Rainey, Bessie Smith, Charlie Patton, Robert Johnson, Muddy Waters, Howlin' Wolf, John Lee Hooker, T-Bone Walker, Professor Longhair, or their estates, legitimate heirs and assigns. But this list, even drawn up on the basis of a liberal reading of "legitimate heirs and assigns," even if *padded,* is not coextensive with "the African American *community.*"

Moreover, these rights can be alienated voluntarily and involuntarily in various ways. They can be purchased, sold, exchanged, wagered, and so on. . . .

Finally, the proprietary argument claims ownership of the blues as genre and style, so that musical and expressive elements as elusive as timbre, diction, vocal inflection, timing, rhythmic "feel," and their imitations become the subjects of dispute. For example, the rock group ZZ Top has obviously imitated or "borrowed from" elements of John Lee Hooker's distinctive style in several of their original compositions. For Baraka this constitutes misappropriation— just another instance of The Great Music Robbery. But where in the notion of music as intellectual property can one find precedent for this? If anything, the history of music provides ample precedent for accepting such borrowings as legitimate forms of tribute and trade in ideas. The modern notion of intellectual property as applied to music can be used to support ownership claims concerning compositions but not musical ideas as ephemeral and problematic for purposes of documentation as these "elements of style."

Arguably this series of objections does very little damage to the proprietary argument. First of all, what the objection grants is important evidence in support of the proprietary argument. The modern notion of intellectual property, insofar as it is applicable to the blues, would seem to warrant at least an indictment of the American music establishment on the offense of Great Music Robbery, just as Baraka maintains. The means whereby the intellectual property rights inherent in the creative work of African American blues musicians were alienated from the artists, later to turn up in various corporate portfolios at greatly appreciated value, were in many cases questionable, to say the least.

But more important, though it may not be entirely inappropriate to apply an 18th Century English legal concept of intellectual property to the blues—after all, the blues *is* modern American music—it's not entirely appropriate either. Approaching the blues via such a conceptual route entails treating the blues as a collection of compositions, discreet pieces of intellectual property, convenient as commodities to the economic apparatus of the 20th century American music and entertainment industries, whereas attention and sensitivity to the social context of the music, its production, presentation and enjoyment disclose phenomena rather more in the nature of real-time event and communally shared experience, in which the roles of performer and audience are nowhere near as sharply delineated as would be suggested by the imposition of the notions of creative artist and consumer upon them. . . .

Finally, in insisting on a contrast between musical compositions as documentable items of intellectual property and relatively problematic ephemera of musical and expressive style, the objection begs a complex set of deeply intriguing questions concerning the ownership and regulation of musical "fragments" as commodified abstract ideas—which, ironically, rap music (particularly in its employment of the technology of digital sampling) has lately elevated to the status of a pressing legal issue. But even more to the point, far from being problematic ephemera, the elements of blues style, when understood within the context of the music's historical origins and the social context of its production, take on crucial semantic and syntactic significance.

On balance, the modern notion of intellectual property as applied to the blues seems little more than an elaborate red herring which in effect obscures crucial facts about the social circumstances of the music's production, appreciation, and indeed, *meaning.* This brings me to what I am calling the "experiential access argument."

THE EXPERIENTIAL ACCESS ARGUMENT

Where the proprietary argument addresses the question of ownership, the experiential access argument addresses the questions of meaning and understanding as these bear centrally on issues of culture, its identity, evolution and transmission. What is the significance of the blues? Who can legitimately claim to understand the blues? Or to speak authoritatively about the blues and its interpretation? Who can legitimately claim fluency in the blues as a musical idiolect? Or the authority to pass it on to the next generation? Who are the real bearers of the blues tradition?

The experiential access argument says in effect that one cannot understand the blues or authentically express oneself in the blues unless one knows what it's like to live as a black person in America, and one cannot know this without being one. To put it more elaborately, the meaning of the blues is deep, hidden and accessible only to those with an adequate grasp of the historically unique experience of the African American community. Members of other communities may take an interest in this experience and even empathize with it, but they have no direct access to the experience and therefore cannot fully comprehend or express it. Hence their attempts to master the blues or to express themselves in the idiom of the blues will of necessity tend to be relatively shallow and superficial, i.e., inauthentic. . . .

In the context of the kinds of questions raised here about culture, its identity, evolution and transmission, the appeal to experience functions as a basis upon which to either establish or challenge authority, based on some such principle as this: Other things equal, the more directly one's knowledge claims are grounded in first hand experience, the more unassailable one's authority. . . . Such a principle as this one seems plausible and reasonable enough.

Nevertheless, stated baldly, and understood literally, the experiential access argument seems to invite the objection that it is either *a priori* or just dubious. The access that most contemporary black Americans have to the experience of slavery or share cropping or life on the Mississippi delta during the twenties and thirties is every bit as remote, mediated, and indirect as that of any white would-be blues player. Does the argument subscribe to some "Myth of Ethnic Memory" whereby mere membership in the ethnic group confers special access to the lived experience of ancestors and other former members? It would be just as facile and fatuous for a Jewish American baby boomer (such as myself) to take the position that only Jews can adequately comprehend the experience of the holocaust.

However the argument is susceptible of a more subtle and defensible reading, namely that the blues is essentially a cryptic language, a kind of secret code. Texts composed in this language typically have multiple layers of meaning, some relatively superficial, some deeper. To gain access to the deeper layers of meaning one must have the keys to the code. But the keys to the code presuppose extensive and detailed familiarity with the historically unique body of experience shared within and definitive of the African American community and are therefore available only to the properly initiated.

There is a certain amount of theoretical and historical material, as well as textual material within the blues, available to support this argument. A general theoretical framework for understanding the development of cryptic devices and systems of communication under repressive circumstances can be found in the work of Leo Strauss. Strauss maintains that where control of the thought and communication of a subjugated population is attempted in order to maintain a political arrangement, even the most violent means of repression are inadequate to the task, for "it is a safe venture to tell the truth one knows to benevolent and trustworthy acquaintances, or . . . to reasonable friends." The human spirit will continue to seek, recognize and communicate the truth privately in defiance of even the most repressive regimes, which moreover cannot even prevent public communication of forbidden ideas, "for a man of independent thought can utter his views in public and remain unharmed, provided he moves with circumspection. He can even utter them in print without incurring any danger, provided he is capable of writing between the lines." Unjust and repressive regimes thus naturally tend to engender covert communication strategies with "all the advantages of private communication without having its greatest disadvantage—that it reaches only the writer's acquaintances, [and] all the advantages of public communication without having its greatest disadvantage—capital punishment for the author."

Evidence of the employment of such strategies within the African American community is fairly well documented. For example, the evolution of "Black English," as well as a number of its salient characteristics, such as crucial ambiguity, understatement, irony, and inversion of meaning ("bad" means "good," and so on), may best be explained as the development of cryptic communicative strategies under repression. . . .

Lyrically the blues are rife with more or less covert allusions to the oppressive conditions of black life in America. . . . Similarly, the blues are full of covert and even overt references, both musical and lyrical, to the esoterica of African religions whose practice on this continent was prohibited and systematically repressed. . . .

The prevalence of such references not only tends to confirm the Straussian hypothesis of a covert communicative strategy, but also begins to suggest what might be involved in a "proper initiation."

Having said all this, it nevertheless remains apparent that neither the proprietary argument nor the experiential access argument quite secures the thesis that white people cannot sing (or play) authentic blues. The experiential access argument has undeniable moral force as a reminder of and warning against the offense of presumptive familiarity, but it distorts the blues in the process by obscuring what is crucially and universally *human* about its central themes. And it leaves open the possibility of the proper initiation of white people and other non-blacks, if not entirely into the African American ethnic community, then at least in the use of the blues as an expressive idiom and so into the blues community. Obvious examples would include Johnny Otis and Dr. John. Given this the force of the proprietary argument is also limited, since initiation into the blues community presumably carries with it legitimate access to the blues as a means of artistic expression.

This of course leaves the authenticity question still open on a case by case basis. Many white attempts at blues certainly come off as inauthentic, as no doubt do some black ones. However if the authenticity question turns not on race but rather on ethnicity, which admits of initiation, and on the achievement and demonstration of genuine understanding and fluency, which are also communicable by other than genetic means, then it is hard to resist the conclusion that Professor Longhair's legitimate cultural and artistic heirs include Dr. John, and that Robert Johnson's legitimate cultural and artistic heirs include John Hammond. It is tempting to conclude on this basis that the answer to the question "Can white people sing (or play) the blues?" is "Yes. Unless you're a racist."

CODA: HOW TO KEEP THE BLUES ALIVE

This isn't very likely to hold up as the last word, however—at least not yet. . . .

I can imagine someone objecting to the line of reasoning I've developed so far: "To dismiss black concerns about white cultural empirialism as 'racist'—to coopt the notion of racism in this way—is the height of disingenuous arrogance. This so-called 'evolution' of the blues community and tradition is just another case of the Great Music Robbery. It's true that the racial makeup of the blues community has evolved over the years, especially if you count these white musicians as blues players (i.e., if you insist on begging the question). Just look at the contemporary blues audience: mostly white people who can't seem to tell the difference between John Lee Hooker (the real thing) and John Hammond (the white imitation)!" Such objections are not hard to come by. Charles Whitaker, in a recent *Ebony Magazine* article entitled "Are Blacks Giving Away the Blues?" goes even further when he notes with alarm the prevalence in the contemporary blues audience of "yuppie-ish white people who clap arrhythmically (sic)." This seems prima facie racist, but is it? What if Whitaker said, "Of course I don't think it's a *genetic* thing, but they (white people) just haven't got it (rhythm). It's an *ethnic* thing." How much does this help? Is ethnocentrism a significant advance beyond racism? Certainly not when measured by the horrors and pointless suffering which have been inflicted over the years in the name of each. This is no way to keep the blues alive.

. . . I think that if we wish to avoid ethnocentrism, as we would wish to avoid racism, what we should say is that the authenticity of a blues performance turns not on the ethnicity of the performer but on the degree of mastery of the idiom and the integrity of the performer's use of the idiom in performance. This last is delicate and can be difficult to discern. But what one is looking for is evidence in and around the performance of the performer's recognition and acknowledgement of indebtedness to sources of inspiration and technique (which as a matter of historical fact *do* have an identifiable ethnicity). In the opening epigram Paul Oliver estimates the blues' chances of survival through these times of ethnic mingling as "unlikely." This kind of "blues purism" is no way to keep the blues alive either. The blues, like any oral tradition, remains alive to the extent that it continues to evolve and things continue to "grow out of it." The way to keep the blues alive is to celebrate such evolutionary developments.

Noël Carroll

THE IMAGE
OF WOMEN
IN FILM

*Noël Carroll is professor of philosophy at the
University of Wisconsin at Madison. He is author of*
Mystifying Movies, Philosophical Problems of Classical
Film Theory, *and* The Philosophy of Horror, or Paradoxes
of the Heart. *In the essay that follows, Carroll takes
issue with those, such as Laura Mulvey, who rely on
psychoanalysis in their critiques of cinematic
portrayals of women, offering an alternative analysis.*

Clearly, the study of the image of women
in film could proceed without commitment
to psychoanalytic theory. However, that is
not what happened. As a participant in the
evolution of film theory and history, my own
sense is that the project of studying the
image of women in film was superseded by
psychoanalysis due to a feeling that this project, as practiced by early feminists, suffered
from being too naively empirical. It
appeared to involve meandering from genre
to genre, from period to period, and even
from film to film, accumulating a mass of
observations which however interesting,
were also thought to be theoretically rag-
tag. Psychoanalysis, in contrast, provided a
means to incorporate many of the scattered
insights of the image of women in film
approach (henceforth, generally called simply "the image approach"), while also sharp-

ening the theoretical direction of feminist
research. That is, psychoanalysis could provide not only a theoretical framework with
which to organize many of the discoveries
of the first wave of film feminism, but also a
powerful program for further research.

This, of course, is not the whole story.
Many film feminists were also interested in
the origins and reinforcement of sexual
difference in our culture, and in this
respect, psychoanalysis, as a putative scientific discipline, had the advantage of having
theories about this, albeit theories whose
patriarchal biases would require modifications by feminists.

The purpose of this paper is to attempt to
defend feminist film studies of the image of
women in film approach, where that is understood as having no necessary commitment to psychoanalysis. In order to carry

Noël Carroll, "The Image of Women in Film: A Defense of a Paradigm," *Journal of Aesthetics and Art
Criticism* 48.4 (1990): 349–60.

out this defense, I will try to sketch some of the shortcomings of the psychoanalytic model, but I will also attempt to indicate that the image approach can be supplied with a respectable theoretical basis drawn from the contemporary philosophy of the emotions. My strategy will be to consider psychoanalytic feminism and the image approach as potentially rival research programs; and I will try to show that the psychoanalytic approach has a number of liabilities which can be avoided by the image approach, while also attempting to show that the image of women in film model need not be thought of as irredeemably sunk in atheoretical naivete. . . .

In summary, Mulvey situates the visual pleasure in Hollywood cinema in the satisfaction of the male's desire to contemplate the female form erotically. This contemplation itself is potentially unmeasurable, however, since contemplation of the female form raises the prospect of castration anxiety. Cinematic strategies corresponding to fetishism and voyeurism—and emblematized respectively by the practices of von Sternberg and Hitchcock—provide visual and narrative means to protect the structure of male visual pleasure, obsessively opting for cinematic conventions and schemata that are subordinated to the neurotic needs of the male ego. Feminist film practice of the sort Mulvey champions seeks to subvert the conventions that support the system of visual pleasure deployed in Hollywood film-making and to depose the hegemony of the male gaze.

I have no doubt that there are conventions of blocking and of posing actresses before the camera that are sexist and that alternative nonsexist styles of composition are worth pursuing. Moreover, as noted earlier, I will not challenge Mulvey's psychoanalytic presuppositions, though I believe that this can and ought to be done. For present purposes, the only comment that I will make about her invocation of psychoanalysis is

that, as already noted, it does not seem methodologically sound. For even if psychoanalysis, or specific psychoanalytic hypotheses, are genuine scientific conjectures, they need to be tested against countervailing hypotheses. Neither Mulvey nor any other contemporary psychoanalytic feminist has performed this rudimentary exercise of scientific and rational inquiry and, as a result, their theories are epistemically suspect.

Moreover, apart from her psychoanalytic commitments, Mulvey's theory of visual pleasure rests on some highly dubitable empirical suppositions. On Mulvey's account, male characters in cinema are active; females are passive, primarily functioning to be seen. She writes that a male movie star's glamorous characteristics are not those of an erotic object of the gaze. It is hard to see how anyone could come to believe this. In our own time, we have Sylvester Stallone and Arnold Schwarzenegger whose star vehicles slow down and whose scenes are blocked and staged precisely to afford spectacles of bulging pectorals and other parts. Nor are these examples from contemporary film new developments in film history. Before Stallone, there was Steve Reeves and Charles Bronson, and before them, Johnny Weismuller. Indeed, the muscle-bound character of Maciste that Steve Reeves often played originated in the 1913 Italian spectacle *Cabiria.*

Nor is the baring of chests for erotic purposes solely the province of second-string male movie stars. Charlton Heston, Kirk Douglas, Yul Brynner—the list could go on endlessly—all have a beefcake side to their star personae. Obviously, there are entire genres that celebrate male physiques, scantily robed, as sources of visual pleasure: biblical epics, ironically enough, as well as other forms of ancient and exotic epics; jungle films; sea-diving films; boxing films; Tarzan adventures; etc.

Nor are males simply ogled on screen for their bodily beauty. Some are renowned for their great facial good looks, for which the action is slowed down so that the audience may take a gander, often in "glamor" close-ups. One thinks of John Gilbert and Rudolph Valentino in the twenties; of the young Gary Cooper, John Wayne, Henry Fonda and Laurence Olivier in the thirties; of Gregory Peck in the forties; Montgomery Clift, Marlon Brando, and James Mason in the fifties; Peter O'Toole in the sixties; and so on. Nor is it useful to suggest a constant correlation between male stars and effective activity. Leslie Howard in *Of Human Bondage* and *Gone With the Wind* seems to have succeeded most memorably as a matinee idol when he was staggeringly ineffectual.

If the dichotomy between male/active images versus female/passive images ill-suits the male half of the formula, it is also empirically misguided for the female half. Many of the great female stars were also great doers. Rosalind Russell in *His Girl Friday* and Katharine Hepburn in *Bringing Up Baby* hardly stop moving long enough to permit the kind of visual pleasure Mulvey asserts is the basis of the female image in Hollywood cinema. Moreover, it seems to me question-begging to say that audiences do not derive visual pleasure from these performances. Furthermore, if one complains here that my counterexamples are from comedies, and that certain kinds of comedies present special cases, let us argue about *The Perils of Pauline*.

After hypothesizing that visual pleasure in film is rooted in presenting the woman as passive spectacle through the agencies of conventional stylization, Mulvey claims that this project contains the seeds of its own destruction, for it will raise castration anxieties in male spectators. Whether erotic contemplation of the female form elicits castration anxiety from male viewers is, I suppose, a psychoanalytic claim, and, as such, not immediately a subject for criticism in this essay. However, as we have seen, Mulvey goes on to say that the ways in which

Hollywood film deals with this purported problem is through cinematic structures that allow the male spectator two particular avenues of escape: fetishism and voyeurism.

One wonders about the degree to which it is appropriate to describe even male viewers as either fetishists or voyeurs. Indeed, Allen Weiss has remarked that real-world fetishists and voyeurs would have little time for movies, preferring to lavish their attentions on actual boots and furs, on the one hand, and living apartment dwellers on the other. Fetishism and voyeurism are literally perversions—involving regression and fixation at an earlier psychosexual stages—in the Freudian system, whereas deriving visual pleasure from movies would not, I take it, be considered a perversion, *ceteris paribus*, by practicing psychoanalysts. Mulvey can only be speaking of fetishism and voyeurism metaphorically. But it is not clear, from the perspective of film theory, that these metaphors are particularly apt.

In general, the idea of voyeurism as a model for all film viewing does not suit the data. Voyeurs require unwary victims for their intrusive gaze. Films are made to be seen and film actors willingly put themselves on display, and the viewers know this. The fanzine industry could not exist otherwise. Mulvey claims that the conventions of Hollywood film give the spectators the illusion of looking in on a *private* world. But what can be the operative force of *private* here? In what sense is the world of *The Longest Day* private rather than public? Surely the invasion of Normandy was public and it is represented as public in *The Longest Day*. Rather one suspects that the use of the concept of private in this context will turn out, if it can be intelligibly specified at all, to be a question-begging dodge that makes it plausible to regard such events as the re-enactment of the battle of Waterloo as a private event.

Also, Mulvey includes under the rubric of *voyeurism* the sadistic assertion of control and the punishment of the guilty. This will allow her to accommodate a lot more filmic material under the category of voyeurism than one might have originally thought that the concept could bear. But is Lee Marvin's punishment of Gloria Grahame in *The Big Heat* voyeurism? If one answers yes to this, mustn't one also admit that the notion of voyeurism has been expanded quite monumentally?

One is driven toward the same conclusions with respect to Mulvey's usage of the concept of fetishism. Extrapolating from the example of von Sternberg, any case of elaborate scenography is to be counted as a fetishization mobilized in order to deflect anxieties about castration. So the elaborate scenography of a solo song and dance number by a female star functions as a containing fetish for castration anxieties. But, then, what are we to make of the use of elaborate scenography in solo song and dance numbers by male stars? If they are fetishizations, what anxiety are they containing? Or, might not the elaborate scenography have some other function? And if it has some other function with respect to male stars, isn't that function something that should be considered as a candidate in a rival explanation of the function of elaborate scenography in the case of the female stars?

In any case, is it plausible to suppose that elaborate composition generally has the function of containing castration anxiety? . . .

Grounding the contrast between fetishistic and voyeuristic strategies of visual pleasure in the contrast between von Sternberg and Hitchcock initially has a strong intuitive appeal because those filmmakers are, pretheoretically, thought to be describable in these terms—indeed, they come pretty close to describing themselves and their interests that way. However, it is important to recall that when commentators speak this way, or even when Hitchcock himself speaks this way, the notions of voyeurism at issue are nontechnical.

Moreover, the important question is even if in some sense these two directors could be interpreted as representing a contrast between cinematic fetishism and voyeurism, does that opposition portend a systematic dichotomy that maps onto all Hollywood cinema? Put bluntly, isn't there a great deal of visual pleasure in Hollywood cinema that doesn't fit into the categories of fetishism and voyeurism, even if those concepts are expanded, metaphorically and otherwise, in the way that Mulvey suggests? Among the things I have in mind here are not only the kind of counterexamples already advanced—male objects of erotic contemplation, female protagonists who are active and triumphant agents, spectacular scenes of the Normandy invasion that are difficult to connect to castration anxieties—but innumerable films that neither have elaborate scenography nor involve male characters as voyeurs, nor subject women characters to male subjugation in a demonstration of sadistic control. . . .

Of course, the real problem that needs to be addressed is Mulvey's apparent compulsion to postulate a general theory of visual pleasure for Hollywood cinema. Why should anyone suppose that a unified theory is available, and why would one suppose that it would be founded upon sexual difference, since in the Hollywood cinema there is pleasure—even visual pleasure—that is remote from issues of sexual difference.

It is with respect to these concerns that I think that the limitations of psychoanalytic film criticism become most apparent. For it is that commitment that drives feminist film critics toward generalizations like Mulvey's that are destined for easy refutation. If one accepts a general theory like psychoanalysis, then one is unavoidably tempted to try to apply its categorical framework to the data of a field like film, come what may, irrespective of the fit of the categories to the data. Partial or glancing correlations of the categorical distinctions to the data will be taken as confirmatory, and all the anomalous data will be regarded as at best topics for further research or ignored altogether as theoretically insignificant. Psychoanalytic-feminists tend to force their "system" on cinema, and to regard often slim correspondences between films and the system as such that one can make vaulting generalizations about how the Hollywood cinema "really" functions. The overarching propensity to fruitless generalization is virtually inherent in the attempt to apply the purported success of general psychoanalytic hypotheses and distinctions, based on clinical practice, to the local case of film. This makes theoretical conjectures like Mulvey's immediately problematic by even a cursory consideration of film history. One pressing advantage, theoretically, of the image approach is that it provides a way to avoid the tendency of psychoanalytic film feminism to commit itself to unsupportable generalizations in its attempt to read all film history through the categories of psychoanalysis. . . .

THE IMAGE OF WOMEN IN FILM

Recent work on the emotions in the philosophy of mind has proposed that we learn to identify our emotional states in terms of paradigm scenarios, which, in turn, also shape our emotions. Ronald de Sousa claims

> my hypothesis is this: We are made familiar with the vocabulary of emotion by association with *paradigm scenarios*. These are drawn first from our daily life as small children and later reinforced by the stories, art and culture to which we are exposed. Later still, in literate cultures, they are supplemented and refined by literature. Paradigm scenarios involve two aspects: first a situation type providing the characteristic *objects* of the specific emotion type, and second, a set of characteristic or "normal" *responses* to the situation, where normality is first a biological matter and then very quickly becomes a cultural one.

Many of the relevant paradigm scenarios are quite primitive, like fear, and some are genetically preprogrammed, though we continue to accumulate paradigm scenarios throughout life and the emotions that they define become more refined and more culturally dependent. Learning to use emotion terms is a matter of acquiring paradigm scenarios for certain situations; i.e., matching emotion terms to situations is guided by fitting paradigm scenarios to the situations that confront us. Paradigm scenarios, it might be said, perform the kind of cognitive role attributed to the formal object of the emotion in preceding theories of mind. However, instead of being conceived of in terms of criteria, paradigm scenarios have a dramatic structure. Like formal objects of given emotions, paradigm scenarios define the type of emotional state one is in. They also direct our attention in the situation in such a way that certain elements in it become salient.

Paradigm scenarios enable us to "gestalt" situations, i.e., "to attend differentially to certain features of an actual situation, to inquire into the presence of further features of the scenario, and to make inferences that the scenario suggests." Given a situation, an enculturated individual attempts, generally intuitively, to fit a paradigm scenario from her repertoire to it. This does not mean that the individual can fully articulate the content of the scenario, but that, in a broad sense, she can recognize that it fits the situation before her. This recognition enables her to batten on certain features of the situation, to explore the situation for further correlations to the scenario, and to make the inferences and responses the scenario suggests. Among one's repertory of love-scenarios, for example, one might have, so to speak, a "West Side Story" scenario which enables one to organize one's thoughts and feelings about the man one has just met. Furthermore, more than one of our scenarios may fit a given situation. Whether one reacts to a situation of public recrimination with anger, humility or fortitude depends on the choice of the most appropriate paradigm scenario.

I will not attempt to enumerate the kinds of considerations that make the postulation of paradigm scenarios attractive except to note that it has certain advantages over competing hypotheses about the best way to characterize the cognitive and conative components in emotional states. Rather, I shall presume that the notion of paradigm scenarios has something to tell us about a component of emotional states in order to suggest how recurring images of women in film may have some influence on spectators, which influence is of relevance to feminists.

Clearly, if we accept the notion of paradigm scenarios, we are committed to the notion that the paradigm scenario we apply to a situation shapes the emotional state we are in. Some paradigm scenarios—for example, those pertaining to the relation of an infant to a caretaker—may be such that recognition of them is genetically endowed. But most paradigm scenarios will be acquired, and even those that start out rather primitively, like rage, may be refined over time by the acquisition of further and more complex paradigm scenarios. There will be many sources from which we derive these paradigm scenarios: observation and memory; stories told us on our caretaker's knee; stories told us by friends and school teachers; gossip, as well, is a rich source of such scenarios; and, of course, so are newspaper articles, self-help books, TV shows, novels, plays, films and so on.

These scenarios may influence our emotional behavior. Male emotional responses to women, for example, will be shaped by the paradigm scenarios that they bring to those relations. Such paradigm scenarios may be derived from films, or, more likely, films may reflect, refine, and reinforce paradigm scenarios already abroad in the culture. One way to construe the study of the image of women in film is as an attempt to isolate widely disseminated paradigm scenarios that contribute to the shaping of emotional responses to women.

The recent film *Fatal Attraction*, for example, provides a paradigm scenario for situations in which a married man is confronted by a woman who refuses to consider their affair as easily terminable as he does. Armed with the *Fatal Attraction* scenario, which isn't so different from the *Crimes and Misdemeanors* scenario, a man might "gestalt" a roughly matching, real life situation, focussing on it in such a way that its object, correlating to Alex (Glenn Close), is, as Dan (Michael Douglas) says, "unreasonable," and "crazy," and, as the film goes on to indicate, pathologically implacable. One might use the scenario to extrapolate other elements of the scenario to the real case; one might leap inductively from Alex's protests that her behavior is justified (you wouldn't accept my calls at the office so I called you at home), which are associated in the film with madness, to the suspicion that a real-life, ex-lover's claims to fair treatment are really insane. Like Dan, one guided by the *Fatal Attraction* scenario may assess his situation as one of paralysing terror, persecution and helplessness that only the death of the ex-lover can alleviate.

I am not suggesting that the *Fatal Attraction* scenario causes someone who matches it to a real life situation to kill his ex-lover, though embracing it may be likely to promote murderous fantasies, in terms of the response component. In any case, matching it to a real life situation will tend to demote the ex-lover to the status of an irrational creature and to regard her claims as a form of persecution. This construal of the woman as persecutrix, of course, was not invented by the makers of *Fatal Attraction*. It finds precedent in other films, like *Play Misty For Me*, and stories, including folklore told among men in the form of gossip.

Fatal Attraction provides a vivid exemplar for emotional attention that reinforces pre-existing paradigm scenarios. However, even if *Fatal Attraction* is not original, studying the image of the woman Alex that it portrays is relevant to feminists because it illuminates one pattern of emotional attention toward women that is available to men, which pattern of emotional attention, if made operational in specific cases, can be oppressive to women, by, for example, reducing claims to fair treatment to the status of persecutory, irrational demands.

That a paradigm scenario like *Fatal Attraction* is available in the culture does not imply that every man or even any man mobilizes it. But it does at least present a potential source or resource for sexist behavior. That such a potential even exists provides a reason for feminists to be interested in it. One aspect of the study of the image of women in film is to identify negative, recurring images of women that may have some influence on the emotional response of men to women. Theoretically, this influence can be understood in terms of the negative, recurring images of women in film as supplying paradigm scenarios that may shape the emotional responses of real men to real women.

Recurring, negative images of women in film may warp the emotions of those who deploy them as paradigm scenarios in several different ways. They may distort the way women are attended to emotionally by presenting wildly fallacious images such as the "spider woman" of *film noir*. Or, the problem may be that the range of images of women available is too impoverished: if the repertoire of images of women is limited in certain cases, for instance, to contraries like mother or whore, then real women who are not perceived via the mother scenario may find themselves abused under the whore scenario. The identification of the range of ways in which negative images of women in film can function cognitively to shape emotional response is a theoretical question that depends on further exploring the variety of

logical/functional types of different images of women in film. That is a project that has hardly begun. Nevertheless, it seems a project worth pursuing.

I began by noting that the image approach might appear to some to be without proper theoretical credentials. I have tried to allay that misgiving by suggesting that the program fits nicely with one direction in the theory of the emotions. From that perspective, the study of the image of women in film might be viewed as the search for paradigm scenarios that are available in our culture and which, by being available, may come to shape emotional responses to women. This aspect of the project should be of special interest to feminists with regard to negative imagery since it may illuminate some of the sources or resources that mobilize sexist emotions. Obviously, the theoretical potentials of the image of women in film model need to be developed. What I have tried to establish is the contention that there is at least a theoretical foundation here upon which to build.

This, of course, is not much of a defense of the image approach. So in my concluding remarks I shall attempt to sketch some of the advantages of this approach, especially in comparison to some of the disadvantages of the psychoanalytic model discussed earlier.

First, the image of women model seems better suited than the psychoanalytic model for accommodating the rich data that film history has bequeathed us. It allows that there will be lots of images of women and lots of images of men and that these may play a role as paradigm scenarios in lots of emotional reactions of all kinds. One need not attempt to limit the ambit of emotional responses to fetishism or voyeurism.

Of course, the image of women model may take particular interest in negative images of women in film, for obvious strategic purposes, but it can also handle the case of positive images as well. Whereas the Rosalind Russell character in *His Girl Friday* may be an inexplicable anomaly in the psychoanalytic system, she can be comprehended in the image approach. For this model allows that there can be positive images of women in film which may play a role in positive emotional responses to real women. It is hard to see how there can be anything of genuine value in Hollywood film in Mulvey's construction. The image approach can identify the good, while acknowledging and isolating the evil.

The image of women in film model is less likely to lead to unsupportable generalizations. What it looks for are recurring images of women in film. It has no commitments about how women always appear in film. Rather it targets images that recur with marked frequency. Moreover, it makes no claims about how all viewers or all male viewers respond to those images. It tracks images of women that reappear in film with some significant degree of probability and, where the images are negative, it can elucidate how they may play a constitutive role in the shaping of oppressive emotional responses to women. It is not committed to the kinds of specific causal laws that Mulvey must accept as underlying her account. It can nevertheless, acknowledge causal efficacy to some paradigm scenarios—indeed, it can acknowledge causal efficacy to paradigm scenarios of all sorts, thereby accommodating the richness of the data.

Mara Miller

DESIRING WOMEN: THE AESTHETICS OF JAPANESE EROTIC ART

Mara Miller has directed the Asian Studies Program at Drew University, in addition to teaching philosophy. She currently teaches at the College of Media Arts and Design, Drexel University. She argues here that certain Japanese depictions of women demonstrate that erotic art need not be sexist.

The very notion of "self" is problematic in the Japanese context, given Japan's history of theory of no-self, its challenges to the apparent isomorphism between body and self (assumed in some Western self-theory) presented by the Buddhist theory of reincarnation, its insistence in the ideological Confucianism in the Tokugawa period on corporate identity and on the undesirability of individualism, and success in equating individualism with selfishness in the popular mind, and recent findings by social scientists that group identity takes precedence over personal identity. Yet in spite of a large body of theory which denies either the existence or the value of the Self, in spite of linguistic structures which problematize and destabilize the "self," and in spite of a wealth of practices which stress group identity at the expense of personal identity, this Self is well-attested—in the history of Japanese arts, in the striking artistic contributions of individuals, in the recurrent self-reflective voicing of subjective experience, and in images of the desiring Subject.

The Japanese Self differs from the Western paradigm in two critical respects: it is constructed intersubjectively, rather than by opposition to an objectified Other, and it is equally feminine and masculine: it does not privilege the male position. The arts not only bear witness to this distinctively Japanese Self, they also play an important role in its constitution. Japanese visual art presents us with evidence of the varieties in types and usages of Selves and Subjects, while literary evidence suggests that practice and appreciation of the arts are integral to the formation of the Self/Subject and crucial to its successful functioning in the world. . . .

KNOWLEDGE, SELF AND SUBJECT IN THE ARTS OF CLASSICAL JAPAN

There is a long history in Japan both of subjective vision and individuality in literature and art, and of ethical actions taken by individuals that run contrary to social expectations. The arts of the classical Heian period (794–1185) have been *both* the champion of what Roland calls the "private self" (challenging philosophical, legal, and religious dictates and countering the evidence of the social sciences) *and* constitutive of the intersubjective Subject, while being themselves intersubjectively constituted. . . .

The Self formed in the Heian period is intensely self-reflective. In her diary . . . as well as her novel, Lady Murasaki, like St. Augustine (who is a favorite forefather of the Modern Self among those who study its history), evinces a fascination with time, a concern over the unreliability of memory, and a keen awareness of the differences between objective knowledge and what the choosing self selects to know. The Heian self is formed (almost as if to fit Western theory of the self) as a response to the Look of the Other, which makes it aware of itself first as an object for the Other's sight, knowledge and judgment. Lady Murasaki, Sie Shōnagon, and other diarists record painfully acute awareness of being judged by others in the act of being observed, of being made the object of others' observation. Now this awareness of the Look of the Other is said, by Sartre and Lacan among others, to be a critical step in the constitution of self-consciousness and the ego. Yet in spite of this thousand-year literary history expressive of the most acute self-consciousness, the arts in Japan, unlike those in the West, have been conditioned by assumptions of intersubjectivity rather than by an idealization of the autonomous self-identical and self-sufficient Self, and have consistently posited—indeed assisted in constructing—the Self as Subject in a context of intersubjectivity rather than by opposition to an Object.

Examples are numerous. Literature of the Heian period (784–1185) establishes the norm; *The Tale of Genji*, the various poetic diaries, and the *renga* or linked verse which develops later all present poetry which does not aim to stand entirely on its own but rather alludes to previous poems via the use of lines and phrases. . . . This is done in two ways. First, the poems alluded to may be part of the generally familiar body of literature. Secondly, as the process is described by Murasaki, new poems are often composed as parts of letters, especially loveletters; in such cases and in *renga*, the poems referred to are poems written by someone the poet knows, someone who shares the same social, literary, and often physical context; they may even be written to (in the case of letters) or for (in the case of *renga*) the poet.

Two implications of this poetic practice are pertinent to our philosophical problem. First, the poet demonstrates his or her participation in the cultural community, and contributes to it, at the same time. Although writers' abilities are acknowledged to vary greatly, poetry writing is an amateur activity and expected of everyone as part of the (aristocrat's) quotidian routine. The poet, like the poem, takes his or her place within the community, and does so by means of the poem, which establishes the poet's identity not as an isolated genius but as a member of a cultural community (part of the "we-self"). Secondly, the works are not meant to stand alone, but to be received as part of a dense network of poetic allusion, a body of literature which they expand even as they mine it. The originality desired of the poet is differently emphasized than in the West; it consists of how s/he brings new pleasures and meanings to a preexisting poetic core. The new work is not intended to be understood as complete, but offers itself for further adumbration to subsequent poets. This means that the author relies upon the audience to complete the meaning, as it were, (foreshadowing current reader-response theory and deconstruction); the fact that the audience can do that reassures the poet that his or her meaning is received within a process that is reciprocal. The success of the poetic project convinces the poets/ lovers of the validity of their assumptions of being understood, of the soundness of their trust in intersubjectivity and of their knowledge of the Other. This ability to trust and take for granted our knowledge of the Other, testified to again and again by modern novelists like Ryunosuke Akutagawa (1892–1927) and Fumiko Enchi (1905–   ), stands of course in the sharpest contrast with Western premises, which in their extreme form insist that we not only do not usually know the other but we *cannot* know the Other.

If we claim, as I believe we may, that poetry is the paradigmatic form of verbal communication in Japan, in that limited but crucial sense in which one might claim that philosophical argument or scientific discourse has become the paradigmatic form in the West, (that is, that it is not just prevalent but in an important sense normative), then its importance in setting up a model that both embodies and validates intersubjectivity and the reliability of our knowledge of the Other cannot be underestimated. Since in this tradition no poem is ever finally complete, objective (independent of the subjectivity of the sender and receiver), or context-free, this precludes the adoption of a poem as an object of knowledge, an unchanging absolute or ideal, in the Western sense. Meaning, on this view, is not independent of the knower, not objective; it is intersubjectively constituted.

This has important consequences not just for how we understand the work of art but, since this model serves as the paradigm for the possibilities of knowing, for how we understand the Other as well. It means, among other things, that the Other can be known (a) accurately and with confidence, and (b) not simply as an Object about whom one infers information but as a Subject, in ways like those by which we know ourselves (when we are not making ourselves into Objects of self-reflection/knowledge),

i.e., pre-reflectively, directly, albeit with gaps. It further implies that knowledge of the Other and of the art work may alter our knowledge of ourselves—may alter what we are. This implication that knowledge of art will change us runs consistently throughout Japanese history. . . .

DESIRE AND THE REPRESENTATION OF THE SUBJECT IN UKIYO-E

The woodblock prints of the Ukiyo-e school of the Edo period (1600–1868) illustrate the major claims of this paper: that the Japanese do have a strong tradition of individual Selfhood, that Selfhood and the Subject position are neither the exclusive privilege of men nor modeled on male experience, that this Selfhood is intersubjectively constituted and premised upon confidence in knowledge of the Other, and that art both illustrates and contributes to the construction of this Self. This section presents a preliminary examination of the first three of these claims in the light of Ukiyo-e.

DEPICTIONS OF THE INDIVIDUAL AS SELF AND AS SUBJECT

Recent studies of Western art and film . . . have analyzed the visual codes of representation that objectify women and establish the position of the viewing Subject as (exclusively) male. In Linda Nochlin's summary:

> representations of women in art are founded upon and serve to reproduce indisputably accepted assumptions held by society in general, artists in particular, and some artists more than others about men's power over, superiority to, difference from, and necessary control of women, assumptions which are manifested in the visual structures as well as the thematic choices of the pictures in question. . . .

Assumptions about women's weakness and passivity; her sexual availability for men's needs; her defining domestic and nurturing function; her identity with the realm of nature; her existence as object rather than creator of art; the patent ridiculousness of her attempts to insert herself actively into the realm of history by means of work or engagement in political struggle—all of these notions, themselves premised on an even more general, more all-pervasive certainty about gender difference itself—all of these notions were shared, if not uncontestedly, to a greater or lesser degree by most people of our period, and as such constitute an ongoing subtext underlying almost all individual images involving women.

Similar assumptions were shared by the neo-Confucianist rulers, educators, and intellectual leaders of Edo Japan. For this reason—and because many of the pictures of women are of courtesans, who made their living by giving pleasure to men—most scholars and interpreters of the prints have assumed that the women pictured function primarily or only as objects for male desire. If we read the prints with eyes trained to the assumptions of Western visual structures, this seems true, but once we base our reading on the Japanese social and artistic contexts, the Ukiyo-e prints give quite a different picture.

There are four ways in which Japanese artistic practices differ from the Western with regard to this paradigmatic correspondence between gender and status as Subject or Object. First, men are depicted not only as Subjects, but as Objects. Second, women are depicted not only as Objects but, far more commonly, as Subjects. In addition, both are shown in intersubjective relation, that is, in the act of mutual acknowledgement of the Subjecthood of the Other (with simultaneous acknowledgement of their own Subjecthood). Finally, the female gaze is recognized and incorporated; men are expected to be able to identify with a female Subject as well as a male one and vice versa. This situation may reflect the realities, if not the statistical

norms, of real life; it certainly does *not* reflect the contemporary Confucianist ideology expounded by the government.

The middle-class Ukiyo-e audiences craved images of the heroes of their new popular culture: actors of the Kabuki theater and *bijin* (literally "beautiful women") and courtesans of the pleasure quarters. Although the stylization of these images is undeniable, so is a fascination with realism. From this realism emerges a type of portraiture distinctly different from that of the West, in that it is primarily interested neither in physical resemblance nor in the character of the person, but in those aspects of the person which reveal what we might call the "intended" self, the self-fashioned self, the self as it has decided to reveal itself to others.

Precursors of this understanding of the Self are found in the portraits of classical poets (male and female) dating from the Kamakura period on, like the portrait of the female poet Ono no Komachi (c. 850) on the cover of this volume by the sixteenth-century Rimpa artist Sakai Hoitsu. The face is turned away from the viewer; it conveys no information of interest. Individuality resides in the set of the body and the costume—the elegance of the twelve-layer kimono is crucial—and in the words of the poet, written alongside the poet's name in expressive calligraphy. Ukiyo-e portraits of contemporary actual people capitalize upon this tradition of indicating Selfhood as a combination of name, posture or deportment, costume, and one's work. They understand the achieved Selfhood of such personages to be a complex comprised of individual identity (identifiable facial features, inscription of the actor's or courtesan's name, etc.), public persona (both as a function of social role—identifying insignia such as the actor's family's crest or the name of the courtesan's house, that help to determine for the viewer the social position—and as a set of choices made by the individual as to how to present herself or himself), and the person's mood or intention at a particular moment.

MEN IN UKIYO-E: DESIRING SUBJECTS OR OBJECTS OF DESIRE

Men in Ukiyo-e, like their counterparts in Western painting and in film, are shown as Subjects—as independent moral and political agents (often as heroes from history or legend), with all indications of their social status and public persona, in poses signifying control. When they are actors this may mean either an anonymous, stylized aggressive pose or one of their (male or female) stage roles. . . .

Yet even as they establish themselves as Subjects, the Kabuki actors, who may play aggressive male heroes or effeminate anti-heroes or women, self-consciously set themselves up as *objects* for the scopophilic gaze of the desiring Subject. This double role as Object functions both in relation to the other characters within the play (who serve as fictive viewing Subjects) and—much to the consternation of the neo-Confucianist government—in relation to the actual viewing Subjects in the audience, male *and* female, who often sought them out as lovers. Not only the prints but the Kabuki plays exploit the theme of the man who is the object of female desire. Prints like Shunko's take this even further to depict men as desirable not merely as Kabuki actors in sublimating spectacle but in their own right, as potential lovers, either male or female, and for either men or women. In his portrait of Danjuro, Shunko exploits this ambiguous status of the actor as both Subject and Object.

WOMEN IN UKIYO-E: THE ACTIVE FEMALE SUBJECT

The complexities and ambiguities of the male Subject/Object are recapitulated in Ukiyo-e portraits of women. Superficially some prints of beautiful women or *bijin* seem to exemplify the woman-as-object model described by Berger, Mulvey, Nochlin and Pollock. In such works the female body is presented as spectacle, an ideal beauty without claims on or by the non-visual reality, a perfect scopophilic object, passively awaiting the male, and with gentle curves that invite completion by the viewer. (Although as indicated above, this is a partial description of many prints of men as well.) Suzuki Harunobu's demure and fragile beauties seem to represent the type. Harunobu, like many other Ukiyo-e artists, virtually invented his own style of female beauty. His is distinguished by the apparent youth, innocence, and daintiness of his subjects, quite different from the mature, majestic, bold styles of women by Kiyonaga and Utamaro. . . .

Yet although among Japanese types of female beauty Harunobu's girl is one of the most compliant and vulnerable, she is not deprived of indicators of autonomy, as a comparable Western fragile beauty would be. The autonomy of Harunobu's innocents is indicated by their position—frequently standing, and often outside, in public space—meeting lovers or . . . visiting shrines. . . . The aesthetic choices in their clothing and environments inform us of their tastes, education, abilities, and preferences. The gentle curves of the subtle kimono designs, each based on nature but alluding also to the season and to a wealth of literary references, suggest their temperaments. Books on the floor bespeak their literacy—which of course would include in this context familiarity with the classical novels, poetry and diaries written by women and men. . . .

Indeed it would seem that the very perfection of the outer image makes the viewer aware of the inner private Self, implied and vividly felt in every image of letter writing, reading of love letters, playing an instrument alone. . . .

SHUNGA: EROTIC ART AND THE INTERSUBJECTIVE SELF

Nowhere does the difference between the Western Self and the Japanese Self emerge more clearly than in erotic art or *Shunga* ("Spring pictures"). This difference is that between the Subject constructed by a relation (of dominance) to an Object and the Subject constructed intersubjectively, in relation to an Other conceived and encountered as a Subject.

In explicitly erotic prints women are *not* restricted to the role of passive object of male desire. They quite clearly appear as active desiring Subjects. Women are sometimes shown in positions of submission, but more often stand and sit upright or lie with a man who is also lying down. Either the woman or the man may be on top; they may be intertwined, with neither dominant. Poses characteristic of Western erotica—the woman lying on her back with her hands behind her head, fully exposed to the viewer, or lying with her head fallen back in abandon, as if her neck were broken—are not seen in Japan until after contact with the West.

These women are not only active, and avoiding either extreme of dominance or submission, but they are desiring. They actively reach out for the man and fondle his genitals. They curl their toes with rapture. It is impossible to mistake their enjoyment.

The disempowerment of the nude Western sex object is missing in the Japanese examples. Nudity is important in the Western context because it signals the permission given the male viewer: deprived of social status, her nudity indicating not merely her agreement to the male gaze/fantasy/act but often a wantonness that makes her agreement beside the point, the woman is vulnerable. In Japan, on the other hand, the vulnerability of nudity is not only unnecessary but undesirable. (And nudity per se is not sexy in Japan; it was common in public bathing.) What is desirable in woman to a Japanese man is a Subject with whom to interact, not an Object on whom to project one's own fantasy. Clothing—the choice and combination of patterns, the colors, the references—is vital to the revelation of one's Subjecthood.

The encounter with the Other as full Subject is signaled by the mutual gaze into each other's eyes. All of these prints show the couple looking at each other. In Shunga, it is not only the male who gazes at the female; the woman gazes back. Or rather, the Gaze (as it is called in representational theory) or the Look (as it is called in philosophy) is mutual—neither looks at an Object, but into another Subject, with a look that creates the other as Subject rather than diminishing her or him to the status of Object. While eye contact is not universal in these prints, it does appear in the Shunga of major artists from the late seventeenth century through Harunobu in the eighteenth century to Hokusai in the mid-nineteenth century.

If, as Western gaze theorists maintain, one's status as Subject is gained partly by the act of looking, both women and men are Subjects here. As indicated by the conventions of representational practice, neither men nor women are seen as Objects, and women are not denied the right to gaze.

THE FEMALE GAZE

Not only in Shunga but generally, Japanese representations differ from Western ones in facilitating the female gaze as well as the male gaze. The Gaze is not only erotic. Ukiyo-e artists thematized perception in countless ways; they were fascinated with the instruments (mirrors, telescopes and eyeglasses) and the phenomena of perception as a process—lantern light and fireflies and moonlight, mist and shadows and veils. They were fascinated with the act of looking.

Women looking is a major theme of Ukiyo-e. The well-known prints by Utamaro of women examining themselves in the mirror . . . exemplify the Self as Subject taking itself as Object, adopting toward itself the stance of the Other. But women assume the right to gaze in other ways as well. They are frequently voyeurs in sexual scenes. They examine other women on the streets, especially in the work of Kiyonaga who is famous for his complex social situations.

CONCLUSIONS

The Japanese representations are shown to depict women with full Subject-hood and in intersubjective sexual relations with men. While Subject-hood is not exclusively male, neither is Object status exclusively female. The impact of such images must be to legitimate the female Subject and the male Object.

María Lugónes

PLAYFULNESS, "WORLD"-TRAVELING, AND LOVING PERCEPTION

María Lugónes is Associate Professor of Comparative Literature and Philosophy, Interpretation, and Culture and of Philosophy and of Women's Studies at the State University of New York—Binghamton. She writes primarily in ethics, social and political philosophy, and feminism. The following selection, from one of her essays on feminism, describes everyday interactions with others in rather aesthetic terms. We perceive others most compassionately when we use our imaginations to "visit" their worlds. Such imaginative travels can yield surprising insights about those whose worlds differ from those that we, personally, inhabit.

... The paper describes the experience of "outsiders" to the mainstream of, for example, white/Anglo organization of life in the U. S. and stresses a particular feature of the outsider's existence: the outsider has necessarily acquired flexibility in shifting from the mainstream construction of life where she is constructed as an outsider to other constructions of life where she is more or less "at home." This flexibility is necessary for the outsider but it can also be willfully exercised by the outsider or by those who are at ease in the mainstream. I recommend this willful exercise, which I call "World"-Traveling, and I also recommend that the willful exercise be animated by an attitude that I describe as playful.

IDENTIFICATION AND LOVE

As a child, I was taught to perceive arrogantly. I have also been the object of arrogant perception. Though I am not a white-Anglo woman, it is clear to me that I can understand both my childhood training as an arrogant perceiver and my having been the object of arrogant perception without any reference to white/Anglo men, which is some indication that the concept of arrogant perception can be used cross-culturally and that white/Anglo men are not the only arrogant perceivers. I was brought up in

María Lugónes, "Playfulness, 'World'-Traveling, and Loving Perception," *Hypatia* 2.2 (1987): 3–19.

Argentina watching men and women of moderate and of considerable means graft the substance of their servants to themselves. I also learned to graft my mother's substance to my own. It was clear to me that both men and women were the victims of arrogant perception and that arrogant perception was systematically organized to break the spirit of all women and of most men. I valued my rural "gaucho" ancestry because its ethos has always been one of independence in poverty through enormous loneliness, courage, and self-reliance. I found inspiration in this ethos and committed myself never to be broken by arrogant perception. I can say all of this in this way only because I have learned from [Marilyn] Frye's "In and Out of Harm's Way: Arrogance and Love." She has given me a way of understanding and articulating something important in my own life.

Frye is not particularly concerned with women as arrogant perceivers but as the objects of arrogant perception. Her concern is, in part, to enhance our understanding of women "untouched by phallocratic machinations" by understanding the harm done to women through such machinations. In this case she proposes that we could understand women untouched by arrogant perception through an understanding of what arrogant perception does to women. She also proposes an understanding of what it is to love women that is inspired by a vision of women unharmed by arrogant perception. To love women is, at least in part, to perceive them with loving eyes. "The loving eye is a contrary of the arrogant eye."

I am concerned with women as arrogant perceivers because I want to explore further what it is to love women. I want to explore two failures of love: my failure to love my mother and white/Anglo women's failure to love women across racial and cultural boundaries in the U.S. As a consequence of exploring these failures I will offer a loving solution to them. My solution modifies

Frye's account of loving perception by adding what I call playful "world"-travel.

It is clear to me that at least in the U.S. and Argentina women are taught to perceive many other women arrogantly. Being taught to perceive arrogantly is part of being taught to be a woman of a certain class in both the U.S. and Argentina, it is part of being taught to be a white/Anglo woman in the U.S. and it is part of being taught to be a woman in both places: to be both the agent and the object of arrogant perception. My love for my mother seemed to me thoroughly imperfect as I was growing up because I was unwilling to become what I had been taught to see my mother as being. I thought that to love her was consistent with my abusing her (using, taking for granted, and demanding her services in a far reaching way that, since four other people engaged in the same grafting of her substance onto themselves, left her little of herself to herself) and was to be in part constituted by my identifying with her, my seeing myself in her: to love her was supposed to be of a piece with both my abusing her and with my being open to being abused. It is clear to me that I was not supposed to love servants: I could abuse them without identifying with them, without seeing myself in them. When I came to the U.S. I learned that part of racism is the internalization of the propriety of abuse without identification: I learned that I could be seen as a being to be used by white/Anglo men and women without the possibility of identification, i.e., without their act of attempting to graft my substance onto theirs, rubbing off on them at all. They could remain untouched, without any sense of loss.

So, women who are perceived arrogantly can perceive other women arrogantly in their turn. To what extent those women are responsible for their arrogant perceptions of other women is certainly open to question, but I do not have any doubt that many women have been taught to abuse women in this particular way. I am not interested in assigning responsibility. I am interested in understanding the phenomenon so as to understand a loving way out of it.

There is something obviously wrong with the love that I was taught and something right with my failure to love my mother in this way. But I do not think that what is wrong is my profound desire to identify with her, to see myself in her; what is wrong is that I was taught to identify with a victim of enslavement. What is wrong is that I was taught to practice enslavement of my mother and to learn to become a slave through this practice. There is something obviously wrong with my having been taught that love is consistent with abuse, consistent with arrogant perception. Notice that the love I was taught is the love that Frye speaks of when she says "We can be taken in by this equation of servitude with love." Even though I could both abuse and love my mother, I was not supposed to love servants. This is because in the case of servants one is and is supposed to be clear about their servitude and the "equation of servitude with love" is never to be thought clearly in those terms. So, I was not supposed to love and could not love servants. But I could love my mother because deception (in particular, self-deception) is part of this "loving." Servitude is called abnegation and abnegation is not analyzed any further. Abnegation is not instilled in us through an analysis of its nature but rather through a heralding of it as beautiful and noble. We are coaxed, seduced into abnegation not through analysis but through emotive persuasion. Frye makes the connection between deception and this sense of "loving" clear. When I say that there is something obviously wrong with the loving that I was taught, I do not mean to say that the connection between this loving and abuse is obvious. Rather I mean that once the connection between this loving and abuse has been unveiled, there is something obviously wrong with the loving given that it is obvious that it is wrong to abuse others.

I am glad that I did not learn my lessons well, but it is clear that part of the mechanism that permitted my not learning well involved a separation from my mother: I saw us as beings of quite a different sort. It involved an abandoning of my mother while I longed not to abandon her. I wanted to love my mother, though, given what I was taught, "love" could not be the right word for what I longed for.

I was disturbed by my not wanting to be what she was. I had a sense of not being quite integrated, my self was missing because I could not identify with her, I could not see myself in her. I could not welcome her world. I saw myself as separate from her, a different sort of being, not quite of the same species. This separation, this lack of love, I saw, and I think that I saw correctly as a lack in myself (not a fault, but a lack). I also see that if this was a lack of love, love cannot be what I was taught. Love has to be rethought, made anew.

◆◆◆

Frye also says that the loving eye is "the eye of one who knows that to know the seen, one must consult something other than one's own will and interests and fears and imagination." This is much more helpful to me so long as I do not understand Frye to mean that I should not consult my own interests nor that I should exclude the possibility that my self and the self of the one I love may be importantly tied to each other in many complicated ways. Since I am emphasizing here that the failure of love lies in part in the failure to identify and since I agree with Frye that one "must consult something other than one's own will and interests and fears and imagination," I will proceed to try to explain what I think needs to be consulted. To love my mother was not possible for me while I retained a sense that it was fine for me and others to see her arrogantly. Loving my mother also required that I see with her eyes, that I go into my mother's world, that I see both of us as we are constructed in her world, that I witness her own sense of herself from within her world. Only through this traveling to her "world" could I identify with her because only then could I cease to ignore her and to be excluded and separate from her. Only then could I see her as a subject even if one subjected and only then could I see at all how meaning could arise fully between us. We are fully dependent on each other for the possibility of being understood and without this understanding we are not intelligible, we do not make sense, we are not solid, visible, integrated; we are lacking. So traveling to each other's "worlds" would enable us to *be* through *loving* each other.

"WORLDS" AND "WORLD" TRAVELING

Some time ago I came to be in a state of profound confusion as I experienced myself as both having and not having a particular attribute. I was sure I had the attribute in question and, on the other hand, I was sure that I did not have it. I remain convinced that I both have and do not have this attribute. The attribute is playfulness. I am sure that I am a playful person. On the other hand, I can say, painfully, that I am not a playful person. I am not a playful person in certain worlds. One of the things I did as I became confused was to call my friends, far away people who knew me well, to see whether or not I was playful. Maybe they could help me out of my confusion. They said to me, "Of course you are playful" and they said it with the same conviction that I had about it. Of course I am playful. Those people who were around me said to me, "No, you are not playful. You are a serious woman. You just take everything seriously." They were just as sure about what they said to me and could offer me every bit of evidence that one could need to conclude that they were right. So I said to myself: "Okay, maybe what's happening here is that there is an attribute that I do have but there are certain worlds in which I am not at ease and it is because I'm not at ease in those worlds that I don't have that attribute in those worlds. But what does that mean?" I was worried both about what I meant by "worlds" when I said "in some worlds I do not have the attribute" and what I meant by saying that lack of ease was what led me not to be playful in those worlds. Because you see, if it was just a matter of lack of ease, I could work on it.

I can explain some of what I mean by a "world." I do not want the fixity of a definition at this point, because I think the term is suggestive and I do not want to close the suggestiveness of it too soon. I can offer some characteristics that serve to distinguish between a "world," a utopia, a possible world in the philosophical sense, and a world view. By a "world" I do not mean a utopia at all. A utopia does not count as a world in my sense. The "worlds" that I am talking about are possible. But a possible world is not what I mean by a "world" and I do not mean a world-view, though something like a world-view is involved here.

For something to be a "world" in my sense it has to be inhabited at present by some flesh and blood people. That is why it cannot be a utopia. It may also be inhabited by some imaginary people. It may be inhabited by people who are dead or people that the inhabitants of this "world" met in some other "world" and now have in this "world" in imagination.

A "world" in my sense may be an actual society given its dominant culture's description and construction of life, including a construction of the relationships of production, of gender, race, etc. But a "world" can also be such a society given a nondominant construction, or it can be such a society or *a* society given an idiosyncratic construction. As we will see it is problematic to say that these are all constructions of the same society. But they are different "worlds."

A "world" need not be a construction of a whole society. It may be a construction of a tiny portion of a particular society. It may be inhabited by just a few people. Some "worlds" are bigger than others.

A "world" may be incomplete in that things in it may not be altogether constructed or some things may be constructed negatively (they are not what "they" are in some other "world.") Or the "world" may be incomplete because it may have references to things that do not quite exist in it, references to things like Brazil, where Brazil is not quite part of that "world." Given lesbian feminism, the construction of "lesbian" is purposefully and healthily still up in the air, in the process of becoming. What it is to be a Hispanic in this country is, in a dominant Anglo construction, purposefully incomplete. Thus one cannot really answer questions of the sort "What is a Hispanic?", "Who counts as a Hispanic?", "Are Latinos, Chicanos, Hispanos, Black Dominicans, white Cubans, Korean-Colombians, Italian-Argentinians, Hispanic?" What it is to be a "Hispanic" in the varied so-called Hispanic communities in the U.S. is also yet up in the air. We have not yet decided whether there is something like a "Hispanic" in our varied "worlds." So, a "world" may be an incomplete visionary nonutopian construction of life or it may be a traditional construction of life. A traditional Hispano construction of Northern New Mexican life is a "world." Such a traditional construction, in the face of a racist, ethnocentrist, money-centered Anglo construction of Northern New Mexican life is highly unstable because Anglo have the means for imperialist destruction of traditional Hispano "worlds."

In a "world" some of the inhabitants may not understand or hold the particular construction of them that constructs them in that "world." So, there may be "worlds" that construct me in ways that I do not even understand. Or it may be that I understand the construction, but do not hold it of myself. I may not accept it as an account of myself, a construction of myself. And yet, I may be *animating* such a construction.

One can "travel" between these "worlds" and one can inhabit more than one of these "worlds" at the very same time. I think that most of us who are outside the mainstream of, for example, the U.S. dominant construction or organization of life, are "world travelers" as a matter of necessity and of survival. It seems to me that inhabiting more than one "world" at the same time and "traveling" between "worlds" is part and parcel of our experience and our situation. One can be at the same time in a "world" that constructs one as stereotypically Latin, for example, and in a "world" that constructs one as Latin. Being stereotypically Latin and being simply Latin are different simultaneous constructions of persons that are part of different "worlds." One animates one or the other or both at the same time without necessarily confusing them, though simultaneous enactment can be confusing if one is not on one's guard.

In describing my sense of a "world," I mean to be offering a description of experience, something that is true to experience even if it is ontologically problematic. Though I would think that any account of identity that could not be true to this experience of outsiders to the mainstream would be faulty even if ontologically unproblematic. Its ease would constrain, erase, or deem aberrant experience that has within it significant insights into nonimperialistic understanding between people.

Those of us who are "world"-travelers have the distinct experience of being different in different "worlds" and of having the capacity to remember other "worlds" and ourselves in them. We can say "That is me there, and I am happy in that 'world.'" So, the experience is of being a different person in different "worlds" and yet of having memory of oneself as different without quite having the sense of there being any underlying

"I." So I can say "That is me there and I am so playful in that 'world.'" I say "That is *me* in that 'world'" not because I recognize myself in that person; rather, the first-person statement is noninferential. I may well recognize that person has abilities that I do not have and yet the having or not having of the abilities is always an "I have . . ." and "I do not have . . ."; i.e., it is always experienced in the first person.

The shift from being one person to being a different person is what I call "travel." This shift may not be willful or even conscious, and one may be completely unaware of being different than one is in a different "world," and may not recognize that one is in a different "world." Even though the shift can be done willfully, it is not a matter of acting. One does not pose as someone else, one does not pretend to be, for example, someone of a different personality or character or someone who uses space or language differently than the other person. Rather one is someone who has that personality or character or uses space and language in that particular way. The "one" here does not refer to some underlying "I." One does not *experience* any underlying "I."

PLAYFULNESS

I had a very personal stake in investigating this topic. Playfulness is not only the attribute that was the source of my confusion and the attitude that I recommend as the loving attitude in traveling across "worlds," I am also scared of ending up a serious human being, someone with no multi-dimensionality, with no fun in life, someone who is just someone who has had the fun constructed out of her. I am seriously scared of getting stuck in a "world" that constructs me that way. A world that I have no escape from and in which I cannot be playful.

I thought about what it is to be playful and what it is to play and I did this thinking in a "world" in which I only remember myself as playful and in which all of those who know me as playful are imaginary beings. A "world" in which I am scared of losing my memories of myself as playful or have them erased from me. Because I live in such a "world," after I formulated my own sense of what it is to be playful and to play I decided that I needed to "go to the literature." I read two classics on the subject: Johan Huizinga's *Homo Ludens* and Hans-Georg Gadamer's chapter on the concept of play in his *Truth and Method*. I discovered, to my amazement, that what I thought about play and playfulness, if they were right, was absolutely wrong. Though I will not provide the arguments for this interpretation of Gadamer and Huizinga here, I understood that both of them have an agonistic sense of "play." Play and playfulness have, ultimately, to do with contest, with winning, losing, battling. The sense of playfulness that I have in mind has nothing to do with those things. So, I tried to elucidate both senses of play and playfulness by contrasting them to each other. The contrast helped me see the attitude that I have in mind as the loving attitude in traveling across "worlds" more clearly.

An agonistic sense of playfulness is one in which *competence* is supreme. You'd better know the rules of the game. In agonistic play there is risk, there is *uncertainty*, but the uncertainty is about who is going to win and who is going to lose. There are rules that inspire hostility. The attitude of *playfulness is conceived as secondary to or derivative from play*. Since play is agon, then the only conceivable playful attitude is an agonistic one (the attitude does not turn an activity into play, but rather presupposes an activity that is play). One of the paradigmatic ways of playing for both Gadamer and Huizinga is role-playing. In role-playing, the person who is a participant in the game has a *fixed conception of him or herself*. I also think that the players are imbued with *self-importance* in agonistic play since they are so keen on winning given their own merits, their very own competence.

When considering the value of "world"-traveling and whether playfulness is the loving attitude to have while traveling, I recognized the agonistic attitude as inimical to traveling across "worlds." The agonistic traveler is a conqueror, an imperialist. Huizinga, in his classic book on play, interprets western civilization as play. That is an interesting thing for Third World people to think about. Western civilization has been interpreted by a white western man as play in the agonistic sense of play. Huizinga reviews western law, art, and many other aspects of western culture and sees agon in all of them. Agonistic playfulness leads those who attempt to travel to another "world" with this attitude to failure. Agonistic travelers fail consistently in their attempt to travel because what they do is to try to conquer the other "world." The attempt is not an attempt to try to erase the other "world." That is what assimilation is all about. Assimilation is the destruction of other people's "worlds." So, the agonistic attitude, the playful attitude given western man's construction of playfulness, is not a healthy, loving attitude to have in traveling across "worlds." Notice that given the agonistic attitude one *cannot* travel across "worlds," though one can kill other "worlds" with it. So for people who are interested in crossing racial and ethnic boundaries, an arrogant western man's construction of playfulness is deadly. One cannot cross the boundaries with it. One needs to give up such an attitude if one wants to travel.

So then, what is the loving playfulness that I have in mind? Let me begin with one example: We are by the river bank. The river is very, very low. Almost dry. Bits of water here and there. Little pools with a few trout hiding under the rocks. But mostly it is wet stones, grey on the outside. We walk on the stones for a while. You pick up a stone and crash it onto the others. As it breaks, it is quite wet inside and it is very colorful, very pretty. I pick up a stone and break it and run toward the pieces to see the colors. They are beautiful. I laugh and bring the pieces back to you and you are doing the same with your pieces. We keep on crashing stones for hours, anxious to see the beautiful new colors. We are playing. The playfulness of our activity does not presuppose that there is something like "crashing stones" that is a particular form of play with its own rules. Rather *the attitude that carries us through the activity, a playful attitude, turns the activity into play.* Our activity has no rules, though it is certainly intentional activity and we both understand what we are doing. The playfulness that gives meaning to our activity includes uncertainty, but in this case the uncertainty is an *openness to surprise.* This is a particular metaphysical attitude that does not expect the world to be neatly packaged, ruly. Rules may fail to explain what we are doing. We are not self-important, we are not fixed in particular constructions of ourselves, which is part of saying that we are *open to self-construction.* We may not have rules, and when we do have rules, *there are no rules that are to us sacred.* We are not worried about competence. We are not wedded to a particular way of doing things. While playful we have not abandoned ourselves to, nor are we stuck in, any particular "world." We *are there creatively.* We are not passive.

Playfulness is, in part, an openness to being a fool, which is a combination of not worrying about competence, not being self-important, not taking norms as sacred and finding ambiguity and double edges a source of wisdom and delight.

So, positively, the playful attitude involves openness to surprise, openness to being a fool, openness to self-construction or reconstruction and to construction or reconstruction of the "worlds" we inhabit playfully. Negatively, playfulness is characterized by uncertainty, lack of self-importance, absence of rules or a not taking rules as sacred, a not worrying about competence, and a lack of abandonment to a particular construction of oneself, others, and one's relation to them. In attempting to take a hold of oneself and of one's relation to others in a particular "world," one may study, examine, and come to understand oneself. One may then see what the possibilities for play are for the being one is in that "world." One may even decide to inhabit that self fully in order to understand it better and find its creative possibilities. All of this is just self-reflection and it is quite different from resigning or abandoning oneself to the particular construction of oneself that one is attempting to take a hold of.

Without knowing the other's "world," one does not know the other, and without knowing the other one is really alone in the other's presence because the other is only dimly present to one.

Through traveling to other people's "worlds" we discover that there are "worlds" in which those who are the victims of arrogant perception are really subjects, lively beings, resistors, constructors of visions, even though in the mainstream construction they are animated only by the arrogant perceiver and are pliable, foldable, file-awayable, classifiable. I always imagine the Aristotelian slave as pliable and foldable at night or after he or she cannot work anymore (when he or she dies as a tool). Aristo-

tle tells us nothing about the slave *apart from the master.* We know the slave only through the master. The slave is a tool of the master. After working hours he or she is folded and placed in a drawer till the next morning. My mother was apparent to me mostly as a victim of arrogant perception. I was loyal to the arrogant perceiver's construction of her and thus disloyal to her in assuming that she was exhausted by that construction. I was unwilling to be like her and thought that identifying with her, seeing myself in her necessitated that I become like her. I was wrong both in assuming that she was exhausted by the arrogant perceiver's construction of her and in my understanding of identification, though I was not wrong in thinking that identification was part of loving and that it involved in part my seeing myself in her. I came to realize through traveling to her "world" that she is not foldable and pliable, that she is not exhausted by the mainstream Argentinian patriarchal construction of her. I came to realize that there are "worlds" in which she shines as a creative being. Seeing myself in her through traveling to her "world" has meant seeing how different from her I am in her "world."

So, in recommending "world"-traveling and identification through "world"-traveling as part of loving other women, I am suggesting disloyalty to arrogant perceivers, including the arrogant perceiver in ourselves, and to their constructions of women. In revealing agonistic playfulness as incompatible with "world"-traveling, I am revealing both its affinity with imperialism and arrogant perception and its incompatibility with loving and loving perception.

DISCUSSION QUESTIONS

1. Should *Huckleberry Finn* be required reading in the high school you attended? Should books that realistically portray racist and sexist attitudes be removed from the canon, or are they an important part of educating students about our tradition? How important is knowledge of the tradition to the average citizen's education?

2. Can you think of examples of films in which women are not portrayed in a sexist manner? How do these films represent women? Can you think of examples of films in which nonwhites are not portrayed in a racist manner? How do these films represent nonwhites?

3. Do you think that women's art is necessarily different in kind from men's art? Explain.

4. Is insight into the historical circumstances of the originators of an art form essential for understanding any kind of art, in your opinion? Is it essential for understanding the blues?

5. Should anything be done to prevent exploitation of artist innovators like "the Great Music Robbery"? If so, what? Should anything retroactively be done to compensate previously exploited artists? If so, what?

6. Does understanding the techniques of racial representation or of gratifying the male audience member undercut their impact? Explain.

7. Can you think of instances of art (either popular or high art) that portray Asian and Middle Eastern cultures in orientalist terms? If so, how is orientalism suggested?

8. Do you agree with Miller's view of how erotic depiction can be nonsexist? Why or why not?

9. Do artistic representations of women dictate our conceptions of female beauty and attractiveness? If so, is this a harmful phenomenon?

10. How are the experiences of minority group members and those of women in connection with the arts similar? How are they different?

FURTHER READING

The Blues

Baraka, Imamu Amiri. *Blues People: Negro Music in White America.* New York: Morrow, 1963.

Keil, Charles. *Urban Blues.* Chicago: U of Chicago P, 1966.

Oliver, Paul. *Blues Fell This Morning: Meaning in the Blues.* 2nd ed. New York: Cambridge UP, 1990.

Feminism

Battersby, Christine. *Gender and Genius: Towards a Feminist Aesthetics.* London: Women's Press, 1989.

Bowers, Jane, and Judith Tick, eds. *Women Making Music: The Western Art Tradition, 1150–1950.* Urbana: U of Illinois P, 1987.

Ecker, Giselda, ed. *Feminist Aesthetics.* Trans. Harriet Anderson. Boston: Beacon, 1985.

Freuh, Joanna, Cassandra L. Langer, and Arlene Raven, eds. *Feminist Art Criticism: An Anthology.* New York: HarperCollins, 1991.

———. *New Feminist Criticism: Art—Identity—Action.* New York: HarperCollins, 1994.

Hein, Hilde, and Carolyn Korsmeyer, eds. *Aesthetics in Feminist Perspective.* Bloomington: Indiana UP, 1993.

Nochlin, Linda. *"Women, Art, and Power" and Other Essays.* London: Thames and Hudson, 1989.

Pendle, Karin, ed. *Women and Music.* Bloomington: Indiana UP, 1992.

Pollock, Griselda. *Framing Feminism: Art and the Women's Movement 1970–1985.* New York: Pandora, 1987.

———. *Vision and Difference: Femininity, Feminism, and Histories of Art.* New York: Routledge, 1988.

Showalter, Elaine, ed. *The New Feminist Criticism: Essays of Women, Literature, and Theory.* New York: Pantheon, 1985.

On Race and Racism

Baker, Houston A. *Black Studies, Rap, and the Academy.* Chicago: U of Chicago P, 1992.

———. "Scene . . . Not Heard." *Reading Rodney King/Reading Urban Uprising.* New York: Routledge, 1993. 38–48.

Frederickson, George. *The Black Image in the White Mind.* Middletown: Wesleyan UP, 1987.

Gates, Henry Louis, Jr., ed. *"Race," Writing, and Difference.* Chicago: U of Chicago P, 1986.

Kochman, Thomas. *Rappin' and Stylin' Out.* Urbana: U of Illinois P, 1972.

Morrison, Toni. *Playing in the Dark: Whiteness and the Literary Imagination.* Cambridge: Harvard UP, 1992.

Moses, Wilson Jeremiah. *Black Messiahs and Uncle Toms: Social and Literary Manipulations of a Religious Myth.* University Park: Pennsylvania State UP, 1982.

Said, Edward W. *Orientalism.* New York: Vintage, 1978.

Sidran, Ben. *Black Talk: How the Music of Black America Created a Radical Alternative to the Values of the Western Literary Tradition.* New York: Holt, 1971.

Thompson, Robert Farris. *Flash of the Spirit: African and Afro-American Art and Philosophy.* New York: Random House, 1983.

POPULAR CULTURE
AND EVERYDAY LIFE

When someone refers to "the arts," what images come to your mind? Do you imagine concert halls, theaters, and museums? Do you think of your favorite radio stations? Are the shows you prefer and your home decorations instances of art as you envision it? Are "the arts" all around you, a part of your everyday life? Do you associate "the arts" with snobs?

Since the eighteenth century, Western philosophy has sharply distinguished between fine art, which is designed to be contemplated, and craft, which, however decorative, is designed for practical use. Perhaps on the basis of this distinction, fine art is associated with the financially well off, who live the proverbial life of leisure and have the resources to invest in impractical things. The popular arts, by contrast, are associated with the less affluent economic classes.

Technological developments have made many of the currently popular arts possible, and the unprecedented artforms that have resulted often follow their own rules. Most of us whose childhoods occurred in the latter half of the twentieth century developed something akin to personal relationships as a consequence of one technological development. Stanley Cavell discusses the nature of cartoon characters and some of the differences between their world and ours. Even basic laws of nature, such as the law of gravity, are altered in the world of cartoons. We accept that the cartoon world is governed by its own laws, according to Cavell, because cartoons succeed in the enterprise of all films—that of projecting a world for our experience.

Walter Benjamin (as noted in Chapter 2) was dubious of the impact that machines would have on our cultural values. Susan Sontag similarly considers the possibility that certain machines—cameras—have eroded our culture's belief in human dignity. Photographs, she contend, allow us to possess and control others. They also involve a kind of magic, evoking the presence of someone who is absent or dead, or distancing us from the reality of what is portrayed. The images produced by cameras have become a world unto themselves, Sontag argues, and the West's psychology of consumption has dictated our response to these images. If we are to improve our relationship to our environment, she contends, we need to revise not only our attitude toward nature, but also toward the world of images as well.

At least since Plato's critique in *The Republic*, intellectuals have often criticized popular art for its depictions of undignified characters and their behavior. Robert C. Solomon addresses the comedy of the Three Stooges, often viewed as childish and vulgar. He considers the standard interpretations of humor and finds all of them applicable to the Three Stooges. The Three Stooges' comedy, he concludes, reflects the basic elements of humor and offers an important enrichment to our lives.

Aesthetics is usually associated with the fine arts and exceptional cases of natural beauty. But our daily lives are filled with countless, if less obvious, encounters with the aesthetic. When we decide what movie to attend or what clothes to wear, we are making judgments of taste. If these decisions are partially in response to advertisements, they are also influenced by aesthetic appeals. The mass media appeal to us constantly, seeking to capture our attention. These efforts, too, address us aesthetically. Likewise, our everyday activities might be pursued in any number of different ways. To the extent that style and taste affect our approach and execution of these activities, they, too, have an aesthetic character.

Most often, philosophers approach questions regarding how we ought to live in the context of ethics. Ethical inquiries into the nature of right and wrong, good and bad, and the like are certainly fundamental to a thoughtful approach to our way of life. But certain aesthetic inquiries are also important. Are some ways of beholding people better than others? Are aesthetic values such as harmony, coherence, and balance appropriate terms in which to evaluate our lives? Are our lives comparable to artworks? In deciding how to live, are we making judgments that resemble those that are made by artists?

American philosopher John Dewey considers aesthetics and ethics to be concerned with the same basic problem. Both ask how we can make the experiences of our lives as significant as possible. Dewey observes that the experiences that we consider most important in our lives are always characterized by aesthetic qualities. The experiences that we most commonly call "aesthetic experiences" are only the clearest cases of what we value in all experience. We should look to aesthetic experience, Dewey argues, to determine what matters in our lives.

Sei Shōnagon, a lady of the Heian dynasty court in Japan around the year 1000 C.E., found sources of aesthetic experience in everyday experiences. Her diary, or "pillow book," records events that she found particularly striking and includes lists that reflect her tastes and sensibilities. The selection from Sei Shōnagon includes some examples.

Garret Sokoloff's "By Pausing before a *Kicho*" analyzes Shōnagon's approach as focused on moments of great charm or delightfulness, typically in contexts that emphasize the nuances of relationships between people. Sokoloff considers these delightful experiences to be intrinsically valuable, but he believes that they enhance interpersonal relationships as well. Although not sought for their instrumental value, such everyday aesthetic experiences serve purposes beyond themselves.

Barbara Sandrisser, like Sokoloff, reflects on Shōnagon's *Pillow Book*. Sandrisser considers Shōnagon's remarks on elegance and compares her perspective to Western attitudes. In the West we often associate elegance, characterized by refinement and simplicity, with superficiality and snobbery. Yet elegant objects and ideas are much more important than we usually realize, Sandrisser argues. They draw us into a more intimate relationship with the rest of our world by enhancing our activities and making us more aesthetically sensitive, which is especially true when we surround ourselves with such objects in our everyday lives.

Janet McCracken considers the home and our selection of decorative objects in her discussion of the "domestic aesthetic." The domestic aesthetic, she argues, is the fundamental sphere in which we develop our ability to make judgments. McCracken maintains that many of the activities conducted around one's home are aesthetic and that they indicate one's fundamental values. Our ability to live a good life depends upon our domestic judgments, according to McCracken, but unfortunately the ability to make good everyday aesthetic judgments has been deteriorating in our culture for some time.

Anna Deavere Smith sees potential for developing our sensitivity in one of the most everyday of our experiences, that of listening to other individuals in the course of everyday conversation. She endorses the aesthetic value of everyday conversation, but she does this through directly artistic methods. In her one-woman shows *Fires in the Mirror* and *Twilight: Los Angeles, 1992*, she crafts theater from statements made by people involved in and affected by recent racial incidents in the United States. Smith believes that ordinary people speak their own poetry when they express their real concerns. Smith's aesthetic lies, literally, in perspective, and her plays attest to her belief in the aesthetic—and artistic—value of everyday speech.

Stanley Cavell

CARTOONS

Stanley Cavell is professor of philosophy at Harvard University. He specializes in American philosophy and film. His books on aesthetics include Disowning Knowledge in Six Plays of Shakespeare, Pursuits of Happiness: The Hollywood Comedy of Remarriage, *and* The World Viewed. *Cavell considers film in general to involve the projection of a world. In the following postscript to* The World Viewed, *he describes the distinctive features of the world of cartoons, which he takes to comprise a specific kind of film.*

There is one whole region of film which . . . explicitly has nothing to do with projections of the real world—the region of animated cartoons. If this region of film counters my insistence upon the projection of reality as essential to the medium of movies, then it counters it completely. Here is what Sesonske says about cartoons (he is thinking specifically of Disney's work, which is fair enough: if any cartoons are obviously to be thought of as movies, even to the point of their containing stars, these are the first candidates):

> . . . neither these lively creatures nor their actions ever existed until they were projected on the screen. Their projected world exists only *now*, at the moment of projection—and when we ask if there is any feature in which it differs from reality, the answer is, "Yes, every feature." Neither space nor time nor the laws of nature are the same. There is *a* world we experience here, but not *the* world—a world I know and see but to which I am nevertheless not present, yet not a world past. For there is no past time at which these events either did occur or purport to have occurred. Surely not the time the drawings were made, or the frames photographed; for the world I know and see had not yet sprung into existence then. It exists only now, when I see it; yet I cannot go to where its creatures are, for there is no access to its space from ours except through vision.

Each of these remarks is the negation or parody of something I claim for the experience of movies. But of course they do not prove that my claims are false except on the assumption that cartoons are movies, and that, therefore, what I said about movies, if it is true, ought to apply to cartoons in the way it applies to movies. But on my assumption (which I should no doubt have made explicit) that cartoons are not movies, these

Stanley Cavell, *The World Viewed*, enl. ed. (Cambridge: Harvard UP, 1979) 167–72.

remarks about their conditions of existence constitute some explanation about *why* they are not.

Since this is merely logic, what is the moral to be drawn from the fact of cartoons? I take the moral to be something like this: A good case can be made out, using the very terms of *The World Viewed* (about a world present to me from which I am absent, about various kinds of succession or motion, about conviction and memory, etc.) that cartoons are movies. It would, therefore, in a sense not be surprising to me if someone likes to think that is what they are. Then there is this asymmetry between his position and mine: He does not have to show that cartoons *are* movies because he has no theory which his taste contradicts. He can simply say "the two are not that different." Whereas I do, apparently, have to show that cartoons are *not* movies, or anyway show that the differences between them are as decisive as my emphasis on reality implies.

And of course I cannot show this, in the sense of prove it—any more than I can show that a robot is not a creature or that a human is not a mouse or a dog or a duck. If someone is convinced that humans are not that different from mice or dogs or ducks, he can bring a great deal of evidence in his support. There are probably more citable similarities between them than differences. To affect someone's conviction that cartoons are movies, all I could do would be to provide some reflections on cartoons. I imagine they would contain considerations of the following sort.

The chief inhabitants of the world of animated cartoons (the ones I am imagining and the ones Sesonske's remarks seem to have in mind) are talking animals—anthropomorphic, we might say, in everything but form. The human figures in them seem, in comparison with the animal figures, out of place or in the way. I think the reason for this is that there is less room, so to speak, in

these human figures for our fulfillment of their animation, i.e., for our anthropomorphizing of them. If it proves to be true that human figures are thus generally problematic, then it becomes of interest to determine how the human figures that occur are made fit to occur, i.e., made to live the laws of animation.

The world inhabited by animated creatures is typically also animated; it may not remain the stable background of the actions of the live figures, but act on its own. It is animistic. There is, of course, no general problem of achieving conviction in such a world; it taps perhaps the most primitive of our convictions about the world. If I say it is essentially a child's world, I hope I will not be taken as belittling it, nor as denying that it remains an ineluctable substratum of our own, and subject to deliberate or unlooked for eruption. The difference between this world and the world we inhabit is not that the world of animation is governed by physical laws or satisfies metaphysical limits which are just different from those which condition us; its laws are often quite similar. The difference is that we are uncertain when or to what extent our laws and limits do and do not apply (which suggests that there are no real *laws* at all).

The most obvious abrogations of our limits and laws concern those governing physical identity or destruction. The possibility of metamorphosis, even a tendency toward it, is familiar enough. The abrogation of gravity is manifested in everything from the touching movement of these creatures as they trace their arabesques in the air or climb upon a friendly petal, to the momentary hesitation before a long fall and the crash which shakes the earth but is never fatal. (The topos of the hesitation suggests that what puts gravity into effect is a consciousness of it.) Or rather, what is abrogated is not gravity (things and creatures *do* fall, and petals are sometimes charmingly difficult to climb up to) but corporeality. The bodies of these creatures never get in their way. Their bodies are indestructible, one might almost say immortal; they are totally subject to will, and perfectly expressive. (Reversing the economy of human expressiveness, their bodies bear the brunt of meaningfulness. Their faces are more or less fixed, confined to two or three attitudes. This condition captures and expresses the condition, the poignance, of real animals.) They are animations, disembodiments, pure spirits.

Apparently it is natural for the animation to be of *small* animals, perhaps because they most immediately convey animateness, quickness; perhaps because they can be given an upright posture without appearing grotesque or parodistic of the human (like chimpanzees dressed in cute clothes). The horse and large dog (the usual principals of movies about animals) either have to be taken seriously or else they are merely comic. (Obvious exceptions here are Bambi—whom I have not seen—and Dumbo. But they are both children, and the former is an animal known for its expressive eyes and the uncanny beauty of its motion, while the latter is redeemed by its almost unbelievable discovery that it can *fly*.) Beasts which are pure spirits, they avoid, or deny, *the* metaphysical fact of human beings, that they are condemned to both souls and bodies. A world whose creatures are incorporeal is a world devoid of sex and death, hence a world apt to be either very sad or very happy. At either extreme its creatures elicit from us a painful tenderness.

If I pursued such thoughts much farther, I would perhaps start sounding theoretical. I would, at any rate, wish to locate the specific moods, emotions, and subjects which are natural to (narrative) animation. Natural is no more than natural, and may change with historical or cultural change. It does not mean that no other art *can* convey the moods and emotions, or employ the subjects, of cartoons; nor that cartoons which compete with movies cannot change. It

means that each art and each change will convey and employ these moods and subjects in its own way. For example, cartoon violence can be funny because while it is very brutal it cannot be bloody. (Silent slapstick can achieve this logic; but its violence is often under-cranked, which feels semi-animated; and it is often more imminent than actual; and where active, often occurs between humans and objects, not between humans; and where between humans, often inadvertently or spasmodically.) Cartoon tenderness and loss is tenderness and loss maximized, or purified. Cartoon terror is absolute, because since the body is not destructible, the threat is to the soul itself. (This is different from horror movies. There the threat is not of isolation through abandonment or annihilation, but of isolation through unacknowledgeable disfigurement. They play upon the fear that cartoons laugh at: irreversible metamorphosis.)—Does Popeye have a soul? Well, does he have a human body? A sailor is nicely suited for exaggerated forearms; and for the rest, Popeye's body survives, or ignores, everything that brute human strength can deliberately inflict upon it—if, that is, it some point receives its magic infusion of canned fuel. His body is not so much fed as stoked, and with a substance for herbivores, anyway for creatures of non-violence, for mythical children. (His timid acquaintance is also associated with a childish food, ground meat, no real amount of which satisfies his need. Which other human figures are indecorous enough to be shown eating?) Steam up, his body acts on its own, unaligned with, and not affecting, other avenues of expression: his face remains, through violence, preternaturally fixed; his voice goes on with its continuous static of undecipherable commentary; at last his pipe releases a whistle or two of satisfaction.

In cartoons, sexuality is apt to be either epicene or caricatured. I suppose this is because cartoons, being fleshless, do not veer toward the pornographic, although, given a chance, they may naturally veer toward the obscene. Of course, overlaps and affinities may be expected among various media. A cartoon of Garbo or Dietrich or Marilyn Monroe will miss what is truly attractive about them—not simply their specific physical presences but the animation of those presences by the human female's exemplification of independence and profundity and wit. A cartoon of Mae West, however, may really capture her genius, because she is already a caricature of sexuality; the caricature of sexuality is her subject. It is the essence of her deflationary comedy that her blatant presence signifies nothing special. She is the woman of *no* mystery, or the woman whose interest has nothing to do with mystery. The invitation of her gait and voice are not suggestive, but epicene—nothing permanent ever happens. The stuffing of her dress is no more revealing than the giant hanging member on the front of an old clown. It is not arousing, but funny and obscene. Her constant self-possession and good humor mock our obsession with the subject of sexuality, both our cravings for it and our evasions of it.

Susan Sontag

ON
PHOTOGRAPHY

Susan Sontag is a literary critic and avant-grade filmmaker and novelist. Sontag opposes the emphasis of many modernist critics on plumbing the deep layers of meaning of an artwork. Instead, she calls for more emphasis on the "sensuous surface" of the artworks and a kind of criticism that would be "an erotics of art." Her books include Against Interpretation and Other Essays, AIDS and its Metaphors, Styles of Radical Will, *and* On Photography. *In this selection from the last, Sontag describes some of photography's functions and emotional appeals.*

Recently, photography has become almost as widely practiced an amusement as sex and dancing—which means that, like every mass art form, photography is not practiced by most people as an art. It is mainly a social rite, a defense against anxiety, and a tool of power.

Memorializing the achievements of individuals considered as members of families (as well as of other groups) is the earliest popular use of photography. For at least a century, the wedding photograph has been as much a part of the ceremony as the prescribed verbal formulas. Cameras go with family life. According to a sociological study done in France, most households have a camera, but a household with children is twice as likely to have at least one camera as a household in which there are no chil-

dren. Not to take pictures of one's children, particularly when they are small, is a sign of parental indifference, just as not turning up for one's graduation picture is a gesture of adolescent rebellion.

Through photographs, each family constructs a portrait-chronicle of itself—a portable kit of images that bears witness to its connectedness. It hardly matters what activities are photographed so long as photographs get taken and are cherished. Photography becomes a rite of family life just when, in the industrializing countries of Europe and America, the very institution of the family starts undergoing radical surgery. As that claustrophobic unit, the nuclear family, was being carved out of a much larger family aggregate, photography came along to memorialize, to restate symbolically, the

Susan Sontag, *On Photography* (New York: Farrar, Straus & Giroux, 1977) 8–21.

imperiled continuity and vanishing extendedness of family life. Those ghostly traces, photographs, supply the token presence of the dispersed relatives. A family's photograph album is generally about the extended family—and, often, is all that remains of it.

As photographs give people an imaginary possession of a past that is unreal, they also help people to take possession of space in which they are insecure. Thus, photography develops in tandem with one of the most characteristic of modern activities: tourism. For the first time in history, large numbers of people regularly travel out of their habitual environments for short periods of time. It seems positively unnatural to travel for pleasure without taking a camera along. Photographs will offer indisputable evidence that the trip was made, that the program was carried out, that fun was had. Photographs document sequences of consumption carried on outside the view of family, friends, neighbors. But dependence on the camera, as the device that makes real what one is experiencing, doesn't fade when people travel more. Taking photographs fills the same need for the cosmopolitans accumulating photograph-trophies of their boat trip up the Albert Nile or their fourteen days in China as it does for lower-middle-class vacationers taking snapshots of the Eiffel Tower or Niagara Falls.

A way of certifying experience, taking photographs is also a way of refusing it—by limiting experience to a search for the photogenic, by converting experience into an image, a souvenir. Travel becomes a strategy for accumulating photographs. The very activity of taking pictures is soothing, and assuages general feelings of disorientation that are likely to be exacerbated by travel. Most tourists feel compelled to put the camera between themselves and whatever is remarkable that they encounter. Unsure of other responses, they take a picture. This gives shape to experience: stop, take a photograph, and move on. The method especially appeals to people handicapped by a ruthless work ethic—Germans, Japanese, and Americans. Using a camera appeases the anxiety which the work-driven feel about not working when they are on vacation and supposed to be having fun. They have something to do that is like a friendly imitation of work: they can take pictures.

People robbed of their past seem to make the most fervent picture takers, at home and abroad. Everyone who lives in an industrialized society is obliged gradually to give up the past, but in certain countries, such as the United States and Japan, the break with the past has been particularly traumatic. In the 1970s, the fable of the brash American tourist of the 1950s and 1960s, rich with dollars and Babbittry, was replaced by the mystery of the group-minded Japanese tourist, newly released from his island prison by the miracle of overvalued yen, who is generally armed with two cameras, one on each hip.

Photography has become one of the principal devices for experiencing something, for giving an appearance of participation. One full-page ad shows a small group of people standing pressed together, peering out of the photograph, all but one looking stunned, excited, upset. The one who wears a different expression holds a camera to his eye; he seems self-possessed, is almost smiling. While the others are passive, clearly alarmed spectators, having a camera has transformed one person into something active, a voyeur: only he has mastered the situation. What do these people see? We don't know. And it doesn't matter: something worth seeing—and therefore worth photographing. The ad copy, white letters across the dark lower third of the photograph like news coming over a teletype machine, consists of just six words: ". . . Prague . . . Woodstock . . . Vietnam . . . Sapporo . . . Londonderry . . . LEICA." Crushed hopes, youth antics, colonial wars, and winter sports are alike—are equalized by the camera. Taking photographs has set up a chronic voyeuristic relation to the world which levels the meaning of all events.

A photograph is not just the result of an encounter between an event and a photographer; picture-taking is an event in itself, and one with ever more peremptory rights—to interfere with, to invade, or to ignore whatever is going on. Our very sense of situation is now articulated by the camera's interventions. The omnipresence of cameras persuasively suggests that time consists of interesting events, events worth photographing. This, in turn, makes it easy to feel that any event, once underway, and whatever its moral character, should be allowed to complete itself—so that something else can be brought into the world, the photograph. After the event has ended, the picture will still exist, conferring on the event a kind of immortality (and importance) it would never otherwise have enjoyed. While real people are out there killing themselves or other real people, the photographer stays behind his or her camera, creating a tiny element of another world: the image-world that bids to outlast us all.

Photographing is essentially an act of non-intervention. Part of the horror of such memorable coups of contemporary photojournalism as the pictures of a Vietnamese bonze reaching for the gasoline can, of a Bengali guerrilla in the act of bayoneting a trussed-up collaborator, comes from the awareness of how plausible it has become, in situations where the photographer has the choice between a photograph and a life, to choose the photograph. The person who intervenes cannot record; the person who is recording cannot intervene. Dziga Vertov's great film, *Man with a Movie Camera* (1929), gives the ideal image of the photographer as someone in perpetual movement, someone moving through a panorama of disparate events with such agility and speed that any intervention is out of the question. Hitchcock's *Rear Window* (1954) gives the complementary image: the photographer played by James Stewart has an intensified relation to one event, through his camera, precisely because he has a broken leg and is confined to a wheelchair; being temporarily immobilized prevents him from acting on what he sees, and makes it even more important to take pictures. Even if incompatible with intervention in a physical sense, using a camera is still a form of participation. Although the camera is an observation station, the act of photographing is more than passive observing. Like sexual voyeurism, it is a way of at least tacitly, often explicitly, encouraging whatever is going on to keep on happening. To take a picture is to have an interest in things as they are, in the status quo remaining unchanged (at least for as long as it takes to get a "good" picture), to be in complicity with whatever makes a subject interesting, worth photographing—including, when that is the interest, another person's pain or misfortune.

"I always thought of photography as a naughty thing to do—that was one of my favorite things about it," Diane Arbus wrote, "and when I first did it I felt very perverse." Being a professional photographer can be thought of as naughty, to use Arbus's pop word, if the photographer seeks out subjects considered to be disreputable, taboo, marginal. But naughty subjects are harder to find these days. And what exactly is the perverse aspect of picture-taking? If professional photographers often have sexual fantasies when they are behind the camera, perhaps the perversion lies in the fact that these fantasies are both plausible and so inappropriate. In *Blowup* (1966), Antonioni has the fashion photographer hovering convulsively over Verushka's body with his camera clicking. Naughtiness, indeed! In fact, using a camera is not a very good way of getting at someone sexually. Between photographer and subject, there has to be distance. The camera doesn't rape, or even possess, though it may presume, intrude, trespass, distort, exploit, and, at the farthest reach of metaphor, assassinate—all activities that, unlike the sexual push and shove, can be conducted from a distance, and with some detachment.

There is a much stronger sexual fantasy in Michael Powell's extraordinary movie *Peeping Tom* (1960), which is not about a Peeping Tom but about a psychopath who kills women with a weapon concealed in his camera, while photographing them. Not once does he touch his subjects. He doesn't desire their bodies; he wants their presence in the form of filmed images—those showing them experiencing their own death—which he screens at home for his solitary pleasure. The movie assumes connections between impotence and aggression, professionalized looking and cruelty, which point to the central fantasy connected with the camera. The camera as phallus is, at most, a flimsy variant of the inescapable metaphor that everyone unselfconsciously employs. However hazy our awareness of this fantasy, it is named without subtlety whenever we talk about "loading" and "aiming" a camera, about "shooting" a film.

The old-fashioned camera was clumsier and harder to reload than a brown Bess musket. The modern camera is trying to be a ray gun. One ad reads:

> The Yashica Electro-35 GT is the spaceage camera your family will love. Take beautiful pictures day or night. Automatically. Without any nonsense. Just aim, focus and shoot. The GT's computer brain and electronic shutter will do the rest.

Like a car, a camera is sold as a predatory weapon—one that's as automated as possible, ready to spring. Popular taste expects an easy, an invisible technology. Manufacturers reassure their customers that taking pictures demands no skill or expert knowledge, that the machine is all-knowing, and responds to the slightest pressure of the will.

It's as simple as turning the ignition key or pulling the trigger.

Like guns and cars, cameras are fantasy-machines whose use is addictive. However, despite the extravagances of ordinary language and advertising, they are not lethal. In the hyperbole that markets cars like guns, there is at least this much truth: except in wartime, cars kill more people than guns do. The camera/gun does not kill, so the ominous metaphor seems to be all bluff—like a man's fantasy of having a gun, knife, or tool between his legs. Still, there is something predatory in the act of taking a picture. To photograph people is to violate them, by seeing them as they never see themselves, by having knowledge of them they can never have; it turns people into objects that can be symbolically possessed. Just as the camera is a sublimation of the gun, to photograph someone is a sublimated murder—a soft murder, appropriate to a sad, frightened time.

Eventually, people might learn to act out more of their aggressions with cameras and fewer with guns, with the price being an even more image-choked world. One situation where people are switching from bullets to film is the photographic safari that is replacing the gun safari in East Africa. The hunters have Hasselblads instead of Winchesters; instead of looking through a telescopic sight to aim a rifle, they look through a viewfinder to frame a picture. In end-of-the-century London, Samuel Butler complained that "there is a photographer in every bush, going about like a roaring lion seeking whom he may devour." The photographer is now charging real beasts, beleaguered and too rare to kill. Guns have metamorphosed into cameras in this earnest comedy, the ecology safari, because nature has ceased to be what it always had been—what people needed protection from. Now nature—tamed, endangered, mortal—needs to be protected from people. When we are afraid, we shoot. But when we are nostalgic, we take pictures.

It is a nostalgic time right now, and photographs actively promote nostalgia. Photography is an elegiac art, a twilight art. Most subjects photographed are, just by virtue of being photographed, touched with pathos. An ugly or grotesque subject may be moving because it has been dignified by the attention of the photographer. A beautiful subject can be the object of rueful feeling, because it has aged or decayed or no longer exists. All photographs are *memento mori*. To take a photograph is to participate in another person's (or thing's) mortality, vulnerability, mutability. Precisely by slicing out this moment and freezing it, all photographs testify to time's relentless melt.

Cameras began duplicating the world at that moment when the human landscape started to undergo a vertiginous rate of change: while an untold number of forms of biological and social life are being destroyed in a brief span of time, a device is available to record what is disappearing. The moody, intricately textured Paris of Atget and Brassaï is mostly gone. Like the dead relatives and friends preserved in the family album, whose presence in photographs exorcises some of the anxiety and remorse prompted by their disappearance, so the photographs of neighborhoods now torn down, rural places disfigured and made barren, supply our pocket relation to the past.

A photograph is both a pseudo-presence and a token of absence. Like a wood fire in a room, photographs—especially those of people, of distant landscapes and faraway cities, of the vanished past—are incitements to reverie. The sense of the unattainable that can be evoked by photographs feeds directly into the erotic feeling of those for whom desirability is enhanced by distance. The lover's photograph hidden in a married woman's wallet, the poster photograph of a rock star tacked up over an adolescent's bed, the campaign-button image of a politician's face pinned on a voter's coat, the snapshots of a cabdriver's children clipped to the visor—all such talismanic uses of photographs express feeling both sentimental and implicitly magical: they are attempts to contact or lay claim to another reality.

Robert C. Solomon

ARE THE THREE STOOGES FUNNY? SOITAINLY!

Robert C. Solomon is Quincy Lee Centennial Professor of Philosophy and Business at the University of Texas at Austin. He has written on a wide range of topics in philosophy. Among his books are The Passions, A Passion for Justice, About Love, Up the University, *and* The Bully Culture. *In the following essay (written in 1990), Solomon defends the antics of the Three Stooges, claiming that humor, even silly humor, offers a key to peace and tolerance.*

Everything is funny so long as it happens to someone else.

—Will Rogers

"Rire est le propre de l'homme," ["To laugh is properly human"] wrote Rabelais. Of course, he never saw the Three Stooges. Would they have given him second thoughts? Can you imagine raunchy Rabelais watching Curly or Shemp doing the dying chicken? Trying to appreciate bowl-coiffured Moe pulling Larry's rag mop of hair, slapping him down while calling him a moron? Of course, Rabelais's countrymen today think that Jerry Lewis is the funniest thing since the invention of the baguette, so there is reason to suppose that an appreciation of idiocy is well settled into the Gallic gene pool. But these are also the people who elevated *logique* to the status of an art, and the juxtaposition is instructive. Although philosophers have long made much of the supposed fact that human beings are the only creatures who "reason," it seems to be just as plausible (with some of the same exceptions) to insist that we are just as unique in our silliness. We are fundamentally creatures who laugh, and these two familiar human functions, reason and humor, are intimately tied together. The bridge between them, as Mark Twain once suggested, is embarrassment.

The Three Stooges have caused considerable embarrassment in the fifty years of their considerable success and popularity. Their humor is chastized as being childish, violent, vulgar and anti-feminist. (Their first film, by way of evidence, was entitled *Women*

Haters.) Few women find them funny—or are willing to admit it, perhaps because they have never spent the requisite time watching the repeat performances that thereby convert idiotic madness into familiar ritual. Educators pontificate about bad influences. The Soviets once wanted to use the shows "to show how Americans had been brutalized . . . in the name of fun." Few adults in their chosen professions would dare attempt a Stooges gesture at risk of being terminally dismissed, but most men carry the secret knowledge around with them, and, in a wild fit of catharsis, display a tell-tale Stooges gesture when the door closes and the boss is out of view. I only hesitate to suggest that it is one of the most basic bonds between men, and perhaps the fact that it mystifies and sometimes horrifies women is far more elemental than the mere phrase "a sense of humor" could ever suggest.

Impropriety is the soul of wit, according to Somerset Maugham, and few wits since the Romans have ever been more improper. But the comedy of the Three Stooges is not just rudeness personified. The comedian John Candy says of the Stooges that "the magic was their subtlety." Film critic Leonard Maltin insists that "their art was artlessness." The stooges were made for television, and they made their mark on television. Their films were originally made and distributed as "shorts" to precede feature length movies, but the Stooges found and still find their largest audience on the small screen. There is nothing special about television humor except, perhaps, that it is so condensed and concise, and it is shared by so many people, across generations and social classes. It lacks, of course, the audience participation that one might enjoy or suffer in a live theatrical performance. There is a drop in the intensity of humor in the conversion of live stage to television screen (e.g., the televised sessions of *Evening at the Improv*) which cannot be explained by appeal to censorship alone. It

is, I believe, that loss of the immediacy that allows stand-up comics to be intimate which allows the Stooges to be safely sealed, like miniatures in a box. But the Stooges excel on television, black and white and basic. Within their little box, they are the heirs of ancient forms of humor, from the theater of Aristophanes and Plautus to the commedia dell'arte to vaudeville, where they started, with their unique combination of wit, slapstick, insult, skill, tomfoolery and stupidity. But their humor and their message, drawn from those ancient sources, are refreshingly up-to-date, primarily aimed at puncturing the pretensions of the rich and powerful.

"Some things just aren't funny," the critics have always complained. (Some of them catch themselves laughing nevertheless.) But why not? No one ever gets hurt in a Three Stooges comedy, and apart from the Dear Departed who may set up a plot with an oddly worded will, no one ever dies. The Stooges make fools of themselves and each other, and they ridicule this profession and that one by their very presence within it. Doctors, plumbers, tailors, soldiers, used chariot salesmen or Nazis, no one is safe from Stoogery. No one is without pretensions. It is slapstick, not the pun, that is the lowest form of humor, although the Stooges make ample use of both. Slapstick humiliates, simply and directly, and the difference between the Stooges and (most of) their unhappy targets is that they respond to that humiliation directly, noisily, and with a dignity that only nonsense provides. This makes us uncomfortable, but it is also something we recognize and admire. This is not "high" humor, nor could it be. The witty come-back line, the deft put-down, the subtle revenge—these are not for the Stooges. The answer to humiliation is a shriek, a "whoop," a little dance, a slap or belly-punch in return. Basic vengeance, and being above (or below) humiliation. Isn't that what we would all like, with our fragile veneers of respectability?

Enjoying slapstick does not require a college education, much less skill or wisdom or philosophical sophistication. There is very little to understand, and that, perhaps, is why so many people find it "beneath" them. Indeed, nothing undermines a philosophical argument so quickly as a belly-laugh, and that, perhaps, is why intellectual life has for so long been suspicious of laughter. But it is not the belly-laugh but rather the attempt to elevate humor to some level of sophistication that is and ought to be suspicious. Shakepeare's puns seem sophisticated to us now, but that is perhaps because only sophisticated people now listen to Shakespeare and some of the language in which he punned now sounds almost foreign to us. His own view was that the pun is as low as one can go, and Shakespeare's humor was often as bawdy as one can imagine, far beyond what is routinely censored from adult television today. So, too, we should remind ourselves, classic Italian opera and much of Mozart are typically riotous, and despite their status in "high culture" today, most of those operas were originally street fare and popular extravaganzas, the low art of their day. One did not and did not need to take them seriously.

It is not just well-fortified cultural snobbery that militates against slapstick humor and the Stooges in particular. There is also the accusation of violence. Never mind that no one ever gets hurt. Never mind that the average television cop-show has a blood and body count far exceeding the modest mayhem of a Stooges film. One argument is that kids will imitate what they see, but do the critics think that kids are idiots? In the context of what little boys try to do to one another—luckily they lack the strength and coordination, the typical Stooge routine, even the infamous eye-poke and familiar slapping are harmless. One of the charms of the Stooges is that their artlessness makes their pretending and their feigning so obvious, so that what kids imitate is not the violence but the imitation of violence, much better than what they learn from *Dirty Harry*. Indeed, in these days when six- to ten-year-olds carry guns to elementary school (and occasionally use them) there is much to be said for the bloodless retaliations of the Stooges. There will still be insults and offenses, but how can we learn that the best and the most effective response is humor? Humor is not "giving in" and it is not weakness. It is a special kind of strength.

Humor is a species of vicarious emotion. Caesar gets stabbed, not once but twenty times, even by his best friend. The audience watches with vicarious horror. They have seen it many times before, this betrayal and multiple stabbing of Caesar. In another theater Othello strangles his struggling but innocent wife. This is called tragedy. (No one laughs.) Nor does anyone comment that the actor playing Caesar isn't really bleeding, or that Desdemona will go out for a cappuccino after the performance. The "willing suspension of disbelief," as Coleridge famously coined it, is alive and well here. No one is "really" hurt so we can allow our emotions their free "make believe" rein. Why, then, is the petty violence of the Three Stooges, equally feigned, in question as comedy? But it is not the word "violence" that best captures the Stooges mutual abuse of their various foils and of each other. It rather falls into the category of ritual humiliation. The Stooges' humor is the humor of humiliation, taking it as well as dishing it out, but one misses the point if they see humiliation as the end in itself. It is humiliation to end all humiliation, for once one accepts oneself as a Stooge, the slings and arrows of outrageous fortune are nothing but fodder for another joke or gesture.

Laughter may indeed be the "best medicine" as one of our more prestigious periodicals proclaims, but laughter at what? We make a rather harsh distinction (at least in polite discourse) between "laughing **at**" and "laughing **with**," and Rule Number One of our ethic of humor is not to laugh at the misfortunes of others. And yet, most of what we find funny in the Stooges is just that, a foolish and frustrated Curly carrying a block of ice up fifteen flights on a hot summer day, Moe wearing a mask of paint or flour, an innocent bystander deprived of his wig, a customer who leaves the shop with a gigantic hole in his pants, a room full of sophisticated diners hit by a battery of pies and, even worse, allowing themselves to join in as well. And then, of course, there is the usual—Moe's ritualized double eye-poke, Curly's equally practiced hand block and Moe's counter-feint. Then Curly's cry and hyperkinetic dance of pain and indignation. (One should not underestimate the importance of **sound** in undermining the seriousness of the Stooges' violence—the kettledrum [stomach punch], the violin pluck [eye poke] and the rachet [ear twist].) "That's not funny," decry the righteous, but they're wrong.

Henri Bergson hypothesized that humor blocks normal emotion, but I think that the opposite is true. It is the sympathetic laughter we enjoy at the Stooges' alleged expense that makes us aware of our own best and least pretentious emotions. Pride, envy and anger all disappear. That sense of status that defines so much of our self-images dissolves. Accordingly, Plato urged censorship of humor as well as poetry to preserve the good judgment and virtue of the guardians of the Republic. I would argue to the contrary that laughter opens up the emotions and it is good humor that makes good judgment possible.

The philosophy of humor is a subject which itself tends to be all too humorless. But that is perhaps because it does not appreciate the extent to which it is itself a ludicrous topic, and my basic belief in these matters is that the basic meaning of humor and "a sense of humor" is ultimately laughter **at oneself**. But for this to be meaningful the laughter will have to be "low humor"

and folly rather than wit and learned cleverness that are the hallmark of humor, quite the contrary of those examples preferred by the most contemporary theorists. Philosophers, in particular, appreciate cleverness, preferably based on some profound linguistic or ontological insight. Freud, by contrast, preferred elephant and fart jokes, but then he was looking for a diagnosis rather than a good laugh. (Did Freud chuckle as he was writing his *Wit and Its Relation to the Unconscious*? Or did he rather insist on maintaining that famous stone face of disapproval, even in the solitude of his study?) The Stooges, by contrast again, were always laughing at themselves, and they invited us to do so too with the understanding that we were laughing at ourselves too. Their shorts are often cited as paradigms of bad taste but have nevertheless dominated television from its earliest days and continue to influence and be imitated by the most talented comedians today. That is why. They are not particularly clever or chauvinist or brutal but they provide a mirror for our own silliness—if only in our laughing at them.

But why are the Three Stooges funny? They would seem to provide an obvious case of **laughing at**. Watching the Three Stooges, what we seem to experience is what the Germans (wonderfully humorous people) describe as *"schadenfreude"*—the enjoyment of other people's pain and suffering, deserved or undeserved. Are we really so cruel? We might note here with some wonder that it is so easy to be funny when there is something to laugh at but hard to be funny when praising or admiring. Critic John Simon is hopeless when (rarely) he likes something. His reviews are memorable when they are offensive. Why? It does not seem to matter whether or not they are deserved. If they are deserved, of course, we can have a clear conscience in laughing, but we find ourselves laughing at insults even when they are not fair. The Stooges, on this easy account, set themselves up to be ridiculed. Their humor is a gift, allowing us to feel wittily superior.

Since ancient times, according to John Morreall in his book on laughter, one can discern three dominant conceptions of humor. First, there is the **Superiority** theory, assumed by Plato and Aristotle, in which laughter expresses one's feeling of sophistication, wisdom and superiority over the poor slob who would get himself entrapped in such a situation. Obviously such humor would be appealing in aristocratic societies or any society that has a more or less clearly delineated inferior class. According to Albert Rapp, in his *Origins of Wit and Humor*, the original laugh was probably roar of triumph of the victor in a fight. Roger Scruton, who is not unsympathetic to Aristocratic thinking, has hypothesized that humor involves de-valuation. The Three Stooges would seem to fit perfectly into this conception of humor, for what losers have ever made themselves more lowly, more ridiculous, more prone to ridicule? In a world in which everyone has the right not to be offended and where everything is becoming offensive, humor by way of superiority is too often inappropriate, "politically incorrect." Laughing at the Stooges, however, is OK. The problem, however, is that we do not just laugh at the Stooges, and much of their humor depends on the humiliation of others. Superiority theory doesn't quite work. One doesn't walk away from the Stooges feeling superior, rather released and relieved.

The second conception might be called the **Relief** theory. It was most famously advocated by Freud, and it renders laughter akin to sport in safely expressing violence and, of course, forbidden sexual impulses. If you can't **do it**, in other words, at least you can laugh about it. But such laughter, so understood, is not just laughing at; it is also a vicarious form of activity, "the world as play." We laugh because the Stooges do what we would like to do, act as we would like to

act, not sexually to be sure but as fools, clowns beyond humiliation, humiliating those who we too would love to humiliate— pompous doctors, overbearing matrons, "tough" bosses, crooked politicians. Humor thus becomes a devious expression of *resentment*, and the release and relief we feel is nothing the less than the catharsis of one of our most poisonous emotions. There is something suspicious, however, about a theory that makes laughter out to be a weakness, a leak in one's psyche, so to speak, and directs itself mainly to one's hostile or immoral thoughts of others. One cannot disprove such a theory, of course, but we should be very cautious about accepting it. Three Stooges humor does not feel particularly vicious, and those who complain that it seems so are easily dismissed as those who have not allowed themselves to "get into it."

Finally, there is the **Incongruity** theory, defended by Kant and Schopenhauer among others and described by the Danish existentialist Kierkegaard as "comedy as painless contradiction." What makes this theory attractive is that it dispenses with any notion of "laughing at" and looks to the language and the humorous situation as such for a clue to the humor. Humor is our reaction to things that don't fit together. We laugh at stupidity not because we feel superior to it but because the juxtaposition of actions and events surprise us. A Woody Allen example: his father gave him a bullet which he carries around in his breast pocket. A fanatical evangelist flings a Bible at him on the street, and "if it weren't for that bullet, the Bible would have gone right through my heart." This is, of course, the favorite conception of humor in academia, where facility with language is a special virtue and puns, wordplay and cleverness is readily appreciated. Similarly, John Morreall suggests that humor involves a "pleasant psychological shift," such as when one is caught off guard. There are, to be sure, any number of unexpected and unusual psychological shifts required to follow the typical Stooges plot, and incongruity is central to much of their humor. But the incongruity theory does not explain why the Stooges get better and better with repetitive viewing, and why imitation is part and parcel of Stooges spectatorship. It also sells the Stooges short, prettifies their humor and ignores or denies its bite. The humor of the Stooges is the humor of mutual humiliation, not mere incongruity or surprise, but neither is it merely relief of our own frustrations or the sense of superiority that comes from laughing at someone else.

No one, to my knowledge, has advocated what we might call the **inferiority** theory of humor, laughter as the great leveler, beyond contempt or indignation, antithetical to pretention and pomp. Sitting on the sofa watching *Malice in the Palace* for the twenty-seventh time, we allow ourselves to fall into a world of miniature mayhem that allows us to feel as foolish as they are. We enjoy these petty plots of ambition, ire and revenge, and not because we feel superior to them or use them for our own catharsis much less because, on the twenty-seventh viewing, we are in any way surprised. Why should we not? Do we still have to pretend with the critics that our own natures are not similarly petty, vengeful, and, viewed from the outside, uproariously slapstick. Larry, Moe, Shemp and Curly capture the silly side of human nature just as surely as Macbeth and Hamlet represent the tragic side, but we can easily understand why the critics would prefer to ennoble themselves with the latter while rejecting the former. Satire and parody may be much more effective for developing individual thought than tragedy and self-righteousness, and in order to avoid the supposed bad taste of enjoying the Three Stooges we encounter the much greater danger of taking ourselves too seriously.

Voltaire once commented that, to combat human misery, we require hope and sleep. It was the moralist Immanuel Kant, of all people, who corrected Voltaire by suggesting that in addition to hope and sleep as palatives for human misery we should also count laughter. But Kant, I presume, would not have found Moe's eye-poke or Curly's clucking chicken chuckle laughable, and Kant's idea of a good joke would no doubt fall flat on television today. Kant, like most intellectuals, thought that a joke should be profound. For the Stooges and their fans, repetitive, mindless silliness was the way to humor. Philosophers, as men of reason, have always found laughter and humor suspicious. (But then, feminists are not much known for their sense of humor either.) As far back as the *Philebus*, Plato warned against the dangers of humor as he had chastized the falsification of poetry in the *Republic*, and he urged censorship to protect the guardians of the republic from the distortions and distractions of laughter. Aristotle, despite his lost treatise on comedy which provides the theme of Umberto Eco's *The Name of the Rose*, shared many of Plato's reservations about comedy. And despite the proliferation of comedy among the "low arts" throughout the ages, comedy as such was never held in high regard. Humor and the commedia dell'arte were strictly the province of the masses, the *hoi polloi*. The most famous "comedy" of the Middle Ages, appropriately, was a thoroughly somber poetic journey through Heaven and Hell, neither place known for its humor.

Among many faults recently raised against the "Western tradition" since Plato—its sexism, racism, Eurocentrism, scientism, its technophilia and obsession with control, its hyper-rationality, myopic universality, asexuality and denial of the body, its ecological mean-spiritedness and wastefulness—surely must be included its lack of humor, its utterly solemn seriousness. Recent defenses of that tradition, e.g., in the fighting words of Alan Bloom, only make that fault even more glaring, and third world and

John Dewey

AESTHETIC QUALITIES

John Dewey (1859–1952), one of the leading philosophers among the American pragmatists, thought that the primary task of philosophy is to assist us in resolving real, practical problems. Aesthetics, too, should focus on the practical function of art and aesthetic experiences in our lives. According to Dewey, art helps us to understand and enhance basic processes of our lives, which consist of our various efforts to interact with and improve our environments.

HAVING AN EXPERIENCE

Experience occurs continuously, because the interaction of live creature and environing conditions is involved in the very process of living. Under conditions of resistance and conflict, aspects and elements of the self and the world that are implicated in this interaction qualify experience with emotions and ideas so that conscious intent emerges. Oftentimes, however, the experience had is inchoate. Things are experienced but in such a way that they are composed into *an* experience. There is distraction and dispersion; what we observe and what we think, what we desire and what we get, are at odds with each other. We put our hands to the plow and turn back; we start and then we stop, not because the experience has reached the end for the sake of which it was initiated but because of extraneous interruptions or of inner lethargy.

In contrast with such experience, we have *an* experience when the material experienced runs its course to fulfillment. Then and then only is it integrated within and demarcated in the general stream of experience from other experiences. A piece of work is finished in a way that is satisfactory; a problem receives its solution; a game is played through; a situation, whether that of eating a meal, playing a game of chess, carrying on a conversation, writing a book, or taking part in a political campaign, is so rounded out that its close is a consummation and not a cessation. Such an experience is a whole and carries with it its own individualizing quality and self-sufficiency. It is *an* experience.

Philosophers, even empirical philosophers, have spoken for the most part of

John Dewey, *Art as Experience* (New York: Capricorn, 1958) 35–43.

experience at large. Idiomatic speech, however, refers to experiences each of which is singular, having its own beginning and end. For life is no uniform uninterrupted march or flow. It is a thing of histories, each with its own plot, its own inception and movement toward its close, each having its own particular rhythmic movement; each with its own unrepeated quality pervading it throughout. A flight of stairs, mechanical as it is, proceeds by individualized steps, not by undifferentiated progression, and an inclined plane is at least marked off from other things by abrupt discreteness.

Experience in this vital sense is defined by those situations and episodes that we spontaneously refer to as being "real experiences"; those things of which we say in recalling them, "that *was* an experience." It may have been something of tremendous importance—a quarrel with one who was once an intimate, a catastrophe finally averted by a hair's breadth. Or it may have been something that in comparison was slight—and which perhaps because of its very slightness illustrates all the better what it is to be an experience. There is that meal in a Paris restaurant of which one say "that *was* an experience." It stands out as an enduring memorial of what food may be. Then there is that storm one went through in crossing the Atlantic—the storm that seemed in its fury, as it was experienced, to sum up in itself all that a storm can be, complete in itself, standing out because marked out from what went before and what came after.

In such experiences, every successive part flows freely, without seam and without unfilled blanks, into what ensues. At the same time there is no sacrifice of the self-identity of the parts. A river, as distinct from a pond, flows. But its flow gives a definiteness and interest to its successive portions greater than exist in the homogenous portions of a pond. In an experience, flow is from something to something. As one part

leads into another and as one part carries on what went before, each gains distinctness in itself. The enduring whole is diversified by successive phases that are emphases of its varied colors.

Because of continuous merging, there are no holes, mechanical junctions, and dead centers when we have *an* experience. There are pauses, places of rest, but they punctuate and define the quality of movement. They sum up what has been undergone and prevent its dissipation and idle evaporation. Continued acceleration is breathless and prevents parts from gaining distinction. In a work of art, different acts, episodes, occurrences melt and fuse into unity, and yet do not disappear and lose their own character as they do so—just as in a genial conversation there is a continuous interchange and blending, and yet each speaker not only retains his own character but manifests it more clearly than is his wont.

An experience has a unity that gives it its name, *that* meal, that storm, that rupture of friendship. The existence of this unity is constituted by a single *quality* that pervades the entire experience in spite of the variation of its constituent parts. This unity is neither emotional, practical, nor intellectual, for these terms name distinctions that reflection can make within it. In discourse *about* an experience, we must make use of these adjectives of interpretation. In going over an experience in mind *after* its occurrence, we may find that one property rather than another was sufficiently dominant so that it characterizes the experience as a whole. There are absorbing inquiries and speculations which a scientific man and philosopher will recall as "experiences" in the emphatic sense. In final import they are intellectual. But in their actual occurrence they were emotional as well; they were purposive and volitional. Yet the experience was not a sum of these different characters; they were lost in it as distinctive traits. No thinker can ply his occupation save as he is lured and rewarded by total integral experiences that are intrinsically worth while. Without them he would never know what it is really to think and would be completely at a loss in distinguishing real thought from the spurious article. Thinking goes on in trains of ideas, but the ideas form a train only because they are much more than what an analytic psychology calls ideas. They are phases, emotionally and practically distinguished, of a developing underlying quality; they are its moving variations, not separate and independent like Locke's and Hume's so-called ideas and impressions, but are subtle shadings of a pervading and developing hue.

We say of an experience of thinking that we reach or draw a conclusion. Theoretical formulation of the process is often made in such terms as to conceal effectually the similarity of "conclusion" to the consummating phase of every developing integral experience. These formulations apparently take their cue from the separate propositions that are premises and the proposition that is the conclusion as they appear on the printed page. The impression is derived that there are first two independent and ready-made entities that are then manipulated so as to give rise to a third. In fact, in an experience of thinking, premises emerge only as a conclusion becomes manifest. The experience, like that of watching a storm reach its height and gradually subside, is one of continuous movement of subject-matters. Like the ocean in the storm, there are a series of waves; suggestions reaching out and being broken in a clash, or being carried onwards by a coöperative wave. If a conclusion is reached, it is that of a movement of anticipation and cumulation, one that finally comes to completion. A "conclusion" is no separate and independent thing; it is the consummation of a movement.

Hence *an* experience of thinking has its own esthetic quality. It differs from those experiences that are acknowledged to be esthetic, but only in its materials. The mater-

ial of the fine arts consists of qualities; that of experience having intellectual conclusion are signs or symbols having no intrinsic quality of their own, but standing for things that may in another experience be qualitatively experienced. The difference is enormous. It is one reason why the strictly intellectual art will never be popular as music is popular. Nevertheless, the experience itself has a satisfying emotional quality because it possesses internal integration and fulfillment reached through ordered and organized movement. This artistic structure may be immediately felt. In so far, it is esthetic. What is even more important is that not only is this quality a significant motive in undertaking intellectual inquiry and in keeping it honest, but that no intellectual activity is an integral event (is *an* experience), unless it is rounded out with this quality. Without it, thinking is inconclusive. In short, esthetic cannot be sharply marked off from intellectual experience since the latter must bear an esthetic stamp to be itself complete.

The same statement holds good of a course of action that is dominantly practical, that is, one that consists of overt doings. It is possible to be efficient in action and yet not have a conscious experience. The activity is too automatic to permit of a sense of what it is about and where it is going. It comes to an end but not to a close or consummation in consciousness. Obstacles are overcome by shrewd skill, but they do not feed experience. There are also those who are wavering in action, uncertain, and inconclusive like the shades in classic literature. Between the poles of aimlessness and mechanical efficiency, there lie those courses of action in which through successive deeds there runs a sense of growing meaning conserved and accumulating toward an end that is felt as accomplishment of a process. Successful politicians and generals who turn statesmen like Caesar and Napoleon have something of the showman about them. This of itself is not art, but it is, I think, a sign that interest is not exclusively, perhaps not mainly, held by the result taken by itself (as it is in the case of mere efficiency), but by it as the outcome of a process. There is interest in completing an experience. The experience may be one that is harmful to the world and its consummation undesirable. But it has esthetic quality.

The Greek identification of good conduct with having proportion, grace, and harmony, the *kalon-agathon*, is a more obvious example of distinctive esthetic quality in moral action. One great defect in what passes as morality is its anesthetic quality. Instead of exemplifying wholehearted action, it takes the form of grudging piecemeal concessions to the demands of duty. But illustrations may only obscure the fact that any practical activity will, provided that it is integrated and moves by its own urge to fulfillment, have esthetic quality.

A generalized illustration may be had if we imagine a stone, which is rolling down hill, to have an experience. The activity is surely sufficiently "practical." The stone starts from somewhere, and moves, as consistently as conditions permit, toward a place and state where it will be at rest— toward an end. Let us add, by imagination, to these external facts, the ideas that it looks forward with desire to the final outcome; that it is interested in the things it meets on its way, conditions that accelerate and retard its movement with respect to their bearing on the end; that it acts and feels toward them according to the hindering or helping function it attributes to them; and that the final coming to rest is related to all that went before as the culmination of a continuous movement. Then the stone would have an experience, and one with esthetic quality.

If we turn from this imaginary case to our own experience, we shall find much of it is nearer to what happens to the actual stone than it is to anything that fulfills the conditions fancy just laid down. For in much of our experience we are not concerned with the connection of one incident with what went before and what comes after. There is no interest that controls attentive rejection or selection of what shall be organized into the developing experience. Things happen, but they are neither definitely included nor decisively excluded; we drift. We yield according to external pressure, or evade and compromise. There are beginnings and cessations, but no genuine initiations and concludings. One thing replaces another, but does not absorb it and carry it on. There is experience, but so slack and discursive that it is not *an* experience. Needless to say, such experiences are anesthetic.

Thus the non-esthetic lies within two limits. At one pole is the loose succession that does not begin at any particular place and that ends—in the sense of ceasing—at no particular place. At the other pole is arrest, constriction, proceeding from parts having only a mechanical connection with one another. There exists so much of one and the other of these two kinds of experience that unconsciously they come to be taken as norms of all experience. Then, when the esthetic appears, it so sharply contrasts with the picture that has been formed of experience, that it is impossible to combine its special qualities with the features of the picture and the esthetic is given an outside place and status. The account that has been given of experience dominantly intellectual and practical is intended to show that there is no such contrast involved in having an experience; that, on the contrary, no experience of whatever sort is a unity unless it has esthetic quality.

The enemies of the esthetic are neither the practical nor the intellectual. They are the humdrum; slackness of loose ends; submission to convention in practice and intellectual procedure. Rigid abstinence, coerced submission, tightness on one side and dissipation, incoherence and aimless indulgence on the other, are deviations in opposite directions from the unity of an experience. Some such considerations perhaps induced Aristotle to invoke the "mean proportional" as the proper designation of what is distinctive of both virtue and the esthetic. He was formally correct. "Mean" and "proportion" are, however, not self-explanatory, nor to be taken over in a prior mathematical sense, but are properties belonging to an experience that has a developing movement toward its own consummation.

I have emphasized the fact that every integral experience moves toward a close, an ending, since it ceases only when the energies active in it have done their proper work. This closure of a circuit of energy is the opposite of arrest, of *stasis*. Maturation and fixation are polar opposites. Struggle and conflict may be themselves enjoyed, although they are painful, when they are experienced as means of developing an experience; members in that they carry it forward, not just because they are there. There is, as will appear later, an element of undergoing, of suffering in its large sense, in every experience. Otherwise there would be no taking in of what preceded. For "taking in" in any vital experience is something more than placing something on the top of consciousness over what was previously known. It involves reconstruction which may be painful. Whether the necessary undergoing phase is by itself pleasurable or painful is a matter of particular conditions. It is indifferent to the total esthetic quality, save that there are few intense esthetic experiences that are wholly gleeful. They are certainly not to be characterized as amusing, and as they bear down upon us they involve a suffering that is none the less consistent with, indeed a part of, the complete perception that is enjoyed.

I have spoken of the esthetic quality that rounds out an experience into completeness and unity as emotional. The reference may cause difficulty. We are given to thinking of emotions as things as simple and compact as are the words by which we name them. Joy, sorrow, hope, fear, anger, curiosity, are treated as if each in itself were a sort of entity that enters full-made upon the scene, an entity that may last a long time or a short time, but whose duration, whose growth and career, is irrelevant to its nature. In fact emotions are qualities, when they are significant, of a complex experience that moves and changes. I say, when they are *significant*, for otherwise they are but the outbreaks and eruptions of a disturbed infant. All emotions are qualifications of a drama and they change as the drama develops. Persons are sometimes said to fall in love at first sight. But what they fall into is not a thing of that instant. What would love be were it compressed into a moment in which there is no room for cherishing and for solicitude? The intimate nature of emotion is manifested in the experience of one watching a play on the stage or reading a novel. It attends the development of a plot; and a plot requires a stage, a space, wherein to develop and time in which to unfold. Experience is emotional but there are no separate things called emotions in it.

By the same token, emotions are attached to events and objects in their movement. They are not, save in pathological instances, private. And even an "objectless" emotion demands something beyond itself to which to attach itself, and thus it soon generates a delusion in lack of something real. Emotion belongs of a certainty to the self. But it belongs to the self that is concerned in the movement of events toward an issue that is desired or disliked. We jump instantaneously when we are scared, as we blush on the instant when we are ashamed. But fright and shamed modesty are not in this case emotional states. Of themselves they are but automatic reflexes. In order to become emotional they must become parts of an inclusive and enduring situation that involves concern for objects and their issues. The jump of fright becomes emotional fear when there is found or thought to exist a threatening object that must be dealt with or escaped from. The blush becomes the emotion of shame when a person connects, in thought, an action he has performed with an unfavorable reaction to himself of some other person.

Physical things from far ends of the earth are physically transported and physically caused to act and react upon one another in the construction of a new object. The miracle of mind is that something similar takes place in experience without physical transport and assembling. Emotion is the moving and cementing force. It selects what is congruous and dyes what is selected with its color, thereby giving qualitative unity to materials externally disparate and dissimilar. It thus provides unity in and through the varied parts of an experience. When the unity is of the sort already described, the experience has esthetic character even though it is not, dominantly, an esthetic experience.

Two men meet; one is the applicant for a position, while the other has the disposition of the matter in his hands. The interview may be mechanical, consisting of set questions, the replies to which perfunctorily settle the matter. There is no experience in which the two men meet, nothing that is not a repetition, by way of acceptance or dismissal, of something which has happened a score of times. The situation is disposed of as if it were an exercise in bookkeeping. But an interplay may take place in which a new experience develops. Where should we look

for an account of such an experience? Not to ledger-entries nor yet to a treatise on economics or sociology or personnel-psychology, but to drama or fiction. Its nature and import can be expressed only by art, because there is a unity of experience that can be expressed only as an experience. The *experience* is of material fraught with suspense and moving toward its own consummation through a connected series of varied incidents. The primary emotions on the part of the applicant may be at the beginning hope or despair, and elation or disappointment at the close. These emotions qualify the experience as a unity. But as the interview proceeds, secondary emotions are evolved as variations of the primary underlying one. It is even possible for each attitude and gesture, each sentence, almost every word, to produce more than a fluctuation in the intensity of the basic emotion; to produce, that is, a change of shade and tint in its quality. The employer sees by means of his own emotional reactions the character of the one applying. He projects him imaginatively into the work to be done and judges his fitness by the way in which the elements of the scene assemble and either clash or fit together. The presence and behavior of the applicant either harmonize with his own attitudes and desires or they conflict and jar. Such factors as these, inherently esthetic in quality, are the forces that carry the varied elements of the interview to a decisive issue. They enter into the settlement of every situation, whatever its dominant nature, in which there are uncertainty and suspense.

Sei Shōnagon

THE PILLOW BOOK

Sei Shōnagon was a lady of the Heian imperial court in tenth-century Japan, a court that was noteworthy for its aesthetic sensibility. The Pillow Book, *one of the classics of Japanese literature, is a diary that records details from Shōnagon's daily life, especially moments of aesthetic delight.*

1. IN SPRING IT IS THE DAWN

In spring it is the dawn that is most beautiful. As the light creeps over the hills, their outlines are dyed a faint red and wisps of purplish cloud trail over them.

In summer the nights. Not only when the moon shines, but on dark nights too, as the fireflies flit to and fro, and even when it rains, how beautiful it is!

In autumn the evenings, when the glittering sun sinks close to the edge of the hills and the crows fly back to their nests in threes and fours and twos; more charming still is a file of wild geese, like specks in the distant sky. When the sun has set, one's heart is moved by the sound of the wind and hum of the insects.

In winter the early mornings. It is beautiful indeed when snow has fallen during the night, but splendid too when the ground is white with frost; or even when there is no snow or frost, but it is simply very cold and the attendants hurry from room to room stirring up the fires and bringing charcoal, how well this fits the season's mood! But as noon approaches and the cold wears off, no one bothers to keep the braziers alight, and soon nothing remains but piles of white ashes.

3. ON THE THIRD DAY OF THE THIRD MONTH

On the third day of the Third Month I like to see the sun shining bright and calm in the spring sky. Now is the time when the peach trees come into bloom, and what a sight it is! The willows too are most charming at this season, with the buds still enclosed like silkworms in their cocoons. After the leaves

Sei Shōnagon, *The Pillow Book of Sei Shōnagon*, trans. Ivan Morris (New York: Viking Penguin, 1967) 21, 24, 51–52, 138, 145, 168, 170, 173, 207.

have spread out, I find them unattractive; in fact all trees lose their charm once the blossoms have begun to scatter.

It is a great pleasure to break off a long, beautifully flowering branch from a cherry tree and to arrange it in a large vase. What a delightful task to perform when a visitor is seated nearby conversing! It may be an ordinary guest, or possibly one of Their Highnesses, the Empress's elder brothers; but in any case the visitor will wear a cherry-coloured Court cloak, from the bottom of which his under-robe emerges. I am even happier if a butterfly or a small bird flutters prettily near the flowers and I can see its face.

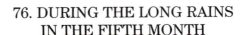

16. THINGS THAT MAKE ONE'S HEART BEAT FASTER

Sparrows feeding their young. To pass a place where babies are playing. To sleep in a room where some fine incense has been burnt. To notice that one's elegant Chinese mirror has become a little cloudy. To see a gentleman stop his carriage before one's gate and instruct his attendants to announce his arrival. To wash one's hair, make one's toilet, and put on scented robes; even if not a soul sees one, these preparations still produce an inner pleasure.

It is night and one is expecting a visitor. Suddenly one is startled by the sound of rain-drops, which the wind blows against the shutters.

17. THINGS THAT AROUSE A FOND MEMORY OF THE PAST

Dried hollyhock. The objects used during the Display of Dolls. To find a piece of deep violet or grape-colored material that has been pressed between the pages of a notebook.

It is a rainy day and one is feeling bored. To pass the time, one starts looking through some old papers. And then one comes across the letters of a man one used to love.

Last year's paper fan. A night with a clear moon.

18. A PALM-LEAF CARRIAGE SHOULD MOVE SLOWLY

A Palm-leaf carriage should move slowly, or else it loses its dignity. A wickerwork carriage, on the other hand, should go fast. Hardly has one seen it pass the gate when it is out of sight, and all that remains is the attendants who run after it. At such moments I enjoy wondering who the passengers may be. But, if a wickerwork carriage moves slowly, one has plenty of time to observe it, and that becomes very dull.

76. DURING THE LONG RAINS IN THE FIFTH MONTH

During the long rains in the Fifth Month, there is something very moving about a place with a pond. Between the dense irises, water-oats, and other plants one can see the green of the water; and the entire garden seems to be the same green color. One stays there all day long, gazing in contemplation at the clouded sky—oh, how moving it is!

I am always moved and delighted by places that have ponds—not only in the winter (when I love waking up to find that the water has frozen over) but at every time of the year. The ponds I like best are not those in which everything is carefully laid out; I much prefer one that has been left to itself so that it is wild and covered with weeds. At night in the green spaces of water one can see nothing but the pale glow of the moonlight. At any time and in any place I find moonlight very moving.

80. THINGS THAT HAVE LOST THEIR POWER

A large boat which is high and dry in a creek at ebb-tide.

A woman who has taken off her false locks to comb the short hair that remains.

A large tree that has been blown down in a gale and lies on its side with its roots in the air.

The retreating figure of a *sumō* wrestler who has been defeated in a match.

A man of no importance reprimanding an attendant.

An old man who removes his hat, uncovering his scanty top-knot.

A woman, who is angry with her husband about some trifling matter, leaves home and goes somewhere to hide. She is certain that he will rush about looking for her; but he does nothing of the kind and shows the most infuriating indifference. Since she cannot stay away for ever, she swallows her pride and returns.

97. THINGS THAT GIVE A CLEAN FEELING

An earthen cup. A new metal bowl.

A rush mat.

The play of the light on water as one pours it into a vessel.

A new wooden chest.

101. SQUALID THINGS

The back of a piece of embroidery.

The inside of a cat's ear.

A swarm of mice, who still have no fur, when they come wriggling out of their nest.

The seams of a fur robe that has not yet been lined.

Darkness in a place that does not give the impression of being very clean.

A rather unattractive woman who looks after a large brood of children.

A woman who falls ill and remains unwell for a long time. In the mind of her love, who is not particularly devoted to her, she must appear rather squalid.

104. THINGS THAT ONE IS IN A HURRY TO SEE OR TO HEAR

Rolled dyeing, uneven shading, and all other forms of dappled dyeing.

When a woman has just had a child, one is in a hurry to find out whether it is a boy or a girl. If she is a lady of quality, one is obviously most curious; but, even if she is a servant or someone else of humble station, one still wants to know.

Early in the morning on the first day of the period of official appointments one is eager to hear whether a certain acquaintance will receive his governorship.

A letter from the man one loves.

134. LETTERS ARE COMMONPLACE

Letters are commonplace enough, yet what splendid things they are! When someone is in a distant province and one is worried about him, and then a letter suddenly arrives, one feels as though one were seeing him face to face. Again, it is a great comfort to have expressed one's feelings in a letter even though one knows it cannot yet have arrived. If letters did not exist, what dark depressions would come over one! When one has been worrying about something and wants to tell a certain person about it, what a relief it is to put it all down in a letter! Still greater is one's joy when a reply arrives. At that moment a letter really seems like an elixir of life.

Garret Sokoloff

BY PAUSING
BEFORE
A <u>KICHO</u>

Garret Sokoloff teaches Japanese in the New York City public schools. In the following essay (written in 1983), Sokoloff analyzes Sei Shōnagon's conception of aesthetic delight. He contends that experiences such as those that Shōnagon describes create a context in which intimate communication can occur.

The Wall that surrounded the Jews of Warsaw preventing escape, changing shape, drawing in, was a Wall that worked. We know that the Wall was made of bricks and houses sealed up, which were thus made into larger bricks. The Wall of bricks, mortar, and sealed up buildings was a carefully used tool that enabled the Germans to murder the people within according to plans. However, the Wall could not have worked as well if there had not already been another Wall pushed against the Jews of Warsaw. One could ask, "What is *that* Wall? What is *that* Wall made of?" Or one could remember that Basho corrected Kikaku.

The story of Basho correcting his student is found in *The Japanese Haiku* of Kenneth Yasuda:

One autumn day when Basho and one of his ten disciples, Kikaku, were going through a rice field, Kikaku composed a haiku on a red dragonfly that caught his fancy. And he showed the following haiku to Basho:

Take a pair of wings
From a dragonfly, you would
Make a pepper pod.

"No," said Basho, "that is not a haiku. You kill the dragonfly. If you want to compose a haiku and give life to it you must say:

Add a pair of wings
To a pepper pod, you would
Make a dragonfly.[1]

The story suggests that focusing too much on the working of a Wall is like writing a haiku about tearing wings off a dragonfly. Such a poem may tell us something about killing, but it does not tell us anything about the dragonfly nor, as haiku can do, let us experience an aspect of dragonfly-ness. The Ghetto Wall was a tearing-off of wings. "But, what was the Dragonfly?"—this is one question that we should ask.

Consider Ivan Morris's translation of *The Pillow Book of Sei Shōnagon*. Whether one has been thinking about what a wall is or not, one will probably pause, in the midst of reading this bewildering assortment of lists, anecdotes, and complaints, to ponder Morris's "note 22" to the text.

> 22. *Kicho* (curtain of state or curtainframe): a piece of furniture that played a most important part in Heian domestic architecture. Analogous to the Indian pardah, it was a portable frame, about six feet high and of variable width, which supported opaque hangings and was mainly aimed at protecting the women of the house from being seen by men and strangers. When reading *The Pillow Book*, we should remember that Shōnagon and her companions spent a good part of their time ensconced behind *kicho*.[2]

Shōnagon gives some additional information about the *kicho* in what is Section 48 of Morris's translation.

> Bright green bamboo blinds are a delight, especially when beneath them one can make out the many layers of a woman's clothes emerging from under brilliantly colored curtains of state. The men who glimpse this sight from the verandah . . . do not as a rule dare enter the room where the woman is seated. . . .
>
> When a three-foot curtain of state has been set up, there is hardly any gap between the top of the frame and the bottom of the head-blind; fortunately the little space that remains always seems to come precisely at the face-level of the man who is standing outside the curtains and of the woman who is conversing with him from inside. What on earth would happen if the man was extremely tall and the woman very short? I really cannot imagine. But, so long as people are of normal height it is satisfactory.[3]

We learn from Shōnagon that the *kicho* itself is shielded from view by bamboo blinds. We also learn that there can be eye contact—assuming that the "people are of normal height"—and that the robes extending out from under the *kicho* are an appreciated part of communication. We learn from

other sections that notes and other small objects are passed back and forth under the *kicho*. As we consider what we know of the *kicho* we begin to wonder how it differs in essence from a Wall. It would not be entirely unexpected or unreasonable for a feminist to label the *kicho*, indeed, a Wall—a tearing-off of wings. However, to label the *kicho* such seems to ignore Shōnagon's own voice heard in phrases as "bright green bamboo blinds are a delight," and "it is satisfactory." The joy heard in Shōnagon's voice seems to proclaim that the *kicho* is not a Wall; the joy heard in her voice seems to say that to read her book is to experience the Dragonfly—not the tearing-off of wings, not the Wall.

The Dragonfly is a relation of you and me.

The Dragonfly is relation. To begin to explain what this means, the dragonfly of haiku poetry should be compared with the Dragonfly of Sei Shōnagon. Yasuda tells us how the haiku dragonfly comes about:

> Let us suppose that a poet is looking at a rye field one sunny afternoon with two friends, one a farmer who owns the field and the other an entomologist. . . . While they are thus talking, a red dragonfly passes before them, and immediately the entomologist notices it. Perhaps he classifies it as an idle mental exercise. . . . The poet, standing beside them, also sees the dragonfly and notices it light on a blade of rye, as do the other two. He is immediately interested in the dragonfly—in its color, form, and quality.
>
> This is a happening shared by the three men. . . .[4]

Yasuda goes on to show that one friend's attitude is "commercial," since he is not moved by the beauty of the insect—he is only thinking about "the price the grain will bring him in the market place." The other friend's attitude is "scientific": "As soon as he sees the red dragonfly, he ceases seeing it directly and sees it only as a part of his system of categories."[5]

Yasuda is much more interested in the poet's attitude, which he calls the "haiku attitude."

> His attention is directed not to his knowledge about the dragonfly, nor to the value of the rye field. He is interested in the object for its own sake. . . . An attitude such as this is aesthetic. I shall call it a haiku attitude.[6]

Presumably the haiku produced by a poet with such an attitude may be one composed by Yasuda himself:

> A crimson dragonfly
> As it lights, sways together
> With a leaf of rye.[7]

When one reads these words one can encounter what Yasuda calls the "haiku moment": "A haiku moment is a kind of aesthetic moment in which the words which created the experience and the experience itself become one." That is, when this poem is read, the mind is filled with the picture of a red flying insect hovering, cellophane wings blurred with motion, keeping the insect motionless above a single stalk of vegetation. Simultaneously, as we read the poem, we experience two feelings—a surprised feeling but also an "of course!" feeling. Of course, we cannot know when the dragonfly ceases its motionless motion, because its landing on the swinging stalk of rye can only happen when it stops moving. When one reads the poem one can feel a sort of disequilibrium for a split second; this disequilibrium tells one that one has indeed experienced the unity of the dragonfly-swaying-with-the-leaf-of-rye.

We can now ask: if Shōnagon were watching the scene in the rye field, what attitude would she have? Shōnagon would have neither a commercial, scientific nor haiku attitude. She would observe the dragonfly as closely as the poet; but what would most interest her is that the dragonfly lighting on a blade of rye is, as Yasuda puts it, "a hap-

pening shared by the three men." She would be most interested in understanding how it is that a "poet is looking at a rye field one sunny afternoon with two friends, one a farmer . . . the other an entomologist." It does seem a rather unlikely threesome. Shōnagon would want to find something in the "happening shared by the three men" that illuminates the fact that these are three friends.

I am not sure if Shōnagon herself knew that she was most interested in the relationship aspect of the scene in the rye field—not in the insect. But it is this aspect of things that she wrote about with her whole being. Shōnagon herself says about her book:

> On the whole I concentrated on things and people that I found charming and splendid; my notes are also full of poems and observations on trees and plants, birds and insects.[8]

Just as the haiku poet gives us a certain kind of experience, so Shōnagon brings us a certain kind or aspect of experience. Some attributes of the haiku are fixed, predictable. The most obvious attribute of this sort is the haiku's 5-7-5 syllable pattern. There are other less obvious attributes, such as the seasonal element. This element is often found in haiku and, as Yasuda says, "expresses a love and kinship with the world of nature which come as naturally to the Japanese as the seventeen syllable poem in which they celebrate their feeling in the language of poetry, and in which they possess it. . . ."[9] Similarly, Shōnagon's prose has certain consistent attributes worthy of discussion.

I prefer to call Shōnagon's form "okashi." Okashi is an adjective often found at the end of Shōnagon's sentences. Usually it is translated as "charming" or "delightful." I will use okashi as a noun designating the kind of experience afforded by Shōnagon's writing. The two most important qualities I find in okashi are **transparency** (tomei in

Japanese) and **overbrim** (*afureru* in Japanese). By transparency I mean a sort of intuitive understanding between people. By overbrim I mean a pregnant sense of occasion that can fill a scene or situation with tension, as the hydrangea fills its space in the following haiku:

> Underneath the eaves
> A blooming large hydrangea
> Overbrims its leaves.[10]

The following section of *The Pillow Book*, as translated by Morris, is a typical *okashi* of Sei Shōnagon.

66. IT WAS A CLEAR, MOONLIT NIGHT

It was a clear, moonlit night a little after the tenth of the Eighth Month. Her Majesty, who was residing in the Empress's Office, sat by the edge of the verandah while Ukon no Naishi played the flute for her. The other ladies in attendance sat together, talking and laughing: but I stayed by myself, leaning against one of the pillars between the main hall and the verandah.

"Why so silent?" said Her Majesty. "Say something. It is sad when you do not speak."

"I am gazing into the autumn moon," I replied.

"Ah yes," she remarked. "That is just what you should have said."[11]

The overbrimming in this section comes from the conjunction of a moonlit night with court ladies playing music and Shōnagon standing by herself, almost off the verandah where the Empress is sitting. There is a tension of gaiety and solemnity. Shōnagon need not add another element to the description of the scene to make it fuller—it overbrims. The tension of the overbrim gives propulsion to a transparency that is revealed when Shōnagon answers the Empress, her answer revealing that each knows the other. Shōnagon's moon in this scene is not that of any of the three friends in Yasuda's rye field. It has no commercial value, yields no scientific data, and it is not appreciated for its

own sake. It is a moon that is appreciated only in so far as it reveals what is in the two women's hearts, and thus it helps to make an occasion into an *okashi*.

An *okashi* does not always require two participants. For example, in the following *okashi*, Shōnagon observes a single individual from afar:

An attractive woman, whose hair tumbles loosely over her forehead, has received a letter in the dark. Evidently she is too impatient to wait for a lamp; instead she takes some fire-tongs, and, lifting a piece of burning charcoal from the brazier, laboriously reads by its pale light. It is a charming scene.[12]

The situation has overbrim; the darkness, the letter, the need for light—these speak of a waiting stillness. When the woman reaches for a coal, the overbrim is released and, in being released, flashes a light that makes transparent the woman's wanting to know *now* what her suitor has to say. Shōnagon can see that transparency from far away. She must know—and we feel too—that each character in the letter will be lit well enough to be read only one at a time, and so will burn like single coals in the woman's memory forever. These words becoming burning coals make an unstated haiku hovering, burning below the crust of the narrative. Shōnagon's point is to show how the desire that creates the woman's haste to read and brings together all those elements—letter, darkness, pale light, burning coal—to give an unforgettable portrait of that desire. Shōnagon finds the scene charming; she would probably do the same.

The following *okashi* is particularly quiet and effective:

60. ONCE IN THE FIFTH MONTH

Once in the Fifth Month during the long spell of rainy weather Captain Tadanobu came and stood next to the bamboo screen by the door leading to the Empress's apartments. He used a most delightful scent, which it was impossible to identify. The air was very damp. Even though nothing noteworthy took place, there was something peculiarly elegant about the entire scene, which makes me feel bound to mention it. The Captain's scent permeated the screen and lingered there till the following day. Small wonder that the younger ladies-in-waiting should have felt this was something unique.[13]

In this *okashi* it is the blinds themselves that make transparency possible. If not for the blinds, there could be no "not noteworthy" noteworthiness. The blinds give the scent a place to stop and hover. It seems that Tadanobu's waiting perfume makes evident an affection that he feels for someone in the Empress's apartments, possibly Shōnagon herself. The scent of Tadanobu—and also his affection—overbrims the blinds into the apartments of the Empress.

Yasuda speaks of "a disinterested awareness" that allows the haiku poet to have a true experience of the contemplated object. He tells a story about a painter to explain.

> The anecdote is told of Seiho, the famous Japanese painter, that in looking at the picture of a chicken drawn by a student he clucked several times. Here awareness of the object was his whole being and he became that chicken. But had he exclaimed on the beauty of the painting, he would have been separated from the object he was observing . . . and would no longer have been one with it.[14]

In *The Pillow Book* a different kind of interest is evidenced. The dog Okinamaro had been flogged by two men for chasing the Emperor's cat. Shōnagon had supposed that Okinamaro was dead, and that the stray dog which had crawled into the Palace was not the pet mentioned. She expresses sorrow that the animal had been killed—"'Poor Okinamaro!' I said. 'He had such a dreadful beating yesterday. How sad to think he is dead! . . . Oh, how he must have suffered!'" In so doing, she provokes a response from

the dog, which becomes indeed something noteworthy. Instead of Shōnagon staring at the dog Okinamaro and becoming one with the dog and his dog nature—as Seiho and the art student apparently did with the chicken—she listens and hears something from the dog that convinces her that the dog has understood *her* nature.

> At that moment the dog lying by the pillar started to shake and tremble, and shed a flood of tears. It was astounding. So this really was Okinamaro! . . .
>
> The news reached His Majesty, and he too came to the Empress's room. "It's amazing," he said with a smile. "To think that even a dog has such deep feelings! . . .
>
> Before long, Okinamaro was granted an Imperial pardon and returned to his former happy state. Yet even now, when I remember how he whimpered and trembled in response to our sympathy, it strikes me as a strange and moving scene; when people talk to me about it, I start crying myself.[15]

I wonder if Yasuda's haiku poet or Seiho, the painter, with their "disinterested awareness," could have brought forth the moving response of Okinamaro. Shōnagon is moved by the dog's own awareness of *her* sympathy. "Disinterested awareness" in this case may have been able to find the dog nature, but it would have entirely missed Okinamaro and *his* nature or soul.

A quality of *The Pillow Book*, which could perhaps be called spiritual, can be ascertained—especially when it is compared to *The Tale of Genji* by Murasaki Shikibu, a contemporary of Sei Shōnagon. The *okashi* of Shōnagon are quite different from Murasaki's long narrative, *The Tale of Genji*. It is ironic that the main character in that narrative is called Hikaru Genji, or "Shining Genji." The fact is that wherever Genji goes, he brings darkness. There is no transparency between him and the women with whom he becomes involved. Indeed, it is because he does not understand them or they him that the plot can move forward. Genji befriends the young Murasaki, not because they understand each other, but because the child amuses him; and Okinamaro understands Shōnagon more than Genji's father understands Genji. Genji is forever involved in affairs that require secrecy and a darkness to hide the Shining Prince. *The Pillow Book*, on the other hand, though its title suggests the darkness of the bedroom, of night, is full of light—the light that goes back and forth between people, illuminating and creating humanity as it illuminates.

There is present tense-ness that permeates *The Pillow Book*, which is connected to the *significance* of *okashi*. One way in which the present tense-ness arises is by means of Shōnagon's apparent insistence in several sections that each year should be a replay of one ideal year. The following section if typical:

9. ON THE FIRST DAY OF THE FIRST MONTH

On the first day of the First Month and on the third of the Third I like the sky to be perfectly clear.

On the fifth of the Fifth Month I prefer a cloudy sky.

On the seventh day of the Seventh Month it should also be cloudy; but in the evening it should be clear. . . .

On the ninth of the Ninth Month there should be a drizzle from early dawn. . . . Sometimes the rain stops early in the morning, but the sky is still overcast, and it looks as if it may start raining again at any moment. This too I find very pleasant.[16]

Another aspect of the book that suggests the present tense is the fact that the events that are recounted take place among conditions that are not in the least remarkable or historic. The sky is cloudy, the moonlight falls on the snow, a dog is beaten, a snow mountain is built—none of these situations is inextricably unique or bound up in a distant past. The recollection of detail in these most mundane situations seems to pull all the events up to the foreground of one large

present. Furthermore, because no time-line is imposed on the events or the sections, the events seem to happen in the relative foreground of time.

The time sense in *The Tale of Genji* is much different. The reader seems always to be directed to look down a long tunnel of time, where the events that have occurred are already far away from the present, a present which is itself rapidly becoming a past. Of course, this structure of time is necessary for a narrative to proceed; but it is especially suited to a concept often associated with *The Tale of Genji*—*mono no aware*, the "pathos of things." *Mono no aware* is a term for the concept or the awareness that youth gets old, that things decay, that the beautiful is no longer beautiful. Hence many of Genji's adventures take place in mansions overgrown with weeds, reminding one of a lost past prosperity. Finally, Genji himself dies, and the reader is left with the impression that his kingdom will never again recover the light that was lost when the Shining Prince left the world.

Shōnagon's *okashi* implicitly deny that the *mono no aware* view of the world is the most valid, the most accurate view. Indeed, we know that things decay, that people die; but when Shōnagon slows us down and makes us notice the moments that make people human, she makes us know that these moments have more significance than the fact of biological finitude.

In fact, these moments when overbrim propels one soul to become transparent to another could be called *okashi* moments. In their present tense-ness, they are somewhat like the haiku moment as Yasuda describes it:

A haiku moment is a kind of aesthetic moment—a moment in which the words which created the experience and the experience itself can become one. The nature of a haiku moment is anti-temporal and its quality is eternal, for in this state man and his environment are one unified whole, in which there is no sense of time.

In the *okashi* moment, the elements in the environment and the feelings in the person become united in the person's soul. The integrity of the unity of an *okashi* can make that moment eternal for the psyche that experiences it—as eternal as the haiku moment—and thus present tense.

Shōnagon does not explicitly set out to stress *mono no aware* in her book. Yet if you consider that the Empress who is *the* woman of *okashi* dies at the age of twenty-four, and that Shōnagon herself is all of thirty-five when she retires from the court life which she writes about, we can feel, if we choose, a more intense *mono no aware* than is afforded us by the sentimental descriptions of people fading out of life in *The Tale of Genji*. By contrast, there is very little *okashi* in that long narrative; rarely are two people simultaneously aware of and in awe of each other's beauty and intelligence. We encounter no Dragonfly.

The Dragonfly of Sei Shōnagon and the dragonfly of the haiku poet reside in what Martin Buber, in his book *I and Thou*, calls "the spheres in which the world of relation arises." Buber describes two "spheres":

> The first: life with nature. Here the relation vibrates in the dark and remains below language. The creatures stir across from us but they are unable to come to us, and the You we say to them sticks to the threshold of language.

The dragonfly of haiku poetry resides in Buber's "first sphere." The Dragonfly of Sei Shōnagon resides in the "second sphere":

> The second: life with men. Here the relation is manifest and enters language. We can give and receive the You.[17]

One enters into relation with the dragonfly of haiku poetry.

Buber suggests that one may sometimes enter into such relation even with beings residing in "the first sphere," a tree, for example.

> I contemplate a tree.
> I can accept it as a picture. . . .
> I can feel it as movement. . . .
> I can assign it to a species. . . .
> I can overcome its uniqueness and form so rigorously that I recognize it only as an expression of the law. . . .
> I can dissolve it into a number. . . .
> But it can also happen, if will and grace are joined, that as I contemplate the tree, I am drawn into a relation, and the tree ceases to be an It. The power of exclusiveness has seized me.[18]

Here Buber describes a haiku moment—the kind of moment when one can, as one reads the haiku about the dragonfly, for example, be seized and made to experience dragonflyness. In Buber's language, one writes a haiku out of the knowledge one gains through engaging in a relationship with the tree—or the dragonfly. One can also come into relation with a human being, even one that is merely being observed, as Shōnagon does when she contemplates the woman reading the letter with the glowing coal. As Buber says, "The relation can obtain even if the human being to whom I say You does not hear it in his experience."

Not all the sections of *The Pillow Book* are *okashi*—many of the sections are merely lists. In the sections that are *okashi*, however, Shōnagon is seen in such relations with people. This is especially true of her relation with the Empress. Buber describes such a relation:

> When I confront a human being as my You and speak the basic word I-You to him, then he is no thing among things nor does he consist of things.
>
> He is no longer He or She, limited by other Hes and Shes, a dot in the world grid of space and time, nor a condition that can be experienced and described, a loose bundle of named qualities. Neighborless and seamless, he is You and fills the firmament. Not as if there were nothing but he; but everything else lives in his light.

When the woman reads the letter by the pale light of the coal there is a literalization of what Buber says. For Shōnagon, at that instant, everything is seen in the light of the woman reading the letter.

Shōnagon seems to agree explicitly with Buber in the following *okashi:*

67. ONE DAY WHEN THERE WERE SEVERAL
PEOPLE IN THE EMPRESS'S PRESENCE

One day when there were several people in the Empress's presence. . . . Her Majesty threw a note at me. "Should I love you or should I not?" it said. "What will you do if I cannot give you first place in my heart?"

No doubt she was thinking of a recent conversation when I had remarked in her hearing, "If I do not come first in people's affections, I had just as soon not be loved at all; in fact I would rather be hated or even maltreated. It is better to be dead than to be loved in the second or third place. Yes, I must be the first." . . .

I wrote the following note and handed it to her: "Among the Nine Ranks of lotus seats even the lowliest would satisfy me."

"Well, well," said the Empress, "You seem to have lost heart completely. That's bad. I prefer you to go on thinking as before."

"My attitude depends on the person in question," I replied.

"That's really bad," she said, much to my delight. "You should try to come first in the affections of even the most important people."

What both Buber and Shōnagon are saying is that where there is *response*—and even rejection is a *response*—there is hope for relation, thus for human life.

Buber *speaks* of relation; Shōnagon presents relation in its vibration, embodiment, and clothing. Her *okashi* give relation form that must be "confronted bodily" like Buber's tree: "The tree is no impression, no aspect of a mood; it confronts me bodily and has to deal with me as I must deal with it— only differently. One should not try to dilute the meaning of the relation: relation is reciprocity."

If we heed Buber and "do not dilute the meaning of the relation" that we have with Shōnagon's *okashi*, then what do we do? In reciprocity to Shōnagon we must watch for, seek, and enter into *okashi* moments. For it is by pausing before a *kicho* that we may restore to the Dragonfly the wings that were torn when the Ghetto Wall and other such walls were built.

[1]Kenneth Yasuda, *The Japanese Haiku* (Tokyo: Tuttle, 1957), p. 170.
[2]Sei Shōnagon, *The Pillow Book of Sei Shōnagon,* trans. Ivan Morris (New York: Penguin, 1967), pp. 271–72.
[3]Ibid., pp. 84–85.
[4]Yasuda, p. 9.
[5]Ibid., pp. 9–10.
[6]Ibid., pp. 9–10.
[7]Ibid., p. 30.
[8]Shōnagon, pp. 263–64.
[9]Yasuda, p. 177.
[10]Ibid., p. 6.
[11]Shōnagon, p. 125.
[12]Ibid., p. 240.
[13]Ibid., pp. 113–14.
[14]Yasudo, p. 23.
[15]Shōnagon, #8, pp. 31–33.
[16]Shōnagon, p. 33.
[17]Martin Buber, *I and Thou,* trans. Walter Kaufmann (New York: Scribner's, 1970), pp. 56–57.
[18]Ibid., pp. 57–58.

Barbara Sandrisser

ON ELEGANCE IN JAPAN

Barbara Sandrisser is a partner of The Paul Partnership, an architectural and site design firm based in New York City. She writes on aesthetic issues, focusing on how traditional Japanese perceive their environment. Sandrisser describes Japanese ideas about elegance in the following essay, taking Sei Shōnagon's list of elegant things as her point of departure.

During the last decade of the 10th Century in Japan, an accomplished, versatile lady-in-waiting, named Sei Shōnagon, wrote about elegance. She described six phenomena she believed to be truly elegant:

1. A white coat worn over a violet waistcoat.
2. Duck eggs.
3. Shaved ice mixed with liana syrup and put in a new silver bowl.
4. A rosary of rock crystal.
5. Wisteria blossoms. Plum blossoms covered with snow.
6. A pretty child eating strawberries.[1]

Today we, and perhaps some Japanese, would find it difficult to understand her interpretation of elegance. Our idea of what constitutes elegance most likely does not include any of Sei Shōnagon's preferences. Yet if we examine her selections carefully, we notice that they have certain attributes in common, and it is this kinship which provides us with a richer understanding of the elusive definition of elegance as perceived by the Japanese.

What strikes us immediately is that all the senses, even taste and sound, intermingle among her selections. We are also unable to dismiss the assuming elegance apparent in natural phenomena. Moreover, a kind of sixth sense emerges, a fusion of an intuitive response and an intellectual one which the Japanese call **kokoro.**[2]

Let us review her small inventory again in order to discover the significance of her selections.

A white coat worn over a violet waistcoat. In one of many highly descriptive vignettes, Sei Shōnagon, sitting in the shadows behind a translucent screen, observes a male caller entering the room:

He looked magnificant as he came towards me. . . . He wore dark grape-colored trousers, boldly splashed with designs of wisteria branches; his crimson under-robe was so glossy that it seemed to sparkle, while underneath one could make out layer upon layer of white and light violet robes.[3]

White, violet and lavender, much admired during Heian times, emit a decided potency, despite their seemingly fragile tones. Sei Shōnagon understood the inherent qualities of purity and cleanliness from her Shinto heritage and she enjoyed observing how brilliant flashes of white reflected neighboring colors.

From her description, one can easily imagine the visual impact. The interplay of color and pattern entices us just as it did one thousand years ago when Sei Shōnagon, Murasaki Shikibu and others carefully noted nuance of hue in their descriptive passages. If we imagine these colors in dim light against unpainted wood, which is how traditional Japanese perceived them indoors, their sensuous qualities become even more apparent. Moreover, we should try not to avoid the sensual aspects of Sei Shōnagon's image as it, too, touches upon the Japanese idea of elegance.

Duck eggs. Normally, Westerners refrain from referring to aspects of the natural world as elegant. We prefer to confine our concept of elegance to human endeavors. Duck eggs exhibit simplicity of form and delicacy of color. Their small and deceptively fragile appearance belies a remarkable inner strength. We imagine that Sei Shōnagon's fingers delighted in stroking their smooth surface as they sat in the palm of her hand. No doubt too they tasted splendid. In her time duck eggs evoked a subtle elegance; beautiful, modest and unequivocal. Their form expressed straightforward honesty and clarity.

Shaved ice mixed with liana syrup and put in a new silver bowl. During the winter ancient Japanese stored ice in special containers to be eaten during the hot, humid summer. Serving it in a silver bowl intensified the sensuous experience, for the melting green ice was beautiful to behold, cool to the touch while refreshing to one's palate. It was most likely the caviar of 10th Century Japan and of subsequent centuries. Smell and sound enhanced the experience of savoring the ice on one's tongue. Although we do not know if liana syrup was particularly fragrant, we know that ice "smells" cold and that the sound of eating can be pleasant to non-Westerners. The anticipation of eating something special and then actually consuming it is generally an accumulated response ultimately encompassing all our sensibilities.[4] Sei Shōnagon delighted in the exquisite taste of a small edible trifle placed in a beautiful but not ostentatious container, especially if the delicate item rapidly changed consistency. Enjoying ice with liana syrup on a hot day is surely a fleeting experience and, thus, to her an elegant moment in time.

A rosary of rock crystal. Possibly due to their flawed yet lovely appearance, Buddhist quartz beads seem to form an intimate relationship with the hand. Small and infinitely tactile, each irregular bead invites touch and contemplation. Thus, one could say that merely by glancing at or holding the rosary, one grasps a profound sense of elegance.

Wisteria blossoms. Plum blossoms covered with snow. The beauty of wisteria vines replete with cascading lavender and white blossoms borders on the erotic. In Sei Shōnagon's time they represented an invitation to one's beloved. Genji refers to the beauty of wisteria blossoms when courting one of his many ladies and we recall Sei Shōnagon's comment about wisteria sprays on the trousers of her male visitor. Traditional Japanese made a point of courting under wisteria arbors, and wisteria images found their way into virtually every art form.

Her image of plum blossoms covered with snow is surely nature's way of seducing us, while simultaneously alerting us to the temporal qualities of beauty. The snow will melt and both the plum blossoms and the wisteria will die. It is, then, again the beauty of the moment in time which is elegant, as well as the beautiful blossoms.

And finally, we wonder about the elegance of **a pretty child eating strawberries.** Possibly this image is the most elusive one to grasp. Indeed, it might be more appropriate to call it charming. Nonetheless, if we permit ourselves to abstract the image for a moment, we notice the harmony of form and color. The innate purity of the child's face is exemplified by its roundness and by the pale, creamy-white skin set against the smooth texture of exceedingly long blue-black hair. To this image of purity, one is compelled to add a touch of sensuousness of color, texture on the palate and flavor, all sensed vicariously: the delicate, red strawberry about to be enjoyed. Once again, it is a special moment in time. Here, too, the idea of **kokoro** emerges, for both the mind and heart realize the aesthetic and sensuous qualities inherent in the images Sei Shōnagon considered elegant.

Her choices are indeed beautiful ones. Beauty and elegance seem to flow into each other, creating a wave of responses. We sense that perhaps the Japanese value the beauty in elegance in ways which we have yet to decipher. Thus, exploring elegance as an aesthetic notion, both as we conceive it in the West and as the Japanese understand it, reveals fundamental yet intriguing truths for us to ponder. Throughout history, elegantly designed objects and expressions of ideas formed an intimate relationship with each of us by extending our knowledge of the world, by enhancing our daily activities and by heightening our aesthetic appreciation. Yet, in our society, this unique aspect of beauty is frequently ignored or misinterpreted. Elegance is oftentimes criticized as a superficial, dispensable quality. If we sense a paradox here, it is probably because one exists.

The etymology of the word elegance is worth exploring from its early Latin origins onward, as it reveals our peculiar cultural prejudices and also a certain Western cultivated egotism. For an idea or object to be considered elegant, it must first be chosen above others.[5] Thus in the etymological sense, it suggests choosing carefully or skillfully. However in early Latin, undoubtedly because of the social climate, the term elegant was used to ridicule those who were overly fastidious and foppish.

During classical times, the meaning of the word expanded to include the ideas of refined luxury and graceful propriety. Cicero, possibly the first true connoisseur of elegance as defined then, had this expanded meaning in mind when he referred to an **elegante vitae,** or elegant life. He found the decadent opulence enjoyed by many powerful Romans, including Julius Caesar, to be in poor taste. Integrity and elegance should not be, but often are, strangers to each other he felt. In his correspondence he refers to the elegant oratory, diction, and writing of others. Yet it was he who set the standard for both elegance and eloquence in this regard.

Sallust, born 20 years after Cicero in 86 BC (and unlike him, a friend of Julius Caesar) suggested that music, specifically melodies from a stringed instrument, and selected forms of dance could be described as elegant. This may be the first reference to elegance in the arts. These ideas of elegance, exemplified by grace of movement and refinement of sound, remain with us today. The fall of the Roman Empire undoubtedly caused the notion of elegance to recede into oblivion. Although difficult to document, the concept apparently remained dormant for centuries, resurfacing again during the Renaissance when the phrase "elegance of speech" returned to favor. Opulence in attire and in one's surrounding re-emerged, and with it, once again, dandyism and grandiosity.

In science the "elegant proof" gained recognition, that is, a scientific solution or theory that exhibits neatness, simplicity and ingenuity, a theory that does not necessarily follow a prescribed mathematical methodology. Indeed, this may be the most profound definition of elegance, one which Cicero would undoubtedly endorse. Unlike other Western thinkers Renaissance scientists comprehended the significance of the relationship between elegance and beauty. Admiration for the elegant theory remains with us today, exemplified by Einstein's theory of relativity. Its supreme elegance and beauty continue to astonish us.

Thus by the 16th Century, elegance reflected early Latin and Classical notions, while simultaneously incorporating new dimensions, such as the notion of height. Tall buildings, statuesque people, high columns, were considered elegant. Graceful movement returned to favor, recalling Sallust's comment on dance. Luxurious attire, correctness of taste and refined manners, resulted in a "high class," in effect a "cultured" minority (the chosen few, one might say) turning back to the original definition of the word.

Today in Western society the word has fallen into disrepute. Elegance is now an affectation, in some ways similar to Roman times and the Renaissance. It is entangled with grandeur, ornateness, wealth, and physical appearance. We seem to have lost sight of the unique qualities inherent in the idea of elegance.

Perhaps we are confusing the **word** elegant with the **idea** of elegance. Oftentimes the word seems to substitute for the idea, image or object. We particularly notice this in advertising copy. Elegance describes virtually everything from clothing and cars to condominiums in Bermuda. But is it an actual component of the product being advertised? Evidence suggests that it is an overused, sexy, superficial word deliberately utilized to sell products, which then, presumably, will make us elegant (chic, tasteful, upper class, cultured) individuals. In short, purchasing such a product relieves us

of our innate clumsiness, our coarseness, and perhaps most significantly, our seeming vulgarity.

Assuming we succumb to this onslaught, this never ending hype, do we then become elegant and if the answer is conceivably "yes," are we then beautiful too? The Latin origin of the word and its subsequent development suggests that in our society the two are completely separate. Generally beauty appears to be missing from elegance; one does not necessarily imply the other, although some, notably theoretical scientists, would suggest that beauty is assumed to be a part of elegance. Einstein frequently reserved his highest praise for an elegant theory by noting its beauty, and others, such as Hideki Yukawa, a Japanese physicist, note that Einstein himself "had a sense of beauty which is given to only a few theoretical physicists."[6]

Articulating how elegance applies to scientific theory is precarious at best. Rollo May interprets it as "The harmony of an internal form, the inner consistency of a theory, the character of beauty that touches your sensibilities."[7] In May's description elegance and beauty unite. Indeed, despite their differing etymologies, it is difficult (and unnecessary) to separate one from the other in order to isolate their parts. To extend this notion outside the realm of science, consider for a moment the elegance and beauty of Mozart's music, which we are told was notated by the composer directly as a unified whole, or Da Vinci's notebooks, Rembrandt's etchings, Rilke's poems: All offer us the exquisite harmony of internal form expressed in a unique way and all touch our sensibilities in a special way.

Yet, despite the creative work of the artists just cited our society appears to be reluctant to unify beauty and elegance overtly except in certain specific situations, such as the "elegant proof" referred to by scientists. Thus it is necessary to look at Japan where elegance is wedded to beauty linguistically and philosophically. One thousand years later, Kawabata, in his Nobel Prize acceptance speech, refers to the elegance of wisteria in much the same way as Shōnagon and Murasaki Shikibu:

> Wisteria sprays, as they trail in the breeze, suggest softness, gentleness, reticence. Disappearing and then appearing again in the early summer greenery, they have in them that feeling for the poignant beauty of things long characterized by the Japanese as *mono no aware.*[8]

Others translate **mono no aware** as the sadness of things, or sensitivity to things. Kawabata's interpretation "The poignant beauty of things" appears closest to Murasaki's idea of elegance. Both agree that our sensibilities and our mind/heart (**kokoro**) must be touched by the experience. Then and today, the phrase epitomizes the feeling which occurs at the precise moment the cherry blossoms are at their peak. Their brief transient glory, beautiful, yet sad, represents an elegant moment, a memorable interval.

The Heian era bequeathed a sophisticated aesthetic vocabulary to future generations due, in large part, to the emphasis placed on elegance. Admittedly, these arbiters of aesthetic nuance were mostly courtiers, the elite in Heian society, not the common people. Yet Sei Shōnagon describes the modest, rustic home of a local governor, lower on the social scale, who happened to be her maternal uncle. Her notion of rustic does not suggest crudeness or coarseness. She implies that the house was carefully designed to give an impression of quiet simplicity rather than ostentatious embellishment. Between the lines, she grudgingly admits that its simple qualities intrigue her. Buried between the snide reference to "poor and cramped" facilities lies a veiled compliment regarding its attractive characteristics.

There are many types of elegant beauty and beautiful elegance, and the Japanese have seemingly innumerable words to depict them. The most common word uniting the two is **miyabi**. How the character links with others suggests that it referred to poetry (**gago,** an elegant word), music (**gagaku,** ceremonial court music) and etiquette (**garyo,** magnanimity of behavior.) Too, it described the kind of elegance Sei Shōnagon appreciated in nature. The word **miyabi** was aristocratic in origin[9] and in application. Refinement of decorum, of costume, of virtually all aspects of daily life, including lovemaking, permeated the Heian Court.

Yubi, another word for elegance prevalent a thousand years ago, suggests a gentle, delicate beauty, exemplified perhaps by the child eating strawberries, the duck eggs, or by the lover who sends a perfectly worded poem, written on beautiful paper accompanied by a small branch of an appropriate blossom. Strength and passion hide behind the tender moment.

It is important then, to distinguish between the self-indulgent foppishness prevalent in Roman times and the ceremonial, almost ritualistic elegance of 10th Century Japan, which continued and expanded over the next centuries. Indeed, the Japanese prized elegance to such a degree that they seemed to nurture it and thus the fundamental notion of what elegance comprises— beauty, integrity of form, dignity, and profundity—intensified over time.

Other words incorporating essential qualities of elegance suggest further insights. During the Medieval period **Yugen** expressed an elegant profundity, an essence beyond words, particularily when referring to an ethereal, often silent, moment in a Nō performance. **Sabi,** and centuries later **Wabi** and **Shibui,** evolved out of the experience encountered in the tea ceremony. These words expressed the subtle nuance of an elegant beauty so profound that it touched the very core of one's being.

Significantly, virtually all Japanese words for beauty incorporating elegance into their meaning (and there are many) evoke an acute awareness of the relationship between time and space. The secret of infinity, then, can be said to be the moment in time when we perceive an elegant truth. Only then do we apprehend the dichotomy between the notion of perfection, which is inert, and the integrity of completeness. Perfection leaves us empty for there is literally nothing more.

Traditional Japanese perceived that, whether created by humans or by nature, objects need not be perfect in the Platonic sense, nor must they express aristocratic ideals. Acquiring the patina of age (**sabi**) exceeds merely becoming old and possibly antique. The modesty (**wabi**) of a simple wood dwelling or of objects used daily over a period of time, elicits an appreciative response. Understatement, even a touch of astringency, exemplified by the aesthetic notion of **shibui,** strongly influenced Japanese design. Less was not necessarily more; it was simply enough.

The Japanese spirit of elegance evokes a unique kind of aesthetic pride which developed from their long tradition of appreciating the grace and dignity inherent in everyday life. Aesthetic pride should not be misconstrued to mean condescension or vanity. Genuine elegance exists in essentiality. Nothing more can be eliminated without violating its meaning and thus everything essential remains and nothing unnecessary is added. Traditional Japanese perceived this essentiality in their environment. They esteemed elegant objects created by humans and elegance discovered in nature.

All cultures interpret themselves in many voices. Still, civilizations tend to echo the fundamental qualities of their cultural development through elegant ideas and through creative endeavors. The fact that animals design their environments, resulting in remarkably elegant solutions (i.e., bird nests, bee hives, beaver dams) only serves to remind us that we as human beings can perceive their elegance while they most likely cannot. The fundamental key which unites utility, comfort and beauty in all three cases is aesthetic appreciation of each as an elegant whole. Discovering elegance is a uniquely human ability, yet we malign the notion. This is merely one side of a paradox. The other side is that we incorporate the **word** elegance, rather than its meaning as evoked here, into a value system which emphasizes selling mediocre products, resulting in what might be called a "valueless system."

Traditional objects designed by the Japanese, such as folding fans, chopsticks, carpenter's tools and movable walls, to name a few, exemplify the concept of elegance in a meaningful way. These deceptively simple things suggest that elegance is not obvious. Occasionally it may even conceal itself, encouraging us to discover its subtleties, for elegance respects the essence of things. Indeed, the continuing value of apprehending and understanding elegance is that it simultaneously intensifies and refines our sensibilities and thus our human experiences.

[1]Sei Shōnagon, *The Pillow Book of Sei Shōnagon,* translated and edited by Ivan Morris, Penguin Books, 1967, pg. 69. In a footnote Ivan Morris tells us that the stems and leaves of the liana vine were used as mild sweeteners.

[2]Literally mind/heart.

[3]*The Pillow Book of Sei Shōnagon,* pg. 94.

[4]To repeat an old aphorism, eating is touch carried to the bitter end, according to Samuel Butler, a 17th Century British poet and satirist.

[5]See *Cassell's Latin Dictionary,* pg. 190.

[6]Hideki Yukawa, *Creativity and Intuition,* Kodansha, 1973, pg. 106.

[7]Rollo May, *The Courage to Create,* Bantam, 1975, pg. 159–160.

[8]Yasuneri Kawabata, *Japan, The Beautiful, and Myself,* Kodansha, 1969, pg. 48.

[9]Originally meaning courtliness.

Janet McCracken

THE DOMESTIC AESTHETIC

Janet McCracken is professor of philosophy at Lake Forest College. She is author of Taste and the Household *as well as a study on* Persian Philosophy, *and she is editor of* Thinking about Gender: A Historical Anthology. *In the following essay (written in 1993), McCracken contends that the aesthetic judgments we make in our everyday lives around our homes develop our abilities to make moral judgments as well.*

WHAT IS THE "DOMESTIC AESTHETIC"?

Domestic aesthetic activities are those whose object—in the sense of their "end" or "goal"—is a beautiful life (where "beautiful" is used both in its modern sense of "the object of aesthetic judgment" and its classical sense of "the object of love"). One's life—at least so far as that life is a physical one—is made livable in the first instance by securing one's survival—by feeding, clothing, and sheltering oneself to the extent made necessary by one's environment—and in the second instance, by securing one's survival pleasantly—i.e., by preparing food, sewing clothes, and building and furnishing houses.

Thus, those things toward which a life is first and foremost directed are those things whose shared locus is "at home," and they are, therefore, "domestic" in the broadest sense. Thus, one's primary choices, the first order of business of one's life, are not what one does for or with one's boss or one's government, but what one does for or with the members of one's household. Domestic aesthetic activities are those in which we engage in order to make and sustain households, i.e., in order to make a pleasant shared life with those with whom we choose to share it.

These activities include, of course, those through which we assert our independence within our personal relationships, as for instance when a man buys a car stereo instead of the set of Revereware his wife would prefer, or when she cuts her hair in the new fashion despite his protests. With these sorts of activities, after all, one maintains onself as a participant in the continuing relationship one deems necessary to the goodness of the life it fills. These gestures are sacrifices just as much as would be refraining from them; one often feels, for instance, that "one can't go on with" a particular person unless she "allows one to be oneself." One insists on "being oneself" in the relationship, then, precisely in order to go on with her.

The domestic aesthetic is the ability to engage in the sorts of activities which will so allow her, an ability whose presence is felt only through engagement in the activities themselves. The ability is of the nature of a skill—and as such is always only a more or less developed ability—and the activities themselves are decorative. As a first effort, then, I will call the domestic aesthetic a skill at decorating the things with which we live, such that we can continue long at living well.

While the word "skill" is often taken to mean good, but unreflective, doing or making—as though the pianist's skill were in her fingers alone—we would not want to call the pianist skillful unless she could recognize good and bad piano-playing, as well as play the piano. In fact, her ability to play the piano well comes from and with the ability to hear her own and others' mistakes, and to hear when they have been corrected. As our pianist becomes better and better at piano-playing, so also does she become a better and better judge of piano-playing.

The situation is the same if we consider something very plebeian, like getting dressed in the morning, or shaving, or making coffee—in other words, domestic aesthetic activities. A person might easily live out her life doing one, two, or all of these things quite badly. But should she ever improve at these basic skills, to that extent she must also be a better judge of her own and of others' achievements. One learns to tie a tie from and as one learns to recognize shabbily and impeccably tied ties; one learns better to shave by and as one notices well and poorly cleaned chins and upper lips; one makes better coffee by and as one taste-tests or polls one's guests.

An idiot-savant, for instance, despite whatever impressive feats she may perform, is not able to make judgments about her performance or the performance of others. We would not want to say, then, that she exhibits a skill, but rather a tremendous talent. This is partly because without reflective judgment, she would not be able to improve or develop the talent; onlooking teachers would be amazed, but helpless towards her. We consider the idiot-savant unfortunate, or sad, or lost to the human community, precisely to the extent that she is unable to reflect critically upon her talent and thereby to learn.

Being a skill, the domestic aesthetic is reminiscent of the Aristotelian notion of virtue, or rather, what underlies virtue, practical wisdom. The domestic aesthetic is not all skills, however, but particular, domestic ones. A moral theory is inadequate if it cannot account for moral learning or moral teaching, i.e., if it cannot account for, nor thereby help initiate, moral improvement in the face of mistakes. That domestic aesthetic activities are skillful, then, is central to their ability to found moral reasoning; for it offers a way of understanding reason as something which one can do well or badly, rather than just as something which one can do or not do. The ancient notion of practical wisdom—on both Aristotle's and Plato's accounts—captures this aspect of moral decision-making. To have a skill, then, is to have both facility and reflective judgment with regard to its performance and, therefore, to be capable of improving or degenerating in one's performance of the activity. In this doubly-aspected sense, the domestic aesthetic is a skill.

Moral education, or education at any skill, requires that a connection be made, in the mind of the agent, between sensory experience and conceptions of ends; in other words, between what the agent takes to be the goal of an action and her interpretation of that action and its consequences. If the agent cannot judge both whether an action achieved what it was supposed to achieve and whether what it was supposed to achieve was really worthwhile after all, the agent cannot improve morally; she cannot either refine and revise her goals, or correct her mistaken actions. This mental connection between concepts and the experience of objects can itself be strong or weak; and part of the process of learning a skill is the forging of a stronger, clearer, such connection.

The first job of a weak moral reasoner is to establish a stronger intimacy between her conception of goodness and the things and actions experienced in the world whose goodness is at issue. This strength can only be achieved through exercise; or in other words, through practice of the skills they support; just as a strong muscle is achieved by doing with it over and over again what one does with strong muscles.

This notion is reminiscent of Aristotle's comparison in *Nicomachean Ethics II*, between learning to be virtuous and learning to play the lyre. This comparison puts in relief the dependence of skillfulness upon physical conditions. For instance, the lyre player cannot be expected to make significant improvement practicing with a warped or water-sogged instrument.

If I am correct in this evaluation, we must look at the domestic aesthetic realm for the basis of judgment's deterioration over recent history, at tastes in food, fashion, and interior decoration in terms of historical, material circumstances. I believe that our options in these matters today give us very weak domestic aesthetic "muscles"; I shall now consider ways they have done so.

SETTLING FOR VAGUENESS IN OUR REPRESENTATIONS OF GOODNESS

The dual desire for the deeply meaningful and the fuzzy (i.e., for purely symbolic sig-

nificance, ungrounded by any natural meaning) marked a person as being without class ten years ago; but it is now the general condition of every American consumer, including the very wealthiest among us. Donald Trump, no less than the lover of velvet paintings of unicorns, falls into this category. He seems to fill his life with portentous yet vague purchases and girlfriends, in a seeming effort to *look* as rich as he is. Similarly, the difference between the foggy profundity of a velvet painting of a mythological creation and that of the futuristic, proto-Nazi, S&M symbolism of En Vogue's *Free Your Mind* video, which has received recent critical acclaim, is scant. In fact, MTV, one long commercial for grotesquely overpriced CD's, is perhaps the pinnacle of "vague and portentous" symbolism.

No longer a symbolism even of upward mobility, the fashion of the day is to symbolize this and that, for no reason and to little effect. One can see quite obviously on MTV a case where a *pretended* system of similarities and differences pretends to make plays of reference; but neither its audience nor its producers have any idea anymore what these symbols are similar *to* or different *from*. They are just symbols we happen to be able to conjure and set to music, to make the music seem meaningful and so seem worth the expense. A society in which even the upper middle class and extremely wealthy put on airs is not a society in which a system controls us; it is a society in which signification has far outstripped what is signified, one in which there is no system at all, but only the vague symbolic gestures of a system.

I believe that this situation has been effected through a mechanism of production wherein symbolic representation of goodness, the projection of the vague inklings of the self-concept of a now quite unskilled consumer/promoter onto objects she can buy, like a bulldozer, flattens and makes obsolete her applied notions of the goodness of the objects she buys. The mechanism gets its originating fuel from the production of lousy domestic aesthetic objects, but it is catalyzed by the adaptation of theory—which filters into the mass-media through textbooks and political activity and marketing strategies—to accommodate this process rather than to reflect upon and improve it.

Through our buying power, we model all production on ourselves without meaning to or realizing that we do. Today, the average American knows only how to be an abstract symbol of herself—a symbol that has rights and possessions—and not how to exercise rights or use those possessions. She is in the market for a role model which is, unbeknownst to her, only a more vague, less powerful, less interesting version of herself—just the person who marketers and promoters take her to be.

The world of such a person cannot help but *seem* structured and systematic and full of meaning, and yet *be* haphazard and confused and insignificant, because the consumer today is a king who feels like a pawn. It is this quite deceived person who "invades" everything without effort, who draws everything to her will, without even having a conscious will by which to draw it. Through her very efforts to make a life that she can be proud of, she keeps getting a life that dissatisfies her—her own, only less so. For the reason the things produced today are so confused is precisely because the consumer *is* the designer of herself and yet does not believe this. It is her own ill-considered, unskillful choices that keep appearing on the shelves, and she doesn't even recognize them.

The domestic aesthetic objects available today are just ill-thought, vague, and careless symbolic versions of our *own* real prior buying trends, funneled through a market analysis and dished back up as a leftover of a now very old meal. Vidal Sassoon's jingle even states, "It's you, amplified. . . ." The increase in TV talk shows, real-life dramas, comedies about death and divorce, and commercials in which the most severely untal-ented "real" people give their anonymous but authentic endorsements or tell their real life stories to the audience-as-therapist, are but more instances of these vague symbolic representations of abstract versions of ourselves offered up as commodities. Nothing we don't know, nothing that will expand our capabilities, nothing in which we are interested, nothing that requires or occasions reflection, appears to us.

In a recent Subaru campaign, for instance, a rather confused, quite inarticulate young gentleman informs us that the new *Impreza* has changed car-making the way punk did music making. The analogy, needless to say, is not fleshed out. Rather, the car is imbued with a vague, "cool" meaningfulness by its association with youth and punk, as though this were what one wanted in a car. In fact, recent car names are perhaps the most blatant of any examples of phenomenologically distant, vague symbolic signification replacing more meaningful, decipherable signification. *Impreza, Integra, Achieva, Vigor, Quattro, Lumina, Probe*—the list goes on—have replaced *Mustang, New Yorker, Cougar, Beetle, Thunderbird.* What were at least real names of icons of strength and speed and urbanity or cuteness have been replaced with made-up names that merely gesture toward mere abstractions, which we may or may not want to see instantiated in a car.

The promotions are based on the assumption that consumers *do not know what is good in their domestic aesthetic products*— a self-fulfilling prophecy. A recent promotion of beef, which gives only the names and cooking times of various dishes, assumes that customers do not know that names and time-consumption are not particularly relevant to good butchery or dining. Or, of course, the marketing of designer clothes and towels and bedclothes—the name is everything. The fit, the softness, the color, the care, whether they are appropriate for the body or the life of the consumer are all now deemed entirely irrelevant.

In all these cases, the objects produced rely on the skill-lessness of the consumer who will use them, and they are marketed so as to make the fact that she doesn't know how to use these things seem like an asset. Over and over again, this wild abandon of production and marketing is geared not just to palming off junk, but to selling junk as a glorification of the consumers' ignorance, gleaned from her very own "buying trends" in her own badly-lived life. This is achieved by the promotion of producers of objects as experts at living, experts because they "bring good things to life," while the consumer can only buy things ready-made.

Anna Deavere Smith

INTRODUCTION TO
FIRES
IN THE
MIRROR

Anna Deavere Smith is an actress and professor of theater at Stanford University. She is renowned for her one-woman plays Fires in the Mirror, *about the Crown Heights incident, and* Twilight: Los Angeles, 1992, *about the Los Angeles riots. In the following selection, she describes the theory on which she has constructed these plays, the view that ordinary people produce their own poetry in everyday speech.*

Fires in the Mirror is a part of a series of theater (or performance) pieces called On the Road: A Search for American Character, which I create by interviewing people and later performing them using their own words. My goal has been to find American character in the ways that people speak. When I started this project, in the early 1980s, my simple introduction to anyone I interviewed was, "If you give me an hour of your time, I'll invite you to see yourself performed." At that time I was not as interested in performance or in social commentary as I was in experimenting with language and its relationship to character.

I was trained as an actress in a conservatory, which at the time placed emphasis on classical training. On the Road is about contemporary life. It's ironic that it was inspired by classical training. Words have always held a particular power for me. I remember leafing through a book of Native American poems one morning while I was waiting for my Shakespeare class to begin and being struck by a phrase from the preface, "The word, the word above all, is truly magical, not only by its meaning, but by its artful manipulation."

This quote, which I added to my journal, reminded me of something my grandfather had told me when I was a girl: "If you say a word often enough it becomes your own." I added that phrase to my journal next to the quote about the magic of words. When I traveled home to Baltimore for my grandfather's funeral a year after my journal entry, I mentioned my grandfather's words to my father. He corrected me. He told me that my

Anna Deavere Smith, *Fires in the Mirror* (New York: Anchor, 1993) xxiii–xli.

grandfather had actually said, "If you say a word often enough, it *becomes* you." I was still a student at the time, but I knew even then, even before I had made a conscious decision to teach as well as act, that my grandfather's words would be important.

I began a series of conversations with my Shakespeare teacher, Juanita Rice, who was brilliant and inspiring. In the first class she talked about speech as an action. She asked us to consider speech in Shakespeare as thought and stressed the importance of thinking on the word, rather than between the words in order to discover the character. She told us to take any fourteen lines of Shakespeare and to repeat the passage over and over again until something happened. No thinking. Just speaking. I chose a speech of Queen Margaret's from Richard III. The Queen says to the Duchess of York:

> From forth the kennel of thy womb hath crept
> A hell hound that doth hunt us all to death
> That dog that had its teeth before his eyes
> To worry lambs and lap their gentle blood
> That foul defacer of God's handiwork
> That excellent grand tyrant of the earth
> That reigns in galled eyes of weeping souls
> Thy womb let loose to chase us to our graves.

I followed Juanita's instructions, saying the fourteen lines over and over well into the wee hours of the morning. I didn't know enough at the time about Queen Margaret, or about Shakespeare to realize that what I had been repeating was very strong language, which was bound to evoke powerful images. In one evening I had traveled to a very dark and decadent world. The speed with which this happened had everything to do with the power of the words. It had everything to do with how the words themselves had worked on *me. I had not controlled the words. I had presented myself as an empty vessel, a repeater, and they had shown their power.* I was soon to learn about the power of rhythm and imagery to evoke the spirit of a character, of a play, of a time.

I then started thinking that if I listened carefully to people's words, and particularly to their rhythms, that I could use language to learn about my own time. If I could find a way to really inhabit the words of those around me, like I had inhabited those of Queen Margaret, that I could learn about the spirit, the imagination, and the challenges of my own time, firsthand.

Actors are very impressionable people, or some would say, suggestible people. We are trained to develop aspects of our memories that are more emotional and sensory than intellectual. The general public often wonders how actors remember their lines. What's more remarkable to me, is how actors remember, recall, and reiterate feelings and sensations. The body has a memory just as the mind does. The heart has a memory, just as the mind does. The act of speech is a physical act. It is powerful enough that it can create, with the rest of the body, a kind of cooperative dance. That dance is a sketch of something that is inside a person, and not fully revealed by the words alone. I came to realize that if I were able to record part of the dance—that is, the spoken part—and reenact it, the rest of the body would follow. I could then create the illusion of being another person by reenacting something they had said *as they had said it.* Using my grandfather's idea that if I said a word often enough it would *become* me, the reenactment, or the reiteration of a person's words would also teach me about that person.

I had been trained in the tradition of acting called "psychological realism." A basic tenet of psychological realism is that characters live inside of you and that you create a character through a process of realizing your own similarity to the character. When I later became a teacher of acting, I began to become more and more troubled by the self-oriented method. I began to look for ways to engage my students in putting themselves in other people's shoes. This went against the grain of the tradition, which was to get the character to walk in the *actor's shoes*. It became less and less interesting intellectually to bring the dramatic literature of the world into a classroom of people in their late teens and twenties, and to explore it within the framework of their real lives. Aesthetically it seemed limited, because most of the times the characters all sounded the same. Most characters spoke somewhere inside the rhythmic range of the students. More troubling was that this method left an important bridge out of acting. The spirit of acting is the *travel* from the self to the other. This "self-based" method seemed to come to a spiritual halt. It saw the self as the ultimate home of the character. To me, the search for character is constantly in motion. It is a quest that moves back and forth between the self and the other.

I needed evidence that you could find a character's psychological reality by "inhabiting" that character's words. I needed evidence of the limitations of basing a character on a series of metaphors from an actor's real life. I wanted to develop an alternative to the self-based technique, a technique that would begin with the other and come to the self, a technique that would empower the other to find the actor rather than the other way around. I needed very graphic evidence that the manner of speech could be a mark of individuality. If we were to inhabit the speech pattern of another, and walk in the speech of another, we could find the individuality of the other and experience that individuality viscerally. I became increasingly convinced that the activity of reenactment could tell us as much, if not more, about another individual than the process of learning about the other by using the self as a frame of reference. The frame of reference for the other would *be* the other. Learning about the other by being the other requires the use of all aspects of memory, the memory of the body, mind, and heart, as well as the words.

The last fifteen to twenty years have given the public consciousness an extended vocabulary for the self. This vocabulary fed the popularity of self-oriented techniques. I think that a vocabulary which is at once political, intellectual, sentimental, visceral, and social would bring life to art. The creation of the On the Road project required that I have a way of thinking that involved multiple vocabularies.

Trying to do other-oriented work also raised some questions which may interest the general public. Any of us who engage in extroverted activities are aware of our inhibitions. I am interested in how inhibitions affect our ability to empathize. If I have an inhibition about *acting* like a man, it may also point to an inhibition I have about *seeing* a man or *hearing* a man. To develop a voice one must develop an ear. To complete an action, one must have a clear vision. Does the inability to empathize start with an inhibition, or a reluctance to see? Do racism and prejudice instruct those inhibitions? If I passed out a piece of poetry to be read by a racially mixed group and I asked them to read it with an English accent, most of them would try. If I passed out a piece of Black poetry written in dialect, many would be inhibited and fearful of offending others. In a playwriting class, I gave an exercise called "gang writing." Students were asked to write short scenes about gangs inspired by gang writing. A student raised the question, "Isn't it offensive for us, here in our privileged environment, to write about gangs?" Does privilege mean one shouldn't *see*? At the same time, the standard for excellence is still a Eurocentric theater written by and for white men. Who else can participate? How? Does it mean new plays? Does it mean rethinking old plays? The mirrors of society do not mirror society.

"Who has the right to see what?" "Who has the right to say what?" "Who has the right to speak for whom?" These questions have plagued the contemporary theater.

These questions address both issues of employment equity and issues of *who is portrayed*. These questions are the questions that unsettle and prohibit a democratic theater in America. If only a man can speak for a man, a woman for a woman, a Black person for all Black people, then we, once again, inhibit the *spirit* of theater, which lives in the *bridge* that makes unlikely aspects *seem* connected. The bridge doesn't make them the same, it merely *displays* how two unlikely *aspects* are *related*. These relationships of the *unlikely*, these connections of things that don't fit together are crucial to American theater and culture if theater and culture plan to help us assemble our obvious differences. The self-centered technique has taken the bridge out of the process of creating character, it has taken metaphor out of acting. It has made the heart smaller, the spirit less gregarious, and the mind less apt to be able to hold on to contradictions or opposition.

At the time that I began my work, celebrity interviews exploded in popular culture. *Interview* magazine began publication at the very moment that I was beginning to experiment with some of these ideas. There were more television talk shows being produced, and real-life drama seemed to be a definite point of fascination for the public. I watched talk shows, and read print interviews, and eventually started to transcribe the television talk shows, and use them along with print interviews as scripts. I staged many of these interviews, looking for the moment in the interview when the celebrity was struggling with the interviewer to free his or her identity from the perception that interviewer had. . . .

Ultimately I began to conduct my own interviews. Talk shows and print interviews of celebrities were often battles between what the interviewer wanted to pretend to be uncovering and what the subject was willing to reveal. Sometimes the battle was authentic, and sometimes it was that the interviewer and the celebrity were in ca-

hoots to give the illusion that something new was on the brink of being uncovered. In fact, it's my experience now that public figures are frequently more difficult to use in my work, because it is less likely that they will say something that they have never said before. It is fully understandable that people who have a relationship to the media learn their way around an interview. The act of speech, then, does become performance rather than discovery. On the other hand, occasionally, public figures are so expert at this kind of performance that they have a greater gift than actors for making what they have said before seem as though they are saying it for the first time. . . .

My goal was to create an atmosphere in which the interviewee would experience his/her own authorship. Speaking teaches us what our natural "literature" is. In fact, everyone, in a given amount of time, will say something that is like poetry. The process of getting to that poetic moment is where "character" lives. If I were to reiterate the person's pursuit of that poetic moment, as well as the poetic moment itself, I could "go into character." The pursuit is frequently filled with *uhs* and *ums* and, in fact, the wrong words, if any words at all, and almost always what would be considered "bad grammar." I suppose much of communication could be narrowed down to "the point." This project is not about a point, it is about a route. It is *on* the road. Character lives in the linguistic road as well as the destination.

In the midst of doing the original experiments with language I became very interested in performing. Some of my students were extremely receptive to this work, and very dedicated. Others didn't see its value, and were very committed to the discovery of themselves. They believed that they couldn't be someone else until they knew themselves. My argument was, and still is, that it doesn't have to be either/or, and that neither comes first. The discovery of human behavior can happen in motion. It can be a process of moving from the self to the other and the other to the self. Nevertheless, my argument didn't always sink in. For example, I arranged to have a student of mine meet a person I had interviewed for her to perform. My student spent the entire evening talking about herself. Ideally, she would have used the time to listen and learn everything she could about the woman she was going to portray. This actor, like others I worked with, was actually awkward when meeting the people she would later portray and frightened to have them come to the performance. Was her talking about herself to her subject a declaration of her own identity? Was it a last-ditch effort to say "I am" before saying "You are"?

I decided to abandon the experiment designed for the classroom, and to work out my hypotheses on myself as a performer. I knew that by using another person's language, it was possible to portray what was invisible about that individual. It struck me that this could work on a social level as well as an individual level. Could language also be a photograph of what was unseen about society just as it reflects what is unseen in an individual?

The project took shape during a time that many institutions were going through identity shifts with regard to gender and ethnicity. I had commissions to create pieces in some institutions that were in transformation. One of the people I interviewed early in the process was a Provost at Princeton University, who pointed out to me that there was a tension between the perception of a place, which is frequently embedded in traditions, and the moment-to-moment identity of a place. For me, the battle between those who prefer the perception of a place and those who claim to experience the reality as different from that, was dramatic. This battle adds up to an identity in motion, but a palpable identity nevertheless. . . .

There is a gap between the perception of a place and the individuals who are responsible for keeping that perception alive. The individuals inside are frequently fighting that their individual voices be heard, while the walls of the place, which are the mask, and the perception, are reluctant to give over to the voices of the individuals. Those in the margins are always trying to get to the center, and those at the center, frequently in the name of tradition, are trying to keep the margins at a distance. Part of the identity of a place is the tension between those in the margins, and those in the center, and they all live behind the walls which wear the tradition. I have been going to the places where this tension is evident to find American character. Can this tension be productive, or will it explode and in the process kill and maim those who happen to be in the wrong place at the wrong time? How can some of us intervene? My answer to the first question is yes, this tension can be productive, in so far as it causes motion, and that we watch and document that motion. To do that, we have to interest those people around us in motion, in moving from one side to the other, in experiencing one hand and the other hand, and to building bridges *between* places. My answer to the second question is that one kind of intervention is the intervention of listening. We can listen for what is inconsistent as well as for what is consistent. We can listen to what the dominant pattern of speech is, and we can listen for the break from that pattern of speech. This applies to individuals, and this applies to groups. The break from the pattern is where character lives, and where dialogue, ironically begins, in the *uh*, in the pause, in the thought as captured for the first time in a moment of speech, rather than in the rehearsed, the proven. Although this is a book, I must conclude by remarking that this project is at its heart, about the act of speech, the physical action of dialogue, and was not originally intended for the printed word. Our effort has been to try to document it in such a way that the act of speech is evident. . . .

During my search for character, I have learned much more than I set out to learn. I am still in the process of learning how the language of groups reflects the character of the group. Some of the same signals that apply with individuals may apply. In these times when we are rethinking cultural identity I am interested in the difficulty people have in talking about race and talking about difference. This difficulty goes across race, class, and political lines. I am interested in the lack of words and mistrustful of the ease with which some people seem to pick up new words and mix them in with the old. The new words seem to get old quickly. This means to me that we do not have a language that serves us as a group. I think that there is a gap between those who are heard and those who speak. Those who really speak in their own communities, to their own people, are not heard as frequently as those who speak on a regular basis with authority. The media most often goes to experts to learn about difference. My sense is that American character lives not in one place or the other, but in the gaps between the places, and in our struggle to be together in our differences. It lives not in what has been fully articulated, but in what is in the process of being articulated, not in the smooth-sounding words, but in the very moment that the smooth-sounding words fail us. It is alive right now. We might not like what we see, but in order to change it, we have to see it clearly.

DISCUSSION QUESTIONS

1. Do you think the distinction between fine and popular art is a useful distinction? How would you differentiate between the two?
2. Why do you think amateur photography is so popular? Do you agree with Sontag's view that we consider photography a magical enterprise? What do you take with you when you take a photograph on a vacation?
3. Is it immoral to laugh at a comedian slipping on a banana peel? Why or why not? Are the Three Stooges a bad influence on their audience? Why or why not?
4. What everyday phenomena are sources of aesthetic experience for you? What about them occasions aesthetic experience?
5. Do you think that your most significant experiences are unified by aesthetic qualities, as Dewey suggests? Do aesthetic criteria like closure and organic structure apply to experiences in everyday life? Think of examples.
6. Do you think that efforts at self-beautification typically reflect our sense of bodily intimacy with our world, or do you think they reflect something else? Are these efforts desirable or undesirable? Explain.
7. Do you think aesthetic delight of the sort Shōnagon expresses and describes is important in a person's life? Why or why not?
8. Do you think that domestic aesthetic judgments are comparable to moral judgments? If so, in what ways? Do you think preferences in food indicate anything about a person or society's character? Explain.
9. Have you ever found a person's everyday speech to be poetically powerful? If so, describe the experience. Why did you find it moving?

FURTHER READING

High Art/Low Art

Cohen, Ted. "High and Low Thinking about High and Low Art." *Journal of Aesthetics and Art Criticism* 51.2 (1993): 151–56.

Collingwood, Robin G. *The Principles of Art.* New York: Oxford UP, 1958.

Kaplan, Abraham. "The Aesthetics of the Popular Arts." *Journal of Aesthetics and Art Criticism* 24 (1966): 351–64.

Novitz, David. *The Boundaries of Art.* Philadelphia: Temple UP, 1992.

Paz, Octavio. *In Praise of Hands: Contemporary Crafts of the World.* Greenwich: New York Graphic Society, 1974.

Shusterman, Richard. *Pragmatist Aesthetics: Living Beauty, Rethinking Art.* Oxford: Basil Blackwell, 1992.

Mundane Life and Aesthetics

Best, David. "The Aesthetic in Sport." *British Journal of Aesthetics* 14 (1974): 197–213.

Betterton, Rosemary. *Looking On: Images of Femininity in the Visual Arts and Media.* New York: Pandora, 1987.

Dewey, John. *Art as Experience.* New York: Capricorn, 1958.

Hollander, Anne. *Seeing through Clothes.* New York: Viking, 1978.

Humble, P. N. "Chess as an Art Form." *British Journal of Aesthetics* 33.1 (1993): 59–66.

Kupfer, Joseph H. *Experience as Art: Aesthetics in Everyday Life.* Albany: State U of New York P, 1983.

McDermott, John. *The Culture of Experience.* New York: New York UP, 1976.

Morreall, John. *Taking Laughter Seriously.* Albany: State U of New York P, 1983.

Novitz, David. "Love, Friendship, and the Aesthetics of Character." *American Philosophical Quarterly* 28.3 (1991): 207–16.

Quinet, Marienne L. "Food as Art: The Problem of Function." *British Journal of Aesthetics* 21.2 (1981): 159–71.

Wolf, Naomi. *The Beauty Myth: How Images of Beauty Are Used against Women.* New York: Vintage, 1990.

Popular Culture and the Mass Media

Cavell, Stanley. *The World Viewed: Reflections on the Ontology of Film.* Enl. ed. Cambridge: Harvard UP, 1979.

Fiske, John. *Television Culture.* London: Routledge, 1987.

Gans, Herbert. *Popular Culture and High Culture.* New York: Basic Books, 1974.

Miller, Mark Crispin. *Boxed In: The Culture of TV.* Evanston: Northwestern UP, 1988.

Newcomb, Horace, ed. *Television: The Critical View.* New York: Oxford University Press, 1994.

Novitz, David. "Ways of Artmaking: The High and the Popular in Art." *British Journal of Aesthetics* 29.3 (1989): 213–29.

Parkes, Graham. "Reflections on Projections: Changing Conditions in Watching Film." *Journal of Aesthetic Education* 21 (1987): 77–82.

Rosenberg, Bernard, and David Manning White, eds. *Mass Culture: The Popular Arts in America.* Glencoe: Free Press, 1957.

Sontag, Susan. *On Photography.* New York: Farrar, Straus, & Giroux, 1977.

Wicke, Peter. *Rock Music: Culture, Aesthetics, and Sociology.* New York: Cambridge UP, 1990.

PART IV

BEYOND
THE
WEST

AESTHETICS AROUND
THE WORLD

Most of this text has been concerned with aesthetics in the Western world. Other societies, however, have their own ideas about aesthetic values, some similar and some quite different from those in our tradition. The articles in this chapter offer introductions to some of the aesthetics of other cultures, including some subcultures within our own society.

Isidore Okpewho indicates some of the artistic standards that inform the creation and criticism of art in Africa. Okpewho takes issue with those anthropologists who, in attempting to connect African art with the African worldview, interpret art primarily in terms of ritualistic function. The playful and imaginative character of African art is at least as prominent as religious function, and ritualistic effectiveness does not necessarily depend on artistic merit. Moreover, African artists infuse their own originality into their art, even when portraying or recounting traditional myths. Art is understood by Africans to be a dynamic project of recreating the life of the myth, not a matter of mere repetition.

Okpewho also observes that imitation is an important value in African art, but imitation is not all focused on everyday appearances. Artists also attempt to depict "the spirit-regarding order" in a realistic and vivid manner. Although somewhat stylized, such representations are imitations of mythic beings, and they are understood to be realistic. The presence of the natural environment is also suggested, if rather subtly.

Christopher Small considers some of the differences between musical aesthetic values of the West and those of Africa. Unlike the music of the Western tradition, which emphasizes harmony and fidelity to precomposed scores, sub-Saharan African music emphasizes rhythm and improvization. In addition, Small observes, African music-making is a matter of community participation, while Western music more typically involves expert musicians performing for audiences.

The philosophical perspective of a culture is often reflected in its aesthetic values. Kuang-Ming Wu describes the relevance of the *yin–yang* distinction, which is basic to Chinese philosophy, for an understanding of Chinese aesthetics. This duality indicates a more dominant (*yang*) and a less dominant (*yin*) member of any particular relationship. This distinction is flexible and adaptable to various types of relationship, and it is used to reflect the fact that a thing or person that is dominant in one relationship may be subordinate in another. *Yin* and *yang* imply the mutuality of a relationship as well as a distinction within it, and Wu emphasizes that Chinese art aims to express the interplay of opposition and mutuality in all things. Even the artist and the subject matter are not considered opposite poles of the process of painting. The painter's own being becomes one with what is painted, and the Chinese see expressions of both within a painting.

Patrick McKee indicates another way that Chinese painting exhibits the mutuality of a person with the world. McKee focuses on a particular type of Chinese painting, that of the mountain landscape. Such landscapes are associated with old age and the wisdom that is supposed to accompany it. McKee observes, for example, that elderly scholars are often portrayed as listening to waterfalls, which combine change and constancy. This image reflects the scholar's insight into the interplay of opposites that is fundamental to reality, according to Chinese philosophy.

Japanese culture is pervaded by a characteristic aesthetic sensibility. Donald Keene describes several tendencies that are typical expressions of the Japanese aesthetic. The Japanese place great aesthetic value on suggestion, irregularity, simplicity, and perishability. Keene sees evidence of these values not only in Japanese art, but in everyday life and ritual as well. Japanese gardens, the famous tea ceremony, even the Japanese style of dining and using flowers reflect these preferences, according to Keene.

As in China and Japan, the conception of aesthetic experience in India is shaped by the culture's philosophical thought. B. N. Goswamy describes the Indian ideal of aesthetic experience. Indian thought considers *rasa*, meaning taste or savor, to be the central component of aesthetic experience. Involving a particular emotional tone, *rasa* is most completely experienced as a state of supreme delight, or bliss. This condition is not achieved by everyone, however. The viewer's own sensitivity, awareness, and imagination determine the extent of an artwork's effect. Ultimately, aesthetic experience depends on the viewer's spiritual condition, which optimally involves a dissolution of one's awareness of self and absorption in supreme reality.

Like the art of many other religious traditions, that of the Islamic world reflects its religious beliefs. Zuheir Al-Faquih explains the artistic tendencies of art throughout the Islamic world by relating them to Islamic doctrine. Of particular importance is the belief in the *tauhid*, or the unity of God, who is manifest everywhere. Islamic art's characteristic decorative pattern, the arabesque, is composed of a single unending line, and it serves as an artistic expression of the *tauhid* doctrine. The abstract character of Islamic art is also religiously motivated. Muslims consider depiction to be a form of prideful competition with God, the Creator, and thus opposed to Islam, which is literally "submission to God."

If cultural and religious belief are commonly expressed through art, perhaps art can help different cultures understand one another. The idea that art can assist cultural dialogue is defended by numerous anthropologists. Steven Feld contends, for instance, that basic cultural tendencies are reflected in the musical aesthetics of the Kaluli tribe in Papua New Guinea. Central to the Kaluli aesthetic is the attempt to achieve *dulugu ganalan,* which Feld translates as *"lift-up-over sounding."* The Kaluli prefer dense textures of overlapping voices, and they consider the sounds of natural forces (such as waterfalls) to be among the voices in a musical texture. These preferences reveal a view of art that contrasts with the Western perspective. The Kaluli do not separate art from the rest of the environment, nor do they take detached contemplation to be an aesthetic ideal. By contrast with Western music that is coordinated under the authoritarian leadership of a conductor, music for the Kaluli is freely participatory. Feld argues that the Kaluli aesthetic reflects the relatively egalitarian social structure of its society, in which individuals are encouraged to engage in activity with others not directed by some central authority.

Besides reflecting and maintaining a society's understanding of itself, art may also reveal a society's basic beliefs about the nature of reality. Inga Clendinnen describes the metaphysical views of the Aztecs of pre-Columbian Mexico, which were profoundly aesthetic in character. The Aztecs considered the world itself to be a painted book, a continual creation of a divine artist. Aesthetic sensitivity to nature, accordingly, was considered to be a kind of worship of the gods, while human art-making was thought to mirror divine creation. In striking contrast with Plato's view that art's emphasis on semblance was a distraction from reality, the Aztecs thought that semblance was the primary vehicle for gaining insight into reality. The philosophical character of artistic representation is reflected in Aztec pictorial style, which reveals a tension between the abstract and the concrete and "a kind of surrealism achieved by dislocation," according to Clendinnen.

Oriana Baddeley and Valerie Fraser also refer to surrealism in connection with Latin America, but they refer directly to the surrealistic art movement of Europe. They observe that the vocabulary of surrealistic art has seemed particularly amenable to many Latin American artists. Surrealistic strategies include the use of juxtapositions to suggest the character of dreams and to suggest simultaneous attraction and antagonism (often by means of male and female imagery). In particular, such strategies seem apt for expressing the inherently contradictory character of Latin America's postcolonial experience and its mixed inheritance of traditions. Surrealistic techniques accommodate the inclusion of elements of indigenous Latin American culture along with cultural influences from other sources.

Navajo aesthetic thought considers art to be continuous with nature. Gary Witherspoon observes that beauty is understood as the nature of all good things, and thus the personal goal of every individual. The Navajo seeks to find beauty in the self and to project it outward. Artistic activity is a part of this larger project. The intimate connection between art and everyday life is evident in such arts as sand-painting and singing (which are believed to have healing powers) and the weaving of blankets (which are worn for warmth, beauty, and power). The Navajo aims to "walk in beauty," conceived as the ideal mode of relationship to the rest of the world.

Isidore Okpewho

PRINCIPLES OF TRADITIONAL AFRICAN ART

*Isidore Okpewho teaches in the English department of
the University of Ibadan, Nigeria. He specializes in
oral literature.*

Those who look for religion or world-view behind everything in traditional art have often ignored the basic *play* interest of the artist. Thus in nearly every study of traditional African art, nothing whatsoever is said about the numerous pieces of phallic or erotic sculpture that can be found in many African villages which have a lively tradition of plastic art. Where mention is made of such pieces, there is usually an effort to connect them with rites of initiation or of fertility, which are happily treated as "religious." Nor, in the countless anthologies with which the market of African folklore is glutted, do we find very much by way of ribald verse; yet ask any youth in a typical African village to recite you his favorite verses, and the chances are the majority of them have to do with sex.

An even more illuminating fact is that, in some of the more popular African tales which have anything to do with traditional religion, the religious element is frequently superseded by the play interest of the narrator, especially in the fervid context of the open performance. A useful illustration of this interest is provided by *The Mwindo Epic*. In fact, this tale gives considerable support to the scepticism of those who have held that there is little connection between myth and religion (or even what Emile Durkheim has called the "collective conscience"). Mwindo's pursuit of his errant father takes him mostly through the underworld regions, and the quest is obstructed by two hostile divinities, Muisa and Sheburungu; the latter of these, as the editors of the epic tell us, is "one of the epithets under which the supreme divinity of fire, Nyamurairi, is known." These are not inconsequential figures of a vague pantheon, but deities accompanied by the full appurtenances of worship. They are grouped along with other gods in the Nyanga cult system, and of them we are told:

> All these divinities, together with the ancestors, are known under the generic term *bashumbu*. Shrines are made and plantains are grown for them, women are dedicated and married to them, sheep and hunting

Isidore Okpewho, "Principles of Traditional African Art," *Journal of Aesthetics and Art Criticism* 35.3 (1977): 301–13.

dogs are consecrated to them, prayers are said to them, and distinctive cultural paraphernalia for each of them are kept by their adepts. They manifest themselves in dreams and oracles and are responsible for good and evil in Nyanga life."

Thus among the Nyanga, at least, it would be considered preposterous for anyone (unless he was himself a divinity, and Mwindo is not a divinity) to be portrayed as contending against and overcoming the gods of the traditional pantheon. But Mwindo gets into a severe physical confrontation with Muisa. In the first round, Muisa levels Mwindo with his magic belt (*karemba*). Mwindo recovers, and with the aid of his own magic *conga*-scepter, smashes Muisa to the ground. With Sheburungu there is only a battle of wits—the *wiki* game. The god wins against Mwindo; but the hero, finding that ordinary human wits are of no use against a divinity, throws his magic *conga*-scepter into the bargain and wins.

For a human character to fight and win against a divinity is, we must agree, contrary to the spirit in which a society' religious life is conducted. Even when Mwindo is translated into the sky by the lightning-god Nkuba and warned against further heroic excesses, the warning is unconnected with his fights and victories against Muisa and Sheburungu, particularly as Nkuba himself had helped Mwindo part of the way in those confrontations. Again, let us look closely at Nkuba's conduct in this connection. Early in the story he takes sides with the enemies of Mwindo, but the hero always wins. Then Nkuba turns and becomes an ally of the hero in his struggles with some of his other enemies including Muisa and Sheburungu. But the final confrontation with Nkuba comes when Mwindo kills a dragon which is sacred to Nkuba, and consequently incurs the anger of his erstwhile ally. Though the denouement of the story seems to portray the hero as an overreacher, it is evident that the case for this rests only on his offense against Nkuba, and does not at all include his earlier acts of ostensible "impiety." The explanation offered by the editors, that "there was an excuse for the hero as long as he was the victim of his father's unjust decisions and actions," is inadequate. Sheburungu, over whom the hero had earlier triumphed, is, as the same editors tell us, the supreme creator-god as well as god of fire; and there is really nothing in the tale or in the editorial notes that puts Nkuba in a superior position to Sheburungu in the Nyanga cult system.

The implications are quite obvious, particularly if we take into consideration, as we should, the lively context of the heroic song. In the live, bubbling atmosphere wherein the Mwindo has been performed, what was normally a matter of serious concern for the community has become subject to the play instincts of the artist. We may not go so far as Lévi-Strauss in maintaining that "myths operate in men's minds without their being aware of the fact"; for those obtrusive "religious" details and strophic comments which punctuate the song argue a certain presence of mind. But it is quite clear that, in this mythopoeic context, both the bard and his audience have been drawn into an experience not altogether germane to the spirit of worship or ritual. The figures of the cult belief have been subjected to patterns of behavior which tend sometimes to detract from the awe in which they are traditionally held, especially in a tale like Mwindo whose dramatic resources are evidently as much comical as serious. An audience treated to such a song will in no way consider its pious instincts offended by the bard's strange picture, particularly when they reflect that the human beings with whom the gods are fabled to be contending are not exactly like their next-door neighbors. True, in their theological beliefs they know that the gods are responsible for evil as well as good, and indeed the whimsical nature of the gods which is revealed by these songs may well mirror some of their convictions. But they are unaccustomed, in their sober theological thinking, to conceive of divinity in the peculiar dramatic circumstances in which the myth-maker puts it, and are well content to grant a heart-warming evening's performance the benefit of its strange content and outlook. Clearly in such a situation, the artistic play-drive has got the better of the religious instinct.

———◆◆◆———

Religion and ritual are not unimportant in the evolution of African art. What is objectionable is the popular notion that religion is always the starting point. In those areas where art of a truly imaginative quality flourished in the environment of ritual, ritual was merely the culminating point of the creative will. The artist had previously been carving tools and ordering his homestead. The people liked what they saw, and thereafter enlisted the artist to arrest for them in a concrete and harmonized manner the myriad forms around which their daily life and thought revolved. There was first the private creative will, which was then harnessed to give concrete meaning to the sacred communal weal; art in fact brought ritual into being. In the verbal arts, the primacy of talent is attested to by observations like the following from Babalola:

> It is only those who have a natural flair for ijala-chanting who successfully go through their period of apprenticeship. Failures are not uncommon among these apprentices. No ijala pupil-artist embarks on this course of training merely because he is ordered to do so by his father or mother or other superior. It is generally assumed that compulsion will merely ensure the failure of a pupil learning ijala-chanting. Over and over again the ijala artists interviewed by the author came out with the declaration . . . "It was because I longed to be able to chant ijala beautifully that I voluntarily went to a master ijala-artist and requested him to take me on as a pupil."

Let us examine briefly some of the dynamic principles and atmosphere determining the productivity of the working artist. To be sure, one cannot be exhaustive in this regard: not the least of our limitation is the fact that we are too far removed from the roots of that art to make any pretentious claims. But we can, at least, reach some tentative conclusions.

THE MIMETIC PRINCIPLE

Much of what we might conjecture to be the creative outlook of the traditional African artist would ultimately depend on what we thought was his society's view of reality. Does reality exist *out there* in some kind of "circumambient air" (to borrow from Hulme), and does the artist place his creative powers at the mercy of a formless infinitude, an intangible world of abstractions? Or does reality exist instead in the realm of human experience, whereby the artist could seek to explain the nature of the unknown and the supernatural? In view of what I have identified as the traditional society's pressing sense of the real, the desire to have "the inapprehensible world grasped," it seems logical to suggest that it has human experience as its fundamental frame of reference. For art this will mean that, though he accepts and respects a metaphysical order, the artist reduces the abstractions to recognizable form in due proportions. The traditional African artist is thus first and foremost a realist artist. But he operates on two levels of realism.

The first level relates to objects of the visible, physical world treated in their just features and characteristics. Under this category can be brought much of the portrait type of art such as Ife and Benin lavishly offer—kings, queens, and queen mothers, and so forth. Portrait art is also known elsewhere in Africa: among the

Bakuba of Zaire and the Baule of the Ivory Coast, to name just a few cases. The element of direct realism in portrait art is employed in the representation of many aspects of experience. There are, for instance, the funeral heads among the Ashanti of Ghana. From Benin again we have several naturalistic portraits of horse soldiers, hunters and their animals, and the like. We need hardly emphasize the overwhelming sense of realism that Benin and Ife reflect: the care taken over facial marks, beads and bangles by their numbers, the insignia of office, coats of mail, stoles in their proper lengths, and so on. No metaphysical qualms here; just plain reality in its striking outlines.

But the artist has a further level of realism for what has been called "the spirit-regarding order." Art critics have repeatedly and erroneously called this kind of art "abstract." But in this category of art, the traditional artist is addressing himself not to ideas as such, or abstractions, but to spirits and deities vividly conceived. The distinction is worth emphasizing, because abstraction properly belongs to an age that has lost considerable faith in the perceptible real—an age, as it were, of disbelief. Those horrendous shapes that feature in the folk myth and the plastic arts are as real as the forests and the sequestered shrines that they inhabit. The *chi wara* of the Bambara is not simply "fecundity" as an abstract idea; it was a spirit sent down by the Creator to promote fecundity. But, although you cannot accurately picture a spirit, the Bambara have too vivid a sense of the real to be lost in imprecisions. So they portray the *chi wara* in the stylized form of a denizen of the fecund environment, the antelope, worn as a mask during their ritual dances.

It would be mistaken to call a figure abstract simply because it combined selective images in a composite form and was treated with some stylization. Those figures are vivid elements of a people's living myth.

Allecto with serpents for her hair is not an abstract idea of fury; she *is* a Fury. The same applies to our ceremonial masks. They are the artist's vivid portrait of an ancestral or a genial presence—the figures, as Senghor tells us in his "Prayer to Masks," *through whom the spirit breathes.* But since the artist cannot claim exact knowledge of the outlines of a spirit's physiognomy, he endeavors to strike a just balance between his limitations and his sense of the real; those masks are a biomorphic response to the various forms and natures of the spirits concerned. It is remarkable how close those portraits of spirits can be. Margaret Trowell has made the following observation on the *Sakapu* society in the Ijo country of southern Nigeria:

> The members performed a most elaborate system of plays in honor of the Owu or water spirits. After sacrifices, with feasting and dancing, the Owu are asked to come forth from their home under the sea and to be present at the rites. The head-dresses are said to represent the Owu when they were last seen.

Surely, to label such an effort as "abstract" is to misunderstand the tremendous closeness and empathy which the traditional artist feels towards his subject. Abstraction is a disengagement—Eliot has the right phrase in "dissociation of sensibility"—and the traditional artist puts hardly a distance between him and the vivid throng of presences that he feels around him. "Abstract," it is true, is only a formal label: but used of traditional art it fails to take due account of the attitude that gave birth to such art.

Something of this kind of realism is also observable in oral literature. On the other hand, there is the vivid, naturalistic portrait of the animal world whose livelihood is so closely tied to that of man. This portrait has a typically anthropomorphic touch to it, especially in the dialogues. But overall, a remarkable pattern of verisimilitude is maintained. The clever tortoise overplays his hand, but has the last laugh on his captors anyway; he swears he loves nothing better than to be dropped in boiling oil, but wails that a cool stream would be the death of him. He is dropped into a cool stream, and escapes. The dog's habit of dillydallying on his way is given a tragic turn when he fails man on a mission of immortality. A misguided sense of kindness brings upon the billy-goat the fate originally intended for the tortoise. The catalog of such tales is endless. The subjects may belong to a non-human realm, but they are treated with such interest and intimacy that the line of distinction virtually disappears.

Man is also observed in his own integral circumstances, and his successes and failures are seen in terms of his courage or of his moral shortcomings. Stories of conflicts between communities abound in this kind of portraiture. There are few metaphysical or theological implications underlying the details, simply an interest in man's grim confrontation with his not-so-gracious fellows. Daniel Kunene bears witness to this category of realism in his study of the oral poetry relating to the legendary world of Moshoeshoe:

> The heroes are not superior beings except in so far as their earthy deeds make them so, least of all are they gods or descendants of gods. They do not possess supernatural powers, or do battle against other worldly creatures such as monsters and demons. They do not go on adventures to worlds beyond that of man. Nor are they wont to provide lavish feasts in palatial mansions. In short, they are ordinary human beings engaged in ordinary human activities. Not seldom, however, the poet, in the vividness of his imagination, uses metaphor, imagery, and symbolism which transport these ordinary activities to a level of extraordinariness, and the hero is often described as fighting against monsters, or as being himself a monster or other terrible creature destroying his opponents. But this is never meant to be more than figurative.

However, a good deal of the traditional literature of Africa—at least the bulk of it in which one might recognize a truly imaginative touch—explores this very idea of "adventure to worlds beyond that of man." We do not need to linger here over the ease with which the artist conceives his setting and peoples it with all manner of shapes, nor the easy spatial links which he establishes between the world of spirits and that of man. What has been said of the plastic arts holds true here: those myriad wraiths and trolls are as germane to the artist's sense of concrete presences as the thicket in the backyard. But perhaps the most significant aspect of the realism in this connection is the tremendous empathy which the bard establishes between himself and the subjects of his tale, especially the hero. In the various epics, for instance, that one reads from diverse reaches of sub-Saharan Africa, one is struck by a pattern of narration in which the pronouns seem happily confused. . . .

THE ECOLOGY OF ART

. . . There is a subtle but discernible relationship between art and the landscape out of which it grows. If we can concede that the earliest art was a response to the immediate pressures of man's living conditions—whether these pressures took the form of hunger, threat to life, or any other form—then it will become clear why the environment would make any difference to the forms or the quality of art. And it would appear that a good deal of the aesthetic nourishment of traditional African art derived from the nature of the surrounding landscape and the concomitant throb of animate company within it.

The griot of old Mali thus spoke well within aesthetic reason when he made a connection between the uncomplicated clarity of the native speech and the lean vegetation of the surrounding savanna. In a rather subtle way, the legends from the savanna country reflect this leanness. A good illustration of this point is the fact that, in these legends, the scope of heroic action is considerably limited. Consider the idea of the entry into the Otherworld. We find something close to this notion in *Sundiata*, at that point where the hero pursues the vanquished Soumaoro until the latter disappears into a "black cavern" in Mount Koulikoro. There the pursuit ends, as Sundiata gapes helplessly at the mouth of the cave. There seems much greater bravado in the forest country. We might safely conjecture that there Sundiata would have been made to carry the fight with Soumaoro into the underworld. There are hardly any restraints on the hero of the forest country, as the extra-terrestrial exploits of Fagunwa's Akara-Ogun, Tutuola's Drinkard, and Rureke's Mwindo witness.

There is also a correspondingly greater belief in life, in forest legends, than in those from the savanna country, as the *Kambili* epic and *Sundiata* indicate. One is struck by a certain haunting and elliptical effect to the whole narrative, an oppressive sense of loss, of decline, and of death. The same effect is noticeable in Northern Nigerian tales when compared with corresponding pieces from the south of the country. There are jinns and daemons, of course, but nothing to compare in extravagance, variety, and ebullience with the figures in , say, Yoruba mythology. In the main, the tales from the forest country tend to explore a victory over death as over its forces, and reflect the throb, lushness, and élan of the organic life and fellowship around them. It is perhaps no accident of detail that, whereas in *Kambili* the dominant sentiment is that "all things that stand eventually lie down," in *Mwindo* it is that "whatever sleeps shall wake." . . .

We can trace a corresponding influence of ecology on traditional African plastic art. There is a certain elegance in the proportionally long and slender antelope figures, masks, and even ancestral figures that dominate the art of the Bambara and the Dogon of the arid Western Sudan, and the landscape has much to do with these forms. The vegetation is thin and low, and the animal as well as human figures stand out in slender relief against the background of scanty bush. This is arguably the underlying principle behind those long, lean horns and headwear; the stylization only heightens the effect. Indeed, there is little in the savanna flora that would supply the kind of stout and lusty wooden material necessary for robust or rotund figures. Yet it is noteworthy what happens as the vegetation begins to thicken. Immediately south of the Bambara are the Senufo, whose representative pieces have a fleshiness somewhat greater than could be found in the art of their northern neighbors. Again, this is largely because the forests are slightly thicker, the organic life fuller. The rotundity becomes complete as we come to the Ngere-Wobe, south toward the Atlantic coast. Ecology thus provides further explanation of the realism of traditional African art. Labels such as "abstract" are therefore misleading in describing the work of artists for whom matter and manner are too starkly unified.

TRADITION AND ORIGINALITY

The problem of tradition and individual talent is one that has engaged several generations of critics, though we have not often drawn the right distinctions between the literate artist's and the unlettered artist's views of tradition. It may, of course, be that scholars have today agreed upon an understanding of tradition as a pattern of growth rather than as a rigid invariable. But though we can reasonably trace the historical origins of literate art, we cannot safely do the same for the unlettered kind; which makes it that much more difficult to establish the relationship which the traditional artist's talent bears to works which his community has come to accept as standards of artistic performance.

We can perhaps trace the artistic portraits of Julius Caesar's life to the records of that life in ancient Roman literature. But since we cannot accurately date the origin of the myths of the *chi wara* of the Bambara, or the *ibeji* of the Yoruba, it becomes something of an academic exercise for us to talk of standards in examining various plastic representations of these myths, however old some of them might happen to be; and how do we tell one version of a tortoise-tale from another, if neither of them contains any details that are historically datable?

The difficulty of judgment is particularly acute with the plastic arts. In an examination of the art surviving from the past, we have no artists' signatures to guide us in making the right distinctions between independent creations and those inspired by a "school" of creative thinking. . . . Artists whose works enjoyed no patronage or adoption were doomed to oblivion, as their pieces crumbled with their homesteads. This situation has led art historians and critics to consider those pieces housed in a shrine or a palace, or else excavated in the vicinities of these, as the definitive output of the community, forgetting that much more that did not conform to the fashionable styles of the "schools" might have been done. It would further appear that the exotic interest shown by foreign collectors of African art—going as far back perhaps as the early trading forays of the fifteenth century—has led to a weakening of the old creative integrity. As a result we can note the growth of a prosperous tourist industry catering to foreign wonder; for the honest creative genius, giving due imaginative expression to the intimate forms of a community's life, has yielded to cheap mercenary interests characterized by an unreflective haste to turn out mere photographic copies of chosen models, dishonestly dated. In his search for the truth, the judge of traditional African art is thus faced with a sore question: is the traditional African artist primarily a slave to model, or does he, like the truly imaginative leader of his people, seek first and foremost to give vitality and meaning to the community's life and myth with the aid of his creative vigor?

Since we cannot have full confidence in the silent pieces that deck the museum shelves, we must turn to the accounts of the careers of traditional artists. In his *Contemporary Art in Africa*, Ulli Beier gives an account of two artists who grew up in the old tradition, one in the service of ritual and the other under the patronage of the royal court. Yemi Bisiri of Oshogbo carves figures for the Ogboni society of the Yoruba, like his father before him. But he has had the courage to make an almost total break from the legacy of his father's days, not only in material (he works with brass instead of wood) but also in style (an almost gothic ornamentation as against the simplicity of the older figures). In Benin, Ovia Idah has made a considerable break from the old ways, using strange materials like ebony and cement instead of the traditional bronze and ivory, and exploring new forms which some of his peers find disturbing.

It is interesting to note that Idah's revolution has not been tolerated as calmly as Bisiri's. The reason for this can be found largely in the economic life of Benin, which depends considerably on the tourist industry. The state government has encouraged the curiosity shops to stock stereotypes of the "Benin head" and copies of antique jewelry. It is therefore understandable that the Benin guild of carvers to which Idah belongs, and the community which benefits so much from their kind of work, should be worried that Idah's originality might harm the tourist economy. Nevertheless, the careers of such representative artists lead us to wonder about the generations before them. Have the patterns of myth undergone alteration as society changed? If so, we would expect the artist to give the new forms due expression, relying on his genius to strike the right selective balance between the new elements and the ancestral legacy. Coming as they do from the old school, Bisiri and Idah attest once again to the restless creative temper of the traditional artist, who has, in fact, a distaste for unintelligent copy.

The problem of tradition and the individual talent is no easier in the oral arts. But if it is recalled that the folk literature is delivered mostly in performance, we can understand why tradition in this regard faces an even more likely risk of change than in the plastic arts. . . . In a context of persistent social and cultural change, and given the fluidity of the medium of music and the unrecorded word, rigid loyalty to received fact would be somewhat difficult, especially in the competitive court atmosphere. "Music," says Djeli Mamoudou in *Sundiata*, "is the griot's soul." And music, especially as an earnest . . . will to please, would seem that much more of a threat to the duty to leave the truth unadjusted.

We can thus imagine what liberties are taken in the area of purely imaginative literature, or at least literature that is considerably free of the tyranny of historical fact. *The Mwindo Epic* is again a good case in point. The editors tells us they have five other versions of the tale, the longest of which is only half the length of the present one. One the whole, the Rureke version seems a thoroughly personal performance: within the fabric of the song, the poor transcribers Biebuyck and Mateene are challenged by repeated, rather formulaic commands of "scribe, move on!" One is left with an overwhelming sense of immediacy, which perhaps vindictes [Albert] Lord's observation that "an oral poem is not composed *for* but *in* performance."

I am not arguing that the traditional African artist has no regard for tradition, assuming tradition to be a hallowed kernel of truth which has to be constantly kept alive by memory. But it seems clear that, in an art form such as this, supported largely by the challenge of ready delivery and the encouragement of ready rewards, the artist is generally forced to rely more on his own creative (i.e., manipulative, among other things) energy than on memory. . . .

Let us now summarize these observations concerning the principles of the traditional African aesthetics. The traditional African artist is a man with a very pressing sense of real and concrete presences, enjoying the closest intimacy with an environment that is both physical and metaphysical. By means of his dynamic sense of form, he tries in all sorts of combinations, with language as with *matériel*, to give tangible meaning to those visible and spiritual presences which give context to his daily life and thought. And as the truly guiding sensibility of his community, he continually leads the way in recreating the progressive forms of the communal myth.

In a society where the means of dissemination of ideas is rather limited, it is often the artist who is responsible for giving a firm foundation to new cultural influences that may otherwise have been treated as passing fancies and thus left to disappear. Let us go back to that example of the traditional hairdresser in Nigeria. The visiting census officials probably spend only a day or two in the allocated village. But the strange hair-styles which they wear make a deep impression on the local hairdresser. She reproduces those styles on the heads of her local customers, and to the styles survive the brief sojourn of those who brought them to the new environment. This may be well worth considering as the major means of infiltration of various lifestyles and influences which most traditional societies acquire. Or take the case of the village sculptor. Most Nigerian villages have no airfields, but every day planes fly above the heads of their citizens. Because he trades in strange modes and novelties, and knows that he attracts attention and custom in that way, the sculptor endeavors to translate his vague impressions of the planes into carvings which he either sells to curious clients or with which he decorates his shop. Whatever happens, he has succeeded in bringing closer to his community what was at best a distant reality.

I have chosen to see the traditional African artist as an active mind operating in a dynamic context. Indeed, it seems to me that we must re-examine the role which the over-simplifying cliches of religion and world-view play in his work. It is all very well to have recourse to the well-known Keatsian principle—"Beauty is truth, truth beauty"—but this is acceptable only insofar as it would illustrate the conviction that the artist manipulates tradition and its values, giving them fresh relevance, fresh meaning, fresh being.

If this is the case, then who is it that supervises this protean exercise and ensures the authenticity of the new forms? In his discussion of the art of the old society, Mace-buh states that, "except on those occasions when expert opinion was called for, the farmer, the hunter, and the winetapper could be relied upon to muster a sufficiently meaningful response to art, and this merely as part of their general awareness as citizens of a community of beings." This portrait of social cohesion is an admirable one, but it is a rather inadequate guide to understanding the growth of art in its context. The situation among the unlettered artists of today cannot be significantly different from what it was ages ago. And I feel convinced that that "meaningful response"—if it means, as

it should, a critical support for the evolution of valid aesthetic standards—can only be supplied by those who, by virtue either of native skill or of long-standing connection with the trade, are qualified to offer intelligent views, not only on the "historic truth" but indeed on the dynamic ingredients of "beauty." In the plastic arts, despite the corrupting influence of tourist demand, only a fellow artist or a man closely connected with the practice of traditional art can make meaningful criticism of a piece of craft; these artists still borrow or condemn each other's styles, and they alone are qualified to suggest whether or not such styles have attained a just balance between old and new. In an oral performance, the masses are not the best critics. As Babalola has amply shown in his work, the performer is perpetually at the mercy of the partisan instincts of the mob, whose occasional heckling may tend to force him to be slavishly loyal—against his better instincts—to the "historic truth." Of course, such distractions may well teach the artist artful ways of negotiating his lines around their interests; which is in one sense a dynamic gain to his art. But such accidental benefits play only a limited part in the actual growth of his art; for true technical excellence he generally depends on the knowledgeable comments of fellow bards and skilled judges who can tell whether or not he has made any improvements on the best performances of more recent memory. For them, indeed, these improvements are the best insurance of tradition.

Christopher Small

AFRICAN
MUSIC

Christopher Small has written several books on music from an ethnomusicological standpoint. These include Music, Society, Education *and* Music of the Common Tongue: Survival and Celebration in Afro-American Music. *In the reading that follows, Small describes some of the ways in which African music is integrated with everyday life.*

. . . As indeed in nearly all non-European societies, music is not separate from everyday life but is an integral part of it; to listen as we do to, say, a symphony, is as unknown in traditional African culture as it is in Bali. That is not to say that Africans do not perform to one another or to themselves purely for entertainment; such music forms an important part of African life. Nor does it mean that everyone is an expert performer or that there are no professional musicians in traditional African culture, but the relation between performer and listener is of an entirely different kind, since both are intimately connected within a community. The detachment with which a western listener contemplates an orchestral performance plays no part in their musical life and customs, and in most music there is opportunity for participation, singing choral parts, handclapping and dancing. Even when listening to a performance the listeners will react loudly and actively to the music with-

out inhibitions, since, as J. H. K. Nketia says, not only does motor response increase enjoyment of the music, but it also provides opportunity for social interaction in a musical context.

Music is found in all the situations of life, from everyday activities to the great rituals of chiefs and kings. Apart from more obvious examples such as cradle songs, work songs and the like, of a kind familiar from western folk song, there are songs which form part of initiation rituals, as well as carrying gossip or news, praise or insult, warnings or exhortations to their listeners. The "songs of the elders" remind people of their past and of the values of a society, chronicle the history of the people and reassure them of the legitimacy of their chiefs and kings. Other songs deal with religious and philosophical matters, while various occupations such as hunters, fishermen or herdsmen have their own songs telling the praises of those whom they hunt or husband. Kings

Christopher Small, *Music, Society, Education* (London: John Calder, 1980) 48–58.

may employ professional singers to tell their praises; these usually belong to an hereditory caste, called *griots*.

Even more than the drum, the human voice is at the heart of African music; few performances lack some part for it. The voice is never "trained" in the western sense to produce sounds remote from those of speech; the vocal music of Africa bears a very intimate relationship to speech (especially is this true of those peoples whose language is tonal, depending for its meanings, as does Chinese, on vocal inflections as well as on actual word forms), and their technique is devoted to as faithful a rendition as possible of heightened speech. They use a dazzling variety of types of singing, depending on the dramatic situation required: head tones, chest tones, grunts, whispers, whistles, amazingly realistic imitations of bird, animal and other natural sounds, ululations and yodels; all are part of their repertory of sounds. Unlike western singers, Africans deliberately cultivate strong differences between the various registers of the voice, even emphasizing the breaks between them, from a growl to a falsetto, even almost a scream, as well as using with virtuosity the various harmonic and non-harmonic sounds of which the human voice is capable.

All writers agree that, to an African, a beautiful voice does not make a good singer; indeed, whether a singer has or has not a beautiful voice is irrelevant. Rather, it is the artistic use he makes of what he has. The nearest parallel in our culture to this concept is perhaps in the orator, who will discover and make use of his own peculiarities of voice, appearance and deportment, not according to any accepted canon of taste or vocal quality but in a way which helps him to communicate what he is as well as what he has to say in the most effective way possible. We find it, too, in popular and folk singers (Bob Dylan, Rod Stewart, and, in another field, Rex Harrison are three who

spring to mind) who may have no "singing voice" in the classical sense but have made their voices into telling and eloquent expressive instruments.

Pre-eminent as the voice undoubtedly is, African musicians also play a wide range of instruments. Most Europeans in thinking of African music think of drumming, but in fact nearly every type of instrument we know in European music, with the exception of the keyboard, has some kind of counterpart in Africa—fiddles, lyres, lutes, a curious and beautiful hybrid harp-lute called the kora, horns, flutes, as well as idiophones such as xylophones, rattles, bells and the like, even metal castanets and tuned stones. There is also an instrument which is unique to Africa (although a Europeanized version has recently been placed on the market) which is indeed almost universal throughout black Africa under various names: mbira, kalimba, sansa, ikembe, or, in English, African piano or thumb piano. This consists of a small sounding board a few inches long to which is attached a number of metal or wooden tines, fixed at one end, passing over a bridge and free at the other. Like the guitar it is a very intimate instrument; the player holds it close to him in both hands and strokes rather than plucks the tines with his thumbs (Europeans trying the instrument for the first time almost invariably pluck too hard and spoil its delicate tone). A small instrument may have only half a dozen tines, but a large mbira may have as many as forty-five, arranged often in two or three manuals; the sounding board may be mounted on a hollow box or placed inside a gourd, both of which act as resonators, and the instrument gives a gentle, haunting sound (there is a great and surprising gentleness in most African music) that is like no other instrument on earth. To take a musical instrument in one's hand will often tell one much about its culture of origin even before one strikes a single sound from it, and the mbira shows this well. First, it personifies the intimate relationship that exists between an African musician and his instrument; the chances are that he will have made it himself, since there are few professional instrument makers, or if he has received it from another it will most likely have been a gift or an inheritance. Selling an instrument is rare; Francis Bebey tells how he tried to buy an instrument from a fine local musician, to be told, coolly, that he, the musician, had come to town to play his drum for the dancing, not to deliver a slave into bondage. The instruments are not mere objects, but colleagues in the work of creation, and symbols, as Bebey says, of the time when God imbued man with life and speech.

Secondly, around each tine of the mbira is wound loosely a piece of metal, which when the tine is plucked buzzes with a non-harmonic sound that lies like a sheen over the music. It is a kind of sound which, if a western classical musician heard it in his instrument, he would take the instrument apart to find and eliminate. Yet Africans seem to love it, as they fill their music with non-harmonic sound, from drums, rattles, scrapers and the like. Even the Chopi of Mozambique, of whom I shall have more to say later, place across the mouths of the gourd resonators under the keys of their xylophones the egg-cases of certain spiders, as thin and flexible as rice paper, to super-impose a buzzing sound on the notes of the instruments. The love of non-harmonic and percussive sounds shows itself too in the predominance of plucked over bowed stringed instruments, and above all in the love of drums and drumming. The love of drum sounds, allied with the emphasis on rhythm as the primary organizing principle, is responsible for some of the most exciting and beautiful of all music.

Thirdly, each individual instrument differs slightly from all others. Instruments do of course fall into broad types, but each is an individual with its own characteristic virtues and defects. Musicians also emerge much

more as individuals than do their western counterparts; this is due partly to the individuality of each instrument but also to the fact that formal training is usually very brief. The musician may be taught the rudiments of his instrument, but after that he pays little attention to technical matters for their own sake. He does not practise; he plays. As Nketia says, "Traditional instruction is not generally organized on a formal institutional basis, for it is believed that natural endowment and a person's natural ability to develop on his own are essentially what is needed. This endowment could include innate knowledge, for, according to the Akan, 'One does not teach the blacksmith's son his father's trade. If he knows it, then it is God who taught him.' The principle . . . seems to be that of learning through social experience. Exposure to musical situations and participation are emphasized more than formal teaching. The organization of traditional music in social life enables the individual to acquire his musical knowledge in slow stages and to widen his experience of the music of his culture through the social groups into which he is slowly absorbed and through the activities in which he takes part." This of course does not mean that the techniques of African music are to be acquired quickly or casually; a man may play his drum for years before he is accepted as a master drummer, if indeed he is ever so accepted. It does, however, mean that the same kind of instrument may be played in a multitude of different styles; as Bebey points out, technique is very much a matter of individual taste. He says, "The absence of technique—in the western sense of the term—does not imply a corresponding absence of artistry. Art is a utility, and, as we have already seen, music is a necessity— a vital function. Music is the outward and audible manifestation of inward biological functions; it is the support and realization of their metaphysical purpose."

The highest achievement of African music is undoubtedly in the field of rhythm.

"Rhythm," says A. M. Jones, whose *Studies in African Music* is the classic of its field, "is to the African what harmony is to the European, and it is in the complex interweaving of contrasting rhythmic patterns that he finds his greatest aesthetic satisfaction. To accomplish this he has built up a rhythmic principle that is quite different from that of Western music and yet is present in his simplest songs. . . . Whatever be the devices used to produce them, in African music there is practically always a *clash of rhythms*; this is a cardinal principle. Even a song which appears to be mono-rhythmic will on investigation turn out to be constructed of two independent but strictly related rhythmic patterns, one inherent in the melody and one belonging to the accompaniment."

It is child's play to an African to sing (to use European terms) in a constantly changing metre while preserving a strict hand-clapping pattern of the type *1 2 1 2 1 2 3 1 2 1 2 3*; often there are anything up to half a dozen or eight different patterns made by drums, handclaps, other instruments and voices, all making not only different patterns but working in different metres with different points of accentuation, so that downbeats do not coincide. Moreover, the master drummer, to whose beat all other musicians must conform, may be continually changing his patterns. The only element holding the performance together is the beat, which is identical for all the lines; around this one constant factor are built complex and fascinating rhythmic structures which most Europeans can scarcely comprehend, much less perform.

The emphasis on rhythm does not, however, mean that African music is melodically deficient. There is a wide variety of scales (though African musicians do not think in those terms), not only of four, five, six or seven tones to the octave (the pentatonic being the most common) but also in a large number of different tunings. Very few, if any, coincide exactly with the tones of the west-

ern tempered scale (which many Africans find intolerably out of tune); each area, even each tribe or village, has its own minute shading of pitch, some even tending towards an equal division of the octave, as in our whole-tone scale. These tunings are not random or accidental, but are argued over, worked on and adjusted with methodical accuracy; a man of the Chopi, for example, moving from one village to another will need to retune his xylophone if he is to play in the orchestra. But the basic pitches, at least in vocal music, are regarded as points of reference from which the singer might move, "bending" the pitches and sliding from one tone to the next as a jazz cornettist might—the real tones are always there by implication.

Melodic phrases tend to be short, and repetition is common; in fact repetition is one of the characteristics of African music. Improvisation is less common than one might imagine, and free improvisation without any framework whatsoever almost unknown. A call-and-response sequence may go on for several hours, with apparently monotonous repetition of the same short phrase sung by a leader and answered by the chorus, but in fact subtle variations are going on all the time, not only in the melodic lines themselves but also in their relation to the complex cross-rhythms in the accompanying drumming or handclapping. It is difficult at first for western listeners to distinguish melodies in much African vocal music; it often seems like mere exaggerated speech inflections with its slides and bendings of pitch and its unfamiliar pitch relations, but that is exactly what the melodies set out to be. The style of most African vocal music is intended "to echo the speech and thoughts of the people as faithfully as possible and without embellishment," and it takes Europeans some time before the different melodic contours become clear, individuated and expressive. Melody is rarely used in a personal expressive way; a poem may lament the death of a child, but it will probably be set to a lively music. "They do not seek to evoke the reflective emotions which we associate with our sentimental ballads composed in some distant theatre land. They seek the trance-like experience of complete participation in music and dance, their own common grief. So they dance together and share together." The repetitions of African music have a function in time which is the reverse of our own music—to dissolve the past and the future into one eternal present, in which the passing of time is no longer noticed. A performance may go on for several hours or all night, and will have no formal beginning or end; rather, it will take some time to gather momentum and probably just fizzle out at the end when the musicians run out of energy or enthusiasm. There is no time limit set.

The music of Africa that is in general most pleasing to European ears is that which functions purely as entertainment; one is haunted by the sound of two Baoulé flutists from Guinea engaging in a polyphony of rhythms as well as of tones, by a single mbira played by a Shona musician of Rhodesia, by the sound of a Hutu shepherd breaking the silence of the night with his flute (and incidentally giving warning to prowlers that the cattle are guarded)—all these sounds and more can be heard on the increasing numbers of fine recordings now available to show the richness of African music. It is of course such contemplative music that comes off best in disc; more active ritual and communal music is reduced on record to a mere shadow of itself through the absence of action and spectacle, and above all of *involvement*.

Before ending this very brief description of African musical culture, it would be worthwhile to examine in a little more detail one group of African musicians whose particular musical skills and attitudes challenge many western notions not only about Af-

rican music but also about the very basis of music and musical technique themselves. These are the Chopi, who live near the coast of Mozambique to the north of the port of Lourenço Marques. Their music was studied thoroughly in the 1940s by the ethnomusicologist Hugh Tracey, whose book *Chopi Musicians* is the source for my information, although the conclusions I draw are my own.

Each of the large Chopi villages has its own *ngodo* or orchestra with singer-dancers, presided over by its own resident composer and musical director, who is responsible for the composition of musical works of symphonic size, lasting up to an hour, for voices and *timbila* or xylophones—both words and music—which are then set to dance by a dance director. These works are in several movements, each lasting up to five or six minutes each, including an orchestral introduction (sometimes more than one) and a finale, and climaxing in the Mzeno, or Great Song, which is the heart of the work. When Dr. Tracey was in Mozambique, in the mid-1940s, there were two outstanding musicians, Katini weNyamombe and Gomukomu weSimbi (to whom, in a touching gesture, he dedicates the book), and he reproduces the texts of several of their works in Chichopi and English, with an elucidation of the local and topical allusions without which even the English would be incomprehensible. These texts are outstanding examples of the allusiveness and obliquity of African poetry, cunning mixtures of mirth and sadness, political comment and protest and just plain gossip, outbursts of vitality which remain indissolubly linked to the concrete lives of the people from whom they arose, and yet at the same time bearing a universally human and spiritual message. Tracey describes the composer's way of working (completely uninfluenced, he insists, by European music), how he builds his text first of all (which, he says, "performs a highly social and cathartic function in a society which has no daily press, no publications, and no stage other than the village yard in which publicly to express its feelings or voice its protests against the rub of the times") then begins the musical settings, first in his mind, then developing the melodic and rhythmic ideas at his timbila, working out counter-melodies and cross-rhythms. He then calls in his fellow-musicians of the orchestra, all of whom are of course fellow-villagers, many of whom in the 40's were conscripted to work in the mines of the Rand; between them they work out the various accompanying figures and textures, usually in the form of variations on a ground, all under the leadership of the composer, who is the final arbiter of which ideas are used, and who puts the final touches to the musical composition. Then the dance leader is called in; the work is played over and he devises the dance routine to fit, calling on occasion, like any other choreographer, for a little more here, a little less there, until agreement is finally arrived at. Thus one movement of the new ngodo is completed, and movement by movement the whole work is created in this way.

The music, to judge from the few available recordings, is by any standards of a noble and satisfying richness of melody, rhythm and texture. It is complex to a degree, full of incident; it is fully composed music, yet not a word or musical sign is written down. The ability of these musicians to imagine a work of symphonic scale without putting pen to paper challenges not only many western notions of the limits of musical memory but also assumptions concerning the necessity for notation: whatever it *is* needed for, it does not seem necessary for the working-out of a composition.

But an even more important challenge to European ideas lies in the way in which these works are used. The new work is inserted into the existing work, movement by movement as it is completed, finally replacing the old completely. The old work is then forgotten; however fine or masterly it might has been (Tracey describes the musical idiom of Gomukomu as "mature and compelling," a view which the recordings bear out), it has served its purpose and can be let go. Tracey says that Katini, who had composed at least ten mgodo, could remember only the last two or three and fragments from earlier ones, and seemed quite unworried by the fact. There was, it seems, plenty more where that came from, and like the Balinese the Chopi see no need for "classics" to keep them in touch with their past, no need to take refuge in the past from the pressures of the present. To these African musicians it is the process of creation that is important; the product is relatively unimportant and can be discarded without compunction, a sign of a self-confidence on the part of these richly creative artists that seems to be lacking in the west.

Finally, although they are greatly admired and respected by the village communities in which they live, these composers do not stand in any way apart from it. They are supported to an extent by the community, it seems, but are certainly not professionals in any European sense. Their function is not to provide completed art works for professionals to play and the community to listen to, but to act as leaders and pacemakers in the communal work of musical and choreographic creation. It is a situation that many European composers might envy.

The two different yet in many ways similar musical cultures of black Africa and of Bali will have to stand as representatives of the innumerable cultures and societies across the world which exhibit features not shared by our own. I must emphasise that my aim in describing these musics and these societies has not been to prove them superior to that of Europe (although they undoubtedly possess features from which we might learn), but to challenge the often unexamined and even unconscious

Kuang-Ming Wu

CHINESE AESTHETICS

Kuang-Ming Wu is professor of philosophy at the University of Wisconsin at Oshkosh. His primary area of research is the philosophy of Chuang Tzu. His books include Thinking through Death, Chuang Tzu: World Philosopher at Play, *and* The Butterfly as Companion: Meditations on the First Three Chapters of Chuang Tzu. *Wu discusses the significance of the Chinese duality of* yin *and* yang, *which he sees as essential background for the understanding of Chinese art.*

. . . For the Chinese, beauty is the constitutive inter-involvement of many into one, and one with many, until the entire unison becomes both concrete-particular and cosmic-universal, both in scale and in substance. Here is a twofold characteristic—distinction and interchange, even on the level of the subject. As a result, beauty is less of a subject to be independently discussed than a pervasive attitude and atmosphere in which one moves and has one's being.

YIN–YANG CONSTITUTIVE INVOLVEMENT

Beauty is something poetic, which is *yin–yang* constitutive involvement. Originally meaning the shaded and the sunny, the *yin* and the *yang* are reciprocals, that is, counterparts and counterpoints. Counterpoints are contraries and contrasts such as yes and no, can and cannot, dark and bright, good and evil, comic and tragic, construction and destruction, and so on. Counterparts are mutuals such as this and that, form and content, will and desires, feeling and reason, body and mind, subject and object, husband and wife, writer and reader, composer, player and audience, the Five Elements (elementary ways of things), and so on.

When these reciprocals are constitutively involved one with another, the situation is "beautiful." It is mutual constitution, in which the one is so much a constituent of the other that when the one is taken away the other disappears. Positively put, these elements—counterpoints and counterparts—constitute together a self-involved unity, presenting a self-recursive integrity.

Kuang-Ming Wu, "Chinese Aesthetics," *Understanding the Chinese Mind*, ed. Robert E. Allinson (Hong Kong: Oxford UP, 1989) 236–264.

Since this is a unity of *counterpoints*, it is always a unity in polar motion; here dwell such phrases as "use of no use," "breath-bone," "the Way that is no way," "self-forgetting," and the like, describing the inscrutable vitality of beauty. Being creative constitution, it is called *poetic*. The entire world comes alive; things dwell therein without attachment, accommodated without being overwhelmed.

By the same token, as *counterparts* are constitutively involved, the form and the content, the natal and the actualized, and the like, realize their self-referential unity and consistency. It is then dispersed, and then realized again, in a dancing rhythm. This is the world of beauty.

In this atmosphere of poetic beauty, the "affective quality," "atmosphere of feeling," the subjective answer to the objective call, and the like, are included and transcended. We need no dichotomy here. . . .

◆◆◆

AESTHETICS AS COSMIC ATTITUDE

. . . What immediately strikes one, on mentioning "Chinese aesthetics," is that there is no such formal discipline in China. The Chinese neither raised theoretical problems (say, whether there is beauty in nature without the artist) and pursued them rigourously, nor erected metaphysical systems about the structure of beauty itself, nor even produced principles of aesthetic activities as a whole. Chinese thinking about beauty is always on the specific and the concrete, never abstract theorization.

Suppose we have a sketch of an apple. We can either stay there and enjoy the freshness of the apple, or leave it for the eternal form of Beauty of which it is a mere pointer and participant, or consider the relation among actuality, the art work and the subjects (the artist's feeling, intuition, sensuality; the viewer's reception through its revealment; adequacy to the apple-actuality), or, finally, classify all such considerations as exclusively in the realm of aesthetics, as the job of the philosopher of art, not of the artist himself or of the philosopher of politics.

In all this what is assumed are the separate entities—the artist, the idea, the art work, the intuition, the revealment or adequacy, the audience, the relation, the harmony, the event, the thing in itself, and all this as separate from other branches of philosophy.

In China such barriers break down. When considering the freshness of an apple, we see how the freshness emanates the breathing energies of the skies and the fields, of the breeze and the sun, of the smell and the colours and the atmosphere. The apple-freshness, glowing in such aura, energies, and smell, enhances the universe, and is enhanced by the universe; the apple and the universe dwell in each other and point to each other. The heaven-and-earth is the fresh apple and the freshness is cosmic, and the fresh is fresh, the cosmic, cosmic.

Without Dürer's sensuous colours and lines or Picasso's jagged abstractions and juxtapositions, the Chinese painting lures us on with rhythm-like natural dynamism, ebbing and flowing through the skies and fields, the cosmic joys and sorrows, the feelings and discernings, and all that amid daily hustle and bustle. The Chinese concrete universality unobtrusively nestles us in our world that is both ordinary and mysterious. The Chinese painterly accuracy is not exactly Italian; it is somehow transparent. In the painting shapes and colours invite us to *their* compellingly actual dynamism that pulses *throughout* the world. There is a diffusion which enhances the concrete. There in diffusion and enhancement is a cosmic significance in the particular. The poet/painter raises the brush, and the heaven-and-earth echo in anticipation. The cosmos-breath flows through the brush's beautiful execution into letters, calligraphy, and paintings, composing the very tapestry (*wen*) of the universe.

And in all this the artist and the viewer are involved. They in turn become the cosmic, while they remain themselves, glowing with the apple-fresh in the sunny autumn hills. They enter and are entered, while they engage in the activities of medicine, cooking, martial arts, politics. Thus every human activity is artistic, and every aesthetic act is cosmic; in everything we do, we utter the "language of ocean, language of sky" which cultivates our cosmic sense of justice, of truth.

All this is to say that we cannot define beauty, because its very definition depends on our attitude. Aesthetics is reflective sensibility, primarily attitude. We can think about aesthetic objects, and we can think about everything aesthetically. In the former our attitude is often that of objective analysis; in the latter, our attitude is not, and cannot be. We can have two attitudes in aesthetics, then: objective analysis and pervasive concord. . . .

Kongzi (Confucius) regarded music as one of the Six Arts to cultivate personality, as Plato regarded music as one of the powerful means of harmonizing personality. But whereas Plato wanted to inundate the soul with music in a planned geometric manner, Confucius wanted music to "perfume" the soul-chamber with its vapour, tuning the soul into a vital flexible whole.

Such natural oneness of the soul with the cosmic rhythm is apparent in painting. People usually say of a Chinese painter that the painter expresses himself, not the mountain, as he paints the mountain; after living in the mountain for months, absorbing it into himself, he goes home and paints.

Not so; the painter is instead at home in self-mountain. He paints as he moves and has his being in the world of the mountain; he neither paints the mountain nor expresses himself. He just is and behaves— he in the mountain and the mountain in him. He goes home because he goes home; have you seen anyone not going home? He neither purposely absorbs the mountain nor is he absorbed by it and disappears in it. He just is; the mountain just is. He paints as naturally as the mountain is there, naturally. He paints as naturally as he eats, sleeps, and dies. To paint is part of himself as he is, in the world as it is, in front of the mountain as it is.

. . . This is not mystical absorption of the self into the world in which the self and the mountain are abolished, or a pre-established harmony of the two, or their mutual reflection. All these descriptions are too fixated, too much categorized, missing that simple naturalness of the painter painting the world, rejoicing and singing the world as he lives at home in it. This is why the painter walks into his own painting; the painting is part of himself and the world. He can go into it because he is it; it is his world in which he lives.

Patrick McKee

OLD AGE
IN THE CHINESE
MOUNTAIN LANDSCAPE

Patrick McKee is professor of philosophy at Colorado State University. His books include Philosophical Foundations of Gerontology *and* The Art of Aging: A Celebration of Old Age in the History of Western Art *(which he coauthored with H. Kauppinen). McKee's interest in aging extends to his discussion of Chinese art. He contends that Chinese painting frequently portrays older scholars in a manner that is consistent both with the Chinese conception of humanity's relationship to nature and with a healthy attitude toward growing old.*

The Chinese mountain landscape is a distinct genre which flourished between the tenth and thirteenth centuries and has had a vigorous history since. It is highly formalized in the sense that each painting is modelled closely on others so that all contain similar elements. Despite differences in style and technique, pictures in this tradition are usually very recognizable. There is a background of mountainous terrain. There is usually a stream flowing from the mountains, often broadening at their base into a wide, quietly flowing river or lake. There is a forest at the foot of the mountains, often containing prominently featured pines. At the edge of the forest, usually at stream side, a small thatched hut with a conspicuous window is seen, and through the window an (always elderly) scholar in quiet contemplation or other contemplative activity such as reading, making tea, or discoursing with another scholar. A path winds past the hut into the high mountains above, often leading to a pagoda or temple. Frequently travelers are shown at various stages along this path or sometimes crossing a rickety bridge over the mountain stream. Equally often the travelers appear in boats, crossing over to (or sometimes from) this world of mountainous seclusion. In addition to scholars and travelers, fishermen and boatmen are sometimes seen. While there are many variations within

Patrick McKee, "Old Age in the Chinese Mountain Landscape," *Journal of Aesthetic Education* 24.4 (1990): 59–73.

this format, the elements just described convey what is more or less "typical" in works of this tradition.

These works are connected to old age by the traditional understanding that the "lofty scholars" who inhabit them can have achieved that status only in advanced age. Also important are the postures, gestures, costume, attendants, walking staffs, and other attributes of age often prominently depicted. That the central figures are often travelers, pilgrims, or scholars shows that these pictures are partly about learning, personal growth, and wisdom. But in many instances it is the learning, growth, and wisdom that come with age that are represented. This is of course directly evident to the extent that the people are shown to be elderly. It is further implied by the use of traditional Chinese symbols of late life, including peaches, the crane, and the pine tree. And, as we shall see in greater detail below, there are frequent allusions to old age in the titles, poetry, and other writings often appearing on these works. Finally, the connection to age is powerfully expressed by the symbolism of the mountain and its upward path. These symbolize the difficult ascent from the limited and confined understanding of youth to the wider, clearer, and more far-reaching perspectives that can be achieved in late life.

Does the artist indicate *what* wisdom comes with age, what insights or understandings are achieved? We are given many clues. First, there are the many bridges and ferry boats symbolizing a "crossing over," the renewal of understanding that comes with transition to a new perspective.

Second, there is the farther shore of such crossings; it is the detachment and solitude symbolized by the mountains, with their real and metaphorical distance from stressful midlife agendas. Finally, there is also the frequent presence of a pagoda in the mountains, symbolizing a philosophical or spiritual rather than worldly wisdom. The same theme is sometimes expressed by a bell in the pagoda or by a depiction of the elderly traveler listening to a distant bell, symbolizing a spiritual awakening. Because of its remote wilderness context, the awakening in question is clearly related to a retreat from the active life of worldly striving and a turn toward contemplation.

The huts and hermitages the scholars live in offer further clues about the nature of the wisdom they seek. These dwellings are always very simple, free of unnecessary adornment. This suggests a certain fundamental nature in the concerns of the inhabitant—a concern with the simplest, most basic questions of life. The same thing is suggested by the window or doorway through which we often view these scholars. For just as a ferry boat or bridge symbolizes a life transition, a dwelling with a window or doorway symbolizes transition from existence in the physical body to existence in the larger cosmos; in short, impending death. This again suggests that the questions being contemplated are the ultimate questions of meaning in life and of our place in the universe. Finally, that it is fundamental rather than prosaic knowledge that is at issue is expressed by the high altitude of the mountains, whose meaning in this respect is alluded to by such typical titles as *Scholars in a Lofty Retreat* or *Lofty Scholars in a Mountain Hermitage*.

Finally, the environment they have chosen to live in implies something about the wisdom these scholars seek. It is an environment whose main features express the basic religious-philosophical thesis of Chinese thought, namely, the reconciliation and harmonious union of contending opposites. In classical Chinese thought the most fundamental of all opposites are permanence and change or process. In these paintings impermanence, change, and process are represented by the rushing waters of the mountain stream as well as by the winds, storms, clouds, and mists often painted into these mountain scenes. Permanence is symbolized by the mountains themselves, the rocky ledges and daunting immovable boulders that are found along the mountain path. It is also expressed by the pine tree, a prominent feature in many of these pictures, or by the quieter, broader expanses of water into which the rushing mountain stream often flows. A frequent image expressive of this theme is that of scholars standing quietly on a rocky precipice and looking at a waterfall. A number of such paintings have the poetically simple title *Listening to the Waterfall*, for the waterfall perfectly expresses the mysterious union of change and constancy. Its steady, even roar and uniformly white cascade express constancy; yet it consists throughout in process and change. The aged scholar's "listening" to the waterfall is a metaphor for the contemplation of the metaphysical union of opposites. Similar ideas are implicit in many titles in these genre, such as *Sitting on a Rock and Watching the Clouds*, a painting by Li Tang, and *A Thatched Hut among Cloud-Filled Trees*, by Wang Fu, in which the evanescence of clouds is counterpointed by the permanence of rocks and trees.

It is interesting to compare the aging Chinese scholar in his mountains to an equally formalized subject in European painting: the aging Saint Jerome in the desert. Like the Chinese mountain recluses, Jerome is a scholar, seeker of truth, an old man in search of understanding. Like them he seeks understanding in a wilderness retreat. Like them, he contemplates ultimates, especially the meaning of life and death and similarly fundamental issues. This is invariably indicated by such items in his study as a Bible, a skull, a burnt-out candle, a crucifix, his nakedness or posture of religious piety, the barren simplicity of his dwelling, and other attributes. Both types of pictures tell of advanced age as a time of withdrawal from worldly concerns and a crossing over to a new agenda which features a contemplative

pursuit of basic insight. And in both traditions, the wisdom attributed to the aging person is understanding the reconciliation of fundamental opposites. In Jerome's case this is a reconciliation of sinful, material man with a holy, spiritual God through Christ's death. In the Chinese scholar's case it is the metaphysical unity of change and permanence.

An interesting question about these Chinese interpretations of age, painted hundreds of years ago in a distant culture, is whether they anticipate any of the discoveries of contemporary Western gerontologists. They clearly do. We have already seen one example in their exploration of the contemplative perspective which understands an underlying unity of opposites. For this is the primary cognitive feature attributed to old age by many contemporary gerontologists. According to Erik Erikson, for example, the development of the ego proceeds through eight successive crises spread across the life span. The eighth and last crisis, if successfully negotiated, leads the aging person to "integrative understanding." This is the ability to transcend the tensions between such conflicting opposites as freedom and authority, affection and anger, life and death, discipline and relaxation, work and play, self and other, and so forth. At other stages of life we tend to experience these polarities as stressful conflicts between irreconcilable opposites. In old age we experience them instead, according to Erikson, as mutually reinforcing and enriching counterpoints of one another. The same idea has been affirmed by other prominent gerontologists. . . .

An important aspect of integrative understanding is related to what recent environmentalists have seen as an advantage of Eastern over Western philosophy, namely, its more holistic or ecological concept of man's place in the natural environment. The environmental philosophy expressed in these painting is not a philosophy of dominance over nature but of harmonious integration with it. This is expressed, for example, by the scale of the human figures in relation to the surrounding natural environment. The human figures and structures are usually shown as a small part of and as integrated with the surrounding environment. Often one has to search to pick out the human figures and structures from their surroundings. The elderly people in these pictures are shown as having achieved what Erik Fromm saw as the ultimate goal of all human striving, namely, overcoming our sense of separateness from the universe and arriving at a feeling of union with it. This again expresses the wisdom of integrative judgment attributed by these artists, and by Erikson and others, to old age. These paintings, then, argue for an understanding of man's place in nature that is consistent with the special mental strength they attribute to old age.

Implicit in what has just been said is a related gerontological thesis anticipated by these pictures, namely, the proposition that late adulthood includes developmental crises or stages. Many gerontologists have argued that developmental crises do occur in late life, in contrast to the traditional Western assumption that human developmental stages end with puberty. The existence of such crises or developmental stages in late life is affirmed by the ferry crossings, bridges over troubled waters, journeys through stormy mountain passes, and by the windows and doorways that are so typical of these works.

A third gerontological theme anticipated by these landscapes is the developmental process which has come to be called "life review" by contemporary gerontologists. According to this prominent idea, reminiscence about the past is an important mental activity characteristic of late life and an important source of insight into fundamental life issues. Central to this developmental stage in elderly people is a process of looking back over one's life in a mood of reverie and reminiscence. According to many

gerontologists, life review is a universal development in elderly persons, a looking-back process in which the content of one's life slowly unfolds and which is reflected in the familiar tendency of elderly persons to talk about their past. This kind of looking-back process occurs at all ages, at stopping points and summing-up intervals as we attempt to get a perspective on where we have been and perhaps on where we are going. But the life review in old age is special, both in being more intensive and in being relatively final. For it is only in the life review of old age that we look over the experience of having lived a whole human life—in an effort to arrive at a settled, final judgment about the ultimate meaning and value of life and the important experiences and relationships it contains.

Life review is prominently depicted in the landscape paintings. It is indicated by the frequent image of the old scholar's "looking back" over the path leading to the mountain or looking into a valley below from a high mountain promontory. The title of a work can indicate that it concerns life review, as with the painting *Returning Boat on Crane Lake*. The image of a boat symbolizes life's voyage, and the theme of "return" suggests the return to the past in memory, as does the symbol of the lake as a reservoir of vital reminiscences beneath the surface of everyday thought. Finally, the name "Crane Lake" indicates that it is an aging person's memory that is referred to by the lake, for in China the crane is a well-known and constantly repeated symbol of longevity and old age.

Another recent gerontological theme explored in these works is the issue of disengagement *versus* activity as general life orientations in old age. Chinese and Japanese cultures derive from India, with strong influence from the early religious and ethical classic, *The Code of Manu*. This work contains the teaching, "When a householder sees his skin wrinkled and his hair white, and the sons of his sons, then he may return to the forest." In this passage and many others the work anticipates the "disengagement theory" discussed by gerontologists in this century. According to this theory, Western culture errs in expecting aging people to "stay active" in the roles, activities, relationships, and goal-seeking of midlife. For, according to this theory, there is a gradual, natural, adaptive-developmental process in late life which urges us to "disengage." In this stage of development the concerns and values of midlife are relinquished, and a new life agenda emerges stressing interiority, detachment, and contemplation. The Chinese mountain landscapes, like *The Code of Manu*, must be taken as endorsements of a disengagement orientation in late life. They affirm both a "psychological" and an "ethical" doctrine of disengagement, the first affirming that a transition to a relatively disengaged posture *does* occur as a natural developmental stage and the second affirming that acceptance of that change, rather than persistence in the orientation proper for midlife, is an ethically correct path.

So far I have described some of the pictorial themes and motifs through which these paintings make statements about aging. The paintings have another important dimension that deserves attention, namely, the calligraphic inscriptions very frequently written on them. These inscriptions include titles, poems, or comments of various kinds made by the artist; poems written by friends of the artists or by successive owners of the works; and other commentary. It is not unusual for a work in this genre—even a great masterpiece—to have a large percentage of its surface covered by such calligraphy. These writing are usually considered part of the work itself because of the aesthetic beauty and expressiveness of Chinese calligraphic figures. I will comment only on what such writings sometimes contribute to the aging motif. To understand this it is important to appreciate their strongly poetic flavor. Their having a poetic dimension is not surprising; it reflects the importance of poetry as a mode of expression and communication in Chinese culture.

Understood in this way, the calligraphic inscriptions are often unmistakably evocative of aging themes. We have already seen this in the title *Listening to the Waterfall* as an allusion to integrative understanding and the title *Returning Boat on Crane Lake* as an allusion to life review. These two titles are typical of many others whose poetic connotations are equally evocative of aging themes. . . .

The agreement between these pictures, painted centuries ago, and concepts of recent Western gerontology suggests that those concepts may have universal application, or at least one wider than to our own time and place. This is a useful confirmation of gerontological theory. But there is a more important value in the congruence of art and theory we have been examining. It reveals the artists who created these paintings as remarkable observers and interpreters of human aging. In a sense this is not surprising, since the culture they lived in attached far more status and importance to old age than our culture does. We may therefore hope that these paintings will yield important further observations and interpretations of late life, still unknown to current theories and waiting to be discovered by aesthetic study. I shall briefly suggest two examples.

First, what is the meaning of the detachment, the absence of intimacy in the people who inhabit these scenes? We get no direct look at their faces or any close-up view of their dwellings. This remoteness contrasts sharply with most Western interpretations of old age in painting, such as Rembrandt's late self-portraits and images of Saint Jerome by Dürer, Leonardo, Rubens and Massys, in which the aging subject's personality is vividly present to the viewer. This impersonal quality may express a view that the contemplative style of late life is or should be directed more at the nonpersonal aspects of the world than at personal relationships. This would differ from the prevailing Western tradition, which tends to see interpersonal relationships, including the relation to a personal God, as indispensable to well-being. But it may be that human beings are oriented toward the impersonal as well as, or even more fundamentally than, toward interpersonal relationships. It is not necessary to assume, as we usually do, that meaning in life is exclusively or even primarily dependent at all stages of life on interpersonal relationships. Freedom from "the other," like freedom from material possessions, may at times have much to recommend it. Abraham Maslow saw the ability to depersonalize as a necessity for creativity: "Certain *prerequisites* of creativeness—in whatever realm—have something to do with this ability to become selfless, outside of . . . society, of history." From this perspective, attachment to the personal may express a dependence which is transcended in late life. This possibility is wholly unexplored in recent gerontology. It is, however, strongly suggested by the paintings we have been discussing.

A second theme in these paintings that might anticipate gerontological theory is the mood of receptivity often expressed in them. What I mean is indicated by such terms and phrases in their titles and accompanying poems as "listening quietly," "sitting and watching the clouds," "brewing tea" (a process of waiting), "gazing at the autumn moon," and is also expressed in the quiet contemplative postures of the scholars depicted. It has been suggested that typically Western cognitive styles are "promethean" or "grasping," in which understanding is sought through the mind's aggressive analytical attack upon its object. There is another mental style, characterized by a willingness to wait for the object to speak to us. This mental style requires not such controlling acts of mind as abstraction and category making, but rather a state of receptivity to the world and to our own inner voice. The aged scholars of the Chinese landscapes, looking calmly out over their rocky precipices or sitting quietly among their waterfalls and soughing pines, may have much to tell us about this that will enrich our theories of late life.

Donald Keene

JAPANESE
AESTHETICS

*Donald Keene is Shincho Professor of Japanese
Literature at Columbia University. He has written
and edited many books on Chinese and Japanese
literature, including* Anthology of Chinese Literature,
Anthology of Japanese Literature, *and* Japanese
Literature: An Introduction for Western Readers. *In the
essay that follows, Keene describes several distinctive
values that characterize the Japanese aesthetic.*

. . . Despite the modernization and the internationalization of standards today, the visitor to Japan never fails to notice the flowers, real or artificial, clustered in a little holder near the bus-driver's head; or the flowers gracefully bending down from a wall-bracket over the toilet; or the artistically brushed signboard in the railway station which proves to mean "Left Luggage Room"; or, for that matter, the maddening artistry with which a parcel is likely to be wrapped in a department store when one is in a hurry. These sights surprise the visitor, who marvels that aestheticism should be so pervasive, but he might equally wonder, of course, why busses, toilets, and left luggage rooms in his own country are not considered the appropriate places for floral or calligraphic embellishment. Or, to take the most famous instance of all, the exquisite appearance of Japanese food, despite its often pallid taste, has been praised by every foreign visitor; indeed, a meal served in the private room of a fine restaurant, where every detail from the color of the cushions of the *tatami* and the flower in the alcove to the last little sauce dish has been artistically planned, tends to make the occasion an aesthetic, rather than a gustatory experience. One has only to know how a first-rate Chinese dinner would be served in Jakarta today or in Shanghai in bygone years to become aware of the special place of aestheticism in Japanese life, as contrasted with other countries of Asia.

These examples may seem facetious, but, however trivial, they should suggest how important is the role played in daily Japanese life today of aesthetic preferences that go back very far in Japanese history. Descriptions in the works of fiction of a thousand years ago, as well as in the diaries and essays, plainly indicate how absorbed the Japanese were with considerations of

Donald Keene, "Japanese Aesthetics," *Philosophy East and West* 19 (1969): 293–326.

beauty. The European knight wore his lady's glove in his helmet, but it would not have occurred to him to examine the glove first to make sure it met his aesthetic standards and confirmed his judgment that his lady was worth dying for; he was quite content to think that the glove had once graced her hand, and an overly fastidious examination of the material, color, pattern and so on would not have endeared him to the lady. The Japanese courtier of the eleventh century, on the other hand, was adamant in his insistence on aesthetic accomplishments in any woman he might offer his love. A note from her in somewhat less than flawless calligraphy, or a disillusioning glimpse of her sleeve that suggested the lady lacked a perfect sensitivity to color harmonies, might easily have dampened his ardor. . . .

. . . A number of headings under which Japanese aesthetics might be discussed come to mind: suggestion, irregularity, simplicity, and perishability. These related concepts point to the most typical forms of Japanese aesthetic expression though . . . exaggeration, uniformity, profusion, and durability are by no means absent.

SUGGESTION

The poet and critic Fujiwara no Kintō (966–1041), dividing poetry into nine categories of excellence, described the highest category thus: "The language is magical and conveys more meanings than the words themselves express." To illustrate this criterion he offered the following poem:

honobono to	Dimly, dimly
Akashi no ura no	The day breaks at Akashi Bay;
asagiri ni	And in the morning mist
shimagakureyuku	My heart follows a vanishing ship
fune wo shi zo omou	As it goes behind an island.

Part of the beauty of this poem lies in the use of language and even the sounds (for example, the o sounds of the first line echoed at the end), but its chief claim to distinction in the eyes of Fujiwara no Kintō was its power of suggesting unspoken implications. The poem would be less if more specific: if, for example, it made clear that the poet's sweetheart was aboard the disappearing ship or that the poet himself for some reason wished he were aboard. The ambiguity, a well-known feature of the Japanese language, which commonly omits the subjects of sentences, is exploited in this poem so as to expand the thirty-one syllables of the tanka to suggest an atmosphere and an emotional state nowhere specifically stated. A sense of mystery is intensified by the mist obscuring the dawn seascape as the ship disappears. What did this sight mean to the poet? Clearly he did not remain impassive, a mere observer. But if the instant when the ship disappeared he felt a stab of parting, he does not choose to explain why.

The reliance of this poem on suggestion, if not a uniquely Japanese phenomenon, is certainly unlike the common European forms of literary expression. Ambiguity was not highly esteemed by, say, Renaissance writers on poetics, who associated it with the humor of the pun. However rich in ambiguity the sonnets of Shakespeare may actually be, some statement of truth or experience is invariably made. But what is the statement in this Japanese poem? Surely it is not the simple recording of the meaningless event of an autumn morning; the sight unquestionably had meaning for the poet, and he assumes it will have meaning for the reader too, but he does not define the nature of this meaning.

The element of suggestion in the poem is the source of its beauty, yet when compared to later Japanese poetry its level of suggestion may seem shallow. By the end of the twelfth century the ideal known as yūgen (or, mystery and depth) was developed by

Fujiwara Shunzei (1114–1204). *Yūgen* as an aesthetic principle has been defined by Brower and Miner in *Japanese Court Poetry* as "The mid-classical ideal of tonal complexity conveyed by the overtones . . . of poems typically in the mode of descriptive symbolism." This ideal may recall Poe's "suggestive indefiniteness of vague and therefore of spiritual effect." The vagueness admired by Poe was easily achieved by Japanese poets, thanks to the Japanese language. The lack of distinctions between singular and plural or between definite and indefinite contributes to the ambiguity, at least to the Western reader who is accustomed to such distinctions. For a Japanese poet precision in language would limit the range of suggestion, as we can easily see from a famous *haiku* by Bashō (1644–1694):

kareeeda ni	On the withered bough
karasu no tomarikeri	A crow has alighted:
aki no kure	Nightfall in autumn.

This English translation represents a possible interpretation of the Japanese words, but the arbitrary nature of its choices of singular and plural is apparent from an eighteenth-century painting illustrating this *haiku* that depicts no less than eight crows alighted on a number of withered branches. This equally possible interpretation of the poem presents a landscape less lonely than that of a single crow on a single withered branch, an interpretation of the poem found in other illustrative paintings, but may convey an even more brooding intensity. Again, the last line of the *haiku*, *aki no kure*, can also be interpreted as meaning "the nightfall of autumn"—that is, the end of autumn. If we were to insist on determining which meaning the poet intended, whether the nightfall of a particular autumn day or the end of the autumnal season, the answer might well be that *both* were intended. If Bashō's phrase were interpreted as meaning nightfall, regardless of whether it were early

or late in autumn, it might suggest that the crow (or crows) were alighting on a withered branch in a tree otherwise filled with bright leaves, producing a disharmonious impression; but if the scene intended had been an unspecified time of day toward the end of autumn, it might mean that the crow was alighting in the full glare of noon, an equally inappropriate possibility. Many meanings and implications may be extracted from the seventeen syllables of this *haiku*, thanks to the ambiguity of the language. However, Bashō's ultimate meaning, what he intended the two elements of the *haiku* to say about each other, and how far beyond the words themselves the suggestions reach, may still elude us.

The *haiku* on the alighting crow exemplifies a related aspect of Japanese aesthetics, the preference for monochromes to bright colors. It is true that magnificent examples of Japanese art—the celebrated *Tale of Genji* scroll among them—are brilliantly colored, but I believe that most Japanese critics would agree that the prevailing preference in Japanese aesthetics has been for the monochrome. The black crow alighting on a withered branch at a time of day and season when all color has vanished suggests the lonely beauty admired by countless Japanese poets, or the severity of Japanese gardens consisting of stones and sand, or the unpainted interiors and exteriors of a Japanese house. The use of color can be brilliant, but it inevitably limits the suggestive range: when a flower is painted red, it can be no other color, but the black outline of a flower of white paper will let us imagine whatever color we choose.

These words may suggest the aesthetics of Zen Buddhism. Indeed, much of what is considered most typical in Japanese aesthetics stems from Zen. Or, it might be more accurate to say, it coincides with Zen. The simplicity of a Shintō shrine building, the bare lines of its architecture and grounds, was an expression of an indigenous preference which coincided with Zen ideals, and made the Japanese receptive to the more sophisticated aesthetics of the continental religion. The Japanese were equally receptive to the aesthetics of the Chinese artists and poets of the Sung dynasty who also favored monochromes. But the principle of suggestion as an aesthetic technique need not have been learned from abroad.

Suggestion as an artistic technique is given one of its most perfect forms of expression in the Nō theatre. The undecorated stage, the absence of props other than bare outlines, the disregard for all considerations of time and space in the drama, the use of a language that is usually obscure and of abstract gestures that scarcely relate to the words, all make it evident that this theatre, unlike representational examples elsewhere (or Kabuki in Japan) was meant to be the outward, beautiful form suggestive of remoter truths or experiences, the nature of which will differ from person to person. The large role played by suggestion, as contrasted with the explicit descriptions of people and situations we more normally encounter in the theatre, gives the Nō an absolute character. It baffles or bores many Japanese, but it moves others in ways that more conventional, dated varieties of drama cannot, and the same holds true of Western spectators. The groans, the harsh music that precedes the entrance of the actors, may irritate a contemporary spectator, but they may also make him sense in a way impossible with words alone the distance separating the world of the dead from the world of the living, the terrible attachment to this world that causes ghosts to return again to suffer the past, or the pain of being born.

Nō can profoundly move even Western spectators totally unfamiliar with Japanese culture, but it can equally repel others who are committed to a representational variety of theatre. Performances staged in Europe and America have been criticized as having insignificant plots and inadequate characterization. After a performance in New York a member of the Actors' Studio complained that the character Tsunemasa did nothing to convince the audience he was indeed a great musician. Such objections, which would be scornfully rejected by admirers of Nō, cannot be attributed merely to the hostility of people ignorant of tradition. Suggestion as an aesthetic method is always open to the charge of deception—of being no more than the Emperor's new clothes. The monk Shōtetsu, writing in the fifteenth century, recognized that the mysterious powers of suggestion designated by the term *yūgen* could not be appreciated by most men:

> *Yūgen* can be apprehended by the mind, but it cannot be expressed in words. Its quality may be suggested by the sight of a thin cloud veiling the moon or by autumn mist swathing the scarlet leaves on a mountainside. If one is asked where in these sights lies the *yūgen*, one cannot say, and it is not surprising that a man who fails to understand this truth is likely to prefer the sight of a perfectly clear, cloudless sky. It is quite impossible to explain wherein lies the interest or the remarkable nature of *yūgen*.

. . . Suggestion depends on a willingness to admit that meanings exist beyond what can be seen or described. In the theatre the Nō actors risk failure if the audience refuses to make this concession, but for the Japanese poet or connoisseur of art the pleasures of suggestion could become an end in themselves to the exclusion of considerations of convincing representation. We can infer this from a famous passage found in *Essays in Idleness* by Kenkō (1283–1350): "Are we to look at cherry blossoms only in full bloom, the moon only when it is cloudless? To long for the moon while looking on the rain, to lower the blinds and be unaware of the passing of the spring—these are even more deeply moving. Branches about to blossom or gardens strewn with faded flowers are worthier of our admiration."

A more common Western conception is that of the climax, the terrible moment when Laocoon and his sons are caught in the serpent's embrace, or the ecstatic moment when the soprano hits high C; but for Kenkō the climax was less interesting than the beginnings and ends, for it left nothing to be imagined. The full moon or the cherry blossoms at their peak do not suggest the crescent or the buds, though the crescent and buds (or the waning moon and the strewn flowers) do suggest the full moon and full flowering. Perfection, like some inviolable sphere, repels the imagination, allowing it no room to penetrate. Bashō's only poem about Mount Fuji describes a day when fog prevented him from seeing the peak. Beginnings that suggest what is to come, or ends that suggest what has been, allow the imagination room to expand beyond the literal facts to the limits of the capacities of the reader of a poem, the spectator at a Nō play, or the connoisseur of a monochrome painting. Beginnings and ends are also of special interest with respect to the development of the form itself: primitive painting or the moderns are more apt to excite people today than the works of Raphael or of Andrea del Sarto, the perfect painter. Here, as so often, a curious coincidence brings traditional Japanese tastes into congruence with those of the contemporary West.

IRREGULARITY

The emphasis on beginnings and ends implied a rejection of regularity as well as of perfection. We know from the earliest literary and artistic remains that the Japanese have generally avoided symmetry and regularity, perhaps finding them constricting and obstructive to the powers of suggestion. Symmetry in Japanese literature and art, whether in the use of parallel prose or architectural constructions arranged along a central axis, almost invariably reflects Chinese or other continental influence. In the *Fudoki*, gazetteers compiled by imperial order early in the eighth century, we find such passages as: "In spring the cherry trees along the shore are a thousand shades of color; in autumn the leaves on the banks are tinted a hundred hues. The warbler's song is heard in the fields, and cranes are seen dancing on the strand. Village boys and fisher girls throng the shore; merchants and farmers pole their boats to and fro." The relentless insistence on parallel expression, so natural to the Chinese, was normally antithetical to the Japanese, despite occasional experimentations. This passage represented an ill-digested emulation of Chinese writing that contrasts with the almost invariable preference for irregularity, and even for prime numbers: for example, the thirty-one syllables of the *tanka*, the classic verse form, are arranged in lines of five, seven, five, seven, and seven syllables. Nothing could be farther removed from the couplets and quatrains that make up normal poetic usage in so many countries. Even when the Japanese intended to take over bodily a Chinese artistic conception, such as the architectural plan of a monastery, they seem to have felt uncomfortable with the stark symmetry prescribed, and before long broke the monotony by moving some buildings to the other side of the central axis. Soper contrasted the regularity of Chinese temple architecture with its subsequent development in Japan: "What remained from the first generation was a sensible irregularity of plan. . . . At the Shingon Kongōbuji on Kōyasan, the central cleared area is a fairly spacious and level one that might have permitted at least a minimal Chinese scheme. Instead, as if by deliberate rejection, the main elements, though they face south, are on independent axes."

Kenkō suggested why the Japanese were so fond of irregularity: "In everything, no matter what it may be, uniformity is undesirable. Leaving something incomplete makes it interesting, and gives one the feeling that there is room for growth." Or again, "People often say that a set of books looks ugly if all volumes are not in the same format, but I was impressed to hear the Abbot Kōyū say, 'It is typical of the unintelligent man to insist on assembling complete sets of everything. Imperfect sets are better.'" Undoubtedly librarians in Kenkō's day were less enthusiastic than he about the desirability of incomplete sets, but as anyone knows who has ever confronted the grim volumes of a complete set of the Harvard Classics, they do not invite browsing. A partiality for irregularity reveals itself also in the ceramics preferred by the Japanese. If you are a guest at a tea ceremony and are offered your choice of bowl—a lovely celadon piece, or a fine porcelain with delicate patterns, or a bumpy, misshapen pot rather suggesting an old shoe—it is easy to prove your appreciation of Japanese aesthetics by unhesitantly selecting the old shoe. A perfectly formed round bowl is boring to the Japanese, for it lacks any trace of the individuality of the potter.

In calligraphy too, copybook perfection is ridiculed or condescendingly dismissed as something best left to the Chinese; Japanese preference tends to favor the lopsided, exaggeratedly individual characters written by a *haiku* or tea ceremony master. In gardens too, the geometrically executed formations of the Alhambra or Versailles would seem to the Japanese less a place to repose the eyes and heart than a rigid mathematical demonstration. The Chinese garden, more natural than the European formal garden, inspired the romanticism of design so dear to the eighteenth-century English landscape architects. But the Japanese went far beyond the Chinese in the irregularity and even eccen-

tricity of their gardens. Derek Clifford, in *A History of Garden Design*, expressed his disapproval of Japanese gardens, contrasting them with the more agreeable Chinese; according to Clifford, "the Chinese stopped short at the extreme lengths of development to which the Japanese went." Clifford seems never to have actually seen a Japanese garden, but he found the famous stone and sand garden of the Ryōanji, the subject of an admiring essay by Sacheverell Sitwell, to be offensive and even dangerous:

> It is the logical conclusion of the refinement of the senses, the precipitous world of the abstract painter, a world in which the stains on the cover of a book can absorb one more utterly than the ceiling of the Sistine chapel; it is the narrow knife edge of art, overthrowing and discarding all that man has ever been and achieved in favour of some mystic contemplative ecstacy, a sort of suspended explosion of the mind, the dissolution of identity. You really cannot go much further than this unless you sit on a cushion like Oscar Wilde and contemplate the symmetry of an orange.

The symmetry of an orange was hardly calculated to absorb the attention of the architects of this exceedingly asymmetrical garden. The marvellous irregularity of the disposition of the stones eludes the analysis of the most sensitive observer. Far from being the artless "stains on the cover of a book," the Ryōanji garden is the product of a philosophical system—that of Zen Buddhism—as serious as that which inspired the ceiling of the Sistine Chapel. And, it might be argued, even a European might derive greater pleasure from daily contemplation of the fifteen stones of the Ryōanji garden than of the Sistine Chapel, without "overthrowing and discarding all that man has ever been and achieved." The Sistine Chapel is magnificent, but it asks our admiration rather than our participation; the stones of the Ryōanji, irregular in shape and position, by allowing us to participate in the creation of the garden may move us even more. But that may be, again, because our own age is closer in artistic expression to that of the Ryōanji than to that of Michelangelo.

SIMPLICITY

The use of the most economical means to obtain the desired effect, the product of Zen philosophy, is another characteristic of the garden of the Ryōanji. The same philosophy affected the creation of many other gardens—the waterless river that swirls through the landscape of the Tenryūji garden, foaming over artfully placed rocks, or the waterless cascade that tumbles through green moss at the Saihōji. But the preference for simplicity in gardens is not restricted to those of Zen temples. The use of a single natural rock for the bridge over a tiny pond or for a water basin suggests the love of the texture of the stone untampered with by human skill. Even the disdain for flowers as a distracting and disruptive element in a garden suggests an insistence on the bare bones of the abstract garden, which has no need for the superficial charm of an herbaceous border or a flower bed that is "a riot of color." Simplicity and the natural qualities of the material employed may have been first emphasized by the Zen teachers, but they are now common ideals of the Japanese people. Soper has pointed out: "A feature of Zen buildings which their origin makes curious is their frequently complete lack of painted decoration, interiors and exteriors alike being left in natural wood. Such austerity is certainly non-Chinese, and must mark a deliberate choice on the part of early Japanese Zen masters . . . in compliance with the spirit of simplicity inherent in Zen teachings." Early Buddhist temples in Japan had been painted on the outside, generally a dull red (as we may see today at the Byōdō-in), but from the thirteenth century onward most temples, regardless of their sect, tended to be built of unpainted wood. The same held true of palaces and private houses.

Kenkō's expression of his own preference for simplicity in the decoration of a house came to be shared by most Japanese: "A house which multitudes of workmen have polished with every care, where strange and rare Chinese and Japanese furnishings are displayed, and even the grasses and trees of the garden have been trained unnaturally, is ugly to look at and most depressing." It is easier for us to assent to this opinion than it would have been for Western writers fifty years ago. Few writers on Japanese aesthetics today would describe the Ginkakuji (Silver Pavilion) in Sansom's words as "an insignificant structure which belies its name . . . simple to the verge of insipidity." The Ginkakuji does not strike me as an insignificant structure. I certainly prefer it to the elaborate mausolea of the Tokugawa at Nikkō, and I believe most other students of Japan would share my views. But traditionally in the West the house which "multitudes of workmen have polished with every care" has been considered the most desirable, as we know from old photographs showing the profusion of treasures with which the drawing rooms of the rich were commonly adorned. Gardens where even the trees and grasses have been trained unnaturally still attract visitors to the great houses of Europe.

Probably the most extreme expression of the Japanese love for unobtrusive elegance is the tea ceremony. The ideal sought by the great tea master Sen no Rikyū (1521–1591) was *sabi*, a word related to *sabi* "rust" or *sabireru* "to become desolate." This may seem to be a curious aesthetic ideal, but it arose as a reaction to the parvenu extravagance of Rikyū's master, the dictator Hideyoshi, who had built a solid gold portable teahouse he doted on so much he took it with him everywhere on his travels. Rikyū's *sabi* was not the enforced simplicity of the man who could not afford better, but a refusal of easily obtainable luxury, a preference for a rusty-looking kettle to one of gold or gleaming newness, a preference for a tiny undecorated hut to the splendors of a palace. This was not the same as Marie Antoinette playing at shepherdess; in fact, it represented a return to the normal Japanese fondness for simplicity and was in no sense an affectation. *Sabi* was accepted because it accorded with deep-seated aesthetic beliefs. The tea ceremony today is sometimes attacked as being a perversion of the ideals it once embodied, but the expense of a great deal of money to achieve a look of bare simplicity is entirely in keeping with Japanese tradition.

The tea ceremony developed as an art concealing art, an extravagance masked in the garb of noble poverty. The Portuguese missionary João Rodrigues (1561–1634) left behind an appreciative description of a tea ceremony he had attended, but he could not restrain his astonishment over the lengths to which the Japanese carried their passion for unobtrusive luxury: "Because they greatly value and enjoy this kind of gathering to drink tea, they spend large sums of money in building such a house, rough though it may be, and in purchasing the things needed for drinking the kind of tea which is offered in these meetings. Thus there are utensils, albeit of earthenware, which come to be worth ten, twenty or thirty thousand *cruzados* or even more—a thing which will appear as madness and barbarity to other nations that know of it."

Madness perhaps, but surely not barbarity! Everything about the tea ceremony was controlled by the most highly developed aesthetic sensibilities. The avoidance of conspicuous wealth was reinforced by an avoidance of color in the hut, of perfume in the flowers displayed, and of taste in the food offered. The interior of the hut, though it embraces many textures of wood and matting, tends to be almost exclusively in shades of brown, with perhaps a pale dot of color in the alcove. There may be incense burnt, generally of an astringent nature, but the typical scents of Western flowers—rose, carnation, or lilac—would be unthinkable. This preference for understatement may stem from the "climate" of Japan. A Japanese teacher once suggested to me that the colors preferred in Japanese art owed their muted hues to the natural colors of seashells. Whether this is strictly true or not, it is certainly easy to distinguish Japanese prints before and after the introduction of Western dyes. But after a brief period of fascination with the screaming purples, crimsons and emeralds of the new, exotic colors, the Japanese returned to the seashells. It is true that the Japanese landscape offers few bright floral colors, and the native flowers have virtually no smell. The aesthetic choices made in the tea hut may owe as much to nature as to deliberate policy.

Japanese food too, and not only that served in the tea ceremony, lacks the intensity of taste found elsewhere. Just as the faint perfume of the plum blossoms is preferred to the heavy odor of the lily, the barely perceptible differences in favor between different varieties of raw fish are prized extravagantly. The Zen monastery vegetarian cuisine, though the subject of much self-adulation, offers a meager range of tastes, and the fineness of a man's palate can be tested by his ability to distinguish virtually tasteless dishes of the same species. The virtuosity is impressive, but it would be hard to convince a Chinese or a European that a lump of cold bean curd dotted with a dash of soy sauce is indeed superior to the supposedly cloying flavors of *haute cuisine*. The early European visitors to Japan, though they praised almost everything else, had nothing good to say about Japanese food. Bernardo de Avila Girón wrote, "I will not praise Japanese food for it is not good, albeit it is pleasing to the eye, but instead I will describe the clean and peculiar way in which it is served." The absence of meat, in conformance with the Buddhist proscription, undoubtedly limited the appeal of Japanese cuisine to the Portuguese and Spanish visitors, but the characteristic preference for simplicity and naturalness—the undisguised flavors of vegetables and fish—was essentially aesthetic.

The insistence on simplicity and naturalness placed a premium on the connoisseur's appreciation of quality. An unpainted wooden column shows the natural quality of the tree from which it was formed just as an uncooked piece of fish reveals its freshness more than one surrounded by sauce. In the Nō theatre too the lack of the usual distractions in a performance—sets, lighting, and the rest—focuses all attention on the actor, and demands a connoisseur to appreciate the slight differences in gesture or voice that distinguish a great actor from a merely competent one. Within the limited ranges permitted in their traditional arts the Japanese prized shadings. Seldom did the painter, poet, or Nō actor take the risks involved in bold statement, as opposed to controlled simplicity; for this reason there is almost nothing of bad taste in traditional Japan. Simplicity is safer than profusion as an aesthetic guide, but if the outsider fails to develop the virtuoso sensibilities of the Japanese he may find that he craves something beyond understatement—whether the brilliance of a chandelier, the depth of taste of a great wine, or the overpowering sound of the Miserere in *Il Trovatore*. By choosing suggestion and simplicity the Japanese forfeited a part of the possible artistic effects, but when they succeeded they created works of art of a beauty unaffected by the shifting tides of taste.

PERISHABILITY

Beyond the preference for simplicity and the natural qualities of things lies what is perhaps the most distinctively Japanese aesthetic ideal, perishability. The desire in the West has generally been to achieve artistic immortality, and this has led men to erect monuments in deathless marble. The realization that even such monuments crumble and disappear has brought tears to the eyes of the poets. The Japanese have built for impermanence, though paradoxically some of the oldest buildings in the world exist in Japan. The Japanese belief that perishability is a necessary element in beauty does not of course mean that they have been insensitive to the poignance of the passage of time. Far from it. Whatever the subject matter of the old poems, the underlying meaning was often an expression of grief over the fragility of beauty and love. Yet the Japanese were keenly aware that without this mortality there could be no beauty. Kenkō wrote, "If man were never to fade away like the dews of Adashino, never to vanish like the smoke over Toribeyama, but lingered on forever in the world, how things would lose their power to move us! The most precious thing in life is its uncertainty." The frailty of human existence, a common theme in literature throughout the world, has rarely been recognized as the necessary condition of beauty. The Japanese not only know this, but expressed their preference for varieties of beauty which most conspicuously betrayed their impermanence. Their favorite flower is of course the cherry blossom, precisely because the period of blossoming is so poignantly brief and the danger that the flowers may scatter even before one has properly seen them is so terribly great. Yet for the day or two of pleasure of the blossoming the Japanese dote on a fruit tree that bears no fruit, but instead attracts a disagreeable quantity of insects. Plum blossoms look much the same and are graced with a scent so faint that even a tea master could not object, but they are less highly prized because they linger so long on the boughs. The samurai was traditionally compared to the cherry blossoms, and his ideal was to drop dramatically, at the height of his strength and beauty, rather than to become an old soldier gradually fading away.

The visible presence of perishability in the cracked tea bowl carefully mended in gold has been appreciated not because it makes the object an indisputable antique, but because without the possibility of aging with time and usage there could be no real beauty. Kenkō quoted with approval the poet Ton'a who said, "It is only after the silk wrapper has frayed at top and bottom, and the mother-of-pearl has fallen from the roller, that a scroll looks beautiful." This delight in shabbiness may suggest the Arabic conception of *barak*, the magical quality an object acquires through long use and care. It is obviously at variance not only with the common Western craving for objects in mint condition, but with the desire to annihilate time by restoring a painting so perfectly that people will exclaim, "It could have been painted yesterday!" An object of gleaming stainless steel that never aged would surely have been repugnant to the Japanese of the past, whose love of old things implied the accretions of time.

The traditional Japanese aesthetics cannot be summed up in a few pages, but even without verbalizing what they were it is easy to sense them at work in the objects created and in the objects for which we will look in vain. The virtuoso connoisseur seems now to have shifted his talents to distinguishing between brands of beer or tobacco, and the perfectionist workman may be replaced by a machine, but it seems safe to say that the aesthetic ideals which have formed Japanese taste over the centuries will find their outlet in media yet undiscovered and maintain their distinctive existence.

B. N. Goswamy

RASA: DELIGHT OF THE REASON

B. N. Goswamy is professor of art history at Panjab University in Chandigarh, India. He has written extensively on Indian art and art theory. Among his works are Essence of Indian Art *and* Stylistic Approach to Indian Miniatures. *Goswamy, in the essay that follows, describes the Indian theory of* rasa, *the emotional savor that art arouses in the appropriately sensitive audience member.*

If one were not so much immersed in it oneself, it could be quite an experience to attend a recital in India of classical Indian music simply to observe the responses of the listeners. We can think of a great Indian vocalist presenting, interpreting, a *raga*, the audience sitting on the floor, not far from him, not far even physically, but quite close, almost within touching distance, accompanists in place, instruments tuned. As the singer opens with the slow, ruminative passage of pure voice movement with no words used, the *alaap*, something that—depending upon which tradition, or *gharana*, he comes from—he can elaborate upon and embellish very considerably (being in no hurry at all, in a deliberate, leisurely fashion), one would notice several persons in the audience closing their eyes, inclining their heads slightly, and slowly, very slowly swaying with a gentle, lyrical movement. An occasional nodding or shaking of the head becomes visible. The listeners open their eyes ever so briefly from time to time to look at the singer when he provides a surprising twist or adds a new flourish or grace, but generally they appear as if they were hearing the note patterns twice over: once physically, through the ears, as being performed at that moment and in that space; but also inwardly at the same time, in the mind's ear, as it were. It is as if they know the pattern well and are seeking some kind of confirmation, a correspondence between what is in their minds and what they are hearing at this moment. The cadenced, almost involuntary motions

B. N. Goswamy, *Essence of Indian Art* (San Francisco: Asian Art Museum of San Francisco, 1986) 17–30.

of the singer's hands vary greatly from performance to performance. As he gets into the body of the *raga*, eyes often close, his gestures lend emphasis, complete a statement, suggest other possibilities, open different kinds of windows. While he does this, a certain number of listeners can also be seen picking up these movements imperceptibly, not matching each gesture of the singer with their own but catching the essence of the motions, for these go with the unheard music within them.

When the opening passage yields to the next, developing the theme of the *raga*, also slow but accompanied by a beat and adding words, the number of people in the audience who seem to become one with the singer increases appreciably, for picking up the pattern of the beat is simpler than getting the nuances of complex unaccompanied arrangements of notes. A palpable excitement enters the atmosphere. The heads begin to nod more surely, the emphasis remaining on the slight downward jerk as it synchronizes with each ending of a cycle in the beat; hands move still faintly but discernibly, now echoing the rhythm in the beat. Occasionally, as the singer introduces a new element, using microtonal graces, catching even the attuned members of the audience with a move that surprises, the hint of a smile passes from singer to listeners. One also picks up short snatches of articulated praise or enthusiasm: they do not disturb the performer in the least and are even acknowledged sometimes with a slight nod of the head.

This goes on for a length of time and, depending upon the abilities of the audience, its *utsaha* or energy, a clear exchange, a rapport, is established between the two. When the singer takes the *raga* into a more complex stage and takes *taans*, those dazzlingly elaborate virtuoso permutations and combinations of notes along the ascending or descending scale, he frequently leaves the audience behind, for it is difficult either to predict what he is going to do or to keep pace with those mercurial, lightning turns and twists of voice.

Then, in a faster tempo, when the theme or the burden of the composition is picked up again, a new energy seems to be released among the listeners. Now two different kinds of exchanges take place, those between the singer and audience, and those between him and his accompanists, the player of a stringed instrument such as the *sarangi*, or the percussionist using a pair of *tabla* drums. The singer suddenly springs surprises of all kinds, uses crossrhythms, while the percussionists try to keep pace, even anticipate him on occasions, as if a game of great sophistication were being played among them, all within the approved, strictly laid-down ambit of a *raga*.

At the same time, between singer and listeners, sometimes even between the instrumental accompanists and the listeners, a new rapport is established. Eyes close and then open again in surprise or admiration; heads sway, and whole bodily movements become accentuated. Since the singer is using poetry that is by this point familiar to the audience (if it were not known to it previously), and the burden of the song is fully understood and identified with, one can hear the last words of a verse sung by the performer being picked up and softly whispered by the more alert listeners.

It is all very spontaneous, the unstudied quality emphasizing the involvement of the audience with the *raga*, with the whole recital. A certain glistening of the eyes becomes evident; a mood seems to pervade. There are no paroxysms of delight, no outbursts that distract the singer: all that these gentle movements of head and hands, the meaningful exchanges between singer and listeners, signify is that they are with the singer, feeling distinct vibrations within themselves, even perfecting the rendering of the song by the force of their own imagination and emotion.

At this point, regardless of the theme of the song incorporated in the *raga*—it could be love-in-union, or love-in-separation, or even a song about death or the final realities of life; this is immaterial—a certain lifting of the spirits among the listeners becomes noticeable. No depression descends, even if the burden of the music is sad; on the other hand, there is an elevation of the mind, a rushing forward. It is as if a spark had jumped from singer to listeners. A particularly graceful or difficult movement of notes, an uncommon elegance improvised and inducted into the structure of the *raga*, a verse that has suddenly assumed the character of a revelation because so ably and creatively interpreted by the singer, send a tingle down the spine of many a listener. The word frequently used in India to describe this sensation is horripilation, hair standing on end. The audience is having an experience of delight: it is tasting *rasa*.

I remember from my childhood—I could not have been more than seven or eight years of age at the time—witnessing a performance by a traveling theatrical troupe that came to a little town called Shakargarh, now in Pakistan. My father, a judicial officer who held court ten days in a month away from his district headquarters, was on a tour of that place, and we children were accompanying him.

The touring company, as it was called, has come and pitched its tents in the open space behind the civil rest-house in which we were staying. They set up a raised stage with the roughest of materials; the curtains with sceneries painted on them were all installed during the day, as we stood around and watched. The musical mixed a great deal of singing by the actors with dialogues which were also mostly in rhyme, following the tradition that I now know to be Parsi theatre, was titled *Wamaq Azra*. None of us understood what the title meant, and it was only much later that I found out that these were the names of two lovers from a famous Persian love legend.

There was excitement when a group of barkers went around the town distributing handbills and making announcements on a horn concerning the performance. There was no entry fee, as the play must have been sponsored by some local patron. A fair crowd gathered in the evening, and we children sneaked out of our rest-house rooms and stood at the back. There were no elaborate lights, no sets but for the painted backdrops, but there was music before the performance began to keep the audience quiet and entertained.

I recall absolutely nothing of the story or the quality of the performance. All that I vividly remember is the sustained music played on traditional instruments throughout the performance, and occasional outbursts of despair from the actors. Clearly, it was an emotion-charged play, full of situations that must have been easy for the spectators to comprehend and identify with. For me, much remained opaque: the language was too high-flown, being some kind of Persianized Urdu, and the plot was outside my reach.

But the music that belonged to the performance apart, what stands out in my mind is the sound of suppressed sobbing that came from the audience. The situation in the play must have been of unbearable grief, arising from some kind of irreversible separation, and several members of the audience seemed to be choked with feeling, silent tears flowing, mouths dry, a lump in their throats that evidently refused to go away. The performance had obviously led to a certain melting of the heart. I remember seeing with a sense of bewilderment grown men wiping tears silently from their eyes and holding their heads between their hands—trying to suppress emotions, anxious not to display them—covering the lower parts of their faces in the coarse cotton sheets that served as wraps around their shoulders in the slight chill of the evening. The spectators seemed to be a rustic, uncouth group of people, but evidently they responded to the performance and were deeply moved by it. Today I would say, recalling that evening, that they were experiencing an aesthetic emotion occasioned by the performance.

The single most important term that figures in the formal theory of art developed in India from very early times is undoubtedly *rasa.* To understand the term outwardly is not difficult, and its several meanings are within easy reach. In its most obvious sense, the sense in which it is still employed most widely in daily parlance in India, it means the sap or juice of plants, extract, fluid. In this physical sense, it is easy to identify: when one speaks thus of the *rasa* of orange or sugarcane, for instance, one is certain that the word means the same thing to everyone. In its secondary sense, *rasa* signifies the nonmaterial essence of a thing, "the best or finest part of it," like perfume, which comes from matter but is not so easy to describe or comprehend. In its tertiary sense, *rasa* denotes taste, flavor, relish related to consuming or handling either the physical object or taking in its nonphysical properties, often yielding pleasure.

In its final and subtlest sense, however— and this is close to the tertiary sense in which the word is applied to art and aesthetic experience—*rasa* comes to signify a state of heightened delight, in the sense of *ananda,* the kind of bliss that can be experienced only by the spirit. As later writers such as Vishwanatha, fourteenth century author of the *Sahitya Darpana,* a celebrated work on poetics, say: *rasa* is an experience akin to ultimate reality, "twin brother to the tasting of Brahma." In Vishwanatha, the very definition of poetry involves invoking the word *rasa.* His dictum is often quoted: "Poetry is a sentence the soul of which is *rasa.*"

The theory of art that centers around the idea of *rasa* was enunciated for the first time, in the form that it has come down to us, by Bharata in the *Natyashastra,* that extraordinary work on the arts of the theater, which is generally placed close to the beginning of the Christian era. But its roots go back still farther, for even as he sets it forth in outline, Bharata acknowledges his debt to older masters. Bharata enunciates and applies the *rasa* theory to the arts of the stage, incorporating dance and music (*natya*), but, as Coomaraswamy says, the theory is "immediately applicable to art of all kinds," much of its terminology specifically employing the concept of color. . . .

So pervasive and widespread is the use of the term *rasa* in the context of the arts in India, so often is it evoked by critics and common viewers or readers, that it forms a central part of the vocabulary of art. A performance of dance or music or of a play often might be criticized as being devoid of *rasa* (*nirasa*), or praised for yielding *rasa* in great measure. The voice of a singer would be acclaimed for being charged with *rasa* (*rasili*), the eyes of the beloved would be described as filled with *rasa,* and so on. Whatever philosophers and theoreticians might have to say of the term and the many complexities that attend its proper understanding when applied to art, the simple appreciator of art knows his mind quite well and uses the term frequently, often with remarkable accuracy. Great and considered works on rhetoric might insist that the justification of art lies in its service of the fourfold purposes of life, its aims (*purusharthas*) as generally understood in India: right action (*dharma*), pleasure (*karma*), wealth (*artha*), and spiritual freedom (*moksha*). At the ordinary level, it is understood that art must result in an experience of *rasa,* must yield delight. Of the four ends of life, as Coomaraswamy says, "the first three represent the proximate and last the ultimate.

The work of art is determined in the same way . . . proximately with regard to immediate use, and ultimately with regard to aesthetic experience." Referring to Vishwanatha, he maintains:

> . . . mere narration, bare utility, are not art, or are only art in a rudimentary sense. Nor has art as such a merely informative value confined to its explicit meaning: only the man of little wit can fail to recognize that art is by nature a well-spring of delight, whatever may have been the occasion of its appearance.

That *rasa* is what art is all about may not be specifically stated in so many words by everyone, but in a very real sense it is what a viewer is looking for in a work of art. I remember quite sharply an occasion when I took some keen doubt of mine, a small inquiry regarding the date or style of a painting, to that great connoisseur of the arts of India, the late Rai Krishna Dasa in Benaras. Rai Sahib, as he was almost universally called, heard my questions with his usual grace and patience, then learned back on the comfortable round bolster on his simple divan and said softly: "These questions I will now leave to you eager historians of art. All that I want to do, at this stage of my life"— he was past seventy years of age then and in frail health—"is to taste *rasa*." Nobody knew more than Rai Sahib about the kinds of questions that I had taken to him at that time, but somehow he had moved on to, or back toward, what the real meaning or purpose of art was, in his eyes.

That in the context of the arts *rasa* is central, something toward which things move and around which they so often revolve, comes through even in Coomaraswamy's brilliant essay, "The Theory of Art in Asia." Bringing a refreshingly different but valid point of view to the average Western reader and critic of his days, Coomaraswamy elaborated upon many Eastern theories in his essay. He explored and attempted to bring within reach many ideas, ranging from the nature and meaning of representation in art as seen though Asian eyes, to the nature of art itself, discussing the issue of ideal types and the six canons of art developed in China and India. He speaks in this essay of symbolism and conventions, of decadence and intellectuality, as understood in the arts of a culture like India, emphasizing how an object of Indian art is a visual symbol, "ideal in the mathematical sense." He also distinguishes between originality and novelty on the one hand, and intensity or energy, on the other. Significantly, the discussion is crowned by, or at least moves in the end toward, the complex notion of *rasa* as forming a part of the "formal theory of art" in India. He seems to say that it is in the context of *rasa*, and with constant reference to it, that art seems to have been viewed in an earlier age in India.

. . . In the performing arts of India, *rasa* is spoken of all too often as being part of the languages of the dancer and the musician, and of the vocabulary of the critic. But in the visual arts, it is not mentioned with as much frequency or self-assurance. It may be useful therefore to begin with understanding the *rasa* experience—not easy to analyze— with reference to its various parts. This will have to be done through the work of writers on the arts of the theater or of poetry, for not much has been written on it with reference to the visual arts. But understanding it in its outline, even if in terms of the world of drama or poetry, would present no serious difficulty. Although the subject bristles with problems, the broad outlines—and these alone interest us here—are reasonably clear.

An impressive amount of literature has been written in India on rhetoric in which ideas on *rasa* figure most prominently. A lively debate seems to have gone on for nearly fifteen hundred years with regard to the true nature of *rasa*: some things are clear, but others remain obscure or elusive. For any understanding of *rasa*, however, a prerequisite is to gain familiarity with some basic terms. The terms had to be expounded at some length by Bharata and some later writers, for the whole understanding of the ideas contained in this theory of art would depend on a precise comprehension of these forms. It needs to be remembered that many of them are not employed in common parlance, certainly not as commonly or easily as *rasa* is, and some writers have been quick to point out that some of these terms were coined or bent toward specific usage by Bharata, so that they are not easily confused with ordinarily employed terms and are seen as possessing special meanings. To this generally difficult situation, we have to add the difficulty of translating them from Sanskrit into Western languages. The difficulty is compounded because different translators of Sanskrit texts in which these terms occur have used different English equivalents for Sanskrit originals. One cannot speak of any standard renderings of these terms: it would serve the interests of clarity, therefore, if the Sanskrit originals are used with some frequency along with their translations.

As we have observed, the word *rasa* is variously rendered. At one point, Coomaraswamy uses for it the term "ideal beauty." While "tincture" or "essence" are not employed in the context of aesthetic experience, the word commonly favored is "flavor." Manmohan Ghosh, in his translation of the text of Bharata's *Natyashastra,* preferred the term "sentiment"; other writers have used the word "relish" for *rasa.* Aesthetic experience is described as the "tasting of flavor" (*rasasvadana*); the taster, in other words the viewer or reader, more specifically a scholar or connoisseur, is referred to as a *rasika.* A work of art possessing *rasa* is often described as being *rasavat,* or *rasavant.* Other terms, a little more difficult to understand because they are used in a very special sense, are: *bhava* (rendered as mood or emotional state), *vibhavas* (determinants), *anub-*

havas (consequents), and *vyabhicharibhavas* (complementary emotional states). A *sthayibhava* is an enduring or durable emotional state; *sattvika bhavas* are involuntary bodily responses in states of emotion. Each of these terms needs to be clearly understood, but to this we can return later.

Some idea of the controversies that obtain in the domain of the *rasa* theory can be gained from the fact that there is no clear agreement even about how many *rasas* there are. Bharata speaks of eight sentiments (to which a widely accepted ninth has been added by later writers): Shringara (the erotic), Hasya (the comic), Karuna (the pathetic), Raudra (the furious), Vira (the heroic), Bhayanaka (the terrible), Bibhatsa (the odious), and Adbhuta (the marvelous). The ninth *rasa* spoken of is Shanta (the quiescent).

These are separately listed because even though *rasa* is defined as one and undivided it is one or the other of these nine *rasas* through which an aesthetic experience takes place, in the language employed by Bharta and later rhetoricians. Because out of these nine, one sentiment or flavor dominates, a work of art propels a spectator toward, or becomes the occasion for, a *rasa* experience.

Aesthetic experience as defined in this context is the act of tasting a *rasa,* "of immersing oneself in it to the exclusion of all else." In essence, Bharata seems to say, with reference to theatrical performance, the focus of his work, "*rasa* is born from the union of the play with the performance of the actors." A great deal of later discussion verges on the interpretation of a terse statement of Bharata's, a *sutra* or aphorism, which reads; "*Rasa* is born out of the union of the determinants (*vibhavas*), the consequents (*anubhavas*) and the complementary emotional states (*vyabhicharibhavas*)." In explanation, Bharata says rather little—later writers were to debate the point with heat and acrimony—but it is appropriate that his exact words be taken in first. After making this brief pronouncement, he asks a rhetorical question: "Is there any instance [parallel to it]?" and proceeds to answer:

> [Yes], it is said that as taste [*rasa*] results from a combination of various spices, vegetables and other articles, and as six tastes are produced by articles, such as raw sugar or spices or vegetables, so the durable emotional states [*sthayibhava*], when they come together with various other psychological states, attain the quality of a sentiment [i.e. become sentiment]. Now one inquires, "What is the meaning of the word *rasa*?" It is said in reply [that *rasa* is so called] because it is capable of being tasted. How is *rasa* tasted? [In reply] it is said that just as well-disposed persons while eating food cooked with many kinds of spices enjoy its taste, and attain pleasure and satisfaction, so the cultured people taste the durable emotional states while they see them represented by an expression of the various emotional states with words, gestures, and derive pleasure and satisfaction. Just as a connoisseur of cooked food [*bhakta*] while eating food which has been prepared from various spices and other articles tastes it, so the learned people taste in their heart [*manas*] the durable emotional states [such as love, sorrow etc.] when they are represented by an expression of the emotional states with gestures. Hence, these durable emotional states in a drama are called sentiments.

Much else follows and several issues arise, but it might be useful first to try to gain a rudimentary understanding of how all this operates. If *rasa* is born of or arises from a combination of determinants, consequents, and complementary emotional states, we begin with these. Determinants (*vibhavas*) are essentially "the physical stimulants to aesthetic reproduction, particularly the theme and its parts, the indications of time and place and other apparatus of representation—the whole *factible*." Of these, too, two different categories are spoken of: *alambana vibhavas* and *uddipana vibhavas*, meaning, respectively, the substantial determinants and the excitant determinants. Taking help from later writers, and taking the example of a specific *rasa* like Shringara, the erotic, its determinants would be of two kinds. The substantial determinants would be a lover and beloved, hero or heroine, or in Sanskrit, a *nayaka* and *nayika*. Without these, the erotic sentiment or mood of love would be difficult to imagine. The excitants would be, among other things, the moon, sandalwood ointment and other unguents, the humming of bees, attractive clothing and jewelry, an empty house or a secluded grove in a garden appropriate as a trysting place. Consequents (*anubhavas*) are "the specific and conventional means of registering emotional states, in particular gestures and glances etc.," something to which the *Natyashastra* pays such wonderfully elaborate attention. Continuing with Shringara, in this case the appropriate consequents (*anubhavas*) could be raising of the eyebrows, sidelong glances, embracing, kissing, holding hands. The range of gestures and movements appropriate to the theme is remarkably rich in both dance and drama, and the performer can draw upon his whole repertoire.

Then there are the complementary (or transitory) emotional states (*vyabhicharibhavas*), of which Bharata lists as many as thirty-three. . . . These range from agitation, depression, weariness, distraction, and stupor to fright, shame, joy, envy, anxiety, and indecision. They are referred to as complementary or transitory because while they arise in the course, say, of a play, and actors interpreting characters go through them, they do not last long and serve eventually only to feed into the dominant mood of a performance. They complement the principal mood or emotional state and do not in themselves leave a lasting impression. Finally, there are listed eight involuntary bodily responses (*sattvikabhavas*) in states of emotions, including perspiration, paralysis, trembling, fainting, change of voice, change of color, and horripilation.

Continuing with Shringara, it is stated that any complementary emotional state could be brought into a work except cruelty, death, indolence, or disgust, because they are opposed to the rise of the principal sentiment, the erotic. In the course of a performance in which the appropriate determinants and consequents and complementary emotional states have been selected, developed, and used, the viewer's heart is constantly and subtly being worked on by these properties, conditions, or representations of states. A "churning of the heart" takes place, at the end of which a dominant emotional state emerges, a *bhava* that is called *sthayi*, or durable. Any one of the nine *bhavas* of this durable kind could come floating to the surface of the mind of the viewer. These nine emotional states are *rati* (love), *hasa* (mirth, playfulness), *shoka* (sorrow), *krodha* (anger), *utsaha* (energy), *bhaya* (fear), *jugupsa* (disgust), *vismaya* (astonishment) and *shama* (equanimity). It would be seen that these durable emotional states (*sthayibhavas*) correspond to the nine *rasas* or sentiments listed earlier. Thus, the emotional state of love has its correspondence in the erotic sentiment, that of laughter or mirth its correspondence in the comic sentiment, and so on. . . .

At this point an elusive, inscrutable element is introduced in the *rasa* theory. It is stated that when, as a result of this churning of the heart, this mixing of the elements, a durable emotional state has emerged, this very state transmutes itself into a *rasa* in a competent person. If the circumstances have been right, if the performance is of the proper order, and if the viewer is cultured and sensitive enough (a *rasika*) a spark would leap from the performance to the viewer, resulting in an experience that would suffuse the entire being of the *rasika*. The experience might possess the suddenness of a flash of lightning, leaving the viewer unprepared for the moment and unaware of the swiftness with which it comes, deeply moved by it. This is the moment when, as a later writer put it, "magical flowers would blossom" in his awareness: *rasa* would be tasted. The experience is genuine and definable, but, it is stated, there are so many variables in the situation that it cannot be predicted or even worked toward. The same viewer may have a *rasa* experience of one level at one time from a performance, and not have it at another; the intensity of one viewer's experience may be different from another's. Many factors intervene, but this at least seems to be the essence of the *rasa* experience.

Aesthetic experience (*rasasvadana*) has been defined by different writers, each in his own terms and according to his own understanding. Bharata's chapter on *rasa* has been commented and elaborated upon by generations of scholars and theoreticians, the most important among them being Abhinavagupta, that great Kashmiri scholar of the eleventh century. After Bharata, an authoritative definition comes from Vishwanatha, author of the celebrated *Sahitya Darpana* (Mirror of Composition). Coomaraswamy regards Vishwanatha's passage defining the nature of aesthetic experience "of such authority and value as to demand translation *in extenso*":

> Flavor [*rasa*] is tasted by men having an innate knowledge of absolute values in exaltation of the pure consciousness as self-luminous in the mode at once of ecstasy and intellect, void of contact with things knowable, twin brother to the tasting of Brahma, whereof the life is a superworldly lightning flash, an intrinsic aspect in indivisibility. . . . Pure aesthetic experience is theirs in whom the knowledge of ideal beauty is innate; it is known intuitively in intellectual ecstasy without accompaniment of ideation, at the highest level of conscious being; born of one mother with the vision of God, its life is as it were a flash of blinding light of transmundane origin, impossible to analyze, and yet in the image of our very being.

Appropriately, Coomaraswamy reminds us that there are two senses in which the word *rasa* is commonly used: first, "relatively, in the plural with reference to the various, usually eight or nine, emotional conditions which may constitute the burden of a given work," and second, "absolutely, in the singular, with reference to the interior act of tasting flavor unparticularized. In the latter sense, the idea of an aesthetic beauty to be tasted, and knowable only in the activity of tasting, is to be clearly distinguished from the relative beauties or loveliness of the separate parts of the work or of the work itself considered merely as a surface."

Aesthetic experience, it has been stated, is "just as a flower born of magic" which has "as its essence, solely the present, it is co-related neither with what came before nor with what comes after." Between the spectator and the experience of *rasa* lie many obstacles, much the same way in which obstacles lie between a meditator and his realization of that supreme bliss that comes from perfect knowledge. These need to be removed, not the easiest of tasks. In fact, long discussions center around this question of the nature of obstacles, and the possibilities of their removal in different kinds and categories of viewers. But once removed, the dust wiped clean from the mirror of the heart, what is experienced is that sense of exalted delight "different from the forms of bliss of practical life, and just because it is devoid of obstacles, it is called Tasting, Delibation, Lysis, Perception, Rest, in the nature of the knowing subject." Aesthetic experience is thus a transformation "not merely of feeling, but equally of understanding," "a condensed understanding in the mode of ecstasy." As Gnoli, paraphrasing Abhinavagupta, puts it:

> The so-called supreme bliss, the lysis, the wonder is . . . nothing but a tasting, that is, a cognitation in all its compact density, of our own liberty. This liberty is *realissima* [that is to say, not metaphorical] and inseparable from the very nature of consciousness. We must not, however, forget that in the tasting of a juice or sweet flavor, etc., there is, between this bliss and us, the separation screen, so to say, of the exterior reality. In poetry, in drama, and so on, this screen is actually missing, but it remains in a latent state. Also in these forms of limited bliss, however, those people whose hearts are carefully devoted to canceling the part which performs the functions of a screen succeed in reaching the supreme bliss.

As would be noticed, there is a marked emphasis in this entire enunciation on the spectator. The words used to denote him are carefully chosen, because the clear assumption behind this entire theory of art is that it is not given to everyone to attain that state, that lightning flash of understanding and delight which is the *rasa* experience. We have to remind ourselves once again that the theory is worked out in the context of drama, and that only the spectator who is a *rasika* will have this experience. For it is he who knows what *rasa* is, and whose mind is prepared to receive the experience. It is clear through several assertions in the *Natyashastra*, and by later writers, that the experience of *rasa* depends a great deal on the energy (*utsaha*) that the spectator brings with him to the experience of a work of art. As is stated, it is his own energy "that is the cause of tasting, just as when children play with clay elephants." The durable emotional state that is subtly brought into being by or through a work of art is one thing: its transmutation into a *rasa* is dependent upon the energy, the inner ability, the singleness of heart of the *rasika*. The faculty of imagination and wonder is greatly emphasized.

It is asserted by several authorities that the *rasa* experience belongs not to the poet or to the actor but exclusively to the viewer. The whole question of where *rasa* lies has been the subject of much debate. Abhinavagupta examines various ideas on the subject and states quite emphatically:

> *Rasa* does not lie in the actor. But where then? You have all forgotten and I remind

you again [of what I have already said]. Indeed I have said that *rasa* is not limited by any difference of space, times, and knowing subjects. Your doubt is then devoid of sense. But what is the actor? The actor, I say, is the means of the tasting, and hence he is called by the name "vessel." The taste of wine, indeed, does not stay in the vessel, which is only a means necessary to the tasting of it. The actor then is necessary and useful only in the beginning.

To the natural question whether the actor or the artist also experience *rasa*, several writers including Vishwanatha maintain that he "may obtain aesthetic experience from the spectacle of his own performance." The actor is understood quite naturally not to be unmoved by "the passions he depicts." Likewise the musician, the dancer, the maker of an image would be involved in the emotion that he brings to his performance or work, but the experiencing of emotion before or during the act of making or performing, it is stated, is of an order different from the *rasa* experience, which has that illuminating, suffusing character, is that lightning flash of delight, and can be experienced by the maker or the performer only when and if he puts himself in the position of a viewer of himself and his work.

There is more cerebration about the *rasa* experience. Is it in the nature of a revelation, an unveiling, of entering a state of manifestness? Or, does it imply the coming into being of a state that did not exist before and is therefore something new and fresh? According to Vishwanatha, when it is said that *rasa* is something brought out into manifestness, what is meant is that it is made manifest "in a different character to which it is changed." Examples from the area of food and tasting—appropriate to the whole question of *asvadana*—illustrate this. It is stated thus that milk and curd are of the same substance, curd being milk presented under a change of character; it is not something previously completed and previously so extant; it is certainly not something only revealed. A change is involved between what one sees and what one experiences, the perception, the act of gustation, identifying the nature of the change. It is along these lines that much of the discussion proceeds, but for our purposes it is not necessary to go at any length into these discussions, except to remind ourselves of an oft-cited aphorism that "*bhava*, the durable emotional state, is the flower, and *rasa* is the fruit thereof." The second is evidently not possible to think of without the first, but this does not mean that the first will, in all cases, result in the second. Flower and fruit are clearly related, being parts of the same plant, but they are different in character and, of course, each flower does not necessarily yield or lead to fruit.

A predictable measure of attention in these discussions is claimed by the question: how does aesthetic experience differ from experience of the kinds of emotions which are part of our real, everyday life? The issue is brought to a head through a relatively simple example. If, as is maintained, the *rasa* experience is one of delight, how is it, it might well be asked, that "things that are painful in reality become, in art, the sources of pleasure?" The states of sorrow, fear, or disgust obviously do not yield pleasure in real life, and yet one speaks of them as leading to an aesthetic experience. As Vishwanatha puts it: "No one possessed of understanding engages—knowingly, and without some ulterior view—in paining himself; and yet we see that everyone enters with engrossing interest into the 'Pathetic' [sentiment]. . . ." He answers himself by stating that the *rasa* experience is not experience at an everyday, mundane level. The nature of *rasa* experience is transcendental, hyperphysical, literally *lokottara*, beyond ordinary experience. If this were not so, who would read the *Ramayana*, that great epic, the leading sentiment of which is Karuna, the pathetic? As it is, we hold it as being one of the most heart-delighting compositions of Indian literature. The distancing from the mundane experience of emotions made possible by a fine work or performance is what makes the difference.

The notion here is different from catharsis. The heart is not lightened through a performance; the *rasa* that it yields is a kind of "delight of the reason," as Coomaraswamy puts it, "an ecstasy in itself inscrutable." Another illuminating instance is that of the *Mahabharata*, that other great epic, in which the unutterably sad adventures of a just and truthful king, Harishchandra, are told at great length, involving the grief of deprivation and tear-shedding. To this it is said that the audience sheds tears not because of the pain that it actually experiences, but because through witnessing the performance of Harishchandra's tale, the heart is melted. This melting of the heart is a matter of moment, and it is from this that further discussion proceeds about why everyone cannot "receive" from a work of art. It is here that the role of imagination, of "cultivated intellectual sensibility," is emphasized. This imagination, this capacity for "conceiving whatever passion is intended to be depicted," is what characterizes a *rasika*.

Another point made is that *rasa* is, essentially, considered unique, indivisible. Its division into eight or nine varieties possesses only limited value and is adopted for the sake of convenience. Were it not so, its universality would come into doubt. The various divisions that we characterize as sentiments are like "rays of different colors, that we perceive when light is passed through a prism." Another image often employed by writers is of the various *rasas* being like different-colored precious stones all strung on the same necklace. *Rasa* is one, we are told; it is only approached or colored differently.

Aesthetic experience is seen, in the final analysis, as

an inscrutable and uncaused spiritual activity, that is virtually ever present and potentially realizable, but not possible to be realized unless and until all effective and mental barriers have been resolved, all knots of the heart undone. . . .

Closely related to *rasa* is the idea of *dhvani*, the reverberation of meaning arising by suggestion. *Dhvani* is referred to as the very soul of poetry. Ordinarily one thinks of a word or other symbol as possessing only two powers, those of denotation (*abhidha*) and connotation (*lakshana*). But Indian thinkers of the brilliant School of Manifestation assume for a word or a symbol "a third power, that of suggestion, the matter suggested, which we should call the real content of the work, being *dhvani*." Here reference is made to the literal, allegorical, and anagogic significance of words and symbols: "*Dhvani*, as overtone of meaning, is thus the immediate vehicle of a single *rasa* and means to aesthetic experience." The heart of the cultivated viewer, the *rasika*, is like "dry wood charged by latent fire": it only needs to be kindled, and the kindling often takes place through a work of art that produces suggestions, "reverberations of meaning."

Coomaraswamy concludes his lucid if relatively brief discussion of the formal Indian theory of art by pointing out that both *rasa* and *dhvani* are essentially metaphysical and vedantic in method and conclusion. The fully evolved Indian theory of beauty, which may have come into being only by the tenth or eleventh century, with all the commentaries on the *Natyashastra* and interpretations added by later writers, evidently drew a great deal upon the philosophical thought of India in which the realization of God was gone into with such extraordinary subtlety and at such length. It is not without reason that writers constantly compare the delight that constitutes the *rasa* experience and is its essence, and the pure bliss experienced by the meditator when he perceives the ultimate reality. In Coomaraswamy's words:

. . . the conception of the work of art as determined outwardly to use and inwardly to a delight of the reason; the view of its operation as not intelligibly causal, but by way of a destruction of the mental and affective barriers behind which the natural manifestation of the spirit is concealed; the necessity that the soul should be already prepared for this emancipation by an inborn or acquired sensibility; the requirement of self-identification with the ultimate theme, on the part of both artist and spectator, as prerequisite to visualization in the first instance and reproduction in the second; finally, the conception of ideal beauty as unconditioned by natural affection, indivisible, supersensual and indistinguishable from the gnosis of God—all these characteristics of the theory demonstrate its logical connection with the predominant trends of Indian thought, and its natural place in the whole body of Indian philosophy.

Clearly in India, as elsewhere, modes of seeing were intimately tied to modes of thought.

Whether the Indian theory is *sui generis* in origins or formulation is a matter of some interest. Coomaraswamy did not see it as being far removed from other points of view in the east (and in the west, up to a point of time), and emphasized only that it differed essentially "from the modern nonintellectual interpretations of art as sensation." In his view, "merely because of the specific idiomatic and mythical form in which it finds expression, it need not be thought of as otherwise than universal." He held that it does not differ, at least in its essentials, from "what is implicit in the Far Eastern view of art, or on the other hand from the scholastic Christian point of view, or what is asserted in the aphorisms of Blake." Other writers do see it as being so strongly rooted in Indian ideas that it is difficult to conceive of it as belonging, even in its essentials, to another culture. In any event its flavor is so Indian, and its presence in the Indian modes of seeing and thinking is so pervasive, that one

would do well to think of it as one of the keys to the code that is Indian culture.

Some relatively lesser matters concerning the theory of *rasa* may be mentioned in passing. In the Indian tradition, concepts are often associated with presiding deities and are assigned colors. The *rasas*, too, have designated colors. Thus: Shringara = *shyama* (bluish-black); Hasya = white; Karuna = dove-colored; Raudra = red; Vira = yellow; Bhayanaka = black; Bibhatsa = blue; Adbhuta = gold; Shanta = the color of jasmine and the moon. Their respective deities are Vishnu, Shiva, Yama, Rudra, Indra, Kala, Mahakala, a gandharva, and Narayana. . . .

Some writers go into the question of which *rasas* are in harmony with each other, and which are opposed or contrary. Jagannatha in his *Rasagangadhara* gives us a list. In his view, Shringara goes with Vira and Adbhuta; likewise Vira goes with Shringara, Raudra, and Adbhuta. But Shringara and Bibhatsa, Shringara and Karuna, and Shringara and Shanta "stand in opposition." Vira and Bhayanaka, and Shanta and Raudra are also opposed to each other. The suggestion is that when in a work one *rasa* is maturing, the experience of *rasa* is broken, so to speak, if its contrary intervenes.

Many authors speak of the faults (*doshas*) that may creep into the process of creating certain moods (*bhavas*) and thus affect their corresponding *rasas*. Taking the example of erotic sentiment based on the durable emotional state of love (*rati*), it is maintained that *bhava* would be improper and/or incomplete if love were made to reside in a secondary hero; if it is directed toward the wife of a sage or teacher; if many heroes are taken as its object; if it does not exist in both the man and the woman; if it exists in a rival hero; or else in low persons, or lower animals. Faults are pointed out, following the practice of emphasizing those virtues and faults in poetical compositions which took up so much of the energy and attention of writers on the subject. There are elaborate discussions on whether love for God, the king, or one's own son can lead to the experience of *rasas* under the category of Shringara, with the emphatic conclusion that this kind of love does not fall properly under the erotic sentiment. Cases of incomplete or imperfect aesthetic experience are cited, and several highly interesting terms are coined and discussed to indicate that imperfect *bhavas* or *rasas* do exist. Again and again it is emphasized that harshness, uselessness, superfluity, affect the soul of art adversely. Essentially, "what does not hope or what is not needed for understanding the principal idea" is understood as a fault and needs to be avoided.

The above outline of the *rasa* theory as part of the formal theory of art in Indian thought takes as its context not the arts of sculpture or painting, but the performing or literary arts. There is reason behind this, for the first enunciation, in a considered form of the "doctrine," is in a text that concerns *natya*, the arts of the stage: the emphasis of most of the later writers who discuss *rasa* remained on poetry. Ideas on *rasa* were scarcely ever applied in detail to sculpture and painting, and certainly no treatise was devoted to the connection. Even examples from sculpture or painting do not seem to have been cited by any of the principal writers and thinkers on the arts in general.

This should not be understood to mean that the ideas on *rasa* do not apply to sculpture and painting. Clearly they do so by implication, and when Coomaraswamy discusses *rasa* he speaks appropriately and firmly of the applicability of this theory to the visual arts as much as to performing or literary arts. That ideas of *rasa* are never far from the thoughts of persons involved in making or seeing images becomes clear whenever any reactions to art are cited in literary works. Praise is accorded to a painting being seen by a character in a poem or play in terms of whether or not it yields an

experience of delight, and details such as the *vibhavas* and *anubhavas* are noted. It remains clear that the enjoyment of a work of sculpture or painting is thought of or described in terms familiar from the complex of ideas that center on *rasa*. At the same time, it must be recalled that a major work on painting and sculpture, one of the principal *shilpa* texts, the *Vishnudharmottaram*, generally dated between the fifth and the seventh centuries A.D. (later than Bharata but considerably earlier than many others whom he have noted, Abhinavagupta or Vishwanatha, for example) speaks of *rasa*. . . . No examples to illustrate the various *rasas* are cited from major works of sculpture or painting—this is not even to be expected, for the principal focus of the work is on "making" in technical terms—but the mere fact that in this highly regarded text, space is taken to expand upon *rasa* is significant. The chapter dealing with *rasa* here opens with the words; "The sentiments represented in painting are said to be nine. . . ." What follows is a brief description of *rasas*, and a discussion of what themes fall under them generally, and even a passage presenting which *rasas* are appropriate for different settings. Thus, it is stated that "pictures to embellish homes should belong to *shringara*, *hasya* and *shanta rasas* alone," and so on. What is suggested directly or by implication, alike to the maker of images and to the person who aims at understanding the ideas underlying the making of works of art, is that *rasa* is as much relevant to these arts as it is to literature and performances. How *rasa* arises is not discussed, but it must have been taken for granted that this is known to the learned.

Yet there are inherent difficulties in demonstrating (not applying) how the *rasa* theory works in the context of sculpture and painting. The intention behind the making of images which can be categorized as "icons" would not be the same as that which lies behind other kinds. Thus, an image to be installed as an object of worship in a sanctum would clearly be approached by the sculptor differently from an image carved or placed on the outer wall of a shrine. The icon, in this rather limited sense, would be the visual equivalent of a *mantra* or a *dhyana*, and would not necessarily be seen as leading to the same kind of experience as does a poetic composition intended to delight. It is easy to concede that this may not always be so, even in the case of icons: thus an image of the Buddha, withdrawn and expressive of the idea of perfect balance, equipoise, could be easily seen as belonging to or falling under quiescence; likewise an image of a *yogini*, or the Devi in one of her many fierce forms, can be easily seen as having been conceived in such a way that it comes close to engendering feelings of fear in the viewer. But in general, icons remains one matter, and the wide range of Indian art another.

The real difficulty in seeing the connection between works of sculpture and painting and the ideas of *rasa* is of a different order. As we see them now, for the most part out of context, on display in museums or private collections, we cannot fully appreciate the impact that these works must have made on viewers of earlier generations, or the ideas that lay behind their making, or their being placed in specific situations. It is one thing to see a sculptured panel in its rightful place on the wall of, say, a standing temple; but quite another to see it, however splendid and elegantly presented, in isolation in a gallery. Originally, each panel must have been visualized in relationship to the monument to which it belonged, as well as conceived as a part of a total scheme and integrally related to other panels of the same monument. It would be unrealistic to expect that such a piece of sculpture, remote from its cultural or programmatic context, would yield the kind of experience it must have yielded when seen in its proper

setting in a binding relationship to other sculptural elements of its series. Unfortunately, very few studies document the sculptural programs of major monuments such as standing temples or *stupas*. Yet, few works of sculpture, barring icons made for the specific purpose of worship at home or installation in a shrine, can have been made singly.

A similar difficulty applies to painting. While here, too, some works must have been produced as icons, or in isolation, it is reasonably certain that most paintings we see today as single folios were originally conceived as elements in a series. This condition is easily demonstrable, for when paintings occur in an illustrated manuscript or belong to a set of painted folios such as the *Gita Govinda*, the *Ramayana*, the *Bhagavata Purana*, or the *Rasamanjari*, their connection is obvious. Even seen in isolation (most sets have been scattered and even illustrated manuscripts taken apart and distributed or sold), we can visualize the connection among folios that once belonged together, whether of a narrative or thematic nature. Even ancestral portraits were frequently made in series: an extraordinary group was produced in the eighteenth century, and a remarkable range of portraits of princes and commoners was painted for Sansar Chand of Kangra in the late eighteenth and early nineteenth centuries. Thus, the fragmented experience they now offer to present-day viewers can only approximate what they must have yielded to viewers of the age to which they first belonged.

Despite all this, the exercise of seeing works of Indian art in the awareness of *rasa*, if not in its exact context, has some merit. At times there may be some advantage in seeing works in isolation, for then we focus upon them more sharply. This apart, it should be possible to gain at least some idea of the effect of images and sculptures in their original contexts and at an earlier time, even when we see them today only in small groups or in specially assembled exhibitions such as the present one. The purpose of viewing in the awareness of *rasa* is to acquaint ourselves with the character of Indian art.

What is presented is not a random selection of significant works of art. No history of Indian art can be reconstructed through these works, no chronology or understanding of the complex world of Indian styles can come within reach, nor is it attempted. All that these works may do is to help the viewer comprehend this part in operation, to assist in learning what it is all about. But the intention of this assembly is not didactic; rather, the attempt is to offer suggestions, especially to Western viewers who are less likely to be familiar with the ways in which these objects and paintings functioned in Indian art in their original contexts.

It is possible, but not necessary, to take each work of art and forcefully point out how its various elements work together in the direction leading toward a *rasa* experience. One is aware that there would be obstacles to taking in what these works of art contain, hindrances of the kinds the texts speak of, such as cluttered minds and imprecise notions, as well as others belonging to the artificial situation in which the objects can only be seen today. Because associations differ and reverberations of meanings cannot be caught in a different cultural context with the same richness, some viewers, both in India and elsewhere, would be inclined to see specific works as possibly relating to a different *rasa* than the one with which they are here associated. Such disparities or preferences are not unexpected, since, as the texts say, we all bring our associations, "impressions from an earlier existence," and our own energies to works of art.

We hope this exhibition will alert viewers to look in Indian works for thing which earlier may have seemed to be of peripheral interest, even extraneous to the works, and thus to become sensitive to details that did not initially impinge upon their awareness. The subsidiary or supporting elements, all those wonderfully elegant and varied stances and gestures, the clouds and lightning in the sky, the rendering of foliage, the inclinations of the head, the direction of glances, all require a quick eye and an eager mind. Even these details have meaning, for they imperceptibly feed the mood, the durable emotional state, that the painter or the sculptor must frequently have had in mind.

It would be a vain labor to try to apply the *rasa* theory in all its complex details to each work of art. Nor would it be possible to point out, in each sculpture and painting, which elements constitute the determinants, consequents, or the complementary emotional states to the letter of the theory. What is of concern is the spirit, and it is hoped that it will come within the viewer's reach. It is especially relevant to point out here that the distribution and application of colors in these paintings need not be examined with reference to the concept of each *rasa* having its given color. That part of the *rasa* theory seems to have followed only a general inconographical concept (like the notion that each *rasa* has a presiding deity) and is not to be seen, perhaps was never intended to be seen, as applying to colors in painting or on polychrome sculptures. The kind of symbolism of color, or the language of color associations, as in the Kathakali dance-drama of Kerala, does not seem to have developed in this context. The paintings are undoubtedly iconographically correct—thus, Krishna and Vishnu are blue or bluish-black; the garments that Krishna wears or the objects that he carries accord with formulas—but neither iconography nor iconology help in understanding the way that colors work in Indian painting, for the most part.

The works in this exhibition are objects of integrity, born of a certain vision, and it is fair to assume that they moved generations of viewers in India. We may not be moved by them in the same manner or in the same degree, but as long as they produce in some measure that melting of the heart of which texts speak, we can be satisfied that we have approached their spirit. Yet it is well to remember that we can take from these works only according to our own energies, our *utsaha.* As Coomaraswamy said: "He who would bring back the wealth of the Indies, must take the wealth of the Indies with him."

Zuheir Al-Faquih

ISLAMIC ART . . .
SUBMISSION TO
DIVINE WILL

Zuheir Al-Faquih was a graduate student in communications at San Francisco State College at the time he wrote this article. In it he explains how artistic practice in the Muslim world reflects Islamic religious doctrines.

BACKGROUND

A vast expanse of land stretching for hundreds of miles without trace of life, *Arabia Deserta*, gave birth to a man and a faith that transformed warring and disunited tribes into a unified nation, and released a new wave of inspiration unknown since the Nazarene 600 years earlier.

Bounded by seas on three sides, the Arabian Peninsula is almost entirely uncultivable. A mountain range lies on its western side, spotted with trees and scrubs. But, underneath its extensive sands are swift moving rivers of sweet water, and here and there oases appear and communities spring up. This wide land is the cradle of the Semitic peoples, including the Babylonians, the Assyrians, the Chaldeans, the Phoenicians, the Amorites, the Aramaeans, the Hebrews, the Abyssinians, and the Arabians themselves, all of whom must have lived at one time as "one people."[1]

The inhabitants of pre-Islamic Arabia, an era referred to by Arab historians as the *Jahiliyya*, or "period of ignorance" (i.e., ignorance of the Word of God), were for the most part nomadic, though there existed many tribal city-fortresses such as Mecca, Yathrib (now known as Medina), Hijr, and in the south, Sana' and Ma'rib. Protected by walls, these communities prospered as trade centers. People had little trust in one another, for a major source of income was the *ghazuw*, or raids, conducted against rival tribes and caravans.

The three marks of the "ideal man" during the *Jahiliyya* were: eloquence (in both poetry and prose), marksmanship in archery, and horsemanship.[2] Though all tribes accepted the *ghazuw* as a way of life, and youths eagerly awaited their turn to assert their manhood, an official truce was observed and peace prevailed for one month each year. During this reprieve, the pagan Arabs would travel to Mecca to perform their pilgrimage at the *Ka'ba* (the Ancient House), said to have been built by Abraham and his son Ishmael,[3] from whom the Arabs trace their descent. Here they made "propitiation sacrifices" and left the meat for the poor.[4]

> At times they indulged in human sacrifices in emulation of Abraham, who had offered his only son to God.[5]

Arab writers have repeatedly criticized the pagans' loose sense of morality, as well as their practice of female infanticide, slavery, greed, drunkenness, general debauchery and their "injustice to women." Nevertheless, the pagans had a concept of Allah, the creator of heaven and hell,[6] though they subscribed to several hundred other idols and committed what the Muslims consider a cardinal sin, *shirk*, or "ascribing plurality to the Deity."[7]

Mecca lies on the western side of the Peninsula, in the mountain range, and connects the Yemen, Africa, and the Red Sea to the Persian and Byzantine Empires. Its location, as well as its religious importance, allowed it to wield great influence in the affairs of Arabia.

The tribe that lived in Mecca and served as the guardian of the shrine was an old and noble people called the Qureish. Into this family in 570 A.D. was born a man destined to bring millions to the worship of the One God.

> Emerging from a bleak background—Arabia Deserta—orphaned in childhood; unfettered and untutored he arose and towered to become an organizer who moulded the warring tribes of his race into a nation which justified him and itself in the verdict of history; a social mentor and law-giver by whose code today one-fifth of the human race is governed; a prophet who led human souls from idolatry and paganism into the simplest and clearest conception of the Creator and His worship; rational and humane, he struck at all fetters and brought forth the first true Reformation by Faith and reason, he opposed slavery and abolished caste, class, color, and race distinction; he encouraged learning and mercy, taught charity and good will.[8]

Through the Prophet's own example and the Revelation, the Muslim tailors his life and conduct to the Will of God. The meaning of *islam* is surrender; i.e., to the will or guidance of God. The term *muslim* means he who surrenders to divine guidance. Thus, through the Prophet's teaching, "Islam cemented the desert peoples into a unity hitherto unknown."[9]

The mosque, the place of worship, is also the center where Muslims meet and, after prayers, decide jointly on matters of civil or religious importance. Here the equality of man before God is practiced, and does not remain just a belief. This had not been the manner of the non-muslim inhabitants of the area, and it may be said that the Prophet, in a word, introduced democracy to Arabia.

> Unity was the great aim of the mission of the Prophet Muhammad, the blessing and peace of God be upon him.[10]

The word in Arabic for the concept of the "unity" of God is *tauhid*.

> The original meaning of *tauhid* is the belief that God is one in indivisible divinity. [It is] the demonstration of the unity of God in Himself and in the act of creation.[11]

The meaning of *tauhid* is well defined by Kenneth Cragg in the introduction to 'Abduh's book:

> *Tauhid* is a causative and intensive noun and never means "unity," still less "unitariness," as an abstract state. It is aggressive, so to speak, antiseptic: it means "unity" intolerant of all pluralism in the ardent subjugation of all that flouts or doubts it.[12]

Tauhid is the greatest single element in Muslim theology, and the *tauhid* of God indicates His transcendental Being. He is all-powerful and all-knowing, and there is none but He. He is everywhere.

> The Qur'an describes the attributes of God, by and large, with a far surer accent of transcendence than the earlier religions.[13]

The relationship between God and man is one of ethics. Izutsu explains:

> It is not a mere matter of human goodness or badness as it used to be in pre-Islamic times; ethics is now an integral part of religion; the whole religion is involved in it, and it is indeed dependent of the ethical response of man.[14]

That God is Merciful and Compassionate is stated in the Quran at the start of each *sura* (chapter) and before and during prayers. The Muslim responds to God's Bounteousness in the manner taught by the Prophet; through prayer, charity, generosity, cleanliness, fairness and a selfless attitude in the service of His Creation. Allah is Compassionate—and Just—so a Muslim resigns himself to His Will.

> God tasketh not a soul beyond its scope. For it is only that which it hath earned, and against it only that which it hath deserved—2:286

To give praise to God is imperative to the Muslim, and indeed the words for thankfulness (*shukr*) and faith (*iman*) are used in the Holy Quran as synonyms.[15]

Allah reveals Himself in two ways: Revelation (*wahy*), and through "signs" (*ayat*), which include such natural phenomena as rain, wind, daylight.[16]

> Verily, in the alternation of the Night and the Day and in all that God hath created; in the heavens and the earth, are signs for those who heed Him.—10:6

> Verily, in the heavens and the earth are signs for those who believe.—45:2

> On the earth are signs for those of assured faith, as also in your own selves: will ye not then see?—51:20

Tauhid may be seen as not a passive "all-inclusiveness," but a dynamic, moving state: infinitely aware and responsive.

The necessary being (Allah) is the source of all harmony and the control of the natural order in undisturbed continuity and this fact must be reckoned within the perfection of existence and so affirmed.[17]

THE QURAN

The Quran is the collection of the messages delivered to Muhammad from God, who in turn revealed God's Will in the missions of the prophets and their equal status as His messengers. Consequently, he taught respect for all "revealed" religions.

. . . The Prophet reported that while at prayer in a cave in Mount Hira' just outside Mecca, a vision appeared and spoke to him. The vision—in the person of the Archangel Gabriel—left words that were written on his heart.

> Read! In the name of thy Lord Who Createth. Createth man from a clot. Read! And it is thy Lord the most Bountiful Who teacheth by the pen. Teacheth man what he knew not!—96:1

> And lo! It is a revelation of the Lord of the worlds which the True Spirit hath brought down upon thy heart, that thou mayst be of the warners.—26:192 . . .

Muhammad's life can only be glossed over here. The Prophet's teachings were, needless to say, the cause of great controversy among the Qureish. He was forced to send some of his early followers away for safety. Soon afterwards, he himself left Mecca, and this flight, termed the *hijra*, or "migration," marks the start of the Muslim calendar. Many Meccans converted to Islam after hearing or reading some of the revelations that the Prophet had set down.

It is reported that when the Muslims returned to Mecca victorious (630 A.D.) after a long and hard struggle, the Prophet ordered the idols in the *Ka'ha* destroyed, except for a painting of the Virgin Mary with the baby Jesus seated on her lap.[18] This he placed his hand over and ordered protected.

The popular Western concept that the knights of Islam offered the Quran in one hand and the sword in the other to the peoples they conquered, is completely unfounded. 'Abduh calls it "great slander" and adds that the Muslims were both tolerant and just.

> The entire world witnessed that Islam counted the proper treatment of conquered peoples as a meritorious and virtuous thing, whereas Europeans regard[ed] such behavior as weak and despicable.[19]

ARAB EXPANSION AND RULE

Immediately following the Prophet's death in 632 A.D., political intrigue started, and after the assassination of the fourth *khalifa* (caliph) Ali, Islam fell under the direction of self-appointed "defenders of the faith." The Umayyad caliphs (661–749 A.D.) made their capital in the old city of Damascus. Here the desert warriors discovered luxuries previously unknown to them, and adopted new manners and customs. The Umayyads were in turn ousted by the ruthless Abbasids (750–1258 A.D.) who built an entirely new capital, Baghdad, on the banks of the Tigris. Islam spread from Arabia to Syria, Egypt and Persia, finally taking Asia Minor from the Byzantines and conquering Spain from the Goths. It spread as far west as France, and as far east as China.

Arab conquerors developed a taste for the finer things in life, and acquired in effect a new culture from the Persians, in the manner of food, dress and "harems." The rich and lavish life of the caliphs in the dazzling city of Baghdad surpasses our unbroken imagination.[20] Though often characterized as a city wherein dwelt the richest of the rich and the poorest of the poor, it was also the center of the "Era of Translation"

(750–850 A.D.) The greatest works in the fields of philosophy and science were translated from Greek, Latin, Persian and Hindi and dealt with philosophy, astronomy, physiology, and chemistry. Hospitals, public baths and centers of learning were built in the city. Their term "Arab" no longer applied exclusively to the former inhabitants of Arabia. So complete was the Arabs' assimilation of the new culture, that all they had left to call their *own* was their language and the Quran, both of which had been accepted by Syrians, Berbers, Numidians, Hispano-Arabs, and Goths. In Baghdad, art flourished under the patronage of nobles and rich merchants.[21] Rugs, tapestries, silk, cotton, woolens, satin, brocade, sofas, cushion covers, furniture and kitchen utensils and most importantly, paper, were produced and exported to Europe. The art of calligraphy was developed and the arabesque form was born. . . .

The art of leatherwork and embossing originally developed by the Moors, spread to Europe where its fineness became well known, and the terms "cordwainer," "cordovan" and "morocco" reflect their origin.[22] Another art developed by the Muslims which gained considerable respect in Europe was metalwork and the inlaying of steel. Damascus was for a long time the leader in this craft as the terms "damascene" and "damask" indicate.[23]

The Moors introduced into the agricultural spectrum rice, apricots, pomegranates, peaches, oranges, sugar cane, cotton and saffron.[24] Most important of all, the Arabs introduced Europe to paper, an art that came to the Arabs from distant China.

PICTORIAL PRESENTATION IN ISLAM

Muslims everywhere accept the Quran as the word of God. But another body of writing, composed of several volumes containing anecdotes on the Prophet Muhammad, including his alleged utterances, his likes and dislikes, manners, and directives, is widely read. This body of literature is known as the *hadith*, or, the traditions. These accounts were gathered long after the Prophet passed away, and each anecdote is usually superseded by a lengthy introduction accrediting the source of information. This collection of sayings and events, constantly reviewed by a body of theologians, cannot be considered as conclusive in determining the Prophet's view on various issues. It does, however, carry a vast influence on Muslims today. That the prejudices of the recorders of the *hadith* may have entered into their writings is not a matter for contention. It obviously has, and this has been well examined by students of Islamic art who have pointed out a number of discrepancies and contradictions between one set of "recollections" and the next.[25] Insofar as art is concerned, Muhammad did warn continuously against idolatry, for fear that the people may revert to their pagan ways of worship after his death. He repeated that he was only a man. As the Quran (3:144) says:

> Muhammad is but a messenger. . . . Will it be that when he dies, you will turn your backs?

In fact, the only passage in the Quran touching upon art is where God warned against statues of worship.

> O believers! Intoxicants and gambling and the dedication of stones and divining arrows are an abomination of Satan's handiwork: avoid them that you may prosper.

It appears as though the writers of the *hadith* should have heeded God's warning themselves, as in *sura* 3:7 where it says:

> He it is Who hath revealed to thee (Muhammad) the Scriptures wherein are clear revelations—they are the substance of the Book—and others which are allegorical. But those in whose hearts is doubt pursue, forsooth, that which is allegorical seeking to cause dissension by seeking to explain

it. None know its explanation save Allah. And those who are of sound instruction say: we believe therein; the whole is from our Lord; but only men of insight can grasp the Message.

The above verse may have been referring to the "mystical" letters recorded at the start of each chapter. Muslims were greatly impressed by the symbols and allegorical qualities in the Quran. One traveler and art critic notes the effect that the above and similar passages had upon the Arabs, saying:

> Islamic thought is, as a rule, of a highly involved and complex nature. . . . Muslims in general, and Arabs in particular, give themselves to thought with a passion. . . .[26]

He adds that in response to a question, an answer "must never be obvious and must tax the ingenuity of the listener."[27] He explains this "complex nature" of the Muslim's thought pattern as a result of his contemplative nature.

> For a Muslim the most important problem of existence is that concerning the being and nature of God, a God Who is transcendent (and not incarnate).[28]

This great pre-occupation with the nature of His Universe, fostered perhaps by the hints in the Quran that only men of "insight" could understand, is reflected in Islamic philosophy, poetry and most especially in that form of design known as "the arabesque." The *tauhid* taught by the Prophet is expressed in the symmetry of the arabesque, while its two-dimensional quality reflects the written form of the Holy Book.

CONSCIOUSNESS IN ART

The large acceptance of art as a product of a people's "innermost feelings" will not be discussed here. However, pure Islamic art expresses more than this. The artist is not the tool of the current, but the devotee, with head bowed in humility before God. The highest aspirations can be seen in the Muslim art, but it also contains hidden meaning. For as in Tibet and China, art is also used to present the Unspoken, to unveil the Unseen.

> Art is that which creates harmony out of chaos . . . art transforms unintelligible multiplicity into intelligible unity . . . art informs, in some degree, every activity that makes clear what was formerly veiled.[29]

Landau traces man's consciousness in art from ancient times to date.[30] From the Greek sculptors and early Christian painters, there is the highest ideal—God in human form. During the Renaissance, man moved to a deification of himself, and it was man who became the central theme and subject. Disillusioned with man, the painters idealized Nature, but even this decayed, and in the artist's struggle for "reality" may be seen only further disillusionment and fragmentation, from the Impressionist school to the "Avant Garde" non-representational artists and culminating, inevitably to "pop" and "op" art. Here the term "art" has suffered immeasurably. It has come to mean a personal fancy, a fleeting moment. The modern artist, when compared to the past masters who cherished a high ideal, is a disillusioned and unforgiving individual.

> Having tried to compete with God, the artist loses touch with man, and floats, an isolated islet, in a sea of abstraction, hardly on speaking terms with the rest of humanity. The word "love" may figure in his vocabulary, but love appears to be the last emotion that inspires him. What we love and have faith in we never abandon. The private abstractions of the Western artist indicate that he has abandoned man and Nature as fashioned by God because he no longer has love for the one or faith in the other.[31]

Abstract art is a means of escape for the disillusioned artist, but for the devotee it signified his "unquestioning submission to God."[32] For the Muslim, representational art

was considered damning, as it was viewed as an attempt to compete with the Creator.[33] Without further consulting the validity of the *hadith*, it should only be noted that tradition did, in fact, carry a strong influence over men's minds at the time.

The fashioners of the arabesque and the calligraphers do not "appear" in their art. They remain for the most part anonymous. Their personality does not project itself into their work as it does, say in a Picasso or a Van Gogh. They are motivated by the "dual wish of worshipping God and of giving pleasure by creating beauty." The Muslim theologists' view of beauty may be very simply summed up:

> Tastes may differ—but things *are* either beautiful or ugly.[34]

This statement may make the art critic with the more indulgent or uncertain "democratic" spirit wince, but it must be remembered that beauty is, to the Muslim, an aspect of his Creator. And He is not subject to earthy qualifications or tastes. 'Abduh writes,

> In the immaterial world of the necessary Being and of the "subtle" spirits and also of the qualities of the human soul, perfection belongs with a beauty accessible only to those who have a mind for it and whose awakened contemplation it quite ravishes.[35]

Artists, travelers and historians have observed the striking contrast in the architecture of the Western Church and of the mosque. The nave directs one to the altar, topped by the Cross which is the central object. In the mosque, God is "invisible" and "all-pervading."[36] The main element in the mosque is the *mihrab*, a niche in the wall which indicates the direction of Mecca and the *Ka'ba*. In many mosques the *mihrab* is set off to one side where it serves its purpose equally well. The austerity of the mosque indicates a "fundamental difference of attitude"[37] between Muslims and Christians, though both acknowledge the One God. For the Muslim, *tauhid* is not merely an intellectual concept, but a secret divulged to him from the Almighty, and towards Whom his thanks must be shown.[38]

> Whatever is in the heaven and on earth—let it declare the Praises and Glory of God: for He is the Exalted in Might, the Wise.—57:1

THE GRAND CALLIGRAPHERS

When examining the art of the calligraphers, it is important to keep in mind that the Quran is believed to have been revealed to Muhammad through the Archangel Gabriel in such a manner that the words were written on his heart.[39] The Quran itself is accepted by the Muslims to contain God's messages "in plain Arabic speech."

> The profession of the calligraphers was one of honour and dignity because he was engaged in copying the Quran, and his labours thereby received a religious sanction.[40]
>
> Even kings did not think it beneath their dignity to compete in this art with professional calligraphers, and sought to win religious merit by writing out copies of the Quran.[41]

The first true calligrapher is said to have been Qutba, who developed four lovely scripts for the Umayyad caliphs.[42]

A story to describe the beauty of Arabic calligraphy says that when an ambassador of the Abbasid caliph al-Wathiq (841–846 A.D.) arrived in Constantinople to see the Byzantine emperor, he saw long scrolls in Arabic writing hung from doorways. When he asked why these scrolls were hung there, he was told that they judged them of such beauty to be worthy of display.[43] The Arab today still considers the language of the Quran to be of the greatest beauty. As the human form was to the Greek sculptor, so the Arabic language was to the Muslim artist.[44]

> Writing seems the direct expression of the spirit of man, and to the mystic the immediate translation of the vision of the Ultimate without the intervention of the objective facts that the illustrator must use."[45]

Calligraphy had a "profound" and "controlling influence" on the other arts and is the main motif in architectural decor. Mosques and homes are decorated with excerpts from the Quran executed in elaborate script; books, furniture, even key chains are embossed with arabesques.

Painters—for the most part scorned by the religious figures, but nonetheless supported by courtiers—tried to gain some respect by referring to themselves as *mudhahib*, or "gilder," with the intention of claiming some of the calligraphers' glory.[46] Writing contributed directly to the development of the arabesques design. The first arabesques were in fact made through the use of calligraphy.

THE ARABESQUE

> He it is Who created you from a single soul—7:189

In the arabesque, *tauhid* received the highest artistic expression. We have seen the development of this high expression in writing, which was viewed as "an immediate transcription of a penetration into Reality,[47] and in the arabesque's symmetry of design— a symmetry so complete as to suggest mathematical precision."[48] It is this mathematical precision which deserves special note in the examination of the arabesque design. Landau writes:

> The arabesque is . . . a statement about formal relations—almost a complex algebraic equation given in correspondingly complex geometric symbols.[49]

He adds that the arrangement of forms in patterns is the essence of the arabesque, and in pattern lies the key to the secret of existence.[50] This exactness, the "mathematical precision" of the arabesque is symbolic of the Creator: the perfection of Beauty, the Unknown (al-gahib).

The Muslims have ninety-nine names for God—each representing a certain aspect of the One whose infinite Self is beyond attributes. These various aspects of the One may be seen in the algebraic equation, x = 1. The Arabs were quite familiar with algebra, having developed it (al-jubr), and it is not surprising that many of the mathematical concepts appear to fit the Muslims' conception of Allah.

An algebraic equation implies perfection. The sum of one side of the equation is exactly matched on the other side, whether it be as simple as x + 1 or as complex as a parametric equation. Symmetry is synonymous with perfection.

Mathematics is the only pure science known—there is no room for subjectivity in the mathematical equations, and all other sciences derive what exactness they possess from mathematical formulae. These formulae can give the correct answer even though it cannot be "shown" to be correct. How can a person be "shown" that the area of a circle is equal to pi r²? One cannot be convinced, but once he accepts the principles underlying the method, then he may set about solving all mathematical problems. To do so, he must accept first the simplest equation: A = A.

Mathematics, too, finds, many answers to puzzling points in the symbol ∞ which represents infinity. An asymptote meets an ordinate at infinity and the largest "quantity" is said to be infinity. Though the term infinity is used as a makeshift boundary for that which is beyond the realm of the mind, it does fit well into the Muslim conception of God: "God is one in indivisible divinity."[51]

Vision comprehendeth Him not, but he comprehendeth all vision. He is the Subtle, the Aware.—6:104

Naught is as His likeness; and He is the Hearer, the Seer.—42:11

Say (O Muslim) : God is One! God is Indivisible! He does not beget, nor is He begotten, and there is naught comparable unto Him!—112:1

The arabesque, then, seeks to make certain statements—but what these statements mean is, as the Quran says, for "men of insight" to conclude (Surah 3:7).

And the arabesque may thus, in spite of all its abstractions, reveal to us—if we but knew how to read it—some of the inmost secrets of existence. And, it may possibly reveal them more accurately than do the superbly "life-like" tragedies and comedies produced by Western art.[52]

What "insight" these artists may have had and how it differs from the Western artists' vision is difficult to presume. For the Muslim, God is the Source, and it is toward Him that all eventually return.

He is the First and the Last, the Evident and the Immanent: and He hath full knowledge of all things.

This can be seen in the structure of the mosque where the different elements demonstrate this point of view. In the vault of the dome is encompassed the Mind ('aql) from whence Creation sprang. In the arches can be seen the arms of the aspirant, reaching up to the Source, and resting on the pillars of Knowledge; the minaret is his struggle to attain his higher self; the running water in the courtyard is symbolic of life, and ablutions performed there is the strengthening of faith through purification. The mihrab which points direction which the Muslim must face when praying represents steadfastness in faith and singularity of purpose in pursuit of God's worship and remembrance.

God the Compassionate!
It is He Who hath taught the Quran;
Who hath created man.
He hath taught him speech.

The sun and the moon follow courses
exactly computed; and the herbs and
the trees—both (alike) bow in adoration;
and the firmament hath He raised high,
and He hath set up the balance of
justice in order that ye may not
transgress balance.
So establish weight with justice
and fall not short in the balance!

MIRRORS OF THE SOUL

During the course of the five daily
prayers, a Muslim kneels, touches his fore-
head to the ground, and says: "Glory unto my
Lord, the Highest!" thirty-four times. In sick-
ness, poverty or death, in birth, health or
prosperity, the Muslim sees the hand of Allah
acting, and accepts his life as a random chapter in the universal book. It is for this reason
that the Muslim artist does not "appear" in
his work. His goal is not simply the presentation of beautiful works but to show his *shukr*
as proof of his *iman* in the Creator. As
Allah is the source of all Beauty, the artist
hopes to suggest the presence of the Hearer
in all he does. Hence, pure Muslim art is non-
representational, and in the pattern of the
design lies the secret of all things.

In Landau's examination of arabesque art,
he points out that certain Muslim philosophers, such as Ibn Arabi, believed God to
contain the forms (*a'yn*) of all things. These
archetypes "underlie all physical manifestation."[53] Mystical interpretation as to the true
meaning behind the written words of the
Quran has been recorded by scholars,[54] and
it is evident that calligraphy and the
arabesque are not merely understood as
"pretty designs," but as containing meaningful discourses on the nature of the God-man

relationship. Izutsu stresses that this relationship demands that the Muslim show
gratitude and thankfulness for his Creator's
beneficiency. But "thankfulness is possible
only when man has grasped the meaning of
the *ayat* (signs)." . . .[55]

In the symmetry of the design—the exactness of the proportion and the repetition of
pattern—lies perfection. The linear quality
of this and like patterns suggests, as does
the writing of the Quran, the Creator Who is
beyond physical form; the Owner of the
ninety-nine names. Even the calligraphic
designs would appear of less significance
had it not been for their symbolic value in
representing God's commands. However,
calligraphic work has been fashioned to suggest this "continuity," . . . where the writing
goes around the minaret and the dome in a
complete circle. The designs on the dome
and minaret suggest the *tauhid* quite clearly
as does most Islamic architectural ornamentation and construction.

What the Muslim artisan—or devotee, to
be accurate—seeks, is to dedicate a "translation of the vision of the Ultimate"[56] as a
symbol of his *shukr* and *iman*.[57] To appreciate his work, it is not necessary to understand "the Muslim mind," but, as 'Abduh
suggests, to have insight into one's own
soul. For beauty belongs "only to those who
have a mind for it and whose awakened contemplation it quite ravishes."[58]

Though 'Abduh was describing the quality of beauty in the human soul, it would not
be an exaggeration to say that the above
applies equally to the quality of arabesque—
certainly, to the source of its conception if
not to the design itself. For art is, after all, a
reflection of the Soul.

[1]Philip K. Hitti, *The Arabs* (Princeton: Princeton
University Press, 1946), page 6.
[2]*Ibid.*, page 21.

[3]Emel Esin, *Mecca the Blessed, Medinah the
Radiant* (New York: Crown Publishers, Inc.,
1963), page 42.

[4]G. I Kheirallah, *Islam and the Arabian Prophet* (New York: Islamic Publishing Co., 1938), page 8.

[5]*Loc. cit.*

[6]Toshihiko Izutsu, *God and Man in the Koran: Semantics of Koranic Weltanschauung* (Tokyo: Keio Institute of Cultural and Linguistic Studies, 1964), page 102.

[7]*A Dictionary of Islam*, ed. Thomas Patrick Hughes (Lahore: Premier Book House, 1964), page 579.

[8]See Kheirallah, Introduction, page i.

[9]Muhammad 'Abduh, *The Theology of Unity*, translated by Ishaq Musa'ad and Kenneth Cragg (London: George Allen and Unwin, Ltd., 1966), page 143.

[10]*Ibid.*, page 29.

[11]*Ibid.*, loc. cit.

[12]*Ibid.*

[13]*Ibid.*, page 31.

[14]*Op. cit.*, page 230

[15]*Ibid.*, page 231.

[16]*Ibid.*, page 134.

[17]See 'Abduh, page 47.

[18]See Azraqi (*ob.* 858 A.D.), a recorder of the Hadith.

[19]See 'Abduh, page 147.

[20]See Hitti, pages 95–97.

[21]*Ibid.*, page 112.

[22]*Ibid.*, page 143.

[23]*Loc. cit.*

[24]*Loc. cit.*

[25]Sir Thomas W. Arnold, *Painting in Islam* (New York: Dover Publications, Inc., 1965), page 6.

[26]Rom Landau, *The Arabesque* ("College of the Pacific: Asian Study Monographs," No. 2; San Francisco: College of the Pacific Press, 1955), page 18.

[27]*Loc. cit.*

[28]*Loc. cit.*

[29]*Ibid.*, page 7.

[30]*Ibid.*, pages 9–12.

[31]*Ibid.*, page 13.

[32]*Loc. cit.*

[33]*Cf.* Bukhari, Ali al Muttaqi.

[34]See 'Abduh, page 67.

[35]*Loc. cit.*

[36]See Landau, page 18.

[37]See Arnold, page 4.

[38]See Izutsu, page 231.

[39]See Kheirallah, pages 24, 25.

[40]See Arnold, page 3.

[41]*Ibid.*, page 1.

[42]See Arthur Upham Pope (ed.), *A Survey of Persian Art: From Prehistoric Times to the Present* (Produced under the auspices of the Asia Institute, New York: Oxford University Press, 1964–5), pages iv, 1716.

[43]*Ibid.*, page 1712. (Ahmad ibn Abi-Khaled, "Al-Ahwal")

[44]See Landau, page 17.

[45]See Pope, page 1708.

[46]See Arnold, page 3.

[47]See Pope, page 1708.

[48]See Landau, page 16.

[49]*Ibid.*, page 14.

[50]*Ibid.*, pages 21–23.

[51]See above, page 5.

[52]See Landau, page 23.

[53]*Ibid.*, pages 21–22.

[54]*Cf.* Titus Burckhardt, *Introduction to Sufi Doctrine*; and Martin Lings, *A Moslem Saint of the Twentieth Century; Shaikh Ahmad Al-'Alawi.*

[55]See Izutsu, page 231.

[56]See above, page 19.

[57]See above, page 6.

[58]See above, page 17.

Steven Field

AESTHETICS
AS ICONICITY
OF STYLE

*Steven Feld is professor of music at Columbia University
and recipient of the MacArthur Prize for his work with
the Kaluli tribe of Papua New Guinea, described in his
book* Sound and Sentiment: Birds, Weeping, Poetics, and
Song in Kaluli Expression. *He is also a practicing jazz
musician. He has recorded Kaluli music, produced as*
Voices of the Rainforest. *In the following excerpts from a
longer essay (recently republished in* Music Grooves, *by
Feld and Charles Keil), Feld describes the basic values at
work in Kaluli music, values that favor participation
and simultaneity and contrast markedly from those
evident in Western classical music.*

The ethnographic materials here focus
on the Kaluli people, who number about
twelve hundred and live in the tropical rain
forest of the Great Papuan Plateau in the
Southern Highlands Province of Papua
New Guinea. . . . On several hundred square
miles of rich land at an altitude of about
two thousand feet they hunt, fish and tend
land-intensive swidden gardens that yield
sweet potatoes, taro, pandanus, pumpkin,
bananas, and many other fruits and vegetables. Their staple food, sago, is processed
from wild palms that grow in shallow
swamps and creeks branching off of larger

river arteries that flow downward from Mt.
Bosavi, the collapsed cone of a volcano
reaching eight thousand feet. Kaluli live in
about twenty distinct longhouse communities; in each, most people still reside in a
single communal house comprising fifteen
families, or about sixty to eighty people. In
recent years, under influence from Papuan
evangelical pastors and government officers, there has been a trend toward smaller
houses occupied by single families, or at
most, two or three famijlies.

This is a classless society that has only
begun to feel the impact of occupational

Steven Feld, "Aesthetics as Iconicity of Style, or 'Lift-Up-Over Sounding': Getting into the Kaluli Groove,"
Yearbook for Traditional Music 20 (1988): 74–113.

specialization, stratification, and socially rewarded differentiation since the intensification of outside contact in the last twenty-five years. Overtly, the tone of everyday Kaluli life is strongly egalitarian in social and political spheres. People hunt, gather, garden and work to produce what they need, taking care of themselves and their families and friends through extensive cooperation in food sharing and labor assistance, all organized informally through networks of obligation and reciprocity. While gender differences are quite overtly marked, there was traditionally little stratification produced by accumulation of goods, rewards or prestige. Traditionally, as E. L. Schieffelin writes, "Kaluli deference is based on such interactional things as intimidation or fear of shame, and is largely situational, and not structural in character" (1988: personal communication). Although that is changing rapidly, there is still, evidenced by our recent ethnographic experiences, a general lack of deference to persons, roles, categories, or groups based on power, position, or material ownership. Obvious recent exceptions include pastors, Aid Post Orderlies, government and mission workers; gender differentials are clearly becoming more pronounced as well.

My use of the term "egalitarian" is not meant to be static and reified. Existing and emerging differentiation, subtle or overt, is a significant historical facet of Kaluli life, as is the emergent character of ranking as a "coordinating device, establishing reciprocal relations within the larger set" (Adams 1975:170). While a full discussion of this issue is not offered here I will attempt to identify ways that Kaluli expressive and interactional style still seem deeply bound up to a local notion of the self and social life that is expressly egalitarian. . . .

The position I assume here on the interface of sound structure and social structure, musical meaning and social meaning, is one that has been stated succinctly by John Shepherd: "Music has meaning only insomuch as the inner-outer, mental-physical dichotomy of verbally referential meaning is transcended by the immanence 'in' music of what we may conceive of as a *abstracted* social structure, and by the articulation of social meaning in individual pieces of music. In this respect music stands in the same relationship to society as does consciousness: society is creatively 'in' each piece of music and articulated by it. . . .

IN A WORD

The Kaluli term *dulugu ganalan* "lift-up-over sounding" is a spatial-acoustic metaphor, a visual image set in sonic form and a sonic form set in visual imagery. The process and idea are familiar enough; for example, in English we speak of the harmonics of a fundamental tone as its "overtones." Similar examples could be cited from musical vocabularies in many languages, as visual-spatial imagery is a common polysemic or metaphoric source of musical terminology. Certainly the verbal figure "lift-up-over sounding" alone provides much for the imagination. "In the case of metaphor," Owen Barfield writes, "it is the pure *content* of the image, not only the *reference*, which delights." . . . The essence of this "pure content" is good to think; an imaginative, delightful figure and ground perfection. Aristotle said that the contemplation of metaphor implies an insight into likeness, an insight that Paul Ricoeur describes as a rapprochement of thinking, sensing, and feeling, "a model for changing our way of looking at things, of perceiving the world." . . .

How might apprehending Kaluli "lift-up-over sounding" change our way of sensing sound? To start that thought-feeling process I'll playfully recycle the dimensionality of Kaluli "lift-up-over sounding" through some personal images, mixing both Freudian cognitive "condensation" and Empsonian poetic "pregnancy" to evoke what cannot readily be adequately glossed or paraphrased. As Roy Wagner says: "A metaphor is at once proposition and resolution; it stands for itself." . . . For me, intuitively, "lift-up-over sounding" feels like:

—continuous layers, sequential but not linear;
—non-gapped multiple presences and densities;
—overlapping chunks without internal breaks;
—a spiralling, arching motion tumbling slightly forward, thinning, and thickening back again

To appropriate a phrase coined by hip-hop rap and scratch DJ's to describe their own layered multitrack soundwork, by "lift-up-over sounding" Kaluli "fix it in the mix." Here the "mix" is the way one creates/perceives horizontal juxtapositions by refiguring vertical ground, and the "fix" is the way the listener manages resultant simultaneous perceptions of part-to-part *and* part-to-whole relationships. "Lift-up-over sounding" is always interactive and relational. By calling attention to both the spatial ("lift-up-over") and temporal ("sound*ing*") axes of experience, the term and process explicitly presuppose each sound to exist in fields of prior and contiguous sounds.

◆◆◆

One morning as Gigio walked alongside my house at dawn he noticed me sitting on the back porch tape recording out into the bush. Quickly he caught my eye, grinned, and called out: . . . "Hearing lift-up-over sounding out there, hey, my Bosavi is really calling out to me!, I'll be thinking like that."

What we were both hearing then was: . . . From the village edge, sounds of mists, winds, waterways, insects, birds, people, pigs, dogs, all located in diffuse but auditorally co-present space. Gigio's comment could have been made at any point during the day. . . .

What did Gigio mean? Most obviously, the rainforest is a tuning fork, providing well-known signals that index, mark and coordinate space, time, and seasons. "The perception of creatures by their voices and movements in the forest gives a peculiar sense of presence and dynamism to things that are unseen, to surrounding but invisible life. . . . It is important to realize the remarkable impression of immediacy of sounds and creatures heard amid the pervading stillness and immobility of the forest" (E. L. Schieffelin). One never knows how many sources are contributing to the passing dense in-sync but out-of-phase textures, but no matter how many there are the quality of forest sound is simultaneously thick and homogenous, multidimensional yet unified, always redundant in the overall but never precisely repetitive from moment to moment.

Canadian composer and soundscape researcher R. Murray Schafer calls soundscapes "hi-fi" when they contain favorable signal to noise ratios, that is, when the full dynamic range of present sounds can be heard clearly and distinctly without crowding, pollution, or masking by intrusive noise sources. . . . Schafer terms "keynote sounds" those continuous, basic, frequent, customary sounds that provide a sense of environmental center. . . . These notions apply well to the Bosavi rainforest soundscape where sounds provide ongoing indexical information about forest height, depth and distance. Kaluli interpret these everpresent sound patterns as clocks of quotidian reality, engaging the soundscape in a continual motion of tuning-in and tuning-out, changing perceptual focus, attending like an auditory zoom lens that scans from micro to wide angle to telephoto angles as forest sound textures shift in figure and ground and change throughout the daily and seasonal cycles.

There also may be a synaesthetic factor here, interrelating, in a sensually involuntary and culturally conventional manner, features of sound, texture, space and motion. In the tropical rainforest height and depth of sound are easily confused. Lack of visual depth cues couple with the ambiguities of different vegetation densities and everpresent sounds (like water hiss) to make depth often sensed as height moving outward, dissipating as it moves. "Lift-up-over sounding" seems to code that ambiguous sensation of upward as outward. My own major adaptation to this environment was learning to feel and distinguish the height and depth of a sound in the absence of visual correlates. Even though I was aware of psychological evidence that humans are better at horizontal than vertical sound localization, and often subjectively sense high tones to be higher in space than they in fact are . . . , I was acoustically disoriented in the forest for months. Kaluli laughed hysterically the first time they saw me *look up* to hear a sound that was deep, whether high or low to the ground. And they quickly learned to reach over and put a hand on mine to move the microphone when I mistakenly was pointing too far up to record a bird of the deep forest.

The forest is also a mystical home of *ane mama*, "gone reflections," spirits of Kaluli dead. The presence of sounds thus implicates spirit presences with bird voices sonically "showing through" to Kaluli. In this sense attending to the forest may engage strong feelings of nostalgia and longing, even though Kaluli attribute no specific mystical power or force to the forest *per se*. There is simultaneously a less cosmic and deeply pleasurable way the forest engages Kaluli as an image of place and of land as a mediator of identity. . . . For Kaluli the forest is both good to listen to and good to sing with; surround sounds provide enjoyment and inspiration. This notion is nicely attested by E. L. Schieffelin: "There is no mistaking the feeling of affection and warmth when two or three men burst into song on arriving back at their own territory after an absence of a few days at another longhouse. Singing is appropriate not only

because it projects the feeling of the singer but also because it is something to be *heard*—of a piece with the sounds of the forest itself. Sound images are much more evocative than visual ones for the Kaluli. . . ."

Becoming part of the forest by singing along with it ultimately intensifies Kaluli sentiments about the comforts of home. . . .

. . . What does *dulugu ganalan* do to help us put aesthetic theory in critical relief? As I continued to meditate on that, Charles Keil sent one answer to both questions, "lifting-up-over" earlier drafts: "Getting into the groove feels so good because it frees us of a lot of abstractions, logics, 'culture,' 'knowledge,' aesthetics, iconicities, etc. and all the forces that both separate and fix music from dance, myth from ritual, recipe from food, etc., etc., etc. Guess I'm suggesting that you push it further downtown and toward applied sociomusicolgy in conclusion rather than saying that we need to think through the fixed concepts in order to grasp the groove. It's the reverse; we need to groove more in order to break open some concepts, drop others, keep all mere ideas at a safe distance" (1986: personal communication).

I accept Keil's version of arch and tumble but also think that as a natural downhome Kaluli stylistic sensibility the *dulugu ganalan* groove feels so right because it accomplishes the social ideal or goal of maximized participation. Each voice in a stream of collaboration is at once a self-referenced "hardness," an attested skill, competence; a presence that is rewarding and revealing. Simultaneously, each voice is socially ratified as cooperative agent, linked and immersed in a myriad of human relations that continually activate the pleasures of identity. What feels good is the familiarity of local ethos—a Kaluli emotional tone that supports as it challenges, agitates as it invites, stimulates as it soothes. *Dulugu ganalan* is about play, about control and letting go, about being loose and being organized, about being poly- and -phonic, together but always open to reconstituting the relationships employed, about being synchronously in and out of time together. Simply: it feels good to know how to feel good.

Getting back to aesthetic theory and Michael Fischer's question, *dulugu ganalan* is, at the least, a forest of trees falling, crashing down and shaking the grounds of any general aesthetics that privileges vision, visual objects, and visualism, privileges product over process, melody and rhythm over timbre and texture, syntax over semantics, structure over emotion, form over participation, linearity over simultaneity, force over flow, transcendental over temporal, top-heavy over egalitarian, vertical harmony over the moving groove. . . .

. . . From the Kaluli perspective, style (as *dulugu ganalan*) is more than the statistical core reflection of the place or time, or patterned choices made within constraints. It is the very human resources that are enacted to constitute the reality of social life in sound. Style is itself the accomplishment, the crystallization of personal and social participation: it is the way performance and engagement endows humanly meaningful shape upon sonic form. Style is an emergence, the means by which newly creative knowledge is developed from playful, rote, or ordinary participatory experience. Style is the way an internalization and naturalization of felt thoughts and thought feelings guides experience; more than just maintaining the *dulugu ganalan* musical order, it creatively produces and sustains it by allowing Kaluli the pleasures of feeling actualized potential, resources, skill, desires, through careful listening no less than actual performance.

With *dulugu ganalan*, the emergent Kaluli camaraderie, sound, and sensation are cognitively and emotionally integrated in the deepest sense, not just as metaphoric equivalents, but as a felt iconic wholeness. In that sense, style is a gloss for the essence of identity; which is why Kaluli *dulugu ganalan* mediates individual creativity and collective experience, and why grooves/styles are universes of discourse (Meyer), pervasive, rigorous unities (Schapiro), assertions of control (Keil), and algorithms of the heart (Bateson) essential to affecting presences (Armstrong).

Inga Clendinnen

AZTEC
AESTHETICS

Inga Clendinnen is reader in history at La Trobe University in Melbourne, Australia. She is a specialist in Mayan and Aztec history, and she received the Bolton Memorial Prize of the Conference of Latin American Studies for her book Ambivalent Conquests: Spaniard and Maya in Yucatan 1517–1577. *The following selection is taken from her most recent book,* The Aztecs. *Clendinnen describes the worldview of the Aztecs as a fundamentally aesthetic vision, in which life in the world was conceived as a divine artwork and art-making as a religious activity.*

. . . A sixteenth-century Mexica song-poem pivots on what we might be tempted to take as no more than an engaging trope: that the experienced world is a painted book, endlessly sung and painted into existence by the Giver of Life; constantly perishing, constantly renewed:

> With flowers you write,
> Giver of Life
> With songs you give color,
>
> With songs you shade
> those who live here on the earth.
>
> Later you will erase eagles and tigers.
> We exist only in your book
> while we are here on the earth.

. . . The experienced world is a representation composed out of representations, the original models in the mind of the divine artificer deriving from the world of the sacred. What we call "nature" is the creation of sacred art. So too are human arrangements. In this painted world men enjoy no priority: they (like everything else) are figments, their brief lives shaped by a divine aesthetic impulse. Even the achieved magnificence of the "eagles" and "tigers" (the "jaguars") of the greatest warrior orders is a fabrication, and fleeting as a flower.

Such a view is subversive of most of our complacencies. Our art-nature distinction lapses where nothing is "natural," the objects of the seen world being themselves the highest art. Our world is not the measure for the "real," but a fiction, a thing constantly made and remade by the divine artificer, its creatures and things called into

Inga Clendinnen, *The Aztecs* (Cambridge: Cambridge UP, 1991) 213–32.

transitory existence through the painting and the singing of an elaborate pictorial text. This might seem not far removed from a "works of Creation" Christian sensibility, but there the crucial mediation of the painted text, with all its implications, is missing, and it is not the giant labour of creation (and the moral burden so placed on man) which is central, but rather a continuing and morally quite neutral divine aesthetic impulse.

The human artist mimics the divine activity. The Mexica born on a propitious daysign who recognized and cultivated his or her implicit talent could come to be acknowledged as "a Toltec," a spiritual descendant of those legendary craftsmen of Tula whose works continued to astonish the artists of imperial Tenochtitlan. The true "Toltec" was one who "converses with his heart, finds things with his mind . . . invents things, works skillfully, creates." Among artists, the scribe—"he who paints in the red and black ink"—was most honoured, as he most closely modelled the activities of the divine painter, in a sense seeking to replicate the original divine text. The scribe's wisdom preceded and defeated history: even before the building of Teotihuacan, the "Cradle of the Gods," there had been a people who had "carried with them the black and the red ink, the manuscripts and painted books, the wisdom. They brought everything with them, the annals, the books of songs, and their flutes." As this sequence makes clear, the poet-singers and musicians who called the painted books to life were only slightly less honoured than the scribes; indeed there is a suggestion in some poems that the processes of chant and inscription were simultaneous, the "text" as much sung as painted. But all arts were intimately interrelated, as all were manifestations or activations or clarifications of the divine text and sustained by the sacred impulse. While human artists could not equal the divine athleticism of the god who moved with absolute freedom across the trivial boundaries within the beauty-making realm, the poet indicated their sacred elevation through metaphor, as we will see, singing of "painting" songs, making drums "blossom": envisioning a sense-transcending, hallucinatory expansion of the possible.

Given such an understanding, "art" among humans become a collective quest for the really real, with men working in paint or song or gold or feathers or stone to approximate the images of the exemplary text, and to retrieve the original unsullied sacred vision from the blurred and shifting images before them. Despite its fragility and inherent instability this uncertain world remains a text: defective, incomplete, chronically mutable to human eyes, yet to be deciphered as a painted book is deciphered by those with the skill to ascertain something of the enduring sacred world it imperfectly mirrors. . . .

Aesthetic responsiveness to things of the world, which are either creations of the divine artist or made by men to approximate those creations, therefore, became worship, as did devoted observation as the signs of the sacred were watched for. Beauty of "natural" appearance (in accordance with the Mexica canon) or some special grace or authority in movement indicated a high precision in replication, the living jaguar or eagle being rendered by that understanding an ambulatory text, worthy of special contemplation, special reverence. In the Templo Mayor caches we find not only masks and figures and incense burners, stone frogs, beads—made things—but the skulls of coyotes, swordfish beaks, whole cadavers of crocodiles, leopards stretched out as if at rest. Considered together these things constitute an "all things living in the empire" category, as I have argued. But they are also individual offerings, to be valued in their own right; the "natural" jaguars and crocodiles the creations of the master artificer, the superb replications in stone man's attempted "realization" of divine models.

Ephemerality, too, becomes an indicator of the sacred when the divine artist "writes with flowers" and "colours with songs." Fugitive beauty hints at the unseen but real world of the sacred and the enduring. Therefore frail and fleeting things are to be cherished precisely because they are evanescent, constantly melting back along that shimmering margin into the invisible and real.

. . . The Mexica passionately prized feathers. . . .

All feathers were passionately valued, but the quetzal plume held a special place in the Mexica (and the Mesoamerican) imagination. It was rare, the shy male bird which grew the two long curing tail feathers living deep in the remote rainforests to the South. The feather filaments are light, long, and glossy, so that the smallest movement sets them shimmering. And the colour, a gilded emerald haunted by a deep singing violet blue, is extraordinary: one of those visual experiences quite impossible to bear in mind, so that each seeing is its own small miracle. . . .

Few Mexica could have seen the majestic bannered flight of this extraordinary bird ripping across the sky, the trailing quetzal plumes sensitive to each shift and movement in the air, but even in stillness their import was clear. The chilli-red underbody, the tail-feathers' constant shift in colour between turquoise and "herb-green," most precious because most divine colours, their lift, curve, colour, and movement like "wide reeds" betrayed their intimate connection with vegetable growth. But they were unlike any reed in their shifting iridescence: such beauty identified this marvellous creation as mediating between the seen and the sacred unseen, so rendering the unseen visible. The Mexica called their most valued feathers and featherwork "the Shadows of the Sacred Ones," the marvellous projections into this dimmed world of the light, colour, and exquisite delicacy of the world of the gods.

The ephemerality theme was everywhere, in the high value placed on the ritual expenditure of flowers and feathers, on fire, on the snuffing out of human life and human beauty. . . .

Poetry, for us one of the most individualistic of art forms, can be said to encapsulate collective understandings among Amerindians, who have a long tradition of song-poems as public, and publicly shaped, performances. While Mexica songs were "made" by individuals, they were more arrangements of shared formulae than full inventions, the symbology and styles within the strongly marked genres (warrior songs, burgeon songs, songs of lamentation) being very much prescribed, and particular songs entering the repertoire only if they won general acceptance. Mexica nobles were especially devoted to song-making. The "friendship" the songs invoked so ardently was less a matter of an exclusivist intimacy between individuals than a collective sympathy, closer to what we would call fellowship or comradeship: a sentiment sufficiently rare in the abraded world of male relations in late-imperial Tenochtitlan. But despite noble commitment, songcraft remained a popularly based art, commoners with talent finding an open way into Moctezoma's favour, the palace, and renown. An early myth tells of the capricious god Tezcatlipoca on one of his earthy visitations as a warrior making ready to sing his triumph song. When all the youths and maidens had gathered, he intoned a song so irresistibly compelling that "right then they answered it. From his lips they took the song." (Unhappily for them, while they were helplessly possessed by the song he lured them to their deaths. The story offers a glimpse not only of Tezcatlipoca's casually malevolent humour, but of the way an individual's song could be publicly taken up in performance—not too difficult a feat given the genre's strong formal patterning—and so prove its power, to the gratification and profit of its original owner. . . .

The songs are . . . sumptuously beautiful and intended to enchant. Sung poetry was called in Nahuatl *xochi-cuicatl*, "flower-song," and in the painted books the speech-scrolls which indicated its speaking were coloured the deep blue-green of jade, of quetzal plumes, and of the incomparably precious. In those which survive the objects of the world and of artifice are spun into the one shimmering web. Separate arts are interwoven, or more correctly identified as aspects of a single activity, melting the human skills of polishing jade, painting, featherworking, or song-making into the "natural" blossoming of a flower.

> I polish jades,
> sparkling in the sun.
> On the paper I am putting
> feathers of the green and black bird.
> I know the origin of songs:
> I only arrange the gold-coloured feathers.
> It is a beautiful song!
> I, the singer, weave precious jades
> show how the blossoms open.
> With this I please
> The Lord of the Close and Near.

The artist does no more than "arrange" natural beauty. The emphasis falls on the poignance of the evanescent: the "weaving" of the fugitive glow of notoriously brittle jade, shattering at a misplaced touch; the delicacy of the opening blossom; sound hanging briefly in air, then fading to silence; while that easy crossing of our divide between the humanly contrived and the natural allows a marvellous concreteness in what we would call "metaphors."

The flower-songs also exhibit an interesting ambiguity of agency, with the god called to be present and in a sense to participate in their making. The songs themselves are invoked as descending from the House of the Sun. More deeply, the singer's activity is presented as an act of reciprocity or, more correctly, of restitution: the song is actual-ized by the singer, but it existed before his actualization as the creation of the divine maker. Bestowed by its creator, it is returned in performance. There is a hint, too, that the divine singer at times invades the human vehicle. Many of the songs are antiphonal, a dialogue between singer and deity in which the god himself, summoned by the song and the singer, "paints" in the flowery patio, singing through the human throat with the human artist become his instrument:

> I appear in this flower court.
> Pictures blossom: they're my drums.
> My words are songs.
> Flowers are the misery I create.

The artist is rewarded by the sacred intoxication of the performance, and the immortality accorded his art. . . .

The flower-songs bring men into reciprocating action with the sacred. They are also, in accordance with the aesthetic imperative, ephemeral, even if constantly recreated existing only in the moment of their performance: "blazing flower words . . . [of] but a moment and a day." After that moment, the "flowers" return to the place of the Sacred Ones. And they further reveal the pathos of the human condition, poignant in its mingling of pain and pleasure. Men, like flowers and song, are in the world only fleetingly: "As a song you're born, O Moctezuma: as a flower you come to bloom on earth." While the songs evoke a daze of images of sound, scent, colour, movement, touch, the world so vividly experienced has no reality. Even moments of rapture and exaltation, like all else in this veiled and shifting world, are no more than a dream. The Mexica conceptualized a universe composed of heavens above and underworlds below, those heavens and underworlds being stable and enduring. This visible world, Tlatlticpactli, "on earth," the layer manifest to the senses, they characterized as "that which changes": for all its vivid actuality, an elaborate deception. . . .

One great poem sums up the principles of human and of aesthetic being. The flesh of the human artist is matter, made from the god-gift of maize, but his art is ordered through the painted sacred book, and through his singing he animates the world and completes his life:

> As white and yellow maize I am born,
> The many-coloured flower of living flesh
>   rises up
> and opens its glistening seeds before the
>   face of our mother.
> In the moisture of Tlalocan, the quetzal
>   water-plants open their corollas.
> I am the work of the only god, his creation.
>
> Your heart lives in the painted page,
> you sing the royal fibres of the book,
> you make the princes dance,
> there you command by the water's
>   discourse.
>
> He created you,
> he uttered you like a flower,
> he painted you like a song:
> a Toltec artist.
> The book has come to the end;
> your heart is now complete.

3

. . . To return to the most inclusive proposition: the notion of the world as painted into existence, with men and all else in it representations, transitory expressions of an enduring, divine sensibility. In such a view the surface appearance and the behaviour of things are "reality," or man's closest access to it. Given such an understanding, characteristics or resemblances in form or making or colour or gait which we would dismiss as "superficial" become of maximum moment, yielding cryptic clues as to the relationships with the sacred world. That earnest focus on "mere" appearance cuts across our preference for establishing likeness through unobvious, often hidden,

indicators of common origin. We have been taught to consider the "structural" as basic, and so—not without effort—categorize dolphins and deer, seahorses and sharks, together. Our ancestors would have found the Mexica obsession with appearance and *semblance* very much more intelligible.

This raises the important but vaporous issue of the sensory mode to which the Mexica were most highly responsive. Dennis Tedlock, in an insightful analysis of the conceptualization of the beginning of the world in the Maya "Popol Yuh," emphasizes the primacy given the aural sense in the Maya imagining of things: in the beginning, there was a murmurous hush which slowly defined itself into the rippling of water, of softly shifting winds, of the tiny noise of insects, as the sounds of the world separated themselves and came into being. In the Mexica beginning-of-the-world story the gods first made light:

> It is told that when yet all was in darkness,
>   when yet no sun had shone . . .
> it is said the gods gathered together and
>   took counsel among themselves there in
>   Teotihuacán.
> They spoke, they said among themselves;
>   "Come hither, O gods!
> Who will carry the burden?
> Who will take it upon himself to be the sun,
>   to bring the dawn?"

There followed the self-immolation of a god, so that light and sight were brought to the world, and men could look about them to fathom the meaning of things.

We have already seen how the correspondences between quetzal plumage and lush foliage excited the Mexica imagination. Recognitions of other likenesses stud the language. Andrew Wiget tells us of a cluster of Nahuatl words centred on precise ways of describing how a flower comes to blossom. Where we are content with "to bloom, to blossom, to flower," Nahuatl distinguishes *mimilhui*, "to bloom in a slow unfolding," *cueponi*, "a more sudden explosion of blossom," and *itzmolinia*, "to regain verdure or greenness after once being brown and dry." All these terms may be applied in other texts, so a new song sung or a bird spreading its feathers was said to be "made to blossom," birds and flower-songs forming a "natural" category for men who studied what they saw, and made their inferences from their observations. Given the cryptic nature of the signs all clues had to be pursued. The rosette markings on a jaguar's skin, taken along with the jaguar fondness for hunting by water, recalled the formal roundness of water lilies. In view of the creature's nocturnal and solitary habits, and its superbly indifferent demeanour, those ambiguous signs also pointed to the stars which studded the night sky, and so to the secret doings of night-walking sorcerers and of their divine patron Tezcatlipoca, the "Smoking Mirror" of the seer's scrying glass. Thus the jaguar was anatomized.

This high concentration on significant appearance helps explain some apparent peculiarities of Mexica sculpture. Mexica "naturalistic" sculptures are to any eye magnificent in their apparently effortless verisimilitude. No concessions were made to the recalcitrance of the medium or the simplicity of the technology (sharpened stone, bird bones, fibrous cords, water, sand): technique was not permitted to be an issue. Stone curves and swells as malleable as clay; the skin of a stone serpent glistens; brittle jade writhes and whirls. Sculptors produced stunningly realistic representations in burnished stone of squashes and shells, gourds and grasshoppers. The vegetable representations have the fanatical attention to detail of botanical models: a squash, for example, displayed with the flower at one end and the species-specific stem immaculately modelled at the other. The "purpose" of these representations has been something of a puzzle. They are commonly explained as ritual "dis-play" objects or offerings. So they probably were. But why the desperate attentiveness to detail in the vegetable representations? And why were small creatures—toads, grasshoppers, frogs, flies, fleas—displayed with equal virtuosity, but commonly in a slightly more schematic, selective, form: the grasshopper missing a pair of legs, the toad huge-headed, huge-eyed? And why this passionate translation into stone of so vast a range of objects—vegetables, insects, drums, bundles of reeds, shields: a translation which seems to have been a particularly Mexica obsession? Pasztory believes the preference "is related to the late position of the Aztecs in Mesoamerican History. They associated stone with the great civilizations of the past and apparently adopted it even for modest objects because of its connotations of permanence and associations with ancient grandeur"; which is true, but does not quite get to the heart of the matter. . . .

An exhortation to Mexica sculptors runs:

> What is carved should be like the original, and have life, for whatever may be the subject which is to be made, the form of it should resemble the original and the life of the original. . . . Take great care to penetrate what the animal you wish to imitate is like, and how its character and appearance can best be shown.

A bland recommendation to verisimilitude? Not quite. This is a matter of "penetrating," of representing "character," of unravelling the implications of "appearance." Vegetable beings offer only their appearance as clues, so appearance must be immaculately reproduced. Creatures which move and act betray their sacred affiliations by behaviour as much as by appearance: both must be studied, and the representation made to incorporate the findings. And animate and inanimate things alike reveal significant relationships by context, and by (not necessarily obvious) resemblance in some detail of appearance.

The descriptions of fauna in the book of the Florentine Codex devoted to "earthly things" make hallucinatory reading, with their precise accounts of the coloration, feeding, and nesting behaviour of a particular bird suddenly riven by a statement of its supernatural powers. All creatures were revelatory, however obscurely. The raccoon, "small, squat, cylindrical; tangle-haired," was called "priestess" or "little old woman," for its human hands and feet and its busy managing ways. . . . The opossum [is] a model of easy fecundity, its multiple children constantly suckling, wreathing its sleek body. It wailed and wept real tears when it was caught and its children taken. Creatures like the deer or the rabbit declared the dangerous futility of unrestrained movement: constantly vulnerable to attack, they had abandoned social restrictions to become restless, nervous wanderers.

If first among birds were those of the greatest beauty, like the quetzal, the raptors also compelled attention: superb hunters, flesh-eaters, moving freely close to the sun. One falcon pierced the throat of its prey to drink the blood. It fed, its human watchers thought, three times a day: "first, before the sun has risen: second, at midday: third, when the sun has set." Therefore, it was concluded, "this falcon gives life to Huitzilopochtli because . . . these falcons, when they eat three times a day . . . give drink to the sun." The eagle, incomparable hunter, was "fearless . . . it can gaze into, it can face, the sun . . . it is brave, daring, a wingbeater, a screamer." Among land animals the jaguar was pre-eminent: "the lord of the animals," a solitary hunter, moving easily through the night; "cleanly, noble . . . cautious, wise, proud." Should an arrow pierce it, "it leaps and then sits up like a man. Its eyes remain open and looking up as it dies." A hunter who missed his shot was dispatched with lordly ease. Both eagle and jaguar revealed by their smutted coats their presence and role in the great moment of

the creation of the Sun, when they had followed the self-immolating deity into the flames, and so were forever participant in his glory. Serpents, also powerful, were more ambiguous. They slid sleekly through the crevices of the earth, moving easily between its dark moist interior and the sun-warmed surface. The road trodden by the traveller, with all its lurking dangers, was a "serpent"; it could "bite" without warning. The snake called "Yellow Lord," yellow as gourd-blossoms, spotted like a jaguar, its rattles marking its age, was said to be the leader of the serpents. Some snakes practised and tested their strike; some shook dance rattles in fury; the jaws of other gaped massively, engulfing whole living creatures, ready to swallow the world.

The vegetable world, if equally significant, was somewhat more opaque. Perfumes, those most ephemeral, evocative, invasive experiences, were so clearly the possessions (or the emanations) of gods that men know to sniff only at the outer edges of bouquets: the deep sweet fragrance at the centre belonged to Tezcatlipoca. (Rather less lyrically, the effluvium of the skunk was identified as "the fart of Tezcatlipoca.") Other plants, scentless and visually unremarkable, signalled their powers by the dreams they induced in men. The mushrooms the Mexica called "the flesh of the gods" grew where they chose, but held riddling visions of what was to come. The small folded buttons of the peyote cactus growing untended in bitter and arid lands enclosed extraordinary experiences in its tough flesh. Infusions of the morning-glory seed or the raw native tobacco flooded him who took them with sensations more vivid and compelling than those of the daylight world. The heart-sap of the maguey cactus thickened and clouded into the sour "milk of the gods," drawing those who drank it to the dangerous threshold of the sacred. Everywhere there was clear experiential evidence of the power of green growing things to move men's minds without their volition, and to precipitate them into contact with the sacred. Their potency, however concealed, must somehow have been signed in the detail of their appearance, which was accordingly most laboriously and precisely recorded.

It is the stone serpents—to me the jewels of Mexica art, and a distinctively Mexica genre—which best exemplify the trajectory from strict realism to intimations of the sacred implied in other animal representations. (They also gloriously bridge the distance between the animal and vegetable worlds.) Along with the magnificently sculpted and precisely observed details of overlapping scales and coils and the precise bifurcations of rattles, some Mexica serpents are grandiosely and implausibly fanged, with the heavy spiral of coils echoing the whorl of a great shell. A line of scales ruffles into feathered or vegetable exuberance, and maize cobs grow obscurely among the tail rattles. Then, still in their serpent form, they writhe upright to become visions of vegetable abundance. These stone serpents, objects-becoming-symbols, mediate between a visible world of imperfect representations and the unseen world of the unchanging. It was, I would argue, that desire to "realize" the unchanging original form which animated the Mexica impulse to model the transitory and the significant in stone regardless of the difficulty and the labour of the task.

There is a further implication of the priority given appearance. Despite the importance of behaviour, for the Mexica—as for Amerindians more generally—it was the skin, that most external and enveloping "appearance," which constituted a creature's essence, and so stored the most formidable symbolic power. When a vision-creature appeared to a Plains Indian as a messenger from the sacred powers, the dreamer secured the skin of the "same" animal as an essential part of his sacred medicine bundle (North-American medicine bundles, with

their withered skins and claws and beaks, look like the detritus of a failed taxidermist). Catlin recorded the costume of a Blackfoot curer as a medley of animal and vegetable, but he noted especially "the skin of the yellow bear . . . skins of snakes, and frogs, and bats." This power of the skin extended through the secondary "skin" of the sacred garment, to face and body paint, masks, and adornments.

Mexica conviction of the transforming capacity of a donned skin or magically charged regalia threads through all their ritual action, and much of their social action too. In the text of the painted world a human being was less than impressive: a featherless biped indeed, with no precedence or privilege. He had to construct himself, to make a "face"; borrowing power through his capacity to "take on" an appearance: a skin, a costume, a mask, insignia, a characteristic movement, a cry. . . .

The warrior costumes of the Mexica, one-piece, forked, gaudily feathered garments facsimilating eagles or jaguars or coyotes, with their elaborate "animal" headpieces, can easily seem absurd in our eyes: items of Disneyesque fancy dress, a very long step from the natural creatures we take to be their models. Here I think we are looking in the wrong direction. They were most deliberate concoctions, the detail of colour and form carefully prescribed. Warrior costumes required as tribute were commonly drawn from regions close to Tenochtitlan, where the protocols would be understood, and featherworkers commonly worked from designs drawn by the scribes. So I suspect the models for the warrior costumes, as for other animal-related regalia, were not the living creatures directly observed but what were deduced to be the original models for those creatures: the stylized jaguar or eagle originally "painted" in the original divine text, and then painted again by the human scribe to guide the featherworkers' realization.

4

While all artists were honoured as "Tolteca," we have seen that it was the scribe or *tlacuilo*, "he who paints in the red and black ink," who was acknowledged supreme, for he was professionally concerned with the mystery of signs. Yet it is with a sense of shock that we turn from the subtle rhythms of the sculpture, powerful in any canon, to the Mexican codices. Maya codices, vase paintings, and figurines offer exuberant celebrations of details of costume and jewellery, marvellously fluid contour lines, practised techniques to suggest three-dimensional space, and precisely observed and rendered human postures—and, through those same inspired brushstrokes, finely nuanced expressions of relationships in a very human "divine" world. Central Mexican codices seem by contrast like awkward cartoons drawn by an obsessive child: the figures vestigial, obdurately two-dimensional; the fields of crude colour sealed with a ferocious black line. We know the ancient Mexica specially cultivated the *cempoalli*, the stiff bright orange and golden marigolds with the vivid green stems and leaves which compete with equally stiff and bold flowers in Mexican markets today. The taste was for clear bright colours: candid reds and yellows jostling deep blues and greens. They were sensitive to the bold colours of their pictured representations, not to "natural" pastels. There is no shading, no modelling. Proportions coherent in the seen world are triumphantly "wrong" in the painted: heads are huge, torsos and limbs short; a solitary eye glares beside a vast nose, or is histrionically sealed by death. Arms jut abruptly from torsos, hands from arms, with a terrible energy which comes as much from unconcern for physical plausibility as from their radical simplifications. The power and control of that black "frame line" declares we are not faced here with drafting incompetence, but with a chosen rejection of "realism."

And a chosen rejection of the human. The pictographic books do not present a human world. Where men and women appear they do so as emblems of (usually naked) humanity, not as individuals. The "painted deities" are schematically human in form, with heads, torsos, limbs, but they are supernatural entities, compiled out of elemental symbols and ciphers and significant colours. Even the representations of named rulers participate in this emblematic quality. Pose, position, and gesture do not catch moments in human life, but declare eternal relationships. Garments do not curve to flesh: they stand stiff as banners, and, like banners, inform. The "human" forms sustaining the complex regalia are mere frames, skeletal structures for the items which constitute the person through constructing the conventional icon. Meaning is stored in the bright precision of garments, paint, accoutrements, and the most simple gestural interactions: snapshots from cosmic narratives; elemental oppositions and conflicts and mergings, with particular objects flagged to trigger recollection. Each figure, like each page, is an idea or an assemblage of ideas, as much writing as picture, or perhaps, given the importance of location and colour, more map than either.

Walter Ong is one among several commentators who have had much to say about the different sensibilities shaped by primary dependence on what he calls the "chirographic" as against the oral mode. One of his key discriminations in distinguishing the sensibility of a literary from an oral culture arises from his claim that writing, by fixing thought, allows "study": the systematic and sequential analysis of ideas. His notion that for study to be systematic "words" need to be arranged sequentially perches on a very narrow cultural base. Mexica pictographs, with their complex iconography and careful distribution on the page, certainly aided thought, and men brooded over them. Like the monumental sculptures they so much resembled, the painted books were a flexible mode, allowing the introduction of novel propositions by the insertion of an unexpected symbol or the use of an unexpected colour in the representation of a particular sacred entity, so inviting speculation on the problematics of the sacred world and its relationship to our visible and defective copy. That is, the pictographs could generate discourse, not merely record received information. The class of specialist priests who painted and expounded them were honoured not as clerkly inscribers of fixed wisdom but as guides, custodians, and exegetes of it. In their form the pictographs resemble an elaborate ritual object—a shaman's bundle, perhaps, with its careful arrangement of "natural" objects rendered symbolic by their significant use. If the painted books could not be "read" as we read a linear sequence of conventionalized representations of sounds, so reconstituting speech, the exegetical voice was cued by the images and their placement and colour. The painted representation was encoded: a system of ciphers, most accessible to the alert and experienced, but never transparent.

Mexica pictorial technique, like Mexica "aesthetics" more generally, seems to have operated through a kind of surrealism achieved by dislocation: the abstraction of objects from their "natural" setting and then their framed juxtapositions and oppositions with other similarly dislocated objects, so that resemblances, differences, possible relationships, and transformations could be reflected upon. In spoken Nahuatl we find a developed predilection for the linking of two words in tension to encapsulate a conventional notion. This often involves a slight but telling shift in perspective, as in the turning of a crystal: "skirt and blouse" for woman as a sexual being; "face and heart" for the person; "flower and song" to mean poetry; "water and hill" for place; "jade and fine plumes" for value; perhaps most poignantly "flower-death" for death in battle or on the killing stone: a habit of mind which sought meaning in the juxtaposition of the superficially unlike. Selected and formally arranged out of a stone of objects-become-symbols, the pictographs function within that same mental field. Straddling the space between concrete and abstract, actual and ideal, they point, as it were, in both directions. This tension lends a quite particular potency and immediacy to Mexica symbolic forms. It also hints at a distinctive understanding of the relations and mediation between thought and the perceived world, the abstract and the actual, the sacred and the mundane.

Oriana Baddeley and Valerie Fraser

THE
SURREALIST
CONTINENT

*Oriana Baddeley teaches at the Camberwell School of
Arts and Crafts in London. Valerie Fraser teaches art
history at the University of Essex. Both are graduates
of the University of Essex and specialists in Latin
American art. In the following chapter from* Drawing
the Line: Art and Cultural Identity in Contemporary
Latin America, *Baddeley and Fraser consider the reasons
why many Latin American artists have made use of
the vocabulary of European surrealist art.*

The formulation of a visual language
capable of encompassing the divergent traditions of representation intrinsic to modern
Latin America has been the goal of many
twentieth-century artists, from the Mexican
muralists through to young Brazilian artists
such as Fernando Lucchesi. However, in
finding a formal signifier of cultural identity
it is difficult, if not impossible, to dislocate
the work of Latin American artists from the
frequently analogous concerns of more traditionally recognized art practice. Throughout the twentieth century the concerns of
artists in Europe and North America have
had an obvious impact on the art of Latin
America, yet it is important to recognize the
particular significance of movements such
as Surrealism or abstraction within a non-
Western context.

Often the ideas of their European contemporaries would themselves contain specific references to issues of particular
relevance to Latin American artists. Nostalgia for lost innocence, for the ritual power
of the art of the past with its mysterious
codes and patterning, had an added political
dimension in many Latin American countries. The pre-conquest past, though often
just as alien to their contemporary life as it
was to a Parisian avant-garde, constantly
served to differentiate Latin American culture from that of Europe. Reference to that
past carried with it the implicit awareness of
the colonial conflict. Interest in the art of

Oriana Baddeley and Valerie Fraser, *Drawing the Line: Art and Cultural Identity in Contemporary
Latin America* (New York: Verso, 1989) 99–117.

the continent's ancient inhabitants was not a simple rejection of accepted tradition of representation as it was for artists such as Picasso; it was also an assertion of the special identity of their own culture.

On another level the incorporation into the practice of fine art of the art forms of subcultures and the whole spectrum of material which falls into the Latin American categorization of "arte popular" called into question not just class and gender but also race. Even in the work of those exiled artists absorbed into the mainstream of Western art, the governing criteria of their art appear different from a Latin American perspective. The processes of cultural syncretism at work are frequently overlooked but can add greatly to the understanding of particular artists' output.

It would be difficult, for example, to locate the work of the Uruguayan artist Joaquín Torres García (1874–1949) without some knowledge of the aesthetic debates of Piet Mondrian and Theo van Doesburg.[1] Yet his paintings are equally dependent on an understanding of the aesthetic conventions of the pre-Columbian civilizations of ancient America. Most of Torres García's creative activity emerged outside of Latin America. At seventeen he had returned with his family to Spain, spending the bulk of his working life in either Barcelona or Paris. His first contact with the pre-Columbian past was probably in the collections of the Musée de l'Homme in Paris rather than in his birthplace.[2] Yet it is equally obvious that the impact of that past on his work was of a very different nature to, say, that of Toltec sculpture on Henry Moore.[3] A work such as his *Indoamérica* of 1938 is a homage to both the Neoplatonic ideals he shared with his Dutch contemporaries and the stylized geometry of ancient America. As such it is not an exploration into the exotic but an attempt to unify the shared characteristics of his separate heritages. Torres García's attempts to find universal proof of the valid-

ity of abstraction as a basis for contemporary art practice were dependent on an awareness of difference and collectivity: the separate traditions of the old and the new world and the need to negotiate the space between the two, to find the space that he himself occupied. The need to explore the past, to locate the distant body of the many-headed Hydra of contemporary culture, remains a strong motivating force for many Latin American artists, whatever the specific idiom of their work.

While the modernist recognition of early forms of abstraction has a specific resonance in Latin America, it is not the most powerful of conjunctions of interest. Surrealism, of all twentieth-century categorizations of artistic form, technique and subject, has had the most pervasive impact on the art of Latin America. The concerns and priorities of the movement, originally formed around the pronouncements of the French poet André Breton[4] were both nourished and consumed by the diverse art practices of Latin America. Breton was initially involved with the anarchic Parisian Dadaists, but from the 1924 publication of his *First Manifesto of Surrealism* he became an increasingly powerful force in the European avant-garde. The relationship of the mainstream of Surrealism to what was perceived as the marginalized, yet truly authentic, world of art production beyond the boundaries of European art represents a complex model of artistic symbiosis.

The doctrines of Surrealism developed out of the European experience of the First World War and the transformations of art and literature engendered by that cataclysmic event. However, its continued survival was at least to some extent based on its claims to be both international and subversive. Breton's search for the fixing of "a certain point of the mind at which life and death, the real and the imagined, past and future, the communicable and the uncommunicable, high and low, cease to be perceived as contradictions"[5] gave Latin America, in particular Mexico, a privileged place within Surrealist writing. He saw Mexico as a "naturally surrealist" location, embodying the very contradictions essential to Surrealism.[6]

The conflicts within the post-colonial cultures of the continent presented fertile new pastures for the Surrealist explorer, who found in the ancient, the popular and the self-consciously political art of Latin America a visual language of opposition. The fascination with Mexico, evidenced by Breton's *Souvenir du Mexique* of 1939, in which both the poet's visit and the place itself take on iconic importance, played upon the country's function as cultural gateway. On one side lay the rational, ordered oppression of the established European civilizations so hated by the Surrealists, on the other the mysterious chaos of the irrational and unknown represented by the native culture of America. The complex blend of race and religion, of native and exile, oppressed and oppressor was seen to manifest itself in the visual culture of Latin America, which like a bilingual text functioned as an access point—that fixed conjunction searched for by Breton between the perceived polarities of human existence.

At the same time Surrealism offered the Latin American artist a place at the high table, welcoming proof of the movement's internationalist aspirations. The Cuban Wifredo Lam (1902–82) and the Chilean Roberto Matta (born 1911), though both working primarily outside of Latin America, embodied those aspects of their native culture most admired by the European exponents of Surrealism. . . .

The international reputations of Lam, Matta and their Mexican contemporary Rufino Tamayo (born 1899) also serve to illustrate some of the generally held stereotypes of the Latin American artist. Surrealism defined itself as primarily preoccupied with "otherness," whether expressed through insanity, social deviancy or the strangeness of differing cultural norms. The function of the Surrealist was to act as a catalyst, transforming banalities into bayonets, seeking out and unleashing subversive tendencies within his own culture, to undermine from within a society seen by Breton as a "petty system of debasement and cretinization."[7] The movement subjected to particular attack the belief in a rational ordered universe governed by an all-seeing beneficent deity, represented by the accumulated heritage of classical philosophy and Christian morality.

Traditional contraventions of this Graeco-Christian model of social order were embraced as revolutionary antecedents of the Surrealists themselves. The perceived opposites of "civilized" values were sought out and adopted as emblems of the Surrealist cause. In Third World countries caught in a battle for some measure of cultural independence, Surrealism offered a validation of their own internal languages of rebellion. Dreams and magic replaced reason and morality, the shaman usurped the priest.

Latin American artists attempting to confront the contradictions of their heritage, to forge a cultural identity which encompassed the divergent strands of colonial history, could find within Surrealism a prioritization of their own concerns. The interest of an artist such as Lam in the Afro-Caribbean roots of his own and Cuba's past, could be easily absorbed into the European avantgarde's fascination with African sculpture and "voodoo" ritual. It is important, however, to distinguish between attempts to consolidate a fragmented culture and the symbolic appropriation of others. Lam's paintings debate the nature of syncretism as a means of understanding his own culture and in that sense have radically different aims to superficially similar works by Picasso. . . .

The angular forms of African sculpture, first encountered by Picasso in the ethnographic collections of the Palais du Trocadéro, continued to permeate his work throughout the century, became a standard component of his visual vocabulary, and were eventually absorbed into the wider languages of twentieth-century art. It is that interest, and the issues raised by the modernist recognition of the existence of culturally divergent forms of visual representation, which serve as the starting point of Lam's aesthetic. In *Luz de arcilla* the tripartite division of the composition presents the spectator with a complex *ménage à trois;* strange creatures with both human and animal characteristics confront each other in an enclosing darkness. The shadowy background has the warm brownness of Velázquez or Goya rather than the deliberately modern cinematic monochrome of *Guernica,* immediately putting Lam's painterly discussion into the past tense. This darkness of the picture surface congeals and evaporates; like primaeval mud it both forms and conceals its inhabitants. These figures seem caught forever in a sexual ritual evoking memories of Marcel Duchamp's *Large Glass*[8] with its fixed coordinates of desire and frustration, yet that work was suffused with the bright light of the scientific laboratory. Here the setting has the mysterious drama of a jungle clearing and the almost sweaty darkness of the tropical night.

The background figure on the left stands alone, a homage to Lam's distant African heritage, the abundantly female buttocks and belly surmounted by an impassively masked head. The sharp lines associated with African sculpture overlay the unmistakable form of the famous "Venus of Lespugue," the prehistoric fertility figure referred to over and over again by Picasso in the 1930s. The combined phallus/vagina imagery of this ancient figure serves to emphasize the antagonistic duality of the principal characters, while simultaneously representing an idealized unification of both physical and cultural divisions. The composite forms of the two central figures are dominated by the recognizably equine char-

acteristics of hoof, tail and muzzle. This horse may belong to the stable of Picasso but it is equally that of the sixteenth-century conquistador, it carries with it the ambivalent relationship of Lam to the European legacy in the Caribbean. The light which both illuminates and activates the protagonists, however, is the ritual light of *santería,* the syncretic Afro-Cuban religion of Lam's childhood memories.

If the iconography of a work such as *Luz de arcilla* is given meaning by the specifics of Latin American history, it is also important to recognize the formal self-consciousness of Lam's visual language, since it is this level of conscious play which is so consistently denied to artists defined as outside the mainstream of the "modern." Lam's painting is as much about painting as it is about history. European conventions interweave with those of Cuba's racially disparate cultures, producing a complex reflection on the nature of representation itself. . . .

While Lam is seen as stylistically derivative, few question the uniqueness of the contribution of Roberto Matta. In fact, the opposite can be said to be true; Matta is, if anything, isolated in his uniqueness. Breton espoused Matta with the fervour of an ageing Don Juan faced with impotency. He initially found in the work of his new protégé all the Surrealist virtues by then perceived as lacking in artists such as Dali. In 1944 he could declare, "It is Matta who holds the star most steadily above the present abyss which has swallowed all the features of life that might make it priceless." At Breton's prompting Matta had produced what amounted to a Surrealist critique of the rationalist strands of modernist practice; his "Mathématique sensible—architecture du temps."[9] In this short written "presentation" piece (which appeared in the spring edition of the Surrealist magazine *Minotaure* in 1938) Matta recanted the teachings of the great modernist architect Le Corbusier in whose architectural practice he had been training since 1934. Deliberately parodying his former teacher's credo of "Mathématique raisonnable,"[10] Matta called for "walls like damp sheets which deform themselves and marry our psychological fears," and offered a denunciation of a logically pure modern architecture.[11]

For fellow Surrealists, Matta's conversion to the movement represented a victory over the forces of scientific law and designed order, but also symbolized the unleashing of his Latin American soul from the constricting body of Eurocentric rationalism. Matta's work, during his decade as Breton's chosen Surrealist painter, exemplifies not only Surrealism but also the values of otherness traditionally imposed upon the colonized subject. Such an elision was intrinsic to the subversive practice of the Surrealist, yet simultaneously reinforced restrictive stereotypes of Latin American culture.

The intrinsic characteristics of post-Renaissance European art were seen to be dependent on the mathematic surety of perspectival space, the painter's skill lying in the ability to manipulate and mask the strict conventions of art's secret geometry. Earlier twentieth-century painters, such as the Cubists, had attacked the European dependence on illusionism, emphasizing the flatness of the canvas and the process of painting as an end in itself. Matta's work of the 1940s broached similar issues but viewed them through the optical distortions of Surrealist automatism. His approach was not to deny the existence of an illusionistic picture space but to create a giddy world of shifting floors, collapsing skies and literally vanishing horizons. To enter into the painted universe of Matta is to lose all certainty in the governing laws of matter, a pun much played upon by the artist himself. A painting such as *A Grave Situation*, 1946, presents the spectator with a series of contradictions; the room without walls, an interior exterior inhabited by strange objects which seem in the process of constant assembly and decon-

struction. Dominating the composition is an authoritative composite figure—a living machine, both insect and human, with the timelessness of an Egyptian deity. It stands like a science-fiction school teacher surrounded by the spinning desks of absent pupils. Matta presents us with the perfect world through the looking glass, where solids dissolve and past and future converge.

In Matta's paintings from this period perspective is not confronted and discussed, as it was by the Cubists, it is inverted. As a Surrealist painter he revealed the parallel universe of contradictions so constantly evoked by his colleagues. Within a Latin American context, however, his imploded and chaotic worlds are typical of the obverse nature of otherness. . . .

For Torres García, . . . Lam and Matta the problem lay in bridging the gap between the current languages of the modernist avantgarde and the requirements of being Latin American artists. The Mexican Rufino Tamayo's work responds to rather different demands. Like his contemporaries Lam and Matta, he has a recognized presence within traditional art history and like them he spent much of his working life outside of Latin America. Admired as a great colourist, Tamayo is seen to unite the concerns of Picasso, whose work has had an acknowledged influence on his own, and Matisse. However, his primary reputation outside Latin America rests upon his opposition to the didactic aims of the Mexican muralists.

At the height of the mural movement in the 1920s and 1930s, Tamayo chose to disassociate himself from his contemporaries. In so doing he initially excluded himself from the mainstream of Mexican art. Opting, as Octavio Paz has put it, "for solitude, criticism. He refused to reduce his art to yet another form of political rhetoric and he decided to pit his own idiom against the so called national style of painting."[12] In the long term this "criticism" has tended to enhance rather than detract from his work.

In terms of the continuing marginalization of the self-consciously political art of Latin America, Tamayo's work is traditionally judged as exemplifying the return to painterly values, a defusing of the threatening aspects of the Mexican aesthetic debates. While the muralists publicly denied the function of painting as a commodity, the work of Tamayo is both decorative and assertive of painting as an object unto itself. His highly collectable works embody, more so than those of any of the other artists being discussed, the acceptable face of Latin American art: not too different to be challenging but manifesting an exoticization of recognizable and familiar painterly forms.

Tamayo's status within Mexico is also helped by the international, particularly North American, approval of his work but his unquestioned pre-eminence is evidence of a more substantial basis to his reputation.[13] Whatever the reasons for Tamayo's popularity abroad, for many Mexicans he also epitomizes vital characteristics of their culture. This is not just by virtue of longevity (although he does represent a physical link with the most dynamic period of art production in Mexico, managing to outlive his exact contemporaries Orozco and Siqueiros, and the younger Kahlo). Probably the most telling of the characteristics of Tamayo's work is his ability to synthesize coherently the prevailing trends of mainstream art practice and the specific concerns of contemporary Latin American culture, while maintaining a formal originality. References to other artists seem strangely distanced from the often subtle yet haunting presence of the paintings, with their dense, worn surfaces. Picasso, Dubuffet and Rothko are all evoked in terms of their formal languages but Tamayo does not appear interested in the more knowing modernist game of deliberate reference. . . .

Like most twentieth-century Mexican artists the pre-Columbian past features prominently in Tamayo's work, not as the specific narrative of the work of Diego Rivera or as the political metaphor of Siqueiros, but as distant archetypes of human behaviour. The dogs featured in *Animales* are related to the famous pre-Columbian clay effigies from Colima but in the final instance they are not to be read as specifically Mexican dogs.[14] They are generic dogs, whose existence outside of Tamayo's painting is not important. Similarly, in a later work such as *Carnavalesca*, 1974, the presence of pre-Columbian sculpture is evoked but never described.

It is in the surface of the paintings themselves that the links between past and present are made most forcibly. However brightly coloured, Tamayo's images seem sun-bleached and weather-beaten, as if discovered by an archaeologist rather than an art critic. The textured surfaces of his paintings have a false patina of age which constantly contradicts the self-conscious modernity of their formal composition. They assert their distance from the conspicuous "newness" of much modern art, claiming a similar appearance of artistic prescience to that of an ancient Cycladic sculpture in a collection of modern art. This formal denial of modernity, deliberate masking of the textures of the industrial world, is a frequently used device among Latin American artists. It serves as a visual proof of the uneasy relationship seen by many Latin Americans to exist between the colonial past and the technological power of their North American neighbour. It reinvokes the divide set out so cogently by Kahlo' *Self-Portrait on the Borderline.*

◆◆◆

The Surrealist perception of Latin America, in which so many European myths about the "New World" coalesced, served to perpetuate the image of the continent as a location of dreams and inversions of rational order. Yet the aesthetic framework of European Surrealism has itself been appropriated by many Latin American artists as a means of articulating their own culture. If the continent dreams, then they are the politically charged revelations of

Antonio Ruiz's *Malinche's Dream*, where the collective memories of the past challenge the realities of the present.

[1] Alfred H. Barr, *Der Stijl, 1917–1921*, New York 1961.

[2] Torres García's son first introduced the artist to pre-Hispanic art, by way of Nazca pots from Peru in the collection of the Musée de l'Homme in Paris, where he was working.

[3] Susan Compton, *Henry Moore* (exhibition catalogue), London 1988.

[4] See Franklin Rosemont, *André Breton and First Principles of Surrealism: Selected Writings of André Breton*, London 1978.

[5] "Second Manifesto of Surrealism," 1930, in André Breton, *Manifestos of Surrealism*, Ann Arbor, Michigan 1972.

[6] In April 1938 Breton and his wife Jacqueline arrived in Mexico, where they stayed with Kahlo and Rivera, socializing and travelling with them and the Trotskys. In the same year Breton and Rivera co-signed the "Manifesto for a Free Revolutionary Art" (which appeared in *Partisan Review*), although it was actually written by Trotsky.

[7] *Manifestos of Surrealism*, p. 125.

[8] See Octavio Paz, *Marcel Duchamp, Appearance Stripped Bare*, Rachel Phillips and Donald Gardener (trans.), New York 1978, p. 125.

[9] *Minotaure*, no. 11, Spring 1938.

[10] C-E. J. Le Corbusier-Saugnier, *Vers une architecture*, Paris 1923. See also *Le Corbusier, Architect of the Century*, exhibition catalogue, London 1988.

[11] Dawn Ades, *Dada and Surrealism Reviewed*, exhibition catalogue, London 1978, p. 315.

[12] *Rufino Tamayo: Myth and Magic*, exhibition catalogue, Solomon R. Guggenheim Museum, 1979, p. 10.

[13] Tamayo's popularity in North America is evidenced by his one-man exhibitions at prestigious locations such as the Guggenheim Museum (1979) and the Phillips Collection (1978).

[14] These pre-Columbian clay vessels from Colima in the shape of plump dogs have been popular throughout this century. There is a particularly fine collection in the Museum of History and Anthropology in Mexico City.

Gary Witherspoon

NAVAJO AESTHETICS: BEAUTIFYING THE WORLD THROUGH ART

Gary Witherspoon is an anthropologist who studies Navajo society. His books include Navajo Kinship and Marriage *and* Language and Art in the Navajo Universe. *In the following excerpt, he describes the Navajo perspective on beauty, which is seen as a model for living well.*

In the Western world, where mind has been separated from body, where man has been extracted from nature, where affect has been divorced from "fact," where the quest for and focus upon the manipulation and accumulation of things has led man to exploit rather than to respect and admire the earth and her web of life, it is not surprising that art would be divorced from the more practical affairs of business and government and the more serious matters of science, philosophy, and theology. In the Navajo world, however, art is not divorced from everyday life, for the creation of beauty and the incorporation of oneself in beauty represent the highest attainment and ultimate destiny of man. *Hózhǫ́* expresses the Navajo concept of beauty or beautiful conditions. But beauty is not separated from good, from health, from happiness, or from harmony. Beauty—*hózhǫ́*—is the combination of all these conditions. It is not an abstractable quality of things or a fragment of experience; it is the normal pattern of nature and the most desirable form of experience.

For the Navajo, beauty is not so much in the eye of the beholder as it is in the mind of its creator and in the creator's relationship to the created (that is, the transformed or the organized). The Navajo does not look for beauty; he generates it within himself and projects it onto the universe. The Navajo says *shił hózhǫ́* "with me there is beauty," *shii' hózhǫ́* "in me there is beauty," and *shaa hózhǫ́* "from me beauty radiates." Beauty is not "out there" in things to be perceived by the perceptive and appreciative

Gary Witherspoon, *Language and Art in the Navajo Universe* (Ann Arbor: U of Michigan P, 1977) 151–78.

viewer; it is a creation of thought. The Navajo experience beauty primarily through expression and creation, not through perception and preservation. Beauty is not so much a perceptual experience as it is a conceptual one.

In the Western world beauty as a quality of things to be perceived is, in essence, static; that is, it is something to be observed and preserved. To the Navajo, however, beauty is an essential condition of man's life and is dynamic. It is not in things so much as it is in the dynamic relationships among things and between man and things. Man experiences beauty by creating it. For the Anglo observer of Navajo sandpaintings, it has always been a source of some bewilderment and frustration that the Navajo "destroy" these sandpaintings in less time than they take to create them. To avoid this overt destruction of beauty and to preserve its artistic value, the Anglo observer always want to take a photograph of the sandpainting, but the Navajo sees no sense and some danger in that. To the Navajo the artistic or aesthetic value of the sandpainting is found in its creation, not in its preservation. Its ritual value is in its symbolic or representational power and in its use as a vehicle of conception. Once it has served that purpose, it no longer has any ritual value.

Navajos take little interest in the display or preservation of their works of art, with the exception of silver and turquoise jewelry. They readily sell them to non-Indians who are looking for beauty in things. Traditionally, they put their works of art to practical use in their daily activities. Now it is more practical to sell them for money and buy stainless steel pots and other more durable but less artistic things. This practice offends the purist's view of aesthetics, but it is, in fact, not a depreciation of aesthetic value at all. It is simply based on the idea that beauty is a dynamic experience in conception and expression, not a static quality of things to be perceived and preserved.

With regard to the two different views of art contrasted above, it is not surprising that Navajo society is one of artists (art creators) while Anglo society consists primarily of nonartists who view art (art consumers). The Navajo find it incomprehensible that we have more art critics than we have artists, and more art collectors than we have art creators. Nearly all Navajos are artists and spend a large part of their time in artistic creation. All Navajos are singers, and most Navajos have composed many songs. Traditionally, over 90 percent of all adult women wove rugs and today, despite limited opportunities to learn this art, a majority of Navajo women over thirty still weave. A large number of Navajo men are skilled at silver work and sandpainting. Some women still make pottery and beautifully designed baskets. Teachers in Navajo schools find that nearly all Navajo students take a special interest in and have an unusual proficiency in the graphic arts. Navajos are also very eloquent and often poetic in their use of language.

In white society it is the exceptional and abnormal person that becomes an artist. The artist is usually associated with marginality and nonconformity with regard to the mainstream of society. From this marginal position the artist dedicates himself almost solely to his artistic creations. The nonartist among the Navajo is a rarity. Moreover, Navajo artists integrate their artistic endeavors into their other activities. Living is not a way of art for them, but art is a way of living.

Navajo artistic interests and talents are enhanced by, if not derived from, the emphasis on the creative nature of thought and the compulsive power of speech. Art is a nondiscursive form of expression, but it involves many of the same processes of symbolic transformation that are found in discursive symbolism. Professor A. D. Richie has noted that "the essential act of thought is symbolization" . . . , and art is as much symbolization as is speech. Art is a symbolic transformation of experience, and, as such, it invests and imbues experience—thus life—with beauty and aesthetic value and meaning.

Navajo culture is not just a food-gathering strategy; it is an artistic way of life. One is admonished to walk in beauty, speak in beauty, act in beauty, sing in beauty, and live in beauty. All things are to be made beautifully, and all activities are to be completed in beauty. The following daily prayer exemplifies the Navajo emphasis on beauty:

> With beauty before me, I walk
> With beauty behind me, I walk
> With beauty above me, I walk
> With beauty below me, I walk
> From the East beauty has been restored
> From the South beauty has been restored
> From the West beauty has been restored
> From the North beauty has been restored
> From the zenith in the sky beauty has been
>   restored
> From the nadir of the earth beauty has
>   been restored
> From all around me beauty has been
>   restored.

The separation of mind and body—or, in the popular idiom, mind and heart—in Western metaphysics has led aesthetic analysis and interpretation into confusion as to what it is that the artist expresses in his work. Experience is divided into fragments which relate to the intellectual realm, the emotional realm, and the aesthetic realm. A major question, then, is whether a particular art work expresses an "idea," whether it expresses the emotions and feelings of the artist who created it, or whether it expresses nothing in the way of ideas or emotions, and simply possesses significant and aesthetic form, a pure expression of beauty.

In the Navajo world, where mind and matter, thought and expression are inseparably connected, the aesthetic experience—the creation of beauty—is simultaneously intellectual, emotional, moral, aesthetic, and biological. Navajo life and culture are based on a unity of experience, and the goal of

Navajo life—the creation, maintenance, and restoration of *hózhó*—expresses that unity of experience. *Hózhó* expresses the intellectual concept of order, the emotional state of happiness, the moral notion of good, the biological condition of health and well-being, and the aesthetic dimensions of balance, harmony, and beauty. In Navajo art we find all these concepts, states, and conditions expressed.

As the essence of the Navajo conception of life is movement or motion, and the experience of beauty is dynamic and flowing, characteristic themes found in Navajo art express this emphasis on movement and activity. . . .

A Navajo often counts his wealth in the songs he knows and especially in the songs he has created. A poor Navajo is one who has no songs, for songs enrich one's experiences and beautify one's activities. Songs accompany and enrich both ceremonial and nonceremonial activities. There are riding songs, walking songs, grinding songs, planting songs, growing songs, and harvesting songs. There are songs to greet the sun in the morning and songs to bid it farewell in the evening. There are songs for horses, for sheep, and for various other animal species. There are songs for blessing a hogan and songs for taking a sweat bath. In the past there were even songs for bidding visitors farewell. And, of course, there are songs of love and romance. But the most powerful songs are those that are essential parts of ceremonial and ritual activities. The former type is a means by which Navajos maintain *hózhó* in their daily life experiences, while the latter type constitutes a means by which Navajos restore *hózhó* when it has been disrupted.

Professor David McAllester, who has spent over twenty-five years studying Navajo music, says Navajo music is characterized by its vigor, its power, and its acrobatic style. It is intense, at times almost "excessive," compared to Pueblo music which is low, controlled, and rehearsed. Navajo music seems to match the cultural emphasis on energy, activity, and motion. There is hardly ever a "held" note, except at the end of a song. . . .

In analyzing the First Snake Song, Professor McAllester finds that one of its chief characteristics is repetition. Repetition is a motif found all through Navajo life and culture. It is associated with the concepts of renewal, regeneration, rejuvenation, revolution, and restoration. Repetition enhances the compulsive power of the song. The repetitive nature of many Navajo songs is adorned with and enlivened by various modes of variation. . . .

In the First Snake Song there is a significant alternation in the *kind* of melodic activity. This is found between level sections based entirely or largely on the tonic, and active sections characterized by rapid and pulsing movement. McAllester considers this to be the quality in Navajo "chanting" that makes the term a misnomer. . . .

The verses of the First Snake Song also exhibit the principle of alternation. Here are found alternations in colors, in sex, in directions, and in jewel symbols. This is a way of presenting pairs of related objects. . . .

McAllester notes that although the First Snake Song is strophic and framed, it is progressive in that the pitch gradually rises from one song to the next. He relates this progression in pitch to a progression in textually expressed ideas where the movement is from mature male to immature female, from animate snake to inanimate hoop, from "holding," "dangling," "lugging" to "trundling." . . . As noted earlier . . . maturity is often thought of as a static and thus male-linked condition, whereas immaturity is associated with activity, process, and growth and is female-linked in the Navajo metaphor. Since the animate snake is obviously active and the inanimate hoop is static, the progression here seems to go from static to active and from active to static. This is con-

trasted by the progression of "holding," "dangling," "lugging," and "trundling," which starts from the static "holding" and gets progressively more active. . . .

Where Navajo music, singing, and poetry are artistic endeavors common to both men and women, the other two major domains of Navajo aesthetics, weaving and sandpainting, are sexually bifurcated. Weaving is primarily an activity of women, and sandpainting is primarily an activity of men. Some Navajo men weave, but this associates them with the category of *nádlééhí*, "transvestite." Such a person, however, is usually held in high esteem and is not normally the object of ridicule or unkind behavior. Reichard notes that Left-Handed Singer or Newcomb was a man who wove. She states that he was highly respected, and a person of superior intelligence combined with extreme gentleness and remarkable independence. As an accomplished singer or "medicine man," he wove primarily sandpainting tapestries. . . . Sandpainting is exclusively a male activity. Even female singers do not do sandpainting, although they may supervise the creation of a sandpainting.

It is relevant to note that the composition and design of Navajo sandpaintings are static; that is, the designs are rigidly established and must be created without significant change or alteration if they are to be an effective part of the particular ritual for which they are used. In contrast, a weaver seldom if ever repeats a design. Each rug woven is designed anew, so designs are always changing, flowing, and moving. Thus the production of design in sandpainting and weaving seems to be appropriately associated with the generally static nature of male-linked endeavors and the dynamic nature of female-linked endeavors.

Before mass-produced retail goods became available to the Navajo, they had to produce their own blankets, garments, and moccasins. Although buckskin and other skins provided the raw materials to satisfy many of these needs, wool from sheep provided the major source of material for clothing and blankets. However, instead of just producing clothing and blankets to satisfy the pragmatic needs of warmth and protection from the elements, Navajo women turned the production of clothing and blankets into an artistic endeavor. Today, Navajo women weave rugs primarily for the use of non-Indians. Although they sell these rugs for cash, it has been estimated that the average weaver gets less than a quarter an hour for her work. Obviously, then, the motivation to weave is aesthetic as well as economic—probably even primarily aesthetic. Weaving is an effort in creative transformation. Navajo women transform the wool on the back of sheep into beautifully designed and delicately woven rugs. This is done through the processes of shearing, cleaning, dyeing, carding, spinning, and weaving. Additional color is added through vegetal dyes.

Navajo women develop and create designs in their minds, and then project them onto the world of external reality through the art of weaving. The intricate and often complex patterns created by Navajo weavers are generated in the mind and kept there through the whole process from dyeing through weaving. She must know exactly how much dye to use or exactly what amounts of black and white wool to mix in order to get the very exact color combinations and contrasts she has in her mind. . . .

. . . A woven rug is a product of the mind and the body. The inner form of the rug is in the mind; the outer form of the rug is projected onto the loom. . . .

In the patterns found on Navajo rugs, movement and activity are expressed by diagonal and zigzag lines (also associated with lightning), by the active colors of yellow (brown), blue (green), and red (pink), by appendages to various "static" centers, and by diamond shapes. In contrast, a static condition is expressed by straight lines and horizontal and vertical stripes, by squares and rectangles, and by the static colors of white, black, and grey. Motion goes in one of two directions: linear, continuative, incomplete motion, or circular, repetitious, complete, cyclical motion. In Navajo language the former is found in the important and extensively used imperfective and progressive modes and in the continuative aspect of Navajo verbs, while the latter is found in iterative and usitive modes and in the repetitive aspect of Navajo verbs. In addition linear and continuative motion is expressed by the verbal prefix *hi* which renders the idea of succession, while circular and repetitious actions and movements are expressed by the verbal prefixes *náá* and *ná* which express the ideas of repetition, revolution, and restoration.

In the language of Navajo weaving, linear, continuative, and incomplete motion is expressed by the successive alternation of static and active symbols—colors, lines, and designs. Linear movement thus follows the pattern or series of static-active-static-active. Circular and cyclical movement is expressed by the sequence already noted: static-active-active-static. This pattern is found in the sequence of color, direction, and growth, and in the daily and annual path of the sun. It is sunwise motion. There is also an opposite sequence, usually associated with witchcraft and its cure, but also associated with protection and with an emphasis on activity, that goes from active to static and static to active.

The former type of cyclical movement is mainly found in Navajo ritual where control and normality are emphasized, whereas the latter type of cyclical movement is often found in Navajo weaving and other art forms where creativity and activity are emphasized. . . .

Navajo sandpainting is a male-linked art form that accompanies most major Navajo ceremonials. The designs are established parts of the ritual and must not be significantly altered if the ritual is to be effective. These designs are made on the earthen floor of the hogan. The surface upon which the painting is made is cleaned and smoothed. The designs vary from a few inches to more than twenty feet in diameter, with most paintings averaging from three to six feet in diameter. The painting is done by letting dry pigments trickle through the thumb and flexed index finger. The dry pigments are made primarily from red, yellow, and white sandstone and various mixtures of these colors, but pigments made from colored corn meal, plant pollens, crushed flower petals, and charcoal are also used.

The sandpaintings are made by several men under the direction of the chanter or medicine man. Just as Reichard learned to weave, on many occasions I have enjoyed the opportunity to help create a sandpainting.

The sandpaintings depict the *Diyin Dine'é* and other sacred entities. They recall significant episodes of mythical drama. The mythical dramas revolve around a cultural hero's unfortunate plight and diseased condition, and his or her ultimate cure through identification with, and sometimes compulsive control of, a deity or deities. The disease is caused by some sort of disruption in the proper and normal order of things and is cured by a restoration of the proper order. The patient in his or her plight is identified with the cultural hero who contracted a similar disease or plight in the same way the patient did. In the curing ritual the patient follows in the footsteps of the hero of the myth, sings the songs he or she sang, prays the prayers he or she prayed, and ultimately acquires and exerts the power to restore health and order to his or her self and world that the hero acquired and exerted.

The myth, retold in the songs and prayers of the ritual, places the patient's illness in a cultural context where it can be understood and eventually cured. From the myth the patient learns that his or her plight and illness is not new, and that both its cause and treatment are known. To be cured, all the patient has to do is to repeat what has been done before. It has to be done sincerely, however, and this sincerity is expressed in concentration and dedication. The sandpainting depicts the desired order of things, and places the patient in this beautiful and ordered world. The patient thus becomes completely identified with the powerful and curing agents of the universe. The patient undresses to the extent modesty permits (men to a G-string and women to a skirt) and sits on the painting. Where appropriate and possible the patient's body parts—feet, knees, legs, etc.—are placed on the corresponding body parts of the deity with whom the patient is identified. In addition, the medicine man applies sand from the body parts of the depicted deity to corresponding body parts of the patient's body. Spectators and family members may also apply the sand to corresponding parts of their bodies as well. This is done for sanctification, blessing, and protection.

After the sandpainting has fulfilled its aesthetic and ritual purpose, the sand is carefully collected and deposited at some out-of-the-way place to the north. The symbolic representation of various sacred beings and things is considered to be effective in attracting them to the ceremonial hogan and thus enabling the patient to absorb their curative power.

Notwithstanding the important ritual functions of the sandpaintings, they also have great aesthetic appeal to Navajos. The painters take a special interest and pride in the quality of their work, and many men travel from ceremony to ceremony mainly to participate in the art forms—singing, poetry, drama, and painting—of the ritual. The ceremonies are really a symphony of the arts and they have great aesthetic appeal to Navajo participants and spectators. Where else can one go to and participate in a symphony of the arts while simultaneously being physically, morally, and intellectually sanctified and blessed?

The aesthetic appeal of the forms and designs of sandpaintings is also demonstrated in their extensive use in other Navajo art forms. This is particularly true in weaving where many designs and forms are taken from sandpaintings. These designs, however, also appear in Navajo silver work and in the oil paintings and drawings of contemporary Navajo artists. Such replications of these sacred designs and forms are potentially dangerous to their creators, and many purists among the Navajos deplore this secularization and profanation of sacred forms and symbols. Nevertheless, the aesthetic appeal of these designs and forms seems to have, in many cases, overriden the fear of the dangers inherent in the secular use of sacred forms. As elsewhere in Navajo culture, movement, repetition, balance and harmony, and controlled or restrained emotion and force are dominant themes in Navajo sandpaintings. . . .

Navajo art thus expresses Navajo experiences, and Navajo experiences are mediated by the concepts of and orientations to the world found in Navajo language and culture. All experiences are directed toward the ideals of *hózhǫ́*, and *hózhǫ́* is the intellectual, moral, biological, emotional, and aesthetic experience of beauty. A Navajo experiences beauty most poignantly in creating it and in expressing it, not in observing it or preserving it. The experience of beauty is dynamic; it flows to one and from one; it is found not in things, but in relationships among things. Beauty is not to be preserved but to be continually renewed in oneself and expressed in one's daily life and activities. To contribute to and be a part of this universal *hózhǫ́* is both man's special blessing and his ultimate destiny.

DISCUSSION QUESTIONS

1. Do the aesthetic values of any of the cultures considered in this chapter resemble values that are present, but not especially emphasized, in the West? Explain.

2. Are the aesthetic values of any of the cultures considered in this chapter contrary to any of the traditional aesthetic values of the West? Explain.

3. Do any of the non-Western aesthetic values considered in this chapter resemble values that Western critics of their own tradition propose as alternatives? Explain.

4. Do you think that our society's aesthetic values mirror other values of our society? If so, how?

5. Can you think of examples of Western art that make use of motifs and ideas from non-Western art? In each case (if so), how closely do you think the artist reflected the aesthetic values of the culture from which he or she borrowed these non-Western elements? What evidence would you use to justify your judgment?

FURTHER READING

Ames, Roger T., and J. Baird Callicott, eds. *Nature in the Asian Tradition of Thought: Essays in Environmental Philosophy.* Albany: State U of New York P, 1989.

Coote, Jeremy, and Anthony Shelton, eds. *Anthropology, Art, and Aesthetics.* Oxford: Clarendon, 1992.

Dutton, Denis, "Tribal Art and Artifact." *Journal of Aesthetics and Art Criticism* 51.1 (1993): 13–22.

Geertz, Clifford. *The Interpretation of Cultures.* New York: Basic Books, 1973.

Jopling, Carol T., ed. *Art and Aesthetics in Primitive Societies: A Critical Anthology.* New York: E. P. Dutton, 1971.

Lomax, Alan. *Folk Song Style and Culture.* American Association for the Advancement of Science, Publication no. 88. Washington, D.C., 1969.

Merriam, Alan P. *The Anthropology of Music.* Evanston: Northwestern UP, 1964.

Otten, Charlotte M., ed. *Anthropology and Art.* Garden City: Natural History Press, 1971.

Small, Christopher. *Music, Society, Education.* London: John Calder, 1980.

Smith, Marion W., ed. *The Artist in Tribal Society.* London: Routledge, 1961.

(See Bibliography for further readings about specific areas and cultures.)

APPENDIX I
LIST OF READINGS
BY MEDIUM

THE RANGE OF MEDIA

Plato, "The Form of Beauty" (1)
Plato, "Beauty's Influence" (1)
David Hume, "Of the Standard of Taste" (1)
Immanuel Kant, "The Four Moments" (1)
Friedrich Nietzsche, "On Beauty and Ugliness" (1)
George Dickie, "Art as a Social Institution" (2)
Robert Plant Armstrong, "The Affecting Presence" (2)
Oscar Wilde, "The Decay of Lying" (3)
Walter Pater, "A Quickened Sense of Life" (4)
Edward Bullough, "Psychical Distance" (4)
José Ortega y Gasset, "The Dehumanization of Art" (4)
George Dickie, "The Myth of the Aesthetic Attitude" (4)
Karsten Harries, "The Ethical Significance of Modern Art" (5)
William H. Gass, "Goodness Knows Nothing of Beauty" (5)
Liza Mundy, "The *New* Critics" (5)
Paul Mattick, Jr., "Arts and the State" (6)
Carole S. Vance, "Misunderstanding Obscenity" (6)
James O. Young, "Destroying Works of Art" (6)
Plato, "Inspiration as Magnetism" (7)
Arthur Schopenhauer, "On Genius" (7)
DeWitt H. Parker, "Aesthetic Form" (8)
Roger Fry, "The Limits of Formal Analysis" (8)
Leo Tolstoy, "What Is Art?" (9)
Clive Bell, "Emotion in Response to Significant Form" (9)
Susanne K. Langer, "The Symbol of Feeling" (9)
Robin G. Collingwood, "Expressing Emotion" (9)
John Hospers, "The Concept of Artistic Expression" (9)
Milan Kundera, "The Nature of Kitsch" (9)
Matei Calinescu, "Kitsch and Hedonism" (9)
G. W. F. Hegel, "The Ages of Art" (11)
Wassily Kandinsky, "Concerning the Spiritual in Art" (11)
Arthur C. Danto, "Approaching the End of Art" (11)
Roland Barthes, "The Structuralist Activity" (12)
Isidore Okpewho, "Principles of Traditional African Art" (15)
Kuang-Ming Wu, "Chinese Aesthetics" (15)

Donald Keene, "Japanese Aesthetics" (15)
B. N. Goswamy, "*Rasa:* Delight of the Reason" (15)
Gary Witherspoon, "Navajo Aesthetics: Beautifying the World through Art" (15)

ARCHITECTURE

Zuheir Al-Faquih, "Islamic Art . . . Submission to Divine Will" (15)

CALLIGRAPHY

Kuang-Ming Wu, "Chinese Aesthetics" (15)
Patrick McKee, "Old Age in the Chinese Mountain Landscape" (15)
Donald Keene, "Japanese Aesthetics" (15)
Zuheir Al-Faquih, "Islamic Art . . . Submission to Divine Will" (15)

DANCE

Friedrich Nietzsche, "Apollo and Dionysus" (1)
David Michael Levin, "Balanchine's Formalism" (8)
D. M. Gruver, "Hawaiian Hula" (11)
Brenda Dixon Gottschild, "Black Dance and Dancers and the White Public—A Prolegomenon to Problems of Definition" (13)

FILM

Mark Crispin Miller, "Advertising—End of Story" (8)
Yuriko Saito, "The Colorization Controversy" (10)
Robert Gooding-Williams, "'Look, a Negro!'" (13)
Noël Carroll, "The Image of Women in Film" (13)

LITERATURE AND POETRY

Plato, "Art and Appearance" (3)
Carlos Fuentes, "Words Apart" (5)
Rainer Maria Rilke, "Letters to a Young Poet" (7)
Christopher Middleton, "On the Mental Image" (7)
David Novitz, "Fiction, Imagination and Emotion" (9)
William K. Wimsatt, Jr., and Monroe C. Beardsley, "The Intentional Fallacy" (10)
P. D. Juhl, "Computer Poems" (10)
Jenene J. Allison, "Deconstruction and the Energizer Bunny Rabbit" (12)
Leo Marx, "Huck at 100" (13)

MONUMENTS

MUSIC

NONSTANDARD MEDIA

PAINTING AND DRAWING

Denis Dutton, "Artistic Crimes: The Problem of Forgery in the Arts" (3)
Rika Burnham, "It's Amazing and It's Profound" (4)
Roger Fry, "The Limits of Formal Analysis" (8)
David Michael Levin, "Balanchine's Formalism" (8)
Leo Steinberg, "Other Criteria" (8)
John Berger, "Oil Painting" (11)
Linda Nochlin, "Why Are There No Great Women Artists?" (13)
Mara Miller, "Desiring Women: The Aesthetics of Japanese Erotic Art" (13)
Patrick McKee, "Old Age in the Chinese Mountain Landscape" (15)
Inga Clendinnen, "Aztec Aesthetics" (15)
Oriana Baddeley and Valerie Fraser, "The Surrealist Continent" (15)

PHOTOGRAPHY

Walter Benjamin, "The Work of Art in the Age of Mechanical Reproduction" (2)
Susan Sontag, "On Photography" (14)

SCULPTURE

Friedrich Nietzsche, "Apollo and Dionysus" (1)
Tom Wolfe, "The Worship of Art: Notes on the New God" (6)
Douglas Stalker and Clark Glymour, "The Malignant Object: Thoughts on Public Sculpture" (6)
Anne Truitt, "Daybook: The Journal of an Artist" (7)
Jerrold Levinson, "Messages in Art" (10)
Kwame Anthony Appiah, "Is the Post- in Postmodernism the Post- in Postcolonial?" (12)

TELEVISION

Alexander Nehamas, "Plato and the Mass Media" (5)
Umberto Eco, "Repetition and the Series" (8)
Stanley Cavell, "Cartoons" (14)
Robert C. Solomon, "Are the Three Stooges Funny? Soitainly!" (14)

THEATER

Aristotle, "The Form of a Tragedy" (1)
Aristotle, "Constructing a Tragedy" (7)
Anna Deavere Smith, "Introduction to *Fires in the Mirror*" (14)
Donald Keene, "Japanese Aesthetics" (15)
B. N. Goswamy, "*Rasa*: Delight of the Reason" (15)

OTHER

Yuriko Saito, "The Japanese Appreciation of Nature" (3)
Tom Wolfe, "The Worship of Art: Notes on the New God" (6)
Eugen Herrigel, "Zen in the Art of Archery" (7)
María Lugónes, "Playfulness, 'World'-Traveling, and Loving Perception" (13)
John Dewey, "Aesthetic Qualities" (14)
Janet McCracken, "The Domestic Aesthetic" (14)

APPENDIX II
LIST OF CASES
DISCUSSED

FILM

Casabalanca (Michael Curtiz, director)—Gooding-Williams
Citizen Kane (Orson Welles, director)—Saito ("Colorization")
Fatal Attraction (Adrian Lyne, director)—Carroll
Ghost (Jerry Zucker, director)—Gooding-Williams
It's a Wonderful Life (Frank Capra, director)—Saito ("Colorization")
The Maltese Falcon (John Huston, director)—Saito ("Colorization")
Missing (Constantin Costa-Gavras, director)—Mark Crispin Miller
Three Stooges, *Malice in the Palace*—Solomon
Three Stooges, *Women Haters*—Solomon

LITERATURE

Robert Browning, "My Last Duchess"—Levinson
Lady Murasaki, *The Tale of Genji*—Mara Miller, Saito ("Japanese"), Sokoloff
Salman Rushdie, *The Satanic Verses*—Fuentes
Sei Shōnagon, *The Pillow Book of Sei Shōnagon*—Mara Miller, Sandrisser,
    Sokoloff, Saito ("Japanese")
Mark Twain, *Huckleberry Finn*—Marx

MONUMENTS

Holocaust Museum—Gourevitch
Vietnam Veterans Memorial—Danto ("Vietnam Veterans Memorial")

MUSIC

J. S. Bach, *St. Matthew Passion*—Kivy
BDP, "Jimmy"—Shusterman
BDP, "Stop the Violence"—Shusterman
The Beatles, "Love Me Do"—Wicke
Bill Haley, "Rock around the Clock"—Wicke
Ice-T, "Drama"—Shusterman
Ice-T, "High Rollers"—Shusterman

Mick Jagger—Bloom
Kool Moe Dee, "Go See the Doctor"—Shusterman
Kool Moe Dee, "Monster Crack"—Shusterman

PAINTING AND DRAWING

Pieter Bruegel the Elder, *The Harvesters*—Parker
Cave Paintings—Lyons
Jean Dubuffet, *Olympia* (1950)—Steinberg
Marcel Duchamp, *LHOOQ*—Binkley
Marcel Duchamp, *LHOOQ Shaved*—Binkley
Giotto, *Pietà*—Fry
Goya, *The Third of May, 1808*—Levinson
El Greco, *Crucifixion*—Parker
Katsushika Hokusai, *36 Views of Mt. Fuji*—Saito ("Japanese")
Andō Hiroshige, *53 Sceneries of Tōkaidō*—Saito ("Japanese")
Frida Kahlo, *Self-Portrait on the Borderline*—Baddeley and Fraser
Wifredo Lam, *Luz de Arcilla*—Baddeley and Fraser
Leonardo da Vinci, *Mona Lisa (La Gioconda)*—Binkley
Roberto Matta, *A Grave Situation*—Baddeley and Fraser
Michelangelo, *Doni Madonna*—Steinberg
Michelangelo, *Last Judgment*—Steinberg
Michelangelo, Sistine Ceiling—Keene, Steinberg
Barnett Newman, *Who's Afraid of Red, Yellow, and Blue?*—Harries
Pablo Picasso, *Guernica*—Baddeley and Fraser
Rafael, *The Transfiguration*—Fry
Robert Rauschenberg, *Chairs* (1968)—Steinberg
Robert Rauschenberg, "Erased De Kooning Drawing"—Binkley
Antonio Ruiz, *Malinche's Dream*—Baddeley and Fraser
Signorelli, *Pan*—Parker
Rufino Tamayo, *Animales*—Baddeley and Fraser
Rufino Tamayo, *Carnavalesca*—Baddeley and Fraser
Tintoretto, *Mercury and the Three Graces*—Parker
Jan Van Meegeren, *Christ and the Disciples at Emmaus*—Dutton

PERFORMANCE ART

Joseph Beuy, *7000 Oaks* (1982–1987)—Heyd
Stuart Brisley, *Artist Project Peterlee* (1976)—Heyd
Bené Fonteles, "Garbage Delivery Performances" (1984, 1986, 1987)—Heyd
Rick Gibson, *Free Art Lesson* (1990)—Heyd
Greenpeace Guerilla Theatre—Heyd

PHOTOGRAPHY

Robert Mapplethorpe's photographs—Mattick

PRINTS, UKIYO-E

Suzuki Harunobu—Mara Miller
Sekidera Komachi—Mara Miller
Okumura Masanobu—Mara Miller
Katsūkawa Shunki, portrait of Danjuro—Mara Miller
Utāmaro—Mara Miller

SCULPTURE

Carl Andre, *36 Stones*—Wolfe, Young
Jean Dubuffet, *Group of Four Trees*—Wolfe
Marcel Duchamp, *Fountain, by R. Mutt*—Binkley
Michael Heizer, *Levitated Mass*—Wolfe
Man with a Bicycle (Yoruba sculpture)—Appiah
Barnett Newman, *Broken Obelisk*—Stalker and Glymour
Claes Oldenberg, *Bat-column*—Stalker and Glymour
Claes Oldenberg, Bed—Danto ("Artworld")
Claes Oldenberg, *Lipstick*—Stalker and Glymour
Jody Pinto, *Heart Chambers for Gertrude*—Stalker and Glymour
Robert Rauschenberg, Bed—Danto ("Artworld")
Richard Serra, *Tilted Arc*—Mattick, Stalker and Glymour, Wolfe, Young
Richard Serra, *Twain*—Young
Anne Truitt, *Landfall*—Truitt
Andy Warhol, Brillo Boxes—Danto ("Artworld")
Women's Coalition for Change, *Rape Piece*—Levinson

TELEVISION

Columbo—Eco
The Lone Ranger—Gooding-Williams
The Three Stooges—Solomon

THEATER

Henrik Ibsen, *An Enemy of the People*—Levinson
Anna Deavere Smith, *Fires in the Mirror*—Anna Deavere Smith

GLOSSARY

◆◆◆

a'yn—(Arabic) forms.

abhidha—(Sanskrit) denotation.

Absolute, the—in Hegel's philosophy, the ultimate aim of Reason and of history. The Absolute is the point at which consciousness has an adequate comprehension of reality in its entirety, recognizing the relationship that each thing has to everything else.

absolute music—music without words, to be enjoyed for its own sake.

adbhuta—(Sanskrit) the wondrous or the marvelous, one of the basic *rasas* in Indian theory.

aesthetic attitude—an attitude that disposes one to have an aesthetic experience, often characterized by disinterestedness. Such an aesthetic attitude is taken by some (such as Kant) to be essential to aesthetic experience.

aesthetic experience—the subjective experience that ideally results from contemplating an object of beauty (or other aesthetic value). Since the eighteenth century in the West, aesthetic experience has often been characterized as disinterested, removed from practical concerns.

aesthetic qualities—in Dewey's philosophy, aesthetic qualities are emotional tones that pervade and unify a given experience. Aesthetic qualities characterize any experience that stands out in a person's life; they also give unity to artworks.

aesthetics—a term coined by Baumgarten in the eighteenth century, literally meaning the science of perception. More broadly, the term is used to indicate the philosophical investigation of such "sensuous" values as beauty, or the entire philosophy of art.

Affektenlehre—(German) a doctrine, current in eithteenth-century Germany, which held that particular emotions were indicated and aroused by particular musical motifs.

afureru—(Japanese) overbrimming.

Ahuitzotl—(Nahuatl, language of the Aztecs) terrifying water creature.

alap, or *alaap*—(Sanskrit) opening improvization without regular meter in Northern Indian (Hindustani) music.

ali'i—(Hawaiian) royal class.

Allah—(Arabic) the Muslim name for God.

almanaque—(Spanish) calendar featuring an image from Mexican folklore.

altares—(Spanish) home religious shrines, popular in Mexican and Chicano culture.

Analects—(Chinese) one of the Confucian classics.

ananda—(Sanskrit) bliss, absorption, identification with the universal consciousness.

anātmatā—(Sanskrit) nonexistence of the self in Buddhist doctrine.

anubhavas—(Sanskrit) responses, physical changes, imitative behavior in the spectator.

aperçu—(French) an insight; a revealing glimpse.

arabesque—a decorative design, common in Islamic art, that intertwines a single line into various flowing patterns.

art for art's sake—the view that art is intrinsically valuable, independently of its impact on social relations or on morality. A movement devoted to this view was prominent in the West in the nineteenth and early twentieth centuries.

artha—(Sanskrit) wealth.

artifact—a humanly made object; an object of art or craft.

artworld—in Danto's theory, the collection of institutions (including journals, museums, galleries, funding agencies, etc.) that determines what counts as art.

asvadaba—(Sanskrit) tasting.

aura—according to Walter Benjamin, the individualizing characteristic of an artwork, which depends on its physical presence.

authentic performance movement—a recent movement concerned with the performance of music. This movement urges that performers should aim to perform in the manner of the work's original performance.

authenticity—genuineness. In the visual arts, a work is authentic if it is the actual work of an artist, not a forgery. In Western theory of the performing arts, a performance is considered authentic when it conforms to the score or text written by the composer. Authenticity is also sometimes taken to require fidelity to the manner of the work's original performance.

autonomy—independence. In this view, autonomous art has value on its own, and its value should not be assessed in terms of how well it promotes moral or other nonartistic values. This position gained prominence in the West in the nineteenth century.

avant-garde—literally, "forward guard," or the vanguard of an army. The avant-garde is the (often self-styled) vanguard or "cutting edge" of art, art that is considered to be ahead of its times by virtue of its unconventionality.

ayat—(Arabic) signs.

ban—(Chinese) stiff.

barak—(Arabic) Arabic conception of a thing's magic, assumed by long use and care.

beauty—a central aesthetic or artistic ideal, characterized by symmetry, balance, and order.

bhakti—(Sanskrit) religious devotion.

bhava—(Sanskrit) affect, emotion, mental state.

bhaya—(Sanskrit) fear; one of the nine durable emotions, according to Indian theory.

bhayanaka—(Sanskrit) the fearful or the terrible; one of the basic *rasas*.

bibhatsa—(Sanskrit) the disgusting or the odious; one of the basic *rasas*.

bonkei—(Japanese) a miniature landscape constructed on a tray.

bonsai—(Japanese) a dwarfed pine.

bricolage—(French) something made haphazardly or in a makeshift fashion.

cadence—literally, "falling." The cadence is the "falling" to a point of rest and relative stability that occurs at the end of a line or phrase of music.

carteles—(Spanish) Mexican theater posters.

catharsis (or katharsis)—purification or purgation (of distressing emotion).

cempoalli—(Nahuatl, language of the Aztecs) stiff orange and gold marigolds with bright green stems, cultivated by the ancient Mexica.

censorship—the forcible suppression of particular kinds of expression (both in art and outside art).

chakras—(Sanskrit) one of the seven vital centers within the human body, according to Indian theory.

ch'i (qi)—(Chinese) vital spirit, moving power, bodily vital energy.

chi wara—(Bambara) a spirit that the Creator has sent to promote fertility. The *chi wara* is believed to have assumed the form of an antelope and taught human beings agriculture. The *chi wara* is often represented as an antelope with a young antelope on its back.

chün-tzu—(Chinese) profound person.

classical art—in Hegel's philosophy, the art that exhibited a balance between the Idea that informed it and its external embodiment. Classical art represented the second stage of his three stages of art; it is typified by ancient Greek sculpture.

closure—the principle that requires an artwork to have clear boundaries, separating it from what is not art.

cognoscenti—(Latin) knowers.

colorization—the introduction of color into film that was originally produced in black and white.

complexity—the property of being composed of a multitude of parts that stand in relation to one another.

conceptual art—art whose primary or only medium is thought and whose sensuous presentation is secondary or nonexistent.

contextualism—the view that art can be properly understood only by considering it in its social or historical context.

craft—(1) skill in making aesthetically pleasing objects that are used for practical purposes, not merely as objects of contemplation; (2) the objects that result from such skill.

cueponi—(Nahuatl, language of the Aztecs) a sudden explosion of blossom.

dadaism—a European art movement of the early twentieth century that emphasized absurdity.

deconstruction—a literary theoretical approach that aims to exhibit and call into question the values presupposed in a literary text.

dehumanization—in Ortega y Gasset's analysis, the tendency of twentieth-century art to forego association with the living concerns of human beings.

demythify—to undercut the power of a myth by exposing the dubious grounds upon which it is based.

dharma—(Sanskrit) in Hinduism, right action, law; in Buddhism, universal truth, the ground principle.

dhvani—(Sanskrit) reverberated meaning that is suggested, for example, by poetry.

dhyana—(Sanskrit) deep meditation.

dialectic—the evolution of new, more complete comprehensions of reality by means of the conflict of less complete perspectives.

discursive symbol—a symbol (such as a sentence of natural language) that is presented in a sequence, not all at once.

disinterestedness—detachment; lack of practical interest. Kant, among others, considers such detachment to be essential to a pure aesthetic judgment.

dislocation—a disruption of one's ordinary sense of location (whether understood literally or figuratively).

dissonance—in music, an interval or set of intervals that suggests tension and the desire for movement.

domestic aesthetic—the arena of aesthetic judgments involved in the home and everyday decoration.

doshas—(Sanskrit) faults.

elegance—refinement; grace in form or style.

elegante vitae—(Latin) elegant life.

emotionalism—the view that art's defining purpose is the expression of emotion.

empathy—emotive appreciation of another's perspectives.

ephebism—depiction of human beings at their optimum maturity, as neither immature nor old.

erh-te—(Chinese) virtue of the ear.

estampas religiosas—(Spanish) holycards with pictures of Catholic saints, commonly used as decoration in Mexican and Chicano households.

ethnocentrism—the tendency to take the standards that one has acquired through one's own ethnic background as universally applicable.

exemplary necessity—the kind of necessity that Kant claims is characteristic of a judgment of the beautiful. On his account, we take an object that we judge beautiful to be an instance of a law that we cannot state. In effect, we suppose that the beautiful object is an example of the sort of thing that others will similarly find beautiful.

existential—relating to or concerned with human beings' actual circumstances.

expression—the transmission or depiction of emotion or other psychological condition by means of art.

expressionism—the early twentieth-century artistic movement that aimed to depict or convey inner, psychological states to the audience.

fauvism—a school of painting that used color in a wild, nonrepresentational manner. (In French, *fauve* means "wild animal.")

feminism—a movement that urges improvements in the status of women. In connection with art, various feminists have urged greater societal recognition of women artists and their work; a rewriting of art history with an emphasis on works by and about women; and inquiry into the possibility that men and women have different perspectives on art and that at least some art is made with the aim of gratifying the male (but not necessarily the female) viewer.

fine art—art that is generally understood to be valuable in its own right, without any utilitarian function; high art, as opposed to popular art.

Five Elements—in Chinese thought, the five basic components that constitute things—earth, wood, fire, metal, and water. These are correlated with other groupings of five basic components, both in nature and in human relationships.

Florentine Codex—a missionary account of the history of pre-Columbian Mexico by Bernandino de Sahagún, one of the chief sources for the history of the pre-Columbian Mexica.

formalism—the view that art's defining purpose, the exclusive basis on which it should be judged, is the display of formal features (e.g., line and color in the case of painting). Formalists urge that critics not concern themselves with an artwork's social, historical, or biographical context or with the subject matter of representational works.

Forms—according to Plato, the realities that occupy another plane of existence and are the prototypes of earthly entities. The Form of Beauty, for instance, is the prototype for all earthly beauties, and the latter are beautiful because they participate in the Form of Beauty.

fortepiano—any of various kinds of early pianos.

found art—art made from natural materials that are not altered or manipulated by the artist.

free play—the mental activity that is fundamental to aesthetic experience, according to Kant. In free play, the mental faculties are active in an open-ended process of contemplation that is not aimed at categorizing the object of contemplation or concerned with the object's potential usefulness in practical projects.

gagku—(Japanese) ceremonial court music.

gago—(Japanese) literally "an elegant word"; poetry.

garyo—(Japanese) magnanimity.

gaze, the—the act of staring or looking, typically without the expectation of having the gaze returned. Feminist theory of art considers the implicitly male audience that gazes at depictions of women.

Gedankenexperiment—(German) thought experiment.

genius—a person of astonishing and original creative talent.

gharana—(Sanskrit) tradition or school (e.g., of performance practice).

griot—professional singer in Africa, usually descended from a family line of other griots.

hadith—(Arabic) "the traditions," a body of writings that includes accounts about Muhammad and his sayings.

haiku—(Japanese) a classic Japanese verse form comprised of 17 syllables.

halau—(Hawaiian) a group of dancers.

happening—a spontaneous theatrical event.

hasa—(Sanskrit) mirth; one of the nine durable emotions according to Indian theory.

hasya—(Sanskrit) the comic; one of the basic *rasas*.

he—(Chinese) harmony; concord.

hijra—(Arabic) Muhammad's flight to Medina from potential persecutors in Mecca. The date of the *hijra* is the beginning of the Muslim calendar.

hip-hop—a type of rap music.

historicism—the view that history determines cultural phenomena (such as art).

hula—(Hawaiian) traditional Hawaiian dance.

i—(Chinese) meaning.

i-pin—(Chinese) unrestrained or untrammeled (in reference to a style of Chinese and Japanese art inspired by Zen).

ibeji—(Yoruba [Nigeria]) twin figures in Yoruban sculpture. Such sculptures are often made when twins are born or when a twin dies. In the case of the death of a twin, the sculpture of the twin that dies is fed, in ritual fashion, when the living twin is fed.

iconography—the study of visual images and symbols in works of art.

iconology—term coined by art historian Erwin Panofsky to refer to the investigation of the points in history at which stylistic transformation occurred.

ijala—(Yoruba [Nigeria]) a traditional type of Nigerian chant that includes improvization on traditional themes.

ikembe—mbira; African thumb piano.

image appropriation—an artist's employment in an artwork of images that were initially produced by others.

iman—(Arabic) faith.

imitation—mimicry; deliberate semblance of the way something or someone appears.

imitation theory of art—the view that art's primary aim is to present likenesses of reality.

impressionism—an art movement of the late nineteenth and early twentieth centuries that aimed to present the overall visual impression, as opposed to the details, of its subject matter.

improvization—spontaneous and unrehearsed performance, especially in music.

indiscernibles—objects that cannot be distinguished from one another.

inspiration—possession by some force outside oneself (such as a muse) or outside one's ego (for example, one's unconscious mind). Artistic creation is described by some artists and philosphers as being a function of inspiration.

installation—an artwork that is constructed inside a gallery or a museum for temporary exhibition.

institutional theory of art—a theory that defines art by reference to the social institutions and practices that confer the status of art on an artifact.

instrumental—having to do with serving as a means.

instrumental theory of art—the view that art serves purposes (e.g., moral, educational, or political purposes) that are not themselves artistic.

intention—a purpose or motivation.

intentional fallacy—taking the inferred intentions of the author or artist to be decisive grounds for interpreting the work. The New Critics held that this strategy in interpretation was a fallacy because it is based on speculation about the inner states of authors and artists.

intentionalism—the view that artworks can be understood only by reference to an artist's intentions.

intertextuality—the property of a text's referring to other texts and having its meaning determined, in part, by the texts to which it refers.

intrinsic—internal to; inherently part of.

intuitionism—the view that the defining purpose of art is to incite nonconceptual knowledge. In Croce's theory, the knowledge to be gained is awareness of the unique individuality of objects.

Islam—(Arabic) the Muslim religion; literally, surrender (to God's guidance or will).

isomorphism—the characteristic of having the same shape or structure.

itzmolinia—(Nahuatl, language of the Aztecs) to regain greenness after being brown.

jen—(Chinese) humanity.

jie—(Chinese) control; knotted.

jing—(Chinese) essence.

judgment, aesthetic—in Kant's theory, intellectual judgment based on apprehension by the senses, without the mediation of concepts.

jugupsa—(Sanskrit) disgust; one of the nine basic emotions, according to Indian theory.

Kabuki theater—(Japanese) a traditional representational form of theater, involving all-male casts. Although highly stylized, Kabuki is more geared toward spectacle than Nō (or Noh) theater, and it employs mime, song, and dance.

kalimba—mbira; African thumb piano.

kama (Sanskrit)—pleasure.

karuna—(Sanskrit) the pathetic; one of the basic *rasas*.

kathakali—(Malaysian) a type of South Indian dance-drama that is based on Hindu literature and often involves mime.

ke—(Chinese) carved.

Kerala—state in southwest India.

kicho—(Japanese) curtain of state or curtain-frame.

kitsch—a type of bad art that is geared to the facile production of emotion in its audience. Kitsch is often associated with mass production.

kokoro—(Japanese) a response that is both intellectual and intuitive, literally, "heart/mind"; essence or spirit.

koto—(Japanese) situations.

krodha—(Sanskrit) anger; one of the nine durable emotions, according to Indian theory.

Krishna—(Sanskrit) an incarnation of the Hindu god Vishnu.

kumu hula—(Hawaiian) traditional Hawaiian dance.

lacuilo—(Nahuatl, language of the Aztecs) literally, an artist who paints in red and black ink. Such artists painted the sacred picture books that recorded Aztec history.

li—(Chinese) decorum; pattern or principle.

lila—(Sanskrit) sportive play.

liu-i—(Chinese) the six classical Confucian arts, believed to cultivate the personality. These include ritual, music, archery, charioteering, calligraphy, and arithmetic.

lokottara—(Sanskrit) beyond ordinary experience.

ludic—having to do with play.

Mahabharata—great Sanskrit epic of 19 volumes that chronicles a war between the Kaurava brothers and the Pāndava.

mantra—(Sanskrit) a Scriptural passage or word that is repeated as a form of prayer or as a stimulus to meditation.

Marxism—ideology based on the philosophy of Karl Marx (1818–1883), who argued that tensions inherent in capitalism would eventually lead to its destruction. Marx believed that art, like all cultural activity, manifests economic conditions and conflicts.

maya—(Sanskrit) illusion.

mbira—African "thumb piano," made of various tines attached to a sounding board and played with the thumbs. This type of instrument is also called the kalimba, the sansa, and the ikembe.

Mexica—(Nahuatl, language of the Aztecs) the name the Aztecs had for themselves.

mihrab—(Arabic) a niche in the wall of a Muslim mosque, which points in the direction of Mecca.

mimesis—(Greek) imitation.

mimilhui—(Nahuatl, language of the Aztecs) to bloom in a slow, unfolding manner.

minimalism—a style in art and music that relies on simple forms or phrases as its exclusive material.

miyabi—(Japanese) beautiful and elegant.

Moctezuma (the younger)—(Nahuatl, language of the Aztecs) Aztec emperor of mythic status, who came to the throne in 1503.

modernism—a movement among artists that rejects classical methods in favor of experimentalism and formal innovation in art. Modernism as an aesthetic sensibility also emphasizes the artwork's autonomy. In art criticism, modernism involves the view that the aim of art is to reveal the intrinsic character of the artistic medium, not to represent reality.

moksa—(Sanskrit) liberation, spiritual freedom.

mono—(Japanese) natural objects.

mono no aware—(Japanese) the sadness of things; according to Kawabata, "the poignant beauty of things"; pathos.

motif—a basic musical melody on which a musical work or section is based.

movidas—(Spanish) coping stategies.

mudhahib—(Arabic) Muslim painters; literally, "gilders."

Musikwissenschaft—(German) scholarship concerned with music; musicology.

Muslim—(Arabic) a follower of Islam, the religion of Muhammad; literally, a person who surrenders to divine guidance.

nada—(Sanskrit) sound.

natya—(Sanskrit) music.

Natyashastra—(Sanskrit) A work by Bharata on the theatrical arts, written around the first century of the Christian era. The *Natyashastra* elaborates on the theory of *rasa* and its relation to drama, dance, and music.

nayoika—(Sanskrit) heroine.

nayoka—(Sanskrit) hero.

NEA—the National Endowment for the Arts, a source of grants in support of artists and exhibitions in the United States.

necessary condition or criterion—a condition or criterion that must be fulfilled in order for a concept to apply.

necessity—inevitability; the condition of being forced or constrained.

ngodo—(Chopi) orchestra, in the language of the Chopi of Africa.

nicho—(Spanish) niche; wall shelf.

nirasa—(Sanskrit) without *rasa*.

Nirvāna—(Sanskrit) in Buddhist doctrine, the simultaneous extinction of greed, hatred, and ignorance; enlightenment; release from the cycle of rebirth.

Nō (or Noh) theater—(Japanese) a form of Japanese theater characterized by sparsity and understatement. Nō evolved from Shinto ritual.

notes inégales—(French) literally, "unequal notes"; a convention in sixteenth- through early nineteenth-century European music that involved dividing the beat unevenly, so that adjacent notes written with the same temporal value would have differing duration. The purpose of this convention was to add lilt to the music.

nuevo arte del Pueblo—(Spanish) new art of the people. A *nuevo arte del Pueblo* was advocated by Male Efe, an art front for Mexican American Liberation in the San Francisco Bay area in 1968.

obscenity—characterized by lewdness and moral offensiveness.

okashi—(Japanese) charming; delightful.

oli—(Hawaiian) Hawaiian chant.

organic model—the model that compares an artwork to an organic body, in which all elements are interrelated and function to sustain the life of the whole.

organicism—the theory that the defining purpose of art is to display the interrelations of parts within a whole.

orientalism—a term coined by Said to describe the ideology of dividing the world into "the West" and "the Orient" in a manner that reinforces attitudes of Western superiority and seems to justify Western imperialism.

originality—the characteristic of being unprecedented or novel.

Owu—(Ijo) water spirits.

pathos—the quality of provoking sentimental sadness.

performance art—a type of art that amalgamates visual elements and dramatic performance.

pétrissage—(French) the molding of a specific medium to articulate strange contents of the imagination.

piece—according to Binkley, the type of thing that an artwork can be said to be. An object becomes on artwork on his account by being "indexed" as art by a person, who becomes an artist by virtue of indexing an object as art.

placas—(Spanish) graffiti.

planes—(Spanish) political programs.

Platonic Ideas—(1) Plato's Forms; (2) in the philosophy of Schopenhauer, the Platonic Forms, which representational art makes visible to the audience.

political correctness—pedantic avoidance of any expression that might be interpreted as giving offense, especially by minority or disadvantaged groups.

Popol Yuh—(Mayan) "Book of the Council" of the Quché Maya, which contains an account of the creation of humanity by the gods.

pornography—depiction that aims to arouse lurid sexual desire in its audience.

postmodernism—a movement in reaction to modernism, which questions universality as a theoretical ideal and the autonomy of art, and urges that artworks be viewed in context.

prana (Sanskrit)—breath.

presentational symbol—a symbol that is presented in its entirety all at once, not sequentially.

psychic distance—detachment; disinterestedness.

psychoanalysis—a method aimed at interpreting and analyzing the unconscious mind. Initially developed by Freud for the treatment of patients with mental disorders, this methodology is applied by some critics to the analysis of literature.

purposiveness—the characteristic of aiming at a resolution or an ultimate purpose.

purusharthas (Sanskrit)—the aims of life.

quetzal—(Nahuatl, language of the Aztecs) a rare male bird with two curving tale feathers, highly valued by the Aztecs.

quetzalli—(Nahuatl, language of the Aztecs) the tail feathers of the quetzal.

quincunx—(Nahuatl, language of the Aztecs) a preferred form in Aztec art. It emphasized four quarters and a central, fifth, direction. Each had its own color, quality, and temporal association. The *quincunx* was understood as the shape of the world.

raga—(Sanskrit) a melody or mode that serves as a basis for improvization in Indian music.

Ramayana—(Sanskrit) great Hindu epic that chronicles the deeds of the hero Rama, an incarnation of Vishnu.

ranfla—(Spanish) low-rider car.

rap—a musical style that originated with young urban blacks in the United States. This style is characterized by rhythmic recitations in rhyme over a strongly rhythmic instrumental background.

rasa—(Sanskrit) literally, flavor or savor; the subtle emotional essence of an artwork that is experienced by the sensitive audience member.

rasavadana—(Sanskrit) aesthetic experience.

rasika—(Sanskrit) literally, "taster"; a member of an artistic audience.

rasili—(Sanskrit) charged with *rasa*.

rasquachismo—(Spanish) an unrestrained sensibility, common in Chicano art, exhibiting the perspective and coping strategies of an underdog.

rati—(Sanskrit) love; one of the nine durable emotions, according to Indian theory.

raudra—(Sanskrit) the furious; one of the basic *rasas*.

readymades—artworks that were "already made," discovered and exhibited by Marcel Duchamp. Examples include a snow shovel, a bottle dryer, and several urinals.

realism—a movement or tendency that aspires to art that closely resembles reality.

relativism—the view that truth and values are not absolute, but instead depend upon cultural context.

representation—an imitation or "stand-in" for something else.

romantic art—in Hegel's theory, art of the third of the three stages of art history. Romantic art aims to embody ideal content that is too fully developed to be adequately presented in sensuous form.

romanticism—a nineteenth-century movement among the arts that emphasized emotion, artistic individuality, fantasy, and grandeur (as opposed to classical proportion).

sabi—(Japanese) rustic simplicity; literally, linked to the words for "rust" and becoming "desolate"; the patina of age.

Sahagún, Bernardino—Franciscan friar who wrote the Florentine Codex, a history of pre-Columbian Mexico.

Samavedic chant—chant based on the Sama Veda, one of four collections of Vedic hymns (in Sanskrit).

sansa—mbira; African thumb piano.

santa—(Sanskrit) the peaceful.

santos—(Spanish) pictures or statues of Catholic saints.

sarangi—(Sanskrit) a stringed instrument used in Indian music.

Schadenfreude—(German) pleasure taken in others' misfortunes.

scopophilia—erotic arousal or pleasure gained primarily from looking; voyeurism.

sforzando—(Italian) a musical term meaning "forced," with accent.

shama—(Sanskrit) equanimity; one of the nine basic emotions, according to Indian theory.

shaman—among North American Indians, a priest, healer, and spiritual guide who is believed to have magical powers and contact with the world of spirits.

shibui—(Japanese) a touch of astringency; understatement and refinement.

shite—(Japanese) the chief character in a Nō play.

shoka—(Sanskrit) sorrow; one of the nine durable emotions, according to Indian theory.

shringara—(Sanskrit) the erotic; one of the basic *rasas*.

shukr—(Arabic) thankfulness.

shunga—(Japanese) "spring pictures"; a type of erotic art.

significant form—the formal quality that makes great art great.

simplicity—the characteristic of being indivisible or of being divisible into only very few components.

slapstick—a type of comedy that is characterized by mock violence, clumsiness, and rude behavior.

Spirit—in the philosophy of Hegel, the collective being of humanity whose experiences are the subject matter of history.

sthayibhavas—(Sanskrit) the permanent emotions.

structuralism—a linguistic theory initiated by Ferdinand de Saussure that treats language as a symbolic system; an anthropological theory initiated by Lévi-Strauss to ascertain the structures of social relations.

style—a characteristic manner of performance; a characteristic form or technique.

sublime—a natural or artistic phenomenon that produces a feeling of awe in its beholder, typically because of the vast size or power of what it is or represents.

sufficient condition or criterion—a condition or criterion that is itself (or in conjunction with other sufficient conditions) enough to warrant the application of a concept.

Sufis—Muslim mystics.

surrealism—an artistic and literary movement of the early twentieth century that aimed to tap and express the contents of the unconscious mind.

symbolic art—in Hegel's philosophy, art of the first stage of the three stages of art history. Symbolic art aims to embody ideal content that is still somewhat inchoate. Typically, the idea seems to be attached symbolically to such art, not to be organically implicit within it.

symmetry—arrangement in regular, balanced proportion.

taan—(Sanskrit) virtuoso elaboration of notes along ascending and descending scales in Northern Indian (Hindustani) music.

tabla—(Sanskrit) Northern Indian double drum.

tala—(Sanskrit) rhythmic section of music (after *alap*) in Northern Indian (Hindustani) music.

tanka—(Japanese) a classic Japanese verse form that involves five lines, of five, seven, five, seven, and seven syllables.

Tao—(Chinese) the Way.

tatami—(Japanese) a floormat made of rice straw with bordered edges.

tauhid—(Arabic) the unity of God; God's all-pervading presence.

techne—(Greek) know-how; practical skill.

Tenochtitlan—(Nahuatl, language of the Aztecs) the Imperial city of the Aztecs (now Mexico City).

Teotihuacan—(Nahuatl, language of the Aztecs) the Cradle of the Gods.

Tezcatlipoca—(Nahuatl, language of the Aztecs) an Aztec god who sometimes took human shape and was characterized by his capriciousness.

timbila— (Chopi) xylophone, in the language of the Chopi of Africa.

Toltec—(Nahuatl, language of the Aztecs) a spiritual descendent of the legendary craftsmen from Tula.

Tolteca—(Nahuatl, language of the Aztecs) artists.

tomli—(Japanese) transparency.

Urbilder—(German) archetypes.

utsaha—(Sanskrit) energy; one of the nine durable emotions, according to Indian theory.

vac—(Sanskrit) speech.

vāsanās—(Sanskrit) in Buddhist thought, memory traces left by experiences.

vedantic—(Sanskrit) having to do with the Hindu system of philosophy based on the *Upanishads*, an ancient philosophical and religious text.

verisimilitude—lifelikeness.

versicle—a short verse; a short sentence or clause.

vibhavas—(Sanskrit) determinants.

vira—(Sanskrit) the heroic; one of the basic *rasas*.

Vishnu—one of the three primary Hindu gods, worshipped as supreme by some Hindus.

vismaya—(Sanskrit) astonishment; one of the nine durable emotions, according to Indian theory.

voluntarism—a philosophical view that takes will or desire to be fundamental.

voyeurism—the achievement of sexual gratification by watching others (who may be actively engaged in erotic or suggestive behavior).

vyabhicharibhavas—(Sanskrit) transient emotions that occasionally flicker during a more stable emotional state.

wabi—(Japanese) modesty.

waki—(Japanese) the secondary character in a Nō play, frequently a traveling priest.

wen—(Chinese) nonmetered writing; a tapestry.

will—in the philosophy of Schopenhauer, the fundamental reality, which is considered to be dynamic and inexhaustible. Virtually all human activity is motivated by the individual's will, which is a manifestation of the cosmic will. In aesthetic experience, however, the individual becomes a purely knowing subject and temporarily experiences a respite from willing.

wu—(Chinese) things.

xin—(Chinese) a unity of thought and emotion; the core of one's being.

xochi cuicatl—(Nahuatl, language of the Aztecs) "flower song" in the Nahuatl language; sung poetry.

yang—(Chinese) the dominant of any two counterparts.

yen-chiao—(Chinese) teaching by words.

yin—(Chinese) the subordinate of any two counterparts.

yin and *yang*—(Chinese) reciprocals that are mutually determining.

yoga—a system of practices (sometimes involving postures and methods of meditation) aimed at achieving union with the Supreme Being.

yogin—(Sanskrit) a male practitioner of yoga.

yogini—(Sanskrit) (1) a female practitioner of yoga; (2) a female demon, often an attendant of Shiva, the Hindu god of destruction, or Durga, a terrifying Hindu goddess.

yubi—(Japanese) elegant in the sense of gentle, delicate beauty.

yue—(Chinese) music.

yūgen—(Japanese) mystery or depth, understood as suggestive and indefinite.

Zeitgeist—(German) the spirit of the time. The notion of a *Zeitgeist* is a central concept in Hegel's philosophy.

BIBLIOGRAPHY

THE WESTERN WORLD

Aesthetics—Classical Texts

Primary Sources

Aristotle. *Basic Works of Aristotle.* Ed. Richard McKeon. New York: Random House, 1941.

Baumgarten, A. G. *Reflections on Poetry.* 1735. Trans. K. Aschenbrenner and W. B. Holthner. Berkeley: U of California P, 1954.

Burke, Edmund. *A Philosophical Enquiry into the Origin of Our Ideas of the Sublime and Beautiful.* 2nd ed. London: Routledge, 1958.

Coleridge, Samuel Taylor. *Aesthetic Essays.* Rpt. in S. T. Coleridge. *Biographia Literaria.* Ed. J. Shawcross. 2 vols. Oxford: Oxford UP, 1907.

Croce, Benedetto. *Aesthetics as Science of Expression and General Linguistic.* Trans. Douglas Ainslie. 2nd ed. London: P. Owen, 1962.

————. *The Essence of Aesthetic.* Trans. Douglas Ainslie. London: William Heinemann, 1921.

Dilthey, Wilhelm. *Dilthey: Selected Writings.* Trans. and ed. H. P. Rickman. Cambridge: Cambridge UP, 1976.

Hegel, G. F. W. *Hegel's Aesthetics: Lectures on Fine Art.* Trans. T. M. Knox. Oxford: Oxford UP, 1975.

Hume, David. *Aesthetics.* Ed. Jerome Stolnitz. London: Macmillan, 1965.

————. *"Of the Standard of Taste" and Other Essays.* Ed. J. W. Linz. New York: Bobbs-Merrill, 1965.

Hutcheson, Francis. *An Inquiry into the Origins of Our Idea of Beauty and Virtue.* London: J. Dabny, 1725.

Kant, Immanuel. *Critique of Judgment.* Trans. Werner S. Pluhar. Indianapolis: Hackett, 1987.

Merleau-Ponty, Maurice. *Phenomenology of Perception.* Trans. C. Smith. New York: Humanities P, 1960.

————. *The Primacy of Perception.* Trans. and ed. J. M. Edie. Evanston: Northwestern UP, 1964.

Nietzsche, Friedrich. *The Birth of Tragedy* [together with *The Case of Wagner*]. Trans. Walter Kaufmann. New York: Random House, 1967.

————. *Twilight of the Idols. The Portable Nietzsche.* Trans. and ed. Walter Kaufmann. New York: Viking, 1968.

Plato. *Collected Dialogues of Plato, Including the Letters.* Ed. Edith Hamilton and Huntington Cairns. Princeton: Princeton UP, 1961.

Sartre, Jean-Paul. *Essays in Aesthetics.* Trans. Wade Baskin. New York: Citadel, 1963.

Schelling, Friedrich Wilhelm Joseph von. *Philosophy of Art.* 1802–1803. Minneapolis: U of Minnesota P, 1988.

Schiller, Friedrich. *Letters on the Aesthetic Education of Man.* 1794. Trans. E. M. Wilkinson and L. A. Willoughby. Oxford: Clarendon, 1967.

Schlegel, August Wilhelm von. *Lectures on Dramatic Art and Literature.* 1809. Trans. J. Black. London: Bell, 1884.

Wilde, Oscar. *Complete Works of Oscar Wilde.* Ed. Vyvyan Holland. London: Collins, 1983.

Wittgenstein, Ludwig. *Lectures and Conversations on Aesthetics, Psychology and Religious Belief.* Ed. C. Barrett. Oxford: Basil Blackwell, 1967.

Secondary Sources

Beardsley, Monroe C. *Aesthetics from Classical Greece to the Present: A Short History.* Montgomery: U of Alabama P, 1975.

Bowie, Andrew. *Aesthetics and Subjectivity: From Kant to Nietzsche.* Manchester: Manchester UP, 1990.

Cohen, Ted, and Paul Guyer, eds. *Essays in Kant's Aesthetics.* Chicago: U of Chicago P, 1982.

Desmond, William. *Art and the Absolute: A Study of Hegel's Aesthetics.* Albany: State U of New York P, 1986.

Gillespie, Michael Allen, and Tracy B. Strong, eds. *Nietzsche's New Seas: Explorations in Philosophy, Aesthetics, and Politics.* Chicago: U of Chicago P, 1988.

Guyer, Paul. *Kant and the Claims of Taste.* Cambridge: Harvard UP, 1979.

Halliwell, Stephen. *Aristotle's Poetics.* London: Duckworth, 1986.

Kivy, Peter, ed. *Essays on the History of Aesthetics.* Rochester: U of Rochester P, 1992.

Krukowski, Lucian. *Aesthetic Legacies.* Philadelphia: Temple UP, 1992.

Martindale, Andrew. *The Rise of the Artist in the Middle Ages and Early Renaissance.* London: Thames and Hudson, 1972.

McCloskey, Mary A. *Kant's Aesthetic.* London: Macmillan, 1987.

Moravcsik, Julius, and Philip Temko, eds. *Plato on Beauty, Wisdom, and the Arts.* Totowa: Rowman and Littlefield, 1982.

Summers, David. *The Judgment of Sense: Renaissance Naturalism and the Rise of Aesthetics.* Cambridge: Cambridge UP, 1987.

Young, Julian. *Nietzsche's Philosophy of Art.* Cambridge: Cambridge UP, 1992.

AESTHETIC THEORY—THE ARTS AND POPULAR CULTURE (GENERAL)

Adorno, Theodor. *Aesthetic Theory.* Trans. C. Lenhardt. London: Routledge, 1984.

Baker, Houston A. *Black Studies, Rap, and the Academy.* Chicago: U of Chicago P, 1992.

———. "Scene . . . Not Heard." *Reading Rodney King/Reading Urban Uprising.* Ed. Robert Gooding-Williams. New York: Routledge, 1993. 38–48.

Battersby, Christine. *Gender and Genius: Towards a Feminist Aesthetics.* London: Women's, 1989.

Beardsley, Monroe C. *The Aesthetic Point of View: Selected Essays*. Ed. Michael J. Wreen and Donald M. Callen. Ithaca: Cornell UP, 1982.

———. "The Definitions of the Arts." *Journal of Aesthetics and Art Criticism* 20 (1960): 175–87.

———, and Wimsatt, William K. "The Intentional Fallacy." *Sewanee Review* 54 (1946): 3–23

Beardsmore, R. W. *Art and Morality*. London: Macmillan, 1971.

Bell, Clive. *Art*. Ed. J. B. Bullen. New York: Oxford UP, 1987.

Benjamin, Walter. *Illuminations*. Ed. Hannah Arendt. Trans. H. Zohn. New York: Schocken, 1969.

Berger, John. *About Looking*. New York: Random House, 1980.

Berleant, Arnold. *Art and Engagement*. Philadelphia: Temple UP, 1991.

Best, David. "The Aesthetic in Sport." *British Journal of Aesthetics* 14 (1974): 197–213.

Best, Steven, and Douglas Kellner. *Postmodern Theory: Critical Interrogations*. New York: Guilford, 1991.

Betterton, Rosemary. *Looking On: Images of Femininity in the Visual Arts and Media*. New York: Pandora, 1987.

Burke, Kenneth. "On Form." *Esthetics Contemporary*. Ed. Richard Kostelanetz. Buffalo: Prometheus, 1978. 132–38.

Calinescu, Matei. *Five Faces of Modernity: Modernism Avant-Garde, Decadence, Kitsch, Postmodernism*. Durham: Duke UP, 1987.

Carroll, Noël. "On Jokes." *Midwest Studies in Philosophy* 16 (1991): 230–310.

———. *The Philosophy of Horror, or Paradoxes of the Heart*. New York: Routledge, 1990.

Cavell, Marcia. "Taste and Moral Sense." *Journal of Aesthetics and Art Criticism* 34.1 (1975): 29–33.

Clifford, Derek. *A History of Garden Design*. London: Faber and Faber, 1962.

Cohen, Ted. "High and Low Thinking about High and Low Art." *Journal of Aesthetics and Art Criticism* 51.2 (1993): 151–56.

Collingwood, R. G. *The Principles of Art*. New York: Oxford UP, 1958.

Coomaraswamy, Ananda K. *The Transformation of Nature in Art*. Cambridge: Harvard UP, 1934.

Cooper, David, ed. *A Companion to Aesthetics*. Cambridge: Basil Blackwell, 1992.

Coote, Jeremy, and Anthony Shelton, eds. *Anthropology, Art, and Aesthetics*. Oxford: Clarendon, 1992.

Cothey, A. L. *The Nature of Art*. New York: Routledge, 1990.

Crick, Philip. "Kitsch." *British Journal of Aesthetics* 23.1 (1983): 48–52.

Crimp, Douglas. *On the Museum's Ruins*. Cambridge: M.I.T. P, 1993.

Danto, Arthur C. "What Happened to Beauty?" *The Nation* 254.12 (1992): 418–21.

Davies, Stephen. *Definitions of Art*. Ithaca: Cornell UP, 1991.

Dewey, John. *Art as Experience*. New York: Capricorn, 1958.

Dickie, George. *Art and the Aesthetics: An Institutional Analysis*. Ithaca: Cornell UP, 1974.

———. *The Art Circle: A Theory of Art*. New York: Haven, 1984.

———. *Evaluating Art*. Philadelphia: Temple UP, 1988.

Dorfles, Gillo. *Kitsch: An Anthology of Bad Taste*. London: Studio Vista, 1969.

Dufrenne, Mikel. *In the Presence of the Sensuous: Essays in Aesthetics*. Ed. and trans. Mark S. Roberts and Dennis Gallagher. Atlantic Highlands: Humanities P International, 1987.

———. *Phenomenology of Aesthetic Experience*. Trans. Edward Casey. Evanston: Northwestern UP, 1973.

Dutton, Denis, ed. *The Forger's Art: Forgery and the Philosophy of Art*. Berkeley: U of California P, 1983.

———. "Tribal Art and Artifact." *Journal of Aesthetics and Art Criticism* 51.1 (1993): 13–22.

Eagleton, Terry. *The Ideology of the Aesthetic*. Oxford: Basil Blackwell, 1990.

Eaton, Marcia Muelder. *Aesthetics and the Good Life*. Madison: F. Dickinson UP, 1989.

———. "Art, Artifacts, and Intentions." *American Philosophical Quarterly* 6 (1969): 165–69.

Ecker, Giselda, ed. *Feminist Aesthetics*. Trans. Harriet Anderson. Boston: Beacon, 1985.

Elkins, James. "From Original to Copy and Back Again." *British Journal Aesthetics* 33.2 (1993): 113–20.

Feagin, Susan L. "On Defining and Interpreting Art Intentionalistically." *The British Journal of Aesthetics* 22 (1982): 65–77.

Fisher, Philip. *Making and Effacing Art: Modern American Art in a Culture of Museums*. New York: Oxford UP, 1991.

Fiske, John. *Television Culture*. London: Routledge, 1987.

Frederickson, George. *The Black Image in the White Mind*. Middletown: Wesleyan UP, 1987.

Freuh, Joanna, Cassandra L. Langer, and Arlene Raven, eds. *Feminist Art Criticism: An Anthology*. New York: HarperCollins, 1991.

———. *New Feminist Criticism: Art—Identity—Action*. New York: HarperCollins, 1994.

Gadamer, Hans-Georg. *The Relevance of the Beautiful and Other Essays*. Trans. Nicholas Walker. Cambridge: Cambridge UP, 1986.

Gans, Herbert. *Popular Culture and High Culture*. New York: Basic, 1974.

Geertz, Clifford. *The Interpretation of Cultures*. New York: Basic Books, 1973.

Goldblatt, David A. "Ventriloquism: Ecstatic Exchange and the History of the Artwork." *Journal of Aesthetics and Art Criticism* 51.3 (1993) 389–98.

Goodman, Nelson. *Languages of Art*. Indianapolis: Hackett, 1976.

———. *Ways of Worldmaking*. Indianapolis: Hackett, 1978.

Graycyk, Theodor A. "Having Bad Taste." *British Journal of Aesthetics* 30.2 (1990): 117–31.

Greenberg, Clement. "Avant-Grade and Kitsch." *Art and Culture*. Boston: Beacon, 1961.

Harrell, Jean Gabbert. *Profundity: A Universal Value*. University Park: Penn State UP, 1992.

Heidegger, Martin. "The Origin of the Work of Art." *Poetry Language, and Thought*. Trans. Albert Hofstadter. New York: Harper & Row, 1971. 17–75.

Hein, Hilde, and Carolyn Korsmeyer, eds. *Aesthetics in Feminist Perspective.* Bloomington: Indiana UP, 1993.

Higgins, Kathleen. "Sweet Kitsch." *Philosophy of the Visual Arts.* Ed. Philip Alperson. New York: Oxford UP, 1992. 568–81.

Hirsch, E. D. *Validity in Interpretation.* New Haven: Yale UP, 1976.

Hollander, Anne. *Seeing through Clothes.* New York: Viking, 1978.

Hoy, David Couzens. *The Critical Circle: Literature, History, and Philosophical Hermeneutics.* Berkeley: U of California P, 1978.

Humble, P. N. "Chess as an Art Form." *British Journal of Aesthetics* 33.1 (1993): 59–66.

Ingarten, Roman. *Ontology of the Work of Art. The Musical Work. The Picture. The Architectural Work. The Film.* Trans. R. Meyer and J. T. Goldwait. Athens: Ohio UP, 1989.

Irwin, Robert. *Being and Circumstances: Notes toward a Conditional Art.* Venice: Lapis, 1985.

Jopling, Carol T., ed. *Art and Aesthetics in Primitive Societies: A Critical Anthology.* New York: E. P. Dutton, 1971.

Kaplan, Abraham. "The Aesthetics of the Popular Arts." *Journal of Aesthetics and Art Criticism* 24 (1966): 351–64.

Kemal, Salim, and Ivan Gaskell, eds. *Landscape, Natural Beauty, and the Arts.* Cambridge: Cambridge UP, 1993.

Királyfahri, Béla. *The Aesthetics of Gyorgy Lukacs.* Princeton: Princeton UP, 1975.

Korsmeyer, Carolyn. "On Distinguishing 'Aesthetic' from 'Artistic.'" *The Journal of Aesthetic Education* 22 (1977): 45–57.

———. "Pleasure: Reflections on Aesthetics and Feminism." *Journal of Aesthetics and Art Criticism* 51.2 (1993): 199–206.

Korthals, Michiel. "Art and Morality: Critical Theory about the Conflict and Harmony between Art and Morality." *Philosophy and Social Criticism* 15.3 (1989): 241–51.

Krukowski, Lucian. *Art and Concept: A Philosophical Study.* Amherst: U of Massachusetts P, 1987.

Kupfer, Joseph H. *Experience as Art: Aesthetics in Everyday Life.* Albany: State U of New York P, 1983.

Lang, Berel, ed. *The Concept of Style.* Ithaca: Cirnell UP, 1987.

Langer, Susanne K. *Feeling and Form.* New York: Routledge, 1953.

———. *Mind: An Essay on Human Feeling.* 3 Vols. Baltimore: Johns Hopkins UP, 1967, 1972, 1982.

———. *Philosophy in a New Key.* 3rd ed. Cambridge: Harvard UP, 1953.

———. *Problems of Art.* New York: Scribner's, 1957.

Lauter, Paul, ed. *Theories of Comedy.* New York: Doubleday, 1964.

Levinson, Jerrold. "Defining Art Historically." *British Journal of Aesthetics* 19 (1979): 232–50.

McDermott, John. *The Culture of Experience.* New York: New York UP, 1976.

Mandelbaum, Maurice. "Family Resemblances and Generalizations Concerning the Arts." *American Philosophical Quarterly* 2 (1965): 219–28.

Marcuse, Herbert. *The Aesthetic Dimension: Towards a Critique of Marxist Aesthetics.* Boston: Beacon, 1978.

Margolis, Joseph. *Art and Philosophy*. Brighton: Havester, 1980.

Marx, Leo. *The Machine in the Garden: Technology and the Pastoral Ideal in America*. New York: Oxford UP, 1964.

Mattick, Paul, Jr. "Aesthetics and Anti-Aesthetics in the Visual Arts." *Journal of Aesthetics and Art Criticism* 51.2 (1993): 253–59.

Miller, Mara. *The Garden as an Art*. Albany: State U of New York P, 1993.

Miller, Mark Crispin. *Boxed In: The Culture of TV*. Evanston: Northwestern UP, 1988.

Monk, Samuel H. *The Sublime*. Ann Arbor: U of Michigan P, 1960.

Morreall, John, ed. *The Philosophy of Laughter and Humor*. Albany: State U of New York P, 1987.

———. *Taking Laughter Seriously*. Albany: State U of New York P, 1983.

———, and Jessica Loy. "Kitsch and Aesthetic Education." *Journal of Aesthetic Education* 23.4 (1989): 63–73.

Morse, Marcia. "Feminist Aesthetics and the Spectrum of Gender." *Philosophy East and West* 42.2 (1992): 287–95.

Mothersill, Mary. *Beauty Restored*. Oxford: Oxford UP, 1984.

Newcomb, Horace, ed. *Television: The Critical View*. New York: Oxford UP, 1994.

Novitz, David. "Art, Life, and Reality." *British Journal of Aesthetics* 30.4 (1990): 301–10.

———. *The Boundaries of Art*. Philadelphia: Temple UP, 1992.

———. "Love, Friendship, and the Aesthetics of Character." *American Philosophical Quarterly* 28.3 (1991): 207–16.

———. "Ways of Artmaking: The High and the Popular in Art." *British Journal of Aesthetics* 29.3 (1989): 213–29.

Osborne, Harold. *Theory of Beauty*. London: Routledge, 1952.

Otten, Charolotte M., ed. Anthropology and Art. Garden City: Natural History, 1971.

Panofsky, Erwin. *Meaning in the Visual Arts*. Chicago: U of Chicago P, 1955.

Passmore, John. *Serious Art: A Study of the Concept in All the Major Arts*. Peru: Open Court, 1991.

Pater, Walter. *The Renaissance: Studies in Art and Poetry*. New York: Oxford UP, 1986.

Paz, Octavio. *Convergences: Essays on Art and Literature*. Trans. Helen Lane. San Diego: Harcourt, 1987.

———. *In Praise of Hands: Contemporary Crafts of the World*. Greenwich: New York Graphic Society, 1974.

Peckham, Morse. *Art and Pornography*. New York: Basic, 1969.

Pole, David. *Aesthetics, Form, and Emotion*. Ed. George Robert. London: Duckworth, 1983.

Pollock, Griselda. *Framing Feminism: Art and the Women's Movement 1970–1985*. New York: Pandora, 1987.

———. *Vision and Difference: Femininity, Feminism, and Histories of Art*. New York: Routledge, 1988.

Prall, David. *Aesthetic Judgment*. New York: Crowell, 1929.

Quinet, Marienne L. "Food as Art: The Problem of Function." *British Journal of Aesthetics* 21.2 (1981): 159–71.

Rosenberg, Bernard, and David Manning White, eds. *Mass Culture: The Popular Arts in America*. Glencoe: Free, 1957.

Sagoff, Mark. "The Aesthetic Status of Forgeries." *The Journal of Aesthetics and Art Criticism* 35 (1976): 169–80.

Santayana, George. *The Sense of Beauty*. New York: Dover, 1896.

Sartwell, Crispin. "The Aesthetics of the Spurious." *The British Journal of Aesthetics* 28 (1988): 360–67.

Savile, Anthony. *The Test Of Time*. Oxford: Clarendon, 1982.

Saw, Ruth L. *Aesthetics: An Introduction*. New York: Doubleday, 1971.

Saxena, Sushil Kumar. "The Aesthetic Attitude." *Philosophy East and West* 28 (1978): 81–90.

Scheman, Naomi. *Engenderings: Construction of Knowledge, Authority, and Privilege*. New York: Routledge, 1993.

Sclafani, Richard J. "'Art,' Wittgenstein, and Open-textured Concepts." *Journal of Aesthetics and Art Criticism* 29 (1971): 333–41.

Seltzer, Mark. *Bodies and Machines*. New York: Routledge, 1992.

Sheppard, Anne. *Aesthetics: An Introduction to the Philosophy of Art*. New York: Oxford UP, 1987.

Showalter, Elaine, ed. *The New Feminist Criticism: Essays of Women, Literature, and Theory*. New York: Pantheon, 1985.

Shusterman, Richard. *Pragmatist Aesthetics: Living Beauty, Rethinking Art*. Oxford: Basil Blackwell, 1992.

Sibley, Frank. "Is Art an Open Concept?—An Unsettled Question." *Contemporary Aesthetics*. Ed. Matthew Lipman. Boston: Allyn and Bacon, 1973. 114–17.

Sircello, Guy. *Mind and Art*. Princeton: Princeton UP, 1972.

Smith, Gary, ed. *Benjamin: Philosophy, Aesthetics, History*. Chicago: U of Chicago P, 1989.

Smith, Marion W., ed. *The Artist in Tribal Society*. London: Routledge, 1961.

Solomon, Robert C. "On Kitsch and Sentimentality." *Journal of Aesthetics and Art Criticism* 49.1 (1990): 1–14.

Sparshott, Francis. *The Theory of the Arts*. Princeton: Princeton UP, 1982.

Stolnitz, Jerome. *Aesthetics*. New York: Macmillan, 1965.

Thompson, Robert Farris. *Flash of the Spirit: African and Afro-American Art and Philosophy*. New York: Random House, 1983.

Tirell, M. Lynne. "Storytelling and Moral Agency." *Journal of Aesthetics and Art Criticism* 48.2 (1990): 115–26.

Tolstoy, Leo. *What Is Art?* Trans. A. Maude. Indianapolis: Bobbs-Merrill, 1960.

Tormey, Alan. *The Concept of Expression*. Princeton: Princeton UP, 1971.

Trilling, Lionel. *Sincerity and Authenticity*. New York: Oxford UP, 1972.

Walton, Kendall. "Categories of Art." *Journal of Aesthetics and Art Criticism* 79 (1970): 334–67.

———. *Mimesis as Make-Believe: On the Foundations of the Representational Arts*. Cambridge: Harvard UP, 1990.

Weitz, Morris. "The Role of Theory in Aesthetics." *Journal of Aesthetics and Art Criticism* 15 (1956): 27–35.

Wolff, Janet. *The Social Production of Art*. London: Macmillan, 1975.

Wolin, Richard. *Walter Benjamin: An Aesthetics of Redemption.* New York: Columbia UP, 1982.

Wollheim, Richard. *Art and Its Objects.* New York: Harper & Row, 1968.

———. *On Art and the Mind: Essays and Lectures.* New York: Penguin, 1973.

Ziff, Paul. *Antiaesthetics: An Appreciation of the Cow with the Subtle Nose.* Dordrecht, Netherlands: D. Reidel, 1984.

———. "The Task of Defining a Work of Art." *The Philosophical Review* 62 (1953): 58–78.

AESTHETIC THEORY—PARTICULAR MEDIA

Architecture

Benedikt, Michael. *Deconstructing the Kimbell: An Essay on Meaning and Architecture.* New York: SITES/Lumen, 1991.

———. *For an Architecture of Reality.* New York: Lumen, 1987.

Crook, J. Mordaunt. *The Dilemma of Style: Architectural Ideas from the Picturesque to the Post-modern.* Chicago: U of Chicago P, 1987.

Frampton, Kenneth. *Modern Architecture and the Critical Present.* London: Architectural Design, 1982.

Goldblatt, David A. "The Dislocation of the Architectural Self." *Journal of Aesthetics and Art Criticism* 49.4 (1991): 337–48.

Harries, Karsten. "The Dream of the Complete Building." *Perspecta* 17 (1980): 36–43.

Kolb, David. *Postmodern Sophistications: Philosophy, Architecture, and Tradition.* Chicago: U of Chicago P, 1990.

Norris, Christopher. *The Concept of Dwelling.* New York: Electra/Rizzoli, 1985.

Risser, James C. "Siting Order at the Limits of Construction: Deconstructing Architectural Place." *Research in Phenomenology* 22 (1992): 62–72.

Scruton, Roger. *The Aesthetics of Architecture.* Princeton: Princeton UP, 1979.

Thalacker, Donald W. *The Place of Art in the World of Architecture.* New York: Chelsea House, 1980.

Wolfe, Tom. *From Bauhaus to Our House.* New York: Farrar, Straus and Giroux, 1981.

Dance

Best, David. *Philosophy and Human Movement.* Boston: Allen and Unwin, 1978.

Lange, Roderyk. *The Nature of Dance: An Anthropological Perspective.* London: Macdonald and Evans. 1975.

McFee, Graham. *Understanding Dance.* New York: Routledge, 1992.

Sparshott, Francis. "Contexts of Dance." *Journal of Aesthetic Education* 24.1 (1990): 73–87.

———. "The Future of Dance Aesthetics." *Journal of Aesthetics and Art Criticism* 51.2 (1993): 227–34.

Whittock, Trevor. "The Role of Metaphor in Dance." *British Journal of Aesthetics* 3.3 (1992): 242–49.

Film

Barwell, Ismay. "Feminine Perspectives and Narrative Points of View." *Hypatia* 5.2 (1990): 63–75.

Bazin, André. *What Is Cinema?* Trans. Hugh Gray. Berkeley: U of California P, 1967–71.

Bordwell, David, and Kristin Thompson. *Film Art: An Introduction.* 4th ed. New York: McGraw-Hill, 1993.

Carroll, Noël. *Mystifying Movies: Fads and Fallacies in Contemporary Film Theory.* New York: Columbia UP, 1988.

———. *Philosophical Problems of Classic Film Theory.* Princeton: Princeton UP, 1988.

Cavell, Stanley. *Pursuits of Happiness: The Hollywood Comedy of Remarriage.* Cambridge: Harvard UP, 1981.

———. *The World Viewed: Reflections on the Ontology of Film.* Enl. ed. Cambridge: Harvard UP, 1979.

Currie, Gregory. "The Long Goodbye: The Imaginary Language of Film." *British Journal of Aesthetics* 33.3 (1993): 207–19.

Daniels, Charles E. "Notes on Colorization." *British Journal of Aesthetics* 30.1 (1990): 68–70.

Fregoso, Rosa Linda. *The Bronze Screen: Chicano and Chicano Film Culture.* Minneapolis: U of Minnesota P, 1993.

Gentile, Mary C. *Film Feminisms: Theory and Practice.* Westport: Greenwood, 1985.

Hollander, Anne. *Moving Pictures.* New York: Knopf, 1989.

Leibowitz, Flo. "Movie Colorization and the Expression of Mood." *Journal of Aesthetics and Art Criticism* 49.4 (1991): 363–65.

Levinson, Jerrold. "Colorization Ill-Defended." *British Journal of Aesthetics* 30.1 (1990): 62–67.

———. "Imaginarily, at the Movies." *Philosophical Quarterly* 43.170 (1993): 70–78.

Mast, Gerlad, and Marshall Cohen, eds. *Film Theory and Criticism: Introductory Readings.* New York: Oxford UP, 1985.

Miller, Mark Crispin. *Seeing through Movies.* New York: Pantheon, 1990.

Panofsky, Erwin. "Style and Medium in the Moving Pictures." *Aesthetics: A Critical Anthology.* Ed. George Dickie, Richard Sclafani, and Ronald Roblin. 1st ed. New York: St. Martin's, 1977.

Parkes, Graham. "Reflections on Projections: Changing Conditions in Watching Film." *Journal of Aesthetic Education* 21 (1987): 77–82.

Penley, Constance. *Feminism and Film Theory.* New York: Routledge, 1988.

Schrage, Laurie. "Feminist Film Aesthetics: A Contextual Approach." *Hypatia* 5.2 (1990): 137–48.

Sesonske, Alexander. "Time And Tense in Cinema." *Journal of Aesthetics and Art Criticism* 38 (1980): 419–26.

Shaviro, Steven. *The Cinematic Body*. Minneapolis: U of Minnesota P, 1993.

Whittock, Trevor. *Metaphor and Film*. New York: Cambridge UP, 1990.

Young, James. "In Defense of Colorization." *British Journal of Aesthetics* 18 (1988): 368–72.

Literature

Abrams, M. H. *The Mirror and the Lamp: Romantic Theory and the Critical Tradition*. New York: Norton, 1958.

Bloom, Harold. *The Anxiety of Influence*. New York: Oxford UP, 1973.

———. *A Map of Misreading*. New York: Oxford UP, 1975.

Eagleton, Terry. *Marxism and Literary Criticism*. London: Methuen, 1976.

Eldridge, Richard. *On Moral Personhood: Philosophy, Literature, Criticism, and Self-Understanding*. Chicago: U of Chicago P, 1989.

Fish, Stanley. *Is There a Text in This Class? The Authority of Interpretive Communities*. Cambridge: Harvard UP, 1980.

Frye, Northrop. *Anatomy of Criticism*. Princeton: Princeton UP, 1957.

Gates, Henry Louis, Jr., ed. *"Race," Writing, and Difference*. Chicago: U of Chicago P, 1986.

Goldberg, S. L. *Agents and Lives: Moral Thinking in Literatures*. New York: Cambridge UP, 1993.

Hartman, Geoffrey. *Saving the Text*. Baltimore: Johns Hopkins UP, 1981.

Ingarden, Roman. *The Literary Work of Art*. Evanston: Northwestern UP, 1973.

Iser, Wolfgang. *The Act of Reading: A Theory of Aesthetic Response*. Baltimore: John Hopkins UP, 1978.

Lukacs, Georg. *The Theory of the Novel*. Trans. Anna Bostock. London: Merlin, 1971.

Lynch, Richard A. "Bakhtin's Ethical Vision." *Philosophy and Literature* 17.1 (1993): 98–109.

Markowitz, Sally. "Guilty Pleasures: Aesthetic Meta-Response and Fiction." *Journal of Aesthetics and Art Criticism* 50.4 (1992): 307–16.

Morrison, Toni. *Playing in the Dark: Whiteness and the Literary Imagination*. Cambridge: Harvard UP, 1992.

Moses, Wilson Jeremiah. *Black Messiahs and Uncle Toms: Social and Literary Manipulations of a Religious Myth*. University Park: Pennsylvania State UP, 1982.

Neill, Alex. "Fiction and the Emotions." *American Philosophical Quarterly* 30.1 (1993): 1–13.

Novitz, David. *Knowledge, Fiction, and Imagination*. Philadelphia: Temple UP, 1987.

Nussbaum, Martha C. *Love's Knowledge: Essays on Philosophy and Literature*. New York: Oxford UP, 1991.

Richards, I. A. *Principles of Literary Criticism*. New York: Harcourt, 1925.

Robinson, Jenefer, and Stephanie Ross. "Women, Morality, and Fiction." *Aesthetics in Feminist Perspective*. Ed. Hilde Hein and Carolyn Korsmeyer. Bloomington: Indiana UP, 1993. 105–18.

Said, Edward W. *Orientalism*. New York: Vintage, 1978.

Sartre, Jean-Paul. *What Is Literature?* Trans. B. Frechtman. London: Methuen, 1950.

Schiller, Friedrich. *"Naive and Sentimental Poetry" (1800) and "On the Sublime" (1801)*. Trans. J. A. Elias. New York: Frederick Ungar, 1966.

Tatum, Charles M. *Chicano Literature*. Boston: Twayne, 1982.

Valéry, Paul. *The Art of Poetry*. New York: Random House, 1958.

Music

Adorno, Theodor. *The Sociology of Music*. Trans. E. B. Ashton. New York: Continuum, 1976.

Alperson, Philip, ed. *What Is Music?* New York: Haven, 1987.

Babbitt, Milton. "Who Cares If You Listen?" *High Fidelity* (1958). Rpt. as "The Composer as Specialist." *Esthetics Contemporary*. Ed. Richard Kostelanetz. Buffalo: Prometheus, 1978. 280–87.

Baraka, Imamu Amiri. *Blues People: Negro Music in White America*. New York: Morrow, 1963.

———. "The Great Music Robbery." *The Music: Reflections on Jazz and the Blues*. New York: Morrow, 1987.

Bowers, Jane, and Judith Tick, eds. *Women Making Music: The Western Art Tradition, 1150–1950*. Urbana: U of Illinois P, 1987.

Budd, Malcolm. *Music and the Emotions*. London: Routledge, 1985.

Campbell, Mark Robin. "John Cage's 4'33": Using Aesthetic Theory to Understand a Musical Notion." *Journal of Aesthetic Education* 26.1 (1992): 83–91.

Cook, Nicholas. *Music, Imagination and Culture*. New York: Oxford UP, 1990.

Cooke, Deryck. *The Language of Music*. Oxford: Oxford UP, 1959.

Dahlhaus, Carl. *The Esthetics of Music*. Trans. William W. Austin. Cambridge: Cambridge UP, 1982.

———. *The Idea of Absolute Music*. Trans. Roger Lustig. Chicago: U of Chicago P, 1989.

Davies, Stephen. "Authenticity in Musical Performance." *The British Journal of Aesthetics* 27 (1987): 39–50.

———. *Musical Meaning and Expression*. Ithaca: Cornell UP, 1994.

Dipert, Randall R. "The Composer's Intentions: An Examination of Their Relevance for Performance." *Musical Quarterly* 66 (1980): 205–18.

Edidin, Aron. "Look What They've Done to My Song: 'Historical Authenticity' and the Aesthetics of Musical Performance." *Midwest Studies in Philosophy* 16 (1991): 194–420.

Ellis, Catherine J. *Aboriginal Music, Education for Living: Cross-Cultural Experience from South Australia*. St. Lucia: U of Queensland P, 1988.

Goehr, Lydia. *The Imaginary Museum of Musical Works: An Essay in the Philosophy of Music*. New York: Oxford UP, 1992.

Hanslick, Eduard. *On the Musically Beautiful*. Trans. Geoffrey Payzant. Indianapolis: Hackett, 1986.

Higgins, Kathleen M. *The Music of Our Lives.* Philadelphia: Temple UP, 1991.

Keil, Charles. *Urban Blues.* Chicago: U of Chicago P, 1966.

Kenyon, Nicholas, ed. *Authenticity and Early Music.* New York: Oxford UP, 1988.

Kerman, Joseph. *Contemplating Music: Challenges to Musicology.* Cambridge: Harvard UP, 1985.

Kivy, Peter. *The Fine Art of Repetition: Essays in the Philosophy of Music.* New York: Columbia UP, 1993.

———. *Music Alone: Philosophical Reflections on the Purely Musical Experience.* Ithaca: Cornell UP, 1990.

———. *Sound and Semblance: Reflections on Musical Representation.* Princeton: Princeton UP, 1984.

———. *Sound Sentiment: An Essay on the Musical Emotions.* Philadelphia: Temple UP, 1989.

Kochman, Thomas. *Rappin' and Stylin' Out.* Urbana: U of Illinois P, 1972.

Krausz, Michael, ed. *The Interpretation of Music: Philosophical Essays.* Oxford: Clarendon, 1993.

Lomax, Alan. *Folk Song Style and Culture.* American Association for the Advancement of Science, Publication no. 88, Washington, D.C., 1969.

Merriam, Alan P. *The Anthropology of Music.* Evanston: Northwestern UP, 1964.

Meyer, Leonard B. *Emotion and Meaning in Music.* Chicago: U of Chicago P, 1956.

———. *Music, the Arts, and Ideas: Patterns and Predictions in Twentieth-Century Culture.* Chicago: U of Chicago P, 1967.

Oliver, Paul. *Blues Fell This Morning: Meaning in the Blues.* 2nd ed. New York: Cambridge: UP, 1990.

Pendle, Karin, ed. *Women and Music.* Bloomington: Indiana UP, 1992.

Radford, Colin. "How Can Music Be Moral?" *Midwest Studies in Philosophy* 16 (1991): 421–38.

Raffman, Diana. *Language, Music, and Mind.* Cambridge: M.I.T. P, 1993.

Rowell, Lewis. *Thinking about Music.* Amherst: U of Massachusetts P, 1983.

Sidran, Ben. *Black Talk: How the Music of Black America Created a Radical Alternative to the Values of the Western Literary Tradition.* New York: Holt, 1971.

Small, Christopher. *Music, Society, Education.* London: John Calder, 1980.

Wicke, Peter. *Rock Music: Culture, Aesthetics, and Sociology.* New York: Cambridge U P, 1990.

Painting

Bell, Clive. *Enjoying Pictures.* London: Chatto and Windus, 1934.

———. *Since Cézanne.* London: Chatto and Windus, 1922.

Clark, Kenneth. *The Nude.* New York: Penguin, 1956.

Gombrich, Ernst H. *Art and Illusion: A Study in the Psychology of Pictorial Representation.* New York: Pantheon, 1960.

————, and Richard Langton Gregory. *Illusion in Nature and Art*. London: Duckworth, 1973.

Greenberg, Clement. *Art and Culture: Critical Essays*. Boston: Beacon, 1961.

McKee, Patrick. "Resemblance: An Account of Realism in Painting." *Philosophical Investigations* 16.4 (1993): 298–306.

Panofsky, Erwin. *Studies in Iconology: Humanistic Themes in the Art of the Renaissance*. New York: Oxford UP, 1962.

Rosenblum, Robert. *Modern Art and the Northern Romantic Tradition*. London: Thames and Hudson, 1975.

Ruskin, John. *Modern Painters*. Ed. and abr. David Barrie. New York: Knopf, 1987.

Schier, Flint. *Deeper into Pictures*. Cambridge: Cambridge UP, 1986.

Steinberg, Leo. *Other Criteria: Confrontation with Twentieth-Century Art*. New York: Oxford UP, 1972.

Ucko, Peter J., and Andrée Rosenfeld. *Paleolithic Cave Art*. London: Wendenfeld and Nicolson, 1967.

Wollheim, Richard. *Painting as an Art*. Princeton: Princeton UP, 1987.

Photography

Adams, Robert. *Beauty in Photography: Essays in Defense of Traditional Values*. Millertown: Aperture, 1981.

Barthes, Roland. *Camera Lucida: Reflections on Photography*. Trans. Richard Howard. London: Flamingo, 1984.

Berger, John. *Another Way of Telling*. London: Writers and Readers, 1982.

————. *Ways of Seeing*. New York: Penguin, 1972.

Brodzky, Anne Grueblood, Rose Danesewich, and Nick Johnson. *An Inquiry into the Aesthetics of Photography*. Toronto: Society for Art, 1975.

Currie, Gregory. "Photography, Painting and Perception." *Journal of Aesthetics and Art Criticism* 49.1 (1991): 23–29.

Gernsheim, Helmut. *Creative Photography: Aesthetic Trends 1939–1960*. London: Faber and Faber, 1962.

Scruton, Roger. "Photography and Representation." *Critical Inquiry* 7 (1981): 577–603.

Sontag, Susan. *On Photography*. New York: Farrar, Straus, and Giroux, 1977.

Sculpture

Read, Herbert. *The Art of Sculpture*. London: Faber and Faber, 1956.

Theater

Read, Alan. *Theatre and Everyday Life: An Ethics of Performance*. New York: Routledge, 1993.

Reinelt, Janelle G., and Joseph R. Roach. *Critical Theory and Performance*. Ann Arbor: U of Michigan P, 1992.

Saltz, David. "How to Do Things on Stage." *Journal of Aesthetics and Art Criticism* 49.1 (1991): 31–45.

Aesthetic Theory—Nature

Ames, Roger T., and J. Baird Callicott, eds. *Nature in the Asian Tradition of Thought: Essays in Environmental Philosophy.* Albany: State U of New York P, 1989.

Coleman, Earle J. "Is Nature Ever Unaesthetic?" *Between Species* 5 (1989): 138–46.

Crawford, Donald. "Nature and Art: Some Dialectical Relationships." *Journal of Aesthetics and Art Criticism* 42 (1983): 49–58.

Hargrove, Eugene C. *Foundations of Environmental Ethics.* Englewood Cliffs: Prentice-Hall, 1989.

Hepburn, Ronald W. "Aesthetic Appreciation of Nature." *Aesthetics in the Modern World.* Ed. Harold Osborne. London: Thames and Hudson, 1968. 49–66.

Kemal, Salim, and Ivan Gaskell, eds. *Landscape, Natural Beauty, and the Arts.* Cambridge: Cambridge UP, 1993.

Sadler, Barry, and Allen Carlson, eds. *Environmental Aesthetics: Essays in Interpretation.* Victoria: U of Victoria P, 1982.

Turner, Frederick, "Cultivating the American Garden: Toward a Secular View of Nature." *Harper's* Aug. 1985: 45–52.

Politics, Law, and Aesthetics

Benjamin, Walter. *Aesthetics and Politics.* Ed. R. Taylor. London: New Left, 1977.

Berger, John. *Ways of Seeing.* New York: Penguin, 1972.

Devereaux, Mary. "Protected Space: Politics, Censorship, and the Arts." *Journal of Aesthetics and Art Criticism* 51.2 (1993): 207–15.

Dubin, Steven C. *Arresting Images: Impolitic Art and Uncivil Actions.* New York: Routledge, 1992.

Duboff, Leonard D. *Art Law: In a Nutshell.* St. Paul: West, 1984.

Feldman, Franklin, and Stephen E. Weil. *Art Law: Rights and Liabilities of Creators and Collectors.* Boston: Little, Brown, 1986.

Gotschalk, D. W. *Art and the Social Order.* Chicago: U of Chicago P, 1947.

Haywood, Ian. *Art and the Politics of Forgery.* Brighton: Harvester, 1983.

Hein, Hilde, and Carolyn Korsmeyer, eds. *Aesthetics in Feminist Perspective.* Bloomington: Indiana UP, 1993.

Hein, Marjorie. *Sex, Sin and Blasphemy: A Guide to America's Censorship Wars.* New York: New, 1993.

Hoffman, Barbara. "Law for Art's Sake in the Public Realm." *Critical Inquiry* 17.3 (1991): 540–73.

Karp, Ivan, and Steven D. Lavine, eds. *Exhibiting Cultures: The Poetics and Politics of Museum Display.* Washington, D. C.: Smithsonian Institution, 1991.

Merryman, John Henry, and Albert E. Elsen. *Law, Ethics, and the Visual Arts.* Philadelphia: U of Pennsylvania P, 1987.

Nochlin, Linda. *"Women, Art, and Power" and Other Essays.* London: Thames and Hudson, 1989.

Senie, Harriet F., and Sally Webster. *Critical Issues in Public Art: Content, Context, and Controversy.* New York: HarperCollins, 1992.

Serra, Richard. "Art and Censorship." *Critical Inquiry* 17.3 (1991): 574–81.

Smith, Ralph A. and Ronald Berman, eds. *Public Policy and the Aesthetic Interest: Critical Essays on Defining Cultural and Educational Relations.* Urbana: U of Illinois P, 1992.

Solomon, Maynard, ed. *Marxism and Art.* New York: Knopf, 1973.

Tolstoy, Leo. *What Is Art?* Trans. A. Maude. Indianapolis: Bobbs-Merrill, 1960.

Wolf, Naomi. *The Beauty Myth: How Images of Beauty Are Used against Women.* New York: Vintage, 1990.

PSYCHOLOGY AND THE ARTS

Arnheim, Rudolf. *Art and Visual Perception: A Psychology of the Creative Eye.* 2nd ed. Berkeley: U of California P, 1974.

Beardsley, Monroe C. "On the Creation of Art." *Journal of Aesthetics and Art Criticism* 23.3 (1965): 291–304.

Boden, Margaret A. *The Creative Mind: Myth and Mechanisms.* London: Weidenfeld and Nicolson, 1990.

Casey, Edward S. *Imagining: A Phenomenological Study.* Bloomington: U of Indiana P, 1976.

Dutton, Denis, and Michael Krausz, eds. *The Concept of Creativity in Science and Art.* The Hague: Martinus Nijhoff, 1981.

Fisher, John, ed. *Perceiving Art.* Philadelphia: Temple UP, 1980.

Freedberg, David. *The Power of Images.* Chicago: Chicago UP, 1989.

Freud, Sigmund. *Jokes and Their Relation to the Unconscious.* Trans. James Strachey. Harmondsworth: Penguin, 1976.

———. *The Standard Edition of the Complete Psychological Works of Sigmund Freud.* Trans. and ed. James Strachey. Vol. 7: *A Case of Hysteria, Three Essays on Sexuality, and Other Works;* vol. 9: *Jensen's "Gradiva" and Other Works;* and vol. 13: *Totem and Taboo and Other Works.* London: Hogarth, 1966–1974. 24 vols.

Hindemith, Paul. *A Composer's World.* Cambridge: Harvard UP, 1952.

Hopkins, Jim, and Anthony Savile, eds. *Psychoanalysis, Mind, and Art.* Cambridge: Basil Blackwell, 1992.

Jung, C. G. *The Collected Works of C. G. Jung.* Trans. R. F. C. Hull. Bollingen Series. Vol. 15: *The Spirit in Man, Art, and Literature.* Princeton: Princeton UP, 1966. 24 vols.

Koestler, Arthur. *The Act of Creation.* New York: Macmillan, 1964.

Kris, Ernst. *Psychoanalytic Explorations in Art.* New York: International UP, 1952.

———, and Otto Kurz. *Legend, Myth, and Magic in the Image of the Artist.* Trans. A. Laing and L. M. Newman. New Haven: Yale UP, 1979.

Kuhns, Richard. *Psychoanalytic Theory of Art: A Philosophy of Art on Developmental Principles.* New York: Columbia UP, 1983.

Scruton, Roger. *Art and Imagination*. London: Metheun, 1979.

Sparshott, Francis. "Imagination—The Very Idea." *Journal of Aesthetics and Art Criticism* 48.1 (1990): 1–8.

Spector, Jack J. *The Aesthetics of Freud: A Study in Psychoanalysis and Art*. New York: Praeger, 1972.

Tomas, V., ed. *Creativity in the Arts*. Englewood Cliffs: Prentice-Hall, 1964.

Warnock, Mary. *Imagination*. Berkeley: U of California P, 1976.

RECENT DEVELOPMENTS IN THE ARTS AND THEORY

Barthes, Roland. *The Elements of Semiology*. Trans. A. Lavers and C. Smith. New York: Hill and Wang, 1967.

———. *The Pleasures of the Text*. Trans. P. Miller. New York: Hill and Wang, 1975.

Battock, Geoffrey, ed. *Minimalist Art*. New York: Dutton, 1968.

Bazin, Germain. *The Museum Age*. New York: Universe, 1967.

Bloom, Harold, et al. *Deconstruction and Criticism*. New York: Seabury, 1979.

Bürger, Peter. *Theory of the Avant-Garde*. Trans. Michael Shaw. Minneapolis: U of Minnesota P, 1984.

Calinescu, Matei. *Five Faces of Modernity: Modernism, Avant-Garde, Decadence, Kitsch, Postmodernism*. Durham: Duke UP, 1987.

Connor, Steven. *Postmodernist Culture: An Introduction to Theories of the Contemporary*. Oxford: Basil Blackwell, 1989.

Culler, Jonathan. *Structuralism and Poetics*. London: Routledge, 1975.

Danto, Arthur C. *The Philosophical Disenfranchisement of Art*. New York: Columbia UP, 1986.

———. *The Transfiguration of the Commonplace*. Cambridge: Harvard UP, 1981.

Derrida, Jacques. *Of Grammatology*. Trans. Gayatri Spivak. Baltimore: John Hopkins UP, 1976.

———. "White Mythology: Metaphor in the Text of Philosophy." *New Literary History* 6 (1974): 5–74.

———. *Writing and Difference*. Trans. Alan Bass. New York: Routledge, 1979.

Eco, Umberto. *The Open Work*. Trans. Anna Cancogni. Cambridge: Harvard UP, 1989.

Foster, Hal. *The Anti-Aesthetic: Essays on Postmodern Culture*. Port Townsend: Bay, 1983.

———, ed. *Postmodern Culture*. London: Pluto, 1985.

Gass, William H. "Vicissitudes of the Avant-Garde." *Harper's* 277.1661 (1988): 64–70.

Goldsmith, Steven. "The Readymades of Marcel Duchamp: The Ambiguities of an Aesthetic Revolution." *The Journal of Aesthetics and Criticism* 42 (1983): 197–308.

Harries, Karsten. *The Meaning of Modern Art: A Philosophical Interpretation*. Evanston: Northwestern UP, 1968.

Hertz, Richard, ed. *Theories of Contemporary Art*. Englewood Cliffs: Prentice-Hall, 1985.

Herwitz, Daniel. *Making Theory/Constructing Art: On the Authority of the Avant-Garde.* Chicago: U of Chicago P, 1993.

Hughes, Robert. *Culture of Complaint: The Fraying of America.* New York: Oxford UP, 1993.

———. *The Shock of the New: Art and the Century of Change.* Rev. and enl. ed. London: Thames and Hudson, 1991.

Hutcheon, Linda. *A Poetics of Postmodernism: History, Theory, Fiction.* New York: Routledge, 1988.

Krauss, Rosalind E. *The Originality of the Avant-Garde and Other Modernist Myths.* Cambridge: M I.T. P, 1987.

Kuspit, Donald. *The Cult of the Avant-Garde.* New York: Cambridge UP, 1993.

Lang, Berel, ed. *The Death of Art.* New York: Haven, 1984.

Lévi-Strauss, Claude. *The Raw and the Cooked: Introduction to a Science of Mythology.* Vol. 1. Trans. John and Doreen Weightman. London: Jonathan Cape, 1969.

———. *The Savage Mind.* London: Weidenfeld and Nicolson, 1966.

Lyotard, Jean-François. *The Postmodern Condition: A Report on Knowledge.* Trans. Geoffrey Bennington and Brian Masumi. Manchester: Manchester UP, 1984.

McCormick, Peter J. *Modernity, Aesthetics, and the Bonds of Art.* Ithaca: Cornell UP, 1990.

Malraux, André. *Museum without Walls.* Trans. Stuart Gilbert and Francis Price. London: Secker and Warburg, 1967.

———. *Voices of Silence: Man and His Art.* New York: Doubleday, 1953.

Norris, Christopher. *The Deconstructive Turn.* New York: Methuen, 1983.

Roberts, David. *Art and Enlightenment: Aesthetic Theory after Adorno.* Lincoln: U of Nebraska P, 1991.

Sayre, Henry. "The Object of Performance: Aesthetics in the '70s." *Georgia Review* 37 (1983): 169–88.

Shattuck, Roger. *The Innocent Eye: On Modern Literature and the Arts.* New York: Farrar, Straus, and Giroux, 1984.

Wolfe, Tom. *The Painted Word.* New York: Bantam, 1976.

THE NON-WESTERN WORLD

AFRICA

Agawu, Kofi. "Representing African Music." *Critical Inquiry* 18 (1992): 245–66.

Blacking, John. *How Musical Is Man?* Seattle: U of Washington P, 1973.

Chernoff, John Miller. *African Rhythm and African Sensibility: Aesthetics and Social Action in African Musical Idioms.* Chicago: U of Chicago P, 1979.

Crowley, Daniel J. "An African Aesthetic." *Journal of Aesthetics and Art Criticism* 24 (1966): 519–24.

D'Azevedo, Warren L., ed. *The Traditional Artist in African Societies.* Bloomington: Indiana UP, 1973.

Duerdon, Dennis. *African Art and Literature: The Invisible Present.* London: Heinemann, 1975.

Fagg, William. *Nigerian Images.* London: Lund Humphries, 1963.

———. *Tribes and Forms in African Art.* New York: Tudor, 1965.

———, and Margaret Plass. *African Sculpture.* New York: Dutton, 1964.

Fraser, Douglas, and Herbert M. Cole, eds. *African Art and Leadership.* Madison: U of Wisconsin P, 1972.

Harrison, Daphne D. "Aesthetic and Social Aspects of Music in African Ritual Settings." *More Than Drumming: Essays on African and Afro-Latin American Music and Musicians.* Ed. Irene V. Jackson. Westport: Greenwood, 1985.

Jones, A. M. *Studies in African Music.* London: Oxford UP, 1959.

Keil, Charles. *Tiv Song.* Chicago: U of Chicago, 1979.

Lawal, Babatunde. "Some Aspects of Yoruba Aesthetics." *British Journal of Aesthetics* 14 (1974): 239–49.

McCall, Daniel T., and Edna G. Bay. *African Images: Essays in African Iconology.* New York: Africana, 1975.

Nketia, J. H. Kwabena. *The Music of Africa.* New York: Norton, 1974.

Oehrle, Elizabeth. "An Introduction to African Views of Music Making." *Journal of Aesthetic Education* 25.3 (1991): 163–74.

Onyewuenyi, Innocent C. "Traditional African Aesthetics: A Philosophical Perspective." *International Philosophical Quarterly* 24 (1984): 237–44.

Sieber, Roy. "The Aesthetic of Traditional African Art." *Seven Metals of Africa.* Ed. Foelich Rainey. Philadelphia: University Museum, 1959.

Thompson, Robert F. "Aesthetics in Traditional Africa." *Art News* 66.9 (1968): 44–66.

———. *African Art in Motion: Icon and Act.* Berkeley: U of California P, 1974.

———. *Flash of The Spirit: African and Afro-American Art and Philosophy.* New York: Random House, 1983.

Willett, Frank. *African Art.* Rev. ed. London: Thames and Hudson, 1993.

———. *Ife and the History of West African Sculpture.* New York: McGraw-Hill, 1967.

CHINA

Allinson, Robert E., ed. *Understanding the Chinese Mind.* Hong Kong: Oxford UP, 1989.

Birch, Cyril, ed. *Anthology of Chinese Literature.* New York: Grove, 1965.

Bush, Susan, and Christian Murck, eds. *Theories of the Arts in China.* Princeton: Princeton UP, 1983.

Cheng, François. *Chinese Poetic Writing.* Bloomington: Indiana UP, 1982.

De Woskin, Kenneth J. *A Song for One or Two: Music and the Concept of Art in Early China.* Ann Arbor: Center for Chinese Studies, 1984.

Fingarette, Herbert. *Confucius—The Secular as Sacred.* New York: Harper & Row, 1972.

Fuguan, Xu. *The Chinese Aesthetics Spirit.* Taipei: Students, 1966.

Higgins, Kathleen. "Music in Confucian and Neo-Confucian Philosophy." *International Philosophical Quarterly* 20 (1980): 433–51.

Liu, James J. Y. *The Art of Chinese Poetry.* Chicago: U of Chicago P, 1962.

———. *Chinese Theories of Literature.* Chicago: U of Chicago P, 1976.

Sullivan, Michael. *An Introduction to Chinese Art.* London: Faber and Faber, 1961.

———. *The Birth of Landscape Painting in China.* London: Routledge, 1962.

Tse-hou, Li. *The Path of Beauty: A Study of Chinese Aesthetics.* Beijing: Morning Glory, 1988.

Yutang, Lin. *The Chinese Theory of Art.* New York: Putnam's, 1967.

INDIA

Basham, A. L. *The Wonder That Was India: A Survey of the Culture of the Indian Sub-Continent before the Coming of the Muslims.* New York: Grove, 1959.

Chaudhury, Pravas Jivan. "Catharsis in the Light of Indian Aesthetics." *Journal of Aesthetics and Art Criticism* 24 (1965): 151–64.

———. "Indian Poetics." *Journal of Aesthetics and Art Criticism* 19 (1961): 289–94.

———. "Psychical Distance in Indian Aesthetics." *Journal of Aesthetics and Art Criticism* 24 (1965): 191–96.

Chethimattam, John Britto, C. M. I. "Rasa, the Soul of Indian Art." *International Philosophical Quarterly* 10 (1970): 44–62.

Coomaraswamy, Ananda Kentisy. *Introduction to Indian Art.* 2nd ed. Delhi: Munshiram Manoharlal, 1969.

Duran, Jane. "The Nagaraja: Symbol and Symbolism in Hindu Art and Iconography." *Journal of Aesthetic Education* 24.2 (1990): 37–47.

Goswamy, B. N. *Essence of Indian Art.* San Francisco: Asian Art Museum of San Francisco, 1986.

Haldar, Asit K. "Symbolism in Indian Art." *Journal of Aesthetics and Art Criticism* 9 (1950): 124–27.

Herman, A. L. "Indian Art and Levels of Meaning." *Philosophy East and West* 15 (1965): 13–30.

Jhanji, Rekha. *The Sensuous in Art: Reflections on Indian Aesthetics.* Delhi: Indian Institute for Advanced Study, in association with Motilal Banarsidass, 1989.

Mukerjee, Radhakamal. "Rasas as Springs of Art in Indian Aesthetics." *Journal of Aesthetics and Art Criticism* 24 (1965): 91–96.

Parthasarathy, R. "Tradition and the Indian Writer." *British Journal of Aesthetics* 32.2 (1992): 134–48.

Raffé, W. G. "Rāgas and Rāginis: A Key to Hindu Aesthetics." *Journal of Aesthetics and Art Criticism* 11 (1952): 105–17.

Zimmer, Heinrich. *The Art of Indian Asia: Its Mythology and Transformations.* Ed. Joseph Campbell. New York: Pantheon, 1955.

———. *Artistic Form and Yoga in the Sacred Images of India.* Trans. Gerald Chapple and James B. Lawson. Princeton: Princeton UP, 1984.

———. *Myths and Symbols in Indian Art and Civilization.* Ed. Joseph Campbell. New York: Pantheon, 1953.

THE ISLAMIC WORLD

Al-Faquih, Zuheir. "Islam and Art." *Studies Islamica* 37 (1973): 81–109.

Al-Faruqi, L. R. "Misconceptions of the Nature of Islamic Art." *Islam and the Modern Age* 1 (1970): 29–49.

Arnold, Sir Thomas W. *Painting in Islam.* New York: Dover, 1965.

Burckhardt, Titus. *Art of Islam: Language and Meaning.* Trans. J. Peter Hobson. London: World of Islam Festival, 1976.

———. "The Spirit of Islamic Art." *The Islamic Quarterly* 1.3–4 (1954): 212–18.

Grabar, Oleg. *The Formation of Islamic Art.* Rev. and enl. ed. New Haven: Yale UP, 1987.

Hill, Derek, and Oleg Grabar. *Islamic Architecture and Its Decoration* A.D. *800–1500.* 2nd ed. London: Faber, 1967.

Hoag, John D. *Islamic Architecture.* New York: Rizzoli, 1987.

Kemal, Salim. *The Poetics of Alfarabi and Avicenna.* Leiden: Brill, 1991.

Kühnel, Ernst. *Islamic Art and Architecture.* Trans. K. Watson. Ithaca: Cornell UP, 1966.

———. *Islamic Arts.* London: Bell, 1970.

Landau, Rom. *The Arabesque.* Asian Study Monographs, No. 2. San Francisco: College of the Pacific Press, 1955.

Madden, Edward H. "Some Characteristics of Islamic Art." *Journal of Aesthetics and Art Criticism* 33.4 (1975): 423–30.

Pope, Arthur Upham, ed., and Phyllis Ackerman, asst. ed. *A Survey of Persian Art: From Prehistoric Times to the Present.* Produced under the auspices of the Asia Institute. New York: Oxford UP, 1964–1965.

———. "On the Nature of the Work of Art in Islam." *Islam and the Modern Age* 1.2 (1970): 68–81.

———. *Persian Architecture: The Triumph of Form and Color.* New York: George Braziller, 1965.

JAPAN

Baker, Joan Stanley. *Japanese Art.* London: Thames and Hudson, 1984.

Benedict, Ruth. *The Chrysanthemum and the Sword: Patterns of Japanese Culture.* Boston: Houghton Mifflin, 1946.

Brower, Robert H., and Earl Miner. *Japanese Court Poetry.* Stanford: Stanford UP, 1961.

Hrdlicka, Z., and V. Hrdlicka. *The Art of Japanese Gardening.* London: Hamlyn, 1989.

Keene, Donald. *Japanese Literature: An Introduction for Western Readers.* New York: Grove, 1955.

Kenkō, Yoshida. *Essays in Idleness: The Tsurezuregusa of Kenkō.* Trans. Donald Keene. New York: Columbia UP, 1967.

Masaharu Anesaki. *Art, Life, and Nature in Japan*. Tokyo: Charles E. Tuttle, 1973.

Miyoshi, Masao. *Accomplices of Silence: The Modern Japanese Novel*. Berkeley: U of California P, 1974.

Murase Miyeko. *Emaki: Narrative Scrolls from Japan*. New York: Asia Society, 1983.

Narazaki, Muneshige. *The Japanese Print: Its Evolution and Essence*. English adpt. C. H. Mitchell. Tokyo: Kodansha, 1966.

Paine, Robert Treat, and Alexander Soper. *The Art and Architecture of Japan*. London: Penguin, 1955.

Sandrisser, Barbara. "Fine Weather—the Japanese View of Rain." *Landscape* 26 (1982): 42–47.

Shūichi, Katō. *A History of Japanese Literature*. Trans. David Chibbett. New York: Kodansha, 1979.

———. *Form, Style, Tradition: Reflections on Japanese Art and Society*. Trans. John Bester. Tokyo: Kodansha, 1981.

Tsunoda, Ryusaku, William Theodore de Bary, and Donald Keene. *Sources of Japanese Tradition*. New York: Columbia UP, 1958.

Ueda, Makoto. *Literary and Art Theories in Japan*. Cleveland: P of Western Reserve U, 1967.

Zeami, Motokiyo. *On the Art of Nō. Drama: The Major Treatises of Zeami*. Trans. J. Thomas Rimer and Yamazaki Masakuzu. Princeton: Princeton UP, 1984.

Meso-America and Latin America

Baddeley, Oriana, and Valerie Fraser. *Drawing the Line: Art and Cultural Identity in Contemporary Latin America*. New York: Verso, 1989.

Clendinnen, Inga. *Aztecs*. Cambridge: Cambridge UP, 1991.

Covarrubias, Miguel. *Indian Art of Mexico and Central America*. New York: Knopf, 1951.

Fernández, Justino. "An Aesthetic of Mexican Art: Ancient and Modern." *Journal of Aesthetics and Art Criticism* 23 (1964): 21–28.

Franco, Jean. *The Modern Culture of Latin America: Society and the Artist*. Rev. ed. Harmondsworth: Penguin, 1970.

Lucie-Smith, Edward. *Latin American Art of the Twentieth Century*. London: Thames and Hudson, 1993.

Miller, Mary Ellen. *The Art of Mesoamerica from Olmec to Aztec*. London: Thames and Hudson, 1986.

Oyarzun, Luis. "Some Aspects of Latin American Poetry." *Journal of Aesthetics and Art Criticism* 21.4 (1963): 433–37.

Paz, Octavio. *Mexican Poetry: An Anthology*. Trans. Samuel Beckett. New York: Grove, 1985.

NATIVE AMERICANS

Braun, Barbara. *Pre-Columbian Art and the Post-Columbian World: Ancient American Sources of Modern Art.* New York: Abrams, 1993.

Callicott, J. Baird. *In Defense of the Land Ethic: Essays in Environmental Philosophy.* Albany: State UP, 1989.

Corarrubias, Miguel. *The Eagle, the Jaguar, and the Serpent: Indian Art of the Americas, North America: Alaska, Canada, the United States.* New York: Knopf, 1954.

Kubler, George. *Esthetic Recognition of Ancient Amerindian Art.* New Haven: Yale UP, 1991.

La Pena, Frank R., and Janice T. Driesbach, eds. *The Extension of Tradition: Contemporary Northern California Native American Art in Cultural Perspective.* Sacramento: Crocker Art Museum, 1985.

Lothrop, Samuel Kirkland. *Essays in Pre-Columbian Art and Archaeology.* Cambridge: Harvard UP, 1961.

McAllester, David P. *Enemy Way Music: A Study of Social and Esthetic Values as Seen in Navaho Music.* Milwood: Kraus, 1973.

Witherspoon, Gary. *Language and Art in the Navajo Universe.* Ann Arbor: U of Michigan P, 1977.

OCEANIA

Ellis, Catherine J. *Aboriginal Music, Education for Living: Cross-Cultural Experience from South Australia.* St. Lucia: U of Queensland P, 1988.

Feld, Steven. *Sound and Sentiment: Birds, Weeping, Poetics, and Song in Kaluli Expression.* 2nd ed. Philadelphia: U of Pennsylvania P, 1990.

———. "Sound Structure as Social Structure." *Ethnomusicology* 28 (1984): 383–410.

Holt, Claire. *Art in Indonesia: Continuities and Change.* Ithaca: Cornell UP, 1967.

Keeler, Ward. *Javanese Shadow Plays, Javanese Selves.* Princeton: Princeton UP, 1987.

———. *Javanese Shadow Puppets.* Princeton: Princeton UP, 1987.

INDEX

◆◆◆

COPYRIGHTS AND ACKNOWLEDGMENTS

The author is indebted to the following for permission to reprint from copyrighted material:

ARAB INFORMATION CENTER   For the excerpt from "Islamic Art . . . Submission to Divine Will" by Zuheir Al-Faquih, which appeared in the July–August issue of *The Arab World* published by the Arab Information Center, New York. Reprinted by permission.

JENENE J. ALLISON   For the excerpt from "Deconstruction and the Energizer Bunny Rabbit." Reprinted by permission of the author.

THE UNIVERSITY OF CHICAGO PRESS   For the excerpt from "Is the Post- in Postmodernism the Post- in Postcolonial?" by Kwame Anthony Appiah, which appeared in *Critical Inquiry* (Winter 1991). Reprinted by permission of the publisher and the author.

UNIVERSITY OF ILLINOIS PRESS   For the excerpt from *The Affecting Presence: An Essay in Humanistic Anthropology* by Robert Plant Armstrong. Copyright © 1971 by the Board of Trustees of the University of Illinois. Used with permission from the University of Illinois Press.

VERSO   For the excerpt from *Drawing the Line: Art and Cultural Identity in Contemporary Latin America* by Oriana Baddeley and Valerie Fraser. Copyright © 1989, Verso. Reprinted by permission.

EDITIONS DU SEUIL   For the excerpt from "The Structuralist Activity" by Roland Barthes, translated by Richard Howard, which appeared in *The Partisan Review*, Volume 34, No. 1 (1967) © 1964 by Editions du Seuil. Reprinted by permission.

HARCOURT BRACE & COMPANY   For excerpts from "The Work of Art in the Age of Mechanical Reproduction" in *Illuminations: Essays and Reflections* by Walter Benjamin, translated by Harry Zohn, copyright © 1955 by Suhrkamp Vrelag, Frankfurt A.M., English translation copyright © 1968 by Harcourt Brace & Company, reprinted by permission of Harcourt Brace & Company.

PENGUIN BOOKS USA INC.   For the excerpt from *Ways of Seeing* by John Berger. Copyright © 1972 by Penguin Books Ltd. Used by permission of Viking Penguin, a division of Penguin Books USA Inc.

STANFORD UNIVERSITY PRESS   For the excerpt from *Cantares Mexicanos: Songs of the Aztecs* translated by John Bierhorst. Reprinted by permission of the publishers.

AMERICAN SOCIETY FOR AESTHETICS   For the excerpt from "Piece: Contra Aesthetics" by Timothy Binkley, which appeared in the *Journal of Aesthetics and Art Criticism*, Volume 35, No. 3 (Spring 1977). Reprinted by permission of the American Society for Aesthetics.

SIMON & SCHUSTER, INC.   For the excerpt from *The Closing of the American Mind* by Allan Bloom. Copyright © 1987 by Allan Bloom. Reprinted by permission of Simon & Schuster, Inc.

THAMES AND HUDSON   For the excerpt from *Image of the New World: The American Continent Portrayed in Native Texts* by Gordon Brotherston with Ed Dorn. Reprinted by permission.

TEACHERS COLLEGE RECORD   For the excerpt from "If You Don't Stop, You Don't See Anything" by Rika Burnham. Reprinted by permission.

UNIVERSITY PRESS OF NEW ENGLAND   For the excerpt from *Silence* by John Cage. Copyright © 1961 by John Cage, Wesleyan University Press. Reprinted by permission of University Press of New England.

DUKE UNIVERSITY PRESS   For the excerpt from *The Faces of Modernity: Avant-Garde, Decadence, Kitsch* by Matei Calinescu. Reprinted by permission.

AMERICAN SOCIETY FOR AESTHETICS   For the excerpt from "The Image of Women in Film: A Defense of the Paradigm" by Noël Carroll, which appeared in the *Journal of Aesthetics and Art Criticism*, Volume 48, No. 4 (Fall 1990). Reprinted by permission of the American Society for Aesthetics.

HARVARD UNIVERSITY PRESS   For the excerpt from *The World Viewed: Reflections on the Ontology of Film* by Stanley Cavell, Cambridge, Mass.: Harvard University Press, Copyright © 1971, 1974, 1979 by Stanley Cavell. Reprinted by permission.

CAMBRIDGE UNIVERSITY PRESS   For the excerpt from *The Aztecs* by Inga Clendinnen. Reprinted by permission of Cambridge University Press.

ARTHUR C. DANTO   For the excerpt from "Approaching the End of Art" by Arthur C. Danto from *The State of the Art* (1987). Reprinted by permission.

THE JOURNAL OF PHILOSOPHY   For the excerpt from "The Artworld" by Arthur C. Danto, which appeared in the 15 October 1964 issue of *The Journal of Philosophy*. Reprinted by permission of the publisher and author.

THE NATION   For the excerpt from "The Vietnam Veterans Memorial" by Arthur C. Danto, which appeared in the 31 August 1985 issue of *The Nation*, copyright © 1985 The Nation Company, Inc. Reprinted by permission of the publisher and author.

CORNELL UNIVERSITY PRESS   For the excerpt from *Musical Meaning and Expression* by Stephen Davies. Copyright © 1994 by Cornell University. Used by permission of the publisher, Cornell University Press.

THE PUTNAM PUBLISHING GROUP   For the excerpt from *Art as Experience* by John Dewey. Reprinted by permission of the Putnam Publishing Group. Copyright © 1934 by John Dewey. Copyright © 1962 by Roberta L. Dewey. Copyright © 1974 by the John Dewey Foundation.

GEORGE DICKIE   For the excerpt from "Art as a Social Institution" by George Dickie from *Aesthetics: An Introduction* (1971). Reprinted by permission.

AMERICAN PHILOSOPHICAL QUARTERLY   For the excerpt from "The Myth of the Aesth
by George Dickie, which appeared in the January 1964 issue of the *American Phil*
Quarterly. Reprinted by permission.

AMERICAN DANCE FESTIVAL   For the excerpt from "Black Dance and Dancers and the Wh
Public—A Prolegomenon to Problems of Definition" by Brenda Dixon-Stowell, which ap,
in *The Black Tradition in American Modern Dance*, ed. Gerald E. Myers (1988). Reprint
permission.

OXFORD UNIVERSITY PRESS   For the exerpt from "Artistic Crimes: The Problems of Forgery in the
Arts" by Denis Dutton, which appeared in the *British Journal of Aesthetics*, Volume 19, No. 4
(Autumn 1979). Reprinted by permission of the publisher and author.

DÆDALUS   For the excerpt from "Innovation and Repetition: Between Modern and Post-Modern
Aesthetics" by Umberto Eco, which appeared in the issue entitled "The Moving Image" Volume
114, No. 4 (Fall 1985). Reprinted by permission of *Dædalus*, Journal of the American Academy
of Arts and Sciences.

INTERNATIONAL COUNCIL FOR TRADITIONAL MUSIC   For the excerpt from "Aesthetics as Iconicity of
Style" by Steven Feld, which appeared in the *Yearbook for Traditional Music*, Volume 20
(1988). Reprinted by permission of the publisher and author.

THE GUARDIAN   For the excerpt from "Words Apart" by Carlos Fuentes, which appeared in the
24 February 1989 issue of *The Guardian*. Reprinted by permission.

HARPER'S MAGAZINE   For the excerpt from "Goodness Knows Nothing of Beauty" by William H.
Gass, which appeared in the April 1987 issue of *Harper's Magazine*. Copyright © 1987 by
Harper's Magazine. All rights reserved. Reprinted from the April issue by special permission.

ROUTLEDGE   For the excerpt from "Look, a Negro!" from *Reading Rodney King/Reading Urban
Uprising* (1993) by Robert Gooding-Williams. Reprinted by permission of the publisher,
Routledge, New York.

B. N. GOSWAMY   For the excerpt from "Rasa: Delight of the Reason" by B. N. Goswamy, which
appeared in *Essence of Indian Art* (Asian Art Museum, San Francisco, 1986). Reprinted by
permission.

HARPER'S MAGAZINE   For the excerpt from "Behold Now Behemoth" by Philip Gourevitch, which
appeared in the July 1993 issue of *Harper's Magazine*. Copyright © 1993 by Harper's Magazine.
All rights reserved. Reprinted from the July issue by special permission.

D. M. GRUVER   For the excerpt from "Hawaiian Hula: An Aesthetic Analysis." Reprinted by
permission.

HACKETT PUBLISHING COMPANY   For the excerpt from *On the Musically Beautiful* by Eduard
Hanslick. Copyright © 1986 by Hackett Publishing Company, Inc. All rights reserved. Reprinted
by permission.

KARSTEN HARRIES   For the excerpt from "The Ethical Significance of Modern Art," which appeared in the July/August 1988 issue of *Design for Arts in Education.* Reprinted by permission.

RANDOM HOUSE   For the excerpt from *Zen in the Art of Archery* by Eugen Herrigel. Copyright © 1953 by Pantheon Books and renewed in 1981 by Random House, Inc. Reprinted by permission of Pantheon Books, a division of Random House, Inc.

OXFORD UNIVERSITY PRESS   For the excerpt from "Understanding Performance Art: Art Beyond Art" by Thomas Heyd, which appeared in the *British Journal of Aesthetics*, Volume 31, No. 1 (1991). Reprinted by permission of the publisher and author.

THE ARISTOTELIAN SOCIETY   For the excerpt from "The Concept of Artistic Expression" by John Hospers, which appeared in the *Proceedings of the Aristotelian Society*, Volume 54 (1954/55). Reprinted courtesy of the Editor of the Aristotelian Society: © 1954.

THE UNIVERSITY OF CHICAGO PRESS   For the excerpt from "Do Computer Poems Show That an Author's Intention Is Irrelevant to the Meaning of a Literary Work?" by P. D. Juhl, which appeared in *Critical Inquiry* (Spring 1979). Reprinted by permission of the publisher and the author.

DOVER PUBLICATIONS, INC.   For the excerpt from *Concerning the Spiritual in Art* by Wassily Kandinsky (1977). Reprinted by permission of the publisher.

HACKETT PUBLISHING COMPANY   For the excerpts from *Critique of Judgment* by Immanuel Kant, translation by Werner S. Pluhar. Copyright © 1987 by Hackett Publishing Company, Inc. All rights reserved. Reprinted by permission.

SMITHSONIAN INSTITUTION PRESS   For the excerpt from *Exhibiting Cultures: The Poetics and Politics of Museum Display*, edited by Ivan Karp and Steven D. Lavine (Washington, DC: Smithsonian Institution Press) pages 128–150. Reprinted by permission of the publisher. Copyright © 1991.

GEORGES BORCHARDT, INC.   For the exerpt from "Japanese Aesthetics" by Donald Keene, which appeared in *Philosophy East and West*, Volume 19 (1969). Copyright © 1969 by Donald Keene. Reprinted by permission of Georges Borchardt, Inc. for the author.

THE MONIST   For the excerpt from "On the Concept of 'The Historically Authentic' Performance" by Peter Kivy, copyright © 1988, *The Monist*, LaSalle, Illinois, 61301. Reprinted by permission.

OXFORD UNIVERSITY PRESS (HONG KONG) LTD.   For the excerpt from "Chinese Aesthetics" by Kuang-Ming Wu, which appeared in *Understanding the Chinese Mind*, edited by Robert E. Allinson. Reprinted by permission.

HARPERCOLLINS PUBLISHERS, INC.   For the excerpt from *The Unbearable Lightness of Being* by Milan Kundera. Copyright © 1984 by Harper & Row, Publishers, Inc. Reprinted by permission of HarperCollins Publishers, Inc.

DONALD KUSPIT   For the excerpt from "Art and the Moral Imperative: Analyzing Activist Art," which appeared in *New Art Examiner,* Volume 18 (January 1991). Reprinted by permission of the author.

SIMON & SCHUSTER   For the excerpt from *Feeling and Form* by Susanne K. Langer. Reprinted with the permission of Simon & Schuster, Inc., from the Macmillan College text. Copyright © 1953 Charles Scribner's Sons; copyright © renewed 1981 Susanne K. Langer.

LATIN AMERICAN INDIAN LITERATURES   For the excerpt from "Translating Amerindian Texts" by Miguel León-Portilla, which appeared in *Latin American Indian Literatures*, Volume 7, No. 2 (Fall 1983). Reprinted by permission.

MARCEL DEKKER, INC.   For the excerpt from "Balanchine's Formalism" by David Michael Levin, which appeared in *Dance Perspectives*, Volume 33 (1973). Reprinted by permission.

AUSTRALASIAN JOURNAL OF PHILOSOPHY   For the excerpt from "Messages in Art" by Jerrold Levinson, which appeared in the *Australasian Journal of Philosophy* (Spring 1995). Reprinted by permission.

MARÍA LUGÓNES   For the excerpt from "Playfulness, 'World'-Traveling, and Loving Perception" by María Lugónes, which appeared in *Hypatia*, Volume 2, No. 2 (1987). Reprinted by permission of the author.

AMERICAN SOCIETY FOR AESTHETICS   For the excerpt from "Paleolithic Aesthetics: The Psychology of Cave Art" by Joseph Lyons, which appeared in the *Journal of Aesthetics and Art Criticism*, Volume 26, No. 1 (1967). Reprinted by permission of the American Society for Aesthetics.

THE NATION   For the excerpt from "Huck at 100" by Leo Marx, which appeared in the 31 August 1985 issue of *The Nation*, copyright © 1985 The Nation Company, Inc. Reprinted by permission of the publisher and author.

THE NATION   For the excerpt from "Arts and the State" by Paul Mattick, Jr., which appeared in the 1 October 1990 issue of *The Nation*, copyright © 1990 The Nation Company, Inc. Reprinted by permission of the publisher and author.

JANET McCRACKEN   For the excerpt from "The Domestic Aesthetic" by Janet McCracken. Reprinted by permission.

UNIVERSITY OF ILLINOIS PRESS   For the excerpt from "Old Age in the Chinese Mountain Landscape" by Patrick McKee, which appeared in the *Journal of Aesthetic Education*, Volume 24, No. 4 (Winter 1990). Copyright © 1990 by the Board of Trustees of the University of Illinois. Used with permission from the University of Illinois Press.

P. N. REVIEW   For the excerpt from "On the Mental Image" by Christopher Middleton, which appeared in the *P. N. Review* (1995). Copyright © 1995 Christopher Middleton. Reprinted by permission.

MARA MILLER   For the excerpt from "Art and the Construction of Self and Subject in Japan." Reprinted by permission of the author.

RANDOM HOUSE   For the excerpt from "Advertising—End of Story," which appeared in *Seeing through Movies* by Mark Crispin Miller. Copyright © 1990 by Mark Crispin Miller. Reprinted by permission of Pantheon Books, a division of Random House, Inc.

LINGUA FRANCA   For the excerpt from "The *New* Critics" by Liza Mundy, which appeared in *Lingua Franca* (September/October 1993). Reprinted from *Lingua Franca*, The Review of Academic Life. Published in New York.

THE MONIST   For the excerpt from "Plato and the Mass Media" by Alexander Nehamas, copyright © 1988, *The Monist*, LaSalle, Illinois, 61301. Reprinted by permission.

RANDOM HOUSE   For the excerpt from *The Birth of Tragedy* by Friedrich Nietzsche, translated by Walter Kaufmann. Copyright © 1967 by Random House, Inc. Reprinted by permission of Random House, Inc.

PENGUIN BOOKS USA, INC.   For the excerpt from *The Portable Nietzsche* by Walter Kaufmann, editor, translated by Walter Kaufmann. Translation copyright © 1954 by the Viking Press, renewed © 1982 by Viking Penguin, Inc. Used by permission of Viking Penguin, a division of Penguin Books USA, Inc.

HARPERCOLLINS PUBLISHERS, INC.   For the excerpt from "Why Are There No Great Women Artists?" by Linda Nochlin, from *Women in Sexist Society* by Vivian Gornick and Barbara K. Moran. Copyright © 1971 by Basic Books, Inc. Reprinted by permission of BasicBooks, a division of HarperCollins Publishers, Inc.

AMERICAN SOCIETY FOR AESTHETICS   For the excerpt from "Fiction, Imagination and Emotion" by David Novitz, which appeared in the *Journal of Aesthetics and Art Criticism*, Volume 38, No. 3 (1980). Reprinted by permission of the American Society for Aesthetics.

AMERICAN SOCIETY FOR AESTHETICS   For the excerpt from "Principles of Traditional African Art" by Isidore Okpewho, which appeared in the *Journal of Aesthetics and Art Criticism*, Volume 35, No. 3 (1977). Reprinted by permission of the American Society for Aesthetics.

PRINCETON UNIVERSITY PRESS   For the excerpt from *The Dehumanization of Art and Other Essays on Art, Culture, and Literature* (1968) by José Ortega y Gasset, translation by Helen Weyl. Copyright © 1968 by Princeton University Press. Renewed 1976. Reprinted by permission of Princeton University Press.

YALE UNIVERSITY PRESS   For the excerpt from *The Analysis of Art* by DeWitt H. Parker. Copyright Yale University Press. Reprinted by permission.

PRINCETON UNIVERSITY PRESS   For the excerpts from *The Collected Dialogues of Plato*, ed. Hamilton & Cairns (1961). Copyright © 1961 by Princeton University Press. Reprinted by permission of Princeton University Press.

RANDOM HOUSE   For the excerpt from *Letters to a Young Poet* by Rainer Maria Rilke, translation by Stephen Mitchell. Copyright © 1984 by Stephen Mitchell. Reprinted by permission of Random House, Inc.

AMERICAN SOCIETY FOR AESTHETICS   For the excerpt from "Race, Ethnicity, Expressive Authenticity: Can White People Sing the Blues?" by Joel Rudinow, which appeared in the *Journal of Aesthetics and Art Criticism*, Volume 52, No. 1 (1994). Reprinted by permission of the American Society for Aesthetics.

UNIVERSITY OF ILLINOIS PRESS   For the excerpt from "Contemporary Aesthetic Issue: The Colorization Controversy" by Yuriko Saito, which appeared in the *Journal of Aesthetic Education*, Volume 23, No. 2 (Summer 1989). Copyright © by the Board of Trustees of the University of Illinois. Used with permission from the University of Illinois Press.

OXFORD UNIVERSITY PRESS   For the excerpt from "The Japanese Appreciation of Nature" by Yuriko Saito, which appeared in the *British Journal of Aesthetics*, Volume 25, No. 3 (1985). Reprinted by permission of the publisher and author.

BARBARA SANDRISSER   For the excerpts from "On Elegance in Japan." Reprinted by permission of the author.

DOVER PUBLICATIONS, INC.   For the excerpt from *The World as Will and Representation*, by Arthur Schopenhauer (1969), translation by Payne. Reprinted by permission of the publisher.

OXFORD UNIVERSITY PRESS   For the excerpt from *The Pillow Book of Sei Shōnagon*, translated and edited by Ivan Morris (1967). Copyright © Ivan Morris 1967. Reprinted by permission of Oxford University Press.

JOHNS HOPKINS UNIVERSITY PRESS   For the excerpt from "The Fine Art of Rap" by Richard Shusterman, which appeared in *New Literary History*. Reprinted by permission of The Johns Hopkins University Press.

RIVERRUN PRESS   For the excerpt from *Music, Society, Education* by Christopher Small. Copyright © 1980 by Christopher Small. Reprinted by permission of Riverrun Press.

DOUBLEDAY   For the excerpt (from The Introduction) from *Fires in the Mirror* by Anna Deavere Smith. Copyright © 1993 by Anna Deavere Smith. Used by permission of Doubleday, a division of Bantam Doubleday Dell Publishing Group, Inc., and the author.

GARRET SOKOLOFF   For the excerpt from "By Pausing Before a *Kicho*" by Garret Sokoloff. Reprinted by permission.

ROBERT C. SOLOMON   For the excerpt from "Are the Three Stooges Funny? Soitainly!" by Robert C. Solomon, which appeared in *Entertaining Ideas* (1992). Reprinted by permission.

FARRAR, STRAUS & GIROUX, INC.   For the excerpt from "In Plato's Cave" from *On Photography* by Susan Sontag. Copyright © 1977 by Susan Sontag. Reprinted by permission of Farrar, Straus & Giroux, Inc.

THE PUBLIC INTEREST   For the excerpt from "The Malignant Object: Thoughts on Public Sculpture" by Douglas Stalker and Clark Glymour, which appeared in *The Public Interest*, No. 66 (Winter 1982). Reprinted with permission.

OXFORD UNIVERSITY PRESS   For the excerpt from "Other Criteria" from *Other Criteria: Confrontations with Twentieth-Century Art* by Leo Steinberg. Reprinted by permission.

MACMILLAN COLLEGE PUBLISHING COMPANY, INC.   For the excerpt from *What Is Art?* by Leo N. Tolstoy, translated by Almyer Maude. Reprinted with the permission of Macmillan College Publishing Company, Inc. Copyright © 1960, renewed in 1985 by Macmillan College Publishing Company, Inc.

RANDOM HOUSE   For the excerpt from *Daybook: The Journal of an Artist* by Anne Truitt. Copyright © 1982 by Anne Truitt. Reprinted by permission of Pantheon Books, a division of Random House, Inc.

BRANT PUBLICATIONS   For the excerpt from "Misunderstanding Obscenity" by Carole S. Vance, which appeared in *Art in America*. Reprinted by permission.

AMERICAN SOCIETY FOR AESTHETICS   For the excerpt from "The Role of Theory in Aesthetics" by Morris Weitz, which appeared in the *Journal of Aesthetics and Art Criticism*, Volume 15, No. 1 (1956). Reprinted by permission of the American Society for Aesthetics.

CAMBRIDGE UNIVERSITY PRESS   For the excerpt from *Rock Music: Culture, Aesthetics and Sociology* by Peter Wicke. Reprinted with the permission of Cambridge University Press.

THE UNIVERSITY PRESS OF KENTUCKY   For the excerpt from *The Verbal Icon: Studies in the Meaning of Poetry* by William K. Wimsatt, Jr., and Monroe C. Beardsley. Copyright © 1954 by the University Press of Kentucky. Reprinted by permission of the publishers.

THE UNIVERSITY OF MICHIGAN PRESS   For the excerpt from "Beautifying the World through Art" from *Language and Art in the Navajo Universe* (1977) by Gary Witherspoon. Reprinted by permission.

HARPER'S MAGAZINE   For the excerpt from "The Worship of Art: Notes on the New God" by Tom Wolfe, which appeared in the October 1984 issue of *Harper's Magazine*. Copyright © 1984 by Harper's Magazine. All rights reserved. Reprinted from the October issue by special permission.